Internet Law in Canada

Michael Geist

University of Ottawa

Captus Press

Internet Law in Canada

The publisher and the author gratefully acknowledge the authors, publishers and organizations for their permission to reproduce their work in this book. Care has been taken to trace ownership of copyright material contained in this book. The publisher will gladly accept any information that will enable the rectification of any reference or credit in subsequent editions and apologizes for any errors or omissions.

Captus Press Inc.
York University Campus, 4700 Keele Street,
North York, Ontario   M3J 1P3   Canada
Telephone: (416) 736–5537   Fax: (416) 736–5793
Email: info@captus.com   Internet: http://www.captus.com

Canadian Cataloguing in Publication Data

Geist, Michael A. (Michael Allen), 1968–
    Internet law in Canada

Includes bibliographical references and index.
ISBN 1-896691-79-X

1. Computer networks – Law and legislation – Canada.
2. Internet (Computer network) – Canada.
3. Electronic commerce – Law and legislation – Canada.   I. Title.

KE452.C6G44 2000   343.7109'944   C00-932071-7
KF390.5.C6G44 2000

Canadä We acknowledge the financial support of the Government of Canada through the Book Publishing Industry Development Program (BPIDP) for our publishing activities.

0 9 8 7 6 5 4 3 2 1
Printed in Canada

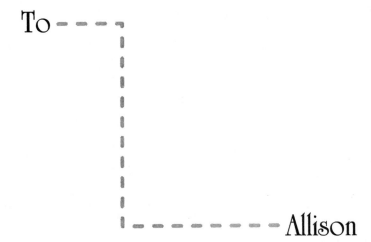

To   Allison

Summary of Contents

Table of Contents

Preface

Internet Law in Canada had a challenge before it right from the start. It had to prove to non-believers that there was indeed such a concept as "Internet law," and once this was accomplished it had to convince doubters that this law consisted of more than just a series of high profile cases emanating from the United States.

This diverse collection of materials certainly illustrates that there is law on the Internet and that there is a uniquely Canadian approach to Internet law. The number of pages absolutely confirms this to be the case. Although the Internet is still in its infancy, it has quickly succeeded in capturing the attention of the legal community. Courts worldwide face cases with an Internet component — from free speech to domain name disputes — on a daily basis. Regulators have turned their attention to the Internet's effect on traditional legislative frameworks, while at the same time seeking to develop new solutions that can keep pace with "Internet speed."

Since law traditionally moves at a relatively slow pace — cases and legislation can take years to wind their way through the courts and legislatures — the Internet presents an exciting and challenging new medium for law. In a single, fairly typical Internet law news day, there are issues related to jurisdiction, defamation, privacy, e-commerce law, copyright, patents, trademarks, and government regulatory policy. Not only is the breadth of coverage noteworthy, but so too is its international scope, with stories from Canada, the United States, Europe, and Australia, as well as several international organizations.

Canadian Internet and e-commerce law and policy is far more advanced than is often realized. With e-commerce and privacy legislation, cases addressing jurisdiction, free speech, spam, domain names, and online securities, as well as policy documents on encryption, Internet taxation, online legal services, and consumer protection, the Canadian Internet law landscape is as broad as that found in any legal system.

In *Internet Law in Canada*, Canadian Internet and e-commerce law and policy has been grouped around five main themes — Jurisdiction and Liability, Internet Speech Regulation, Internet Privacy, Intellectual Property, and Internet Commerce.

Jurisdiction and Liability (Part I) considers the question that underlies virtually every Internet law issue — who is entitled to apply their laws to online activity? Included are chapters that introduce the Internet, assess competing visions of what Internet law ought to be, analyze case law on Internet jurisdiction, and consider what responsibility Internet service providers (ISPs) should bear for the conduct of their users.

Internet Speech Regulation (Part II) considers how free speech principles map onto the online environment. Included are a comparative chapter on Internet speech regulatory approaches, specific analysis of online obscenity, hate speech, defamation, and commercial speech, as well as a chapter on private regulators of speech such as filters and computer code of conduct policies.

Internet Privacy (Part III) considers Canadian and international approaches to privacy regulation, an issue that has emerged as one of the most contentious among Internet users and businesses. Included are chapters that examine whether online privacy raises unique concerns, Canada's new private sector privacy legislation, privacy approaches found in the United States and the European Union, as well as a chapter on the role technology and anonymity play within the privacy debate.

Intellectual Property (Part IV) considers a range of issues that are at the very forefront of Internet law and policy. The trademarks and domain names chapter analyzes the first major source of Internet law disputes, while the Intellectual Property chapter assesses several new copyright challenges including linking, framing, meta-tags, and spidering. Two timely issues are accorded their own chapters — digital music and e-commerce patents.

Internet Commerce (Part V) is the largest section, outlining a very broad range of online commercial issues including online contracting, digital signatures, electronic cash, consumer protection, Internet taxation, securities regulation, and the online provision of services such as legal and health care services. The role played by the Canadian Radio-television and Telecommunications Commission (CRTC), Canada's lead regulator on broadcast and telecommunications issues is also examined in a chapter that focuses on CRTC Internet regulation, Internet telephony, and access issues.

Each chapter functions independently and therefore, much like navigating the Internet itself, the reader need not proceed in a linear fashion. Indeed, the Web version of this book will allow readers to effortlessly hyperlink between chapters.

Given the rapid pace of change in this field and the electronic nature of the Internet, the publication of a traditional text may admittedly seem somewhat anachronistic. As a longtime user of technology within the pedagogical process, I certainly appreciate these sentiments. In fact, when I first began teaching Internet law at the University of Ottawa in 1998, all my materials could be found online. Over the years, however, I found that relying exclusively on online materials is somewhat limiting — content changes or disappears, readings become burdensome as I am unable to "cut and paste" materials, and in the end students often print out the materials in any event. Moreover, the absence of a tangible set of materials leaves some uneasy, as if the absence of a book makes the entire subject matter somehow ephemeral.

The most obvious advantage of relying on electronic materials is that I am able to update those materials in response to new developments instantly. Books are updated far less frequently than Web sites, and a major concern of any Internet law author is that their work will be outdated before it hits the shelves.

This book seeks to combine the strengths of a traditional law text with the advantages of electronic publication by doing both. The book is current to July 2000, which suggests that most of the materials should remain relevant for the foreseeable future. The book is accompanied by a Web edition, that features all of the printed materials in electronic format as well as an update section containing references and materials to new developments.

ACKNOWLEDGEMENTS

Although my name alone appears on the cover, a book of this scope would not be possible without the assistance and support of a great number of people.

The University of Ottawa, Faculty of Law, particularly former Dean Sanda Rodgers and Dean Bruce Feldthusen, deserve sincere thanks for their support and vision in developing Internet and e-commerce law as a specialty at the law school.

Captus Press, particularly Randy Hoffman, Pauline Lai, Lily Chu, and the Captus Press editors, worked tirelessly to bring this book to fruition. They provided me with unmitigated support whenever needed and exhibited extraordinary patience while the project was in development.

Sundeep Chauhan and Chad Bayne, two students at the University of Ottawa, Faculty of Law provided outstanding assistance in tracking down materials and carefully proofreading the manuscript.

As always, thanks to Rene Geist, whose timely editorial assistance demonstrated that her expertise and energy knows no bounds.

Most of all, thanks to my wife Allison and my two children Jordan and Ethan. When this project began, we were just settling into a new community and Jordan was only a few months old. Not the best time to take on a major new writing project, but Allison provided me with her unconditional love and support to see it through. Today, we're proud to be part of the Ottawa community and Jordan is nearly two years old and a big sister to her brother Ethan. While the Internet can provide an online equivalent for many offline things, nothing can be a substitute for a wonderful family.

Michael Geist
Ottawa, Ontario
Summer 2000

Acknowledgements

I acknowledge the copyright holders who kindly granted me permission to include portions of their work within the text. They include:

John Perry Barlow, "A Declaration of the Independence of Cyberspace".

The Honorable Michel Bastarache and the Manitoba Law Journal, The Honorable Michel Bastarache, "The Challenge of Law in the New Millennium", 25 Man. L. J. 411 (1997–98).

Canadian Association of Internet Providers, Canadian Association of Internet Providers Privacy Code.

Canadian Marketing Association, Canadian Marketing Association Code of Ethics.

Gay and Lesbian Alliance Against Defamation, Access Denied: An Impact of Internet Filtering Software in the Gay and Lesbian Community (1997).

Jack L. Goldsmith and the University of Chicago Law School, Jack L. Goldsmith, "Against Cyberanarchy", 65 U. Chi. L. Rev. 1199 (1998).

Jerry Kang and American Bar Association, Jerry Kang, "Cyberspace Privacy: A Primer and Proposal", 26 Human Rights 3 (1999).

Mark Lemley and Southern California Law Review, Mark Lemley, "Intellectual Property and Shrinkwrap Licenses", 68 S. Cal. L. Rev. 1239 (1995).

Minister of Public Works and Government Services Canada,

- Gerry Miller et al., "Regulation of the Internet: A Technological Perspective"
- Heather De Santis, "Combating Hate on the Internet: An International Comparative Review of Policy Approaches"
- Privacy Commissioner of Canada Annual Report, 1997–98
- Roger Tasse and Kathleen Lemieux, "Consumer Protection Rights in the Context of Electronic Commerce"
- Canada's Health Infoway: Paths to Better Health

South Carolina Law Review, Jane K. Winn, "Couriers Without Luggage: Negotiable Instruments and Digital Signatures", 49 S. Car. L. Rev. 739 (1998).

Stanford Law Review, David R. Johnson and David Post, "Law and Borders — The Rise of Law in Cyberspace", 48 Stan. L. Rev. 1367 (1996).

Stanford Law Review, Jerry Kang, "Information Privacy in Cyberspace Transactions", 50 Stan. L. Rev. 1193 (1998).

Uniform Law Conference of Canada, D. Bruce Farrend, "Policy Considerations Behind Legislation Recognizing Electronic Signatures".

Uniform Law Conference of Canada, Uniform Electronic Commerce Act.

University of Pittsburgh Journal of Law and Commerce, A. Michael Froomkin, "Flood Control on the Information Ocean: Living With Anonymity, Digital Cash, and Distributed Databases", 15 U. Pitt. J. of Law & Comm. 395 (1996).

Washington Law Review, Michael Geist, "The Reality of Bytes: Regulating Economic Activity in the Age of the Internet", 73 Wash. L. Rev. 521 (1998).

Jonathan Weinberg, "Rating the Net", 19 Hastings Comm/Ent. L.J. 453 (1997).

PART ONE

INTERNET JURISDICTION AND LIABILITY

1

Introduction to the Internet

The study of Internet law is distinguishable from other areas of legal study for several reasons, not the least of which is the prominent role played by technology. Detailed analysis of Internet law issues, whether privacy, electronic commerce, or freedom of speech, frequently results in a debate on the merits of technological regulation versus traditional legal regulation. Accordingly, a key aspect of rulemaking online is an understanding of the technology that underlies the Internet. There are many instances of courts struggling with complex Internet cases due, in large measure, to their lack of understanding of the technology that underlies the issue. Without such an understanding, lawyers, regulators and judges simply cannot be expected to prescribe realistic solutions to Internet problems or to identify instances where a hands-off approach is warranted.

That is not to say, however, that Internet law need be an arena occupied only by the technologically adept. In fact, quite the opposite is true. Unlike other technology law areas long dominated by lawyers with a technology or engineering background (such as patent law), Internet law demands the creativity and divergent perspectives that a multiplicity of backgrounds yields. This is particularly true given the breadth of topics covered in Internet law, including aspects of property, contracts, torts, criminal, constitutional, intellectual property and business law.

This chapter provides the building blocks for understanding the technology and the history behind the Internet. It begins with an excerpt from an article by the author that summarizes the historical development of the Internet.

The Reality of Bytes: Regulating Economic Activity in the Age of the Internet[†]

MICHAEL GEIST

Frequently characterized as a network of networks, the Internet grew out of two concerns: the high cost of computing and the potential vulnerability of the U.S. communications network to nuclear attack. Founded in 1958 by President Eisenhower, the Advanced Research Projects Agency (ARPA) was created to consolidate some of the country's most advanced research. In the 1960s, the agency found that there was a significant shortage of costly computer equipment. In particular, researchers working on similar issues at different institutions were all requesting their own computers. Bob Taylor, director of ARPA's Information Processing Techniques Office (IPTO), noted the rising costs and wasted duplication and suggested developing electronic linkages between computers to enable researchers to pool their efforts and make more efficient use of precious computer resources. The ARPA cost concerns coincided with security concerns voiced at the RAND Corporation regarding the vulnerability of the national communications network. RAND researchers noted that the country's ability to launch a counterstrike against an attack depended upon the operational survival of the national long-distance networks.

The design of the initial network, dubbed ARPANET, reflected these joint concerns and helps explain the structure and limitations of today's Internet. The first distinguishing characteristic of ARPANET was the use of a distributed network. Responding to the need for a network that could withstand nuclear attack, the distributed network model avoided using a central command. The network consisted of numerous stand alone computers or nodes, each connected to a neighboring node, with the graphical appearance of a fish net or spider web. The distributed model ensured that a single message could take many different routes to get from point A to point B. If part of the network was incapacitated, a message could still travel through an alternate route.

The second distinguishing characteristic of the network was the use of fractured messages, later known as packet switching. Packet switching broke single messages into a series of smaller blocks or packets. When a message was sent, the computer created a series of packets, each containing a final address, which would be transported using different routes and then reassembled at their final destination. Along the way, each node would use packet switchers to direct the packet toward its destination, using whichever path was quickest based on current data traffic patterns. This approach added security to avoid interception of the entire message and allowed for network resources to be more efficiently allocated by maximizing use of the various routes.

In 1968, the consulting firm of Bolt Beranek and Newman (BBN) was commissioned to develop packet switchers called Interface Message Processors (IMPs). Within two years, ARPANET was a reality with IMPs installed at four institutions: UCLA, Stanford, UC Santa Barbara, and the University of Utah. The network grew

---

† Originally published in 73 Washington Law Review (1998) 521 at 526–30. Notes omitted. Reproduced by permission of the publisher.

at a pace of roughly one new node per month in the early 1970s with additional IMPs installed at institutions on both coasts including MIT, Harvard, and Carnegie Mellon.

The transformation of ARPANET into today's Internet began with the development of the Transmission Control Protocol/Internet Protocol (TCP/IP) networking protocol in 1972. Prior to TCP/IP, networks such as ARPANET could only communicate internally. The TCP/IP protocol, universally adopted in 1983, enabled different networks to interchange data without making any internal changes to the network. The protocol used global addressing, which allowed computers to find network addresses by numeric address with no correlation to geographic location.

Foreshadowing the potential uses of the modern-day Internet, email and site information quickly became the network's most popular uses. In fact, a 1973 ARPA study found that three quarters of network traffic was email, a major surprise given the original purpose of resource sharing. An IPTO study later in the decade concluded:

> The largest single surprise of the ARPANET program has been the incredible popularity and success of network mail. There is little doubt that the techniques of network mail developed in connection with the ARPANET program are going to sweep the country and drastically change the techniques used for intercommunication in the public and private sectors.

Early users of the network began to look for news and other information online. As early as 1973, the Stanford node was connected to the Associated Press newswire, which attracted visitors throughout the network. In response to the growing availability of resources, an industry publication, ARPANET News, began to include a "Featured Site" series in which system managers from host computers could describe what was available at their site.

The new network resembled today's Internet in certain respects, but network security was not one of them. In the early 1970s, a computer scientist at Stanford's Artificial Intelligence Lab created a "FINGER" command that allowed users to identify the last time another user had logged on to the network and whether the user had read his or her mail. When some users began to express privacy concerns, the command was altered to enable users to prevent others from using FINGER to access such information. Viewed through today's prism of widespread concern for online privacy, it is somewhat ironic that the creator of the altered command was strongly criticized as being "spineless" and "socially irresponsible" for limiting the network's openness.

The Internet might have remained the province of scientists and the academic community were it not for Tim Berners-Lee, a researcher at the CERN atomic research center in Switzerland. Weary of the trial and error process of finding information on the CERN network, in 1989, Berners-Lee proposed a series of software and network protocols that created the power to browse and navigate among documents by point-and-click commands of the mouse. The new protocol, called Hyper-Text Markup Language (HTML) used hyperlinks to enable users to click on highlighted text and immediately "jump" to a new document. By applying the hyperlinks protocol to the Internet, users could transparently jump between documents on the same computer or on a computer located at the other end of the world — hence the label, World Wide Web.

The final critical innovation in the Internet's growth came in 1993 with the development of advanced (for the time) Web browsing software. Although Web browsers, which enable computers to read HTML, began circulating around the Internet soon after the appearance of the World Wide Web, most were quite primitive and inaccessible to the average computer user. Marc Andreessen, a University of Illinois student, worked at the National Center for Supercomputing Applications (NCSA) to develop a browser with widespread appeal. The result was Mosaic, a browser far more stable and advanced than its predecessors, which allowed incorporation of images onto the Web (until that point the Web had been text only). Mosaic employed an intuitive graphical interface that allowed users to easily scroll up and down pages, return to previously viewed pages, and more easily jump between hyperlinks. Mosaic, available on the UNIX, Windows, and Macintosh operating systems within a year, quickly became the most commonly used Web browser, igniting interest in the Internet that continues to grow unabated.

The Internet has grown from the initial four host computers to nearly thirty million host computers in 240 countries and territories, with an annual growth rate of forty to fifty percent. In the United States alone, there are an estimated sixty-six million Internet users, fifty million of whom have used the World Wide Web. Although the Internet now supports audio, video, and software enhancements such as Java, the underlying structure remains relatively unchanged from its initial design as a communication and resource sharing tool for the scientific community.

This initial design, featuring an open, distributed network, packet switching, and a universal communications protocol, is responsible for both the power and limitations of the Internet. A regulatory structure designed to operate effectively in the virtual environment must take this design into account. Regulators constrained by current technologies should consider the Internet's gradual technological changes, including the development of HTML and the Web browser, and appreciate that today's Internet may not be tomorrow's Internet. As the founders of the Internet themselves admitted in a recent paper:

> One should not conclude that the Internet has now finished changing. The Internet, although a network in name and geography, is a creature of the computer, not the traditional network of the telephone or television industry. It will, indeed it must, continue to change and evolve at the speed of the computer industry if it is to remain relevant.

Notes

As we enter the new millennium, the Internet continues to evolve in several important ways. First, while still expanding upon its central role as an interpersonal communication and information sharing tool (indeed controversial sites such as Napster use peer-to-peer technologies to extend the Internet's information sharing capabilities), the Internet has also begun to dramatically extend its functionality into other services. Using the Internet for banking, education, entertainment, and the selection and purchase of a broad variety of goods and services is well established and growing at a remarkable pace. On the horizon are Application Service Providers (ASPs) that use the Internet to deliver services online by effectively replacing the need to install both simple and complex software programs on a personal computer. One of the earliest and most successful implementations of this technology is Web-based email services such as Hotmail, which enrolled millions of users.

Alongside the growing trend toward Internet-based services is the Internet's convergence with other media, particularly television and wireless communications. Surfing the Web on a television has been available for several years as Web TV enables html and other Web content to be transmitted in an unused segment of the broadcast signal and appear on the television screen. A very simple user interface allows browsing, email and, of course, commerce.

The convergence of wireless services and the Internet serves a similar purpose. With the increasing popularity of wireless phones, pagers, and other devices, suppliers of Internet connectivity embraced the opportunity to provide access without the necessity of a fixed connection. The distinction between online and offline is rapidly blurring as the Internet becomes integrated into every aspect of our daily lives.

Discussion Questions

1. The historical development of the Internet is marked by open systems and the absence of centralized control. Do you think this characterization will remain valid in five years? Ten years? How will attempts to develop proprietary standards impact the Internet's development?

2. Who will exert the greatest influence over the Internet's development? The technologists? Governments? Corporations? Individual Internet users? Might the answer not be a "who" but rather a "what", such as changes in social structure, or new technological developments?

As noted in the following study commissioned by Industry Canada, the Canadian Internet experience closely mirrors the American experience. In recent years, the Canadian Internet infrastructure has grown at an incredible rate with the expectation that the latest Internet backbone, CA*Net3, will provide Canadians with the fastest network in the world.

Regulation of the Internet: A Technological Perspective[†]

GERRY MILLER, GERRI SINCLAIR,
DAVID SUTHERLAND & JULIE ZILBER

THE CANADIAN EXPERIENCE (FROM R&D TO COMMERCIAL)
The history of the Canadian Internet closely parallels the American experience. In the 1970's, there were regional networks in a number of locations interconnecting Universities in the region.

---

† (March 1999), online: Industry Canada Homepage <http://strategis.ic.gc.ca/SSG/it05082e.html>. Source of Information: Industry Canada. Reproduced with the permission of the Minister of Public Works and Government Services Canada, 1999.

These networks used proprietary communications protocols, and, typically, interconnected large mainframe computers. The main use was for transferring large files of information.

At the start of the 1980's, newer networking technologies started to appear. CDNnet, a research network founded to develop email standards was established and connected a number of Universities in the country. NETNORTH, the Canadian equivalent of BITNET in the US, was established with the help of funding from IBM Canada by the University community as a national network, and was connected to similar networks in other countries.

Email became a way of life for the academic community. Towards the end of that decade, the first TCP/IP networks were established in Canadian Universities in Ontario and British Columbia. These were connected directly to the US backbone with cross-border links, and part of the Canadian academic community became members of the burgeoning Internet community.

In 1989 the NETNORTH board of directors, made up of representatives from the Canadian University community, developed a strategic plan to carry NETNORTH forward and transform it to a TCP/IP technology. Funding was sought from the federal government and a $2,000,000 start-up grant was awarded by the National Research Council (NRC). In-kind contributions were also received from IBM Canada.

The NETNORTH community incorporated a not-for-profit organization to operate the network, called CA*Net Networking Inc. The board of directors was made up of one representative from each province in the country as well as representatives from the University of Toronto, the network operator and from NRC. Most of the board members were from the University community.

At the same time, regional academic networks were established in each province:

- British Columbia: BCNet
- Alberta: ARNet
- Saskatchewan: SASKNet
- Manitoba: MBNet
- Ontario: Onet
- Quebec: RISQ
- New Brunswick: NBNet
- Prince Edward Island: PEINet
- Nova Scotia: NSTN
- Newfoundland: NLNet

CA*Net interconnected these regional networks and provided three connections to the NSFNet in the US through Vancouver, Toronto and Montreal. The original connections were 56 Kbps, but the rapid growth of Internet traffic in 1990 and 1991 drove the need for increased network capacity.

In January of 1993, the federal government announced the formation of CANARIE, an organization created to stimulate industrial research and development on broadband network facilities and applications. One of its first initiatives was the upgrading of the CA*Net backbone to T1 speeds, or 1.54 Mbps. Similar upgrades were done in regional networks. At the same time, CANARIE funded the connection of Canada's north by funding links to regional networks in the Northwest Territories and the Yukon.

Internet growth in Canada paralleled the experience in other countries. It became exponential, and further upgrades were required to T3 speeds or 45 Mbps. In some cases multiple T3 connections were needed, particularly on the US links.

In 1995, the University of Toronto stopped operating the network, and, after a tender process, network operations were awarded to Bell Advanced Communications.

In 1996, it became evident to the CA*Net board of directors that the Canadian Internet had evolved beyond its origins as an academic research and development network to a fast-growing commercial network. The board then decided the time had come to transition the Canadian Internet to a commercial one, and after another tender process Bell Canada was awarded the network. It now operates as a commercial Bell offering. In recognition of the work of the founding CA*Net community, CA*Net and Bell Canada created the CA*Net Institute, a funding organization dedicated to promoting the use of the Internet in the spirit of the original CA*net. This organization is in place and the first awards have been given to a wide variety of Internet-related projects.

At the present time, this backbone network is one of many in Canada. Companies such as Sprint, BCT.Telus, and MetroNet as well as Bell are installing and upgrading national Internet backbone networks, connecting to the global Internet through a number of locations. Speeds of these backbones are up to 655 Mbps, 12,000 times faster than the original CA*Net nine years ago.

Theoretical speeds using new broadband network technologies are up to 1.5 Tbps, another large increase. Since the unit cost of bandwidth becomes cheaper as overall network speeds increase, the availability of higher speeds encourages network growth and its use by a widening clientele in both the public and private sectors.

These networks are connected to the global Internet through cross-border connections to the US, Europe and Asia. As well, there are many private connections outside Canada for corporate Intranets. While the number of cross-border Internet connections is not easily determined, it is large and growing.

The volume of traffic on the Canadian Internet is growing at typical rates, doubling every 4–6 months. Since there are a number of national Internet backbones, and since such information is proprietary for competitive reasons, determining total traffic is difficult. However, it is certainly now in the hundreds of gigabits per second, and is rapidly approaching terabits per second. The other fundamental change in the Canadian Internet has been the shift from research traffic to commercial use. Just a few years ago, the majority of the traffic was for research and education purposes. Now, of course, the traffic is overwhelmingly commercial.

Notes

For a detailed look at the Internet's development, consider *A Brief History of the Internet*, an essay written by several of the Internet's founders. The essay can be found on the Internet Society's Web site at <http://www.isoc.org/internet-history/brief.html>.

ACLU v. *Reno*, the well-known challenge to the *Communications Decency Act*, marked the first time the U.S. Supreme Court faced the issue of Internet regulation. As the case wound its way through the U.S. court system, the district court provided a helpful review of Internet access and activities that provided both the litigants and the judiciary with the background necessary to effectively adjudicate the case.

American Civil Liberties Union v. Reno[†]

How Individuals Access the Internet

Individuals have a wide variety of avenues to access cyberspace in general, and the Internet in particular. In terms of physical access, there are two common methods to establish an actual link to the Internet. First, one can use a computer or computer terminal that is directly (and usually permanently) connected to a computer network that is itself directly or indirectly connected to the Internet. Second, one can use a "personal computer" with a "modem" to connect over a telephone line to a larger computer or computer network that is itself directly or indirectly connected to the Internet. As detailed below, both direct and modem connections are made available to people by a wide variety of academic, governmental, or commercial entities.

Students, faculty, researchers, and others affiliated with the vast majority of colleges and universities in the United States can access the Internet through their educational institutions. Such access is often via direct connection using computers located in campus libraries, offices, or computer centers, or may be through telephone access using a modem from a student's or professor's campus or off-campus location. Some colleges and universities install "ports" or outlets for direct network connections in each dormitory room or provide access via computers located in common areas in dormitories. Such access enables students and professors to use information and content provided by the college or university itself, and to use the vast amount of research resources and other information available on the Internet worldwide.

Similarly, Internet resources and access are sufficiently important to many corporations and other employers that those employers link their office computer networks to the Internet and provide employees with direct or modem access to the office network (and thus to the Internet). Such access might be used by, for example, a corporation involved in scientific or medical research or manufacturing to enable corporate employees to exchange information and ideas with academic researchers in their fields.

Those who lack access to the Internet through their schools or employers still have a variety of ways they can access the Internet. Many communities across the country have established "free-nets" or community networks to provide their citizens with a local link to the Internet (and to provide local-oriented content and discussion groups). The first such community network, the Cleveland Free-Net Community Computer System, was established in 1986, and free-nets now exist in scores of communities as diverse as Richmond, Virginia, Tallahassee, Florida, Seattle, Washington, and San Diego, California. Individuals typically can access free-nets at little or no

---

[†] 929 F. Supp. 824 (E.D. Pa. 1996).

cost via modem connection or by using computers available in community buildings. Free-nets are often operated by a local library, educational institution, or non profit community group.

Individuals can also access the Internet through many local libraries. Libraries often offer patrons use of computers that are linked to the Internet. In addition, some libraries offer telephone modem access to the libraries' computers, which are themselves connected to the Internet. Increasingly, patrons now use library services and resources without ever physically entering the library itself. Libraries typically provide such direct or modem access at no cost to the individual user.

Individuals can also access the Internet by patronizing an increasing number of storefront "computer coffee shops," where customers — while they drink their coffee — can use computers provided by the shop to access the Internet. Such Internet access is typically provided by the shop for a small hourly fee.

Individuals can also access the Internet through commercial and non-commercial "Internet service providers" that typically offer modem telephone access to a computer or computer network linked to the Internet. Many such providers — including the members of plaintiff Commercial Internet Exchange Association — are commercial entities offering Internet access for a monthly or hourly fee. Some Internet service providers, however, are non-profit organizations that offer free or very low cost access to the Internet. For example, the International Internet Association offers free modem access to the Internet upon request. Also, a number of trade or other non-profit associations offer Internet access as a service to members.

Another common way for individuals to access the Internet is through one of the major national commercial "online services" such as America Online, CompuServe, the Microsoft Network, or Prodigy. These online services offer nationwide computer networks (so that subscribers can dial-in to a local telephone number), and the services provide extensive and well organized content within their own proprietary computer networks. In addition to allowing access to the extensive content available within each online service, the services also allow subscribers to link to the much larger resources of the Internet. Full access to the online service (including access to the Internet) can be obtained for modest monthly or hourly fees. The major commercial online services have almost twelve million individual subscribers across the United States.

In addition to using the national commercial online services, individuals can also access the Internet using some (but not all) of the thousands of local dial-in computer services, often called "bulletin board systems" or "BBSs." With an investment of as little as $2,000.00 and the cost of a telephone line, individuals, non-profit organizations, advocacy groups, and businesses can offer their own dial-in computer "bulletin board" service where friends, members, subscribers, or customers can exchange ideas and information. BBSs range from single computers with only one telephone line into the computer (allowing only one user at a time), to single computers with many telephone lines into the computer (allowing multiple simultaneous users), to multiple linked computers each servicing multiple dial-in telephone lines (allowing multiple simultaneous users). Some (but not all) of these BBS systems offer direct or indirect links to the Internet. Some BBS systems charge users a nominal fee for access, while many others are free to the individual users.

Although commercial access to the Internet is growing rapidly, many users of the Internet — such as college students and staff — do not individually pay for access (except to the extent, for example, that the cost of computer services is a component of college tuition). These and other Internet users can access the Internet without paying for such access with a credit card or other form of payment.

Methods to Communicate Over the Internet

Once one has access to the Internet, there are a wide variety of different methods of communication and information exchange over the network. These many methods of communication and information retrieval are constantly evolving and are therefore difficult to categorize concisely. The most common methods of communications on the Internet (as well as within the major online services) can be roughly grouped into six categories:

(1) one-to-one messaging (such as "e-mail"),
(2) one-to-many messaging (such as "listserv"),
(3) distributed message databases (such as "USENET newsgroups"),
(4) real time communication (such as "Internet Relay Chat"),
(5) real time remote computer utilization (such as "telnet"), and
(6) remote information retrieval (such as "ftp," "gopher," and the "World Wide Web").

Most of these methods of communication can be used to transmit text, data, computer programs, sound, visual images (i.e., pictures), and moving video images.

One-to-one messaging. One method of communication on the Internet is via electronic mail, or "e-mail," comparable in principle to sending a first class letter. One can address and transmit a message to one or more other people. E-mail on the Internet is not routed through a central control point, and can take many and varying paths to the recipients. Unlike postal mail, simple e-mail generally is not "sealed" or secure, and can be accessed or viewed on intermediate computers between the sender and recipient (unless the message is encrypted).

One-to-many messaging. The Internet also contains automatic mailing list services (such as "listservs"), [also referred to by witnesses as "mail exploders"] that allow communications about particular subjects of interest to a group of people. For example, people can subscribe to a "listserv" mailing list on a particular topic of interest to them. The subscriber can submit messages on the topic to the listserv that are forwarded (via e-mail), either automatically or through a human moderator overseeing the listserv, to anyone who has subscribed to the mailing list. A recipient of such a message can reply to the message and have the reply also distributed to everyone on the mailing list. This service provides the capability to keep abreast of developments or events in a particular subject area. Most listserv-type mailing lists automatically forward all incoming messages to all mailing list subscribers. There are thousands of such mailing list services on the Internet, collectively with hundreds of thousands of subscribers. Users of "open" listservs typically can add or remove their names from the mailing list automatically, with no direct human involvement. Listservs may also be "closed," i.e., only allowing for one's acceptance into the listserv by a human moderator.

Distributed message databases. Similar in function to listservs — but quite different in how communications are transmitted — are distributed message databases such as "USENET newsgroups." User-sponsored newsgroups are among the most popular and widespread applications of Internet services, and cover all imaginable topics of interest to users. Like listservs, newsgroups are open discussions and exchanges on particular topics. Users, however, need not subscribe to the discussion mailing list in advance, but can instead access the database at any time. Some USENET newsgroups are "moderated" but most are open access. For the moderated newsgroups, all messages to the newsgroup are forwarded to one person who can screen them for relevance to the topics under discussion. USENET newsgroups are disseminated using ad hoc, peer to peer connections between approximately 200,000 computers (called USENET "servers") around the world. For unmoderated newsgroups, when an individual user with access to a USENET server posts a message to a newsgroup, the message is automatically forwarded to all adjacent USENET servers that furnish access to the newsgroup, and it is then propagated to the servers adjacent to those servers, etc. The messages are temporarily stored on each receiving server, where they are available for review and response by individual users. The messages are automatically and periodically purged from each system after a time to make room for new messages. Responses to messages, like the original messages, are automatically distributed to all other computers receiving the newsgroup or forwarded to a moderator in the case of a moderated newsgroup. The dissemination of messages to USENET servers around the world is an automated process that does not require direct human intervention or review.

There are newsgroups on more than fifteen thousand different subjects. In 1994, approximately 70,000 messages were posted to newsgroups each day, and those messages were distributed to the approximately 190,000 computers or computer networks that participate in the USENET newsgroup system. Once the messages reach the approximately 190,000 receiving computers or computer networks, they are available to individual users of those computers or computer networks. Collectively, almost 100,000 new messages (or "articles") are posted to newsgroups each day.

Real time communication. In addition to transmitting messages that can be later read or accessed, individuals on the Internet can engage in an immediate dialog, in "real time", with other people on the Internet. In its simplest forms, "talk" allows one-to-one communications and "Internet Relay Chat" (or IRC) allows two or more to type messages to each other that almost immediately appear on the others' computer screens. IRC is analogous to a telephone party line, using a computer and keyboard rather than a telephone. With IRC, however, at any one time there are thousands of different party lines available, in which collectively tens of thousands of users are engaging in conversations on a huge range of subjects. Moreover, one can create a new party line to discuss a different topic at any time. Some IRC conversations are "moderated" or include "channel operators."

In addition, commercial online services such as America Online, CompuServe, the Microsoft Network, and Prodigy have their own "chat" systems allowing their members to converse.

Real time remote computer utilization. Another method to use information on the Internet is to access and control remote computers in "real time" using "telnet." For example, using telnet, a researcher at a university would be able to use the computing power of a supercomputer located at a different university. A student can use telnet to connect to a remote library to access the library's online card catalog program.

Remote information retrieval. The final major category of communication may be the most well known use of the Internet — the search for and retrieval of information located on remote computers. There are three primary methods to locate and retrieve information on the Internet.

A simple method uses "ftp" (or file transfer protocol) to list the names of computer files available on a remote computer, and to transfer one or more of those files to an individual's local computer.

Another approach uses a program and format named "gopher" to guide an individual's search through the resources available on a remote computer.

The World Wide Web

A third approach, and fast becoming the most well-known on the Internet, is the "World Wide Web." The Web utilizes a "hypertext" formatting language called hypertext markup language (HTML), and programs that "browse" the Web can display HTML documents containing text, images, sound, animation and moving video. Any HTML document can include links to other types of information or resources, so that while viewing an HTML document that, for example, describes resources available on the Internet, one can "click" using a computer mouse on the description of the resource and be immediately connected to the resource itself. Such "hyperlinks" allow information to be accessed and organized in very flexible ways, and allow people to locate and efficiently view related information even if the information is stored on numerous computers all around the world.

Purpose. The World Wide Web (W3C) was created to serve as the platform for a global, online store of knowledge, containing information from a diversity of sources and accessible to Internet users around the world. Though information on the Web is contained in individual computers, the fact that each of these computers is connected to the Internet through W3C protocols allows all of the information to become part of a single body of knowledge. It is currently the most advanced information system developed on the Internet, and embraces within its data model most information in previous networked information systems such as ftp, gopher, wais, and Usenet.

History. W3C was originally developed at CERN, the European Particle Physics Laboratory, and was initially used to allow information sharing within internationally dispersed teams of researchers and engineers. Originally aimed at the High Energy Physics community, it has spread to other areas and attracted much interest in user support, resource recovery, and many other areas which depend on collaborative and information sharing. The Web has extended beyond the scientific and academic community to include communications by individuals, non-profit organizations, and businesses.

Basic Operation. The World Wide Web is a series of documents stored in different computers all over the Internet. Documents contain information stored in a variety of formats, including text, still images, sounds, and video. An essential element of the Web is that any document has an address (rather like a telephone number). Most Web documents contain "links." These are short sections of text or image which refer to another document. Typically the linked text is blue or underlined when displayed, and when selected by the user, the referenced document is automatically displayed, wherever in the world it actually is stored. Links for example are used to lead from overview documents to more detailed documents, from tables of contents to particular pages, but also as cross-references, footnotes, and new forms of information structure.

Many organizations now have "home pages" on the Web. These are documents which provide a set of links designed to represent the organization, and through links from the home page, guide the user directly or indirectly to information about or relevant to that organization.

As an example of the use of links, if these Findings were to be put on a World Wide Web site, its home page might contain links such as those:

> THE NATURE OF CYBERSPACE
> CREATION OF THE INTERNET AND THE DEVELOPMENT
> OF CYBERSPACE
> HOW PEOPLE ACCESS THE INTERNET
> METHODS TO COMMUNICATE OVER THE INTERNET

Each of these links takes the user of the site from the beginning of the Findings to the appropriate section within this Adjudication. Links may also take the user from the original Web site to another Web site on another computer connected to the Internet. These links from one computer to another, from one document to another across the Internet, are what unify the Web into a single body of knowledge, and what makes the Web unique. The Web was designed with a maximum target time to follow a link of one tenth of a second.

Publishing. The World Wide Web exists fundamentally as a platform through which people and organizations can communicate through shared information. When information is made available, it is said to be "published" on the Web. Publishing on the Web simply requires that the "publisher" has a computer connected to the Internet and that the computer is running W3C server software. The computer can be as simple as a small personal computer costing less than $1500 dollars or as complex as a multi-million dollar mainframe computer. Many Web publishers choose instead to lease disk storage space from someone else who has the necessary computer facilities, eliminating the need for actually owning any equipment oneself.

The Web, as a universe of network accessible information, contains a variety of documents prepared with quite varying degrees of care, from the hastily typed idea, to the professionally executed corporate profile. The power of the Web stems from the ability of a link to point to any document, regardless of its status or physical location.

Information to be published on the Web must also be formatted according to the rules of the Web standards. These standardized formats assure that all Web users who want to read the material will be able to view it. Web standards are sophisticated and flexible enough that they have grown to meet the publishing needs of many large corporations, banks, brokerage houses, newspapers and magazines which now publish "online" editions of their material, as well as government agencies, and even courts, which use the Web to disseminate information to the public. At the same time, Web publishing is simple enough that thousands of individual users and small community organizations are using the Web to publish their own personal "home pages," the equivalent of individualized newsletters about that person or organization, which are available to everyone on the Web.

Web publishers have a choice to make their Web sites open to the general pool of all Internet users, or close them, thus making the information accessible only to those with advance authorization. Many publishers choose to keep their sites open to all in order to give their information the widest potential audience. In the event that the publishers choose to maintain restrictions on access, this may be accomplished by assigning specific user names and passwords as a prerequisite to access to the site. Or, in the case of Web sites maintained for internal use of one organization, access will only be allowed from other computers within that organization's local network.

Searching the Web. A variety of systems have developed that allow users of the Web to search particular information among all of the public sites that are part of the Web. Services such as Yahoo, Magellan, Altavista, Webcrawler, and Lycos are all services known as "search engines" which allow users to search for Web sites that contain certain categories of information, or to search for key words. For example, a Web user looking for the text of Supreme Court opinions would type the words "Supreme Court" into a search engine, and then be presented with a list of World Wide Web sites that contain Supreme Court information. This list would actually be a series of links to those sites. Having searched out a number of sites that might contain the desired information, the user would then follow individual links, browsing through the information on each site, until the desired material is found. For many content providers on the Web, the ability to be found by these search engines is very important.

Common standards. The Web links together disparate information on an ever-growing number of Internet-linked computers by setting common information storage formats (HTML) and a common language for the exchange of Web documents (HTTP). Although the information itself may be in many different formats, and stored on computers which are not otherwise compatible, the basic Web standards provide a basic set of standards which allow communication and exchange of information. Despite the fact that many types of computers are used on the Web, and the fact that many of these machines are otherwise incompatible, those who "publish" information on the Web are able to communicate with those who seek to access information with little difficulty because of these basic technical standards.

A distributed system with no centralized control. Running on tens of thousands of individual computers on the Internet, the Web is what is known as a distributed system. The Web was designed so that organizations with computers containing information can become part of the Web simply by attaching their computers to the Internet and running appropriate World Wide Web software. No single organization controls any membership in the Web, nor is there any single centralized point from which individual Web sites or services can be blocked from the Web. From a user's perspective, it may appear to be a single, integrated system, but in reality it has no centralized control point.

Contrast to closed databases. The Web's open, distributed, decentralized nature stands in sharp contrast to most information systems that have come before it. Private information services such as Westlaw, Lexis/Nexis, and Dialog, have contained large storehouses of knowledge, and can be accessed from the Internet with the appropriate passwords and access software. However, these databases are not linked together into a single whole, as is the World Wide Web.

Success of the Web in research, education, and political activities. The World Wide Web has become so popular because of its open, distributed, and easy-to-use nature. Rather than requiring those who seek information to purchase new software or hardware, and to learn a new kind of system for each new database of information they seek to access, the Web environment makes it easy for users to jump from one set of information to another. By the same token, the open nature of the Web makes it easy for publishers to reach their intended audiences without having to know in advance what kind of computer each potential reader has, and what kind of software they will be using.

Discussion Questions

1. Consider that this judgment is now about four years old. How much has the Internet changed during the course of those four years?

2. When this judgment was written, most judgments and articles written about the Internet began with an introduction to the Internet (much like this book). Is this still necessary? Has the Internet become sufficiently integrated into our everyday routine that we should be able to assume ready knowledge of the Internet?

2

Competing Visions of Internet Law

In the early days of the Internet, discussion of Internet law centered largely on whether the Internet could or should be regulated. The Internet of those days bore little resemblance to the Internet of today. Rather, the Internet of the 1980s and early 1990s had a communal feel, where users generally trusted one another and commercial activities were frowned upon. Longtime Internet users often yearn for that Internet of old — a space governed by the inhabitants, where the Internet genuinely constituted a place separate and apart from real space.

Today the Internet has emerged as an integral part of our communications and social infrastructure, with millions of users and companies online. This growth resulted in critical changes to the legal regulation of Internet-based activity. Legal scholars have now advanced beyond the issue of whether to regulate Internet activity and are instead focusing on the more challenging question of *how* to regulate such activity.

Notwithstanding these developments, the hope that the Internet can return to its roots remains firmly in place for many users. This view is best illustrated by John Perry Barlow's *Declaration of the Independence of Cyberspace*. Barlow, a co-founder of the influential Electronic Frontier Foundation, first published the declaration on the Internet in the wake of the U.S. Congress enacting the *Communications Decency Act*, which was the first U.S. national attempt at Internet content regulation. The declaration attracted widespread attention, as it captured the frustration of thousands of Internet users who felt helpless as they witnessed the profound change enveloping the Internet legal landscape.

"A Declaration of the Independence of Cyberspace"†

JOHN PERRY BARLOW

Date: Fri, 9 Feb 1996 17:16:35 +0100
To: barlow@eff.org
From: John Perry Barlow
Subject: A Cyberspace Independence Declaration

Yesterday, that great invertebrate in the White House signed into the law the Telecom "Reform" Act of 1996, while Tipper Gore took digital photographs of the proceedings to be included in a book called "24 Hours in Cyberspace."

I had also been asked to participate in the creation of this book by writing something appropriate to the moment. Given the atrocity that this legislation would seek to inflict on the Net, I decided it was as good a time as any to dump some tea in the virtual harbor.

After all, the Telecom "Reform" Act, passed in the Senate with only 5 dissenting votes, makes it unlawful, and punishable by a $250,000 to say "shit" online. Or, for that matter, to say any of the other 7 dirty words prohibited in broadcast media. Or to discuss abortion openly. Or to talk about any bodily function in any but the most clinical terms.

It attempts to place more restrictive constraints on the conversation in Cyberspace than presently exist in the Senate cafeteria, where I have dined and heard colorful indecencies spoken by United States senators on every occasion I did.

This bill was enacted upon us by people who haven't the slightest idea who we are or where our conversation is being conducted. It is, as my good friend and Wired Editor Louis Rossetto put it, as though "the illiterate could tell you what to read."

Well, fuck them.

Or, more to the point, let us now take our leave of them. They have declared war on Cyberspace. Let us show them how cunning, baffling, and powerful we can be in our own defense.

I have written something (with characteristic grandiosity) that I hope will become one of many means to this end. If you find it useful, I hope you will pass it on as widely as possible. You can leave my name off it if you like, because I don't care about the credit. I really don't.

But I do hope this cry will echo across Cyberspace, changing and growing and self-replicating, until it becomes a great shout equal to the idiocy they have just inflicted upon us.

I give you...

A DECLARATION OF THE INDEPENDENCE OF CYBERSPACE
Governments of the Industrial World, you weary giants of flesh and steel, I come from Cyberspace, the new home of Mind. On behalf of the future, I ask you of the past to leave us alone. You are not welcome among us. You have no sovereignty where we gather.

---

† Online: <http://www.eff.org/~barlow/Declaration-Final.html>. Reproduced with permission.

We have no elected government, nor are we likely to have one, so I address you with no greater authority than that with which liberty itself always speaks. I declare the global social space we are building to be naturally independent of the tyrannies you seek to impose on us. You have no moral right to rule us nor do you possess any methods of enforcement we have true reason to fear.

Governments derive their just powers from the consent of the governed. You have neither solicited nor received ours. We did not invite you. You do not know us, nor do you know our world. Cyberspace does not lie within your borders. Do not think that you can build it, as though it were a public construction project. You cannot. It is an act of nature and it grows itself through our collective actions.

You have not engaged in our great and gathering conversation, nor did you create the wealth of our marketplaces. You do not know our culture, our ethics, or the unwritten codes that already provide our society more order than could be obtained by any of your impositions.

You claim there are problems among us that you need to solve. You use this claim as an excuse to invade our precincts. Many of these problems don't exist.

Where there are real conflicts, where there are wrongs, we will identify them and address them by our means. We are forming our own Social Contract. This governance will arise according to the conditions of our world, not yours.

Our world is different.

Cyberspace consists of transactions, relationships, and thought itself, arrayed like a standing wave in the web of our communications. Ours is a world that is both everywhere and nowhere, but it is not where bodies live.

We are creating a world that all may enter without privilege or prejudice accorded by race, economic power, military force, or station of birth.

We are creating a world where anyone, anywhere may express his or her beliefs, no matter how singular, without fear of being coerced into silence or conformity.

Your legal concepts of property, expression, identity, movement, and context do not apply to us. They are all based on matter, and there is no matter here.

Our identities have no bodies, so, unlike you, we cannot obtain order by physical coercion. We believe that from ethics, enlightened self-interest, and the commonweal, our governance will emerge. Our identities may be distributed across many of your jurisdictions. The only law that all our constituent cultures would generally recognize is the Golden Rule. We hope we will be able to build our particular solutions on that basis. But we cannot accept the solutions you are attempting to impose.

In the United States, you have today created a law, the Telecommunications Reform Act, which repudiates your own Constitution and insults the dreams of Jefferson, Washington, Mill, Madison, DeToqueville, and Brandeis. These dreams must now be born anew in us.

You are terrified of your own children, since they are natives in a world where you will always be immigrants. Because you fear them, you entrust your bureaucracies with the parental responsibilities you are too cowardly to confront yourselves. In our world, all the sentiments and expressions of humanity, from the debasing to the angelic, are parts of a seamless whole, the global conversation of bits. We cannot separate the air that chokes from the air upon which wings beat.

In China, Germany, France, Russia, Singapore, Italy and the United States, you are trying to ward off the virus of liberty by erecting guard posts at the frontiers of Cyberspace. These may keep out the contagion for a small time, but they will not work in a world that will soon be blanketed in bit-bearing media.

Your increasingly obsolete information industries would perpetuate themselves by proposing laws, in America and elsewhere, that claim to own speech itself throughout the world. These laws would declare ideas to be another industrial product, no more noble than pig iron. In our world, whatever the human mind may create can be reproduced and distributed infinitely at no cost. The global conveyance of thought no longer requires your factories to accomplish.

These increasingly hostile and colonial measures place us in the same position as those previous lovers of freedom and self-determination who had to reject the authorities of distant, uninformed powers. We must declare our virtual selves immune to your sovereignty, even as we continue to consent to your rule over our bodies. We will spread ourselves across the Planet so that no one can arrest our thoughts.

We will create a civilization of the Mind in Cyberspace. May it be more humane and fair than the world your governments have made before.

Is cyberspace a place? That question was a central theme of early Internet scholarship as leading academics and practitioners debated the merits of an Internet-specific legal structure and the viability of applying traditional, real space rules to online activity.

The leading proponent of the "cyberspace is a place" camp is Professor David Post, a law professor at Temple University in Philadelphia. His 1996 article, *Law and Borders — The Rise of Law in Cyberspace*, co-authored with David Johnson, is one of the most widely read Internet law articles, attracting the attention of legal scholars worldwide.

Law And Borders — The Rise Of Law In Cyberspace[†]

DAVID R. JOHNSON & DAVID POST

Global computer-based communications cut across territorial borders, creating a new realm of human activity and undermining the feasibility — and legitimacy — of laws based on geographic boundaries. While these electronic communications play havoc with geographic boundaries, a new boundary, made up of the screens and passwords that separate the virtual world from the "real world" of atoms, emerges. This new boundary defines a distinct Cyberspace that needs and can create its own law and legal institutions. Territorially based law-makers and law-enforcers find this new environment deeply threatening. But established territorial authorities may yet learn to defer to the self-regulatory efforts of Cyberspace participants who care most deeply about this new digital trade in ideas, information, and services. Separated from doctrine tied to territorial jurisdictions, new rules will emerge to govern a wide range of new phenomena that have no clear parallel in the nonvirtual world. These new rules will play the role of law by defining legal personhood and property, resolving

---

† (1996) 48:5 Stan. L. Rev. 1367. Notes omitted. Republished with permission of the Stanford Law Review, 559 Nathan Abbott Way, Palo Alto, CA 94305. Reproduced by permission of the publisher via Copyright Clearance Center.

disputes, and crystallizing a collective conversation about online participants' core values.

We take for granted a world in which geographical borders — lines separating physical spaces — are of primary importance in determining legal rights and responsibilities. Territorial borders, generally speaking, delineate areas within which different sets of legal rules apply. There has until now been a general correspondence between borders drawn in physical space (between nation states or other political entities) and borders in "law space." For example, if we were to superimpose a "law map" (delineating areas where different rules apply to particular behaviors) onto a political map of the world, the two maps would overlap to a significant degree, with clusters of homogeneous applicable law and legal institutions fitting within existing physical borders.

. . . .

Physical borders are not, of course, simply arbitrary creations. Although they may be based on historical accident, geographic borders for law make sense in the real world. Their logical relationship to the development and enforcement of legal rules is based on a number of related considerations.

Power. Control over physical space, and the people and things located in that space, is a defining attribute of sovereignty and statehood. Law-making requires some mechanism for law enforcement, which in turn depends on the ability to exercise physical control over, and impose coercive sanctions on, law-violators. For example, the U.S. government does not impose its trademark law on a Brazilian business operating in Brazil, at least in part because imposing sanctions on the Brazilian business would require assertion of physical control over business owners. Such an assertion of control would conflict with the Brazilian government's recognized monopoly on the use of force over its citizens.

Effects. The correspondence between physical boundaries and "law space" boundaries also reflects a deeply rooted relationship between physical proximity and the effects of any particular behavior. That is, Brazilian trademark law governs the use of marks in Brazil because that use has a more direct impact on persons and assets within Brazil than anywhere else. For example, a large sign over "Jones' Restaurant" in Rio de Janeiro is unlikely to have an impact on the operation of "Jones' Restaurant" in Oslo, Norway, for we may assume that there is no substantial overlap between the customers, or competitors, of these two entities. Protection of the former's trademark does not — and probably should not — affect the protection afforded the latter's.

Legitimacy. We generally accept the notion that the persons within a geographically defined border are the ultimate source of law-making authority for activities within that border. The "consent of the governed" implies that those subject to a set of laws must have a role in their formulation. By virtue of the preceding considerations, those people subject to a sovereign's laws, and most deeply affected by those laws, are the individuals who are located in particular physical spaces. Similarly, allocation of responsibility among levels of government proceeds on the assumption that, for many legal problems, physical proximity between the responsible authority and those most directly affected by the law will improve the quality of decision making, and that it is easier to determine the will of those individuals in physical proximity to one another.

Notice. Physical boundaries are also appropriate for the delineation of "law space" in the physical world because they can give notice that the rules change when the boundaries are crossed. Proper boundaries have signposts that provide warning that we will be required, after crossing, to abide by different rules, and physical boundaries — lines on the geographical map — are generally well-equipped to serve this signpost function.

Cyberspace radically undermines the relationship between legally significant (online) phenomena and physical location. The rise of the global computer network is destroying the link between geographical location and: (1) the power of local governments to assert control over online behavior; (2) the effects of online behavior on individuals or things; (3) the legitimacy of a local sovereign's efforts to regulate global phenomena; and (4) the ability of physical location to give notice of which sets of rules apply. The Net thus radically subverts the system of rule-making based on borders between physical spaces, at least with respect to the claim that Cyberspace should naturally be governed by territorially defined rules.

Cyberspace has no territorially based boundaries, because the cost and speed of message transmission on the Net is almost entirely independent of physical location. Messages can be transmitted from one physical location to any other location without degradation, decay, or substantial delay, and without any physical cues or barriers that might otherwise keep certain geographically remote places and people separate from one another. The Net enables transactions between people who do not know, and in many cases cannot know, each other's physical location. Location remains vitally important, but only location within a virtual space consisting of the "addresses" of the machines between which messages and information are routed. The system is indifferent to the physical location of those machines, and there is no necessary connection between an Internet address and a physical jurisdiction. Although the domain name initially assigned to a given machine may be associated with an Internet Protocol address that corresponds to that machine's physical location (for example, a ".uk" domain name extension), the machine may be physically moved without affecting its domain name. Alternatively, the owner of the domain name might request that the name become associated with an entirely different machine, in a different physical location. Thus, a server with a ".uk" domain name need not be located in the United Kingdom, a server with a ".com" domain name may be anywhere, and users, generally speaking, are not even aware of the location of the server that stores the content that they read.

The power to control activity in Cyberspace has only the most tenuous connections to physical location. Nonetheless, many governments' first response to electronic communications crossing their territorial borders is to try to stop or regulate that flow of information. Rather than permitting self-regulation by participants in online transactions, many governments establish trade barriers, attempt to tax border-crossing cargo, and respond especially sympathetically to claims that information coming into the jurisdiction might prove harmful to local residents. As online information becomes more important to local citizens, these efforts increase. In particular, resistance to "transborder data flow" (TDF) reflects the concerns of sovereign nations that the development and use of TDF's will undermine their "informational sovereignty," will impinge upon the privacy of local citizens, and will upset private property interests in information. Even local governments in the United States have expressed concern about their loss of control over information and transactions flowing across their borders.

But efforts to control the flow of electronic information across physical borders — to map local regulation and physical boundaries onto Cyberspace — are likely to prove futile, at least in countries that hope to participate in global commerce. Individual electrons can easily, and without any realistic prospect of detection, "enter" any sovereign's territory. The volume of electronic communications crossing territorial boundaries is just too great in relation to the resources available to government authorities.

.   .   .   .

Traditional legal doctrine treats the Net as a mere transmission medium that facilitates the exchange of messages sent from one legally significant geographical location to another, each of which has its own applicable laws. But trying to tie the laws of any particular territorial sovereign to transactions on the Net, or even trying to analyze the legal consequences of Net-based commerce as if each transaction occurred geographically somewhere in particular, is most unsatisfying. A more legally significant, and satisfying, border for the "law space" of the Net consists of the screens and passwords that separate the tangible from the virtual world.

Many of the jurisdictional and substantive quandaries raised by border-crossing electronic communications could be resolved by one simple principle: conceiving of Cyberspace as a distinct "place" for purposes of legal analysis by recognizing a legally significant border between Cyberspace and the "real world." Using this new approach, we would no longer ask the unanswerable question "where" in the geographical world a Net-based transaction occurred. Instead, the more salient questions become: What procedures are best suited to the often unique characteristics of this new place and the expectations of those who are engaged in various activities there? What mechanisms exist or need to be developed to determine the content of those rules and the mechanisms by which they can enforced? Answers to these questions will permit the development of rules better suited to the new phenomena in question, more likely to be made by those who understand and participate in those phenomena, and more likely to be enforced by means that the new global communications media make available and effective.

Treating Cyberspace as a separate "space" to which distinct laws apply should come naturally. There is a "placeness" to Cyberspace because the messages accessed there are persistent and accessible to many people. Furthermore, because entry into this world of stored online communications occurs through a screen and (usually) a password boundary, you know when you are "there." No one accidentally strays across the border into Cyberspace. To be sure, Cyberspace is not a homogenous place; groups and activities found at various online locations possess their own unique characteristics and distinctions, and each area will likely develop its own set of distinct rules. But the line that separates online transactions from our dealings in the real world is just as distinct as the physical boundaries between our territorial governments — perhaps more so.

Crossing into Cyberspace is a meaningful act that would make application of a distinct "law of Cyberspace" fair to those who pass over the electronic boundary. As noted, a primary function and characteristic of a border or boundary is its ability to be perceived by the one who crosses it. As regulatory structures evolve to govern Cyberspace-based transactions, it will be much easier to be certain which of those rules apply to your activities online than to determine which territorial-based authority might apply its laws to your conduct. For example, you would know to abide by the "terms of service" established by CompuServe or America Online when you are in their online territory, rather than guess whether Germany, or Tennessee, or the SEC will succeed in asserting their right to regulate your activities and those of the "placeless" online personae with whom you communicate.

.   .   .   .

Even if we agree that new rules should apply to online phenomena, questions remain about who sets the rules and how they are enforced. We believe the Net can develop its own effective legal institutions.

In order for the domain name space to be administered by a legal authority that is not territorially based, new law-making institutions will have to develop. Many questions that arise in setting up this system will need answers: Should a new top level domain be created? Do online addresses belong to users or service providers? Does one name impermissibly interfere with another, thus confusing the public and diluting the value of the pre-existing name? The new system must also include procedures to give notice in conflicting claims, to resolve these claims, and to assess appropriate remedies (including, possibly, compensation) in cases of wrongful use. If the Cyberspace equivalent of eminent domain develops, questions may arise over how to compensate individuals when certain domain names are destroyed or redeployed for the public good of the Net community. Someone must also decide threshold membership issues for Cyberspace citizens, including how much users must disclose (and to whom) about their real-world identities to use e-mail addresses and domain names for commercial purposes. Implied throughout this discussion is the recognition that these rules will be meaningful and enforceable only if Cyberspace citizens view whoever makes these decisions as a legitimate governing body.

Experience suggests that the community of online users and service providers is up to the task of developing a self-governance system. For example, the current domain name system evolved from decisions made by engineers and the practices of Internet service providers. Now that trademark owners are threatening the company that administers the registration system, the same engineers who established the original domain name standards are again deliberating whether to alter the domain name system to take these new policy issues into account.

Every system operator who dispenses a password imposes at least some requirements as conditions of continuing access, including paying bills on time or remaining a member of a group entitled to access (for example, students at a university). System operators (sysops) have an extremely powerful enforcement tool at their disposal to enforce such rules — banishment. Moreover, communities of users have marshaled plenty of enforcement weapons to induce wrongdoers to comply with local conventions, such as rules against flaming, shunning, mailbombs, and more. And both sysops and users have begun explicitly to recognize that formulating and enforcing such rules should be a matter for principled discussion, not an act of will by whoever has control of the power switch.

While many of these new rules and customs apply only to specific, local areas of the global network, some standards apply through technical protocols on a nearly universal basis. And widespread agreement already exists about core principles of "netiquette" in mailing lists and discussion groups — although, admittedly, new users have a slow learning curve and the Net offers little formal "public education" regarding applicable norms. Moreover, dispute resolution mechanisms suited to this new environment also seem certain to prosper. Cyberspace is anything but anarchic; its distinct rule sets are becoming more robust every day.

Perhaps the most apt analogy to the rise of a separate law of Cyberspace is the origin of the Law Merchant — a distinct set of rules that developed with the new, rapid boundary-crossing trade of the Middle Ages. Merchants could not resolve their disputes by taking them to the local noble, whose established feudal law mainly concerned land claims. Nor could the local lord easily establish meaningful rules for a sphere of activity that he barely understood and that was executed in locations beyond his control. The result of this jurisdictional confusion was the development of a new legal system — Lex Mercatoria. The people who cared most about and best understood their new creation formed and championed this new law, which did not destroy or replace existing law regarding more territorially based transactions (e.g., transferring land ownership). Arguably, exactly the same type of phenomenon is developing in Cyberspace right now.

Governments cannot stop electronic communications from coming across their borders, even if they want to do so. Nor can they credibly claim a right to regulate the Net based on supposed local harms caused by activities that originate outside their borders and that travel electronically to many different nations. One nation's legal institutions should not monopolize rule-making for the entire Net. Even so, established authorities will likely continue to claim that they must analyze and regulate the new online phenomena in terms of some physical locations. After all, they argue, the people engaged in online communications still inhabit the material world, and local legal authorities must have authority to remedy the problems created in the physical world by those acting on the Net. The rise of responsible law-making institutions within Cyberspace, however, will weigh heavily against arguments that describe the Net as "lawless" and thus connect regulation of online trade to physical jurisdictions. As noted, sysops, acting alone or collectively, have the power to banish those who commit wrongful acts online. Thus, for online activities that minimally affect the vital interests of sovereigns, the self-regulating structures of Cyberspace seem better suited to dealing with the Net's legal issues.

· · · ·

Global electronic communications have created new spaces in which distinct rule sets will evolve. We can reconcile the new law created in this space with current territorially based legal systems by treating it as a distinct doctrine, applicable to a clearly demarcated sphere, created primarily by legitimate, self-regulatory processes, and entitled to appropriate deference — but also subject to limitations when it oversteps its appropriate sphere.

The law of any given place must take into account the special characteristics of the space it regulates and the types of persons, places, and things found there. Just as a country's jurisprudence reflects its unique historical experience and culture, the law of Cyberspace will reflect its special character, which differs markedly from anything found in the physical world. For example, the law of the Net must deal with persons who "exist" in Cyberspace only in the form of an e-mail address and whose purported identity may or may not accurately correspond to physical characteristics in the real world. In fact, an e-mail address might not even belong to a single person. Accordingly, if Cyberspace law is to recognize the nature of its "subjects," it cannot rest on the same doctrines that give geographically based sovereigns jurisdiction over "whole," locatable, physical persons. The law of the Net must be prepared to deal with persons who manifest themselves only by means of a particular ID, user account, or domain name.

Moreover, if rights and duties attach to an account itself, rather than to an underlying real world person, traditional concepts such as "equality," "discrimination," or even "rights and duties" may not work as we normally understand them. For example, when AOL users joined the Net in large numbers, other Cyberspace users often ridiculed them based on the ".aol" tag on their email addresses — a form of "domainism" that might be discouraged by new forms of Netiquette. If a doctrine of Cyberspace law accords rights to users, we will need to decide whether those rights adhere only to particular types of online appearances, as distinct from those attaching to particular individuals in the real world.

Similarly, the types of "properties" that can become the subject of legal discussion in Cyberspace will differ from real world real estate or tangible objects. For example, in the real world the physical covers of a book delineate the boundaries of a "work" for purposes of copyright law; those limits may disappear entirely when the same materials are part of a large electronic database. Thus, we may have to change the "fair use" doctrine in copyright law that previously depended on calculating what portion of the physical work was copied. Similarly, a web page's "location" in Cyberspace may take on a value unrelated to the physical place where the disk holding that Web page resides, and efforts to regulate web pages by attempting to control physical objects may only cause the relevant bits to move from one place to another. On the other hand, the boundaries set by "URLs" (Uniform Resource Locators, the location of a document on the World Wide Web) may need special protection against confiscation or confusingly similar addresses. And, because these online "places" may contain offensive material, we may need rules requiring (or allowing) groups to post certain signs or markings at these places' outer borders.

The boundaries that separate persons and things behave differently in the virtual world but are nonetheless legally significant. Messages posted under one e-mail name will not affect the reputation of another e-mail address, even if the same physical person authors both messages. Materials separated by a password will be accessible to different sets of users, even if those materials physically exist on the very same hard drive. A user's claim to a right to a particular online identity or to redress when that identity's reputation suffers harm, may be valid even if that identity does not correspond exactly to that of any single person in the real world.

Clear boundaries make law possible, encouraging rapid differentiation between rule sets and defining the subjects of legal discussion. New abilities to travel or exchange information rapidly across old borders may change the legal frame of reference and require fundamental changes in legal institutions. Fundamental activities of lawmaking — accommodating conflicting claims, defining property rights, establishing rules to guide conduct, enforcing those rules, and resolving disputes — remain very much alive within the newly defined, intangible territory of Cyberspace. At the same time, the newly emerging law challenges the core idea of a current law-making authority — the territorial nation state, with substantial but legally restrained powers.

If the rules of Cyberspace thus emerge from consensually based rule sets, and the subjects of such laws remain free to move among many differing online spaces, then considering the actions of Cyberspace's system administrators as the exercise of a power akin to "sovereignty" may be inappropriate. Under a legal framework where the top level imposes physical order on those below it and depends for its continued effectiveness on the inability of its citizens to fight back or leave the territory, the legal and political doctrines we have evolved over the centuries are essential to constrain such power. In that situation, where exit is impossible, costly, or painful, then a right to a voice for the people is essential. But when the "persons" in question are not whole people, when their "property" is intangible and portable, and when all concerned may readily escape a jurisdiction they do not find empowering, the relationship between the "citizen" and the "state" changes radically. Law, defined as a thoughtful group conversation about core values, will persist. But it will not, could not, and should not be the same law as that applicable to physical, geographically-defined territories.

Discussion Questions

1. The authors argue that logging onto the Internet involves moving from the physical to the virtual — with the consequence that we can treat cyberspace as a place separate from the physical world. Such an approach would enable us (consider who the "us" is) to craft laws specific to cyberspace and to place significant limitations on traditional regulatory approaches. Do you agree with this characterization? Do you think that recent technological change impacts the authors' analysis? Has the Internet become sufficiently ingrained into daily life that it now functions as part of real space?

2. How much of Post and Johnson's arguments rest upon the technological limitations of their day? In view of the rapid progress of Internet development, might the arguments pertaining to enforcement limitations be rendered moot someday soon?

The most direct response to the Law and Borders article comes from Professor Jack Goldsmith of the University of Chicago Law School. His 1998 article, *Against Cyberanarchy*, tackles the "cyberspace is a place" argument with a forceful case for the belief that existing law can adapt to the Internet.

Against Cyberanarchy†

JACK L. GOLDSMITH

The Supreme Court's partial invalidation of the Communications Decency Act on First Amendment grounds raises the more fundamental question of whether the state can regulate cyberspace at all. Several commentators, whom I shall call "regulation skeptics," have argued that it cannot. Some courts have also expressed skepticism. The popular and technical press are full of similar claims.

† (1998) 65 U. Chi. L. Rev. 1199. Notes omitted. Reproduced by permission of University of Chicago Law School and the author.

The regulation skeptics make both descriptive and normative claims. On the descriptive side, they claim that the application of geographically based conceptions of legal regulation and choice of law to a-geographical cyberspace activity either makes no sense or leads to hopeless confusion. On the normative side, they argue that because cyberspace transactions occur " simultaneously and equally" in all national jurisdictions, regulation of the flow of this information by any particular national jurisdiction illegitimately produces significant negative spillover effects in other jurisdictions. They also claim that the architecture of cyberspace precludes notice of governing law that is crucial to the law's legitimacy. In contrast, they argue, cyberspace participants are much better positioned than national regulators to design comprehensive legal rules that would both internalize the costs of cyberspace activity and give proper notice to cyberspace participants. The regulation skeptics conclude from these arguments that national regulators should "defer to the self-regulatory efforts of Cyberspace participants."

. . . .

This Section argues that the skeptics' claims about the infeasibility of national regulation of cyberspace rest on an underappreciation of the realities of modern conflict of laws, and of the legal and technological tools available to resolve multijurisdictional cyberspace conflicts. From the perspective of jurisdiction and choice of law, regulation of cyberspace transactions is no less feasible than regulation of other transnational transactions.

A.   DEFAULT LAWS AND PRIVATE ORDERING IN CYBERSPACE

Cyberspace transactions that implicate default laws, like other transnational transactions that implicate such laws, are subject to private legal ordering. The architecture of cyberspace facilitates this private ordering and thus enables cyberspace participants to avoid many transnational conflicts of law.

At the most basic level, private ordering is facilitated by the technical standards that define and limit cyberspace. To participate in the Internet function known as the World Wide Web, users must consent to the TCP/IP standards that define the Internet as well as to the HTML standards that more particularly define the Web. Similarly, sending e-mail over the Internet requires the sender to use TCP/IP standards and particular e-mail protocols. One's experience of cyberspace is further defined and limited by the more particular communication standards embedded in software. For example, within the range of what TCP/IP and HTML permit, an individual's communication via the World Wide Web will be shaped and limited by (among many other things) her choice of browsers and search engines. These and countless other technical standard choices order behavior in cyberspace. In this sense, access to different cyberspace networks and communities is always conditioned on the accessors' consent to the array of technical standards that define these networks and communities.

Technical standards cannot comprehensively specify acceptable behavior in cyberspace. Within the range of what these standards permit, information flows might violate network norms or territorial laws. Many network norms are promulgated and enforced informally. A more formal method to establish private legal orders in cyberspace is to condition access to particular networks on consent to a particular legal regime.

This regime could take several forms. It could be a local, national, or international law. When you buy a Dell computer through the company's web page from anywhere in the world, you agree that "(a)ny claim relating to, and the use of, this Site and the materials contained herein is governed by the laws of the state of Texas." Alternatively, the chosen law could be a free-standing model law attached to no particular sovereign but available to be incorporated by contract. For example, parties to a commercial transaction over the Internet could agree that their transaction is governed by UNIDROIT Principles or the Uniform Customs and Practice for Documentary Credits. Or the governing law could be the contractual terms themselves. Waivers and exclusions operate as private law in this way. So too do chat rooms, discussion lists, and local area networks that condition participation on the user's consent to community norms specified in a contract.

Cyberspace architecture can also help to establish other aspects of a private legal order. Through conditioned access, cyberspace users can consent to have subsequent disputes resolved by courts, arbitrators, systems operators, or even "virtual magistrates." They can also establish private enforcement regimes. Technical standards operate as an enforcer of sorts by defining and limiting cyberspace activity. For example, software filters can block or condition access to certain information, and various technologies perform compliance monitoring functions. In addition, the gatekeeper of each cyberspace community can cut off entry for noncompliance with the community rules, or punish a user for bad acts by drawing on a bond (perhaps simply a credit card) put up as a condition on the user's entry.

Many have proposed a structure for private legal ordering of cyberspace along the lines just sketched. There is nothing remarkable about this structure. It differs little from the legal structure of other private groups, such as churches, merchants, families, clubs, and corporations, which have analogous consent based governing laws, dispute resolution mechanisms, and private enforcement regimes. But just as private ordering is often not a comprehensive solution to the regulation of "real-space" private groups, it will not be a comprehensive solution to the regulation of cyberspace either.

In part this is because it remains an open question how to generate consent across cyberspace networks. Conditioning access on consent to a governing legal regime is relatively easy at the entry point of a cyberspace network. In theory, it is just as easy to generate such consent at the interface between networks. It is commonplace to click on a hypertext link and be greeted by a message that conditions further access on presentation of an identification code, or credit card number, or personal information such as age and address. A similar demand for consent to a particular legal regime could be added as a condition for access. However, this process might become confusing; the technological and conceptual details of consenting to and coordinating different legal regimes as one works one's way through dozens of cyberspace networks remain to be worked out. In addition, the generation of legal consent across networks will impose time and other costs that are anathema to many cyberspace users.

An important additional difficulty is that many cyberspace activities affect non-cyberspace participants with whom ex ante consent to a private legal regime will not be possible. Cyberspace is not, as the skeptics often assume, a self-enclosed regime. A communication in cyberspace often has consequences for persons outside the computer network in which the communication took place. For example: a book uploaded on the Net can violate an author's copyright; a chat room participant can defame someone outside the chat room; terrorists can promulgate bomb making or kidnapping tips; merchants can conspire to fix prices by e-mail; a corporation can issue a fraudulent security; a pornographer can sell kiddie porn; Internet gambling can decrease in-state gambling revenues and cause family strife; and so on. In these and many other ways, communications via cyberspace produce harmful, real-world effects on those who have not consented to the private ordering of the cyberspace community.

Finally, even if the hurdles to consent can be surmounted, consent-based legal orders are limited by a variety of national mandatory law restrictions. These mandatory laws define who may consent to these private regimes. For example, they prevent persons of certain ages from entering into certain types of contracts. They also limit the form and scope of such consent. The consideration requirement and limitations on liquidated damages clauses fall into this category, as do requirements that the law chosen by the parties have a reasonable relationship to the subject matter of the contract. Some mandatory laws also limit the internal and external activities of the group's activities. Criminal law, for example, falls in this category.

Private legal ordering thus has the potential to resolve many, but not all, of the challenges posed by multijurisdictional cyberspace activity. Cyberspace activities for which ex ante consent to a governing legal regime is either infeasible or unenforceable are not amenable to private ordering. Such activities remain subject to the skeptics' concerns about multiple or extraterritorial national regulation.

B. THE LIMITS OF ENFORCEMENT JURISDICTION

The skeptics' concerns are further attenuated, however, by limitations on every nation's ability to enforce its laws. A nation can purport to regulate activity that takes place anywhere. The Island of Tobago can enact a law that purports to bind the rights of the whole world. But the effective scope of this law depends on Tobago's ability to enforce it. And in general a nation can only enforce its laws against: (i) persons with a presence or assets in the nation's territory; (ii) persons over whom the nation can obtain personal jurisdiction and enforce a default judgment against abroad; or (iii) persons whom the nation can successfully extradite.

A defendant's physical presence or assets within the territory remains the primary basis for a nation or state to enforce its laws. The large majority of persons who transact in cyberspace have no presence or assets in the jurisdictions that wish to regulate their information flows in cyberspace. Such regulations are thus likely to apply primarily to Internet service providers and Internet users with a physical presence in the regulating jurisdiction. Cyberspace users in other territorial jurisdictions will indirectly feel the effect of the regulations to the extent that they are dependent on service or content providers with a presence in the regulating jurisdiction. But for almost all users, there will be no threat of extraterritorial legal liability because of a lack of presence in the regulating jurisdictions.

A nation or state can also enforce its laws over an entity with no local presence or assets if it can obtain personal jurisdiction over the entity and enforce a local default judgment against that entity abroad. The domestic interstate context presents a much greater threat in this regard than does the international context. This is because the Full Faith and Credit Clause requires a state to enforce the default judgment of a sister state that had personal jurisdiction over the defendant. This threat is attenuated, however, by constitutional limits on a state's assertion of personal jurisdiction. The Due Process Clauses prohibit a state from asserting personal jurisdiction over an entity with no local presence unless the entity has purposefully directed its activities to the forum state and the assertion of jurisdiction is reasonable.

Application of this standard to cyberspace activities presents special difficulties. Under standard assumptions about cyberspace architecture, persons can upload or transmit information knowing that it could reach any and all jurisdictions, but not knowing which particular jurisdiction it might reach. Can every state where these transmissions appear assert specific personal jurisdiction over the agent of the information under the purposeful availment and reasonableness tests?

Full consideration of this issue is far beyond this Article's scope. I simply wish to point out why there is relatively little reason at present, and even less reason in the near future, to believe that the mere introduction of information into cyberspace will by itself suffice for personal jurisdiction over the agent of the transmission in every state where the information appears. Most courts have required something more than mere placement of information on a web page in one state as a basis for personal jurisdiction in another state where the web page is accessed. For a variety of reasons, these decisions have limited specific personal jurisdiction to cases in which there are independent indicia that the out-of-state defendant knowingly and purposefully directed the effects of out-of-state conduct to a particular state where the acts were deemed illegal.

Given the skeptics' assumptions about cyberspace architecture, this conclusion appears appropriate. It seems unfair to expose a content provider to personal jurisdiction in all fifty states for the mere act of uploading information on a computer if she cannot take affordable precautions to avoid simultaneous multi-jurisdictional effects. But we shall see below that the skeptics' architectual assumptions are inaccurate. It is already possible for content providers to take measures to achieve significant control over information flows. And filtering and identification technology promise greater control at less cost. In cyberspace as in real space, the ultimate meaning of "purposeful availment" and "reasonableness" will depend on the cost and feasibility of information flow control. As such control becomes more feasible and less costly, personal jurisdiction over cyberspace activities will become functionally identical to personal jurisdiction over real-space activities.

This detour into the technicalities of personal jurisdiction was necessitated by a worry about the extraterritorial enforcement of local default judgments against nonlocal cyberspace users within the American federal system. Such concerns are less pronounced in the international context. In contrast to the domestic interstate context, customary international law imposes few enforceable controls on a country's assertion of personal jurisdiction, and there are few treaties on the subject. However, also in contrast to domestic law, there is no full faith and credit obligation to enforce foreign judgments in the international sphere. If one country exercises personal jurisdiction on an exorbitant basis, the resulting judgment is unlikely to be enforced in another country. In addition, local public policy exceptions to the enforcement of foreign judgments are relatively commonplace in the international sphere, especially when the foreign judgment flies in the face of the enforcing state's regulatory regime. For these reasons, there is little concern that a foreign default judgment will be enforceable against cyberspace users who live outside the regulating jurisdiction.

The final way that a nation can enforce its regulations against persons outside its jurisdiction is by seeking extradition. In the United States, extradition among the several states is regulated by Article IV of the Constitution and the federal extradition law. As a general matter, State A must accede to the proper demand of State B for the surrender of a fugitive who committed an act in State B that State B considers a crime. Nonetheless, a person who in State A transmits information flows that appear in and constitute a crime in State B will not likely be subject to extradition to State B under these provisions. This is because the extradition obligation only extends to fugitives who have fled State B, and these terms have long been limited to persons who were physically present in the demanding state at the time of the crime's commission. A different, but equally forceful, limitation applies to international extradition. International extradition is governed largely by treaty. A pervasive feature of modern extradition treaties is the principle of double criminality. This principle requires that the charged offense be criminal in both the requesting and the requested jurisdictions. This principle, and its animating rationale, make it unlikely that there will be international cooperation in the enforcement of exorbitant unilateral criminal regulations of cyberspace events.

This review of transnational enforcement jurisdiction makes clear that the skeptics exaggerate the threat of multiple regulation of cyberspace information flows. This threat must be measured by a regulation's enforceable scope, not by its putative scope. And the enforceable scope is relatively narrow. It extends only to individual users or system operators with presence or assets in the enforcement jurisdiction, or (in the U.S.) to entities that take extra steps to target cyberspace information flows to states where such information flows are illegal. Such regulatory exposure is a significant concern for cyberspace participants. But it is precisely how regulatory exposure operates in "real space." And it is far less significant than the skeptics' hyperbolic claim that all users of the Web will be simultaneously subject to all national regulations.

Even with these limitations, the skeptics worry that an individual cyberspace content provider in one jurisdiction faces potential liability in another jurisdiction when she places information on the Internet. This potential liability can become an unforeseen reality when the provider travels to the regulating jurisdiction, or moves assets there. Such potential liability in turn affects the providers' activities at home and thus can be viewed as a weak form of extraterritorial regulation. This form of regulation is a theoretical possibility, but it should not be exaggerated. No nation has as yet imposed liability on a content provider for unforeseen effects in an unknown jurisdiction. The threat of such liability will lessen as content providers continue to gain means to control information flows. It is also conceivable that weak normative limitations might exist or develop to prevent a jurisdiction from regulating local effects that were truly unforeseeable or uncontrollable. The point for now is that even in the absence of such limits, this potential threat of liability is relatively insignificant and does not come close to the skeptics' broad descriptive claims about massive multiple regulation of individual users.

C. INDIRECT REGULATION OF EXTRATERRITORIAL ACTIVITY

Indeed, if the limits on enforcement jurisdiction support any of the skeptics' descriptive claims, it is their somewhat different claim that because of the potential for regulation evasion, cyberspace transactions are beyond the regulatory powers of territorial governments. Cyberspace content providers can, at some cost, shift the source of their information flows to jurisdictions beyond the enforceable scope of national regulation and thus continue information transmissions into the regulating jurisdiction. For example, they can relocate in geographical space, or employ telnet or anonymous remailers to make the geographical source of their content difficult to discern. These and related regulatory evasion techniques can make it difficult for a nation to regulate the extraterritorial supply side of harmful cyberspace activity.

Regulation evasion of this sort is not limited to cyberspace. For example, corporations reincorporate to avoid mandatory laws and criminals launder money offshore. Closer to point, offshore regulation evasion has been a prominent characteristic of other communication media. For example, Radio-Free Europe broadcast from western Europe into the former Soviet Union but lacked a regulatable presence there. Similarly, television signals are sometimes broadcast from abroad by an entity with no local presence. The extraterritorial source of these and many other non-cyberspace activities is beyond the enforceable scope of local regulation. But this does not mean that local regulation is inefficacious. In cyberspace as in real space, offshore regulation evasion does not prevent a nation from regulating the extraterritorial activity.

This is so because a nation can regulate people and equipment in its territory to control the local effects of the extraterritorial activity. Such indirect regulation is how nations have, with varying degrees of success, regulated local harms caused by other communications media with offshore sources and no local presence. And it is how nations have begun to regulate local harms caused by offshore Internet content providers. For example, nations penalize in-state end users who obtain and use illegal content or who otherwise participate in an illegal cyberspace transaction. They also regulate the local means through which foreign content is transmitted. For example, they impose screening obligations on in-state Internet service providers and other entities that supply or transmit information. Or they regulate in-state hardware and software through which such transmissions are received. Or they regulate the local financial intermediaries that make commercial transactions on the Internet possible.

These and related regulations of domestic persons and property make it more costly, and thus more difficult, for in-state users to obtain content from, or transact with, regulation evaders abroad. In this fashion a nation can indirectly regulate the extraterritorial supply of prohibited content even though the source of the content is beyond its enforcement jurisdiction and even though it cannot easily stop transmission at the border. These various forms of indirect regulation will not be perfect in the sense of eliminating regulation evasion. But few regulations are perfect in this sense, and regulation need not be perfect in this sense to be effective. The question is always whether the regulation will heighten the costs of the activity sufficiently to achieve its acceptable control from whatever normative perspective is appropriate.

In the cyberspace regulation context, the answer to this question depends on empirical and technological issues that are unresolved and that will vary from context to context. The prodigious criticism of and lobbying efforts against proposed regulation of (among other things) digital goods, Internet gambling, and encryption technology suggest that governments can raise the costs of many cyberspace transactions to a significant degree. And of course unilateral national regulation is one of many regulation strategies at a nation's disposal. The point for now is simply that offshore regulation evasion does not, as the skeptics think, undermine a nation's ability to regulate cyberspace transactions. Although a nation will sometimes have difficulty in imposing liability on extraterritorial content providers, it can still significantly regulate the local effects of these providers' activities through laws aimed at local persons and entities.

. . . .

E. INTERNATIONAL HARMONIZATION

Private legal ordering, the limitations on enforcement jurisdiction, indirect regulation, and effective information flow control, taken together, go a long way toward redressing the skeptics' descriptive claims about the infeasibility of cyberspace regulation. These techniques will not resolve all conflict of laws in cyberspace any more than they do in real space. Nor will they definitively resolve the problem of the relative ease by which information suppliers can "relocate" into a safe haven outside of the regulating jurisdiction, a problem that also has many real-space analogies. When similar spillover and evasion problems have occurred with respect to non-cyberspace transactions, nations have responded with a variety of international harmonization strategies.

The same harmonization strategies are being used today to address the challenges presented by cyberspace transactions. A few examples will suffice. Several recent treaties and related multinational edicts have strengthened digital content owners' right to control the distribution and presentation of their property online. These harmonization efforts grow out of an international copyright regime that is over one hundred years old. The G8 economic powers have recently begun to coordinate regulatory efforts concerning cyberspace-related crimes in five areas: pedophilia and sexual exploitation; drug-trafficking; money-laundering; electronic fraud; and industrial and state espionage. These initiatives mirror similar efforts to redress similar regulatory leakage problems in real-space contexts such as environmental policy, banking and insurance supervision, and antitrust regulation. Several international organizations have drafted model laws and guidelines to facilitate Internet commerce and related digital certification issues. There are scores of other international efforts in a variety of cyberspace-related contexts.

International harmonization is not always (or even usually) the best response to the spillovers and evasions that result from unilateral regulation. And harmonization is often not easy to achieve. However, the proliferation of international organizations, in combination with modern means of communication and transportation, has helped to facilitate international harmonization. Harmonization is especially likely in those contexts — like many aspects of criminal law enforcement — where nations' interests converge and the gains from cooperation are high. But nations sometimes lack the incentive to participate in international regimes, and there are often international and domestic political economy obstacles to harmonization. It is too early to tell how successful international efforts will be in addressing the challenges of cyberspace. It is clear, however, that international harmonization will play an important role in nations' overall cyberspace-regulation strategy.

F. RESIDUAL CHOICE-OF-LAW TOOLS

The skeptics' implicit goal of eliminating all conflicts of laws that arise from cyberspace transactions is unrealistic. Private legal ordering, the limits of enforcement jurisdiction, indirect regulation of extraterritorial activity, filtering and identification technology, and international cooperation facilitate and rationalize legal regulation of cyberspace. These tools, however, will not eliminate all conflicts of laws in cyberspace any more than they do in real space. Transnational activity is too complex. As mentioned above, the elimination of conflict of laws would require the elimination of decentralized lawmaking or of transnational activity. In this light, the enormous increases in the pervasiveness and complexity of conflict of laws in this century can be viewed as an acceptable cost to a world that wishes to expand transnational activity while retaining decentralized lawmaking. As persistent conflicts become prohibitively costly to private parties and regulating nations, public or private international coordination or technological innovation becomes more attractive and thus more likely.

Short of these developments, transnational transactions in cyberspace, like transnational transactions mediated by telephone and mail, will continue to give rise to disputes that present challenging choice-of-law issues. For example: "Whose substantive legal rules apply to a defamatory message that is written by someone in Mexico, read by someone in Israel by means of an Internet server located in the United States, injuring the reputation of a Norwegian?" Similarly, (w)hich of the many plausibly applicable bodies of copyright law do we consult to determine whether a hyperlink on a World Wide Web page located on a server in France and constructed by a Filipino citizen, which points to a server in Brazil that contains materials protected by German and French (but not Brazilian) copyright law, which is downloaded to a server in the United States and reposted to a Usenet newsgroup, constitutes a remediable infringement of copyright?

It would be silly to try to formulate a general theory of how such issues should be resolved. One lesson of this century's many failures in top-down choice-of-law theorizing is that choice-of-law rules are most effective when they are grounded in and sensitive to the concrete details of particular legal contexts. This does not mean that standards are better than rules in this context. It simply means that in designing choice-of-law rules or standards, it is better to begin at the micro rather than macro level, and to examine recurrent fact patterns and implicated interests in discrete legal contexts rather than devise a general context-transcendent theory of conflicts.

With these caveats in mind, I want to explain in very general terms why the residual choice-of-law problems implicated by cyberspace are not significantly different from those that are non-cyberspace conflicts. Cyberspace presents two related choice-of-law problems. The first is the problem of complexity. This is the problem of how to choose a single governing law for cyberspace activity that has multijurisdictional contacts. The second problem concerns situs. This is the problem of how to choose a governing law when the locus of activity cannot easily be pinpointed in geographical space. Both problems raise similar concerns. The choice of any dispositive geographical contact or any particular law in these cases will often seem arbitrary because several jurisdictions have a legitimate claim to apply their law. Whatever law is chosen, seemingly genuine regulatory interests of the nations whose laws are not applied may be impaired.

The problems of complexity and situs are genuine. They are not, however, unique to cyberspace. Identical problems arise all the time in real space. In fact, they inhere in every true conflict of laws. Consider the problem of complexity. The hypotheticals concerning copyright infringements and multistate libels in cyberspace are no more complex than the same issues in real space. They also are no more complex or challenging than similar issues presented by increasingly prevalent real-space events such as airplane crashes, mass torts, multistate insurance coverage, or multinational commercial transactions, all of which form the bread and butter of modern conflict of laws. Indeed, they are no more complex than a simple products liability suit arising from a two-car accident among residents of the same state, which can implicate the laws of several states, including the place of the accident, the states where the car and tire manufacturers are headquartered, the states where the car and tires were manufactured, and the state where the car was purchased.

Resolution of choice-of-law problems in these contexts is challenging. But the skeptics overstate the challenge. Not every geographical contact is of equal significance. For example, in the copyright hypothetical above, the laws of the source country and the end-use countries have a much greater claim to governing the copyright action than the laws of the country of the person who built the server and the country of the server whose hyperlink pointed to the server that contained the infringing material. The limits on enforcement jurisdiction may further minimize the scope of the conflict. In addition, even in extraordinarily complex cases where numerous laws potentially apply, these laws will often involve similar legal standards, thus limiting the actual choice of law to two or perhaps three options. Finally, these complex transactions need not be governed by a single law. Applying different laws to different aspects of a complex transaction is a perfectly legitimate choice-of-law technique.

The application of a single law to complex multijurisdictional conflicts will sometimes seem arbitrary and will invariably produce spillover effects. But as explained above, the arbitrariness of the chosen law, and the spillovers produced by application of this law, inhere in all conflict situations in which two or more nations, on the basis of territorial or domiciliary contacts, have a legitimate claim to apply their law. When in particular contexts the arbitrariness and spillovers become too severe, a uniform international solution remains possible. Short of such harmonization, the choice-of-law issues implicated by cyberspace transactions are no more complex than the issues raised by functionally identical multijurisdictional transactions that occur in real space all the time.

Like the problem of complexity, the situs problem is a pervasive and familiar feature of real-space jurisdictional conflicts. A classic difficulty is the situs of intangibles like a debt or a bank deposit. More generally, the situs problem arises whenever legally significant activity touches on two or more states. For example, when adultery committed in one state alienates the affections of a spouse in another, the situs of the tort is not self-evident. It depends on what contact the forum's choice-of-law rule deems dispositive. Similar locus difficulties arise when the tort takes place over many states, such as when poison is administered in one state, takes effect in another, and kills in a third. The situs problem even arises when a bodily injury occurs in one state based on negligence committed in another, for there is no logical reason why the place of injury should be viewed as the place of the tort any more than should the place of negligence. In all of these situations, the importance of any particular geographical contact is never self-evident; it is a legal rather than a factual consideration that is built into the forum's choice-of-law rules. As the geographical contacts of a transaction proliferate, the choice of any one contact as dispositive runs the risk of appearing arbitrary. But again, this problem pervades real-space conflicts of law and is not unique to cyberspace conflicts.

So the complexity and situs problems inhere to some degree in all transnational conflicts, and are exacerbated in real space and cyberspace alike as jurisdictional contacts proliferate. No choice-of-law rule will prove wholly satisfactory in these situations. However, several factors diminish the skeptics' concerns about the infeasibility of applying traditional choice-of- law tools to cyberspace. For example, the skeptics are wrong to the extent that they believe that cyberspace transactions must be resolved on the basis of geographical choice-of-law criteria that are sometimes difficult to apply to cyberspace, such as where events occur or where people are located at the time of the transaction. But these are not the only choice-of-law criteria, and certainly not the best in contexts where the geographical locus of events is so unclear. Domicile (and its cognates, such as citizenship, principal place of business, habitual residence, and so on) are also valid choice-of-law criteria that have particular relevance to problems, like those in cyberspace, that involve the regulation of intangibles or of multinational transactions.

The skeptics are further mistaken to the extent that their arguments assume that all choice-of-law problems must be resolved by multilateral choice-of-law method-ologies. A multilateral methodology asks which of several possible laws governs a transaction, and selects one of these laws on the basis of specified criteria. Multi-lateral methods accentuate the situs and complexity problems. But the regulatory issues that are most relevant to the cyberspace governance debate almost always involve unilateral choice-of-law methods that alleviate these problems. A unilateral method considers only whether the dispute at issue has close enough connections to the forum to justify the application of local law. If so, local law applies; if not, the case is dismissed and the potential applicability of foreign law is not considered. For example, a jurisdiction typically does not apply foreign criminal law. If a Tennes-see court has personal jurisdiction over someone from across the Virginia border who shot and killed an in-stater, the court does not consider whether Tennessee or Virginia law applies. It considers only whether Tennessee law applies. If so, the case proceeds; if not, it is dismissed.

Unilateral choice-of-law methods make the complexity and situs problems less significant. They do not require a determination of which of a number of possible laws apply. Nor do they require a court to identify where certain events occurred. What matters is simply whether the activity has local effects that are significant enough to implicate local law. By failing to recognize that courts can and will use unilateral rather than multilateral choice-of-law methods to resolve cyberspace conflicts, the skeptics again exaggerate the challenge of cyberspace regulation.

G. NUMBER AND VELOCITY OF TRANSACTIONS

The skeptics' final descriptive claim is that even if cyberspace transactions appear like real-space transnational transactions in other respects, they differ significantly with respect to the velocity and number of transactions. Cyberspace dramatically low-ers the costs of multinational communication. With only a computer and Internet access, anyone in the world can communicate with anyone, and potentially everyone, in the world. The skeptics believe communications via cyberspace will be so prevalent that governments will not find it cost-effective to regulate them.

A dramatic increase in the number and speed of transactions might well multi-ply the aggregate harms from such transactions. But this increases rather than decreases a nation's incentives to regulate. Consider Internet gambling. In pre-Internet days, individuals in the United States could gamble from home or work via telephone with domestic and offshore bookies. Although this form of gambling was regulated by a variety of state and federal statutes, the statutes were filled with loop-holes and rarely enforced because transactions were relatively infrequent. Internet gambling makes it significantly easier to gamble from home or work. This has led to a dramatic increase in gambling and a related rise in the costs of gambling that governments worry about: fraud, diminution in local gambling and other entertain-ment expenditures, loss of tax revenues, decreased productivity, gambling by children, and so on. Not surprisingly, federal and state governments are beginning to regulate gambling much more extensively, and seriously, than ever.

Even with governments' heightened incentives to regulate Internet transactions, some believe that the sheer number of transactions will overwhelm governments' ability to regulate. A related argument is that because individuals can so easily engage in transnational communications via the Internet, governmental regulation will be less effective; for individuals operating on the Internet are hard to identify, isolate, and thus sanction. Once again, the conclusion that regulation is infeasible simply does not follow from these premises. The mistake here is the belief that governments regulate only through direct sanctioning of individuals. But of course this is not the only way, or even the usual way, that regulation works. Governments regulate an activity by raising the activity's costs in a manner that achieves desired ends. This can be accomplished through several means other than individual sanctions. Governments can, for example, try to alter the social meaning of the activity, regulate the hardware and software through which the activity takes place, make individual penalties severe and notorious, or impose liability on intermediaries like Internet service providers or credit card companies.

In short, a dramatic increase in the number and velocity of transactions by itself says very little about the feasibility of governmental regulation. Numerous communication advances, beginning with the telegraph, dramatically increased the velocity and number of communications, and lowered their costs. The skeptics have provided no reason to think that the differences between cyberspace and prior communication technology are so much greater than the differences between pre- and post-telegraph technology (which reduced communication time from weeks and months to hours and minutes), or between pre- and post-telephone technology (which also dramatically reduced the cost and enhanced the frequency and privacy of transjurisdictional communication) to justify the conclusion that governmental regulation will be nonefficacious.

Discussion Question

Goldsmith argues that the spillover effects in cyberspace mirror those found in real space. Do you agree? Does the interconnected nature of the Internet alter the analysis in any way?

Notes

A third vision of regulating Internet activity comes from those who argue that technology is rapidly replacing law as the regulator of choice. Proponents of this view argue that in real space, law sets the traditional parameters for conduct. For example, copyright law sets the rules for use of content, privacy law sets the rules for the use of private data, and consumer protection law sets the rules for consumer retail transactions. In electronic commerce, technology is rapidly usurping the role traditionally played by law by providing a quicker and more effective means of recourse. Digital watermarking and technologies that limit repeated uses of digital information may soon replace law as the tool of choice for content creators anxious to protect their rights. Similarly, digital signatures are replacing law as the gatekeeper to contractual certainty. Consumers, cognizant of the limitations of the traditional consumer protection legal framework, now look to private protections such as private insurance and online escrow services.

For more on this "software code as law" approach, see Lawrence Lessig, *Code and Other Laws of Cyberspace* (Basic Books, 1999); Joel Reidenberg, *Lex Informatica: The Formulation of Information Policy Rules Through Technology*, 76 Texas L. Rev. 553 (1998); or James Boyle, *Foucault in Cyberspace: Surveillance, Sovereignty, and Hard-Wired Censors*, 66 U Cin L Rev. 177 (1997) available on the Internet at <http://www.wcl.american.edu/ pub/faculty/boyle/foucault.htm>.

The issue of Internet regulation has not escaped the notice of members of the Canadian Supreme Court. Consider this excerpt from Justice Michel Bastarache. With which perspective do you think Bastarache most closely identified?

The Challenge of the Law in the New Millennium[†]

THE HONORABLE MICHEL BASTARACHE

As with aboriginal legal norms, developments in international law raise the question of whether a pluralistic structure of normativity can be accommodated in a single, coherent legal order. Individual issues will come and go, but that structural issue will remain. Will our legal system really evolve from an essentially unitary doctrinal structure to a much more pluralistic one, with competing valid normative orders? That is a question which underlies the specific challenges inherent in the enhanced status which has been — and may be granted over time — to aboriginal and international law.

That larger question is also posed by the dramatic emergence of what I would reluctantly describe as cyberspace. It is perhaps the most stunning example of a technological innovation which defies traditional legal models and which will probably continue to do so for many years. I say I am "reluctant" because to concede that the medium of computer-assisted communication is a "space" is immediately to accept certain premises about the separateness of that realm from real world models of spatial jurisdiction. If it really is cyberspace, then doesn't that imply that there should be separate jurisdiction of cyber-courts, with cyber-rules, cyber-citizenry, and cyber normativity? There are legal academics who argue just that. And probably the majority of cyberspace participants are excited at the prospect of an Eden unspoiled by insidious legal regulation, and insist on the viability of self regulation based on technological borders rather than the frontiers of states.

Searching for the right metaphors which relate cyberspace to conventional law is a huge challenge precisely because there are no precise analogies to cyberspace in the real world. Moreover, many questions are implicated by the nature of cyberspace which have never been previously raised and which pose insoluble problems for legal doctrine as currently constituted. Questions such as: [w]hen users are in different countries, where is a contract made over the Internet for jurisdictional purposes? When a defamatory statement is made on the Internet, does every state where the

---

† (1997–98) 25 Manitoba Law Journal 411. Reproduced by permission of the author and the publisher.

statement is accessible have jurisdiction over that tort? Are criminal sanctions against, for example, hate speech, gambling, or pornography subject to the authority of any jurisdiction in which that speech is accessible? What type of communication on the Internet should be considered private and what should be considered public? Is a "chat-room" public or private? How private does the "chat-room" have to be before it is considered analogous to the privacy of one's home? Does, for example, the delicate balancing required under the Charter apply with equal force to all forms of speech on the Internet, even though that speech and the opportunity for response, rebuttal, control, and tuning-out are greater than in any other "public" forum?

The Internet raises a host of other issues which I have not canvassed here, particularly in the realm of intellectual property law. In fact, it is hardly an exaggeration to say that cyberspace is sufficiently distinct from any other model of communication and human interaction that almost every important issue in civil law, and many in the criminal context, may need to be reviewed according to the particular circumstances of this new technology. Moreover, courts will need to be aware as in no other domain of developments in other jurisdictions and the dictates of inter-jurisdictional comity. But this will be an elusive task for a medium where a message posted onto the Internet can simultaneously be available in every country in the world. The borders of cyberspace do not map onto the borders of real space, which poses a fundamental problem for courts whose jurisdiction is based on geography. New tools and new doctrines will need to be developed, and perhaps certain doctrines that have been developed heretofore, particularly in the realm of conflict of laws, will need to be revisited. While this challenge may not require the acceptance of a new normative order, as in the case of aboriginal or international law, it does present a whole area of such rapid technological change that it will be a challenge for legal models to adapt quickly and yet remain coherent and comprehensible over time. And depending on the response of other jurisdictions and users of cyberspace, what amounts to an independent normative code could develop and demand deference from Canadian courts.

Discussion Question

Consider this excerpt from Michael Geist, *The Reality of Bytes: Regulating Economic Activity in the Age of the Internet*:

> While the Internet may change the manner in which commerce is conducted, it will not alter the state's interest in regulating such activity. The rationales for regulating commercial activity — shifting costs to those parties who can best afford to bear the external costs created by the activity, addressing market imperfections such as informational inequalities, and implementing social regulation such as worker rights — remain unchanged in the age of the Internet.

Do you agree with this perspective? What, if anything, does the Internet change with regard to legal regulation?

3

Jurisdiction on the Internet

Lurking in the background of virtually every Internet law issue is the question of jurisdiction. Given the borderless nature of the Internet, the matter of who is entitled to regulate or assert jurisdiction quickly becomes as important as what is being regulated and how. As we have already discovered, some experts consider the jurisdictional dilemma unresolvable through traditional legal jurisdictional means and thus advocate a unique, Internet-specific solution.

As Internet law has developed, a two-step analytical approach has emerged. First, courts, regulators and legal practitioners must determine what law applies. In many instances it is unclear if traditional legal rules can be readily adapted to Internet activity. Although the common law is based on the laws' ability to adapt to changing circumstances, in certain fields the Internet represents a paradigm shift of a magnitude not previously contemplated by legislators, thus leaving existing law ill-equipped to handle these emerging legal issues.

Assuming the applicable law can be identified, the analysis then shifts to a second step consisting of determining who is entitled to apply the law. The effects of Internet activity are global in nature, such that online activity — be it fraudulent conduct or defamatory postings — can be accessed worldwide and, therefore, theoretically, subject the party to the legal system of any country worldwide.

From a practical perspective, however, there is little risk of being hauled into court in far off jurisdictions where the likelihood of enforcing a judgment is practically nil. For multinational corporations and others operating or traveling within multiple jurisdictions, the concern that Internet activity can be subject to legal proceedings in several jurisdictions is nevertheless worrisome, as legal proceedings can be costly and reputationally damaging.

In certain respects, these concerns are not new. Regulators and courts must always be cognizant of the limitations on their regulatory reach, striving to craft regulations that meet their policy needs yet simultaneously adhering to limitations of their jurisdiction. Whether in real space or online, legal regulations often have a cross-border element that frequently results in some degree of uncertainty as to which rules apply.

As academics and policy makers consider the Internet jurisdiction issue, courts worldwide have been confronted with many cases requiring resolution, resulting in the gradual development of a series of principles for determining Internet-based jurisdiction.

The examination of the law begins with a trilogy of cases from the United States, whose courts have played the leading role in developing Internet jurisdiction jurisprudence.

Inset Systems, Inc. v. Instruction Set, Inc.†

The plaintiff, Inset Systems, Inc. ("Inset"), is a corporation organized under the laws of the state of Connecticut, with its office and principal place of business in Brookfield, Connecticut. Inset develops and markets computer software and other related services throughout the world. The defendant, Instruction Set, Inc. ("ISI"), is a corporation organized under the laws of the state of Massachusetts, with its office and principal place of business in Natick, Massachusetts. ISI provides computer technology and support to thousands of organizations throughout the world. ISI does not have any employees, nor offices within Connecticut, and it does not conduct business in Connecticut on a regular basis.

On August 23, 1985, Inset filed for registration as the owner of the federal trademark INSET. On October 21, 1986, Inset received registration number 1,414,031.

Thereafter, ISI obtained "INSET.COM" as its Internet domain address. ISI uses this domain address to advertise its goods and services.... Inset first learned of ISI's Internet domain address in March, 1995 when attempting to obtain the same Internet domain address. ISI also uses the telephone number "1-800-US-INSET" to further advertise its goods and services. Inset did not authorize ISI's use of its trademark, "INSET", in any capacity. ISI continues to use "INSET" in relation to both its Internet domain address and its toll-free number. On June 30, 1995, the plaintiff filed the within action.

· · · ·

The Connecticut long-arm statute, C.G.S. §33-411(c)(2) states that "Every foreign corporation shall be subject to suit in this state, by a resident of this state ... on any cause of action arising ... (2) out of any business solicited in this state ... if the corporation has repeatedly so solicited business, whether the orders or offers relating thereto were accepted within or without the state ..." ... since March, 1995,

---

† 937 F. Supp. 161 (D. Conn. 1996).

ISI has been continuously advertising over the Internet, which includes at least 10,000 access sites in Connecticut. Further, unlike hard-copy advertisements noted in the above two cases, which are often quickly disposed of and reach a limited number of potential consumers, Internet advertisements are in electronic printed form so that they can be accessed again and again by many more potential consumers.

The court concludes that advertising via the Internet is solicitation of a sufficient repetitive nature to satisfy subsection (c)(2) of the Connecticut long-arm statute, C.G.S. §33-411, thereby conferring Connecticut's long-arm jurisdiction upon ISI.

. . . .

The defendant claims that personal jurisdiction is lacking here because it does not have sufficient minimum contacts within Connecticut to satisfy constitutional precepts concerning due process. Minimum contacts are lacking, according to the defendant, because it is a Massachusetts corporation with its office and principal place of business in Natick, Massachusetts, "it does not conduct business in Connecticut on a regular basis," and it "does not maintain an office in Connecticut, nor does it have a sales force or employees in the State."

The plaintiff responds that minimum contacts comporting with due process have been satisfied because the defendant has used the Internet, as well as its toll-free number to try to conduct business within the state of Connecticut.

"[Due Process] limitations require that a nonresident corporate defendant have 'minimum contacts' with the forum state such that it would reasonably anticipate being haled into court there. [Further], [m]aintenance of the suit in the forum state cannot offend traditional notions of fair play and substantial justice."

The essence of the minimum contacts test is "that there be some act by which the defendant purposefully avails itself of the privilege of conducting activities within the forum State, thus invoking the benefits and protections of its laws." This "due process inquiry rests upon the totality of the circumstances rather than any mechanical criteria ..."

In Whelen Eng'g Co., the court concluded that because "[the defendant] readily supplied interested potential customers with catalogs advertised in periodicals having Connecticut circulation, provided products on order ..., and demonstrated its readiness to initiate telephone solicitation of Connecticut customers," it purposefully availed itself of the privilege of doing business within the state and therefore, could reasonably be expected to be hailed [sic] into court.

In the present case, Instruction has directed its advertising activities via the Internet and its toll-free number toward not only the state of Connecticut, but to all states. The Internet as well as toll-free numbers are designed to communicate with people and their businesses in every state. Advertisement on the Internet can reach as many as 10,000 Internet users within Connecticut alone. Further, once posted on the Internet, unlike television and radio advertising, the advertisement is available continuously to any Internet user. ISI has therefore, purposefully availed itself of the privilege of doing business within Connecticut.

The court concludes that since ISI purposefully directed its advertising activities toward this state on a continuing basis since March, 1995, it could reasonably anticipate the possibility of being hailed [sic] into court here.

Bensusan Restaurant Corp. v. King[†]

Bensusan, a New York corporation, is the creator of a jazz club in New York City known as "The Blue Note." It also operates other jazz clubs around the world. Bensusan owns all rights, title and interest in and to the federally registered mark "The Blue Note." King is an individual who lives in Columbia, Missouri and he owns and operates a "small club" in that city which is also called "The Blue Note."

In April of 1996, King posted a "site" on the World Wide Web of the Internet to promote his club. This Web site, which is located on a computer server in Missouri, allegedly contains "a fanciful logo which is substantially similar to the logo utilized by [Bensusan]." The Web site is a general access site, which means that it requires no authentication or access code for entry, and is accessible to anyone around the world who has access to the Internet. It contains general information about the club in Missouri as well as a calendar of events and ticketing information. The ticketing information includes the names and addresses of ticket outlets in Columbia and a telephone number for charge-by-phone ticket orders, which are available for pick-up on the night of the show at the Blue Note box office in Columbia.

At the time this action was brought, the first page of the Web site contained the following disclaimer: "The Blue Note's Cyberspot should not be confused with one of the world's finest jazz club[s] [the] Blue Note, located in the heart of New York's Greenwich Village. If you should find yourself in the big apple give them a visit." Furthermore, the reference to Bensusan's club in the disclaimer contained a "hyperlink" which permits Internet users to connect directly to Bensusan's Web site by "clicking" on the link. After Bensusan objected to the Web site, King dropped the sentence "If you should find yourself in the big apple give them a visit" from the disclaimer and removed the hyperlink.

Bensusan brought this action asserting claims for trademark infringement, trademark dilution and unfair competition. King has now moved to dismiss the action for lack of personal jurisdiction pursuant to Fed. R. Civ. P. 12(b)(2).

. . . .

...[t]he issue that arises in this action is whether the creation of a Web site, which exists either in Missouri or in cyberspace — i.e., anywhere the Internet exists — with a telephone number to order the allegedly infringing product, is an offer to sell the product in New York.

Even after construing all allegations in the light most favorable to Bensusan, its allegations are insufficient to support a finding of long-arm jurisdiction over plaintiff. A New York resident with Internet access and either knowledge of King's Web site location or a "search engine" capable of finding it could gain access to the Web site and view information concerning the Blue Note in Missouri.

It takes several affirmative steps by the New York resident, however, to obtain access to the Web site and utilize the information there. First, the New York resident has to access the Web site using his or her computer hardware and software. Then, if the user wished to attend a show in defendant's club, he or she would have to telephone the box office in Missouri and reserve tickets. Finally, that user would need to pick up the tickets in Missouri because King does not mail or other-

---

† 937 F. Supp. 296 (S.D. N.Y. 1996).

wise transmit tickets to the user. Even assuming that the user was confused about the relationship of the Missouri club to the one in New York, such an act of infringement would have occurred in Missouri, not New York. The mere fact that a person can gain information on the allegedly infringing product is not the equivalent of a person advertising, promoting, selling or otherwise making an effort to target its product in New York.

Zippo Mfg. Co. v. Zippo Dot Com, Inc.[†]

The facts relevant to this motion are as follows. Manufacturing is a Pennsylvania corporation with its principal place of business in Bradford, Pennsylvania. Manufacturing makes, among other things, well known "Zippo" tobacco lighters. Dot Com is a California corporation with its principal place of business in Sunnyvale, California. Dot Com operates an Internet Web Site and an Internet news service and has obtained the exclusive right to use the domain names "zippo.com", "zippo.net" and "zipponews.com" on the Internet.

Dot Com's Web site contains information about the company, advertisements and an application for its Internet news service. The news service itself consists of three levels of membership — public/free, "Original" and "Super." Each successive level offers access to a greater number of Internet newsgroups. A customer who wants to subscribe to either the "Original" or "Super" level of service fills out an on-line application that asks for a variety of information including the person's name and address. Payment is made by credit card over the Internet or the telephone. The application is then processed and the subscriber is assigned a password which permits the subscriber to view and/or download Internet newsgroup messages that are stored on the Defendant's server in California.

Dot Com's contacts with Pennsylvania have occurred almost exclusively over the Internet. Dot Com's offices, employees and Internet servers are located in California. Dot Com maintains no offices, employees or agents in Pennsylvania. Dot Com's advertising for its service to Pennsylvania residents involves posting information about its service on its Web page, which is accessible to Pennsylvania residents via the Internet. Defendant has approximately 140,000 paying subscribers worldwide. Approximately two percent (3,000) of those subscribers are Pennsylvania residents. These subscribers have contracted to receive Dot Com's service by visiting its Web site and filling out the application. Additionally, Dot Com has entered into agreements with seven Internet access providers in Pennsylvania to permit their subscribers to access Dot Com's news service. Two of these providers are located in the Western District of Pennsylvania.

The basis of the trademark claims is Dot Com's use of the word "Zippo" in the domain names it holds, in numerous locations in its Web site and in the heading of Internet newsgroup messages that have been posted by Dot Com subscribers. When an Internet user views or downloads a newsgroup message posted by a Dot Com subscriber, the word "Zippo" appears in the "Message-Id" and "Organization" sections of the heading. The news message itself, containing text and/or pictures,

---

[†] 952 F. Supp. 1119 (W.D. Pa. 1997).

follows. Manufacturing points out that some of the messages contain adult oriented, sexually explicit subject matter.

. . . .

The Internet and Jurisdiction

In *Hanson* v. *Denckla*, the Supreme Court noted that "[a]s technological progress has increased the flow of commerce between States, the need for jurisdiction has undergone a similar increase." Twenty seven years later, the Court observed that jurisdiction could not be avoided "merely because the defendant did not physically enter the forum state."

The Court observed that:

[I]t is an inescapable fact of modern commercial life that a substantial amount of commercial business is transacted solely by mail and wire communications across state lines, thus obviating the need for physical presence within a State in which business is conducted.

Enter the Internet, a global "'super-network' of over 15,000 computer networks used by over 30 million individuals, corporations, organizations, and educational institutions worldwide." "In recent years, businesses have begun to use the Internet to provide information and products to consumers and other businesses." The Internet makes it possible to conduct business throughout the world entirely from a desktop. With this global revolution looming on the horizon, the development of the law concerning the permissible scope of personal jurisdiction based on Internet use is in its infant stages. The cases are scant. Nevertheless, our review of the available cases and materials reveals that the likelihood that personal jurisdiction can be constitutionally exercised is directly proportionate to the nature and quality of commercial activity that an entity conducts over the Internet. This sliding scale is consistent with well developed personal jurisdiction principles. At one end of the spectrum are situations where a defendant clearly does business over the Internet. If the defendant enters into contracts with residents of a foreign jurisdiction that involve the knowing and repeated transmission of computer files over the Internet, personal jurisdiction is proper.

At the opposite end are situations where a defendant has simply posted information on an Internet Web site which is accessible to users in foreign jurisdictions. A passive Web site that does little more than make information available to those who are interested in it is not grounds for the exercise personal jurisdiction. The middle ground is occupied by interactive Web sites where a user can exchange information with the host computer. In these cases, the exercise of jurisdiction is determined by examining the level of interactivity and commercial nature of the exchange of information that occurs on the Web site.

Traditionally, when an entity intentionally reaches beyond its boundaries to conduct business with foreign residents, the exercise of specific jurisdiction is proper. Different results should not be reached simply because business is conducted over the Internet. In *Compuserve, Inc.* v. *Patterson*, the Sixth Circuit addressed the significance of doing business over the Internet. In that case, Patterson, a Texas resident, entered into a contract to distribute shareware through Compuserve's Internet server located in Ohio. From Texas, Patterson electronically uploaded thirty-two master software files to Compuserve's server in Ohio via the Internet. One of

Patterson's software products was designed to help people navigate the Internet. When Compuserve later began to market a product that Patterson believed to be similar to his own, he threatened to sue. Compuserve brought an action in the Southern District of Ohio, seeking a declaratory judgment. The District Court granted Patterson's motion to dismiss for lack of personal jurisdiction and Compuserve appealed. The Sixth Circuit reversed, reasoning that Patterson had purposefully directed his business activities toward Ohio by knowingly entering into a contract with an Ohio resident and then "deliberately and repeatedly" transmitted files to Ohio.

In *Maritz, Inc.* v. *Cybergold, Inc.*, the defendant had put up a Web site as a promotion for its upcoming Internet service. The service consisted of assigning users an electronic mailbox and then forwarding advertisements for products and services that matched the users' interests to those electronic mailboxes. The defendant planned to charge advertisers and provide users with incentives to view the advertisements. Although the service was not yet operational, users were encouraged to add their address to a mailing list to receive updates about the service. The court rejected the defendant's contention that it operated a "passive Web site." The court reasoned that the defendant's conduct amounted to "active solicitations" and "promotional activities" designed to "develop a mailing list of Internet users" and that the defendant "indiscriminately responded to every user" who accessed the site.

Inset Systems, Inc. v. *Instruction Set*, represents the outer limits of the exercise of personal jurisdiction based on the Internet. In Inset Systems, a Connecticut corporation sued a Massachusetts corporation in the District of Connecticut for trademark infringement based on the use of an Internet domain name. The defendant's contacts with Connecticut consisted of posting a Web site that was accessible to approximately 10,000 Connecticut residents and maintaining a toll free number. The court exercised personal jurisdiction, reasoning that advertising on the Internet constituted the purposeful doing of business in Connecticut because "unlike television and radio advertising, the advertisement is available continuously to any Internet user."

Bensusan Restaurant Corp. v. *King*, reached a different conclusion based on a similar Web site. In Bensusan, the operator of a New York jazz club sued the operator of a Missouri jazz club for trademark infringement. The Internet Web site at issue contained general information about the defendant's club, a calendar of events and ticket information. However, the site was not interactive. If a user wanted to go to the club, she would have to call or visit a ticket outlet and then pick up tickets at the club on the night of the show. The court refused to exercise jurisdiction based on the Web site alone, reasoning that it did not rise to the level of purposeful availment of that jurisdiction's laws. The court distinguished the case from Compuserve, where the user had "'reached out' from Texas to Ohio and 'originated and maintained' contacts with Ohio."

Pres-Kap, Inc. v. *System One Direct Access, Inc.*, is not inconsistent with the above cases. In Pres-Kap, a majority of a three-judge intermediate state appeals court refused to exercise jurisdiction over a consumer of an on-line airline ticketing service. Pres-Kap involved a suit on a contract dispute in a Florida court by a Delaware corporation against its New York customer. The defendant had leased computer equipment which it used to access an airline ticketing computer located in Florida. The contract was solicited, negotiated, executed and serviced in New York. The defendant's only contact with Florida consisted of logging onto the computer located in Florida and mailing payments for the leased equipment to Florida. Pres-Kap is distinguishable from the above cases and the case at bar because it addressed the exercise of jurisdiction over a consumer of on-line services as opposed to a provider. When a consumer logs onto a server in a foreign jurisdiction he is engaging in a fundamentally different type of contact than an entity that is using the Internet to sell or market products or services to residents of foreign jurisdictions. The Pres-Kap court specifically expressed concern over the implications of subjecting users of "on-line" services with contracts with out-of-state networks to suit in foreign jurisdictions.

Application to this Case

First, we note that this is not an Internet advertising case in the line of Inset Systems and Bensusan. Dot Com has not just posted information on a Web site that is accessible to Pennsylvania residents who are connected to the Internet. This is not even an interactivity case in the line of Maritz. Dot Com has done more than create an interactive Web site through which it exchanges information with Pennsylvania residents in hopes of using that information for commercial gain later. We are not being asked to determine whether Dot Com's Web site alone constitutes the purposeful availment of doing business in Pennsylvania. This is a "doing business over the Internet" case in the line of Compuserve. We are being asked to determine whether Dot Com's conducting of electronic commerce with Pennsylvania residents constitutes the purposeful availment of doing business in Pennsylvania. We conclude that it does. Dot Com has contracted with approximately 3,000 individuals and seven Internet access providers in Pennsylvania. The intended object of these transactions has been the downloading of the electronic messages that form the basis of this suit in Pennsylvania.

We find Dot Com's efforts to characterize its conduct as falling short of purposeful availment of doing business in Pennsylvania wholly unpersuasive. At oral argument, Defendant repeatedly characterized its actions as merely "operating a Web site" or "advertising." Dot Com also cites to a number of cases from this Circuit which, it claims, stand for the proposition that merely advertising in a forum, without more, is not a sufficient minimal contact. This argument is misplaced. Dot Com has done more than advertise on the Internet in Pennsylvania. Defendant has sold passwords to approximately 3,000 Subscribers in Pennsylvania and entered into seven contracts with Internet access providers to furnish its services to their customers in Pennsylvania.

Discussion Questions

1. The *Inset* decision is still referred to by some courts seeking support for the assertion of jurisdiction. Did the court ask the right questions? Is the number of hits or visits to a Web site relevant when considering jurisdiction? What problems can you envision with using hits as a determining factor for the assertion of jurisdiction?

2. The use of analogies or metaphors plays an important role in developing our understanding of the Internet and its application to the legal system. Do you agree with the *Inset* court's characterization of the Internet as a continuous advertisement? Can you think of a better analogy? Is the use of analogies dangerous in this context given the proclivity to overlook the actual online activity and instead work to neatly characterize the Internet into a pre-existing legal approach?

3. The *Zippo* analysis set the tone for future Internet jurisdiction cases with most citing the approach with approval. Do you think that the passive vs. active distinction is clear? What factors do you think should be considered as part of the analysis?

    Consider, for example, the sale of an everyday consumer product such as a lawnmower. Few would contest jurisdiction where the lawnmower manufacturer uses its Web site to sell its product directly to consumers. However, what if the Web site only advertises the lawnmower, with no direct sales? What if the site provides an email address for direct customer contact but still no direct sales? What if the site includes an online catalogue but still no direct sales? What if the site does not sell directly online but directs purchasers to an 800 toll free number where lawnmowers can be purchased? Does the wide range of possibilities suggest that there may be less certainty to the jurisdiction test than the *Zippo* court implies?

Canadian firms have not been immune to the prospect of facing litigation in the United States for Internet-based activity. Colorworks Reproduction & Design, Inc., a Vancouver-based firm, was forced to defend its right to the "colorworks.com" domain name in this 1999 proceeding in Pennsylvania.

Desktop Technologies, Inc. v. Colorworks Reproduction & Design, Inc.[†]

Plaintiff is a corporation organized under the laws of Pennsylvania with its principal place of business in Boyertown, Pennsylvania. Defendant is a corporation organized under the laws of Canada with its principal place of business in Vancouver, British Columbia. Defendant contends, and Plaintiff does not contest, that its business is carried out exclusively in the British Columbia lower mainland and that Defendant has not transacted any business, provided any services, contracted to provide any services, earned any income, or entered into any contracts in Pennsylvania.

The general nature of the parties' businesses are the same: both companies prepare and print color reproductions. Plaintiff is the owner of a U.S. trademark, COLORWORKS, which was registered in the United States on June 4, 1996. Defendant is the owner of the trademark, "ColorWorks," which was registered in Canada on March 25, 1997.

Since August 21, 1995, Defendant has operated a web site on the Internet with the domain name of "colorworks.com." Defendant's web site is accessible to all Internet users, including those in Pennsylvania at http://www.colorworks.com. In its complaint, Plaintiff alleges that Defendant's use of the word "ColorWorks" as its domain name on the Internet infringes Plaintiff's trademark rights and enables Defendant to compete unfairly with Plaintiff in the United States.

---

† U.S. Dist. Lexis 1934 (E.D. Pa. 1999).

Defendant's web site contains information about the company, advertisements about the company, and employment opportunities at the company. The site specifically states that it services clients in British Columbia, Alberta, and Yukon. It lists its local telephone and facsimile numbers, and provides an order form and instructions for entering orders. The site also allows a reader to send a message via e-mail and to exchange files via Internet File Transfer Protocol ("FTP"). However, the site indicates that Defendant does not conduct sales, accept orders, or receive payments through its web site. The site also indicates that receiving a file via Internet FTP or an e-mail is not a sales transaction and does not constitute placing an order. To place an order, a reader can print up a copy of the fax order form, complete the form, and fax it to Defendant. Notably, the order form cannot be completed on-line.

I.   General Jurisdiction

In analyzing a defendant's contacts through the use of the Internet, the probability that personal jurisdiction may be constitutionally exercised is "directly proportionate to the nature and quality of commercial activity that an entity conducts over the Internet." *Grutkowski* v. *Steamboat Lake Guides & Outfitters, Inc.*, (quoting *Blackburn* v. *Walker Oriental Rug Galleries, Inc.*). Courts have established three categories of Internet contacts, each with its own standards governing the propriety of personal jurisdiction based on those contacts. As explained in Blackburn: The first type of contact is when the defendant clearly does business over the Internet. If the defendant enters into contracts with residents of a foreign jurisdiction that involve the knowing and repeated transmission of computer files over the Internet, personal jurisdiction is proper. The second type of contact occurs when a user can exchange information with the host computer. In these cases, the exercise of jurisdiction is determined by examining the level of interactivity and commercial nature of the exchange of information that occurs on the Web site. The third type of contact involves the posting of information or advertisements on an Internet Web site which is accessible to users in foreign jurisdictions. Personal jurisdiction is not exercised for this type of contact because a finding of jurisdiction ... based on an Internet web site would mean that there would be nationwide (indeed worldwide) personal jurisdiction over anyone and everyone who establishes an Internet Web site. Such nationwide jurisdiction is not consistent with personal jurisdiction case law.

The nature of Defendant's contacts with this District falls into the third category, which consists of a passive web site. Defendant's web site contains several pages of advertisements and employment opportunities at Colorworks. Thus, the interactivity of Defendant's web site is plainly limited to exchanging files with Defendant via Internet FTP or e-mail. The web site also indicates that receiving a file via Internet FTP or e-mail does not constitute an order or sale; the site does not permit a reader to place an order over the Internet and thus, does not permit Defendant to "transact business" over the Internet. Instead, the site specifically directs the reader to print out a copy of the fax order form provided and to fax it into Defendant to place an order. Defendant will not begin working on the order until it has verified the order by telephone.

Defendant's web site is tantamount to a passive advertisement. Though commercial in nature, Plaintiff has failed to establish that Defendant has maintained either systematic or continuous contacts necessary to establish general personal jurisdiction. The Internet FTP and the e-mail links are the only interactive elements of these pages. The Internet FTP is merely a system which allows a user to transfer a file to Defendant via the Internet. The e-mail links are, as stated by the court in

Grutkowski, "the electronic equivalents of advertisements' response cards" and are insufficient to make these pages more than advertisements (holding that an e-mail link was insufficient to establish personal jurisdiction). Because advertising on the Internet is similar to advertising in national publications, and advertising in national publications is not a basis for asserting personal jurisdiction, this Court finds that Defendant's Internet advertisements do not subject Defendant to general personal jurisdiction in Pennsylvania.

II. Specific Jurisdiction

As there is no general personal jurisdiction over Defendant under the facts of this case, if personal jurisdiction exists, it must be specific. "Specific jurisdiction is invoked when the cause of action arises from the defendant's forum related activities ... 'such that the defendant should reasonably anticipate being haled into court there.'" To establish specific jurisdiction, "the plaintiff must show that the defendant has constitutionally sufficient 'minimum contacts' with the forum." In applying the minimum contacts standard, it is clear that a "defendant will not be haled into a jurisdiction solely as a result of 'random,' fortuitous,' or 'attenuated' contacts." Rather, the plaintiff must establish that the defendant "purposefully availed itself" of the privilege of conducting activities within the forum.

The likelihood that personal jurisdiction can be constitutionally exercised is directly proportionate to the nature and quality of commercial activity that an entity conducts over the Internet. This sliding scale approach is similar to the approach used to determine whether general jurisdiction can be exercised. At one end of the spectrum are situations where a defendant clearly does business over the Internet. If the defendant enters into contracts with residents of a foreign jurisdiction that involve the knowing and repeated transmission of computer files over the Internet, personal jurisdiction is proper. At the opposite end are situations where a defendant has simply posted information on a web site which is accessible to users in foreign jurisdictions. Thus, "[a] passive Web site that does little more than make information available to those who are interested in it is not grounds for the exercise [of] personal jurisdiction." The middle ground is occupied by interactive web sites where a user can exchange information with the host computer. In these cases, the exercise of jurisdiction is determined by examining the level of interactivity and the commercial nature of the exchange of information that occurs on the web site.

Because the parties have agreed that Defendant's business is carried out exclusively in the British Columbia lower mainland, any claim that this Court has specific jurisdiction over Defendant must be based on the allegation that Defendant's domain name, colorworks.com, and its web site infringe Plaintiff's trademark in Pennsylvania and that Defendant's web site can be accessed in Pennsylvania. Upon review of recent cases that have addressed the issue of whether a forum can exercise specific jurisdiction over a non-resident defendant based upon a claim that the defendant's web site or domain name infringes the trademark rights of a resident plaintiff, a basic principal emerges:

> [S]imply registering someone else's trademark as a domain name and posting a web site on the Internet is not sufficient to subject a party domiciled in one state to jurisdiction in another ... [T]here must be "something more" to demonstrate that the defendant directed his activity towards the forum state.

Thus, publication of a page on the web, without more, is not an act by which a party purposefully avails itself of the privilege of conducting business in the forum state.

The level of interactivity in this case is insufficient to justify exercising specific personal jurisdiction over Defendant. Courts have repeatedly recognized that there must be "something more" than simply registering someone else's trademark as a domain name and posting a web site on the Internet to demonstrate that the defendant directed its activity towards the forum state. In Zippo Mfg. Co., the court characterized the litigation as a "doing business over the Internet case" and found that the defendant had "done more than advertise on the Internet in Pennsylvania. The fact that defendant had sold passwords to approximately 3,000 subscribers in Pennsylvania and entered into seven contracts with Internet access providers to furnish its services to its customers in Pennsylvania constituted purposeful availment of doing business in Pennsylvania. In the present case, which this Court characterizes as an Internet advertising case, Plaintiff has failed to prove that Defendant purposefully availed itself of the privilege of conducting business in Pennsylvania.

Defendant's Internet presence and e-mail link are its only contacts with Pennsylvania. As established earlier, Defendant maintains the web site to advertise and post information about its services and employment opportunities. The web site does not exist for the purpose of entering into contracts with customers outside of Canada or for the purpose of attracting customers from Pennsylvania. Instead, its web site specifically states that it is servicing clients in British Columbia, Alberta and Yukon. Defendant has never entered into any contracts in Pennsylvania, made sales or earned income in Pennsylvania, or sent messages over the Internet to users in Pennsylvania. While visitors to the web site are able to exchange information over the web site via Internet FTP and e-mail, receiving a file through Internet FTP or an e-mail does not constitute placing an order. Thus, while Defendant is exchanging information over the Internet, it is not doing business over the Internet with residents of Pennsylvania. Accordingly, this Court finds that Defendant's registration of "ColorWorks" as a domain name and posting a web site on the Internet are insufficient to subject Defendant to specific personal jurisdiction in Pennsylvania.

Postscript

Colorworks filed for bankruptcy protection during this proceeding. In early 2000, the domain name was sold to a New Jersey-based company.

Following several years of speculation, the Canadian courts finally ruled on an Internet jurisdiction case in the spring of 1999. Although the case involved a judgment enforcement action, the B.C. Court of Appeal nevertheless provided the Canadian legal community with a clear sense of the Canadian approach to Internet jurisdiction.

Braintech, Inc. v. Kostiuk†

On 7 May 1997 the respondent ("Braintech") obtained a default judgment in the District Court of Harris County in the State of Texas against the appellant ("Kostiuk"). On 9 May 1997 Braintech commenced an action on this judgment in the Supreme Court of British Columbia. On 2 April 1998, after a summary trial Braintech obtained a judgment in its favour from which the present appeal is taken.

Braintech described itself in its first pleading (the "Original Petition") filed in the District Court:

> BrainTech, Inc. is a developmental stage company with corporate offices located in Vancouver, British Columbia and research and development facilities located in Austin, Texas. BrainTech is involved in design and development of advanced recognition systems based on its patented and highly adaptable set of computer-based pattern matching algorithms.
>
> As a corporation in the "developmental stage" it makes no claim it produces and sells its systems.

It asserts itself to be a publicly held company whose stock is bought and sold via OTC Bulletin Board trading. The location of the OTC exchange is not stated. From other references it may be inferred it is not in Canada.

In 1996 Kostiuk is alleged to have used the Internet to transmit and publish defamatory information about BrainTech. Specifically, the means of dissemination was alleged in Braintech's amended pleading (the "Amended Petition") as follows:

> A discussion group or bulletin board has been established on the Internet to facilitate discussion and exchange of information regarding technology stocks and investments. This discussion group, which is operated under the name Silicon Investor, allows those interested in technology companies like BrainTech to exchange information relevant to possible investments in such companies.

I will refer to this bulletin board as "Silicon Investor".

.   .   .   .

The Standard of Review of a Foreign Judgment by a Canadian Court

The starting point is the judgment of the Supreme Court of Canada in Morguard. In that case De Savoye (the appellant) owned land in Alberta subject to two mortgages. When the mortgages fell into arrears the mortgagees commenced proceedings in Alberta. Meanwhile the appellant had left that province and service was effected in accordance with the rules for service ex juris of the Alberta court. The appellant took no steps to appear or to defend the actions.

The mortgagees obtained judgments nisi and, at the expiration of the redemption period, orders for judicial sale of the mortgaged properties to themselves. Judgments were entered against the appellant for the deficiencies. Each mortgagee then commenced a separate action in the Supreme Court of British Columbia to enforce the Alberta judgments for the deficiencies. The issue in the Supreme Court of Canada was the recognition to be given by the courts in province A to an in personam

---

† [1999] 171 D.L.R. (4th) 46 (B.C. C.A.).

judgment of the courts in province B granted in default of appearance of the non-resident defendant.

Mr. Justice La Forest, speaking for the Court, concluded that considerations which reflected modern requirements of commerce and the reality of modern means of communication justified a departure from 19th century standards:

> These concerns, however, must be weighed against fairness to the defendant. The taking of jurisdiction by a court in one province and its recognition in another must be viewed as correlatives and recognition in other provinces should be dependent on the fact that the court giving judgment "properly" or "appropriately" exercised jurisdiction. It may meet the demands of order and fairness to recognize a judgment given in a jurisdiction that had the greatest or at least significant contacts with the subject matter of the action. But it hardly accords with principles of order and fairness to permit a person to sue another in any jurisdiction, without regard to the contacts that jurisdiction may have to the defendant or the subject matter of the suit. If the courts of one province are to be expected to give effect to judgments given in another province, there must be some limit to the exercise of jurisdiction against persons outside the province. If it is reasonable to support the exercise of jurisdiction in one province, it is reasonable that the judgment be recognized in other provinces.
>
> The approach of permitting suit where there is a real and substantial connection with the action provides a reasonable balance between the rights of the parties. It affords some protection against being pursued in jurisdictions having little or no connection with the transaction or the parties.

As to the difficulties which may be experienced with the new test, Mr. Justice La Forest said:

> I am aware, of course, that the possibility of being sued outside the province of his residence may pose a problem for a defendant. But that can occur in relation to actions in rem now. In any event, this consideration must be weighed against the fact that the plaintiff under the English rules may often find himself subjected to the inconvenience of having to pursue his debtor to another province, however just, efficient or convenient it may be to pursue an action where the contract took place or the damage occurred.

and:

> There are as well other discretionary techniques that have been used by courts for refusing to grant jurisdiction to plaintiffs whose contact with the jurisdiction is tenuous or where entertaining the proceedings would create injustice, notably the doctrine of forum non conveniens and the power of a court to prevent an abuse of its process; for a recent discussion, see Elizabeth Edinger, "Discretion in the Assumption and Exercise of Jurisdiction in British Columbia."
>
> There may also be remedies available to the recognizing court that may afford redress to the defendant in certain cases such as fraud or conflict with the law or public policy of the recognizing jurisdiction. Here, too, there may be room for the operation of s. 7 of the Charter. None of these questions, however, are relevant to the facts of the present case and I have not given them consideration.

In the case before him he observed Alberta was the place where the real properties were situate; where the contracts were entered into and where the affinity between a foreclosure proceeding and an action on the covenant was most apparent.

The trial judge in the case at bar instructed himself with respect to the Morguard test, namely, whether there was a real and substantial connection to Texas, and concluded that the evidence strongly supported there being such a connection. For reasons I will next discuss I am of the view he erred.

Real and Substantial Connection

I will consider first the connection between Texas and the injury alleged.

It is here the judgment of the Supreme Court of Canada in Amchem is helpful. It does not appear to have been drawn to the attention of the trial judge.

In Morguard the fairness of the process in a foreign jurisdiction was not directly in issue as the proceedings were wholly within the Canadian federation. On the other hand, in respect of a true foreign judgment fairness to the non-resident defendant required that the judgment be issued by a court acting through fair process with properly restrained jurisdiction.

Comity thus becomes an element in the case at bar.

In Amchem its importance arose in the context of an anti-suit injunction issued by the Supreme Court of British Columbia restraining those subject to it from pursuing a tort remedy in Texas for asbestos related injuries. Although the facts are complex, in its simplest form the action in Texas was commenced by plaintiffs resident in British Columbia against corporations unconnected with this province but which were alleged, as to some of them, to do business in Texas. Upon being served most of the corporate defendants specially appeared in the Texas court to claim Texas was not a convenient forum. The doctrine or rule commonly known as forum non conveniens has been abolished in Texas. The application for a stay of proceedings failed.

In the British Columbia court the corporate defendants sought a declaration this province was the "natural forum" as most of the plaintiffs were residents claiming damages for injuries suffered here. Actions had been commenced here and the right to maintain an action which included an alleged conspiracy on the part of defendants who did not do business here had been confirmed by the Supreme Court of Canada. As well, many of the plaintiffs here were in receipt of compensation from the Workers' Compensation Board of this province giving rise in the latter to subrogated rights.

A major reason why the chambers judge in Amchem granted the anti-suit injunction was the abolition of the rule of forum non conveniens in Texas. This was regarded as oppressive, arising from the defendants' need to defend parallel actions in two jurisdictions.

As has been seen it was unnecessary in Morguard to consider the case of competing jurisdictions to which the recognized principle of comity applied with full force. This was the situation in Amchem.

Mr. Justice Sopinka, speaking for the Court in Amchem, adopted the same definition of comity as was adopted in Morguard, namely, the following from the judgment in the Supreme Court of the United States in *Hilton* v. *Guyot*:

> "Comity" in the legal sense, is neither a matter of absolute obligation, on the one hand, nor of mere courtesy and good will, upon the other. But it is the recognition which one nation allows within its territory to the legislative, executive or judicial acts of another nation, having due regard both to international duty and convenience, and to the rights of its own citizens or of other persons who are under the protection of its laws ...

He identified the principle of forum non conveniens as the means of implementing the balancing of interests called for in the last clause of this definition. But, he expressly held its abolition in Texas did not have the conclusive weight adopted in the British Columbia courts. He said:

> With due respect to the trial judge, the principle of comity to which I have referred does not require that the decision of the foreign court be based on the doctrine of forum non conveniens. Many states in the United States and other countries do not apply that principle. Indeed, until comparatively recent times, it was not applied in England. Does this mean that a decision of the courts of one of these countries which, in the result, is consistent with the application of our rules would not be entitled to respect? The response must be in the negative. It is the result of the decision when measured against our principles that is important and not necessarily the reasoning that leads to that decision. Moreover, while the Texas courts do not apply a forum non conveniens test as such, they are required to comply with Section 1 of the Fourteenth Amendment to the Constitution of the United States which operates to limit the power of a state to assert in personam jurisdiction over a non-resident defendant. ... The due process requirements are satisfied when in personam jurisdiction is asserted over a non-resident corporate defendant that has "certain minimum contacts with [the forum] such that the maintenance of the suit does not offend 'traditional notions of fair play and substantial justice';

If the obligation to defer to the comity which is to be accorded the default judgment of the District Court of Harris County pronounced 7 May 1997 is to be tested by the principle of forum non conveniens some flesh must be put on the bare bones of "real and substantial connection".

That this is the task of the courts of the jurisdiction of the resident against whom the judgment is sought to be enforced seems clear from what was said in Amchem:

> While the above scenario is one we should strive to attain, it has not yet been achieved. Courts of other jurisdictions do occasionally accept jurisdiction over cases that do not satisfy the basic requirements of the forum non conveniens test. Comity is not universally respected. In some cases a serious injustice will be occasioned as a result of the failure of a foreign court to decline jurisdiction. It is only in such circumstances that a court should entertain an application for an anti-suit injunction. This then indicates the general tenor of the principles that underlie the granting of this form of relief. In order to arrive at more specific criteria, it is necessary to consider when a foreign court has departed from our own test of forum non conveniens to such an extent as to justify our courts in refusing to respect the assumption of jurisdiction by the foreign court and in what circumstances such assumption amounts to a serious injustice. The former requires an examination of the current state of the law relating to the stay of proceedings on the ground of forum non conveniens, while the latter, the law with respect to injunctions and specifically anti-suit injunctions.

It is apparent the "real and substantial connection" relied upon for the assumption of jurisdiction by the Texas court is the alleged publication there of a libel which affected the interests of resident present and potential investors. This is true only if the mode of communication through the Internet supports this conclusion.

It is trite law that a libel is only committed when the defamatory material is published to at least one person other than the complainant.

I earlier referred to the constitutional limitation in the United States on the exercise of personal jurisdiction. In *Zippo Manufacturing Company* v. *Zippo DotCom, Inc.* the following occurs....

From what is alleged in the case at bar it is clear Kostiuk is not the operator of Silicon Investor. It is equally clear the bulletin board is "passive" as posting information volunteered by people like Kostiuk, accessible only to users who have the means of gaining access and who exercise that means.

In these circumstances the complainant must offer better proof that the defendant has entered Texas than the mere possibility that someone in that jurisdiction might have reached out to cyberspace to bring the defamatory material to a screen in Texas. There is no allegation or evidence Kostiuk had a commercial purpose that utilized the highway provided by Internet to enter any particular jurisdiction.

It would create a crippling effect on freedom of expression if, in every jurisdiction the world over in which access to Internet could be achieved, a person who posts fair comment on a bulletin board could be haled before the courts of each of those countries where access to this bulletin could be obtained.

In the default judgment it is recited that the allegations of the Original and Amended Petitions "have been admitted". This simply reflects the convention in Texas that if a defendant who has been properly served does not appear the allegations in the petition are admitted as proven. This is a deemed admission which does not assist the respondent in establishing a real and substantial connection between the appellant and the Texas court.

In the circumstance of no purposeful commercial activity alleged on the part of Kostiuk and the equally material absence of any person in that jurisdiction having "read" the alleged libel all that has been deemed to have been demonstrated was Kostiuk's passive use of an out of state electronic bulletin. The allegation of publication fails as it rests on the mere transitory, passive presence in cyberspace of the alleged defamatory material. Such a contact does not constitute a real and substantial presence. On the American authorities this is an insufficient basis for the exercise of an in personam jurisdiction over a non-resident.

Discussion Questions

1. Why do you think Braintech launched the action in Texas? Is this an illustration of the perils of forum shopping in the age of the Internet?

2. Do you agree that postings to a discussion forum are passive in nature? What would be needed to change your mind?

3. Internet jurisdiction discussion often focuses on the location of the Web server with many arguing that jurisdiction can be avoided by placing a Web site on a server outside the jurisdiction. Do you think this is correct? Should parties avoid legal rules through mechanisms as simple as this?

   Consider that courts in several other countries have faced this question and ruled that the "server is elsewhere" is not an effective excuse for avoiding local jurisdiction. For example, individuals in both Japan and the U.K. have been convicted under local pornography laws despite the fact that the materials in question were located on a Web server in the United States.

In Canada, a criminal libel case winding its way through the Canadian court system as of July 2000 will also test this question. In May 1999 Gregory Barrett became the first Canadian to be charged with criminal libel for materials posted on a Web site. Barrett moved the offending materials to a Web site based in El Salvador as means of avoiding Canadian jurisdiction.

4. A 1998 Newfoundland case also addressed the issue of Internet jurisdiction, albeit indirectly. *Alteen* v. *Informix Corp.* ([1998] N.J. No. 122 1997 (Newfoundland T.D.)) involved a securities tort action where the stock issuer had no offices or contacts within the province. Its disclosure documents were readily available to provincial residents via the Internet, however, a fact that the court used to find that jurisdiction within the province was foreseeable. Does this reasoning sound strikingly similar to that found in the *Inset* approach? Should it similarly be rejected?

5. The cross-border nature of the Internet frequently creates confusing litigation. Consider the confusion in the Mecklermedia Internet World case in England where a U.S. company's U.K. subsidiary brought an action against a German company for trademark infringement based on Internet World trade shows that occurred in Germany and Austria. Which court should have jurisdiction over such a complex (but increasingly common) set of facts? See [1998] Ch 40, [1998] 1 All ER 148, [1997] 3 WLR 479, [1997] FSR 627.

The Alberta Securities Commission faced a similarly complex set of facts in a case involving an Internet-based stock exchange called the World Stock Exchange. The venture originated in Alberta but was incorporated in the Cayman Islands and used a Web server in Antigua. The Commission addressed the issue of its jurisdiction in February 2000.

World Stock Exchange (Re)[†]

At all relevant times, Orest Rusnak and Tom Seto both resided in Edmonton, Alberta. Tom Seto described himself as a salesman, business consultant and the founder of the WSE. Orest Rusnak, a former lawyer, is president of Academy Financial Planners & Consultants Inc. ("Academy Financial"). The letterhead of Academy Financial says, "International Business, Legal & Financial Consulting".

In September or October of 1997, Tom Seto came up with the idea of setting up an Internet stock exchange. He discussed the idea with Orest Rusnak, who prepared most of the written material relating to the WSE, with editorial input from Tom Seto. Mr. Rose, an Edmonton businessman, also provided some comments on the material.

At that time, there was no formal organization to the WSE. Tom Seto described Mr. Rose as an "extremely competent and conscientious type businessman" whose advice he respected. Tom Seto described Orest Rusnak's role with the WSE

---

† Alberta Securities Commission Decision, February 15, 2000.

"basically as a consultant and advisor, and in some ways a friend and business cohort".

In late October of 1997, Tom Seto registered a domain name (worldstock.com) and opened a website under the name "World Stock Exchange on the Internet". A website is a collection of web pages stored on a single computer that is connected to, and accessible through, the Internet. The WSE website was stored on and accessible through an Internet service provider whose computer was located in Edmonton, Alberta.

At that time, the website was still under construction and, although it is clear that no companies were then listed, the website included information on how a company could become listed on the WSE. Not all the information on the website was consistent, but it appeared to include a requirement that the listing company purchase shares in the WSE. A printed copy of the website as it existed on November 5, 1997 was entered in evidence.

By November 5, 1997 Commission staff had learned of the website and issued an Investigation Order pursuant to section 28 of the Act. On November 10, 1997 a Commission investigator, Mr. Kimak, met with Tom Seto and advised him to "take the website down" pending further investigation. Tom Seto removed everything except the title page, and advised Mr. Kimak that he was going to the Cayman Islands the next day to set up the website there.

On November 11, 1997, Tom Seto, Orest Rusnak and Mr. Rose went to the Cayman Islands. On that trip, WSE was incorporated in the Cayman Islands, as were Valle Los Reyes Island Resort Ltd. ("Valle Los Reyes") and Canroc International Ltd. ("Canroc"), two of the companies to be listed on the WSE.

Tom Seto was named as a director of WSE. Mr. Rose was, as he described it, "a director and the nominal president". According to Mr. Rose, Orest Rusnak was essentially running the show during their time in the Cayman Islands, while Mr. Rose "sort of toddled around behind everybody". Mr. Rose resigned his positions with the WSE in May 1998 because, as he described it:

> I was concerned that Orest Rusnak was doing some things, and even though I was nominal president and director I wanted to know what was going on. And I didn't know that our website had been shut down, I didn't know that our lawyer had ceased to act for us and things like that that had to do with this problem with the Cayman Stock Exchange and with the government getting on our case. And a month had gone by and Orest who had all of this information didn't pass it on to me. I thought there is no communication here and, therefore, I can't be left in a position where I am a director of a company and I don't know what is happening. So that is when I resigned.

The WSE website was stored on and accessible on the Internet through a computer located in the Cayman Islands for some time. The Cayman Island authorities had some problems with the WSE website and, as Mr. Rose described it, "the government, the police shut it down". The WSE website was then moved to a computer located in Antigua. Mr. Kimak downloaded a copy of the Antigua website as it existed on September 28, 1998 and the printed version of that was entered in evidence.

.   .   .   .

The WSE is active in and has connections to many jurisdictions, including Alberta. Our jurisdiction under the Securities Act is basically territorial, and we must consider whether the WSE's activities fall within that jurisdiction.

We find that the same territoriality considerations apply in this case as discussed by the Supreme Court of Canada in *Libman* v. *The Queen*. Libman involved a fraud charge under the Criminal Code where the accused conducted activities in several countries, including Canada. La Forest J. reviews the history of English and Canadian law in relation to transnational offences and distills it down to a concise rationale and conclusion which we find directly applicable to the case at hand.

La Forest J. describes the basic rationale for territoriality as follows:

> [T]he territorial principle in criminal law was developed by the courts to respond to two practical considerations, first, that a country has generally little direct concern for the actions of malefactors abroad, and secondly, that other states may legitimately take umbrage if a country attempts to regulate matters taking place wholly or substantially within their territories. For these reasons the courts adopted a presumption against the application of laws beyond the realm....

. . . .

La Forest J. summarized his approach to the limits of territoriality as follows:

> As I see it, all that is necessary to make an offence subject to the jurisdiction of our courts is that a significant portion of the activities constituting that offence took place in Canada. As it is put by modern academics, it is sufficient that there be a "real and substantial link" between an offence and this country, a test well known in public and private international law....

La Forest J. also described the need to adopt an evolving concept of comity, saying:

> Just what may constitute a real and substantial link in a particular case, I need not explore. There were ample links here. The outer limits of the test may, however, well be coterminous with the requirements of international comity.
>
> As I have already noted, in some of the early cases the English courts tended to express a narrow view of the territorial application of English law so as to ensure that they did not unduly infringe on the jurisdiction of other states. However, even as early as the late 19th century, following the invention and development of modern means of communication, they began to exercise criminal jurisdiction over transnational transactions as long as a significant part of the chain of action occurred in England. Since then means of communications have proliferated at an accelerating pace and the common interests of states have grown proportionately. Under these circumstances, the notion of comity, which means no more nor less than "kindly and considerate behaviour towards others", has also evolved. How considerate is it of the interests of the United States in this case to permit criminals based in this country to prey on its citizens? How does it conform to its interests or to ours for us to permit such activities when law enforcement agencies in both countries have developed cooperative schemes to prevent and prosecute those engaged in such activities? To ask these questions is to answer them. No issue of comity is involved here. In this regard, I make mine the words of Lord Diplock in *Treacy* v. *Director of Public Prosecutions* cited earlier. I also agree with the sentiments expressed by Lord Salmon in *Director of Public Prosecutions* v. *Doot*, supra, that we should not be indifferent to the protection of the public in other countries. In a shrinking world, we are all our brother's keepers. In the criminal arena this is underlined by the international cooperative schemes that have been developed among national law enforcement bodies.

Although the Libman decision addresses territoriality in the context of criminal law, in our view the same principles are applicable to the Act, including section 52(1).

(g) Conclusion

We find that the WSE did carry on business as an exchange in Alberta, contrary to section 52(1) of the Act.

We find that any similarity between the activities in Alberta of the WSE and of regulated exchanges is entirely superficial. The most important distinguishing characteristic of the WSE is its general lack of regulation, manifested in business practices that are contrary to the public interest. We find that the purpose of section 52(1) is [sic] protect the public interest by prohibiting such practices.

We interpret the phrase "carry on business as an exchange in Alberta" to mean, in effect, "conduct any exchange activity in Alberta that requires the Commission to act to protect the public interest". Although this makes the application of section 52(1) somewhat nebulous, that is a natural consequence of the fact that it is impossible to precisely define the public interest in the context of innovative or evolving exchange activity. While the public interest remains relatively constant, and is quite clearly reflected in the regulatory requirements imposed upon the actual activities of recognized exchanges, exchange activities are almost infinitely variable. Every exchange must be assessed individually and it is the combined effect of all its activities that must be weighed against the public interest to determine whether section 52(1) should apply. It would be inappropriate to focus on particular operations or activities as determinative because these are easily manipulated (as this case shows), and to do so would enable such manipulation to succeed in avoiding public-interest regulation.

.   .   .   .   .

With the passage of physical trading floors and the evolution of technology, the location of exchange operations has become increasingly flexible and notional. That makes the location of exchange operations less significant, and the functional linkage between an exchange and its recognizing regulator more significant, in determining where that exchange carries on business. To some extent, exchanges may choose where they want to be regulated and so assert where they believe that they carry on business within the meaning of the Act, as CDNX did recently when it sought recognition from the Commissions in both Alberta and British Columbia. In our view, as long as the connection between a regulated exchange and its home jurisdiction is reasonable and substantial, and the exchange's activities do not raise public interest concerns in Alberta (generally, by the home jurisdiction maintaining regulatory standards comparable to ours), section 52(1) should be interpreted to say that the regulated exchange carries on business only in its home jurisdiction.

We see clear distinctions between the connection of a typical regulated exchange to its home jurisdiction and the situation of the WSE. The WSE tried to choose its regulator by deliberately seeking the minimum possible amount of regulation. When the authorities in the Cayman Islands shut down the WSE's operations there, it moved to Antigua. In our view, this flag-of-convenience approach demonstrates the lack of any substantial connection between the WSE and either of its purported home jurisdictions. Even if the WSE had much closer links to its purported home jurisdictions, the lack of significant regulation by those jurisdictions would, in our view, preclude them from being considered home jurisdictions comparable to those of regulated exchanges. In this sense, unregulated exchanges are homeless. They may therefore be seen as carrying on business wherever they set foot and subject to enforcement action by any jurisdiction with standards comparable to ours.

The WSE has real and substantial links to Alberta, more than sufficient to justify the application of Alberta law. The WSE was established in and run from Alberta. Tom Seto and Orest Rusnak were both Alberta residents who spent much of their time here promoting the WSE to Albertans. The real and substantial nature of these links is evident by comparing them to the artificial and insignificant links between the WSE and the Cayman Islands (place of incorporation) or Antigua (location of computer).

We also find that the Commission has a legitimate interest in applying Alberta law to the WSE merely because its activities have unlawful consequences here. If the WSE had operated entirely "offshore", as it wanted to, we would still have jurisdiction to take enforcement action against anyone in Alberta with a sufficient connection to the WSE. Similar considerations would apply in every other jurisdiction with securities laws comparable to ours. As a practical issue, it may be necessary to wait until someone comes from offshore to such a jurisdiction before effective enforcement action can be taken. The prospect of such action by any of a number of major commercial jurisdictions should be a deterrent to anyone associated with offshore entities who conduct unlawful securities market activities through the Internet. Such deterrent is only effective if individual jurisdictions take action wherever possible, and we see no reason in comity to prevent that. There would be no purpose in having an elaborate framework of securities regulation to protect the public interest if the law permitted entities like the WSE to circumvent it all by using modern technology and communications to step beyond our jurisdiction.

The WSE's potential victims include anyone with Internet access so, in this situation, comity encourages us to apply Alberta law because the WSE's links to Alberta allow us to act and because we would want other jurisdictions to take a similar approach.

Discussion Questions

Do you agree with the characterization of the place of incorporation as insignificant? If place of incorporation matters for tax treatment and other purposes, should it be ignored from an Internet law perspective?

Although Internet jurisdiction issues are typically global in nature, Canadians must also factor Canadian constitutional issues into the equation. In recent years, debate over whether the Internet is best viewed as a federal or provincial matter has created considerable controversy nationwide.

The Province of Quebec's French language policies in particular have generated heated debate and anger. That anger escalated in June 1999 when the province applied its laws to an English-only Web site maintained by a Quebec based photographer, Mike Calomiris. Calomiris, who vowed to fight the language authorities, was ordered to either remove the site or provide a French version. The incident spawned a series of angry editorials, as many questioned the legality of Quebec asserting its language laws over the Internet.

Interestingly, this was the second instance of Quebec applying its language laws to the Internet. In 1997, the province similarly ordered MicroBytes-Logiciels Inc., a Montreal-based software developer, to either remove its site from the Web or provide a French version. The company complied with the order, indicating that it acquiesced for business rather than legal reasons.

The Office de la Langue Française released the following document in 1997 to clarify its position with regard to language regulation of commercial speech on the Internet.

The Position of the Office de la Langue Française with Regard to Language Regulation of Commercial Speech[†]

It is standard procedure for the Office de la Langue Française to follow up on complaints regarding non-compliance with various provisions of the Charter of the French language. The Office thus decided to intervene in the case of complaints with respect to commercial advertising on the Internet.

Commercial advertising, as a whole, is dealt with in the Charter regardless of the medium used. The Office thus considers that commercial advertising posted on a Web site, as well as advertising material sent by fax or electronic mail, fall under section 52, which means that the use of French is compulsory. A translation may be provided as long as French is given equal prominence. Section 52 applies to all advertising documentation made available to the public by a firm which has a place of business in Québec. Non-commercial messages or those of a political or ideological nature are consequently excluded.

The Office considers that a firm which has an address in Québec falls under section 52. Under the law, commercial advertising posted on the Web pages of firms must include a French translation. Let us remember that, in Québec, consumers have a right to be informed and served in French.

The Office applies to Web sites the same rules and exceptions as those concerning commercial advertising. English media Web sites could thus use English exclusively without violating the Charter. In addition, products of a cultural or educative nature may be advertised exclusively in the language of the product, without a French version.

Aware of the fact that the Internet is now used by companies as a means of advertising products on the global market, which products are often destined only for exportation, the Office de la 7ise will apply a simple rule: a French version must be provided only in the case of advertisements posted on the Web site of a company located in Québec for products available in Québec.

It is noteworthy to specify that "cyber-inspectors" will not be surfing the Net for possible language violations. The Office does not have the time nor the resources to dedicate to such task. In practice, OLF almost exclusively follows up on complaints received from the public.

---

† Online: <http://olf.gouv.qc.ca/charte/english/charter.html>.

Discussion Questions

Under what set of circumstances do you think Quebec is entitled to apply its language laws to Internet Web sites? Should the company require a physical presence and a Web server? Should either a Web server or a physical presence suffice? Can a Quebec company avoid the laws by moving the Web site out of the province? Should the laws affect multinational companies who happen to maintain a branch office in the province?

Notes

Although portrayed by the Canadian media as unique, Quebec is not the only jurisdiction to attempt to enforce language laws on the Internet. In 1996, two French language protection groups filed a complaint charging that Georgia Tech University's French campus English language Web site violated a law requiring all public communications in France to be in French. The original case was dismissed on procedural grounds, and on retrial the court held that the English-only site was permissible. The final decision came after the University established a trilingual site, effectively rendering the issue moot. The site can be found at <http://www.georgiatech-metz.fr/>.

At the federal level, the issue of federal jurisdiction over the Internet played a prominent role in an interesting 1999 decision of the Canadian Industrial Relations Board (*Re City-TV*, [1999] C.I.R.B.D. No. 22). Members of CITY-TV's CityInteractive, the company's Internet services division, petitioned the Board to join the Communications, Energy and Paperworkers Union of Canada, the union that represents CITY-TV's broadcast workers. CITY-TV argued those workers in its CityInteractive unit were functionally separate from workers in its broadcasting division and thus fell outside of the union. It also argued that the matter was outside of the Board's constitutional jurisdiction, which is limited to employees in federally regulated businesses. In CITY-TV's view, the creation of Web content and promotion was strictly a provincial matter. The Board considered the jurisdictional issue and ruled as follows.

Re City-TV[†]

The respondent sought to show CityInteractive as separate from CHUM's broadcasting business by arguing that CityInteractive was not engaged in broadcasting. CHUM Television argued that CityInteractive's role on the Internet was similar to that of a publisher. In support of this contention, the respondent relied on the fact that the core of CityInteractive's work was the design, production and marketing of Web sites and that these activities were carried on by CityInteractive without a CRTC-issued broadcasting license. Mr. Lewis testified that in his capacity as Legal Advisor for the

---

[†] [1999] C.I.R.B.D. No. 22.

CHUM organization, he had determined that there was no class of licence presently issued by the CRTC, nor were there any broadcasting regulations pertaining to the operation of Internet Web sites. Mr. Lewis stated that he had reviewed the operations of CityInteractive and determined that the operation of Web sites was not a broadcasting undertaking, as defined in the Broadcasting Act, S.C. 1991, c. 11. He stressed that the requirement under the Broadcasting Act for any television station (such as CITY-TV or MuchMusic) to be licensed turned on the threshold question of whether there was a "broadcasting undertaking" being carried on. The relevant definitions of the Broadcasting Act read as follows:

> (a)(1) In this Act,
>
> "broadcasting" means any transmission of programs, whether or not encrypted, by radio waves or other means of telecommunication for reception by the public by means of broadcasting receiving apparatus, but does not include any such transmission of programs that is made solely for performance or display in a public place;
>
> "broadcasting undertaking" includes a distribution undertaking, a programming undertaking and a network;
>
> "distribution undertaking" means an undertaking for the reception of broadcasting and the retransmission thereof by radio waves or other means of telecommunication to more than one permanent or temporary residence or dwelling unit or to another such undertaking;
>
> "licence" means a licence to carry on a broadcasting undertaking issued by the Commission under this Act;
>
> "program" means sounds or visual images, or a combination of sounds and visual images, that are intended to inform, enlighten or entertain, but does not include visual images, whether or not combined with sounds, that consist predominantly of alphanumeric text;
>
> "programming undertaking" means an undertaking for the transmission of programs, either directly by radio waves or other means of telecommunication or indirectly through a distribution undertaking, for reception by the public by means of broadcasting receiving apparatus;

(2) For the purposes of this Act, "other means of telecommunication" means any wire, cable, radio, optical or other electromagnetic system, or any similar technical system.

As appears from the above definitions, the determination of whether a service is "broadcasting" under the Broadcasting Act does not depend on the type of technology that is used for its transmission, but rather, on whether it consists of "programs" that are "transmitted for reception by the public." In this regard, Mr. Lewis stressed that the definition of "programs" in section 2 of the Broadcasting Act excluded "visual images, whether or not combined with sounds, that consist predominantly of alphanumeric text," and there was little doubt that the data transmitted by CityInteractive by digital means consisted predominantly of alphanumeric text.

The argument that an undertaking does not exist until a licence is granted and until the activity is carried into effect, or is capable of being lawfully carried out, was expressly rejected by the Privy Council in Winner, supra. Furthermore, the determination of CityInteractive's jurisdictional status does not turn on whether it is engaged in broadcasting in a statutory sense or, in any particular sense. It is well established that all aspects of a company's work need not be of the same type in order to come under the same operation. That principle was reiterated recently in Westcoast Energy, supra, in the context of the single enterprise test. The Court observed that a number of cases stated that a single federal undertaking could exist notwithstanding that it was engaged in different activities and one of them was not transportation or communication:

In Empress Hotel, the Privy Council stated in obiter dicta that a hotel set up exclusively to serve the railway's passengers could form part of a federal railway undertaking. In *The King* v. *Eastern Terminal Elevator Co.*, Duff J. stated in obiter dicta that a grain elevator could form part of a federal railway or shipping undertaking. In Dome Petroleum, supra, underground storage caverns were held to form part of an interprovincial pipeline undertaking. This was also the view of Gerard V. La Forest in *Water Law in Canada: The Atlantic Provinces* (1973), at pp. 49–50:

> ... there may be situations where a single business enterprise may carry on several undertakings. This is evident from *Canadian Pacific Railway* v. *Attorney-General of British Columbia* where the Empress Hotel operated by the C.P.R. like any other large hotel was held to be a separate undertaking from the company's railway operations. This by no means indicates that all aspects of a company's work must be of the same kind, as in Bell Telephone Co. and Winner cases, to come within the same operation. In the Empress Hotel case the court conceded that a hotel or restaurant maintained as an adjunct to the company's railway business for the benefit of passengers travelling on its lines could certainly be part of its railway undertaking. [Emphasis added.]
>
> In our opinion, the fact that an activity or service is not of a transportation or communications character does not preclude a finding that it forms part of a single federal undertaking for the purposes of s. 92(10) (a) under the first test in Central Western, supra. The test remains a fact-based one ...

In any event, in the Board's opinion, the argument that CityInteractive does not broadcast is unfounded. The absence of licencing requirements for carrying on CityInteractive's activities does not persuade us that some of CityInteractive's activities do not amount to a form of broadcasting, i.e., the transmission of programs by means of telecommunication for reception by the public. Webcasts, for example, involve the transmission of audio/visual signals to members of the public situated anywhere in the world.

On the other hand, to conclude that CityInteractive does not engage in broadcasting does not fully answer the question, since some of its Internet-related activities may amount to communication activities extending beyond the limits of a province, pursuant to section 92(10)(a) of the Constitution Act, 1867. Indeed, whether CityInteractive's activities on the digital platform meet or do not meet the existing statutory definition of broadcasting does not necessarily mean that CityInteractive does not engage in "broadcasting" in a non-statutory sense, or that it does not otherwise carry on interprovincial communications activities. The general exclusion of the on-line platform from the regulating scope of the CRTC, due to the definition of "program" in the Broadcasting Act, reflects policy considerations; not the extent of Parliament's constitutional jurisdiction over novel forms of telecommunications and broadcasting. The broadcasting and telecommunications fields are being rapidly transformed by the technological advances witnessed in the digital arena and the emergence of new media services, and the precise nature of these services has yet to be determined.

The CRTC has implicitly acknowledged this, as well as the fact that to date, there has been uncertainty about whether services delivered over the Internet constitute broadcasting or telecommunications services. On July 31, 1998, in Broadcasting Public Notice CRTC 1998-2 and Telecom Public Notice CRTC 98-20 ("the Public Notice"), the CRTC announced that it was initiating a proceeding under both the Broadcasting Act and the Telecommunications Act calling for comments on the rapidly expanding and increasingly available range of communications services collectively referred to as "new media." In the Public Notice, the CRTC proposed the following working definition of the notion of new media:

> New media can be described as encompassing, singly or in combination, and whether interactive or not, services and products that make use of video, audio, graphics and alphanumeric text; and involving, along with other, more traditional means of distribution, digital delivery over networks interconnected on a local or global scale.

While noting that "under such a description, virtually all services found on the Internet could be considered as forms of new media," the CRTC requested submissions for the purpose of answering the following questions:

(a) In what ways, and to what extent, do new media affect, or are they likely to affect, the broadcasting and telecommunications undertakings now regulated by the Commission?

(b) In what ways, and to what extent, are some or any of the new media either broadcasting or telecommunications services?

(c) To the extent that any of the new media are broadcasting or telecommunications, to what extent should the Commission regulate and supervise them pursuant to the Broadcasting Act and the Telecommunications Act?

(d) Do the new media raise any other broad policy issues of national interest?

Thus, apart from the Board's finding that CityInteractive is a non-severable part of CHUM's federal broadcasting operation whether or not it itself carries on broadcasting activities or communication activities that extend beyond the limits of a province, there is more support for concluding that CityInteractive properly falls within the federal realm.

Based on the evidence, in the Board's respectful opinion, there is little doubt that, even if the respondent's interactive business could be viewed as a separate operation, severable from CHUM's core broadcasting undertaking, that operation would also come under federal jurisdiction on its own account. In the Board's view, the webcasting services currently performed by CityInteractive amount to a form of broadcasting, and the other interactive services it provides are interprovincial in nature. All of these services are performed on a regular and continuous basis as an integral part of CityInteractive's new media services operation. The fact that the design and marketing of Web sites and the posting of information on the Web constitute CityInteractive's primary activity, and that such an activity may not itself be federally regulated, is not determinative. What is significant, is that the extra-provincial activities performed by CityInteractive as an integral part of its operation are regular and continuous. Authorities have rejected a quantitative approach which would determine the result based upon a comparison of the extra-provincial business to the business carried on within the province (see Re Ottawa-Carleton Regional transit Commission and Amalgamated Transit Union, Local 279 et al., [1983] 4 D.L.R. (4th) 452 (O.C.A.)).

The test for determining whether CityInteractive is an interprovincial undertaking on its own account boils down to the question of "what is the ordinary business of CityInteractive?" The answer to that question leads to the conclusion that CityInteractive's ordinary business connects provinces on a regular and continuous basis, rendering it federal in nature. CityInteractive is not a mere publisher on the Web. It carries on activities that in effect take television on-line and the Internet to the air. The scope and complexity of the Internet as "a network of computer networks interconnected by means of telecommunications facilities using common protocols and standards that allow for the exchange of information between each connected computer" (C. Pinsky, supra, page 3), and the instantaneous, ubiquitous, and borderless nature that characterizes digital communications, lead to the natural conclusion that these activities, viewed functionally and realistically, bear a clear interprovincial communication stamp.

Discussion Question

Consider the implications of the *City-TV* decision. Does the Board's view of federal jurisdiction over Webcasting suggest that Quebec and the other provinces are precluded from regulating such Internet activity? Can Quebec's application of its language laws be reconciled with federal authority over Internet broadcasts?

The Board returned to the issue of the Internet and federal jurisdiction in a February 2000 decision involving the Internet services division of Prince Edward Island's Island Telecom. The decision is likely to have a significant impact on the regulation of Internet Service Providers (ISPs) in Canada and therefore merits serious consideration. See pp. 83–86, below for an excerpt from that decision.

Perhaps the most significant implication of the classification of Webcasting as broadcasting is what it may mean for the application of federal laws and tribunals, such as the *Personal Information Protection and Electronic Documents Act*, Canada's new privacy and electronic commerce law formerly known as Bill C-6. Due primarily to jurisdictional concerns, the law applies only to federally regulated businesses, such as banks, airlines or broadcasters, during its first three years in force. Assuming that activities such as Webcasting constitute broadcasting, however, businesses and organizations that Webcast could find themselves subject to the law immediately.

4

Internet Service Provider Liability

Once the domain of small operations and university institutions, Internet Service Providers (ISPs) have become big business, with providers like America Online (AOL) and Bell Sympatico boasting thousands of users coast to coast. As gatekeepers to the Internet, ISPs have received particular attention with regard to their legal liability for civil and criminal violations that take place under their "watch."

With governments and regulators generally frustrated with their lack of control over Internet activities, the potential for ISPs to carry out the regulatory function is viewed by some as a possible solution to Internet regulation. Particularly if one accepts the important role that technology can play in regulating Internet activity, then the role of the ISP becomes quite crucial. Although certain technologies can be implemented at the level of the individual browser or by an individual Web site, there are times technological implementation falls to the ISP, if to anyone at all.

The issue is further complicated by the considerable confusion surrounding precisely what ISPs are actually capable of doing. ISPs prefer to characterize their activities as akin to common carriers. They argue that they transport data but have no control over it, don't know (and don't want to know) what it contains, and should not be held accountable where such information proves to be illegal in nature. Others prefer alternative analogies, including that of a distributor or a publisher, both of which may carry a higher level of responsibility than that of a mere conduit of information.

Notwithstanding their protestations, the information possessed by ISPs appears to belie their claims of helplessness. For example, in a two week span in early April 1999, two suspects were apprehended for virus and stock hoaxes. In each instance, it was an ISP (AOL) that played an integral role in the investigation by providing law enforcement officials with access data records. The ISP's ability to cooperate under circumstances mandated by legal necessity suggests that they may possess greater access to data than they might have the public believe.

The changing role of the ISP must also be factored into the equation. In the early 1990s, ISPs were limited almost exclusively to providing public Internet access. Today, ISPs provide several types of access (dial up, high speed), often provide content (discussion forums, Internet guides, AOL's merger with Time Warner), software (AOL purchase of Netscape), and even phone service. Accordingly, ISPs defy easy categorization, and their responsibility in the overall regulatory framework must reflect their evolving role.

Our examination of ISP liability begins with two seemingly conflicting U.S. cases, which illustrate the tension between holding ISPs accountable for content passing through their system and acknowledging their lack of control over such content.

Cubby, Inc. v. Compuserve, Inc.[†]

CompuServe develops and provides computer-related products and services, including CompuServe Information Service ("CIS"), an on-line general information service or "electronic library" that subscribers may access from a personal computer or terminal. Subscribers to CIS pay a membership fee and online time usage fees, in return for which they have access to the thousands of information sources available on CIS. Subscribers may also obtain access to over 150 special interest "forums," which are comprised of electronic bulletin boards, interactive online conferences, and topical databases.

One forum available is the Journalism Forum, which focuses on the journalism industry. Cameron Communications, Inc. ("CCI"), which is independent of CompuServe, has contracted to "manage, review, create, delete, edit and otherwise control the contents" of the Journalism Forum "in accordance with editorial and technical standards and conventions of style as established by CompuServe."

One publication available as part of the Journalism Forum is Rumorville USA ("Rumorville"), a daily newsletter that provides reports about broadcast journalism and journalists. Rumorville is published by Don Fitzpatrick Associates of San Francisco ("DFA"), which is headed by defendant Don Fitzpatrick. CompuServe has no employment, contractual, or other direct relationship with either DFA or Fitzpatrick; DFA provides Rumorville to the Journalism Forum under a contract with CCI. The contract between CCI and DFA provides that DFA "accepts total responsibility for the contents" of Rumorville. The contract also requires CCI to limit access to Rumorville to those CIS subscribers who have previously made membership arrangements directly with DFA.

CompuServe has no opportunity to review Rumorville's contents before DFA uploads it into CompuServe's computer banks, from which it is immediately available to approved CIS subscribers. CompuServe receives no part of any fees that DFA charges for access to Rumorville, nor does CompuServe compensate DFA for providing Rumorville to the Journalism Forum; the compensation CompuServe receives for

---

† 776 F. Supp. 135 (S.D.N.Y. 1991).

making Rumorville available to its subscribers is the standard online time usage and membership fees charged to all CIS subscribers, regardless of the information services they use. CompuServe maintains that, before this action was filed, it had no notice of any complaints about the contents of the Rumorville publication or about DFA.

In 1990, plaintiffs Cubby, Inc. ("Cubby") and Robert Blanchard ("Blanchard") (collectively, "plaintiffs") developed Skuttlebut, a computer database designed to publish and distribute electronically news and gossip in the television news and radio industries. Plaintiffs intended to compete with Rumorville; subscribers gained access to Skuttlebut through their personal computers after completing subscription agreements with plaintiffs.

Plaintiffs claim that, on separate occasions in April 1990, Rumorville published false and defamatory statements relating to Skuttlebut and Blanchard, and that CompuServe carried these statements as part of the Journalism Forum. The allegedly defamatory remarks included a suggestion that individuals at Skuttlebut gained access to information first published by Rumorville "through some back door"; a statement that Blanchard was "bounced" from his previous employer, WABC; and a description of Skuttlebut as a "new start-up scam."

. . . .

Plaintiffs base their libel claim on the allegedly defamatory statements contained in the Rumorville publication that CompuServe carried as part of the Journalism Forum. CompuServe argues that, based on the undisputed facts, it was a distributor of Rumorville, as opposed to a publisher of the Rumorville statements. CompuServe further contends that, as a distributor of Rumorville, it cannot be held liable on the libel claim because it neither knew nor had reason to know of the allegedly defamatory statements. Plaintiffs, on the other hand, argue that the Court should conclude that CompuServe is a publisher of the statements and hold it to a higher standard of liability.

Ordinarily, "one who repeats or otherwise republishes defamatory matter is subject to liability as if he had originally published it." With respect to entities such as news vendors, book stores, and libraries, however, "New York courts have long held that vendors and distributors of defamatory publications are not liable if they neither know nor have reason to know of the defamation."

The requirement that a distributor must have knowledge of the contents of a publication before liability can be imposed for distributing that publication is deeply rooted in the First Amendment, made applicable to the states through the Fourteenth Amendment. "[T]he constitutional guarantees of the freedom of speech and of the press stand in the way of imposing" strict liability on distributors for the contents of the reading materials they carry. In Smith, the Court struck down an ordinance that imposed liability on a bookseller for possession of an obscene book, regardless of whether the bookseller had knowledge of the book's contents. The Court reasoned that "Every bookseller would be placed under an obligation to make himself aware of the contents of every book in his shop. It would be altogether unreasonable to demand so near an approach to omniscience." And the bookseller's burden would become the public's burden, for by restricting him the public's access to reading matter would be restricted. If the contents of bookshops and periodical stands were restricted to material of which their proprietors had made an inspection, they might be depleted indeed. Although Smith involved criminal liability, the First Amendment's guarantees are no less relevant to the instant action: "What a State may not constitutionally bring about by means of a criminal statute is likewise beyond the reach of its civil law of libel. The fear of damage awards ... may be markedly more inhibiting than the fear of prosecution under a criminal statute."

CompuServe's CIS product is in essence an electronic, for-profit library that carries a vast number of publications and collects usage and membership fees from its subscribers in return for access to the publications. CompuServe and companies like it are at the forefront of the information industry revolution. High technology has markedly increased the speed with which information is gathered and processed; it is now possible for an individual with a personal computer, modem, and telephone line to have instantaneous access to thousands of news publications from across the United States and around the world. While CompuServe may decline to carry a given publication altogether, in reality, once it does decide to carry a publication, it will have little or no editorial control over that publication's contents. This is especially so when CompuServe carries the publication as part of a forum that is managed by a company unrelated to CompuServe.

With respect to the Rumorville publication, the undisputed facts are that DFA uploads the text of Rumorville into CompuServe's data banks and makes it available to approved CIS subscribers instantaneously. CompuServe has no more editorial control over such a publication than does a public library, book store, or newsstand, and it would be no more feasible for CompuServe to examine every publication it carries for potentially defamatory statements than it would be for any other distributor to do so. "First Amendment guarantees have long been recognized as protecting distributors of publications.... Obviously, the national distributor of hundreds of periodicals has no duty to monitor each issue of every periodical it distributes. Such a rule would be an impermissible burden on the First Amendment."

Technology is rapidly transforming the information industry. A computerized database is the functional equivalent of a more traditional news vendor, and the inconsistent application of a lower standard of liability to an electronic news distributor such as CompuServe than that which is applied to a public library, book store, or newsstand would impose an undue burden on the free flow of information. Given the relevant First Amendment considerations, the appropriate standard of liability to be applied to CompuServe is whether it knew or had reason to know of the allegedly defamatory Rumorville statements.

B. CompuServe's Liability as a Distributor

CompuServe contends that it is undisputed that it had neither knowledge nor reason to know of the allegedly defamatory Rumorville statements, especially given the large number of publications it carries and the speed with which DFA uploads Rumorville into its computer banks and makes the publication available to CIS subscribers. The burden is thus shifted to plaintiffs, who "must set forth specific facts showing that there is a genuine issue for trial." Plaintiffs have not set forth anything other than conclusory allegations as to whether CompuServe knew or had reason to know of the Rumorville statements, and have failed to meet their burden on this issue. Plaintiffs do contend that CompuServe was informed that persons affiliated with Skuttlebut might be "hacking" in order to obtain unauthorized access to Rumorville, but that claim is wholly irrelevant to the issue of whether CompuServe was put on notice that the Rumorville publication contained statements accusing the Skuttlebut principals of engaging in "hacking."

Plaintiffs have not set forth any specific facts showing that there is a genuine issue as to whether CompuServe knew or had reason to know of Rumorville's contents. Because CompuServe, as a news distributor, may not be held liable if it neither knew nor had reason to know of the allegedly defamatory Rumorville statements, summary judgment in favor of CompuServe on the libel claim is granted.

Stratton Oakmont, Inc. v. Prodigy Services Co.[†]

Plaintiffs commenced this action against PRODIGY, the owner and operator of the computer network on which the statements appeared, and the unidentified party who posted the aforementioned statement. The second amended complaint alleges ten causes of action, including claims for per se libel. On this motion, "in order to materially advance the outcome of this litigation" Plaintiffs seek partial summary judgment on two issues, namely: (1) whether PRODIGY may be considered "publisher" of the aforementioned statements; and, (2) whether Epstein, the Board Leader for the computer bulletin board on which the statements were posted, acted with actual and apparent authority as PRODIGY's "agent" for the purpose of the claims in this action.

By way of background, it is undisputed that PRODIGY's computer network has at least two million subscribers who communicate with each other and with the general subscriber population on PRODIGY's bulletin boards. "Money Talk" the board on which the aforementioned statements appeared, in allegedly the leading and most widely read financial computer bulletin board in the United States, where members can post statements regarding stocks, investments and other financial matters. PRODIGY contracts with bulletin Board Leaders, who, among other things, participate in board discussions and undertake promotional efforts to encourage usage and increase users. The Board Leader for "Money Talk" at the time the alleged libelous statements were posted was Charles Epstein.

PRODIGY commenced operations in 1990. Plaintiffs base their claims that PRODIGY is a publisher in large measure on PRODIGY's stated policy, starting in 1990, that it was a family oriented computer network. In various national newspaper articles written by Geoffrey Moore, PRODIGY's Director of Market Programs and Communications, PRODIGY held itself out as an online service that exercised editorial control over the content of messages posted on its computer bulletin boards, thereby expressly differentiating itself from its competition and expressly likening itself to a newspaper.

.   .   .   .

A finding that PRODIGY is a publisher is the first hurdle for Plaintiffs to overcome in pursuit of their defamation claims because one who repeats or otherwise republishes a libel is subject to liability as if he had originally published it. In contrast, distributors such as bookstores and libraries may be liable for defamatory statements of others only if they knew or had reason to know of the defamatory statement at issue. A distributor or deliverer of defamatory material is considered a passive conduit and will not be found liable in the absence of fault. However, a

---

[†] 23 Med. L.R. 1794 (N.Y. Sup. Ct. 1995).

newspaper, for example, is more than a passive receptacle or conduit for news, comment and advertising. The choice of material to go into a newspaper and the decisions made as to the content of the paper constitute the exercise of editorial control and judgment and with this editorial control comes increased liability. In short, the critical issue to be determined by this Court is whether the foregoing evidence established a prime [sic] facie case that PRODIGY exercised sufficient editorial control over its computer bulletin boards to render it a publisher with the same responsibilities as a newspaper.

Again, PRODIGY insists that its former policy of manually reviewing all messages prior to posting was changed "long before the messages complained of by Plaintiffs were posted". However, no documentation or detailed explanation of such a change, and the dissemination of news of such a change, has been submitted. In addition, PRODIGY argues that in terms of sheer volume — currently 60,000 messages a day are posted on PRODIGY bulletin boards — manual review of messages is not feasible. While PRODIGY admits that Board Leaders may remove messages that violate its Guidelines, it claims in conclusory manner that Board Leaders do not function as "editors". Furthermore, PRODIGY argues generally that this Court should not decide issues that can directly impact this developing communications medium without the benefit of a full record, although it fails to describe what further facts remain to be developed on this issue of whether it is a publisher.

As for legal authority, PRODIGY relies on the Cubby case, ...

The key distinction between CompuServe and PRODIGY is two fold. First, PRODIGY held itself out to the public and its members as controlling the content of its computer bulletin boards. Second, PRODIGY implemented this control through its automatic software screening program, and the Guidelines which Board Leaders are required to enforce. By actively utilizing technology and manpower to delete notes from its computer bulletin boards on the basis of offensiveness and "bad taste", for example, PRODIGY is clearly making decisions as to content, and such decisions constitute editorial control. That such control is not complete and is enforced both as early as the notes arrive and as late as a complaint is made, does not minimize or eviscerate the simple fact that PRODIGY has uniquely arrogated to itself the role of determining what is proper for its members to post and read on its bulletin boards. Based on the foregoing, this Court is compelled to conclude that for the purposes of Plaintiffs' claims in the action, PRODIGY is a publisher rather than a distributor.

An interesting comparison may be found in *Auvil* v. *CBS 60 Minutes*, where apple growers sued a television network and local affiliates because of an allegedly defamatory investigative report generated by the network and broadcast by the affiliates. The record established that the affiliates exercised no editorial control over the broadcast although they had the power to do so by virtue of their contract with CBS, they had the opportunity to do so by virtue of a three hour hiatus for the west coast differential, they had the technical capability to do so, and they in fact had occasionally censored network programming in the past, albeit never in connection with "60 Minutes." The Auvil court found:

> It is argued that these features, coupled with the power to censor, triggered the duty to censor. That is a leap which the Court is not prepared to join in ... plaintiffs' construction would force the creation of full time editorial boards at local stations throughout the country which possess sufficient knowledge, legal acumen and access to experts to continually monitor incom-

ing transmissions and exercise on-the-spot discretionary calls or face $75 million dollar lawsuits at every turn. That is not realistic.

... More than merely unrealistic in economic terms, it is difficult to imagine a scenario more chilling on the media's right of expression and the public's right to know.

Consequently, the court dismissed all claims against the affiliates on the basis of "conduit liability", which could not be established therein absent fault, which was not shown.

In contrast, here PRODIGY has virtually created an editorial staff of Board Leaders who have the ability to continually monitor incoming transmissions and in fact do spend time censoring notes. Indeed, it could be said that PRODIGY's current system of automatic scanning, Guidelines and Board Leaders may have a chilling effect on freedom of communication in Cyberspace, and it appears that this chilling effect is exactly what PRODIGY wants, but for the legal liability that attaches to such censorship.

Let it be clear that this Court is in full agreement with Cubby and Auvil, Computer bulletin boards should generally be regarded in the same context as bookstores, libraries and network affiliates. It is PRODIGY's own policies, technology and staffing decisions which have altered the scenario and mandated the finding that it is a publisher.

PRODIGY's conscious choice, to gain the benefits of editorial control, has opened it up to a greater liability than CompuServe and other computer networks that make no such choice. For the record, the fear that this Court's finding of publisher status for PRODIGY will compel all computer networks to abdicate control of their bulletin boards, incorrectly presumes that the market will refuse to compensate a network for its increased control and the resulting increased exposure.

Discussion Questions

Can you reconcile these two cases? How would you characterize today's ISPs — are they more like Prodigy, Compuserve or something else entirely?

The Supreme Court of New York revisited the liability of ISPs in another case involving Prodigy in 1998. In *Lunney* v. *Prodigy*, the court adopted the Cubby approach and found no liability on the part of Prodigy for allegedly defamatory postings.

Lunney v. Prodigy[†]

[The Court acknowledged the *Stratton Oakmont* decision and reasoned as follows:]

We are aware, of course, of the decision in Stratton Oakmont, Inc. v Prodigy Services Co. In that case, the Supreme Court held that Prodigy had been shown to have

---

† 683 N.Y.S. 2d 557 (N.Y. App. Div. 1998).

exercised editorial control over a financial bulletin board to the extent that it could be considered the publisher of a defamatory posting, which contained defamatory statements concerning the plaintiff, and which had been placed on the bulletin board by a third party. For several reasons, Stratton Oakmont is not controlling here.

First, it is obvious that the Stratton Oakmont rationale would apply, if at all, only to the portion of the plaintiff's amended complaint which related to the bulletin board postings. Whatever editorial control over such postings might have been possible, it is clear from the present record that a service provider such a [sic] Prodigy cannot screen all of the e-mail sent by its subscribers.

Second, the evidence in the record in Stratton Oakmont describes the efforts at editorial control which, according to the evidence in the present record, Prodigy in fact abandoned in January 1994, prior to the events underlying the present complaint. Thus, the decision in Stratton Oakmont was made in an entirely different factual context.

Third, the Anderson decision, discussed at length above, states that a telecommunications company can be considered a publisher of those messages in whose transmission it actually participates. It does not hold that such a company, if it were to participate in the formulation of the text of one or two messages, would thereupon expose itself to liability based on the text contained in the millions of other messages in whose transmission it did not participate. It is, in other words, irrelevant if Prodigy, in the case at hand, is shown to have exercised the power to exclude certain vulgarities from the text of certain messages. What matters is that there is no proof that any such control was exercised in connection with the transmission of the messages complained of by the plaintiff.

Fourth, as outlined above, the Anderson case establishes the rule that even a telecommunications company which in some measure participates in the transmission of a libelous message cannot be held liable unless it knew that the message was in fact libelous, a circumstance which will rarely, if ever, be proved. The common law privilege which benefits telegraph companies must apply to internet service providers as well. E-mail is, in substance, nothing but an updated version of the telegraph.

Our disagreement with the holding in Stratton Oakmont is not only compelled by our understanding of the holding of the Court of Appeals in Anderson, but is also dictated by at least one simple consideration of fairness. The Stratton Oakmont court itself acknowledged that a purely passive on-line service provider would face no liability based on the transmission of defamatory material through its services. Liability was imposed on Prodigy in that case solely because Prodigy had attempted, to some extent, to control the text of the various messages placed on its bulletin boards. The Stratton Oakmont holding "appears to encourage systems operators to ignore the content of their bulletin boards in order to attain 'distributor' status." Thus, in Stratton Oakmont, Prodigy was punished for allegedly performing in an inadequate way the very conduct (exercise of editorial control) which, initially, it had no legal duty to perform at all. The rule of law announced in Stratton Oakmont discourages the very conduct which the plaintiff in Stratton Oakmont argued should be encouraged.

The plaintiff in this case argues that Prodigy exposed itself to tort liability by parties with whom it had no contractual relationship when it allegedly failed to adhere to the commitments it made to its subscribers in its Service Member Agreement (hereinafter the agreement). This argument fails for several reasons. Most basically, the text of this agreement actually provides that "Prodigy reserves the right (but is not obligated) to review and edit any material submitted for display." This provision negates any possible extension of tort liability to third parties based on any alleged failure, on the part of Prodigy, to monitor its bulletin boards.

Our application of the holding of the Court of Appeals in Anderson results in our being in complete harmony with the expanding body of case law which supports the general proposition that an on-line service company such as Prodigy is not liable for damages when its services are misused by a third party who transmits an offensive or libelous text.

Postscript

The *Lunney* v. *Prodigy* decision was affirmed by the New York Court of Appeals in December 1999.

In the context of illegal or defamatory content, the case law suggests that there are several possible approaches to the ISP liability issue. These include (from most lenient to least lenient):

1. No liability or responsibility for content or activities.
2. An obligation to act only under a court order.
3. An obligation to act if made aware of illegal or defamatory content.
4. An obligation to actively monitor content or activities for illegal or defamatory content.
5. An obligation to control content.
6. An obligation to control content with personal liability attached to the obligation.

The United States eliminated any doubts of where they fall on this spectrum with the passage of the *Communications Decency Act* (CDA). Although the CDA is best known for the content-related provisions which were struck down as unconstitutional by the U.S. Supreme Court, other provisions within the Act endure, including a section devoted to ISP liability.

Communications Decency Act[†]

(c) Protection for "good samaritan" blocking and screening of offensive material.

(1) Treatment of publisher or speaker. No provider or user of an interactive computer service shall be treated as the publisher or speaker of any information provided by another information content provider.

(2) Civil liability. No provider or user of an interactive computer service shall be held liable on account of —

(A) any action voluntarily taken in good faith to restrict access to or availability of material that the provider or user considers to be obscene,

---

† 47 USCS §230.

lewd, lascivious, filthy, excessively violent, harassing, or otherwise objectionable, whether or not such material is constitutionally protected; or

(B) any action taken to enable or make available to information content providers or others the technical means to restrict access to material described in paragraph (1).

(f) Definitions. As used in this section:

(2) Interactive computer service. The term "interactive computer service" means any information service, system, or access software provider that provides or enables computer access by multiple users to a computer server, including specifically a service or system that provides access to the Internet and such systems operated or services offered by libraries or educational institutions.

Zeran v. America Online Inc.[†]

Kenneth Zeran brought this action against America Online, Inc. ("AOL"), arguing that AOL unreasonably delayed in removing defamatory messages posted by an unidentified third party, refused to post retractions of those messages, and failed to screen for similar postings thereafter.

. . . .

Because §230 was successfully advanced by AOL in the district court as a defense to Zeran's claims, we shall briefly examine its operation here. Zeran seeks to hold AOL liable for defamatory speech initiated by a third party. He argued to the district court that once he notified AOL of the unidentified third party's hoax, AOL had a duty to remove the defamatory posting promptly, to notify its subscribers of the message's false nature, and to effectively screen future defamatory material. Section 230 entered this litigation as an affirmative defense pled by AOL. The company claimed that Congress immunized interactive computer service providers from claims based on information posted by a third party.

The relevant portion of §230 states: "No provider or user of an interactive computer service shall be treated as the publisher or speaker of any information provided by another information content provider." 47 U.S.C. §230(c)(1). By its plain language, §230 creates a federal immunity to any cause of action that would make service providers liable for information originating with a third-party user of the service. Specifically, §230 precludes courts from entertaining claims that would place a computer service provider in a publisher's role. Thus, lawsuits seeking to hold a service provider liable for its exercise of a publisher's traditional editorial functions — such as deciding whether to publish, withdraw, postpone or alter content — are barred.

The purpose of this statutory immunity is not difficult to discern. Congress recognized the threat that tort-based lawsuits pose to freedom of speech in the new and burgeoning Internet medium. The imposition of tort liability on service providers for the communications of others represented, for Congress, simply another form of

---

† 958 F. Supp. 1124 (Ed. Va. 1997).

intrusive government regulation of speech. Section 230 was enacted, in part, to maintain the robust nature of Internet communication and, accordingly, to keep government interference in the medium to a minimum. In specific statutory findings, Congress recognized the Internet and interactive computer services as offering "a forum for a true diversity of political discourse, unique opportunities for cultural development, and myriad avenues for intellectual activity." It also found that the Internet and interactive computer services "have flourished, to the benefit of all Americans, with a minimum of government regulation." Congress further stated that it is "the policy of the United States ... to preserve the vibrant and competitive free market that presently exists for the Internet and other interactive computer services, unfettered by Federal or State regulation."

None of this means, of course, that the original culpable party who posts defamatory messages would escape accountability. While Congress acted to keep government regulation of the Internet to a minimum, it also found it to be the policy of the United States "to ensure vigorous enforcement of Federal criminal laws to deter and punish trafficking in obscenity, stalking, and harassment by means of computer." Congress made a policy choice, however, not to deter harmful online speech through the separate route of imposing tort liability on companies that serve as intermediaries for other parties' potentially injurious messages.

Congress' purpose in providing the §230 immunity was thus evident. Interactive computer services have millions of users. The amount of information communicated via interactive computer services is therefore staggering. The specter of tort liability in an area of such prolific speech would have an obvious chilling effect. It would be impossible for service providers to screen each of their millions of postings for possible problems. Faced with potential liability for each message republished by their services, interactive computer service providers might choose to severely restrict the number and type of messages posted. Congress considered the weight of the speech interests implicated and chose to immunize service providers to avoid any such restrictive effect.

Another important purpose of §230 was to encourage service providers to self-regulate the dissemination of offensive material over their services. In this respect, §230 responded to a New York state court decision, *Stratton Oakmont, Inc.* v. *Prodigy Servs. Co.* ...

Congress enacted §230 to remove the disincentives to self-regulation created by the Stratton Oakmont decision. Under that court's holding, computer service providers who regulated the dissemination of offensive material on their services risked subjecting themselves to liability, because such regulation cast the service provider in the role of a publisher. Fearing that the specter of liability would therefore deter service providers from blocking and screening offensive material, Congress enacted §230's broad immunity "to remove disincentives for the development and utilization of blocking and filtering technologies that empower parents to restrict their children's access to objectionable or inappropriate online material." In line with this purpose, §230 forbids the imposition of publisher liability on a service provider for the exercise of its editorial and self-regulatory functions.

Zeran argues, however, that the §230 immunity eliminates only publisher liability, leaving distributor liability intact. Publishers can be held liable for defamatory statements contained in their works even absent proof that they had specific knowledge of the statement's inclusion. According to Zeran, interactive computer service providers like AOL are normally considered instead to be distributors, like traditional news vendors or book sellers. Distributors cannot be held liable for defamatory statements contained in the materials they distribute unless it is proven at a minimum that they have actual knowledge of the defamatory statements upon which liability is predicated.

Zeran contends that he provided AOL with sufficient notice of the defamatory statements appearing on the company's bulletin board. This notice is significant, says Zeran, because AOL could be held liable as a distributor only if it acquired knowledge of the defamatory statements' existence.

Because of the difference between these two forms of liability, Zeran contends that the term "distributor" carries a legally distinct meaning from the term "publisher." Accordingly, he asserts that Congress' use of only the term "publisher" in §230 indicates a purpose to immunize service providers only from publisher liability. He argues that distributors are left unprotected by §230 and, therefore, his suit should be permitted to proceed against AOL. We disagree. Assuming arguendo that Zeran has satisfied the requirements for imposition of distributor liability, this theory of liability is merely a subset, or a species, of publisher liability, and is therefore also foreclosed by §230.

The terms "publisher" and "distributor" derive their legal significance from the context of defamation law. Although Zeran attempts to artfully plead his claims as ones of negligence, they are indistinguishable from a garden variety defamation action. Because the publication of a statement is a necessary element in a defamation action, only one who publishes can be subject to this form of tort liability. Publication does not only describe the choice by an author to include certain information. In addition, both the negligent communication of a defamatory statement and the failure to remove such a statement when first communicated by another party — each alleged by Zeran here under a negligence label — constitute publication. In fact, every repetition of a defamatory statement is considered a publication.

In this case, AOL is legally considered to be a publisher. "Every one who takes part in the publication ... is charged with publication." Even distributors are considered to be publishers for purposes of defamation law: Those who are in the business of making their facilities available to disseminate the writings composed, the speeches made, and the information gathered by others may also be regarded as participating to such an extent in making the books, newspapers, magazines, and information available to others as to be regarded as publishers. They are intentionally making the contents available to others, sometimes without knowing all of the contents — including the defamatory content — and sometimes without any opportunity to ascertain, in advance, that any defamatory matter was to be included in the matter published. AOL falls squarely within this traditional definition of a publisher and, therefore, is clearly protected by §230's immunity.

Discussion Questions

What is your view of the U.S. approach? Does it apportion risk/liability in a fair manner?

Notes

The Zeran approach has been used on several other occasions since the enactment of the CDA. One of the most infamous cases involved well-known cyber-gossip Matt Drudge. Drudge, who maintains a personal and AOL based Web site devoted to breaking news stories, falsely published a report that Sidney Blumenthal, an aide to President Bill Clinton, had a history of spousal abuse. Drudge retracted the story within hours of its release; however, Blumenthal was not satisfied and launched a defamation action against both Drudge and AOL. A federal court dismissed the action against AOL, citing the Zeran case and the protection afforded by §230 of the CDA. As of July 2000, the case against Drudge was unresolved. Updates can be found at the Matt Drudge Information Center at <http://cspc.org/drudge/mdinfo.htm>.

Several European cases illustrate the opposite end of the liability spectrum. Consider the following British case, which many experts believe provides a model for how the Canadian courts would address ISP liability if confronted with the issue.

Godfrey v. Demon Internet[†]

The Plaintiff is a lecturer in physics, mathematics and computer science resident in England.

The Defendant is an Internet Service Provider (I.S.P.) carrying on a business in England and Wales.

The Defendant ISP carries the Newsgroup "soc.culture.thai" and stores postings within that hierarchy for about a fortnight during which time the posting is available to be read by its customers.

On the 13th January 1997 someone unknown made a posting in the U.S.A. in the Newsgroup "soc.culture.thai". The posting followed a path from its originating American ISP to the Defendants' news server in England. This posting was squalid, obscene and defamatory of the Plaintiff. It is set out in Tab 1 page 1 of the Court Bundle. It purports to come from the Plaintiff although "Lawrence" is misspelt with a "W". It invites replies by giving the Plaintiff's Email address. It was a forgery.

On the 17th January 1997 the Plaintiff sent a letter by "fax" to Mr. Stanford, the Defendant's Managing Director, informing him that the posting was a forgery, and that he was not responsible for it and requesting that the Defendants remove the posting from its Usenet news server.

Although denying that Mr. Stanford personally received the fax, the Defendants admit its receipt and that the posting was not removed as requested but remained available on its news-server until its expiry on about the 27th January 1997. There is no dispute that the Defendants could have obliterated the posting from its news-server after receiving the Plaintiff's request.

As is clear from the prayer for relief in the Statement of Claim the Plaintiff only claims damages for libel in respect of the posting after the 17th January 1997 when the Defendants had knowledge it was defamatory.

The governing statute is the Defamation Act 1996. Section 1 is headed "Responsibility for Publication".

---

† (March 26, 1999), Case No. 1998-G-No 30 (High Court of Justice (Queen's Bench Division)).

The relevant words are as follows:

> **1(1)** In defamation proceedings a person has a defence if he shows that
>
> (a) he was not the author, editor or publisher of the statement complained of,
> (b) he took reasonable care in relation to its publication, and
> (c) he did not know, and had no reason to believe, that what he did caused or contributed to the publication of a defamatory statement.

It should be noted that for the defence to succeed (a) and (b) and (c) have to be established by the Defendant.

> **1(2)** For this purpose ... "publisher" have the following meanings, which are further explained in sub-section (3)
>
> "publisher" means a commercial publisher, that is, a person whose business is issuing material to the public, or a section of the public, who issues material containing the statement in the course of that business.
>
> **1(3)** A person shall not be considered the author, editor or publisher of a statement if he is only involved
>
> (a) in printing, producing, distributing or selling printed material containing the statement
> (c) in processing, making copies of, distributing or selling any electronic medium in or on which the statement is recorded, or in operating or providing any equipment, system or service by means of which the statement is retrieved, copied, distributed or made available in electronic form;
> (e) as the operator of or provider of access to a communications system by means of which the statement is transmitted, or made available, by a person over whom he has no effective control.

In a case not within paragraphs (a) to (e) the court may have regard to those provisions by way of analogy in deciding whether a person is to be considered the author, editor or publisher of a statement.

> **1(5)** In determining for the purposes of this section whether a person took reasonable care, or had reason to believe that what he did caused or contributed to the publication of a defamatory statement, regard shall be had to
>
> (a) the extent of his responsibility for the content of the statement or the decision to publish it,
> (b) the nature or circumstances of the publication, and
> (c) the previous conduct or character of the author, editor or publisher.

In my judgment the Defendants were clearly not the publisher of the posting defamatory of the Plaintiff within the meaning of Section 1(2) and 1(3) and incontrovertibly can avail themselves of Section 1(1)(a).

However the difficulty facing the Defendants is Section 1(1)(b) and 1(1)(c). After the 17th January 1997 after receipt of the Plaintiff's fax the Defendants knew of the defamatory posting but chose not to remove it from their Usenet news servers. In my judgment this places the Defendants in an insuperable difficulty so that they cannot avail themselves of the defence provided by Section 1.

Notes

1. Godfrey had a history of provocative postings, the ones in this case being particularly inflammatory. Do you think the nature of Godfrey's conduct should factor into the legal analysis? You may be interested to learn that the British court issued a subsequent ruling taking note of Godfrey's conduct in the case and providing a strong indication that no damages would be forth-coming. As a result of that decision, Demon Internet chose not to appeal this decision, leaving many troubled by the precedent it established. In fact, in the aftermath of a settlement between Demon Internet and Godfrey in April 2000, several British ISPs increased the monitoring activities and removed content from their servers under the fear of similar defamation actions.

2. Several other European cases have gone even further than Godfrey. In one German case, Felix Somm, a CompuServe executive, was held criminally liable for CompuServe's failure to block access to pornographic materials on a newsgroup. That decision, which sparked international condemnation, was overturned by an appellate court in November 1999.

   In the 1998 French case *Lefebure* v. *Lacambre*, Tribunal de Grande Instance de Paris, Ref. 551B1/98. No.1/JP (June 1998), an ISP was held responsible for the morality of the content distributed via the client-operated Web sites it hosted. A French model claimed that the ISP violated her privacy and damaged her professional reputation by allowing a subscriber to publish nude photographs of her on a Web site. The court held that an ISP was obligated to guarantee the morality of those to whom it provides service and that those parties respect the rules governing the Internet as well as national laws and regulations. In the aftermath of the case, the offending site was shut down, damages awarded, and the ISP was required to ensure the photos in question were not distributed from any site under its control.

The Canadian Copyright Board addressed ISP liability within the context of copyright in an October 1999 decision popularly referred to as the *Re Tariff 22, Internet* decision. The Board was asked to rule on a wide range of Internet issues, including ISP liability, content creator responsibility for online content and online linking.

Re Tariff 22, Internet[†]

[The Board reviewed the availability of a legislative exemption for ISPs for copyright liability and found as follows:]

---

† *SOCAN Statement of Royalties, Public Performance of Musical Works 1996, 1997, 1998 (sub nom. Re Tariff 22, Internet)* 1 C.P.R. 4th 417.

> Persons who can avail themselves of paragraph 2.4(1)(b) of the Act
> with respect to a given communication of a work do not communi-
> cate the work.

Generally speaking, this includes all entities acting as Internet intermediaries such as
the ISP of the person who makes the work available, persons whose servers acts as
a cache or mirror, the recipient's ISP and those who operate routers used in the
transmission

Paragraph 2.4(1)(b) of the Act provides that "a person whose only act in respect
of the communication of a work ... to the public consists of providing the means of
telecommunication necessary for another person to so communicate the work ... does
not communicate the work ... to the public". Proponents and opponents of Tariff 22
view this provision in diametrically different ways.

Opponents of Tariff 22 argue that anyone who operates equipment or facilities
used for Internet transmissions is not involved in the communication which may
occur. These Internet intermediaries include, in their view, those who operate routers, provide equipment or software that are used to provide connectivity, or operate
a server on which another party posts content, anyone in fact, except the person
responsible for the contents and the end user. In effect, their view is that only the
sender and recipient are legally involved in the communication.

For their part, proponents of Tariff 22 contend that paragraph 2.4(1)(b) applies
only to the provision of physical facilities used by others to communicate a work to
the public. They contend that the expression "means of telecommunication" refers to
the means of transmission, not to any service or other means of communication.
They argue that "means of telecommunication" connotes equipment or physical
systems or facilities, as opposed to a "service", being the provision of professional or
other assistance. The decision interpreted the expression "telecommunication facility"
in section 287.1 of the Criminal Code, which the proponents of Tariff 22 argue
connotes much the same thing.

SOCAN also cites as authority for its interpretation of the term "service" the
case of *Bartholomew Green 1751 Assn. Inc.* v. *Canada (Attorney General)*, and various
definitions from the *Telecommunications Act*, S.C. 1993, c. 38, s. 23, in support of
the distinction it draws between "means" and "services".

Proponents of Tariff 22 suggest that by contrasting the provision of means and
that of services, one should be led to the conclusion, for example, that paragraph
2.4(1)(b) applies to a telephone company if it supplies lines and facilities for an ISP
but not connectivity or other Internet services. They contend that these services are
not necessary for a communication to occur and that, therefore, the exemption does
not apply.

The interpretation favored by proponents of Tariff 22 is too narrow. "Means"
has a broader meaning than "facilities". The "means" that are necessary to effect an
Internet transmission and to which paragraph 2.4(1)(b) refers are not limited to routers and other hardware. They include all software connection equipment, connectivity
services, hosting and other facilities and services without which such communications
would not occur, just as much as the switching equipment, software and other facilities that are used as part of the infrastructure of a common carrier for the transmission of voice, data or other information.

Moreover, an Internet intermediary is not precluded from relying on paragraph
2.4(1)(b) simply because it provides services that are ancillary to providing the means
of communication or because it performs certain steps or procedures (such as cach-

ing) to improve performance. Paragraph 2.4(1)(b) does not contain any wording excluding its applicability when "telecommunications" are provided as part of a service offering. Neither does the exemption cease to apply for the sole reason that the intermediary may have a contractual relationship with its subscribers. As long as its role in respect of any given transmission is limited to providing the means necessary to allow data initiated by other persons to be transmitted over the Internet, and as long as the ancillary services it provides fall short of involving the act of communicating the work or authorizing its communication, it should be allowed to claim the exemption.

Proponents of Tariff 22 also argue that the Michelin decision *Cie Generale des Etablissements Michelin — Michelin & Cie* v. *C.A.W. — Canada* (1996), at 379.31 stands for the proposition that exceptions in the Act such as paragraph 2.4(1)(b) should be narrowly construed. This is incorrect. The proposition for which Michelin stands is that courts should not read exceptions into the Act. Furthermore, there is no reason to believe that any individual provision of the Act should be construed narrowly. Instead, recent decisions make it clear that the Act should be interpreted in accordance with the ordinary meaning of the words used in the statute, in the context in which the particular language is found and consistent with the many related portions of the statute and with the view to make it as technologically neutral as possible.

Much insistence was also put on the Electric Despatch decision. In some way, the decision anticipated the rationale of paragraph 2.4(1)(b) of the Act in that it held that the party whose wires were used to send a message should not be held contractually liable for the transmission, and interpreted the notion of transmission as involving the person who sends the message and the one who received it, but not the technical intermediary. However, the decision is not otherwise relevant to the issue at hand, if only because it revolved around the interpretation of a clause in a contract according to the rules generally applicable to the interpretation of contracts.

In the end, each transmission must be looked at individually to determine whether in that case, an intermediary merely acts as a conduit for communications by other persons, or whether it is acting as something more. Generally speaking, however, it is safe to conclude that with respect to most transmissions, only the person who posts a musical work communicates it. Both the WIPO Treaty and the draft European directive contain provisions which have a similar effect to paragraph 2.4(1)(b). American legislation now contains detailed requirements that ISPs must meet in order to claim immunity from liability, even though earlier decisions went some way to ensure that they would not be held liable in most cases. To date, the Canadian Parliament has given no indication that it intends to resort to such a detailed, sui generis regime.

Internet intermediaries cannot always claim the benefit of paragraph 2.4(1)(b)
The liability of an entity participating in any Internet transmission must be assessed as a function of the role the entity plays in that transmission, and not as a function of what it generally does over the Internet. Consequently, Internet intermediaries can rely on paragraph 2.4(1)(b) of the Act only with respect to communications in which they limit themselves to acting as intermediaries. In some cases, as a result of business relationships or other factors, intermediaries will act in concert with others in a different manner. Such is the case where an ISP posts content, associates itself with others to offer content, creates embedded links or moderates a newsgroup. In these cases, these entities are no longer acting as intermediaries; their liability will be

assessed according to the general rules dealing with copyright liability. The fact that there may be multiple parties engaged in the transmission does not preclude a finding that each is communicating the work. Thus, where a site owner, through a mirroring arrangement, grants a second party the right to operate a mirror site in its own name, both the original site owner and the person who operates the mirror site jointly communicate works that are posted on the original site when they are transmitted from the mirror site. The same will hold true where an ISP creates a cache for reasons other that [sic] improving system performance, modifies the contents of the cached material or interferes with any means of obtaining information as to the number of "hits" or "accesses" to the cached material.

Thus, entities whose routers handle only some of the transmitted packets will always be able to argue that they do not handle a substantial part of the work. By contrast, attempts at relying on notions of volition or causation to avoid liability will be met with the same scepticism as in other situations, as there is no "prerequisite of knowledge of the existence of the violated copyright or that the action in question amounts to infringement. Infringement is the single act of doing something which 'only the owner of the copyright has the right to do' ".

In the same vein, entities wishing to rely on decisions dealing with the notion of authorization to argue that they should not be held liable will probably find it difficult to do so, if only because their liability would flow not from their authorizing the communication, but from being an active and direct participant in it.

Postscript

As of July 2000, the Copyright Board's Tariff 22 decision was under appeal.

Discussion Question

Should ISP be held accountable for facilitating copyright infringement? Contrast the Canadian Copyright Board's Tariff 22 decision with a U.S. court's characterization of Northwest's (an ISP) role in a copyright infringement case.

Marobie-FL, Inc. v. National Association of Fire Equipment Distributors[†]

Northwest argues it cannot be held liable for the direct infringement of plaintiff's copyrights for two reasons. First, Northwest argues that the transmission of the information in a requested file in electronic form through the RAM of its computer does not constitute "copying" as a matter of law. Under the Copyright Act (the "Act") "copies" are defined as "material objects ... in which a work is fixed by any method now known or later developed, and from which the work can be perceived, reproduced, or otherwise communicated, either directly or with the aid of a machine or

---

† 983 F. Supp. 1167 (N.D.Ill. 1997).

device." 17 U.S.C. §101. "A work is 'fixed' in a tangible medium of expression when its embodiment in a copy ... is sufficiently permanent or stable to permit it to be perceived, reproduced, or otherwise communicated for a period of more than transitory duration." Northwest claims it made no "copy" because the information from plaintiff's clip art files was never "fixed" in its computer's RAM.

The court finds Northwest's argument unpersuasive in light of several cases that discuss the nature of information in RAM. In *MAI Systems Corp.* v. *Peak Computer, Inc.*, the Court of Appeals for the Ninth Circuit held that a "copy" for the purposes of the Act is made when a computer program is transferred from a computer storage device such as Read Only Memory ("ROM") to RAM. The MAI court found that the copyrighted software program at issue was "fixed" in RAM because the computer user was able to view a representation of the program's information, including the system error log, after loading the program into the computer's RAM. In *Religious Technology Center* v. *Netcom On-Line Communication Services, Inc.*, the district court applied the reasoning of MAI to a scenario analogous to that presented in the instant case. In Religious Technology Center, plaintiffs brought an infringement action against the operator of a computer bulletin board service (the "operator") and an Internet access provider (the "provider") because an individual bulletin board subscriber (the "subscriber") was posting portions of their copyrighted work onto his local bulletin board where it could be read and from which it was distributed to other bulletin boards. The subscriber posted his messages in the following manner. First, the subscriber connected to the operator's bulletin board using a telephone and modem. The subscriber then transmitted his messages to the operator's computer. According to a prearranged pattern established by the provider's software, the subscriber's initial act of posting a message resulted in the automatic copying of the subscriber's message from the operator's computer onto the provider's computer and onto other computers in the community of electronic bulletin board services, commonly known as the Usenet. Relying on MAI, the court in Religious Technology Center determined that "copies" within the meaning of the Act were created on both the operator's computer and the provider's computer in the course of transmission.

In the instant case, plaintiff claims its copyrighted information was transmitted from the hard drive of Northwest's computer to Internet users. Northwest does not claim that the copy that existed in its hard drive was the copy sent to an Internet user. On the contrary, Northwest itself asserts that its computer "automatically serves up a copy of the requested file" when a file is asked for by an Internet user. It is that copy in the RAM of Northwest's computer that is transmitted to the Internet user. Northwest argues that this copy is not a "copy" under the Act because it is not "fixed." Northwest argues that it is not "fixed" because the information is transmitted "through" RAM and over the Internet at high speed in the electronic form of bytes. According to Northwest, this process of duplication and transmission happens so quickly that "typically only a portion of a file is in RAM at any one time."

"A work is 'fixed' in a tangible medium of expression when its embodiment in a copy ... is sufficiently permanent or stable to permit it to be perceived, reproduced, or otherwise communicated for a period of more than transitory duration." 17 U.S.C. §101. Yet, a "copy" under the Act need not be potentially perceptible with the naked eye. On the contrary, a "copy" is a "material object ... in which a work is fixed by any method now known or later developed, and from which the work can be perceived, reproduced, or otherwise communicated, either directly or with the aid of a machine or device." 17 U.S.C. §101. In the instant case, the copy created by

Northwest's computer can be perceived with the aid of a machine or device, namely, the Internet user's computer. Although the information in a file is transmitted in pieces, Northwest itself states that "the smaller units are reunited, and the files arrive at the requester's Internet address," and that the Internet user may then view the information by "loading the graphic images into some computer program capable of displaying the formatted image."

Northwest argues that the copying element was found satisfied in Religious Technology Center because the electronic data at issue remained on the computer for days and in MAI because the electronic data at issue remained on the computer long enough to check an error log by viewing it on the computer screen. In the instant case, the information does not remain in the RAM of Northwest's computer, but is immediately transmitted over the Internet. Nevertheless, Northwest's argument fails. The fact that a copy is transmitted after it is created, or even as it is created, does not change the fact that once an Internet user receives a copy, it is capable of being perceived and thus "fixed." Accordingly, the court rejects Northwest's argument that its computer did not "copy" plaintiff's files when they were requested by Internet users.

ISPs' desire to be treated as akin to common carriers, such as telephone companies, was granted in a February 2000 decision of the Canadian Industrial Relations Board. The decision highlights the need to be careful about what you wish for — although ISPs may have obtained liability protection through the common carrier classification, they also face a series of new federal rules (including the *Personal Information Protection and Electronic Documents Act*, Canada's new e-commerce privacy legislation) as federally regulated entities.

Re Island Telecom Inc.[†]

On October 23, 1997, the CEP Local 401 filed an application pursuant to sections 35 and 44 of the Canada Labour Code, seeking a declaration that Island Telecom Inc. ("Island Tel") and Island Tel Advanced Solutions Inc. ("ITAS") are a single undertaking or business for all purposes of Part I of the Code. In the alternative, it seeks a declaration that there has been a sale of business within the meaning of section 44(1) of the Code from Island Tel to ITAS. On May 4, 1998, Local 902 filed a similar application.

In reply to the application, ITAS raised the Board's constitutional jurisdiction, alleging that it is not operating a federal work, undertaking or business.

It was conceded by the parties at the hearing that if the Board finds that ITAS falls within federal jurisdiction, Island Tel and ITAS would meet the test of single employer within the meaning of section 35 of the Code. Accordingly, the remaining issues can be succinctly stated as follows.

1. Do the services provided by ITAS, as an ISP, constitute a federal work, undertaking or business, either by virtue of (a) the fact that the nature of the services provided by an ISP and its mode of operation in relation to the

† [2000] C.I.R.B.D. No. 12.

"Internet/Cyberspace," in and of itself, falls within federal jurisdiction, or (b) the fact that the work done by ITAS is so functionally integrated with that of Island Tel that it forms a single undertaking for jurisdictional purposes?
2. If the answer to the first question is affirmative, should the Board exercise its discretion with respect to the single employer application?

Dr. Vincent Mosco, an acknowledged authority in information technology, was qualified by the Board to testify as an expert in Telecommunications and the role of the Internet in Telecommunications in Canada....

Central to the convergence of electronic and digital communication networks is the ISP. Dr. Mosco described, in detail, the function and operation of an ISP:

> ...a company that, for a fee, provides you with the means to go out over the Internet; that is, it's a company that will have, lets say more sophisticated computers, more powerful computers than you have at home, and a set of devices, modems, that will link your connection to the outside world; that is the world beyond the Internet service provider to other computers that you may want to reach in order to secure information or communicate with other people.

Dr. Mosco described an ISP as a value-added service. It adds value to the telecommunications system by permitting customers to use that system to connect to the Internet. In doing so, the customer can do much more than simply speak to someone on the telephone. With their computers, users can search and secure information from other computers. Users can also communicate with other users through services like electronic mail (e-mail) or chat rooms.

In order to provide access to the Internet, ITAS put together several services. ITAS provides its customers with a software package (Sympatico), which the customer installs on a PC. Customers will then have direct access to the Internet via telephone lines. How does the signal travel through from the PC to reach the Internet? The process was described in the testimony of both Mr. Colin Affleck, ITAS's Information Systems Manager, and Dr. Mosco. Reduced to its essence it can be described as follows.

Users direct their computers to connect with the Internet. The signal is converted into digital bits by the PC users' modem and, in the present case, travels through the telephone lines. The modem within the users' PC dials up the modem pool at Island Tel. The modem pool sends a request to ITAS's authentication server. The ISP's server is a computer that holds a list of authorized users and their password. If users are members of the ISP, the PC can access the Internet. Once the signal has reached the ISP, the ISP's server will identify the users. If those users are members of Sympatico, then ITAS's authentication server sends a message to Bell's authentication server. Bell's server will respond whether or not users are allowed access to the Internet. If members are approved, Bell's authentication server sends a message to ITAS's authentication server, which in turn sends a message back to Island Tel's modem to give users access. The door is then opened to give the customer access to Island Tel's router. Users are now connected to the Internet. The actual "signals" go from Island Tel's router to the line connected to Maritime Telegraph and Telephone Company Ltd. (MT&T) in Halifax. The signals go through a router in Halifax and connect to a line that consolidates the traffic coming from Newfoundland and goes to Fredericton. From there it goes to Québec City where a router sends the signal to Montréal. From there, "the access to the rest of the world is through Toronto on Bell's service into MCI across the border" (I/95).

At this point, on the home computer screen there appears the Sympatico home page, which is delivered from ITAS server. Users now have the ability to get on the Internet. According to Mr. Affleck, "The door is open so that (the user) can get on the Net."

Then, in order to access any of the sites on the Internet users wish to contact, their PCs must make use of ITAS Domain Name Server ("DNS"). The DNS provides the equivalent of a phone book or a 411 service for ITAS's subscribers. ITAS has its own DNS located in Charlottetown and, according to Mr. Affleck, most ISPs will have a server within their local realm. Mr. Affleck described the function of a DNS as follows:

> The function of the server is really to translate the request of a name, so as a user you look for www.microsoft.com ... DNS translates that into a physical number or an IP number, Internet Protocol Number.... And at that point, that's the destination you want to go to is the Internet Protocol Number. The DNS server is doing the look-up on that name. It delivers it back to the host work station or your PC at home, it says, tells your computer to now go to this nine-digit number.

If the ITAS's DNS does not have the number of the address requested, "it will refer the request off to another DNS server within a family of DNS servers around the world."

Whether access to the Internet is sought by a home or business computer, the ISP's authorization is absolutely necessary to access the Internet. As Mr. Affleck pointed out, the ISP's functions are integral to the Internet process. The ISP gives the connection itself, that is, the addresses or the "phone numbers" that allow users to communicate with other users and connect with other Internet sites. In order to achieve this, the ISP complies with international regulations and protocols when it supplies addresses to a user. Without the proper Internet Protocol Address or Domain Name, there is no possible electronic communication.

In short, an ISP is the "gatekeeper" to the Internet. For general users, access can only be obtained through an ISP.

According to Dr. Mosco, in order to operate locally, provincially, nationally or internationally, an ISP must use a telecommunications system, be it telephone, cable or satellite. Overwhelmingly today, the connections to the ISP, and from the ISP to its outside services, are done via a telephone line.

ITAS is principally an ISP. In 1997, 80% of its revenues came from its ISP business; in 1998, it was 60%. Approximately 20% comes from its consulting business to Island Tel.

ITAS purchases the "Sympatico" software from Bell Global Solutions (BGS). It does not own any of the assets necessary to "transport" the signals. It purchases the use of telephone lines owned by Island Tel and pays for the use of its modem pool and its router. In that sense, Stephen Murray described ITAS's activities as being "primarily a reseller of other people's services" that are provided to ITAS (I/83). ITAS buys access from Island Tel to the Canadian net or, in other words, the capacity to connect to the national — and international — network. "It's like buying blocks of long distance time."

ITAS pays monthly fees to Island Tel and BGS for services they provide. The payment of these tariffs constitutes about 50% of ITAS's budget (II/15). In addition,

ITAS and Island Tel entered into a service agreement, by which Island Tel provides ITAS with the following operational services and facilities: market development; network repair and maintenance; corporate development; accounting; rates and regulatory affairs; investor services/internal affairs; business services in sales and support; and treasury. The costs of these services and facilities are determined by the Profit Centre Reporting system of Island Tel.

Although, ITAS provides a number of services to Island Tel, and to a lesser extent, other clients, (e.g., Sympatico Help Desk, Virtual Business Centre, Internet Facsimile, Remote Secure Access, Advantage Internet, Web hosting, Intranet, Extranet), the vast majority of its work revolves around providing telecommunication access for its clients to the Internet or services available therefrom.

General Principles

The Board's jurisdiction over the labour relations of a federal work, undertaking or business is described in section 4 of the Code:

> 4. This Part applies in respect of employees who are employed on or in connection with the operation of any federal work, undertaking or business, in respect of the employers of all such employees in their relations with those employees and in respect of trade unions and employers' organizations composed of those employees or employers.

The relevant definition of "federal work, undertaking or business" is set out in section 2(b) of the Code and is to the same effect as section 92(10)(a) of the Constitution Act, 1867. Section 2(b) of the Code reads as follows:

> 2. In this Act,
>
> "federal work, undertaking or business" means any work, undertaking or business that is within the legislative authority of Parliament, including, without restricting the generality of the foregoing,
>
> (b) a railway, canal, telegraph or other work or undertaking connecting any province with any other province, or extending beyond the limits of a province, ...

It is well established that labour relations fall within the provinces' exclusive jurisdiction. Parliament may only assert exclusive jurisdiction over labour relations if it is shown that it is an integral part of its primary competence over some other single federal subject. In respect of works or undertakings extending beyond the limits of a province, or connecting a province with any other province, the combined effect of sections 91(29) and 92(10)(a) of the Constitution Act, 1867, creates an exception whereby Parliament has exclusive jurisdiction over interprovincial transportation and communication works and undertakings.

As stated in *United Transportation Union* v. *Central Western Railway Corp.*, [1990], there are two ways in which an undertaking may be found to fall within federal jurisdiction. First, it can constitute a federal undertaking if it carries on activities that are within the exclusive competence of Parliament under section 92 of the Constitution Act, 1867. Secondly, if it is not a federal undertaking, it may still fall under federal jurisdiction if it is integral to a core federal undertaking. As noted in *Westcoast Energy Inc.* v. *Canada (National Energy Board)*, [1998], an enterprise may be found to constitute a federal undertaking in two different ways: an undertaking may fall under federal jurisdiction in its own right, or it may be operated as a single enterprise, in common with one or more other undertakings, which together fall under federal jurisdiction.

In the present case, ITAS would constitute a federal undertaking if its activities are found to be interprovincial communications or, alternatively, if it operates a single interprovincial communications enterprise in common with Island Tel. If ITAS does not constitute a federal undertaking pursuant to either of these tests, it may still fall under federal jurisdiction if its operation is integral to a core federal undertaking.

How do these constitutional principles apply to cases concerning new computer technologies and new media? There is very little jurisprudence that deals with the Internet. In fact, apart from the Board's recent decision in CITY-TV, CHUM City Productions Limited, MuchMusic Network and BRAVO!, Division of CHUM Limited, [1999] CIRB no. 22, there is none. In that case, the Board had to decide whether CityInteractive's business, which designs and markets Web sites and provides interactive services, such as taking the Internet to television — thus allowing live on-line chats — and taking television on-line (webcasting), fell within federal or provincial jurisdiction. The Board found that CityInteractive operated in common with one or more federal enterprises. It also concluded, albeit in obiter, that CityInteractive's business was a federal business on its own. It concluded as follows ...

What flows from these decisions, and particularly from the Alberta Government Telephone and the Téléphone Guèvremont cases, is that the use of the physical equipment of telecommunications is not in itself sufficient to bring the business under federal jurisdiction. Conversely, the ownership or operation of the physical equipment is not a prerequisite for a business to fall within federal jurisdiction. In other words, it is not because a business does not do the "switching" or does not operate the "router" that it is automatically excluded from federal jurisdiction. One must examine the nature of the services provided and the mode of operation of the undertaking.

In the present case, ITAS is not itself a carrier or a physical link in the "transport domain." It does not operate a "router," nor any piece of "physical" equipment. The Board heard from Stephen Murray that the telephone company was responsible for the physical transmission of information along the telephone network. That is part of what is called the "transport domain." In the respondent's view, ITAS cannot constitute a federal undertaking because its services are restricted to the "application domain," which are the sets of software and protocols that allow computers to communicate with others.

However useful it is to understand the complexities of the technical aspects of Internet communication, this categorization does not answer the fundamental question: "what is the ordinary business of ITAS."

Counsel for the unions argued that ITAS, as an ISP, falls within the definition of "telecommunications" or "broadcasting", its "business" is that of telecommunications and it is therefore subject to the Board's jurisdiction in the present case. They note that pursuant to section 2(1) of the Telecommunications Act, c. 38, 1993, "telecommunications":

> Means the emission, transmission or reception of intelligence by any wire, cable, radio, optical or other electromagnetic system, or by any similar technical system;

> "telecommunications services":

> Means a service provided by means of telecommunications facilities and includes the provision in whole or in part of telecommunication facilities and any related equipment, whether by sale, lease or otherwise; ...

Finally, section 23 provides:

> For the purposes of this Part and Part IV, "telecommunications service" has the same meaning as in section 2 and includes any service that is incidental to the business of providing telecommunications service.

ITAS' authentication server and its Domain Name Server are specifically designed to provide screening and access in order to permit interprovincial and international telecommunications. The very nature of the service that ITAS delivers is to provide critical access to local, national and international telecommunications. Counsel for the unions argues that even if that service is determined to be "incidental" to the business of providing telecommunications, by section 23 of the Telecommunications Act, it falls within the definition of "telecommunications service."

Although it appears from the facts and the above noted sections that ITAS falls within the regulatory authority of the Telecommunications Act, a determination in that respect, even if we were inclined to make it, would not be determinative of our constitutional jurisdiction over ITAS for the purposes of the Code. Our focus, as indicated earlier, is the ordinary business of ITAS and the service it provides.

Because of the functions carried out by its authentication server and its DNS server, ITAS is an integral part of the process of transmission of digital bits from one province to another, and from one country to another, via telephones lines, for interconnected computers. As Dr. Mosco stressed, any computer may be loaded with software such as Netscape, a graphical user interface. However, this "does not give the connection itself"; that is, the addresses or the phone numbers that allow users to connect to others. The primary concern, from our perspective, is not the physical structures or their actual location, but rather the service that is provided by the undertaking.

The ISP allows those computers connected through the networks to communicate, transmit and receive information across the world. Once access to the Internet is guaranteed, there are no geographical boundaries to the movement of digital bits. Once ITAS's authentication authorizes P.E.I. Sympatico or P.E.I. Advantage Internet users to access Island Tel's router, users have access to the international network.

The fact that ITAS is involved in the "application domain" as opposed to the "transport domain," as argued by the Respondents, is irrelevant in terms of constitutional findings. What is essential is that the nature of the services provided by ITAS is critical for PC users in P.E.I. to access the international networks. In essence, what ITAS does is enable and permit telecommunications via the Internet. Without ITAS and its authentication and domain name servers, these users could not telecommunicate. The word that, everyone agreed, best described ITAS's role as an ISP is that of "gatekeeper" to the Internet. That word by itself, in our view, speaks descriptive volumes of the nature of the services provided by ITAS as well as its mode of operation. At the risk of gilding that descriptive lily, ITAS, as an ISP, provides access to telecommunications. Without it, users could not telecommunicate via the Internet, Island Tel's transport domain notwithstanding.

The nature of the work done by ITAS — which, as the facts above disclose, clearly extends beyond the limits of Prince Edward Island — brings it within the definition of a federal work as defined in section 2(b) of the Code. In the Board's view, ITAS, because of the nature of the service it provides and its mode of operation as an ISP, is a federal business on its own account.

Australia is the latest country to put forth its own proposal for content regulation and ISP liability. In late June 1999, it enacted the following legislation, which took effect in January 2000.

Broadcasting Services Amendment (Online Services) Act 1999†

s. 80 Online provider determinations

(1) The ABA may make a written determination setting out rules that apply to Internet service providers in relation to the supply of Internet carriage services.
(2) The ABA may make a written determination setting out rules that apply to Internet content hosts in relation to the hosting of Internet content in Australia.
(3) A determination under subclause (1) or (2) is called an *online provider determination*.

s. 81 Exemptions from online provider determinations

(1) The Minister may, by written instrument, determine that a specified Internet service provider, or a specified Internet content host, is exempt from online provider determinations.
(2) The Minister may, by written instrument, determine that a specified Internet service provider, or a specified Internet content host, is exempt from a specified online provider determination.
(3) A determination under this clause may be unconditional or subject to such conditions (if any) as are specified in the determination.
(4) A determination under this clause has effect accordingly.
(5) A determination under this clause is a disallowable instrument for the purposes of section 46A of the *Acts Interpretation Act 1901*.

s. 82 Compliance with online provider rules
A person is guilty of an offence if:

(a) an online provider rule is applicable to the person; and
(b) the person contravenes the rule.

s. 83 Remedial directions — breach of online provider rules

(1) This clause applies if an Internet service provider, or an Internet content host, has contravened, or is contravening, an online provider rule.
(2) The ABA may give the provider or host a written direction requiring the provider or host to take specified action directed towards ensuring that the pro-

---

† (1999), No. 90.

vider or host does not contravene the rule, or is unlikely to contravene the rule, in the future.

(3) The following are examples of the kinds of direction that may be given to an Internet service provider, or an Internet content host, under subclause (2):

(a) a direction that the provider or host implement effective administrative systems for monitoring compliance with an online provider rule;

(b) a direction that the provider or host implement a system designed to give the provider's or host's employees, agents and contractors a reasonable knowledge and understanding of the requirements of an online provider rule, in so far as those requirements affect the employees, agents or contractors concerned.

(4) A person is guilty of an offence if:

(a) the person is subject to a direction under subclause (2); and

(b) the person contravenes the direction.

s. 84 Formal warnings — breach of online provider rules

The ABA may issue a formal warning if a person contravenes an online provider rule.

s. 85 Federal Court may order a person to cease supplying Internet carriage services or cease hosting Internet content

(1) If the ABA is satisfied that:

(a) a person who is an Internet service provider is supplying an Internet carriage service otherwise than in accordance with an online provider rule; or

(b) a person who is an Internet content host is hosting Internet content in Australia otherwise than in accordance with an online provider rule;

the ABA may apply to the Federal Court for an order that the person cease supplying that Internet carriage service or cease hosting that Internet content in Australia, as the case requires.

(2) If the Federal Court is satisfied, on such an application, that the person is:

(a) supplying an Internet carriage service otherwise than in accordance with the online provider rule; or

(b) hosting Internet content in Australia otherwise than in accordance with the online provider rule;

the Federal Court may order the person to cease supplying that Internet carriage service or cease hosting that Internet content in Australia, as the case requires.

Discussion Questions

1. The wide range of approaches to ISP liability suggests that this issue is far from settled. Is there middle ground to be found between the United States and Australian approaches?

2. Canada has yet to develop its own legislative framework for ISP liability. Does it risk harming its Internet industries and infrastructure if it fails to

provide a greater level of certainty on this issue? Alternatively, is this matter best left to the courts and tribunals to decide?

For more on Canadian ISP issues, see the Canadian Association of Internet Providers Web site at <http://www.caip.ca> or the RISC (Responsible Internet Service Companies) Web site at <http://www.risc.ca>.

PART TWO

INTERNET SPEECH REGULATION

5

Internet Speech Regulation — A Comparative Perspective

As one of democracy's most cherished rights, the right of free speech is at the foundation of the rights enjoyed by citizens in a free society. Contrary to popular belief, however, it is not an absolute right, as all countries establish some limitations to free speech.

Certain limitations, such as criminal speech consisting of death threats or defamatory speech, are relatively uncontroversial. Other forms of speech, such as hate speech or obscenity, are subject to differing rules in different countries. At one end of the spectrum, the United States has adopted perhaps the most permissive free speech legal framework, with even the most hateful material enjoying constitutional protection. By contrast, Canada and many European countries have set limitations on hate speech, rendering certain forms illegal.

Given the free flow of information on the Internet, these differing approaches to speech regulation assume a heightened level of importance, since speech legal in one jurisdiction may be illegal in a neighboring jurisdiction, even though the material is readily available in both places via the Internet. An understanding of the different approaches to speech regulation is therefore essential within the context of Internet law, since a harmonized international legal framework for much of the controversial speech is highly unlikely.

This chapter canvasses several international approaches to Internet speech regulation. Canadian approaches are examined in Chapters 6 and 7.

THE UNITED STATES

U.S. restrictions to free speech on the Internet have primarily targeted the accessibility of pornographic materials. After the *Communications Decency Act* was struck down as unconstitutional by the U.S. Supreme Court in 1997, the U.S. Congress revisited the issue by enacting the *Child Online Protection Act (COPA)*. The statute was challenged in federal court in February 1999, with indications that the case may also work its way up to the Supreme Court.

American Civil Liberties Union v. Reno[†]

The First Amendment to the United States Constitution provides that "Congress shall make no law ... abridging the freedom of speech." Although there is no complete consensus on the issue, most courts and commentators theorize that the importance of protecting freedom of speech is to foster the marketplace of ideas. If speech, even unconventional speech that some find lacking in substance or offensive, is allowed to compete unrestricted in the marketplace of ideas, truth will be discovered. Indeed, the First Amendment was designed to prevent the majority, through acts of Congress, from silencing those who would express unpopular or unconventional views.

But with freedom come consequences. Many of the same characteristics which make cyberspace ideal for First Amendment expression — ease of participation and diversity of content and speakers — make it a potentially harmful media for children. A child with minimal knowledge of a computer, the ability to operate a browser, and the skill to type a few simple words may be able to access sexual images and content over the World Wide Web. For example, typing the word "dollhouse" or "toys" into a typical Web search engine will produce a page of links, some of which connect to what would be considered by many to be pornographic Web sites. These Web sites offer "teasers," free sexually explicit images and animated graphic image files designed to entice a user to pay a fee to browse the whole site.

Intending to address the problem of children's access to these teasers, Congress passed the Child Online Protection Act ("COPA"), which was to go into effect on November 29, 1998. On October 22, 1998, the plaintiffs, including, among others, Web site operators and content providers, filed this lawsuit challenging the constitutionality of COPA under the First and Fifth Amendments and seeking injunctive relief from its enforcement. Two diametric interests — the constitutional right of freedom of speech and the interest of Congress, and indeed society, in protecting children from harmful materials — are in tension in this lawsuit.

This is not the first attempt of Congress to regulate content on the Internet. Congress passed the Communications Decency Act of 1996 ("CDA") which purported to regulate the access of minors to "indecent" and "patently offensive" speech on the Internet. The CDA was struck down by the Supreme Court in *ACLU* v. *Reno*, ("Reno I") as violative of the First Amendment. COPA represents congressional efforts to remedy the constitutional defects in the CDA.

Plaintiffs attack COPA on several grounds: (1) that it is invalid on its face and as applied to them under the First Amendment for burdening speech that is constitutionally protected for adults, (2) that it is invalid on its face for violating the First Amendment rights of minors, and (3) that it is unconstitutionally vague under the

---

[†] 31 F. Supp. 2d 473 (E.D. Pa. 1999).

First and Fifth Amendments. The parties presented evidence and argument on the motion of plaintiffs for a temporary restraining order on November 19, 1998. This Court entered a temporary restraining order on November 20, 1998, enjoining the enforcement of COPA until December 4, 1998. The defendant agreed to extend the duration of the TRO through February 1, 1999. The parties conducted accelerated discovery thereafter. While the parties and the Court considered consolidating the preliminary injunction hearing with a trial on the merits, the Court, upon due consideration of the arguments of the parties, ultimately decided that it would proceed only on the motion for preliminary injunction. There necessarily remains a period for completion of discovery and preparation before a trial on the merits.

The defendant filed a motion to dismiss the entire action pursuant to Federal Rule of Civil Procedure 12(b)(1) for lack of standing in addition to her arguments in response to the motion for preliminary injunction. The plaintiffs filed a response to the motion to dismiss, to which the defendant filed a reply.

Based on this evidence and for the reasons that follow, the motion to dismiss will be denied and the motion for a preliminary injunction will be granted.

IV. THE CHILD ONLINE PROTECTION ACT
In what will be codified as 47 U.S.C. 231, COPA provides that:

(1) PROHIBITED CONDUCT. — Whoever knowingly and with knowledge of the character of the material, in interstate or foreign commerce by means of the World Wide Web, makes any communication for commercial purposes that is available to any minor and that includes any material that is harmful to minors shall be fined not more than $50,000, imprisoned not more than 6 months, or both.

(2) INTENTIONAL VIOLATIONS. — In addition to the penalties under paragraph (1), whoever intentionally violates such paragraph shall be subject to a fine of not more than $50,000 for each violation. For purposes of this paragraph, each day of violation shall constitute a separate violation.

(3) CIVIL PENALTY. — In addition to the penalties under paragraphs (1) and (2), whoever violates paragraph (1) shall be subject to a civil penalty of not more than $50,000 for each violation. For purposes of this paragraph, each day of violation shall constitute a separate violation.

. . . .

II. ARGUMENTS OF THE PARTIES
The arguments of the parties are plentiful and will be only summarized here for purposes of the motion for a preliminary injunction. Plaintiffs argue that COPA is unconstitutional on its face and as applied to them because the regulation of speech that is "harmful to minors" burdens or threatens a large amount of speech that is protected as to adults. According to the plaintiffs, the fact that COPA is vague, overbroad, and a direct ban on speech that provides only affirmative defenses to prosecution contributes to the burden COPA places on speech. The plaintiffs argue that the affirmative defenses provided in COPA do not alleviate the burden on speech because their implementation imposes an economic and technological burden on speakers which results in loss of anonymity to users and consequently loss of users to its Web sites. The plaintiffs contend that the defendant cannot justify the burden on speech by showing that COPA is narrowly tailored to a compelling

government interest or the least restrictive means to accomplish its ends. Alternatively, plaintiffs frame their facial attack to the statute as an overbreadth challenge, arguing that speech will be chilled on the Web because the statute covers more speech than it was intended to cover, even if it can be constitutionally applied to a narrow class of speakers. The plaintiffs also challenge COPA as being unconstitutionally vague under the First and Fifth Amendments and facially unconstitutional as to speech protected for minors.

Defendant argues that COPA passes constitutional muster because it is narrowly tailored to the government's compelling interest in protecting minors from harmful materials. The defendant argues that the statute does not inhibit the ability of adults to access such speech or the ability of commercial purveyors of materials that are harmful to minors to make such speech available to adults. The defendant points to the presence of affirmative defenses in the statute as a technologically and economically feasible method for speakers on the Web to restrict the access of minors to harmful materials. As to the plaintiffs' argument that COPA is overbroad, the defendant argues that the definition of "harmful to minors" material does not apply to any of the material on the plaintiffs' Web sites, and that the statute only targets commercial pornographers, those who distribute harmful to minors material "as a regular course" of their business. The defendant contends that plaintiffs cannot succeed on their motion for a preliminary injunction because they cannot show a likelihood of success on their claims and that their claim of irreparable harm is merely speculative.

. . . .

VI. ANALYSIS OF THE MOTION FOR PRELIMINARY INJUNCTION AND CONCLUSIONS OF LAW

A. Substantial Likelihood of Success on the Merits

For the purposes of the motion for preliminary injunction, the Court will focus its analysis on the claim of plaintiffs that COPA is unconstitutional on its face for violating the First Amendment rights of adults.

1. Standard of Scrutiny

COPA is a content-based regulation of speech which is protected at least as to adults. Although there are lower standards of scrutiny where the regulation of general broadcast media or "commercial" speech, that is, speech that proposes a commercial transaction, are involved, neither is appropriate here.

As a content-based regulation of such expression, COPA is presumptively invalid and is subject to strict scrutiny by this Court. "As a matter of constitutional tradition, in the absence of evidence to the contrary, we presume that governmental regulation of the content of speech is more likely to interfere with the free exchange of ideas than to encourage it." Thus, the content of such protected speech may be regulated in order to promote a compelling governmental interest "if it chooses the least restrictive means to further the articulated interest. Attempts of Congress to serve compelling interests must be narrowly tailored to serve those interests without unnecessarily interfering with First Amendment freedoms. Thus, the burden imposed on speech must be outweighed by the benefits gained by the challenged statute. The Supreme Court has repeatedly stated that the free speech rights of adults may not be reduced to allow them to read only what is acceptable for children.

2. Burden on Speech Imposed by COPA

A statute which has the effect of deterring speech, even if not totally suppressing speech, is a restraint on free expression. One such deterrent can be a financial disincentive created by the statute. "A statute is presumptively inconsistent with the First Amendment if it imposes a financial burden on speakers because of the content of their speech."

Evidence presented to this Court is likely to establish at trial that the implementation of credit card or adult verification screens in front of material that is harmful to minors may deter users from accessing such materials and that the loss of users of such material may affect the speakers' economic ability to provide such communications. The plaintiffs are likely to establish at trial that under COPA, Web site operators and content providers may feel an economic disincentive to engage in communications that are or may be considered to be harmful to minors and thus, may self-censor the content of their sites. Further, the uncontroverted evidence showed that there is no way to restrict the access of minors to harmful materials in chat rooms and discussion groups, which the plaintiffs assert draw traffic to their sites, without screening all users before accessing any content, even that which is not harmful to minors, or editing all content before it is posted to exclude material that is harmful to minors. This has the effect of burdening speech in these fora that is not covered by the statute. I conclude that based on the evidence presented to date, the plaintiffs have established a substantial likelihood that they will be able to show that COPA imposes a burden on speech that is protected for adults.

3. Compelling Government Interest

It is clear that Congress has a compelling interest in the protection of minors, including shielding them from materials that are not obscene by adult standards. There is nothing in the legislative history of COPA that indicates that the intention of Congress was anything but the protection of minors. Congress expressed that its intent in COPA was to require "the commercial pornographer to put sexually explicit messages 'behind the counter'" on the Web, similar to existing requirements in some states that such material to be held behind the counter or sold in a paper wrapper in a physical store.

4. Narrow Tailoring and Least Restrictive Means

While the plaintiffs have the burden in the context of the motion for preliminary injunction of showing success on the merits of their claims, the defendant ultimately will bear the burden of establishing that COPA is the least restrictive means and narrowly tailored its objective, which the defendant argues is the regulation of commercial pornographers.

Here, this Court's finding that minors may be able to gain access to harmful to minors materials on foreign Web sites, non-commercial sites, and online via protocols other than http demonstrates the problems this statute has with efficaciously meeting its goal. Moreover, there is some indication in the record that minors may be able to legitimately possess a credit or debit card and access harmful to minors materials despite the screening mechanisms provided in the affirmative defenses. These factors reduce the benefit that will be realized by the implementation of COPA in preventing minors from accessing such materials online.

On the record to date, it is not apparent to this Court that the defendant can meet its burden to prove that COPA is the least restrictive means available to achieve the goal of restricting the access of minors to this material. The plaintiffs suggest that an example of a more efficacious and less restrictive means to shield minors from harmful materials is to rely upon filtering and blocking technology. Evidence was presented that blocking and filtering software is not perfect, in that it is possible that some appropriate sites for minors will be blocked while inappropriate sites may slip through the cracks. However, there was also evidence that such software blocks certain sources of content that COPA does not cover, such as foreign sites and content on other protocols. The record before the Court reveals that blocking or filtering technology may be at least as successful as COPA would be in restricting minors' access to harmful material online without imposing the burden on constitutionally protected speech that COPA imposes on adult users or Web site operators. Such a factual conclusion is at least some evidence that COPA does not employ the least restrictive means.

Beyond the debate over the relative efficacy of COPA compared to blocking and filtering technology, plaintiffs point to other aspects of COPA which Congress could have made less restrictive. Notably, the sweeping category of forms of content that are prohibited — "any communication, picture, image, graphic image file, article, recording, writing, or other matter of any kind" (emphasis added) — could have been less restrictive of speech on the Web and more narrowly tailored to Congress' goal of shielding minors from pornographic teasers if the prohibited forms of content had included, for instance, only pictures, images, or graphic image files, which are typically employed by adult entertainment Web sites as "teasers." In addition, perhaps the goals of Congress could be served without the imposition of possibly excessive and serious criminal penalties, including imprisonment and hefty fines, for communicating speech that is protected as to adults or without exposing speakers to prosecution and placing the burden of establishing an affirmative defense on them instead of incorporating the substance of the affirmative defenses in the elements of the crime.

B.   Irreparable Harm

The plaintiffs have uniformly testified or declared that their fears of prosecution under COPA will result in the self-censorship of their online materials in an effort to avoid prosecution, and this Court has concluded in the resolution of the motion to dismiss that such fears are reasonable given the breadth of the statute. Such a chilling effect could result in the censoring of constitutionally protected speech, which constitutes an irreparable harm to the plaintiffs. "It is well established that the loss of First Amendment freedoms, for even minimal periods of time, unquestionably constitutes irreparable injury." For plaintiffs who choose not to self-censor their speech, they face criminal prosecution and penalties for communicating speech that is protected for adults under the First Amendment, which also constitutes irreparable harm.

C.   Balance of Interests

In deciding whether to issue injunctive relief, this Court must balance the interests and potential harm to the parties. It is well established that no one, the government included, has an interest in the enforcement of an unconstitutional law. It follows in this context that the harm to plaintiffs from the infringement of their rights under the First Amendment clearly outweighs any purported interest of the defendant.

VII. CONCLUSION

The protection of children from access to harmful to minors materials on the Web, the compelling interest sought to be furthered by Congress in COPA, particularly resonates with the Court. This Court and many parents and grandparents would like to see the efforts of Congress to protect children from harmful materials on the Internet to ultimately succeed and the will of the majority of citizens in this country to be realized through the enforcement of an act of Congress. However, the Court is acutely cognizant of its charge under the law of this country not to protect the majoritarian will at the expense of stifling the rights embodied in the Constitution.

Despite the Court's personal regret that this preliminary injunction will delay once again the careful protection of our children, I without hesitation acknowledge the duty imposed on the Court and the greater good such duty serves. Indeed, perhaps we do the minors of this country harm if First Amendment protections, which they will with age inherit fully, are chipped away in the name of their protection.

Based on the foregoing analysis, the motion to dismiss the plaintiffs for lack of standing will be denied.

Based on the foregoing findings and analysis, the Court concludes that the plaintiffs have established a likelihood of success on the merits, irreparable harm, and that the balance of interests, including the interest of the public, weighs in favor of enjoining the enforcement of this statute pending a trial on the merits, and the motion of plaintiffs for a preliminary injunction will be granted.

Discussion Questions

1. The court seems almost reluctant to rule against the statute. Can you suggest what alterations might persuade a court that the law is constitutionally valid?

2. Consider the technology discussion from the court, which suggests that the technology is not presently available to provide a sufficiently effective alternative. Should the validity of a law depend upon technology? Does this create time-limited effectiveness of the laws?

Postscript

The District Court decision was upheld by the 3rd Circuit Court of Appeal in June 2000. The court ruled that the statute was overly broad and would require even non-offensive sites to censor content or implement an age verification system.

Internet regulation in other parts of the world can make the approaches in Canada and the United States appear very permissive. Consider the new legislative framework in Australia, as well as the more repressive legal frameworks in force in Singapore and China.

AUSTRALIA

Broadcasting Services Amendment (Online Services) Act 1999[†]

s. 10 Prohibited content
Internet content hosted in Australia
(1) For the purposes of this Schedule, Internet content hosted in Australia is *prohibited content* if:

(a) the Internet content has been classified RC or X by the Classification Board; or
(b) both:
  (i) the Internet content has been classified R by the Classification Board; and
  (ii) access to the Internet content is not subject to a restricted access system.

Internet content hosted outside Australia
(2) For the purposes of this Schedule, Internet content hosted outside Australia is *prohibited content* if the Internet content has been classified RC or X by the Classification Board.

s. 11 Potential prohibited content
(1) For the purposes of this Schedule, Internet content is *potential prohibited content* if:

(a) the Internet content has not been classified by the Classification Board; and
(b) if the Internet content were to be classified by the Classification Board, there is a substantial likelihood that the Internet content would be prohibited content.

(2) In determining whether particular Internet content is potential prohibited content, it is to be assumed that this Schedule authorised the Classification Board to classify the Internet content.

s. 14 Reclassification of Internet content
(1) If Internet content has been classified by the Classification Board (otherwise than because of subclause 12(1)):

(a) the Classification Board must not reclassify the content within the 2-year period beginning on the day on which the classification occurred; and
(b) after that 2-year period, the Classification Board may reclassify the content.

(2) The Classification Board may act under paragraph (1)(b):

(a) if required to do so by the Minister or the ABA; or
(b) on the Classification Board's own initiative.

(3) If the Minister or the ABA requires the Classification Board to act under paragraph (1)(b), the Classification Board must do so.

(4) If Internet content is reclassified by the Classification Board, the Classification Board must notify the ABA accordingly.

---

† (1999), No. 90.

s. 15 Notice of intention to reclassify Internet content

(1) If:

(a) Internet content has been classified by the Classification Board (otherwise than because of subclause 12(1)); and

(b) the Classification Board intends to reclassify the content;
then:

(c) the Director of the Classification Board must give notice of that intention, inviting submissions about the matter; and

(d) the Director of the Classification Board must cause the contents of the notice to be published, in such manner as the Director decides, at least 30 days before the Classification Board proposes to consider the matter; and

(e) the Director of the Classification Board must give a copy of the notice to the Minister and to the ABA at least 30 days before the Classification Board proposes to consider the matter.

(2) A notice under paragraph (1)(c) must specify the day on which the Board proposes to consider the matter.

. . . .

(4) The matters that the Classification Board is to take into account in reclassifying the Internet content include issues raised in submissions made to the Classification Board about the matter.

s. 22 Complaints about prohibited content or potential prohibited content

Complaints about access to prohibited content or potential prohibited content

(1) If a person has reason to believe that end-users in Australia can access prohibited content or potential prohibited content using an Internet carriage service, the person may make a complaint to the ABA about the matter.

Complaints relating to Internet content hosts

(2) If a person has reason to believe that an Internet content host is:

(a) hosting prohibited content in Australia; or

(b) hosting potential prohibited content in Australia;
the person may make a complaint to the ABA about the matter.

Content of complaint

(3) A complaint under subclause (1) or (2) about particular Internet content must:

(a) identify the Internet content; and

(b) set out how to access the Internet content (for example: set out a URL, a password, or the name of a newsgroup); and

(c) if the complainant knows the country or countries in which the Internet content is hosted — set out the name of that country or those countries; and

(d) set out the complainant's reasons for believing that the Internet content is prohibited content or potential prohibited content; and

(e) set out such other information (if any) as the ABA requires.

(4) The rule in paragraph (3)(b) does not apply to a complaint to the extent (if any) to which finding out how to access the Internet content would cause the complainant to contravene a law of a State or Territory.

(5) A person is not entitled to make a complaint under subclause (1) or (2) about something that occurs before 1 January 2000.

s. 30 Action to be taken in relation to a complaint about prohibited content hosted in Australia

Prohibited content

(1) If, in the course of an investigation under Division 2, the ABA is satisfied that Internet content hosted in Australia is prohibited content, the ABA must give the relevant Internet content host a written notice (a *final take-down notice*) directing the Internet content host not to host the prohibited content.

Potential prohibited content

(2) The following provisions have effect if, in the course of an investigation under Division 2, the ABA is satisfied that Internet content hosted in Australia is potential prohibited content:

(a) if the ABA is satisfied that, if the Internet content were to be classified by the Classification Board, there is a substantial likelihood that the Internet content would be classified RC or X — the ABA must:
    (i) give the relevant Internet content host a written notice (an *interim take-down notice*) directing the Internet content host not to host the Internet content until the ABA notifies the host under subclause (4) of the Classification Board's classification of the Internet content; and
    (ii) request the Classification Board to classify the Internet content;

(b) if the ABA is satisfied that, if the Internet content were to be classified by the Classification Board, there is a substantial likelihood that the Internet content would be classified R — the ABA must request the Classification Board to classify the Internet content.

(3) If the Classification Board receives a request under paragraph (2)(a) or (b) to classify particular Internet content, the Classification Board must:

(a) classify the content; and
(b) inform the ABA, in writing, of its classification.

(4) If the ABA is informed under paragraph (3)(b) of the classification of particular Internet content, the ABA must:

(a) give the relevant Internet content host a written notice setting out the classification; and
(b) in a case where the effect of the classification is that the Internet content is prohibited content — give the Internet content host a written notice (a *final take-down notice*) directing the host not to host the prohibited content.

(5) If the ABA requests the Classification Board to classify particular Internet content:

(a) the ABA must give the Classification Board:
    (i) sufficient information about the content to enable the Classification Board to access the content; or
    (ii) a copy of the content; and
(b) the ABA must give the Classification Board sufficient information about the content to enable the Classification Board to classify the content; and

(c) the ABA may, at the request of the Classification Board or on its own initiative, give the Classification Board additional information about the content if the ABA is of the opinion that the additional information would be likely to facilitate the classification of the content.

(6) If the ABA makes a decision under paragraph (2)(b) to request the Classification Board to classify Internet content, the ABA must give the relevant Internet content host a written notice setting out the decision.

s. 40 Action to be taken in relation to a complaint about prohibited content hosted outside Australia

(1) If, in the course of an investigation under Division 2, the ABA is satisfied that Internet content hosted outside Australia is prohibited content or potential prohibited content, the ABA must:

(a) if the ABA considers the content is of a sufficiently serious nature to warrant referral to a law enforcement agency (whether in or outside Australia) — notify the content to:
   (i) a member of an Australian police force; or
   (ii) if there is an arrangement between the ABA and the chief (however described) of an Australian police force under which the ABA is authorised to notify the content to a [sic] another person or body (whether in or outside Australia) — that other person or body; and
(b) if a code registered, or standard determined, under Part 5 of this Schedule deals with the matters referred to in subclause 60(2) — notify the content to Internet service providers under the designated notification scheme set out in the code or standard, as the case may be; and
(c) if paragraph (b) does not apply — give each Internet service provider known to the ABA a written notice (a *standard access-prevention notice*) directing the provider to take all reasonable steps to prevent end-users from accessing the content.

(2) For the purposes of paragraph (1)(c), in determining whether particular steps are reasonable, regard must be had to:

(a) the technical and commercial feasibility of taking the steps; and
(b) the matters set out in subsection 4(3).

(3) Subclause (2) does not, by implication, limit the matters to which regard must be had.

Recognised alternative access-prevention arrangements

(4) An Internet service provider is not required to comply with a standard access-prevention notice in relation to a particular end-user if access by the end-user is subject to a recognised alternative access-prevention arrangement (as defined by subclause (5)) that is applicable to the end-user.

(5) The ABA may, by written instrument, declare that a specified arrangement is a *recognised alternative access-prevention arrangement* for the purposes of the application of this Division to one or more specified end-users if the ABA is satisfied that the arrangement is likely to provide a reasonably effective means of preventing access by those end-users to prohibited content and potential prohibited content.

(6) The following are examples of arrangements that could be declared to be recognised alternative access-prevention arrangements under subclause (5):

(a) an arrangement that involves the use of regularly updated Internet content filtering software;

(b) an arrangement that involves the use of a "family-friendly" filtered Internet carriage service.

SINGAPORE

Internet Code of Practice[†]

It is hereby notified for general information that, in exercise of the powers conferred by section 18 of the Singapore Broadcasting Authority Act, the Singapore Broadcasting Authority has issued, with effect from 1st November 1997, the Internet Code of Practice as set out in the Schedule.

2. Notification no. 2400/96 of 15th July 1996 is cancelled.

The Schedule
Internet Code Of Practice
Foreword

1.(1) The Singapore Broadcasting Authority Act (Cap. 297) makes it the duty of the Singapore Broadcasting Authority to ensure that nothing is included in any broadcasting service which is against public interest or order, national harmony or which offends against good taste or decency. This Code of Practice has been produced by the Singapore Broadcasting Authority for this purpose.

(2) All Internet Service Providers and Internet Content Providers licensed under the Singapore Broadcasting Authority (Class Licence) Notification 1996 are required to comply with this Code of Practice. Under the Singapore Broadcasting Authority Act, the Authority has the power to impose sanctions, including fines, on licensees who contravene this Code of Practice.

Internet Code of Practice

2. A licensee shall use his best efforts to ensure that prohibited material is not broadcast via the Internet to users in Singapore.

Obligations under this Code

3.(1) An Internet Access Service Provider or Reseller discharges his obligations under this Code, in relation to programmes on the World Wide Web, when he denies access to sites notified to him by the Authority as containing prohibited material, under clause 4 below.

---

† Singapore Broadcasting Authority Act, Ch. 297. Online: <http://www.sba.gov.sg/work/sba/internet.nsf/pages/code>.

(2) An Internet Access Service Provider or Reseller discharges his obligations under this Code, in relation to Internet Newsgroups, when it: —

(a) refrains from subscribing to any newsgroup if, in his opinion, it is likely to contain prohibited material; and
(b) unsubscribes from any newsgroups that the Authority may direct.
   (3) An Internet Content Provider discharges his obligation under this Code: —

(a) in relation to private discussion fora hosted on his service (eg. chat groups), when the licensee chooses discussion themes which are not prohibited under the guidelines in clause 4 below;
(b) in relation to programmes on his service contributed by other persons who are invited to do so on the licensee's service for public display (eg. bulletin boards), when the licensee denies access to any contributions that contain prohibited material that he discovers in the normal course of exercising his editorial duties, or is informed about; and
(c) in relation to all other programmes on his service, if the licensee ensures that such programmes do not include material that would be considered to be prohibited under the guidelines in clause 4 below*.

(4) An Internet Content Provider shall deny access to material considered by the Authority to be prohibited material if directed to do so by the Authority.
   (5) Paragraph (3) does not apply to any web publisher or web server administrator in respect of programmes on his service for which he has no editorial control.

Prohibited Material

4.(1) Prohibited material is material that is objectionable on the grounds of public interest, public morality, public order, public security, national harmony, or is otherwise prohibited by applicable Singapore laws.
   (2) In considering what is prohibited material, the following factors should be taken into account:

(a) whether the material depicts nudity or genitalia in a manner calculated to titillate;
(b) whether the material promotes sexual violence or sexual activity involving coercion or non-consent of any kind;
(c) whether the material depicts a person or persons clearly engaged in explicit sexual activity;
(d) whether the material depicts a person who is, or appears to be, under 16 years of age in sexual activity, in a sexually provocative manner or in any other offensive manner;
(e) whether the material advocates homosexuality or lesbianism, or depicts or promotes incest, paedophilia, bestiality and necrophilia;
(f) whether the material depicts detailed or relished acts of extreme violence or cruelty;
(g) whether the material glorifies, incites or endorses ethnic, racial or religious hatred, strife or intolerance.

(3) A further consideration is whether the material has intrinsic medical, scientific, artistic or educational value.
   (4) A licensee who is in doubt as to whether any content would be considered prohibited may refer such content to the Authority for its decision.

CHINA

Computer Information Network and Internet Security, Protection and Management Regulations[†]

Chapter One Comprehensive Regulations

Section One — In order to strengthen the security and the protection of computer information networks and of the Internet, and to preserve the social order and social stability, these regulations have been established on the basis of the "PRC Computer Information Network Protection Regulations", the "PRC Temporary Regulations on Computer Information Networks and the Internet" and other laws and administrative regulations.

Section Two — The security, protection and management of all computer information networks within the borders of the PRC fall under these regulations.

Section Three — The computer management and supervision organization of the Ministry of Public Security is responsible for the security, protection and management of computer information networks and the Internet. The Computer Management and Supervision organization of the Ministry of Public Security should protect the public security of computer information networks and the Internet as well as protect the legal rights of Internet service providing units and individuals as well as the public interest.

Section Four — No unit or individual may use the Internet to harm national security, disclose state secrets, harm the interests of the State, of society or of a group, the legal rights of citizens, or to take part in criminal activities.

Section Five — No unit or individual may use the Internet to create, replicate, retrieve, or transmit the following kinds of information:

(1) Inciting to resist or breaking the Constitution or laws or the implementation of administrative regulations;
(2) Inciting to overthrow the government or the socialist system;
(3) Inciting division of the country, harming national unification;
(4) Inciting hatred or discrimination among nationalities or harming the unity of the nationalities;
(5) Making falsehoods or distorting the truth, spreading rumors, destroying the order of society;
(6) Promoting feudal superstitions, sexually suggestive material, gambling, violence, murder,
(7) Terrorism or inciting others to criminal activity; openly insulting other people or distorting the truth to slander people;
(8) Injuring the reputation of state organs;
(9) Other activities against the Constitution, laws or administrative regulations.

Section Six — No unit or individual may engage in the following activities which harm the security of computer information networks:

---

† Approved by the State Council on December 11 1997 and promulgated by the Ministry of Public Security on December 30, 1997.

(1) No-one may use computer networks or network resources without getting proper prior approval

(2) No-one may without prior permission may change network functions or to add or delete information

(3) No-one may without prior permission add to, delete, or alter materials stored, processed or being transmitted through the network.

(4) No-one may deliberately create or transmit viruses.

(5) Other activities which harm the network are also prohibited.

Section Seven — The freedom and privacy of network users is protected by law. No unit or individual may, in violation of these regulations, use the Internet to violate the freedom and privacy of network users.

Chapter 2 Responsibility for Security and Protection

Section 8 — Units and individuals engaged in Internet business must accept the security supervision, inspection, and guidance of the Public Security organization. This includes providing to the Public Security organization information, materials and digital document, and assisting the Public Security organization to discover and properly handle incidents involving law violations and criminal activities involving computer information networks.

Section 9 — The supervisory section or supervisory units of units which provide service through information network gateways through which information is imported and exported and connecting network units should, according to the law and relevant state regulations assume responsibility for the Internet network gateways as well as the security, protection, and management of the subordinate networks.

Section 10 — Connecting network units, entry point units and corporations that use computer information networks and the Internet and other organizations must assume the following responsibilities for network security and protection:

(1) Assume responsibility for network security, protection and management and establish a thoroughly secure, protected and well managed network.

(2) Carry out technical measures for network security and protection. Ensure network operational security and information security.

(3) Assume responsibility for the security education and training of network users

(4) Register units and individuals to whom information is provided. Provide information according to the stipulations of article five.

(5) Establish a system for registering the users of electronic bulletin board systems on the computer information network as well as a system for managing bulletin board information.

(6) If a violation of articles four, five, six or seven is discovered than an unaltered record of the violation should be kept and reported to the local Public Security organization.

(7) According to the relevant State regulations, remove from the network and address, directory or server which has content in violation of article five.

Section 11 — The network user should fill out a user application form when applying for network services. The format of this application form is determined by Public Security.

Section 12 — Connecting network units, entry point units, and corporations that use computer information networks and the Internet and other organizations (including connecting network units that are inter-provincial, autonomous region, municipalities directly under the Central Government or the branch organization of these units) should, within 30 days of the opening of network connection, carry out the proper registration procedures with a unit designated by the Public Security organization of the provincial, autonomous region, or municipality directly under the Central Government peoples' government.

The units mentioned above have the responsibility to report for the record to the local public security organization information on the units and individuals which have connections to the network. The units must also report in a timely manner to Public Security organization any changes in the information about units or individuals using the network.

Section 13 — People who register public accounts should strengthen their management of the account and establish an account registration system. Accounts may not be lent or transferred.

Section 14 — Whenever units involved in matters such as national affairs, economic construction, building the national defense, and advanced science and technology are registered, evidence of the approval of the chief administrative section should be shown.

Appropriate measures should be taken to ensure the security and protection of the computer information network and Internet network links of the units mentioned above.

Chapter Three Security and Supervision

Section 15 — The provincial, autonomous region or municipal Public Security agency or bureau, as well as city and county Public Security organizations should have appropriate organizations to ensure the security, protection and management of the Internet.

Section 16 — The Public Security organization computer management and supervision organization should have information on the connecting network units, entry point unit, and users, establish a filing system for this information, maintain statistical information on these files and report to higher level units as appropriate.

Section 17 — The Public Security computer management and supervision organization should have establish a system for ensuring the security, protection and good management of the connecting network units, entry point unit, and users. The Public Security organization should supervise and inspect network security, protection and management and the implementation of security measures.

Section 18 — If the Public Security computer management and supervision organization discovers an address, directory or server with content in violation of section five, then the appropriate units should be notified to close or delete it.

Section 19 — The Public Security computer management and supervision organization is responsible for pursuing and dealing with illegal computer information network activities and criminal cases involving computer information networks. Criminal activities in violation of sections four or section seven should according to the relevant State regulations, be handed over to the relevant department or to the legal system for appropriate disposition.

Chapter Four Legal Responsibility

Section 20 — For violations of law, administrative regulations or of section five or section six of these regulations, the Public Security organization gives a warning and if there income from illegal activities, confiscates the illegal earnings.

For less serious offenses a fine not to exceed 5000 RMB to individuals and 15,000 RMB to work units may be assessed.

For more serious offenses computer and network access can be closed down for six months, and if necessary Public Security can suggest that the business operating license of the concerned unit or the cancellation of its network registration. Management activities that constitute a threat to public order can be punished according to provisions of the public security management penalties articles. Where crimes have occurred, prosecutions for criminal responsibility should be made.

Section 21 — Where one of the activities listed below has occurred, the Public Security organization should order that remedial action should be taken with a specific period and give a warning; if there has been illegal income, the income should be confiscated; if remedial action is not taken within the specified period, then a fine of not more than 5000 RMB may be assessed against the head of the unit and persons directly under the unit head and a fine of not more than 15,000 RMB against the unit; in the case of more offenses, the network and equipment can be closed for up to six months. In serious cases Public Security may suggest that the business license of the organization be canceled and its network registration canceled.

1. Not setting up a secure system;
2. Not implementing security techniques and protection measures;
3. Not providing security education and training for network users;
4. Not providing information, materials or electronic documentation needed for security, protection and management or providing false information;
5. For not inspecting the content of information transmitted on behalf of someone else or not registering the unit or individual on whose behalf the information was transmitted;
6. Not establishing a system for registering users and managing the information of electronic bulletin boards;
7. Not removing web addresses and directories or not closing servers according to the relevant state regulations;
8. Not establishing a system for registering users of public accounts;
9. Lending or transferring accounts.

Section 22 — Violation of section four or section seven of these regulations shall be punished according to the relevant laws and regulations.

Section 23 — Violations of section eleven or section twelve of these regulations or not fulfilling the responsibility or registering users shall be punished by a warning from Public Security or suspending network operations for six months.

Notes

The following Web sites provide useful resources on online free speech issues:

- Electronic Frontier Canada — <http://www.efc.ca>
- Electronic Frontier Foundation — <http://www.eff.org>
- Electronic Frontier Australia — <http://www.efa.org.au>
- Global Internet Liberty Campaign — <http://www.gilc.org>
- Center for Democracy and Technology — <http://www.cdt.org>
- Cyber Rights and Cyber Liberties (U.K.) — <http://www.cyber-rights.org/>

6

Regulation of Online Obscenity

Few areas of speech regulation evoke as much controversy and diversity of opinion as obscenity. Although most people agree that some obscene material should be regulated, few can agree on what actually constitutes obscenity. The Internet magnifies this issue, since it allows for relatively easy distribution of illegal materials such as child pornography. Unlike the corner store, where pornographic content is found on the top shelf, often wrapped in plastic, such content is easily accessible online. In fact, there is often nothing to distinguish between a pornographic site and a legitimate site, as illustrated by the fact that accessing <www.whitehouse.gov> yields the official White House site, whereas accessing <www.whitehouse.com> yields a pornography site.

The problem is particularly difficult in the context of child pornography. Illegal in virtually every jurisdiction worldwide, the Internet provides a new, quick means to distribute child pornography. Interestingly, the Internet also provides law enforcement authorities with new tools to track down creators of child pornography, since many digitized documents leave electronic clues that can be used to trace materials to their originating source.

The crucial issue for Canadian lawmakers is whether existing Canadian law meets the challenge posed by the Internet. We begin our examination of the issue with the relevant Criminal Code provisions and an excerpt from *R. v. Jorgensen*, the Supreme Court of Canada's most recent ruling on the obscenity section of the Criminal Code.

Canada Criminal Code[†]

163.(1) Every one commits an offence who

(a) makes, prints, publishes, distributes, circulates, or has in his possession for the purpose of publication, distribution or circulation any obscene written matter, picture, model, phonograph record or other thing whatever; or

(b) makes, prints, publishes, distributes, sells or has in his possession for the purpose of publication, distribution or circulation a crime comic.

(2) Every one commits an offence who knowingly, without lawful justification or excuse,

(a) sells, exposes to public view or has in his possession for such a purpose any obscene written matter, picture, model, phonograph record or other thing whatever;

(b) publicly exhibits a disgusting object or an indecent show;

(c) offers to sell, advertises or publishes an advertisement of, or has for sale or disposal, any means, instructions, medicine, drug or article intended or represented as a method of causing abortion or miscarriage; or

(d) advertises or publishes an advertisement of any means, instructions, medicine, drug or article intended or represented as a method for restoring sexual virility or curing venereal diseases or diseases of the generative organs.

. . . .

(5) For the purposes of this section, the motives of an accused are irrelevant.

. . . .

(8) For the purposes of this Act, any publication a dominant characteristic of which is the undue exploitation of sex, or of sex and any one or more of the following subjects, namely, crime, horror, cruelty and violence, shall be deemed to be obscene.

163.1(1) In this section, "child pornography" means

(a) a photographic, film, video or other visual representation, whether or not it was made by electronic or mechanical means,

(i) that shows a person who is or is depicted as being under the age of eighteen years and is engaged in or is depicted as engaged in explicit sexual activity, or

(ii) the dominant characteristic of which is the depiction, for a sexual purpose, of a sexual organ or the anal region of a person under the age of eighteen years; or

(b) any written material or visual representation that advocates or counsels sexual activity with a person under the age of eighteen years that would be an offence under this Act.

---

† R.S., c. C-34.

(2) Every person who makes, prints, publishes or possesses for the purpose of publication any child pornography is guilty of

. . . .

(b) an offence punishable on summary conviction.

(3) Every person who imports, distributes, sells or possesses for the purpose of distribution or sale any child pornography is guilty of

(a) an indictable offence and liable to imprisonment for a term not exceeding ten years; or

(b) an offence punishable on summary conviction.

(4) Every person who possesses any child pornography is guilty of

(a) an indictable offence and liable to imprisonment for a term not exceeding five years; or

(b) an offence punishable on summary conviction.

(5) It is not a defence to a charge under subsection (2) in respect of a visual representation that the accused believed that a person shown in the representation that is alleged to constitute child pornography was or was depicted as being eighteen years of age or more unless the accused took all reasonable steps to ascertain the age of that person and took all reasonable steps to ensure that, where the person was eighteen years of age or more, the representation did not depict that person as being under the age of eighteen years.

(6) Where the accused is charged with an offence under subsection (2), (3) or (4), the court shall find the accused not guilty if the representation or written material that is alleged to constitute child pornography has artistic merit or an educational, scientific or medical purpose.

R. v. Jorgensen†

This appeal concerns the interpretation of s. 163(2)(a) of the Criminal Code, R.S.C., 1985, c. C-46, which deals with "knowingly" selling obscene material "without lawful justification or excuse". Does s. 163(2)(a) of the Code require that the retailer have knowledge of the specific acts which make the material obscene in law or, is it sufficient to show that this retailer had a general knowledge that the material deals with the exploitation of sex?

II. FACTUAL BACKGROUND

The appellant, Randy Jorgensen, is the sole officer of 913719 Ontario Limited which owns and operates a store in Scarborough under the name of "Adults Only Video and Magazine". Acting in an undercover capacity, members of the Metropolitan Toronto Police Force and the Pornography and Hate Literature Section purchased eight videotapes from the appellant's store. Despite the fact that the

---

† [1995] 4 S.C.R. 55.

Ontario Film Review Board ("OFRB") had approved the videotapes, members of the Pornography and Hate Literature Section viewed the videotapes and concluded that they were obscene. The appellants were charged with eight counts of selling obscene material without lawful justification or excuse contrary to s. 163(2)(a) of the Criminal Code.

.   .   .   .

V.   ANALYSIS

A.   Knowingly

The central issue in this appeal is the nature of the mens rea requirement in s. 163(2)(a) of the Criminal Code when it states that it must be shown that the accused acted "knowingly" in selling obscene material. Is an accused acting knowingly when he or she is aware only of the general nature or the subject matter of the work in question? The Crown responds in the affirmative and submits that it is sufficient that it is established that the accused was aware that the dominant characteristic is the exploitation of sex. On the other hand, the accused appellants contend that the term "knowingly" should extend to all factual elements of the actus reus. On the basis of this submission, it must be shown that the accused was aware of particular content of the material which makes it criminal. Material, the dominant characteristic of which is the exploitation of sex, crosses the line and becomes criminal only when it is shown that the exploitation of sex is undue. The appellants contend that the prosecution must establish knowledge on the part of the accused of the content of the material which renders the exploitation undue in law.

I therefore conclude that in using the word "knowingly" in s. 163(2) Parliament did not intend to restrict its meaning. In all the circumstances it would make little sense to conclude that Parliament required proof of knowledge but limited the requirement to proof of the aspect of the actus reus that is perfectly lawful. Although, as a constitutional imperative, a blameworthy mental element need not extend to all aspects of the actus reus, Parliament can choose to legislate beyond minimum constitutional limits. In my view, in choosing the term "knowingly", it has done so in this case.

Having reviewed these cases, I would suggest that the jurisprudence supports the conclusion that for the Crown to convict on a charge of "knowingly" selling obscene materials, it must show more than that the accused had a general knowledge of the nature of the film as a sex film. Although the cases have been few and are by no means clear on this point, cases such as McFall and Metro News illustrate that courts have looked for some indication that the seller of the obscene material was aware of the relevant facts that made the material obscene. In the case of displaying paintings or posters, it could be inferred that the person selling these paintings or posters had knowledge of what made them obscene. The obscene material is plainly in view and its contents and knowledge of the specific nature of its contents can be assumed "known." The same cannot be said concerning films, videos and other media involving a collection of images and where it takes some time and active steps to observe and "know" the contents. In the case of pornographic films and videos, it cannot be easily inferred that those selling these materials "know" their contents. As noted above, it may be inferred that the retailer is aware that the materials are erotic or pornographic and deal with the exploitation of sex. But selling films which deal with the exploitation of sex is not an illegal activity in itself. There must be something in the material that transports it into the realm of obscenity. Not only must the dominant characteristic of the material be the exploitation of sex, but the exploitation of sex must be undue.

If we relate these observations to the application of s. 163(2)(a), it suggests that merely showing that a retailer knows that the material that he or she is selling deals generally with the exploitation of sex fails to link the retailer to the offence of "knowingly" selling obscene material. In my view, the law requires that in order to make the necessary link it must be shown that the retailer knew of the specific acts or set of facts which led the courts to the conclusion that the material in question was obscene under s. 163(8). If, for example, the offensive part of the video was that which showed a male spanking the female and forcing her to have sexual relations, then for an accused to be convicted under s. 163(2)(a), it must be shown that the retailer was aware or wilfully blind that the video being sold contained this scene.

This is not, of course, to suggest that a retailer must know that the materials being sold were obscene in law. If the retailer says he viewed the films and saw the particular spanking or noticed the underlying degradation but thought that it was harmless and inoffensive, this will not provide a defence. The retailer will not be immune from charges merely because he or she does not know how the law defines obscenity. Nor will a retailer be immune from conviction because he or she is unaware that there are any laws against selling obscene material. This would amount to the defence of mistake of law and it is well established that ignorance of the law is no defence. What is required is that the Crown prove beyond a reasonable doubt the retailer's knowledge that the materials being sold have the qualities or contain the specific scenes which render such materials obscene in law.

B. Wilful Blindness

The second response to the concerns expressed by the Crown relates to the principles of wilful blindness. It is well established in criminal law that wilful blindness will also fulfil a mens rea requirement. If the retailer becomes aware of the need to make further inquiries about the nature of the videos he was selling yet deliberately chooses to ignore these indications and does not make any further inquiries, then the retailer can be nonetheless charged under s. 163(2)(a) for "knowingly" selling obscene materials. Deliberately choosing not to know something when given reason to believe further inquiry is necessary can satisfy the mental element of the offence.

Discussion Questions

Consider the application of the court's analysis regarding the standard for "knowingly" to the various participants in the Internet service chain. Under what circumstances would an ISP face liability? A Web site owner? A site that links to obscene materials? A search engine that indexes the materials? A user?

The issue of the standard for "knowingly" within the context of the Internet was addressed in *ACLU* v. *Johnson*, a November 1999 challenge to a New Mexico state law prohibiting the distribution of obscene materials to minors.

ACLU v. Johnson[†]

In its 1998 session, the New Mexico Legislature enacted section 30-37-3.2(A), which provides as follows.

DISSEMINATION OF MATERIAL THAT IS HARMFUL TO A MINOR BY COMPUTER (N.M. STAT. ANN. S 30-37-3.2(C))

A. Dissemination of material that is harmful to a minor by computer consists of the use of a computer communications system that allows the input, output, examination or transfer of computer data or computer programs from one computer to another, to knowingly and intentionally initiate or engage in communication with a person under eighteen years of age when such communication in whole or in part depicts actual or simulated nudity, sexual intercourse or any other sexual conduct. Whoever commits dissemination of material that is harmful to a minor by computer is guilty of a misdemeanor.

The statute provides the following defenses:

In a prosecution for dissemination of material that is harmful to a minor by computer, it is a defense that the defendant has:

(1) in good faith taken reasonable, effective and appropriate actions under the circumstances to restrict or prevent access by minors to indecent materials on computer, including any method that is feasible with available technology;
(2) restricted access to indecent materials by requiring the use of a verified credit card, debit account, adult access code or adult personal identification number; or
(3) in good faith established a mechanism such as labeling, segregation or other means that enables indecent material to be automatically blocked or screened by software or other capability reasonably available to persons who wish to effect such blocking or screening and the defendant has not otherwise solicited a minor not subject to such screening or blocking capabilities to access the indecent material or to circumvent screening or blocking.

N.M. Stat. Ann. s 30-37-3.2(C).

.   .   .   .

Defendants also argue that the intent clause ("knowingly and intentionally initiate or engage in communication with a person under eighteen") appropriately narrows the statute. But the statutory definition of "knowingly" only requires "having general knowledge of, or reason to know, or a belief or ground for belief which warrants further inspection or inquiry of ... the age of the minor." N.M. Stat. Ann. s 30-37-1(G). As the Supreme Court acknowledged in Reno, "[g]iven the size of the potential audience for most messages [on the Internet], in the absence of a viable age verification process, the sender must be charged with knowing that one or more minors will likely view it." Reno, 521 U.S. at 876. Thus, virtually all communication on the Internet would meet the statutory definition of "knowingly" and potentially be subject to liability under section 30-37-3.2(A). Indeed, the Supreme Court unequivo-

---

† 1999 WL 992744 (10th Cir. (N.M.))

cally rejected this very argument in Reno: "[t]he Government's assertion that the knowledge requirement somehow protects the communications of adults is ... untenable. Even the strongest reading of the 'specific person' requirement of s 223(d) cannot save the statute."

Do you agree with the Court's conclusion that virtually all communication on the Internet would meet the statutory definition of "knowingly"? Are there precautions open to a Web site owner that would allow for a successful use of the "knowingly" defence?

R. v. Hurtubise[†]

These are appeals from convictions registered against the appellants after a joint trial on several counts laid under section 163(1)(a) and section 163.1(2) of the Criminal Code ...

The facts giving rise to the charges are set out concisely in the reasons for judgment of the trial judge as follows:

> In 1992, Gerald Hurtubise started a local computer bulletin board, YOUR Neighbourhood BBS, as a hobby. Gerald Hurtubise was the system operator, looking after the technical aspects. His wife, Brenda Hurtubise, began to assist him and became responsible for the public relations side. A local computer bulletin board is a computer information sharing system with modem access. YOUR Neighborhood BBS was a family oriented bulletin board for general access without INTERNET access. Running YOUR Neighbourhood BBS took a considerable amount of effort but Gerald and Brenda Hurtubise testified they obtained a great deal of satisfaction from running the local bulletin board.
>
> In 1993 in response to requests from their users, the Hurtubise's set up another computer bulletin board, CYBER Playground BBS, for adult users which was to contain pornography. Gerald and Brenda Hurtubise made some efforts with other operators of adult bulletin boards to determine how to operate the adult bulletin board within the law to restrict access to adult users. Although there were no clear guidelines from any regulatory body, the Hurtubise's restricted access by requiring verification that the user was an adult. Only on being satisfied that the user was an adult, would he or she be allowed access to CYBER Playground.
>
> CYBER Playground became quite popular. By March, 1995, Gerald Hurtubise estimates that over 1000 users had access to CYBER Playground. Approximately 250 users had been verified as adult by the Hurtubise's but access was given to others who had been verified by other adult local bulletin boards. (There were some 6 to 10 other local adult bulletin boards by March, 1995.) According to Gerald Hurtubise, CYBER Playground was the biggest and most noticeable.
>
> In November, 1994, Detective Tiessen located CYBER Playground and accessed it on his computer. Initially, he was denied access to the local bulletin board until he sent in proof of age which he did by using an alias.

---

† [1997] B.C.J. No. 40 (BCCA).

He also made a donation of $15.00 to have more than 60 minutes usage per day. In December, 1994, after receiving the password, Detective Tiessen began to download files from CYBER Playground to his personal computer. He downloaded files on several occasions in December 1994 and January and February, 1995 finding the offensive material which is the subject matter of the counts before the Court.

On March 1, 1995, Detective Tiessen and Constable Kirby obtained a search warrant for the Hurtubise residence. Upon executing it, the police officers found the system that was operating CYBER Playground. The Hurtubise's were operating the local bulletin board with 1 personal computer with a CD ROM and 2 modems. The CD ROM contained the CD "T&A2THEMAXX", which made its contents available through CYBER Playground to users of CYBER Playground and the other local adult bulletin boards. The CD contained 3100 graphic files in 11 directories and 800 text files in 8 directories. All users with access could scan the CD's directories and access the files or graphics including downloading the files or graphics to their computers. Once the files or graphics were downloaded to individual computers, they could be copied to disk or uploaded to other computer bulletin boards.

On the first ground of appeal, counsel for the appellants argued that the trial judge erred in concluding that the appellants were "distributors" of obscenity within s. 163(1)(a). He conceded that the materials in question are obscene and contended that the trial judge should have concluded that the appellants were "sellers" or persons exposing the obscenity to public view within the provisions of s. 163(2)(a).

If the appellants were sellers within s. 163(2)(a), they could not be found guilty unless the Crown proved knowledge that the material was obscene, whereas a distributor of obscenity may be found guilty in the absence of due diligence.

Appellants' counsel referred in argument to R. v. Dorosz for the proposition that the appellants were in a position analogous to that of the operator of a retail video store who would be, as a matter of law, a seller and not a distributor of obscenity. I do not read Dorosz to support that proposition. The issue there was whether, as a matter of law, evidence of the possession of obscene material for the purpose of sale by a book store proprietor constituted evidence of possession for the purpose of distribution. The Court held that such evidence would not justify a finding of possession for the purpose of distribution in the absence of further supporting evidence.

The Court in Dorosz reasoned that, in amending the Code in 1949 to make distribution a strict liability offence, Parliament's purpose was to control the proliferation of obscenity by making it easier to obtain a conviction for that offence. Brooke, J.A., writing for the majority, said:

> The obvious [evil to be remedied] was the problem of proving the state of mind of persons to be charged and so to control the proliferation of obscene matter at which the section was directed. The remedy was to reclassify certain of the activities in the previous section as being of such moment as to require for their control not only the removal of the necessity of proof of the element of mens rea, but the denial as a defence to the accused of his ignorance as to the nature or presence of the matter in relation to which the offence was said to have been committed.
>
> Accordingly, Parliament drew a line through the chain from production to consumption. It drew the line immediately preceding those who may sell to the ultimate consumer and left only that conduct and related conduct as it stood before the change.

Who is the "ultimate consumer" and where the accused stands in the produc-tion-consumption chain, however, are questions of fact in each case and do not depend on whether the accused is a "retailer" or a "wholesaler". Brooke, J.A. alluded to that at p. 209 of his reasons where he approved of the application of the authorities referred to by the trial judge, and said:

> The facts in each of those cases are quite different from the facts in the case at bar. In the cases referred to, each accused was found to be a distrib-utor not because he engaged in the sale of books which were found in his possession, but rather because the nature of his business was characterized as being that of one who is a distributor of books whether by sale or other-wise.

Accordingly, I do not agree with the submission that, if they were in a position analogous to an operator of a retail video store, as a matter of law the appellants cannot be considered to be distributors of obscenity. Whether they were or were not distributors must be determined by examining their conduct in the light of the pre-vailing circumstances. The objective of the inquiry is not to identify the status of the appellants in the production-consumption chain, although that status may be a help-ful guide, but to determine whether their activities were of the type leading to the proliferation of obscenity that were the target of the 1949 amendment.

The trial judge focused on the conduct of the appellants and its effect on the proliferation of obscenity, and recognized that their status in the production-con-sumption chain was not necessarily determinative. She said:

> The Concise Oxford Dictionary (1982) defines "distribute" amongst others as:
>> "deal out, give share of to each of a number; spread about, scatter, put at different points, divide into parts, arrange, classify"

The local bulletin board, CYBER Playground, which allowed access to over 1,000 users, although not at one time, must clearly fall within this definition of dis-tribute. The dichotomy described in Regina v. Dorosz, between the last person in the chain to the consumer, between a retailer and a wholesaler, is a distinction which is applicable to and makes sense with print material, but not one which is necessarily applicable to computer technology.

A look at the purpose of the legislation does not suggest this is a case where the clear dictionary meaning of 'distribution' should not be applied. By making a CD accessible through a local computer bulletin board, the contents of the CD become readily accessible to multiple computers. Around each computer, there could be mul-tiple users. The contents of each file on the CD can, of course, be downloaded, kept on computer, copied to another disk, uploaded to other systems, or put into hard print. This is not, in my view, analogous to an individual retailer who is selling indi-vidual copies, even if multiple copies, of books or movie video cassettes.

In my view, she dealt with this issue correctly.

Discussion Questions

The question of obscenity in the context of the Internet raises particular concerns in defining community standards. A challenge under ordinary circumstances, defining community standards is particularly more complicated online, where it is unclear which community should be the standard — the local community where the materials were viewed? The community where the materials were posted? The entire Internet community?

Consider the analysis of the U.S. Court of Appeals, 6th Circuit in *U.S.* v. *Thomas*, 74 F.3d 701 (6th Cir. 1996) in which bulletin board operators in California faced trial in Tennessee for distribution of pornographic materials.

> Defendants and Amicus Curiae appearing on their behalf argue that the computer technology used here requires a new definition of community, i.e., one that is based on the broad-ranging connections among people in cyberspace rather than the geographic locale of the federal judicial district of the criminal trial. Without a more flexible definition, they argue, there will be an impermissible chill on protected speech because BBS operators cannot select who gets the materials they make available on their bulletin boards. Therefore, they contend, BBS operators like Defendants will be forced to censor their materials so as not to run afoul of the standards of the community with the most restrictive standards.
>
> Defendants' First Amendment issue, however, is not implicated by the facts of this case. This is not a situation where the bulletin board operator had no knowledge or control over the jurisdictions where materials were distributed for downloading or printing. Access to the Defendants' AABBS was limited. Membership was necessary and applications were submitted and screened before passwords were issued and materials were distributed. Thus, Defendants had in place methods to limit user access in jurisdictions where the risk of a finding of obscenity was greater than that in California. They knew they had a member in Memphis; the member's address and local phone number were provided on his application form. If Defendants did not wish to subject themselves to liability in jurisdictions with less tolerant standards for determining obscenity, they could have refused to give passwords to members in those districts, thus precluding the risk of liability.

A further complication involves the issue of what it means to publish to the public in the context of the Internet. A Hong Kong court considered the issue in *Hksar* v. *Cheung Kam Keung* (1998-2 HKC 156), a 1998 case involving online distribution of pornography.

> The prosecution case was that publication was complete when appellant uploaded the computer files to the newsgroup because the pictures then became available to other persons with access. Whether someone chose to download them or not, the articles had been published. The magistrate found that appellant, by uploading the computer files or electronic data to the newsgroup, had distributed and circulated the pictures they contained thus 'publishing' within s 2(4)(a). Further, since the images could be seen on screen in the process of downloading, they were also shown and projected within limb (b) of s 2(4). He found publication proved.
>
> Counsel for the appellant argued that as recipients had to take an active role to download files and could only receive the transmission of the files privately, they did not therefore form the public, or a section of the public, as contemplated by the Ordinance.
>
> The magistrate found that once the files were uploaded to the Internet, they were available to other Internet users with access, not only to subscribers, eg Asiaonline, but to all those who could access the files through other newsgroups, whether in Hong Kong or overseas. He found there was no requirement that publication was confined to publication 'in public' and considered, with good reason, that the size of the potential group with access certainly constituted the public or section of the public.

Proof can also pose a significant problem in the context of obscenity cases and the Internet. Since one person may own a computer, yet it may be accessed by others, prosecutors must often assemble a compelling collection of circumstantial to prove that the accused was responsible for the offending materials. Review the *Pecciarich* case below and consider whether you think possession can be used to impute knowledge.

R. v. Pecciarich[†]

The accused Joseph Pecciarich is charged that (1) between the 20th day of August, 1993 and the 28th day of August 1993 he unlawfully did distribute obscene pictures, to wit a series of files of computer images, and (2) between the 7th day of August 1993 and the 30th day of September 1993 he unlawfully distribute child pornography, to wit a series of computer images and text files. In short, he is accused of using his personal computer to send the obscene texts and images to one or more computer distribution centres referred to as bulletin boards, where they can be accessed by or sent to other computer users.

Proof that the Accused is Recent Zephyr

In my view, the fact that many documents in the accused's computer exhibit the name "Recent Zephyr" in a place where one would expect the name of the creator to be tends to indicate that the alias is his.

Generally, documents found in the possession of the accused are admissible if relevant; they may show acceptance of the truth of the contents, and most likely will at least show knowledge of the contents. The law is also summarized in Phipson on Evidence:

> Documents which are, or have been, in the possession of a party will, as we have seen, generally be admissible against him as original (circumstantial) evidence to show his knowledge of their contents, his connection with, or complicity in, the transactions to which they relate, or his state of mind with reference thereto. They will further be receivable against him as admissions (i.e., exceptions to the hearsay rule) to prove the truth of their contents if he has in any way recognized, adopted or acted upon them.

Defence counsel argues that the documents could have been downloaded to his client's computer, without his knowledge; however, according to Detective Sweeney, the documents on the backup tape could not have arrived there without being directly accepted by the operator of the computer unless a special configuration of software was used, and no such configuration was located when the tape was seized by the police. Therefore, I find as fact that the accused knew he had documents stored in his computer containing reference to child pornography with the name Recent Zephyr in areas normally indicative of authorship or proprietorship, which fact contributes to the inferences to be discussed below.

---

† [1995] 22 O.R. (3d) 748 (Ont. Gen. Div.).

In determining whether the accused is "Recent Zephyr", it is also necessary to consider the purported signature of the accused on one image which forms part of ex. 9(e), being according to Detective Sweeney a series of steps in the creation of ex. 9(d), a depiction of a man performing oral sex on a child. The image is titled "Forestwood Kids Part 3". As noted above, 9(d), located on both the backup tape and according to Detective Sweeney on the "Scruples" bulletin board, had the name "Recent Zephyr" in the corner; the image in 9(e) has the signature "J. Pecciarich". Although usage of the signature to strictly indicate authorship would violate the hearsay rule, the fact that it is in the same place as the name "Recent Zephyr" on a matching image allows me to consider it as a piece of original, or real circumstantial evidence that J. Pecciarich and Recent Zephyr are one. Furthermore, like all of the "Exhibit Nine" documents, his possession indicates knowledge — in this case, knowledge and even complicity in being portrayed as the author of a piece of pornography. It is logical to assume that someone would not leave his purported signature or name on illegal material stored on a backup tape if he were not somehow connected to it, or even involved in its creation.

In determining if the accused is Recent Zephyr it is also necessary to look at evidence establishing that he is the creator of some of the pornographic files enumerated in count 2. Regarding ex. 9(d), the image is located on both the accused's backup tape as well as a bulletin board, and as stated above its development as a "work in progress" is evidenced by ex. 9(e) from the backup tape. According to Detective Sweeney, ex. 1(e), found in the accused's briefcase, is the original drawing which became the computer image, and examination of it tends to confirm the likeness. Mr. Blumberg explained how images such as this, being a drawing of central body parts attached to the head and legs from a catalogue picture, can be placed on a computer with a device known as a scanner, and further altered with software. Given that the accused was found in possession of a scanner, and given that the drawing matches the images found on the backup tape and the bulletin board, it is reasonable to conclude that he created exs. 9(d) and (e), which, as detailed above, demonstrate the names "Recent Zephyr" and "RZ," as well as "J. Pecciarich." It is also reasonable to conclude that he created the narrative entitled "Forestwood Kids" found in the manila folder, given that it is part of the same file containing the image ex. 9(e) which was viewed by Detective Sweeney on the Gateway.

In my view, original evidence also establishes that the accused created the "Moppett" files enumerated in count 2. Mr. Blumberg testified as to how ex. 1(c) on argument, a computer image of two naked girls, could have been a catalogue picture transported to computer by the scanner, with the clothing removed and genitalia added by computer software. Exhibit 1(a), a catalogue picture of little girls wearing clothes, found in the accused's briefcase was stated to be identical to the pornographic computer image except for the clothing. A cursory viewing confirms Mr. Blumberg's evidence in this regard. The nude image downloaded by him from the Gateway Bulletin Board, has the words "Recent Zephyr Scan" across the top, and the word "Moppett" at the bottom. The logical inference to be drawn is that the accused created this image, and that the name "Recent Zephyr" stamped on the computer image is therefore associated with him and with the "Moppett" series.

Mr. Blumberg also reviewed ex. 1(b) on argument, another "Moppett" series photo of a nude boy on top of a little girl in a pool, with the words "Recent Zephyr Scan" beside it. He explained how ex. 1(b), a catalogue photo of children in a pool, found in the briefcase, could have been altered to create the final image. In my view, his evidence and my own observations confirm that the accused created this image which is strongly linked to the name "Recent Zephyr". Exhibits 1(a) and (d), other pornographic images from the Gateway, also feature the words "Moppett" and "Recent Zephyr Scan", indicating a link suggestive of creation by Recent Zephyr. Again, in my view, evidence that the accused created pornographic images featuring the name "Recent Zephyr" is strong evidence that they are one and the same person.

In considering ex. 8, the bulletin board user list, however, I agree with defence counsel that it cannot be used to show that the accused and Recent Zephyr have the same telephone number and city of residence. Such use would clearly be for the truth of the contents, and thus would violate the hearsay rule.

Defence counsel argues that proof of authorship is not possible unless the documents are used in violation of the hearsay rule — namely to prove the truth of their message that the creator is "Recent Zephyr". However, rather than for truth, I have used the documents as pieces of original circumstantial evidence that the accused and the name "Recent Zephyr" are so frequently linked in a meaningful way as to create the logical inference that they are the same person. A similar exercise was undertaken in R. v. Bastien, a decision of the British Columbia County Court in which an intercepted parcel (ex. 1) exhibiting the name and return address of the accused was admitted as proof that he lived at the address and sent the parcel containing stolen money. A pad which contained an imprint of the writing on the parcel, ex. E, was also admitted. The judge states:

> The fact that "F. Cote, 831 Hamilton Street, Vancouver", appears on the outside of ex. I is evidence from which a jury could conclude this to be a return address and the identity of the sender or mailer was Cote, who was in possession of the five $100 bills contained in ex. I.
>
> The submission concedes the hearsay rule, but although not so expressly stated by Crown counsel, is founded on the proposition that, having regard to evidence adduced and the circumstances of the case, exs. E and I, respectively, are original, circumstantial, evidence, not hearsay, and, therefore, admissible.
>
> ... it is my opinion that the registered package or parcel, ex. I, intercepted in mail, constitutes some evidence capable of inference or conclusion that a name and address endorsed thereon is that of Cote and that Cote was the sender or mailer and had possession of Ex. I and its contents.
>
> ...
>
> Admissibility thereof does not infringe upon the hearsay rule since exs. E and I, respectively, are not admitted to prove the truth of the matters stated thereon or therein; that each constitutes original, circumstantial, evidence tending to link, connect or identify Cote with possession of ex. I and, in particular, the five $100 bills enclosed therein. Each has, therefore, a limited evidentiary use and probative value, as indicated above.

I also rely upon the recent decision of the Supreme Court of Canada in R. v. Evans, dealing with a statement made by an alleged robber to the vendors of the getaway car. The vendors testified that the purchase mentioned that he had a pregnant dog and worked in chain link fencing; and it was proven by other evidence that he had a pregnant dog and worked in chain link fencing. The majority of the court held that the statements were admissible merely for the fact that they were even made. Sopinka J. states:

That being said, the statements still have some probative value as non-hearsay. Quite apart from the truth of the contents, the statements have some probative value on the issue of identity. On the issue of identity, the fact that certain representations are made is probative as it narrows the identity of the declarant to the group of people who are in a position to make similar representations. The more unique or unusual the representations, the more probative they will be on the issue of identity. I emphasize that the statements are not being used as truth of their contents at this stage.

In my view, the references to "Recent Zephyr" discussed above are admissible on a similar basis; namely, that, taken in their entirety and their context, they narrow or point strongly to the accused as the person capable of being "Recent Zephyr". Although previously reviewed, the references to the name which point to the accused should be summarized as follows:

(1) Pornographic images from the "Moppett" series, downloaded from the Gateway and referred to in count two, which feature the name Recent Zephyr.
(2) documents containing narrative from the backup tape of his computer which he is deemed to know about, and which feature the name Recent Zephyr in a position usually designating authorship;
(3) a pornographic image on his backup tape, labeled Forestwood Kids 3 which features his purported signature on one copy and the name Recent Zephyr on another copy;
(4) a file folder in the accused's possession, containing lewd stories, labeled in pen "Recent Zephyr Software". The stories bear the same title as the "Recent Zephyr" image referred to in (2) above — "Forestwood Kids".

Recently, the Ontario Court of Appeal in the decision of R. v. Morrissey summarized the law related to the drawing of inferences as follows:

> A trier of fact may draw factual inferences from the evidence. The inferences must, however, be ones which can be reasonable and logically drawn from a fact or group of facts established by the evidence. An inference which does not flow logically and reasonably from established facts cannot be made and is condemned as conjecture and speculation. As Chipman J.A. put it in R. v. White:
>
>> These cases establish that there is a distinction between conjecture and speculation on the one hand and rational conclusions from the whole of the evidence on the other. The failure to observe the distinction involves an error on a question of law.

In applying this principle, I reiterate that substantial documentary evidence in the possession of the accused and on bulletin boards points to him as "Recent Zephyr". This evidence, combined with testimony of Mr. Blumberg that most users of bulletin boards have code names or aliases, and the fact that all of the documents seized from his home, described in the "Facts" section, demonstrates that he is generally a creator of child pornography who therefore would have need of an alias leads to the rational conclusion that the accused and Recent Zephyr are on and the same person.

Proof that Recent Zephyr uploaded the Files
Having found that the accused used the name "Recent Zephyr", I also conclude that the documents on his backup tape purportedly authored by him are his creations

and are as such admissions that he uploaded the files enumerated in count 2. To suggest, in all the circumstances, that they were created by an imposter, but knowingly stored by him on a backup tape is in my view conjecture. The admissions can be summarized as follows:

(1) Exhibits 9(f) and (c), lists of files created by him which according to the text he intended to deliver to bulletin boards. The files in count 2 were all ultimately located by Mr. Blumberg on bulletin boards, and are found on the lists.

(2) Exhibit 9(g), a statement of Recent Zephyr indicating his intention to have his "software", "files", and "stories" distributed at no cost.

When determining who uploaded the files, these admissions must be considered along with the following additional evidence:

(1) His admission to the police that he left his name when some programs were uploaded, and that he was the "Co-Sys-Op" at the Gateway bulletin board. Although I agree with defence counsel that the admissions are not totally clear, and that the term "Co-Sys-Op" was not well explained, the first statement leads to an inference that he uploaded files, and the second establishes a clear link to the Gateway where some of his products were proved to be found. In considering the term "Co-Sys-Op" on such a limited basis, I need not deal with defence argument that it should have been defined by an expert, or with the effect of his failure to object until the time of his submissions;

(2) His possession of a Gateway "user list", exhibit 8, which when considered not for its truth but for the fact of possession indicates a strong link to the Gateway;

(3) Evidence that he is the creator of "Moppett" and "Forestwood Kid" files which were found on the Gateway and other bulletin boards, which was reviewed above;

(4) Other exhibits, which lead to an inference that he is a creator of the type of child pornography found with his name on it on bulletin boards. These include 1(f), the catalogue of characters who appear in the Forestwood Kid stories found in the "Recent Zephyr" manila file, and in 9(h) a list of his files; 1(a) and 1(b), story drafts marked with file names including "Young Fun", and the catalogue cutouts and lewd drawings contained in his briefcase; and

(5) Evidence of his fascination with child pornography, as exhibited (a) in his discussion with Andy Dabydeen found on his computer, and at the bulletin board, and (b) the scrapbook of newspaper articles on the subject, as well as articles about sexual assault cases and related legalities.

Defence counsel argues that all the evidence reviewed may well indicate that the accused created child pornography and even some of the files enumerated; however, he contends that uploading is not proved, as despite the evidence referred to above an imposter could have uploaded the material under his name, and/or downloaded materials to his computer. This position, however, is not borne out by the evidence. As stated earlier, Detective Sweeney clarified that such downloading could not occur without his knowledge, unless special software was configured, and no such materials were located. Although Mr. Blumberg admired [sic] that uploading by an imposter was a remote possibility, it is not a suggestion genuinely supported by evidence, given the absence of any indication that the materials created by him were transmitted through a third party. The law in this area is summarized in R. v. McCrum:

It is firmly established law that conclusions or references based on facts, established by evidence only, can be considered in applying the rule. Possible explanations based on conjecture or assumption, not supported by the evidence, but advanced as mere possibilities in argument should not be considered by the Court: see Wild v. The Queen, wherein Martland, J., stated [quoting from the judgement of Smith, C.J.A., in the Appelate Division]:

I agree with and consider that the following statement of Evans, J.A., for the Court of Appeal of Ontario in R. v. Torrie is applicable to the case at bar. That statement is as follows:

With the greatest respect, I am of the opinion that the learned trial Judge misapplied the rule in Hodge's Case, as to circumstantial evidence in that he based his finding of reasonable doubt on nonexistent evidence. In R. v. McIver, McRuer, C.J.H.C., said:

The rule (in Hodge's Case) makes it clear that the case is to be decided on the facts, that is, the facts proved in evidence and the conclusions alternative to the guilt of the accused must be rational conclusions based on inferences drawn from proven facts. No conclusions can be a rational conclusion that is not founded on evidence. Such a conclusion would be a speculative, imaginative conclusions, not a rational one.

The statement was approved on appeal to this Court, and an appeal therefrom to the Supreme Court of Canada was dismissed.

I recognized that the onus of proof must rest with the Crown to establish the guilt of the accused beyond a reasonable doubt, but I do not understand this proposition to mean that the Crown must negative every possible conjecture, no matter how irrational or fanciful, which might be consistent with the innocence of the accused.

I do, however, agree with defence counsel that the statements from the bulletin "uploaded by Recent Zephyr", accompanied by a date in August or September 1993, are pure hearsay and therefore not evidence of uploading or of the date specified.

The Crown argued that, given the other admissible evidence of uploading, the statements "uploaded by Recent Zephyr" have probative value and should therefore be admitted for their truth. Although not specifically referred to by him, the second ratio in R. v. Evans, supra, lends some support to this theory, in providing for a two-stage test for admissibility of declarations of the accused. The test is described by Sopinka J. as follows:

If there is some evidence to permit the issue to be submitted to the trier of fact, the matter must be considered in two stages. First, a preliminary determination must be made as to whether, on the basis of evidence admissible against the accused, the Crown has established on a balance of probabilities that the statement is that of the accused. If this threshold is met, the trier of fact should then consider the contents of the statement along with other evidence to determine the issue of innocence or guilt. While the contents of this statement may only be considered for the limited purpose to which I have referred above in the first stage, in the second stage the contents are evidence of the truth of the assertions contained therein.

Detective Sweeney, however, gave the following testimony concerning the statement "uploaded by Recent Zephyr", as it appeared along with the files on the bulletin board:

> "Uploaded by RECENT ZEPHYR" is predominantly put on by the actual computer system itself automatically. So, you have no control over the particular message. It is changeable by the system operator or the co system operator but that would be an automatic product to put that on.

That testimony, in my view, is less than crystal clear and does not permit me to find on a balance of probabilities that the accused produced the alleged admission of uploading. In addition, I question whether the ratio from Evans referred to above is applicable to a case such as this, when the ultimate issue is whether or not the contents of the statement, namely, "Uploaded by Recent Zephyr", are true. In applying Evans, if I decided that the statement was that of the accused on only a balance of probabilities, I would then be permitted to consider whether it was true on a higher standard of beyond a reasonable doubt. Thus the analysis at the second stage would lead to the finding of guilt or innocence, despite the fact that the accused was proved to be the maker of the statement on the basis of non-hearsay evidence weighed only on the balance of probabilities. With all due respect, I question whether Evans was meant to provide for access to a statement for its truth in this manner when the statement alone could lead to a conviction or acquittal, rather than simply forming part of a greater body of evidence for total consideration as was the situation in Evans.

It is my conclusion, however, that despite the inadmissibility of the phrase "uploaded by Recent Zephyr", the Crown has proved uploading of the files in count 2 by the accused beyond a reasonable doubt on the basis of the evidence summarized above.

Law Relating to Distribution

I agree with the Crown that the evidence of the uploading of the files onto bulletin boards, which the public can access through an application process, is clear evidence of distribution. The various cases referred to deal with the distinction between sale and distribution, making it clear that more than retail sale to the public is required for the latter charge. However, in this case the evidence of uploading by the accused along with his statements in exs. 9(b), (c), (b) and (f) about his intent to have them widely dispersed is clear evidence of intent to distribute.

Notes

1. In 1997 Industry Canada released a detailed report on Internet liability issues, entitled the *Internet Content-Related Liability Study*. The study was one of the first comprehensive examinations of the application of Canadian law to Internet-based activities. The study's coverage of obscene materials and child pornography is particularly useful, as it canvasses the potential liability of many parties providing Internet services. The study can be obtained from the Industry Canada Web site at <http://strategis.ic.gc.ca/SSG/it03117e.html>.

2. The impact of the Internet on differing approaches to free speech became readily apparent during the Paul Bernardo murder trial in 1993. When the Ontario court hearing the case issued a prohibition on media publication of trial details in Canada, Web sites in the United States began to carry the

banned details. For a copy of the media ban decision, see <http://www.cs.indiana.edu/canada/MediaBan>. For an example of a Bernardo trial Web site, see <http://www.cs.indiana.edu/canada/karla.html>.

3.   For a pre-Web review of liability for obscene content online, see *Illegal and Offensive Content on the Information Highway*, a 1995 report prepared for Industry Canada available online at <http://insight.mcmaster.ca/org/efc/pages/doc/offensive.html>.

4.   Canadian courts have faced several pornography cases involving the Web. These include *R. v. Lowes* ([1997] M.J. No. 549), a 1997 Manitoba case, *R. v. Ritchie* ([1997] O.J. No. 5564), a 1997 Ontario case, as well as *R. v. Weir* ([1998] A.J. No. 155) and *R. v. Rideout*, ([1998] A.J. No. 199) two 1998 Alberta cases.

5.   Although not an Internet case *per se*, the *R. v. Sharpe* (BCCA 1999 416) case, a British Columbia Court of Appeal decision which attracted international attention deserves some consideration. The case, which struck down as unconstitutional elements of the child pornography section of the Criminal Code, has particular relevance given the increasing use of the Internet as a means of disseminating child pornography. The Supreme Court is likely to rule on an appeal sometime in 2000. For more on the issue of Internet child pornography, see:
   • Pedowatch — <http://www.pedowatch.org/>
   • Cyberangels — <http://cyberangels.org/>
   • UNESCO — <http://www.unesco.org/webworld/child_screen/conf_index.html>.

7

Regulation of Online Hate

The Internet provides purveyors of hate materials with a new method of distribution, and has left some questioning whether current laws are obsolete. Hate groups around the world have embraced the potential of the Internet, with current estimates of over 1,000 hate sites online.

Legal approaches to hate vary considerably in real space, and those differences are reflected online. Canada's hate speech laws, which include provisions in both the Criminal Code and Human Rights Codes at the federal and provincial levels, are among the strongest worldwide. They have been the focus of several landmark Supreme Court decisions, and their application continues to stir controversy among free speech advocates, who point to the more permissive approaches to hate speech found in the United States.

Canada Criminal Code[†]

318.(1) Every one who advocates or promotes genocide is guilty of an indictable offence and liable to imprisonment for a term not exceeding five years.

(2) In this section, "genocide" means any of the following acts committed with intent to destroy in whole or in part any identifiable group, namely,

(a) killing members of the group; or
(b) deliberately inflicting on the group conditions of life calculated to bring about its physical destruction.

---

† R.S., c. C-34.

---

(3) No proceeding for an offence under this section shall be instituted without the consent of the Attorney General.

(4) In this section, "identifiable group" means any section of the public distinguished by colour, race, religion or ethnic origin.

319.(1) Every one who, by communicating statements in any public place, incites hatred against any identifiable group where such incitement is likely to lead to a breach of the peace is guilty of

(a) an indictable offence and is liable to imprisonment for a term not exceeding two years; or
(b) of an offence punishable on summary conviction.

(2) Every one who, by communicating statements, other than in a private conversation, wilfully promotes hatred against any identifiable group is guilty of

(a) an indictable offence and is liable to imprisonment for a term not exceeding two years; or
(b) an offence punishable on summary conviction.

(3) No person shall be convicted of an offence under subsection (2)

(a) if he establishes that the statements communicated were true;
(b) if, in good faith, he expressed or attempted to establish by argument an opinion on a religious subject;
(c) if the statements were relevant to any subject of public interest, the discussion of which was true for public benefit, and if on reasonable grounds be believed them to be true; or
(d) if, in good faith, he intended to point out, for the purpose of removal, matters producing or tending to produce feelings of hatred toward an identifiable group in Canada.

(4) Where a person is convicted of an offence under section 318 or subsection (1) or (2) of this section, anything by means of or in relation to which the offence was committed, on such conviction, may, in addition to any other punishment imposed, be ordered by the presiding provincial court judge or judge to be forfeited to Her Majesty in right of the province in which that person is convicted, for disposal as the Attorney General may direct.

(5) Subsections 199(6) and (7) apply with such modifications as the circumstances require to section 318 or subsection (1) or (2) of this section.

(6) No proceeding for an offence under subsection (2) shall be instituted without the consent of the Attorney General.

(7) In this section,

"communicating" includes communicating by telephone, broadcasting or other audible or visible means;

"identifiable group" has the same meaning as in section 318;

"public place" includes any place to which the public have access as of right or by invitation, express or implied;

"statements" include words spoken or written or recorded electronically or electromagnetically or otherwise, and gestures, signs, or other visible representations.

320.(1) A judge who is satisfied by information on oath that there are reasonable grounds for believing that any publication, copies of which are kept for sale or distribution in premises within the jurisdiction of the court, is hate propaganda, shall issue a warrant under his hand authorizing seizure of the copies.

(2) Within seven days of the issue of the warrant under subsection (1), the judge shall issue a summons to the occupier of the premises requiring him to appear before court and show cause why the matter seized should not be forfeited to Her Majesty.

(3) The owner and the author of the matter seized under subsection (1) and alleged to be hate propaganda may appear and be represented in the proceedings in order to oppose the making of an order of forfeiture of the matter.

(4) If the court is satisfied that the publication referred to in subsection (1) is hate propaganda, it shall make an order declaring the matter forfeited to Her Majesty in right of the province in which the proceedings take place, for disposal as the Attorney General may direct.

(5) If the court is not satisfied that the publication referred to in subsection (1) is hate propaganda, it shall order the matter restored to the person from whom it was seized forthwith after the time for the final appeal has expired.

(6) An appeal lies from an order made under subsection (4) or (5) by any person who appeared in the proceedings

(a) on any ground of appeal that involves a question of law alone,
(b) on any ground of appeal that involves a question of fact alone, or
(c) on any ground of appeal that involves a question of mixed law and fact,

as if it were an appeal against conviction or against a judgement or verdict of acquittal, as the case may be, on a question of law alone under Part XXI, and sections 673 to 696 apply with such modifications as the circumstances require.

(7) No proceeding for an offence under this section shall be instituted without the consent of the Attorney General.

R. v. *Keegstra*, the seminal Supreme Court of Canada case on the Criminal Code's hate speech provisions, is worth considering within the context of our examination of Internet law. Do any of the Court's holdings pose a problem in the online environment?

R. v. Keegstra[†]

This appeal was heard in conjunction with the appeals in R. v. Andrews, and Canada (Human Rights Commission) v. Taylor. Along with Andrews it raises a delicate and highly controversial issue as to the constitutional validity of s. 319(2) of the Criminal Code, R.S.C., 1985, c. C-46, a legislative provision which prohibits the wilful promotion of hatred, other than in private conversation, towards any section of the

---

† [1990] 3 S.C.R. 697.

public distinguished by colour, race, religion or ethnic origin. In particular, the Court must decide whether this section infringes the guarantee of freedom of expression found in s. 2(b) of the Canadian Charter of Rights and Freedoms in a manner that cannot be justified under s. 1 of the Charter. A secondary issue arises as to whether the presumption of innocence protected in the Charter's s. 11(d) is unjustifiably breached by reason of s. 319(3)(a) of the Code, which affords a defence of "truth" to the wilful promotion of hatred, but only where the accused proves the truth of the communicated statements on the balance of probabilities.

I.   FACTS

Mr. James Keegstra was a high school teacher in Eckville, Alberta from the early 1970s until his dismissal in 1982. In 1984 Mr. Keegstra was charged under s. 319(2) (then s. 281.2(2)) of the Criminal Code with unlawfully promoting hatred against an identifiable group by communicating anti-semitic statements to his students. He was convicted by a jury in a trial before McKenzie J. of the Alberta Court of Queen's Bench.

Mr. Keegstra's teachings attributed various evil qualities to Jews. He thus described Jews to his pupils as "treacherous", "subversive", "sadistic", "money-loving", "power hungry" and "child killers". He taught his classes that Jewish people seek to destroy Christianity and are responsible for depressions, anarchy, chaos, wars and revolution. According to Mr. Keegstra, Jews "created the Holocaust to gain sympathy" and, in contrast to the open and honest Christians, were said to be deceptive, secretive and inherently evil. Mr. Keegstra expected his students to reproduce his teachings in class and on exams. If they failed to do so, their marks suffered.

Prior to his trial, Mr. Keegstra applied to the Court of Queen's Bench in Alberta for an order quashing the charge on a number of grounds, the primary one being that s. 319(2) of the Criminal Code unjustifiably infringed his freedom of expression as guaranteed by s. 2(b) of the Charter. Among the other grounds of appeal was the allegation that the defence of truth found in s. 319(3)(a) of the Code violates the Charter's presumption of innocence. The application was dismissed by Quigley J., and Mr. Keegstra was thereafter tried and convicted. He then appealed his conviction to the Alberta Court of Appeal, raising the same Charter issues. The Court of Appeal unanimously accepted his argument, and it is from this judgment that the Crown appeals.

The Attorneys General of Canada, Quebec, Ontario, Manitoba and New Brunswick, the Canadian Jewish Congress, Interamicus, the League for Human Rights of B'nai Brith, Canada, and the Women's Legal Education and Action Fund (L.E.A.F.) have intervened in this appeal in support of the Crown. The Canadian Civil Liberties Association has intervened in support of striking down the impugned legislation.

.   .   .   .

VI.   SECTION 2(B) OF THE CHARTER — FREEDOM OF EXPRESSION

The first step in the Irwin Toy analysis involves asking whether the activity of the litigant who alleges an infringement of the freedom of expression falls within the protected s. 2(b) sphere.

Apart from rare cases where expression is communicated in a physically violent form, the Court thus viewed the fundamental nature of the freedom of expression as ensuring that "if the activity conveys or attempts to convey a meaning, it has expressive content and prima facie falls within the scope of the guarantee." In other words, the term "expression" as used in s. 2(b) of the Charter embraces all content of expression irrespective of the particular meaning or message sought to be conveyed.

The second step in the analysis outlined in Irwin Toy is to determine whether the purpose of the impugned government action is to restrict freedom of expression. The guarantee of freedom of expression will necessarily be infringed by government action having such a purpose. If, however, it is the effect of the action, rather than the purpose, that restricts an activity, s. 2(b) is not brought into play unless it can be demonstrated by the party alleging an infringement that the activity supports rather than undermines the principles and values upon which freedom of expression is based.

Having reviewed the Irwin Toy test, it remains to determine whether the impugned legislation in this appeal — s. 319(2) of the Criminal Code — infringes the freedom of expression guarantee of s. 2(b). Communications which wilfully promote hatred against an identifiable group without doubt convey a meaning, and are intended to do so by those who make them. Because Irwin Toy stresses that the type of meaning conveyed is irrelevant to the question of whether s. 2(b) is infringed, that the expression covered by s. 319(2) is invidious and obnoxious is beside the point. It is enough that those who publicly and wilfully promote hatred convey or attempt to convey a meaning, and it must therefore be concluded that the first step of the Irwin Toy test is satisfied.

Moving to the second stage of the s. 2(b) inquiry, one notes that the prohibition in s. 319(2) aims directly at words — in this appeal, Mr. Keegstra's teachings — that have as their content and objective the promotion of racial or religious hatred. The purpose of s. 319(2) can consequently be formulated as follows: to restrict the content of expression by singling out particular meanings that are not to be conveyed. Section 319(2) therefore overtly seeks to prevent the communication of expression, and hence meets the second requirement of the Irwin Toy test.

In my view, through s. 319(2) Parliament seeks to prohibit communications which convey meaning, namely, those communications which are intended to promote hatred against identifiable groups. I thus find s. 319(2) to constitute an infringement of the freedom of expression guaranteed by s. 2(b) of the Charter.

VII. SECTION 1 ANALYSIS OF SECTION 319(2)

. . . .

C. Objective of Section 319(2)

I now turn to the specific requirements of the Oakes approach in deciding whether the infringement of s. 2(b) occasioned by s. 319(2) is justifiable in a free and democratic society. According to Oakes, the first aspect of the s. 1 analysis is to examine the objective of the impugned legislation. Only if the objective relates to concerns which are pressing and substantial in a free and democratic society can the legislative limit on a right or freedom hope to be permissible under the Charter.

In my opinion, it would be impossible to deny that Parliament's objective in enacting s. 319(2) is of the utmost importance. Parliament has recognized the substantial harm that can flow from hate propaganda, and in trying to prevent the pain suffered by target group members and to reduce racial, ethnic and religious tension in Canada has decided to suppress the wilful promotion of hatred against identifiable groups. The nature of Parliament's objective is supported not only by the work of numerous study groups, but also by our collective historical knowledge of the potentially catastrophic effects of the promotion of hatred. Additionally, the international commitment to eradicate hate propaganda and the stress placed upon equality and multiculturalism in the Charter strongly buttress the importance of this objective. I consequently find that the first part of the test under s. 1 of the Charter is easily satisfied and that a powerfully convincing legislative objective exists such as to justify some limit on freedom of expression.

D.   Proportionality

The second branch of the Oakes test — proportionality — poses the most challenging questions with respect to the validity of s. 319(2) as a reasonable limit on freedom of expression in a free and democratic society. It is therefore not surprising to find most commentators, as well as the litigants in the case at bar, agreeing that the objective of the provision is of great importance, but to observe considerable disagreement when it comes to deciding whether the means chosen to further the objective are proportional to the ends.

.   .   .   .

(ii) Rational Connection

Section 319(2) makes the wilful promotion of hatred against identifiable groups an indictable offence, indicating Parliament's serious concern about the effects of such activity. Those who would uphold the provision argue that the criminal prohibition of hate propaganda obviously bears a rational connection to the legitimate Parliamentary objective of protecting target group members and fostering harmonious social relations in a community dedicated to equality and multiculturalism. I agree, for in my opinion it would be difficult to deny that the suppression of hate propaganda reduces the harm such expression does to individuals who belong to identifiable groups and to relations between various cultural and religious groups in Canadian society.

In sum, having found that the purpose of the challenged legislation is valid, I also find that the means chosen to further this purpose are rational in both theory and operation, and therefore conclude that the first branch of the proportionality test has been met. Accordingly, I move now to the issue of whether s. 319(2) minimally impairs the s. 2(b) guarantee of freedom of expression.

(iii) Minimal Impairment of the Section 2(b) Freedom

The criminal nature of the impugned provision, involving the associated risks of prejudice through prosecution, conviction and the imposition of up to two years imprisonment, indicates that the means embodied in hate propaganda legislation should be carefully tailored so as to minimize impairment of the freedom of expression. It therefore must be shown that s. 319(2) is a measured and appropriate response to the phenomenon of hate propaganda, and that it does not overly circumscribe the s. 2(b) guarantee.

The main argument of those who would strike down s. 319(2) is that it creates a real possibility of punishing expression that is not hate propaganda. It is thus submitted that the legislation is overbroad, its terms so wide as to include expression which does not relate to Parliament's objective, and also unduly vague, in that a lack of clarity and precision in its words prevents individuals from discerning its meaning with any accuracy. In either instance, it is said that the effect of s. 319(2) is to limit the expression of merely unpopular or unconventional communications. Such communications may present no risk of causing the harm which Parliament seeks to prevent, and will perhaps be closely associated with the core values of s. 2(b). This overbreadth and vagueness could consequently allow the state to employ s. 319(2) to infringe excessively the freedom of expression or, what is more likely, could have a chilling effect whereby persons potentially within s. 319(2) would exercise self-censorship. Accordingly, those attacking the validity of s. 319(2) contend that vigorous debate on important political and social issues, so highly valued in a society that prizes a diversity of ideas, is unacceptably suppressed by the provision.

. . . .

D. CONCLUSION AS TO MINIMAL IMPAIRMENT

To summarize the above discussion, in light of the great importance of Parliament's objective and the discounted value of the expression at issue I find that the terms of s. 319(2) create a narrowly confined offence which suffers from neither overbreadth nor vagueness. This interpretation stems largely from my view that the provision possesses a stringent mens rea requirement, necessitating either an intent to promote hatred or knowledge of the substantial certainty of such, and is also strongly supported by the conclusion that the meaning of the word "hatred" is restricted to the most severe and deeply-felt form of opprobrium. Additionally, however, the conclusion that s. 319(2) represents a minimal impairment of the freedom of expression gains credence through the exclusion of private conversation from its scope, the need for the promotion of hatred to focus upon an identifiable group and the presence of the s. 319(3) defences. As for the argument that other modes of combatting hate propaganda eclipse the need for a criminal provision, it is eminently reasonable to utilize more than one type of legislative tool in working to prevent the spread of racist expression and its resultant harm. It will indeed be more difficult to justify a criminal statute under s. 1, but in my opinion the necessary justificatory arguments have been made out with respect to s. 319(2).

(iv) Effects of the Limitation

The third branch of the proportionality test entails a weighing of the importance of the state objective against the effect of limits imposed upon a Charter right or guarantee. Even if the purpose of the limiting measure is substantial and the first two components of the proportionality test are satisfied, the deleterious effects of a limit may be too great to permit the infringement of the right or guarantee in issue.

I have examined closely the significance of the freedom of expression values threatened by s. 319(2) and the importance of the objective which lies behind the criminal prohibition. It will by now be quite clear that I do not view the infringement of s. 2(b) by s. 319(2) as a restriction of the most serious kind. The expressive activity at which this provision aims is of a special category, a category only tenuously connected with the values underlying the guarantee of freedom of speech. Moreover, the narrowly drawn terms of s. 319(2) and its defences prevent the prohibition of expression lying outside of this narrow category. Consequently, the suppression of hate propaganda affected by s. 319(2) represents an impairment of the individual's freedom of expression which is not of a most serious nature.

It is also apposite to stress yet again the enormous importance of the objective fueling s. 319(2), an objective of such magnitude as to support even the severe response of criminal prohibition. Few concerns can be as central to the concept of a free and democratic society as the dissipation of racism, and the especially strong value which Canadian society attaches to this goal must never be forgotten in assessing the effects of an impugned legislative measure. When the purpose of s. 319(2) is thus recognized, I have little trouble in finding that its effects, involving as they do the restriction of expression largely removed from the heart of free expression values, are not of such a deleterious nature as to outweigh any advantage gleaned from the limitation of s. 2(b).

E. Analysis of Section 319(2) Under Section 1 of the Charter: Conclusion

I find that the infringement of the respondent's freedom of expression as guaranteed by s. 2(b) should be upheld as a reasonable limit prescribed by law in a free and democratic society. Furthering an immensely important objective and directed at expression distant from the core of free expression values, s. 319(2) satisfies each of the components of the proportionality inquiry. I thus disagree with the Alberta Court of Appeal's conclusion that this criminal prohibition of hate propaganda violates the Charter, and would allow the appeal in this respect.

Canada Human Rights Act[†]

Hate messages

13.(1) It is a discriminatory practice for a person or a group of persons acting in concert to communicate telephonically or to cause to be so communicated, repeatedly, in whole or in part by means of the facilities of a telecommunication undertaking within the legislative authority of Parliament, any matter that is likely to expose a person or persons to hatred or contempt by reason of the fact that that person or those persons are identifiable on the basis of a prohibited ground of discrimination.

(2) Subsection (1) does not apply in respect of any matter that is communicated in whole or in part by means of the facilities of a broadcasting undertaking.

(3) For the purposes of this section, no owner or operator of a telecommunication undertaking communicates or causes to be communicated any matter described in subsection (1) by reason only that the facilities of a telecommunication undertaking owned or operated by that person are used by other persons for the transmission of that matter.

Zundel v. Canada (Attorney General)[‡]

The complainants alleged that Mr. Zundel was violating s. 13 of the Canadian Human Rights Act, R.S.C. 1985, c. H-6 by causing hate messages to be communicated through a computer website known as the "Zundelsite", which can be readily accessed through the internet. The server for the website, and the person who

---

† 1976–77, c. 33.

‡ (F.C.T.D., 1999) 67 C.R.R. (2d) 54.

manages it and posts material on it, are located in California. The complainants took objection to material on the "Zundelsite" claiming that the scale of the holocaust has been greatly exaggerated; they alleged that this material was likely to expose persons of the Jewish faith or ethnicity to hatred or contempt.

In this application for judicial review Mr. Zundel challenges on five grounds the commission's decision to request the appointment of a tribunal, and the jurisdiction of the tribunal to inquire into the complaints. First, the commission's decision to request the appointment of a tribunal is vitiated by bias as a result of statements made by the Deputy Chief Commissioner prior to the filing of the complaints and to her subsequent participation in the commission's decision to refer them for adjudication. Second, the tribunal has no jurisdiction to inquire into these complaints because material posted on the website in the form of text and graphics is not communicated "telephonically" as required by s. 13. Third, a tribunal has no jurisdiction to hear and determine these complaints because the server for the website is located outside Canada, as is the person responsible for selecting what is posted on it, who is the only person able to enter the material.

. . . .

The issues raised by Mr. Zundel challenge the legal authority of the commission and the tribunal to regulate material available on the internet, which is fast becoming one of the most powerful media of mass communication. The benefits to be obtained from awaiting the tribunal's considered determination of questions of this complexity, novelty and importance clearly outweigh the costs to Mr. Zundel, and to the public purse, of permitting the administrative process to run its course before the matter is fully reviewed by the court.

(i)   "Communicate telephonically"

It is a discriminatory practice under s. 13(1) for a person or a group of persons "to communicate telephonically or to cause to be so communicated ... by means of the facilities of a telecommunication undertaking within the legislative authority of Parliament" material commonly known as hate messages.

Counsel for Mr. Zundel submitted that material was only "communicated telephonically", and so capable of falling within the scope of s. 13(1), if the communication involved the transmission of the human voice through the medium of the telephone and telephone wires. He relied heavily on dictionary definitions of "telephone" and "telephonic" to support this interpretation. While sounds can be transmitted between computers, it was agreed that only text and graphics were available on the "Zundelsite".

Furthermore, it was argued, an interpretation of s. 13(1) that includes messages heard on the telephone, but not material obtained by computer from a website, is also supported by policy considerations. In particular, those who access the "Zundelsite" have available to them there material that challenges the "revisionist" view of the holocaust advanced by Mr. Zundel. In other words, the "Zundelsite" is a less powerful medium of communication than a pre-recorded message on a telephone answering machine because it allows those interested to enter into an active exchange of views, and to gain access to a range of opinions.

Counsel for Ms. Citron, on the other hand, submitted that the adverb "telephonically" should be interpreted broadly so as to include the internet, on the ground that most users gain access to it by dialling up and using a modem that is plugged into a telephone line outlet, and that information passes in digital form along telephone wires from the "Zundelsite" server to the computer of the person accessing it. The fact that sound, including the human voice, is not being transmitted should not be conclusive.

In support of her position counsel relied on a broader definition of the word "telephonically" contained in Newton's Telecom Dictionary, a not particularly authoritative source. In addition, counsel pointed out that if "telephonically" were given the meaning for which the respondent contended, its presence in the Act would still serve a purpose because it would, for example, exclude communication via satellite.

More importantly, counsel relied on the principle that human rights legislation, being quasi-constitutional in nature, should be given a broad and liberal interpretation. Accordingly, in order to tackle the mischief at which s. 13 is aimed, namely the dissemination of hate messages, s. 13(1) should be interpreted in a manner that accomplishes this goal by including this powerful new medium which relies in part on the telephone system. Section 13(2) specifically exempts from s. 13(1) material that is communicated by the facilities of a broadcasting undertaking. This is because broadcasting is regulated by another federal agency, the CRTC.

There is little doubt that when s. 13 was first enacted in 1977 Parliament almost certainly did not intend the adverb "telephonically" to include communication via the internet because it was not then a widely available medium. However, on a progressive, as opposed to a static interpretation of the Act, a court could conclude that "telephonically" should be construed in light of both the overall purpose of the legislation as set out in s. 2, and technological developments.

In Canada (Attorney General) v. Mossop (1993), it is true, the court refused to interpret "family status" as including same sex couples, largely because a contemporaneous amendment to include sexual orientation as a prohibited ground of discrimination had been defeated in the House of Commons. However, there is no evidence that Parliament considered the application of s. 13 to the internet, and rejected it.

Dictionaries, no doubt, still have their place in assisting in the interpretation of statutory language, particularly in identifying the range of meanings that words are capable of bearing in the ordinary use of the English language. However, it is a place of diminishing importance, as courts have increasingly sought to attribute meaning to the text of legislation by placing more weight on the statutory context in which the words are used, and the purposes underlying the legislative scheme.

Indeed, the Supreme Court of Canada has regularly endorsed a broad and purposive approach to the interpretation of human rights legislation in recognition of its quasi-constitutional status. This is another important reason for no longer regarding Bell v. Ontario (Human Rights Commission), supra, as a reliable precedent; in 1970 the court attached at least as much weight to the respondent's proprietary rights as to the complainant's right not to be the subject of discrimination, which at that time had no quasi-constitutional status.

Therefore, on a consideration of the language of the Act, the evidence and the interpretative approach to be taken to human rights legislation, it cannot be said that the position adopted by the commission on the interpretation of the word "telephonically" lacks a rational basis. Whether it is correct in law is not for me to decide in this proceeding; that will be for the court before which any application for judicial review of the tribunal's decision is brought. Meanwhile, the tribunal must be permitted to make findings of fact about technical aspects of internet communication on the evidence before it, and to give its considered interpretation of s. 13 in light of the arguments of counsel and its own understanding of the purposes of the Act.

(ii) The extraterritorial issue

Counsel for Mr. Zundel submitted that s. 13 does not permit the commission and the tribunal to regulate material posted on websites that are located beyond Parliament's geographic reach, when the person in control of the selection and posting of the material is also outside Canada. The fact that interested individuals may access the "Zundelsite" from within Canada was, he submitted, insufficient to justify the extraterritorial reach that the commission was purporting to give to the Canadian Human Rights Act.

The position of the respondents and of the commission on this issue was simple. They submitted that s. 13(1) prohibits people in Canada from communicating hate messages or causing them to be communicated. Mr. Zundel is present in Canada, and the commission maintains that, while he may not have posted material on the "Zundelsite" himself, and indeed, may be incapable technically of so doing, in fact he controlled the selection of the material that was posted, including many of his own writings, some of which had originally appeared in printed form.

Evidence was tendered to show that the "Zundelsite" was under the supervision of Dr. Ingrid Rimland, "the webmaster", who not only shared Mr. Zundel's views of the Holocaust, but also was paid for her services. The commission argued that it could be inferred from the communications between Mr. Zundel and Dr. Rimland, from the nature of the relationship between them, and from Mr. Zundel's references to "our 'Zundelsite'", and "my webmaster", that Mr. Zundel in fact exercised such a substantial degree of control over what Dr. Rimland posted on the "Zundelsite" that he could be said to be causing the material on the "Zundelsite" to be communicated.

I agree with the proposition that a person in Canada causes material to be communicated for the purpose of s. 13 if that person effectively controls the content of material posted on a website that is maintained from outside Canada.

Whether Mr. Zundel exercised the requisite degree of control over the content of the "Zundelsite" to bring him within s. 13 is a question with a very significant factual component. There was sufficient evidence before the commission on this issue to enable it to conclude that an inquiry into the complaints by a Human Rights Tribunal was warranted. It should be left to the tribunal to decide whether the evidence adduced at the hearing by the parties is sufficient to establish that Mr. Zundel was causing the material to be communicated for the purpose of s. 13.

(iii) "Cause to be communicated"

Counsel argued on behalf of Mr. Zundel that he could not be found to be in violation of s. 13(1) by reason of having caused the communication of material on the website to which the complaints related. His argument was that those who accessed the "Zundelsite" from their computers and called up the material that they wished to see caused it to be communicated; until then it was simply stored in electronic files.

This is the merest sophistry and provides no basis for the court to intervene in the proceedings now before the tribunal. It would follow from counsel's submission that the person who opens the morning's newspaper causes its content to be communicated to her, rather than the journalists who wrote the items that are published and printed in the newspaper.

Discussion Questions

1. Should it matter where the site is located? How can one prove who controls the site?

2. Consider the following excerpt from the Supreme Court decision in the Canadian Liberty Net case. Does this case provide further support for the suggestion that the "server is elsewhere" excuse will not succeed in the context of the *Canadian Human Rights Act*?

    Canada (Human Rights Commission) v. *Canadian Liberty Net*
    [1998] 1 S.C.R. 626.

    In December 1991, the Canadian Human Rights Commission (the "Commission") received five complaints regarding telephone messages made available by an organization advertising itself as "Canadian Liberty Net". Callers to the Liberty Net phone number were offered a menu of telephone messages to choose from, by subject area. These messages included denials of the existence or extent of the Holocaust; assertions that non-white "aliens" are importing crime and problems into Canada, and the implicit suggestion that violence could be helpful to "set matters straight"; criticism of an alleged "Kosher tax" on some foods to ensure that some percentage can be certified as Kosher; complaints about the alleged domination of the entertainment industry by Jews; and a number of messages decrying the alleged persecution of well-known leaders of the white supremacist movement. After having investigated the content of the messages, the Commission requested on January 20, 1992 that a Human Rights Tribunal (the "Tribunal") be empanelled to decide whether these messages were in violation of s. 13(1) of the *Human Rights Act*, which makes it a "discriminatory practice ... to communicate telephonically ... any matter that is likely to expose a person or persons to hatred or contempt ... on the basis of a prohibited ground of discrimination". Section 3 of the Act includes race, national or ethnic origin, colour, and religion as prohibited grounds of discrimination.

    On January 27, 1992, one week after the request to the Tribunal, the Commission filed an originating notice of motion before the Federal Court of Canada, Trial Division, seeking an injunction, enjoining Liberty Net, including Tony McAleer and any other associates in the Liberty Net organization, from making available any phone messages "that are likely to expose persons to hatred or contempt by reason of the fact that those persons are identifiable on the basis of race, national or ethnic origin, colour or religion", until a final order of the Tribunal is rendered. On February 5 and 6, the motion was argued, and on March 3, 1992, Muldoon J. granted the injunction sought. Upon further submissions of the parties, Muldoon J. varied the content of his order slightly, although those changes are not germane to any controversy in this appeal.

    A Tribunal was empanelled in response to the Commission's request and held hearings for a total of five days in May and August 1992. The panel reserved its decision for more than a year, finally rendering a decision on September 9, 1993. Thus, the injunction order of Muldoon J. was in effect for almost 18 months, from March 3, 1992 until September 9, 1993.

    On June 5, 1992, a Commission investigator telephoned the Liberty Net phone number and heard a message referring callers to a new number of the Canadian Liberty Net "in exile" where they could "say exactly what we want without officious criticism and sanction". This new number was rented from a telephone company in the State of Washington, in the United States. Callers to that number then had access to a similar menu of messages as had been available prior to the issuance of Muldoon J.'s order of March 3. Indeed, Liberty

Net admitted before the Court of Appeal that some of those messages were specifically covered by the injunction, but they contended that the messages were not in breach of the order because they emanated from a source outside Canada, and thus outside the jurisdiction of the Federal Court.

. . . .

The appellants' second ground of attack is that the contempt order is inapplicable because it seeks to restrain conduct taking place outside of Canada, and, therefore, beyond the territorial jurisdiction of the Federal Court of Canada. This argument is misguided. The violation being impugned here is not the existence of the phone number in the United States without more, but rather the combined effect of that American phone number with the offending messages, and the referral message to that phone number on Liberty Net's old line. The gravamen of the violation of the order is the communication of the offending messages; that communication takes place by virtue of the advertisement on the Canadian phone line and the broadcast of the message on the American phone line. The former element took place "by means of the facilities of a telecommunication undertaking within the legislative authority of Parliament", as provided for under s. 13 of the *Human Rights Act*. As long as at least part of an offence has taken place in Canada, Canadian courts are competent to exert jurisdiction.

What shortcomings can you identify in the federal Human Rights Code in applying it to the Internet? Consider whether the Saskatchewan version of the code eliminates some of the federal code's problems.

The Saskatchewan Human Rights Code[†]

14(1) No person shall publish or display, or cause or permit to be published or displayed, on any lands or premises or in a newspaper, through a television or radio broadcasting station or any other broadcasting device or in any printed matter or publication or by means of any other medium that he owns, controls, distributes or sells, any representation, including, without restricting the generality of the foregoing, any notice, sign, symbol, emblem, article, statement or other representation:

(a) tending or likely to tend to deprive, abridge or otherwise restrict the enjoyment by any person or class of persons of any right to which he is or they are entitled under law; or

(b) which exposes, or tends to expose, to hatred, ridicules, belittles or otherwise affronts the dignity of any person, any class of persons or a group of persons;

because of his or their race, creed, religion, colour, sex, sexual orientation, family status, marital status, disability, age, nationality, ancestry, place of origin or receipt of public assistance.

(2) Nothing in subsection (1) restricts the right to freedom of speech under the law upon any subject.

---

† S.S. 1979, c. S.-24.1, as amended by S.S. 1980–81, c.c. 41, 81, S.S. 1989–90, c. 23, S.S. 1993, c.c. 51, 61.

Faced with growing hate online worldwide, countries have turned to a wide variety of solutions in trying to combat the problem. Heather De Santis provides a helpful overview of some initiatives around the world in this 1998 report prepared for the Department of Canadian Heritage and Industry Canada.

Combating Hate on the Internet: An International Comparative Review of Policy Approaches[†]

HEATHER DE SANTIS

It has been estimated that only about 150 individuals in Canada post hate propaganda on the Internet, yet their "voice is disproportionate to their numbers." The nature of this specific medium allows the dissemination of propaganda to a more diverse, international audience. The Web expands the traditionally narrow means of spreading hate literature (through pamphlets for example) into a forum which allows them a level of credibility and influence which does not exist off-line.

Initially, numerous white supremacists, racists and Holocaust deniers were extremely active in USENET discussion groups and chat rooms to stir up emotional debate. Such fora allow users to engage in discussions with extremists in order to counter their attacks. Increasingly, however, extremists are retreating to non-interventionist Web sites which do not allow room for discussion through which users can dispute extremist views. Such sites have been compared to electronic magazines which hate mongers, as the publishers, can make to look reputable and credible by posting pseudoscholarly arguments. The user may not have the experience or knowledge to distinguish between legitimate sites and those which have the intent to mislead. Such content is available off-line as well, but the Internet broadens both the accessibility to, and dissemination of, hate-oriented content. Hate sites further expand the network of hate by offering Internet E-mail lists and dial-in bulletin board systems.

The Internet allows a great deal of anonymity which allows extremists to hide behind their words on Web sites and in E-mail messages. It is not only difficult to trace hate messages, but the transboundary nature of the flow of information on the Internet raises the question of national and international jurisdictions.

For these reasons, all of the countries and multilateral organizations surveyed in this report have placed the issue of controversial content on the Internet high on their agendas for discussion and action. Much like in the Canadian context, the problematic issues of freedom of expression, access to information, applicable legislation and national/international jurisdiction are themes repeated in the debate about the Internet in each case study. Yet, policy-makers in each country and organization reviewed in this report agree that some kind of organized response to hate on the Internet is warranted.

---

† Online: Department of Canadian Heritage <http://policyresearch.schoolnet.ca/networks/kbes/sra-350.pdf> [Excerpts]. Source of Information: Canadian Heritage — Multiculturalism Program. Reproduced with the permission of the Minister of Public Works and Government Services Canada, 1999 and the Minister of Canadian Heritage.

The rapid expansion of online services has presented new challenges to regulators. All of the countries surveyed in this report are exploring various new measures to control the dissemination of illegal/controversial content on the Internet. They are struggling to reconcile the freedom of expression with control over the access to controversial content. Measures span both ends of the spectrum: legislation (Germany) to complete self-regulation (the Netherlands). It would seem that compromise and cooperation between government and Internet service providers (ISPs) which avoids cumbersome, ill-defined legislation in favour of self-regulation, user-educational programs and preventative measures, offers the greatest potential for the Canadian situation. Existing legislation needs to be better defined in terms of Internet applicability; however, to create completely new legislation at this stage appears to be premature.

Another main problem which eludes resolution is the effort of legislators to locate a legislative "virtual jurisdiction." The transnational flow of information on the Internet makes out-of-country prosecution almost impossible for national governments. Therefore, the numerous studies being conducted by the multilateral organizations reviewed in this report may offer solutions to this jurisdictional problem. One example may be an internationally accepted ISP code of conduct. It is in the Government of Canada's interest to monitor the outcomes of these international research projects and discussions.

The Government of Canada accepts that existing legislation (Criminal Code, Canadian Human Rights Act) also applies to Internet communication (although it is still in the process of being interpreted by the courts). Similarly, most countries surveyed in this report have relied on existing laws to cover illegal content on the Internet. It is generally accepted that the Internet is not operating in a legal vacuum; rather it falls under the auspices of existing hate or content legislation. In other words, content which is illegal "off-line" is also illegal online.

Applicability

To determine which legislation is applicable to the Internet, it is crucial to understand how each country defines Internet content. This varies greatly from country to country. It can be understood as one of, or a combination of the following: telecommunications (France, Germany); broadcasting (Australia); publishing (New Zealand); writing (Germany); and/or audiovisual materials (New Zealand, UK). In the US, the debate over which definition to use has yet to be settled. This issue of defining Internet content will become increasingly problematic as telecommunications technologies continue to converge. Confusion regarding under which category of media the Internet actually falls may further complicate the ability of law enforcement authorities to apply appropriate legislation to controversial online activity.

Further to the debate, the categorisation of "illegal" content reflects how a state deals with hate generally. For example, Germany has quite strict laws about what content it considers prohibited (Nazi symbols, hate mongering) while New Zealand's laws are rather vague (hostility or ill-will against persons). Regardless, all countries surveyed in this report have existing legislation which criminalizes hate activities and are all signatory to the United Nations International Convention on the Elimination of Racial Discrimination. Yet, certain states (specifically the US) place more emphasis on the protection of free speech, which has resulted in failed attempts to limit the dissemination of content on the Internet.

It is important to note that in most discussions about Internet regulation in these surveyed countries, pornography appears to be the main concern of regulators, with particular emphasis on its availability to minors. That is not to say, however, that the protection of human dignity is not a priority. Rather, innovative measures to combat illegal content are generally driven by the desire to restrict pornography, but also include provisions for the regulation of hate.

Existing Legislation

Some countries have resorted to minor amendments to increase the scope of exiting [sic] laws to cover electronically disseminated information. For example, the UK updated its Obscene Publications Act 1956 in 1994 to include the transmission of electronically stored information under the umbrella of "publication." Further, the Protection of Children Act 1978, which contains provisions against child pornography, was amended to apply to computer generated "pseudo-photographs."

Germany as well has amended its penal law to include writings which are stored or disseminated electronically. France attempted to amend its Telecommunications Act 1986 to determine liability but failed when the Constitutional Council considered the proposals too vague for ISPs to follow.

New Legislation

Three states reviewed in this report have passed or have attempted to pass legislation to regulate the flow of content on the Internet (Germany, New Zealand, US). Germany, however, is the only country to have created entirely new telecommunications legislation to deal with the Internet. Both the United States and New Zealand failed to pass sweeping Internet-specific legislation. In the US, the Communications Decency Act 1996 was struck down by the US Supreme Court as a violation of freedom of expression and because it limited adult accessibility to legal materials. The Technology and Crimes Reform Bill in New Zealand stagnated at the Committee level (then died due to an election) because it was considered to be too restrictive even after numerous liberalizing amendments.

Confusion and vagueness about liability, restricted access and freedom of speech (for adults) seem to be the major impediments to the creation of workable and well-defined legislation. Perhaps, it is also premature for national governments to attempt to control an emerging technology, due to its rapid development, international nature and high accessibility.

Censorship

Classification bodies are also held responsible for monitoring content, and determining what should/should not be restricted to the public via the Internet. Both Australia and New Zealand consider the Internet to fall under the watch of their respective censorship bodies, which apply existing conventional media censorship laws to the Internet.

In Australia, it appears that existing censorship laws would apply to materials published, exhibited, sold or rented (and possibly even imported) using the Internet, where the resulting materials were expressed in hard-copy form, or stored in a disk-file. Currently, Australia is concerned with both hard core pornography and the incitement of, or instruction in crime. Materials of this nature are described as "Refused Classification" (RC) by determination of the Office of Film and Literature Classification (OFLC), a statutory authority. It is an offence to publish, exhibit, import, sell or rent materials that have been or would be given an RC classification code.

In New Zealand, the Office of Film and Literature Classification in the Ministry of Internal Affairs oversees the enforcement of the Films, Videos, Publications Classifications Act of 1993, which determines what is and is not "objectionable" material. Materials posted on the Internet are considered to be publications and are subject to two categories of illegal content: restricted materials (which can be distributed legally under certain conditions, such as age restrictions) and objectionable material. For the most part, in public discourse, "objectionable material" has referred to blatant child pornography, torture, bondage, and other materials that the community (through Parliament) has decided should not be available to the public. There are provisions for racist-related behaviour as well, although, to date, in both countries various convictions have had to do with the dissemination of pornography and not hate.

Censorship is a highly contentious issue in the debates surrounding Internet regulation, and is generally avoided directly as a new option to deal with controversial content. Australia and New Zealand have asked existing censorship bodies to apply the same criteria used to rate content on existing media to a new medium. In Canada, laws regarding indecent material also seem to apply to content on the Internet. New or increased censorship activity is, therefore, not warranted.

Innovative Industry Action
Most governments have worked (or are working) in tandem with ISPs to promote the development of ISP codes of practice and other non-regulatory measures to protect consumers. Generally, most major ISPs have attempted in their codes to protect the right to free speech and access to content, but at the same time, have established procedures intended to protect users from accessing inappropriate or objectionable material. Self-regulation offers an approach which avoids government involvement in the highly contentious area of censorship in both the national and international Internet community. Therefore, several states have cooperated with industry to create an almost a [sic] completely preventative self-regulatory approach (Netherlands, UK). Other states have chosen to combine government legislation and industry regulation for a two-pronged approach (Australia, France, and New Zealand).

Codes of Practice
A code is an agreement through which ISPs accept their responsibility to follow a process which limits or restricts access to "illegal" material in compliance with national or state laws.

Ultimately, ISPs must determine for themselves where the balance lies between the protection of user accessibility and the right to free speech, and their responsibility to "protect" a user from accessing inappropriate or objectionable material.

In most nations, ISP codes of practice, which have emerged from industry associations, have been endorsed by national governments as a means to promote ethical industry self-regulation and self-policing. In most nations surveyed in this report, ISPs have already established or are working to establish an Industry Code of Practice in compliance with existing laws defining illegal materials. Usually the codes attempt to clarify liability, define a handling process for content complaints, and establish procedures for the removal of (or restriction of access to) illegal material. Often there are provisions for a standard industry contract with content providers, which include a policy to inform content providers of their legal obligations, as well as confirm their agreement to cooperate with the appropriate authorities about content investigations. Codes often include the requirement that ISPs provide information to their users about how to lodge a complaint on content to the appropriate body. They can also give advice on technological options for user controlled filtering of content (such as Net Nanny see blocking section).

This approach has been endorsed by a number of governments and multilateral organizations because it is a front-line mechanism for addressing content issues and promotes cooperation between the user, ISP and the appropriate authorities. There remains and [sic] issue, however, regarding the appropriateness of industry associations acting as representatives of service providers, specifically in circumstances where the service providers are international and industry organizations are based on national memberships. However, associations which represent only Canadian ISPs may be able to come to a consensus on a code of practice according to shared national standards.

Hotlines

The Netherlands, Germany, the UK have established hotlines (via fax, phone and E-mail) to help enable citizens, police and ISPs monitor the presence of (potentially) illegal content on the Internet. (France and Australia are also considering similar courses of action). Initial experiences with hotlines have proven to be very successful; over 200 complaints have been recorded to date in the UK. For the most part, complaints have involved pornography on newsgroups, but hate mongering would be treated in the same manner.

In the Netherlands, the hotline allows service providers to warn content providers to remove their material. If they decide to ignore the warning, the complaint is forwarded to the Justice Department and the police are contacted. In the UK, the Internet Watch Foundation (the ISP-run, government-supported group which is responsible for Internet self-regulation) distributes details about offending sites simultaneously to all subscribing ISPs, which then remove such material from their individual news feeds. This is executed regardless of the origin of the offending material. For a UK site, the IWF informs the host ISP which then will take the appropriate steps to remove the material. Details are passed to the police for enforcement action against the originator. Unfortunately, incident reports involving out-of-country providers are problematic and therefore cannot fall within the parameters of complaints which will be investigated by a national body.

Even with local content, there is the possibility that mirror sites may spring up with the same content based in another state. In the UK, the National Criminal Intelligence Service (NCIS), which is the body responsible for the liaison between UK police forces and their international counterparts, passes the information onto the appropriate foreign authority. It is hoped that eventually links will be developed between national self-regulatory bodies.

The use of hotlines appears to be an effective preventative tool (which depends on the collaboration among users, ISPs and the police) that may be applicable to the Canadian situation. The OECD warns though that it is important to consider that hotline operators may be placed in positions of having to make decisions about the legality of particular content when dealing with a complaint. An established set of clear guidelines would be necessary to prepare operators for complaints about specific types of content. Therefore, if this initiative were to be adopted in Canada, hotline operators would need to be well versed about what types of content violate the Criminal Code or Human Rights Act.

"No Hate Page" Policy

HateWatch, a US based organization that monitors the growing and evolving treatment of hate group activity on the Internet, has indexed a list of US ISPs that have a "no hate page" policy.

Servers retain the right to terminate a subscription without compensation if the subscriber abuses the account, specifically by disseminating illegal, racist, and/or pornographic material. While there are only 9 ISPs listed to date, this self-regulating approach offers a promising alternative to government intervention. The Government of Canada could, however, actively encourage ISPs and their national associations to adopt such a policy.

Domain Names
In New Zealand, the Internet Society is the main association of ISPs which is responsible for the allocation of domain names (i.e. sites with the name ".nz"), will refuse to register a name if it considers that it may be offensive. While this is not specifically directed at hate sites, it is an interesting means through which to monitor new sites which may contain offensive or illegal content. Consistency in the process which delegates domain names also makes it easier for authorities to locate the origin of content providers. Not all governments, however, want this responsibility: the US recently announced that control over domain names will be handed back to the private sector from a government appointed body. This demonstrates the general US trend of government withdrawal from direct involvement in the regulation of the Internet.

Technological Solutions (and User Participation)
There are a number of industry initiatives designed to empower the user through rating, filtering and/or blocking certain sites according to different criteria. Certain countries have endorsed such standards to be used in conjunction with (or in the absence of) other non- and legislative measures (Australia, Netherlands, UK, US). These endorsements can be seen as encouragement to promote responsible user activity, such as parental supervision, which is important in the use of any media. It can be argued that user participation, one of the most fascinating and unique aspects of the Internet, has the potential to empower users to combat hate on an individual level.

Technological solutions have been criticized for being expensive and unwieldy. It is also feared that their use may lead to censorship or at least further regulation of content. There is the risk that certain types of valuable content cannot be accommodated by these technologies: the screening criteria may filter out "good" content with the "bad." Cultural differences may also complicate the criteria used to screen content.

These types of initiatives would be useful for Canadian users provided that they are aware of the difficulties encountered when trying to determine acceptable blocking/filtering criteria.

More importantly, it must be ensured that it remains the choice of the user as to whether or not content is screened or their access to certain types of content is limited.

Rating and Filtering
The Platform for Internet Content Selection (PICS) is an example of user-friendly technical standards for creating filtering software and ratings which provide for self-labelling (by the author or the publisher) and third-party labelling to indicate certain types of content. The system was developed as a result of a merger between the Information Highway Parental Empowerment Group (IHPEG) and the World Wide Web Consortium (including Netscape, Microsoft and Progressive Networks). It

is not a rating system itself, but provides an infrastructure for content labelling which is done by using either embedded ratings tags conforming to a particular rating system or by reference to a third party server, which independently rates content. It is an open industry standard, which has been, or is being implemented by both major (US) web browser developers and by developers of other leading access control software.

PICS can be used in conjunction with a number of independent rating systems, such as the one devised by the Recreation Software Advisory Council (RSAC), a Washington DC based non-profit organisation. Specifically, it can provide consumers with information about the level of offensive (hate motivated) language and other violence in software games and Web sites. It has been incorporated into Microsoft's browser, Internet Explorer and Compuserve.

Blocking

The United States is extremely vocal about the importance of parental supervision to restrict access to controversial sites. While this does not directly combat hate sites on the Web, software which restricts access to extremist views cannot be discounted in the overall effort to limit the reach of hate propaganda. Sites/Newsgroups with specific themes considered unsuitable by parents/caregivers or otherwise, can be blocked with numerous software packages such as Cyber Patrol, CYBERsitter, The Internet Filter, Net Nanny, Parental Guidance, SurfWatch, Netscape Proxy Server, WebTrack and SurfWatch. A problem with some software packages however is that they often are not able to discriminate "good" content from "bad" content, thus blocking access to useful material in their sweep of unwanted words or concepts.

Furthermore, several US non-profit organizations have established informative websites aimed at educating parents/caregivers about their content control options.

NGOs

Just as the Internet is widely open to those promoting hate, it is a valuable educational tool for those active in countering hate and hate propaganda. Anti-racism NGOs, such as the Nizkor Project and B'nai Brith, and individual volunteers have been able to counter extremist views through informative anti-racism web sites and through participation in debate in virtual fora (USENET, chat groups) where racist opinions can be challenged. Karen Mock of B'nai Brith has argued that,

> The problem of hate did not begin with the Internet ... The best way to attack the problem is to offer an even stronger counterbalance. It is important to remember that just as hate can be transmitted over the Net, so can good education and positive messages of tolerance.

While the activities of these groups are outside the scope of this report, the importance of their role in the overall fight against hate should not be discounted. Continued government support, dialogue and cooperation with anti-racism NGOs can only further strengthen this particular front in the fight against racism and hate.

International Cooperation

Numerous multilateral organizations have recognized the importance of the issue of Internet regulation and have undertaken internal studies to explore different legislative and self-regulatory options to deal with controversial content. The Council of

Europe, European Union, OECD, UN and UNESCO have all identified the Internet to be a rapidly developing means of communication which requires some form of monitoring or regulation (self-regulating or otherwise).

The key problem with an approach to any form of national or international reg-ulation is jurisdiction and enforcement in the global network environment. The trans-national nature of the Internet creates liability questions that have thus far defied national solutions to controlling out-of-state content providers. For this reason, an international collaborative agreement would seem to be the only viable, long term approach. However, different cultural attitudes, values and beliefs may impede an agreement on the definition of "controversial content" and suitable "punishments" for offenders. Specifically, the reconciliation of freedom of expression and the pro-tection of human dignity appears to be a highly contentious issue, particularly in those organisations which focus on the preservation of human rights (UN, Council of Europe).

The following recurring themes, which also may inhibit international agreement and cooperation, have been identified as key areas for consideration by governments in the contemplation of their approaches to Internet regulation

* identification of primary actors;
* the importance of the role of industry in terms of technical development and self-regulation;
* the implications of liability and responsibility;
* the role of fundamental rights and values in balancing the various interests;
* the need to focus on education and individual user responsibilities; and
* the question of appropriate international cooperation.

Similar to the situation in individual countries, these matters are currently being researched and evaluated by each multilateral organization reviewed in this report. At this time there have been no concrete international agreements in this area, although many organizations have established recommendations, resolutions and proposed plans of action. It is of great importance to the Government of Canada to monitor the developments in each body, both to identify options for future action and to identify opportunities for international cooperation. Furthermore, Canada should take a proactive role in these discussions through participation in debate in international fora.

Given the generally permissive approach to hate speech found in the United States, prosecutors have been forced to rely on civil rights and terrorism statutes in order to combat online hatred. The following case brought by the Attorney General of Pennsylvania succeeded in removing some hate materials from the Internet.

Commonwealth of Pennsylvania v. Alpha HQ[†]

AND NOW comes the Commonwealth of Pennsylvania, acting by Attorney General D. Michael Fisher, (hereinafter referred to as the "Commonwealth"), and brings this

---

† In The Court Of Common Pleas Of Berks County, Pennsylvania Civil Action — Equity.

action pursuant to the State Civil Redress Statute, 42 Pa. C.S. Sec. 8309, to request injunctive or other equitable relief from the conduct and activity which constitutes a violation of 18 Pa. C.S. Sec. 2710. In support thereof, the Commonwealth represents the following:

Plaintiff is the Commonwealth of Pennsylvania, acting by Attorney General D. Michael Fisher, on behalf of the citizens of the Commonwealth.

Defendants are ALPHA HQ, Ryan Wilson, Tim DeLaire, Bluelantern, Inc., Stormfront, Inc., Nevada Business Resources — Deepwell Internet Services, Network Solutions, Inc., and all other unnamed individuals acting in concert with, or in furtherance of the conduct of said named Defendants, (hereinafter referred to as "Defendants").

Defendant, ALPHA HQ is a white supremacist group with its main headquarters located at 2439 Memphis Street, Philadelphia, PA 19125.

Defendant, Ryan Wilson, located at 2439 Memphis Street, Philadelphia, Pennsylvania 19125, is the founder of ALPHA HQ and the registered owner and controller of the alpha.org domain which is an Internet site.

Defendant, Tim DeLaire, located at P.O. Box 6180, St. Charles, Missouri, is the registered technical contact of ALPHA HQ and as such is in a position of control over the alpha.org domain.

Defendant, Bluelantern, Inc., located at 7393 W. Jefferson, Lakewood, Colorado 80235, is the named owner of the Internet domain wpww.com and the website entitled WPWW, or White Power World Wide, which is the host of the alpha.org domain, and as such has control over the content of the alph.org domain.

Defendant, Stormfront, Inc., located at P.O. Box 6637, West Palm Beach, Florida, 33405, offers domain services (address and direction services) to alpha.org and wpww.com and thus has control over access to the alpha.org website.

Defendant, Nevada Business Resources — Deepwell Internet Services, located at 7949 California Avenue, Suites 8&9, Fair Oaks, California 95628, provides the same address and direction services to alph.org that Defendant Stormfront provides thus also has control over access to the alpha.org website.

Defendant, Network Solutions, Inc., is located at 505 Huntmar Park Drive, Herndon, Virginia 20170, and engages in the following:

   a. provides core registration services to alpha.org;
   b. is involved in domain name disputes; and
   c. has control over the access to the domain of alpha.org.

At all times relevant hereto, Bonnie Jouhari was employed as a Fair Housing Specialist with the Reading-Berks Human Relations Council. Her duties included fair housing enforcement and chairing the Berks County Conflict Resolution Task Force. In these positions her responsibilities included planning anti-hate activities in the community, addressing issues of hate crime and racial hatred, and the activities of local hate groups.

At all times relevant hereto, Ann Van Dyke was employed as the Assistant to the Director of the Education and Community Services Division at the Pennsylvania Human Relations Commission. Her duties included responding to public acts of organized hate groups and addressing issues of racial hatred and intolerance. She is known to members of various hate groups in the Commonwealth of Pennsylvania to be vocal in the community about issues of race relations, hate crimes and racial intolerance and bigotry.

Count I, Terroristic Threats

Paragraphs 1 through 11, inclusive are incorporated herein by reference as if more fully set forth herein.

Upon information and belief, during February and March of 1998, and at other subsequent times, Defendants engages in conduct which constitutes a violation of 18 Pa. C.S. Sec. 2706, by publishing on the Internet webpage http://www.alpha.org/ stateofhate/stateofhate.html threatening material, with intent to terrorize and/or with reckless disregard for the risk of causing terror to Bonnie Jouhari, all employees of the Reading-Berks Human Relations Council, and Ann Van Dyke as follows:

a. A picture of Bonnie Jouhari, stating "[she] has received warnings in the mail that she is a race traitor ... Traitors like this should beware, for in our day, they will be hung from the neck from the nearest tree or lamp post";
b. A picture depicting the bombing of the Reading-Berks Human Relations Council Office. (A disclaimer was subsequently added to this exploding image);
c. A picture of Ann Van Dyke, stating that she is "more attractive than she is intelligent" and that "Pennsylvania has all the characteristics of Germany prior to World War II".

See Attached Exhibits 2&3, Downloaded Images and Print-outs.

The aforementioned pictures and messages communicated and received through the Internet constitute explicit and overt threats of violence within the purview of 42 Pa. C.S. Sec. 8309(b).

In the context of the circumstances, the pictures and messages as communicated through the Internet constitute threats of murder and arson; cause psychological distress; terrorize Bonnie Jouhari, all employees of the Reading-Berks Human Relations Council, and Ann Van Dyke and invade their personal sense of security.

Prayer For Relief

Wherefore, the Commonwealth respectfully requests that this Court issue the following Orders:

A. Permanently enjoin Defendants ALPHA HQ and Ryan Wilson, and/or others, from publishing, posting, or distributing on the Internet, and/or website http:// www.alpha.org and/or webpage, http://www.alpha.org/stateofhate.html, the aforementioned pictures and/or messages, in violation of 18 Pa. C.S. Sec. 2706, which constitute terroristic threats, threats of violence, and cause psychological distress to Bonnie Jouhari, all employees of the Reading-Berks Human Relations Council, and Ann Van Dyke and invades their personal sense of security.

If Defendants ALPHA HQ or Ryan Wilson and/or others, fail to cease and desist from publishing, posting, or distributing on the Internet, and/or website http:// www.alpha.org and/or webpage, http://www.alpha.org/stateofhate.html, the aforementioned pictures and/or messages:

B. Permanently enjoin Defendants Tim DeLaire, Bluelantern, Inc., Stormfront, Inc., Nevada Business Resources — Deepwell Internet Services from providing, operating, or running Domain Name Service (hereinafter referred to as "DNS") for the ALPHA HQ website or any other host on which the aforementioned webpage appears.

If Defendants Tim DeLair, Bluelantern, Inc., Stormfront, Inc., Nevada Business Resources — Deepwell Internet Services fail to cease and desist from providing, operating, or running DNS for the ALPHA HQ website at www.alph.org, alpha.org, or any other host on which the aforementioned webpage appears:

C. Permanently enjoin Network Solutions Inc., from providing, operating, or running root DNS for the ALPHA HQ domain of alph.org.

D. Permanently enjoin Defendants ALPHA HQ and Ryan Wilson from engaging in the aforementioned acts or other practices in violation of 18 Pa. C.S. Sec. 2706.

E. Grant the Commonwealth costs of investigation and costs of filing this action against Defendants.

F. Provide any and all other such relief as the Court may deem just and necessary.

Notes

1. Civil rights statutes were also used in two California cases involving threatening email. In one instance (*State* v. *Quon*), the accused sent threatening email to many Latin American students on a college campus. The perpetrator pled guilty to violating the students' civil rights and was sentenced to two years imprisonment.

   In January 2000, Federal prosecutors launched another action against ALPHA HQ, this time for violating the *Fair Housing Act*. The charges stemmed from threats made to an individual who helped people file discrimination complaints under the housing act. A federal judge awarded U.S.$1.1 million in July 2000 in the case, the largest award ever against a hate Web site.

2. European countries have also been active in prosecuting individuals using the Internet to spread hate speech regardless of where the speech is hosted. In Denmark, a district court found a defendant guilty of posting racist slurs on the Danish Usenet newsgroup dk.politik. The individual was originally charged with posting slurs via DigiWeb, a U.S.-based ISP, but realizing the difficulty in overcoming the U.S. First Amendment protection of hate speech, authorities brought the second charge based on the Danish newsgroup.

   In Germany, prosecutors faced no such concerns in bringing charges in the spring of 1999 against Australian Fredrick Töben, a well-known Holocaust denier for materials found on an Australian-based Web site. The case was dismissed on jurisdictional grounds. Interestingly, despite a call by Germany's Justice Minister in June 2000 for a global ban on online hate, one month later another German minister admitted that his country had conceded defeat in its battle against foreign hate Web sites.

   In France, anti-racism groups launched a pair of legal actions in the spring of 2000 arising out of online hate materials. In one action, a French anti-racism group launched a lawsuit against Yahoo! over the sale of Nazi memorabilia on the portal's auction site. In another case, the French Jewish

Students Association launched a lawsuit against MultiMania, a French portal, for the accidental display of Nazi materials. The two cases resulted in conflicting decisions. The case against Yahoo! resulted in a court order against the Internet giant to ensure that Nazi memorabilia would not be available to French residents. Yahoo! immediately appealed the decision arguing that compliance was impossible. The case against MultiMania, conversely, was dismissed.

3. Several Web sites provide comprehensive resources for learning more about hate on the Internet. The best include:
    - Nizkor — <http://www.nizkor.org>
    - Hatewatch — <http://hatewatch.org>
    - Media Awareness Centre — <http://www.media-awareness.ca/eng/issues/internet/hintro.htm>

8

Regulation of Online
Defamation

Online defamation — often referred to as cybersmearing or cyberlibel — is one of the fastest growing areas of Internet law. Defamatory speech, whether in the form of email postings to mailing lists or defamatory Web sites, has become commonplace as disgruntled ex-employees or consumers find that the Internet is an easy and effective way to distribute their message. As a result, the Internet is now home to hundreds of Web sites verbalizing why companies ranging from America Online (AOL) to Nike "suck." As well, thousands of email postings disparage people, politicians, companies and virtually any other available target.

In addition to facilitating defamatory speech, the Internet also introduces several complications to the application of traditional defamation law. First, the Internet provides users with the power of anonymity, which may allow a speaker to remain unknown and possibly unaccountable. This is particularly problematic in the case of chat room postings, where users are not only difficult to trace but may also believe that there are no legal ramifications to their activity.

The anonymous[7] nature of chat room postings has led to numerous legal actions against John and Jane Does, designed simply to uncover who is responsible for the utterance For example, in 1998, Philip Services Corp. went to an Ontario court in order to identify several individuals who, it claimed, were using pseudonyms to post libelous and defamatory messages on a Yahoo! chat board. The company used a court order to obtain the IP numbers associated with the accounts on the dates and times the offending messages were posted. Aided by that information, they were able to track down the Internet service provider through which the offending messages were posted. Once that information was secured, the company obtained a second court order to acquire the ISP's logs and to identify the individuals from whose accounts the offending messages were posted. As this example illustrates, although it is possible to track down posters of defamatory speech, it is a long, arduous and costly process to do so.

The Internet also alters the traditional defamation paradigm with respect to the speed of dissemination of defamatory speech. Traditional libel law affords an opportunity to correct a false assertion, premised on the belief that the harm caused by the defamation can be remedied with a quick retraction. However, Internet based defamation is far more difficult to retract, since the materials can be distributed worldwide with such rapidity that retraction may prove insufficient.

Conversely, the power of speech provided by the Internet provides the defamed party with an unparalleled opportunity to respond quickly and directly to the allegations. This also alters traditional libel law, which was designed to assist people without a voice, who had no guarantees that they could disseminate their side of the story in print.

For example, consider the ongoing battle between the Church of Scientology and Ron Newman. Newman believes strongly that the Church of Scientology is a dangerous cult that must be exposed. Newman has used his Web site to chronicle the church's many activities (<http://www2.thecia.net/users/rnewman/scientology/home.html>). In response, an organization called Parishioners.org has posted a Newman exposé which claims that Newman harasses Scientologists (<http://www.parishioners.org/Intolerance/newman.html>). Although neither side is behaving particularly admirably, the dispute illustrates how the Internet provides both Newman and the Church of Scientology with the opportunity to publicly air their perspective.

Our examination of libel law and the Internet begins with another case involving the Church of Scientology. This case, a 1995 Supreme Court decision, is the court's most recent pronouncement on the issue of Canadian libel law.

Hill v. Church of Scientology of Toronto[†]

Cory J. — On September 17, 1984, the appellant Morris Manning, accompanied by representatives of the appellant Church of Scientology of Toronto ("Scientology"), held a press conference on the steps of Osgoode Hall in Toronto. Manning, who was wearing his barrister's gown, read from and commented upon allegations contained in a notice of motion by which Scientology intended to commence criminal contempt proceedings against the respondent Casey Hill, a Crown attorney. The notice of motion alleged that Casey Hill had misled a judge of the Supreme Court of Ontario and had breached orders sealing certain documents belonging to Scientology. The remedy sought was the imposition of a fine or the imprisonment of Casey Hill.

. . . . .

   ii. At the contempt proceedings, the allegations against Casey Hill were found to be untrue and without foundation. Casey Hill thereupon commenced this action for damages in libel against both Morris Manning and Scientology. On October

---

† [1995] 2 S.C.R. 1130.

3, 1991, following a trial before Carruthers J. and a jury, Morris Manning and Scientology were found jointly liable for general damages in the amount of $300,000 and Scientology alone was found liable for aggravated damages of $500,000 and punitive damages of $800,000. Their appeal from this judgment was dismissed by a unanimous Court of Appeal.

.   .   .   .

III.   ANALYSIS

Two major issues are raised in this appeal. The first concerns the constitutionality of the common law action for defamation. The second relates to the damages that can properly be assessed in such actions.

Let us first review the appellants' submissions pertaining to defamation actions. The appellants contend that the common law of defamation has failed to keep step with the evolution of Canadian society. They argue that the guiding principles upon which defamation is based place too much emphasis on the need to protect the reputation of plaintiffs at the expense of the freedom of expression of defendants. This, they say, is an unwarranted restriction which is imposed in a manner that cannot be justified in a free and democratic society. The appellants add that if the element of government action in the present case is insufficient to attract *Charter* scrutiny under s.32, the principles of the common law ought, nevertheless, to be interpreted, even in a purely private action, in a manner consistent with the *Charter*. This, the appellants say, can only be achieved by the adoption of the "actual malice" standard of liability articulated by the Supreme Court of the United States in the case of *New York Times* v. *Sullivan*.

.   .   .   .

(b)   The Nature of Actions for Defamation: The Values to Be Balanced

There can be no doubt that in libel cases the twin values of reputation and freedom of expression will clash. As Edgerton J. stated in *Sweeney* v. *Patterson*, whatever is "added to the field of libel is taken from the field of free debate". The real question, however, is whether the common law strikes an appropriate balance between the two. Let us consider the nature of each of these values.

(i)   Freedom of Expression

Much has been written of the great importance of free speech. Without this freedom to express ideas and to criticize the operation of institutions and the conduct of individual members of government agencies, democratic forms of government would wither and die. More recently, in *Edmonton Journal*, at p. 1336, it was said:

> It is difficult to imagine a guaranteed right more important to a democratic society than freedom of expression. Indeed a democracy cannot exist without that freedom to express new ideas and to put forward opinions about the functioning of public institutions. The concept of free and uninhibited speech permeates all truly democratic societies and institutions. The vital importance of the concept cannot be over-emphasized.

However, freedom of expression has never been recognized as an absolute right. Duff C.J. emphasized this point in *Reference re Alberta Statutes*, at p. 133:

The right of public discussion is, of course, subject to legal restrictions; those based upon considerations of decency and public order, and others conceived for the protection of various private and public interests with which, for example, the laws of defamation and sedition are concerned. <u>In a word, freedom of discussion means ... "freedom governed by law."</u> [Emphasis added.]

Similar reasoning has been applied in cases argued under the *Charter*. Although a *Charter* right is defined broadly, generally without internal limits, the *Charter* recognizes, under s.1, that social values will at times conflict and that some limits must be placed even on fundamental rights. As La Forest J. explained in *United States of America* v. *Cotroni* at p. 1489, this Court has adopted a flexible approach to measuring the constitutionality of impugned provisions wherein "the underlying values [of the *Charter*] must be sensitively weighed in a particular context against other values of a free and democratic society ...".

Certainly, defamatory statements are very tenuously related to the core values which underlie s. 2(*b*). They are inimical to the search for truth. False and injurious statements cannot enhance self-development. Nor can it ever be said that they lead to healthy participation in the affairs of the community. Indeed, they are detrimental to the advancement of these values and harmful to the interests of a free and democratic society. This concept was accepted in *Globe and Mail Ltd.* v. *Boland* at pp. 208–9, where it was held that an extension of the qualified privilege to the publication of defamatory statements concerning the fitness for office of a candidate for election would be "harmful to that 'common convenience and welfare of society'". Reliance was placed upon the text *Gatley on Libel and Slander in a Civil Action: With Precedents of Pleadings* (4th ed. 1953), at p. 254, wherein the author stated the following:

It would tend to deter sensitive and honourable men from seeking public positions of trust and responsibility, and leave them open to others who have no respect for their reputation.

(ii)   The Reputation of the Individual

The other value to be balanced in a defamation action is the protection of the reputation of the individual. Although much has very properly been said and written about the importance of freedom of expression, little has been written of the importance of reputation. Yet, to most people, their good reputation is to be cherished above all. A good reputation is closely related to the innate worthiness and dignity of the individual. It is an attribute that must, just as much as freedom of expression, be protected by society's laws. In order to undertake the balancing required by this case, something must be said about the value of reputation.

Democracy has always recognized and cherished the fundamental importance of an individual. That importance must, in turn, be based upon the good repute of a person. It is that good repute which enhances an individual's sense of worth and value. False allegations can so very quickly and completely destroy a good reputation. A reputation tarnished by libel can seldom regain its former lustre. A democratic society, therefore, has an interest in ensuring that its members can enjoy and protect their good reputation so long as it is merited.

The character of the law relating to libel and slander in the 20th century is essentially the product of its historical development up to the 17th century, subject to a few refinements such as the introduction and recognition of the defences of privilege and fair comment. From the foregoing we can see that a central theme through the ages has been that the reputation of the individual is of fundamental importance. As Professor R. E. Brown writes in *The Law of Defamation in Canada* (2nd ed. 1994), at p. 1–4:

> "(N)o system of civil law can fail to take some account of the right to have one's reputation remain untarnished by defamation." Some form of legal or social constraints on defamatory publications "are to be found in all stages of civilization, however imperfect, remote, and proximate to barbarism." [Footnotes omitted.]

Though the law of defamation no longer serves as a bulwark against the duel and blood feud, the protection of reputation remains of vital importance. As David Lepofsky suggests in "Making Sense of the Libel Chill Debate: Do Libel Laws 'Chill' the Exercise of Freedom of Expression?" (1994), 4 *N.J.C.L.* 169, at p. 197, reputation is the "fundamental foundation on which people are able to interact with each other in social environments". At the same time, it serves the equally or perhaps more fundamentally important purpose of fostering our self-image and sense of self-worth. This sentiment was eloquently expressed by Stewart J. in *Rosenblatt* v. *Baer* (1966), who stated at p. 92:

> The right of a man to the protection of his own reputation from unjustified invasion and wrongful hurt reflects no more than our basic concept of the essential dignity and worth of every human being — a concept at the root of any decent system of ordered liberty.

Although it is not specifically mentioned in the *Charter*, the good reputation of the individual represents and reflects the innate dignity of the individual, a concept which underlies all the *Charter* rights. It follows that the protection of the good reputation of an individual is of fundamental importance to our democratic society.

Further, reputation is intimately related to the right to privacy which has been accorded constitutional protection. As La Forest J. wrote in *R.* v. *Dyment*, at p. 427, privacy, including informational privacy, is "[g]rounded in man's physical and moral autonomy" and "is essential for the well-being of the individual". The publication of defamatory comments constitutes an invasion of the individual's personal privacy and is an affront to that person's dignity. The protection of a person's reputation is indeed worthy of protection in our democratic society and must be carefully balanced against the equally important right of freedom of expression.

Reform Party Of Canada v. Western Union Insurance Co.[†]

The petitioner is a national political party. As many organizations do these days, it maintains various websites on the internet. Its main website is found at www.reform.ca. The website is navigated by clicking on various titles or "links", which include a Senate Reform page website at www.senate-reform.ca. In the Spring of 1998, as internet users scrolled down the Senate Reform website, a list of topics appeared which included "Senators on the Need for an Elected Senate", "Retirement Dates of Sitting Senators", and one called "Senate Scandals".

---

† [1999] B.C.J. No. 2794 (B.C. Sup. Ct. 1999).

On July 15, 1998, Edward M. Lawson issued a Writ of Summons and Statement of Claim in this court (Vancouver Registry No. C983019) claiming damages against the petitioner and others. It is alleged that through the Senate Reform website the defendants falsely and maliciously published, or caused to be published, concerning the plaintiff the following defamatory words:

REFORM

Senate Scandals

Several Senators have been involved in scandals of varying degrees. Below is a list of the names and details of the 'top ten' Senate scandals.

...

Senator Edward Lawson (Ind., British Columbia)

(March 1989) Lawson, former Canadian Teamsters union leader, was involved in the US government's anti-corruption lawsuit against the Teamsters. Lawson and two other high Teamster officials, were removed as defendants from the case after coming to an agreement with the government. The Senator agreed not to obstruct the case at hand and to support efforts to clean up the union by endorsing electoral reform and disciplinary reform.

(March 1988) Lawson's name was used in one of the many alleged stock manipulation tactics employed by promoters Ed Carter and David Howard Ward in 1984–85. It was alleged the promoters manipulated 15 stocks on the VSE in 84–85 and then paid $1.4 million in bribes to fund money to buy the stocks. It was mentioned in court that in exchange for free trips on the Teamster union jet, Lawson received free stocks in companies Carter and Ward promoted.

The plaintiff Lawson claims an injunction, punitive and aggravated damages, and special costs, in addition to damages for defamation.

At the relevant times, a commercial general liability insurance policy made between the petitioner and the respondent was in full force and effect. The respondent denies coverage under the policy for the cost of providing a defence to the claim on the basis the allegations do not fall within the coverage provided for "personal injury" or "advertising injury". The definition of "personal injury" indicates coverage is provided for the publication of a libel or other defamatory material, "except publications or utterances in the course of or related to advertising, publishing, broadcasting or telecasting activities conducted by or on behalf of the Named Insured". The respondent says that the posting of allegedly defamatory material on a website constituted or was related to "advertising, publishing, broadcasting or telecasting activities", and therefore falls outside coverage afforded for "personal injury".

·   ·   ·   ·

In deciding whether there is a duty to defend, it is necessary to determine whether the pleadings on their face disclose any allegation that possibly falls within the coverage provided by the policy.

The first issue is whether the allegations fall within the coverage provided for "personal injury". The petitioner relies on *P.C.S. Investments Ltd.* v. *Dominion of Canada General Insurance Co.* (1994); varied on other grounds at (1996) 37 Alta.L.R. (3d) 38 (Alta.C.A.). There the policy afforded similar coverage for personal injury, also "excluding advertising, publishing, broadcasting or telecasting". An action against the insured claimed that it had mailed a defamatory letter to 130 members of the insurance industry. Medhurst J. concluded that distribution to 130 persons was not a widespread or public distribution to a broad audience, and was therefore not "publication" excluded by the policy. He stated at pp. 278 to 279:

> ... Three principles of interpretation, two specific to insurance contracts and one of general usage are of assistance. Firstly, as a general principle, terms of a policy of insurance which allow coverage should be read broadly for the benefit of the insured, while terms limiting coverage should be interpreted strictly or narrowly against the insurer. ...
>
> Next, if there is ambiguity in interpreting a provision in the policy then an interpretation which would render the endeavour on the part of the insured to obtain insurance protection nugatory should be avoided. ...
>
> Finally, the rule expressed by the Latin term noscitur a sociis states that the meaning of a word is revealed by words with which it is associated. This rule would influence the interpretation placed on the word "publishing", where it exists within in the phrase "advertising, publishing, broadcasting and telecasting ..." The other words in this phrase denote communication with a broad audience.
>
> The implications of these three rules are that the coverage clause which allows indemnity for the publication of libel and slander material should be interpreted as broadly as possible to allow for an encompassing definition of "publication". The definition of "publishing" in the clause limiting coverage should be read as narrowly as possible, so as to limit the circumstances in which coverage may be denied. This would permit the word "publish" to have a similar meaning to the words with which it is associated.
>
> In considering the exact meaning of "publishing" two decisions of Courts in the United States are of interest. The phrase "advertising, broadcasting and telecasting" was considered in interpreting an exclusion clause similar to the one here under review. Both decisions concluded that the word in issue, "advertising", denoted a widespread and public distribution, because of the presence of the other two words. ...
>
> It would appear that the definition of "publication" in the clause granting coverage should be read as broader than the definition of "publishing" in the clause which limits coverage. Clause 13 of the Statement of Claim alleges that the Defendants "... caused the alleged letter to be published by mailing or delivering the letter to approximately one hundred thirty employers, managers and adjusters in the insurance industry in Calgary, Alberta."
>
> The allegations indicate that publication was made so this would trigger the coverage provided by the policy. Is it then excluded by the clause limiting coverage?
>
> In my view, it is reasonable to conclude that a distribution to one hundred thirty persons does not exceed the coverage afforded by the policy. The duty to defend then does arise with respect to the allegation of libel and defamation.

The petitioner compares the number of mailings with the number of "hits" to the Senate Scandals webpage, that is, the number of times a page is accessed by internet users. In a period of 12 weeks, there were 738 successful hits to the main Senate Reform website, but just 173 hits to the Senate Scandals page, for an average of about two users per day. The petitioner argues that the 173 hits is similar to the 130 letters mailed in P.C.S. Investments Ltd. and that unlike that case, it did not actively distribute printed material in the mail. Instead, the Senate Scandals page was only accessible to those who became aware of the site and were interested enough to browse the site.

The respondent focuses on the fact that there are potentially millions of internet users searching the World Wide Web. As of 1999, 12.7 million users access the internet in Canada, another 106.3 million users access the internet in the United States, and there are 129 million English-speaking users globally. The respondent says the internet has become so pervasive that it is increasingly being used to access news, and some polls suggest that eventually the internet may eclipse newspapers as a primary source of news.

In my view, whether the internet may or may not replace newspapers is of little assistance in determining whether the material was published or broadcast. Similarly, in my view the number of "hits" is of little assistance in determining whether posting the material on the website was a publication "in the course of or related to publishing" activities conducted by or on behalf of the petitioner. To accept the petitioner's argument means that if the same article were placed in a newspaper but only 173 persons actually turned to and read the page, it would not be "publishing".

The petitioner relies on the general principles of interpretation for insurance policies. Those being that terms allowing coverage should be read broadly and terms limiting coverage should be interpreted narrowly. Therefore, unless a website is "visited", there has been no communication and no publication. It says there must be proof of communication. But there has been communication. The petitioner admits the site has been visited by 173 users.

Next, the petitioner refers to a decision of the United States Supreme Court in *Reno* v. *American Civil Liberties Union* (1997), which details the explosive growth of the internet and the World Wide Web. The court in that case said that the internet is not as invasive as radio or television. Instead of simply pressing a button or turning a knob like a radio or television, a series of affirmative steps is needed to access specific material. In my view, *Reno* v. *American Civil Liberties Union* is distinguishable. The Court affirmed a lower court decision that legislation prohibiting transmission of obscene or indecent material over the internet to minors abridged freedom of speech. In arriving at its decision, the court took into account the fact that it was highly unlikely that a minor could accidentally stumble upon a sexually explicit internet site because the images are preceded by a contents warning, and the sites are difficult to access without a series of affirmative steps.

There is no evidence in the case at bar that public access to the petitioner's website was restricted or difficult to access. As distinct from *P.C.S. Investments Ltd.* and *Reno* v. *American Civil Liberties Union*, by posting the Senate Scandals material over the internet, the petitioner made the material available to a vast audience. The number of potential recipients who could access the Senate Scandals site was not limited or restricted.

"Publish" is defined in Black's Law Dictionary, 6th ed. (St. Paul, Minn.: West Publishing Co., 1990) as "[t]o make public; to circulate; to make known to people in general. To issue; to put into circulation", and in The Shorter Oxford English Dictionary, 3rd ed. (Oxford: Clarendon Press) as "[t]o make publicly or generally known; to declare openly or publicly; ... To make generally accessible or available; to place before or offer to the public".

"Broadcast" is defined in Webster's Ninth New Collegiate Dictionary (Philippines: Merriam-Webster Inc., 1983) as "to make widely known" and in The Oxford Paperback Dictionary, 4th ed. (Oxford: Oxford University Press, 1994) as to "make generally known".

The Statement of Claim in the underlying action alleges as follows:

7. The defendant, Brad Farquhar arranged for the publication of the words set out in paragraph 6 by and on behalf of the defendant, the Reform Party of Canada.

8. The defendant, E. Preston Manning approved of the content and method of publication of the words set out in paragraph 6.

9. The defendant, Telnet Canada Enterprises Ltd. is an Internet domain server.

10. The words set out in paragraph 6 were published by the defendant, Telnet Canada Enterprises Ltd. through the defendant, the Reform Party of Canada's website on the Internet at www.senate-reform.org/scandals.html.

14. ...

(b) the defendants abused their positions by publishing the words knowing that the statements about the plaintiff were false and defamatory or alternatively were wilfully and recklessly blind as to the truth of those words;

(c) the defendants published words in furtherance of a partisan political agenda and without any regard to the truth or accuracy of the statements or the damage that would inure to the plaintiff's character, reputation and standing; and

...

(g) the defendants published the words through a forum and venue where the statements were calculated to do the most harm to the plaintiff's reputation, character and standing;

In paragraphs 6 and 7 of the Statement of Defence in the underlying action, the petitioner alleges that the words complained to be defamatory are "... accurate summaries or verbatim repetitions of previously published media reports concerning two different court proceedings", and that the media reports were privileged publications. Paragraph 8 of the Statement of Defence sets out the "previously published media reports", and in paragraph 16 the petitioner says that "the statement of principles" set out in its constitution includes an affirmation of the need to establish a "Triple-E Senate," and:

[a]ccordingly, the words that were posted by this Defendant to its website were published by this Defendant to advance its view of the best interest of the Canadian people and therefore constituted fair and reasonable comment on matters involving the public interest.

The Statement of Defence supports my view that the posting of the material over the website constituted, or was related to, "publishing" or "broadcasting" activities conducted by the petitioner, and I therefore find the allegations in the underlying action fall outside the coverage afforded for personal injury.

Notes

In addition to the *Philip Services Corp.* and the *Reform Party* cases discussed above, there have been several other Canadian cases involving libel and the Internet. The most prominent such case is *Braintech Inc.* v. *Kostiuk*, the 1999 B.C. Court of Appeal decision best known for its discussion of Internet jurisdiction.

However, the case also provides a helpful illustration of the ease with which alleg-edly defamatory speech can be posted on the Internet and the difficulty in finding an appropriate legal response.

The first Canadian defamation case with an Internet component was *Egerton* v. *Finucan* ([1995] O.J. No. 1653 (Gen. Div.)). The case involved a defamatory email posting in which a professor suffered the embarrassment of having his performance evaluation and termination letter distributed throughout the entire college network on the school's email system. The Ontario court ruled that the professor's defamation action was a separate and distinct cause of action from his wrongful termination claim.

In late 1998, the Investors Group, Canada's largest mutual fund company, obtained an injunction forcing a former employee to remove allegedly defamatory materials from his Web site. The injunction came as part of a $450,000 lawsuit against the former employee for damages arising out of the site.

In early 1999, Thomson Kernaghan, a Canadian brokerage house, sued both Yahoo and a series of posters for allegedly defamatory postings. The case had not been resolved as of July 2000.

In the spring of 1999, Caroll Daniels and Mountaintop Legal Services, a legal services provider, succeeded in obtaining a court order against several individuals to remove some allegedly defamatory material from a Web site. What distinguished this case was the breadth of the court order and the obligations that arose as a result. The court ordered that not only should the offending material be removed, but that the hosting ISP (Easynet) arrange the removal of any links to the sites found on the databases of all Internet search engines.

Cyberlibel on a smaller scale arose in October 1999 when Tasleeem Suleman, a B.C. resident, filed a libel lawsuit against Shaine Varini for statements made in an email distributed to four people. The case raised the question of whether a small email distribution constituted publication for the purposes of a libel action.

Stockwell Day, leader of the Canadian Alliance party, illustrated the power of the Web in responding to libel allegations when he created a Web site in November 1999 with the intent of publicizing his version of events in a $600,000 lawsuit. The site, <www.stockwellday.org>, provided background information on the case as well as links to related information.

Canada was also home to the world's first criminal libel action involving the Internet. The case involved an ongoing battle between Gregory Barrett and Darla Lofranco. Barrett had posted some allegedly defamatory materials on his Web site regarding the dog breeding expertise of Lofranco. When Lofranco succeeded in getting Barrett's Canadian-based ISP to remove the material, Barrett moved the site to El Salvador. In response, Barrett was charged with criminal libel. As of July 2000, the case had yet to go to trial.

Perhaps the most important Internet defamation case took place in the spring of 1999 in the United Kingdom, when Laurence Godfrey succeeded in his libel action against ISP Demon Internet. For more on the case, see pp. 81–82, above.

An additional concern in applying traditional defamation laws to the Internet is the potential for a strict interpretation of the libel and defamation statutes. For example, some statutes refer specifically to "newspapers, magazines, or periodi-cals." How would you characterize a Webzine? How about an online chat room or bulletin board?

Libel is often treated as the more serious version of defamation (as opposed to slander) since it involves the written word. How should email be treated? Although written, many email users are more casual in their email correspondence than in traditional written correspondence, treating the medium as akin to an electronic conversation. Should this impact the application of the libel and slander laws?

A March 1999 Ontario defamation action involving allegedly defamatory postings in an Internet Relay Chat room may answer some of these questions, as it addresses the issue of the proper characterization of real time online conversations. The plaintiff in *Kirikos* v. *Nicks* alleged that a series of postings in the chat room constituted defamation. The case had not gone to trial as of July 2000.

There is also some question as to when the defamation occurs. A defamatory letter is treated as published when opened, while a postcard is deemed read by the post office. When should an email be deemed read? Should the sender be held responsible for subsequent transmissions of the email?

Rindos v. Hardwick[†]

The plaintiff is an anthropologist. He obtained a doctorate from Cornell University in the United States of America in August 1981 and worked for several years at universities in the USA as assistant professor and in other capacities as an anthropologist. In about 1988 he emigrated to Australia. In June 1989 he commenced employment as a senior lecturer in the Department of Archaeology at the University of Western Australia. In November 1989 he was appointed temporary acting head of the Department of Archaeology and in February 1990 he became the acting head of the Department. From March 1991 until June 1993 he was attached to the Geography Department of the University of Western Australia as senior lecturer in archaeology. He ceased being engaged at the University after June 1993.

Numerous publications of the plaintiff's works have appeared throughout the world, including translations into languages other than English. He has given papers at numerous national and international conferences and has given lectures at different universities around the world. His work has been cited regularly in papers by other academics. He is well known internationally in the areas of anthropology and archaeology.

While the plaintiff was employed at the University of Western Australia, a review took place as to whether he should be granted tenure. In early March 1993 the Tenure Review Committee recommended that he be denied tenure on the ground of insufficient productivity. This was made formal in June 1993 and the plaintiff was dismissed by the Vice Chancellor of the University with effect from 13 June 1993.

There was a large amount of interest, internationally, about the actions of the University of Western Australia in denying the plaintiff tenure and in dismissing him.

On 23 June 1993 a message appeared on a worldwide computer network bulletin board, inserted by one Hugh Jarvis, an anthropologist in the United States of America. The message criticised the University of Western Australia for refusing to grant tenure to the plaintiff and for dismissing him.

[†] No 1994 of 1993 (Unreported Judgement 940164) (Sup. Ct. W. Aus.).

The computer bulletin board on which the message appeared is devoted to "science anthropology". It is part of an international computer news service to which persons can have access through computers and by which users of computers can communicate with each other.

Subscribers to or participants in the network utilise their computers to communicate and receive items of interest concerning anthropology. Most major universities throughout the world are participants in the network, which is also used by other persons. The main users are academics and students. There are approximately 23 000 persons worldwide whose computers have access to the bulletin board in question.

The bulletin board has a wide international readership.

The messages that appear on the bulletin board can remain on the computer of a subscriber or participant for a number of days or weeks, depending on the storage capacity of the computer in question. The types of messages vary. Examples include information on anthropological issues and personalities, debates on anthropological topics and personal messages between anthropologists. The messages come from persons all round the world, but particularly from the United States of America, the United Kingdom, Canada and Australia. Most of the persons who send messages and who view the bulletin board on a regular basis are persons who are working or studying in the general field of anthropology.

Items of interest on the bulletin board can be printed on hard copy. Such print outs can be and at times, no doubt, are circulated. Persons who read the contents of the bulletin board and cause messages to be printed include not only the owner of the particular computer, but any person who has access to it, such as academics and university students.

On 26 June 1993, in reply to the message published by Hugh Jarvis, the defendant caused a message to be published on the bulletin board. According to the material supplied by the defendant to the computer, it was transmitted by him from a computer in Derby, Western Australia. The distribution was to "the world", which means that the message was visible, and would have been able to have been read, on every computer around the world able to receive the science anthropology news bulletin.

The relevant passages in the message that the defendant so sent, are as follows:

> "Well, here we have my old mate Hugh Jarvis, the guy responsible for the first anthropologist (myself) being denied access to ANTHRO-L, now crying over one of his fellow Americans being the first to be denied tenure at an Australian University."

> "Sorry, UWA is my own turf, Hugh. I know very well that problems there are associated with the Anthropology Department there (now including the Archaeology Department) but I am also well aware of the wider social and political issues associated with our discipline here in Western Australia centrally focussed around Aboriginal Affairs."

> "The first matter I would raise in comment here, is the very public difference between myself and Dr Rhindos (sic) on the matter of categories in Aboriginal culture, played out on this very news group. In that case Dr Rhindos (sic) quite openly attempted to discredit my own lifetime's experience with Aboriginal people on the basis of his one phone call apparently to an outstation!"

> "I have met the man myself, and my impression is that his entire career has been built not on field research at all, but on his ability to berate and bully all and sundry on the logic of his own evolutionary theories. In the local pub, drinking and chain smoking all the while for that matter."

"Secondly, and this is rumours passed to me by several reputable and long-standing Western Australian anthropologists as to Dr Rhindos' (sic) 'Puppy Parties' focussed I am told on a local boy they called 'Puppy'. Hmm, strange dicey behaviour indeed, especially here in an environment dominated by conservative fundamentalists."

"Thirdly, and far more substantially, there are extremely serious questions arising here concerning an ongoing political campaign here against the Anthropology Department, most notably targetting (sic) the department's long-standing support for Aboriginal Land Rights against powerful international mining lobbies. This particular episode comes of great interest right in the midst of our national debate over the effects of the High Court's finding last year in favour of Eddie Mabo."

"I am sorry Hugh, but if someone for whom I might have a little more respect than yourself had posted what you did, I would have hesitated to post my own reply to your scurrilous attack on the University of Western Australia, I can only imagine prompted by the powerful vested interests lacking the guts and integrity to come out and speak honestly on important issues deeply affecting Western Australia. If you are on their payroll, I detest your involvement in this matter; if you are not on their payroll I can only assume you are a complete fool."

"As has been Dr Rhindos (sic), apparently believing that since he is an American he is somehow immune from the criticism of his non-American colleagues in *their* country."

"In the meantime your hysteria, in my case earlier when you decided unilaterally to deny me access to ANTHRO-L, and in this present case now, does not in any way bring you credibility."

"The rest of you professors, lecturers, staff, students, professionals and sundry lurkers and lookers-on, I do ask that you think critically about what is going on here. Please be a little more intelligent than to be swayed by grossly exaggerated and one-sided campaigns by a media to which only one party has ready access. Please think about which powerful politicians and vested interests might be behind this whole business."

"Please think that the real victims are the Aboriginal people here."

Thank you.

Gil Hardwick

It was submitted that the publication of 26 June 1993 contained five defamatory imputations, namely:

(a) The plaintiff engaged in sexual misconduct, in particular paedophilia with a "local boy" called "Puppy".
(b) The plaintiff has no genuine academic ability in his field and has not based his theories on appropriate research but has simply depended upon berating and bullying others.
(c) The plaintiff "is against Aboriginal land rights and Aboriginal people" and is a racist person.
(d) The plaintiff is not a genuine anthropologist but a tool of mining corporations.
(e) The plaintiff drinks to excess and spends most of his time "in the local pub".

I accept that words in the message published by the defendant give rise to an imputation that the plaintiff engaged in sexual misconduct with a "local boy".

I also accept that the message contains the imputation that the plaintiff's professional career and reputation has not been based on appropriate academic research "but on his ability to berate and bully all and sundry". This seriously denigrates his academic competence.

I do not accept that the other paragraphs give rise to the imputations alleged. In the course of argument these other imputations were not pressed.

The imputation of sexual misconduct, and that relating to the plaintiff's career being based on the ability to "berate and bully" and lack of professional competence are, in my opinion, seriously defamatory of the plaintiff. The inference is that these matters had some bearing on the failure of Dr Rindos to be awarded tenure and his dismissal from the University.

These defamatory remarks were published in academic circles throughout the world. I accept the submission made by counsel for the plaintiff that the nature of the remarks is such that they are likely to be repeated, and that any rumours of a like kind that had circulated previously were likely to gain strength from their publication.

. . . .

I accept that the defamation caused serious harm to the plaintiff's personal and professional reputation. I am satisfied that the publication of these remarks will make it more difficult for him to obtain appropriate employment. He suffered a great deal of personal hurt. The damages awarded must compensate the plaintiff for all these matters and must vindicate his reputation to the public.

The Rindos case was the first widely reported legal case involving libel and the Internet. For more on the Rindos case, see the Rindos Case Web site at <http://wings.buffalo.edu/anthropology/Rindos/Law/>.

Perhaps the best known case of Internet libel involved cyber-gossip Matt Drudge. The case, discussed in Chapter 4 as part of the ISP liability analysis, also provides an interesting perspective on libel issues.

Drudge v. Blumenthal[†]

This is a defamation case revolving around a statement published on the Internet by defendant Matt Drudge. On August 10, 1997, the following was available to all having access to the Internet:

> The DRUDGE REPORT has learned that top GOP operatives who feel there is a double-standard of only reporting republican shame believe they are holding an ace card: New White House recruit Sidney Blumenthal has a spousal abuse past that has been effectively covered up.
>
> ...Late at night on the evening of Sunday, August 10, 1997 (Pacific Daylight Time), defendant Drudge wrote and transmitted the edition of the Drudge Report that contained the alleged defamatory statement about the Blumenthals. Drudge transmitted the report from Los Angeles, California by e-mail to his direct subscribers and by posting both a headline and the full

† 992 F. Supp. 44 (D.D.C. 1998).

text of the Blumenthal story on his world wide web site. He then transmitted the text but not the headline to AOL, which in turn made it available to AOL subscribers.

After receiving a letter from plaintiffs' counsel on Monday, August 11, 1997, defendant Drudge retracted the story through a special edition of the Drudge Report posted on his web site and e-mailed to his subscribers. At approximately 2:00 a.m. on Tuesday, August 12, 1997, Drudge e-mailed the retraction to AOL which posted it on the AOL service. Defendant Drudge later publicly apologized to the Blumenthals.

Following a discussion of s.230 of the CDA, the court remarked:

The purpose of this statutory immunity is not difficult to discern. Congress recognized the threat that tort-based lawsuits pose to freedom of speech in the new and burgeoning Internet medium. The imposition of tort liability on service providers for the communications of others represented, for Congress, simply another form of intrusive government regulation of speech. Section 230 was enacted, in part, to maintain the robust nature of Internet communication and, accordingly, to keep government interference in the medium to a minimum.

. . . .

None of this means, of course, that the original culpable party who posts defamatory messages would escape accountability. While Congress acted to keep government regulation of the Internet to a minimum, it also found it to be the policy of the United States "to ensure vigorous enforcement of Federal criminal laws to deter and punish trafficking in obscenity, stalking, and harassment by means of computer." Congress made a policy choice, however, not to deter harmful online speech through the separate route of imposing tort liability on companies that serve as intermediaries for other parties' potentially injurious messages.

The proliferation of Web sites that target companies using monikers such as AOLsucks.com has become a major source of concern for many image-conscious companies. This practice can be surprisingly difficult to stop, as Bally's Total Fitness and Lucent Technologies learned to their detriment.

Bally Total Fitness v. Faber[†]

Bally Total Fitness Holding Corp. ("Bally") brings this action for trademark infringement, unfair competition, and dilution against Andrew S. Faber ("Faber") in connection with Bally's federally registered trademarks and service marks in the terms "Bally," "Bally's Total Fitness," and "Bally Total Fitness," including the name and distinctive styles of these marks. Bally is suing Faber based on his use of Bally's marks in a web site he designed.

Faber calls his site "Bally sucks." The web site is dedicated to complaints about Bally's health club business. When the web site is accessed, the viewer is presented with Bally's mark with the word "sucks" printed across it. Immediately under this, the web site states "Bally Total Fitness Complaints! Un-Authorized."

[†] 29 F. Supp. 2d 1161 (C.D. Cal. 1998).

. . . .

The Lanham Act provides the basic protections that a trademark owner receives. To find that Faber has infringed Bally's marks the Court would have to find that Bally has valid protectable trademarks and that Faber's use creates a likelihood of confusion ... Faber's site states that it is "unauthorized" and contains the words "Bally sucks." No reasonable consumer comparing Bally's official web site with Faber's site would assume Faber's site "to come from the same source, or thought to be affiliated with, connected with, or sponsored by, the trademark owner." Therefore, Bally's claim for trademark infringement fails as a matter of law.

Lucent Technologies, Inc. v. Lucentsucks.Com[†]

Plaintiff Lucent Technologies, Inc. is a Delaware Corporation with its principal place of business in Murray Hill, New Jersey. It has filed this in rem action against the domain name lucentsucks.com under the Anti-Cybersquatting Consumer Protection Act ("ACPA"), *15 U.S.C. §1125.*

. . . .

Defendant maintains that dismissal of this complaint is also warranted because, as a matter of law, plaintiff could not make out a violation of trademark rights without infringing the registrant's free speech rights. We need not rule on this argument, because we have found other grounds for dismissal. Nevertheless, we note that defendant's position has some merit.

The likelihood of confusion is a key element when determining whether trademark infringement or dilution has occurred. The Fourth Circuit has acknowledged that effective parody "diminishes any risk of consumer confusion," and can therefore not give rise to a cause of action under the Trademark Act. Defendant argues persuasively that the average consumer would not confuse lucentsucks.com with a web site sponsored by plaintiff.

Moreover, no civil action for trademark infringement or dilution lies under the ACPA unless the registrant's bad faith intent is demonstrated. Courts may consider nine factors when determining whether a bad faith intent exists, including "the person's bona fide noncommercial or fair use of the mark in a site accessible under the domain name." The House Judiciary Committee explained that this provision is intended to:

> Balance the interests of trademark owners with the interests of those who would make the lawful noncommercial or fair uses of others' marks online, such as in comparative advertising, comment, criticism, parody, newsreporting, etc. ... The fact that a person may use a mark in a site in such a lawful manner may be an appropriate indication that the person's registration or use of the domain name lacked the required element of bad-faith.

---

† 95 F. Supp. 2d 528 (E.D. Va. 2000).

H.R. Rep. No. 106-412, at 9 (1999). As one federal court has explained, "'sucks' has entered the vernacular as a word loaded with criticism." *Bally Total Fitness Holding Corp. v. Faber.* A successful showing that lucentsucks.com is effective parody and/or a cite for critical commentary would seriously undermine the requisite elements for the causes of action at issue in this case.

One of the most infamous libel sites on the Web belongs to Bill Sheehan, a very angry individual who resides in the Pacific Northwest. The site, which can be found at <http://billsheehan.com>, includes numerous examples of unsubstantiated allegations alongside highly personal information. Notwithstanding the libelous nature of the site, a 1998 attempt by several credit agencies to force the site off the Web failed.

Sheehan v. King County Experian aka TRW[†]

The record shows that the plaintiff's web site has contained grievances against government officials, credit reporting agencies, and debt collection services; scurrilous expressions of opinion (e.g., referring to Experian as "criminally insane" and to named persons as "assholes," "jerkoffs," and "scumbags"); and other allegations that are claimed to be defamatory. It has also contained information about credit agency employees and attorneys (including home addresses, street maps, home telephone numbers, fax numbers, and social security numbers); as to their category, plaintiff declares that he obtained the information lawfully from public information such as the Washington Secretary of State and other Internet sites.

Plaintiff has stated that the purpose of his web site is to hold the credit companies "accountable." He argues that the addresses and telephone numbers would make it easier for others aggrieved by credit reports to serve process. With regard to one attorney, he has printed the words, in quotation marks, "please medicate these guys!" But the web site has not suggested that readers take any specific action, or that they put the information to any particular use. There is no showing that lawless action was either asked for or imminent. In fact, information of this nature has been available on plaintiff's web site since early 1997, and there is no evidence that anyone has ever been harassed, approached, or contacted by a person who viewed the site.

The First Amendment is renowned for protecting speech we deplore as thoroughly as the speech we admire. Plaintiff's verbal pyrotechnics have surely been offensive, but they have had a theme — his belief (whether false or overblown does not matter) that he and others are victims of credit reporting agencies. Offensive speech — even if it "stirs people to anger" — is ordinarily protected.... The Internet is a modern version of the leaflets distributed in Keefe. In the absence of incitement to imminent unlawful action, the motion for a preliminary injunction must be denied.

---

† 26 Media L. Rep. 2340 (W.D. Wa. 1998).

For more on cyberlibel in Canada, see the following resources:

- Cyberlibel — <http://www.cyberlibel.com>
- Defamation in Canadian Cyberspace — <http://www.angelfire.com/ca2/defamation/>

9

Regulation of Online Commercial Speech

Few aspects of the Internet raise the ire of users as much as unsolicited commercial email, better known as spam. Promoting pornography, get rich quick schemes, magazine subscriptions, and the like, spam is the electronic equivalent of junk mail. Unlike junk mail, which can be left in the trash without ever entering your home, spam is sent directly to your email box and downloaded into your computer.

Interestingly, one of the first incidents of spam involved the legal profession. Canter and Seigel, an immigration law firm based in Arizona, sent spam to (or "spammed") a USENET group advertising their green card services in 1993. The incident sparked widespread anger among Internet users, who viewed the practice as a violation of "netiquette," or network etiquette. The lawyers were unapologetic, however, and they proceeded to send further spam messages, an action that later resulted in the disciplinary action against one of the firm's partners.

Opponents of spam raise several arguments to explain why spam is a problem. First, the cost of spam is borne by the individual Internet user and the ISP, not the party sending the spam. Since sending email is virtually free, spammers incur minimal costs in targeting thousands of users. There is a cost to spam, however, in the form of network time for Internet users who pay for usage based on time online, as well as wasted network resource costs incurred by ISPs. Second, a large percentage of spam is criminal or quasi-criminal in nature, with many of the emails advertising fraudulent schemes or pornographic materials. Third, spam creates confusion, as it leaves Internet users unsure about the legitimacy of their email. Fourth, spam frequently violates personal privacy standards, since users rarely consent to the receipt of such materials.

In recent years, ISPs have taken their opposition to spam to the courts and legislatures. Spam cases have become increasingly common in the United States, and there have been numerous legislative initiatives to curtail and punish spamming activity. Although Canada has lagged behind in this regard, two spam cases from the spring of 1999 indicate that the issue has begun to attract significant interest among Canadian Internet users.

There are several options available to those engaged in the battle against spam. At one end of the spectrum, users and ISPs may choose to do nothing, relying instead on the delete button or software filters to rid themselves of a mild annoyance. Legal solutions, however, have become increasingly the approach of choice for ISPs, who estimate that more than 25 percent of emails may be spam. These legal solutions include the use of contracts, trademarks, property law and criminal law.

CONTRACT LAW

1267623 Ontario Inc. v. Nexx Online Inc.†

The plaintiff 1267623 Ontario Inc. (1267623) is an Oakville based home furnishing company that sells directly to customers using the Internet. The plaintiff Codes Communications Inc. (Codes) is a web page design company that works exclusively for and acts as agent on behalf of 1267623.

The defendant Nexx Online, Inc. (Nexx) is an Internet service provider based in Toronto. Its primary business is hosting web pages, also called websites, on the Internet, which is also known as the "World Wide Web". For a fee, a web host provides shared computer space on its server to allow businesses, organizations and individual clients to have websites available for viewing by Internet users. A web page is identified and located using a domain name, beginning with "www" (the short form for "world wide web"), followed by a unique identifier (often the business name), and concluding with the highest sub-domain (such as "com", "ca" or "org").

On August 6, 1998, Nexx entered into a one-year service agreement (the Contract) with Codes to host the plaintiffs' website: www.beaverhome.com.

Beginning January 27, 1999, Nexx began to receive complaints from Internet users concerning the distribution of unsolicited bulk e-mail. In February 1999 Nexx informed the plaintiff that unsolicited bulk e-mail was not permitted, and that continuation with such activity could lead to the termination of service. The plaintiffs then retained a third party to send the bulk e-mail on their behalf. Beginning March 31, 1999, 1267623 through a third party service provider in California began sending out unsolicited bulk commercial e-mail at the rate of 200,000 per day in an attempt to promote their products and encourage potential customers to visit their website. The bulk e-mail was sent randomly to any Internet users. Nexx clients were not specifically targeted, but some Nexx clients on a random basis were receiving the unsolicited e-mail.

---

† [1999] O.J. No. 2246 (Ont. Sup. Ct.).

On April 5, 1999, Nexx deactivated the company's web page as a result of the plaintiff's alleged breach of Contract which included a breach of Netiquette.

The plaintiffs claim that the deactivation by Nexx was a breach of the Contract. They further assert that their entire business is Internet-dependant, and that a mandatory order is required pending the outcome of the litigation to prevent 1267623 from going out of business.

Nexx argues that it was in fact the plaintiffs who breached the Contract and the established rules of Netiquette by sending out junk e-mail or "spam". This activity was endangering Nexx's business, both by irritating its other clients, who began complaining, and by explicitly, violating Nexx's agreement with Exodus Communications Inc. (Exodus), the service provider that provides Nexx with its connection to the Internet.

The Terms of the Contract

The plaintiffs allege that Nexx is in breach of the Contract for having disconnected the beaverhome.com website, several months prior to the expiry of the service agreement between the parties. The full yearly fee of $352.51 had been paid in advance by the plaintiffs.

There is a factual dispute as to what was specifically discussed with respect to bulk e-mail prior to the Contract being executed. The plaintiffs claim to have been told by Nexx before signing the Contract that there were no provisions prohibiting the sending of bulk commercial e-mail. In sharp contrast, the president of Nexx states:

> Prior to entering into this agreement [the Contract], Damir Zovic, the principal of Codes, specifically discussed with me the proposed distribution of unsolicited commercial e-mail, also known in the industry as "junk mail" or "Spam". The distribution of such e-mail, usually distributed completely at random and without regard for whether the recipient has any interest in receiving the e-mail, is considered a breach of the code of conduct, or rules of etiquette known as "Netiquette", governing the use of the Internet/World Wide Web system. I specifically informed Mr. Zoric in August of 1998 that Nexx Online did not, and would not, permit the distribution of unsolicited commercial e-mail on or through its system.

Although several contractual issues were argued, in my view, there are two relevant provisions of the Contract:

> The Account Holder agrees to follow generally accepted "Netiquette" when sending e-mail messages or posting newsgroup messages ... The undersigned Account Holder agrees to abide by the following provisions of this service contract and may have to agree to additional provisions from Nexx Online covering this agreement and/or any future services added to this agreement. If Account Holder refuses to accept any future provisions, Account Holder will have the option to cancel service and receive a pro-rated refund of any moneys pre-paid for this agreement. The pro-rated refund will be calculated after the normal monthly cost for the service has been deducted from any amounts pre-paid by Account Holder.

Does Unsolicited Bulk E-Mail Offend the Rules of "Netiquette"

The governing Contract does not specifically forbid bulk e-mail advertising. It does provide, however, that the "Account Holder agrees to follow generally accepted 'Netiquette' when sending e-mail messages or posting newsgroup messages ...". It is the position of the defendant that sending out unsolicited bulk e-mail is in breach of established rules of Netiquette, and hence the defendants were entitled to disconnect the plaintiffs' website services without a pro-rata reimbursement of the prepaid balance of the Contract. The plaintiffs argue the sending out bulk e-mail through a third party is not a breach of "Netiquette".

What then are the rules of Netiquette? It is acknowledged that there is no written Netiquette policy. It appears that a code is evolving based upon good neighbour principles for the orderly development of the Internet, and to prevent potential Internet abuse.

The defendant has provided copies of reports on bulk e-mail advertising that lead to the inevitable conclusion that the sending of unsolicited bulk commercial e-mail is considered an inappropriate and unacceptable use of the Internet by most users and service providers. Few if any Internet service providers allow unsolicited bulk e-mail. In the United States several states have prohibited the practice or severely restricted its use. John Levine, author of The Internet for Dummies, has posted a paper entitled "Why is Spam Bad?" at http://spam.abuse.net/spambad.html, in which he summarizes six important problems with spam advertising and why it is considered unacceptable:

1) the recipient pays far more, in time and trouble as well as money, than the sender does, unlike advertising through the postal service;
2) the recipient must take the time to request removal from the mailing list, and most spammers claim to remove names on request but rarely do so;
3) many spammers use intermediate systems without authorization to avoid blocks set up to avoid spam;
4) many spam messages are deceptive and partially or entirely fraudulent;
5) spammers often use false return addresses to avoid the cost of receiving responses;
6) some forms of spam are illegal in various jurisdictions in the United States.

The complaints received by the defendant were included in the motion material. There is a consistent flavour to the responses. The complaints received by Nexx regarding the plaintiffs' unsolicited advertising e-mail were often intense and to the point of outrage. This negative public response from internet users is an indication that unsolicited commercial bulk e-mail advertising is not an accepted internet practice. Some of the complaints also pointed out apparently forged return addresses and e-mail headers on e-mail sent out by the plaintiffs: one had the return address "catholic.org", implying the existence of a religious affiliation, but was advertising the beaverhome.com website.

Caselaw Relevant to the Issue of "Netiquette"

Not surprisingly, there are no Canadian cases on point defining rules of "netiquette" or with respect to unsolicited bulk e-mail. However, several American cases have dealt with disputes over unsolicited bulk e-mail. None are factually similar to this case. The issue of "netiquette" was not an issue specifically discussed in the decisions. However, principles relevant to use of the internet are discussed and are helpful.

An important case is *Cyber Promotions Inc.* v. *American Online Inc.* The District Court held that the right to freedom of expression under the First Amendment did not give the defendant the right to send unsolicited bulk e-mail over the internet to subscribers of a private online company. Weiner J. confirms the paucity of rules with respect to internet use at p. 1:

... while the Internet provides the opportunity to disseminate vast amounts of information, the Internet does not, at least at the present time, have any means to police the dissemination of that information.

Cyber Promotions Inc. v. *American Online Inc.* was followed in *CompuServe Inc.* v. *Cyber Promotions Inc.* Again, the defendant, Cyber Promotions Inc., tried to use the First Amendment as a defence to an action for trespass to personal property. The plaintiff, CompuServe, was a company that provided Internet access to subscribers for a fee. The defendant was an advertising agency that used bulk e-mail as its method of promoting its clients. The action arose because the defendant sent unsolicited bulk e-mails to the plaintiff's subscribers, and continued to do so, even after the plaintiff demanded the defendant terminate its practice. The court granted an injunction prohibiting the defendant from sending bulk unsolicited e-mails to the plaintiff's subscribers.

In *CompuServe Inc.* v. *Cyber Promotions Inc.*, the court concluded that the practice of sending unsolicited e-mails to the plaintiff's subscribers was an unwanted intrusion into the plaintiff's computer systems. The court found that the defendant's practice commanded the disk space and processing power of the plaintiff's computer equipment, diverting its resources away from paying subscribers. The value of the equipment was thereby diminished, even though it was not physically damaged. The court also found the defendant's practice to be harmful to the plaintiff's business reputation and goodwill. Since subscribers paid according to the amount of time they accessed the Internet, the cost of processing and deleting the e-mails fell on them. As a result, subscribers threatened to discontinue their accounts. Some actually did terminate their accounts. The court held that the public interest was advanced by granting the injunction. The high volumes of e-mail slowed down data transfer between computers connected to the Internet and congested the electronic paths through which they travel. As well, bulk e-mails caused recipients to spend time and money processing unwanted messages.

In another case concerning trespass and bulk e-mailing, *Parker* v. *C.N. Enterprises*, the court found that the unauthorized use of Ms. Parker's e-mail address constituted common law nuisance and trespass and granted a permanent injunction against the defendants, C.N. Enterprises.

A relevant but distinguishable case is *Cyber Promotions, Inc.* v. *Apex Global Information Services, Inc.* The plaintiff, Cyber Promotions, was also seeking a preliminary injunction directing the defendant, Apex Global Information Services, to restore the plaintiff's Internet access for 30 days. The defendant terminated the plaintiff's connection to the Internet without notice due to technical problems known as "pinging". The governing contract between the parties acknowledged that the plaintiff Cyber was in the business of sending unsolicited bulk e-mails. It also provided for a minimum period on 30 days notice before termination of internet services. The defendant provided internet services to various promoters of unsolicited bulk e-mail. The court granted the injunction on the basis that the plaintiff had a valid claim for breach of contract, and that it would be irreparably harmed by a failure to grant the injunction. The public interest lay in insuring that parties live up to their legal contracts. The court does comment, on the unpopularity of commercial bulk e-mail.

> ... it is undisputed that Cyber's business of sending unsolicited bulk e-mail is a controversial one. Many computer users find the receipt of bulk e-mail annoying and intrusive.

The Internet is a potent legitimate means of advertising, selling on the Internet benefiting retailers and consumers alike. The use of the internet is in its relative infancy. In the words of counsel, it is "an unruly beast". Or so it will certainly become without a foundation of good neighbour commercial principles. The unrestricted use of unsolicited bulk commercial e-mail appears to undermine the integrity and utility of the Internet system. Network systems become blocked. The user expends time and expense reviewing or deleting unwanted messages. Of fundamental importance is the distortion of the essentially personal nature of an e-mail address.

I conclude after reviewing the principles that emerge in the American caselaw, the excerpts from the literature provided, and the reaction of individual internet users that unless a service provider specifically allows in the contract for unsolicited commercial bulk e-mail to be distributed, it appears clear that sending out unsolicited bulk e-mail for commercial advertising purposes is contrary to the emerging principles of "Netiquette". This conclusion is further reinforced by the admission by the plaintiff that they are unable to find another service provider which will permit bulk e-mail advertising through a third party.

Nexx's Right to Add Provisions to the Contract

Although the Contract does not include a specific provision against bulk commercial e-mail, it does permit Nexx to add terms to the Contract with the requirement to reimburse for the balance owing under the Contract if the client is not in agreement with the new term. There is no dispute between the parties that Nexx informed the plaintiffs that they were not permitted to send bulk e-mail advertising prior to terminating their website. By the terms, of the Contract, the defendants were entitled to add a term to the Contract prohibiting unsolicited commercial bulk e-mail, upon payment of the prorated balance of the fees that were prepaid for the one year term of the Contract.

The Contract between Nexx and Exodus

The contract between the defendant Nexx and Exodus, Nexx's service provider is relevant in assessing irreparable harm and the balance of convenience as between the parties. The Nexx/Exodus contract specifically precludes the sending of unsolicited bulk advertising e-mail. The contract includes an "Online Conduct Policy", which begins:

> Customer [here, Nexx] will not, and will not permit any persons using Customer's online facilities (including but not limited to Customer's Web site(s) and transmission capabilities), to do any of the following:
>
> * Send Spam (unsolicited commercial messages or communications in any form).

The Nexx/Exodus contract also includes a clear "Anti-Spamming Policy Statement here reproduced in full:

> As a provider of Internet network services and management, Exodus considers it an obligation to put an end to Spam. We respect your need for efficient, cost-effective and interruption-free services, and we pride ourselves on offering you one of the most scaleable, reliable and redundant networks available today. Exodus is committed to a Zero-tolerance, anti-Spamming policy. Under this policy, we protect you and your customers by prohibiting Spam, or any, unsolicited commercial e-mail, from being sent either:

- Over the Exodus network, by customers or any other users of the Exodus network (including customers' customers); AND/OR
- Over ANY network B if the message sent advertises or mentions a site hosted on the Exodus network.

    We react quickly and seriously to violations, and we further reserve the right to terminate the network services of any customer willfully disregarding this policy.

    If you have any complaints or comments regarding Spam on our network, please direct them via e-mail to abuse@exodus.net.

At the time of disconnection, the plaintiffs did not send out bulk commercial e-mail from their website hosted by Nexx. Rather they did so through a separate company not a party to this action. The bulk commercial e-mail did direct recipients to the beaverhome.com website hosted by Nexx, which is in turn hosted by Exodus. Clearly retaining a third party to send the bulk e-mail is in contravention of the anti-spamming policy enunciated in the Nexx/Exodus contract.

Both Nexx and Exodus received multiple complaints about the unsolicited bulk e-mails received from the plaintiff company. Exodus warned Nexx that the unsolicited bulk e-mail was prohibited by their Anti-Spamming Policy. Exodus warned Nexx that the Nexx/Exodus contract would be enforced if Nexx did not take timely action to prevent another such occurrence. It is clear that if the injunction requested is granted, Nexx will be in breach of the terms of the Nexx/Exodus contract creating serious business risk including potential termination of services.

Conclusions

In addressing the questions with respect to the granting of an injunction I conclude as follows:

1) Is there a serious question to be tried?

For the reasons previously given, I conclude that there is no serious question to be tried. Firstly, I conclude that sending unsolicited bulk commercial e-mail is in breach of the emerging principles of Netiquette, unless it is specifically permitted in the governing contract. As the rules of Netiquette govern the parties' Contract, the plaintiff is in breach of its terms justifying disconnection of service. Secondly, in the alternative, Nexx is permitted to add terms to the Contract precluding a Nexx client sending unsolicited bulk e-mail directly, or through a third party. If the plaintiffs do not concur with the new term, they are entitled to a rebate of the pro-rated balance of the Contract price, and the defendant is entitled to disconnect service. The defendant has agreed to repay the prorated balance owing under the Contract from April 5, 1999 to August 5, 1999.

Postscript

Notwithstanding their claim that they could not find an alternate ISP, Beaverhome.com did find another ISP and was online as of July 2000.

Discussion Questions

1. Does the use of "netiquette" as a legal standard create any problems? Could the judge have reached the same result without relying on the netiquette analysis?

2. Although Beaverhome.com did not spam directly through Nexx Online (following an initial warning), the judge still found that they violated their user agreement and thus breached their contract. Do you agree with this interpretation of the facts?

This case marked the second spam case faced by the Ontario courts in 1999. Earlier that year, an Ontario court ruled in favour of I.D. Internet Direct Ltd., a local ISP, in their legal battle against spammer, Corey Altelaar ([1999] O.J. No. 1804 (Ont. Sup. Ct.)). The court granted the ISP's motion for a restraint against Altelaar for further spamming, since the court agreed that Altelaar was in breach of the terms of his email use agreement with the provider

TRADEMARK LAW

AOL v. CN Productions, Inc.[†]

Findings Of Fact

America Online's (AOL) Business
In connection with its products and online services, AOL has used the initials "AOL" as a trademark and as a service mark since October 1989. AOL has registered this mark with the United States Patent and Trademark Office and has invested substantial resources to promote and protect its products and services using this mark. AOL has also registered its mark with the InterNIC as part of its registration of the "aol.com" Internet domain name. AOL uses the domain name "aol.com" as a source identifier of its online services.

Defendants' Business
Defendants Jay Nelson and CN Productions, Inc. ("'CN Productions") own and operate Internet web sites, registered with InterNIC, at which they make available, for a fee, a variety of adult entertainment products and services.

Defendants' Transmission of UBE to AOL Members
Defendants have repeatedly and knowingly transmitted unsolicited bulk e-mail [UBE] messages advertising their products and services through AOL's mail servers to AOL Meters. These UBE advertisements contain embedded hyper-text links that, when clicked upon, cause a viewer to be taken to one of Defendants' web sites.

Defendants have repeatedly and knowingly transmitted UBE containing false information regarding the source, transmission path and subject of the message in order to evade AOL's bulk e-mail filtering system. Defendants used "aol.com" in the "to," "from" and "reply to" lines, placed invalid user names in the "from" and "reply to" lines (such as "XmasSantaX"), used non-existent domain names (such as "blahblahblah.com"), inserted false transmission dates, relayed their messages through

---

† Civil Action No.: 98-552-A (E.D. Va. 1998).

third party Internet Service Providers (such as dialsprint.net), and identified the subject of their messages with greetings that did not reflect the nature of their messages (such as "Happy Holidays!").

Defendants' use of the aol.com domain name caused AOL Members to believe that AOL was connected to, affiliated with, approved of, or condoned Defendants' transmission or the adult entertainment products and services advertised in their messages. AOL Members forwarded Defendants' advertisements to TOSSpam, with the following complaints attached:

> Lovely Crap from Santa, who apparently has become a degenerate thanks to AMERICA ONLINE!!!!!

> I would think you could at least track down the sender who is a member of AOL who is using a Santa name to forward this smut through your system.

> More smut in my account and this is from an AOL address. Now you HAVE to be able to stop this one, don't you?

> Unless you guys can figure a way to block this type of stuff from an aol.com site I will be forced to cancel my membership.

> WHY DO YOU LET THESE PERVERTS USE AOL? WHY DO PEOPLE LIKE THIS EVEN HAVE AN ACCOUNT WITH YOUR COMPANY? HAVE YOU NO DECENCY??????????? I DO NOT WANT ANYMORE OF THIS JUNK IN MY PERSONAL MAILBOX. IF THIS CRAP CONTINUES, I WILL CANCEL MY AOL ACCOUNT SOON — I DON'T EVEN RECEIVE SEXUALLY EXPLICIT MAIL IN MY POSTAL MAILBOX. WHY SHOULD I PUT UP WITH IT HERE?????????

Defendants knew their transmission of UBE to AOL Members was not authorized by AOL, and was prohibited by AOL's Terms of Service and UBE Policy. On December 8, 1997, AOL notified Defendants Jay Nelson and CN Productions that they, along with their agents, were prohibited from transmitting UBE to AOL and its Members. After this date, Defendants continued to transmit unsolicited e-mail advertisements to AOL and its Members, and continued to use aol.com in the "from" and "reply to" lines.

A reasonable calculation of the total number of unsolicited bulk e-mail messages transmitted by Defendants to AOL and its Members between June 26, 1997 and April 18, 1998 is in excess of 212 million (717,608 messages per day multiplied by 297 days).

Between early December 1998 and January 4, 1999, TOSSpam has received over 190,000 Member complaints regarding e-mail messages that contain hypertext links that lead to web sites owned and maintained by the Defendants.

Order

It is hereby

ORDERED that the defendants, CN Productions, Inc. and Jay Nelson, their agents, assignees and those in privity with them, are enjoined from directly or indirectly engaging in any of the following activities:

(1) using any images, designs, logos or marks which copy, imitate or simulate any trade or service mark of America Online, Inc. (AOL) for any purpose, and/or using "aol" in any Internet domain name or any Internet Web site for any purpose, including but not limited to any advertisement, promotion, sale or use of any products or services;

(2) performing any action or using any images, designs, logos or marks that are likely to cause confusion, to cause mistake, to deceive, or to otherwise mislead the trade or public into believing that AOL and Defendants, or any of them, are in any way connected, or that AOL sponsors Defendants; or that Defendants, or any of them, are in any manner affiliated or associated with or under the supervision or control of AOL, or that Defendants and AOL or AOL's services are associated in any way;

(3) using any images, designs, logos or marks or engaging in any other conduct that creates a likelihood of injury to the business reputation of AOL or a likelihood of misappropriation and/or dilution of AOL's distinctive marks and the goodwill associated therewith;

(4) sending or transmitting to any destination, or directing, aiding, or conspiring with others. to send or transmit to any destination, electronic mail or electronic communication bearing any false, fraudulent, anonymous, inactive, deceptive, or invalid return information, or containing the domain "aol.com," or otherwise using any other artifice, scheme or method of transmission that would prevent the automatic return of undeliverable electronic mail to its original and true point of origin or that would cause the e-mail return address to be that of anyone other than the actual sender;

(5) using, or directing, aiding, or conspiring with others to use AOL's computers or computer networks in any manner, directly or indirectly, in connection with the transmission or transfer of any form of electronic information across the Internet;

(6) opening, creating, obtaining access to, and/or using in any way, or directing, aiding, or conspiring with others to open, create, obtain access to, and/or use in any way, any AOL membership or account;

(7) acquiring, compiling or transferring AOL member email addresses or email addresses that contain "aol" in the domain; and,

(8) sending or transmitting, or directing, aiding, facilitating or conspiring with others to send or transmit, any electronic mail message, or any electronic communication of any kind, to or through AOL or its members.

PROPERTY LAW

CompuServe Incorporated v. Cyber Promotions, Inc.[†]

This case presents novel issues regarding the commercial use of the Internet, specifically the right of an online computer service to prevent a commercial enterprise from sending unsolicited electronic mail advertising to its subscribers.

Plaintiff CompuServe Incorporated ("CompuServe") is one of the major national commercial online computer services. This allows its subscribers to send and receive electronic messages, known as "e-mail," by the Internet. Defendants Cyber Promotions, Inc. and its president Sanford Wallace are in the business of sending unsolicited e-mail advertisements on behalf of themselves and their clients to hun-

---

† 962 F. Supp. 1015 (S.D. Ohio 1997).

dreds of thousands of Internet users, many of whom are CompuServe subscribers. CompuServe has notified defendants that they are prohibited from using its computer equipment to process and store the unsolicited e-mail and has requested that they terminate the practice. Instead, defendants have sent an increasing volume of e-mail solicitations to CompuServe subscribers. CompuServe has attempted to employ technological means to block the flow of defendants' e-mail transmissions to its computer equipment, but to no avail.

This matter is before the Court on the application of CompuServe for a preliminary injunction which would extend the duration of the temporary restraining order issued by this Court on October 24, 1996 and which would extend and in addition prevent defendants from sending unsolicited advertisements to CompuServe subscribers.

For the reasons which follow, this Court holds that where defendants engaged in a course of conduct of transmitting a substantial volume of electronic data in the form of unsolicited e-mail to plaintiff's proprietary computer equipment, where defendants continued such practice after repeated demands to cease and desist, and where defendants deliberately evaded plaintiff's affirmative efforts to protect its computer equipment from such use, plaintiff has a viable claim for trespass to personal property and is entitled to injunctive relief to protect its property.

I.

In an effort to shield its equipment from defendants' bulk e-mail, CompuServe has implemented software programs designed to screen out the messages and block their receipt. In response, defendants have modified their equipment and the messages they send in such a fashion as to circumvent CompuServe's screening software. Allegedly, defendants have been able to conceal the true origin of their messages by falsifying the point-of-origin information contained in the header of the electronic messages. Defendants have removed the "sender" information in the header of their messages and replaced it with another address. Also, defendants have developed the capability of configuring their computer servers to conceal their true domain name and appear on the Internet as another computer, further concealing the true origin of the messages. By manipulating this data, defendants have been able to continue sending messages to CompuServe's equipment in spite of CompuServe's protests and protective efforts.

Defendants assert that they possess the right to continue to send these communications to CompuServe subscribers. CompuServe contends that, in doing so, the defendants are trespassing upon its personal property.

. . . .

IV.

This Court will now address the second aspect of plaintiff's motion in which it seeks to enjoin defendants Cyber Promotions, Inc. and its president Sanford Wallace from sending any unsolicited advertisements to any electronic mail address maintained by CompuServe.

CompuServe predicates this aspect of its motion for a preliminary injunction on the common law theory of trespass to personal property or to chattels, asserting that defendants' continued transmission of electronic messages to its computer equipment constitutes an actionable tort.

Trespass to chattels has evolved from its original common law application, concerning primarily the asportation of another's tangible property, to include the unauthorized use of personal property:

> Its chief importance now, is that there may be recovery ... for interferences with the possession of chattels which are not sufficiently important to be classed as conversion, and so to compel the defendant to pay the full value of the thing with which he has interfered. Trespass to chattels survives today, in other words, largely as a little brother of conversion.
>
> Prosser & Keeton, Prosser and Keeton on Torts, (1984).

The scope of an action for conversion recognized in Ohio may embrace the facts in the instant case. The Supreme Court of Ohio established the definition of conversion under Ohio law in *Baltimore & O. R. Co.* v. *O'Donnell*, (1892) by stating that:

> In order to constitute a conversion, it was not necessary that there should have been an actual appropriation of the property by the defendant to its own use and benefit. It might arise from the exercise of a dominion over it in exclusion of the rights of the owner, or withholding it from his possession under a claim inconsistent with his rights. If one take the property of another, for a temporary purpose only, in disregard of the owner's right, it is a conversion. Either a wrongful taking, an assumption of ownership, an illegal use or misuse, or a wrongful detention of chattels will constitute a conversion.

Both plaintiff and defendants cite the Restatement (Second) of Torts to support their respective positions. In determining a question unanswered by state law, it is appropriate for this Court to consider such sources as the restatement of the law and decisions of other jurisdictions.

The Restatement §217(b) states that a trespass to chattel may be committed by intentionally using or intermeddling with the chattel in possession of another. Restatement §217, Comment e defines physical "intermeddling" as follows:

> ... intentionally bringing about a physical contact with the chattel. The actor may commit a trespass by an act which brings him into an intended physical contact with a chattel in the possession of another[.]

Electronic signals generated and sent by computer have been held to be sufficiently physically tangible to support a trespass cause of action. *State* v. *McGraw*, (Ind. 1985) (Indiana Supreme Court recognizing in dicta that a hacker's unauthorized access to a computer was more in the nature of trespass than criminal conversion); and *State* v. *Riley*, (1993) (computer hacking as the criminal offense of "computer trespass" under Washington law). It is undisputed that plaintiff has a possessory interest in its computer systems. Further, defendants' contact with plaintiff's computers is clearly intentional. Although electronic messages may travel through the Internet over various routes, the messages are affirmatively directed to their destination.

Defendants, citing Restatement (Second) of Torts §221, which defines "dispossession", assert that not every interference with the personal property of another is actionable and that physical dispossession or substantial interference with the chattel is required. Defendants then argue that they did not, in this case, physically dispossess plaintiff of its equipment or substantially interfere with it. However, the Restatement (Second) of Torts §218 defines the circumstances under which a trespass to chattels may be actionable:

> One who commits a trespass to a chattel is subject to liability to the possessor of the chattel if, but only if,
>
>   (a)   he dispossesses the other of the chattel, or
>
>   (b)   the chattel is impaired as to its condition, quality, or value, or
>
>   (c)   the possessor is deprived of the use of the chattel for a substantial time, or
>
>   (d)   bodily harm is caused to the possessor, or harm is caused to some person or thing in which the possessor has a legally protected interest.

Therefore, an interference resulting in physical dispossession is just one circumstance under which a defendant can be found liable.

A plaintiff can sustain an action for trespass to chattels, as opposed to an action for conversion, without showing a substantial interference with its right to possession of that chattel. Harm to the personal property or diminution of its quality, condition, or value as a result of defendants' use can also be the predicate for liability. Restatement §218(b).

An unprivileged use or other intermeddling with a chattel which results in actual impairment of its physical condition, quality or value to the possessor makes the actor liable for the loss thus caused. In the great majority of cases, the actor's intermeddling with the chattel impairs the value of it to the possessor, as distinguished from the mere affront to his dignity as possessor, only by some impairment of the physical condition of the chattel. There may, however, be situations in which the value to the owner of a particular type of chattel may be impaired by dealing with it in a manner that does not affect its physical condition.... In such a case, the intermeddling is actionable even though the physical condition of the chattel is not impaired.

In the present case, any value CompuServe realizes from its computer equipment is wholly derived from the extent to which that equipment can serve its subscriber base. Michael Mangino, a software developer for CompuServe who monitors its mail processing computer equipment, states by affidavit that handling the enormous volume of mass mailings that CompuServe receives places a tremendous burden on its equipment. Defendants' more recent practice of evading CompuServe's filters by disguising the origin of their messages commandeers even more computer resources because Compuserve's computers are forced to store undeliverable e-mail messages and labor in vain to return the messages to an address that does not exist. To the extent that defendants' multitudinous electronic mailings demand the disk space and drain the processing power of plaintiff's computer equipment, those resources are not available to serve CompuServe subscribers. Therefore, the value of that equipment to CompuServe is diminished even though it is not physically damaged by defendants' conduct.

Next, plaintiff asserts that it has suffered injury aside from the physical impact of defendants' messages on its equipment. Restatement §218(d) also indicates that recovery may be had for a trespass that causes harm to something in which the possessor has a legally protected interest. Plaintiff asserts that defendants' messages are largely unwanted by its subscribers, who pay incrementally to access their e-mail, read it, and discard it. Also, the receipt of a bundle of unsolicited messages at once can require the subscriber to sift through, at his expense, all of the messages in order to find the ones he wanted or expected to receive. These inconveniences decrease the utility of CompuServe's e-mail service and are the foremost subject in recent complaints from CompuServe subscribers.

Many subscribers have terminated their accounts specifically because of the unwanted receipt of bulk e-mail messages. Defendants' intrusions into CompuServe's computer systems, insofar as they harm plaintiff's business reputation and goodwill with its customers, are actionable under Restatement §218(d).

Defendants argue that plaintiff made the business decision to connect to the Internet and that therefore it cannot now successfully maintain an action for trespass to chattels. Their argument is analogous to the argument that because an establishment invites the public to enter its property for business purposes, it cannot later restrict or revoke access to that property, a proposition which is erroneous under Ohio law.

Further, CompuServe expressly limits the consent it grants to Internet users to send e-mail to its proprietary computer system by denying unauthorized parties the use of CompuServe equipment to send unsolicited electronic mail messages. This policy statement, posted by CompuServe online, states as follows:

> CompuServe is a private online and communications services company. CompuServe does not permit its facilities to be used by unauthorized parties to process and store unsolicited e-mail. If an unauthorized party attempts to send unsolicited messages to e-mail addresses on a CompuServe service, CompuServe will take appropriate action to attempt to prevent those messages from being processed by CompuServe. Violations of CompuServe's policy prohibiting unsolicited e-mail should be reported to....

Defendants Cyber Promotions, Inc. and its president Sanford Wallace have used plaintiff's equipment in a fashion that exceeds that consent. The use of personal property exceeding consent is a trespass. It is arguable that CompuServe's policy statement, insofar as it may serve as a limitation upon the scope of its consent to the use of its computer equipment, may be insufficiently communicated to potential third-party users when it is merely posted at some location on the network. However in the present case the record indicates that defendants were actually notified that they were using CompuServe's equipment in an unacceptable manner. To prove that a would-be trespasser acted with the intent required to support liability in tort it is crucial that defendant be placed on notice that he is trespassing.

CRIMINAL LAW

Canada Criminal Code[†]

(1) Every one who, fraudulently and without colour of right,

(a) obtains, directly or indirectly, any computer service
(b) by means of an electro-magnetic, acoustic, mechanical or other device, intercepts or causes to be intercepted, directly or indirectly, a function of a computer system

---

† R.S., c. C-34, s. 342.1

(c) uses or causes to be used, directly or indirectly, a computer system with intent to commit an offence under paragraph (a) or (b) or an offence under section 430 in relation to data or a computer system, or

(d) uses, possesses, traffics in or permits another person to have access to a computer password that would enable a person to commit an offence under paragraph (a), (b) or (c)

is guilty of an indictable offence and liable for imprisonment for a term not exceeding ten years, or is guilty of an offence punishable on summary conviction.

(2) In this section,

"computer password" means any data by which a computer service or computer system is capable of being obtained or used;

"computer program" means data representing instructions or statements that, when executed in a computer system, causes the computer system to perform a function;

"computer service" includes data processing and the storage or retrieval of data;

"computer system" means a device that, or a group of interconnected or related devices one or more of which,

(a) contains computer programs or other data, and
(b) pursuant to computer programs,
    (i) performs logic and control, and
    (ii) may perform any other function;

"data" means representations of information or of concepts that are being prepared or have been prepared in a form suitable for use in a computer system;

"electro-magnetic, acoustic, mechanical or other device" means any device or apparatus that is used or is capable of being used to intercept any function of a computer system, but does not include a hearing aid used to correct subnormal hearing of the user to not better than normal hearing;

"function" includes logic, control, arithmetic, deletion, storage and retrieval and communication or telecommunication to, from or within a computer system;

"intercept" includes listen to or record a function of a computer system, or acquire the substance, meaning or purport thereof. R.S.C. 1985, c.27 (1st Supp.), s.45.

"traffic" means, in respect of a computer password, to traffic, sell, export from or import into Canada, distribute or deal in any other way. R.S.C. 1985, c.27 (1st Supp), s.45; 1997, c.18, s.18.

AOL v. LCGM, Inc.[†]

AOL, an Internet service provider located in the Eastern District of Virginia, provides a proprietary, content-based online service that provides its members (AOL members) access to the Internet and the capability to receive as well as send e-mail messages. AOL registered "AOL" as a trademark and service mark in 1996 and has registered its domain name "aol.com" with the InterNIC. At the time this cause of

---

† 46 F. Supp. 2d 444 (E.D. Va. 1998).

action arose, defendant LCGM, Inc. was a Michigan corporation which operated and transacted business from Internet domains offering pornographic web sites. Plaintiff alleges that defendant Web Promo is a d/b/a designation for FSJD, Inc., a Michigan corporation that operates Internet domains offering pornographic web sites. Defendant Francis Sharrak was the vice-president of Web Promo and the sole shareholder and president of LCGM. Defendant James Drakos was the president of Web Promo. Defendants Francis Sharrak and James Drakos have participated in the transmission of the bulk e-mails.

AOL alleges that defendants, in concert, sent unauthorized and unsolicited bulk e-mail advertisements ("spam") to AOL customers. AOL's Unsolicited Bulk E-mail Policy and its Terms of Service bar both members and nonmembers from sending bulk e-mail through AOL's computer systems. Plaintiff estimates that defendants, in concert with their "site partners," transmitted more than 92 million unsolicited and bulk e-mail messages advertising their pornographic Web sites to AOL members from approximately June 17, 1997 to January 21, 1998. Plaintiff bases this number on defendants' admissions that they sent approximately 300,000 e-mail messages a day at various intervals from their Michigan offices. Plaintiff asserts that defendants provided AOL with computer disks containing a list of the addresses of 820,296 AOL members to whom defendants admitted to transmitting bulk e-mail.

Plaintiff alleges that defendants harvested, or collected, the e-mail addresses of AOL members in violation of AOL's Terms of Service. Defendants have admitted to maintaining AOL memberships to harvest or collect the e-mail addresses of other AOL members.

Defendants have admitted to maintaining AOL accounts and to using the AOL Collector and E-mail Pro/Stealth Mailer extractor programs to collect the e-mail addresses of AOL members, alleging that they did so in targeted adult AOL chat rooms. Defendants have admitted to using this software to evade AOL's filtering mechanisms.

Plaintiff alleges that defendants forged the domain information "aol.com" in the "from" line of e-mail messages sent to AOL members. Defendants have admitted to creating the domain information "aol.com" through an e-mail sending program, and to causing the AOL domain to appear in electronic header information of its commercial e-mails.

Plaintiffs assert that as a result, many AOL members expressed confusion about whether AOL endorsed defendants' pornographic Web sites or their bulk e-mailing practices. Plaintiff also asserts that defendants e-mail messages were sent through AOL's computer networks. Defendants have admitted to sending e-mail messages from their computers through defendants' network via e-mail software to AOL, which then relayed the messages to AOL members.

Plaintiff alleges that AOL sent defendants two cease and desist letters, dated respectively December 8, 1997 and December 30, 1997, but that defendants continued their e-mailing practices to AOL members after receiving those letters. Defendants have admitted to receiving those letters, contending that any e-mails sent after such receipt were "lawful."

Plaintiff alleges that defendants paid their "site partners" to transmit unsolicited bulk e-mail on their behalf and encouraged these site partners to advertise. Plaintiff further alleges that defendants conspired with CN Productions, another pornographic e-mailer, to transmit bulk e-mails to AOL members. Plaintiff alleges that many e-mails sent by defendants contained Hyper-Text Links both to defendants' web sites and CN Production's web sites.

Plaintiff alleges that defendants' actions injured AOL by consuming capacity on AOL's computers, causing AOL to incur technical costs, impairing the functioning of AOL's e-mail system, forcing AOL to upgrade its computer networks to process authorized e-mails in a timely manner, damaging AOL's goodwill with its members, and causing AOL to lose customers and revenue. Plaintiff asserts that between the months of December 1997 and April 1998, defendants' unsolicited bulk e-mails generated more than 450,000 complaints by AOL members.

Count I: False Designation of Origin Under the Lanham Act
The undisputed facts establish that defendants violated 15 U.S.C. §1l25(a)(1) of the Lanham Act, which makes it unlawful to use in commerce:

> any false designation of origin ... which ... is likely to cause confusion, or to cause mistake, or to deceive as to the affiliation, connection, or association of such person with another person, or as to the origin, sponsorship, or approval of his or her goods, services, or commercial activities by another person.

The unauthorized sending of bulk a-mails has been held to constitute a violation of this section of the Lanham Act. The elements necessary to establish a false designation violation under the Lanham Act are as follows:

> (1) a defendant uses a designation; (2) in interstate commerce; (3) in connection with goods and services; (4) which designation is likely to cause confusion, mistake or deception as to origin, sponsorship, or approval of defendant's goods or services; and (5) plaintiff has been or is likely to be damaged by these acts.

Each of the false designation elements has been satisfied. First, defendants clearly used the "aol.com" designation, incorporating the registered trademark and service mark AOL in their e-mail headers. Second, defendants' activities involved interstate commerce because all e-mails sent to AOL members were routed from defendants' computers in Michigan through AOL's computers in Virginia. Third, the use of AOL's designation was in connection with goods and services as defendants' e-mails advertised their commercial web sites. Fourth, the use of "aol.com" in defendants' e-mails was likely to cause confusion as to the origin and sponsorship of defendants' goods and services. Any e-mail recipient could logically conclude that a message containing the initials "aol.com" in the header would originate from AOL's registered Internet domain, which incorporates the registered mark "AOL." The recipient of such a message would be led to conclude the sender was an AOL member or AOL, the Internet Service Provider. Indeed, plaintiff alleges that this designation did cause such confusion among many AOL members, who believed that AOL sponsored and authorized defendants' bulk e-mailing practices and pornographic web sites.

Finally, plaintiff asserts that these acts damaged AOL's technical capabilities and its goodwill. The defendants are precluded from opposing these claims due to their failure to comply with discovery orders. Therefore, there is no genuine issue of material fact in regards to this Count, and the Court holds the plaintiff is entitled to summary judgment on Count I.

Count III: Exceeding Authorized Access in Violation of the Computer Fraud and Abuse Act

The facts before the Court establish that defendants violated 18 U.S.C. §1030(a) (2)(c) of the Computer Fraud and Abuse Act, which prohibits individuals from "intentionally access[ing] a computer without authorization or exceed[ing] authorized access, and thereby obtain[ing] information from any protected computer if the conduct involved an interstate or foreign communication." Defendants' own admissions satisfy the Act's requirements. Defendants have admitted to maintaining an AOL membership and using that membership to harvest the e-mail addresses of AOL members. Defendants have stated that they acquired these e-mail addresses by using extractor software programs. Defendants' actions violated AOL's Terms of Service, and as such was unauthorized. Plaintiff contends that the addresses of AOL members are "information" within the meaning of the Act because they are proprietary in nature. Plaintiff asserts that as a result of defendants' actions, it suffered damages exceeding $5,000, the statutory threshold requirement.

Count IV: Impairing Computer Facilities In Violation of the Computer Fraud and Abuse Act

The undisputed facts establish that defendants violated 18 U.S.C. §1030(a) (5)(C) of the Computer Fraud and Abuse Act, which prohibits anyone from "intentionally access[ing] a protected computer without authorization, and as a result of such conduct, causes damage." Another court found that spamming was an actionable claim under this Act. Defendants have admitted to utilizing software to collect AOL members' addresses. These actions were unauthorized because they violated AOL's Terms of Service. Defendants' intent to access a protected computer, in this case computers within AOL's network, is clear under the circumstances. Defendants' access of AOL's computer network enabled defendants to send large numbers of unsolicited bulk e-mail messages to AOL members.

In addition to defendants' admissions, plaintiff alleges that by using the domain information "aol.com" in their e-mails, defendants and their "site partners" camouflaged their identities, and evaded plaintiff's blocking filters and its members' mail controls. Defendants have admitted to using extractor software to evade AOL's filtering mechanisms. As a result of these actions, plaintiff asserts damages to its computer network, reputation and goodwill in excess of the minimum $5,000 statutory requirement.

Count V: Violations of the Virginia Computer Crimes Act

The facts presented to the Court establish that defendants violated the Virginia Computer Crimes Act, Va. Code §18.2-152.3(3), which provides that "[a]ny person who uses a computer or computer network without authority and with the intent to [c]onvert the property of another shall be guilty of the crime of computer fraud." Section 18.2-152.12 authorizes a private right of action for violations of the Act. Defendants have admitted to causing "aol.com" to appear in the electronic header information of e-mail messages which they sent. Sending such messages through AOL's computer network was unauthorized. Plaintiff alleges chat defendants intended to obtain services by false pretenses and to convert AOL's property. Plaintiff alleges that the inclusion of false domain information in defendants' e-mails enabled defendants to escape detection by plaintiff's blocking filters and its members' mail controls. Plaintiff argues that as a result, defendants illegitimately obtained the unauthorized service of plaintiff's mail delivery system and obtained free advertising from AOL because AOL, not defendants, bore the costs of sending these messages. There are no genuine issues for trial with respect to this Count. As such, plaintiff's Motion for Summary Judgment must be granted on Count V.

Notes

For an interesting view on the anti-spam legal process, visit the Localhost.com Legal Web site at <http://www.cs.colorado.edu/~seidl/lawsuit/>, which chronicles a legal action against spammers.

Notwithstanding the success ISPs have enjoyed in bringing legal actions against spammers, the cost of such litigation does not enable individual Internet users to seek recourse. In response, several U.S. states, including California, Virginia and Washington, have enacted anti-spam legislation.

State of Washington Bill 2752[†]

AN ACT Relating to electronic mail; adding a new chapter to Title 19 RCW; creating a new section; prescribing penalties; and providing an expiration date.

BE IT ENACTED BY THE LEGISLATURE OF THE STATE OF WASHINGTON:

Sec. 1. The legislature finds that the volume of commercial electronic mail is growing, and the consumer protection division of the attorney general's office reports an increasing number of consumer complaints about commercial electronic mail. Interactive computer service providers indicate that their systems sometimes cannot handle the volume of commercial electronic mail being sent and that filtering systems fail to screen out unsolicited commercial electronic mail messages when senders use a third party's internet domain name without the third party's permission, or otherwise misrepresent the message's point of origin. The legislature seeks to provide some immediate relief to interactive computer service providers by prohibiting the sending of commercial electronic mail messages that use a third party's internet domain name without the third party's permission, misrepresent the message's point of origin, or contain untrue or misleading information in the subject line.

The legislature also finds that the utilization of electronic mail messages for commercial purposes merits further study. A select task force should be created to explore technical, legal, and cost issues surrounding the usage of electronic mail messages for commercial purposes and to recommend to the legislature any potential legislation needed for regulating commercial electronic mail messages.

---

† (1998) (as enacted).

Sec. 2. The definitions in this section apply throughout this chapter unless the context clearly requires otherwise.

(1) "Commercial electronic mail message" means an electronic mail message sent for the purpose of promoting real property, goods, or services for sale or lease.

(2) "Electronic mail address" means a destination, commonly expressed as a string of characters, to which electronic mail may be sent or delivered.

(3) "Initiate the transmission" refers to the action by the original sender of an electronic mail message, not to the action by any intervening interactive computer service that may handle or retransmit the message.

(4) "Interactive computer service" means any information service, system, or access software provider that provides or enables computer access by multiple users to a computer server, including specifically a service or system that provides access to the internet and such systems operated or services offered by libraries or educational institutions.

(5) "Internet domain name" refers to a globally unique, hierarchical reference to an internet host or service, assigned through centralized internet naming authorities, comprising a series of character strings separated by periods, with the right-most string specifying the top of the hierarchy.

Sec. 3.(1) No person, corporation, partnership, or association may initiate the transmission of a commercial electronic mail message from a computer located in Washington or to an electronic mail address that the sender knows, or has reason to know, is held by a Washington resident that:

(a) Uses a third party's internet domain name without permission of the third party, or otherwise misrepresents any information in identifying the point of origin or the transmission path of a commercial electronic mail message; or
(b) Contains false or misleading information in the subject line.

(2) For purposes of this section, a person, corporation, partnership, or association knows that the intended recipient of a commercial electronic mail message is a Washington resident if that information is available, upon request, from the registrant of the internet domain name contained in the recipient's electronic mail address.

Sec. 4.(1) It is a violation of the Consumer Protection Act, chapter 19.86 RCW, to initiate the transmission of a commercial electronic mail message that:

(a) Uses a third party's internet domain name without permission of the third party, or otherwise misrepresents any information in identifying the point of origin or the transmission path of a commercial electronic mail message; or
(b) Contains false or misleading information in the subject line.

(2) The legislature finds that the practices covered by this chapter are matters vitally affecting the public interest for the purpose of applying the Consumer Protection Act, chapter 19.86 RCW. A violation of this chapter is not reasonable in relation to the development and preservation of business and is an unfair or deceptive act in trade or commerce and an unfair method of competition for the purpose of applying the Consumer Protection Act, chapter 19.86 RCW.

Sec. 5.(1) Damages to the recipient of a commercial electronic mail message sent in violation of this chapter are five hundred dollars, or actual damages, whichever is greater.

(2) Damages to an interactive computer service resulting from a violation of this chapter are one thousand dollars, or actual damages, whichever is greater.

Sec. **6.**(1) An interactive computer service may, upon its own initiative, block the receipt or transmission through its service of any commercial electronic mail that it reasonably believes is, or will be, sent in violation of this chapter.

(2) No interactive computer service may be held liable for any action voluntarily taken in good faith to block the receipt or transmission through its service of any commercial electronic mail which it reasonably believes is, or will be, sent in violation of this chapter.

In March 2000, a Washington state judge dismissed an action against an Oregon man brought under that state's anti-spam law. The judge ruled that the statute in question was unduly restrictive and burdensome. The case was under appeal as of July 2000.

In addition to the state-level initiatives, several members of Congress have attempted to pass national anti-spam legislation. One recent attempt, from March 1999, is the following Senate bill, sponsored by Senator Murkowski.

Senate Bill, s. 759

To regulate the transmission of unsolicited commercial electronic mail on the Internet, and for other purposes.

IN THE SENATE OF THE UNITED STATES
March 25, 1999
Mr. MURKOWSKI (for himself, Mr. TORRICELLI, Mr. BURNS, and Mr. REID) introduced the following bill; which was read twice and referred to the Committee on Commerce, Science, and Transportation.

A BILL
To regulate the transmission of unsolicited commercial electronic mail on the Internet, and for other purposes.

> Be it enacted by the Senate and House of Representatives of the United
> States of America in Congress assembled,

Sec. 1. Short Title.
This Act may be cited as the 'Inbox Privacy Act of 1999'.

Sec. 2. Transmissions Of Unsolicited Commercial Electronic Mail.
(a) PROHIBITION ON TRANSMISSION TO PERSONS DECLINING RECEIPT—

(1) IN GENERAL — A person may not initiate the transmission of unsolicited commercial electronic mail to another person if such other person submits to the person a request that the initiation of the transmission of such mail by the person to such other person not occur.
(2) FORM OF REQUEST — A request under paragraph (1) may take any form appropriate to notify a person who initiates the transmission of unsolicited commercial electronic mail of the request, including an appropriate reply to a notice specified in subsection (d)(2).

(3) CONSTRUCTIVE AUTHORIZATION —

(A) IN GENERAL — Subject to subparagraph (B), for purposes of this subsection, a person who secures a good or service from, or otherwise responds electronically to an offer in a commercial electronic mail message shall be deemed to have authorized the initiation of transmissions of unsolicited commercial electronic mail from the person who initiated transmission of the message.

(B) NO AUTHORIZATION FOR REQUEST FOR TERMINATION — A reply to a notice specified in subsection (d)(2) shall not constitute authorization for the initiation of transmissions of unsolicited commercial electronic mail under this paragraph.

(b) PROHIBITION ON TRANSMISSION TO DOMAIN OWNERS DECLINING RECEIPT —

(1) IN GENERAL — Except as provided in paragraph (2), a person may not initiate the transmission of unsolicited commercial electronic mail to any electronic mail addresses served by a domain if the domain owner has elected not to receive transmissions of such mail at the domain in accordance with subsection (c).

(2) EXCEPTIONS — The prohibition in paragraph (1) shall not apply in the case of the following:

(A) A domain owner initiating transmissions of commercial electronic mail to its own domain.

(B) Any customer of an Internet service provider or interactive computer service provider included on a list under subsection (c)(3)(C).

(c) DOMAIN-WIDE OPT-OUT SYSTEM —

(1) IN GENERAL — A domain owner may elect not to receive transmissions of unsolicited commercial electronic mail at its own domain.

(2) NOTICE OF ELECTION — A domain owner making an election under this subsection shall —

(A) notify the Federal Trade Commission of the election in such form and manner as the Commission shall require for purposes of section 4(c); and

(B) if the domain owner is an Internet service provider or interactive computer service provider, notify the customers of its Internet service or interactive computer service, as the case may be, in such manner as the provider customarily employs for notifying such customers of matters relating to such service, of —

(i) the election; and

(ii) the authority of the customers to make the election provided for under paragraph (3).

(3) CUSTOMER ELECTION TO CONTINUE RECEIPT OF MAIL —

(A) ELECTION — Any customer of an Internet service provider or interactive computer service provider receiving a notice under paragraph (2)(B) may elect to continue to receive transmissions of unsolicited commercial electronic mail through the domain covered by the notice, notwithstanding the election of the Internet service provider or interactive computer service provider under paragraph (1) to which the notice applies.

(B) TRANSMITTAL OF MAIL — An Internet service provider or interactive computer service provider may not impose or collect any fee for the receipt of unsolicited commercial electronic mail under this paragraph (other than the usual and customary fee imposed and collected for the receipt of commercial electronic mail by its customers) or otherwise discriminate against a customer for the receipt of such mail under this paragraph.

(C) LIST OF CUSTOMERS MAKING ELECTION —

    (i) REQUIREMENT — An Internet service provider or interactive computer service provider shall maintain a list of each of its current customers who have made an election under subparagraph (A).

    (ii) AVAILABILITY OF LIST — Each such provider shall make such list available to the public in such form and manner as the Commission shall require for purposes of section 4(c).

    (iii) PROHIBITION ON FEE — A provider may not impose or collect any fee in connection with any action taken under this subparagraph.

(d) INFORMATION TO BE INCLUDED IN ALL TRANSMISSIONS — A person initiating the transmission of any unsolicited commercial electronic mail message shall include in the body of such message the following information:

(1) The name, physical address, electronic mail address, and telephone number of the person.

(2) A clear and obvious notice that the person will cease further transmissions of commercial electronic mail to the recipient of the message at no cost to that recipient upon the transmittal by that recipient to the person, at the electronic mail address from which transmission of the message was initiated, of an electronic mail message containing the word 'remove' in the subject line.

(e) ROUTING INFORMATION — A person initiating the transmission of any commercial electronic mail message shall ensure that all Internet routing information contained in or accompanying such message is accurate, valid according to the prevailing standards for Internet protocols, and accurately reflects the routing of such message.

Sec. 3. Deceptive Acts Or Practices In Connection With Sale Of Goods Or Services Over The Internet.

(a) AUTHORITY TO REGULATE —

(1) IN GENERAL — The Federal Trade Commission may prescribe rules for purposes of defining and prohibiting deceptive acts or practices in connection with the promotion, advertisement, offering for sale, or sale of goods or services on or by means of the Internet.

(2) COMMERCIAL ELECTRONIC MAIL — The rules under paragraph (1) may contain specific provisions addressing deceptive acts or practices in the initiation, transmission, or receipt of commercial electronic mail.

(3) NATURE OF VIOLATION — The rules under paragraph (1) shall treat any violation of such rules as a violation of a rule under section 18 of the Federal Trade Commission Act (15 U.S.C. 57a), relating to unfair or deceptive acts or practices affecting commerce.

(b) PRESCRIPTION — Section 553 of title 5, United States Code, shall apply to the prescription of any rules under subsection (a).

Sec. 4. Federal Trade Commission Activities With Respect To Unsolicited Commercial Electronic Mail.

(a) INVESTIGATION —

(1) IN GENERAL — Subject to paragraph (2), upon notice of an alleged violation of a provision of section 2, the Federal Trade Commission may conduct an investigation in order to determine whether or not the violation occurred.

(2) LIMITATION — The Commission may not undertake an investigation of an alleged violation under paragraph (1) more than 2 years after the date of the alleged violation.

(3) RECEIPT OF NOTICES — The Commission shall provide for appropriate means of receiving notices under paragraph (1). Such means shall include an Internet web page on the World Wide Web that the Commission maintains for that purpose.

(b) ENFORCEMENT POWERS — If as a result of an investigation under subsection (a) the Commission determines that a violation of a provision of section 2 has occurred, the Commission shall have the power to enforce such provision as if such violation were a violation of a rule prescribed under section 18 of the Federal Trade Commission Act (15 U.S.C. 57a), relating to unfair or deceptive acts or practices affecting commerce.

(c) INFORMATION ON ELECTIONS UNDER DOMAIN-WIDE OPT-OUT SYSTEM —

(1) INITIAL SITE FOR INFORMATION — The Commission shall establish and maintain an Internet web page on the World Wide Web containing information sufficient to make known to the public for purposes of section 2 the domain owners who have made an election under subsection (c)(1) of that section and the persons who have made an election under subsection (c)(3) of that section.

(2) ALTERNATIVE SITE — The Commission may from time to time select another means of making known to the public the information specified in paragraph (1). Any such selection shall be made in consultation with the members of the Internet community.

(d) ASSISTANCE OF OTHER FEDERAL AGENCIES — Other Federal departments and agencies may, upon request of the Commission, assist the Commission in carrying out activities under this section.

Sec. 5. Actions By States.

(a) IN GENERAL — Whenever the attorney general of a State has reason to believe that the interests of the residents of the State have been or are being threatened or adversely affected because any person is engaging in a pattern or practice of the transmission of electronic mail in violation of a provision of section 2, or of any rule prescribed pursuant to section 3, the State, as parens patriae, may bring a civil action on behalf of its residents to enjoin such transmission, to enforce compliance with such provision or rule, to obtain damages or other compensation on behalf of its residents, or to obtain such further and other relief as the court considers appropriate.

(b) NOTICE TO COMMISSION —

(1) NOTICE — The State shall serve prior written notice of any civil action under this section on the Federal Trade Commission and provide the Commission with a copy of its complaint, except that if it is not feasible for the State to provide such prior notice, the State shall serve written notice immediately after instituting such action.

(2) RIGHTS OF COMMISSION — On receiving a notice with respect to a civil action under paragraph (1), the Commission shall have the right —
    (A) to intervene in the action;
    (B) upon so intervening, to be heard in all matters arising therein; and
    (C) to file petitions for appeal.

(c) ACTIONS BY COMMISSION — Whenever a civil action has been instituted by or on behalf of the Commission for violation of a provision of section 2, or of any rule prescribed pursuant to section 3, no State may, during the pendency of such action, institute a civil action under this section against any defendant named in the complaint in such action for violation of any provision or rule as alleged in the complaint.

(d) CONSTRUCTION — For purposes of bringing a civil action under subsection (a), nothing in this section shall prevent an attorney general from exercising the powers conferred on the attorney general by the laws of the State concerned to conduct investigations or to administer oaths or affirmations or to compel the attendance of witnesses or the production of documentary or other evidence.

(e) VENUE; SERVICE OF PROCESS — Any civil action brought under subsection (a) in a district court of the United States may be brought in the district in which the defendant is found, is an inhabitant, or transacts business or wherever venue is proper under section 1391 of title 28, United States Code. Process in such an action may be served in any district in which the defendant is an inhabitant or in which the defendant may be found.

(f) DEFINITIONS — In this section:

(1) ATTORNEY GENERAL — The term 'attorney general' means the chief legal officer of a State.

(2) STATE — The term 'State' means any State of the United States, the District of Columbia, Puerto Rico, Guam, American Samoa, the United States Virgin Islands, the Commonwealth of the Northern Mariana Islands, the Republic of the Marshall Islands, the Federated States of Micronesia, the Republic of Palau, and any possession of the United States.

Sec. 6. Actions By Internet Service Providers And Interactive Computer Service Providers.

(a) ACTIONS AUTHORIZED — In addition to any other remedies available under any other provision of law, any Internet service provider or interactive computer service provider adversely affected by a violation of section 2(b)(1) may, within 1 year after discovery of the violation, bring a civil action in a district court of the United States against a person who violates such section.

(b) RELIEF —

(1) IN GENERAL — An action may be brought under subsection (a) to enjoin a violation referred to in that subsection, to enforce compliance with the provision referred to in that subsection, to obtain damages as specified in paragraph (2), or to obtain such further and other relief as the court considers appropriate.

(2) DAMAGES —

  (A) IN GENERAL — The amount of damages in an action under this section for a violation specified in subsection (a) may not exceed $50,000 per day in which electronic mail constituting such violation was received.

  (B) RELATIONSHIP TO OTHER DAMAGES — Damages awarded under this subsection for a violation under subsection (a) are in addition to any other damages awardable for the violation under any other provision of law.

  (C) COST AND FEES — The court may, in issuing any final order in any action brought under subsection (a), award costs of suit, reasonable costs of obtaining service of process, reasonable attorney fees, and expert witness fees for the prevailing party.

(c) VENUE; SERVICE OF PROCESS — Any civil action brought under subsection (a) in a district court of the United States may be brought in the district in which the defendant or in which the Internet service provider or interactive computer service provider is located, is an inhabitant, or transacts business or wherever venue is proper under section 1391 of title 28, United States Code. Process in such an action may be served in any district in which the defendant is an inhabitant or in which the defendant may be found.

Sec. 7. Preemption.

This Act preempts any State or local laws regarding the transmission or receipt of commercial electronic mail.

Sec. 8. Definitions.

In this Act:

(1) COMMERCIAL ELECTRONIC MAIL — The term 'commercial electronic mail' means any electronic mail or similar message whose primary purpose is to initiate a commercial transaction, not including messages sent by persons to others with whom they have a prior business relationship.

(2) INITIATE THE TRANSMISSION —

  (A) IN GENERAL — The term 'initiate the transmission', in the case of an electronic mail message, means to originate the electronic mail message.

  (B) EXCLUSION — Such term does not include any intervening action to relay, handle, or otherwise retransmit an electronic mail message, unless such action is carried out in intentional violation of a provision of section 2.

(3) INTERACTIVE COMPUTER SERVICE PROVIDER — The term 'interactive computer service provider' means a provider of an interactive computer service (as that term is defined in section 230(e)(2) of the Communications Act of 1934 (47 U.S.C. 230(e)(2)).

(4)   INTERNET — The term 'Internet' has the meaning given that term in section 230(e)(1) of the Communications Act of 1934 (47 U.S.C. 230(e)(1)).

Discussion Questions

1.   What elements are necessary for effective spam legislation? Spam advocates point to the need for individual actions, penalties, and a prohibition against any unsolicited email. Is this sufficient?

2.   Some politicians have advocated using a national opt-out list, whereby Internet users could request that they not receive further spam. Would this approach work? Consider the fact that most invitations to be removed from a solicitation list are treated by spammers as a confirmation of a valid email address.

3.   Another popular proposal is the "one kick at the can" approach. This would provide spammers with the opportunity to send one unsolicited email and only send further materials if the user provides consent. Do you think this approach has merit?

4.   The Canadian government has suggested that the *Personal Information Protection and Electronic Documents Act*, Canada's new electronic commerce and privacy legislation, will help to curtail spam. Do you agree?

5.   In a fall 1999 study, Canada's Electronic Commerce Task Force concluded that spam legislation was unnecessary, arguing that current legal remedies were sufficient. That study can be found online at <http://www.e-com.ic.gc.ca/using/en/spam.html>.

6.   One of the most challenging aspects of developing effective spam legislation is the definition of spam itself. Consider the definitions adopted in the two statutes discussed above. What email do you consider to be spam?

7.   The Canadian Direct Marketing Association has responded to anti-spam sentiment by developing several guidelines to marketing on the Internet. Are these guidelines sufficient?

   Canadian Marketing Association Code of Ethics[†]

   E4. Internet and Other Electronic Media

   E4.1 Application: The general provisions of these standards of practice apply to all other forms of electronic media. In addition, the following media specific standards of practice apply to electronic media including (but not limited to) the Internet, electronic mail, interactive kiosks, databases and computer-based information services.

   E4.2 Consent: Marketers shall not transmit marketing e-mail without the consent of the recipient or unless the marketer has an existing relationship with the recipient.

---

† CMA Web site: <http://www.the-cma.org/main.html>. Published with the permission of the Canadian Marketing Association.

E4.3 Reply: Every e-mail message shall clearly identify the marketer and pro-vide the recipient with a simple and easy-to-use e-mail means to reply to the marketer.

Marketers shall not send e-mail to recipients who have indicated they wish not to receive further communications from that marketer.

E4.4 Protection of the Virtual Environment: Marketers acknowledge that their continuing responsibility to manage their businesses to reduce unwanted mar-keting offers applies also to the maintenance of the electronic distribution envi-ronment, including e-mail and the Internet.

E4.5 Disclosure: When gathering data from individual consumers that could identify the consumer, and which will be linked with 'clickstream' data, market-ers shall advise consumers:

(a) what information is being collected; and,

(b) how the information will be used. The marketer shall provide access to this advisory before consumers submit data that could identify them. Marketers shall also provide a meaningful opportunity for con-sumers to decline to have information that identifies them collected, or transferred, for marketing purposes. In addition, access to this ad-visory shall be provided in every location, site or page from which the marketer is collecting such data.

Definition: Within this document, the term 'clickstream' is defined as data de-rived from an individual's behaviour, pathway, or choices expressed during the course of visiting a World Wide Web site.

For more coverage of the spam issue, see the following resources:

- Coalition Against Unsolicited Commercial Email — <http://www.cauce.org>
- Fight Spam on the Internet — <http://spam.a77buse.net/>
- Junk Email — <http://www.junkemail.org>
- Junkbusters — <http://www.junkbusters.com>
- Spam Recycling Center — <http://www.chooseyourmail.com/spamindex.cfm>

10

Private Regulation of Online Speech

With the law often unable to adequately protect or regulate online speech, Internet users are increasingly turning to technology or private contracts in place of law. The shocking murders at a Littleton, Colorado high school in the spring of 1999 provided an excellent illustration of the growing popularity of technology-based solutions, as in the aftermath of the killings, the Federal Communications Commission launched the Parents Information Page, designed to provide advice on using software filters (<http://www.fcc.gov/parents_information/>).

The use of filtering technology as a replacement for law is not without controversy, however. The primary concern pertains to the potential for filtering technologies to censor perfectly legal and acceptable materials. Many filtering software programs use keyword identification systems that may block legitimate sites together with objectionable ones. For example, a program that blocks access to pornographic sites might also block access to sex education sites since similar keywords would appear on both sites. With filtering software companies loath to provide a list of the sites they block, many speech advocates are also concerned about the possibility of political agendas entering into the evaluation process.

Filtering or rating online materials is problematic, since the process is inherently subjective. There are numerous rating systems currently in use, leaving prospective users uncertain about which materials are being blocked and why. This concern is heightened within the context of publicly funded Internet access. For example, library use of filtering software could well be equated with state-sponsored censorship and thus violate constitutional safeguards in many countries.

Platform for Internet Content Selection, or PICS, is one proposal that has attracted worldwide attention. PICS, developed by the World Wide Web Consortium (W3C), is a plan to allow Web site creators to self-rate their own material. Although the plan effectively eliminates the concerns of censorship emanating from software companies, self-rating creates a series of new concerns, including enforcement issues and the power for intermediaries such as states and large ISPs to engage in their own censorship practices based on the PICS standard.

Rating The Net†

JONATHAN WEINBERG

Background

Internet rating services respond to parents' and governments' concerns about children's access to sexually explicit material, and other adult content, available on the net. The services focus greatest attention on children's access to the World Wide Web (Web). The Web consists of a vast collection of documents, each residing on a computer linked to the Internet. These documents may contain text, pictures, sound, and/or video. Any Web document may contain links to other Web documents or other Internet resources, so that a user with a Web browser can jump from one document to another with a single mouse click. It is easy for users without sophisticated equipment or expensive Internet connections to create Web pages that are then accessible to any other user with access to the Web.

Rating services have also paid special attention to Usenet newsgroups. Usenet newsgroups allow any user to post text, pictures, sound, or video to one of more than 15,000 different open fora, each devoted to a different topic. About 200,000 computer networks worldwide participate in the Usenet news system. A small number of Usenet newsgroups are devoted to sexually explicit material.

It is fairly easy for software to screen access to Usenet news. Because each newsgroup has a name describing its particular topic (such as rec.music.folk, soc.culture.peru, or alt.tv.x-files), software writers can do a reasonably effective job of blocking access to sexually explicit material by simply blocking access to those newsgroups (such as alt.sex.stories) whose names indicate that they include sexually explicit material.

Blocking access to sexually explicit material on the Web is much more difficult. There are millions of individual pages on the Web, and the number is increasing every day. An astonishingly small fraction of those pages contain sexually explicit material. Every Web page (indeed, every document accessible over the Internet) has a unique address, or "URL," and the URLs of some Web pages do contain clues as to their subject matter. Because nothing in the structure or syntax of the Web requires Web pages to include labels advertising their content, though, identifying pages with sexually explicit material is not an easy task.

First-generation blocking software compiled lists of off-limits Web pages through two methods. First, the rating services hired raters to work through individual Web

---

† Reproduced from 19 Hastings Comm/Ent L.J. 453 (1997), by permission. Notes omitted.

pages by hand, following links to sexually explicit sites and compiling lists of URLs to be deemed off-limits to children. Second, they used string-recognition software to automatically proscribe any Web page that contained a forbidden word (such as "sex" or "xxx") in its URL.

The PICS specifications contemplate that a ratings system can be more sophisticated. A rating service may rate a document along multiple dimensions. Instead of merely rating a document as "adult" or "child-safe," it might give it separate ratings for violence, sex, nudity, and adult language. Further, along any given dimension, the rating service may choose from any number of values. Instead of simply rating a site "block" or "no-block" for violence, a rating service might assign it a rating of between one and ten for increasing amounts of violent content. These features are important because they allow the creation of filtering software that is customizable by parents. A parent subscribing to such a rating service, for example, might seek to block only sites rated over 3 for violence and 8 for sex. Finally, the PICS documents note that ratings need not be assigned by the authors of filtering software. They can be assigned by the content creators themselves or by third parties. One of the consequences of the PICS specifications is that varying groups — the Christian Coalition, say, or the Boy Scouts — can seek to establish rating services reflecting their own values, and these ratings can be implemented by off-the-shelf blocking software.

Most rating services today follow the PICS specifications. Their particular approaches, however, differ. The Recreational Software Advisory Council (RSAC) has developed an Internet rating system called RSACi. Participating content providers rate their own sites along a scale of 0 through 4 on four dimensions: violence, nudity, sex, and language. RSAC does not itself market blocking software; instead, it licenses its service to software developers. Safesurf is another system in which content providers rate their own speech. In that system, content providers choose from nine values in each of nine categories, from "profanity" through "gambling."

Rating services associated with individual manufacturers of blocking software include Cyber Patrol, Specs for Kids, and CYBERSitter. Cyber Patrol rates sites along fifteen dimensions, from "violence/profanity" to "alcohol & tobacco," but assigns only two values within each of those categories: CyberNOT and CyberYES. Specs for Kids rates documents along eleven dimensions, including "advertising," "alternative lifestyles," "politics," and "religion," and assigns up to five values (including "no rating") in each of those categories. CYBERSitter, by contrast, maintains a single list of objectionable sites; it affords users no opportunity to block only portions of the list.

Accuracy

Since blocking software first came on the market, individual content providers have complained about the ratings given to their sites. Not all of those complaints relate to problems inherent to filtering software. For example, some programs tend to block entire directories of Web pages simply because they contain a single "adult" file. That means that large numbers of innocuous Web pages are blocked merely because they are located near some other page with adult content. Some programs block entire domains, including all of the sites hosted by particular Internet service providers. This may be a temporary glitch, though; over time, it is possible that the most successful rating services will — properly — label each document separately.

Other problems arise from the wacky antics of string-recognition software. America Online's software, ever alert for four-letter words embedded in text, refused to let users register from the British town of "Scunthorpe." The University of Kansas Medical Center installed Surfwatch in its Internet kiosk, and discovered that users could not see the Web page of their own Archie R. Dykes Medical Library. For sheer wackiness, nothing can match a CYBERSitter feature that causes Web browsers to white out selected words but display the rest of the page (so that the sentence "President Clinton opposes homosexual marriage" would be rendered "President Clinton opposes marriage"). These problems too, though, may be addressed through proper software design.

Controversies over sites actually rated by humans are less amenable to technological solution. One dispute arose when Cyber Patrol blocked animal-rights web pages because of images of animal abuse, including syphillis-infected monkeys; Cyber Patrol classed those as "gross depiction" CyberNOTs. The situation was aggravated because Cyber Patrol, following the entire-directory approach described above, blocked all of the hundred or so animal welfare, animal rights, and vegetarian pages hosted at the Animal Rights Resource Site. An officer of Envirolink, which had provided the web space, responded:

> "Animal rights is usually the first step that children take in being involved in the environment. Ignoring companies like Mary Kay that do these things to animals and allowing them to promote themselves like good corporate citizens is a 'gross depiction.'"

Sites discussing gay and lesbian issues are commonly blocked, even if they contain no references to sex. Surfwatch, in its initial distribution, blocked a variety of sites including the Queer Resources Directory, an archive of material on homosexuality in America, and the International Association of Gay Square Dance Clubs. Surfwatch responded to protests by unblocking most of the contested sites. Other blocking programs, on the other hand, still exclude them: Cyber Patrol blocks a mirror of the Queer Resources Directory, along with Usenet newsgroups including clari.news.gays (which carries AP and Reuters dispatches) and alt.journalism.gaypress. CYBERSitter is perhaps the most likely to block any reference to sexual orientation, forbidding such newsgroups as alt.politics.homosexual. In the words of a CYBERSitter representative: "I wouldn't even care to debate the issues if gay and lesbian issues are suitable for teenagers .... We filter anything that has to do with sex. Sexual orientation [is about sex] by virtue of the fact that it has sex in the name."

The list of blocked sites is sometimes both surprising and alarming. Cyber Patrol blocks Usenet newsgroups including alt.feminism, soc.feminism, clari.news.women, soc.support.pregnancy. loss, and alt.support.fat-acceptance. It blocks gun and Second Amendment Web pages (including one belonging to the NRA Members' Council of Silicon Valley). It blocks the Web site of the League for Programming Freedom (a group opposing software patents). It blocked the Electronic Frontier Foundation's censorship archive. It blocked a site maintained by the U.S. Naval Academy Weapon Systems Engineering Department. CYBERSitter blocks the National Organization of Women web site. It blocks the Penal Lexicon, an encyclopedic British site concerned with prisons and penal affairs. It blocks some Web pages that criticize its blocking decisions, and at one point demanded that a critic's Internet service provider terminate the critic's account or see all of the sites on its server blocked. After the Netly News — a component of Time Warner Pathfinder — posted a search engine allowing viewers to find out whether the software blocked particular sites, CYBERSitter blocked the more than 150,000 pages on pathfinder.com.

One might think that a better answer lies in rating systems, such as RSACi and SafeSurf, in which content providers evaluate their own sites. An author, one might assume, could hardly disagree with a rating he chose himself. The matter, though, is not so clear. When an author evaluates his site in order to gain a rating from any PICS-compliant rating service, he must follow the algorithms and rules of that service. Jonathan Wallace, thus, in an article called Why I Will Not Rate My Site, asks how he is to rate "An Auschwitz Alphabet," his powerful and deeply chilling work of reportage on the Holocaust. The work contains descriptions of violence done to camp inmates' sexual organs. A self-rating system, Wallace fears, would likely force him to choose between the unsatisfactory alternatives of labeling the work as suitable for all ages, on the one hand, or "lump[ing it] together with the Hot Nude Women page" on the other.

At least some of the rating services' problems in assigning ratings to individual documents are inherent. It is the nature of the process that no ratings system can classify documents in a perfectly satisfactory manner. Consider first how a ratings system designer might construct a ratings algorithm. She might provide an algorithm made up entirely of simple, focused questions, in which each question has a relatively easily ascertainable "yes" or "no" answer. (Example: "Does the file contain a photographic image depicting exposed male or female genitalia?") Alternatively, she might seek to afford evaluators more freedom to apply broad, informal, situationally sensitive guidelines so as to capture the overall feel of each site. (Example: "Is the site suitable for a child below the age of 13?")

In jurisprudential terms, the first approach relies on "rules" and the second on "standards." The RSACi system attempts to be rule-based. In coding its violence levels, for example, to include "harmless conflict; some damage to objects"; "creatures injured or killed; damage to objects, fighting"; "humans injured or killed with small amount of blood"; "humans injured or killed; blood and gore"; and "wanton and gratuitous violence; torture; rape," its designers have striven to devise simple, hard-edged rules, with results turning mechanically on a limited number of facts. Not all RSAC categories are hard-edged — the "revealing attire" nudity level requires a rater to decide whether a "reasonable person" would consider particular clothing sexually suggestive and alluring — but the system overall aims for rules.

Other rating systems rely more heavily on standards. The SafeSurf questionnaire, for example, requires the self-rater to determine whether nudity is "artistic" (levels 4 through 6), "erotic" (level 7), "pornographic" (level 8), or "explicit and crude" pornographic (level 9). The Voluntary Content Rating self-rating system promoted by CYBERSitter is almost the model of a standards-based regime: it offers as its only guidance the instructions that self-raters should determine whether their sites are "not suitable for children under the age of 13," and whether they include material "intended for an audience 18 years of age or older." Specs for Kids raters are instructed to distinguish between sites that: (1) refer to homosexuality "[i]mpartial[ly]"; (2) discuss it with "acceptance or approval"; or (3) "[a]ctive[ly] promot[e]" it or "attempt to recruit the viewer." Each of these classifications requires more judgment on the part of the evaluator, and is not so hard-edged as the RSACi categories. Individuals with different perspectives and values may disagree as to where the lines fall. With respect to the Specs treatment of references to homosexuality, individuals disagree as to whether the categories are even coherent. These categories work only within a community of shared values, so that evaluators can draw on the same norms and assumptions in applying the value judgments embedded in the standards.

This distinction follows the more general rules-standards dichotomy in law, which focuses on the instructions lawmakers give to law-appliers in a variety of contexts. Legal thought teaches that rules and standards each have disadvantages. A problem with standards is that they are less constraining; relatively speaking, a standards-based system will lack consistency and predictability. Rules become increasingly necessary as the universe of law-appliers becomes larger, less able to rely on shared culture and values as a guide to applying standards in a relatively consistent and coherent way. One can see a parallel in problems the Yahoo! indexing service faces in seeking to classify the increasing number of Web sites. Yahoo!'s taxonomy embodies editorial judgments; the job is not amenable to resolution simply through rules. Consistent application of the taxonomy "comes from having the same 20 people classify every site, and by having those people crammed together in the same building where they are constantly engaged in a discussion of what belongs where." As a result, Yahoo! is faced with an unforgiving trade-off between the size and the quality of its directory. If Yahoo! hires another 50 or 60 classifiers to examine every last site on the Web, the catalog will become less consistent.... On the other hand, if Yahoo! stays with a small number of classifiers, the percentage of sites Yahoo! knows about will continue to shrink.

For this reason, the designers of RSACi attempted to be rule-like. They contemplate that the universe of ratings evaluators will include every content provider on the Web; that group can claim no shared values and culture. To accomodate [sic] that heterogeneous group, RSAC offers a rules-based questionnaire that (it hopes) all can understand in a similar manner. This, RSAC explains, will "provide fair and consistent ratings by eliminating most of the subjectivity inherent in alternative rating systems." It seems plain that with a relatively large universe of evaluators — and it is hard to see how one could seek to map the entire Net without one — a ratings system relying too heavily on standards just won't work. The dangers of arbitrariness and inconsistency will be too great.

Rules, though, have their own problems. They direct law-appliers to treat complex and multifaceted reality according to an oversimplified schematic. The point of rules, after all, is that by simplifying an otherwise complex inquiry, they "screen off from a decisionmaker factors that a sensitive decision maker would otherwise take into account." They may thus generate results ill-serving the policies behind the rules. Consider the task of deciding which citizens are mature enough to vote. A rule that any person can vote if he or she has reached the age of 18 has the advantage of administrability and avoids biased enforcement. Few of us would welcome a system in which a government bureaucrat examined each of us individually to determine whether we were mature enough to vote. Because the rule is much simpler than the reality it seeks to govern, though, it is both over and under — inclusive: it bars from the franchise some people under 18 who are mature, and grants the franchise to some people over 18 who are not. Rules thus give rise to their own arbitrariness. At best, a rule-based filtering system will miss nuances; at worst, it will generate absurd results — as when America Online, enforcing a rule forbidding certain words in personal member profiles, barred subscribers from identifying themselves as "breast" cancer survivors. Given this theoretical critique, one might think that the challenge facing ratings system designers is to devise really good rules-based systems, ones that track reality as well as possible, minimizing the difficulties noted above. That is what RSAC claims to have done in RSACi. I think the product of any such effort, though, necessarily will be flawed. The next few pages attempt to explain why.

Let's return to the choices facing a ratings system designer as she constructs blocking software. So far, this Article has not addressed the most basic question confronting her: what sort of material should trigger ratings consequences? Should children have access to material about weapons making? How about hate speech? Or artistic depictions of nudity? Again, she can take two different approaches. First, she can decide all such questions herself, so that the home user need only turn the system on and all choices as to what is blocked are already made. CYBERSitter adopts this approach. This has the benefit of simplicity, but seems appropriate only if members of the target audience are in basic agreement with the rating service (and each other) respecting what sort of speech should and should not be blocked.

Alternatively, she can leave those questions for the user to answer. The ratings system designer need not decide whether to block Web sites featuring bomb-making recipes or hate speech. She can instead design the system so that the user has the power to block those sites if he chooses. Microsoft's implementation of the RSACi labels allows parents to select the levels of adult language, nudity, sex and violence that the browser will let through. Cyber Patrol allows parents to select which of the twelve CyberNOT categories to block.

Either approach, though, imposes restrictions on the categories chosen by the ratings system designer. If the system designer wishes to leave substantive choices to parents, she must create categories that correspond to the different sides of the relevant substantive questions. That is, if the designer wishes to leave users the choice whether to block sites featuring hate speech, she must break out sites featuring hate speech into a separate category or categories. If she wishes to leave the user the choice whether to block sites that depict explicit sexual behavior but nonetheless have artistic value, she must categorize those sites differently from those that do not have artistic value. On the other hand, if the system designer makes those substantive decisions herself, making her own value choices as to what material should and should not be blocked, she must create categories that correspond to those value choices.

The problem is that many of these questions cleave on lines defined by standards. Many users, for example, might like to block "pornography," but allow other, more worthy, speech, even if it is sexually explicit. SafeSurf responds to that desire when it requires self-raters to determine whether nudity is "artistic," "erotic," "pornographic," or "explicit and crude" pornographic. It gets high marks for attempting to conform its system to user intuitions, but its lack of rulishness means problems in application. Similarly, Specs' distinction between "impartial reference," "acceptance or approval," and "active promotion" of homosexuality may well correspond to the intuitions of much of its target audience but will hardly be straightforward in actual application. The problem increases with the heterogeneity of the service's audience: the more heterogeneous the audience, the more categories a rating system must include to accomodate [sic] different user preferences.

With this perspective, one can better appreciate the limitations of RSAC's attempt to be rule-bound. RSACi ignores much content that some other ratings systems classify as potentially unsuitable, including speech relating to drug use, alcohol, tobacco, gambling, scatology, computer hacking and software piracy, devil worship, religious cults, militant or extremist groups, weapon making, tatooing and body piercing, and speech "grossly deficient in civility or behavior." For many observers (myself included), RSACi's narrow scope is good news because it limits the ability to block access to controversial political speech. My point, though, is that RSACi had to confine its reach if it was to maintain its rule-bounded nature.

The problem appears as well in connection with the categories RSACi does address. Consider RSACi's treatment of sex. It divides up sexual depictions into "romance, no sex," "passionate kissing," "clothed sexual touching," "non-explicit sexual activity," and "explicit sexual activity; sex crimes." But RSACi, in contrast to some other ratings systems, does not seek to distinguish educational, artistic, or crude depictions from others. There is no way, consistent with rulishness, that it can seek to distinguish the serious or artistic from the titilating. It achieves rule-boundedness, and ease of administration, at the expense of nuance; it achieves consistent labeling but in categories that do not correspond to the ones many people want.

In sum, rating system designers face a dilemma. If a rating service seeks to map the Web in a relatively comprehensive manner, it must rely on a relatively large group of evaluators. Such a group of evaluators can achieve fairness and consistency only if the ratings system uses simple, hard-edged categories relying on a few, easily ascertainable characteristics of each site. Such categories, though, will not categorize the Net along the lines that home users will find most useful, and will not empower those users to heed their own values in deciding what speech should and should not be blocked. To the extent that ratings system designers allow evaluators to consider more factors in a more situationally specific manner to capture the essence of each site, they will ensure inconsistency and hidden value choices as the system is applied.

Unrated Sites

Blocking software can work perfectly only if all sites are rated. Otherwise, the software must either exclude all unrated sites, barring innocuous speech, or allow unrated sites, letting in speech that the user would prefer to exclude. What are the prospects that a rating service will be able to label even a large percentage of the millions of pages on the Web? What are the consequences if it cannot?

First, consider rating services associated with individual manufacturers of blocking software, such as CYBERSitter and Cyber Patrol. These services hire raters to label the entire Web, site by site. The limits on their ability to do so are obvious. As the services get bigger, hiring more and more employees to rate sites, their consistency will degrade; that was one of the lessons of Part II of this Article. Moreover, no service could be big enough to rate the entire Web. Too many new pages come on-line every day. The content associated with any given page is constantly changing. Further, some of the sites most likely to be ephemeral are also among the most likely to carry sexually explicit material. A ratings service simply cannot keep tabs on every college freshman who gets to school and puts up a Web page, notwithstanding that college freshmen are of an age to be more interested in dirty pictures than most. A ratings service certainly cannot keep tabs on every Web page put up by a college freshman in Osaka, say, or in Amsterdam. So any such rating service must take for granted that there will be a huge number of unrated sites.

As a practical matter, providing access to all unrated sites is not an option for these rating services; it would let through too much for them to be able to market themselves as reliable screeners. Instead, they must offer users other options, dealing with unrated sites in one of two ways. First, they can seek to catch questionable content through string-recognition software. CYBERSitter, for example, offers this option. The problem with this approach, though, is that at least under current technology, string-recognition software simply doesn't work very well. This article has already mentioned America Online's travails with the town of Scunthorpe and the word "breast"; other examples are easy to find. Surfwatch, for example, blocked a page on the White House web site because its URL contains the forbidden word "couples" (http://www.whitehouse.gov/WH/kids/html/couples.html).The second option is for the rating services simply to block all unrated sites. Industry members seem to contemplate this as the necessary solution. Microsoft, for example, cautions Internet content providers that "[f]or a rating system to be useful, the browser application must deny access to sites that are unrated." Other observers reach the same result.

What about self-rating approaches, like those of SafeSurf and RSACi? These services have the potential for near-universal reach, since they can draw on the services of an effectively unlimited number of evaluators. While the evaluators will be a diverse group (to say the least), rating service designers can try to cope with that diversity by constructing rule-bound questionnaires. While some evaluators may misrepresent their sites, rating services can try to devise enforcement mechanisms to cope with that as well. On the other hand, self-rating services will not achieve their potential unless content providers have a sufficient incentive to participate in the ratings process in the first place.

That incentive is highly uneven. Mass-market commercial providers seeking to maximize their audience reach will participate in any significant self-rating system, so as not to be shut out of homes in which parents have configured their browsers to reject all unrated sites. Many noncommercial site owners, though, may not participate. They may be indifferent to their under-18 visitors and may not wish to incur the costs of self-rating. It is still early to predict what those costs may be. For the owner of a large site containing many documents, supplying a rating for each page may be a time-consuming pain in the neck.

RSAC appears to have abandoned plans to charge web sites for using its ratings, but there may be other disincentives. Some content providers may not self-rate because they are philosophically opposed to the censorship a rating system enables or are dissatisfied with the choices a rating system provides. More generally, why should a college or graduate student with a Web page bother to self-rate? He's not necessarily writing for people concerned about ratings, and if those people exclude him, the author may not much care.

It may be that the only way to ensure participation in a self-rating system even in a single country (let alone internationally) would be for the government to compel content providers to self-rate (or to compel Internet access providers to require their customers to do so). It is not obvious how such a requirement would work. The drafters of such a law would face the choice of forcing content providers to score their sites with reference to a particular rating system specified in the law, or allowing them leeway to choose one of a variety of PICS-compliant ratings systems. Neither approach seems satisfactory. The first, mandating use of a particular rating system, would freeze technological development by eliminating competitive pressures leading to the introduction and improvement of new searching, filtering, and organizing techniques. It would leave consumers unable to choose the rating system that best served their needs. The second would be little better.

Some government organ would have to assume the task of certifying particular self-rating systems as adequately singling out material unsuitable for children. It is hard to imagine how that agency could ensure that every approved system yielded ratings useful to most parents, while nonetheless maintaining a healthy market and allowing innovation.

Access Denied: An Impact Of Internet Filtering Software In The Gay & Lesbian Community[†]

For over a decade, GLAAD has been promoting fair, accurate and inclusive representations based on sexual orientation or identity in all forms of media. As the Internet has become a mainstream reality, GLAAD has been a leader in ensuring equal access for gay and lesbian people.

In 1995, GLAAD became aware of a new technology that affected gay and lesbian presence on the Internet. Filtering software was being developed to help parents filter the Internet for "indecent" materials. Through keyword blocking (the use of descriptors to block sites) and outright censoring, the world found gay and lesbian sites being filtered off the Internet. SurfWatch Software, Inc. had just released a software program called "SurfWatch" that "helps you deal with the flood of sexually explicit material on the Internet. By helping you to be responsible for blocking what is being received at any individual computer, children and others using your computer have less chance of accidentally or deliberately being exposed to unwanted materials."

Online activist Christopher Kryzan noted that SurfWatch's database of censored sites had included many that "clearly do not contain sexually explicit materials, but rather provide information, education, resources and calendars of events." Among the blocked information services were those provided by the International Association of Gay Square Dance Clubs, the Queer Resources Directory, the Lesbian/Gay/Bisexual Association of the University of California at Berkeley, and the Maine Gay Network.

GLAAD joined !OutProud! in its criticism of the software, notifying its members and the gay, lesbian, bisexual and transgender community of SurfWatch's discriminatory database. Within a few days, a representative from SurfWatch contacted Kryzan and assured him that the informational, educational and support sites would not be blocked in the next release of the software. SurfWatch also put together a site review advisory board that would include members of the gay, lesbian, bisexual and transgender community.

In November, 1995, GLAAD criticized the Massachusetts-based Microsystems Software, Inc. for its software "Cyber Patrol," which was also blocking gay, lesbian, bisexual and transgender resources. Some of the sites that were being blocked were the San Jose gay and lesbian newspaper, OutNOW!; gay and lesbian community center sites around the country; and resource guides for gay student and employee groups.

GLAAD promptly encouraged its members to write Microsystems Software with concerns that important resources were being blocked. Almost immediately, Richard Gorgens, Microsystems' Chief Executive Officer, contacted GLAAD to discuss Cyber Patrol and how it affects the gay and lesbian community. Gorgens explained that their Internet researchers, made up of educators and parents, chose sites blocked following a criteria of "12 well-defined sections based on their opinion." He assured GLAAD that gay and lesbian sites would not be considered a part of that criteria.

[†] 1997 Report of Gay and Lesbian Alliance Against Defamation (Posted at GLAAD Web site: <http://www.glaad.org/glaad/access_denied/index.html>). Reproduced by permission.

Taking from what was learned during its work with SurfWatch, GLAAD's suggestion that Microsystems Software invite gay, lesbian, bisexual and transgender people to be part of the Internet research committee was received with much enthusiasm. In February 1996, Microsystems Software held true to its word and developed a CyberNOT Oversight Committee for Cyber Patrol, appointing GLAAD as a charter member to act as an advocate for gay, lesbian, bisexual and transgender sites up for review. The CyberNOT Oversight Committee is comprised of representatives from different areas of experience and expertise, including groups such as parents, teachers, clergy, the National Rifle Association, Anti-Defamation League, ACLU, GLAAD and women's rights groups.

In December 1996, online service provider CompuServe deleted more than 200 Internet newsgroups from its worldwide system after a request made by a German prosecutor who was investigating "illegal" material being transmitted through CompuServe. While GLAAD's research indicated that CompuServe was not asked to ban or censor gay and lesbian newsgroups, CompuServe did use the words "gay," "lesbian" and "homosexual" as part of their blocking criteria. As such, groups such as the gay, lesbian and bisexual youth support newsgroup, soc.support.youth.gay-lesbian-bi, and gay and lesbian journalism newsgroup, clari.news.gay, were blocked.

GLAAD then received a statement issued by CompuServe CEO Bob Massey that said, "I want to make it clear that regardless of how this issue is resolved, there are certain newsgroups that will not be added to our index." William Giles, a spokesman for CompuServe, said the provider was working on a way to resume broadcasting a full range of Internet content to its subscribers. While the statement GLAAD received did not specifically name which newsgroups would continue to be banned, GLAAD was troubled that CompuServe continued to confuse legitimate lesbian and gay newsgroups with child pornography and erotic newsgroups. In the meantime, GLAAD launched a campaign that alerted its members and the gay and lesbian community to consider other Internet service providers. CompuServe was also barraged by e-mails and letters, urging the company to reinstate gay and lesbian newsgroups.

"Our gay membership is an important segment of our audience, and that was reflected by the activities that we saw in light of the suspension of access...It showed that this is an active, vocal segment of our [subscriber] population," acknowledged CompuServe spokesperson Jeff Shafer to The Washington Blade.

After a month and a half of deleted gay and lesbian newsgroups, CompuServe finally reinstated all but five of the 200 newsgroups. The five that remained blocked were not gay and lesbian, but dealt with child pornography. CompuServe also installed free parental controls in the form of Internet filtering software Cyber Patrol.

In February 1996, the Telecommunications Reform Bill, which contained the highly controversial Communications Decency Act (CDA), was passed into law. The CDA would place heavy restriction on Internet publishing by making it illegal to post "indecent" materials. However, the CDA's wording was so vague that it had the potential to make information about AIDS, safe-sex, abortion and information relevant to the gay and lesbian community illegal. It was now clear. GLAAD had to become the leader of ensuring equal access for the gay and lesbian community.

While the CDA was found unconstitutional by both a three-judge panel of the Federal Court in Philadelphia and by the United States Supreme Court, GLAAD has warned of the danger of censoring gay, lesbian, bisexual and transgender information and stepped up its fight against Internet censorship.

In January 1997, GLAAD criticized the manufacturer of the Internet filtering software NetNanny for its "audit trail" feature, which allows parents to check what sites and newsgroups their children have tried to access in their absence. While this may sound harmless, GLAAD finds this auditing feature particularly dangerous to youth, particularly to those wrestling with their sexual orientation, but indeed for all youth. This kind of digital paper trail can lead to the accidental disclosure of a young person's sexual orientation before she or he is ready, potentially causing tension and isolation within the family.

NetNanny did not block on the basis of sexual orientation or identity, however.

GLAAD informed its members and the gay and lesbian community of this auditing feature. After several e-mails and letters, Gordon Ross, Chief Executive Officer of Net Nanny, called GLAAD to discuss how NetNanny works and committed himself to working with GLAAD to finding solutions that would benefit both parents and all communities.

At the same time that it challenged NetNanny, GLAAD also criticized Solid Oak software company and Cybersitter, its Internet filtering software. Like NetNanny, CyberSitter provides parents with an audit trail function, but went a step further. CyberSitter actually blocks keywords such as "gay," "lesbian," "homosexual" and other words. While the software allows parents to choose whatever information they want to block from their children, gay and lesbian information is blocked regardless, a fact that is not made available in any literature for CyberSitter.

CyberSitter's owners have made their anti-gay agenda public on several occasions. When Bennett Haselton from the teen online free-speech group Peacefire discovered various sites that were being blocked by CyberSitter, one of the sites that was mentioned was the National Organization for Women's (NOW) Web site. Solid Oak president Brian Milburn told News.com, "The NOW site has a bunch of lesbian stuff on it, and our users don't want it."

While Solid Oak denies allegiance with any organization, CyberSitter was at one point the favored Internet filtering software of religious radical group Focus on the Family, most probably due to Milburn's alleged membership with the organization.

GLAAD is not only appalled by CyberSitter's wholesale censorship of gay, lesbian, bisexual and transgender information, but also by Solid Oak's gross misrepresentation of itself in not making buyers aware of its automatic blocking in its literature.

In June 1997, GLAAD became aware that, for the first time since CyberSitter, a new content filtering program outright discriminated against the gay, lesbian, bisexual and transgender community. PlanetWeb, the Web browser of the highly popular Sega Saturn game console, offered the option of blocking what was originally termed as "alternative lifestyles." This category offered three filtering levels: "1) Mention of alt.lifestyle: Impartial references to homosexuality, bisexuality, transvestites and transgender issues or lifestyles. 2) Approval of alt.lifestyle: Acceptance or approval of alternative lifestyles. 3) Ads for alt.lifestyle: Promotes alternative lifestyle or attempts to recruit the viewer into that lifestyle."

GLAAD contacted both PlanetWeb and Sega of America, Inc. Both companies defended the content filtering program; claiming that since as it allows parents the right of choice, the program did not automatically filter out gay and lesbian information. While GLAAD respects and supports a parent's right to choose what information his or her child sees, PlanetWeb and Sega do not provide parents the option to choose to block out other entire classes of people, on such traits as race, gender, age, national origin or physical or mental ability. By singling out the gay community among these groups, these companies perpetuate the misconception that gay, lesbian, bisexual and transgender people are a "controversial ideology," sending a message that there is something implicitly wrong with being lesbian, gay, bisexual or transgender. GLAAD challenged PlanetWeb and Sega to ask themselves if the same technology had existed before the civil rights movement, would they have offered the option to filter out civil rights information or positive representation of people of color. PlanetWeb founder Ken Soohoo told News.com that "he never would filter out a certain racial or ethnic groups. 'We're not in the business of selling prejudice here.'"

A week after GLAAD contacted PlanetWeb and Sega, PlanetWeb took a step forward. While it did not remove the option or provide more options, it did reword the anti-gay language of the filter. So, instead of "alternative lifestyles," it now offers the option to block "Gay, Lesbian and Transgender subjects." While it still offers filters of "positive" and "impartial" gay representations, it has added the option of blocking sites with "a negative representation of gay, lesbian, bisexual and transgender subjects." At the same time, Sega of America's Chief Operating Officer, Bernard Stolar, sent GLAAD a letter explaining its position and asking GLAAD to put its suggestions in writing.

GLAAD has since written letters to both the companies, offering itself as a resource, and awaits a response.

In August 1997, GLAAD learned that InterGO Communication's search engine, SafeSearch, designed to assist families to "explore and enjoy the Internet without being exposed to objectionable sources." However, when GLAAD conducted searches for gay and lesbian sites that contained no sexually explicit materials and for those that offered important educational, informational and support resources about the community, it was shocked to see the results. Gay and lesbian youth support sites, such as the Web site for !OutProud!, The National Coalition for Gay, Lesbian, Bisexual and Transgender Youth, and Youth Assistance Online, were rated for "Mature" viewing only (17 years and older). National gay and lesbian organizations such as GLAAD and Parents, Families and Friends of Lesbians and Gays (PFLAG) were rated for "Adults Only" (21 years and older).

GLAAD has tried to contact InterGO. As of this printing the company has not returned any calls or e-mail.

The Internet remains a concern for GLAAD. Access to it by the community is vitally important. GLAAD will continue to monitor developments in the Internet filtering and rating industry and will work with any industry leader that believes in equality for all communities on the information superhighway.

Discussion Questions

Critics of filtering software and ratings point to a number of deficiencies with both approaches. Filtering software is perceived to be over-inclusive, judgmental, and ineffective, while self-rating is subject to misuse, is imprecise and may result in a filtered Internet. Notwithstanding these shortcomings, do you have a preferred approach? Is an imperfect solution better than no solution?

The importance filtering software companies attach to their lists of blocked sites became readily apparent in a spring 2000 battle between Mattel, the maker of the

Cyber Patrol filtering program, and two computer science students. The students created a software hack program, known as "CP4break.zip," that enabled users to view which sites Cyber Patrol blocked.

The company moved swiftly to ban distribution of the program. First, it obtained the following temporary injunction on March 17, 2000:

> Upon the Verified Complaint, the Memorandum in Support of Ex Parte Motion for Expedited Discover, Affidavit of Irwin B. Schwartz and for good cause shown, it is hereby ORDERED that:
>
> 1. Plaintiffs shall serve as rapidly as possible the Summons, Verified Complaint, and the discovery attached hereto as Exhibit A, and that defendants shall deliver all documents responsive to the document requests to the office of plaintiffs' counsel no later than twenty-four hours after service upon them.
> 2. A Temporary Restraining Order immediately shall issue, and the defendants, their officers, agents, servants, employees, attorneys, and those persons in active concert or participation with them, shall discontinue publishing defendants' Cyber Patrol bypass source code and binaries (known as "CP4break.zip" or cphack.exe or any derivative thereof).
> 3. In addition, all defendants shall preserve inviolate the software and information that makes up all such Web sites, source or object code and documents relating to Cyber Patrol as well as all records which reflect the identity or number of persons who downloaded "CP4break.zip" or "cphack.exe" from the Web sites;

When copies of the program spread to mirror sites around the world, the company obtained a second injunction prohibiting others from posting the program.

Microsystems Software Inc. v. Scandanavia Online AB.[†]

Upon the stipulation and agreement of Plaintiffs Microsystems Software, Inc and Mattel, Inc. and Defendants Eddy L.O. Jansson ("Jansson") and Matthew Skala ("Skala"), the verified Complaint, the Affidavit of Irwin B. Schwartz in Further Support of Application for Temporary Restraining Order filed March 17, 2000, and the Findings of Fact and Conclusions of Law. It is hereby ordered that:

> Defendants Jansson and Skala, their agents, employees, and all persons in active concert or participation with Defendant Jansson and/or Defendant Skala, shall discontinue and be permanently enjoined from publishing the software source code and binaries known as "CP4break.zip" or "cphack.exe" or any derivative thereof.

The Federal Rules of Civil Procedure allow a Court to accomplish service and notice of injunctive orders by "personal service or otherwise." Fed R.Civ.P. 65(d). This Order shall be served on Defendants Jansson and Skala, their agents, employees, and all persons in active concert or participation with Jansson and/or Skala by certified mail to last known address.

---

† Civil Action NO. 00-10488-EFH (D. Mass 2000).

Any violation of this Injunction shall be determined by the Court only on the filing by Plaintiffs of a Motion for to Show Cause Why a Certain Person or Entity Should Not be Held in Contempt and after a full hearing thereon.

All remaining claims in this action shall be and are hereby dismissed with prejudice.

This case involves a dispute between private parties relating to the federal copyright law and has been resolved by a stipulation entered into by the parties.

The federal law of copyright gives exclusive ownership of and the right to make use of written and literary works and material, protected by law for a specified period of time. This federal law has been a prodigious and inexhaustable stimulator of rich creative thought and the firm protector of free individual expression. It is the exclusive province of the federal court to insure that the law's protections are enforced and an owner's rights to his creation secured.

Yet this case involves more than a complex and significant legal issue relating to copyright law. It raises a most profound societal issue, namely, who is to control the educational and intellectual nourishment of young children — the parents or the purveyors of pornography and the merchants of death and violence.

Ideas bear consequences, fruitful and also destructive. The pernicious idea that all men are not created equal is the philosophic bais [sic] which incited the degradations of slavery and the genocidal slaughter of the Holocaust.

Under our Constitution all have the right to disseminate even evil ideas and such ideas cannot by law be suppressed by the government. On the other hand, parents, in the exercise of their parental obligation to educate their young children, have the equal right to screen and, thus, prevent noxious and insidious ideas from corrupting their children's fertile and formative minds.

Although filtering software and ratings anger many free speech advocates, few dispute the rights of parents or other individuals to install such software on their personal computers at home. The issue becomes contentious, however, once such programs are used in combination with publicly funded Internet access, such as Internet access in libraries.

Mainstream Loudoun v. Board of Trustees of the Loudoun County Library†

At issue in this civil action is whether a public library may enact a policy prohibiting the access of library patrons to certain content-based categories of Internet publications. Plaintiffs are Loudoun County non-profit organization, suing on its own behalf and on behalf of its members, and individual Loudoun County residents who claim to have had their access to Internet sites blocked by the defendant library board's Internet policy. They, along with plaintiff-intervenors ("intervenors"), individuals and other entities who claim that defendant's Internet policy has blocked their websites or other materials they placed on the Internet, allege that this Policy infringes their

---

† 24 F. Supp. 2d 552 (E.D. Va. 1998).

right to free speech under the First Amendment. Defendant, the Board of Trustees of the Loudoun County Library, contends that a public library has an absolute right to limit what it provides to the public and that any restrictions on Internet access do not implicate the First Amendment.

The background of this action is fully summarized in this Court's April 7, 1998 Memorandum Opinion and will not be repeated in depth here. On October 20, 1997, defendant passed a "Policy on Internet Sexual Harassment" ("Policy") stating that the Loudoun County public libraries would provide Internet access to its patrons subject to the following restrictions: (1) the library would not provide e-mail, chat rooms, or pornography; (2) all library computers would be equipped with site-blocking software to block all sites displaying: (a) child pornography and obscene material, and (b) material deemed harmful to juveniles; (3) all library computers would be installed near and in full view of library staff; and (4) patrons would not be permitted to access pornography and, if they do so and refuse to stop, the police may be called to intervene. It is the second restriction in the Policy that lies at the heart of this action.

To effectuate the second restriction, the library has purchased X-Stop, commercial site-blocking software manufactured by Log-On Data Corporation. While the method by which X-Stop chooses sites to block has been kept secret by its developers, it is undisputed that it has blocked at least some sites that do not contain any material that is prohibited by the Policy.

If a patron is blocked from accessing a site that she feels should not be blocked under the Policy, she may request that defendant unblock the site by filing an official, written request with the librarian stating her name, the site she wants unblocked, and the reason why she wants to access the site. The librarian will then review the site and manually unblock it if he determines that the site should not be blocked under the Policy. There is no time limit in which a request must be handled and no procedure for notifying the patron of the outcome of a request. All unblocking requests to date have been approved.

Plaintiffs and intervenors both allege that the Policy, as written and as implemented, violates their First Amendment rights because it impermissibly discriminates against protected speech on the basis of content and constitutes an unconstitutional prior restraint. In response, defendant contends: (1) intervenors do not have standing; (2) the Policy does not implicate the First Amendment and is reasonable; (3) the Policy is the least restrictive means to achieve two compelling government interests; and (4) the library has statutory immunity from this action.

.   .   .   .

Constitutionality of the Policy

Defendant contends that even if we conclude that strict scrutiny is the appropriate standard of review, the Policy is constitutional because it is the least restrictive means to achieve two compelling government interests: "1) minimizing access to illegal pornography; and 2) avoidance of creation of a sexually hostile environment...."

A content-based limitation on speech will be upheld only where the state demonstrates that the limitation "is necessary to serve a compelling state interest and that it is narrowly drawn to achieve that end." This test involves three distinct inquiries: (1) whether the interests asserted by the state are compelling; (2) whether the limitation is necessary to further those interests; and (3) whether the limitation is narrowly drawn to achieve those interests.

A. Whether the Defendant's Interests Are Compelling

Although plaintiffs and intervenors argue that these interests were not really the motivating factors behind the Policy and that they are not furthered by the Policy, they do not argue that the interests themselves are not compelling. For the purposes of this analysis, therefore, we assume that minimizing access to illegal pornography and avoidance of creation of a sexually hostile environment are compelling government interests.

B. Whether the Policy is Necessary to Further Those Interests

The only evidence to which defendant can point in support of its argument that the Policy is necessary consists of a record of a single complaint arising from Internet use in another Virginia library and reports of isolated incidents in three other libraries across the country. In the Bedford County Central Public Library in Bedford County, Virginia, a patron complained that she had observed a boy viewing what she believed were pornographic pictures on the Internet. This incident was the only one defendant discovered within Virginia and the only one in the 16 months in which the Bedford County public library system had offered unfiltered public access to the Internet. After the incident, the library merely installed privacy screens on its Internet terminals which, according to the librarian, "work great".

The only other evidence of problems arising from unfiltered Internet access is described by David Burt, defendant's expert, who was only able to find three libraries that allegedly had experienced such problems, one in Los Angeles County, another in Orange County, Florida, and one in Austin, Texas. There is no evidence in the record establishing that any other libraries have encountered problems; rather, Burt's own statements indicate that such problems are practically nonexistent. Significantly, defendant has not pointed to a single incident in which a library employee or patron has complained that material being accessed on the Internet was harassing or created a hostile environment. As a matter of law, we find this evidence insufficient to sustain defendant's burden of showing that the Policy is reasonably necessary.

C. Whether the Policy is Narrowly Tailored to Achieve the Compelling Government Interests

Even if defendant could demonstrate that the Policy was reasonably necessary to further compelling state interests, it would still have to show that the Policy is narrowly tailored to achieve those interests.

1. WHETHER LESS RESTRICTIVE MEANS ARE AVAILABLE

We find that the Policy is not narrowly tailored because less restrictive means are available to further defendant's interests and, as in Sable, there is no evidence that defendant has tested any of these means over time. First, the installation of privacy screens is a much less restrictive alternative that would further defendant's interest in preventing the development of a sexually hostile environment. Second, there is undisputed evidence in the record that charging library staff with casual monitoring of Internet use is neither extremely intrusive nor a change from other library policies. Third, filtering software could be installed on only some Internet terminals and minors could be limited to using those terminals. Alternately, the library could install filtering software that could be turned off when an adult is using the terminal. While we find that all of these alternatives are less restrictive than the Policy, we do not find that any of them would necessarily be constitutional if implemented. That question is not before us.

2. WHETHER THE POLICY IS OVERINCLUSIVE

In examining the specific Policy before us, we find it overinclusive because, on its face, it limits the access of all patrons, adult and juvenile, to material deemed fit for juveniles. It is undisputed that the Policy requires that "[i]f the Library Director considers a particular website to violate ... [the Virginia Harmful to Juveniles Statute], the website should be blocked under the policy for adult as well as juvenile patrons." It has long been a matter of settled law that restricting what adults may read to a level appropriate for minors is a violation of the free speech guaranteed by the First Amendment and the Due Process Clause of the Fourteenth Amendment.

Because we have found that less alternatives are available to defendant and that defendant has not sufficiently tried to employ any of them, the Policy's limitation of adult access to constitutionally protected materials cannot survive strict scrutiny.

3. WHETHER X-STOP IS THE LEAST RESTRICTIVE FILTERING SOFTWARE

Defendant claims that X-Stop is the least restrictive filtering software currently available and, therefore, the Policy is narrowly tailored as applied. Our finding that the Policy is unconstitutional on its face makes this argument moot. A facially overbroad government policy may nevertheless be saved if a court is able to construe government actions under that policy's narrowly along the lines of their implementation, if the policy's text or other sources of government intent demonstrate "a clear line" to draw. We find no such clear line here. Defendant has asserted an unconditional right to filter the Internet access it provides to its patrons and there is no evidence in the record that it has applied the Policy in a less restrictive way than it is written. Therefore, our finding that the Policy is unconstitutional on its face makes any consideration of the operation of X-Stop moot.

VII. CONCLUSION

Although defendant is under no obligation to provide Internet access to its patrons, it has chosen to do so and is therefore restricted by the First Amendment in the limitations it is allowed to place on patron access. Defendant has asserted a broad right to censor the expressive activity of the receipt and communication of information through the Internet with a Policy that (1) is not necessary to further any compelling government interest; (2) is not narrowly tailored; (3) restricts the access of adult patrons to protected material just because the material is unfit for minors; (4) provides inadequate safeguards for restricting access; and (5) provides inadequate procedural safeguards to ensure prompt judicial review. Such a policy offends the guarantee of free speech in the First Amendment and is, therefore, unconstitutional.

Discussion Questions

1. The judge lists several alternative options to blocking software, including acceptable use policies, privacy screens, adjustable filters, education and time limits. Do you think these options are as effective as the technological solution?

2. Does this case suggest that filtering in libraries would be constitutional under certain circumstances?

3. How do you think these facts would be treated by a Canadian court? The issue of filters in libraries has arisen in Canada in the town of Burlington, Ontario. Assuming that a public library would be classified a government agency for the purposes of the Charter, do you think that a filtering policy would survive a Charter analysis?

4. Some U.S. states have enacted legislation mandating the use of filters. For example, consider this provision from an Indiana legislative proposal.

    Sec. 7.(a) The board of a public library that offers Internet access to library patrons shall do the following:

    (1) Adopt a written policy identifying:

    (A) Internet sites; or
    (B) types of Internet sites;

    that may not be accessed by library patrons who are using library software to access the Internet.

    (2) Install and maintain functioning filtering software on computers located in the public library to block access by library patrons to Internet sites identified by the policy adopted under subdivision (1).

    (b) The state library and historical board may not distribute state money to a public library that does not comply with the requirements of subsection (a).

5. Part of the problem associated with filtering programs is the lack of transparency in what sites are being blocked. Consider the claims made by Solid Oak Software, the makers of Cybersitter (<http://www.solidoak.com/>) and then contrast it with this page from Professor Peter Junger who lists the sites blocked by the program (<http://samsara.law.cwru.edu/comp_law/cybersit.html>).

6. For more on the filtering issue, see the following resources:
    - The Censorware Project — <http://censorware.org>
    - Peacefire — <http://www.peacefire.org>
    - Filtering Facts — <http://www.filteringfacts.org>

In addition to technological solutions, private contract can also go a long way in solving speech issues. Virtually every ISP now employs an acceptable use policy (AUP) that provides it with the power to remove a subscriber if he or she violates its use policies.

Blaber v. University of Victoria[†]

The petitioner, a computing science student at the University of Victoria, avers *inter alia* that his right to freedom of expression as guaranteed by section 2(b) of the Canadian Charter of Rights and Freedoms has been unconstitutionally infringed by

---

[†] [1995] B.C.J. No. 558 (B.C. S.C.).

the University of Victoria, Dr. Michael Miller and Ms. K. Susan Shaw (hereinafter referred to collectively as the "respondents") in so far as they have curtailed, or threatened to curtail, the petitioner's access to and use of a computer account that provides the petitioner with access to the Internet. The petitioner further claims that the process by which the respondents seek to limit his computer access violates his rights enshrined in s. 7 of the *Charter* not to be deprived of liberty except in accordance with the principles of fundamental justice.

The petitioner asks this Court to issue an interim injunction pursuant to s. 10 of the *Judicial Review Procedure Act* R.S.B. 1979, c. 209 (hereinafter referred to as the "Act") enjoining the respondents from interfering with his computer account. S. 10 of the Act reads as follows:

> 10. On an application for judicial review, the court may make an interim order it considers appropriate pending the final determination of the application.

In addition, the petitioner seeks a declaration pursuant to s. 24(1) of the Charter that the impugned "orders" restricting computer access and the policy referenced in these "orders", namely, section 2.2 c. of the University's Harassment Policy (cited below) be declared of no force or effect.

Findings of Fact pertaining to the application for interim injunctive relief

Students enrolled in the University of Victoria's computing science program are provided with access to a computing services account. This account, paid for by the University, enables students to conduct their academic work and also provides students with a means of accessing E-mail, the Internet and various electronic "newsgroups". The petitioner's university paid account is "rblaber[at]sol" (hereinafter referred to as the "sol account").

In his affidavit, Dr. Michael Miller, Chair, Computing Science, Faculty of Engineering (hereinafter referred to as "Dr. Miller") states that:

> ... the University and its Department of Computer Science limits the use of the University-paid accounts by students in accordance with the policy of use which is specifically agreed to and accepted by the students before issuance of account privileges.

The policy referred to by Dr. Miller is the University of Victoria Policy Guide — Computer Use Responsibilities (Authorized April 14, 1986; Revised November 10, 1992). I find that Dr. Miller's statement is a true and accurate reflection of the conditions pertaining to the issuance of computer accounts.

I further find that the petitioner agreed to this policy of use prior to obtaining his computer privileges.

On or about December 8, 1994 the petitioner, using his sol account, posted a message entitled "Open Letter to Beth Hardy" on an electronic school newsgroup. Ms. Hardy, also a student at the University, had earlier in the year been elected to sit on the University's Board of Governors. As this letter provides the focal point for the events that follow, I set out its contents in full. It reads:

> Dear Miss Hardy,
>
> Since being elected to the Board of Governors, I charge that you have done virtually nothing to benefit the student body other than to create an atmosphere of gender hatred.

You have not used this medium, the internet to inform we the students of UVic of any of your sundry albeit useless exploits in the realm of student politics.

I charge that you are not only incompetent as a member of the board of governors, but a waste of space on the ballot. It sickens me to think that you will use this position on your resume without explaining how inept you actually were.

Pheh!

Robyn Blaber.

"And I will execute great vengeance upon them with furious rebukes, and they shall know that I am the LORD, when I shall may [sic] my vengeance upon them."
Ezekiel 25:17

Ms. Hardy, in her affidavit filed January 17, 1995, deposed that upon reading this letter she was "immediately distressed and frightened". Ms. Hardy contacted Ms. Sheldon Collyer, the University Secretary, and, acting on Ms. Collyer's advice, met with K. Susan Shaw (hereinafter referred to as Ms. Shaw), the University's Anti-Harassment Officer.

On or about December 15, 1994, Ms. Shaw sent an E-mail letter to Dr. Michael Miller and Mr. Herb Widdifield, Director, Computing and Systems Services. Ms. Shaw's letter, which is reproduced in part below, was accompanied by two of the petitioner's electronic messages, namely: the December 8 letter to Ms. Hardy and a June 30 message posted on the E-mail system by the petitioner in his role as president of the "Men's Club." The June 30 message consisted of crude and sometimes violent "pick-up lines". Ms. Shaw felt that both the June 30 message and the December 8 message violated the University's Harassment Policy and Procedure. She opined:

> In addition, according to student Usage Guidelines, Computing Science Department, #5 (enclosed), "You will not distribute or maintain material in violation of the University's Harassment Policy", Mr. Blaber has violated these Guidelines ... further violated University policy according to the "Computing User Responsibilities" ... "Not to harass other users of computing service of facilities" and section 3.1, "Abuse or misuse of computing services or facilities may not only be a violation of user responsibilities but also of the Criminal Code. ... Therefore the University will take appropriate action in response to user abuse or misuse of computing services of [sic] facilities, which may include, but not necessarily be limited to:
>
> 3.1.1.
> withdrawal of computing privileges;
> 3.2.2.
> laying of charges under the Criminal Code;
>
> ... It is my recommendation that Mr. Blaber have his computing privileges ... withdrawn for a reasonable period of time and that he be given clear instructions that his behaviour is unacceptable and must stop immediately. If there is to be any reinstatement of those privileges at any time, I recommend that Mr. Blaber be required to re-apply only under the conditions that any further violation of University policies will result in permanent withdrawal of all computer user privileges and possibly further disciplinary action. [emphasis added]

The final letter that is of concern is that sent by Dr. Miller to the petitioner on or about December 18, 1994 via E-mail. In this, Dr. Miller informs the petitioner that he is aware of the December 8 message to Ms. Hardy and states that the message "constitutes an inappropriate use of a Departmental account." Dr. Miller then writes:

> I require you to do three things:
> a)   Write to Ms. Shaw in her capacity as Anti-Harassment Officer with a copy to me, and explain the reason for the inclusion of the biblical quote, acknowledge that your letter could have had the effect of being seriously threatening or intimidating and assure her, and me, that you will not use your computer account to that end.
> b)   Review the Department account usage guidelines on the departmental gopher and send me a signed letter that you agree to abide by them.
> c)   Take care to moderate the tone of all messages, postings and other forms of communication that originate from your Departmental account.
>
> I consider that you have been put on notice that we expect a higher level of responsible behaviour in the use of accounts issued by the Department. Adherence to (a),(b) and (c) is required for you to retain your Departmental account.
>
> Any subsequent episode of this or a related nature will leave me no choice but to shut-off your account pending an investigation of the behaviour.
>
> I expect to receive copies of the communications mentioned in (a) and (b) above within three working days of your receipt of this message.

The petitioner responded to Dr. Miller's letter by initiating these court proceedings.

Issues

1. Whether the so called orders of Ms. Shaw and Dr. Miller are orders or decisions within the meaning of the *Judicial Review Procedure Act*? In other words, has the petitioner properly invoked the *Judicial Review Procedure Act*?
2. Can it be said that there is a fair question to be tried on the claim that the respondents, by their actions, have infringed the petitioner's rights to freedom of speech and fundamental justice?
3. Is there a fair question to be tried on the issues that the harassment policy of the respondent University violates the Canadian *Charter of Rights and Freedoms* and is not justified under s.1 of the Charter, as being a reasonable limit prescribed by law as can be demonstrably justified in a free and democratic society?

The Appropriateness of the Invocation of the *Judicial Review Procedure Act*

As noted, the petitioner brings his case to this court by way of petition pursuant to section 10 of the *Judicial Review Procedure Act* (hereinafter referred to as the "Act"). I am assured by counsel for the petitioner that the Attorney General has been given proper notice pursuant to s. 16 of the Act. I turn then to consider whether the Act has been properly invoked.

Before the Court can be asked to exercise its jurisdiction to make an interim order under s. 10 of the Act, it is incumbent upon the petitioner to demonstrate that the actions of the respondents which he seeks to impugn were made pursuant to functions in the categories of decision making within the ambit of the Act. In other words, the subject of the petition vis a vis Ms. Shaw, Dr. Miller, and the University, must relate to a "statutory power of decision" or the exercise of a "statutory power" as defined in s. 1 of the Act.

The petitioner characterizes both Ms. Shaw's and Dr. Miller's letters as "orders", but that is an assumption in itself. It is for the Court to decide whether or not that is a correct assumption in law and in fact. I therefore turn to consider each of the respondents' letters in turn, commencing with the December 15 letter sent by Ms Shaw to Dr. Miller.

Ms. Shaw's letter consists of a review of policy, an opinion that the petitioner's conduct was in breach of that policy and recommendations for action. There is no evidence before this Court to suggest that Dr. Miller was in any way bound by the content of Ms. Shaw's letter. In other words, Ms. Shaw's recommendations were merely a communication of what she thought was desirable in the circumstances. They did not directly affect the legal rights of either the petitioner or Dr. Miller.

I accept, as Macdonald J. observed in *Save Richmond Farmland Society* v. *Richmond (Township)*: The power to merely advise does not amount to a power to order or determine ... For the Judicial Review Procedure Act to apply, there must be a power to decide in respect of a legal right or duty. " The fact that Dr. Miller decided to follow these recommendations does not alter their true nature. In the result, I find that Ms. Shaw's letter is not subject to judicial review.

Dr. Miller's letter is *prima facie* in the nature of an "order" in so far as the petitioner's failure to comply with the letter's directives results in negative consequences for the petitioner, namely, the termination of his departmental account. Can it be said, however, that the consequences flowing from a failure to comply with this ostensible "order" affects the petitioner's "legal rights"?

The petitioner submits that the legal right affected is his right to free speech as guaranteed by the *Charter*. Based on the evidence I am unable to conclude that the petitioner's freedom of speech has been infringed or denied. It is clear from the evidence that the petitioner has access to a variety of computer accounts at the University, all of which provide him with the same access to the Internet that his sol account provided. In any event, free speech has never meant "free" in the sense that it must be paid for by the state or, in this case, by the University.

The petitioner also claims that his rights under section 7 of the *Charter* have been infringed in that Dr. Miller's letter presumes guilt, denies any form of impartial trial, and administers punishment without or before a hearing. Further, it demands admission of guilt as a condition of further use of the computer system. There is nothing in the evidence to suggest that these concerns could not properly be addressed within the existing administrative framework. It is a fundamental principle of administrative law that the internal adjudicative processes available to the petitioner ought to be exhausted prior to coming to court.

If the matter at bar is anything, it is a matter of student academic discipline. As such it comes within the ambit of s. 36 of the *University Act* and, in particular, s. 36(s) which reads:

> 36. The academic governance of the university is vested in the senate and it has power

...

(s)   to establish a standing committee of final appeal for students in matters of academic discipline;

In the result, I dismiss his application for the interim order pursuant to s. 10 of the *Judicial Review Procedure Act*.

Whether the Petitioner is entitled to a remedy under s. 24(1) of the Canadian Charter of Rights and Freedoms

The petitioner seeks a declaration under s. 24(1) of the Charter that Ms. Shaw's "order" is a violation of s. 2(b) and s. 7 of the Charter and is not saved by section 1 thereof and hence is inoperative and of no force or effect. In other words, the petitioner contends that Ms. Shaw's letter amounts to an unreasonable restriction of the petitioner's freedom of speech and denies the petitioner his guaranteed right to fundamental justice. The identical claim is made with respect to Dr. Miller's letter.

This claim must stand or fall on whether or not the Charter applies to the activities in question. Both counsel accept that the authority on this question is *McKinney* v. *University of Guelph*. However, the application of *McKinney* to the case at bar is a contentious matter left to the determination of this court.

The majority of the court held that dismissal of academic staff pursuant to a mandatory retirement policy was not subject to the *Charter*. On the evidence before me, I have not been persuaded that different reasoning should apply to the discipline of a student especially in this case where the internal decision making procedures have not been exhausted and the "ultimate decision" of the university on this matter is unknown. It is not for this court to speculate upon what the outcome of such a hearing might be.

I find support for my conclusion that the *Charter* does not apply to the case at bar in the wording of section 46.1 of the *University Act* which reads:

> 46.1(1) The minister shall not interfere in the exercise of powers conferred on a university, its board, senate and other constituent bodies by this Act respecting
> (a)   the formation and adoption of academic policies and standards,
>
> ...

In the result, I do not find it necessary to consider the merits of arguments regarding the infringement of the petitioner's *Charter* rights finding, as I do, that the petitioner is not entitled to interim injunctive relief, either under the *Judicial Review Procedure Act* or the *Charter* neither of which apply to the letters written by Ms. Shaw and Dr. Miller. However, I observe that on the whole of the evidence I am not persuaded that the conduct of the respondents constitutes an infringement of the petitioner's right to "life, liberty and security of the person" or his right to "freedom of expression" as guaranteed by the *Charter*. I make this observation subject to my reasoning on the final issue, namely, whether the harassment policy of the University is contrary to s. 2(b) of the Charter.

The Matter of the University's Harassment Policy and s. 2(b) of the *Charter*

The goal of the Harassment Policy, as set out in the preamble, is to ensure that:

... all members of the University community — its faculty, staff, students and visitors — have the right to participate equally in activities at the University without fear of harassment.

Two threshold questions arise in respect of the Harassment Policy. Firstly, whether the *Charter* applies to the Harassment Policy and, secondly, whether the petitioner has standing to challenge the Policy pursuant to the *Charter*. The respondent, relying on *McKinney*, maintains that the University is not subject to the *Charter*. It is further contended by the respondent that the petitioner has, by contract, agreed to adhere to the terms of the Harassment Policy at the University of Victoria thereby rendering a *Charter* challenge to the Policy irrelevant. The petitioner, on the other hand, contends that the majority in *McKinney* held that the Charter does apply to Universities in some circumstances. In response to the claim that this is merely a matter of contract, the petitioner avers that no waiver of *Charter* rights can be accomplished unless expressly stated and that there is nothing in evidence to suggest that the petitioner waived his *Charter* rights.

I am in agreement with the petitioner's reading of *McKinney*. Indeed, in that case La Forest J. observed:

> There may be situations in respect of specific activities where it can fairly be said that the decision is that of the government, or that the government sufficiently partakes in the decision as to make it an act of government, but there is nothing here to indicate any participation in the decision by the government and, as noted, there is no statutory requirement imposing mandatory retirement on the universities.

In the case at bar, the Harassment Policy is really best characterized as a set of rules establishing the boundaries of acceptable behaviour for all members of the University community, including visitors. In essence, the Policy defines the limits of "academic freedom".

There is no evidence before me regarding how the Policy came into existence or what the government's role was, if any, in the creation of the policy. Neither the evidence nor the argument makes clear the statutory provisions by which this Policy was developed. There is no evidence as to whether the Policy was created pursuant to the powers granted to the Board of Governors (s. 27), the Senate (s. 36) or the President (s.56).

It would be imprudent of this Court, in the absence of such evidence and argument, to determine whether or not the Charter applies to the University's Harassment Policy. Accordingly, I do not find it necessary to consider the issue of standing or engage in a s. 1 analysis of s. 2.2 c. of the University's Harassment Policy.

I note, however, that on its face the wording of s. 2.2 c., referring as it does to such treatment having "the effect or purpose of seriously threatening or intimidating a person" (my emphasis), does appear to fall outside the ambit of constitutionally acceptable infringements of Charter rights. However, I make no ruling on the matter for the reasons noted above.

A similar set of circumstances arose in the U.S. decision, *Loving* v. *Boren* 956 F. Supp. 953 (W.D. Okla., 1997) aff'd. 133 F. 3d 771 (10th Cir. 1998), with a similar outcome.

The enforceability of AUPs is particularly relevant in the context of combating spam. For more on the Canadian approach to the issue, see *1267623 Ontario Inc.*

v. *Nexx Online Inc.* ([1999] O.J. No. 2246) (Ont. Sup. Ct.) discussed at pp. 178–183 in Chapter 9. A U.S. example with a similar set of circumstances is found in this case involving a well-known spammer and an ISP.

Cyber Promotions, Inc. v. Apex Global Information Services, Inc.[†]

Plaintiff Cyber Promotions Inc. ("Cyber") moves under Fed R. Civ. P. 65(a) for a preliminary injunction directing the defendant Apex Global Information Services ("AGIS") to restore Internet access services to Cyber for 30 days under the terms of a contract between Cyber and AGIS. Cyber is a promoter of unsolicited bulk commercial e-mail (known as "spam"); AGIS is an Internet Service Provider.

The controversy began on September 16, 1997 when AGIS terminated Cyber's connection to the Internet without prior notice. The termination followed a massive "ping attack" on AGIS's network which it maintains appeared to be directed at Cyber's computers. On October 25, 1996, AGIS had contracted in writing with Cyber to grant Cyber full Internet access through one T-1 line. On March 10, 1997, the parties entered into a second contract providing Cyber with two additional T-1 lines. The only difference between the two contracts was the addition to the second contract of two paragraphs: one restricting AGIS from terminating Cyber's service without 30 days notice and the other acknowledging that Cyber was in the business of sending unsolicited bulk commercial e-mail. The first additional paragraph was added because Cyber wanted AGIS to acknowledge in writing that it was aware that Cyber was in the business of sending unsolicited bulk commercial e-mail over AGIS's system; the second was added because Cyber wanted 30 days notice in the event that AGIS terminated Cyber's service to enable it to find an alternate carrier.

On September 22, 1997, Cyber filed a complaint seeking damages, specific performance and moved for a temporary restraining order and a preliminary injunction. The motions for injunctive relief sought the compelling of AGIS to restore Internet access services to Cyber of the two additional T-1 lines for a 30 day period as required by the second contract. I denied Cyber's request for a temporary restraining order and scheduled a hearing on the preliminary injunction. On September 25, 1997, I held a hearing on the preliminary injunction to prove that it has a reasonable probability of eventual success on the merits and it will be irreparably harmed if the injunction is not granted. *Opticians Ass'n* v. *Independent Opticians*. The harm to the moving party, especially if financial, must be "immediate." I must consider the granting or denial of a preliminary injunction in terms of the possibility of harm to the defendant and other interested persons and the potential impact on the public.

Cyber has a valid claim for breach of contract. Paragraph #1 of both contracts provides the following:

> AGIS'S DUTIES AND OBLIGATIONS: During the terms hereof, AGIS shall, subject to the terms & conditions hereof, provide CUSTOMER with access to the INTERNET through AGIS. Any and all access to other networks via AGIS must be in compliance with all policies and rules of those networks.... No Guarantee of end-to-end bandwidth on the Internet is made

---

[†] 1997 U.S. Dist. LEXIS 15344 (E.D. Pa.).

... AGIS makes no guarantee of service on full routing and/or peering. If AGIS is requested to provide full routing to a customer, that decision is at the complete and total option of AGIS. This full routing service is subject to termination at any time without prior notice. AGIS cannot guarantee the peering sessions between our customers and other non-AGIS companies and/ or networks.

Although Cyber did not persuade me that it did not receive full routing service — the paragraph captioned "AGIS'S DUTIES AND OBLIGATIONS" can be interpreted as simply a disclaimer for AGIS if it fails to provide full routing service and not a basis for total avoidance of the contract. More importantly, since the parties specifically bargained for the 30 day notice provision in the second contract it controls the other provisions and will be enforced.

Paragraph #9 of both contracts provides that AGIS will not be responsible for delays or failure to perform due to "strikes, inclimate weather, acts of god or other causes beyond AGIS's reasonable control." AGIS claims that the ping attacks on its router was a factor beyond its reasonable control and thus excused AGIS's failing to reconnect Cyber without prior notice. The ping attacks on AGIS's router did not constitute a factor beyond AGIS's reasonable control that excused AGIS's failure to perform. The testimony indicated that AGIS was aware that its grant of access to Cyber might result in ping attacks on its system. Furthermore AGIS gave assurances to Cyber that it would be able to cope with such attacks. AGIS can cope with attacks albeit at some cost to the quality of the service it provides to others. Also AGIS's chief technician testified that AGIS continues to provide Internet connectivity to other promoters of unsolicited bulk commercial e-mail and that AGIS continued to be attacked with pings after it disconnected Cyber. Thus the language of paragraph #9 in no way entitled AGIS to disconnect Cyber without notice.

Cyber has demonstrated that it will be irreparably harmed by a failure to grant the injunction. An irreparable injury is a "potential harm which cannot be addressed by a legal or equitable remedy following a trial." A showing that a plaintiff may suffer a substantial loss of business or bankruptcy if relief is not granted meets the standards for interim relief. Cyber's business will be irreparably harmed by being forced into dissolution or bankruptcy unless it is reconnected by AGIS immediately.

Cyber's business reputation is based on its ability to provide a continuous connection to the Internet. Cyber's customer good will is being destroyed and it is losing customers permanently. It has already received demands from its clients seeking damages or refunds. If Cyber is not restored to the Internet immediately, Cyber will not have the capital to commit to a contract with another Internet service provider.

The public interest also tips toward the issuance of a preliminary injunction although it is undisputed that Cyber's business of sending unsolicited bulk E-mail is a controversial one. Many computer users find the receipt of bulk e-mail annoying and intrusive. However, the fact that Cyber is an unpopular citizen of the Internet does not mean that Cyber is not entitled to have its contracts enforced in a court of law or that Cyber is not entitled to such injunctive relief as any similarly situated business. Cyber specifically bargained for the 30 day notice provision with AGIS because both parties knew the pressures AGIS would face to cut off Cyber. It is in the public interest that parties live up to their legal contracts even if they are unpopular.

PART THREE

INTERNET PRIVACY

11

Online Privacy —
Is There a Problem?

The popularity of the Internet has created a new awareness of threats of personal privacy. The collection and use of personal data has evolved into a major industry, with companies willing to pay thousands of dollars for consumer databases that provide contact information and personal preference data. Computers have fundamentally altered the collection and processing of such facts and figures, as data mining software can be used to provide marketers with the "targeted" information they seek. The growth of the personal information industry has left many concerned about the loss of personal privacy and annoyed by the growing mountain of marketing material that arrives by mail, telephone or email.

The issue of personal privacy is particularly acute in the context of the Internet, since it provides a new source of data collection that is "database ready", enabling quick processing and sale by data collection agencies. Moreover, Internet users have experienced a steady increase in the number of Web sites that request personal information. In some instances, the information requested is limited to a name and email address, though Web sites have been known to ask for the completion of detailed marketing surveys including financial information and personal preferences.

The issue of online privacy captured national headlines in early 1999 when it was revealed that a security breach in the Air Miles Web site allowed anyone to access data on thousands of Air Miles members. The security leak was quickly fixed, but the incident left many questioning whether existing legislative protections were sufficient. Although characterized as an isolated incident, similar occurrences in the United States have led many to believe that the current privacy legal framework must be strengthened. Those views are in accord with the arguments of Bruce Phillips, Canada's former Privacy Commissioner, who argued for years that the Internet presents a new privacy threat to all Canadians.

Privacy Commissioner of Canada Annual Report, 1997–98[†]

Internet — still no privacy

The 1995–96 Annual Report gave readers some tips on how to protect their privacy on electronic networks (*Privacy in Cyberspace: a Surfer's Guide*). Two years later, the Internet has become much more commercial (to the point that some governments are looking at ways to tax on-line purchases!), and privacy is at even greater risk. There are currently four main types of privacy invasions on the Internet:

On the World Wide Web

The biggest Internet privacy invasion is the collection of your personal information without your knowledge — information that can be used, rented or sold to on-line and other direct marketers. And this applies to both information about yourself and about your activities on the Web ...

• Your electronic mail ("e-mail") address, sometimes your name, your Internet Protocol ("IP") address (from which your rough geographical location can be inferred using a domain name lookup service), the type of browsing software you use (and by implication, the operating system of your computer). Fortunately, most of this information can be withheld from Web sites if you first surf through such sites as the Anonymizer, at [www.anonymizer.com].

• Information about your activities on the Web (also known as "click-stream information"): who you are, when you enter a site, the last page you accessed (required for the BACK function of your browser), which sections of a site you go to and how much time you spend on each, what documents (or pictures) you download onto your own computer, and what information you search for with such well-known tools as AltaVista or Yahoo. As above, your clickstream information can be also be anonymized by first going through certain sites. Web sites may also store some of this information on your own computer in the form of a "cookie" file. This allows the site to retrieve the information at your next visit, and "personalize" its greetings. However, you can instruct your computer to refuse such cookie files.

As well, some municipalities and government institutions are increasingly interested in using the World Wide Web to post information for the general public. While the intended convenience is usually laudable, the end result can be disastrous. The cities of Victoria, B.C. and Aylmer, Québec (among others) had to remove sensitive financial information from the Web following the public outcry that ensued. While tax rolls are usually publicly available information, it is a quantum leap from a personal consultation of tax records at a local city hall to providing over 40 million

---

† Online: <http://infoweb.magi.com/~privcan/pubs/e_ar97.pdf> at pp. 65–68. Source of Information: Privacy Commissioners of Canada. Reproduced with permission of the Minister of Public Works and Government Services Canada, 1999.

computer users worldwide a person's address, property value, taxes owing and (in some jurisdictions) religious affiliation — all from the comfort of their homes. Similarly, Manitoba Telephone Systems had to remove billing information from the Web following protests by its subscribers.

On the Usenet

Participating in discussion groups on the Usenet can lead to a second, less well known privacy invasion. Every message you post to a discussion group is archived for others to search. Not only are your personal views on a given topic stored permanently, it is also possible to search the Usenet to find out which discussion groups you participate in, and thus determine your interests (DejaNews — the message archivist — does allow you to delete selected messages). Even worse, it is also possible to find out who is looking at a message at a given moment!

Writing e-mail

You will never hear it enough: e-mail on the Internet is as private and secure as a post card in the "snail mail". Everyone from your Internet provider staff to your correspondent's friends or colleagues can read your electronic message from the moment you click "SEND" on your computer. Unless you and your correspondent use encryption, avoid including sensitive information such as credit card numbers, vacation dates or medical information in your electronic messages. You could also use anonymous remailers which forward your message, and sometimes the reply, without including any personal information. Among others, you can find a good list of those remailers at our Web site.

Another privacy invasion prompted by e-mail is junk electronic messages, better known as "spam." Once an on-line direct marketer gets hold of your e-mail address, you will find unsolicited electronic advertising in your mail box. Because junk e-mail is as much a nuisance as regular junk mail, and because it is costly to you (keeping you connected while you receive, read and delete the junk messages), most Internet Service Providers (ISPs) have devised ways to block spam from your e-mail box. Inquire!

Hacking

Hacking is the unauthorized access to computer systems and files. And the best electronic protections (such as "gateways" and "firewalls") can, and do, fail. Because the Internet is nothing more (and nothing less) than a worldwide electronic computer network, it is a hacker's paradise. Getting access to your ISP's file listing of all of its users' names and passwords would be a dream for a hacker who could then read, redirect, change or delete your e-mail without your knowledge. Some hackers prefer shopping and try to hack ISP or Web site files containing credit card numbers. Others are more interested in company or personal secrets and will look for interesting business or personal information they could resell or misuse.

This is not just the stuff of movies: last year alone the best protected computers in the world; those of the Pentagon, the FBI and NASA were successfully hacked hundreds of times! And if you think your information is of little interest, think again: some hackers specialize in stealing enough information about you to impersonate you; ordering credit cards in your name, renting or buying in your name, holding a job in your name — leaving all the bills and income tax to pay (not to mention a reputation to rebuild) also all in your name! This is the growing problem of "identity theft" which is exacerbated by electronic transactions.

Are there solutions to all of these privacy invasions?

Aside from these tips, there is little to protect your privacy on the Internet. Laws would be of little use because laws change from one country to the next, and the Internet knows no borders. Codes of ethics (like the December 1996 Code of the Canadian Association of Internet Providers) are nice statements of intent but they are voluntary and useless if they are breached. Yet, two new solutions have recently appeared which could make a difference — if they work.

The first is TRUSTe. Launched by a group of American companies and advocacy groups in June 1997, the program encourages Web sites to tell surfers about their privacy protection practices and what they do with the personal information they collect. Sites that subscribe to TRUSTe display the program logo or "trustmark" on their welcome page (and can be audited at random for compliance). Unfortunately, few sites have joined the program — by April 1998 it had attracted only 75 participants. Apparently one major factor in companies' hesitation is TRUSTe's sanctions for those which do not comply with the guidelines. However, businesses that are serious about gaining clients' trust by protecting their privacy in an electronic environment should embrace this attempt at self-regulation, rather than waiting for legislation to force them to comply.

The second solution is the Platform for Privacy Preferences Project (or "P3P" for short). Begun in May 1997 by the consortium that oversees the development of the Web, the project allows surfers to specify their privacy protection preferences (through their browser), and Web sites their privacy protection practices. Surfers can then access compatible sites, and choose to either stay away from, or negotiate with, incompatible sites. P3P is still under development, however, and will not become fully operational for several months. Its future is uncertain, as is its popularity with Web site owners.

When it comes to the Internet, the sad truth is that there still more money to be made by invading your privacy than by protecting it. Until that changes, beware!

While privacy advocates maintain that privacy protection without the backing of legislation is ineffective, a powerful lobby of U.S. companies argues for self-regulation of privacy protections. The effectiveness of a self-regulatory system was called into serious question by the following two incidents involving GeoCities, one of the most popular Web sites on the Internet (now part of Yahoo!), and AOL, the world's largest ISP.

In The Matter Of GeoCities, A Corporation[†]

AGREEMENT CONTAINING CONSENT ORDER

The Federal Trade Commission has conducted an investigation of certain acts and practices of GeoCities, a corporation ("proposed respondent"). Proposed respondent, having been represented by counsel, is willing to enter into an agreement containing a consent order resolving the allegations contained in the attached draft complaint. Therefore,

---

† U.S. Federal Trade Commission, FILE NO. 9823015.

IT IS HEREBY AGREED by and between GeoCities, by its duly authorized officer, and counsel for the Federal Trade Commission that:

ORDER

DEFINITIONS

For purposes of this order, the following definitions shall apply:

1. "Child" or "children" shall mean a person of age twelve (12) or under.
2. "Parents" or "parental" shall mean a legal guardian, including, but not limited to, a biological or adoptive parent.
3. "Personal identifying information" shall include, but is not limited to, first and last name, home or other physical address (e.g., school), e-mail address, telephone number, or any information that identifies a specific individual, or any information which when tied to the above becomes identifiable to a specific individual.
4. "Disclosure" or "disclosed to third party(ies)" shall mean (a) the release of information in personally identifiable form to any other individual, firm, or organization for any purpose or (b) making publicly available such information by any means including, but not limited to, public posting on or through home pages, pen pal services, e-mail services, message boards, or chat rooms.
5. "Clear(ly) and prominent(ly)" shall mean in a type size and location that are not obscured by any distracting elements and are sufficiently noticeable for an ordinary consumer to read and comprehend, and in a typeface that contrasts with the background against which it appears.
6. "Archived" database shall mean respondent's off-site "back-up" computer tapes containing member profile information and GeoCities Web site information.
7. "Electronically verifiable signature" shall mean a digital signature or other electronic means that ensures a valid consent by requiring: (1) authentication (guarantee that the message has come from the person who claims to have sent it); (2) integrity (proof that the message contents have not been altered, deliberately or accidentally, during transmission); and (3) non-repudiation (certainty that the sender of the message cannot later deny sending it).
8. "Express parental consent" shall mean a parent's affirmative agreement that is obtained by any of the following means: (1) a signed statement transmitted by postal mail or facsimile; (2) authorizing a charge to a credit card via a secure server; (3) e-mail accompanied by an electronically verifiable signature; (4) a procedure that is specifically authorized by statute, regulation, or guideline issued by the Commission; or (5) such other procedure that ensures verified parental consent and ensures the identity of the parent, such as the use of a reliable certifying authority.
9. Unless otherwise specified, "respondent" shall mean GeoCities, its successors and assigns and its officers, agents, representatives, and employees.
10. "Commerce" shall mean as defined in Section 4 of the Federal Trade Commission Act, 15 U.S.C. §44.

I.

IT IS ORDERED that respondent, directly or through any corporation, subsidiary, division, or other device, in connection with any online collection of personal identifying information from consumers, in or affecting commerce, shall not make any misrepresentation, in any manner, expressly or by implication, about its collection or use of such information from or about consumers, including, but not limited to, what information will be disclosed to third parties and how the information will be used.

II.

IT IS FURTHER ORDERED that respondent, directly or through any corporation, subsidiary, division, or other device, in connection with any online collection of personal identifying information from consumers, in or affecting commerce, shall not misrepresent, in any manner, expressly or by implication, the identity of the party collecting any such information or the sponsorship of any activity on its Web site.

III.

IT IS FURTHER ORDERED that respondent, directly or through any corporation, subsidiary, division, or other device, in connection with the online collection of personal identifying information from children, in or affecting commerce, shall not collect personal identifying information from any child if respondent has actual knowledge that such child does not have his or her parent's permission to provide the information to respondent. Respondent shall not be deemed to have actual knowledge if the child has falsely represented that (s)he is not a child and respondent does not knowingly possess information that such representation is false.

IV.

IT IS FURTHER ORDERED that respondent, directly or through any corporation, subsidiary, division, or other device, in connection with the online collection of personal identifying information, in or affecting commerce, shall provide clear and prominent notice to consumers, including the parents of children, with respect to respondent's practices with regard to its collection and use of personal identifying information. Such notice shall include, but is not limited to, disclosure of:

A. what information is being collected (e.g., "name," "home address," "e-mail address," "age," "interests");

B. its intended use(s);

C. the third parties to whom it will be disclosed (e.g., "advertisers of consumer products," "mailing list companies," "the general public");

D. the consumer's ability to obtain access to or directly access such information and the means by which (s)he may do so;

E. the consumer's ability to remove directly or have the information removed from respondent's databases and the means by which (s)he may do so; and

F. the procedures to delete personal identifying information from respondent's databases and any limitations related to such deletion.

Such notice shall appear on the home page of respondent's Web site(s) and at each location on the site(s) at which such information is collected.

Provided that, respondent shall not be required to include the notice at the locations at which information is collected if such information is limited to tracking information and the collection of such information is described in the notice required by this Part.

Provided further that, for purposes of this Part, compliance with all of the following shall be deemed adequate notice: (a) placement of a clear and prominent hyperlink or button labeled PRIVACY NOTICE on the home page(s), which directly links to the privacy notice screen(s); (b) placement of the information required in this Part clearly and prominently on the privacy notice screen(s), followed on the same screen(s) with a button that must be clicked on to make it disappear; and (c) at each location on the site at which any personal identifying information is collected, placement of a clear and prominent hyperlink on the initial screen on which the collection takes place, which links directly to the privacy notice and which is accompanied by the following statement in bold typeface:

NOTICE: We collect personal information on this site. To learn more about how we use your information click here.

V.

IT IS FURTHER ORDERED that respondent, directly or through any corporation, subsidiary, division, or other device, in connection with the online collection of personal identifying information from children, in or affecting commerce, shall maintain a procedure by which it obtains express parental consent prior to collecting and using such information.

Provided that, respondent may implement the following screening procedure that shall be deemed to be in compliance with this Part. Respondent shall collect and retain certain personal identifying information from a child, including birth date and the child's and parent's e-mail addresses (hereafter "screening information"), enabling respondent to identify the site visitor as a child and to block the child's attempt to register with respondent without express parental consent. If respondent elects to have the child register with it, respondent shall: (1) give notice to the child to have his/her parent provide express parental consent to register; and/or (2) send a notice to the parent's e-mail address for the purpose of obtaining express parental consent. The notice to the child or parent shall provide instructions for the parent to: (1) go to a specific URL on the Web site to receive information on respondent's practices regarding its collection and use of personal identifying information from children and (2) provide express parental consent for the collection and use of such information. Respondent's collection of screening information shall be by a manner that discourages children from providing personal identifying information in addition to the screening information. All personal identifying information collected from a child shall be held by respondent in a secure manner and shall not be used in any manner other than to effectuate the notice to the child or parent, or to block the child from further attempts to register or otherwise provide personal identifying information to respondent without express parental consent. The personal identifying information collected shall not be disclosed to any third party prior to the receipt of express parental consent. If express parental consent is not received by twenty (20) days after respondent's collection of the information from the child, respondent shall remove all such personal identifying information from its databases, except such screening information necessary to block the child from further attempts to register or otherwise provide personal identifying information to respondent without express parental consent.

VI.

IT IS FURTHER ORDERED that respondent GeoCities, and its successors and assigns, shall provide a reasonable means for consumers, including the parents of children, to obtain removal of their or their children's personal identifying information collected and retained by respondent and/or disclosed to third parties, prior to the date of service of this order, as follows:

A. Respondent shall provide a clear and prominent notice to each consumer over the age of twelve (12) from whom it collected personal identifying information and disclosed that information to CMG Information Services, Inc., describing such consumer's options as stated in Part VI.C and the manner in which (s)he may exercise them.

B. Respondent shall provide a clear and prominent notice to the parent of each child from whom it collected personal identifying information prior to May 20, 1998, describing the parent's options as stated in Part VI.C and the manner in which (s)he may exercise them.

C. Respondent shall provide the notice within thirty (30) days after the date of service of this order by e-mail, postal mail, or facsimile. Notice to the parent of a child may be to the e-mail address of the parent and, if not known by respondent, to the e-mail address of the child. The notice shall include the following information:

1. the information that was collected (e.g., "name," "home address," "e-mail address," "age," "interests"); its use(s) and/or intended use(s); and the third parties to whom it was or will be disclosed (e.g., "advertisers of consumer products," "mailing list companies," "the general public") and with respect to children, that the child's personal identifying information may have been made public through various means, such as by publicly posting on the child's personal home page or disclosure by the child through the use of an e-mail account;
2. the consumer's and child's parents right to obtain access to such information and the means by which (s)he may do so;
3. the consumer's and child's parent's right to have the information removed from respondent's or a third party's databases and the means by which (s)he may do so;
4. a statement that children's information will not be disclosed to third parties, including public posting, without express parental consent to the disclosure or public posting;
5. the means by which express parental consent may be communicated to the respondent permitting disclosure to third parties of a child's information; and
6. a statement that the failure of a consumer over the age of twelve (12) to request removal of the information from respondent's databases will be deemed as approval to its continued retention and/or disclosure to third parties by respondent.

D. Respondent shall provide to consumers, including the parents of children, a reasonable and secure means to request access to or directly access their or their children's personal identifying information. Such means may include direct access through password protected personal profile, return e-mail bearing an electronically verifiable signature, postal mail, or facsimile.

E. Respondent shall provide to consumers, including the parents of children, a reasonable means to request removal of their or their children's personal identifying information from respondent's and/or the applicable third party's databases or an assurance that such information has been removed. Such means may include e-mail, postal mail, or facsimile.

F. The failure of a consumer over the age of twelve (12) to request the actions specified above within twenty (20) days after his/her receipt of the notice required in Part VI.A shall be deemed to be consent to the information's continued retention and use by respondent and any third party.

G. Respondent shall provide to the parent of a child a reasonable means to communicate express parental consent to the retention and/or disclosure to third parties of his/her child's personal identifying information. Respondent shall not use any such information or disclose it to any third party unless and until it receives express parental consent.

H. If, in response to the notice required in Part VI.A, respondent has received a request by a consumer over the age of twelve (12) that respondent should remove from its databases the consumer's personal identifying information or has not received the express consent of a parent of a child to the continued retention and/or disclosure to third parties of a child's personal identifying information by respondent within twenty (20) days after the parent's receipt of the notice required in Part VI.B, respondent shall within ten (10) days:

1. Discontinue its retention and/or disclosure to third parties of such information, including but not limited to (a) removing from its databases all such information, (b) removing all personal home pages created by the child, and (c) terminating all e-mail accounts for the child; and
2. Contact all third parties to whom respondent has disclosed the information, requesting that they discontinue using or disclosing that information to other third parties, and remove the information from their databases.

With respect to any consumer over the age of twelve (12) or any parent of a child who has consented to respondent's continued retention and use of personal identifying information pursuant to this Part, such consumer's or parent's continuing right to obtain access to his/her or a child's personal identifying information or removal of such information from respondent's databases shall be as specified in the notice required by Part IV of this order.

I. Within thirty (30) days after the date of service of this order, respondent shall obtain from a responsible official of each third party to whom it has disclosed personal identifying information and from each GeoCities Community Leader a statement stating that (s)he has been advised of the terms of this order and of respondent's obligations under this Part, and that (s)he agrees, upon notification from respondent, to discontinue using or disclosing a consumer's or child's personal identifying information to other third parties and to remove any such information from its databases.

J. As may be permitted by law, respondent shall cease to do business with any third party that fails within thirty (30) days of the date of service of this order to provide the statement set forth in Part VI.I or whom respondent knows or has reason to know has failed at any time to (a) discontinue using or disclosing a child's personal identifying information to other third parties, or (b) remove any such information from their databases. With respect to any GeoCities Community Leader, the respondent shall cease the Community Leader status of any person who fails to provide the statement set forth in Part VI.I or whom respondent knows or has reason to know has failed at any time to (a) discontinue using or disclosing a child's personal identifying information to other third parties, or (b) remove any such information from their databases.

For purposes of this Part: "third party(ies)" shall mean each GeoCities Community Leader, CMG Information Services, Inc., Surplus Software, Inc. (Surplus Direct/ Egghead Computer), Sage Enterprises, Inc. (GeoPlanet/Planetall), Netopia, Inc. (Netopia), and InfoBeat/Mercury Mail (InfoBeat).

VII.

IT IS FURTHER ORDERED that for the purposes of this order, respondent shall not be required to remove personal identifying information from its archived database if such information is retained solely for the purposes of Web site system maintenance, computer file back-up, to block a child's attempt to register with or otherwise provide personal identifying information to respondent without express parental consent, or to respond to requests for such information from law enforcement agencies or pursuant to judicial process.

Except as necessary to respond to requests from law enforcement agencies or pursuant to judicial process, respondent shall not disclose to any third party any information retained in its archived database. In any notice required by this order, respondent shall include information, clearly and prominently, about its policies for retaining information in its archived database.

VIII.

IT IS FURTHER ORDERED that for five (5) years after the date of this order, respondent GeoCities, and its successors and assigns, shall place a clear and prominent hyperlink within its privacy statement which states as follows in bold typeface:

NOTICE: Click here for important information about safe surfing from the Federal Trade Commission.

The hyperlink shall directly link to a hyperlink/URL to be provided to respondent by the Commission. The Commission may change the hyperlink/URL upon thirty (30) days prior written notice to respondent.

IX.

IT IS FURTHER ORDERED that respondent GeoCities, and its successors and assigns, shall maintain and upon request make available to the Federal Trade Commission for inspection and copying the following:

A. For five (5) years after the last date of dissemination of a notice required by this order, a print or electronic copy in HTML format of all documents relating to compliance with Parts IV through VIII of this order, including, but not limited to, a sample copy of every information collection form, Web page, screen, or document containing any representation regarding respondent's information collection and use practices, the notice required by Parts IV through VI, any communication to third parties required by Part VI, and every Web page or screen linking to the Federal Trade Commission Web site. Each Web page copy shall be accompanied by the

URL of the Web page where the material was posted online. Electronic copies shall include all text and graphics files, audio scripts, and other computer files used in presenting information on the World Wide Web; and

Provided that, after creation of any Web page or screen in compliance with this order, respondent shall not be required to retain a print or electronic copy of any amended Web page or screen to the extent that the amendment does not affect respondent's compliance obligations under this order.

B. For five (5) years after the last collection of personal identifying information from a child, all materials evidencing the express parental consent given to respondent.

X.

IT IS FURTHER ORDERED that respondent GeoCities, and its successors and assigns, shall deliver a copy of this order to all current and future principals, officers, directors, and managers, and to all current and future employees, agents, and representatives having responsibilities with respect to the subject matter of this order. Respondent shall deliver this order to current personnel within thirty (30) days after the date of service of this order, and to future personnel within thirty (30) days after the person assumes such position or responsibilities.

XI.

IT IS FURTHER ORDERED that respondent GeoCities, and its successors and assigns, shall establish an "information practices training program" for any employee or GeoCities Community Leader engaged in the collection or disclosure to third parties of consumers' personal identifying information. The program shall include training about respondent's privacy policies, information security procedures, and disciplinary procedures for violations of its privacy policies. Respondent shall provide each such current employee and GeoCities Community Leader with information practices training materials within thirty (30) days after the date of service of this order, and each such future employee or GeoCities Community Leader such materials and training within thirty (30) days after (s)he assumes his/her position or responsibilities.

McVeigh v. Cohen†

The Plaintiff, Senior Chief Timothy R. McVeigh, is a highly decorated seventeen-year veteran of the United States Navy who has served honorably and continuously since he was nineteen years old. At the time of the Navy's decision to discharge him, he was the senior-most enlisted man aboard the United States nuclear submarine U.S.S. Chicago.

On September 2, 1997, Ms. Helen Hajne, a civilian Navy volunteer, received an electronic mail ("email") message through the America Online Service ("AOL") regarding the toy-drive that she was coordinating for the Chicago crew members' children. The message box stated that it came from the alias "boysrch," but the text of the email was signed by a "Tim." Administrative Record ("AR"). Through an option available to AOL subscribers, the volunteer searched through the "member

---

† 983 F. Supp. 215, (D.D.C. 1998).

profile directory" to find the member profile for this sender. The directory specified that "boysrch" was an AOL subscriber named Tim who lived in Honolulu, Hawaii, worked in the military, and identified his marital status as "gay." Although the profile included some telling interests such as "collecting pics of other young studs" and "boy watching," it did not include any further identifying information such as full name, address, or phone number. However, on other occasions, Hajne had communicated with the Plaintiff about his participation in the drive.

Ms. Hajne proceeded to forward the email and directory profile to her husband, who, like Plaintiff, was also a noncommissioned officer aboard the U.S.S. Chicago. The material eventually found its way to Commander John Mickey, the captain of the ship and Plaintiff's commanding officer. In turn, Lieutenant Karin S. Morean, the ship's principal legal adviser and a member of the Judge Advocate General's ("JAG") Corps was called in to investigate the matter. By this point, the Navy suspected the "Tim" who authored the email might be Senior Chief Timothy McVeigh. Before she spoke to the Plaintiff and without a warrant or court order, Lieutenant Morean requested a Navy paralegal on her staff, Legalman First Class Joseph M. Kaiser, to contact AOL and obtain information from the service that could "connect" the screen name "boysrch" and accompanying user profile to McVeigh. Legalman Kaiser called AOL's toll-free customer service number and talked to a representative at technical services. Legalman Kaiser did not identify himself as a Naval serviceman. According to his testimony at the administrative hearing, he stated that he was "a third party in receipt of a fax sheet and wanted to confirm the profile sheet, [and] who it belonged to." The AOL representative affirmatively identified Timothy R. McVeigh as the customer in question.

Upon verification from AOL, Lieutenant Morean notified Senior Chief McVeigh that the Navy had obtained "some indication[ ] that he made a statement of homosexuality" in violation of §654(b)(2) of "Don't Ask, Don't Tell." In light of the Uniform Code of Military Justice prohibition of sodomy and indecent acts, she then advised him of his right to remain silent. Shortly thereafter, in a memorandum dated September 22, 1997, the Navy advised Plaintiff that it was commencing an administrative discharge proceeding (termed by the Navy as an "administrative separation") against him. The reason stated was for "homosexual conduct, as evidenced by your statement that you are a homosexual."

On November 7, 1997, the Navy conducted an administrative discharge hearing before a three-member board. At the hearing, the Plaintiff made an unsworn oral statement that explained the substance of his email to Ms. Hajne, and thus by inference confirmed his authorship of the correspondence. The Plaintiff presented evidence of a prior engagement to a woman and several other heterosexual relationships to rebut the presumption of homosexuality, pursuant to §654(b)(2). This evidence was rejected by the Board. At the conclusion of the administrative hearing, the board held that the government had sufficiently shown by a preponderance of the evidence that Senior Chief McVeigh had engaged in "homosexual conduct," a dischargeable offense.

. . . .

Certainly, the public has an inherent interest in the preservation of privacy rights as advanced by Plaintiff in this case. With literally the entire world on the world-wide web, enforcement of the ECPA is of great concern to those who bare the most personal information about their lives in private accounts through the

Internet. In this case in particular, where the government may well have violated a federal statute in its zeal to brand the Plaintiff a homosexual, the actions of the Navy must be more closely scrutinized by this Court. It is disputed in the record exactly as to how the Navy represented itself to AOL when it requested information about the Plaintiff. The Defendants contend that Legalman Kaiser merely asked for confirmation of a fax sheet bearing Plaintiff's account. Plaintiff contends, and AOL confirms, however, that the Naval officer "mislead" AOL's representative by "both failing to disclose the identity and purpose [of his request] and by portraying himself as a friend or acquaintance of Senior Chief McVeigh's." At the final injunction hearing, this issue should be fully explored.

The Court believes that when this case is finally determined, it will become clear that the case will be able to be disposed on the basis of the "Don't Ask, Don't Tell, Don't Pursue" policy. This provision draws a fine balance between the interests of gay service members and the Armed Forces. It is a way of permitting gay women and men to serve in the Armed Forces, a right that the military did not provide them prior to the adoption of "Don't Ask, Don't Tell, Don't Pursue."

To make the policy work requires each of the parties to refrain from taking certain actions. Under the provisions of the policy, if the gay member agrees to remain silent about his or her sexual orientation, he or she is permitted to serve. For its part under the policy, the military is required to refrain from asking any of its members about their sexual orientation or pursuing an inquiry into a member's sexual orientation without a reasonable basis in fact. So far, pursuant to the record developed in this case, while Plaintiff complied with the requirements imposed upon him under "Don't Ask, Don't Tell, Don't Pursue," the Defendant went further than the policy permits. Although Officer McVeigh did not publicly announce his sexual orientation, the Navy nonetheless impermissibly embarked on a search and "outing" mission. Therefore, when this case is finally heard, if the record remains as it is now, the Plaintiff will likely prevail. It is accordingly for this reason that a preliminary injunction will issue. An appropriate order follows.

Discussion Questions

Consider the terms of agreement reached in the GeoCities settlement. Do you think the terms could form the basis for privacy legislation? What do you see as the key elements in a legislative solution for privacy protection?

Notes

1. For more on the McVeigh case, see Timothy McVeigh's personal Web site at <http://www.geocities.com/Pentagon/9241/>.

2. Recent studies on online privacy provide conflicting conclusions on whether the situation is gradually improving. In 1998, the Federal Trade Commission, the U.S. agency responsible for consumer protection issues, released a study that indicated that the majority of commercial Web sites did not have adequate privacy protections. Moreover, sites targeting children were particularly problematic, since many collected personal data without parental supervision. A year later, a Georgetown University study found that 66% of sites included a privacy policy on their Web site. A December 1999 study of the top 100

Internet shopping sites by the Electronic Privacy Information Center found that all sites collected personal information, yet the majority did not provide users with access to their personal data and or provide sufficient information about the use of collected data. The FTC report can be found online at <http://www.ftc.gov/privacy/reports.htm>; the Georgetown study can be found at <http://www.gsb.georgetown.edu/faculty/culnanm/gippshome.html>; and the EPIC report can be found at <http://www.epic.org/reports/surfer-beware3.html>.

Cyberspace Privacy: A Primer and a Proposal[†]

JERRY KANG

Human ingenuity has provided us a great gift, cyberspace. This blooming network of computing-communication technologies is quickly changing the world and our behavior in it. Already, it has become cliche to catalog cyberspace's striking benefits, its endless possibilities. But great gifts often come with a great price. Congress thinks that the price will be sexual purity due to easy access to pornography. Industry thinks it will be our economy due to easy copying of Hollywood's and Silicon Valley's programs. I worry that it will be our privacy.

When I mention "privacy," lawyers naturally think of privacy as used in the historic case, *Roe* v. *Wade*. Others think of the privacy of their own homes and back-yards, largely in territorial terms. I use "privacy" differently. Instead of emphasizing privacy in a decisional or spatial sense, I mean it in an information sense. Information privacy is an individual's claim to control the terms under which personal information is acquired, disclosed, and used.

My thesis is that cyberspace threatens information privacy in extraordinary ways, and without much thought or collective deliberation, we may be in the process of surrendering our privacy permanently as we enter the next century.

Why Care About Privacy?
Some people do not understand what the big deal is about privacy. They assume that privacy is important only for those who have something to hide. This view is misguided. Let me articulate why individuals should enjoy meaningful control over the acquisition, disclosure, and use of their personal information.

Use of personal data. Personal data are often misused. For example, personal data can be used to commit identity theft, in which an impostor creates fake financial accounts, runs up enormous bills, and disappears leaving only a wrecked credit report behind. Personal data, such as home addresses and telephone numbers, can be used to harass and stalk. Personal data, such as one's sexual orientation, can be used to deny employment because of unwarranted prejudice.

Disclosure of personal data. Sometimes, even if such data will not be "used" against us, its mere disclosure may lead to embarrassment. In any culture, certain conditions are embarrassing even when they are not blameworthy. Take impotency for example. In most cases, impotency will not affect whether one receives a job, a loan, or a promotion. In this sense, the data will not be misused in the allocation of rewards and opportunities. However, the mere disclosure of this medical condition would cause intense embarrassment for most men.

In addition to causing embarrassment, the inability to control the disclosure of personal data can hamper the building of intimate relationships. We construct many intimacies not only by sharing experiences but also by sharing secrets about ourselves, details not broadcast to a mass audience. If we have information privacy, we can regulate the outflow of such private information to others. By reducing this flow to a trickle (for example, to your boss), we maintain aloofness; by releasing a more telling stream (for example, to your former college roommate living afar) we invite and affirm intimacy. If anyone could find out anything about us, secrets would lose their ability to help construct intimacy.

Acquisition of personal data. Finally, consider the fact that personal information is acquired by observing who we are and what we do. When such observation is nonconsensual and extensive, we have what amounts to surveillance, which is in tension with human dignity. Human beings have dignity because they are moral persons — beings capable of self-determination, with the capacity to reflect upon and choose personal and political projects. Extensive, undesired observation interferes with this exercise of choice because we act differently when we are being watched. Simply put, surveillance leads to self-censorship. When we do not want to be surveilled, it disrespects our dignity to surveil us nonetheless, unless some important social justification exists. This insult to individual dignity has social ramifications. It chills out-of-the-mainstream behavior. It corrodes private experimentation and reflection. It threatens to leave us with a bland, unoriginal polity, characterized by excessive conformity.

The Difference That Cyberspace Makes

So now that we know why privacy matters, we must ask what difference does cyberspace make? My claim is that cyberspace makes broad societal surveillance possible and, if we do nothing, likely. To see the greater threat that cyberspace poses, imagine the following two visits to a mall — one in real space, the other in cyberspace.

In real space, you drive to a mall, walk its corridors, peer into numerous shops, and stroll through the aisles of inviting stores. You walk into a bookstore and flip through a few magazines. Finally, you stop at a clothing store and buy a friend a scarf with a credit card. In this narrative, numerous persons interact with you and collect information along the way. For instance, while walking through the mall, fellow visitors visually collect information about you, if for no other reason than to avoid bumping into you. But such information is general, e.g., it does not pinpoint the geographical location and time of the sighting, is not in a format that can be processed by a computer, is not indexed to your name or any unique identifier, and is impermanent, residing in short-term human memory. You remain a barely noticed stranger. One important exception is the credit card purchase.

By contrast, in cyberspace, the exception becomes the norm: Every interaction may soon be like the credit card purchase. The best way to grasp this point is to take seriously, if only for a moment, the metaphor that cyberspace is an actual place, a virtual reality. In this alternate universe, you are invisibly stamped with a bar code as soon as you venture outside your home. There are entities called "road providers" (your Internet Service Provider), who supply the streets and ground you walk on, who track precisely where, when, and how fast you traverse the lands, in order to charge you for your wear on the infrastructure. As soon as you enter the cyber-mall's domain, the mall tracks you through invisible scanners focused on your bar code. It automatically records which stores you visit, which windows you browse, in which order, and for how long. The specific stores collect even more detailed data when you enter their domain. For example, the cyber-bookstore notes which magazines you skimmed, recording which pages you have seen and for how long, and notes the pattern, if any, of your browsing. It notes that you picked up a health magazine featuring an article on Viagra, read for seven minutes a newsweekly detailing a politician's sex scandal, and flipped ever-so-quickly through a tabloid claiming that Elvis lives. Of course, whenever any item is actually purchased, the store, as well as the credit, debit, or virtual cash company that provides payment through cyberspace, takes careful notes of what you bought — in this case, a silk scarf, red, expensive, a week before Valentine's Day.

All these data generated in cyberspace are detailed, computer-processable, indexed to the individual, and permanent. While the mall example may not concern data that appear especially sensitive, the same extensive data collection can take place as we travel through other cyberspace domains — for instance, to research health issues and politics; to communicate to friends, businesses, and the government; and to pay our bills and manage our finances. Moreover, the data collected in these various domains can be aggregated to produce telling profiles of who we are, as revealed by what we do and with whom we associate. The very technology that makes cyberspace possible also makes detailed, cumulative, invisible observation of ourselves possible. One need only sift through the click streams generated by our cyber-activity.

It turns out that few laws limit what can be done with this data collected in cyberspace. Unlike Europe, the United States has no omnibus privacy law covering the private sector's processing of personal information. Instead, U.S. law features a legal patchwork that regulates different types of personal information in different ways, depending on how it is acquired, by whom, and how it will be used. To be sure, there are numerous statutes that govern specific sectors, such as consumer credit, education, cable programming, electronic communications, videotape rentals, motor vehicle records, and the recently enacted Children's Online Privacy Protection Act. But it turns out that in toto, information collectors can largely do what they want.

The Market Solution

Let me restate the problem. All cyber-activity, even simply browsing a Webpage, involves a "transaction" between an individual and potential information collectors. These collectors not only include the counterparty to the transaction but also intermediaries (transaction facilitators) that support the electronic communications (telephone company, cable company, Internet service provider) and sometimes payment (credit card company, electronic cash company). In these transactions, personal information is inevitably generated as either necessary or incidental by-products. Privacy enthusiasts insist that the individual owns this data; information collectors vigorously disagree. What shall be done?

Perhaps the market might solve the problem. One might reasonably view personal information as a commodity, whose pricing and consumption can and should be governed by the laws of supply and demand. Through offers and counteroffers between individual and information collector, the market will move the correctly priced personal data to the party that values it most. Economists love this approach because it appears to be economically efficient. The private sector loves this approach because it staves off regulation. Regulators love this approach for the same reason in the current antiregulatory environment.

The problem is that in practice, individuals and information collectors do not negotiate express privacy contracts before engaging in each transaction. Although privacy notices have become more frequent on Webpages, it is a stretch to say that there is a "meeting of the minds" on privacy terms each time an individual browses a Webpage. What is necessary, then, is a clear articulation of the default rules governing personal data collected in a cyberspace transaction, when parties have not agreed explicitly otherwise.

There are two default rules that society might realistically adopt. First, there is the status quo's "plenary" default rule: Unless the parties agree otherwise, the information collector may process the personal data anyway it likes. Second, there is the "functionally necessary" default rule: Unless the parties agree otherwise, the information collector may process the personal data only in functionally necessary ways. This rule allows the information collector to process personal data on a need-only basis to complete the transaction in which the information was originally collected.

A one-size-fits-all default rule is efficient for some transactions but inefficient for others. Those parties for whom the default is inefficient will either contract around the rule — "flip" — or they will "stick" with the rule and accept the inefficiencies. Thus, the social cost of a default rule equals the sum of the transaction costs of contracting around the rule — the "flip cost" — plus the inefficiency cost of not contracting around the rule even when it would be more efficient to do so — the "stick cost." We seek the rule that minimizes social costs.

If we implement the plenary rule, most parties will stick because it is hard for a consumer to flip out of the default rule. First, she would face substantial research costs to determine what information is being collected and how it is used. That is because individuals today are largely clueless about how personal information is processed through cyberspace. Sometimes, they are deceived by the information collectors themselves, as the Federal Trade Commission recently charged against the Internet Service Provider, Geocities. Second, the individual would run into a collective action problem. Realistically, the information collector would not entertain one person's idiosyncratic request to purchase back personal information because the costs of administering such an individually tailored program would be prohibitive. Therefore, to make it worth the firm's while, the individual would have to band together with other like-minded individuals to renegotiate the privacy terms of the underlying transaction. These individuals would suffer the collective action costs of locating each other, then coming to a mutually acceptable proposal to deliver to the information collector, — all the while discouraging free riders.

By contrast, the "functionally necessary" rule would not be sticky at all. With this default, if the firm valued personal data more than the individual, then the firm would have to buy permission to process the data in functionally unnecessary ways. Note, however, two critical differences in contracting around this default. First, unlike the individual who has to find out how information is processed, the collector need not bear such research costs since it already knows what its information practices are. Second, the collector does not confront collective action problems. It need not seek out other like-minded firms and reach consensus before coming to the individual with a request. This is because an individual would gladly entertain an individualized, even idiosyncratic, offer to purchase personal information.

Now, the task is to compare the costs of the equilibrium generated by each default rule. For the "plenary" equilibrium, the cost of the default rule is approximately the stick cost because few parties will flip. By contrast, for the "functionally necessary" equilibrium, the cost of the default rule is approximately the flip cost; almost all parties who care to flip will flip. Which cost is higher? We lack the data to be confident in our answer. However, we do know that given how seriously many individuals feel about their privacy, the stick cost of the plenary rule will not be trivial. Many individuals who care deeply about their privacy will not be able to get it. By contrast, the flip cost of the functionally necessary rule will be small because cyberspace makes communications cheap. The information collector can ask in a simple dialog box whether the individual will allow some unnecessary use of personal data, in exchange for some benefit. What is more, this inequality will increase over time. As information processing becomes more sophisticated, people will feel less in control of their personal information; accordingly they will value control more (making the cost of "sticking" greater). Simultaneously, the cost of communication will decrease as cyberspace improves (making the cost of "flipping" less).

In conclusion, I think it is more likely than not that a functionally necessary rule will be less costly to society than the plenary rule we currently have. Putting economic efficiency aside, the functionally necessary rule also better respects human dignity by respecting an individual's desire not to be surveilled.

Notes

1. For an excellent Canadian survey of privacy issues, see Ontario Privacy Commissioner Ann Cavoukian's *Privacy: The Key To Electronic Commerce*, available online at <http://www.ipc.on.ca/web_site.eng/matters/sum_pap/PAPERS/e-comm.htm>.

2. Online privacy concerns are best appreciated through experience. Consider this Web page (<http://www.ece.jhu.edu/class/213/grades>) from Johns Hopkins University. Is this a problem? How common do you think using social security numbers as student identification numbers is? You can find out by going to the Altavista search engine and running the boolean search "host.*edu and grades and SSN".

    Next, visit the following page from Anonymizer.com, a site that enables you to browse the Web anonymously (<http://privacy.net/anonymizer/>). Did you know that this information was so readily available to the Web sites you visit? Is this a problem?

    Now visit (<http://www.reversephonedirectory.com/>) and pick the reverse telephone lookup. If you call your local operator with only a phone number would they provide you with this information? Is this a cause for concern?

Finally, consider (<http://www.digicrime.com/>). Did you realize that an external Web site could exert this level of control over your computer? Is this a problem?

3. For more about online privacy issues, see the following Web resources:
    • Electronic Privacy Information Center (EPIC) — <http://www.epic.org>
    • Privacy Rights Clearinghouse — <http://www.privacyrights.org/>
    • The Privacy Page — <http://www.privacy.org/>

12

Canadian Approaches to Online Privacy

In response to the Canadian public's growing concern with personal privacy, the government has passed a major legislative initiative that, for the first time, creates national private sector privacy protections. Although the legislative process was slowed by opposition from various constituencies, the *Personal Information Protection and Electronic Documents Act*, popularly known as Bill C-6, received Royal Assent on April 13, 2000 and is scheduled to take effect on January 1, 2001.

The heart of the legislation is the Canadian Standards Association Model Code for the Protection of Personal Information. The subject of intense negotiation between business, consumer groups, and government in the early and mid-1990s, the Code represents a compromise between the need to protect individual privacy and the desire of organizations to collect personal data for marketing and other commercial purposes. This compromise remains intact in the new law, and is reflected in its purpose clause, which explicitly refers to the balance between the competing interests of individuals and business. (An early version of the bill referred only to personal privacy.)

Given the privacy dangers discussed in Chapter 11, the most disappointing aspect of the law is the long delay in its application to most Canadian businesses. Once the law comes into effect, it will initially only apply to federally regulated organizations such as airlines, broadcasters, and banks. For the vast majority of organizations, the law takes effect only three years after it comes into force, which effectively means that it will not have widespread impact on Canadian Internet use until at least 2004.

Despite the long delay, the new law represents the cornerstone of the Canadian privacy legal framework and is worthy of detailed examination. This chapter canvasses the law's key provisions while providing references to the federal *Privacy Act* and the common law.

THE CSA MODEL CODE

The heart of the new law is the Canadian Standards Association Model Code for the Protection of Personal Information. Based on the OECD's 1981 Model Code on Privacy, the CSA Code contains 10 principles that have emerged as the basis for good privacy practices. The Code is granted legal effect by virtue of its attachment to the law as Schedule One.

The Personal Information Protection and Electronic Documents Act[†]

4.1 Principle 1 — Accountability

An organization is responsible for personal information under its control and shall designate an individual or individuals who are accountable for the organization's compliance with the following principles.

4.1.1 Accountability for the organization's compliance with the principles rests with the designated individual(s), even though other individuals within the organization may be responsible for the day-to-day collection and processing of personal information. In addition, other individuals within the organization may be delegated to act on behalf of the designated individual(s).

4.1.2 The identity of the individual(s) designated by the organization to oversee the organization's compliance with the principles shall be made known upon request.

4.1.3 An organization is responsible for personal information in its possession or custody, including information that has been transferred to a third party for processing. The organization shall use contractual or other means to provide a comparable level of protection while the information is being processed by a third party.

4.1.4 Organizations shall implement policies and practices to give effect to the principles, including

  (a) implementing procedures to protect personal information;
  (b) establishing procedures to receive and respond to complaints and inquiries;
  (c) training staff and communicating to staff information about the organization's policies and practices; and
  (d) developing information to explain the organization's policies and procedures.

---

† S.C. 2000, c. 5, Schedule One.

4.2   Principle 2 — Identifying Purposes

The purposes for which personal information is collected shall be identified by the organization at or before the time the information is collected.

4.2.1 The organization shall document the purposes for which personal information is collected in order to comply with the Openness principle (Clause 4.8) and the Individual Access principle (Clause 4.9).

4.2.2 Identifying the purposes for which personal information is collected at or before the time of collection allows organizations to determine the information they need to collect to fulfil these purposes. The Limiting Collection principle (Clause 4.4) requires an organization to collect only that information necessary for the purposes that have been identified.

4.2.3 The identified purposes should be specified at or before the time of collection to the individual from whom the personal information is collected. Depending upon the way in which the information is collected, this can be done orally or in writing. An application form, for example, may give notice of the purposes.

4.2.4 When personal information that has been collected is to be used for a purpose not previously identified, the new purpose shall be identified prior to use. Unless the new purpose is required by law, the consent of the individual is required before information can be used for that purpose. For an elaboration on consent, please refer to the Consent principle (Clause 4.3).

4.2.5 Persons collecting personal information should be able to explain to individuals the purposes for which the information is being collected.

4.2.6 This principle is linked closely to the Limiting Collection principle (Clause 4.4) and the Limiting Use, Disclosure, and Retention principle (Clause 4.5).

4.3   Principle 3 — Consent

The knowledge and consent of the individual are required for the collection, use, or disclosure of personal information, except where inappropriate.

Note: In certain circumstances personal information can be collected, used, or disclosed without the knowledge and consent of the individual. For example, legal, medical, or security reasons may make it impossible or impractical to seek consent. When information is being collected for the detection and prevention of fraud or for law enforcement, seeking the consent of the individual might defeat the purpose of collecting the information. Seeking consent may be impossible or inappropriate when the individual is a minor, seriously ill, or mentally incapacitated. In addition, organizations that do not have a direct relationship with the individual may not always be able to seek consent. For example, seeking consent may be impractical for a charity or a direct-marketing firm that wishes to acquire a mailing list from another organization. In such cases, the organization providing the list would be expected to obtain consent before disclosing personal information.

4.3.1 Consent is required for the collection of personal information and the subsequent use or disclosure of this information. Typically, an organization will seek consent for the use or disclosure of the information at the time of collection. In certain circumstances, consent with respect to use or disclosure may be sought after the information has been collected but before use (for example, when an organization wants to use information for a purpose not previously identified).

4.3.2 The principle requires "knowledge and consent". Organizations shall make a reasonable effort to ensure that the individual is advised of the purposes for which the information will be used. To make the consent meaningful, the purposes must be stated in such a manner that the individual can reasonably understand how the information will be used or disclosed.

4.3.3 An organization shall not, as a condition of the supply of a product or service, require an individual to consent to the collection, use, or disclosure of information beyond that required to fulfil the explicitly specified, and legitimate purposes.

4.3.4 The form of the consent sought by the organization may vary, depending upon the circumstances and the type of information. In determining the form of consent to use, organizations shall take into account the sensitivity of the information. Although some information (for example, medical records and income records) is almost always considered to be sensitive, any information can be sensitive, depending on the context. For example, the names and addresses of subscribers to a newsmagazine would generally not be considered sensitive information. However, the names and addresses of subscribers to some special-interest magazines might be considered sensitive.

4.3.5 In obtaining consent, the reasonable expectations of the individual are also relevant. For example, an individual buying a subscription to a magazine should reasonably expect that the organization, in addition to using the individual's name and address for mailing and billing purposes, would also contact the person to solicit the renewal of the subscription. In this case, the organization can assume that the individual's request constitutes consent for specific purposes. On the other hand, an individual would not reasonably expect that personal information given to a health-care professional would be given to a company selling health-care products, unless consent were obtained. Consent shall not be obtained through deception.

4.3.6 The way in which an organization seeks consent may vary, depending on the circumstances and the type of information collected. An organization should generally seek express consent when the information is likely to be considered sensitive. Implied consent would generally be appropriate when the information is less sensitive. Consent can also be given by an authorized representative (such as a legal guardian or a person having power of attorney).

4.3.7 Individuals can give consent in many ways. For example:

(a) an application form may be used to seek consent, collect information, and inform the individual of the use that will be made of the information. By completing and signing the form, the individual is giving consent to the collection and the specified uses;

(b) a checkoff box may be used to allow individuals to request that their names and addresses not be given to other organizations.
   Individuals who do not check the box are assumed to consent to the transfer of this information to third parties;

(c) consent may be given orally when information is collected over the telephone; or

(d) consent may be given at the time that individuals use a product or service.

4.3.8 An individual may withdraw consent at any time, subject to legal or contractual restrictions and reasonable notice. The organization shall inform the individual of the implications of such withdrawal.

4.4 Principle 4 — Limiting Collection

The collection of personal information shall be limited to that which is necessary for the purposes identified by the organization. Information shall be collected by fair and lawful means.

4.4.1 Organizations shall not collect personal information indiscriminately. Both the amount and the type of information collected shall be limited to that which is necessary to fulfil the purposes identified. Organizations shall specify the type of information collected as part of their information-handling policies and practices, in accordance with the Openness principle (Clause 4.8).

4.4.2 The requirement that personal information be collected by fair and lawful means is intended to prevent organizations from collecting information by misleading or deceiving individuals about the purpose for which information is being collected. This requirement implies that consent with respect to collection must not be obtained through deception.

4.4.3 This principle is linked closely to the Identifying Purposes principle (Clause 4.2) and the Consent principle (Clause 4.3).

4.5 Principle 5 — Limiting Use, Disclosure, and Retention

Personal information shall not be used or disclosed for purposes other than those for which it was collected, except with the consent of the individual or as required by law. Personal information shall be retained only as long as necessary for the fulfilment of those purposes.

4.5.1 Organizations using personal information for a new purpose shall document this purpose (see Clause 4.2.1).

4.5.2 Organizations should develop guidelines and implement procedures with respect to the retention of personal information. These guidelines should include minimum and maximum retention periods. Personal information that has been used to make a decision about an individual shall be retained long enough to allow the individual access to the information after the decision has been made. An organization may be subject to legislative requirements with respect to retention periods.

4.5.3 Personal information that is no longer required to fulfil the identified purposes should be destroyed, erased, or made anonymous. Organizations shall develop guidelines and implement procedures to govern the destruction of personal information.

4.5.4 This principle is closely linked to the Consent principle (Clause 4.3), the Identifying Purposes principle (Clause 4.2), and the Individual Access principle (Clause 4.9).

4.6 Principle 6 — Accuracy

Personal information shall be as accurate, complete, and up-to-date as is necessary for the purposes for which it is to be used.

4.6.1 The extent to which personal information shall be accurate, complete, and up-to-date will depend upon the use of the information, taking into account the interests of the individual. Information shall be sufficiently accurate, complete, and up-to-date to minimize the possibility that inappropriate information may be used to make a decision about the individual.

4.6.2 An organization shall not routinely update personal information, unless such a process is necessary to fulfil the purposes for which the information was collected.

4.6.3 Personal information that is used on an ongoing basis, including information that is disclosed to third parties, should generally be accurate and up-to-date, unless limits to the requirement for accuracy are clearly set out.

4.7   Principle 7 — Safeguards
Personal information shall be protected by security safeguards appropriate to the sensitivity of the information.

4.7.1 The security safeguards shall protect personal information against loss or theft, as well as unauthorized access, disclosure, copying, use, or modification. Organizations shall protect personal information regardless of the format in which it is held.

4.7.2 The nature of the safeguards will vary depending on the sensitivity of the information that has been collected, the amount, distribution, and format of the information, and the method of storage. More sensitive information should be safeguarded by a higher level of protection. The concept of sensitivity is discussed in Clause 4.3.4.

4.7.3 The methods of protection should include

  (a) physical measures, for example, locked filing cabinets and restricted access to offices;
  (b) organizational measures, for example, security clearances and limiting access on a "need-to-know" basis; and
  (c) technological measures, for example, the use of passwords and encryption.

4.7.4 Organizations shall make their employees aware of the importance of maintaining the confidentiality of personal information.

4.7.5 Care shall be used in the disposal or destruction of personal information, to prevent unauthorized parties from gaining access to the information (see Clause 4.5.3).

4.8   Principle 8 — Openness
An organization shall make readily available to individuals specific information about its policies and practices relating to the management of personal information.

4.8.1 Organizations shall be open about their policies and practices with respect to the management of personal information. Individuals shall be able to acquire information about an organization's policies and practices without unreasonable effort. This information shall be made available in a form that is generally understandable.

4.8.2 The information made available shall include

  (a) the name or title, and the address, of the person who is accountable for the organization's policies and practices and to whom complaints or inquiries can be forwarded;
  (b) the means of gaining access to personal information held by the organization;

(c) a description of the type of personal information held by the organization, including a general account of its use;

(d) a copy of any brochures or other information that explain the organization's policies, standards, or codes; and

(e) what personal information is made available to related organizations (e.g., subsidiaries).

4.8.3 An organization may make information on its policies and practices available in a variety of ways. The method chosen depends on the nature of its business and other considerations. For example, an organization may choose to make brochures available in its place of business, mail information to its customers, provide online access, or establish a toll-free telephone number.

4.9 Principle 9 — Individual Access

Upon request, an individual shall be informed of the existence, use, and disclosure of his or her personal information and shall be given access to that information. An individual shall be able to challenge the accuracy and completeness of the information and have it amended as appropriate.

Note: In certain situations, an organization may not be able to provide access to all the personal information it holds about an individual. Exceptions to the access requirement should be limited and specific. The reasons for denying access should be provided to the individual upon request. Exceptions may include information that is prohibitively costly to provide, information that contains references to other individuals, information that cannot be disclosed for legal, security, or commercial proprietary reasons, and information that is subject to solicitor-client or litigation privilege.

4.9.1 Upon request, an organization shall inform an individual whether or not the organization holds personal information about the individual. Organizations are encouraged to indicate the source of this information. The organization shall allow the individual access to this information. However, the organization may choose to make sensitive medical information available through a medical practitioner. In addition, the organization shall provide an account of the use that has been made or is being made of this information and an account of the third parties to which it has been disclosed.

4.9.2 An individual may be required to provide sufficient information to permit an organization to provide an account of the existence, use, and disclosure of personal information. The information provided shall only be used for this purpose.

4.9.3 In providing an account of third parties to which it has disclosed personal information about an individual, an organization should attempt to be as specific as possible. When it is not possible to provide a list of the organizations to which it has actually disclosed information about an individual, the organization shall provide a list of organizations to which it may have disclosed information about the individual.

4.9.4 An organization shall respond to an individual's request within a reasonable time and at minimal or no cost to the individual. The requested information shall be provided or made available in a form that is generally understandable. For example, if the organization uses abbreviations or codes to record information, an explanation shall be provided.

4.9.5 When an individual successfully demonstrates the inaccuracy or incompleteness of personal information, the organization shall amend the information as required. Depending upon the nature of the information challenged, amendment involves the correction, deletion, or addition of information. Where appropriate, the amended information shall be transmitted to third parties having access to the information in question.

4.9.6 When a challenge is not resolved to the satisfaction of the individual, the substance of the unresolved challenge shall be recorded by the organization. When appropriate, the existence of the unresolved challenge shall be transmitted to third parties having access to the information in question.

4.10 Principle 10 — Challenging Compliance

An individual shall be able to address a challenge concerning compliance with the above principles to the designated individual or individuals accountable for the organization's compliance.

4.10.1 The individual accountable for an organization's compliance is discussed in Clause 4.1.1.

4.10.2 Organizations shall put procedures in place to receive and respond to complaints or inquiries about their policies and practices relating to the handling of personal information. The complaint procedures should be easily accessible and simple to use.

4.10.3 Organizations shall inform individuals who make inquiries or lodge complaints of the existence of relevant complaint procedures. A range of these procedures may exist. For example, some regulatory bodies accept complaints about the personal-information handling practices of the companies they regulate.

4.10.4 An organization shall investigate all complaints. If a complaint is found to be justified, the organization shall take appropriate measures, including, if necessary, amending its policies and practices.

Discussion Questions

1. Does the Code read like a traditional piece of legislation or more like a statement of best practices? Can you identify potential interpretation problems within the Code, since it has now become law?

2. The Consent principle (Principle 3) is the core of the Code. Do you think it affords sufficient protection?

3. One of the most common methods of obtaining consent online is the use of the negative option check box, which requires a user to check the box if they do not wish to receive further information or have their data collected and used. This approach places the onus on the individual to opt-out of a data collection scheme rather than forcing an organization to obtain an individual's

opt-in. How does the Code view the use of negative option check boxes? Would the use of such a consent mechanism, buried at the bottom of a Web page, meet the standard set by the new law?

DEFINITIONS

An effective legal framework requires more than simply attaching the CSA Model Code to the law. Definitional provisions, enforcement provisions, jurisdictional issues, and policy exceptions all work to create a framework much larger than Code itself.

The Personal Information Protection and Electronic Documents Act[†]

The definitions in this subsection apply in this Part.

"commercial activity" means any particular transaction, act or conduct or any regular course of conduct that is of a commercial character, including the selling, bartering or leasing of donor, membership or other fundraising lists.

"Commissioner" means the Privacy Commissioner appointed under section 53 of the Privacy Act.

"Court" means the Federal Court-Trial Division.

"federal work, undertaking or business" means any work, undertaking or business that is within the legislative authority of Parliament. It includes

(a) a work, undertaking or business that is operated or carried on for or in connection with navigation and shipping, whether inland or maritime, including the operation of ships and transportation by ship anywhere in Canada;
(b) a railway, canal, telegraph or other work or undertaking that connects a province with another province, or that extends beyond the limits of a province;
(c) a line of ships that connects a province with another province, or that extends beyond the limits of a province;
(d) a ferry between a province and another province or between a province and a country other than Canada;
(e) aerodromes, aircraft or a line of air transportation;
(f) a radio broadcasting station;
(g) a bank;
(h) a work that, although wholly situated within a province, is before or after its execution declared by Parliament to be for the general advantage of Canada or for the advantage of two or more provinces;

---

† S.C. 2000, c. 5, s. 2(1).

(i) a work, undertaking or business outside the exclusive legislative authority of the legislatures of the provinces; and

(j) a work, undertaking or business to which federal laws, within the meaning of section 2 of the Oceans Act, apply under section 20 of that Act and any regulations made under paragraph 26(1)(k) of that Act.

"personal information" means information about an identifiable individual, but does not include the name, title or business address or telephone number of an employee of an organization.

"record" includes any correspondence, memorandum, book, plan, map, drawing, diagram, pictorial or graphic work, photograph, film, microform, sound recording, videotape, machine-readable record and any other documentary material, regardless of physical form or characteristics, and any copy of any of those things.

Notes

1. Note that the law provides an exhaustive definition for federal work, undertaking, or business. This definition becomes important due to the transitional provisions found in the law. They include:

    30.(1) This Part does not apply to any organization in respect of personal information that it collects, uses or discloses within a province whose legislature has the power to regulate the collection, use or disclosure of the information, unless the organization does it in connection with the operation of a federal work, undertaking or business or the organization discloses the information outside the province for consideration.

    (2) Subsection (1) ceases to have effect three years after the day on which this section comes into force.

    As noted above, the effect of s. 30 is to limit the applicability of the law to federal undertakings during the law's first three years.

2. In December 1999, the Senate sought to add the following definition for personal health information:

    "Personal health information", with respect to an individual, whether living or deceased means:

    (a) information concerning the physical or mental health of the individual;
    (b) information concerning any health service provided to the individual;
    (c) information concerning the donation by the individual of any body part or any bodily substance of the individual or information derived from the testing or examination of a body part or bodily substance of the individual;
    (d) information that is collected in the course of providing health services to the individual; or
    (e) information that is collected incidentally to the provision of health services to the individual.

    The Senate proposed that personal health information be exempted from the law during its first year in force. The changes were accepted by Industry Minister John Manley in February 2000 and became part of the new law when it received royal assent in April 2000.

Discussion Questions

Compare the definition of personal information in the new law with that found in the federal *Privacy Act*. Which do you prefer? Why do you think the drafters of the new law opted for the shorter approach?

Privacy Act, C. P-21, s. 3

"personal information" means information about an identifiable individual that is recorded in any form including, without restricting the generality of the foregoing,

(a) information relating to the race, national or ethnic origin, colour, religion, age or marital status of the individual,

(b) information relating to the education or the medical, criminal or employment history of the individual or information relating to financial transactions in which the individual has been involved,

(c) any identifying number, symbol or other particular assigned to the individual,

(d) the address, fingerprints or blood type of the individual,

(e) the personal opinions or views of the individual except where they are about another individual or about a proposal for a grant, an award or a prize to be made to another individual by a government institution or a part of a government institution specified in the regulations,

(f) correspondence sent to a government institution by the individual that is implicitly or explicitly of a private or confidential nature, and replies to such correspondence that would reveal the contents of the original correspondence,

(g) the views or opinions of another individual about the individual,

(h) the views or opinions of another individual about a proposal for a grant, an award or a prize to be made to the individual by an institution or a part of an institution referred to in paragraph (e), but excluding the name of the other individual where it appears with the views or opinions of the other individual, and

(i) the name of the individual where it appears with other personal information relating to the individual or where the disclosure of the name itself would reveal information about the individual,

but, for the purposes of sections 7, 8 and 26 and section 19 of the Access to Information Act, does not include

(j) information about an individual who is or was an officer or employee of a government institution that relates to the position or functions of the individual including,

(i) the fact that the individual is or was an officer or employee of the government institution,

(ii) the title, business address and telephone number of the individual,

(iii) the classification, salary range and responsibilities of the position held by the individual,

(iv) the name of the individual on a document prepared by the individual in the course of employment, and

(v) the personal opinions or views of the individual given in the course of employment,

(k) information about an individual who is or was performing services under contract for a government institution that relates to the services performed, including the terms of the contract, the name of the individual and the opinions or views of the individual given in the course of the performance of those services,

(l) information relating to any discretionary benefit of a financial nature, including the granting of a licence or permit, conferred on an individual, including the name of the individual and the exact nature of the benefit, and

(m) information about an individual who has been dead for more than twenty years;

PURPOSE OF THE LAW

The purpose clause of the new law was the subject of considerable debate during House of Commons hearings. Privacy advocates noted that the original purpose clause focused on e-commerce, with privacy treated merely as an element within an e-commerce legal framework. Business interests noted that the purpose clause referred solely to the individual right to privacy without referencing the need of organizations to collect personal information in a reasonable manner. The revised purpose clause better reflects the compromise approach of the CSA Model Code, with privacy protection and data collection afforded equal billing.

> **3.** The purpose of this Part is to establish, in an era in which technology increasingly facilitates the circulation and exchange of information, rules to govern the collection, use and disclosure of personal information in a manner that recognizes the right of privacy of individuals with respect to their personal information and the need of organizations to collect, use or disclose personal information for purposes that a reasonable person would consider appropriate in the circumstances.

Discussion Questions

1. Compare the new law's purpose clause with that found in the *Privacy Act*. Which do you prefer? Was it necessary to include both privacy protection and data collection within the law?

   > Privacy Act, Ch. P-21, s. 2
   >
   > The purpose of this Act is to extend the present laws of Canada that protect the privacy of individuals with respect to personal information about themselves held by a government institution and that provide individuals with a right of access to that information.

2. Consider the words of Justice La Forest in *R.* v. *Dyment*, [1988] 2 S.C.R. 417, one of the Supreme Court's leading privacy decisions. Does the purpose clause found in the new law reflect the same urgency and importance of privacy protection found in the judgment?

   > Finally, there is privacy in relation to information. This too is based on the notion of the dignity and integrity of the individual. As the Task Force put it (p. 13): "This notion of privacy derives from the assumption that all information about a person is in a fundamental way his own, for him to communicate or retain for himself as he sees fit." In modern society, especially, retention of information about oneself is extremely important. We may, for one reason or another, wish or be compelled to reveal such information, but situations abound

where the reasonable expectations of the individual that the information shall remain confidential to the persons to whom, and restricted to the purposes for which it is divulged, must be protected. Governments at all levels have in recent years recognized this and have devised rules and regulations to restrict the uses of information collected by them to those for which it was obtained; see, for example, the Privacy Act, S.C. 1980-81-82-83, c. 111.

One further general point must be made, and that is that if the privacy of the individual is to be protected, we cannot afford to wait to vindicate it only after it has been violated. This is inherent in the notion of being secure against unreasonable searches and seizures. Invasions of privacy must be prevented, and where privacy is outweighed by other societal claims, there must be clear rules setting forth the conditions in which it can be violated. (429–30)

APPLICATION OF THE ACT

The Personal Information Protection and Electronic Documents Act[†]

(1) This Part applies to every organization in respect of personal information that

  (a) the organization collects, uses or discloses in the course of commercial activities; or

  (b) is about an employee of the organization and that the organization collects, uses or discloses in connection with the operation of a federal work, undertaking or business.

(2) This Part does not apply to

  (a) any government institution to which the Privacy Act applies;

  (b) any individual in respect of personal information that the individual collects, uses or discloses for personal or domestic purposes and does not collect, use or disclose for any other purpose; or

  (c) any organization in respect of personal information that the organization collects, uses or discloses for journalistic, artistic or literary purposes and does not collect, use or disclose for any other purpose.

(3) Every provision of this Part applies despite any provision, enacted after this subsection comes into force, of any other Act of Parliament, unless the other Act expressly declares that that provision operates despite the provision of this Part.

---

† S.C. 2000, c. 5, s. 4.

Discussion Questions

1. The Act does not include a definition of personal or domestic purposes. How broad an exclusion do you think this is?

2. The journalistic exception was opposed by some groups who feared that press activity could undermine the law's privacy protections. Journalists, which once included the federal Privacy Commissioner, pointed out that freedom of the press was a freedom equally cherished in a free and democratic society. Does the law provide an effective balance between freedom of the press and privacy? Should the journalist exception be subject to certain limitations?

3. Subsection 3, which grants the new law supremacy over other federal legislation, was not included in the initial draft of the bill, but rather was added after privacy groups lobbied for its inclusion.

4. The CSA Model Code contains numerous references to "must" and "should." The law clarifies the effect of those words in Section 5.

    5.(1) Subject to sections 6 to 9, every organization shall comply with the obligations set out in Schedule 1.
    (2) The word "should", when used in Schedule 1, indicates a recommendation and does not impose an obligation.

5. Unlike the European Union Data Privacy directive (discussed at pp. 280–285 in Chapter 13), which provides that certain types of data may never be collected, used, or disclosed, the only such limitation found in the new law is the following:

    5.(3) An organization may collect, use or disclose personal information only for purposes that a reasonable person would consider are appropriate in the circumstances.

    Do you think certain types of information should receive a higher level of protection or perhaps be barred from collection or disclosure?

EXCEPTIONS TO THE CSA MODEL CODE

The Personal Information Protection and Electronic Documents Act[†]

7.(1) For the purpose of clause 4.3 of Schedule 1, and despite the note that accompanies that clause, an organization may collect personal information without the knowledge or consent of the individual only if

(a) the collection is clearly in the interests of the individual and consent cannot be obtained in a timely way;

---

† S.C. 2000, c. 5.

(b) it is reasonable to expect that the collection with the knowledge or consent of the individual would compromise the availability or the accuracy of the information and the collection is reasonable for purposes related to investigating a breach of an agreement or a contravention of the laws of Canada or a province; or

(c) the collection is solely for journalistic, artistic or literary purposes; or

(d) the information is publicly available and is specified by the regulations.

(2) For the purpose of clause 4.3 of Schedule 1, and despite the note that accompanies that clause, an organization may, without the knowledge or consent of the individual, use personal information only if

(a) in the course of its activities, the organization becomes aware of information that it has reasonable grounds to believe could be useful in the investigation of a contravention of the laws of Canada, a province or a foreign jurisdiction that has been, is being or is about to be committed, and the information is used for the purpose of investigating that contravention;

(b) it is used for the purpose of acting in respect of an emergency that threatens the life, health or security of an individual;

(c) it is used for statistical, or scholarly study or research, purposes that cannot be achieved without using the information, the information is used in a manner that will ensure its confidentiality, it is impracticable to obtain consent and the organization informs the Commissioner of the use before the information is used;

(c.1) it is publicly available and is specified by the regulations; or

(d) it was collected under paragraph (1)(a) or (b).

(3) For the purpose of clause 4.3 of Schedule 1, and despite the note that accompanies that clause, an organization may disclose personal information without the knowledge or consent of the individual only if the disclosure is

(a) made to, in the Province of Quebec, an advocate or notary or, in any other province, a barrister or solicitor who is representing the organization;

(b) for the purpose of collecting a debt owed by the individual to the organization;

(c) required to comply with a subpoena or warrant issued or an order made by a court, person or body with jurisdiction to compel the production of information, or to comply with rules of court relating to the production of records;

(c.1) made to a government institution or part of a government institution that has made a request for the information, identified its lawful authority to obtain the information and indicated that

    (i) it suspects that the information relates to national security, the defence of Canada or the conduct of international affairs,

    (ii) the disclosure is requested for the purpose of enforcing any law of Canada, a province or a foreign jurisdiction, carrying out an investigation relating to the enforcement of any such law or gathering intelligence for the purpose of enforcing any such law, or

    (iii) the disclosure is requested for the purpose of administering any law of Canada or a province;

(d) made on the initiative of the organization to an investigative body, a government institution or a part of a government institution and the organization

      (i) has reasonable grounds to believe that the information relates to a breach of an agreement or a contravention of the laws of Canada, a province or a foreign jurisdiction that has been, is being or is about to be committed, or

      (ii) suspects that the information relates to national security, the defence of Canada or the conduct of international affairs;

(e) made to a person who needs the information because of an emergency that threatens the life, health or security of an individual and, if the individual whom the information is about is alive, the organization informs that individual in writing without delay of the disclosure;

(f) for statistical, or scholarly study or research, purposes that cannot be achieved without disclosing the information, it is impracticable to obtain consent and the organization informs the Commissioner of the disclosure before the information is disclosed;

(g) made to an institution whose functions include the conservation of records of historic or archival importance, and the disclosure is made for the purpose of such conservation;

(h) made after the earlier of

      (i) one hundred years after the record containing the information was created, and

      (ii) twenty years after the death of the individual whom the information is about;

(h.1) of information that is publicly available and is specified by the regulations;

(h.2) made by an investigative body and the disclosure is reasonable for purposes related to investigating a breach of an agreement or a contravention of the laws of Canada or a province; or

(i) required by law.

    (4) Despite clause 4.5 of Schedule 1, an organization may use personal information for purposes other than those for which it was collected in any of the circumstances set out in subsection (2).

    (5) Despite clause 4.5 of Schedule 1, an organization may disclose personal information for purposes other than those for which it was collected in any of the circumstances set out in paragraphs (3)(a) to (h.2).

9.(1) Despite clause 4.9 of Schedule 1, an organization shall not give an individual access to personal information if doing so would likely reveal personal information about a third party. However, if the information about the third party is severable from the record containing the information about the individual, the organization shall sever the information about the third party before giving the individual access.

    (2) Subsection (1) does not apply if the third party consents to the access or the individual needs the information because an individual's life, health or security is threatened.

Discussion Questions

1. The exceptions found in Section 7(1) have been particularly controversial. Can you envision a scenario that would meet the "clearly in the interests" exception found in subsection 7(1)(a)? Is this legislative drafting sufficiently precise?

2. Section 7(1)(b) initially referred only to the accuracy of the information. Given the propensity for Internet users to provide inaccurate data to protect their privacy, might an organization have been justified in citing this exception for Web-based collection of data?

3. What information do you expect will be included in the public domain exception found in subsection 7(1)(d)?

4. The *Privacy Act* also includes a long list of consent exceptions, an issue that has raised the ire of the Privacy Commissioner for many years.

> The Privacy Act, C. P-21, s. 8
>
> (1) Personal information under the control of a government institution shall not, without the consent of the individual to whom it relates, be disclosed by the institution except in accordance with this section.
>
> (2) Subject to any other Act of Parliament, personal information under the control of a government institution may be disclosed
>> (a) for the purpose for which the information was obtained or compiled by the institution or for a use consistent with that purpose;
>> (b) for any purpose in accordance with any Act of Parliament or any regulation made thereunder that authorizes its disclosure;
>> (c) for the purpose of complying with a subpoena or warrant issued or order made by a court, person or body with jurisdiction to compel the production of information or for the purpose of complying with rules of court relating to the production of information;
>> (d) to the Attorney General of Canada for use in legal proceedings involving the Crown in right of Canada or the Government of Canada;
>> (e) to an investigative body specified in the regulations, on the written request of the body, for the purpose of enforcing any law of Canada or a province or carrying out a lawful investigation, if the request specifies the purpose and describes the information to be disclosed;
>> (f) under an agreement or arrangement between the Government of Canada or an institution thereof and the government of a province, the government of a foreign state, an international organization of states or an international organization established by the governments of states, or any institution of any such government or organization, for the purpose of administering or enforcing any law or carrying out a lawful investigation;
>> (g) to a member of Parliament for the purpose of assisting the individual to whom the information relates in resolving a problem;
>> (h) to officers or employees of the institution for internal audit purposes, or to the office of the Comptroller General or any other person or body specified in the regulations for audit purposes;
>> (i) to the National Archives of Canada for archival purposes;
>> (j) to any person or body for research or statistical purposes if the head of the government institution
>>> (i) is satisfied that the purpose for which the information is disclosed cannot reasonably be accomplished unless the information is provided in a form that would identify the individual to whom it relates, and
>>> (ii) obtains from the person or body a written undertaking that no subsequent disclosure of the information will be made in a form that could reasonably be expected to identify the individual to whom it relates;

    (k) to any association of aboriginal people, Indian band, government institution or part thereof, or to any person acting on behalf of such association, band, institution or part thereof, for the purpose of researching or validating the claims, disputes or grievances of any of the aboriginal peoples of Canada;

    (l) to any government institution for the purpose of locating an individual in order to collect a debt owing to Her Majesty in right of Canada by that individual or make a payment owing to that individual by Her Majesty in right of Canada; and

    (m) for any purpose where, in the opinion of the head of the institution,

        (i) the public interest in disclosure clearly outweighs any invasion of privacy that could result from the disclosure, or

    (ii) disclosure would clearly benefit the individual to whom the information relates.

5. The historic exception found in subsection 7(3)(h)(ii) faced opposition from several Senators who argued that it was unnecessary and potentially damaging. Do you agree?

FILING COMPLAINTS

The Personal Information Protection and Electronic Documents Act[†]

(1) An individual may file with the Commissioner a written complaint against an organization for contravening a provision of Division 1 or for not following a recommendation set out in Schedule 1.

(2) If the Commissioner is satisfied that there are reasonable grounds to investigate a matter under this Part, the Commissioner may initiate a complaint in respect of the matter.

(3) A complaint that results from the refusal to grant a request under section 8 must be filed within six months, or any longer period that the Commissioner allows, after the refusal or after the expiry of the time limit for responding to the request, as the case may be.

(4) The Commissioner shall give notice of a complaint to the organization against which the complaint was made.

---

† S.C. 2000, c. 5, s. 11.

COMMISSIONER'S POWERS AND DUTIES

The Personal Information Protection and Electronic Documents Act[†]

12.(1) The Commissioner shall conduct an investigation in respect of a complaint and, for that purpose, may

(a) summon and enforce the appearance of persons before the Commissioner and compel them to give oral or written evidence on oath and to produce any records and things that the Commissioner considers necessary to investigate the complaint, in the same manner and to the same extent as a superior court of record;

(b) administer oaths;

(c) receive and accept any evidence and other information, whether on oath, by affidavit or otherwise, that the Commissioner sees fit, whether or not it is or would be admissible in a court of law;

(d) at any reasonable time, enter any premises, other than a dwelling-house, occupied by an organization on satisfying any security requirements of the organization relating to the premises;

(e) converse in private with any person in any premises entered under paragraph (d) and otherwise carry out in those premises any inquiries that the Commissioner sees fit; and

(f) examine or obtain copies of or extracts from records found in any premises entered under paragraph (d) that contain any matter relevant to the investigation.

(2) The Commissioner may attempt to resolve complaints by means of dispute resolution mechanisms such as mediation and conciliation.

(3) The Commissioner may delegate any of the powers set out in subsection (1) or (2).

(4) The Commissioner or the delegate shall return to a person or an organization any record or thing that they produced under this section within ten days after they make a request to the Commissioner or the delegate, but nothing precludes the Commissioner or the delegate from again requiring that the record or thing be produced.

(5) Any person to whom powers set out in subsection (1) are delegated shall be given a certificate of the delegation and the delegate shall produce the certificate, on request, to the person in charge of any premises to be entered under paragraph (1)(d).

13.(1) The Commissioner shall, within one year after the day on which a complaint is filed or is initiated by the Commissioner, prepare a report that contains

(a) the Commissioner's findings and recommendations;

(b) any settlement that was reached by the parties;

---

† S.C. 2000, c. 5.

(c) if appropriate, a request that the organization give the Commissioner, within a specified time, notice of any action taken or proposed to be taken to implement the recommendations contained in the report or reasons why no such action has been or is proposed to be taken; and

(d) the recourse, if any, that is available under section 14.

(2) The Commissioner is not required to prepare a report if the Commissioner is satisfied that

(a) the complainant ought first to exhaust grievance or review procedures otherwise reasonably available;

(b) the complaint could more appropriately be dealt with, initially or completely, by means of a procedure provided for under the laws of Canada, other than this Part, or the laws of a province;

(c) the length of time that has elapsed between the date when the subject-matter of the complaint arose and the date when the complaint was filed is such that a report would not serve a useful purpose; or

(d) the complaint is trivial, frivolous or vexatious or is made in bad faith.

If a report is not to be prepared, the Commissioner shall inform the complainant and the organization and give reasons.

(3) The report shall be sent to the complainant and the organization without delay.

14.(1) A complainant may, after receiving the Commissioner's report, apply to the Court for a hearing in respect of any matter in respect of which the complaint was made, or that is referred to in the Commissioner's report, and that is referred to in clause 4.1.3, 4.2, 4.3.3, 4.4, 4.6, 4.7 or 4.8 of Schedule 1, in clause 4.3, 4.5 or 4.9 of that Schedule as modified or clarified by Division 1, in subsection 5(3) or 8(6) or 7) or in section 10.

(2) The application must be made within forty-five days after the report is sent or within any further time that the Court may, either before or after the expiry of those forty-five days, allow.

15. The Commissioner may, in respect of a complaint that the Commissioner did not initiate,

(a) apply to the Court, within the time limited by section 14, for a hearing in respect of any matter described in that section, if the Commissioner has the consent of the complainant;

(b) appear before the Court on behalf of any complainant who has applied for a hearing under section 14; or

(c) with leave of the Court, appear as a party to any hearing applied for under section 14.

16. The Court may, in addition to any other remedies it may give,

(a) order an organization to correct its practices in order to comply with sections 5 to 10;

(b) order an organization to publish a notice of any action taken or proposed to be taken to correct its practices, whether or not ordered to correct them under paragraph (a); and

(c) award damages to the complainant, including damages for any humiliation that the complainant has suffered.

18.(1) The Commissioner may, on reasonable notice and at any reasonable time, audit the personal information management practices of an organization if the Commissioner has reasonable grounds to believe that the organization is contravening a provision of Division 1 or is not following a recommendation set out in Schedule 1, and for that purpose may

(a) summon and enforce the appearance of persons before the Commissioner and compel them to give oral or written evidence on oath and to produce any records and things that the Commissioner considers necessary for the audit, in the same manner and to the same extent as a superior court of record;

(b) administer oaths;

(c) receive and accept any evidence and other information, whether on oath, by affidavit or otherwise, that the Commissioner sees fit, whether or not it is or would be admissible in a court of law;

(d) at any reasonable time, enter any premises, other than a dwelling-house, occupied by the organization on satisfying any security requirements of the organization relating to the premises;

(e) converse in private with any person in any premises entered under paragraph (d) and otherwise carry out in those premises any inquiries that the Commissioner sees fit; and

(f) examine or obtain copies of or extracts from records found in any premises entered under paragraph (d) that contain any matter relevant to the audit.

Notes

1. With the Commissioner's audit powers extending to situations where the Commissioner has reason to believe that privacy violations may be occurring, the law ensures that the Commissioner's office is not restricted to reactive investigations. Provincial privacy commissioners urged the inclusion of this power by arguing that compliance was far better where the Commissioner could act in a proactive manner.

    The powers have sparked controversy, however, as some privacy advocates argued that the powers included few restrictions on the right to enter any premises, a situation that might result in Commissioner-instigated privacy violations.

2. Public education has long been regarded by the Commissioner's office as an integral aspect of its duties. Those duties are now enshrined within the law, which should ease budgetary commitments to education programs.

    24. The Commissioner shall

    (a) develop and conduct information programs to foster public understanding, and recognition of the purposes, of this Part;

    (b) undertake and publish research that is related to the protection of personal information, including any such research that is requested by the Minister of Industry;

    (c) encourage organizations to develop detailed policies and practices, including organizational codes of practice, to comply with sections 5 to 10; and

(d) promote, by any means that the Commissioner considers appropriate, the purposes of this Part.

3. As part of its Privacy Act duties, the Commissioner's office produces an annual privacy report. Those duties are extended in the new law with an annual reporting requirement.

> 25.(1) The Commissioner shall, as soon as practicable after the end of each calendar year, submit to Parliament a report concerning the application of this Part, the extent to which the provinces have enacted legislation that is substantially similar to this Part and the application of any such legislation.
>
> (2) Before preparing the report, the Commissioner shall consult with those persons in the provinces who, in the Commissioner's opinion, are in a position to assist the Commissioner in reporting respecting personal information that is collected, used or disclosed interprovincially or internationally.

4. At the urging of privacy groups, the government added whistleblower protection provisions to the law. They ensure that employees who report potential privacy violations will not face retribution from within their organization.

> 27.(1) Any person who has reasonable grounds to believe that a person has contravened or intends to contravene a provision of Division 1, may notify the Commissioner of the particulars of the matter and may request that their identity be kept confidential with respect to the notification.
>
> (2) The Commissioner shall keep confidential the identity of a person who has notified the Commissioner under subsection (1) and to whom an assurance of confidentiality has been provided by the Commissioner.
>
> 27.1(1) No employer shall dismiss, suspend, demote, discipline, harass or otherwise disadvantage an employee, or deny an employee a benefit of employment, by reason that
>
> (a) the employee, acting in good faith and on the basis of reasonable belief, has disclosed to the Commissioner that the employer or any other person has contravened or intends to contravene a provision of Division 1;
>
> (b) the employee, acting in good faith and on the basis of reasonable belief, has refused or stated an intention of refusing to do anything that is a contravention of a provision of Division 1;
>
> (c) the employee, acting in good faith and on the basis of reasonable belief, has done or stated an intention of doing anything that is required to be done in order that a provision of Division 1 not be contravened; or
>
> (d) the employer believes that the employee will do anything referred to in paragraph (a), (b) or (c).

5. Privacy legislation is not strictly a federal matter. Several provinces, including Ontario, British Columbia, and Alberta, have provincial equivalents of the *Privacy Act*. Moreover, in 1994 Quebec became the first North American jurisdiction to enact private sector privacy legislation. For more information on Canadian privacy legislation, see <http://aix1.uottawa.ca/~geist/privacy.html.>

Privacy self-regulation models are not limited to the United States. Several Canadian associations, including the Canadian Association of Internet Providers (CAIP) and the Canadian Bankers Association (CBA), have developed their own privacy codes. As you review the CAIP Code, consider whether you think it as effective as a legislation solution. If not, why not? Does the new law render industry codes meaningless?

Canadian Association Of Internet Providers (CAIP) Privacy Code†

Purpose of the CAIP Privacy Code
In October 1996, CAIP released its voluntary Code of Conduct which stated that privacy was of fundamental importance to its members and that they would respect and protect the privacy of their users and would disclose personal information to law enforcement authorities only as required by law.

CAIP supports industry self-regulatory efforts in several areas, including privacy. The CAIP Privacy Code is based on the new Canadian Standards Association Model Code for the Protection of Personal Information, CAN/CSA-Q830-96 (the "CSA Code"), which was published as a National Standard of Canada. CAIP has attempted to apply the principles of the CSA Code specifically to the online environment in developing its own CAIP Privacy Code.

CAIP will continue to review the CAIP Privacy Code (the "Code") at least every year to make sure it is relevant and remains current with changing technologies, current regulatory regimes and the evolving needs of its members and their users.

Scope and Application
The CAIP Privacy Code is a voluntary code that represents a formal statement of principles and guidelines concerning the minimum protection that CAIP members will provide to their users regarding the protection of personal information.

The Code applies to the management of personal information about a member's users in any form whether oral, electronic or written that is collected, used or disclosed by the member.

This model is intended to help members develop their own privacy code and policies. The Code consists of ten principles that are closely related. Where a member chooses to adopt the principles of the CAIP Privacy Code, the member undertakes to follow all ten principles.

In addition, a member may define how it subscribes to each principle, modify details to provide specific examples, and include additional measures for the protection of privacy.

Definitions
Because the following words have specific meanings, they have been defined at the beginning of the Code.

clickstream data — data derived from a user's navigational choices expressed during the course of visiting a World Wide Web site or other online areas.

---

† Online: <http://www.caip.ca/privacy/privacy1.htm>. Reproduced by permission of Canadian Association of Internet Providers.

collect — to gather, acquire, record or obtain personal information, from any source, by any means.

consent — voluntary agreement with the collection, use and disclosure of personal information. Consent can be expressed, implied, or provided through an authorized representative. Express consent can be given orally, electronically or in writing, but is always unequivocal and does not require any inference by the member seeking consent. Implied consent arises where consent may reasonably be inferred from the action or inaction of the user.

disclose — to make personal information available outside the member to a third party.

Member — individual, organization or entity that belongs to CAIP and agrees to adhere to the CAIP Privacy Code. Each member may further tailor the CAIP Privacy Code and define clearly what affiliates, if any, are included in its definition of "the member" and bound by its code.

personal information — information about a user that is recorded in an individually identifiable form, but does not include aggregated information that cannot be associated with a specific user.

Personal information includes but is not limited to information such as a user's name, postal and electronic addresses, age, gender, income, employment, credit information, billing records, and the like. Clickstream data is only considered personal information if it is linked to other personal information about a user.

third party — an individual or organization outside the member.

use — to manage personal information by and within the member.

user — an individual who uses, or applies to use, a member's products or services.

The Ten Privacy Principles
The following ten principles seek to balance the application of information age technologies with the privacy concerns of users.

1. Accountability
Members are responsible for personal information under their control.

Members are also responsible for any personal information transferred to third parties for processing on their behalf and should use contractual or other means to provide a comparable level of protection.

Members will designate one or more persons to be accountable for compliance with these principles.

Members will identify internally the person, or persons to be accountable for compliance.

Members will identify to users a method to contact such person or persons. Depending on the size of the organization, other individuals within the member may act on behalf of the designated person or take responsibility for the day-to-day collection and management of personal information.

Members will establish necessary policies and procedures implement and comply with their own privacy codes, such as procedures for the collection, handling, storage and destruction of personal information, to train staff and to deal with complaints.

2. Identifying the purposes for collection of personal information

Members will identify the purposes of collecting personal information, before or at the time the information is collected.

Members may collect personal information for any specified purpose. Generally, members collect personal information for the following purposes:

   i) to establish and maintain responsible commercial relations with users and to provide ongoing service;
  ii) to understand user needs;
 iii) to develop, enhance, market or provide products and services;
  iv) to manage and develop the member's business and operations;
   v) to meet legal and regulatory requirements.

Members will identify their purposes for the collection, use and disclosure of personal information electronically, in writing or orally, and in language that users can easily understand.

Members will not use or disclose personal information for any purpose beyond that for which it was originally collected without first identifying the new purpose and getting the user's consent.

3. Getting the user's consent

The knowledge and consent of the user are required for the collection, use or disclosure of personal information, except where inappropriate.

Members, however, may collect, use or disclose personal information without the user's consent for legal, urgent medical, or security reasons.

Members will make a reasonable effort to inform users how the personal information collected will be used and disclosed.

Generally, a member will seek consent to use and disclose personal information at the same time it collects it. Sometimes, however, a member may identify a new purpose and seek consent to use and disclose personal information after it has been collected.

A user's consent can be expressed, implied, or given through an authorized representative. In determining the appropriate form of consent, the member will take into account the sensitivity of the information and reasonable expectations of a user.

Members will provide full and fair disclosure of its collection use and disclosure pursuant to these principles and will not deceive a user into giving consent.

A user can withdraw consent to use personal information at any time, subject to legal or contractual restrictions and reasonable notice.

Members should inform users of the implications of withdrawing consent and how to do so.

4. Limits for collecting personal information

Members will collect only the amount and type of personal information needed for the purposes they have identified.

Members will collect personal information using procedures that are fair and lawful.

When a member collects clickstream data that will be linked with personal information, the member will advise users what information is being collected and how it will be used. Otherwise, the collection, use or disclosure of clickstream data is not restricted.

Although a member will collect personal information primarily from users, it may also collect personal information from other sources including credit bureaus, or other third parties who represent that they have the right to disclose the information.

5. Limits for using, disclosing, and keeping personal information

Members will use or disclose personal information only for the purposes it was collected, unless a user gives consent or as required by law.

A member may disclose personal information without consent when required to do so by law, e.g. subpoenas, search warrants, other court and government orders, or demands from other parties who have a legal right to personal information, or to protect the security and integrity of its network or system. In such circumstances, a member will protect the interests of its users by making sure that:

i) orders or demands appear to comply with the laws under which they were issued; and

ii) it discloses only the personal information that is legally required, and nothing more.

A member may notify users that an order has been received, if the law allows it.

Only a member's employees with a business need to know, or whose duties so require, should be granted access to users' personal information.

Members will keep personal information only as long as necessary to fulfill the identified purposes.

Depending on the circumstances, personal information used to make a decision about a user should be kept long enough to allow the user access to the information after the decision has been made.

Members will keep reasonable controls, schedules and practices for information and records retention, and will destroy, erase or make anonymous within a reasonable period of time any personal information no longer needed for its identified purposes or for legal requirements.

6. Keeping personal information accurate

Members will keep personal information as accurate, complete and up-to-date as necessary for the purposes for which it is to be used.

Members may rely exclusively on the representation provided by their users in determining the completeness, accuracy, and timeliness of the personal information. This Principle does not imply any obligation on the member to seek independent verification of any personal information supplied by the user.

7. Safeguarding personal information

Members will protect personal information with safeguards appropriate to the sensitivity of the information.

Members will use appropriate safeguards to protect personal information against such risks as loss or theft, unauthorized access, disclosure, copying, use, modification or destruction.

8. Making information about policies and procedures available to users

Members will be open about the policies and procedures they use to manage personal information. Users will have access to information about these policies and procedures and the information will be easy to understand.

Members will make reasonable efforts so that users are made aware of the existence and location of their policies. Such efforts may include posting the policy online and making available information on how to access and correct personal information.

9. *Providing user access to personal information*

When users request it, members will tell them what personal information the member has, what it is being used for, and to whom it has been disclosed, and will give them access to their information.

In certain situations, however, members may not be able to give users access to all personal information they hold about the user, e.g. the information is unreasonably costly to provide, the information contains references to other users, the information cannot be disclosed for legal, security or commercial proprietary reasons, the information is subject to solicitor-client or litigation privilege. Members will explain the reasons for denying access when users ask.

In providing an account of the use and disclosure of personal information, members should state the source of the personal information where reasonably possible. Members will provide a list of the third parties to which it may have disclosed the user's personal information when it is not possible to provide an actual list.

In responding to a user's request, members will provide personal information in an understandable form, within a reasonable time and at minimal or no cost to the user.

Users will be able to challenge the accuracy and completeness of the information and have it amended as appropriate.

Members should keep records of any unresolved challenges to a user's personal information. Members will ensure that all subsequent transmissions of personal information shall include any amended information or the existence of any unresolved challenges. Where appropriate, members will transmit to third parties having access to the personal information in question any amended information and the existence of any unresolved challenges.

10. Handling users' complaints and questions

Users may challenge a member's compliance with its own privacy code. Members will have policies and procedures to receive, investigate and respond to users' complaints and questions.

Members will respond to all complaints and questions in a timely manner under the circumstances. Members will make their complaint escalation process known to their users.

13

International Approaches to Online Privacy

Despite widespread agreement on the need for privacy protection, there is no agreement among world leaders on how this can be best achieved. At one end of the spectrum lies the European Union, which has adopted an aggressive privacy law that impacts data transfers within the E.U. and abroad. At the other end of the spectrum lies the United States, which has resisted a legislative solution in favour of a self-regulation model. Canada finds itself somewhere in the middle, with the *Personal Information Protection and Electronic Documents Act* providing Canadians with a less stringent legislative solution.

The importance of these differing perspectives extends beyond the privacy protections enjoyed by residents of their respective countries. Trade in data is a critical component of modern business, and the differing approaches could well escalate into a global trade war. In fact, until agreement was reached in March 2000, the United States. and the E.U. were embroiled in a major dispute over data protection, with both sides suggesting that trade sanctions were a distinct possibility.

At the heart of the dispute is the E.U. Data Privacy directive, which has influenced data privacy laws around the world through provisions within the directive that mandate the blockage of data transfer to countries that do not employ adequate privacy protections. Many countries have responded to the directive by enacting new legislation in the hope of meeting the E.U. standard. In fact, Canada's new privacy legislation is perceived by many to be a direct response to the directive.

This chapter explores the growing rift over data privacy by examining portions of the E.U. directive and assessing the U.S. response.

Directive 95/46/EC of the European Parliament and of the Council of 24 October 1995 on the protection of individuals with regard to the processing of personal data and on the free movement of such data[†]

Article 1   Object of the Directive

1. In accordance with this Directive, Member States shall protect the fundamental rights and freedoms of natural persons, and in particular their right to privacy with respect to the processing of personal data.

2. Member States shall neither restrict nor prohibit the free flow of personal data between Member States for reasons connected with the protection afforded under paragraph 1.

· · · ·

Article 3   Scope

1. This Directive shall apply to the processing of personal data wholly or partly by automatic means, and to the processing otherwise than by automatic means of personal data which form part of a filing system or are intended to form part of a filing system.

2. This Directive shall not apply to the processing of personal data:

  i) in the course of an activity which falls outside the scope of Community law, such as those provided for by Titles V and VI of the Treaty on European Union and in any case to processing operations concerning public security, defence, State security (including the economic well-being of the State when the processing operation relates to State security matters) and the activities of the State in areas of criminal law,

  ii) a natural person in the course of a purely personal or household activity.

· · · ·

SECTION II — CRITERIA FOR MAKING DATA PROCESSING LEGITIMATE

Article 7

Member States shall provide that personal data may be processed only if:

  (a) the data subject has unambiguously given his consent; or
  (b) processing is necessary for the performance of a contract to which the data subject is party or in order to take steps at the request of the data subject prior to entering into a contract; or
  (c) processing is necessary for compliance with a legal obligation to which the controller is subject; or

---

† Official Journal of the European Communities No L. 281 (23 November 1995) at 31.

(d) processing is necessary in order to protect the vital interests of the data subject; or

(e) processing is necessary for the performance of a task carried out in the public interest or in the exercise of official authority vested in the controller or in a third party to whom the data are disclosed; or

(f) processing is necessary for the purposes of the legitimate interests pursued by the controller or by the third party or parties to whom the data are disclosed, except where such interests are overridden by the interests for fundamental rights and freedoms of the data subject which require protection under Article 1 (1).

SECTION III — SPECIAL CATEGORIES OF PROCESSING

Article 8   The processing of special categories of data

1. Member States shall prohibit the processing of personal data revealing racial or ethnic origin, political opinions, religious or philosophical beliefs, trade-union membership, and the processing of data concerning health or sex life.

2. Paragraph 1 shall not apply where:

(a) the data subject has given his explicit consent to the processing of those data, except where the laws of the Member State provide that the prohibition referred to in paragraph 1 may not be lifted by the data subject's giving his consent; or

(b) processing is necessary for the purposes of carrying out the obligations and specific rights of the controller in the field of employment law in so far as it is authorized by national law providing for adequate safeguards; or

(c) processing is necessary to protect the vital interests of the data subject or of another person where the data subject is physically or legally incapable of giving his consent; or

(d) processing is carried out in the course of its legitimate activities with appropriate guarantees by a foundation, association or any other non-profit-seeking body with a political, philosophical, religious or trade-union aim and on condition that the processing relates solely to the members of the body or to persons who have regular contact with it in connection with its purposes and that the data are not disclosed to a third party without the consent of the data subjects; or

(e) the processing relates to data which are manifestly made public by the data subject or is necessary for the establishment, exercise or defence of legal claims.

3. Paragraph 1 shall not apply where processing of the data is required for the purposes of preventive medicine, medical diagnosis, the provision of care or treatment or the management of health-care services, and where those data are processed by a health professional subject under national law or rules established by national competent bodies to the obligation of professional secrecy or by another person also subject to an equivalent obligation of secrecy.

4. Subject to the provision of suitable safeguards, Member States may, for reasons of substantial public interest, lay down exemptions in addition to those laid down in paragraph 2 either by national law or by decision of the supervisory authority.

5. Processing of data relating to offences, criminal convictions or security measures may be carried out only under the control of official authority, or if suitable specific safeguards are provided under national law, subject to derogations which may be granted by the Member State under national provisions providing suitable specific safeguards. However, a complete register of criminal convictions may be kept only under the control of official authority.

Member States may provide that data relating to administrative sanctions or judgements in civil cases shall also be processed under the control of official authority.

6. Derogations from paragraph I provided for in paragraphs 4 and 5 shall be notified to the Commission

7. Member States shall determine the conditions under which a national identification number or any other identifier of general application may be processed.

. . . .

SECTION V — THE DATA SUBJECT'S RIGHT OF ACCESS TO DATA

Article 12   Right of access
Member States shall guarantee every data right to obtain from the controller:

(a) without constraint at reasonable intervals and without excessive delay or expense:
   i) confirmation as to whether or not data relating to him are being processed and information at least as to the purposes of the processing, the categories of data concerned, and the recipients or categories of recipients to whom the data are disclosed,
   ii) communication to him in an intelligible form of the data undergoing processing and of any available information as to their source,
   iii) knowledge of the logic involved in any automatic processing of data concerning him at least in the case of the automated decisions referred to in Article 15 (1);
(b) as appropriate the rectification, erasure or blocking of data the processing of which does not comply with the provisions of this Directive, in particular because of the incomplete or inaccurate nature of the data;
(c) notification to third parties to whom the data have been disclosed of any rectification, erasure or blocking carried out in compliance with (b), unless this proves impossible or involves a disproportionate effort.

. . . .

CHAPTER IV — TRANSFER OF PERSONAL DATA TO THIRD COUNTRIES

Article 25   Principles

1. The Member States shall provide that the transfer to a third country of personal data which are undergoing processing or are intended for processing after transfer may take place only if, without prejudice to compliance with the national provisions adopted pursuant to the other provisions of this Directive, the third country in question ensures an adequate level of protection,

2. The adequacy of the level of protection afforded by a third country shall be assessed in the light of all the circumstances surrounding a data transfer operation or set of data transfer operations; particular consideration shall be given to the nature of the data, the purpose and duration of the proposed processing operation or operations, the country of origin and country of final destination, the rules of law, both general and sectoral, in force in the third country in question and the professional rules and security measures which are complied with in that country.

3. The Member States and the Commission shall inform each other of cases where they consider that a third country does not ensure an adequate level of protection within the meaning of paragraph 2.

4. Where the Commission finds, under the procedure provided for in Article 31 (2), that a third country does not ensure an adequate level of protection within the meaning of paragraph 2 of this Article, Member States shall take the measures necessary to prevent any transfer of data of the same type to the third country in question.

5. At the appropriate time, the Commission shall enter into negotiations with a view to remedying the situation resulting from the finding made pursuant to paragraph 4.

6. The Commission may find, in accordance with the procedure referred to in Article 31 (2), that a third country ensures an adequate level of protection within the meaning of paragraph 2 of this Article, by reason of its domestic law or of the international commitments it has entered into, particularly upon conclusion of the negotiations referred to in paragraph 5, for the protection of the private lives and basic freedoms and rights of individuals.

Member States shall take the measures necessary to comply with the Commission's decision.

Article 26 Derogations

1. By way of derogation from Article 25 and save where otherwise provided by domestic law governing particular cases, Member States shall provide that a transfer or a set of transfers of personal data to a third country which does not ensure an adequate level of protection within the meaning of Article 25 (2) may take place on condition that:

(a) the data subject has given his consent unambiguously to the proposed transfer; or
(b) the transfer is necessary for the performance of a contract between the data subject and the controller or the implementation of precontractual measures taken in response to the data subject's request; or
(c) the transfer is necessary for the conclusion or performance of a contract concluded in the interest of the data subject between the controller and a third party; or
(d) the transfer is necessary or legally required on important public interest grounds, or for the establishment, exercise or defence of legal claims; or
(e) the transfer is necessary in order to protect the vital interests of the data subject; or
(f) the transfer is made from a register which according to laws or regulations is intended to provide information to the public which is open to consultation either by the public in general or by any person who can demonstrate legiti-

mate interest, to the extent that the conditions laid down in law for consultation are fulfilled in the particular case.

2. Without prejudice to paragraph 1, a Member State may authorize a transfer or a set of transfers of personal data to a third country which does not ensure an adequate level of protection within the meaning of Article 25 (2), where the controller adduces adequate safeguards with respect to the protection of the privacy and fundamental rights and freedoms of individuals and as regards the exercise of the corresponding rights; such safeguards may in particular result from appropriate contractual clauses.

3. The Member State shall inform the Commission and the other Member States of the authorizations it grants pursuant to paragraph 2.

If a Member State or the Commission objects on justified grounds involving the protection of the privacy and fundamental rights and freedoms of individuals, the Commission shall take appropriate measures in accordance with the procedure laid down in Article 31 (2).

Member States shall take the necessary measures to comply with the Commission's decision.

4. Where the Commission decides, in accordance with the procedure referred to in Article 31 (2), that certain standard contractual clauses offer sufficient safeguards as required by paragraph 2, Member States shall take the necessary measures to comply with the Commission's decision.

Discussion Questions

1. Contrast the object of the directive with that found in Canada's privacy law. Which do you prefer — a law about privacy, or a law about electronic commerce with a privacy component?

2. Consider the exceptions contained in Article 3. What circumstances do you think the provision is addressing?

3. Compare the consent provision found in Article 7 with that found in Canada's privacy law. Are they equivalent? Do you think the Canadian provision is sufficiently strong to meet the adequate protection provision found at Article 25?

4. Article 8 contains a series of categories of information that cannot be processed under any circumstances. Do you think this provision is necessary?

5. Articles 25 and 26 are at the centre of the controversy over data protection. Does the provision provide a sufficient level of ambiguity such that negotiated standards are possible?

6. Many E.U. countries have explicit, constitutionally based privacy protections in addition to the E.U. data privacy directive. This approach to privacy is rooted in history. In the wake of World War II, many Western European countries enshrined privacy protections, and then, following the collapse of the Berlin Wall, many Eastern European countries followed suit. This historical background is in sharp contrast to the North American perspective on privacy, which is based largely on commercial considerations. What effect do you think this will have on global privacy developments?

7. The E.U. directive provides that member states must meet or exceed the standards established within the directive. In light of the constitutional squabbling in Canada over privacy jurisdiction, do you think this model provides Canada with an effective approach?

Safe Harbor Privacy Principles[†]

The European Union's comprehensive privacy legislation, the Directive on Data Protection (the Directive), became effective on October 25, 1998. It requires that transfers of personal data take place only to non-EU countries that provide an "adequate" level of privacy protection. While the United States and the European Union share the goal of enhancing privacy protection for their citizens, the United States takes a different approach to privacy from that taken by the European Union. The United States uses a sectoral approach that relies on a mix of legislation, regulation, and self regulation. Given those differences, many U.S. organizations have expressed uncertainty about the impact of the EU-required "adequacy standard" on personal data transfers from the European Union to the United States.

To diminish this uncertainty and provide a more predictable framework for such data transfers, the Department of Commerce is issuing this document and Frequently Asked Questions ("the Principles") under its statutory authority to foster, promote, and develop international commerce. The Principles were developed in consultation with industry and the general public to facilitate trade and commerce between the United States and European Union. They are intended for use solely by U.S. organizations receiving personal data from the European Union for the purpose of qualifying for the safe harbor and the presumption of "adequacy" it creates. Because the Principles were solely designed to serve this specific purpose, their adoption for other purposes may be inappropriate. The Principles cannot be used as a substitute for national provisions implementing the Directive that apply to the processing of personal data in the Member States.

Decisions by organizations to qualify for the safe harbor are entirely voluntary, and organizations may qualify for the safe harbor in different ways. Organizations that decide to adhere to the Principles must comply with the Principles in order to obtain and retain the benefits of the safe harbor and publicly declare that they do so. For example, if an organization joins a self-regulatory privacy program that adheres to the Principles, it qualifies for the safe harbor. Organizations may also qualify by developing their own self-regulatory privacy policies provided that they conform with the Principles. Where in complying with the Principles, an organization relies in whole or in part on self-regulation, its failure to comply with such self-regulation must also be actionable under Section 5 of the Federal Trade Commission Act prohibiting unfair and deceptive acts or another law or regulation prohibiting

---

[†] U.S. Department of Commerce, July 2000. Online: <http://www.ita.doc.gov/td/ecom/SHPRINCIPLESFINAL.htm>.

such acts. (See the annex for the list of U.S. statutory bodies recognized by the EU.) In addition, organizations subject to a statutory, regulatory, administrative or other body of law (or of rules) that effectively protects personal privacy may also qualify for safe harbor benefits. In all instances, safe harbor benefits are assured from the date on which each organization wishing to qualify for the safe harbor self-certifies to the Department of Commerce (or its designee) its adherence to the Principles in accordance with the guidance set forth in the Frequently Asked Question on Self-Certification.

Adherence to these Principles may be limited: (a) to the extent necessary to meet national security, public interest, or law enforcement requirements; (b) by statute, government regulation, or case law that create conflicting obligations or explicit authorizations, provided that, in exercising any such authorization, an organization can demonstrate that its non-compliance with the Principles is limited to the extent necessary to meet the overriding legitimate interests furthered by such authorization; or (c) if the effect of the Directive or Member State law is to allow exceptions or derogations, provided such exceptions or derogations are applied in comparable contexts. Consistent with the goal of enhancing privacy protection, organizations should strive to implement these Principles fully and transparently, including indicating in their privacy policies where exceptions to the Principles permitted by (b) above will apply on a regular basis. For the same reason, where the option is allowable under the Principles and/or U.S. law, organizations are expected to opt for the higher protection where possible.

Organizations may wish for practical or other reasons to apply the Principles to all their data processing operations, but they are only obligated to apply them to data transferred after they enter the safe harbor. To qualify for the safe harbor, organizations are not obligated to apply these Principles to personal information in manually processed filing systems. Organizations wishing to benefit from the safe harbor for receiving information in manually processed filing systems from the EU must apply the Principles to any such information transferred after they enter the safe harbor. An organization that wishes to extend safe harbor benefits to human resources personal information transferred from the EU for use in the context of an employment relationship must indicate this when it self-certifies to the Department of Commerce (or its designee) and conform to the requirements set forth in the Frequently Asked Question on Self-Certification. Organizations will also be able to provide the safeguards necessary under Article 26 of the Directive if they include the Principles in written agreements with parties transferring data from the EU for the substantive privacy provisions, once the other provisions for such model contracts are authorized by the Commission and the Member States.

U.S. law will apply to questions of interpretation and compliance with the Safe Harbor Principles (including the Frequently Asked Questions) and relevant privacy policies by safe harbor organizations, except where organizations have committed to cooperate with European Data Protection Authorities. Unless otherwise stated, all provisions of the Safe Harbor Principles and Frequently Asked Questions apply where they are relevant.

"Personal data" and "personal information" are data about an identified or identifiable individual that are within the scope of the Directive, received by a U.S. organization from the European Union, and recorded in any form.

NOTICE: An organization must inform individuals about the purposes for which it collects and uses information about them, how to contact the organization with any inquiries or complaints, the types of third parties to which it discloses the information, and the choices and means the organization offers individuals for limiting its use and disclosure. This notice must be provided in clear and conspicuous language when individuals are first asked to provide personal information to the organization or as soon thereafter as is practicable, but in any event before the organization uses such information for a purpose other than that for which it was originally collected or processed by the transferring organization or discloses it for the first time to a third party.

CHOICE: An organization must offer individuals the opportunity to choose (opt out) whether their personal information is (a) to be disclosed to a third party or (b) to be used for a purpose that is incompatible with the purpose(s) for which it was originally collected or subsequently authorized by the individual. Individuals must be provided with clear and conspicuous, readily available, and affordable mechanisms to exercise choice.

For sensitive information (i.e. personal information specifying medical or health conditions, racial or ethnic origin, political opinions, religious or philosophical beliefs, trade union membership or information specifying the sex life of the individual), they must be given affirmative or explicit (opt in) choice if the information is to be disclosed to a third party or used for a purpose other than those for which it was originally collected or subsequently authorized by the individual through the exercise of opt in choice. In any case, an organization should treat as sensitive any information received from a third party where the third party treats and identifies it as sensitive.

ONWARD TRANSFER: To disclose information to a third party, organizations must apply the Notice and Choice Principles. Where an organization wishes to transfer information to a third party that is acting as an agent, as described in the endnote, it may do so if it first either ascertains that the third party subscribes to the Principles or is subject to the Directive or another adequacy finding or enters into a written agreement with such third party requiring that the third party provide at least the same level of privacy protection as is required by the relevant Principles. If the organization complies with these requirements, it shall not be held responsible (unless the organization agrees otherwise) when a third party to which it transfers such information processes it in a way contrary to any restrictions or representations, unless the organization knew or should have known the third party would process it in such a contrary way and the organization has not taken reasonable steps to prevent or stop such processing.

SECURITY: Organizations creating, maintaining, using or disseminating personal information must take reasonable precautions to protect it from loss, misuse and unauthorized access, disclosure, alteration and destruction.

DATA INTEGRITY: Consistent with the Principles, personal information must be relevant for the purposes for which it is to be used. An organization may not process personal information in a way that is incompatible with the purposes for which it has been collected or subsequently authorized by the individual. To the extent necessary for those purposes, an organization should take reasonable steps to ensure that data is reliable for its intended use, accurate, complete, and current.

ACCESS: Individuals must have access to personal information about them that an organization holds and be able to correct, amend, or delete that information where it is inaccurate, except where the burden or expense of providing access would be disproportionate to the risks to the individual's privacy in the case in question, or where the rights of persons other than the individual would be violated.

ENFORCEMENT: Effective privacy protection must include mechanisms for assuring compliance with the Principles, recourse for individuals to whom the data relate affected by non-compliance with the Principles, and consequences for the organization when the Principles are not followed. At a minimum, such mechanisms must include

(a) readily available and affordable independent recourse mechanisms by which each individual's complaints and disputes are investigated and resolved by reference to the Principles and damages awarded where the applicable law or private sector initiatives so provide;

(b) follow up procedures for verifying that the attestations and assertions businesses make about their privacy practices are true and that privacy practices have been implemented as presented; and

(c) obligations to remedy problems arising out of failure to comply with the Principles by organizations announcing their adherence to them and consequences for such organizations. Sanctions must be sufficiently rigorous to ensure compliance by organizations.

Notes

The Online Privacy Alliance has taken the lead in promoting the self-regulation model. The organization's Web site provides details on its members, activities, and perspectives. It can be found at <http://www.privacyalliance.org>.

Discussion Questions

1. As discussed in Chapter 11, the U.S. self-regulation model of privacy protection has enjoyed mixed results. What is your view of the principles found in the U.S. proposal? Is the concern focused primarily on the availability of privacy policy or on the effectiveness of privacy protection?

2. An increasingly popular self-regulatory privacy approach is the use of third party privacy certifications. TRUSTe (<http://www.truste.com>) and the Better Business Bureau Online (<http://www.bbbonline.org>) are two of the leading organizations that permit companies to obtain a privacy "seal of approval."

   TRUSTe is arguably the best known seal programme on the Web. Similar to many other programmes, it provides what is described as an "online branded seal" to sites that meet TRUSTe criteria relating to a number of matters, including the disclosure, choice, access and security of personal information. Members of the seal programme are entitled to display a TRUSTe image on their Web site. The easy identification of a TRUSTe approved site is intended to provide consumers with increased assurance that their privacy and security is adequately protected.

   TRUSTe provides users with easy access to the programme participant's privacy policy, since access can be obtained by simply clicking on the

TRUSTe image on the site. TRUSTe also provides an online dispute resolution process for its members, acting as a mediator in disputes that cannot be readily remedied without third-party assistance between the original parties. Finally, TRUSTe performs on-site compliance reviews of programme participants when necessary.

Seal assurance programmes such as TRUSTe effectively create a self-regulatory model of Web privacy and security, thereby theoretically reducing the need for government involvement. TRUSTe establishes standards, assists companies with their implementation, and even acts as an arbiter by facilitating appropriate remedies when disputes arise.

Although this type of self-regulatory scheme may provide an effective alternative to regulation, some concerns remain. Most consumers are unaware of the role that seal programmes play with respect to a Web site. The programmes themselves vary tremendously in scope and effect. This potentially leads to confusion among users, who are likely unaware of specific details relating to every seal programme that they encounter on the Web. Moreover, it appears that the number of seal programmes on the Web is increasing with time. Entrepreneurs see profit potential, while various industry groups, non-profit organisations, and professional associations are attempting to allay government and consumer based concerns relating to privacy and security on the Web by implementing their own seal programmes. In a sense, the proliferation of programmes tends to dilute the effectiveness of any single programme by creating excessive "noise" on a Web site, leaving consumers unable to discern which seal programmes they can trust.

Consumer trust is further hampered as awareness of a potential conflict between seal programmes and their participants grows. Since many seal programmes are affiliated with major corporate interests, the essential "third-party and independent" characteristic of such programmes is called into question. Furthermore, unlike government-backed bodies, seal programmes are unable to exact punitive measures against delinquent participants in their programme.

Take a few moments to view these organizations' sites and consider the standards necessary to obtain their privacy seal of approval. Are the standards sufficient? Contrast the TRUSTe and BBBOnline standards with those used by the Canadian Institute of Chartered Accountants in the CAWebTrust program, the only Canadian-based certification program (<http://www.cica.ca/WebTrust/ee_index.htm>). Which do you prefer? Are the CAWebTrust standards too demanding? Can the conflict described above be effectively reconciled? Is government intervention needed?

Although the United States has developed a reputation for adopting a regulatory hands-off approach to privacy, Congress has enacted several privacy laws that have had a significant impact on online privacy. Foremost among these is the *Children's Online Privacy Protection Act of 1998*, better known as COPPA. COPPA came into effect in the spring of 2000 and had a major effect on numerous U.S. Web sites, which were forced to obtain parental consent for the collection and use of children's private data.

Children's Online Privacy Protection Act of 1998[†]

SEC. 1302.   DEFINITIONS.

In this title:

(1) CHILD. — The term "child" means an individual under the age of 13.

(2) OPERATOR. — The term "operator" —

(A) means any person who operates a website located on the Internet or an online service and who collects or maintains personal information from or about the users of or visitors to such website or online service, or on whose behalf such information is collected or maintained, where such website or online service is operated for commercial purposes, including any person offering products or services for sale through that website or online service, involving commerce —

(i) among the several States or with 1 or more foreign nations;
(ii) in any territory of the United States or in the District of Columbia, or between any such territory and —
(I) another such territory; or
(II) any State or foreign nation; or
(iii) between the District of Columbia and any State, territory, or foreign nation; but

(B) does not include any nonprofit entity that would otherwise be exempt from coverage under section 5 of the Federal Commission Act (15 U.S.C. 45).

(3) COMMISSION. — The term "Commission" means the Federal Trade Commission.

(4) DISCLOSURE. — The term "disclosure" means, with respect to personal information —

(A) the release of personal information collected from a child in identifiable form by an operator for any purpose, except where such information is provided to a person other than the operator who provides support for the internal operations of the website and does not disclose or use that information for any other purpose; and

(B) making personal information collected from a child by a website or online service directed to children or with actual knowledge that such information was collected from a child, publicly available in identifiable form, by any means including by a public posting, through the Internet, or through —

(i) a home page of a website;
(ii) a pen pal service;
(iii) an electronic mail service;
(iv) a message board; or
(v) a chat room.

(5) FEDERAL AGENCY. — The term "Federal agency" means an agency, as that term is defined in section 551(1) of title 5, United States Code.

---

† 15 U.S.C. §6501, et seq.

(6) INTERNET. — The term "Internet" means collectively the myriad of computer and telecommunications facilities, including equipment and operating software, which comprise the interconnected world-wide network of networks that employ the Transmission Control Protocol/Internet Protocol, or any predecessor or successor protocols to such protocol, to communicate information of all kinds by wire or radio.

(7) PARENT. — The term "parent" includes a legal guardian.

(8) PERSONAL INFORMATION. — The term "personal information" means individually identifiable information about an individual collected online, including —
    (A) a first and last name;
    (B) a home or other physical address including street name and name of a city or town;
    (C) an e-mail address;
    (D) a telephone number;
    (E) a Social Security number;
    (F) any other identifier that the Commission determines permits the physical or online contacting of a specific individual; or
    (G) information concerning the child or the parents of that child that the website collects online from the child and combines with an identifier described in this paragraph.

(9) VERIFIABLE PARENTAL CONSENT. — The term "verifiable parental consent" means any reasonable effort (taking into consideration available technology), including a request for authorization for future collection, use, and disclosure described in the notice, to ensure that a parent of a child receives notice of the operator's personal information collection, use, and disclosure practices, and authorizes the collection, use, and disclosure, as applicable, of personal information and the subsequent use of that information before that information is collected from that child.

(10) WEBSITE OR ONLINE SERVICE DIRECTED TO CHILDREN. —
    (A) IN GENERAL. — The term "website or online service directed to children" means —

  (i) a commercial website or online service that is targeted to children; or
  (ii) that portion of a commercial website or online service that is targeted to children.

    (B) LIMITATION. — A commercial website or online service, or a portion of a commercial website or online service, shall not be deemed directed to children solely for referring or linking to a commercial website or online service directed to children by using information location tools, including a directory, index, reference, pointer, or hypertext link.

(11) PERSON. — The term "person" means any individual, partnership, corporation, trust, estate, cooperative, association, or other entity.

(12) ONLINE CONTACT INFORMATION. — The term "online contact information" means an e-mail address or another substantially similar identifier that permits direct contact with a person online.

SEC. 1303. REGULATION OF UNFAIR AND DECEPTIVE ACTS AND PRACTICES IN CONNECTION WITH THE COLLECTION AND USE OF PERSONAL INFORMATION FROM AND ABOUT CHILDREN ON THE INTERNET.

(a) ACTS PROHIBITED. —

(1) IN GENERAL. — It is unlawful for an operator of a website or online service directed to children, or any operator that has actual knowledge that it is collecting personal information from a child, to collect personal information from a child in a manner that violates the regulations prescribed under subsection (b).

(2) DISCLOSURE TO PARENT PROTECTED. — Notwithstanding paragraph (1), neither an operator of such a website or online service nor the operator's agent shall be held to be liable under any Federal or State law for any disclosure made in good faith and following reasonable procedures in responding to a request for disclosure of personal information under subsection (b)(1)(B)(iii) to the parent of a child.

(b) REGULATIONS. —

(1) IN GENERAL. — Not later than 1 year after the date of the enactment of this Act, the Commission shall promulgate under section 553 of title 5, United States Code, regulations that —
　(A) require the operator of any website or online service directed to children that collects personal information from children or the operator of a website or online service that has actual knowledge that it is collecting personal information from a child —

　(i) to provide notice on the website of what information is collected from children by the operator, how the operator uses such information, and the operator's disclosure practices for such information; and
　(ii) to obtain verifiable parental consent for the collection, use, or disclosure of personal information from children;

　(B) require the operator to provide, upon request of a parent under this subparagraph whose child has provided personal information to that website or online service, upon proper identification of that parent, to such parent —

　(i) a description of the specific types of personal information collected from the child by that operator;
　(ii) the opportunity at any time to refuse to permit the operator's further use or maintenance in retrievable form, or future online collection, of personal information from that child; and
　(iii) notwithstanding any other provision of law, a means that is reasonable under the circumstances for the parent to obtain any personal information collected from that child;

　(C) prohibit conditioning a child's participation in a game, the offering of a prize, or another activity on the child disclosing more personal information than is reasonably necessary to participate in such activity; and

(D) require the operator of such a website or online service to establish and maintain reasonable procedures to protect the confidentiality, security, and integrity of personal information collected from children.

(2) WHEN CONSENT NOT REQUIRED. — The regulations shall provide that verifiable parental consent under paragraph (1)(A)(ii) is not required in the case of —

(A) online contact information collected from a child that is used only to respond directly on a one-time basis to a specific request from the child and is not used to recontact the child and is not maintained in retrievable form by the operator;

(B) a request for the name or online contact information of a parent or child that is used for the sole purpose of obtaining parental consent or providing notice under this section and where such information is not maintained in retrievable form by the operator if parental consent is not obtained after a reasonable time;

(C) online contact information collected from a child that is used only to respond more than once directly to a specific request from the child and is not used to recontact the child beyond the scope of that request —

(i) if, before any additional response after the initial response to the child, the operator uses reasonable efforts to provide a parent notice of the online contact information collected from the child, the purposes for which it is to be used, and an opportunity for the parent to request that the operator make no further use of the information and that it not be maintained in retrievable form; or

(ii) without notice to the parent in such circumstances as the Commission may determine are appropriate, taking into consideration the benefits to the child of access to information and services, and risks to the security and privacy of the child, in regulations promulgated under this subsection;

(D) the name of the child and online contact information (to the extent reasonably necessary to protect the safety of a child participant on the site) —

(i) used only for the purpose of protecting such safety;

(ii) not used to recontact the child or for any other purpose; and

(iii) not disclosed on the site, if the operator uses reasonable efforts to provide a parent notice of the name and online contact information collected from the child, the purposes for which it is to be used, and an opportunity for the parent to request that the operator make no further use of the information and that it not be maintained in retrievable form; or

(E) the collection, use, or dissemination of such information by the operator of such a website or online service necessary —

(i) to protect the security or integrity of its website;

(ii) to take precautions against liability;

(iii) to respond to judicial process; or

(iv) to the extent permitted under other provisions of law, to provide information to law enforcement agencies or for an investigation on a matter related to public safety.

(3) TERMINATION OF SERVICE. — The regulations shall permit the operator of a website or an online service to terminate service provided to a child whose parent has refused, under the regulations prescribed under paragraph (1)(B)(ii), to permit the operator's further use or maintenance in retrievable form, or future online collection, of personal information from that child.

14

Online Anonymity and Technology

The power of anonymity, one of the Internet's defining characteristics, presents users and legal officials with both great opportunity and significant challenges. The famous New Yorker cartoon depicting a dog, at a computer screen, commenting that on the Internet no one knows you're a dog is an effective illustration of how the Internet allows users to role play online by creating alter egos. Knowing that an online persona need not be the same as a real person can be a liberating experience that enables individuals to speak freely without fear of reputational harm or repercussions.

The freedom accorded by anonymity also has a darker side. Some have used their anonymity as a license to verbalize things they would never say if held accountable for their speech. While this may be acceptable in certain situations, at times such speech crosses the border into illegal speech. For example, stock hyping and cyberlibel, two forms of speech that carry stiff penalties in real space, have proliferated on the Internet in recent years, as some users act under the misconception that there are no limits to anonymous speech.

As the increasing number of court cases illustrate, laws applicable in real space will be applied to online speech, albeit with some difficulty. Unlike real space incidents, where the speaker is easily identifiable and the legal proceedings are able to examine the contested speech, online anonymous speech creates an additional burden, whereby the party seeking to curtail the speech must first identify the responsible party.

Online anonymity also nicely illustrates the tension between law and technology. Although law can be applied to anonymous speech, technology such as anonymous remailers or third party proxy servers are increasingly capable of rendering the responsible party virtually unidentifiable. Further complicating the issue is the positive contribution made by remailers and proxy servers to the cause of free speech. Many people worldwide are subject to legal regimes where free speech is not permitted. These technological solutions are frequently the only means of safely communicating without fear of criminal liability. For example, during the Kosovo conflict in the spring of 1999, Anonymizer.com established the Kosovo Privacy Project to enable those in the midst of the conflict to communicate with the rest of the world.

Professor Michael Froomkin of the University of Miami Law School has written extensively on the issue of anonymity, from both a free speech and a commercial perspective. This excerpt provides a helpful introduction to the technology and legal issues that underlie online anonymity.

Flood Control on the Information Ocean: Living with Anonymity, Digital Cash, And Distributed Databases[†]

A. MICHAEL FROOMKIN

There is no consensus, nor is there likely to be, as to whether, on balance, anonymity is a good. Anonymity has both valuable and harmful consequences, and different persons weigh these differently. Some, perhaps focussing on anonymity's contribution to many freedoms, argue that anonymity's benefits outweigh any likely harms it may cause, or that the harms (e.g., censorship) associated with trying to ban anonymity are not worth any benefits that could ensue. Others, perhaps focussing on the victims of harmful actions that can be accomplished anonymously, look at anonymity and often see dangerous license. Their conclusion is that at least some forms of anonymity should be banned.

A. Costs of Anonymity

Anonymous communication is a great tool for evading detection of illegal and immoral activity. Conspiracy, electronic hate-mail and hate-speech in general, electronic stalking, libel, general nastiness, disclosure of trade secrets and other valuable intellectual property, all become lower-risk activities if conducted via anonymous communications. These activities are merely low-risk rather than no-risk because it always remains possible to infer the identity of the author of some messages from clues intrinsic to the message itself. For example, by analyzing the manifesto issued by the "unabomber," the FBI concluded that he went to class or "hovered around" a major university in the late 1970's to mid-1980's, most probably Northwestern University, the Chicago Circle campus of the University of Illinois, the University of Utah, Brigham Young University or University of California at Berkeley. Similarly, the leaker of proprietary or classified data can sometimes be identified if the circle of people who had access to the information was small.

An anonymous author suggests that the most serious argument against anonymous speech is that "disclosure advances the search for truth," because when propaganda is anonymous it "makes it more difficult to identify the self interest or bias

---

† (1996) 15 U. Pitt. J. of Law & Comm. 395 at 402–27. Notes omitted. Reproduced by permission of the publisher.

underlying an argument." The author notes, however, that this argument assumes the validity of the metaphor of the marketplace of ideas, and that whether the benefit of increased information from the ban on anonymous speech outweighs the loss of the ideas whose expression the anonymity ban discourages is an empirical question that is unanswerable. Justice Black, the First Amendment absolutist, thought identity disclosure requirements might enhance the freedom of speech, and suggested Congress could require the disclosure of foreign agents "so that hearers and readers may not be deceived by the belief that the information comes from a disinterested source. Such legislation implements rather than detracts from the prized freedoms guaranteed by the First Amendment."

To an economist who treats markets in ideas as more concrete than a metaphor, the desire to control information about oneself can be either a final or an intermediate good. Treating privacy as a final good, however, limits the power of economic analysis, since privacy is no more than one of many elements of consumer preferences that determine her purchases when faced with the purchases that the market has to offer. Judge Posner has suggested that privacy can usefully be analyzed as an intermediate good. Using this simplifying assumption, Posner concluded that personal privacy is generally inefficient, since it allows persons to conceal disreputable facts about themselves. This failure to disclose disreputable facts shifts costs of information acquisition (or the cost of failing to acquire information) on to those who are not the least-cost avoiders. On the other hand, Posner argues that concealment by businesses is generally efficient, since allowing businesses to conceal trade secrets and other forms of intellectual property will tend to spur innovation. Posner's formulation, however, has been criticized for neglecting the strategic aspects of the individual's desire to control the release of personal information that is not disreputable.

Anonymous communication also poses particularly stark enforcement problems for libel law and intellectual property law. While it may be true that a signed defamatory message carries more credibility and thus is more damaging than an anonymous one, it does not necessarily follow that an unsigned message is harmless. Most people would probably be upset to discover a series of unsigned posters accusing them of pedophilia tacked to trees or lampposts in their neighborhood. Perhaps aware that some people believe that where there is smoke there must be fire, the victim of such a libel is unlikely to be soothed by the suggestion that anonymous attacks lack credibility. An Internet libel can be spread world-wide, and may be effectively indelible since it may be reproduced, and stored, in countless and untraceable numbers of computers. Anonymity can also be used to reveal a trade secret. For example, on September 9, 1994 an anonymous poster sent source code purporting to be RC4, a proprietary cryptographic algorithm of RSA Data Security, Inc., to the cypherpunks Internet mailing list. In most cases, a public posting will tend to reduce the value of a trade secret.

Sissela Bok has argued that a society in which "everyone can keep secrets impenetrable at will" be they "innocuous ... [or] lethal plans," noble acts or hateful conspiracies, would be undesirable because "[i]t would force us to disregard the legitimate claims of those persons who might be injured, betrayed, or ignored as the result of secrets inappropriately kept." Justice Scalia believes anonymity is generally dishonorable because it eliminates accountability. This damage to society's ability to redress legitimate claims is, I believe, the strongest moral objection to the increase in anonymous interaction. It is also clearly an objection with popular resonance, as a recent Wall Street Journal column critiquing the growth of anonymous communication on the Internet illustrates. Even a more moderate writer, while admitting that anonymity has its place, suggests that "[p]ermitting anonymity for the purpose of removing any vestige of accountability for abusive behavior ... is not likely to be tolerated in the Networld."

Anonymity has another serious consequence. Digital anonymity exacerbates the trends that are producing a society of strangers. Strangers are people who lack the mutual and continuous monitoring associated with life in a small town. Another way of putting the same point is that strangers are people about whom one has little or no information; in effect strangers engage each other as if they had complete informational privacy. A society of strangers may be one in which trust may be more difficult. "He who stands by what he has allowed to be known about himself, whether consciously or unconsciously, is worthy of trust." People about whom one knows little or nothing are harder to trust; they can be feared.

Anonymous communication can thus be viewed as one part of a more general debate over the extent to which individuals should control the dissemination of information about themselves. The problem is more complex than the loss of some imagined rural idyll. Urbanization itself does not necessarily breed mistrust. Georg Simmel suggested that in many cases "external facts" about people and goods suffice to create interpersonal confidence which therefore "no longer needs any properly personal knowledge." Certainly, the prevalence of trust is valuable: "Trust is not the sole foundation of the world; but a ... fairly complex society ... could not be established without trust." Anonymity, like other forms of personal control over information, threatens to make access to those "external facts" on which people rely more difficult. Unwillingness to trust strangers leads to the growth of social institutions designed to compensate for, or eliminate, anonymity — walled and monitored communities, credit checks, lie detectors, drug tests and on-the-job monitoring. "Surveillance is the cost of privacy." The reinterpretation of Fourth Amendment privacy rights via so-called regulatory searches in recent decisions such as *National Treasury Employees Union* v. *Von Raab*, and *Vernonia School District 47J* v. *Acton*, may be in part a response to perceived social consequences of privacy. A similar impulse may motivate legislative initiatives such as Megan's Law.

The objection to communicative anonymity with the most popular resonance may blend all these concerns. The combination of communicative anonymity with a powerful, global, poorly understood new medium seems to threaten people because the Internet allows strangers to reach into the same homes that are being turned into fortresses against strangers, and to allow those strangers to interact with its inhabitants (especially its children) without any risk of being held accountable for their communications. It may be that the idea of the home as a secure fortress is an illusion, but it is a powerful hope.

B.   Advantages of Anonymity

Ironically, the same anonymity that is blamed for undermining the accountability necessary for the security of the home/fortress may turn out to be the tool that the inhabitants of that home need to level the playing field against corporations and governments that might seek to use new data processing and data collection tools in ways that constrain the citizen's transactional or political freedom. Larger and faster database processing techniques combined with the ever-increasing quantity of personal data available on individuals makes it possible for both governments and private organizations to construct personal profiles based on transactions, demographics, and even reading habits of most citizens. Since most people lack the ability to contract for privacy on affordable terms, their main line of defense against being profiled is likely to be anonymous communication and anonymous transactions.

Anonymous communication may be particularly deserving of protection for its own sake. Not everyone is so courageous as to wish to be known for everything they say, and some timorous speech deserves encouragement. Corporate whistle-blowers, even junior professors, may fear losing their jobs. People criticizing a religious cult or other movement from which they might fear retaliation may fear losing their lives. In some countries, even this one in some times and places, it is unsafe to be heard to criticize the government. Persons who wish to criticize a repressive government or foment a revolution against it may find anonymity invaluable. Indeed, given the ability to broadcast messages widely using the Internet, anonymous e-mail may become the modern replacement of the anonymous handbill.

Communicative anonymity encourages people to post requests for information to public bulletin boards about matters they may find too personal to discuss if there were any chance that the message might be traced back to its origin. In addition to the obvious psychological benefits to people who thus find themselves enabled to communicate, there may be external benefits to the entire community. To pick just one example, public health is enhanced by the provision of information regarding communicable diseases, but many people would feel uncomfortable asking signed questions about sexually transmitted diseases, and might be especially cautious about being identified as a potential sufferer of AIDS. This caution may be particularly reasonable as data-collection technology improves: any post to a public newsgroup or bulletin board is liable to be archived and searchable, perhaps for all eternity.

Anonymous communication, whether traceable or not, fosters the development of digital personae, which may be experienced as liberating by some. The option of creating such personae is likely to increase and enhance the quantity, if not inevitably the quality, of speech. In addition to increasing the quantity of speech, anonymous communication may also enhance the quality of speech and debate. Communications that give no hint of the age, sex, race, or national origin of the writer must be judged solely on their content as there is literally nothing else to go by. This makes bigotry and stereotyping very difficult, and also should tend to encourage discussions that concentrate on the merits of the speech rather than the presumed qualities of the speakers.

In the U.S., anonymous speech may be guaranteed by the First Amendment or whatever right to privacy exists in the Constitution. In the U.S., anonymous speech also benefits from its association with well-remembered incidents in which political actors holding unpopular views that many now accept benefited from the ability to hide their identity. The Federalist Papers, the nation's most influential political tracts, were published pseudonymously under the name "Publius." More recently, the Supreme Court held the guarantee of free speech in the Constitution protects a right of anonymous association and that a state therefore lacked the power to compel a local chapter of the NAACP to disclose the names of its members. In so doing, the Court protected the NAACP members from danger at the hands of bigots who would have had access to their identities if the state had prevailed. Anonymity basks in the glow of association with good causes.

. . . .

How the Internet Enables Anonymous Communication

Thanks in large part to the easy availability of powerful cryptographic tools, the Internet provides the ability to send anonymous electronic messages at will. As described in more detail below, the anonymously remailed e-mail cannot, if properly implemented, be traced to its sender. In addition, two or more persons can communicate without knowing each other's identity, while preserving the 'untraceable' nature of their communications. As detailed below, the availability of strong cryptography vastly enhances communicative privacy and anonymity.

Currently the Internet makes it easy to send an anonymous message. Although no tangible goods can be exchanged, this communicative anonymity allows users to engage in political speech without fear of retribution, to engage in whistle-blowing while greatly reducing the risk of detection, and to seek advice about embarrassing personal problems without fear of discovery — things that are hard to do by telephone in this age of caller ID.

The traditional anonymous leaflet required a printing and distribution strategy that avoided linking the leaflet with the author. If the leaflet risked attracting the attention of someone armed with modern forensic techniques, great pains were required to avoid identifying marks such as distinctive paper or fingerprints. In contrast, on the Internet communications are all digital; the only identifying marks they carry are information inserted by the sender, the sender's software, or by any intermediaries who may have relayed the message while it was in transit. Ordinarily, an e-mail message, for example, arrives with the sender's return address and routing information describing the path it took to get from sender to receiver; were it not for that information, or perhaps for internal clues in the message itself ("hi mom!"), there would be nothing about the message to disclose the sender's identity.

Enter the anonymous remailer. Remailers vary, but all serious remailing programs share the common feature that they delete all the identifying information about incoming e-mails, substitute a predefined header identifying the remailer as the sender or using a cute tag such as nobody@nowhere. By employing easily automated cryptographic precautions widely available on the Internet, and routing a message through a series of remailers, a user can ensure three things conducive to high-security anonymity: (1) none of the remailer operators will be able to read the text of the message because it has been multiply encrypted in a fashion that requires the participation of each operator in turn before the message can be read; (2) neither the recipient nor any remailer operators in the chain (other than the first in line) can identify the sender of the text without the cooperation of every prior remailer's operator; (3) therefore it is impossible for the recipient of the message to connect the sender to the text unless every single remailer in the chain both keeps a log of its message traffic and is willing to share this information with the recipient (or is compelled to do so by a court or other authority). Since some remailer operators refuse to keep logs as a matter of principle, there is a good chance that the necessary information does not exist. Even if logs exist, it could be prohibitively expensive to compel all the operators to divulge their logs when remailers are located in different countries.

Any electronic communication, even live two-way 'chat' communication, can theoretically be made anonymous. In current practice, anonymous remailer technology applies to e-mail, and hence is used for communication to individuals, mailing lists, and 'newsgroup' discussions. E-mail offers the simplest case, and although e-mail remailer technology may not yet be as user-friendly as it could be, it is available to anyone who knows where to look and can even be found on an easy-to-use World Wide Web page.

It is useful to distinguish between four types of communication in which the sender's physical (or "real") identity is at least partly hidden: (1) traceable anonymity, (2) untraceable anonymity, (3) untraceable pseudonymity, and (4) traceable pseudonymity. These categories allow one to disentangle concepts that are otherwise conflated: whether and how an author identifies herself as opposed to whether and how the real identity of the author can be determined by others.

To make the examples that follow clearer, in each case Alice will be the person sending an e-mail message to Bob. Ted, Ursula, and Victor will be remailer operators, and Carol a judge with subpoena power.

1. Electronic Anonymity

Electronic anonymity can be "traceable" or "untraceable." Only the latter offers real security to the speaker.

A. TRACEABLE ANONYMITY

A remailer that gives the recipient no clues as to the sender's identity, but leaves this information in the hands of a single intermediary, is a system of traceable anonymity. In the simplest example, Alice sends an unencrypted e-mail to a remailer operated by Ted, with instructions to forward the e-mail to Bob. Ted's remailer deletes Alice's identifying return address and sends the message on to Bob purporting to be from "nobody@remailer.com."

Alice has no way of knowing whether Ted has logged the message, keeping a record of Alice and Bob's e-mail addresses, or indeed the entire text of the message. If Ted has done this, then Bob can find out who sent him the message by persuading Ted to tell him or, in some cases, if the message appears to violate a law, by enlisting the aid of Carol, a judge with subpoena power. Of course, if Ted lives in another country, outside Carol's jurisdiction, there may be little that Carol can do to assist Bob in his quest to persuade Ted to reveal Alice's identity. Many countries do have agreements for judicial assistance, but these can be costly, difficult, and in many cases require that the act complained of be illegal in both nations.

Although traceable anonymity offers the lowest security, it suffices for many purposes. Some messages do not require any more security than a new header. There have been occasions when I have posted messages to newsgroups and received a great deal of unwanted e-mail in reply because my e-mail signature identifies me as a law professor. One way to avoid getting requests for free legal advice, or long and vicious notes attempting to re-educate me about gun control, is to delete the signature and route comments through a remailer. That simple expedient suffices because the consequences of my being discovered as the author of my posts on legal topics are not terribly severe.

In general, however, sending a message with sensitive information directly to a remailer for immediate forwarding to the intended recipient requires an inordinate amount of trust that the remailer operator will not read or copy the message or report the sender to the appropriate authorities. I have often thought that a nice novel could be written using a crooked remailer operator as its central character: imagine that Ted opens up for business, runs a fine remailer for a few years, collects many guilty secrets, and then retires on his blackmail profits.

Much greater security, and nearly iron-clad anonymity, can be achieved at the price of somewhat greater complexity through the use of "untraceable anonymity."

B. UNTRACEABLE ANONYMITY

By "untraceable anonymity" I mean a communication for which the author is simply not identifiable at all. For example, if Alice drops an unsigned leaflet with no fingerprints on Bob's doorstep in the dead of night when no one is looking, her leaflet is "untraceably anonymous."

Current Internet technology allows this form of anonymity by the routing of messages through a series of anonymous remailers. This technique is called "chained remailing" and is about as anonymous as directed communication gets these days. Nothing is foolproof, however: as explained below, if Alice has the bad luck to use only compromised remailers whose operators are willing to club together to reveal her identity, she is just out of luck. If one member of the chain performs, however, Alice can ensure that no one can connect her to the message Bob receives so long as she uses both encryption and chaining. Even these two techniques together may not be enough to foil a determined eavesdropper who is able to track messages going in and out of multiple remailers over a period of time. To foil this level of surveillance, which has nothing to do with the bad faith of the remailer operators, requires even more exotic techniques including having the remailers alter the size of messages and ensuring that they are not remailed in the order they are received.

At the simplest level, encryption ensures that the first remailer operator cannot read the message and effortlessly connect Alice to Bob and/or the contents of the message. But encryption also has a far more important and subtle role to play. Suppose that Alice decides to route her anonymous message via Ted, Ursula, and Victor, each of whom operates a remailer and each of whom has published a public key in a public-key encryption system such as PGP. Alice wants to ensure that no member of the chain knows the full path of the other remailers handling the message; anyone who knew the full path would be able to identify Alice from the message Bob will receive. On the other hand, each member of the chain will necessarily know the identity of the immediately previous remailer from which the message came, and of course the identity of the next remailer to which the message will be sent.

Alice thus wants Ted, the first member of the chain, to remove all the information linking her to the message; she is particularly anxious that Ted not be able to read her message since he is the one party in the chain who will know that Alice sent it. Alice also wants Ted to know only that the message should go to Ursula, and to remain ignorant of the message's route thereafter. Alice wants Ursula, the second member of the chain, to know only that the message came from Ted and should go to Victor; Victor should know only that it came from Ursula and should go to Bob, although by the time the message reaches Victor, Alice may not care as much whether Victor can read the message since her identity has been well camouflaged.

Alice achieves these objectives by multiply encrypting her message, in layers, using Ted, Ursula and Victor's public keys. As each remailer receives the message, it discards the headers identifying the e-mail's origins and then decrypts the message with its private key, revealing the next address, but no more.

. . . .

Chaining the message through Ted, Ursula, and Victor means that no remailer operator alone can connect Alice to either the text of the message or Bob. Of course, if Ted, Ursula and Victor are in a cabal, or all in Carol's jurisdiction and keep logs that could be the subject of a subpoena, Alice may find that Bob is able to learn her identity. All it takes to preserve Alice's anonymity, however, is a single remailer in the chain that is both honest and either erases her logs or is outside Carol's jurisdiction. In theory, there is no limit to the number of remailers in the chain, and Alice can, if she wishes, loop the message through some remailers more than once to throw off anyone attempting traffic analysis.

2. Electronic Pseudonymity

Suppose Alice is a repeat participant in a broadcast medium such as USENET or a mailing list. She may not wish to sign her name to her messages, but she desires to engage in discussion and debate with other list members and she wishes to do so under a continuous identity. Alice decides to sign her messages as "Andrea." Alice could, however, have chosen to sign her messages as "Frank," on the theory that this might allow her to avoid anti-female discrimination. Indeed, either sex can masquerade as the other; children as adults (and vice-versa). If nothing else, this creates some potential for embarrassment, and concerns some parents.

Like fully anonymous messages, pseudonymous messages come in two varieties: traceable and untraceable. The advantage of traceable pseudonymity is that it gives the sender a consistent name that allows other parties to send replies far more easily than is possible with any untraceable system.

A. TRACEABLE PSEUDONYMITY

Traceable pseudonymity is communication with a nom de plume attached which can be traced back to the author (by someone), although not necessarily by the recipient. While a traceable pseudonymous system makes it much easier for someone to discover Alice's identity, it usually offers one large compensating advantage: the recipients of Alice's message can usually reply to it by sending e-mail directly to the pseudonymous e-mail address in the "From:" field of the message. The message will then either go to Ted, the remailer operator, who keeps an index of the addresses that link Andrea to Alice, or in the case of commercial service providers who allow subscribers to use pseudonymous IDs, directly to Alice's account.

Anon.penet.fi, probably the best-known "anonymous" remailer, is in fact merely a very user-friendly traceable pseudonymous remailer:

> [Anon.penet.fi] provides a front for sending mail messages and posting news items anonymously. As you send your very first message to the server, it automatically allocates you an id of the form anNNN , and sends you a message containing the allocated id. This id is used in all your subsequent anon posts/mails. Any mail messages sent to your-id@anon.penet.fi gets redirected to your original, real address. Any reply is of course anonymized in the same way, so the server provides a double-blind. You will not know the true identity of any user, unless she chooses to reveal her identity explicitly.

The anon.penet.fi system keeps a record of each user's e-mail address. The security of the approximately 8,000 messages that pass through anon.penet.fi daily thus depends critically on the willingness of the operator, Johan Helsingius, a Finnish computer scientist, to refuse to disclose the contents of his index which maps each pseudonymous ID to an e-mail address. In February 1995, the Church of Scientology successfully enlisted the aid of the Finnish police, via Interpol, to demand the identity of a person who had, the Church of Scientology claimed, used anon.penet.fi to post the contents of a file allegedly stolen from a Scientology computer to a USENET group called "alt.religion.scientology." In compliance with

Finnish law, Helsingius surrendered the information, believing that the only alternative would have been to have the entire database seized by the police.

The social institution of traceable pseudonymity, which is permitted by a number of commercial Internet providers, is likely to generate some interesting lawsuits. Many commercial ISPs and on-line service providers, such as America OnLine for example, allow users to use any unique name they like as their "user ID," their on-line identifier. When my brother opened an account with an ISP, he used our family name for his account. As a result, when my parents set up an Internet account with the same service provider they were forced to select something different. Their ID is an amalgam of their first names. They could, however, have chosen any combination of letters and numbers they wanted so long as their ISP had not already assigned that name to someone else. Whether the ISP will release my parents' actual name to anyone who asks is primarily a question of contract law until a subpoena is involved. When people think they have been defamed or otherwise injured by the actions of a user who employs a pseudonym, the party claiming injury is likely to ask courts to require the ISPs to disclose the identity of the subscriber, at least when the ISP is in an accessible jurisdiction.

B. UNTRACEABLE PSEUDONYMITY

Untraceable pseudonymity works just like untraceable anonymity, except that Alice chooses to sign her message as Andrea, a pseudonym. If Alice is worried that someone else may try to masquerade as Andrea, she can sign her message with a digital signature generated specially for "Andrea," which will uniquely and unforgeably distinguish an authentic signed message from any counterfeit. By participating in discussions under a consistent pseudonym (often abbreviated to "nym" on the Internet) Alice can establish Andrea as a digital persona:

> [N]yms allow for continuity of identity to be maintained over a period of time. A person posting under a nym can develop an image and a reputation just like any other online personality. Most people we interact with online are just a name and an e-mail address, plus whatever impression we have formed of them by what they say. The same thing can be true of nyms. Cryptography can also help maintain the continuity of the nym, by allowing the user to digitally sign messages under the name of the nym. The digital signature cannot be forged, nor can it be linked to the True Name of the user. But it makes sure that nobody can send a message pretending to be another person's nym.

Strictly speaking, a digital persona does not require untraceable anonymity: it is sufficient to have a system that allows one to communicate under a "nym" and to digitally sign one's messages in order to prevent anyone else from masquerading as the nym. "Publius," the author of the Federalist Papers, was known to "his" publisher, and a digital persona can exist even if the persona's ISP knows the persona's real identity. Nevertheless, a nym may have more value, or at least may be experienced as more liberating, if the identity of the person(s) behind the persona is untraceable.

3. The Human Element: Remailer Operators

While the technological alternatives described above have their own interest, the most important point for present purposes is that very effective Internet anonymity requires only two things: cryptographic tools, and willing remailer operators. The cryptographic tools are in ready supply. If the user deploys the cryptographic tools properly, the remailer operators need not be known to be trustworthy; since the message is untraceably anonymous if any single operator in a chain is honest, it will ordinarily suffice to route the message through several remailers. The more remailers in the chain, however, the longer it may take the message to get to its destination, and the greater the chance that an operator in the chain will fail to pass the message on down the line.

The supply of remailer operators is the major potential constraint on Internet anonymity. Remailer programs are currently operated by a relatively small number of volunteers located in a few countries; at present they receive no compensation for this service, and in the absence of anonymous electronic cash or the equivalent it is difficult to see how an electronic payment system could be constructed that would not risk undermining the very anonymity the remailers are designed to protect.

The remailer operator's problem is a simple one. No remailer operator can control the content of the messages that flow through the remailer. Furthermore, the last remailer operator in a chain has no reliable way of concealing the identity of the sending machine from the message's ultimate recipient. Suppose, to return to the example above, Alice wants to send an anonymous death threat to Bob via remailers operated by Ted, Ursula, and Victor. If Victor does nothing to mask his e-mail address, Bob will know he was the last to remail the message. Victor can make any attempt to identify him more difficult by forging his e-mail address in the message to Bob, but Victor cannot be certain that this will work. Indeed, he can be almost certain that over time it will fail.

The last remailer in a chain thus risks being identified by an unhappy recipient. An identifiable person is a potential target for regulation. If the remailer operators were made strictly liable for the content of messages that passed through their hands, even though they were unable to learn the content of those encrypted messages, most reasonable people probably would find running a remailer to be an unacceptable risk if they resided in a jurisdiction capable of enforcing such a rule.

Remailer operators already have come under various forms of attack, most recently lawsuits or subpoenas instigated by officials of the Church of Scientology who sought to identify the person they allege used remailers to disseminate copyrighted and secret Church teachings. As a result, operating a remailer is not a risk-free activity today. Indeed, one can imagine a number of creative lawsuits that might reasonably be launched at the operator of a remailer. Examples include a new tort of concealment of identity, a claim of conspiracy with the wrong-doer, and a RICO claim. A remailer operator whose remailer was used to harass someone might face a common law tort claim of harassment. A conspiracy charge would be difficult since it would be difficult to prove the element of agreement that is a necessary part of a conspiracy. It is difficult to say that Bob conspires with a stranger, even if he leaves a tool lying in plain sight, knowing that criminals are likely but not certain to come by and use it. If Bob is really ignorant of the identity, content, and purposes of the messages he retransmits, he can plausibly say that there is no agreement between him and the conspirator, and that he should no more be liable for the misuse of his remailer than the rental car company that leases a car to a terrorist. A RICO claim against a remailer could also founder on the lack of agreement. Although it is far from obvious that any of these legal theories would or should succeed, some raise non-frivolous issues and thus would be expensive to defend.

At some point, if the number of remailers becomes small, it becomes technically (if not necessarily politically or legally) feasible for the authorities to conduct traffic analysis on all the remailers and make deductions about who sent what to whom. In the absence of a compensation mechanism, or a jurisdiction capable of offering a safe haven for remailers, the cornerstone of Internet anonymity currently relies entirely on the kindness of strangers.

Notes

1. Anonymous Web browsing became considerably easier in December 1999, when Montreal-based software developer Zero-Knowledge Systems released its Freedom browser. The browser, which allows users to surf completely anonymously, quickly raised concerns in the law enforcement communities. Additional information on the browser can obtained at the company Web site at <http://www.zeroknowledge.com>.

2. For free anonymous Web browsing, visit Anonymizer.com at <http://www.anonymizer.com>.

3. To see how easy it is to send anonymous email, visit My Email at <http://www.myemail.net/anonymous.html>.

The Canadian courts faced the issue of online anonymity in the summer of 1998 in *Phillips Services Corp.* v. *John Doe*. The case involved a demand that an ISP release the identity of several of its users who had allegedly made fraudulent postings to a stock chat room. The court granted the motion to release the names, illustrating that anonymity on the Internet is not as absolute as some might otherwise believe.

Philip Services Corp. v. Joe Doe†

Philip Services Corp.

and

JOHN DOE 1 a.k.a. Addicted2PHV,
JOHN DOE 2 a.k.a. alreadygored,
JOHN DOE 3 a.k.a. Angelofthelaw,
JOHN DOE 4 a.k.a. Ben_Hurr98,
JOHN DOE 5 a.k.a. brokerr39 and Broker39,
JOHN DOE 6 a.k.a. Coma_Cozy,
JOHN DOE 7 a.k.a. CountBuster,
JOHN DOE 8 a.k.a. cstew,
JOHN DOE 9 a.k.a. Imm1tya,
JOHN DOE 10 a.k.a. Imshort65,
JOHN DOE 11 a.k.a. inthebunker,
JOHN DOE 12 a.k.a. mobhit,

---

† (1998) Court file no. 4582/98 (Ont. Ct. (Gen. Div.)).

JOHN DOE 13 a.k.a. mreecs,
JOHN DOE 14 a.k.a. Paul Palango,
JOHN DOE 15 a.k.a. PJ_21,
JOHN DOE 16 a.k.a. Realdic,
JOHN DOE 17 a.k.a. sava_urasa,
JOHN DOE 18 a.k.a. scrappym,
JOHN DOE 19 a.k.a. skeptic666 and skeptik666,
JOHN DOE 20 a.k.a. somnific_no_more,
JOHN DOE 21 a.k.a. Stucklikeglue and stucklikeglue,
JOHN DOE 22 a.k.a. SunTzu22,
JOHN DOE 23 a.k.a. THEPHVPOSTMAN,
JOHN DOE 24 a.k.a. tigerstar666,
JOHN DOE 25 a.k.a. twickewnbam,
JOHN DOE 26 a.k.a. wentworth_guy,
AND PERSONS UNKNOWN

Defendants/Respondents

ORDER to Weslink Datalink Corporation

THIS MOTION, made by Philip Services Corp. for a preservation order, for the answers to questions and for the sealing of this file, made ex parte without notice, was heard this day at Hamilton, Ontario.

ON READING the Motion Record filed in these proceedings and on hearing the submissions of counsel for the Applicant Philip Services Corp. appearing in person,

1. THIS COURT ORDERS Weslink Datalink Corporation to preserve all electronic, computerized, and computer produced data, or data in any other form — whether printed, recorded, copied, or electronic — related to the persons who were using the Internet Protocol addresses at the dates and times listed on Schedule A including without limitation:

   (a) logs of calls or log-ons made,
   (b) names, addresses, modem telephone numbers, bills, records, and data about the persons sending the messages listed and for all other messages sent by such persons through the internet providers,
   (c) names, addresses, modem telephone numbers, bills, records, and data about the persons with the e-mail addresses listed on Schedule A,
   (d) names, models, registration numbers, serial numbers, and other identifying information concerning the computers and modems used by the persons.

Notes

Online anonymity issues have not been confined to allegedly defamatory Internet postings. The right to online anonymity has also been challenged in the political arena. In 1997 Elections Canada ordered the removal of a Green Party Web site from the Internet, since the site violated the *Canada Elections Act* by not disclosing the person responsible for the site. In response numerous mirror sites were launched across the Internet, rendering the Elections Canada order completely ineffective. For more on the case, see the Electronic Frontier Canada Web site at http://insight.mcmaster.ca/org/efc/pages/pr/efc-pr.22may97.html.

Discussion Questions

1. Although legal actions of this nature have been relatively rare in Canada, they have proliferated in the United States. In most instances ISPs have indicated their willingness to provide whatever records they possess when presented with a court order. Should an ISP bear some measure of responsibility even without such an order?

2. Given the ease with which court orders mandating the disclosure of ISP records have been issued, some free speech advocates fear that the pendulum has swung too far. They argue that an anonymous poster is virtually without rights in the face of a legal proceeding, since contesting the action will often necessitate surrendering their anonymous persona. Do you agree? Can an effective middle ground be found? If yes, what would you suggest it is?

   In one June 1999 case, Xircom, a modem manufacturer, launched an action to expose the person behind several email postings on a stock chat Web site. The poster challenged the action, but wished to maintain his or her anonymity. The parties eventually settled on an agreement whereby senior corporate executives of Xircom were informed of the poster's identity, but the name was not released to the public.

3. The right to anonymity is also found in the *Copyright Act*, which references anonymity rights in Section 6.1. Can you effectively reconcile that right with the limitations imposed by the *Canada Elections Act*?

The Canadian Supreme Court has yet to face the issue of online anonymity. In recent years, it has grappled with several cases involving the issue of anonymity that provide a sense of the court's views on the issue.

R. v. Plant[†]

The purpose of s. 8 is to protect against intrusion of the state on an individual's privacy. The limits on such state action are determined by balancing the right of citizens to have respected a reasonable expectation of privacy as against the state interest in law enforcement. Section 8 protects people and not property. It is, therefore, unnecessary to establish a proprietary interest in the thing seized. In this respect, I must disagree with the Court of Appeal which relied on the absence of a proprietary interest on the part of the appellant in the computer information.

In balancing the reasonable expectation of privacy of the individual with the interests of the state in law enforcement, this Court has determined that electronic taping of private communication by state authorities violates the personal sphere pro-

---

† [1993] 3 S.C.R. 281.

tected by s. 8. Similarly, such investigative practices as videotaping of events in a private hotel room and seizure by state agents of a blood sample taken by medical personnel for medical purposes have been found to run afoul of the s. 8 right against unreasonable search and seizure in that the dignity, integrity and autonomy of the individual are directly compromised. While this Court has considered the possibility of violations of s. 8 in relation to informational privacy, we have not previously considered whether state inspection of computer records implicates s. 8 of the Charter.

Some indication of the parameters of the protection afforded by s. 8 with respect to informational privacy can be derived from the following passage from the reasons of La Forest J. in *Dyment*, commenting on the Report of the Task Force on Privacy and Computers:

> In modern society, especially, retention of information about oneself is extremely important. We may, for one reason or another, wish or be compelled to reveal such information, but situations abound where the reasonable expectations of the individual that the information shall remain confidential to the persons to whom, and restricted to the purposes for which it is divulged, must be protected.

Consideration of such factors as the nature of the information itself, the nature of the relationship between the party releasing the information and the party claiming its confidentiality, the place where the information was obtained, the manner in which it was obtained and the seriousness of the crime being investigated allow for a balancing of the societal interests in protecting individual dignity, integrity and autonomy with effective law enforcement. It is, then, necessary to apply this contextual approach to the facts of the case at bar.

Godbout v. Longueuil (City)[†]

La Forest J. — In modern times, the ability of individuals to make decisions free from unwelcome external interference is increasingly under pressure. Whether that pressure finds its roots in changing patterns of social organization, in technological advancements, in governmental action, or in some other source, its net effect has largely been to whittle down the scope of personal freedom. While the exigencies of community life clearly preclude the possibility that individuals could ever be guaranteed an untrammeled right to do as they please, the basic ability to make fundamentally private choices unfettered by undesired restrictions demands protection under law, such that it can only be overridden where other pressing concerns so dictate. The central issue raised in this appeal is whether the choice of where to establish one's home falls within that narrow sphere of personal decision-making deserving of the law's protection and whether, even if it does, other important considerations might nevertheless take precedence over it. More specifically, the appeal raises the question whether, on pain of termination, the appellant municipality can legitimately require all its permanent employees — including the respondent — to live within the territorial limits of the city and to maintain their homes there for the duration of their employment.

---

† [1997] 3 S.C.R. 844.

Issue 2: Whether the Residence Requirement Violates Section 5 of
the Quebec *Charter* and Whether, if it Does, it Can Be Saved by
Section 9.1

(A) THE RIGHT TO PRIVACY IN SECTION 5

Unlike the Canadian Charter, the scope of the Quebec *Charter* is not restricted
to "government action". Consequently, no issues of application need be discussed.
Furthermore, given that I have already addressed the nature of the right asserted by
the respondent in my discussion of s. 7 of the Canadian *Charter* (i.e., by finding that
it is a "right to choose where to live" and not a "right to work" as contended by the
appellant), it is unnecessary to revisit that question here. Nor do I consider it necessary to make any further comments with respect to the issue of waiver, for while the
appellant pointed out that this Court's decision in *Frenette* v. *Metropolitan Life Insurance Co.*, establishes the possibility of waiving rights to privacy under s. 5 of the
Quebec *Charter* in some circumstances, those circumstances do not exist in this case
for the reasons given earlier in relation to waiver under the Canadian *Charter*.

As regards s. 5, the respondent contended that choosing where to live is a
fundamentally personal decision, falling within the ambit of the "private life" protected by that provision. As regards s. 1, the respondent similarly alleged that
the right to choose where to establish one's home falls within the scope of the right
to "freedom".

Were there not another provision of the Quebec *Charter* aimed more directly at
guaranteeing protection for individuals' private spheres of life, I would have had considerable sympathy for the respondent's s. 1 argument. It seems to me, however, that
in enacting s. 5 in addition to s. 1, the Quebec legislator expressly contemplated the
importance of protecting matters of a fundamentally private or personal nature, and
deemed it appropriate to provide specific protection for them. In light of this, I am
of the view that matters involving personal autonomy and privacy — such as choosing
where to establish one's home — will normally be more appropriately addressed under s. 5. This is not necessarily to say that s. 1 does not protect personal autonomy
at all; rather, it is simply to say that since s. 5 is, by its very terms, aimed directly at
protecting individuals' private lives, matters that implicate privacy and personal autonomy will generally be better dealt with there. Since I am of the view that the
right asserted by the respondent in this case is protected by s. 5, I find it unnecessary to address the arguments made in respect of s. 1.

For all these reasons, I am of the view that the residence requirement imposed
by the appellant violates the respondent's right to respect for her private life, enshrined in s. 5 of the Quebec *Charter*.

Aubry v. Éditions Vice-Versa†

L'Heureux-Dubé and Bastarache JJ. — This appeal concerns the scope of the right to
one's image as an element of the more general right to privacy. It also involves a
balancing of the right to privacy and freedom of expression.

It should be noted at the outset that since the events on which this case is
based occurred in 1988, the matter is governed by the Civil Code of Lower Canada.

---

† [1998] 1 S.C.R. 591.

Facts

The respondent, Pascale Claude Aubry, brought an action in civil responsibility against the appellants, Gilbert Duclos and Les Éditions Vice-Versa inc., for taking and publishing a photograph showing the respondent sitting on a step in front of a building on Ste-Catherine Street in Montreal. Both sides accept that the photograph was taken in a public place and published without the respondent's consent. According to the evidence, it was the appellant Gilbert Duclos who took the respondent's photograph. The photograph was published by the appellant Les Éditions Vice-Versa inc. in the June issue of Vice-Versa, a magazine dedicated to the arts, and 722 copies of the issue in question were sold. The photograph was drawn to the respondent's attention by a friend who had purchased a copy of the magazine. The respondent, who was 17 at the time, brought this action for damages in the amount of $10,000, half as compensatory damages and the other half as exemplary damages.

· · · ·

Analysis

The case at bar raises a problem of civil law and it is in light of that law that it must be resolved. The infringement of a right guaranteed by the Charter of Human Rights and Freedoms (hereinafter the "Quebec Charter") gives rise, under s. 49 para. 1, to an action for moral and material prejudice. Such an action is subject to the civil law principles of recovery. As a result, the traditional elements of liability, namely fault, damage and causal connection, must be established..

It should be mentioned at the outset that our analysis will be limited to the sole issue before this Court, namely publication of a photograph taken without permission.

There is a debate in French law, and a corresponding uncertainty in Quebec law, as to whether the right to one's image is a separate right of personality or an element of the right to privacy. In our view, the right to one's image, which has an extrapatrimonial and a patrimonial aspect, is an element of the right to privacy under s. 5 of the Quebec Charter. This is consistent with the liberal interpretation given to the concept of privacy in the recent decision *Godbout* v. *Longueuil (City)*, and in past judgments of this Court.

Since the right to one's image is included in the right to respect for one's private life, it is axiomatic that every person possesses a protected right to his or her image. This right arises when the subject is recognizable. There is, thus, an infringement of the person's right to his or her image, and therefore fault, as soon as the image is published without consent and enables the person to be identified.

The right to respect for one's private life should not be confused with the right to one's honour and reputation under s. 4 of the Quebec *Charter* even though, in certain cases, wrongful publication of an image may in itself result in an injury to one's honour and reputation. Since every person is entitled to protection of his or her privacy, and since the person's image is protected accordingly, it is possible for the rights inherent in the protection of privacy to be infringed even though the published image is in no way reprehensible and has in no way injured the person's reputation. In the case at bar, the judges at trial and on appeal found that the photograph was in no way reprehensible and did not injure the respondent's honour or reputation. The Court of Appeal also found that the manner in which the photograph was juxtaposed with the text did not make it possible to associate the two elements and that, at any rate, the text was serious and not open to ridicule.

The right to respect for one's private life comes into conflict here with another right protected by the Quebec *Charter*, in s. 3, namely the right to freedom of expression. LeBel J.A. and Biron J. stated that Quebec law does not yet consider artistic expression to be a separate right. It is our view that freedom of expression includes freedom of artistic expression. It is, therefore, unnecessary to create a special category to take freedom of artistic expression into account. Artistic expression does not require a special category to be effective. Nor is there any justification for giving it a status superior to that of general freedom of expression. An artist can assert his or her right to freedom of expression under the same conditions as any other person. There is, thus, no need to distinguish freedom of artistic expression from journalistic reporting, as we have been asked to do.

The right to respect for one's private life, like freedom of expression, must be interpreted in accordance with the provisions of s. 9.1 of the Quebec *Charter*. For this purpose, it is necessary to balance these two rights.

The public's right to information, supported by freedom of expression, places limits on the right to respect for one's private life in certain circumstances. This is because the expectation of privacy is reduced in certain cases. A person's right to respect for his or her private life may even be limited by the public's interest in knowing about certain traits of his or her personality. In short, the public's interest in being informed is a concept that can be applied to determine whether impugned conduct oversteps the bounds of what is permitted.

The public interest so defined is thus conclusive in certain cases. The balancing of the rights in question depends both on the nature of the information and on the situation of those concerned. This is a question that depends on the context. Thus, it is generally recognized that certain aspects of the private life of a person who is engaged in a public activity or has acquired a certain notoriety can become matters of public interest. This is true, in particular, of artists and politicians, but also, more generally, of all those whose professional success depends on public opinion. There are also cases where a previously unknown individual is called on to play a high-profile role in a matter within the public domain, such as an important trial, a major economic activity having an impact on the use of public funds, or an activity involving public safety. It is also recognized that a photographer is exempt from liability, as are those who publish the photograph, when an individual's own action, albeit unwitting, accidentally places him or her in the photograph in an incidental manner. The person is then in the limelight in a sense. One need only think of a photograph of a crowd at a sporting event or a demonstration.

In the case at bar, the appellants are liable *a priori*, since the photograph was published when the respondent was identifiable. In our view, the artistic expression of the photograph, which was alleged to have served to illustrate contemporary urban life, cannot justify the infringement of the right to privacy it entails. It has not been shown that the public's interest in seeing this photograph is predominant. The argument that the public has an interest in seeing any work of art cannot be accepted, especially because an artist's right to publish his or her work, no more than other forms of freedom of expression, is not absolute. The wording of s. 9.1 of the Quebec Charter should be borne in mind here, together with the fact that this Court has stated on a number of occasions that freedom of expression must be defined in light of the other values concerned.

None of the exceptions mentioned earlier based on the public's right to information is applicable here. Accordingly, there appears to be no justification for giving precedence to the appellants other than their submission that it would be very difficult in practice for a photographer to obtain the consent of all those he or she photographs in public places before publishing their photographs. To accept such an exception would, in fact, amount to accepting that the photographer's right is unlimited, provided that the photograph is taken in a public place, thereby extending the photographer's freedom at the expense of that of others. We reject this point of view. In the case at bar, the respondent's right to protection of her image is more important than the appellants' right to publish the photograph of the respondent without first obtaining her permission.

The appeal is dismissed with costs.

Notes

A recent Alberta case considered the right of a litigant to remain anonymous during the course of the court proceedings. The court granted the motion for anonymity, ruling that:

> The applicant is, provisionally, entitled to an order that prohibits his identification. The factors I have taken into account in granting this interim ban are:
> - the ban creates symmetry, in civil proceedings, with the protection given to complainants in criminal proceedings for several offences;
> - the ban will be fully assessed, after giving all potentially affected parties a chance to support their positions;
> - at this stage, there appears to be no prejudice to the defendants because the credibility of the plaintiff is not in issue; and
> - at this stage, there also appears to be no prejudice to the justice system.
>
> No person is entitled to publish the identity of the plaintiff. This ban applies not only to the media, but also to any individuals present in the courtroom or who in a similar fashion might come to learn of the plaintiff's identity. Not only can the plaintiff's identity not be published or broadcast, but, for greater certainty, his identity cannot be disclosed, for example, on the Internet.
>
> For the reasons given above, until the plaintiff chooses to sue, there is a temporary, renewable, publication ban on the identity of the defendants. This publication ban applies to all persons including the plaintiff.
>
> In order to ensure the integrity of the system, the court hearing the application may consider whether it should require an undertaking from the applicant to initiate contempt proceedings against any person who breaches the non-publication order.
>
> **Use of pseudonym**
>
> For the same reasons as those set out in relation to the application for a publication ban the applicant is, provisionally, entitled to an order allowing him to use a pseudonym.
>
> Indeed, although it may not always be so in every case where proceedings take place in an open courtroom, the use of a pseudonym, without a publication ban as to a litigant's identity, would be potentially ineffective.

For more on the case, *see*, *John Doe* v. *Roe*, [1999] A.J. No. 411 (Alta. QB 1999).

The U.S. courts addressed the issue of anonymity within the context of the Internet in *ACLU of Georgia* v. *Miller*. The case involved the constitutionality of a Georgia state legislative provision that prohibited the use of an anonymous persona online.

ACLU v. Miller[†]

Plaintiffs bring this action for declaratory and injunctive relief challenging the constitutionality of Act No. 1029, Ga. Laws 1996, p. 1505, codified at O.C.G.A. §16-9-93.1 ("act" or "statute"). The act makes it a crime for

> any person ... knowingly to transmit any data through a computer network ... for the purpose of setting up, maintaining, operating, or exchanging data with an electronic mailbox, home page, or any other electronic information storage bank or point of access to electronic information if such data uses any individual name ... to falsely identify the person ...

and for

> any person ... knowingly to transmit any data through a computer network ... if such data uses any ... trade name, registered trademark, logo, legal or official seal, or copyrighted symbol ... which would falsely state or imply that such person ... has permission or is legally authorized to use [it] for such purpose when such permission or authorization has not been obtained.

The parties vigorously dispute the scope of the act. Plaintiffs, a group of individuals and organization members who communicate over the Internet, interpret it as imposing unconstitutional content-based restrictions on their right to communicate anonymously and pseudonymously over the internet, as well as on their right to use trade names, logos, and other graphics in a manner held to be constitutional in other contexts.

Plaintiffs argue that the act has tremendous implications for internet users, many of whom "falsely identify" themselves on a regular basis for the purpose of communicating about sensitive topics without subjecting themselves to ostracism or embarrassment. Plaintiffs further contend that the trade name and logo restriction frustrates one of the Internet's unique features — the "links" that connect web pages on the World Wide Web and enable users to browse easily from topic to topic through the computer network system. Plaintiffs claim that the act's broad language is further damaging in that it allows for selective prosecution of persons communicating about controversial topics.

Defendants contend that the act prohibits a much narrower class of communications. They interpret it as forbidding only fraudulent transmissions or the appropriation of the identity of another person or entity for some improper purpose. Defendants ask the Court to abstain from exercising jurisdiction in this case in order to give the Georgia Supreme Court an opportunity to definitively interpret the act.

· · · ·

[†] 977 F. Supp. 1288 (N.D. Ga. 1997).

Having addressed defendants' affirmative defenses, the Court concludes that plaintiffs are likely to prevail on the merits of their claim. It appears from the record that plaintiffs are likely to prove that the statute imposes content-based restrictions which are not narrowly tailored to achieve the state's purported compelling interest. Furthermore, plaintiffs are likely to show that the statute is overbroad and void for vagueness.

First, because "the identity of the speaker is no different from other components of [a] document's contents that the author is free to include or exclude," the statute's prohibition of Internet transmissions which "falsely identify" the sender constitutes a presumptively invalid content-based restriction. The state may impose content-based restrictions only to promote a "compelling state interest" and only through use of "the least restrictive means to further the articulated interest." Thus, in order to overcome the presumption of invalidity, defendants must demonstrate that the statute furthers a compelling state interest and is narrowly tailored to achieve it.

Defendants allege that the statute's purpose is fraud prevention, which the Court agrees is a compelling state interest. However, the statute is not narrowly tailored to achieve that end and instead sweeps innocent, protected speech within its scope. Specifically, by its plain language the criminal prohibition applies regardless of whether a speaker has any intent to deceive or whether deception actually occurs.

For similar reasons, plaintiffs are likely to succeed on their overbreadth claim because the statute "sweeps protected activity within its proscription." In the first amendment context, the overbreadth doctrine, which invalidates overbroad statutes even when some of their applications are valid, is based on the recognition that "the very existence of some broadly written laws has the potential to chill the expressive activity of others not before the Court."

The Court concludes that the statute was not drafted with the precision necessary for laws regulating speech. On its face, the Act prohibits such protected speech as the use of false identification to avoid social ostracism, to prevent discrimination and harassment, and to protect privacy, as well as the use of trade names or logos in non-commercial educational speech, news, and commentary — a prohibition with well-recognized first amendment problems. Therefore, even if the statute could constitutionally be used to prosecute persons who intentionally "falsely identify" themselves in order to deceive or defraud the public, or to persons whose commercial use of trade names and logos creates a substantial likelihood of confusion or the dilution of a famous mark, the statute is nevertheless overbroad because it operates unconstitutionally for a substantial category of the speakers it covers.

Finally, plaintiffs are likely to succeed on their claim that the statute is unconstitutionally vague. The void-for-vagueness doctrine requires a criminal statute to "define the criminal offense with sufficient definiteness that ordinary people can understand what conduct is prohibited and in a manner that does not encourage arbitrary and discriminatory enforcement." Like the overbreadth doctrine, the policies underlying the vagueness rule apply with special force where the statute at issue restricts speech. The Court concludes that plaintiffs are likely to prove that the statute is void for vagueness because it 1) does not give fair notice of the scope of conduct it proscribes; 2) is conducive to arbitrary enforcement; and 3) infringes upon plaintiffs' free expression.

First, the Act fails to give fair notice of proscribed conduct to computer network users by failing to define the following terms and phrases: "falsely identify," "use," "falsely imply," and "point of access to electronic information." These undefined terms provide inadequate notice of the scope of proscribed conduct to persons of ordinary intelligence and thus void the act for vagueness.

The statute criminalizes computer transmissions which "falsely identify" the sender, yet fails to state whether or not proof of specific intent to deceive, or proof of actual deception, is required.

Similarly, the portion of the Act relating to trade names and logos fails to define or adequately limit the word "use." Other statutes protecting intellectual property expressly limit the definition of "use" to use in a commercial context. In contrast, the only limiting concept of "use" in the Act is that such use must "falsely imply" that permission to use the mark has been obtained. This restriction, which is also undefined and suffers from the same vagueness problems as the term "falsely identify," fails to provide sufficiently specific notice of proscribed conduct.

Finally, the Act fails to explain the phrase "any data ... over the transmission facilities or through the network facilities of a local telephone network for the purpose of ... exchanging data with ... a point of access to electronic information." Plaintiffs contend that this phrase could mean that the act applies not only to computer transmissions *per se*, but also to transmissions by telephone, fax machine, answering machine, voice mail system, pager, or any other electronic device which might be connected to computer network facilities. The act provides no guidance about these potential applications.

Second, the Act's vague provisions create a risk of arbitrary and discriminatory enforcement. The Act's failure to specifically articulate proscribed conduct affords prosecutors and police officers substantial room for selective prosecution of persons who express minority viewpoints.

Third, the Act's vagueness is particularly harmful because it chills protected expression. Plaintiffs' affidavits indicate that they have already altered what they believe to be innocent and legitimate behavior because of their inability to discern what exactly the Act proscribes. Without court intervention, this self-censorship will continue until the act is amended, revoked, or definitively interpreted by the state supreme court.

For all of these reasons, the Court concludes that plaintiffs are likely to succeed on their claim that the Act is void for vagueness, overbroad, and not narrowly tailored to promote a compelling state interest.

Discussion Questions

Do you think a Canadian court would reach a similar conclusion? On what grounds?

Online music has emerged as one of the most popular uses of the Internet, featuring thousands of songs freely available in digital format. The recording industry has reacted to the proliferation of online, unlicensed music with alarm, particularly since many sites distribute unlicensed music under the veil of anonymity. The following case illustrates one method of countering anonymous Web sites that provide access to unlicensed or pirated music. Note that the court asserts jurisdiction over the case based on the location of the Web server hosting the pirated music.

A&M Records, Inc. v. Internet Site Known As Fresh Kutz[†]

This case involves the infringement of Plaintiffs' copyrighted sound recordings by Defendants via the Internet. Defendants have created and maintain an Internet site know as Fresh Kutz ("Defendants Site"), the sole purpose of which is the reproduction, distribution, and exchange of unauthorized copies of copyrighted sound recordings. Without permission of the copyright holders, Defendants have copied hundreds of full-length sound recordings to a computer file server connected to the Internet. The vast majority of these sound recordings are owned by Plaintiffs or their affiliates. Defendants then make these infringing recordings available at Defendants' Site for reproduction and distribution to millions of Internet users worldwide. Indeed, Defendants boast that theirs is the "biggest and best" such site on the Internet, with new songs added every day. Moreover, as part of their infringement scheme, Defendants actively encourage Internet users to download the infringing materials — and thus create additional copies in the users' computers. Defendants even provide software which users can download to their computers to enable them to play the infringing recordings in high-fidelity stereo. In addition, upon information and belief, Defendants encourage Internet users visiting their site to contribute additional copies of unauthorized sound recordings to Defendants' Site for copying by and distribution to countless other Internet users.

A fledgling industry in pirated copies of sound recordings thus is emerging on the Internet. In this way, commercially released recordings which otherwise are available for purchase through legitimate channels (e.g., records stores) are being pirated online. Because the Internet offers near instantaneous access worldwide, this conduct is causing and threatens to continue to cause severe and irreparable harm to the Plaintiffs, and to the recording industry generally. This action seeks an injunction against the Defendants' unauthorized copying and distribution, and seeks damages for the infringements which have occurred to date.

Jurisdiction and Venue

The true names and capacities of Defendants Does I-X, inclusive, are unknown to Plaintiffs at this time. Plaintiffs therefore sue said Defendants by such fictitious names. As soon as the true names of Does I-X have been ascertained, Plaintiffs will amend this Complaint accordingly. On information and belief, Does I-X own, operate and maintain Defendant Internet Site Known as Fresh Kutz.

This is an action for copyright infringement under 17 U.S.C. §101 *et seq.* Pursuant to 28 U.S.C. §§1331 and 1338, this Court has original and exclusive jurisdiction over all claims herein.

Venue is proper in this Court under 28 U.S.C. §§1391(b) and 1400(a). Defendants' Internet Site Known as Fresh Kutz and Does I-X maintain Defendants' Site on a computer server located in this District. Defendants therefore may be found in this District within the meaning of 28 U.S.C. §1400(a), and their infringement of Plaintiffs' copyright occurs in this District within the meaning of 28 U.S.C. §1391(b).

[†] Case No. 97-CV-1099H (JFS) (S.D. Cal. 1997).

. . . .

Temporary Restraining Order and Order to Show Cause
Re: Preliminary Injunction
Upon consideration of Plaintiffs' Motion for a Temporary Restraining Order and Preliminary Injunction, and entire record herein, it is this 10th day of June 1997,

ORDERED, that for a period of ten (10) days from the issuance of this Order, good cause having been shown pursuant to Rule 65 of the Federal Rules of Civil Procedure that immediate and irreparable injury and damage will result to plaintiffs before the motion for a preliminary injunction can be heard and decided, Defendants, their agents, servants and employees, and all persons acting in concert with them or assisting them through the provision of services for or in the maintenance of the Internet site known as "http://www.avalon.simplenet.com/coolmp3/music.htm" and/or "http://www.avalon.simplenet.com//bossnetsux/music.htm" (hereinafter "Defendants' Site"):

1. are temporarily enjoined from:
    (a) copying, reproducing, duplicating, disseminating, distributing, selling or in any way exploiting any unauthorized copies of Plaintiffs' Recordings or any copyrighted sound recording;
    (b) otherwise infringing any sound recording copyright by permitting, supervising, enabling, encouraging, contributing to, aiding or abetting any of the acts in subparagraph (a) above; and
    (c) destroying, discarding, transferring, or modifying any documents, software, hardware, equipment, or data used in connection with defendants' Site, including but not limited to, (i) business records that pertain to the copying, reproduction, duplication, dissemination, or distribution of any sound recordings, or any revenues or remuneration (monetary or otherwise) derived therefrom, (ii) computer files contained on Defendants' Site, (iii) Defendants' site itself, or (iv) documents or other materials relating to Plaintiffs' Recordings; and

2. shall immediately block access to all unauthorized sound recordings which are copies of or otherwise substantially similar to any of the Subject Recordings at Defendants' Site and at every other computer site over which Defendants have control;

As the law struggles to catch up with the rapid development of technology, many frustrated Internet users are turning to technology to protect their interests. In many aspects of Internet use — from copyright to privacy — technology is usurping the role traditionally played by law by providing a quicker and more effective means of recourse.

Leading the way is cryptography, which has the potential to play an important role in safeguarding privacy and enabling private speech. As lawmakers debate the merits of legislated privacy protections, cryptography software enables users to send encrypted email that remains inaccessible to all except those with the requisite code.

Bernstein v. United States Department Of Justice[†]

Bernstein is currently a professor in the Department of Mathematics, Statistics, and Computer Science at the University of Illinois at Chicago. As a doctoral candidate at the University of California, Berkeley, he developed an encryption method — "a zero-delay private-key stream encryptor based upon a one-way hash function" — that he dubbed "Snuffle." Bernstein described his method in two ways: in a paper containing analysis and mathematical equations (the "Paper") and in two computer programs written in "C," a high-level computer programming language ("Source Code"). Bernstein later wrote a set of instructions in English (the "Instructions") explaining how to program a computer to encrypt and decrypt data utilizing a one-way hash function, essentially translating verbatim his Source Code into prose form.

Seeking to present his work on Snuffle within the academic and scientific communities, Bernstein asked the State Department whether he needed a license to publish Snuffle in any of its various forms. The State Department responded that Snuffle was a munition under the International Traffic in Arms Regulations ("ITAR"), and that Bernstein would need a license to "export" the Paper, the Source Code, or the Instructions. There followed a protracted and unproductive series of letter communications between Bernstein and the government, wherein Bernstein unsuccessfully attempted to determine the scope and application of the export regulations to Snuffle.

Bernstein ultimately filed this action, challenging the constitutionality of the ITAR regulations. The district court found that the Source Code was speech protected by the First Amendment, see *Bernstein* v. *Department of State*, ("Bernstein I"), and subsequently granted summary judgment to Bernstein on his First Amendment claims, holding the challenged ITAR regulations facially invalid as a prior restraint on speech, see *Bernstein* v. *Department of State*, ("Bernstein II").

In December 1996, President Clinton shifted licensing authority for nonmilitary encryption commodities and technologies from the State Department to the Department of Commerce. The Department of Commerce then promulgated regulations under the EAR to govern the export of encryption technology, regulations administered by the Bureau of Export Administration ("BXA"). Bernstein subsequently amended his complaint to add the Department of Commerce as a defendant, advancing the same constitutional objections as he had against the State Department. The district court, following the rationale of its earlier Bernstein opinions, once again granted summary judgment in favor of Bernstein, finding the new EAR regulations facially invalid as a prior restraint on speech. The district court enjoined the Commerce Department from future enforcement of the invalidated provisions, an injunction that has been stayed pending this appeal.

B. Overview of Cryptography

Cryptography is the science of secret writing, a science that has roots stretching back hundreds, and perhaps thousands, of years. For much of its history, cryptography has been the jealously guarded province of governments and militaries. In the past twenty years, however, the science has blossomed in the civilian sphere, driven on the one hand by dramatic theoretical innovations within the field, and on the other by the needs of modern communication and information technologies. As a re-

---

† 176 F. 3d 1132 (9th Cir, 1999).

sult, cryptography has become a dynamic academic discipline within applied mathematics. It is the cryptographer's primary task to find secure methods to encrypt messages, making them unintelligible to all except the intended recipients.

The applications of encryption, however, are not limited to ensuring secrecy; encryption can also be employed to ensure data integrity, authenticate users, and facilitate non-repudiation (e.g., linking a specific message to a specific sender).

It is, of course, encryption's secrecy applications that concern the government. The interception and deciphering of foreign communications has long played an important part in our nation's national security efforts.

As increasingly sophisticated and secure encryption methods are developed, the government's interest in halting or slowing the proliferation of such methods has grown keen. The EAR regulations at issue in this appeal evidence this interest.

C. The EAR regulations

The EAR contain specific regulations to control the export of encryption software, expressly including computer source code. Encryption software is treated differently from other software in a number of significant ways. First, the term "export" is specifically broadened with respect to encryption software to preclude the use of the internet and other global mediums if such publication would allow passive or active access by a foreign national within the United States or anyone outside the United States. Second, the regulations governing the export of nonencryption software provide for several exceptions that are not applicable to encryption software. In addition, although printed materials containing encryption source code are not subject to EAR regulation, the same materials made available on machine-readable media, such as floppy disk or CD-ROM, are covered.

If encryption software falls within the ambit of the relevant EAR provisions, the "export" of such software requires a prepublication license. When a prepublication license is requested, the relevant agencies undertake a "case-by-case" analysis to determine if the export is "consistent with U.S. national security and foreign policy interests." All applications must be "resolved or referred to the President no later than 90 days" from the date an application is entered into the BXA's electronic license processing system. There is no time limit, however, that applies once an application is referred to the President. Although the regulations do provide for an internal administrative appeal procedure, such appeals are governed only by the exhortation that they be completed "within a reasonable time." Final administrative decisions are not subject to judicial review.

DISCUSSION

I. Prior Restraint

The parties urge a number of theories on us. We limit our attention here, for the most part, to only one: whether the EAR restrictions on the export of encryption software in source code form constitute a prior restraint in violation of the First Amendment. We review de novo the district court's affirmative answer to this question.

The Supreme Court has treated licensing schemes that act as prior restraints on speech with suspicion because such restraints run the twin risks of encouraging self-censorship and concealing illegitimate abuses of censorial power. As a result, "even if the government may constitutionally impose content-neutral prohibitions on a particular manner of speech, it may not condition that speech on obtaining a license or permit from a government official in that official's boundless discretion." We follow the lead of the Supreme Court and divide the appropriate analysis into two parts. The threshold question is whether Bernstein is entitled to bring a facial challenge against the EAR regulations. If he is so entitled, we proceed to the second question: whether the regulations constitute an impermissible prior restraint on speech.

A. Is Bernstein entitled to bring a facial attack?

A licensing regime is always subject to facial challenge as a prior restraint where it "gives a government official or agency substantial power to discriminate based on the content or viewpoint of speech by suppressing disfavored speech or disliked speakers," and has "a close enough nexus to expression, or to conduct commonly associated with expression, to pose a real and substantial threat of ... censorship risks."

The EAR regulations at issue plainly satisfy the first requirement — "the determination of who may speak and who may not is left to the unbridled discretion of a government official." BXA administrators are empowered to deny licenses whenever export might be inconsistent with "U.S. national security and foreign policy interests." No more specific guidance is provided.

The more difficult issue arises in relation to the second requirement — that the challenged regulations exhibit "a close enough nexus to expression." We are called on to determine whether encryption source code is expression for First Amendment purposes.

We begin by explaining what source code is. "Source code," at least as currently understood by computer programmers, refers to the text of a program written in a "high-level" programming language, such as "PASCAL" or "C." The distinguishing feature of source code is that it is meant to be read and understood by humans and that it can be used to express an idea or a method.

Also important for our purposes is an understanding of how source code is used in the field of cryptography. Bernstein has submitted numerous declarations from cryptographers and computer programmers explaining that cryptographic ideas and algorithms are conveniently expressed in source code. That this should be so is, on reflection, not surprising. As noted earlier, the chief task for cryptographers is the development of secure methods of encryption. While the articulation of such a system in layman's English or in general mathematical terms may be useful, the devil is, at least for cryptographers, often in the algorithmic details. By utilizing source code, a cryptographer can express algorithmic ideas with precision and methodological rigor that is otherwise difficult to achieve. This has the added benefit of facilitating peer review — by compiling the source code, a cryptographer can create a working model subject to rigorous security tests. The need for precisely articulated hypotheses and formal empirical testing, of course, is not unique to the science of cryptography; it appears, however, that in this field, source code is the preferred means to these ends.

In light of these considerations, we conclude that encryption software, in its source code form and as employed by those in the field of cryptography, must be viewed as expressive for First Amendment purposes, and thus is entitled to the protections of the prior restraint doctrine. If the government required that mathematicians obtain a prepublication license prior to publishing material that included mathematical equations, we have no doubt that such a regime would be subject to scrutiny as a prior restraint. The availability of alternate means of expression, moreover, does not diminish the censorial power of such a restraint — that Adam Smith wrote Wealth of Nations without resorting to equations or graphs surely would not justify governmental prepublication review of economics literature that contain these modes of expression.

The government, in fact, does not seriously dispute that source code is used by cryptographers for expressive purposes. Rather, the government maintains that source code is different from other forms of expression (such as blueprints, recipes, and "how-to" manuals) because it can be used to control directly the operation of a computer without conveying information to the user. In the government's view, by targeting this unique functional aspect of source code, rather than the content of the ideas that may be expressed therein, the export regulations manage to skirt entirely the concerns of the First Amendment. This argument is flawed for at least two reasons.

First, it is not at all obvious that the government's view reflects a proper understanding of source code. As noted earlier, the distinguishing feature of source code is that it is meant to be read and understood by humans, and that it cannot be used to control directly the functioning of a computer. While source code, when properly prepared, can be easily compiled into object code by a user, ignoring the distinction between source and object code obscures the important fact that source code is not meant solely for the computer, but is rather written in a language intended also for human analysis and understanding.

Second, and more importantly, the government's argument, distilled to its essence, suggests that even one drop of "direct functionality" overwhelms any constitutional protections that expression might otherwise enjoy. This cannot be so. The distinction urged on us by the government would prove too much in this era of rapidly evolving computer capabilities. The fact that computers will soon be able to respond directly to spoken commands, for example, should not confer on the government the unfettered power to impose prior restraints on speech in an effort to control its "functional " aspects. The First Amendment is concerned with expression, and we reject the notion that the admixture of functionality necessarily puts expression beyond the protections of the Constitution.

B. Are the regulations an impermissible prior restraint?

"[T]he protection even as to previous restraint is not absolutely unlimited." (Near). The Supreme Court has suggested that the "heavy presumption" against prior restraints may be overcome where official discretion is bounded by stringent procedural safeguards. As our analysis above suggests, the challenged regulations do not qualify for this First Amendment safe harbor. In *Freedman* v. *Maryland*, the Supreme Court set out three factors for determining the validity of licensing schemes that impose a prior restraint on speech: (1) any restraint must be for a specified brief period of time; (2) there must be expeditious judicial review; and (3) the censor must bear the burden of going to court to suppress the speech in question and must bear the burden of proof. The district court found that the procedural protections provided by the EAR regulations are "woefully inadequate" when measured against these requirements. We agree.

We conclude that the challenged regulations allow the government to restrain speech indefinitely with no clear criteria for review. As a result, Bernstein and other scientists have been effectively chilled from engaging in valuable scientific expression. Bernstein's experience itself demonstrates the enormous uncertainty that exists over the scope of the regulations and the potential for the chilling of scientific expression. In short, because the challenged regulations grant boundless discretion to government officials, and because they lack the required procedural protections set forth in Freedman, we find that they operate as an unconstitutional prior restraint on speech.

C. Concluding comments.

We emphasize the narrowness of our First Amendment holding. We do not hold that all software is expressive. Much of it surely is not. Nor need we resolve whether the challenged regulations constitute content-based restrictions, subject to the strictest constitutional scrutiny, or whether they are, instead, content-neutral restrictions meriting less exacting scrutiny. We hold merely that because the prepublication licensing regime challenged here applies directly to scientific expression, vests boundless discretion in government officials, and lacks adequate procedural safeguards, it constitutes an impermissible prior restraint on speech.

We will, however, comment on two issues that are entwined with the underlying merits of Bernstein's constitutional claims. First, we note that insofar as the EAR regulations on encryption software were intended to slow the spread of secure encryption methods to foreign nations, the government is intentionally retarding the progress of the flourishing science of cryptography. To the extent the government's efforts are aimed at interdicting the flow of scientific ideas (whether expressed in source code or otherwise), as distinguished from encryption products, these efforts would appear to strike deep into the heartland of the First Amendment. In this regard, the EAR regulations are very different from content-neutral time, place and manner restrictions that may have an incidental effect on expression while aiming at secondary effects.

Second, we note that the government's efforts to regulate and control the spread of knowledge relating to encryption may implicate more than the First Amendment rights of cryptographers. In this increasingly electronic age, we are all required in our everyday lives to rely on modern technology to communicate with one another. This reliance on electronic communication, however, has brought with it a dramatic diminution in our ability to communicate privately. Cellular phones are subject to monitoring, email is easily intercepted, and transactions over the internet are often less than secure. Something as commonplace as furnishing our credit card number, social security number, or bank account number puts each of us at risk. Moreover, when we employ electronic methods of communication, we often leave electronic "fingerprints" behind, fingerprints that can be traced back to us. Whether we are surveilled by our government, by criminals, or by our neighbors, it is fair to say that never has our ability to shield our affairs from prying eyes been at such a low ebb. The availability and use of secure encryption may offer an opportunity to reclaim some portion of the privacy we have lost. Government efforts to control encryption thus may well implicate not only the First Amendment rights of cryptographers intent on pushing the boundaries of their science, but also the constitutional rights of each of us as potential recipients of encryption's bounty. Viewed from this perspective, the government's efforts to retard progress in cryptography may implicate the Fourth Amendment, as well as the right to speak anonymously, the right against compelled speech, and the right to informational privacy. While we leave for another day the resolution of these difficult issues, it is important to point out that Bernstein's is a suit not merely concerning a small group of scientists laboring in an esoteric field, but also touches on the public interest broadly defined.

CONCLUSION

Because the prepublication licensing regime challenged by Bernstein applies directly to scientific expression, vests boundless discretion in government officials, and lacks adequate procedural safeguards, we hold that it constitutes an impermissible prior restraint on speech. We decline the invitation to line edit the regulations in an attempt to rescue them from constitutional infirmity, and thus endorse the declaratory relief granted by the district court.

Notes

A rehearing of the Bernstein case was granted by the 9th Circuit Court of Appeals in July 1999. The rehearing took place in December 1999. For a complete archive of Bernstein legal documents, see the Electronic Frontier Foundation's archive at <http://www.eff.org/pub/Privacy/ITAR_export/Bernstein_case/>.

While technology has the power to protect privacy, it can also hinder privacy. Internet users are becoming increasingly familiar with terms such as cookies and digital identifiers that allow outsiders to track their movement on the Web to develop a consumer preference profile.

Information Privacy In Cyberspace Transactions†

JERRY KANG

A cookie is a piece of information sent by the server to the client to store for some time. Its purpose is to store information about the client's state, so as to personalize the browsing experience. For example, various Web servers provide movie listings by zip code. Because it is inefficient to require the user to reenter her zip code at each visit, the server saves the zip code and other "state information" on the client's hard drive in the form of a cookie. Thereafter, by accessing the cookie, the server can automatically present local movie features without querying the user for her location. Many personalized news services operate this way. One's preferences — for example, sports scores in Chicago or the weather in Boston — can be saved in a cookie.

Recently, there has been great public anxiety that cookies can be freely accessed by all Web servers we contact, thereby disclosing details about our browsing history. This fear is somewhat overblown: A client does not serve up cookies simply to anyone who asks. In other words, not all servers have access to all cookies. Each cookie, when initially set, circumscribes the range of servers to whom the cookie may be subsequently given. The default range is the domain name of the server that initially set the cookie itself. So, if the server hollywood.movienews.com set a cookie

---

† (1998) 50:4 Stanford L. Rev. 1193 at 1227–30. Notes omitted. Republished with permission of the Stanford Law Review, 559 Nathan Abbott Way, Palo Alto, CA 94305. Reproduced by permission of the publisher via Copyright Clearance Center.

identifying my zip code as 90210 and did not specify a domain name range in the cookie, then, by default, the cookie would be presented only to holly-wood.movienews.com in the future. While it is true that hollywood.movienews.com could have set the domain range to a larger set of servers, by setting the domain name range to the tail portion of its name, i.e., movienews.com, it could not have set the range to an entirely different domain name, say, blockbuster.com. Recipro-cally, the client will only disclose a cookie to a server if the domain name range for the cookie "tail-matches" the server's domain name. In other words, a cookie with the domain name range movienews.com will not be disclosed to any server that has the tail of blockbuster.com. As a result, cookies can usually be read only by those entities that wrote the cookie in the first place.

That said, there is nothing to keep companies like movienews.com and block-buster.com from sharing with each other the browsing history of a given individual recorded through their respective cookies. In effect, this is what is done by various Internet advertising companies that target advertisement banners to individuals based on their browsing profile. These advertising companies establish relationships with numerous Web servers. Whenever a client browses one of these Web pages, the cli-ent is fed an in-line image that invisibly connects it to the advertising company's server without the individual user's explicit knowledge or command. Once connected, the advertiser retrieves the identity information described above. On the one hand, if the client's IP address or domain name has not been seen before, the advertiser cre-ates a unique identification number and saves it in a cookie on the client's hard drive. On the other hand, if the IP address/domain name has been seen already, then the advertiser accesses the previously set cookie, which contains a unique iden-tification number, and updates the extant database record indexed by that number with the browsing activity of the client. Based on this database of browsing activity collected from all affiliated Web sites, the advertiser delivers a targeted ad banner. These transactions occur within a fraction of a second.

To summarize, a client's browsing behavior at a particular site can be tracked with detail. Through, for instance, the use of cookies, this tracking can continue over multiple visits, over an indefinite period of time, with all browsing information com-piled into a database. This does not mean, however, that any other site has auto-matic access to this information — with the following critical exception: Sites may be linked together through a data sharing relationship, the most prominent of which is affiliation with a common advertiser. These three types of disclosures — identity, computer configuration, and browsing activity — are not software bugs or security loopholes that will be corrected momentarily. Rather, they are the standard, albeit unpopular, elements of the Web browsing process. Further, these personal informa-tion flows can be leveraged to produce additional information, often cheaply and rapidly, through cyberspace. For example, an e-mail address or domain name may be reverse-indexed, using national computerized White Pages, to find, in many cases, the individual's name, telephone number, and physical address. Even unlisted information can sometimes be located through the use of national lookup databases.

Notes

1. In February 2000, a controversy involving Doubleclick, an Internet advertising giant, graphically illustrated the danger of cookies. The problem began with the 1999 merger of Doubleclick and Abacus Direct. The merger was a

marketer's dream with the combined entity featuring Doubleclick's network of over 11,000 Web sites (the sites used by the company to serve up online advertising) and Abacus Direct's database of more than 2 billion consumer catalogue transactions.

Privacy advocates immediately became concerned with the prospect for detailed consumer profiling by the new company and lobbied the Federal Trade Commission in the United States to block the merger. Although sympathetic to the privacy advocates' concerns, the FTC granted its approval in November 1999.

Doubleclick wasted little time in taking advantage of its marketing muscle. The company proceeded to introduce a new service that provided advertisers with the opportunity to target their message more precisely than ever. By matching offline spending history with online browsing habits through the use of cookies, Doubleclick had the capability of developing detailed, personally identifiable consumer profiles.

Although the company defended the practice by noting that users were provided notice about the potential collection and use of their private data, few users were aware of the full implications. In fact, a California woman launched a lawsuit against Doubleclick, alleging that it misrepresented its intention not to collect personal and identifying information and arguing that the company has created a "sophisticated and highly intrusive means of collecting and cross-referencing private personal information without the knowing consent of Internet users." The company backed down on its marketing plans following a major outcry by privacy advocates.

2. The technological threat to privacy extends beyond cookies. In February 1999 a boycott of Intel, the world's largest semiconductor manufacturer, was organized in response to the release of the Pentium III, a chip that contained a digital identifier known as a PSN or processor serial number. The PSN, which provided each computer with a unique identifier, could be used by Web site owners to collect data on every visitor who accessed their site. This information could be collected without the user's knowledge, since the PSN operated transparently. Moreover, Web sites could, conceivably, share data to create a detailed consumer profile.

    Initially Intel configured the PSN to activate every time at startup. When privacy groups objected, the company agreed to release a software utility that automatically turned off the PSN function. Privacy groups were unimpressed, however, as they pointed out that the PSN remained on the system and was potentially subject to manipulation.

    For more on the boycott, see Big Brother Inside at <http://www.bigbrotherinside.com>.

3. Sun Microsystems CEO Scott McNealy was quoted in early 1999 as saying, "There is no privacy online. Get over it." Do you agree? If this is the prevailing attitude among leading technology executives, can we expect technology to develop in a manner that protects or hinders personal privacy?

PART FOUR

INTERNET AND INTELLECTUAL
PROPERTY

15

Domain Names and Trademarks

Domain name disputes have become one of the most contentious Internet legal issues. As many businesses realized the economic potential of the Internet and the importance of acquiring a memorable domain name, a virtual real estate market boom began, with demand quickly outstripping supply. Prices increased exponentially as a result.

Domain names became an extremely valuable commodity. In addition to many potentially valuable generic terms, various Internet users realized that the domain name equivalent of many trademarks had not been registered. The lack of initial interest by trademark holders created economic opportunities for domain name speculators. These names were registered with the expectation that they would be sold at a later date to the "rightful" holder at a substantial premium.

With millions of names now registered, many trademark holders find themselves at a disadvantage since their most obvious access points to the World Wide Web have already been claimed by other parties. Characterized as squatters and pirates, trademark holders claim that domain name speculators do not have a legitimate right to register their trademarks as domain names. When legal threats do not succeed in extracting the domain name, trademark holders frequently turn to the court system to resolve their disputes, suing both the domain name registrant and the registrar.

Domain names present a unique problem in that they raise several competing issues. First, domain names serve a two-fold purpose. From a purely technological perspective, they simplify the identification of host systems on the Internet. For example, when a user types in a domain name such as <www.lawbytes.com>, that domain name is translated into the Internet protocol number equivalent

208.231.177.24. Since it is very difficult to remember lengthy IP addresses, the domain name approach makes it easier to access content on the Web. In addition to their identification role, domain names have developed secondary characteristics that are very similar to trademarks, since they have emerged as a critical component of Internet marketing.

Second, domain names are unique. As a result, United Airlines, United Postal Service, United Van Lines and the United Way may all stake a claim to "united.com," but in reality, none of these entities owns the domain (Mail.com does, and it uses the domain name to redirect Web users to the mail.com site). This state of affairs can be contrasted with trademark law, which permits the registration of identical marks provided there is no confusion.

Third, the domain name system creates perpetual monopolies in cyberspace. Trademark registration requirements are not applied when registering a domain name. Due to weak registration requirements, registrants have the ability to create a monopoly in generic terms such as "mail," "toys" or "books."

Our examination of the legal aspects of domain names begins with a review of how courts understand the technological aspects of the domain name system.

Thomas v. Network Solutions†

Individuals generally obtain access to the Internet through these host computers, each of which has a numerical address, or Internet Protocol number, such as "98.37.241.30," that allows other host computers to identify and locate it. When the Internet was in its infancy, Internet Protocol numbers were assigned and maintained by the late Dr. Jon Postel, then a UCLA graduate student working under a contract between the Defense Department and the university. When Dr. Postel moved from UCLA to the Information Sciences Institute at the University of Southern California, he continued to maintain the lists pursuant to contracts with the Defense Department. As the lists grew, Dr. Postel delegated certain aspects of the list maintenance to what eventually became known as the Internet Assigned Numbers Authority.

Because many numerical sequences are difficult to remember, the Internet community created a system allowing an Internet computer to be identified by a "domain name." The domain name system is a hierarchy. Top-level domains are divided into second-level domains, and so on. More than 200 national, or country-code, top-level domains — e.g., ".us" for the United States, ".pa" for Panama, ".uk" for the United Kingdom, and so on — are administered by their corresponding governments or by private entities with the government's permission. A small set of generic top-level domains carry no national identifier, but denote the intended function of that portion of the domain space: ".com" for commercial users; ".org" for non-profit organizations; ".net" for network service providers; ".edu" for educational; institutions; ".gov" for United States government institutions; ".mil" for United States military institutions; and ".int" for international institutions.

---

† (May 14, 1999) WL 300619 (D.C. Cir.).

Domain names — e.g., bettyandnicks.com — consist of at least two groups of alphanumeric characters, each known as a string, separated by a period or dot. The last string — the farthest to the right — denotes the top-level domain. The second-to-last string is the second-level domain name and identifies the person's or organization's Internet computer site. Each string may contain up to 63 characters but the overall domain name must be less than 256 characters. For the domain name system to function, each domain name must be unique and correspond to a unique Internet Protocol number. A new user who wishes to have an Internet site with a domain name address first obtains an Internet Protocol number (e.g., 1.23.456.7). The user then registers a domain name and it becomes linked with that Internet Protocol number.

Before using a domain name to locate an Internet computer site in "cyberspace," a computer must match the domain name to the domain name's Internet Protocol number. The match information is stored on various Internet-connected computers around the world known as domain name servers. The computer attempts to find the match information by sending out an address query. The goal of the address query is to find the particular domain name server containing the match information the user seeks. When ordered to translate an unknown domain name into an Internet Protocol number, a computer will ask its Internet Service Provider's server if it knows the domain name and corresponding Internet Protocol number. If that server lacks the information, it will pass the query to a "root server," also called a "root zone" file, the authoritative and highest level of the domain name system database. The root zone file directs the query to the proper top-level domain zone file, which contains the domain names in a given domain and their corresponding Internet Protocol numbers. In the case of someone searching for the "bettyandnicks.com" home page, the root zone file sends the query to the top-level domain zone file with information about ".com" domain names. The ".com" zone file then refers the query to a second-level domain name file with all the second-level domain names under ".com." This is where the "bettyandnicks.com" query ends: the second-level domain name file has the information matching the domain name to its associated Internet Protocol number. With the Internet Protocol number, the user's computer can connect the user to the requested Internet site. The "bettyandnicks.com" home page will appear, just as if the user had typed in the Internet Protocol number instead of the domain name.

Initially, the Internet Assigned Numbers Authority retained responsibility for both Internet Protocol number allocation and domain name registration. In 1991 and 1992, NSF, an independent agency of the federal government, assumed responsibility for coordinating and funding the management of the nonmilitary portion of the Internet infrastructure. In March 1992, NSF solicited competitive proposals to provide a variety of infrastructure services, including domain name registration services. NSF issued the solicitation pursuant to the National Science Foundation Act of 1950, 42 U.S.C. ss 1861–1887, as amended, and the Federal Grant and Cooperative Agreement Act, 31 U.S.C. ss 6301–6308. In December 1992, after an independent review of the proposals responsive to the solicitation, NSF selected the bid from, and entered into a cooperative agreement with, Network Solutions, Inc., a private company.

Peinet Inc. v. O'Brien (c.o.b. Island Services Network (ISN))[†]

The plaintiff seeks an interlocutory injunction preventing the defendants from using the name PEI.NET or any similar name or address which may be confused by the public with the corporate name of the plaintiff. The action is one of "passing off". Throughout this decision I shall refer to the two named defendants as "the defendant".

FACTS

The parties are in agreement on most of the facts. The plaintiff was incorporated on July 30, 1993. It provides network services to its clients including access to Internet. Internet is a world-wide computer network. In order to gain access to Internet, it is necessary to obtain a 'feed' from a national distributor such as CA Net in Canada or some other national access provider.

The plaintiff is a member of CA Net. All subscribers to Internet obtain a 'domain name', which is really an electronics address. CA Net provides domain names to its customers using the following format: name.province.ca. This would mean the regional internet provider in Nova Scotia would have the name: nsnet.ns.ca. The plaintiff as the regional Internet provider in Prince Edward Island was given the name: peinet.pe.ca.

After becoming incorporated, the plaintiff alleges it took extensive steps to develop public awareness of itself. The defendant, Kevin O'Brien, was one of the plaintiff's employees. He remained with the plaintiff until October, 1994 when he was dismissed. Mr. O'Brien then formed his own business as an Internet provider under the name Island Services Network. He was assigned the domain name pei.net from a United States provider. In the affidavit of James Hill, President of the plaintiff, it is stated the defendant was assigned the domain name PEI.NET using upper case letters. The destination is stated to be important according to the defendant.

. . . .

The plaintiff asks for an injunction restraining the defendant from using the domain name of PEI.NET. The plaintiff uses upper case letters. There is no evidence that the defendant used such a domain name, rather the name pei.net was used. The plaintiff also states that the defendant by using the domain name PEI.NET confused the public as to the identity of the plaintiff and defendant, however, it is to be noted that the plaintiff's name is PEINET INC. and the plaintiff does not use a period to separate PEI and NET.

The defendant states that anyone using the internet network would not confuse the plaintiff and the defendant. The defendant states anyone intending to contact the plaintiff using its domain name would not be able to contact the defendant and vice versa. The plaintiff did not answer that allegation.

The whole area of the use of the internet network and its conventions is new to the Court. I find that the plaintiff has only made superficial submissions without explaining the Internet system. The plaintiff merely filed a short affidavit of its president, which leaves much to be desired insofar as an explanation of Internet is concerned. The plaintiff's president did not give viva voce evidence to further

---

† [1995] P.E.I.J. No. 68.

expand on his affidavit. The defendant, Kevin O'Brien, did give direct evidence. He raised sufficient concerns to cast doubt on the plaintiff's case. It must be remembered that the burden is upon the plaintiff to prove its case.

Even if the plaintiff had proven that the defendant's use of the domain name pei.net was an infringement of the plaintiff's use of the name PEINET Inc., I am of the opinion that the plaintiff has not established all of the elements of a passing off action. The Supreme Court of Canada in *Ciba-Geigy Canada Ltd.* v. *Apoten Inc.* [1992] 3 S.C.R. 120, 95 D.L.R. (4th) 385 has recently stated that the three components of a passing off action are; (1) the existence of goodwill; (2) deception of the public due to a misrepresentation; and (3) actual or potential damage to the plaintiff.

The plaintiff has failed to establish that the defendants had misrepresented the public. I do not consider the limited use the defendants had of pei.net to be sufficient to meet the component of deception of the public due to misrepresentation. It must be remembered that the defendants did not operate or use the plaintiff's company name of PEINET. Basically all the defendants did was, for a very short period of time, use a "telephone" number that was the same as the plaintiff's name. This use of the same name consisted of a reference to it in a newspaper article, not an advertisement, and a listing on Internet, also for a very short period of time.

The misrepresentation must lead or likely lead the public to believe that the goods or services offered by the defendant are the goods and services of the plaintiff. That has not been established.

The plaintiff has shown no actual damage loss. Neither will there be a potential loss to the plaintiff as the defendant has agreed to delist the domain name pei.net from its Internet server.

Neither am I satisfied that the plaintiff has established himself in business under its trade name for such a reasonable time and to such a reasonable extent that it has acquired a reputation under that trade name that would prevent the defendants from using a similar name: Remedies in Tort, Klar, Linden, Cherniak, Kryworuk, pp. 19–21.

In the circumstances I would dismiss the application. There shall be no order for costs.

Discussion Question

The previous two decisions demonstrate the enormous difference in the level of understanding of Internet technology and, specifically, domain names. Does the Canadian court understand what domain names are all about?

Do domain names even fall within the scope of the *Trademarks Act*? Should a trademark registration confer automatic rights to a domain name? Consider these two fundamental questions as you review the relevant provisions in the Canadian trademark statute.

Trade-marks Act[†]

2. In this Act,

"confusing", when applied as an adjective to a trade-mark or trade-name, means a trade-mark or trade-name the use of which would cause confusion in the manner and circumstances described in section 6;

"trade-mark" means

(a) a mark that is used by a person for the purpose of distinguishing or so as to distinguish wares or services manufactured, sold, leased, hired or performed by him from those manufactured, sold, leased, hired or performed by others,

(b) a certification mark,

(c) a distinguishing guise, or

(d) a proposed trade-mark;

"trade-name" means the name under which any business is carried on, whether or not it is the name of a corporation, a partnership or an individual;

"use", in relation to a trade-mark, means any use that by section 4 is deemed to be a use in association with wares or services;

4.(1) A trade-mark is deemed to be used in association with wares if, at the time of the transfer of the property in or possession of the wares, in the normal course of trade, it is marked on the wares themselves or on the packages in which they are distributed or it is in any other manner so associated with the wares that notice of the association is then given to the person to whom the property or possession is transferred.

(2) A trade-mark is deemed to be used in association with services if it is used or displayed in the performance or advertising of those services.

(3) A trade-mark that is marked in Canada on wares or on the packages in which they are contained is, when the wares are exported from Canada, deemed to be used in Canada in association with those wares.

6.(1) For the purposes of this Act, a trade-mark or trade-name is confusing with another trade-mark or trade-name if the use of the first mentioned trade-mark or trade-name would cause confusion with the last mentioned trade-mark or trade-name in the manner and circumstances described in this section.

(2) The use of a trade-mark causes confusion with another trade-mark if the use of both trade-marks in the same area would be likely to lead to the inference that the wares or services associated with those trade-marks are manufactured, sold, leased, hired or performed by the same person, whether or not the wares or services are of the same general class.

(3) The use of a trade-mark causes confusion with a trade-name if the use of both the trade-mark and trade-name in the same area would be likely to lead to the inference that the wares or services associated with the trade-mark and those associated with the business carried on under the trade-name are manufactured, sold, leased, hired or performed by the same person, whether or not the wares or services are of the same general class.

---

† R.S.C., c. T-13.

(4) The use of a trade-name causes confusion with a trade-mark if the use of both the trade-name and trade-mark in the same area would be likely to lead to the inference that the wares or services associated with the business carried on under the trade-name and those associated with the trade-mark are manufactured, sold, leased, hired or performed by the same person, whether or not the wares or services are of the same general class.

(5) In determining whether trade-marks or trade-names are confusing, the court or the Registrar, as the case may be, shall have regard to all the surrounding circumstances including

(a) the inherent distinctiveness of the trade-marks or trade-names and the extent to which they have become known;
(b) the length of time the trade-marks or trade-names have been in use;
(c) the nature of the wares, services or business;
(d) the nature of the trade; and
(e) the degree of resemblance between the trade-marks or trade-names in appearance or sound or in the ideas suggested by them.

7. No person shall

(a) make a false or misleading statement tending to discredit the business, wares or services of a competitor;
(b) direct public attention to his wares, services or business in such a way as to cause or be likely to cause confusion in Canada, at the time he commenced so to direct attention to them, between his wares, services or business and the wares, services or business of another;
(c) pass off other wares or services as and for those ordered or requested;
(d) make use, in association with wares or services, of any description that is false in a material respect and likely to mislead the public as to
    (i) the character, quality, quantity or composition,
    (ii) the geographical origin, or
    (iii) the mode of the manufacture, production or performance
    of the wares or services; or
(e) do any other act or adopt any other business practice contrary to honest industrial or commercial usage in Canada.

12.(1) Subject to section 13, a trade-mark is registrable if it is not

(a) a word that is primarily merely the name or the surname of an individual who is living or has died within the preceding thirty years;
(b) whether depicted, written or sounded, either clearly descriptive or deceptively misdescriptive in the English or French language of the character or quality of the wares or services in association with which it is used or proposed to be used or of the conditions of or the persons employed in their production or of their place of origin;
(c) the name in any language of any of the wares or services in connection with which it is used or proposed to be used;
(d) confusing with a registered trade-mark;
(e) a mark of which the adoption is prohibited by section 9 or 10;
(f) a denomination the adoption of which is prohibited by section 10.1.
(g) in whole or in part a protected geographical indication, where the trade-mark is to be registered in association with a wine not originating in a territory indicated by the geographical indication; and

(h) in whole or in part a protected geographical indication, where the trade-mark is to be registered in association with a spirit not originating in a territory indicated by the geographical indication.

(2) A trade-mark that is not registrable by reason of paragraph (1)(a) or (b) is registrable if it has been so used in Canada by the applicant or his predecessor in title as to have become distinctive at the date of filing an application for its registration.

14.(1) Notwithstanding section 12, a trade-mark that the applicant or the applicant's predecessor in title has caused to be duly registered in or for the country of origin of the applicant is registrable if, in Canada,

(a) it is not confusing with a registered trade-mark;
(b) it is not without distinctive character, having regard to all the circumstances of the case including the length of time during which it has been used in any country;
(c) it is not contrary to morality or public order or of such a nature as to deceive the public; or
(d) it is not a trade-mark of which the adoption is prohibited by section 9 or 10.

(2) A trade-mark that differs from the trade-mark registered in the country of origin only by elements that do not alter its distinctive character or affect its identity in the form under which it is registered in the country of origin shall be regarded for the purpose of subsection (1) as the trade-mark so registered.

19. Subject to sections 21, 32 and 67, the registration of a trade-mark in respect of any wares or services, unless shown to be invalid, gives to the owner of the trade-mark the exclusive right to the use throughout Canada of the trade-mark in respect of those wares or services.

20.(1) The right of the owner of a registered trade-mark to its exclusive use shall be deemed to be infringed by a person not entitled to its use under this Act who sells, distributes or advertises wares or services in association with a confusing trade-mark or trade-name, but no registration of a trade-mark prevents a person from making

(a) any bona fide use of his personal name as a trade-name, or
(b) any bona fide use, other than as a trade-mark,
   (i) of the geographical name of his place of business, or
   (ii) of any accurate description of the character or quality of his wares or services,
   in such a manner as is not likely to have the effect of depreciating the value of the goodwill attaching to the trade-mark.

22.(1) No person shall use a trade-mark registered by another person in a manner that is likely to have the effect of depreciating the value of the goodwill attaching thereto.

Given the global nature of the Internet and the national nature of trademark law, the intersection of these two issues raises some significant jurisdictional questions. Colorworks Reproduction & Design, a B.C. based company, confronted precisely this issue as it faced a domain name lawsuit in the United States in a contest between competing trademarks.

Desktop Technologies, Inc v. ColorWorks Reproduction & Design, Inc.†

I.   BACKGROUND

Plaintiff is a corporation organized under the laws of Pennsylvania with its principal place of business in Boyertown, Pennsylvania. Defendant is a corporation organized under the laws of Canada with its principal place of business in Vancouver, British Columbia. Defendant contends, and Plaintiff does not contest, that its business is carried out exclusively in the British Columbia lower mainland and that Defendant has not transacted any business, provided any services, contracted to provide any services, earned any income, or entered into any contracts in Pennsylvania.

The general nature of the parties' businesses are the same: both companies prepare and print color reproductions. Plaintiff is the owner of a U.S. trademark, COLORWORKS, which was registered in the United States on June 4, 1996. Defendant is the owner of the trademark, "ColorWorks," which was registered in Canada on March 25, 1997.

Since August 21, 1995, Defendant has operated a web site on the Internet with the domain name of "colorworks.com." Defendant's web site is accessible to all Internet users, including those in Pennsylvania at http://www.colorworks.com. In its complaint, Plaintiff alleges that Defendant's use of the word "ColorWorks" as its domain name on the Internet infringes Plaintiff's trademark rights and enables Defendant to compete unfairly with Plaintiff in the United States.

Defendant's web site contains information about the company, advertisements about the company, and employment opportunities at the company. The site specifically states that it services clients in British Columbia, Alberta, and Yukon. It lists its local telephone and facsimile numbers, and provides an order form and instructions for entering orders. The site also allows a reader to send a message via e-mail and to exchange files via Internet File Transfer Protocol ("FTP"). However, the site indicates that Defendant does not conduct sales, accept orders, or receive payments through its web site. The site also indicates that receiving a file via Internet FTP or an e-mail is not a sales transaction and does not constitute placing an order. To place an order, a reader can print up a copy of the fax order form, complete the form, and fax it to Defendant. Notably, the order form cannot be completed on-line.

.   .   .   .

Because the parties have agreed that Defendant's business is carried out exclusively in the British Columbia lower mainland, any claim that this Court has specific jurisdiction over Defendant must be based on the allegation that Defendant's domain name, colorworks.com, and its web site infringe Plaintiff's trademark in Pennsylvania and that Defendant's web site can be accessed in Pennsylvania. Upon review of recent cases that have addressed the issue of whether a forum can exercise specific jurisdiction over a non-resident defendant based upon a claim that the defendant's web site or domain name infringes the trademark rights of a resident plaintiff, a basic principal emerges:

> Simply registering someone else's trademark as a domain name and posting
> a web site on the Internet is not sufficient to subject a party domiciled in

---

† 1999 U.S. Dist. LEXIS 1934 (E.D. Pa. 1999).

one state to jurisdiction in another ... There must be "something more" to demonstrate that the defendant directed his activity towards the forum state.

Thus, publication of a page on the web, without more, is not an act by which a party purposefully avails itself of the privilege of conducting business in the forum state.

The level of interactivity in this case is insufficient to justify exercising specific personal jurisdiction over Defendant. Courts have repeatedly recognized that there must be "something more" than simply registering someone else's trademark as a domain name and posting a web site on the Internet to demonstrate that the defendant directed its activity towards the forum state. In Zippo Mfg. Co., the court characterized the litigation as a "doing business over the Internet case" and found that the defendant had "done more than advertise on the Internet in Pennsylvania." The fact that defendant had sold passwords to approximately 3,000 subscribers in Pennsylvania and entered into seven contracts with Internet access providers to furnish its services to its customers in Pennsylvania constituted purposeful availment of doing business in Pennsylvania. In the present case, which this Court characterizes as an Internet advertising case, Plaintiff has failed to prove that Defendant purposefully availed itself of the privilege of conducting business in Pennsylvania.

Defendant's Internet presence and e-mail link are its only contacts with Pennsylvania. As established earlier, Defendant maintains the web site to advertise and post information about its services and employment opportunities. The web site does not exist for the purpose of entering into contracts with customers outside of Canada or for the purpose of attracting customers from Pennsylvania. Instead, its web site specifically states that it is servicing clients in British Columbia, Alberta and Yukon. Defendant has never entered into any contracts in Pennsylvania, made sales or earned income in Pennsylvania, or sent messages over the Internet to users in Pennsylvania. While visitors to the web site are able to exchange information over the web site via Internet FTP and e-mail, receiving a file through Internet FTP or an e-mail does not constitute placing an order. Thus, while Defendant is exchanging information over the Internet, it is not doing business over the Internet with residents of Pennsylvania. Accordingly, this Court finds that Defendant's registration of "ColorWorks" as a domain name and posting a web site on the Internet are insufficient to subject Defendant to specific personal jurisdiction in Pennsylvania.

At the heart of domain name disputes is the question of confusion. Trademark holders are concerned with whether the public will be confused by a domain name that employs their trademark held by someone other than the trademark holder, while domain name holders argue that the two are distinct. The following case is one of the leading U.S. opinions on the matter.

Brookfield Communications, Inc. v. West Coast Entertainment Corporation[†]

We must venture into cyberspace to determine whether federal trademark and unfair competition laws prohibit a video rental store chain from using an entertainment-industry information provider's trademark in the domain name of its web site [...].

---

† 174 F. 3d 1036 (9th Cir. 1999).

I

Brookfield Communications, Inc. ("Brookfield") appeals the district court's denial of its motion for a preliminary injunction prohibiting West Coast Entertainment Corporation ("West Coast") from using in commerce terms confusingly similar to Brookfield's trademark, "MovieBuff." Brookfield gathers and sells information about the entertainment industry. Founded in 1987 for the purpose of creating and marketing software and services for professionals in the entertainment industry, Brookfield initially offered software applications featuring information such as recent film submissions, industry credits, professional contacts, and future projects. These offerings targeted major Hollywood film studios, independent production companies, agents, actors, directors, and producers.

Brookfield expanded into the broader consumer market with computer software featuring a searchable database containing entertainment industry related information marketed under the "MovieBuff" mark around December 1993. Brookfield's "MovieBuff" software now targets smaller companies and individual consumers who are not interested in purchasing Brookfield's professional level alternative, The Studio System, and includes comprehensive, searchable, entertainment-industry databases and related software applications containing information such as movie credits, box office receipts, films in development, film release schedules, entertainment news, and listings of executives, agents, actors, and directors. This "MovieBuff" software comes in three versions — (1) the MovieBuff Pro Bundle, (2) the MovieBuff Pro, and (3) MovieBuff — and is sold through various retail stores, such as Borders, Virgin Megastores, Nobody Beats the Wiz, The Writer's Computer Store, Book City, and Samuel French Bookstores.

Sometime in 1996, Brookfield attempted to register the World Wide Web ("the Web") domain name "moviebuff.com" with Network Solutions, Inc. ("Network Solutions"), but was informed that the requested domain name had already been registered by West Coast. Brookfield subsequently registered "brookfieldcomm.com" in May 1996 and "moviebuffonline.com" in September 1996. Sometime in 1996 or 1997, Brookfield began using its web sites to sell its "MovieBuff" computer software and to offer an Internet-based searchable database marketed under the "MovieBuff" mark. Brookfield sells its "MovieBuff" computer software through its "brookfieldcomm.com" and "moviebuffonline.com" web sites and offers subscribers online access to the MovieBuff database itself at its "inhollywood.com" web site.

On August 19, 1997, Brookfield applied to the Patent and Trademark Office (PTO) for federal registration of "MovieBuff" as a mark to designate both goods and services. Its trademark application describes its product as "computer software providing data and information in the field of the motion picture and television industries." Its service mark application describes its service as "providing multiple-user access to an on-line network database offering data and information in the field of the motion picture and television industries." Both federal trademark registrations issued on September 29, 1998. Brookfield had previously obtained a California state trademark registration for the mark "MovieBuff" covering "computer software" in 1994.

In October 1998, Brookfield learned that West Coast — one of the nation's largest video rental store chains with over 500 stores — intended to launch a web site at "moviebuff.com" containing, inter alia, a searchable entertainment database similar to "MovieBuff." West Coast had registered "moviebuff.com" with Network Solutions on February 6, 1996 and claims that it chose the domain name because the term "Movie Buff" is part of its service mark, "The Movie Buff's Movie Store," on which a federal registration issued in 1991 covering "retail store services featuring video cassettes and video game cartridges" and "rental of video cassettes and video game cartridges." West Coast notes further that, since at least 1988, it has also used various phrases including the term "Movie Buff" to promote goods and services available at its video stores in Massachusetts [...].

On November 10, Brookfield delivered to West Coast a cease-and-desist letter alleging that West Coast's planned use of the "moviebuff.com" would violate Brookfield's trademark rights; as a "courtesy" Brookfield attached a copy of a complaint that it threatened to file if West Coast did not desist.

The next day, West Coast issued a press release announcing the imminent launch of its web site full of "movie reviews, Hollywood news and gossip, provocative commentary, and coverage of the independent film scene and films in production." The press release declared that the site would feature "an extensive database, which aids consumers in making educated decisions about the rental and purchase of" movies and would also allow customers to purchase movies, accessories, and other entertainment-related merchandise on the web site.

Brookfield fired back immediately with a visit to the United States District Court for the Central District of California, and this lawsuit was born. In its first amended complaint filed on November 18, 1998, Brookfield alleged principally that West Coast's proposed offering of online services at "moviebuff.com" would constitute trademark infringement and unfair competition in violation of sections 32 and 43(a) of the Lanham Act, 15 U.S.C. §§1114, 1125(a). Soon thereafter, Brookfield applied ex parte for a temporary restraining order ("TRO") enjoining West Coast "from using ... in any manner ... the mark MOVIEBUFF, or any other term or terms likely to cause confusion therewith, including moviebuff.com, as West Coast's domain name, ... as the name of West Coast's website service, in buried code or metatags on their home page or web pages, or in connection with the retrieval of data or information on other goods or services."

On November 27, West Coast filed an opposition brief in which it argued first that Brookfield could not prevent West Coast from using "moviebuff.com" in commerce because West Coast was the senior user. West Coast claimed that it was the first user of "MovieBuff" because it had used its federally registered trademark, "The Movie Buff's Movie Store," since 1986 in advertisements, promotions, and letterhead in connection with retail services featuring videocassettes and video game cartridges. Alternatively, West Coast claimed seniority on the basis that it had garnered common-law rights in the domain name by using "moviebuff.com" before Brookfield began offering its "MovieBuff" Internet-based searchable database on the Web. In addition to asserting seniority, West Coast contended that its planned use of "moviebuff.com" would not cause a likelihood of confusion with Brookfield's trademark "MovieBuff" and thus would not violate the Lanham Act.

The district court heard arguments on the TRO motion on November 30. Later that day, the district court issued an order construing Brookfield's TRO motion as a motion for a preliminary injunction and denying it. The district court concluded that West Coast was the senior user of the mark "MovieBuff" for both of the reasons asserted by West Coast. The court also determined that Brookfield had not established a likelihood of confusion.

Brookfield responded by filing a notice of appeal from the denial of preliminary injunction followed by a motion in the district court for injunction pending appeal, which motion the district court denied. On January 16, 1999, West Coast launched its web site at "moviebuff.com." Fearing that West Coast's fully operational web site would cause it irreparable injury, Brookfield filed an emergency motion for injunction pending appeal with this court a few days later.

· · · ·

III

We review the district court's denial of preliminary injunctive relief for an abuse of discretion. Under this standard, reversal is appropriate only if the district court based its decision on clearly erroneous findings of fact or erroneous legal principles. "A district court would necessarily abuse its discretion if it based its ruling on an erroneous view of the law," so we review the underlying legal issues injunction de novo.

"A plaintiff is entitled to a preliminary injunction in a trademark case when he demonstrates either (1) a combination of probable success on the merits and the possibility of irreparable injury or (2) the existence of serious questions going to the merits and that the balance of hardships tips sharply in his favor." To establish a trademark infringement claim under section 32 of the Lanham Act or an unfair competition claim under section 43(a) of the Lanham Act, Brookfield must establish that West Coast is using a mark confusingly similar to a valid, protectable trademark of Brookfield's. The district court denied Brookfield's motion for preliminary injunctive relief because it concluded that Brookfield had failed to establish [...] West Coast's use of the "moviebuff.com" domain name created a likelihood of confusion.

· · · ·

V

[...] Brookfield must also show that the public is likely to be somehow confused about the source or sponsorship of West Coast's "moviebuff.com" web site — and somehow to associate that site with Brookfield. The Supreme Court has described "the basic objectives of trademark law" as follows: "trademark law, by preventing others from copying a source-identifying mark, 'reduces the customer's costs of shopping and making purchasing decisions,' for it quickly and easily assures a potential customer that this item — the item with this mark — is made by the same producer as other similarly marked items that he or she liked (or disliked) in the past. At the same time, the law helps assure a producer that it (and not an imitating competitor) will reap the financial, reputation-related rewards associated with a desirable product." Where two companies each use a different mark and the simultaneous use of those marks does not cause the consuming public to be confused as to who makes what, granting one company exclusive rights over both marks does nothing to further the objectives of the trademark laws; in fact, prohibiting the use of a mark that the public has come to associate with a company would actually contravene the intended purposes of the trademark law by making it more difficult to identify and to distinguish between different brands of goods.

"The core element of trademark infringement is the likelihood of confusion, i.e., whether the similarity of the marks is likely to confuse customers about the source of the products." We look to the following factors for guidance in determining the likelihood of confusion: similarity of the conflicting designations; relatedness or proximity of the two companies' products or services; strength of Brookfield's mark; marketing channels used; degree of care likely to be exercised by purchasers in selecting goods; West Coast's intent in selecting its mark; evidence of actual confusion; and likelihood of expansion in product lines. These eight factors are often referred to as the Sleekcraft factors.

A word of caution: this eight-factor test for likelihood of confusion is pliant. Some factors are much more important than others, and the relative importance of each individual factor will be case-specific. Although some factors — such as the similarity of the marks and whether the two companies are direct competitors — will always be important, it is often possible to reach a conclusion with respect to likelihood of confusion after considering only a subset of the factors. Moreover, the foregoing list does not purport to be exhaustive, and non-listed variables may often be quite important. We must be acutely aware of excessive rigidity when applying the law in the Internet context; emerging technologies require a flexible approach.

A

We begin by comparing the allegedly infringing mark to the federally registered mark. The similarity of the marks will always be an important factor. Where the two marks are entirely dissimilar, there is no likelihood of confusion. "Pepsi" does not infringe Coca-Cola's "Coke." Nothing further need be said. Even where there is precise identity of a complainant's and an alleged infringer's mark, there may be no consumer confusion — and thus no trademark infringement — if the alleged infringer is in a different geographic area or in a wholly different industry. Nevertheless, the more similar the marks in terms of appearance, sound, and meaning, the greater the likelihood of confusion. In analyzing this factor, "the marks must be considered in their entirety and as they appear in the marketplace," with similarities weighed more heavily than differences.

In the present case, the district court found West Coast's domain name "moviebuff.com" to be quite different than Brookfield's domain name "moviebuffonline.com." Comparison of domain names, however, is irrelevant as a matter of law, since the Lanham Act requires that the allegedly infringing mark be compared with the claimant's trademark, which here is "MovieBuff," not "moviebuffonline.com." Properly framed, it is readily apparent that West Coast's allegedly infringing mark is essentially identical to Brookfield's mark "MovieBuff." In terms of appearance, there are differences in capitalization and the addition of ".com" in West Coast's complete domain name, but these differences are inconsequential in light of the fact that Web addresses are not caps-sensitive and that the ".com" top-level domain signifies the site's commercial nature.

Looks aren't everything, so we consider the similarity of sound and meaning. The two marks are pronounced the same way, except that one would say "dot com" at the end of West Coast's mark. Because many companies use domain names comprised of ".com" as the top-level domain with their corporate name or trademark as the second-level domain, the addition of ".com" is of diminished importance in distinguishing the mark. The irrelevance of the ".com" becomes further apparent once we consider similarity in meaning. The domain name is more than a mere address: like trademarks, second-level domain names communicate information as to source. As we explained in Part II, many Web users are likely to associate "moviebuff.com" with the trademark "MovieBuff," thinking that it is operated by the company that makes "MovieBuff" products and services. Courts, in fact, have routinely concluded that marks were essentially identical in similar contexts. As "MovieBuff" and "moviebuff.com" are, for all intents and purposes, identical in terms of sight, sound, and meaning, we conclude that the similarity factor weighs heavily in favor of Brookfield.

The similarity of marks alone, as we have explained, does not necessarily lead to consumer confusion. Accordingly, we must proceed to consider the relatedness of the products and services offered. Related goods are generally more likely than unrelated goods to confuse the public as to the producers of the goods. In light of the virtual identity of marks, if they were used with identical products or services likelihood of confusion would follow as a matter of course. If, on the other hand, Brookfield and West Coast did not compete to any extent whatsoever, the likelihood of confusion would probably be remote. A Web surfer who accessed "moviebuff.com" and reached a web site advertising the services of Schlumberger Ltd. (a large oil drilling company) would be unlikely to think that Brookfield had entered the oil drilling business or was sponsoring the oil driller. At the least, Brookfield would bear the heavy burden of demonstrating (through other relevant factors) that consumers were likely to be confused as to source or affiliation in such a circumstance.

The district court classified West Coast and Brookfield as non-competitors largely on the basis that Brookfield is primarily an information provider while West Coast primarily rents and sells videotapes. It noted that West Coast's web site is used more by the somewhat curious video consumer who wants general movie information, while entertainment industry professionals, aspiring entertainment executives and professionals, and highly focused moviegoers are more likely to need or to want the more detailed information provided by "MovieBuff." This analysis, however, overemphasizes differences in principal lines of business, as we have previously instructed that "the relatedness of each company's prime directive isn't relevant." Instead, the focus is on whether the consuming public is likely somehow to associate West Coast's products with Brookfield. Here, both companies offer products and services relating to the entertainment industry generally, and their principal lines of business both relate to movies specifically and are not as different as guns and toys or computer circuit boards and the Rocky Horror Picture Show. Thus, Brookfield and West Coast are not properly characterized as non-competitors.

Not only are they not non-competitors, the competitive proximity of their products is actually quite high. Just as Brookfield's "MovieBuff" is a searchable database with detailed information on films, West Coast's web site features a similar searchable database, which Brookfield points out is licensed from a direct competitor of Brookfield. Undeniably then, the products are used for similar purposes. "The rights of the owner of a registered trademark ... extend to any goods related in the minds of consumers," and Brookfield's and West Coast's products are certainly so related to some extent. The relatedness is further evidenced by the fact that the two companies compete for the patronage of an overlapping audience. The use of similar marks to offer similar products accordingly weighs heavily in favor of likelihood of confusion.

In addition to the relatedness of products, West Coast and Brookfield both utilize the Web as a marketing and advertising facility, a factor that courts have consistently recognized as exacerbating the likelihood of confusion. Both companies, apparently recognizing the rapidly growing importance of Web commerce, are maneuvering to attract customers via the Web. Not only do they compete for the patronage of an overlapping audience on the Web, both "MovieBuff" and "moviebuff.com" are utilized in conjunction with Web-based products.

Given the virtual identity of "moviebuff.com" and "MovieBuff," the relatedness of the products and services accompanied by those marks, and the companies' simultaneous use of the Web as a marketing and advertising tool, many forms of consumer confusion are likely to result. People surfing the Web for information on "MovieBuff" may confuse "MovieBuff" with the searchable entertainment database at "moviebuff.com" and simply assume that they have reached Brookfield's web site. In the Internet context, in particular, entering a web site takes little effort — usually one click from a linked site or a search engine's list; thus, Web surfers are more likely to be confused as to the ownership of a web site than traditional patrons of a brick-and-mortar store would be of a store's ownership. Alternatively, they may incorrectly believe that West Coast licensed "MovieBuff" from Brookfield or that Brookfield otherwise sponsored West Coast's database. Other consumers may simply believe that West Coast bought out Brookfield or that they are related companies.

Yet other forms of confusion are likely to ensue. Consumers may wrongly assume that the "MovieBuff" database they were searching for is no longer offered, having been replaced by West Coast's entertainment database, and thus simply use the services at West Coast's web site. And even where people realize, immediately upon accessing "moviebuff.com," that they have reached a site operated by West Coast and wholly unrelated to Brookfield, West Coast will still have gained a customer by appropriating the goodwill that Brookfield has developed in its "MovieBuff" mark. A consumer who was originally looking for Brookfield's products or services may be perfectly content with West Coast's database (especially as it is offered free of charge); but he reached West Coast's site because of its use of Brookfield's mark as its second-level domain name, which is a misappropriation of Brookfield's goodwill by West Coast.

The district court apparently assumed that likelihood of confusion exists only when consumers are confused as to the source of a product they actually purchase. It is, however, well established that the Lanham Act protects against the many other forms of confusion that we have outlined.

The factors that we have considered so far — the similarity of marks, the relatedness of product offerings, and the overlap in marketing and advertising channels — lead us to the tentative conclusion that Brookfield has made a strong showing of likelihood of confusion. Because it is possible that the remaining factors will tip the scale back the other way if they weigh strongly enough in West Coast's favor, we consider the remaining likelihood of confusion factors, beginning with the strength of Brookfield's mark. The stronger a mark — meaning the more likely it is to be remembered and associated in the public mind with the mark's owner — the greater the protection it is accorded by the trademark laws. Marks can be conceptually classified along a spectrum of generally increasing inherent distinctiveness as generic, descriptive, suggestive, arbitrary, or fanciful. West Coast asserts that Brookfield's mark is "not terribly distinctive," by which it apparently means suggestive, but only weakly so. Although Brookfield does not seriously dispute that its mark is only suggestive, it does defend its (mark's) muscularity.

We have recognized that, unlike arbitrary or fanciful marks which are typically strong, suggestive marks are presumptively weak. As the district court recognized, placement within the conceptual distinctiveness spectrum is not the only determinant of a mark's strength, as advertising expenditures can transform a suggestive mark into a strong mark, see id., where, for example, that mark has achieved actual marketplace recognition. Brookfield, however, has not come forth with substantial evidence establishing the widespread recognition of its mark; although it argues that its strength is established from its use of "MovieBuff" for over five years, its federal and California state registrations, and its expenditure of $100,000 in advertising its mark, the district court did not clearly err in classifying "MovieBuff" as weak. Some weak marks are weaker than others, and although "MovieBuff" falls within the weak side of the strength spectrum, the mark is not so flabby as to compel a finding of no likelihood of confusion in light of the other factors that we have considered. Importantly, Brookfield's trademark is not descriptive because it does not describe either the software product or its purpose. Instead, it is suggestive — and thus strong enough to warrant trademark protection — because it requires a mental leap from the mark to the product. Because the products involved are closely related and West Coast's domain name is nearly identical to Brookfield's trademark, the strength of the mark is of diminished importance in the likelihood of confusion analysis.

We thus turn to intent. "The law has long been established that if an infringer 'adopts his designation with the intent of deriving benefit from the reputation of the trade-mark or trade name, its intent may be sufficient to justify the inference that there are confusing similarities.'" The district court found that the intent factor favored West Coast because it did not adopt the "moviebuff.com" mark with the specific purpose of infringing Brookfield's trademark. The intent prong, however, is not so narrowly confined.

This factor favors the plaintiff where the alleged infringer adopted his mark with knowledge, actual or constructive, that it was another's trademark. In the Internet context, in particular, courts have appropriately recognized that the intentional registration of a domain name knowing that the second-level domain is another company's valuable trademark weighs in favor of likelihood of confusion. There is, however, no evidence in the record that West Coast registered "moviebuff.com" with the principal intent of confusing consumers. Brookfield correctly points out that, by the time West Coast launched its web site, it did know of Brookfield's claim to rights in the trademark "MovieBuff." But when it registered the domain name with Network Solutions, West Coast did not know of Brookfield's rights in "MovieBuff" (at least Brookfield has not established that it did). Although Brookfield asserts that West Coast could easily have launched its web site at its alternate domain address, "westcoastvideo.com," thereby avoiding the infringement problem, West Coast claims that it had already invested considerable sums in developing its "moviebuff.com" web site by the time that Brookfield informed it of its rights in the trademark. Considered as a whole, this factor appears indeterminate.

Importantly, an intent to confuse consumers is not required for a finding of trademark infringement. Instead, this factor is only relevant to the extent that it bears upon the likelihood that consumers will be confused by the alleged infringer's mark (or to the extent that a court wishes to consider it as an equitable consideration). Here, West Coast's intent does not appear to bear upon the likelihood of confusion because it did not act with such an intent from which it is appropriate to infer consumer confusion.

The final three Sleekcraft factors — evidence of actual confusion, likelihood of expansion in product lines, and purchaser care — do not affect our ultimate conclusion regarding the likelihood of confusion. The first two factors do not merit extensive comment. Actual confusion is not relevant because Brookfield filed suit before West Coast began actively using the "moviebuff.com" mark and thus never had the opportunity to collect information on actual confusion. The likelihood of expansion in product lines factor is relatively unimportant where two companies already compete to a significant extent. In any case, it is neither exceedingly likely nor unlikely that West Coast will enter more directly into Brookfield's principal market, or vice versa.

Although the district court did not discuss the degree of care likely to be exercised by purchasers of the products in question, we think that this issue deserves some consideration. Likelihood of confusion is determined on the basis of a "reasonably prudent consumer." What is expected of this reasonably prudent consumer depends on the circumstances. We expect him to be more discerning — and less easily confused — when he is purchasing expensive items and when the products being sold are marketed primarily to expert buyers. We recognize, however, that confusion may often be likely even in the case of expensive goods sold to discerning customers. On the other hand, when dealing with inexpensive products, customers are likely to exercise less care, thus making confusion more likely.

The complexity in this case arises because we must consider both entertainment professionals, who probably will take the time and effort to find the specific product they want, and movie devotees, who will be more easily confused as to the source of the database offered at West Coast's web site. In addition, West Coast's site is likely to be visited by many casual movie watchers. The entertainment professional, movie devotee, and casual watcher are likely to exercise high, little, and very little care, respectively. Who is the reasonably prudent consumer? Although we have not addressed the issue of purchaser care in mixed buyer classes, another circuit has held that "the standard of care to be exercised by the reasonably prudent purchaser will be equal to that of the least sophisticated consumer." This is not the only approach available to us, as we could alternatively use a weighted average of the different levels of purchaser care in determining how the reasonably prudent consumer would act. We need not, however, decide this question now because the purchaser confusion factor, even considered in the light most favorable to West Coast, is not sufficient to overcome the likelihood of confusion strongly established by the other factors we have analyzed.

. . . .

In light of the foregoing analysis, we conclude that Brookfield has demonstrated a likelihood of success on its claim that West Coast's use of "moviebuff.com" violates the Lanham Act. We are fully aware that although the question of "whether confusion is likely is a factual determination woven into the law," we nevertheless must review only for clear error the district court's conclusion that the evidence of likelihood of confusion in this case was slim. Here, however, we are "left with the definite and firm conviction that a mistake has been made."

Discussion Questions

1. Does the sophistication of the Internet user play a role in determining whether a domain name is causing confusion? How can we characterize the expectations of a typical "Web surfer" when a site is accessed? Do surfers always correlate the domain name with a particular trademark?

2. Do the availability of search engines and the ability to bookmark Web sites reduce the likelihood of confusion?

3. In many instances, domain names are used to forward Web users to a particular site. Would confusion occur if the domain name never appeared in the browser's uniform resource locator window?

Bell Actimedia Inc. v. Puzo[†]

This is a motion by the plaintiff for an interlocutory injunction. This motion is part of a trade-mark infringement action.

FACTS

The plaintiff company produces and distributes trade and telephone directories in Canada. It also provides business listings on the Internet.

The plaintiff also owns the Canadian rights to the trade-marks YELLOW PAGES and PAGES JAUNES.

These trade-marks were registered in Canada at the registration office under the numbers:

> (i) the mark YELLOW PAGES: nos. TMA 246988; TMA 205312; and TMA 495876;
>
> (ii) the mark PAGES JAUNES: nos. TMA 246989 and TMA 266549.

The plaintiff has been using these trade-marks in Canada since as long ago as 1948.

The defendants, Andrea Puzo and Philip Armand, do business as a partnership under the name Communications Globe Tete. The partnership was registered on August 16, 1996.

www.lespagesjaunes.com is an electronic address that Globe Tete Communications uses in connection with an international communication system called the Internet.

An organization called INTERNIC assigns electronic Internet addresses using a Universal Resource Locator (URL). INTERNIC gave Globe Tete Communications the address www.lespagesjaunes.com. This address is used worldwide for a site that is marketed as the [TRANSLATION] "business directory of the French-speaking world".

.   .   .   .

According to the submissions of both counsel, it appears the defendants do not dispute the plaintiff's right to have an injunction maintained under the circumstances.

The defendants' objection is that if the injunction has to be maintained, it should be "trimmed" to cover Canada only, and should not under any circumstances prevent the defendants from using their Internet site outside Canada.

With respect to the argument that the plaintiff supposedly consented to the use of the trade-mark PAGES JAUNES because one of its salespeople apparently accepted an advertisement in the PAGES JAUNES, I must dismiss this argument.

The plaintiff's salespeople have to deal with tens of thousands of clients every year to sell advertising in the PAGES JAUNES. Quite obviously, the salespeople examine the insets placed in the plaintiff's directories before they are printed, but it is clear that it was an unfortunate mistake by one of the plaintiff's salespeople to allow the reference to www.lespagesjaunes.com to appear in the corporate advertisement of the defendants' business Globe Tete Communications, and that it would be unreasonable to find based on that fact alone that the plaintiff waived its rights in the trade-marks it legally holds.

---

† 1999 Fed. Ct. Trial LEXIS 554 (F.C.T.D.).

It must also be noted that on the face of the contract between the two parties, the defendants had to know when they negotiated the purchase of advertising in the PAGES JAUNES directory that they did not own the rights to use the words PAGES JAUNES, and they certainly cannot argue good faith under the circumstances.

As in its previous actions before the courts to prevent the illegal use of its trade-marks, the plaintiff's vigilance on discovering that the defendants were using its trade-marks and the speed with which it took action before the Court show that it has never accepted its trade-marks being used by anyone, including the defendants.

Having examined the issues, I have no hesitation in deciding that the plaintiff is entitled to an interlocutory injunction.

In my view, a *prima facie* case for this entitlement was clearly made out, as had previously been done before my colleague Mr. Justice Dube.

Considering the amounts at issue and the particular problem for a business that has been using a trade-mark for over 50 years, I have no hesitation in recognizing that there is a serious issue to be tried.

Nor do I have any hesitation in recognizing that the plaintiff has clearly established that it will suffer irreparable harm if the interlocutory injunction is not granted.

The balance of convenience clearly favours the plaintiff, considering its 500-million-dollar sales and dealings with tens of thousands of businesses for over 50 years.

I am also of the view that there is urgency in the case at bar, and that the plaintiff acted as promptly as possible as soon as it learned that the defendants were infringing its rights in the trade-marks.

For all these reasons, the interlocutory injunction sought is maintained, and the defendants have raised no ground sufficient for me to alter the terms of the injunction the Honourable Mr. Justice Dube has already issued. The injunction will thus be granted based on the wording the plaintiff submitted in English.

Discussion Question

The previous decision along with *ITV Technologies, Inc.* v. *WIC Television, Ltd.*, 1999 Fed. Ct. Trial LEXIS 1039 (F.C.T.D.) provide an adequate gauge of the Canadian courts' treatment of the domain name issue. Are the Canadian courts obliged to apply the existing trademark legislation in an attempt to resolve domain name disputes?

Should a court accept responsibility for transferring a domain name to its "rightful" owner? Consider this Canadian case and its implications for the interaction between domain name administration and the legal system.

Molson Breweries v. Kuettner[†]

This application arises in the context of an action commenced by the plaintiff on January 25, 1999, for infringement, passing off and depreciation of goodwill of the

---

† 3 C.P.R. 4th 479 (F.C.T.D. 1999).

registered trade-marks MOLSON and MOLSON'S. Within the relief sought, is an order requiring the defendants to transfer ownership of the Internet domain names molsons.com and molsonbeer.com.

NSI, an American company based in Herndon, Virginia, is responsible for the registration of "second-level" Internet domain names, in this case, "molson" and "molsonbeer" in the "top-level" .com, .org, .net and .edu domains.

Through the affidavit of Barry E. Hutsell, the plaintiff tenders in evidence, NSI's Domain Name Dispute Policy, as well as the "Frequently Asked Questions" page from NSI's Domain Name Dispute Policy.

The following summarizes the provisions of the dispute policy. NSI registers domain names on a "first come, first served" basis. It does not determine the legality of the domain names' registration, or otherwise evaluate whether that registration or use may infringe the rights of a third party.

Pursuant to the policy, NSI has the right to revoke, suspend, transfer or otherwise modify a domain name registration upon notice, or at such time as it receives a properly authenticated order from a Court of competent jurisdiction requiring same.

While NSI neither acts as an arbiter nor provides resolution of disputes arising out of the registration and use of domain names, if presented with information that a domain name may be violating the trade-mark rights of a trade-mark owner, it applies a process stipulated in some detail in the policy. Thus, where it receives a complaint with satisfactory evidence of trade-mark ownership and the potential for legal harm that the owner may be suffering, it has the authority to put the impugned domain name on "hold".

In the instant case, the policy having been engaged by notice on behalf of the plaintiff, the disputed domain names, molson.com and molsonbeer.com, are currently on "hold" and their use and registration is sought to be tendered to the Court by way of the deposit of the declaration of Mr. Orentas.

According to the declaration, NSI's records indicate the defendant SAYCAN Industries as the registrant of the molsons.com and molsonbeer.com, domain names. Having placed the domain names on "hold", NSI declares that it will not allow any change to the registration record or change the status of the domain names until either: the Court renders a temporary or final decision regarding the interests of the above-named party in the domain name; or, NSI receives a voluntary dismissal filed by the plaintiff.

In the meantime, through the deposit of this declaration with the Registry of the Court, NSI purports to "tender to the Court complete control and authority regarding the disposition of the registration" of the molsons.com and molsonbeer.com domain names.

The declaration, by its terms, expires automatically and in the event the Court declines to accept the tender of the declaration, control and authority regarding the registration and use of the domain names in question reverts to NSI one hundred and twenty (120) days from the date of the declaration, namely, October 5, 1999.

. . . .

The plaintiff suggests in argument, that "an element of the transfer of beneficial property in the domain names would occur by way of the deposit of the declaration". Counsel for SAYCAN, explains that whatever the statement in the declaration purporting to transfer control of the domain names may mean, such rights as his client may have in the domain names, would "travel with the deposit into the Court" and would accordingly be safeguarded.

Admittedly, the law in respect of domain names, their registration, the rights and property which they confer is merely nascent. Having said that, the plaintiff seeks to have the Court take into custody and order the preservation of rights or property, the nature, an effect of which is unclear to the parties themselves. Among the questions outstanding and unanswered, whether the acceptance of the tender, by the Court, may give rise to rights in third parties or may be challenged by these and whether there may be a potential burden or responsibility to the Court as a result. It would appear that NSI is seeking to devolve its responsibility in favour of the Court where a more appropriate mechanism might be by way of a third party escrow arrangement. Certainly, it is not apparent that the tender is in any way necessary for the Court's determination of the rights of the parties in the litigation.

Cybersquatting is a term used to describe a variety of domain name registration practices. Generally, a "cybersquatter" is someone who purchases domain names with the future intention of selling the names for profit. This practice includes the act of "warehousing" domain names for speculative purposes and the bad faith, abusive registration practices of attempting to extort money from holders of famous trademarks or intentionally attempting to block competitors from securing the most logically obvious domain name. The bad faith, abusive registration practices have also been characterized as "cyberpiracy."

The British courts have attempted to address the issue by applying the doctrine of passing-off to disputes involving abusive registrations.

British Telecommunications plc and another v. One In A Million Ltd[†]

The appellants are dealers in Internet domain names. They register them and sell them. They have made a speciality of registering domain names for use on the Internet comprising well-known names and trade marks without the consent of the person or company owning the goodwill in the name or trade mark. Examples are the registration and subsequent offer for sale to Burger King by the second defendant of the domain name burgerking.co.uk for £25,000 plus value added tax and of bt.org to British Telecommunications plc for £4,700 plus value added tax.

The plaintiffs Marks & Spencer plc, J Sainsbury plc, Virgin Enterprises Ltd, British Telecommunications plc, Telecom Securicor Cellular Radio Ltd, Ladbrokes plc are well-known companies. In the actions brought by them, they allege that the activities of the appellants amount to passing off, to infringement of their well-known registered trade marks, to threats of passing off and infringement, and to wrongful acts such as to entitle them to injunctive relief. Their complaints stem from the registration by One In A Million Ltd of ladbrokes.com; sainsbury.com; sainsburys.com; j-sainsbury.com; marksandspencer.com; cellnet.net; bt.org and virgin.org; by Global Media Communications of marksandspencer.co.uk; britishtelecom.co.uk; britishtelecom.net; and by Junic of britishtelecom.com.

· · · ·

[†] [1998] 4 All ER 476.

Passing off — the law

Lord Diplock in Erven Warnink BV v J Townend & Sons (Hull) Ltd [1979] 2 All ER 927 at 932–933, [1979] AC 731 at 742 identified, from the cases decided before 1980, five characteristics which had to be present. He said:

> My Lords, AG Spalding & Bros v AW Gamage Ltd (1915) 84 LJ Ch 449, [1914–15] All ER Rep 147 and the later cases make it possible to identify five characteristics which must be present in order to create a valid cause of action for passing off: (1) a misrepresentation (2) made by a trader in the course of trade, (3) to prospective customers of his or ultimate consumers of goods or services supplied by him, (4) which is calculated to injure the business or goodwill of another trader (in the sense that this is a reasonably foreseeable consequence) and (5) which causes actual damage to a business or goodwill of the trader by whom the action is brought or (in a quia timet action) will probably do so.

. . . .

In my view there was clear evidence of systematic registration by the appellants of well-known trade names as blocking registrations and a threat to sell them to others. No doubt the primary purpose of registration was to block registration by the owner of the goodwill. There was, according to Mr Wilson nothing unlawful in doing that. The truth is different. The registration only blocks registration of the identical domain name and therefore does not act as a block to registration of a domain name that can be used by the owner of the goodwill in the name. The purpose of the so-called blocking registration was to extract money from the owners of the goodwill in the name chosen. Its ability to do so was in the main dependent upon the threat, expressed or implied, that the appellants would exploit the goodwill by either trading under the name or equipping another with the name so he could do so.

The judge rightly analysed the position in his judgment. He said ([1998] FSR 265 at 269):

> For a dealer in Internet domain names there are in principle only four uses to which the names can be put. The first and most obvious is that it may be sold to the enterprise whose name or trade mark has been used, which may be prepared to pay a high price to avoid the inconvenience of there being a domain name comprising its own name or trade mark which is not under its control. Secondly, it may be sold to a third party unconnected with the name, so that he may try to sell it to the company whose name is being used, or else use it for purposes of deception. Thirdly, it may be sold to someone with a distinct interest of his own in the name, for example a solicitor by the name of John Sainsbury or the government of the British Virgin Islands, with a view to its use by him. Fourthly, it may be retained by the dealer unused and unsold, in which case it serves only to block the use of that name as a registered domain name by others, including those whose name or trade mark it comprises.

In my view there was evidence that the appellants registered the domain names in issue in this case with all those forms of use in mind.

Conclusion — passing off

The judge considered first the action brought by Marks & Spencer plc and then went on to deal with the other actions. I will adopt the same approach as the Marks & Spencer case raises slightly different issues to those raised in the other cases.

It is accepted that the name Marks & Spencer denotes Marks & Spencer plc and nobody else. Thus anybody seeing or hearing the name realises that what is being referred to is the business of Marks & Spencer plc. It follows that registration by the appellants of a domain name including the name Marks & Spencer makes a false representation that they are associated or connected with Marks & Spencer plc. This can be demonstrated by considering the reaction of a person who taps into his computer the domain name marksandspencer.co.uk and presses a button to execute a 'whois' search. He will be told that the registrant is One In A Million Ltd. A substantial number of persons will conclude that One In A Million Ltd must be connected or associated with Marks & Spencer plc. That amounts to a false representation which constitutes passing off.

Mr Wilson submitted that mere registration did not amount to passing off. Further, Marks & Spencer plc had not established any damage or likelihood of damage. I cannot accept those submissions. The placing on a register of a distinctive name such as marksandspencer makes a representation to persons who consult the register that the registrant is connected or associated with the name registered and thus the owner of the goodwill in the name. Such persons would not know of One In A Million Ltd and would believe that they were connected or associated with the owner of the goodwill in the domain name they had registered. Further, registration of the domain name including the words Marks & Spencer is an erosion of the exclusive goodwill in the name which damages or is likely to damage Marks & Spencer plc.

Mr Wilson also submitted that it was not right to conclude that there was any threat by the appellants to use or dispose of any domain name including the words Marks & Spencer. He submitted that the appellants, Mr Conway and Mr Nicholson, were two rather silly young men who hoped to make money from the likes of the respondents by selling domain names to them for as much as they could get. They may be silly, but their letters and activities make it clear that they intended to do more than just retain the names. Their purpose was to threaten use and disposal sometimes explicitly and on other occasions implicitly. The judge was right to grant quia timet relief to prevent the threat becoming reality.

I also believe that domain names comprising the name Marks & Spencer are instruments of fraud. Any realistic use of them as domain names would result in passing off and there was ample evidence to justify the injunctive relief granted by the judge to prevent them being used for a fraudulent purpose and to prevent them being transferred to others.

The other cases are slightly different. Mr Wilson pointed to the fact that there are people called Sainsbury and Ladbroke and companies, other than Virgin Enterprises Ltd, who have as part of their name the word Virgin and also people or firms whose initials would be BT. He went on to submit that it followed that the domain names which the appellants had registered were not inherently deceptive. They were not instruments of fraud. Further there had been no passing off and none was threatened and a transfer to a third party would not result in the appellants becoming joint tortfeasors in any passing off carried out by the person to whom the registrations were transferred. Thus, he submitted, there was no foundation for the injunctive relief in the actions brought by four of the respondents.

I believe that, for the same reasons I have expressed in relation to the Marks & Spencer plc action, passing off and threatened passing off has been demonstrated. The judge (at 273) was right to conclude:

> The history of the defendants' activities shows a deliberate practice followed over a substantial period of time of registering domain names which are chosen to resemble the names and marks of other people and are plainly intended to deceive. The threat of passing off and trade mark infringement, and the likelihood of confusion arising from the infringement of the mark are made out beyond argument in this case, even in which (sic) it is possible to imagine other cases in which the issue would be more nicely balanced.

I also believe that the names registered by the appellants were instruments of fraud and that injunctive relief was appropriate upon this basis as well. The trade names were well-known 'household names' denoting in ordinary usage the respective respondent. The appellants registered them without any distinguishing word because of the goodwill attaching to those names. It was the value of that goodwill, not the fact that they could perhaps be used in some way by a third party without deception, which caused them to register the names. The motive of the appellants was to use that goodwill and threaten to sell it to another who might use it for passing off to obtain money from the respondents. The value of the names lay in the threat that they would be used in a fraudulent way. The registrations were made with the purpose of appropriating the respondents' property, their goodwill, and with an intention of threatening dishonest use by them or another. The registrations were instruments of fraud and injunctive relief was appropriate just as much as it was in those cases where persons registered company names for a similar purpose.

Note

It is highly likely that the Canadian courts will follow the *One in a Million* decision if faced with similar cybersquatting issues. Other common law jurisdictions have accepted and applied the *One in a Million* decision. In New Zealand, it was applied in *OGGI Advertising, Ltd.* v. *McKenzie and others*, [1999] 1 NZLR 631 (H.C. Auck.). In India, the decision was relied upon in *Yahoo! Inc.* v. *Akash Arora*, [1999] FSR 931 (H.C. Delhi).

It is important to remember that many U.S. decisions rely on trademark dilution to resolve issues of alleged cybersquatting/cyberpiracy. Canadian courts should be cautious when considering them.

U.S. Federal Dilution Act of 1995†

§1127. Construction and definitions; intent of chapter
The term "dilution" means the lessening of the capacity of a famous mark to identify and distinguish goods or services, regardless of the presence or absence of —

(1) competition between the owner of the famous mark and other parties, or

---

† 15 USCS (1999)

(2) likelihood of confusion, mistake, or deception.

The term "use in commerce" means the bona fide use of a mark in the ordinary course of trade, and not made merely to reserve a right in a mark. For purposes of this Act, a mark shall be deemed to be in use in commerce —
(1) on goods when —
    (A) it is placed in any manner on the goods or their containers or the displays associated therewith or on the tags or labels affixed thereto, or if the nature of the goods makes such placement impracticable, then on documents associated with the goods or their sale, and
    (B) the goods are sold or transported in commerce, and
(2) on services when it is used or displayed in the sale or advertising of services and the services are rendered in commerce, or the services are rendered in more than one State or in the United States and a foreign country and the person rendering the services is engaged in commerce in connection with the services.

§1125. False designations of origin and false descriptions forbidden
(c) Remedies for dilution of famous marks.
    (1) The owner of a famous mark shall be entitled, subject to the principles of equity and upon such terms as the court deems reasonable, to an injunction against another person's commercial use in commerce of a mark or trade name, if such use begins after the mark has become famous and causes dilution of the distinctive quality of the mark, and to obtain such other relief as is provided in this subsection. In determining whether a mark is distinctive and famous, a court may consider factors such as, but not limited to —
        (A) the degree of inherent or acquired distinctiveness of the mark;
        (B) the duration and extent of use of the mark in connection with the goods or services with which the mark is used;
        (C) the duration and extent of advertising and publicity of the mark;
        (D) the geographical extent of the trading area in which the mark is used;
        (E) the channels of trade for the goods or services with which the mark is used;
        (F) the degree of recognition of the mark in the trading areas and channels of trade used by the marks' owner and the person against whom the injunction is sought;
        (G) the nature and extent of use of the same or similar marks by third parties; and
        (H) whether the mark was registered under the Act of March 3, 1881, or the Act of February 20, 1905, or on the principal register.

    (2) In an action brought under this subsection, the owner of the famous mark shall be entitled only to injunctive relief as set forth in section 34 [15 USCS §1116] unless the person against whom the injunction is sought willfully intended to trade on the owner's reputation or to cause dilution of the famous mark. If such willful intent is proven, the owner of the famous mark shall also be entitled to the remedies set forth in sections 35(a) and 36 [15 USCS §§1117(a), 1118], subject to the discretion of the court and the principles of equity.

(3) The ownership by a person of a valid registration under the Act of March 3, 1881, or the Act of February 20, 1905, or on the principal register shall be a complete bar to an action against that person, with respect to that mark, that is brought by another person under the common law or a statute of a State and that seeks to prevent dilution of the distinctiveness of a mark, label, or form of advertisement.

(4) The following shall not be actionable under this section:
  (A) Fair use of a famous mark by another person in comparative commercial advertising or promotion to identify the competing goods or services of the owner of the famous mark.
  (B) Noncommercial use of a mark.
  (C) All forms of news reporting and news commentary.

Panavision International, L.P. v. Toeppen[†]

Panavision holds registered trademarks to the names "Panavision" and "Panaflex" in connection with motion picture camera equipment. Panavision promotes its trademarks through motion picture and television credits and other media advertising.

In December 1995, Panavision attempted to register a web site on the Internet with the domain name Panavision.com . It could not do that, however, because Toeppen had already established a web site using Panavision's trademark as his domain name. Toeppen's web page for this site displayed photographs of the City of Pana, Illinois.

On December 20, 1995, Panavision's counsel sent a letter from California to Toeppen in Illinois informing him that Panavision held a trademark in the name Panavision and telling him to stop using that trademark and the domain name Panavision.com . Toeppen responded by mail to Panavision in California, stating he had the right to use the name Panavision.com on the Internet as his domain name. Toeppen stated:

> If your attorney has advised you otherwise, he is trying to screw you. He wants to blaze new trails in the legal frontier at your expense. Why do you want to fund your attorney's purchase of a new boat (or whatever) when you can facilitate the acquisition of 'PanaVision.com' cheaply and simply instead?

Toeppen then offered to "settle the matter" if Panavision would pay him $13,000 in exchange for the domain name. Additionally, Toeppen stated that if Panavision agreed to his offer, he would not "acquire any other Internet addresses which are alleged by Panavision Corporation to be its property."

After Panavision refused Toeppen's demand, he registered Panavision's other trademark with NSI as the domain name Panaflex.com. Toeppen's web page for Panaflex.com simply displays the word "Hello."

Toeppen has registered domain names for various other companies including Delta Airlines, Neiman Marcus, Eddie Bauer, Lufthansa, and over 100 other marks.

---

† 141 F. 3d 1316 (9th Cir. 1998).

Toeppen has attempted to "sell" domain names for other trademarks such as intermatic.com to Intermatic, Inc. for $10,000 and americanstandard.com to American Standard, Inc. for $15,000.

Panavision filed this action against Toeppen in the District Court for the Central District of California. Panavision alleged claims for dilution of its trademark under the Federal Trademark Dilution Act of 1995, 15 U.S.C. §1125(c), and under the California Anti-dilution statute, California Business and Professions Code §14330. Panavision alleged that Toeppen was in the business of stealing trademarks, registering them as domain names on the Internet and then selling the domain names to the rightful trademark owners. The district court determined it had personal jurisdiction over Toeppen, and granted summary judgment in favor of Panavision on both its federal and state dilution claims. This appeal followed.

. . . .

B. TRADEMARK DILUTION CLAIMS

The Federal Trademark Dilution Act provides:

> The owner of a famous mark shall be entitled ... to an injunction against another person's commercial use in commerce of a mark or trade name, if such use begins after the mark has become famous and causes dilution of the distinctive quality of the mark....

The California Anti-dilution statute is similar. It prohibits dilution of "the distinctive quality" of a mark regardless of competition or the likelihood of confusion. The protection extends only to strong and well recognized marks. Panavision's state law dilution claim is subject to the same analysis as its federal claim.

In order to prove a violation of the Federal Trademark Dilution Act, a plaintiff must show that (1) the mark is famous; (2) the defendant is making a commercial use of the mark in commerce; (3) the defendant's use began after the mark became famous; and (4) the defendant's use of the mark dilutes the quality of the mark by diminishing the capacity of the mark to identify and distinguish goods and services.

Toeppen does not challenge the district court's determination that Panavision's trademark is famous, that his alleged use began after the mark became famous, or that the use was in commerce. Toeppen challenges the district court's determination that he made "commercial use" of the mark and that this use caused "dilution" in the quality of the mark.

1. Commercial Use

Toeppen argues that his use of Panavision's trademarks simply as his domain names cannot constitute a commercial use under the Act. Case law supports this argument.

Developing this argument, Toeppen contends that a domain name is simply an address used to locate a web page. He asserts that entering a domain name on a computer allows a user to access a web page, but a domain name is not associated with information on a web page. If a user were to type Panavision.com as a domain name, the computer screen would display Toeppen's web page with aerial views of Pana, Illinois. The screen would not provide any information about "Panavision," other than a "location window" which displays the domain name. Toeppen argues that a user who types in Panavision.com, but who sees no reference to the plaintiff

Panavision on Toeppen's web page, is not likely to conclude the web page is related in any way to the plaintiff, Panavision.

Toeppen's argument misstates his use of the Panavision mark. His use is not as benign as he suggests. Toeppen's "business" is to register trademarks as domain names and then sell them to the rightful trademark owners. He "acts as a 'spoiler,' preventing Panavision and others from doing business on the Internet under their trademarked names unless they pay his fee." This is a commercial use.

As the district court found, Toeppen traded on the value of Panavision's marks. So long as he held the Internet registrations, he curtailed Panavision's exploitation of the value of its trademarks on the Internet, a value which Toeppen then used when he attempted to sell the Panavision.com domain name to Panavision.

In a nearly identical case involving Toeppen and Intermatic Inc., a federal district court in Illinois held that Toeppen's conduct violated the Federal Trademark Dilution Act. There, Intermatic sued Toeppen for registering its trademark on the Internet as Toeppen's domain name, intermatic.com. It was "conceded that one of Toeppen's intended uses for registering the Intermatic mark was to eventually sell it back to Intermatic or to some other party." The court found that "Toeppen's intention to arbitrage the 'intermatic.com' domain name constituted a commercial use."

Toeppen's reliance on *Holiday Inns, Inc.* v. *800 Reservation, Inc.* is misplaced. In *Holiday Inns*, the Sixth Circuit held that a company's use of the most commonly misdialed number for Holiday Inns' 1-800 reservation number was not trademark infringement.

Holiday Inns is distinguishable. There, the defendant did not use Holiday Inns' trademark. Rather, the defendant selected the most commonly misdialed telephone number for Holiday Inns and attempted to capitalize on consumer confusion.

A telephone number, moreover, is distinguishable from a domain name because a domain name is associated with a word or phrase. A domain name is similar to a "vanity number" that identifies its source. Using Holiday Inns as an example, when a customer dials the vanity number "1-800-Holiday," she expects to contact Holiday Inns because the number is associated with that company's trademark. A user would have the same expectation typing the domain name HolidayInns.com. The user would expect to retrieve Holiday Inns' web page.

Toeppen made a commercial use of Panavision's trademarks. It does not matter that he did not attach the marks to a product. Toeppen's commercial use was his attempt to sell the trademarks themselves. Under the Federal Trademark Dilution Act and the California Anti-dilution statute, this was sufficient commercial use.

2. Dilution

"Dilution" is defined as "the lessening of the capacity of a famous mark to identify and distinguish goods or services, regardless of the presence or absence of (1) competition between the owner of the famous mark and other parties, or (2) likelihood of confusion, mistake or deception."

Trademark dilution on the Internet was a matter of Congressional concern. Senator Patrick Leahy (D-Vt.) stated:

> It is my hope that this anti-dilution statute can help stem the use of deceptive Internet addresses taken by those who are choosing marks that are associated with the products and reputations of others.

To find dilution, a court need not rely on the traditional definitions such as "blurring" and "tarnishment." Indeed, in concluding that Toeppen's use of

Panavision's trademarks diluted the marks, the district court noted that Toeppen's conduct varied from the two standard dilution theories of blurring and tarnishment. The court found that Toeppen's conduct diminished "the capacity of the Panavision marks to identify and distinguish Panavision's goods and services on the Internet."

This view is also supported by *Teletech*. There, TeleTech Customer Care Management Inc., ("TCCM"), sought a preliminary injunction against Tele-Tech Company for use of TCCM's registered service mark, "TeleTech," as an Internet domain name. The district court issued an injunction, finding that TCCM had demonstrated a likelihood of success on the merits on its trademark dilution claim. The court found that TCCM had invested great resources in promoting its servicemark and Teletech's registration of the domain name teletech.com on the Internet would most likely dilute TCCM's mark.

Toeppen argues he is not diluting the capacity of the Panavision marks to identify goods or services. He contends that even though Panavision cannot use Panavision.com and Panaflex.com as its domain name addresses, it can still promote its goods and services on the Internet simply by using some other "address" and then creating its own web page using its trademarks.

We reject Toeppen's premise that a domain name is nothing more than an address. A significant purpose of a domain name is to identify the entity that owns the web site. "A customer who is unsure about a company's domain name will often guess that the domain name is also the company's name." "[A] domain name mirroring a corporate name may be a valuable corporate asset, as it facilitates communication with a customer base."

Using a company's name or trademark as a domain name is also the easiest way to locate that company's web site. Use of a "search engine" can turn up hundreds of web sites, and there is nothing equivalent to a phone book or directory assistance for the Internet.

Moreover, potential customers of Panavision will be discouraged if they cannot find its web page by typing in "Panavision.com," but instead are forced to wade through hundreds of web sites. This dilutes the value of Panavision's trademark. We echo the words of Judge Lechner, quoting Judge Wood: "Prospective users of plaintiff's services who mistakenly access defendant's web site may fail to continue to search for plaintiff's own home page, due to anger, frustration or the belief that plaintiff's home page does not exist."

Toeppen's use of Panavision.com also puts Panavision's name and reputation at his mercy.

We conclude that Toeppen's registration of Panavision's trademarks as his domain names on the Internet diluted those marks within the meaning of the Federal Trademark Dilution Act, 15 U.S.C. §1125(c), and the California Anti-dilution statute, Cal.Bus. & Prof. Code §14330.

Avery Dennison Corporation v. Sumpton[†]

Sumpton is the president of Freeview, an Internet e-mail provider doing business as "Mailbank." Mailbank offers "vanity" e-mail addresses to users for an initial fee

---

† 189 F. 3d 868 (9th Cir. 1999).

of $19.95 and $4.95 per year thereafter, and has registered thousands of domain-name combinations for this purpose. Most SLDs that Mailbank has registered are common surnames, although some represent hobbies, careers, pets, sports interests, favorite music, and the like. One category of SLDs is titled "Rude" and includes lewd SLDs, and another category, titled "Business," includes some common trademark SLDs. Mailbank's TLDs consist mainly of <.net> and <.org>, but some registered domain name combinations, including most in the "Business" and "Rude" categories, use the TLD <.com>. Mailbank's surname archives include the domain-name combinations <avery.net> and <dennison.net>.

Avery Dennison sells office products and industrial fasteners under the registered trademarks "Avery" and "Dennison," respectively. "Avery" has been in continuous use since the 1930s and registered since 1963, and "Dennison" has been in continuous use since the late 1800s and registered since 1908. Avery Dennison spends more than $5 million per year advertising its products, including those marketed under the separate "Avery" and "Dennison" trademarks, and the company boasts in the neighborhood of $3 billion in sales of all of its trademarks annually. No evidence indicates what percentage of these dollar figures apply to the "Avery" or "Dennison" trademarks. Avery Dennison maintains a commercial presence on the Internet, marketing its products at <avery.com> and <averydennison.com>, and maintaining registrations for several other domain-name combinations, all using the TLD <.com>.

Avery Dennison sued Appellants, alleging trademark dilution under the Federal Trademark Dilution Act and California Business and Professional Code §14330. Avery Dennison also sued NSI, alleging contributory dilution and contributory infringement. The district court granted summary judgment to NSI on Avery Dennison's claims. The district court then concluded as a matter of law that the disputed trademarks were famous and denied summary judgment to Appellants and granted summary judgment to Avery Dennison on its dilution claims, entering an injunction requiring Appellants to transfer the registrations to Avery Dennison.

III   TRADEMARK LAW

Trademark protection is "the law's recognition of the psychological function of symbols." Two goals of trademark law are reflected in the federal scheme. On the one hand, the law seeks to protect consumers who have formed particular associations with a mark. On the other hand, trademark law seeks to protect the investment in a mark made by the owner.

Until recently, federal law provided protection only against infringement of a registered trademark, or the unregistered trademark analog, unfair competition. These causes of action require a plaintiff to prove that the defendant is using a mark confusingly similar to a valid, protectable trademark of the plaintiff's.

Many states, however, have long recognized another cause of action designed to protect trademarks: trademark dilution. With the 1995 enactment of the Federal Trademark Dilution Act, dilution became a federal-law concern. Unlike infringement and unfair competition laws, in a dilution case competition between the parties and a likelihood of confusion are not required to present a claim for relief. Rather, injunctive relief is available under the Federal Trademark Dilution Act if a plaintiff can establish that (1) its mark is famous; (2) the defendant is making commercial use of the mark in commerce; (3) the defendant's use began after the plaintiff's mark became famous; and (4) the defendant's use presents a likelihood of dilution of the distinctive value of the mark.

California's dilution cause of action is substantially similar, providing relief if the plaintiff can demonstrate a "likelihood of injury to business reputation or of dilution of the distinctive quality of a mark ..., notwithstanding the absence of competition between the parties or the absence of confusion as to the source of goods or services." We have interpreted §14330, like the Federal Trademark Dilution Act, to protect only famous marks.

. . . .

V   DILUTION PROTECTION

We now turn to the dilution causes of action at issue in this case, brought under the Federal Trademark Dilution Act and California Business and Professional Code §14330.

In *Panavision*, we held that both the Federal Trademark Dilution Act and §14330 were implicated when the defendant registered domain-name combinations using famous trademarks and sought to sell the registrations to the trademark owners. Three differences made *Panavision* easier than the instant case. First, the defendant did not mount a challenge on the famousness prong of the dilution tests. Second, the *Panavision* defendant did not challenge the factual assertion that he sought to profit by arbitrage with famous trademarks. Third, the diluting registrations in *Panavision* both involved the TLD <.com>. In the instant case, by contrast, Appellants contest Avery Dennison's claim of famousness, Appellants contend that the nature of their business makes the trademark status of "Avery" and "Dennison" irrelevant, and the complained-of registrations involve the TLD <.net>.

A.   Famousness

The district court considered evidence submitted by Avery Dennison regarding marketing efforts and consumer association with its marks and concluded as a matter of law that "Avery" and "Dennison" were famous marks entitled to dilution protection. We hold that Avery Dennison failed to create a genuine issue of fact on the famousness element of both dilution statutes.

Dilution is a cause of action invented and reserved for a select class of marks — those marks with such powerful consumer associations that even non-competing uses can impinge on their value. Dilution causes of action, much more so than infringement and unfair competition laws, tread very close to granting "rights in gross" in a trademark. In the infringement and unfair competition scenario, where the less famous a trademark, the less the chance that consumers will be confused as to origin, a carefully-crafted balance exists between protecting a trademark and permitting non-infringing uses. In the dilution context, likelihood of confusion is irrelevant. If dilution protection were accorded to trademarks based only on a showing of inherent or acquired distinctiveness, we would upset the balance in favor of over-protecting trademarks, at the expense of potential non-infringing uses.

We view the famousness prong of both dilution analyses as reinstating the balance — by carefully limiting the class of trademarks eligible for dilution protection, Congress and state legislatures granted the most potent form of trademark protection in a manner designed to minimize undue impact on other uses.

Therefore, to meet the "famousness" element of protection under the dilution statutes, " 'a mark [must] be truly prominent and renowned.' " In a 1987 report, which recommended an amendment to the Lanham Act to provide a federal dilution cause of action, the Trademark Review Commission of the United States Trademark

Association emphasized the narrow reach of a dilution cause of action: "We believe that a limited category of trademarks, those which are truly famous and registered, are deserving of national protection from dilution."

The Federal Trademark Dilution Act lists eight non-exclusive considerations for the famousness inquiry, 15 U.S.C. §1125(c)(1)(A)–(H), which are equally relevant to a famousness determination under Business and Professional Code §14330. These are:

. . . .

We note the overlap between the statutory famousness considerations and the factors relevant to establishing acquired distinctiveness, which is attained "when the purchasing public associates the [mark] with a single producer or source rather than just the product itself." Proof of acquired distinctiveness is a difficult empirical inquiry which a factfinder must undertake, considering factors including:

> [1] whether actual purchasers ... associate the [mark] with [the plaintiff]; [2] the degree and manner of [the plaintiff's] advertising; [3] the length and manner of [the plaintiff's] use of the [mark]; and [4] whether [the plaintiff's] use of the [mark] has been exclusive.

Furthermore, registration on the principal register creates a presumption of distinctiveness — in the case of a surname trademark, acquired distinctiveness.

However, the Federal Trademark Dilution Act and Business and Professional Code §14330 apply "only to those marks which are both truly distinctive *and* famous, and therefore most likely to be adversely affected by dilution." The Trademark Review Commission stated that "a higher standard must be employed to gauge the fame of a trademark eligible for this extraordinary remedy." Thus, "to be capable of being diluted, a mark must have a degree of distinctiveness and 'strength' beyond that needed to serve as a trademark." We have previously held likewise under California Business and Professional Code §14330.

Applying the famousness factors from the Federal Trademark Dilution Act to the facts of the case at bench, we conclude that Avery Dennison likely establishes acquired distinctiveness in the "Avery" and "Dennison" trademarks, but goes no further. Because the Federal Trademark Dilution Act requires a showing greater than distinctiveness to meet the threshold element of fame, as a matter of law Avery Dennison has failed to fulfill this burden.

1 DISTINCTIVENESS

We begin with the first factor in the statutory list: "inherent or acquired distinctiveness." §1125(c)(1)(A). No dispute exists that "Avery" and "Dennison" are common surnames — according to evidence presented by Appellants, respectively the 775th and 1768th most common in the United States. A long-standing principle of trademark law is the right of a person to use his or her own name in connection with a business. This principle was incorporated into the Lanham Act, which states that a mark that is "primarily merely a surname" is not protectable unless it acquires secondary meaning. Avery Dennison cannot claim that "Avery" and "Dennison" are inherently distinctive, but must demonstrate acquired distinctiveness through secondary meaning.

The drafters of the Federal Trademark Dilution Act continued the concern for surnames when adding protection against trademark dilution to the federal scheme. On early consideration of the Act, the report from the Senate Judiciary Committee emphasized: "The committee intended to give special protection to an individual's ability to use his or her own name in good faith." The Federal Trademark Dilution Act imports, at a minimum, the threshold secondary-meaning requirement for registration of a surname trademark.

Avery Dennison maintains registrations of both "Avery" and "Dennison" on the principal register, prima facie evidence that these marks have achieved the secondary meaning required for protection from infringement and unfair competition. We reject Appellants' argument that the distinctiveness required for famousness under the Federal Trademark Dilution Act is inherent, not merely acquired distinctiveness. However, because famousness requires a showing greater than mere distinctiveness, the presumptive secondary meaning associated with "Avery" and "Dennison" fails to persuade us that the famousness prong is met in this case.

2   OVERLAPPING CHANNELS OF TRADE

We next consider the fifth and sixth factors of the statutory inquiry: the channels of trade for the plaintiff's goods and the degree of recognition of the mark in the trading areas and channels of trade used by plaintiff and defendant. §1125(c)(1)(E), (F). The drafters of the Federal Trademark Dilution Act broke from the Trademark Review Commission's recommendation that only marks "which have become famous throughout a substantial part of the United States" could qualify for protection.

Instead, fame in a localized trading area may meet the threshold element under the Act if plaintiff's trading area includes the trading area of the defendant. The rule is likewise for specialized market segments: specialized fame can be adequate only if the "diluting uses are directed narrowly at the same market segment." No evidence on the record supports Avery Dennison's position on these two prongs of the famousness inquiry.

In *Teletech*, fame in a narrow market segment was present when the plaintiff showed "that the Teletech Companies may be the largest provider of primarily inbound integrated telephone and Internet customer care nationwide." The defendant was "a contractor providing engineering and installation services to the telecommunications industry," and maintained the domain-name combination, <teletech.com>. The court held that the showing on the threshold element under the Federal Trademark Dilution Act was adequate to qualify for a preliminary injunction. In *Washington Speakers*, both the plaintiff and defendant were in the business of scheduling speaking engagements for well-known lecturers. In the instant case, by contrast, Appellants' sought-after customer base is Internet users who desire vanity e-mail addresses, and Avery Dennison's customer base includes purchasers of office products and industrial fasteners. No evidence demonstrates that Avery Dennison possesses any degree of recognition among Internet users or that Appellants direct their e-mail services at Avery Dennison's customer base.

3   USE OF THE MARKS BY THIRD PARTIES

The seventh factor, "the nature and extent of use of the same ... marks by third parties," undercuts the district court's conclusion as well. All relevant evidence on the record tends to establish that both "Avery" and "Dennison" are commonly used as trademarks, both on and off of the Internet, by parties other than Avery Dennison. This evidence is relevant because, when "a mark is in widespread use, it may not be famous for the goods or services of one business."

The record includes copies of five trademark registrations for "Avery" and "Averys," a computer printout of a list of several businesses with "Avery" in their names who market products on the Internet, and a list of business names including "Avery," which, according to a declaration submitted by NSI, is a representative sample of over 800 such businesses. The record also contains a computer printout of a list of several businesses with "Dennison" in their names which market products on the Internet and a list of business names including "Dennison," a representative sample of over 200 such businesses. Such widespread use of "Avery" and "Dennison" makes it unlikely that either can be considered a famous mark eligible for the dilution cause of action.

4 OTHER FAMOUSNESS FACTORS

Avery Dennison argues that evidence of extensive advertising and sales, international operations, and consumer awareness suffices to establish fame. We agree that the remaining four statutory factors in the famousness inquiry likely support Avery Dennison's position. Both "Avery" and "Dennison" have been used as trademarks for large fractions of a century and registered for decades. Avery Dennison expends substantial sums annually advertising each mark, with some presumable degree of success due to Avery Dennison's significant annual volume of sales. In addition, Avery Dennison markets its goods internationally. However, we disagree that Avery Dennison's showing establishes fame.

Avery Dennison submitted three market research studies regarding perceptions of the "Avery" and "Avery Dennison" brands. Discussion groups through which one study was conducted were formed "using Avery client lists," and produced the conclusion that the "Avery" name has "positive associations ... among current customers." Surveyed persons in the other two studies were mostly "users and purchasers of office products" and "office supply consumers." The one consumer group that did not necessarily include office supply purchasers for businesses was still required to be "somewhat" or "very" familiar with Avery products in order to be counted.

Avery Dennison's marketing reports are comparable to a survey we discussed in *Anti-Monopoly, Inc.* v. *General Mills Fun Group, Inc.* proving only the near tautology that consumers already acquainted with Avery and Avery Dennison products are familiar with Avery Dennison. The marketing reports add nothing to the discussion of whether consumers in general have any brand association with "Avery" and "Avery Dennison," and no evidence of product awareness relates specifically to the "Dennison" trademark. Although proper consumer surveys might be highly relevant to a showing of fame, we reject any reliance on the flawed reports submitted by Avery Dennison.

Finally, Avery Dennison — like any company marketing on the Internet — markets its products worldwide. By itself, this factor carries no weight; worldwide use of a non-famous mark does not establish fame. Because famousness requires more than mere distinctiveness, and Avery Dennison's showing goes no further than establishing secondary meaning, we hold that Avery Dennison has not met its burden to create a genuine issue of fact that its marks are famous. Avery Dennison's failure to fulfill its burden on this required element of both dilution causes of action mandates summary judgment for Appellants.

5 LIKELIHOOD OF CONFUSION REMAINS IRRELEVANT

We recognize that our discussion of the breadth of fame and overlapping market segments begins to sound like a likelihood of confusion analysis, and we agree with Avery Dennison that likelihood of confusion should not be considered under either the Federal Trademark Dilution Act or Business and Professional Code §14330. However, as we discuss above, the famousness element of the dilution causes of action serves the same general purpose as the likelihood of confusion element of an infringement or unfair competition analysis — preventing the trademark scheme from granting excessively broad protection at the expense of legitimate uses. The close parallels between the two analyses are therefore not surprising; nor do they cause us concern.

B Commercial Use

Addressing the second element of a cause of action under the Federal Trademark Dilution Act, the district court held that Appellants' registration of <avery.net> and <dennison.net> constituted commercial use. We disagree.

Commercial use under the Federal Trademark Dilution Act requires the defendant to be using the trademark as a trademark, capitalizing on its trademark status. Courts have phrased this requirement in various ways. In a classic "cybersquatter" case, one court referenced the defendants "intention to arbitrage" the registration which included the plaintiff's trademark. Another court, whose decision we affirmed, noted that the defendant "traded on the value of marks as marks." In our *Panavision* decision, we considered the defendant's "attempt to sell the trademarks themselves."

All evidence in the record indicates that Appellants register common surnames in domain-name combinations and license e-mail addresses using those surnames, with the consequent intent to capitalize on the surname status of "Avery" and "Dennison." Appellants do not use trademarks qua trademarks as required by the caselaw to establish commercial use. Rather, Appellants use words that happen to be trademarks for their non-trademark value. The district court erred in holding that Appellants' use of <avery.net> and <dennison.net> constituted commercial use under the Federal Trademark Dilution Act, and this essential element of the dilution causes of action likewise mandates summary judgment for Appellants.

C Dilution

The district court then considered the dilution requirement under both statutes, holding that Appellants' use of <avery.net> and <dennison.net> caused dilution, or a likelihood of dilution, of "Avery" and "Dennison." We hold that genuine issues of fact on this element of the causes of action should have precluded summary judgment for Avery Dennison.

Two theories of dilution are implicated in this case. First, Avery Dennison argues that Appellants' conduct is the cybersquatting dilution that we recognized in *Panavision*. Second, Avery Dennison argues that Appellants' conduct in housing the <avery.net> and <dennison.net> domain names in the same database as various lewd SLDs causes tarnishment of the "Avery" and "Dennison" marks.

1 CYBERSQUATTING

Cybersquatting dilution is the diminishment of "'the capacity of the [plaintiff's] marks to identify and distinguish the [plaintiff's] goods and services on the Internet.'" We recognized that this can occur if potential customers cannot find a web page at <trademark.com>. Dilution occurs because "'prospective users of plaintiff's services ... may fail to continue to search for plaintiff's own home page, due to anger, frustration or the belief that plaintiff's home page does not exist.'"

In the instant case, Appellants registered the TLD <.net>, rather than <.com>, with the SLDs <avery> and <dennison>. As we recognized in *Panavision*, <.net>

applies to networks and <.com> applies to commercial entities. Evidence on the record supports this distinction, and courts applying the dilution cause of action to domain-name registrations have universally considered <trademark.com> registrations. Although evidence on the record also demonstrates that the <.com> and <.net> distinction is illusory, a factfinder could infer that dilution does not occur with a <trademark.net> registration. This genuine issue of fact on the question of cybersquatting dilution should have prevented summary judgment for Avery Dennison.

2 TARNISHMENT

Tarnishment occurs when a defendant's use of a mark similar to a plaintiff's presents a danger that consumers will form unfavorable associations with the mark. The district court did not reach Avery Dennison's claims regarding tarnishment.

Avery Dennison offers, as an alternative ground for affirming the district court, the fact that Appellants house <avery.net> and <dennison.net> at the same web site as lewd domain-name registrations. However, the evidence likewise indicates that to move from <avery.net> or <dennison.net> to a lewd SLD requires "linking" through the Mailbank home page, which might remove any association with the "Avery" and "Dennison" trademarks that the Internet user might have had. Whether Appellants' use of the registrations presents a danger of tarnishment is an issue of fact that could not be decided on summary judgment.

D Injunction

Under the Federal Trademark Dilution Act and Business and Professional Code §14330, an injunction may issue if Appellants' conduct dilutes, or is likely to dilute, Avery Dennison's trademarks. Actual success on the merits of a claim is required for a permanent injunction. Because we conclude that the district erred as a matter of law in finding "Avery" and "Dennison" to be famous and Appellants' use of <avery.net> and <dennison.net> to be commercial use, and because genuine issues of material fact existed as to whether Appellants' use of the domain-name registrations dilutes or is likely to dilute Avery Dennison's marks, the district court necessarily erred in granting Avery Dennison an injunction.

. . . .

VII CONCLUSION

We reverse the district court's summary judgment in favor of Avery Dennison and remand with instructions to enter summary judgment for Sumpton and Freeview. [...]

Discussion Questions

1. Has trademark dilution been consistently applied in both cases? Are the courts stretching the definition of "commercial use" in order to catch Mr. Toeppen's activities?

2. Is *male fides* (bad faith) a fundamental element of cybersquatting/cyberpiracy? Consider the *Avery* decision.

3. Do you think it would be prudent for Canada to enact legislation similar to that of the United States? What are the policy arguments on either side of the debate?

In 1993, the U.S. government entered an agreement with Network Solutions Inc. ("NSI"). NSI was transferred control over all non-military Internet registration services for a period of five years. NSI implemented a "first-come, first-served" policy of domain name registration with the ".com", ".net", and ".org" generic top-level domains. This open registration policy quickly resulted in heated disputes once the business world realized the economic advantages of the Internet.

In response to the unrest created by trademark holders, NSI implemented a dispute resolution policy. This policy had many flaws and caused considerable problems. The US government did not renew their five-year agreement with NSI. Instead, they became the principal force behind the creation of the new Internet Corporation for Assignment of Names and Numbers (ICANN). ICANN established a new dispute resolution policy, hoping to address the previous shortcomings of the NSI policy.

World Wrestling Federation Entertainment, Inc. v. Michael Bosman[†]

1. The Parties
The complainant is World Wrestling Federation Entertainment, Inc., f/k/a Titan Sports, Inc., a corporation organized under the laws of the State of Delaware, United States of America, having its principal place of business at Stamford, Connecticut, United States of America. The respondent is Michael Bosman, an individual resident in Redlands, California, United States of America.

2. The Domain Name(s) and Registrar(s)
The domain name at issue is <worldwrestlingfederation.com>, which domain name is registered with MelbourneIT, based in Australia.

3. Procedural History
A Complaint was submitted electronically to the World Intellectual Property Organization Arbitration and Mediation Center (the "WIPO Center") on December 2, 1999, and the signed original together with four copies forwarded by express courier under cover of a letter of the same date. An Acknowledgment of Receipt was sent by the WIPO Center to the complainant, dated December 3, 1999. On December 3, 1999 a Request for Registrar Verification was transmitted to the registrar, Melbourne IT requesting it to: (1) confirm that the domain name at issue is registered with MelbourneIT; (2) confirm that the person identified as the respondent is the current registrant of the domain name; (3) provide the full contact details (i.e., postal address(es), telephone number(s), facsimile number(s), e-mail address(es)) available in the registrar's Whois database for the registrant of the disputed domain name, the technical contact, the administrative contact and the billing contact; (4) provide a copy of the registration agreement that was in effect at the time of the original registration of the domain name, as well as any subsequent amendments to the agreement; (5) provide a copy of the domain name dispute policy (if different from ICANN's Uniform Domain Name Dispute Resolution Policy) that was in effect at the time of the original registration of the domain name, as well as any subse-

---

[†] Case No. D99-0001 (WIPO Arbitration and Mediation Center).

quent amendments to the policy. On December 8, 1999, MelbourneIT confirmed by reply e-mail that the domain name <worldwrestlingfederation.com> is registered with MelbourneIT and that the respondent, Michael Bosman, was the current registrant of the name. The registrar also forwarded the requested Whois details, as well as copies of the registration agreement and applicable dispute resolution policy.

The policy in effect at the time of the original registration of the domain name at issue provided that "Registrant agrees to be bound by the terms and conditions of this Registration Agreement." MelbourneIT Domain Name Registration Agreement, effective as of October 7, 1999, para. 1. Paragraph 7 of the Registration Agreement, entitled, "Dispute Policy," provides in pertinent part:

> Registrant agrees, as a condition to submitting this Registration Agreement, and if the Registration Agreement is accepted by MelbourneIT, that the Registrant is bound by MelbourneIT's current Dispute Policy ("Dispute Policy"). Registrant agrees that MelbourneIT, in its sole discretion, may change or modify the Dispute Policy, incorporated by reference herein, at any time. Registrant agrees that Registrant's maintaining the registration of a domain name after changes or modifications to the Dispute Policy become effective constitutes Registrant's continued acceptance of these changes or modifications. Registrant agrees that if Registrant considers any such changes or modifications to be unacceptable, Registrant may request that the domain name be deleted from the domain name database. Registrant agrees that any dispute relating to the registration or use of its domain name will be subject to the provisions specified in the Dispute Policy.

Effective December 1, 1999, MelbourneIT adopted the Uniform Domain Name Dispute Resolution Policy, adopted by the Internet Corporation for Assigned Names and Numbers ("ICANN") on August 26, 1999 (the "Policy"). There is no evidence that respondent ever requested that the domain name at issue be deleted from the domain name database. Accordingly, respondent is bound by the provisions of the Policy.

On December 6, 1999, having received written permission from the WIPO Center, the complainant submitted (electronically and in hardcopy) a Supplemental Complaint under cover of a letter of the same date. The Complaint and Supplemental Complaint will hereafter be referred to as the "Complaint."

A Formal Requirements Compliance Checklist was completed by the assigned WIPO Center Case Administrator on December 8, 1999. The Panel has independently determined and agrees with the assessment of the WIPO Center that the Complaint is in formal compliance with the requirements of the Policy, the Rules for Uniform Domain Name Dispute Resolution Policy, as approved by ICANN on October 24, 1999 (the "Uniform Rules"), and the WIPO Supplemental Rules for Uniform Domain Dispute Resolution Policy, in effect as of December 1, 1999 (the "WIPO Supplemental Rules"). The required fees for a single-member Panel were paid on time and in the required amount by the complainant. No formal deficiencies having been recorded, on December 9, 1999, a Notification of Complaint and Commencement of Administrative Proceeding (the "Commencement Notification") was transmitted to the respondent (with copies to the complainant, MelbourneIT and ICANN), setting a deadline of December 28, 1999, by which the respondent could file a Response to the Complaint. The Commencement Notification was transmitted to the respondent by e-mail to the e-mail addresses indicated in the Complaint and specified in MelbourneIT's Whois confirmation, as well as to <postmster@worldwrestlingfederation.com>; no e-mail addresses were found at any web page relating to the disputed domain name. In addition, the complaint was sent by express courier to all available postal addresses. Having reviewed the communications records in the case file, the Administrative Panel finds that the WIPO Center has discharged its responsibility under Paragraph 2(a) of the Uniform Rules "to employ reasonably available means calculated to achieve actual notice to Respondent." In any event, evidence of proper notice is provided by the evidence in the record of the respondent's participation in the settlement negotiations with the complainant.

On December 14, 1999, in view of the complainant's designation of a single panelist (but without prejudice to any election to be made by the respondent) the WIPO Center invited M. Scott Donahey to serve as a panelist in Case No. D99-0001, and transmitted to him a Statement of Acceptance and Request for Declaration of Impartiality and Independence.

On December 29, 1999, having received no Response from the designated respondent, using the same contact details and methods as were used for the Commencement Notification, the WIPO Center transmitted to the parties a Notification of Respondent Default. Having received on December 14, 1999, M. Scott Donahey's Statement of Acceptance and Declaration of Impartiality and Independence, also on December 29, 1999, the WIPO Center transmitted to the parties a Notification of Appointment of Administrative Panel and Projected Decision Date, in which M. Scott Donahey was formally appointed as the Sole Panelist. The Projected Decision Date was January 11, 2000. The Sole Panelist finds that the Administrative Panel was properly constituted and appointed in accordance with the Uniform Rules and WIPO Supplemental Rules.

Following these transmittals, the WIPO Center received a series of emails from the respondent and the complainant's representative, indicating that the parties intended to settle and had reached a settlement in principle. On January 6, 2000, the WIPO Center received a copy of an unsigned settlement agreement, with assurances that a signed copy would be transmitted by facsimile. On January 6, 2000, in view of the settlement negotiations between the parties, the Case Administrator notified the parties that the time in which the Panel was to issue a decision on the merits had been extended to January 15, 2000.

Following repeated requests from the WIPO Center for a copy of the fully executed final settlement agreement, on January 12, 2000, a copy of an agreement, signed only by respondent, was received. While the Panel is aware that the parties are close to completing their settlement, the Panel is also mindful of its responsibility to issue a timely decision, and one in compliance with the deadlines established by the Uniform Rules, the WIPO Supplemental Rules, and those established by the WIPO Center in accordance with those rules. See, e.g., Uniform Rules, paras. 10(c) and 15(b). Accordingly, this decision is issued prior to having received completely executed settlement documents, and, as such, does not rely on any purported settlement agreement. The Administrative Panel shall issue its Decision based on the Complaint, the e-mails exchanged, the Policy, the Uniform Rules, the WIPO Supplemental Rules, and without the benefit of any Response from respondent.

4.   Factual Background

The complainant has provided evidence of the registration of the following marks:

1. Service Mark — WORLD WRESTLING FEDERATION, registered for a term of 20 years from January 29, 1985, with the United States Patent and Trademark Office;

2. Trademark — WORLD WRESTLING FEDERATION, registered for a term of 20 years from November 7, 1989, with the United States Patent and Trademark Office.

The respondent registered the domain name <worldwrestlingfederation.com> for a term of two years from October 7, 1999. E-mail dated December 7, 1999, from Jan Webster to the WIPO Center Case Administrator, providing Whois details. The respondent is not a licensee of complainant, nor is he otherwise authorized to use complainant's marks.

Complainant is authorized to use and has used its service mark in connection with entertainment services, namely the provision of sporting events such as wrestling exhibitions for television. Complainant is authorized to use and has used its trademark in connection with metal key chains, phonograph records, prerecorded audio and video cassettes, switch plates, computer programs concerning the sport of wrestling, watches, stickers, book markers, book plates, collection books, pictorial biographies, blowouts, paper napkins, paper table covers, memo boards, posters, stationery-type portfolios, memo pads, book covers, calendars, trading cards, pens, pencils, magazines, decals, umbrellas, backpacks, roll bags, seat cushions, towels, shoes, bibs, children's pajamas, T-shirts, sweatshirts, ties, caps, sweaters, sports shirts, headbands, sweatbands, belts, fleece sets comprising warm-up pants and warm-up jacket, puzzles, board games, workout sets comprising exercise equipment in the nature of barbells, dumbbells, handgrips, wristbands. Charts, and/or audio cassette tapes. Complainant has also used its mark in connection with the promotion of wrestling entertainment services on its internet web site which may be found at <wwf.com>.

On October 10, 1999, three days after registering the domain name at issue, respondent contacted complainant by e-mail and notified complainant of the registration and stated that his primary purpose in registering the domain name was to sell, rent or otherwise transfer it to complainant for a valuable consideration in excess of respondent's out-of-pocket expenses. By e-mail dated December 3, 1999, respondent contacted complainant's representative and offered to sell the complainant the domain name at issue for the sum of US$1,000.00. In his e-mail, respondent stated that cybersquatting cases "typically accomplish very little and end up costing the companies thousands of dollars in legal fees, wasted time and energy." The payment of US$1,000 would represent more than payment for respondent's time and money, but also and "most important" [sic] would serve as consideration for "the right of current ownership of the domain name 'worldwrestlingfederation.com.'" Respondent has not developed a Web site using the domain name at issue or made any other good faith use of the domain name. The domain name at issue is not, nor could it be contended to be, a nickname of respondent or other member of his family, the name of a household pet, or in any other way identified with or related to a legitimate interest of respondent.

5.   Parties' Contentions

A. Complainant

Complainant contends that respondent has registered as a domain name a mark which is identical to the service mark and trademark registered and used by complainant, that respondent has no rights or legitimate interests in respect to the domain name at issue, and that respondent has registered and is using the domain name at issue in bad faith.

B. Respondent
Respondent has not contested the allegations of the Complaint.

6. Discussion and Findings

Paragraph 15(a) of the Rules instructs the Panel as to the principles the Panel is to use in determining the dispute: "A Panel shall decide a complaint on the basis of the statements and documents submitted in accordance with the Policy, these Rules and any rules and principles of law that it deems applicable." Since both the complainant and respondent are domiciled in the United States, and since United States' courts have recent experience with similar disputes, to the extent that it would assist the Panel in determining whether the complainant has met its burden as established by Paragraph 4(a) of the Policy, the Panel shall look to rules and principles of law set out in decisions of the courts of the United States. Paragraph 4(a) of the Policy directs that the complainant must prove each of the following:

1) that the domain name registered by the respondent is identical or confusingly similar to a trademark or service mark in which the complainant has rights; and,

2) that the respondent has no legitimate interests in respect of the domain name; and,

3) the domain name has been registered and used in bad faith.

It is clear beyond cavil that the domain name <worldwrestlingfederation.com> is identical or confusingly similar to the trademark and service mark registered and used by complainant, WORLD WRESTLING FEDERATION. It is also apparent that the respondent has no rights or legitimate interests in respect of the domain name. Since the domain name was registered on October 7, 1999, and since respondent offered to sell it to complainant three days later, the Panel believes that the name was registered in bad faith.

However, the name must not only be registered in bad faith, but it must also be used in bad faith. The issue to be determined is whether the respondent used the domain name in bad faith. It is not disputed that the respondent did not establish a Web site corresponding to the registered domain name. Accordingly, can it be said that the respondent "used" the domain name?

It is clear from the legislative history that ICANN intended that the complainant must establish not only bad faith registration, but also bad faith use. "These comments point out that cybersquatters often register names in bulk, but do not use them, yet without use the streamlined dispute-resolution procedure is not available. While that argument appears to have merit on initial impression, it would involve a change in the policy adopted by the Board. The WIPO report, the DNSO recommendation, and the registrars-group recommendation all required both registration and use in bad faith before the streamlined procedure would be invoked. Staff recommends that this requirement not be changed without study and recommendation by the DNSO." Second Staff Report on Implementation Documents for the Uniform Dispute Resolution Policy, submitted for Board meeting of October 24, 1999, para. 4.5,a.

Paragraph 4,b,i of the Policy, provides that "the following circumstances ... shall be evidence of the registration and use of a domain name in bad faith: ... circumstances indicating that you have registered or you have acquired the domain name primarily for the purpose of selling, renting or otherwise transferring the domain name registration to the complainant who is the owner of the trademark or service mark ... for valuable consideration in excess of the documented out-of-pocket costs directly related to the domain name." (Emphasis added.)

Because respondent offered to sell the domain name to complainant "for valuable consideration in excess of" any out-of-pocket costs directly related to the domain name, respondent has "used" the domain name in bad faith as defined in the Policy. Although it is therefore unnecessary to consult decisions of United States' courts, the panel notes that decisions of those courts in cases which determine what constitutes "use" where the right to a domain name is contested by a mark owner support the panel's conclusion. For example, in the case of *Panavision International, L.P.* v. *Dennis Toeppen, et al.*, the Court of Appeals held that the defendant's intention to sell the domain name to the plaintiff constituted "use" of the plaintiff's mark:

> Toeppen's argument misstates his use of the Panavision mark. His use is not as benign as he suggests. Toeppen's 'business' is to register trademarks as domain names and then sell them to the rightful trademark owners. He 'acts as a 'spoiler,' preventing Panavision and others from doing business on the Internet under their trademarked names unless they pay his fee.' ... As the district court found, Toeppen traded on the value of Panavision's marks. So long as he held the Internet registrations, he curtailed Panavision's exploitation of the value of its trademarks on the Internet, a value which Toeppen then used when he attempted to sell the panavision.com domain name to Panavision.

To the same effect is the decision in *Intermatic Inc.* v. *Toeppen*. In that case the Federal District Court determined that "Toeppen's intention to arbitrage the 'intermatic.com' domain name constitutes a commercial use.... Toeppen's desire to resell the domain name is sufficient to meet the 'commercial use' requirement of the Lanham Act. Id., 1239.

The Panel notes with approval that the Policy and Rules set out by ICANN encourage settlement and that the parties in this case have engaged in extensive settlement negotiations. It was noted by the complainant in an email to the respondent regarding possible settlement that, while it was not the complainant's policy to pay individuals to stop infringing its intellectual property, it was also complainant's policy not to litigate against its fans. Email from Complainant's Representative to Respondent, dated December 09, 1999. Complainant acknowledged that it could have proceeded to litigation under the United States "Anticybersquatting Consumer Protection Act," but that it elected not to. By engaging in this proceeding, complainant has sought to protect complainant's intellectual property interests while preserving the relationship between complainant and its fans at a minimal cost to all concerned.

7. Decision

For all of the foregoing reasons, the Panel decides that the domain name registered by respondent is identical or confusingly similar to the trademark and service mark in which the complainant has rights, and that the respondent has no rights or legitimate interests in respect of the domain name, and that the respondent's domain name has been registered and is being used in bad faith. Accordingly, pursuant to Paragraph 4,i of the Policy, the Panel requires that the registration of the domain name <worldwrestlingfederation.com> be transferred to the complainant.

Notes

1. The ICANN Uniform Domain Name Dispute Resolution Policy can be found at <http://www.icann.org/udrp/udrp-policy-24oct99.htm>. The associated rules can be found at <http://www.icann.org/udrp/udrp-rules-24oct99.htm>.

    The World Wrestling Federation case excerpted above was the first ICANN domain name dispute resolution decision. It has been followed by hundreds more in a matter of months.

    The ICANN process is based on the premise that dot-com disputes are global in nature (anyone anywhere can own a dot-com domain), that resolution of disputes must be fast and inexpensive, and that the rights of trademark holders may sometimes trump the rights of an individual to own a particular domain name.

    The ICANN rules entitle anyone, regardless of country of residence, to contest a top-level generic domain name registration (this includes dot-com, dot-net, and dot-org registrations). To move the process along speedily, once a claim is launched, the responding party has 20 days to file its side of the story, and the arbitrator (either one or a panel of three) has another two weeks to render a decision.

    As the excerpt illustrates, for a trademark holder to succeed, they must prove three elements. First, the contested domain name is identical or confusingly similar to a trademark or service mark to which they have rights. Second, the current holder has no rights or legitimate interests in the domain name. Third, the domain name was registered and is being used in bad faith.

    The most critical of these elements is bad faith. It may include evidence which suggests that the holder acquired the domain with the intent of selling it to the rightful trademark holder, to create confusion, or to transfer the domain to a competitor of the trademark holder.

    Unfortunately, many decisions have been rendered in an inconsistent manner with sparse reasoning behind them. Consider this case involving two Canadian river boat companies, located within walking distance of one another. Is the reasoning sufficient? (The entire decision is posted below.) Do cases such as these call the validity of the entire process into question?

    Rockport Boat Line (1994) Limited (Complainant) v. *Gananoque Boat Line LTD (Respondent)*[†]

    Respondent registered the domain name, ROCKPORTBOATLINE.COM with Network Solutions on March 13, 2000. The domain name is in active status with Network Solutions.

    Both the Complainant and the Respondent operate passenger boat lines in Ontario, Canada. Complainant operates its business out of Rockport Ontario and Respondent operates its business in Gananoque and Ivy Lea. These locations are the village of Rockport, Ivy Lea being two miles west of Rockport.

    Both of the businesses service the 1000 Islands area by providing cruises and related activities.

    Respondent adopted a business plan five years ago that provided for aggressive expansion. Pursuant to that plan, the second departure location for its

---

† (Forum File No.: FA0004000094653).

boats was established in the village of Ivy Lea and a 300-passenger vessel added to the fleet.

In 1997, Complainant established an internet presence as www.rockportcruises.com from which they currently operate. Respondent's acquisition of the domain name rockportboatline.com was in accordance with its expansion plans which include utilizing a federally owned wharf in the city of Rockport should such a wharf become available.

Conclusions

The undersigned certifies that he has acted independently and has no known conflict of interest to serve as the arbitrator in this proceeding. Having been duly selected, and being impartial, the undersigned makes the following findings and conclusions.

There is no evidence that Respondent registered and is using the domain name rockportboatline.com in bad faith. While the circumstances listed in Paragraph 4(b) of the Dispute Resolution Policy are not exclusive, it is the finding of the Arbitrator that the registration and use by Respondent does not meet the criteria of any of the four circumstances listed in ICANN Policy 4(b).

The ICANN Dispute Resolution Policy 4(a) requires that each of the three elements listed therein must be proven to be present for the Complainant to prevail and the evidence does not lead to a conclusion that any of the elements are present in this case.

Decision

Based upon the findings and conclusions, it is decided as follows:

> THE UNDERSIGNED DIRECTS THAT THE COMPLAINT BE DISMISSED AND THAT THE DOMAIN NAME ROCKPORTBOATLINE.COM NOT BE TRANSFERRED FROM RESPONDENT, GANANOQUE BOAT LINE LTD, TO COMPLAINANT, ROCKPORT BOAT LINE (1994) LIMITED.

2. Do you think the ICANN Uniform Domain Name Dispute Resolution process will be effective in the long run? Does it adequately address the issue of cybersquatting?

The U.S. government, in an attempt to protect interests within its jurisdiction, enacted the *Anticybersquatting Consumer Protection Act.* Initially the Act contained criminal sanctions as a deterrent for cybersquatting activities; however, they are absent from the final enacted legislation. The liability created under the Act threatens to jeopardize the newly established ICANN Domain Name Dispute Resolution process by providing a more comprehensive choice of remedies, including damages.

Anticybersquatting Consumer Protection Act[†]

SEC. 3002. CYBERPIRACY PREVENTION.

(a) In General.
Section 43 of the Trademark Act of 1946 (15 U.S.C. 1125) is amended by inserting at the end the following:

---

† P.L. 106–113.

(d)(1)(A) A person shall be liable in a civil action by the owner of a mark, including a personal name which is protected as a mark under this section, if, without regard to the goods or services of the parties, that person —

(i) has a bad faith intent to profit from that mark, including a personal name which is protected as a mark under this section; and

(ii) registers, traffics in, or uses a domain name that —

(I) in the case of a mark that is distinctive at the time of registration of the domain name, is identical or confusingly similar to that mark;

(II) in the case of a famous mark that is famous at the time of registration of the domain name, is identical or confusingly similar to or dilutive of that mark; or

(III) is a trademark, word, or name protected by reason of section 706 of title 18, United States Code, or section 220506 of title 36, United States Code.

(B)(i) In determining whether a person has a bad faith intent described under subparagraph (A), a court may consider factors such as, but not limited to —

(I) the trademark or other intellectual property rights of the person, if any, in the domain name;

(II) the extent to which the domain name consists of the legal name of the person or a name that is otherwise commonly used to identify that person;

(III) the person's prior use, if any, of the domain name in connection with the bona fide offering of any goods or services;

(IV) the person's bona fide noncommercial or fair use of the mark in a site accessible under the domain name;

(V) the person's intent to divert consumers from the mark owner's online location to a site accessible under the domain name that could harm the goodwill represented by the mark, either for commercial gain or with the intent to tarnish or disparage the mark, by creating a likelihood of confusion as to the source, sponsorship, affiliation, or endorsement of the site;

(VI) the person's offer to transfer, sell, or otherwise assign the domain name to the mark owner or any third party for financial gain without having used, or having an intent to use, the domain name in the bona fide offering of any goods or services, or the person's prior conduct indicating a pattern of such conduct;

(VII) the person's provision of material and misleading false contact information when applying for the registration of the domain name, the person's intentional failure to maintain accurate contact information, or the person's prior conduct indicating a pattern of such conduct;

(VIII) the person's registration or acquisition of multiple domain names which the person knows are identical or confusingly similar to marks of others that are distinctive at the time of registration of such domain names, or dilutive of famous marks of others that are famous at the time of registration of such domain names, without regard to the goods or services of the parties; and

(IX) the extent to which the mark incorporated in the person's domain name registration is or is not distinctive and famous within the meaning of subsection (c)(1) of section 43.

(ii) Bad faith intent described under subparagraph (A) shall not be found in any case in which the court determines that the person believed and had reasonable grounds to believe that the use of the domain name was a fair use or otherwise lawful.

(C) In any civil action involving the registration, trafficking, or use of a domain name under this paragraph, a court may order the forfeiture or cancellation of the domain name or the transfer of the domain name to the owner of the mark.

(D) A person shall be liable for using a domain name under subparagraph (A) only if that person is the domain name registrant or that registrant's authorized licensee.

(E) As used in this paragraph, the term 'traffics in' refers to transactions that include, but are not limited to, sales, purchases, loans, pledges, licenses, exchanges of currency, and any other transfer for consideration or receipt in exchange for consideration.

(2)(A) The owner of a mark may file an in rem civil action against a domain name in the judicial district in which the domain name registrar, domain name registry, or other domain name authority that registered or assigned the domain name is located if —

  (i) the domain name violates any right of the owner of a mark registered in the Patent and Trademark Office, or protected under subsection (a) or (c); and

  (ii) the court finds that the owner —

    (I) is not able to obtain in personam jurisdiction over a person who would have been a defendant in a civil action under paragraph (1); or

    (II) through due diligence was not able to find a person who would have been a defendant in a civil action under paragraph (1) by —

      (aa) sending a notice of the alleged violation and intent to proceed under this paragraph to the registrant of the domain name at the postal and e-mail address provided by the registrant to the registrar; and

      (bb) publishing notice of the action as the court may direct promptly after filing the action.

(B) The actions under subparagraph (A)(ii) shall constitute service of process.

(C) In an in rem action under this paragraph, a domain name shall be deemed to have its situs in the judicial district in which —

  (i) the domain name registrar, registry, or other domain name authority that registered or assigned the domain name is located; or

  (ii) documents sufficient to establish control and authority regarding the disposition of the registration and use of the domain name are deposited with the court.

(D)(i) The remedies in an in rem action under this paragraph shall be limited to a court order for the forfeiture or cancellation of the domain name or the transfer of the domain name to the owner of the mark. Upon receipt of written notification of a filed, stamped copy of a complaint filed by the owner of a mark in a United States district court under this paragraph, the domain name registrar, domain name registry, or other domain name authority shall —

  (I) expeditiously deposit with the court documents sufficient to establish the court's control and authority regarding the disposition of the registration and use of the domain name to the court; and

  (II) not transfer, suspend, or otherwise modify the domain name during the pendency of the action, except upon order of the court.

(ii) The domain name registrar or registry or other domain name authority shall not be liable for injunctive or monetary relief under this paragraph except in the case of bad faith or reckless disregard, which includes a willful failure to comply with any such court order.

(3) The civil action established under paragraph (1) and the in rem action established under paragraph (2), and any remedy available under either such action, shall be in addition to any other civil action or remedy otherwise applicable.

(4) The in rem jurisdiction established under paragraph (2) shall be in addition to any other jurisdiction that otherwise exists, whether in rem or in personam.

(b) Cyberpiracy Protections for Individuals.

(1) In general.

(A) Civil liability. Any person who registers a domain name that consists of the name of another living person, or a name substantially and confusingly similar thereto, without that person's consent, with the specific intent to profit from such name by selling the domain name for financial gain to that person or any third party, shall be liable in a civil action by such person.

(B) Exception. A person who in good faith registers a domain name consisting of the name of another living person, or a name substantially and confusingly similar thereto, shall not be liable under this paragraph if such name is used in, affiliated with, or related to a work of authorship protected under title 17, United States Code, including a work made for hire as defined in section 101 of title 17, United States Code, and if the person registering the domain name is the copyright owner or licensee of the work, the person intends to sell the domain name in conjunction with the lawful exploitation of the work, and such registration is not prohibited by a contract between the registrant and the named person. The exception under this subparagraph shall apply only to a civil action brought under paragraph (1) and shall in no manner limit the protections afforded under the Trademark Act of 1946 (15 U.S.C. 1051 et seq.) or other provision of Federal or State law.

(2) Remedies. In any civil action brought under paragraph (1), a court may award injunctive relief, including the forfeiture or cancellation of the domain name or the transfer of the domain name to the plaintiff. The court may also, in its discretion, award costs and attorneys fees to the prevailing party.

(3) Definition. In this subsection, the term "domain name" has the meaning given that term in section 45 of the Trademark Act of 1946 (15 U.S.C. 1127).

(4) Effective date. This subsection shall apply to domain names registered on or after the date of the enactment of this Act.

SEC. 3003. DAMAGES AND REMEDIES.

(a) Remedies in Cases of Domain Name Piracy.

(1) Injunctions. Section 34(a) of the Trademark Act of 1946 (15 U.S.C. 1116(a)) is amended in the first sentence by striking "(a) or (c)" and inserting "(a), (c), or (d)".

(2) Damages. Section 35(a) of the Trademark Act of 1946 (15 U.S.C. 1117(a)) is amended in the first sentence by inserting ", (c), or (d)" after "section 43(a)".

376 / Part Four: Internet and Intellectual Property

(b) Statutory Damages. Section 35 of the Trademark Act of 1946 (15 U.S.C. 1117) is amended by adding at the end the following:

(d) In a case involving a violation of section 43(d)(1), the plaintiff may elect, at any time before final judgment is rendered by the trial court, to recover, instead of actual damages and profits, an award of statutory damages in the amount of not less than $1,000 and not more than $100,000 per domain name, as the court considers just.

SEC. 3004. LIMITATION ON LIABILITY.

Section 32(2) of the Trademark Act of 1946 (15 U.S.C. 1114) is amended —

(1) in the matter preceding subparagraph (A) by striking "under section 43(a)" and inserting "under section 43(a) or (d)"; and

(2) by redesignating subparagraph (D) as subparagraph (E) and inserting after subparagraph (C) the following:

(D)(i)(I) A domain name registrar, a domain name registry, or other domain name registration authority that takes any action described under clause (ii) affecting a domain name shall not be liable for monetary relief or, except as provided in subclause (II), for injunctive relief, to any person for such action, regardless of whether the domain name is finally determined to infringe or dilute the mark.

(II) A domain name registrar, domain name registry, or other domain name registration authority described in subclause (I) may be subject to injunctive relief only if such registrar, registry, or other registration authority has —

    (aa) not expeditiously deposited with a court, in which an action has been filed regarding the disposition of the domain name, documents sufficient for the court to establish the court's control and authority regarding the disposition of the registration and use of the domain name;

    (bb) transferred, suspended, or otherwise modified the domain name during the pendency of the action, except upon order of the court; or

    (cc) willfully failed to comply with any such court order.

(ii) An action referred to under clause (i)(I) is any action of refusing to register, removing from registration, transferring, temporarily disabling, or permanently canceling a domain name —

    (I) in compliance with a court order under section 43(d); or

    (II) in the implementation of a reasonable policy by such registrar, registry, or authority prohibiting the registration of a domain name that is identical to, confusingly similar to, or dilutive of another's mark.

(iii) A domain name registrar, a domain name registry, or other domain name registration authority shall not be liable for damages under this section for the registration or maintenance of a domain name for another absent a showing of bad faith intent to profit from such registration or maintenance of the domain name.

(iv) If a registrar, registry, or other registration authority takes an action described under clause (ii) based on a knowing and material misrepresentation by any other person that a domain name is identical to, confusingly similar to, or dilutive of a mark, the person making the knowing and material misrepresentation shall be liable for any damages, including costs and attorney's fees, incurred by the domain name registrant as a result of such action. The court may also grant injunctive relief to the domain name registrant, including the reactivation of the domain name or the transfer of the domain name to the domain name registrant.

(v) A domain name registrant whose domain name has been suspended, disabled, or transferred under a policy described under clause (ii)(II) may, upon notice to the mark owner, file a civil action to establish that the registration or use of the domain name by such registrant is not unlawful under this Act. The court may grant injunctive relief to the domain name registrant, including the reactivation of the domain name or transfer of the domain name to the domain name registrant.

SEC. 3005. DEFINITIONS.

Section 45 of the Trademark Act of 1946 (15 U.S.C. 1127) is amended by inserting after the undesignated paragraph defining the term "counterfeit" the following:

The term 'domain name' means any alphanumeric designation which is registered with or assigned by any domain name registrar, domain name registry, or other domain name registration authority as part of an electronic address on the Internet.

The term 'Internet' has the meaning given that term in section 230(fSec.)(1) of the Communications Act of 1934 (47 U.S.C. 230(fSec.)(1)).

SEC. 3006. STUDY ON ABUSIVE DOMAIN NAME REGISTRATIONS INVOLVING PERSONAL NAMES.

(a) In General.
Not later than 180 days after the date of the enactment of this Act, the Secretary of Commerce, in consultation with the Patent and Trademark Office and the Federal Election Commission, shall conduct a study and report to Congress with recommendations on guidelines and procedures for resolving disputes involving the registration or use by a person of a domain name that includes the personal name of another person, in whole or in part, or a name confusingly similar thereto, including consideration of and recommendations for —

(1) protecting personal names from registration by another person as a second level domain name for purposes of selling or otherwise transferring such domain name to such other person or any third party for financial gain;

(2) protecting individuals from bad faith uses of their personal names as second level domain names by others with malicious intent to harm the reputation of the individual or the goodwill associated with that individual's name;

(3) protecting consumers from the registration and use of domain names that include personal names in the second level domain in manners which are intended or are likely to confuse or deceive the public as to the affiliation, connection, or association of the domain name registrant, or a site accessible under the domain name, with such other person, or as to the origin, sponsorship, or approval of the goods, services, or commercial activities of the domain name registrant;

(4) protecting the public from registration of domain names that include the personal names of government officials, official candidates, and potential official candidates for Federal, State, or local political office in the United States, and the use of such domain names in a manner that disrupts the electoral process or the public's ability to access accurate and reliable information regarding such individuals;

(5) existing remedies, whether under State law or otherwise, and the extent to which such remedies are sufficient to address the considerations described in paragraphs (1) through (4); and

(6) the guidelines, procedures, and policies of the Internet Corporation for Assigned Names and Numbers and the extent to which they address the considerations described in paragraphs (1) through (4).

(b) Guidelines and Procedures.
The Secretary of Commerce shall, under its Memorandum of Understanding with the Internet Corporation for Assigned Names and Numbers, collaborate to develop guidelines and procedures for resolving disputes involving the registration or use by a person of a domain name that includes the personal name of another person, in whole or in part, or a name confusingly similar thereto.

The frustration of domain name holders has often led to legal actions against domain registrars such as NSI. The courts have been generally unsympathetic, however, with registrars succeeding in avoiding liability. Is this a fair approach? Should some responsibility for the domain name mess fall to the registrars who implement domain name policy and often seem to encourage multiple registrations without regard for intellectual property rights?

Lockheed Martin Corporation v. Network Solutions, Inc.†

At all relevant times, NSI was the sole National Science Foundation contractor in charge of registering domain-name combinations for the top-level domains <.gov>, <.edu>, <.com>, <.org>, and <.net>. (For clarity, we set off Internet-related character strings with the caret symbols ("< >").) After registration, NSI entered the combination and the corresponding IP Address in its database, permitting automatic translation when an Internet user entered a domain-name combination. NSI is no longer the exclusive registrar. Since oral argument on this appeal, a new competitive scheme has been implemented.

When registering with NSI to receive a domain-name combination, an applicant submits NSI's "template" electronically over the Internet. On approval, NSI puts the domain-name combination in its database in conjunction with the correct IP Address. NSI then routes Internet users who enter a certain domain-name combination to the registrant's computer. At the time of argument on this appeal, NSI was receiving approximately 130,000 registrations per month, although evidence indicates that the number of monthly registrations has been increasing steadily and is possibly much larger today. Ninety percent of templates are processed electronically, and the entire registration process for each application requires between a few minutes and a few hours. Ten percent of the time, an employee of NSI reviews the application. Human intervention might occur because of an error in filling out the form or because the applied-for domain name includes a "prohibited" character string — such as specific variations on the words Olympic, Red Cross, or NASA, and certain "obscene" words.

---

† 194 F. 3d 980 (9th Cir. 1999).

NSI also performs a conflict check on all applications, which compares an application to other registered domain-name combinations. However, NSI does not consult third parties during the registration process, check for a registrant's right to use a particular word in a domain-name combination, or monitor the use of a combination once registered. NSI is also not an Internet Service Provider. It performs none of the "hosting" functions for a web site.

NSI does maintain a post-registration dispute-resolution procedure. Anyone who feels that his or her rights are violated by the domain-name combination maintained by a registrant can submit a certified copy of a trademark registration to NSI. NSI then requires the registrant to obtain a declaratory judgment of the right to maintain the domain-name combination. If the registrant fails to do so, its registration is terminated.

B

Lockheed owns and operates "The Skunk Works," an aircraft design and construction laboratory. Since 1943, The Skunk Works has developed prototypes of this country's first jet fighter, the U-2 and SR-71 spy planes, and the F-117 and F-22 fighter planes. The Skunk Works is currently involved in designing a possible replacement for the space shuttle. "Skunk Works" is a registered and incontestable service mark.

II

Third parties, not involved in this litigation, have registered domain-name combinations with NSI which are variations on the phrase "skunk works." These include: <skunkworks.com>, <skunkworks.net>, <skunkwrks.com>, <skunkwerks.com>, <skunkworx.com>, <theskunkworks.com>, <skunkworks1.com>, <skunkworks.org>, <skunkwear.com,> <the-skunkwerks.com>, <skunkwurks.com>, and <theencryptedskunkworks.com>. Lockheed alleges that many of these registrations infringe and dilute its "Skunk Works" service mark.

Lockheed sent two letters, on May 7 and June 18, 1996, bringing the <skunkworks.com> and <skunkworks.net> registrations to NSI's attention. Lockheed's letters informed NSI of its belief that the third-party registrants were infringing or diluting Lockheed's service mark. Lockheed requested that NSI cancel the allegedly offending registrations. Lockheed also requested that NSI cease registering domain-name combinations that included "Skunk Works" or variations on the phrase and report to Lockheed all such domain-name combinations contained in its registry. NSI took no action on Lockheed's requests, informing Lockheed by letter that Lockheed had failed to comply with the terms of NSI's dispute resolution policy. Due to Lockheed's dealings with the third-party registrants, <skunkworks.com> and <skunkworks.net> ceased being used, but NSI did not immediately cancel the registrations and later permitted a new registrant to register <skunkworks.com>.

Lockheed sued NSI on October 22, 1996, claiming contributory service mark infringement, infringement, unfair competition, and service mark dilution, all in violation of the Lanham Act, and also seeking declaratory relief. The complaint alleged that four specific domain-name registrations infringed or diluted Lockheed's "Skunk Works" service mark. [...]

. . . .

Contributory infringement occurs when the defendant either intentionally induces a third party to infringe the plaintiff's mark or supplies a product to a third party with actual or constructive knowledge that the product is being used to infringe the service mark. Lockheed alleges only the latter basis for contributory infringement liability and therefore must prove that NSI supplies a product to third parties with actual or constructive knowledge that its product is being used to infringe "Skunk Works."

The district court assumed for purposes of summary judgment that third parties were infringing Lockheed's "Skunk Works" service mark, and NSI does not ask us to affirm on the alternate ground that no genuine issue of material fact exists as to infringement. We are thus left to consider two issues on Lockheed's contributory infringement cause of action: (1) whether NSI supplied a product to third parties and (2) whether NSI had actual or constructive knowledge of any infringement. Because we accept the district court's excellent analysis on the first question, we affirm summary judgment without reaching the second.

A

Under the plain language of the Inwood Lab. formulation, to be liable for contributory infringement, NSI must supply a "product" to a third party with which the third party infringes Lockheed's service mark. In Inwood Lab., the Supreme Court considered an action against a manufacturer of generic pharmaceuticals. Non-party pharmacists packaged the defendant's less-expensive generic pills, but labeled them with the plaintiff's brand name. The plaintiff stated a cause of action for contributory infringement by alleging that the defendant "continued to supply [the product] to pharmacists whom the petitioners knew were mislabeling generic drugs."

Inwood Lab. has been applied in the broader context of renting booth space at a flea market.

Rock, the Seventh Circuit explicitly addressed the distinction between a product and a service, noting that while the pharmaceutical company in Inwood Lab. clearly supplied a product to the third-party pharmacists, a "temporary help service ... might not be liable if it furnished [to the defendant] the workers he employed to erect his stand. The court then held that space at a flea market was more comparable to pharmaceuticals than to manpower, in part because of the close comparison between the legal duty owed by a landlord to control illegal activities on his or her premises and by a manufacturer to control illegal use of his or her product. We adopted the Hard Rock analysis in *Fonovisa, Inc.* v. *Cherry Auction, Inc.*, holding that a flea market could be liable for contributory infringement if it "supplied the necessary marketplace" for the sale of infringing products.

Hard Rock and Fonovisa teach us that when measuring and weighing a fact pattern in the contributory infringement context without the convenient "product" mold dealt with in Inwood Lab., we consider the extent of control exercised by the defendant over the third party's means of infringement. Direct control and monitoring of the instrumentality used by a third party to infringe the plaintiff's mark permits the expansion of Inwood Lab.'s "supplies a product" requirement for contributory infringement.

B

The case at bench involves a fact pattern squarely on the "service" side of the product/service distinction suggested by Inwood Lab and its offspring. All evidence in the record indicates that NSI's role differs little from that of the United States Postal Service: when an Internet user enters a domain-name combination, NSI translates the domain-name combination to the registrant's IP Address and routes the information or command to the corresponding computer. Although NSI's routing service is only available to a registrant who has paid NSI's fee, NSI does not supply the domain-name combination any more than the Postal Service supplies a street address by performing the routine service of routing mail. As the district court correctly observed,

> Where domain names are used to infringe, the infringement does not result from NSI's publication of the domain name list, but from the registrant's use of the name on a web site or other Internet form of communication in connection with goods or services.... NSI's involvement with the use of domain names does not extend beyond registration.

The "direct control and monitoring" rule established by Hard Rock and Fonovisa likewise fails to reach the instant situation. The district court correctly recognized that NSI's rote translation service does not entail the kind of direct control and monitoring required to justify an extension of the "supplies a product" requirement. Such a stretch would reach well beyond the contemplation of Inwood Lab. and its progeny.

In an attempt to fit under Fonovisa's umbrella, Lockheed characterizes NSI's service as a licensing arrangement with alleged third-party infringers. Although we accept Lockheed's argument that NSI licenses its routing service to domain-name registrants, the routing service is just that — a service. In Fonovisa and Hard Rock, by contrast, the defendants licensed real estate, with the consequent direct control over the activity that the third-party alleged infringers engaged in on the premises.

. . . .

NSI is not liable for contributory infringement as a matter of law. [...]

16

Intellectual Property and the Internet

Intellectual property law, the law that governs copyright, trademarks, and patents, has long been closely associated with Internet law. E-commerce businesses and their legal advisors have aggressively targeted software and music piracy (which clearly violates copyright laws) and domain name cybersquatting (which may violate trademark law) and have begun to register e-commerce business method patents to obtain a competitive advantage in a fierce marketplace.

With IP issues frequently dominating Internet law news headlines, Canadians must be careful to distinguish between U.S. and Canadian law. Although the principles are similar, notable differences include the absence of contributory copyright infringement from Canadian copyright law and the inclusion of moral rights within the Canadian *Copyright Act*.

This chapter surveys some of the most interesting legal intersections between IP and the Internet. These involve linking, framing, meta-tags, and spidering.

LINKING

Ease of copying materials and transferring them digitally presents a tremendous challenge to existing copyright laws. For Internet users and Web site designers, copyright issues such as the use of hyperlinks and frames go to the very heart of what the Web is all about. At its most fundamental, these concerns raise the question of how copyright can be enforced and whether it can survive in the digital age.

The following three cases illustrate the struggle that courts and tribunals have had in coming to a legal determination on the legality of linking. Each case originates from a different jurisdiction — beginning with Scotland, followed by the United States and Canada.

Shetland Times Limited v. Dr Jonathan Wills[†]

The pursuers own and publish The Shetland Times, a newspaper which carries local, national and international news. The second defenders provide a news reporting service and trade under the name "The Shetland News". The first defender is the managing director of the second defenders.

In The Shetland Times there appear news items comprising texts under relative headlines. Photographs also appear.

In the Issue of The Shetland Times printed on Friday, October 11, 1996, there appeared an item, running to several paragraphs, concerning financial difficulties about the Fraser Peterson Centre in Shetland. It appeared under the headline "Bid to save centre after council funding 'cock up'". A number of other items also appeared in that issue, each under a relative headline.

. . . .

The pursuers have recently established such a web site. By this means they make available on the Internet items, including photographs, which appear in printed editions of The Shetland Times. Such items are stored electronically by reference to an index of relative headlines, being the headlines which appear above those items in the printed issues. Access to the text of the printed items is gained by the caller clicking on the relative headline which appears on a "front page". The front page is the display which first appears on access being gained to the pursuers' web site. The pursuers' front page bears the heading "The Shetland Times". On an item being accessed there appears below the text a note in the following terms:

CONTACTING THE SHETLAND TIMES
Comments or suggestions on this server [sic] please to webmaster@shetland-times.co.uk.

The pursuers have expended resources in establishing this web site. It is their expectation that, once this information service becomes known to and is used by Internet users, the pursuers will be able to sell advertising space on the front page on their web site.

The defenders also operate a web site with a relative web address. The front page accessed by callers at that web address is headed "The Shetland News" and sub-headed "Main Headline Page". A number of advertisements appear on that page. Beneath those are a number of news headlines.

Since about October 14, 1996 the defenders have included among the headlines on their front page a number of headlines appearing in recent issues of The Shet-

---

† [1997] FSR 604 (Ct. Sess.).

land Times as reproduced on the pursuers' web site. These headlines are verbatim reproductions of the pursuers' headlines as so reproduced. A caller accessing the defenders' web site may, by clicking on one of those headlines appearing on the defenders' front page, gain access to the relative text as published and reproduced by the pursuers. Access is so gained and subsequent access to other such headlines also gained without the caller requiring at any stage to access the pursuers' front page. Thus, access to the pursuers' items (as published in printed editions and reproduced by them on their web site) can be obtained by by-passing the pursuers' front page and accordingly missing any advertising material which may appear on it.

In this action the pursuers seek declarator that the defenders' actings constitute an infringement of copyright owned by them. The case came before me on the pursuers' motion for interim interdict.

The grounds of action are twofold. The pursuers maintain that the headlines made available by them on their web site are cable programmes within the meaning of section 7 of the Copyright, Designs and Patents Act 1988 ("the Act"), that the facility made available by the defenders on their web site is a cable programme service within the meaning of section 7 and that the inclusion of those items in that service constitutes an infringement of copyright under section 20 of the Act. The pursuers also maintain that the headlines are literary works owned by them and that the defenders' activities constitute infringement by copying under section 17 of the Act, the copying being in the form of storing the works by electronic means.

Miss Milligan for the pursuers maintained that in respect of each of those grounds of action the pursuers had a prima facie case and that the balance of convenience favoured the grant of interim interdict. Mr MacLeod for the defenders maintained that the pursuers had no prima facie case on either ground and that the balance of convenience favoured the refusal of interim interdict.

Mr MacLeod did not dispute that copyright subsisted in the pursuers in the text of items appearing in the printed editions of The Shetland Times and in such texts therefrom as appeared on the pursuers' web site. It was acknowledged that these were literary works. It was, however, maintained that no copyright subsisted in the headlines. I shall return to that issue in due course.

The principal argument before me related to the alleged infringement under section 20. This turned essentially on an interpretation of section 7. That section, by subsection (1), defines "cable programme" as meaning "any item included in a cable programme service" and defines "cable programme service" as meaning —

> a service which consists wholly or mainly in sending visual images, sounds or other information by means of a telecommunications system, otherwise than by wireless telegraphy, for reception —
>
> (a)   at two or more places (whether for simultaneous reception or at different times in responses to requests by different users), or
> (b)   for presentation to members of the public,
>
> and which is not, or so far as it is not, excepted by or under the following provisions of this section.

Subsection (2) provides:

> The following are excepted from the definition of "cable programme service"
>
> (a)   a service or part of a service of which it is an essential feature that while visual images, sounds or other information are being conveyed by the person providing the service there will or may be sent from

each place of reception, by means of the same system or (as the case may be) the same part of it, information (other than signals sent for the operation or control of the service) for reception by the person providing the service or other persons receiving it ...

Mr MacLeod for the defenders submitted (1) that the process involved in Internet communication did not involve "sending" information, (2) that, if it did, the sending was in the circumstances done not by the pursuers but by the defenders, and (3) that, in any event, the service was an "interactive" service excepted by sub-section (2)(a). No detailed technical information was put before me in relation to the electronic mechanisms involved. It was simply submitted that there was not "sending" in an ordinary sense and that a contrast could be made with cable television where there was sending by transmission from the provider to the customer. On the Internet a caller electronically accessed information which was provided entirely passively.

In my view the pursuers' contention that the service provided by them involves the sending of information is prima facie well founded. Although in a sense the information, it seems, passively awaits access being had to it by callers, that does not, at least prima facie, preclude the notion that the information, on such access being taken, is conveyed to and received by the caller. If that is so, the process may arguably be said to involve the sending of that information.

If the information is being sent, it prima facie is being sent by the pursuers on whose web site it has been established. The fact that the information is provided to the caller by his accessing it through the defenders' web site does not, in my view, result in the defenders being the persons sending the information.

As to the argument founded on section 7(2)(a), the contention was that, because it was possible for a caller to contact the pursuers by the Internet and because comments and suggestions were encouraged by the note below the text to be transmitted by this means, any cable programme service was interactive and fell within the exception. It was also submitted that information by way of comment and suggestion could also be sent by this means to the defenders' web site. In my view, it is plainly arguable that the exception does not apply. While the facility to comment or make suggestions via the Internet exists, this does not appear to me to be an essential element in the service, the primary function of which is to distribute news and other items. In any event, it is arguable that this facility is a severable part of the pursuers' cable programme service.

The resolution of the above issues may in the end turn on technical material not available to me at the hearing on interim interdict. On the information that was available and on the basis of the arguments presented, the pursuers have, in my opinion, a prima facie case that the incorporation by the defenders in their web site of the headlines provided at the pursuers' web site constitutes an infringement of section 20 of the Act by the inclusion in a cable programme service of protected cable programmes.

As to section 17, Mr MacLeod submitted that headlines such as "Bid to save centre after council funding 'cock up'" and the other headlines complained of in the Summons were not original literary works within the meaning of the Act and that accordingly there was no infringement in copying them by any means. It was submitted that there was not such expenditure of skill or labour as to make any of them original literary works; they were "ordinary in the extreme". Mr MacLeod did not go so far as to submit that no newspaper headline could ever attract copyright. His position was that those complained of did not.

I was not referred to any authority on this aspect. While literary merit is not a necessary element of a literary work, there may be a question whether headlines, which are essentially brief indicators of the subject matter of the items to which they relate, are protected by copyright. However, in light of the concession that a headline could be a literary work and since the headlines at issue (or at least some of them) involve eight or so words designedly put together for the purpose of imparting information, it appeared to me to be arguable that there was an infringement, at least in some instances, of section 17.

The balance of convenience clearly, in my view, favoured the grant of interim interdict subject to certain amendments in the formulation of the conclusion. The defenders' activities of which complaint is made have just begun. It was not suggested that they would sustain any loss if prevented ad interim from making use of the pursuers' material in this way. It was fundamental to the setting up by the pursuers of their web site that access to their material should be gained only by accessing their web directly. While there has been no loss to date, there is a clear prospect of loss of potential advertising revenue in the foreseeable future. The extent of any loss will be difficult to quantify. There was, in the circumstances, no substance, in my view, in the suggestion that the pursuers were gaining an advantage by their newspaper items being made available more readily through the defenders' web site.

Certain amendments having been made to the second conclusion, I granted interim interdict in terms of that conclusion as amended.

Intellectual Reserve, Inc. v. Utah Lighthouse Ministry, Inc.[†]

The United States Copyright Act allows a court to "grant temporary and final injunctions on such terms as it may deem reasonable to prevent or restrain infringement of a copyright." Here, in determining whether plaintiff is now entitled to the injunctive relief, the following factors are to be considered:

> (1) substantial likelihood that the movant will eventually prevail on the merits; (2) a showing that the movant will suffer irreparable injury unless the injunction issues; (3) proof that the threatened injury to the movant outweighs whatever damage the proposed injunction may cause the opposing party; and (4) a showing that the injunction, if issued, would not be adverse to the public interest.

I.   LIKELIHOOD OF PLAINTIFF PREVAILING ON THE MERITS

First, the court considers whether there is a substantial likelihood that plaintiff will eventually prevail on the merits. Plaintiff alleges that the defendants infringed its copyright directly by posting substantial portions of its copyrighted material on defendants' website, and also contributed to infringement of its copyright by inducing, causing or materially contributing to the infringing conduct of another. To determine the proper scope of the preliminary injunction, the court considers the likelihood that plaintiff will prevail on either or both of its claims.

[†] 75 F. Supp. 2d 1290 (C.D. Utah 1999).

A. Direct Infringement

To prevail on its claim of direct copyright infringement, "plaintiff must establish both: (1) that it possesses a valid copyright and (2) that defendants copied protectable elements of the copyrighted work." Defendants initially conceded in a hearing, for purposes of the temporary restraining order and preliminary injunction, that plaintiff has a valid copyright in the Handbook, and that defendants directly infringed plaintiff's copyright by posting substantial portions of the copyrighted material. Defendants changed their position, in a motion to dismiss, claiming that plaintiff has failed to allege facts necessary to show ownership of a valid copyright. Despite the defendants' newly-raised argument, the court finds, for purpose of this motion, that the plaintiff owns a valid copyright on the material defendants posted on their website. Plaintiff has provided evidence of a copyright registration certificate and the certificate "constitutes prima facie evidence of the validity of the copyright." Defendants have not advanced any additional affirmative defenses to the claim of direct infringement. Therefore, the court finds that there is a substantial likelihood that plaintiff will prevail on its claim of direct infringement.

B. Contributory Infringement

According to plaintiff, after the defendants were ordered to remove the Handbook from their website, the defendants began infringing plaintiff's copyright by inducing, causing, or materially contributing to the infringing conduct of others. It is undisputed that defendants placed a notice on their website that the Handbook was online, and gave three website addresses of websites containing the material defendants were ordered to remove from their website. Defendants also posted e-mails on their website that encouraged browsing those websites, printing copies of the Handbook and sending the Handbook to others.

Although the copyright statute does not expressly impose liability for contributory infringement, the absence of such express language in the copyright statute does not preclude the imposition of liability for copyright infringements on certain parties who have not themselves engaged in the infringing activity. For vicarious liability is imposed in virtually all areas of the law, and the concept of contributory infringement is merely a species of the broader problem of identifying the circumstances in which it is just to hold one accountable for the actions of another.

Liability for contributory infringement is imposed when "one who, with knowledge of the infringing activity, induces, causes or materially contributes to the infringing conduct of another." Thus, to prevail on its claim of contributory infringement, plaintiff must first be able to establish that the conduct defendants allegedly aided or encouraged could amount to infringement. Defendants argue that they have not contributed to copyright infringement by those who posted the Handbook on websites nor by those who browsed the websites on their computers.

1. Can the Defendants Be Liable Under a Theory of Contributory Infringement for the Actions of Those Who Posted the Handbook on the Three Websites?

A. DID THOSE WHO POSTED THE HANDBOOK ON THE WEBSITES INFRINGE PLAINTIFF'S COPYRIGHT?

During a hearing on the motion to vacate the temporary restraining order, defendants accepted plaintiff's proffer that the three websites contain the material which plaintiff alleges is copyrighted. Therefore, plaintiff at trial is likely to establish that those who have posted the material on the three websites are directly infringing plaintiff's copyright.

B. DID THE DEFENDANTS INDUCE, CAUSE OR MATERIALLY CONTRIBUTE TO THE INFRINGEMENT?

The evidence now before the court indicates that there is no direct relationship between the defendants and the people who operate the three websites. The defendants did not provide the website operators with the plaintiff's copyrighted material, nor are the defendants receiving any kind of compensation from them. The only connection between the defendants and those who operate the three websites appears to be the information defendants have posted on their website concerning the infringing sites. Based on this scant evidence, the court concludes that plaintiff has not shown that defendants contributed to the infringing action of those who operate the infringing websites.

2. *Can the Defendants Be Liable Under a Theory of Contributory Infringement for the Actions of Those Who Browse the Three Infringing Websites?*

Defendants make two arguments in support of their position that the activities of those who browse the three websites do not make them liable under a theory of contributory infringement. First, defendants contend that those who browse the infringing websites are not themselves infringing plaintiff's copyright; and second, even if those who browse the websites are infringers, defendants have not materially contributed to the infringing conduct.

A. DO THOSE WHO BROWSE THE WEBSITES INFRINGE PLAINTIFF'S COPYRIGHT?

The first question, then, is whether those who browse any of the three infringing websites are infringing plaintiff's copyright. Central to this inquiry is whether the persons browsing are merely viewing the Handbook (which is not a copyright infringement), or whether they are making a copy of the Handbook (which is a copyright infringement).

"Copy" is defined in the Copyright Act as: "material objects ... in which a work is fixed by any method now known or later developed, and from which the work can be perceived, reproduced, or otherwise communicated, either directly or with the aid of a machine or device." "A work is fixed ... when it's ... sufficiently permanent or stable to permit it to be perceived, reproduced, or otherwise communicated for a period of more than transitory duration."

When a person browses a website, and by so doing displays the Handbook, a copy of the Handbook is made in the computer's random access memory (RAM), to permit viewing of the material. And in making a copy, even a temporary one, the person who browsed infringes the copyright. Additionally, a person making a printout or re-posting a copy of the Handbook on another website would infringe plaintiff's copyright.

B. DID THE DEFENDANTS INDUCE, CAUSE OR MATERIALLY CONTRIBUTE TO THE INFRINGEMENT?

The court now considers whether the defendants' actions contributed to the infringement of plaintiff's copyright by those who browse the three websites.

The following evidence establishes that defendants have actively encouraged the infringement of plaintiff's copyright. After being ordered to remove the Handbook from their website, defendants posted on their website: "Church Handbook of

Instructions is back online!" and listed the three website addresses. Defendants also posted e-mail suggesting that the lawsuit against defendants would be affected by people logging onto one of the websites and downloading the complete handbook. One of the e-mails posted by the defendants mentioned sending a copy of the copyrighted material to the media. In response to an e-mail stating that the sender had unsuccessfully tried to browse a website that contained the Handbook, defendants gave further instruction on how to browse the material. At least one of the three websites encourages the copying and posting of copies of the allegedly infringing material on other websites.

Based on the above, the court finds that the first element necessary for injunctive relief is satisfied.

· · · ·

Therefore, for the reasons stated, the court orders the following preliminary injunction:

1. Defendants, their agents and those under their control, shall remove from and not post on defendants' website the material alleged to infringe plaintiff's copyright;
2. Defendants, their agents and those under their control, shall not reproduce or distribute verbatim, in a tangible medium, material alleged to infringe plaintiff's copyright;
3. Defendants, their agents and those under their control, shall remove from and not post on defendants' website, addresses to websites that defendants know, or have reason to know, contain the material alleged to infringe plaintiff's copyright;

Re Tariff 22, Internet[†]

I. INTRODUCTORY REMARKS
Pursuant to section 67 of the Copyright Act, R.S.C. 1985, c. C-42 (the "Act"), the Society of Composers, Authors and Publishers of Music of Canada (SOCAN) filed with the Board statements of proposed royalties for the public performance, or the communication to the public by telecommunication, in Canada, of musical or dramatico-musical works for the years 1996 to 1998. The statements were published in the Canada Gazette on September 30, 1995, October 19, 1996 and October 18, 1997, respectively. The Board also gave notice to users of their right to file objections to the proposed tariffs.

The proposed tariffs included an item 22 (Transmission of Musical Works to Subscribers Via a Telecommunications Service Not Covered under Tariff Nos. 16 or 17). As drafted, Tariff 22 targets the communication of musical works by means of computers or other devices connected to a telecommunications network where the transmission of those works can be accessed by a person independently of any other person. "Telecommunications service" is defined as including operations that provide

---

† *SOCAN Statement of Royalties, Public Performance of Musical Works 1996, 1997, 1998 (sub nom. Re Tariff 22, Internet)* 1 C.P.R. 4th 417.

for or authorize the digital encoding, random access and/or storage of musical works for transmission via a telecommunications network, or that provide access to such a network. The tariff as drafted is therefore sufficiently broad to cover almost any computer network. However, the record of these proceedings deals almost exclusively with the Internet, which SOCAN says ought to be the primary target of the tariff. Accordingly, this is the primary focus of the decision.

Some of the objections to the proposed tariff raised issues of a preliminary nature. The Board opted to conduct the hearings in two phases. The first would determine which activities on the Internet, if any, constitute a protected use targeted in the tariff. The second would deal with who should pay the tariff as well as the tariff structure.

On November 12, 1996, the Board raised with participants a number of issues, including:

(a) whether there is a communication by telecommunication to the public when a musical work is electronically transmitted, made available, uploaded, downloaded or browsed;
(b) if there is a communication, who effects it, who is liable for it and whether anyone can claim the exemption in subsection 2.4(1)(b) of the Act;
(c) whether the answers would be different where a musical work is embedded in a radio or television signal;
(d) whether any of the uses outlined above are covered by the retransmission regime;
(e) whether a communication over a network for which access is restricted is a communication to the public;
(f) the circumstances in which a communication occurs in Canada;
(g) whether the Board may approve a tariff applicable to persons located outside of Canada; and
(h) whether there are any tariff structures that the Board is prohibited from adopting.

The Canadian Motion Picture Distributors Association (CMPDA), the Canadian Recording Industry Association (CRIA), the Canadian Association of Internet Providers (CAIP), the Canadian Cable Television Association (CCTA), AT&T Canada, MCI Communications Corporation, ExpressVu, the Canadian Association of Broadcasters (CAB), Time Warner, Stentor Telecom Policy Inc. and the Canadian Broadcasting Corporation participated in the proceedings as objectors or intervenors. CMPDA and CRIA supported the tariff, while everyone else opposed it or argued that the people they represent should not be liable for it.

What follows are the Board's reasons on Phase I issues. The hearings dealing with this matter required eleven days which ended on May 15, 1998. Filing of arguments and replies was completed on October 13, 1998.

· · · ·

III. ANALYSIS

The Board's conclusions on the issues raised in these proceedings can be summarized as follows:

1) A musical work is not communicated when it is made available on a server.

2) A musical work is communicated by telecommunication when a server containing the work responds to a request and packets are transmitted over the Internet for the purpose of allowing the recipient to hear, see or copy the work.

3) The public or private character of a communication over the Internet can be determined according to established legal and jurisprudential principles.

4) A communication need not be instantaneous or simultaneous to be a communication to the public.

5) By making a work available, a person authorizes its communication.

6) The person who made a work available communicates it when it is transmitted from any server (host, cache, mirror).

7) Persons who can avail themselves of paragraph 2.4(1)(b) of the Act with respect to a given communication of a work do not communicate the work. Generally speaking, this includes all entities acting as Internet intermediaries such as the ISP of the person who makes the work available, persons whose servers acts as a cache or mirror, the recipient's ISP and those who operate routers used in the transmission.

8) An entity cannot claim the benefit of paragraph 2.4(1)(b) with respect to a given communication of a work if the relationships it entertains with the person who made the work available are such that it can be said to act in concert with that person or if it does not confine itself to the role of an Internet intermediary.

9) The person that creates an embedded hyperlink to a work authorizes its communication. The person that merely supplies a link which must be activated by the user does not.

10) Communications occur at the site of the server from which the work is transmitted, without regard to the origin of the request or the location of the original Web site. Therefore, to occur in Canada, a communication must originate from a server located in Canada on which content has been posted. In the same vein, the communication triggered by an embedded hyperlink occurs at the site to which the link leads.

The foregoing conclusions flow from the answers the Board has given to the following questions:

1) What do "communication", "telecommunication", "public" and "musical work" mean in the context of Internet transmissions?

2) When does a communication to the public occur on the Internet?

3) Who communicates on the Internet? In particular, who can benefit from paragraph 2.4(1)(b) of the Act?

4) When does the act of authorizing a communication on the Internet occur?

5) When does a communication on the Internet occur in Canada?

Most of the answers to these questions can be derived from recent decisions of the Federal Court of Appeal dealing with the nature of television and cable transmissions. A few other issues that were raised during the course of these proceedings are addressed at the end of these reasons.

For their part, American precedents are numerous. However, the important distinctions that exist between American and Canadian copyright law on issues such as distribution rights and contributory infringement, coupled with the detailed statutory provisions that now address the liability of ISPs mean that American cases are of little relevance in determining the application of Canadian legal principles in these matters.

· · · ·

2. *The person that creates an automatic or embedded hyperlink to a work authorizes the communication of the work from the site to which the link leads. The person that merely supplies a link which must be activated by the user does not.*

In itself, the creation of hyperlinks does not involve a communication to the public of any works contained at the linked sites. In their simplest form, hyperlinks represent an electronic directory of addresses.

However, the content provider who includes into a Web page an automatic link which effects the transmission of a musical work to the recipient without the need for further action by the end user holds itself out as responsible for the material at the linked sites and therefore, authorizes its communication. This will be true even in the [page 459] absence of a business relationship with the owner of the linked sites. By creating such automatic hyperlinks, the site owner makes itself "a party in interest to the [communication] by warranting the right to [communicate]".

Discussion Questions

1. Although the judge in *Shetland Times* granted an injunction on the links, does the judgment actually suggest that hyperlinks infringe upon copyright? Is the analogy of the Internet to a "cable program" an effective analogy? The *Shetland Times* case eventually settled minutes before a full trial was set to commence.

2. Does posting material on the Internet create an implied licence for other Web users to link to it unless otherwise stipulated? By prohibiting linking through copyright protection, has the law sterilized the original purpose of the World Wide Web — the creation a web of information?

3. Consider the situation where a patented device is commercially made available. At common law, the purchaser has an implied licence to use the goods upon purchase. It was stated in *Badische-Anilin und Soda Fabrik* v. *Isler*, [1906] 23 R.P.C. 173 that:

   > If a patentee sells the patented article to a purchaser and the purchaser uses it, he, of course, does not infringe. But why? By reason of the fact that the law presumes from the sale of an implied licence given by the patentee to the purchaser that he shall use that which he bought, and in the absence of condition, this implied licence is a licence to use or sell or deal with the goods as the purchaser pleases.

   This concept has been held to be equally applicable to the sale of copyrighted material. See *North American Systemshops Ltd.* v. *King* (1989), 27 C.P.R. (3d) 367 (Alta. Q.B.). Should a similar concept be applied to Web links?

4. The *Utah Lighthouse* case suggests that courts can prohibit linking in certain circumstances. Is there an effective alternative? Given the widespread practice of mirroring content on multiple Web sites, is a prohibition on display of content rendered meaningless if linking is not also included in the prohibition?

5. The Tariff 22 decision refers to "imbedded hyperlinks." This is a relatively un-
    common type of link that executes automatically without requiring the user to
    actually click on the link.

6. How important is the technology that underpins linking? From a technological
    perspective, a link is a little more than a request to view an electronic docu-
    ment. It is actually the copyright owner that "chooses" to provide the docu-
    ment by responding to the request. Viewed in this way, the link is little more
    than a "speedy citation." Since there is no prohibition on citing documents,
    should an electronic citation be treated differently?

7. One of the most contentious linking issues has involved "deep linking," the
    practice of linking to a document found within a Web site rather than to its
    "front page." The first legal action involving deep linking pitted Microsoft
    against Ticketmaster. Microsoft maintained a Web city guide called Sidewalk.
    In the events section of the site, it allowed visitors to purchase tickets to
    events online by linking directly to the event itself within the Ticketmaster
    site. Ticketmaster objected, arguing that all users should access its site from
    the front page and navigate to the desired event.

    The case settled before going to trial, but raised many interesting
    questions. Is there such a thing as a "deep link?" Can a Web site force users
    to enter through its front page? Why would a Web site object to the additional
    traffic and sales created by the deep link? Would a technological solution,
    such as coding Web pages to "bounce" to the front page, or placing content
    in a database and creating new pages on the fly, not solve this issue?

    Since the Microsoft-Ticketmaster dispute, several similar cases have
    arisen. In Canada, a 20 year old Ottawa resident, Jean-Pierre Bazinet, was
    asked in 1999 to remove deep links from his Movie List site (<www.movie-
    list.com>) to movie trailers on the Universal Studios Web site on the grounds
    that the studio preferred users to access the site through its front page.
    Bazinet complied with the request after the studio contacted his ISP, who
    then threatened to shut him down.

    Ticketmaster found itself embroiled in another linking dispute in March
    2000, this time with competitor Tickets.com. A request for a preliminary
    injunction against the deep linking practice was rejected, with the court
    stating the following.

    Ticketmaster Corp. v. Tickets.Com, Inc.[†]

    The web site of plaintiffs Ticketmaster Corporation and Ticketmaster Online-
    CitySearch, Inc. (hereafter collectively in the singular Ticketmaster) operates to
    allow customers to purchase tickets to various events (concerts, ball games,
    etc.) through an internet connection with its customers. On the Ticketmaster
    home page, there are instructions and a directory to subsequent pages (one
    per event). The event pages provide basic information (short description of the
    event, date, time, place, and price) and a description of how to order tickets by
    either internet response, telephone, mail, or in person. Each of these subse-
    quent pages is identifiable with an electronic address. The home page further
    contains (if a customer scrolls to the bottom) "terms and conditions" which pro-
    scribe, among other things, copying for commercial use. However, the customer

† 2000 U.S. Dist. LEXIS 4553 (C.D. Cal. 2000).

need not view the terms and conditions to proceed straight to the event page which interests him. Ticketmaster has exclusive agreements with the events it carries on its web pages so that tickets are not generally available to those events except through Ticketmaster (or reserved for sale by the event itself, or available from premium ticket brokers who generally charge higher than face value).

Tickets also operates a web site (Tickets.Com) which performs a somewhat different ticketing service. While Tickets does sell some tickets to certain events on its own, it also provides information as to where and how tickets which it does not sell may be purchased. A short factual description as to event, time, date, place and price is listed. Where Tickets does not itself sell the tickets, a place is given the customers to click for a reference to another ticket broker, or to another on-line ticket seller. Here is where the unique feature of this case — hyperlinks or deep linking — comes in. Where the exclusive ticket broker is Ticketmaster, and the customer clicks on "Buy this ticket from another on-line ticketing company", the customer is instantly transferred to the interior web page of Ticketmaster (bypassing the home page) for the particular event in question, where the customer may buy the tickets (from Ticketmaster, not Tickets) on-line. An explanation is generally given by Tickets as follows: "These tickets are sold by another ticketing company. Although we can't sell them to you, the link above will take you directly to the other company's web site where you can purchase them." The interior web page contains the Ticketmaster logo and the customer must know he is dealing with Ticketmaster, not Tickets.

In order to obtain the basic information on Ticketmaster events, Tickets is alleged to copy the interior web pages and extract the basic information (event, place, time, date, and price) from them. That information is then placed in Tickets format on its own interior web pages. Tickets no longer (if it once did as alleged) merely copies the Ticketmaster event page on its own event page. However, by the use of hyper-linking (i.e. electronic transfer to the particularly numbered interior web page of Ticketmaster), the customer is transferred directly to the Ticketmaster interior event page.

. . . .

Further, hyperlinking does not itself involve a violation of the Copyright Act (whatever it may do for other claims) since no copying is involved, the customer is automatically transferred to the particular genuine web page of the original author. There is no deception in what is happening. This is analogous to using a library's card index to get reference to particular items, albeit faster and more efficiently.

FRAMING

"Framing" is a very common design feature incorporated into many pages on the Web. Originally conceived by Netscape Communications Corporation as a proprietary feature to its Web browser, framing allows the Web page designer to split the viewer screen into multiple windows ("frames"). Each frame operates as an independent browser window containing an individual Web page. Unlike linking, the concept of framing permits the designer to incorporate entire sites within another Web page.

The Federal Court of Canada had the opportunity to consider the legal implications of framing in a copyright and trademark dispute between Imax and Showmax, two large screen movie companies. The court was sympathetic to the framed party, issuing a temporary injunction barring the practice.

Imax Corp. v. Showmax Inc.[†]

On March 30, 1999 the plaintiff [Imax] commenced this action against Showmax Inc. for trade-mark infringement, passing off, depreciation of goodwill, and statutory trade libel under the Trade-marks Act R.S.C. 1985, c. T-13, as amended, and for copyright infringement.

The action is based on the defendant's use of the trade-mark and trade name Showmax in association with a large-format motion picture theatre to be opened at the Forum Entertainment Centre in Montréal, and the advertisements for this theatre on banners, magazines and through an internet website which all bear the name Showmax.

The plaintiff states that since as early as November 1996, Showmax has provided real estate development and consulting services in relation to the development and operation of large-format motion picture in Canada in association with the trademark SHOWMAX.

In July 1998, Showmax announced publicly that it had entered into an agreement with Canderel to open a 450-seat large-format motion picture theatre under the name Showmax in Montréal, Québec at the Forum Entertainment Center (the site of the hockey arena formerly known as The Montréal Forum) which is scheduled to open in late 1999.

On July 23, 1998, Canderel Properties Limited SDG Montreal Forum Company, and Société RECP de Montréal registered a partnership in Québec under the name "The Forum Entertainment Center G.P." with the object of developing the Montréal Forum into a fully integrated multi-tenant entertainment and retail centre.

In October 1998, Canderel Properties Limited announced that construction on the Forum Entertainment Centre had begun, that Showmax would be a major tenant, and that it had formed the Montréal Forum Entertainment Company with partners, Simon Property Group, DJL Real Estate Capital Partners, and Madison Marquette to fund and develop the complex.

Showmax is responsible for an internet website with the following address, or Universal Resource Locator (URL): http://www.showmax.com. Showmax has used this site to advertise the opening of the Showmax large-format theatre at the Forum Entertainment Centre.

The plaintiff states that the technology page on the Showmax website offers further links, including one which leads the viewer to the Old Port of Montréal website, which appears still framed within the framing page of the Showmax website. The Old Port of Montréal website, as framed, contains information and advertising regarding the Imax theatre at the Old Port of Montreal and displays the Imax trade-mark.

---

† [2000] F.C.J. No. 69.

The plaintiff states that the arrangement of framing and linking causes the viewer to be likely to infer that Imax is responsible for, or is connected with Showmax, for the purposes of the proposed large-format Showmax theatre.

. . . .

... [I]n my view there may be evidence of confusion between the trade-marks of Imax and Showmax to satisfy the first part of the test, that is, a serious issue to argue. Firstly, the affidavit of G. Mary Ruby states at page 3, paragraph 7, that Showmax is exhibiting an image of an Imax theatre in its promotional materials. Specifically, the image from the film Skyward on screen at the Bradford Imax theatre at the National Museum of Photography, Film and Television in Bradford, England.

Secondly, I am satisfied that the Showmax website does contain images of the Imax theatre at the Old Port of Montreal and that it is reasonable to conclude that consumers would infer that the proposed Showmax theatre is operated and controlled by the same entity as the Imax theatre.

Futuredontics, Inc. v. Applied Anagramics, Inc.†

Plaintiff's FAC in general alleges that Plaintiff operates a dental referral business utilizing the anagramatic phone number "1-800-DENTIST." AAI owns the registered service mark, "1-800-DENTIST." AAI has granted Plaintiff exclusive use of the telephone number and service mark throughout the United States. "The current 1-800-DENTIST dental referral service has been entirely designed and developed by Futuredontics, which is solely responsible for its success."

In early 1996, Plaintiff decided to establish an Internet site to advertise its dental referral business. Plaintiff's site consists of a number of web pages containing graphics and text, which are copyrightable subject matter. Plaintiff registered its copyrighted web pages.

AAI established its own site sometime after March 25, 1997.

The AAI web site includes a "link" through which AAI reproduces web pages from the Futuredontics Site within a "frame" ("AAI Frame Page"). The AAI Frame Page includes a frame around a reproduction of the web page from the Futuredontics Site. The frame includes AAI's logo, information on AAI, and links to all of AAI's other web pages.... Futuredontics has never authorized AAI to reproduce the Futuredontics Site on the AAI Frame Page.

With respect to the Third Claim for relief, Plaintiff specifically, alleges that Futuredontics is the owner of the copyrighted material comprising the web pages on the Futuredontics Site. Plaintiff also alleges that AAI and the other defendants "are willfully infringing Futuredontics' copyright in the material on its web pages by copying that material to the AAI Frame Page and reproducing it there without the permission of Futuredontics."

. . . .

---

† 45 U.S. P.Q. 2D (BNA) 2005 (C.D. Ca. 1998).

To establish copyright infringement, Plaintiff must prove (1) that Plaintiff owned the copyrights, and (2) that Defendants copied Plaintiff's copyrighted work. A copyright is infringed when a person other than the owner violates any of the exclusive rights conferred by copyright. A copyright owner has several exclusive rights, including the exclusive right to "prepare derivative works based upon the copyrighted works."

Defendants contend that Plaintiff's copyright infringement claim should be dismissed because the framed link, does not create a derivative work.

The Copyright Act defines a "derivative work" as:

> a work based upon one or more preexisting works such as ... art reproduction, abridgment, condensation, or any other form in which a work may be recast, transformed, or adapted. A work consisting of editorial revisions, annotations, elaborations, or other modifications which, as a whole, represent an original work of authorship, is a "derivative work."

The parties sharply dispute what function AAI's framed link serves. Defendants contend that AAI's window or frame provides a "lens" which enables Internet users to view the information that Plaintiff itself placed on the Internet. Plaintiff's complaint, however, alleges that defendants reproduce its copyrighted web page by combining AAI material and Plaintiff's web site. ("The AAI web site includes a 'link' through which AAI reproduces web pages from the Futuredontics Site within [the AAI Frame Page]. The AAI Frame Page includes a frame around a reproduction of the web page from the Futuredontics Site.")

The parties cite to several cases which purportedly support their interpretation of the function AAI's framed link serves. None of these cases, however, is directly on point.

The parties discuss the applicability of *Mirage Editions, Inc.* v. *Albuquerque A.R.T. Co.* In *Mirage*, the Ninth Circuit held that transferring and affixing art images with glue to ceramic tiles constituted "the creation of a derivative work in violation of the copyright laws." As this Court noted, in its Order denying Plaintiff's request for a preliminary injunction, Mirage is distinguishable from the present case. In this case, AAI has not affixed an image to a ceramic tile, rather AAI appears to have placed an electronic frame or border around Plaintiff's web page.

Defendants primarily rely on *Louis Galoob Toys, Inc.* v. *Nintendo of America, Inc.* In that case, the Ninth Circuit held that a Game Genie which merely enhances audiovisual displays which originate in Nintendo game cartridges does not constitute a derivative work because, in part, it does "not incorporate a portion of a copyrighted work in some concrete or permanent form." The Court also noted that the Game Genie could not duplicate or recast a Nintendo game's output. Galoob did distinguish Mirage and noted that the Mirage decision would have been different had the plaintiff "distributed lenses that merely enabled users to view several art works simultaneously."

Nevertheless, Galoob, like Mirage, is distinguishable from the instant case. Galoob does not foreclose Plaintiff from establishing that AAI's web page, incorporates Futuredontic's web page in some "concrete or permanent form" or that AAI's framed link duplicates or recasts Plaintiff's web page.

For these reasons, the Court finds that the cases cited by the parties do not conclusively determine whether Defendants' frame page constitutes a derivative work. Therefore, the Court determines that Plaintiff's Third Claim for Relief sufficiently alleges a claim for copyright infringement.

The best known framing case to date involves TotalNews (<www.totalnews.com>), a online news provider, and several major media companies, including Washington Post, CNN, Entertainment Weekly, Los Angeles Times and Reuters (see *Washington Post Co. and others* v. *Total News*, 97 Cv. 1990 (PKL) (S.D.N.Y.)). TotalNews is a search engine dedicated to news articles posted on the Web. It had been the practice of TotalNews to link to the individual stories by displaying them within a frame. The use of the frame gave the appearance that the content from the media sites was actually that of TotalNews. The following is an excerpt from the settlement between the involved parties:

Screen Shot of the TotalNews™ Web Site†

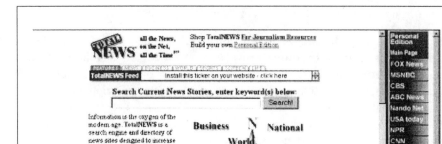

3. Subject to any modification of the terms of this stipulation and order pursuant to paragraph 10 below, Defendants agree permanently not to directly or indirectly cause any Plaintiff's website to appear on a user's computer screen with any material (e.g., Universal Resource Locator ("URL"), text, graphics, pop-up window, audio, video or other) supplied by or associated with Defendants or any third party, such as an advertiser, acting in privity with Defendants or under Defendants' direct or indirect control; in particular, Defendants agree permanently to cease the practice of "framing" Plaintiffs' websites as that practice is described in the complaint in this case.

4. Plaintiffs agree that Defendants may link from the totalnews.com website or any other website to any Plaintiff's website, provided that:

(a) Defendants may link to Plaintiffs' websites only via hyperlinks consisting of the names of the linked sites in plain text, which may be highlighted;

(b) Defendants may not use on any website, as hyperlinks or in any other way, any of Plaintiffs' proprietary logos or other distinctive graphics, video or audio material, nor may Defendants otherwise link in any manner reasonably likely to: (i) imply affiliation with, endorsement or sponsorship by any Plaintiff; (ii) cause confusion, mistake or deception; (iii) dilute plaintiffs' marks; or (iv) otherwise violate state or federal law;

. . . .

6. Nothing in this stipulation and order restricts Defendants from linking to any website page that (a) does not include any of a Plaintiff's proprietary content and (b) is part of any website not owned or operated by a Plaintiff, provided that Defendants may not link to any page of any website in any way that purposefully or overtly encourages users, once at the non-Plaintiff's site, to link to any Plaintiff's website in a manner forbidden by paragraph 2 above. As an illustrative example, not intended to describe the full scope of this subparagraph, it would be a violation of this subparagraph for Defendants to state on their website that a Plaintiff's website could be reached with two clicks — the first click taking the user to a third-party website, and the second click taking the user, via a hyperlink supplied by the third party, to a Plaintiff's website that would then be seen through Defendants' frame. As a second illustrative example, not intended to describe the full scope of this paragraph, it would not be a violation of this stipulation and order if Defendants simply provide a hypertext link, using frames technology, to a website page other than a Plaintiff's website, from which the user on her own is able to, and does, link to a Plaintiff's website in a manner permitted by law.

Discussion Questions

1. Is there a right of display on the Web? If competing browsers render Web pages differently and some users access pages with different screen resolutions, with the graphics disabled, or without Java, is it reasonable for a Web designer to expect that their page will be viewed in precisely the same manner by everyone accessing the page? Might the approach to framing be different in Canada by using moral rights arguments?

2. "Inlining" or embedded linking is a design technique that falls in between hyperlinks and frames. Inlining creates the opportunity to embed content in the form of text, clip art, photos, sound clips and even video clips within a Web page. Is inlining or framing any different than linking?

META-TAGS

Brookfield Communications, Inc. v. West Coast Entertainment Corporation[†]

We must venture into cyberspace to determine whether federal trademark and unfair competition laws prohibit a video rental store chain from using an entertainment-in-

---

[†] 174 F. 3d 1036 (9th Cir. 1999).

dustry information provider's trademark in the domain name of its web site and in its web site's metatags.

[The facts of case can be found at pp. 337–345 in Chapter 15 on Domain names.]

II

To resolve the legal issues before us, we must first understand the basics of the Internet and the World Wide Web. Because we will be delving into technical corners of the Internet — dealing with features such as domain names and metatags — we explain in some detail what all these things are and provide a general overview of the relevant technology.

. . . .

A Web surfer's second option when he does not know the domain name is to utilize an Internet search engine, such as Yahoo, Altavista, or Lycos. When a keyword is entered, the search engine processes it through a self-created index of web sites to generate a (sometimes long) list relating to the entered keyword. Each search engine uses its own algorithm to arrange indexed materials in sequence, so the list of web sites that any particular set of keywords will bring up may differ depending on the search engine used. Search engines look for keywords in places such as domain names, actual text on the web page, and metatags. Metatags are HTML code intended to describe the contents of the web site. There are different types of metatags, but those of principal concern to us are the "description" and "keyword" metatags. The description metatags are intended to describe the web site; the keyword metatags, at least in theory, contain keywords relating to the contents of the web site. The more often a term appears in the metatags and in the text of the web page, the more likely it is that the web page will be "hit" in a search for that keyword and the higher on the list of "hits" the web page will appear.

. . . .

So far we have considered only West Coast's use of the domain name "moviebuff.com." Because Brookfield requested that we also preliminarily enjoin West Coast from using marks confusingly similar to "MovieBuff" in metatags and buried code, we must also decide whether West Coast can, consistently with the trademark and unfair competition laws, use "MovieBuff" or "moviebuff.com" in its HTML code.

At first glance, our resolution of the infringement issues in the domain name context would appear to dictate a similar conclusion of likelihood of confusion with respect to West Coast's use of "moviebuff.com" in its metatags. Indeed, all eight likelihood of confusion factors outlined in Part V-A — with the possible exception of purchaser care, which we discuss below — apply here as they did in our analysis of domain names; we are, after all, dealing with the same marks, the same products and services, the same consumers, etc. Disposing of the issue so readily, however, would ignore the fact that the likelihood of confusion in the domain name context resulted largely from the associational confusion between West Coast's domain name "moviebuff.com" and Brookfield's trademark "MovieBuff." The question in the metatags context is quite different. Here, we must determine whether West Coast can use "MovieBuff" or "moviebuff.com" in the metatags of its web site at "westcoastvideo.com" or at any other domain address other than "moviebuff.com" (which we have determined that West Coast may not use).

Although entering "MovieBuff" into a search engine is likely to bring up a list including "westcoastvideo.com" if West Coast has included that term in its metatags, the resulting confusion is not as great as where West Coast uses the "moviebuff.com" domain name. First, when the user inputs "MovieBuff" into an Internet search engine, the list produced by the search engine is likely to include both West Coast's and Brookfield's web sites. Thus, in scanning such list, the Web user will often be able to find the particular web site he is seeking. Moreover, even if the Web user chooses the web site belonging to West Coast, he will see that the domain name of the web site he selected is "westcoastvideo.com." Since there is no confusion resulting from the domain address, and since West Coast's initial web page prominently displays its own name, it is difficult to say that a consumer is likely to be confused about whose site he has reached or to think that Brookfield somehow sponsors West Coast's web site.

Nevertheless, West Coast's use of "moviebuff.com" in metatags will still result in what is known as initial interest confusion. Web surfers looking for Brookfield's "MovieBuff" products who are taken by a search engine to "westcoastvideo.com" will find a database similar enough to "MovieBuff" such that a sizeable number of consumers who were originally looking for Brookfield's product will simply decide to utilize West Coast's offerings instead. Although there is no source confusion in the sense that consumers know they are patronizing West Coast rather than Brookfield, there is nevertheless initial interest confusion in the sense that, by using "moviebuff.com" or "MovieBuff" to divert people looking for "MovieBuff" to its web site, West Coast improperly benefits from the goodwill that Brookfield developed in its mark. Recently in Dr. Seuss, we explicitly recognized that the use of another's trademark in a manner calculated "to capture initial consumer attention, even though no actual sale is finally completed as a result of the confusion, may be still an infringement."

The Dr. Seuss court, in recognizing that the diversion of consumers' initial interest is a form of confusion against which the Lanham Act protects, relied upon Mobil Oil. In that case, Mobil Oil Corporation ("Mobil") asserted a federal trademark infringement claim against Pegasus Petroleum, alleging that Pegasus Petroleum's use of "Pegasus" was likely to cause confusion with Mobil's trademark, a flying horse symbol in the form of the Greek mythological Pegasus. Mobil established that "potential purchasers would be misled into an initial interest in Pegasus Petroleum" because they thought that Pegasus Petroleum was associated with Mobil. But these potential customers would generally learn that Pegasus Petroleum was unrelated to Mobil well before any actual sale was consummated. See id. Nevertheless, the Second Circuit held that "such initial confusion works a sufficient trademark injury."

Mobil Oil relied upon its earlier opinion in *Grotrian, Helfferich, Schulz, Th. Steinweg Nachf.* v. *Steinway & Sons*. Analyzing the plaintiff's claim that the defendant, through its use of the "Grotrian-Steinweg" mark, attracted people really interested in plaintiff's "Steinway" pianos, the Second Circuit explained:

> We decline to hold, however, that actual or potential confusion at the time of purchase necessarily must be demonstrated to establish trademark infringement under the circumstances of this case.

> The issue here is not the possibility that a purchaser would buy a Grotrian-Steinweg thinking it was actually a Steinway or that Grotrian had some connection with Steinway and Sons. The harm to Steinway, rather, is the likelihood that a consumer, hearing the "Grotrian-Steinweg" name and thinking it had some connection with "Steinway," would consider it on that basis. The "Grotrian-Steinweg" name therefore would attract potential customers based on the reputation built up by Steinway in this country for many years.

Both Dr. Seuss and the Second Circuit hold that initial interest confusion is actionable under the Lanham Act, which holdings are bolstered by the decisions of many other courts which have similarly recognized that the federal trademark and unfair competition laws do protect against this form of consumer confusion.

Using another's trademark in one's metatags is much like posting a sign with another's trademark in front of one's store. Suppose West Coast's competitor (let's call it "Blockbuster") puts up a billboard on a highway reading — "West Coast Video: 2 miles ahead at Exit 7" — where West Coast is really located at Exit 8 but Blockbuster is located at Exit 7. Customers looking for West Coast's store will pull off at Exit 7 and drive around looking for it. Unable to locate West Coast, but seeing the Blockbuster store right by the highway entrance, they may simply rent there. Even consumers who prefer West Coast may find it not worth the trouble to continue searching for West Coast since there is a Blockbuster right there. Customers are not confused in the narrow sense: they are fully aware that they are purchasing from Blockbuster and they have no reason to believe that Blockbuster is related to, or in any way sponsored by, West Coast. Nevertheless, the fact that there is only initial consumer confusion does not alter the fact that Blockbuster would be misappropriating West Coast's acquired goodwill.

The few courts to consider whether the use of another's trademark in one's metatags constitutes trademark infringement have ruled in the affirmative. For example, in a case in which Playboy Enterprises, Inc. ("Playboy") sued AsiaFocus International, Inc. ("AsiaFocus") for trademark infringement resulting from AsiaFocus's use of the federally registered trademarks "Playboy" and "Playmate" in its HTML code, a district court granted judgment in Playboy's favor, reasoning that AsiaFocus intentionally misled viewers into believing that its Web site was connected with, or sponsored by, Playboy.

In a similar case also involving Playboy, a district court in California concluded that Playboy had established a likelihood of success on the merits of its claim that defendants' repeated use of "Playboy" within "machine readable code in Defendants' Internet Web pages, so that the PLAYBOY trademark [was] accessible to individuals or Internet search engines which attempted to access Plaintiff under Plaintiff's PLAYBOY registered trademark" constituted trademark infringement. The court accordingly enjoined the defendants from using Playboy's marks in buried code or metatags.

In a metatags case with an interesting twist, a district court in Massachusetts also enjoined the use of metatags in a manner that resulted in initial interest confusion. In that case, the defendant Radiation Monitoring Devices ("RMD") did not simply use Niton Corporation's ("Niton") trademark in its metatags. Instead, RMD's web site directly copied Niton's web site's metatags and HTML code. As a result, whenever a search performed on an Internet search engine listed Niton's web site, it also listed RMD's site. Although the opinion did not speak in terms of initial consumer confusion, the court made clear that its issuance of preliminary injunctive relief was based on the fact that RMD was purposefully diverting people looking for Niton to its web site.

Consistently with Dr. Seuss, the Second Circuit, and the cases which have addressed trademark infringement through metatags use, we conclude that the Lanham Act bars West Coast from including in its metatags any term confusingly similar with Brookfield's mark. West Coast argues that our holding conflicts with Holiday Inns, in which the Sixth Circuit held that there was no trademark infringement where an alleged infringer merely took advantage of a situation in which confusion was likely to exist and did not affirmatively act to create consumer confusion. Unlike the defendant in Holiday Inns, however, West Coast was not a passive figure; instead, it acted affirmatively in placing Brookfield's trademark in the metatags of its web site, thereby creating the initial interest confusion. Accordingly, our conclusion comports with Holiday Inns.

C

Contrary to West Coast's contentions, we are not in any way restricting West Coast's right to use terms in a manner which would constitute fair use under the Lanham Act. It is well established that the Lanham Act does not prevent one from using a competitor's mark truthfully to identify the competitor's goods.

In Welles, the case most on point, Playboy sought to enjoin former Playmate of the Year Terri Welles ("Welles") from using "Playmate" or "Playboy" on her web site featuring photographs of herself. Welles's web site advertised the fact that she was a former Playmate of the Year, but minimized the use of Playboy's marks; it also contained numerous disclaimers stating that her site was neither endorsed by nor affiliated with Playboy. The district court found that Welles was using "Playboy" and "Playmate" not as trademarks, but rather as descriptive terms fairly and accurately describing her web page, and that her use of "Playboy" and "Playmate" in her web site's metatags was a permissible, good faith attempt to index the content of her web site. It accordingly concluded that her use was permissible under the trademark laws.

We agree that West Coast can legitimately use an appropriate descriptive term in its metatags. But "MovieBuff" is not such a descriptive term. Even though it differs from "Movie Buff" by only a single space, that difference is pivotal. The term "Movie Buff" is a descriptive term, which is routinely used in the English language to describe a movie devotee. "MovieBuff" is not. The term "MovieBuff" is not in the dictionary. Nor has that term been used in any published federal or state court opinion. In light of the fact that it is not a word in the English language, when the term "MovieBuff" is employed, it is used to refer to Brookfield's products and services, rather than to mean "motion picture enthusiast." The proper term for the "motion picture enthusiast" is "Movie Buff," which West Coast certainly can use. It cannot, however, omit the space.

Moreover, West Coast is not absolutely barred from using the term "MovieBuff." As we explained above, that term can be legitimately used to describe Brookfield's product. For example, its web page might well include an advertisement banner such as "Why pay for MovieBuff when you can get the same thing here for FREE?" which clearly employs "MovieBuff" to refer to Brookfield's products. West Coast, however, presently uses Brookfield's trademark not to reference Brookfield's products, but instead to describe its own product (in the case of the domain name) and to attract people to its web site in the case of the metatags. That is not fair use.

. . . .

VII

[...] Similarly, using a competitor's trademark in the metatags of such web site is likely to cause what we have described as initial interest confusion. [...]

Notes

1. Canada had its own high profile meta-tag dispute in the battle between its two leading online bookstores, Chapters.ca and Indigo.ca. In the summer of 1999 it was revealed that Chapters had inserted the term "Indigo" into its meta-tags. The company removed the term after Indigo threatened legal action.

2. Superior Radiant Products, a Canadian heating equipment supplier, faced a lawsuit in the United States based on its insertion of a competitor's name into its meta-tags. A federal court in New York asserted jurisdiction over the case in February 2000 with the case scheduled for trial later in the year. The jurisdictional decision can be found as *Roberts-Gordon, LLC* v. *Superior Radiant Products, Ltd.*, 2000 U.S. Dist. LEXIS 2475 (W.D.N.Y., 2000).

SPIDERING

With millions of Web pages online, finding relevant information on the Internet is often a challenge. The primary resource for uncovering content are search engines such as Altavista and Google, which catalogue millions of pages in huge databases. Search engines employ a technology known as "spidering" to index Web pages. Spiders are automated software programs that track millions of Web pages and copy their content.

The use of spiders has grown increasingly controversial as new graphical search engines track graphics rather than text, and companies establish business models based on the aggregation of information obtained by spidering other sites.

Kelly v. Arriba Soft Corp†

Defendant Ditto (formerly known as Arriba) operates a "visual search engine" on the Internet. Like other Internet search engines, it allows a user to obtain a list of related Web content in response to a search query entered by the user. Unlike other Internet search engines, Defendant's retrieves images instead of descriptive text. It produces a list of reduced, "thumbnail" pictures related to the user's query.

---

† 1999 WL 1210918 (C.D. Cal. 1999).

During the period when most of the relevant events in this case occurred, Defendant's visual search engine was known as the Arriba Vista Image Searcher. By "clicking" on the desired thumbnail, an Arriba Vista user could view the "image attributes" window displaying the full-size version of the image, a description of its dimensions, and an address for the Web site where it originated. By clicking on the address, the user could link to the originating Web site for the image.

Ditto's search engine (in both of its versions) works by maintaining an indexed database of approximately two million thumbnail images. These thumbnails are obtained through the operation of Ditto's "crawler," a computer program that travels the Web in search of images to be converted into thumbnails and added to the index. Ditto's employees conduct a final screening to rank the most relevant thumbnails and eliminate inappropriate images.

Plaintiff Kelly is a photographer specializing in photographs of California gold rush country and related to the works of Laura Ingalls Wilder. He does not sell the photographs independently, but his photographs have appeared in several books. Plaintiff also maintains two Web sites, one of which (www.goldrush1849.com) provides a "virtual tour" of California's gold rush country and promotes Plaintiff's book on the subject, and the other (www.showmethegold.com) markets corporate retreats in California's gold rush country.

In January 1999, around thirty five of Plaintiff's images were indexed by the Ditto crawler and put in Defendant's image database. As a result, these images were made available in thumbnail form to users of Defendant's visual search engine. After being notified of Plaintiff's objections, Ditto removed the images from its database, though due to various technical problems some of the images reappeared a few times. Meanwhile Plaintiff, having sent Defendant a notice of copyright infringement in January, filed this action in April. Plaintiff argues its copyrights in the images were infringed by Defendant's actions and also alleges Defendant violated the Digital Millennium Copyright Act (DMCA) by removing or altering the copyright management information associated with Plaintiff's images.

A.   FAIR USE

In order to show copyright infringement, Plaintiff must show ownership of a valid copyright and invasion of one of the exclusive rights of copyright holders. Defendant does not dispute the validity of Plaintiff's copyrights or his ownership of them. Defendant also does not dispute it reproduced and displayed Plaintiff's images in thumbnail form without authorization. Plaintiff thus has shown a prima facie case of copyright infringement unless the fair use doctrine applies.

"Fair use" is a limitation on copyright owners' exclusive right "to reproduce the copyrighted work in copies." It is codified at 17 U.S.C. s 107, which provides:

> Notwithstanding the provisions of sections 106 and 106A, the fair use of a copyrighted work, including such use by reproduction in copies or phonorecords or by any other means specified by that section, for purposes such as criticism, comment, news reporting, teaching (including multiple copies for classroom use), scholarship, or research, is not an infringement of copyright.

In determining whether the use made of a work in any particular case is a fair use the factors to be considered shall include —

(1) the purpose and character of the use, including whether such use is of a commercial nature or is for nonprofit educational purposes;
(2) the nature of the copyrighted work;
(3) the amount and substantiality of the portion used in relation to the copyrighted work as a whole; and
(4) the effect of the use upon the potential market for or value of the copyrighted work.

The fact that a work is unpublished shall not itself bar a finding of fair use if such finding is made upon consideration of all the above factors. Fair use is an affirmative defense, and defendants carry the burden of proof on the issue. Based on an analysis of the factors, the Court finds there is fair use here.

1. Purpose and Character Of The Use

The first factor considers the nature of the use, including whether the use is commercial or educational. This, however, does not end the inquiry. "Purpose and character" also involve an assessment of whether "the new work merely supersedes the objects of the original creation, or instead adds something new, with a further purpose or different character, altering the first with new expression, meaning, or message; it asks, in other words, whether and to what extent the new work is transformative." *Campbell* v. *Acuff-Rose Music*, 510 U.S. 569, 579 (1994) (citation omitted). "[T]he more transformative the new work, the less will be the significance of other factors, like commercialism, that may weigh against a finding of fair use."

There is no dispute Defendant operates its Web site for commercial purposes. Plaintiff's images, however, did not represent a significant element of that commerce, nor were they exploited in any special way. They were reproduced as a result of Defendant's generally indiscriminate method of gathering images. Defendant has a commercial interest in developing a comprehensive thumbnail index so it can provide more complete results to users of its search engine. The Ditto crawler is designed to obtain large numbers of images from numerous sources without seeking authorization. Plaintiff's images were indexed as a result of these methods. While the use here was commercial, it was also of a somewhat more incidental and less exploitative nature than more traditional types of "commercial use."

The most significant factor favoring Defendant is the transformative nature of its use of Plaintiff's images. Defendant's use is very different from the use for which the images were originally created. Plaintiff's photographs are artistic works used for illustrative purposes. Defendant's visual search engine is designed to catalog and improve access to images on the Internet. The character of the thumbnail index is not esthetic, but functional; its purpose is not to be artistic, but to be comprehensive.

To a lesser extent, the Arriba Vista image attributes page also served this purpose by allowing users to obtain more details about an image. The image attributes page, however, raises other concerns. It allowed users to view (and potentially download) full-size images without necessarily viewing the rest of the originating Web page. At the same time, it was less clearly connected to the search engine's purpose of finding and organizing Internet content for users. The presence of the image attributes page in the old version of the search engine somewhat detracts from the transformative effect of the search engine. But, when considering purpose and character of use in a new enterprise of this sort, it is more appropriate to consider the transformative purpose rather than the early imperfect means of achieving that purpose. The Court finds the purpose and character of Defendant's use was on the whole significantly transformative.

The Court finds the first factor weighs in favor of fair use.

2. Nature of the Copyrighted Work

The second factor in s 107 is an acknowledgment "that some works are closer to the core of intended copyright protection than others, with the consequence that fair use is more difficult to establish when the former works are copied." Artistic works like Plaintiff's photographs are part of that core. The Court finds the second factor weighs against fair use.

3. Amount And Substantiality of the Portion Used

The third fair use factor assesses whether the amount copied was "reasonable in relation to the purpose of the copying." The analysis focuses on "the persuasiveness of a [copier's] justification for the particular copying done, and the enquiry will harken back to the first of the statutory factors, for ... the extent of permissible copying varies with the purpose and character of the use."

In the thumbnail index, Defendant used Plaintiff's images in their entirety, but reduced them in size. Defendant argues it is necessary for a visual search engine to copy images in their entirety so users can be sure of recognizing them, and the reduction in size and resolution mitigates damage that might otherwise result from copying. As Defendant has illustrated in its brief, thumbnails cannot be enlarged into useful images. Use of partial images or images further reduced in size would make images difficult for users to identify, and would eliminate the usefulness of Defendant's search engine as a means of categorizing and improving access to Internet resources.

As with the first factor, the Arriba Vista image attributes page presents a greater problem because it displayed a full-size image separated from the surrounding content on its originating Web page. Image attributes (e.g. dimensions and the address of the originating site) could have been displayed without reproducing the full-size image, and the display of the full image was not necessary to the main purposes of the search engine. If only the thumbnail index were at issue, Defendant's copying would likely be reasonable in light of its purposes. The image attributes page, however, was more remotely related to the purposes of the search engine. The Court finds the third factor weighs slightly against fair use.

4. Effect of the Use On The Potential Market or Value

The fourth factor inquiry examines the direct impact of the defendant's use and also considers "whether unrestricted and widespread conduct of the sort engaged in by the defendant ... would result in a substantially adverse impact on the potential market for the original." The relevant market is Plaintiff's Web sites as a whole. The photographs are used to promote the products sold by Plaintiff's Web sites (including Plaintiff's books and corporate tour packages) and draw users to view the additional advertisements posted on those Web sites. The fourth factor addresses not just the potential market for a particular photo, but also its "value." The value of Plaintiff's photographs to Plaintiff could potentially be adversely affected if their promotional purposes are undermined.

Defendant argues there is no likely negative impact because its search engine does not compete with Plaintiff's Web sites and actually increases the number of users finding their way to those sites. Plaintiff argues the market for his various products has been harmed. Defendant's conduct created a possibility that some users might improperly copy and use Plaintiff's images from Defendant's site. Defendant's search engine also enabled users to "deep link" directly to the pages containing retrieved images, and thereby bypass the "front page" of the originating Web site. As a result, these users would be less likely to view all of the advertisements on the Web sites or view the Web site's entire promotional message. However, Plaintiff has shown no evidence of any harm or adverse impact.

In the absence of any evidence about traffic to Plaintiff's Web sites or effects on Plaintiff's businesses, the Court cannot find any market harm to Plaintiff. The Defendant has met its burden of proof by offering evidence tending to show a lack of market harm, and Plaintiff has not refuted that evidence. The Court finds the fourth factor weighs in favor of fair use.

5.   Conclusion — Fair Use

The Court finds two of the four factors weigh in favor of fair use, and two weigh against it. The first and fourth factors (character of use and lack of market harm) weigh in favor of a fair use finding because of the established importance of search engines and the "transformative" nature of using reduced versions of images to organize and provide access to them. The second and third factors (creative nature of the work and amount or substantiality of copying) weigh against fair use.

The first factor of the fair use test is the most important in this case. Defendant never held Plaintiff's work out as its own, or even engaged in conduct specifically directed at Plaintiff's work. Plaintiff's images were swept up along with two million others available on the Internet, as part of Defendant's efforts to provide its users with a better way to find images on the Internet. Defendant's purposes were and are inherently transformative, even if its realization of those purposes was at times imperfect. Where, as here, a new use and new technology are evolving, the broad transformative purpose of the use weighs more heavily than the inevitable flaws in its early stages of development.

The Court has weighed all of the s 107 factors together. The Court finds Defendant's conduct constituted fair use of Plaintiff's images. There is no triable issue of material fact remaining to be resolved on the question of fair use, and summary adjudication is appropriate. Defendant's motion is GRANTED and Plaintiff's motion is DENIED as to the copyright infringement claims.

Ebay v. Bidder's Edge Inc.[†]

BACKGROUND

eBay is an Internet-based, person-to-person trading site. eBay offers sellers the ability to list items for sale and prospective buyers the ability to search those listings and bid on items. The seller can set the terms and conditions of the auction. The item is sold to the highest bidder. The transaction is consummated directly between the buyer and seller without eBay's involvement. A potential purchaser looking for a particular item can access the eBay site and perform a key word search for relevant

---

† 2000 U.S. Dist. LEXIS 7287 (N.D. Cal. 2000).

auctions and bidding status. eBay has also created category listings which identify items in over 2500 categories, such as antiques, computers, and dolls. Users may browse these category listing pages to identify items of interest.

Users of the eBay site must register and agree to the eBay User Agreement. Users agree to the seven page User Agreement by clicking on an "I Accept" button located at the end of the User Agreement. The current version of the User Agreement prohibits the use of "any robot, spider, other automatic device, or manual process to monitor or copy our web pages or the content contained herein without our prior expressed written permission." It is not clear that the version of the User Agreement in effect at the time BE began searching the eBay site prohibited such activity, or that BE ever agreed to comply with the User Agreement.

eBay currently has over 7 million registered users. Over 400,000 new items are added to the site every day. Every minute, 600 bids are placed on almost 3 million items. Users currently perform, on average, 10 million searches per day on eBay's database. Bidding for and sales of items are continuously ongoing in millions of separate auctions.

A software robot is a computer program which operates across the Internet to perform searching, copying and retrieving functions on the web sites of others. A software robot is capable of executing thousands of instructions per minute, far in excess of what a human can accomplish. Robots consume the processing and storage resources of a system, making that portion of the system's capacity unavailable to the system owner or other users. Consumption of sufficient system resources will slow the processing of the overall system and can overload the system such that it will malfunction or "crash." A severe malfunction can cause a loss of data and an interruption in services.

The eBay site employs "robot exclusion headers." A robot exclusion header is a message, sent to computers programmed to detect and respond to such headers, that eBay does not permit unauthorized robotic activity. Programmers who wish to comply with the Robot Exclusion Standard design their robots to read a particular data file, "robots.txt," and to comply with the control directives it contains.

To enable computers to communicate with each other over the Internet, each is assigned a unique Internet Protocol ("IP") address. When a computer requests information from another computer over the Internet, the requesting computer must offer its IP address to the responding computer in order to allow a response to be sent. These IP addresses allow the identification of the source of incoming requests. eBay identifies robotic activity on its site by monitoring the number of incoming requests from each particular IP address. Once eBay identifies an IP address believed to be involved in robotic activity, an investigation into the identity, origin and owner of the IP address may be made in order to determine if the activity is legitimate or authorized. If an investigation reveals unauthorized robotic activity, eBay may attempt to ignore ("block") any further requests from that IP address. Attempts to block requests from particular IP addresses are not always successful.

Organizations often install "proxy server" software on their computers. Proxy server software acts as a focal point for outgoing Internet requests. Proxy servers conserve system resources by directing all outgoing and incoming data traffic through a centralized portal. Typically, organizations limit the use of their proxy servers to local users. However, some organizations, either as a public service or because of a failure to properly protect their proxy server through the use of a "firewall," allow their proxy servers to be accessed by remote users. Outgoing requests from remote users can be routed through such unprotected proxy servers and appear to originate from the proxy server. Incoming responses are then received by the proxy server and routed to the remote user. Information requests sent through such proxy servers cannot easily be traced back to the originating IP address and can be used to circumvent attempts to block queries from the originating IP address. Blocking queries from innocent third party proxy servers is both inefficient, because it creates an endless game of hide-and-seek, and potentially counterproductive, as it runs a substantial risk of blocking requests from legitimate, desirable users who use that proxy server.

BE is a company with 22 employees that was founded in 1997. The BE web site debuted in November 1998. BE does not host auctions. BE is an auction aggregation site designed to offer on-line auction buyers the ability to search for items across numerous on-line auctions without having to search each host site individually. As of March 2000, the BE web site contained information on more than five million items being auctioned on more than one hundred auction sites. BE also provides its users with additional auction-related services and information. The information available on the BE site is contained in a database of information that BE compiles through access to various auction sites such as eBay. When a user enters a search for a particular item at BE, BE searches its database and generates a list of every item in the database responsive to the search, organized by auction closing date and time. Rather than going to each host auction site one at a time, a user who goes to BE may conduct a single search to obtain information about that item on every auction site tracked by BE. It is important to include information regarding eBay auctions on the BE site because eBay is by far the biggest consumer to consumer on-line auction site.

· · · ·

In late August or early September 1999, eBay requested by telephone that BE cease posting eBay auction listings on its site. BE agreed to do so. In October 1999, BE learned that other auction aggregations sites were including information regarding eBay auctions. On November 2, 1999, BE issued a press release indicating that it had resumed including eBay auction listings on its site. On November 9, 1999, eBay sent BE a letter reasserting that BE's activities were unauthorized, insisting that BE cease accessing the eBay site, alleging that BE's activities constituted a civil trespass and offering to license BE's activities. eBay and BE were again unable to agree on licensing terms. As a result, eBay attempted to block BE from accessing the eBay site; by the end of November, 1999, eBay had blocked a total of 169 IP addresses it believed BE was using to query eBay's system. BE elected to continue crawling eBay's site by using proxy servers to evade eBay's IP blocks.

Approximately 69% of the auction items contained in the BE database are from auctions hosted on eBay. BE estimates that it would lose one-third of its users if it ceased to cover the eBay auctions.

The parties agree that BE accessed the eBay site approximately 100,000 times a day. eBay alleges that BE activity constituted up to 1.53% of the number of requests received by eBay, and up to 1.10% of the total data transferred by eBay during certain periods in October and November of 1999. BE alleges that BE activity constituted no more than 1.11% of the requests received by eBay, and no more than 0.70% of the data transferred by eBay. eBay alleges that BE activity had fallen 27%, to 0.74% of requests and 0.61% of data, by February 20, 2000. eBay alleges damages due to BE's activity totaling between $45,323 and $61,804 for a ten month period including seven months in 1999 and the first three months in 2000. However, these calculations appear flawed in that they assume the maximal BE usage of eBay resources continued over all ten months. Moreover, the calculations attribute a pro rata share of eBay expenditures to BE activity, rather than attempting to calculate the incremental cost to eBay due to BE activity. eBay has not alleged any specific incremental damages due to BE activity.

It appears that major Internet search engines, such as Yahoo!, Google, Excite and AltaVista, respect the Robot Exclusion Standard.

eBay now moves for preliminary injunctive relief preventing BE from accessing the eBay computer system based on nine causes of action: trespass, false advertising, federal and state trademark dilution, computer fraud and abuse, unfair competition, misappropriation, interference with prospective economic advantage and unjust enrichment. However, eBay does not move, either independently or alternatively, for injunctive relief that is limited to restricting how BE can use data taken from the eBay site.

. . . .

I.   Trespass

Trespass to chattels "lies where an intentional interference with the possession of personal property has proximately caused injury." *Thrifty-Tel* v. *Bezenek*, 46 Cal. App. 4th 1559, 1566 (1996). Trespass to chattels "although seldom employed as a tort theory in California" was recently applied to cover the unauthorized use of long distance telephone lines. Specifically, the court noted "the electronic signals generated by the [defendants'] activities were sufficiently tangible to support a trespass cause of action." Thus, it appears likely that the electronic signals sent by BE to retrieve information from eBay's computer system are also sufficiently tangible to support a trespass cause of action.

In order to prevail on a claim for trespass based on accessing a computer system, the plaintiff must establish: (1) defendant intentionally and without authorization interfered with plaintiff's possessory interest in the computer system; and (2) defendant's unauthorized use proximately resulted in damage to plaintiff. Here, eBay has presented evidence sufficient to establish a strong likelihood of proving both prongs and ultimately prevailing on the merits of its trespass claim.

a. BE's Unauthorized Interference

eBay argues that BE's use was unauthorized and intentional. eBay is correct. BE does not dispute that it employed an automated computer program to connect with and search eBay's electronic database. BE admits that, because other auction aggregators were including eBay's auctions in their listing, it continued to "crawl" eBay's web site even after eBay demanded BE terminate such activity.

BE argues that it cannot trespass eBay's web site because the site is publicly accessible. BE's argument is unconvincing. eBay's servers are private property, conditional access to which eBay grants the public. eBay does not generally permit the type of automated access made by BE. In fact, eBay explicitly notifies automated visitors that their access is not permitted. "In general, California does recognize a trespass claim where the defendant exceeds the scope of the consent." *Baugh* v. *CBS, Inc.*, 828 F. Supp. 745, 756 (N.D. Cal. 1993).

Even if BE's web crawlers were authorized to make individual queries of eBay's system, BE's web crawlers exceeded the scope of any such consent when they began acting like robots by making repeated queries.

Moreover, eBay repeatedly and explicitly notified BE that its use of eBay's computer system was unauthorized. The entire reason BE directed its queries through proxy servers was to evade eBay's attempts to stop this unauthorized access. The court concludes that BE's activity is sufficiently outside of the scope of the use permitted by eBay that it is unauthorized for the purposes of establishing a trespass.

eBay argues that BE interfered with eBay's possessory interest in its computer system. Although eBay appears unlikely to be able to show a substantial interference at this time, such a showing is not required. Conduct that does not amount to a substantial interference with possession, but which consists of intermeddling with or use of another's personal property, is sufficient to establish a cause of action for trespass to chattel.

Although the court admits some uncertainty as to the precise level of possessory interference required to constitute an intermeddling, there does not appear to be any dispute that eBay can show that BE's conduct amounts to use of eBay's computer systems. Accordingly, eBay has made a strong showing that it is likely to prevail on the merits of its assertion that BE's use of eBay's computer system was an unauthorized and intentional interference with eBay's possessory interest.

b. Damage to eBay's Computer System

A trespasser is liable when the trespass diminishes the condition, quality or value of personal property. The quality or value of personal property may be "diminished even though it is not physically damaged by defendant's conduct." The Restatement offers the following explanation for the harm requirement:

The interest of a possessor of a chattel in its inviolability, unlike the similar interest of a possessor of land, is not given legal protection by an action for nominal damages for harmless intermeddlings with the chattel. In order that an actor who interferes with another's chattel may be liable, his conduct must affect some other and more important interest of the possessor. Therefore, one who intentionally intermeddles with another's chattel is subject to liability only if his intermeddling is harmful to the possessor's materially valuable interest in the physical condition, quality, or value of the chattel, or if the possessor is deprived of the use of the chattel for a substantial time, or some other legally protected interest of the possessor is affected .... Sufficient legal protection of the possessor's interest in the mere inviolability of his chattel is afforded by his privilege to use reasonable force to protect his possession against even harmless interference.

eBay is likely to be able to demonstrate that BE's activities have diminished the quality or value of eBay's computer systems. BE's activities consume at least a portion of plaintiff's bandwidth and server capacity. Although there is some dispute as to the percentage of queries on eBay's site for which BE is responsible, BE admits that it sends some 80,000 to 100,000 requests to plaintiff's computer systems per day.

Although eBay does not claim that this consumption has led to any physical damage to eBay's computer system, nor does eBay provide any evidence to support the claim that it may have lost revenues or customers based on this use, eBay's claim is that BE's use is appropriating eBay's personal property by using valuable bandwidth and capacity, and necessarily compromising eBay's ability to use that capacity for its own purposes.

BE argues that its searches represent a negligible load on plaintiff's computer systems, and do not rise to the level of impairment to the condition or value of eBay's computer system required to constitute a trespass. However, it is undisputed that eBay's server and its capacity are personal property, and that BE's searches use a portion of this property. Even if, as BE argues, its searches use only a small amount of eBay's computer system capacity, BE has nonetheless deprived eBay of the ability to use that portion of its personal property for its own purposes. The law recognizes no such right to use another's personal property. Accordingly, BE's actions appear to have caused injury to eBay and appear likely to continue to cause injury to eBay. If the court were to hold otherwise, it would likely encourage other auction aggregators to crawl the eBay site, potentially to the point of denying effective access to eBay's customers. If preliminary injunctive relief were denied, and other aggregators began to crawl the eBay site, there appears to be little doubt that the load on eBay's computer system would qualify as a substantial impairment of condition or value. California law does not require eBay to wait for such a disaster before applying to this court for relief. The court concludes that eBay has made a strong showing that it is likely to prevail on the merits of its trespass claim, and that there is at least a possibility that it will suffer irreparable harm if preliminary injunctive relief is not granted. eBay is therefore entitled to preliminary injunctive relief.

. . . .

3. PUBLIC INTEREST

The traditional equitable criteria for determining whether an injunction should issue include whether the public interest favors granting the injunction. The parties submit a variety of declarations asserting that the Internet will cease to function if, according to eBay, personal and intellectual property rights are not respected, or, according to BE, if information published on the Internet cannot be universally accessed and used. Although the court suspects that the Internet will not only survive, but continue to grow and develop regardless of the outcome of this litigation, the court also recognizes that it is poorly suited to determine what balance between encouraging the exchange of information, and preserving economic incentives to create, will maximize the public good. Particularly on the limited record available at the preliminary injunction stage, the court is unable to determine whether the general public interest factors in favor of or against a preliminary injunction.

BE makes the more specific allegation that granting a preliminary injunction in favor of eBay will harm the public interest because eBay is alleged to have engaged in anticompetitive behavior in violation of federal antitrust law. The Ninth Circuit has noted that in evaluating whether to issue a preliminary injunction, the district court is under no obligation to consider the merits of any antitrust counterclaims once the plaintiff has demonstrated a likelihood of success on the merits. Although anticompetitive behavior may be appropriately considered in the context of a preliminary injunction based on trademark infringement, where misuse is an affirmative defense, it does not appear to be appropriately considered here, because there is no equivalent affirmative defense to trespass to chattels. Accordingly, the court concludes the public interest does not weigh against granting a preliminary injunction.

Discussion Questions

1. Do you agree with the court's characterization of computing system resources and its belief that its use can result in a legal right of action?

2. Should the court have taken the public interest more seriously? If so, where do you think the public interest lies on this issue?

3.   Should Web sites control who can access a publicly available site and how many times they can access it? Should all search engines be required to follow standards such as the Robot Exclusion Standard?

17

Digital Music and the Internet

The emergence of the MP3 as the standard for digital music transfer has created enormous upheaval within the music industry. Swapping songs online has become one of the most popular Internet activities, with companies such as Napster and MP3.com becoming household names. The popularity of MP3s is perceived by much of the music industry as a major threat. Leading the charge has been the Recording Industry Association of America, which has launched a series of high profile lawsuits against companies associated with the dissemination and playback of MP3s.

Recording Industry Association Of America v. Diamond Multimedia Systems Inc.[†]

In this case involving the intersection of computer technology, the Internet, and music listening, we must decide whether the Rio portable music player is a digital audio recording device subject to the restrictions of the Audio Home Recording Act of 1992.

---

† 180 F. 3d 1072 (9th Cir. 1999).

I

This appeal arises from the efforts of the Recording Industry Association of America and the Alliance of Artists and Recording Companies (collectively, "RIAA") to enjoin the manufacture and distribution by Diamond Multimedia Systems ("Diamond") of the Rio portable music player. The Rio is a small device (roughly the size of an audio cassette) with headphones that allows a user to download MP3 audio files from a computer and to listen to them elsewhere. The dispute over the Rio's design and function is difficult to comprehend without an understanding of the revolutionary new method of music distribution made possible by digital recording and the Internet; thus, we will explain in some detail the brave new world of Internet music distribution.

A

The introduction of digital audio recording to the consumer electronics market in the 1980's is at the root of this litigation. Before then, a person wishing to copy an original music recording — e.g., wishing to make a cassette tape of a record or compact disc — was limited to analog, rather than digital, recording technology. With analog recording, each successive generation of copies suffers from an increasingly pronounced degradation in sound quality. For example, when an analog cassette copy of a record or compact disc is itself copied by analog technology, the resulting "second-generation" copy of the original will most likely suffer from the hiss and lack of clarity characteristic of older recordings. With digital recording, by contrast, there is almost no degradation in sound quality, no matter how many generations of copies are made. Digital copying thus allows thousands of perfect or near perfect copies (and copies of copies) to be made from a single original recording. Music "pirates" use digital recording technology to make and to distribute near perfect copies of commercially prepared recordings for which they have not licensed the copyrights.

Until recently, the Internet was of little use for the distribution of music because the average music computer file was simply too big: the digital information on a single compact disc of music required hundreds of computer floppy discs to store, and downloading even a single song from the Internet took hours. However, various compression algorithms (which make an audio file "smaller" by limiting the audio bandwidth) now allow digital audio files to be transferred more quickly and stored more efficiently. MPEG-1 Audio Layer 3 (commonly known as "MP3") is the most popular digital audio compression algorithm in use on the Internet, and the compression it provides makes an audio file "smaller" by a factor of twelve to one without significantly reducing sound quality. MP3's popularity is due in large part to the fact that it is a standard, non-proprietary compression algorithm freely available for use by anyone, unlike various proprietary (and copyright-secure) competitor algorithms. Coupled with the use of cable modems, compression algorithms like MP3 may soon allow an hour of music to be downloaded from the Internet to a personal computer in just a few minutes.

These technological advances have occurred, at least in part, to the traditional music industry's disadvantage. By most accounts, the predominant use of MP3 is the trafficking in illicit audio recordings, presumably because MP3 files do not contain codes identifying whether the compressed audio material is copyright protected. Various pirate websites offer free downloads of copyrighted material, and a single pirate site on the Internet may contain thousands of pirated audio computer files.

RIAA represents the roughly half-dozen major record companies (and the artists on their labels) that control approximately ninety percent of the distribution of recorded music in the United States. RIAA asserts that Internet distribution of serial digital copies of pirated copyrighted material will discourage the purchase of legitimate recordings, and predicts that losses to digital Internet piracy will soon surpass the $300 million that is allegedly lost annually to other more traditional forms of piracy. RIAA fights a well-nigh constant battle against Internet piracy, monitoring the Internet daily, and routinely shutting down pirate websites by sending cease-and-desist letters and bringing lawsuits. There are conflicting views on RIAA's success — RIAA asserts that it can barely keep up with the pirate traffic, while others assert that few, if any, pirate sites remain in operation in the United States and illicit files are difficult to find and download from anywhere online.

In contrast to piracy, the Internet also supports a burgeoning traffic in legitimate audio computer files. Independent and wholly Internet record labels routinely sell and provide free samples of their artists' work online, while many unsigned artists distribute their own material from their own websites. Some free samples are provided for marketing purposes or for simple exposure, while others are teasers intended to entice listeners to purchase either mail order recordings or recordings available for direct download (along with album cover art, lyrics, and artist biographies). Diamond cites a 1998 "Music Industry and the Internet" report by Jupiter Communications which predicts that online sales for pre-recorded music will exceed $1.4 billion by 2002 in the United States alone.

Prior to the invention of devices like the Rio, MP3 users had little option other than to listen to their downloaded digital audio files through headphones or speakers at their computers, playing them from their hard drives. The Rio renders these files portable. More precisely, once an audio file has been downloaded onto a computer hard drive from the Internet or some other source (such as a compact disc player or digital audio tape machine), separate computer software provided with the Rio (called "Rio Manager") allows the user further to download the file to the Rio itself via a parallel port cable that plugs the Rio into the computer. The Rio device is incapable of effecting such a transfer, and is incapable of receiving audio files from anything other than a personal computer equipped with Rio Manager.

Generally, the Rio can store approximately one hour of music, or sixteen hours of spoken material (e.g., downloaded newscasts or books on tape). With the addition of flash memory cards, the Rio can store an additional half-hour or hour of music. The Rio's sole output is an analog audio signal sent to the user via headphones. The Rio cannot make duplicates of any digital audio file it stores, nor can it transfer or upload such a file to a computer, to another device, or to the Internet. However, a flash memory card to which a digital audio file has been downloaded can be removed from one Rio and played back in another.

B

RIAA brought suit to enjoin the manufacture and distribution of the Rio, alleging that the Rio does not meet the requirements for digital audio recording devices under the Audio Home Recording Act of 1992, 17 U.S.C. §1001 et seq. (the "Act"), because it does not employ a Serial Copyright Management System ("SCMS") that sends, receives, and acts upon information about the generation and copyright status of the files that it plays. RIAA also sought payment of the royalties owed by Diamond as the manufacturer and distributor of a digital audio recording device.

. . . .

Under the plain meaning of the Act's definition of digital audio recording devices, computers (and their hard drives) are not digital audio recording devices because their "primary purpose" is not to make digital audio copied recordings. Unlike digital audio tape machines, for example, whose primary purpose is to make digital audio copied recordings, the primary purpose of a computer is to run various programs and to record the data necessary to run those programs and perform various tasks. The legislative history is consistent with this interpretation of the Act's provisions, stating that "the typical personal computer would not fall within the definition of 'digital audio recording device,'" because a personal computer's "recording function is designed and marketed primarily for the recording of data and computer programs." Another portion of the Senate Report states that "[i]f the 'primary purpose' of the recording function is to make objects other than digital audio copied recordings, then the machine or device is not a 'digital audio recording device,' even if the machine or device is technically capable of making such recordings." The legislative history thus expressly recognizes that computers (and other devices) have recording functions capable of recording digital musical recordings, and thus implicate the home taping and piracy concerns to which the Act is responsive. Nonetheless, the legislative history is consistent with the Act's plain language — computers are not digital audio recording devices.

In turn, because computers are not digital audio recording devices, they are not required to comply with the SCMS requirement and thus need not send, receive, or act upon information regarding copyright and generation status. And, as the district court found, MP3 files generally do not even carry the codes providing information regarding copyright and generation status. Thus, the Act seems designed to allow files to be "laundered" by passage through a computer, because even a device with SCMS would be able to download MP3 files lacking SCMS codes from a computer hard drive, for the simple reason that there would be no codes to prevent the copying.

Again, the legislative history is consistent with the Act's plain meaning. As the Technical Reference Document that describes the SCMS system explains, "[d]igital audio signals ... that have no information concerning copyright and/or generation status shall be recorded by the [digital audio recording] device so that the digital copy is copyright asserted and original generation status." Thus, the incorporation of SCMS into the Rio would allow the Rio to copy MP3 files lacking SCMS codes so long as it marked the copied files as "original generation status." And such a marking would allow another SCMS device to make unlimited further copies of such "original generation status" files, despite the fact that the Rio does not permit such further copies to be made because it simply cannot download or transmit the files that it stores to any other device. Thus, the Rio without SCMS inherently allows less copying than SCMS permits.

In fact, the Rio's operation is entirely consistent with the Act's main purpose — the facilitation of personal use. As the Senate Report explains, "[t]he purpose of [the Act] is to ensure the right of consumers to make analog or digital audio recordings of copyrighted music for their private, noncommercial use." The Act does so through its home taping exemption, which "protects all noncommercial copying by consumers of digital and analog musical recordings". The Rio merely makes copies in order to render portable, or "space-shift," those files that already reside on a user's hard drive. Such copying is paradigmatic noncommercial personal use entirely consistent with the purposes of the Act.

UMG Recordings Inc. et. al. v. MP3.com[†]

The complex marvels of cyberspatial communication may create difficult legal issues; but not in this case. Defendant's infringement of plaintiff's copyrights is clear. Accordingly, on April 28, 2000, the Court granted defendant's motion for partial summary judgment holding defendant liable for copyright infringement. This opinion will state the reasons why.

The pertinent facts, either undisputed or, where disputed, taken most favorably to defendant, are as follows:

The technology known as "MP3" permits rapid and efficient conversion of compact disc recordings ("CDs") to computer files easily accessed over the Internet. Utilizing this technology, defendant MP3.com, on or around January 12, 2000, launched its "My.MP3.com" service, which it advertised as permitting subscribers to store, customize, and listen to the recordings contained on their CDs from any place where they have an internet connection. To make good on this offer, defendant purchased tens of thousands of popular CDs in which plaintiffs held the copyrights, and, without authorization, copied their recordings onto its computer servers so as to be able to replay the recordings for its subscribers.

Specifically, in order to first access such a recording, a subscriber to MP3.com must either "prove" that he already owns the CD version of the recording by inserting his copy of the commercial CD into his computer CD-Rom drive for a few seconds (the "Beam-it Service") or must purchase the CD from one of defendant's cooperating online retailers (the "Instant Listening Service"). Thereafter, however, the subscriber can access via the Internet from a computer anywhere in the world the copy of plaintiffs' recording made by defendant. Thus, although defendant seeks to portray its service as the "functional equivalent" of storing its subscribers' CDs, in actuality defendant is re-playing for the subscribers converted versions of the recordings it copied, without authorization, from plaintiffs' copyrighted CDs. On its face, this makes out a presumptive case of infringement under the Copyright Act of 1976 ("Copyright Act"), 17 U.S.C. @ 101 et seq.

Defendant argues, however, that such copying is protected by the affirmative defense of "fair use." In analyzing such a defense, the Copyright Act specifies four factors that must be considered: "(1) the purpose and character of the use, including whether such use is of a commercial nature or is for nonprofit educational purposes; (2) the nature of the copyrighted work; (3) the amount and substantiality of the portion used in relation to the copyrighted work as a whole; and (4) the effect of the use upon the potential market for or value of the copyrighted work." Id. Other relevant factors may also be considered, since fair use is an "equitable rule of reason" to be applied in light of the overall purposes of the Copyright Act.

Regarding the first factor — "the purpose and character of the use" — defendant does not dispute that its purpose is commercial, for while subscribers to My.MP3.com are not currently charged a fee, defendant seeks to attract a sufficiently large subscription base to draw advertising and otherwise make a profit. Consideration of the first factor, however, also involves inquiring into whether the new use essentially repeats the old or whether, instead, it "transforms" it by infusing it with new meaning, new understanding, or the like. Here, although defendant recites that

---

† 92 F. Supp. 2d 349 (S.D. N.Y. 2000).

My.MP3.com provides a transformative "space shift" by which subscribers can enjoy the sound recordings contained on their CDs without lugging around the physical discs themselves, this is simply another way of saying that the unauthorized copies are being retransmitted in another medium — an insufficient basis for any legitimate claim of transformation.

Here, defendant adds no new "new aesthetics, new insights and understandings" to the original music recordings it copies, but simply repackages those recordings to facilitate their transmission through another medium. While such services may be innovative, they are not transformative.

Regarding the second factor — "the nature of the copyrighted work" — the creative recordings here being copied are "close to the core of intended copyright protection," and, conversely, far removed from the more factual or descriptive work more amenable to "fair use."

Regarding the third factor — "the amount and substantiality of the portion [of the copyrighted work] use [by the copier] in relation to the copyrighted work as a whole" — it is undisputed that defendant copies, and replays, the entirety of the copyrighted works here in issue, thus again negating any claim of fair use.

Regarding the fourth factor — "the effect of the use upon the potential market for or value of the copyrighted work" — defendant's activities on their face invade plaintiffs' statutory right to license their copyrighted sound recordings to others for reproduction. Defendant, however, argues that, so far as the derivative market here involved is concerned, plaintiffs have not shown that such licensing is "traditional, reasonable, or likely to be development." Moreover, defendant argues, its activities can only enhance plaintiffs' sales, since subscribers cannot gain access to particular recordings made available by MP3.com unless they have already "purchased" (actually or purportedly), or agreed to purchase, their own CD copies of those recordings.

Such arguments — though dressed in the garb of an expert's "opinion" (that, on inspection, consists almost entirely of speculative and conclusory statements) — are unpersuasive. Any allegedly positive impact of defendant's activities on plaintiffs' prior market in no way frees defendant to usurp a further market that directly derives from reproduction of the plaintiffs' copyrighted works. This would be so even if the copyrightholder had not yet entered the new market in issue, for a copyrightholder's "exclusive" rights, derived from the Constitution and the Copyright Act, include the right, within broad limits, to curb the development of such a derivative market by refusing to license a copyrighted work or by doing so only on terms the copyright owner finds acceptable.

Finally, regarding defendant's purported reliance on other factors, this essentially reduces to the claim that My.MP3.com provides a useful service to consumers that, in its absence, will be served by "pirates." Copyright, however, is not designed to afford consumer protection or convenience but, rather, to protect the copyrightholders' property interests. Moreover, as a practical matter, plaintiffs have indicated no objection in principle to licensing their recordings to companies like MP3.com; they simply want to make sure they get the remuneration the law reserves for them as holders of copyrights on creative works. Stripped to its essence, defendant's "consumer protection" argument amounts to nothing more than a bald claim that defendant should be able to misappropriate plaintiffs' property simply because there is a consumer demand for it. This hardly appeals to the conscience of equity.

In sum, on any view, defendant's "fair use" defense is indefensible and must be denied as a matter of law.

A&M Records, Inc. et. al. v. Napster Inc.[†]

Napster — a small Internet start-up based in San Mateo, California — makes its pro-prietary MusicShare software freely available for Internet users to download. Users who obtain Napster's software can then share MP3 music files with others logged-on to the Napster system. MP3 files, which reproduce nearly CD-quality sound in a compressed format, are available on a variety of websites either for a fee or free-of-charge. Napster allows users to exchange MP3 files stored on their own computer hard-drives directly, without payment, and boasts that it "takes the frustration out of locating servers with MP3 files."

Although the parties dispute the precise nature of the service Napster pro-vides, they agree that using Napster typically involves the following basic steps: After downloading MusicShare software from the Napster website, a user can access the Napster system from her computer. The MusicShare software interacts with Napster's server-side software when the user logs on, automatically connecting her to one of some 150 servers that Napster operates. The MusicShare software reads a list of names of MP3 files that the user has elected to make available. This list is then added to a directory and index, on the Napster server, of MP3 files that users who are logged-on wish to share. If the user wants to locate a song, she enters its name or the name of the recording artist on the search page of the MusicShare program and clicks the "Find It" button. The Napster software then searches the current directory and generates a list of files responsive to the search request. To download a desired file, the user highlights it on the list and clicks the "Get Selected Song(s)" button. The user may also view a list of files that exist on another user's hard drive and select a file from that list. When the requesting user clicks on the name of a file, the Napster server communicates with the requesting user's and host user's MusicShare browser software to facilitate a connection between the two users and initiate the downloading of the file without any further action on either user's part.

According to Napster, when the requesting user clicks on the name of the desired MP3 file, the Napster server routes this request to the host user's browser. The host user's browser responds that it either can or cannot supply the file. If the host user can supply the file, the Napster server communicates the host's address and routing information to the requesting user's browser, allowing the requesting user to make a connection with the host and receive the desired MP3 file. The parties dis-agree about whether this process involves a hypertext link that the Napster server-side software provides. However, plaintiffs admit that the Napster server gets the necessary IP address information from the host user, enabling the requesting user to connect to the host. The MP3 file is actually transmitted over the Internet, but the steps neces-sary to make that connection could not take place without the Napster server.

The Napster system has other functions besides allowing users to search for, request, and download MP3 files. For example, a requesting user can play a downloaded song using the MusicShare software. Napster also hosts a chat room.

Napster has developed a policy that makes compliance with all copyright laws one of the "terms of use" of its service and warns users that:

> Napster will terminate the accounts of users who are repeat infringers of the copyrights, or other intellectual property rights, of others. In addition,

---

[†] 54 U.S. P.Q. 2d 1746 (N.D. Cal. 2000).

> Napster reserves the right to terminate the account of a user upon any single infringement of the rights of others in conjunction with use of the Napster service.

However, the parties disagree over when this policy was instituted and how effectively it bars infringers from using the Napster service. Napster claims that it had a copyright compliance policy as early as October 1999, but admits that it did not document or notify users of the existence of this policy until February 7, 2000.

.　.　.　.

Plaintiffs' principal argument against application of the 512(a) safe harbor is that Napster does not perform the passive conduit function eligible for protection under this subsection. As defendant correctly notes, the words "conduit" or "passive conduit" appear nowhere in 512(a), but are found only in the legislative history and summaries of the DMCA. The court must look first to the plain language of the statute, "construing the provisions of the entire law, including its object and policy, to ascertain the intent of Congress." If the statute is unclear, however, the court may rely on the legislative history. The language of subsection 512(a) makes the safe harbor applicable, as a threshold matter, to service providers "transmitting, routing or providing connections for, material through a system or network controlled or operated by or for the service provider...." According to plaintiffs, the use of the word "conduit" in the legislative history explains the meaning of "through a system."

Napster has expressly denied that the transmission of MP3 files ever passes through its servers. Indeed, Kessler declared that "files reside on the computers of Napster users, and are transmitted directly between those computers." MP3 files are transmitted "from the Host user's hard drive and Napster browser, through the Internet to the recipient's Napster browser and hard drive." The Internet cannot be considered "a system or network controlled or operated by or for the service provider," however. To get around this problem, Napster avers (and plaintiffs seem willing to concede) that "Napster's servers and Napster's MusicShare browsers on its users' computers are all part of Napster's overall system." Defendant narrowly defines its system to include the browsers on users' computers. In contrast, plaintiffs argue that either (1) the system does not include the browsers, or (2) it includes not only the browsers, but also the users' computers themselves.

Even assuming that the system includes the browser on each user's computer, the MP3 files are not transmitted "through" the system within the meaning of subsection 512(a). Napster emphasizes the passivity of its role — stating that "[a]ll files transfer directly from the computer of one Napster user through the Internet to the computer of the requesting user." It admits that the transmission bypasses the Napster server. This means that, even if each user's Napster browser is part of the system, the transmission goes from one part of the system to another, or between parts of the system, but not "through" the system. The court finds that subsection 512(a) does not protect the transmission of MP3 files.

The prefatory language of subsection 512(a) is disjunctive, however. The subsection applies to "infringement of copyright by reason of the provider's transmitting, routing, or providing connections through a system or network controlled or operated by or for the service provider." The court's finding that transmission does not occur "through" the system or network does not foreclose the possibility that subsection 512(a) applies to "routing" or "providing connections." Rather, each of these functions must be analyzed independently.

Napster contends that providing connections between users' addresses "constitutes the value of the system to the users and the public." This connection cannot be established without the provision of the host's address to the Napster browser software installed on the requesting user's computer. The central Napster server delivers the host's address. See id. While plaintiffs contend that the infringing material is not transmitted through the Napster system, they provide no evidence to rebut the assertion that Napster supplies the requesting user's computer with information necessary to facilitate a connection with the host.

Nevertheless, the court finds that Napster does not provide connections "through" its system. Although the Napster server conveys address information to establish a connection between the requesting and host users, the connection itself occurs through the Internet. The legislative history of section 512 demonstrates that Congress intended the 512(a) safe harbor to apply only to activities "in which a service provider plays the role of a 'conduit' for the communications of others." Drawing inferences in the light most favorable to the non-moving party, this court cannot say that Napster serves as a conduit for the connection itself, as opposed to the address information that makes the connection possible. Napster enables or facilitates the initiation of connections, but these connections do not pass through the system within the meaning of subsection 512(a).

Neither party has adequately briefed the meaning of "routing" in subsection 512(a), nor does the legislative history shed light on this issue. Defendant tries to make "routing" and "providing connections" appear synonymous — stating, for example, that "the central Napster server routes the transmission by providing the Host's address to the Napster browser that is installed on and in use by User's computer." However, the court doubts that Congress would have used the terms "routing" and "providing connections" disjunctively if they had the same meaning. It is clear from both parties' submissions that the route of the allegedly infringing material goes through the Internet from the host to the requesting user, not through the Napster server. The court holds that routing does not occur through the Napster system. Because Napster does not transmit, route, or provide connections through its system, it has failed to demonstrate that it qualifies for the 512(a) safe harbor. The court thus declines to grant summary adjudication in its favor.

III. Copyright Compliance Policy

Even if the court had determined that Napster meets the criteria outlined in subsection 512(a), subsection 512(i) imposes additional requirements on eligibility for any DMCA safe harbor. This provision states:

> The limitations established by this section shall apply to a service provider only if the service provider —
>
> (A) has adopted and reasonably implemented, and informs subscribers and account holders of the service provider's system or network of, a policy that provides for the termination in appropriate circumstances of subscribers and account holders of the service provider's system or network who are repeat infringers; and
>
> (B) accommodates and does not interfere with standard technical measures.
>
> 17 U.S.C. §512(i).

Plaintiffs challenge Napster's compliance with these threshold eligibility requirements on two grounds. First, they point to evidence from Kessler's deposition that

Napster did not adopt a written policy of which its users had notice until on or around February 7, 2000 — two months after the filing of this lawsuit. Kessler testified that, although Napster had a copyright compliance policy as early as October 1999, he is not aware that this policy was reflected in any document, or communicated to any user. Congress did not intend to require a service provider to "investigate possible infringements, monitor its service or make difficult judgments as to whether conduct is or is not infringing," but the notice requirement is designed to insure that flagrant or repeat infringers "know that there is a realistic threat of losing [their] access."

Napster attempts to refute plaintiffs' argument by noting that subsection 512(i) does not specify when the copyright compliance policy must be in place. Although this characterization of subsection 512(i) is facially accurate, it defies the logic of making formal notification to users or subscribers a prerequisite to exemption from monetary liability. The fact that Napster developed and notified its users of a formal policy after the onset of this action should not moot plaintiffs' claim to monetary relief for past harms. Without further documentation, defendant's argument that it has satisfied subsection 512(i) is merely conclusory and does not support summary adjudication in its favor.

Summary adjudication is also inappropriate because Napster has not shown that it reasonably implemented a policy for terminating repeat infringers. If Napster is formally notified of infringing activity, it blocks the infringer's password so she cannot log on to the Napster service using that password. Napster does not block the IP addresses of infringing users, however, and the parties dispute whether it would be feasible or effective to do so.

Plaintiffs aver that Napster wilfully turns a blind eye to the identity of its users — that is, their real names and physical addresses — because their anonymity allows Napster to disclaim responsibility for copyright infringement. Hence, plaintiffs contend, "infringers may readily reapply to the Napster system to recommence their infringing downloading and uploading of MP3 music files." Plaintiffs' expert, computer security researcher Daniel Farmer, declared that he conducted tests in which he easily deleted all traces of his former Napster identity, convincing Napster that "it had never seen me or my computer before." Farmer also cast doubt on Napster's contention that blocking IP addresses is not a reasonable means of terminating infringers. He noted that Napster bans the IP addresses of users who runs "bots" on the service.

Hence, plaintiffs raise genuine issues of material fact about whether Napster has reasonably implemented a policy of terminating repeat infringers. They have produced evidence that Napster's copyright compliance policy is neither timely nor reasonable within the meaning of subparagraph 512(i)(A).

A&M Records, Inc. v. Napster, Inc.[†]

The matter before the court concerns the boundary between sharing and theft, personal use and the unauthorized worldwide distribution of copyrighted music and sound recordings. On December 6, 1999, A & M Records and seventeen other re-

---

† No. C 99-5183 (N.D. Cal, July 26, 2000).

cord companies ("record company plaintiffs") filed a complaint for contributory and vicarious copyright infringement, violations of the California Civil Code section 980(a)(2), and unfair competition against Napster, Inc., an Internet start-up that enables users to download MP3 music files without payment. On January 7, 2000, plaintiffs Jerry Leiber, Mike Stoller, and Frank Music Corporation filed a complaint for vicarious and contributory copyright infringement on behalf of a putative class of similarly-situated music publishers ("music publisher plaintiffs") against Napster, Inc. and former CEO Eileen Richardson. The music publisher plaintiffs filed a first amended complaint on April 6, 2000, and on May 24, 2000, the court entered a stipulation of dismissal of all claims against Richardson. Now before this court is the record company and music publisher plaintiffs' joint motion to preliminarily enjoin Napster, Inc. from engaging in or assisting others in copying, downloading, uploading, transmitting, or distributing copyrighted music without the express permission of the rights owner. In opposition to this motion, defendant seeks to expand the "fair use" doctrine articulated in Sony Corp. of America v. Universal City Studios, Inc., 464 U. S. 417 (1984), to encompass the massive downloading of MP3 files by Napster users. Alternatively, defendant contends that, even if this third-party activity constitutes direct copyright infringement, plaintiffs have not shown probable success on the merits of their contributory and vicarious infringement claims. Defendant also asks the court to find that copyright holders are not injured by a service created and promoted to facilitate the free downloading of music files, the vast majority of which are copyrighted.

Having considered the parties' arguments, the court grants plaintiffs' motion for a preliminary injunction against Napster, Inc. The court makes the following Findings of Fact and Conclusions of Law to support the preliminary injunction under Federal Rules of Civil Procedure 65(d).

I.   FINDINGS OF FACT

A.   MP3 Technology
Digital compression technology makes it possible to store audio recordings in a digital format that uses less memory and may be uploaded and downloaded over the Internet. MP3 is a popular, standard format used to store such compressed audio files. Compressing data into MP3 format results in some loss of sound quality. However, because MP3 files are smaller, they require less time to transfer and are therefore better suited to transmission over the Internet.

Consumers typically acquire MP3 files in two ways. First, users may download audio recordings that have already been converted into MP3 format by using an Internet service such as Napster. Second, "ripping" software makes it possible to copy an audio compact disc ("CD") directly onto a computer hard-drive; ripping software compresses the millions of bytes of information on a typical CD into a smaller MP3 file that requires a fraction of the storage space.

B.   Defendant's Business
Napster, Inc. is a start-up company based in San Mateo, California. It distributes its proprietary file-sharing software free of charge via its Internet website. People who have downloaded this software can log-on to the Napster system and share MP3 music files with other users who are also logged-on to the system. It is uncontradicted that Napster users currently upload or download MP3 files without payment to each other, defendant, or copyright owners. According to a Napster, Inc. executive sum-

mary, the Napster service gives its users the unprecedented ability to "locate music by their favorite artists in MP3 format." Defendant boasts that it "takes the frustration out of locating servers with MP3 files" by providing a peer-to-peer file-sharing system that allows Napster account holders to conduct relatively sophisticated searches for music files on the hard drives of millions of other anonymous users.

Although Napster was the brainchild of a college student who wanted to facilitate music-swapping by his roommate, it is far from a simple tool of distribution among friends and family. According to defendant's internal documents, there will be 75 million Napster users by the end of 2000. At one point, defendant estimated that even without marketing, its "viral service" was growing by more than 200 percent per month. Approximately 10,000 music files are shared per second using Napster, and every second more than 100 users attempt to connect to the system.

Napster, Inc. currently collects no revenues and charges its clientele no fees; it is a free service. However, it has never been a non-profit organization. It plans to delay the maximization of revenues while it attracts a large user base. The value of the system grows as the quantity and quality of available music increases. Defendant's internal documents reveal a strategy of attaining a "critical mass" of music in an "ever-expanding library" as new members bring their MP3 collections online. Defendant eventually plans to "monetize" its user base. Potential revenue sources include targeted email; advertising; commissions from links to commercial websites; and direct marketing of CDs, Napster products, and CD burners and rippers. Defendant also may begin to charge fees for a premium or commercial version of its software. The existence of a large user base that increases daily and can be "monetized" makes Napster, Inc. a potentially attractive acquisition for larger, more established firms.

Napster Inc.'s value — which is measured, at least in part, by the size of its user base — lies between 60 and 80 million dollars. Defendant obtained substantial capital infusions after the onset of this litigation. For example, in May 2000, the venture firm Hummer Winblad purchased a twenty-percent ownership interest in the company for 13 million dollars; other investors simultaneously invested 1.5 million dollars.

The evidence shows that virtually all Napster users download or upload copyrighted files and that the vast majority of the music available on Napster is copyrighted. Eighty-seven percent of the files sampled by plaintiffs' expert, Dr. Ingram Olkin, "belong to or are administered by plaintiffs or other copyright holders." After analyzing Olkin's data, Charles J. Hausman, anti-piracy counsel for the RIAA, determined that 834 out of 1,150 files in Olkin's download database belong to or are administered by plaintiffs; plaintiffs alone own the copyrights to more than seventy percent of the 1,150 files. Napster users shared these files without authorization.

Napster, Inc. has never obtained licenses to distribute or download, or to facilitate others in distributing or downloading, the music that plaintiffs own.

Defendant's internal documents indicate that it seeks to take over, or at least threaten, plaintiffs' role in the promotion and distribution of music.

Defendant's internal documents also demonstrate that its executives knew Napster users were engaging in unauthorized downloading and uploading of copyrighted music. Several Napster executives admitted in their depositions that they believed many of the millions of MP3 music files available on Napster were copyrighted.

At least on paper, the promotion of new artists constituted an aspect of defendant's plan as early as October 1999. New or unsigned artists now may promote their works and distribute them in MP3 format via the Napster service. Napster, Inc. has sought business alliances and developed both Internet-and software-based technologies to support its New Artist Program. However, the court finds that the New Artist Program accounts for a small portion of Napster use and did not become central to defendant's business strategy until this action made it convenient to give the program top billing. An early version of the Napster website advertised the ease with which users could find their favorite popular music without "wading through page after page of unknown artists." Defendant did not even create the New Artist Program that runs on its Internet website until April 2000 — well after plaintiffs filed this action. Moreover, in Olkin's sample of 1,150 files (which were randomly selected from over 550,000), only 232 files matched any of the 19,440 names that were listed in defendant's new artist database as of July 2000. An RIAA representative who analyzed the data also noted that the list of so-called new artists actually contained many popular stars represented by major record labels — among them teen sensation Britney Spears and the legendary alternative rock band Nirvana. Once established artists were eliminated from the results, only eleven new artists and fourteen of their music files remained in Olkin's sample of 1,150 files.

Defendant employs the term "space-shifting" to refer to the process of converting a CD the consumer already owns into MP3 format and using Napster to transfer the music to a different computer — from home to office, for example. The court finds that space-shifting accounts for a de minimis portion of Napster use and is not a significant aspect of defendant's business. According to the court's understanding of the Napster technology, a user who wanted to space-shift files from her home to her office would have to log-on to the system from her home computer, leave that computer online, commute to work, and log-on to Napster from her office computer to access the desired file. In the meantime, many users might download it before she reached the office. Common sense dictates that this use does not draw users to the system. Defendant fails to cite a single Napster, Inc. document indicating that the company saw space-shifting as an attraction for its user base, and survey evidence shows that almost half of college-student survey respondents previously owned less than ten percent of the songs they have downloaded.

. . . .

D. Plaintiffs' Business

The music publisher plaintiffs compose music and write songs. They depend financially upon the sale of sound recordings because they earn royalties from such sales. However, they do not get a royalty when a Napster user uploads or downloads an MP3 file of their compositions without payment or authorization. The record company plaintiffs' sound recordings also result from a substantial investment of money, time, manpower, and creativity. In contrast, defendant invests nothing in the content of the music which means that, compared with plaintiffs, it incurs virtually no costs in providing a wide array of music to satisfy consumer demand.

To make a profit, the record company plaintiffs largely rely on the success of "hit" or popular recordings, which may constitute as little as ten or fifteen percent of albums released. Many, or all, of their top recordings have been available for free on Napster.

The record company plaintiffs have invested substantial time, effort, and funds in actual or planned entry into the digital downloading market. BMG Music ("BMG") began to explore digital downloading in early 1996 and has made more than twenty tracks commercially available for downloading through the digital service providers ("DSPs") Amplified. com and the Liquid Music Network. BMG has entered several business partnerships, strategic marketing agreements, and clearinghouse relationships to develop a plan for secure, commercial digital downloading; July 2000 was the target date for BMG's launch. Plaintiffs Capitol Record, Inc. and Virgin Records America are affiliated with EMI Recorded Music, North America ("EMI"). EMI has developed business plans to distribute its music through several DSPs which represent more than 800 retail websites. All digital downloads that EMI offers will be encrypted and watermarked. Sony Music Entertainment ("Sony") has already begun to make selected singles available through its websites and those of its artists; to obtain a permanent copy of this music, consumers must pay for the download.

As of May 31, 2000, Sony also began selling downloadable music through a distribution network of about thirty-five retail sites. Plaintiffs A & M Records, Geffen Records, Interscope Records, Island Records, MCA Records, Motown Records, UMG Records, and Universal Records (collectively, "Universal") have spent millions of dollars preparing a secure digital distribution system scheduled for launch in mid-summer 2000. Warner Music Group and its associated labels — plaintiffs Atlantic Recording Corp., London-Sire Records Inc. (f/ k/ a Sire Records Group Inc.), Elektra Entertainment Group Inc., and Warner Bros. Records (collectively, "Warner") — have done due diligence and dedicated a substantial budget to digital distribution. Warner expects to launch its commercial digital distribution of hundreds of recordings by the fourth quarter of 2000.

Promotional samples offered by plaintiffs and other retail sites differ significantly from using Napster to decide whether to buy a CD. The record company plaintiffs have made some free downloads available but have limited them in amount and duration. They have not provided entire albums, and the downloads typically have been "timed-out" so that users can only play them for a finite period of time — often less than a month.

Although plaintiffs have not been completely successful in managing the rights to promotional downloads, record company executives accord importance to the security of music distributed in this manner. Retail sites, such as Amazon. com, offer thirty-to-sixty-second song samples in streaming audio format, rather than as downloads. Unlike downloading, streaming does not copy the music onto the listener's computer hard drive; it merely allows her to hear it. Because companies like DiscoverMusic that provide song samples to these Internet retailers enter licensing agreements, rights holders earn royalties from this form of sampling. In contrast, persons who obtain MP3 files for free using Napster can retain and play them indefinitely — and, even if they download a song to make a purchasing decision, they may decide not to buy the music. While Napster users can burn CDs comprised of unauthorized downloads they obtained to "sample" new songs, sampling on sites affiliated with plaintiffs does not substitute for purchasing the entire disc.

E. Effect of Napster on the Market for Plaintiffs' Copyrighted Works

The court finds that Napster use is likely to reduce CD purchases by college students, whom defendant admits constitute a key demographic. Plaintiffs' expert, Dr. E. Deborah Jay, opined that forty-one percent of her college-student survey respondents "gave a reason for using Napster or described the nature of its impact on their music purchases in a way which either explicitly indicated or suggested that Napster displaces CD sales." She also found that twenty-one percent of the college students surveyed revealed that Napster helped them make a better selection or decide what to buy. However, Jay's overall conclusion was that "[t] he more songs Napster users have downloaded," the more likely they are to admit or imply that such use has reduced their music purchases. The report of Soundscan CEO Michael Fine lends support to Jay's findings. After examining data culled from three types of retail stores near college or university campuses, Fine concluded that "on-line file sharing has resulted in a loss of album sales within college markets." For the reasons discussed in the court's separate order, the report by defendant's expert, Dr. Peter S. Fader, does not provide credible evidence that music file-sharing on Napster stimulates more CD sales than it displaces. Nor do the recording industry documents that defendant cites reliably show increased music sales due to Napster use. One such memorandum deals with the effect of Warner's promotional downloads, which are "timed-out" and thus differ from MP3 files obtained using Napster. However, the court has too little information about this survey to rely on it, and the deponent, Universal representative Lawrence Kenswil, declined to vouch for the survey's accuracy.

Because plaintiffs entered the digital download market very recently, or plan to enter it in the next few months, they are especially vulnerable to direct competition from Napster, Inc. The court finds that, in choosing between the free Napster service and pay-per-download sites, consumers are likely to choose Napster. Defendant's economic expert, Dr. Robert E. Hall, opines that plaintiffs' music could still command a high price after a period when the price has been zero due to Napster use; thus, he concludes, plaintiffs will not suffer irreparable harm between now and a trial verdict against defendant. This argument does not square with Hall's assertion that preliminarily enjoining defendant will put it out of business because users will switch to services offered by "kindred spirits." If this is true, consumers will not necessarily resume buying music if Napster is enjoined; rather, they will go to other sites offering free MP3 files. Indeed, as Dr. David J. Teece avers, defendant has contributed to a new attitude that digitally-downloaded songs ought to be free — an attitude that creates formidable hurdles for the establishment of a commercial downloading market.

Hall also maintains that Napster, Inc. will increase the volume of plaintiffs' online sales by stimulating consumer investment in the hardware and software needed to obtain and play MP3 files. However, he ignores evidence of reduced CD-buying among college students due to Napster use, and the data upon which he relies to argue that Napster has enhanced sales is either weak (in the case of the Fader Report) or unavailable for the court's review. The court therefore finds that the barriers to commercial distribution posed by an emerging sense of entitlement to free music probably outweigh the benefits that defendant purports to confer.

Downloading on Napster also has the potential to disrupt plaintiffs' promotional efforts because it does not involve any of the restrictions on timing, amount, or selection that plaintiffs impose when they offer free music files. Even if Napster users sometimes download files to determine whether they want to purchase a CD, sampling on Napster is vastly different than that offered by plaintiffs. On Napster, the user — not the copyright owner — determines how much music to sample and how long to keep it.

II. CONCLUSIONS OF LAW

A. Legal Standard

The Ninth Circuit authorizes preliminary injunctive relief for "a party who demonstrates either (1) a combination of probable success on the merits and the possibility of irreparable harm, or (2) that serious questions are raised and the balance of hardships tips in its favor."

The standard is a sliding scale which requires a greater degree of harm the lesser the probability of success. In a copyright infringement case, demonstration of a reasonable likelihood of success on the merits creates a presumption of irreparable harm.

B.   Proof of Direct Infringement
To prevail on a contributory or vicarious copyright infringement claim, a plaintiff must show direct infringement by a third party. As a threshold matter, plaintiffs in this action must demonstrate that Napster users are engaged in direct infringement.

Plaintiffs have established a prima facie case of direct copyright infringement. As discussed above, virtually all Napster users engage in the unauthorized downloading or uploading of copyrighted music; as much as eighty-seven percent of the files available on Napster may be copyrighted, and more than seventy percent may be owned or administered by plaintiffs

C.   Affirmative Defense of Fair Use and Substantial Non-Infringing Use
Defendant asserts the affirmative defenses of fair use and substantial non-infringing use. The latter defense is also known as the staple article of commerce doctrine. Sony stands for the rule that a manufacturer is not liable for selling a "staple article of commerce" that is "capable of commercially significant noninfringing uses." The Supreme Court also declared in Sony, "Any individual may reproduce a copyrighted work for a 'fair use'; the copyright holder does not possess the exclusive right to such a use." Defendant bears the burden of proving these affirmative defenses.

For the reasons set forth below, the court finds that any potential non-infringing use of the Napster service is minimal or connected to the infringing activity, or both. The substantial or commercially significant use of the service was, and continues to be, the unauthorized downloading and uploading of popular music, most of which is copyrighted.

Section 107 of the Copyright Act provides a non-exhaustive list of fair use factors. These factors include:

(1)   the purpose and character of the use, including whether such use is of a commercial nature or is for nonprofit educational purposes;
(2)   the nature of the copyrighted work;
(3)   the amount and substantiality of the portion used in relation to the copyrighted work as a whole; and
(4)   the effect of the use upon the potential market for or value of the copyrighted work. 17 U.S.C. §107.

In the instant action, the purpose and character of the use militates against a finding of fair use. Ascertaining whether the new work transforms the copyrighted material satisfies the main goal of the first factor. Plaintiff persuasively argues that downloading MP3 files does not transform the copyrighted music.

Under the first factor, the court must also determine whether the use is commercial. In Acuff-Rose, the Supreme Court clarified that a finding of commercial use weighs against, but does not preclude, a determination of fairness.

If a use is non-commercial, the plaintiff bears the burden of showing a meaningful likelihood that it would adversely affect the potential market for the copyrighted work if it became widespread.

Although downloading and uploading MP3 music files is not paradigmatic commercial activity, it is also not personal use in the traditional sense. Plaintiffs have not shown that the majority of Napster users download music to sell — that is, for profit.

However, given the vast scale of Napster use among anonymous individuals, the court finds that downloading and uploading MP3 music files with the assistance of Napster are not private uses. At the very least, a host user sending a file cannot be said to engage in a personal use when distributing that file to an anonymous requester. Moreover, the fact that Napster users get for free something they would ordinarily have to buy suggests that they reap economic advantages from Napster use.

The court finds that the copyrighted musical compositions and sound recordings are creative in nature; they constitute entertainment, which cuts against a finding of fair use under the second factor.

With regard to the third factor, it is undisputed that downloading or uploading MP3 music files involves copying the entirety of the copyrighted work. The Ninth Circuit held prior to Sony that "wholesale copying of copyrighted material precludes application of the fair use doctrine." Even after Sony, wholesale copying for private home use tips the fair use analysis in plaintiffs' favor if such copying is likely to adversely affect the market for the copyrighted material.

The fourth factor, the effect on the potential market for the copyrighted work, also weighs against a finding of fair use. Plaintiffs have produced evidence that Napster use harms the market for their copyrighted musical compositions and sound recordings in at least two ways. First, it reduces CD sales among college students. Second, it raises barriers to plaintiffs' entry into the market for the digital downloading of music.

Defendant asserts several potential fair uses of the Napster service — including sampling, space-shifting, and the authorized distribution of new artists' work. Sampling on Napster is not a personal use in the traditional sense that courts have recognized — copying which occurs within the household and does not confer any financial benefit on the user. Instead, sampling on Napster amounts to obtaining permanent copies of songs that users would otherwise have to purchase; it also carries the potential for viral distribution to millions of people. Defendant ignores critical differences between sampling songs on Napster and VCR usage in Sony. First, while "time-shifting [TV broadcasts] merely enables a viewer to see ... a work which he ha[s] been invited to witness in its entirety free of charge," plaintiffs in this action almost always charge for their music — even if it is downloaded song-by-song. They only make promotional downloads available on a highly restricted basis. Copyright owners also earn royalties from streamed song samples on retail websites like Amazon.com. Second, the majority of VCR purchasers in Sony did not distribute taped television broadcasts, but merely enjoyed them at home. In contrast, a Napster user who downloads a copy of a song to her hard drive may make that song available to millions of other individuals, even if she eventually chooses to purchase the CD. So-called sampling on Napster may quickly facilitate unauthorized distribution at an exponential rate.

Defendant's argument that using Napster to sample music is akin to visiting a free listening station in a record store, or listening to song samples on a retail website, fails to convince the court because Napster users can keep the music they download. Whether or not they decide to buy the CD, they still obtain a permanent copy of the song. In contrast, many retail sites only offer thirty-to-sixty-second samples in streaming audio format and promotional downloads from the record company plaintiffs are often "timed-out." The global scale of Napster usage and the fact that users avoid paying for songs that otherwise would not be free militates against a determination that sampling by Napster users constitutes personal or home use in the traditional sense.

Even if the type of sampling supposedly done on Napster were a non-commercial use, plaintiffs have demonstrated a substantial likelihood that it would adversely affect the potential market for their copyrighted works if it became widespread. Plaintiffs claim three general types of harm: a decrease in retail sales, especially among college students; an obstacle to the record company plaintiffs' future entry into the digital downloading market; and a social devaluing of music stemming from its free distribution. With regard to sampling, twenty-one percent of the Jay survey respondents indicated that Napster helps them decide what music to purchase. Nevertheless, Jay reached the overarching conclusion that the more songs Napster users download, the more likely they are to reveal that such use reduces their music buying. Jay's evidence suggests that sampling and building a free music library through unauthorized downloading are not mutually exclusive: it is likely that survey respondents who sample are primarily direct infringers. Napster users — not the record companies — control the music selection, the amount and the timing of the sampling activity, and they may keep many songs after deciding not to purchase the entire CD. Defendant maintains that sampling does not decrease retail music sales and may even stimulate them. To support this assertion, it relies heavily on the Fader Report, which concludes that consumers do not view MP3 files as perfect substitutes for CDs. Fader cites a survey that he did not conduct for the assertion that "60% of on-line users who download free digital music do so to preview music before buying the CD." Examining the results of a different survey that he purportedly designed, but did not carefully supervise, he reports that about twenty-eight percent of Napster users indicate that their music purchases have increased since they began using the Napster software. For reasons explained in the court's evidentiary order, the Fader Report is unreliable and fails to rebut plaintiffs' showing of harm. Plaintiffs have demonstrated a meaningful likelihood that the activity defendant calls sampling actually decreases retail sales of their music.

Any potential enhancement of plaintiffs' sales due to sampling would not tip the fair use analysis conclusively in favor of defendant. Indeed, courts have rejected the suggestion that a positive impact on sales negates the copyright holder's entitlement to licensing fees or access to derivative markets.

The MP3.com opinion is especially instructive. Although MP3.com's activities arguably stimulated CD sales, the plaintiffs "adduced substantial evidence that they ... [had] taken steps to enter [the digital downloading market]." The fourth factor thus weighed against a finding of fair use. Plaintiffs in the instant action similarly allege that Napster use impedes their entry into the online market. The record company plaintiffs have already expended considerable funds and effort to commence Internet sales and licensing for digital downloads. Plaintiffs' economic expert opined that the availability of free MP3 files will reduce the market for authorized, commercial downloading. This point is corroborated by the fact that all forty-nine songs available for purchase on Sony's website can be obtained for free using Napster. If consumers choose to buy, rather than burn, entire CDs they are still more likely to obtain permanent copies of songs on Napster than buy them from Sony's site or listen to streamed samples at other online locations.

The court concludes that, even assuming the sampling alleged in this case is a non-commercial use, the record company plaintiffs have demonstrated a meaningful likelihood that it would adversely affect their entry into the online market if it became widespread. Moreover, it deprives the music publisher plaintiffs of royalties for individual songs. The unauthorized downloading of plaintiffs' music to sample songs would not constitute a fair use, even if it enhanced CD sales.

The court is also unconvinced that Sony applies to space-shifting. Defendant erroneously relies on the Ninth Circuit's assertion, in a case involving an inapplicable statute, that space-shifting constitutes non-commercial personal use. Defendant also implies that space-shifting music is sufficiently analogous to time-shifting television broadcasts to merit the protection of Sony. According to the gravely flawed Fader Report, space-shifting — like time-shifting — leaves the value of the copyrights unscathed because it does not displace sales. Defendant again cites Fader for the statistic that seventy percent of Napster users at least sometimes engage in space-shifting. In contrast, Jay opined that approximately forty-nine percent of her college-student survey respondents previously owned less than ten percent of the songs they downloaded, and about sixty-nine percent owned less than a quarter. The court has already held that the Jay Report bears greater indicia of reliability than the Fader Report. Moreover, under either analysis, the instant matter is distinguishable from Sony because the Supreme Court determined in Sony that time-shifting represented the principal, rather than an occasional use of VCRs.

Defendant argues that, if space-shifting is deemed a fair use, the staple article of commerce doctrine precludes liability for contributory or vicarious infringement. Under Sony, the copyright holder cannot extend his monopoly to products "capable of substantial noninfringing uses." Defendant fails to show that space-shifting constitutes a commercially significant use of Napster. Indeed, the most credible explanation for the exponential growth of traffic to the website is the vast array of free MP3 files offered by other users — not the ability of each individual to space-shift music she already owns. Thus, even if space-shifting is a fair use, it is not substantial enough to preclude liability under the staple article of commerce doctrine.

This court also declines to apply the staple article of commerce doctrine because, as paragraphs (D)(6) and (E)(2) of the legal conclusions explain, Napster exercises ongoing control over its service. In Sony, the defendant's participation did not extend past manufacturing and selling the VCRs: "[t] he only contact between Sony and the users of the Betamax ... occurred at the moment of sale." Here, in contrast, Napster, Inc. maintains and supervises an integrated system that users must access to upload or download files. Courts have distinguished the protection Sony offers to the manufacture and sale of a device from scenarios in which the defendant continues to exercise control over the device's use. Napster, Inc.'s facilitation of unauthorized file-sharing smacks of the contributory infringement in these cases, rather than the legitimate conduct of the VCR manufacturers. Given defendant's control over the service, as opposed to mere manufacturing or selling, the existence of a potentially unobjectionable use like space-shifting does not defeat plaintiffs' claims.

Nor do other potential non-infringing uses of Napster preclude contributory or vicarious liability. Defendant claims that it engages in the authorized promotion of independent artists, ninety-eight percent of whom are not represented by the record company plaintiffs. However, the New Artist Program may not represent a substantial or commercially significant aspect of Napster. The evidence suggests that defendant initially promoted the availability of songs by major stars, as opposed to "page after page of unknown artists." Its purported mission of distributing music by artists unable to obtain record-label representation appears to have been developed later. Other facts point to the conclusion that the New Artists Program was an afterthought, not a major aspect of the Napster business plan. Former CEO Eileen Richardson claimed in her deposition that she told the press Napster is not about known artists like Madonna. But, tellingly, discovery related to downloads by Napster executives reveals that Richardson's own computer contained about five Madonna files obtained using Napster. Defendant did not launch the website aspect of its New Artist Program until after plaintiffs filed suit, and as recently as July 2000, bona fide new artists constituted a very small percentage of music available on Napster. In any event, Napster's primary role of facilitating the unauthorized copying and distribution established artists' songs renders Sony inapplicable.

Plaintiffs do not object to all of the supposedly non-infringing uses of Napster. They do not seek an injunction covering chat rooms or message boards, the New Artist Program or any distribution authorized by rights holders. Nor do they seek to enjoin applications unrelated to the music recording industry. Because plaintiffs do not ask the court to shut down such satellite activities, the fact that these activities may be non-infringing does not lessen plaintiffs' likelihood of success. The court therefore finds that plaintiffs have established a reasonable probability of proving third-party infringement.

D. Contributory Copyright Infringement

Once they have shown direct infringement by Napster users, plaintiffs must demonstrate a likelihood of success on their contributory infringement claim. A contributory infringer is "one who, with knowledge of the infringing activity, induces, causes or materially contributes to the infringing conduct of another." Courts do not require actual knowledge; rather, a defendant incurs contributory copyright liability if he has reason to know of the third party's direct infringement.

Plaintiffs present convincing evidence that Napster executives actually knew about and sought to protect use of the service to transfer illegal MP3 files. For example, a document authored by co-founder Sean Parker mentions the need to remain ignorant of users' real names and IP addresses "since they are exchanging pirated music." The same document states that, in bargaining with the RIAA, defendant will benefit from the fact that "we are not just making pirated music available but also pushing demand." These admissions suggest that facilitating the unauthorized exchange of copyrighted music was a central part of Napster, Inc.'s business strategy from the inception. Plaintiff also demonstrate that defendant had actual notice of direct infringement because the RIAA informed it of more than 12,000 infringing files. Although Napster, Inc. purportedly terminated the users offering these files, the songs are still available using the Napster service, as are the copyrighted works which the record company plaintiffs identified in Schedules A and B of their complaint.

The law does not require actual knowledge of specific acts of infringement. Accordingly, the court rejects defendant's argument that titles in the Napster directory cannot be used to distinguish infringing from non-infringing files and thus that defendant cannot know about infringement by any particular user of any particular musical recording or composition.

Defendant's reliance on Religious Technology Center v. Netcom Online Communication Services, Inc., 907 F. Supp. 1361 (N. D. Cal. 1995), does not alter the court's conclusion that plaintiffs have a reasonable likelihood of proving contributory liability. The cited passage from Religious Technology Center states: Where a BBS [bulletin board service] operator cannot reasonably verify a claim of infringement, either because of a possible fair use defense, the lack of copyright notices on the copies, or the copyright holder's failure to provide the necessary documentation to show that there is likely infringement, the operator's lack of knowledge will be found reasonable and there will be no liability for contributory infringement for allowing the continued distribution of the works on its system.

This language is dicta because the plaintiffs in Religious Technology Center raised a genuine issue of material fact regarding knowledge. More importantly, Napster is not an Internet service provider that acts as a mere conduit for the transfer of files. Rather, it offers search and directory functions specifically designed to allow users to locate music, the majority of which is copyrighted. Thus, even if dicta from another federal district court were binding, Religious Technology Center would not mandate a determination that Napster, Inc. lacks the knowledge requisite to contributory infringement.

At the very least, defendant had constructive knowledge of its users' illegal conduct. Some Napster executives boast recording industry experience, and defendant does not dispute that it possessed enough sophistication about intellectual property laws to sue a rock band that copied its logo. The evidence indicates that Napster executives downloaded infringing material to their own computers using the service and promoted the website with screen shots listing infringing files. Such conduct satisfies the objective test for constructive knowledge — defendant had reason to know about infringement by third parties.

Plaintiffs have also shown that defendant materially contributed to the infringing activity. In Fonovisa, the owners of copyrights for musical recordings stated a contributory infringement claim against the operators of a swap meet at which independent vendors sold counterfeit recordings. The Ninth Circuit held the copyright owners' allegations were "sufficient to show material contribution" because "it would have been difficult for the infringing activity to take place in the massive quantities alleged without the support services provided by the swap meet." According to plaintiffs in the instant action, "Napster is essentially an Internet swap meet — more technologically sophisticated but in many ways indistinguishable from the [defendant] in Fonovisa." The court largely agrees with this characterization.

Unlike the swap meet vendors, Napster users offer their infringing music for free. However, defendant's material contribution is still analogous to that of the swap meet in Fonovisa. The swap meet provided support services like parking, booth space, advertising, and clientele. Here, Napster, Inc. supplies the proprietary software, search engine, servers, and means of establishing a connection between users' computers. Without the support services defendant provides, Napster users could not find and download the music they want with the ease of which defendant boasts. Several contributory infringement cases involving online services are in accord with the court's conclusion that defendant materially contributes to the infringing activity. For example in Sega II, an electronic bulletin board service acted as a central depository for unauthorized copies of computer games and materially contributed to infringement because it provided software, hardware, and phone lines needed for uploading and downloading copyrighted material.

Similarly, in Religious Technology Center, a case defendant ignores when convenient, a court in this district stated that an Internet access provider is not a mere landlord; rather, it exerts control akin to a radio station replaying infringing broadcasts. Defendant marshals two district court cases in an attempt to rebut plaintiffs' argument about material contribution. See Intellectual Reserve, Inc. v. Utah Lighthouse Ministry, 75 F. Supp. 2d 1290, 1293 (D. Utah 1999) (holding that posting links to infringing websites did not contribute to infringement by those websites' operators); Bernstein v. J. C. Penny, Inc., 50 U. S. P. Q. 2d 1063 (C. D. Cal. 1998) (paraphrasing defendant's apparently successful argument that "multiple linking does not constitute substantial participation in any infringement where the linking website does not mention the fact that Internet users could, by following the links, find infringing material on another website"). The Bernstein court offered no reasoning for its dismissal of the complaint. Neither case is factually apposite, for Napster provides its users with much more than hyperlinking; Napster is an integrated service designed to enable users to locate and download MP3 music files. In keeping with its view that Napster, Inc. plays a more active role in facilitating file-sharing than an Internet service provider acting as a passive conduit, this court finds it probable that defendant materially contributed to unlawful conduct.

Because they have made a convincing showing with regard to both the knowledge and material contribution elements, plaintiffs have established a reasonable likelihood of success on their contributory infringement claims.

E. Vicarious Copyright Infringement

Even in the absence of an employment relationship, a defendant incurs liability for vicarious copyright infringement if he "has the right and ability to supervise the infringing activity and also has a direct financial interest in such activities."

In Fonovisa, the swap meet operator satisfied the first element of vicarious liability because it had the right to terminate vendors at will; it also controlled customers' access and promoted its services. Although Napster, Inc. argues that it is technologically difficult, and perhaps infeasible, to distinguish legal and illegal conduct, plaintiffs have shown that defendant supervises Napster use. Indeed, Napster, Inc. itself takes pains to inform the court of its improved methods of blocking users about whom rights holders complain. This is tantamount to an admission that defendant can, and sometimes does, police its service.

Moreover, a defendant need not exercise its supervisory powers to be deemed capable of doing so. The court therefore finds that Napster, Inc. has the right and ability to supervise its users' infringing conduct.

Plaintiffs have shown a reasonable likelihood that Napster, Inc. has a direct financial interest in the infringing activity. Citing several non-governing cases from other districts, they contend that direct financial benefit does not require earned revenue, so long as the defendant has economic incentives for tolerating unlawful behavior. For instance, in Major Bob Music v. Stubbs, 851 F. Supp. 475 (S.D. Ga. 1994), a bar derived direct financial benefit from infringing musical performances on its premises. The court noted that "an enterprise is considered to be 'profit-making' even if it never actually yields a profit."

Although Napster, Inc. currently generates no revenue, its internal documents state that it "will drive [sic] revenues directly from increases in userbase." The Napster service attracts more and more users by offering an increasing amount of quality music for free. It hopes to "monetize" its user base through one of several generation revenue models noted in the factual findings. This is similar to the type of direct financial interest the Ninth Circuit found sufficient for vicarious liability in Fonovisa, where the swap meet's revenues flowed directly from customers drawn by the availability of music at bargain basement prices. Napster, Inc.'s cursory discussion of the second element of vicarious liability does little to rebut this line of reasoning. Relying on Religious Technology Center, 907 F. Supp. at 1376–77, defendant maintains that it does not have a policy of ignoring infringement, and that even if it did, its non-infringing uses lure consumers to its service. The latter contention, for which it provides no factual support, does not square with its prediction that "the requested injunction would effectively put Napster out of business." If many of defendant's commercially significant uses were non-infringing, an injunction limited to unlawful activity would not have such a dire impact. Defendant's representations about the primacy of its legitimate uses thus appear disingenuous. The ability to download myriad popular music files without payment seems to constitute the glittering object that attracts Napster's financially-valuable user base.

Plaintiffs has shown a reasonable likelihood of success on their vicarious infringement claims.

F. Defendant's First Amendment Challenge

According to Napster, Inc., the requested injunction would impose a prior restraint on its free speech, as well as that of its users and the unsigned artists that depend upon its service. This First Amendment argument centers on the fact that defendant offers an electronic directory, which does not itself contain copyrighted material. Directories have been accorded First Amendment protection.

Although an overbroad injunction might implicate the First Amendment, free speech concerns "are protected by and coextensive with the fair use doctrine." This court has already determined that plaintiffs do not seek to enjoin any fair uses of the Napster service that are not completely contrived or peripheral to its existence.

The parties dispute the extent to which infringing and non-infringing aspects of the service are separable. Napster, Inc.'s interim CEO Hank Barry and Vice President of Engineering Edward Kessler both opine that the requested injunction would have the practical effect of compelling defendant to exclude all songs from its system, including those which plaintiffs do not own. In this view, the injunction would destroy the Napster service, or if the service did not shut down completely, forcibly supplant peer-to-peer file-sharing with a model under which defendant dictated the content. Barry avers that, as a result of the injunction, Napster would lose its competitive edge vis-a-vis similar services.

In contrast, plaintiffs contend that Napster's New Artist Program, message boards, chat rooms, and file-sharing applications for business and scientific research would remain viable if the court granted the requested relief. Plaintiffs expert Daniel Farmer suggests several potentially viable methods of limiting the Napster service to music files authorized for sharing. First, defendant could compile a database of authorized music and then write a software program to read the files on users' hard drives when they log-on to the Napster service. The program would compare those file names with the authorized list, and only those files that matched could be uploaded onto Napster. Alternatively, defendant could write a software program that prevented users from successfully searching for file names excluded from the authorized list. In the event that Napster, Inc. cannot separate the infringing and non-infringing aspects of its service, its First Amendment argument still fails. Courts will not sustain a First Amendment challenge where the defendant entraps itself in an "all-or-nothing predicament." Even if it is technologically impossible for Napster, Inc. to offer such functions as its directory without facilitating infringement, the court still must take action to protect plaintiffs' copyrights.

.   .   .   .

For the foregoing reasons, the court GRANTS plaintiffs' motion for a preliminary injunction against Napster, Inc. Defendant is hereby preliminarily ENJOINED from engaging in, or facilitating others in copying, downloading, uploading, transmitting, or distributing plaintiffs' copyrighted musical compositions and sound recordings, protected by either federal or state law, without express permission of the rights owner. This injunction applies to all such works that plaintiffs own; it is not limited to those listed in Schedules A and B of the complaint.

Discussion Questions

1. The RIAA has enjoyed mixed success in bringing these actions against new MP3 companies. Might they ultimately win the battle but lose the war? Can the popularity of MP3s be stopped in the courtroom?

2. Clearly, all MP3s are not pirated, as many enjoy free distribution unencumbered by copyright limitations. How does this affect the legal analysis when considering services such as MP3.com and Napster?

Musicians appear to be of mixed minds regarding MP3s and services like Napster. Some, such as rock band Metallica, have openly challenged Napster to follow through with its copyright compliance policy. Others, such as punk group The Offspring, have voiced support for the service.

Soon after the MP3.com decision, the company negotiated settlements with several major music labels and negotiated licensing fees for distribution of copyrighted music.

Since most litigation over digital music has occurred in the United States, Canadian must be careful to distinguish between our differing approaches to copyright law. In fact, had these cases been argued in Canada, the arguments, and potentially the outcomes might have been different. For example, legal concepts such as contributory copyright infringement and the non-infringing uses of a technology, critical to the RIAA and Napster legal arguments, are not found in Canadian copyright law.

In Canada, the legal framework for digital music downloading on the Internet has been addressed largely through two decisions of the Copyright Board. The Tariff 22 decision, introduced earlier in this chapter within the context of linking, considered whether music transmissions on the Internet fall within the regulatory framework, and the Private Copying decision addressed how private copying of music would be treated under the *Copyright Act*. Both decisions are excerpted below.

Re Tariff 22, Internet[†]

A. WHAT DO "COMMUNICATION", "TELECOMMUNICATION", "PUBLIC" AND "MUSICAL WORK" MEAN IN THE CONTEXT OF INTERNET TRANSMISSIONS?

1.   Internet transmissions are communications

To communicate is to make known or convey information. A musical work is information. It is communicated when it is conveyed or made known to someone. For example, a musical work is communicated when its notation is published in a news-

---

[†] *SOCAN Statement of Royalties, Public Performance of Musical Works 1996, 1997, 1998 (sub nom. Re Tariff 22, Internet)* 1 C.P.R. 4th 417.

paper. It is also communicated when packets of data are transmitted over the Internet so that once reassembled, they allow the work to be performed, copied or otherwise conveyed or made known to the recipient.

Internet transmissions remain communications within the meaning of the Act even though they also involve, or result in, one or more transitory or permanent reproductions. A single activity may give rise to liability under more than one head of subsection 3(1) of the Act. Thus, a facsimile transmission results in a communication even though it involves a reproduction.

2. Internet transmissions are communications by telecommunication

Section 2 of the Act defines "telecommunication" as "any transmission of signs, signals, writing, images or sounds or intelligence [page 444] of any nature by wire, radio, visual, optical or other electromagnetic system". Packets of information transmitted on the Internet meet that definition.

A distinction should be made between the words "communicate" and "by telecommunication". "Communicate" refers to the act of making known, while the term "by telecommunication" refers to the physical means used to communicate.

3. The public or private character of a communication over the Internet can be determined according to established legal and jurisprudential principles

Most court decisions dealing with the meaning of "public" in the Act addressed the expression "performance in public", not "to communicate to the public". Nevertheless, since the Federal Court of Appeal has ruled that the expression "to the public" is broader than "in public", it can safely be assumed that a telecommunication is to the public every time a performance would be public in similar circumstances. These decisions also make it clear that expressions such as "in public" and "to the public" are to be interpreted by taking a realistic view of the impact and effect of technological developments and in a manner consistent with their plain and usual meaning "that is to say openly, without concealment and to the knowledge of all".

Consequently, a communication intended to be received by members of the public in individual private settings is a communication to the public. The same holds true of a communication intended only for a segment of the public, whether it be through e-mail, to a newsgroup, a bulletin board service or a service offered on a subscription basis, or of a communication over a network for which access is restricted, as long as the transmission occurs outside a purely domestic setting, and even though only certain members of the public may be willing to pay a fee or take other steps to subscribe to the service.

For example, a newsgroup communication will be to the public if the newsgroup constitutes a public. If any customer of an IAP that carries the newsgroup can access it, then any transmission that occurs when a member of the newsgroup gains access to a work will ordinarily be a communication to the public.

Having said this, the person posting a file must intend it to be accessed by some segment of the public, and certainly more than a single recipient, in order for its transmission to constitute a communication to the public. Consequently, an e-mail communication between a single sender and a single recipient is not a communication to the public for the sole reason that it is sent outside the context of a domestic setting.

4. A communication need not be instantaneous or simultaneous to be a communication to the public

Opponents of Tariff 22 argue that a communication to the public implies an immediacy of experience by the recipient which is necessary in order to distinguish it from reproduction. They contrast what occurs over the Internet with the broadcast radio and television, where signal reception and listening or viewing are simultaneous, and conclude from this that Internet transmissions are not communications to the public.

The Board disagrees. To communicate is to convey information, whether or not this is done in a simultaneous fashion. The private or public nature of the communication should be assessed as a function of the intended target of the act. In other words, the time frame within which the communication takes place is irrelevant; a facsimile transmission to ten thousand randomly selected persons is a communication to the public even though the transmission can only occur sequentially.

Musical works are made available on the Internet openly and without concealment, with the knowledge and intent that they be conveyed to all who might access the Internet. Accordingly, a communication may be to the public when it is made to individual members of the public at different times, whether chosen by them (as is the case on the Internet) or by the person responsible for sending the work (as is the case with facsimile transmissions).

Nothing in the Act requires that a communication be sent simultaneously to the intended recipients to be a communication to the public. Nevertheless, opponents of Tariff 22 rely on a statement found in the Trial Division decision in CCTA, to the effect that "one may communicate to the public by a series of simultaneous individual communications to numerous people in different locations", to conclude that such a requirement exists.

For several reasons, the opponents' position is not supported by the above referenced passage. First, the only kinds of communication at issue in CCTA were simultaneous communications. Consequently, it is not surprising that the decision should focus on them. Second, the decision expressly refers to the possibility of communicating a work to the public by facsimile, something which necessarily involves a non-simultaneous transmission. Third, the decision on appeal is absolutely devoid of any reference to simultaneity. Fourth, both the Trial Division and the Court of Appeal clearly stated the need to "take a realistic view of the impact and effect of technological developments". To require simultaneity would run contrary to this admonition.

Such an interpretation must also be set aside because it might render nugatory all Canadian copyright legislation in the world of telecommunications, by putting future advances in interactivity, addressability and transmission on demand outside of the realm of copyright protection. As was pointed out by proponents of Tariff 22, the fact that the Internet is interactive and fully addressable by members of the public who choose to access the work does not change its underlying purpose of allowing the transmission of the work to anyone who is provided with access to the Internet and who wishes to receive the work.

5. Musical works can be communicated by telecommunication over the Internet

Opponents of Tariff 22 argue that the various operations and technologies involved in making music available over the Internet mean that musical works, within the meaning of the Act, are not communicated over the Internet. The Board disagrees.

Opponents of Tariff 22 state that the process of compression and decompression means that something other than a musical work is transmitted. Yet, the result of these operations is that information is provided that allows a lay recipient to recognize the work. That, in itself, is sufficient. If such operations, or others such as modulation or encoding, could somehow change the nature of what is being communicated, then it would be impossible to communicate a musical work through a digital transmission. This would result in the rather absurd situation that commercial radio stations would no longer need to pay royalties to SOCAN as soon as they switched to digital technology.

The Board also disagrees with the argument that a communication of the work does not occur because the work is broken into packets, each of which may not contain a substantial part of a musical work. The work is so broken down solely to respond to the technical exigencies of the Internet. What is transmitted in response to a request is not one, but a series of packets of data resulting in a communication of the work. While some intermediaries may not be transmitting the entire work or a substantial part of a work, all of the packets required to communicate the work are transmitted from the server on which the work is located to the end user. Consequently, the work is communicated.

In the same vein, the fact that packets may be sent or received out of order is also irrelevant. A copy of a work is on a hard drive even if the relevant data is stored in separate sectors located throughout the hard drive.

Opponents of Tariff 22 also argue that what is transmitted over the Internet is not the work itself, but instructions that allow the end user to reconstitute the work. The Board's view is that what is transmitted is a musical work in various formats in accordance with the technological exigencies of the Internet. Be that as it may, the end result is the reconstitution on the end user's hardware of all that is required to view, play or store the work, and therefore a communication of the work. Again, any other interpretation would run contrary to the admonition of the Federal Court of Appeal and make the rights of authors dependent on the technology employed.

Opponents of Tariff 22 rely on earlier decisions of the Federal and Supreme courts to argue that what is communicated over the Internet is not works, but performances of works. This argument fails to take into account the legislative evolution that has taken place since these decisions were rendered, the cumulative effect of which is that musical works can be communicated by telecommunication.

Thus paragraph 3(1)(f) of the Act has included since 1989 "the right ... to communicate the work to the public by telecommunication". At the same time, "telecommunication" was defined as "any transmission of signs, signals, writings, images or sounds or intelligence of any nature by wire, radio, visual, optical or other electromagnetic system".

Notwithstanding these amendments, the Federal Court of Appeal, relying on the definition of musical work as "any combination of melody and harmony, or either of them, printed, reduced to writing [page 448] or otherwise graphically produced or reproduced", ruled that the musical work exists in the form in which it is fixed. Therefore, a communication to the public by telecommunication of musical works, as opposed to the communication of a performance thereof, occurred only if sheet music was shown in front of a camera or faxed to a segment of the public.

Parliament responded to this decision, by changing the definition of "musical work" to "any work of music or musical composition". As a result, the transmission of music by cable operators (and others) was transformed from a public performance to a public telecommunication. Finally, on January 1, 1994, a provision came into force that made it clear that the person who communicates a work does not perform it.

Consequently, it is no longer the case that a musical work exists in the form in which it is fixed, and CTV 1968, CTV 1993 and CCTA (C.A.) are no longer authorities on this issue. Furthermore, the ruling that musical works can be communicated over the Internet is the only one consonant with the rules of interpretation that earlier court decisions have applied when interpreting the Act.

Significantly, in CAB 1994, the Court carefully avoided passing any judgment on the situation as of September 1, 1993: see p. 197.

B. WHEN IS A COMMUNICATION TO THE PUBLIC EFFECTED ON THE INTERNET?

A work is communicated not when it is made available, but when it is transmitted.

Those who argue that a work is communicated when it is made available, for example, by storing it on a host server where it can be accessed by members of the public, rely both on an international treaty and on Canadian court decisions.

They quote Article 8 of the World Intellectual Property Organization (WIPO) Copyright Treaty adopted in December 1996. It provides that the right to authorize the communication to the public of a work includes making it available in such a way that members of the public may access it from a place and at a time individually chosen by them. However, the Treaty is not binding in Canada since it has been signed but not ratified by the Canadian Government.

They also refer to the CCTA (C.A.) and CAB 1994 decisions. Again, these are of little help as support for the argument put forward by proponents of Tariff 22.

The first decision rejected the argument that cable operators do not perform musical works in public because subscribers must turn on their television sets before a work may be heard:

> ...the appellant transmits directly to the public ... the fact that the subscriber has to turn on the television set in no way alters the nature of the transmission. The appellant is more than a mere facilitator of a public performance ... it is the actual performer through an innocent agent or with the assistance of a third party who completes the final and missing link by turning on the television set.

The second decision endorsed the following statement by the Board:

> The Federal Court of Appeal recently stated that "the transmission of non-broadcast services by [cable operators] ... is a performance in public". This statement, which the board finds equally applicable to the transmission of a broadcast signal by a television station, highlights two further characteristics of a broadcaster's performance.
>
> First, it establishes that the performance occurs at the time of the transmission. As a result, the existence of the performance is not even dependent on anyone viewing the program....

These decisions do not state that a work is communicated when it is made available. Instead, they deal with the nature of what occurs when the signal of a cable operator or of a conventional television station is transmitted. Incidentally, they also clarify the fact that a protected act can occur without the need to prove that any person actually viewed or heard the work being transmitted.

Consequently, a work is not communicated when it is made available.

Having said this, the CCTA (C.A.) and CAB 1994 decisions are useful in deciding the time at which a communication occurs over the Internet in at least three respects.

First, given that the performance occurs at the time of transmission, it is easy to conclude by analogy that the communication of a work over the Internet occurs at the same time. As a result, a communication to the public occurs each time that any member of the public uses a browser to access the work from the source computer.

Second, a work is communicated to the public even if it is transmitted only once, as long as it is made available on a site that is accessible to a segment of the public. As was stated earlier, a communication is to the public if its intended target is a public. The degree to which the person wishing to communicate the work succeeds in doing so is irrelevant.

Third, the communication occurs at the time the work is transmitted whether or not it is played or viewed upon receipt, is stored for use at a later date or is never used at all. A communication by facsimile is no less a communication if the message is stored in computer memory for later retrieval rather than immediately printed to paper.

C. WHO EFFECTS COMMUNICATIONS ON THE INTERNET? IN PARTICULAR, WHO CAN BENEFIT FROM PARAGRAPH 2.4(1)(B) OF THE ACT?

1. When a work is transmitted, it is the person who posted it who communicates it

The person who posts a work (usually the content provider) does so for the sole purpose that it be accessed by others. Since Internet transmissions are communications, one should look at the source of the transmission to find out who is responsible for it. Any communication of a work occurs because a person has taken all the required steps to make the work available for communication. The fact that this is achieved at the request of the recipient or through an agent neither adds to, nor detracts from the fact that the content provider effects the communication.

The fact that the communication is automated is irrelevant. If the system is programmed to operate automatically once certain actions are taken by persons other that the content provider, it is because the Internet is so designed and because the person who posts content wishes to avail his/herself of the advantages inherent in that design. Returning again to our analogy, the person who programs a facsimile to transmit a message while he/she is asleep nevertheless effects the communication.

The fact that the hardware that actually transmits the work in any given communication may not be the hardware on which it was originally posted is just as irrelevant. The person who posted the work communicates it even if the transmission originates from a source, cache or mirror server. In the case of source or mirror sites, the responsibility is obvious: the work is being stored as a result of formal arrangements taken by the person posting the work. But the responsibility is just as clear in the case of transmissions originating from cache or proxy servers, even though these operations occur without the authorization of the person posting the work. These are part of the facilities of the Internet. The person posting content avails his/herself of these facilities. Indeed, he/she can prevent caching through the use of various devices such as meta-tags.

2. Persons who can avail themselves of paragraph 2.4(1)(b) of the Act with respect to a given communication of a work do not communicate the work.

Generally speaking, this includes all entities acting as Internet intermediaries such as the ISP of the person who makes the work available, persons whose servers acts [sic] as a cache or mirror, the recipient's ISP and those who operate routers used in the transmission

Paragraph 2.4(1)(b) of the Act provides that "a person whose only act in respect of the communication of a work ... to the public consists of providing the means of telecommunication necessary for another person to so communicate the work ... does not communicate the work ... to the public". Proponents and opponents of Tariff 22 view this provision in diametrically different ways.

Opponents of Tariff 22 argue that anyone who operates equipment or facilities used for Internet transmissions is not involved in the communication which may occur. These Internet intermediaries include, in their view, those who operate routers, provide equipment or software that are used to provide connectivity, or operate a server on which another party posts content, anyone in fact, except the person responsible for the contents and the end user. In effect, their view is that only the sender and recipient are legally involved in the communication.

For their part, proponents of Tariff 22 contend that paragraph 2.4(1)(b) applies only to the provision of physical facilities used by others to communicate a work to the public. They contend that the expression "means of telecommunication" refers to the means of transmission, not to any service or other means of communication. They argue that "means of telecommunication" connotes equipment or physical systems or facilities, as opposed to a "service", being the provision of professional or other assistance.

SOCAN also cites as authority for its interpretation of the term "service" the case of Bartholomew Green 1751 Assn. Inc. v. Canada (Attorney General) and various definitions from the Telecommunications Act in support of the distinction it draws between "means" and "services".

Proponents of Tariff 22 suggest that by contrasting the provision of means and that of services, one should be led to the conclusion, for example, that paragraph 2.4(1)(b) applies to a telephone company if it supplies lines and facilities for an ISP but not connectivity or other Internet services. They contend that these services are not necessary for a communication to occur and that, therefore, the exemption does not apply.

The interpretation favored by proponents of Tariff 22 is too narrow. "Means" has a broader meaning than "facilities". The "means" that are necessary to effect an Internet transmission and to which paragraph 2.4(1)(b) refers are not limited to routers and other hardware. They include all software connection equipment, connectivity services, hosting and other facilities and services without which such communications would not occur, just as much as the switching equipment, software and other facilities that are used as part of the infrastructure of a common carrier for the transmission of voice, data or other information.

Moreover, an Internet intermediary is not precluded from relying on paragraph 2.4(1)(b) simply because it provides services that are ancillary to providing the means of communication or because it performs certain steps or procedures (such as caching) to improve performance. Paragraph 2.4(1)(b) does not contain any wording excluding its applicability when "telecommunications" are provided as part of a service offering. Neither does the exemption cease to apply for the sole reason that the intermediary may have a contractual relationship with its subscribers. As long as its role in respect of any given transmission is limited to providing the means necessary to allow data initiated by other persons to be transmitted over the Internet, and as long as the ancillary services it provides fall short of involving the act of communicating the work or authorizing its communication, it should be allowed to claim the exemption.

Proponents of Tariff 22 also argue that the Michelin decision stands for the proposition that exceptions in the Act such as paragraph 2.4(1)(b) should be narrowly construed. This is incorrect. The proposition for which Michelin stands is that courts should not read exceptions into the Act. Furthermore, there is no reason to believe that any individual provision of the Act should be construed narrowly. Instead, recent decisions make it clear that the Act should be interpreted in accordance with the ordinary meaning of the words used in the statute, in the context in which the particular language is found and consistent with the many related portions of the statute and with the view to make it as technologically neutral as possible.

Much insistence was also put on the Electric Despatch decision. In some way, the decision anticipated the rationale of paragraph 2.4(1)(b) of the Act in that it held that the party whose wires were used to send a message should not be held contractually liable for the transmission, and interpreted the notion of transmission as involving the person who sends the message and the one who received it, but not the technical intermediary. However, the decision is not otherwise relevant to the issue at hand, if only because it revolved around the interpretation of a clause in a contract according to the rules generally applicable to the interpretation of contracts.

In the end, each transmission must be looked at individually to determine whether in that case, an intermediary merely acts as a conduit for communications by other persons, or whether it is acting as something more. Generally speaking, however, it is safe to conclude that with respect to most transmissions, only the person who posts a musical work communicates it.

3. Internet intermediaries cannot always claim the benefit of paragraph 2.4(1)(b)

The liability of an entity participating in any Internet transmission must be assessed as a function of the role the entity plays in that transmission, and not as a function of what it generally does over the Internet. Consequently, Internet intermediaries can rely on paragraph 2.4(1)(b) of the Act only with respect to communications in which they limit themselves to acting as intermediaries. In some cases, as a result of business relationships or other factors, intermediaries will act in concert with others in a different manner. Such is the case where an ISP posts content, associates itself with others to offer content, creates embedded links or moderates a newsgroup. In these cases, these entities are no longer acting as intermediaries; their liability will be assessed according to the general rules dealing with copyright liability. The same will hold true where an ISP creates a cache for reasons other than improving system performance, modifies the contents of the cached material or interferes with any means of obtaining information as to the number of "hits" or "accesses" to the cached material.

Thus, entities whose routers handle only some of the transmitted packets will always be able to argue that they do not handle a substantial part of the work. By contrast, attempts at relying on notions of volition or causation to avoid liability will be met with the same scepticism as in other situations, as there is no "prerequisite of knowledge of the existence of the violated copyright or that the action in question amounts to infringement. Infringement is the single act of doing something which only the owner of the copyright has the right to do'".

In the same vein, entities wishing to rely on decisions dealing with the notion of authorization to argue that they should not be held liable will probably find it difficult to do so, if only because their liability would flow not from their authorizing the communication, but from being an active and direct participant in it.

4. **Paragraph 2.4(1)(c) of the Act is of limited use, if any, with respect to Internet transmissions**

Paragraph 2.4(1)(c) of the Act provides that

> where a person, as part of ... any programming undertaking whose operations result in the communication of works ... to the public, transmits by telecommunication a work ... that is communicated to the public by another person ... the transmission and communication of the work ... constitutes a single communication to the public for which those persons are jointly and severally liable.

Pursuant to subsection 2.4(2) the Governor in Council has defined the expression "programming undertaking" as:

> 2. ... a network, other than a network within the meaning of the Broadcasting Act, consisting of
>
> (a) a person who transmits by telecommunication all or part of the person's programs or programming directly or indirectly to the person referred to in paragraph (b); and
> (b) a person who communicates all or part of the programs or programming referred to in paragraph (a) to the public by telecommunication.

SOCAN argued that musical works on a Web site come within the term "programs" or "programming" and that the provision applies:

(a) when a Web site operator transmits programming to an IAP who then transmits it to its subscribers;
(b) when the operator of a Web site transmits content which is mirrored or cached on an IAP server;
(c) when one entity provides content for inclusion on the Web site of an IAP or on-line service which transmits the content to its subscribers.

Opponents of Tariff 22 correctly point out that paragraph 2.4(1) (c) imposes liability on the originator of a communication of a musical work in circumstances where the initial communication was not to the public. This provision is of little use, if any, in the context of the Internet. First, the provision is unnecessary to impose liability on the person who posts the work, since that person communicates the work. Second, so long as the "other persons" referred to in the provision can avail themselves of paragraph 2.4(1)(b), they do not communicate and therefore, the conditions set out in the provision are not met.

Furthermore, paragraph 2.4(1)(c) is aimed only at programming undertakings as defined in the regulations. Whether this can be said to include anyone other than television and radio networks, specialty services and cable operators remains to be determined.

As to whether material transmitted over the Internet constitutes programming, the CRTC has determined that for purposes of the Broadcasting Act, various digital and video and audio services would come within the definition of programs and broadcasting under that Act. Whether this is sufficient also remains to be seen.

D. WHEN DOES THE ACT OF AUTHORIZING A COMMUNICATION ON THE INTERNET OCCUR?

1. By making a work available to the public on a server, a person authorizes its communication

A musical work is not communicated when it is made available, but only when it is transmitted. However, its communication is authorized as soon as the work is made available.

"Authorization" constitutes a separate protected use under the Act. To authorize is to sanction, approve and countenance. The person who makes a musical work available on an Internet-accessible site authorizes its communication. The work is posted for the sole purpose of being communicated and with full knowledge and intention that such a communication would occur. The person who makes the work available does more than merely provide the means to communicate the work; he/she either controls or purports to control the right to communicate it.

Viewed from another angle, by making a musical work available on a site, a person asks that his/her ISP (who is contractually required to comply with the request) transmit the work at the request of end users, thereby effecting the communication intended by the content provider. Under these circumstances, the person who supplies the work must be taken as purporting to have authority to put it to the use for which it is intended.

This is in clear contrast with decisions that have refused to find that the supply of equipment or facilities that may be used to infringe copyright does not constitute the act of authorization, which focussed on the lack of control exercised by the person alleged to have authorized a protected use.

Thus, in Vigneux, the Court found that the person renting out a record playing machine was not liable for authorizing musical performances in the restaurant where the machine was being used because it had no control over that use, and "no voice as to whether at any particular time it was to be available to the restaurant customers or not." In Muzak, the defendant provided recordings of music to third parties who used them to perform musical works in public. Kellock J. equated the fact situation with that in Vigneux, and found that Muzak authorized the use of its recordings in performances, but did not authorize the performances. Similarly, in de Tervagne, the Court, having found that the person who leased a theatre in which an infringing performance had taken place exercised no control on the use of the theatre, had to conclude that the theatre operator did not authorize an infringing performance that had taken place in the theatre. The defendant had done nothing more than approve the use of the hall and was entitled to presume that the person renting it would present the play in a lawful manner. By contrast, where works are posted to a Web site, the content provider controls the choice of music, including whether that includes or not protected music.

English decisions are to the same effect. In CBS Inc., the Court concluded that the defendant retailer, who rented records and sold blank audio tapes which the customers used to make copies of the rented records, was not liable for authorizing infringement. The defendant had not provided recording equipment or facilities and had not purported to grant its customers permission to copy the records. The Court found that merely assisting a third party to undertake an act that is an infringement of copyright does not constitute authorization of the infringement. In CBS Songs, the Court concluded that the manufacturer of twin-deck cassette recorders that conferred on the purchaser the ability to copy was nevertheless not liable because it had not sanctioned, approved or countenanced an infringing use of the cassette decks. The purchaser of the cassette deck decided whether to copy recorded cassette tapes and what to copy, and the supplier of the cassette decks had no control over the use of the machines.

As can be seen, these cases focus on supplying facilities or means by which another person infringes copyright. Under these circumstances, authorization occurs only when a person exerts a degree of actual or apparent control over the activities of "the grantee" sufficient for the person to be said to purport to have the authority to grant to another person the right to use the work in a manner that comes within the exclusive rights of the copyright owner. The likelihood of such an occurrence increases with the extent to which the commercial interests of the parties are linked to the protected use and the actual or imputed knowledge of the probability of a protected use. That likelihood decreases when the tools or means can be used to use unprotected works or effect unprotected uses.

The situation at hand is in stark contrast with all situations contemplated in those cases. Content providers do not provide tools for the use to occur; they provide the work. They dictate content. They determine whether the site will contain musical works. They select those works, protected or unprotected. They know and expect that the materials they post will serve to effect a use which is protected if the work is not in the public domain, something which it is incumbent upon them to verify: their contractual arrangements with the person whose services they retain to ensure transmission of the work clearly contemplate that the sole use of the posted content is to be the production of audible and visual messages on the recipient's hardware. In fact, once posted, the music, assuming it is protected, cannot be used without infringing copyright.

Moreover, it is the act of posting that constitutes authorization. By doing so, a person invites anyone with Internet access to have the work communicated to them. Consequently, when dealing with the Internet, authorization occurs before communication. This is not as surprising as it may seem. For example, SOCAN clearly authorizes a station to broadcast music when it issues a licence, and not when the broadcast takes place. Given what has been said with respect to paragraph 2.4(1)(b) of the Act, there is no need to debate at length whether Internet intermediaries authorize. In fact, to do so would be to look at the issue from the wrong end of the telescope. Even knowledge by an ISP that its facilities may be employed for infringing purposes does not make the ISP liable for authorizing the infringement if it does not purport to grant to the person committing the infringement a license or permission to infringe. An intermediary would have to sanction, approve or countenance more than the mere use of equipment that may be used for infringement. Moreover, an ISP is entitled to presume that its facilities will be used in accordance with law.

Having said this, other persons may be authorizing communications over the Internet. Where certain relationships exist between a person and the content provider, or where the person's conduct displays certain characteristics, an "authorization" will have occurred. The question of whether someone other than a content provider may be liable for authorizing the communication of a work will require an analysis of whether in the particular circumstances, one party is granting or purporting to grant to another party the right to communicate the work. Thus, while a person who contributes material to a newsgroup may be liable both as authorizing the communication and effecting it, the entity acting as a moderator may be liable for either authorizing the communication of any message that it allows to reach the newsgroup or that it edits, or as jointly communicating it.

. . . .

E. WHEN DOES A COMMUNICATION ON THE INTERNET OCCUR IN CANADA?

To occur in Canada, a communication must originate from a server located in Canada on which content has been posted. CAB 1994 makes it clear that communications occur where the transmission originates. The place of origin of the request, the location of the person posting the content and the location of the original Web site are irrelevant. [As a result, the right to authorize must be obtained from the person administering the right in Canada only when the information is posted on a Canadian server, and the right to communicate must be obtained from that same person only when the transmission originates from a server located in Canada. Conversely, a foreign resident posting a musical work on a Canadian server requires a licence from that same person.

Posting includes not only posting to the original site, but also posting to any mirror site. A mirror site is but another site on which the content provider has posted content. Consequently, when a work is transmitted from a server operating as a mirror located in Canada, the communication occurs in Canada.

For the same reasons, communications triggered by an embedded hyperlink occur at the site to which the link leads. As a result, the person who creates an embedded link to a foreign site from a Canadian site does not require a licence from SOCAN. Conversely, the person who creates an embedded link to a site on a server located in Canada authorizes its communication in Canada, irrespective of where the person is.

By contrast, when a transmission involves a cache, the communication occurs at the location of the host or mirror site from which the cache originally obtained the information. The cache, just as the router, is but an intrinsic element of the telecommunications system that is the Internet. Data resides in a cache only for a limited period of time, at the initiative of the person operating the equipment on which the cache is located. The information, and the means taken to communicate it, reside elsewhere. This is in contrast with mirror sites, which exist with the knowledge and consent of the content provider.

The previous analysis is subject to one proviso, however, since the issue of whether an entity that provides content outside Canada with the intention to communicate it specifically to recipients in Canada is communicating it in Canada remains open.

Difficulties in determining where protected activities take place for the purposes of copyright law are not unique to Canada. In Europe, it is generally thought that communications occur at the point of transmission, even though some European courts have held that communications occur in the country of destination where broadcasters specifically target an audience in that second country.

By contrast, the WIPO Treaty and the draft European directive that would implement it do not speak to the issue of the locus of the act of authorization.

Copyright Act[†]

79. In this Part,

"audio recording medium" means a recording medium, regardless of its material form, onto which a sound recording may be reproduced and that is of a kind ordinarily used by individual consumers for that purpose, excluding any prescribed kind of recording medium;

"blank audio recording medium" means

(a) an audio recording medium onto which no sounds have ever been fixed, and

(b) any other prescribed audio recording medium;

"collecting body" means the collective society, or other society, association or corporation, that is designated as the collecting body under subsection 83(8);

"eligible author" means an author of a musical work, whether created before or after the coming into force of this Part, that is embodied in a sound recording, whether made before or after the coming into force of this Part, if copyright subsists in Canada in that musical work;

"eligible maker" means a maker of a sound recording that embodies a musical work, whether the first fixation of the sound recording occurred before or after the coming into force of this Part, if

(a) both the following two conditions are met:

    (i) the maker, at the date of that first fixation, if a corporation, had its headquarters in Canada or, if a natural person, was a Canadian citizen or permanent resident of Canada within the meaning of the Immigration Act, and

    (ii) copyright subsists in Canada in the sound recording, or

(b) the maker, at the date of that first fixation, if a corporation, had its headquarters in a country referred to in a statement published under section 85 or, if a natural person, was a citizen, subject or permanent resident of such a country;

"eligible performer" means the performer of a performer's performance of a musical work, whether it took place before or after the coming into force of this Part, if the performer's performance is embodied in a sound recording and

(a) both the following two conditions are met:

    (i) the performer was, at the date of the first fixation of the sound recording, a Canadian citizen or permanent resident of Canada within the meaning of the Immigration Act, and

    (ii) copyright subsists in Canada in the performer's performance, or

(b) the performer was, at the date of the first fixation of the sound recording, a citizen, subject or permanent resident of a country referred to in a statement published under section 85;

"prescribed" means prescribed by regulations made under this Part.

80.(1) Subject to subsection (2), the act of reproducing all or any substantial part of

(a) a musical work embodied in a sound recording,

(b) a performer's performance of a musical work embodied in a sound recording, or

---

† R.S.C. 1985, c. C-42, as amended.

(c) a sound recording in which a musical work, or a performer's performance of a musical work, is embodied

onto an audio recording medium for the private use of the person who makes the copy does not constitute an infringement of the copyright in the musical work, the performer's performance or the sound recording.

(2) Subsection (1) does not apply if the act described in that subsection is done for the purpose of doing any of the following in relation to any of the things referred to in paragraphs (1)(a) to (c):

(a) selling or renting out, or by way of trade exposing or offering for sale or rental;

(b) distributing, whether or not for the purpose of trade;

(c) communicating to the public by telecommunication; or

(d) performing, or causing to be performed, in public.

81.(1) Subject to and in accordance with this Part, eligible authors, eligible performers and eligible makers have a right to receive remuneration from manufacturers and importers of blank audio recording media in respect of the reproduction for private use of

(a) a musical work embodied in a sound recording;

(b) a performer's performance of a musical work embodied in a sound recording; or

(c) a sound recording in which a musical work, or a performer's performance of a musical work, is embodied.

(2) Subsections 13(4) to (7) apply, with such modifications as the circumstances require, in respect of the rights conferred by subsection (1) on eligible authors, performers and makers.

82.(1) Every person who, for the purpose of trade, manufactures a blank audio recording medium in Canada or imports a blank audio recording medium into Canada

(a) is liable, subject to subsection (2) and section 86, to pay a levy to the collecting body on selling or otherwise disposing of those blank audio recording media in Canada; and

(b) shall, in accordance with subsection 83(8), keep statements of account of the activities referred to in paragraph (a), as well as of exports of those blank audio recording media, and shall furnish those statements to the collecting body.

(2) No levy is payable where it is a term of the sale or other disposition of the blank audio recording medium that the medium is to be exported from Canada, and it is exported from Canada.

Re Private Copying 1999–2000, Tariff of Levies to be Collected by CPCC†

On March 19, 1998, Part VIII of the Copyright Act (the "Act") came into force. Part VIII was one of the highlights of the long-awaited Phase II reform of the Act. Until then, copying any sound recording for almost any purpose infringed copyright.

---

† 4 C.P.R. 4th 15.

Private copying never was fair dealing within the meaning of the Act. Arguments to the contrary confuse the Canadian concept of fair dealing and the American notion of fair use. In Canada, fair dealing is a defence to copyright infringement. It is triggered when a protected work is used fairly for research, private study, criticism, review or news reporting. Copying a musical work for any other purpose infringes the copyright holder's reproduction right. Also, exceptions should not be read into the Act where there are none. Consequently, there is no implied exemption for those who copy music to listen to in the car or while jogging. This makes it unnecessary to debate whether copying of a whole work can constitute fair dealing. In practice, that prohibition was largely unenforceable. Part VIII legalizes one such activity: copying of sound recordings of musical works onto recording media for the private use of the person who makes the copy (hereafter "private copying"). At the same time, a levy is imposed on blank audio recording media to compensate authors, performers and makers who own copyright in those sound recordings.

The structure of Part VIII eloquently highlights the purpose of the regime.

Section 79 sets the scene by providing a number of definitions. These determine who benefits from the levy, and what is subject to it.

Section 80 legalizes private copying onto audio recording media.

Section 81 creates the right to remuneration for copying activities outlined in section 80. It also determines who shares in the remuneration: authors of musical works in which copyright subsists in Canada (which means virtually any author throughout the world), as well as performers and makers who are citizens or residents of Canada or of a country referred to in a ministerial statement made pursuant to section 85 of the Act.

Section 82 sets out how the remuneration is to be paid, when, to whom, and for what. The remuneration takes the form of a levy. Manufacturers and importers of blank audio recording media ordinarily used by individual consumers to copy sound recordings pay the levy when they sell or otherwise dispose of such media in Canada. The payment is made for the benefit of eligible copyright owners to a single collecting body designated by the Board.

Section 83 outlines how the levy is to be set. Collective societies (or "collectives") must file proposed tariffs for the benefit of their members or lose their right to remuneration. Anyone can object to the proposals. After hearing from collectives and objectors, the Board sets a fair and equitable tariff and designates the collecting body. It also allows rights owners who are not members of a collective to claim their share of the levy.

Sections 84 to 88 deal with various incidental aspects of the regime. They determine that the levy is to be shared amongst collectives in the proportions fixed by the Board and outline how the Minister can add to, or subtract from, the eligible repertoire of performers and makers. They exempt from the levy any entity that represents persons with a perceptual disability and set out Cabinet's regulatory powers. Finally, they specify what the collecting body's rights are against those who do not pay the levy.

. . . .

III. STATUTORY INTERPRETATION AND ISSUES OF MIXED FACT AND LAW

A. The Validity of CPCC's Claim to All of the Eligible Repertoire

Objectors argue that CPCC cannot claim royalties for all the eligible repertoire for at least two reasons. First, some or all of the entities that filed proposed tariffs did not qualify. Second, those that did can only claim royalties for the repertoire they actually administer. CPCC counters that even a collective that does not yet administer some rights holders' private copying rights can validly file a tariff, as long as it has secured the appropriate corporate authority to do so.

The evidence filed on these subjects concerning the nature of the relationships between the various collectives and their members as regards private copying was at best fragmentary. Nevertheless, it demonstrates that as of March 31, 1998 (the date by which proposed tariffs were to be filed), AVLA Audio-Video Licensing Agency Inc. (AVLA), the Societe de gestion collective des droits des producteurs de phonogrammes et de videogrammes du Quebec (SOPROQ), the Societe de gestion collective de l'Union des artistes (ArtistI), SOGEDAM and SODRAC had executed written instruments which expressly referred to the administration of private copying rights with at least some of their members. SOCAN, ACTRA Performers' Rights Society (APRS), the American Federation of Musicians (AFM) and CMRRA had not, but their internal corporate rules had been amended to allow them to administer those rights. Those changes had been made by bodies (e.g., a board of directors) on which some rights holders sat. The Board also believes it is reasonable to infer that each organization recruited new members after these changes intervened and before March 31, 1998. By that same date, NRCC's member collectives had empowered it to act as a collective of collectives. CPCC's creation occurred several months later, and the collectives that had filed proposed tariffs authorized CPCC to act on their behalf. Finally, no one claiming to represent rights holders took issue with the claims made by CPCC or its member collectives.

What was sometimes referred to as the "chain of title" issue raises two questions. First, is the Board properly seized of the private copying matter? Second, to what extent is the eligible repertoire entitled to remuneration?

1. Is the Board properly seized of the private copying matter?

The answer to this question depends on whether CMRRA, NRCC, SOGEDAM, SODRAC and SOCAN, who filed proposed tariffs on March 31, 1998, were private copying collectives at that time.

A collective that does not administer at least some private copying rights cannot validly file a proposed tariff pursuant to subsection 83(1) of the Act. This remains true even though the wording of that provision does not expressly state that filing collectives must be private copying collectives. It states that the societies must have been "authorized to act for that purpose", adding that the authorization must take the form of an assignment, grant of licence, appointment as one's agent or other form of authorization.

In interpreting this provision, it is clear that the "purpose" referred to must be the administration of private copying rights. Since such a purpose must be something that can be achieved through "assignment, grant of licence, appointment as one's agent or otherwise", it cannot be a reference to the authority to file proposed tariffs as such. No licence or agency agreement is required to authorize the filing of a tariff. By contrast, assignments, licences and agency agreements are how the administration of copyright is usually secured. Furthermore, the transaction must relate to private copying rights. A collective that has secured the administration of performing rights cannot use this mandate to claim the power to act as a private copying collective.

In addition, the necessary authorizations from right holders must be secured by the time set in the Act for filing proposed tariffs (in this case, March 31, 1998). The only way rights holders can be remunerated for private copying is through the collection of levies by the collecting body under the authority of a certified tariff. The Board cannot certify a tariff for a given year if no proposed tariff is filed by March 31, of the previous year; absent such a filing, it is not seized of the matter. Consequently, lack of filing results in the loss of the right to remuneration. Viewed another way, manufacturers and importers are entitled to sell audio recording media without having to pay anything if no proposed tariff is filed on time. To allow rights holders to retroactively alter the state of the matter to the prejudice of importers and manufacturers would be contrary to the scheme of the Act. Common law rules cannot be invoked to achieve a result contrary to that scheme, and ratification cannot retroactively change the natural consequences of the statutory regime set out in the Act. Consequently, unless a collective acts as a private copying collective (that is, for the benefit of rights owners who have already authorized it to act on their behalf) when it files the proposed tariff of royalties, the filing is invalid.

However, the authorization can be secured by any implicit or explicit means available at common law. For example, rules governing implicit contract agency or agency by ratification may very well work in a putative collective's favour where some rights holders were instrumental in getting the entity to file the tariff or to acquire the necessary corporate authority to administer rights. Thus, CMRRA's directors, who are also music publishers and therefore rights holders under Part VIII, granted CMRRA an implicit mandate to administer their private copying rights when they voted in favour of the collective becoming a private copying collective.

Based on these principles, all entities that filed proposed tariffs were authorized to do so pursuant to subsection 83(1) of the Act. AFM, CMRRA, APRS and SOCAN had received implicit mandates to act on behalf of rights holders who sit on their board of directors. SOGEDAM and SODRAC had clearly secured proper authorizations from at least some of their members, as had AVLA, SOPROQ and ArtistI for the benefit of NRCC. Moreover, as stated earlier, each member recruited after changes were made to the collectives' adhesion contracts and before March 31, 1998, formally authorized them to administer their private copying rights. In any event, proposed tariffs were properly filed by SODRAC with respect to eligible authors, by SOGEDAM and NRCC with respect to eligible performers, and by NRCC with respect to eligible makers. All colleges of rights holders are therefore properly before the Board.

2. The share of the eligible repertoire entitled to remuneration
In the Board's view, certified tariffs must account for all eligible subject matters of a type for which proposed tariffs were validly filed.

The repertoire cannot be limited to the filing collectives' repertoire at the time of filing, or at any other particular date during or after the certification process. This would run against the essentially prospective nature of the tariff and render subsection 83(11) of the Act (the orphans' provision) meaningless. The only interpretation consistent with that provision is that the eligible repertoire includes all works, performer's performances or sound recordings of a kind for which a proposed tariff was filed.

As already stated, proposed tariffs were properly filed for all three eligible colleges. Moreover, the Board is satisfied that at the time of filing proposed tariffs, SODRAC, SOGEDAM and NRCC had secured a sufficient number of authorizations from rights owners to administer private copying rights in each and every possible type of works, performers' performances and sound recordings comprising the eligible repertoire. This is only reinforced by the Board's conclusion that all proposed tariffs were properly filed.

Subsection 83(1) of the Act provides that a tariff is filed "for the benefit of" a collective's rights owners. That proviso must not be read as limiting the ambit of the tariff a collective can file. First, the French version is less restrictive; it only requires that a collective, act "au nom" of its rights owners. Second, to limit the repertoire before the Board to that of the members of the eligible societies either would again render subsection 83(11) of the Act meaningless or would require rights holders to bear the burden of compensating orphans out of their own share of the remuneration. Third, the proviso should not be interpreted in a way that impinges on the prospective nature of the regime. Fourth, subsection 83(8), combined with the requirement to designate a single collecting body, clearly contemplates a single tariff structure; to require that collectives file proposed tariffs dealing only with their own repertoire would run against the scheme of the Act. Consequently, a collective that files a proposed tariff, while doing so for the benefit of its rights holders, may take all of the eligible repertoire into account, including the part belonging to members of other collectives, non-members and unknown persons.

B.   The Importance of the Eligible Repertoire in Private Copying
CPCC relies on a report based upon a radio airplay survey prepared by its experts Paul Audley and Stephen Stohn (Stohn/Audley) to ask that the eligible repertoire be set at 100 per cent for authors, 37 per cent for performers and 31 per cent for makers. At the request of the Board, CPCC subsequently offered an analysis of record sales which set the percentages at 30 per cent for performers and 25 per cent for makers. In both cases, CPCC takes into account foreign performers and makers who it argues are potentially eligible. CPCC asks that the Board rely on both surveys to determine the share of eligible repertoire, suggesting that radio airplay receive three times the weight of sales.

CSMA argues that the radio survey results are biased in favour of eligible rights holders because of Canadian content rules imposed by the Canadian Radio-television and Telecommunications Commission (CRTC) on radio broadcasters. It asks that the Board rely only on the record sales study, adding that even those estimates are overstated. It requests that no account be taken of foreign performers and makers.

The two studies do not give a perfect indication of the performers' and makers' repertoire used for private copying, but contain sufficient information to enable the Board to reach a conclusion. The Board hopes that more complete sales data will be made available when future tariffs are filed. For the purposes of the present tariff, and for the reasons given by CSMA, the Board agrees that the radio airplay survey probably overstates eligibility rates for performers and makers. For one thing, their share of air time is much higher than their share of sales, and nothing indicates that the former is a better predictor of private copying than the latter. On the other hand, the sales study probably understates the amount of private copying attributable to Canadian recordings by focusing only on the top 250 selling albums in Canada and by not fully taking into account French language sales in Quebec. For these reasons, the Board uses a simple average of the results obtained from the two surveys.

No account is taken of foreign performers and makers. Section 79 of the Act is clear: only Canadian performers and makers are entitled to share in the levy until the Minister issues a statement pursuant to section 85 of the Act. Should such a statement take effect before this tariff expires, CPCC will be free to ask that the tariff be varied pursuant to section 66.52 of the Act.

Based on these considerations, the Board concludes that 28 per cent of private copies are made using the repertoire of eligible performers, while 23 per cent use the repertoire of eligible makers.

Some account has to be taken of the musical works that are no longer protected by copyright. CSMA argues it is five per cent; CPCC argues it is three. Based on the little information it was provided, the Board concludes that 96 per cent of private copies are made using the repertoire of eligible authors.

On a related issue, ICRMC argues that the "maker" of a sound recording is not the record company but the person (sometimes called the "artistic producer") who directs the artistic and creative work leading to the production of the sound recording. The Board does not accept this interpretation. According to section 2 of the Act, the maker of a sound recording is the person who undertakes the arrangements necessary for the first fixation of the sounds. Section 2.11 adds that these include arrangements for entering into contracts with performers, financial arrangements and technical arrangements required for the first fixation of the sounds for a sound recording. The mention of contractual and financial arrangements is clearly meant to refer to those who take on the financial risk of producing records, not to the person who shapes the sounds of the record and provides artistic advice to the performers.

C.   The Meaning of "Ordinarily Used by Individual Consumers"

Section 79 of the Act defines "audio recording medium" as "a recording medium, regardless of its material form, onto which a sound recording may be reproduced and that is of a kind ordinarily used by individual consumers for that purpose ...". No one questions whether it is possible to reproduce sound recordings onto the media targeted by CPCC, or the concept of an individual consumer. The meaning of the phrase "ordinarily used", however, is at issue.

CPCC submits that if a medium is regularly, commonly or normally used by individuals for private copying, then it qualifies, adding that there can be more than one common use for a type of medium. CSMA argues that the levy should apply only to the media that are most often used for private copying, and would exclude media (e.g., Mini Discs) whose share of the market is marginal, even if most or all are used to make private copies.

Although the word "ordinarily" is broad, context sensitive and "very fluid", dictionaries and case law greatly help in understanding its meaning. "Ordinary" is used to describe anything from that which is regular, normal or average, to what is merely recurring or consistent. Therefore, the ordinary character of an occurrence is not necessarily a function of quantity, but rather a matter of consistency. One can ordinarily spend Christmas with one's family even though this only occurs once a year: the regularity of a person's visit with kin makes it "ordinary".

Court decisions also tend to emphasize consistency rather than frequency. An ordinary activity need not be a person's main activity, as long as it is one which is not rare or abnormal or minimal, that is, not trivial or insignificant. The use of a secondary residence by a family needs to be consistent, not frequent, in order for it to be ordinary.

Modern statutory interpretation generally gives to an expression the meaning that a reasonable individual would ascribe to it, taking into account the context, linguistic conventions and what we know of the world, including the purpose of the legislation where the expression is found and the policy considerations motivating its use. So the purpose of the regime is of primary importance in interpreting as fluid a notion as "ordinary". One of the purposes of the regime is to legalize private copying. Another is to adequately compensate eligible authors, performers and producers of musical works. This will not happen if the definition of "blank audio recording medium" is interpreted restrictively. Too restrictive an interpretation will strip the regime of any meaning. A broad interpretation of the definition helps to level the playing field for importers and manufacturers by ensuring that only those media that clearly are not used to make private copies are not subject to the levy. Consequently, ordinary use, as that expression is found in the definition of "audio recording medium", ought to be interpreted as including all non-negligible uses.

Therefore, a person who made two copies of sound recordings onto a type of medium in each of the last two years ordinarily uses that type of medium for private copying, even though that same person may well use many more such media for other purposes: a medium can have more than one ordinary use.

Furthermore, since the definition speaks of ordinary use by individual consumers, the analysis must focus on the person who uses the medium for her own enjoyment, to the exclusion of others. Thus, the fact that only five per cent of a given type of medium is sold to individual consumers does not mean that it does not qualify. In fact, all those media, including the 95 per cent sold to "non-consumers", will be subject to the levy as long as a non-marginal number of consumers use them for private copying in a fashion that is not marginal.

By contrast, media essentially reserved for corporate or professional uses will not qualify even if a few individuals use the technology to make private copies of music. The "personal consumer use" must involve more than a few eccentrics.

Based on these principles, the Board concludes that all audio cassettes with a playing time of 40 minutes or more qualify. The evidence suggests that C-45 cassettes are the shortest standard length that can conveniently be used to make private copies of music. Anything else is simply not convenient; total sales of these and shorter length cassettes are in fact minimal. However, the Board uses the 40-minute threshold to ensure that manufacturers do not adjust cassette length for the sole purpose of avoiding the tariff.

The Board notes CPCC's opposition to such a determination. The CPCC fears that the market might try to evade the levy by manufacturing different cassette lengths, or by placing pre-recorded sounds on otherwise blank media. Nevertheless, for the reasons stated above, the Board considers that audio cassettes of a length of 40 minutes or less are not audio recording media ordinarily used by individual consumers to copy music.

No distinction will be made between Type I and other cassettes. Type I cassettes represent 72 per cent of the market. If, as the Board concludes later, close to two-thirds of all cassettes are used for private copying, then a large number of Type I cassettes must be used for that purpose. Furthermore, the testimony and demonstration of Mr. David Basskin, President of CMRRA, clearly showed that the quality of copies now made onto Type I cassettes is for all intents and purposes the same as for those made onto other types.

Neither will the Board distinguish between standard length and custom length cassettes or cassettes with other characteristics (e.g., record protect tabs removed) that may make them less suited to private copying. Too much specificity may open the door to levy avoidance by marketing new lengths and types of cassettes to consumers.

Mini Disc, CD-R Audio and CD-RW Audio also qualify. Even though these media account for only one per cent of total sales, they are mostly, if not exclusively, targeted at consumers and sold for the purpose of copying music.

Finally CD-R and CD-RW qualify. The proportion of these media used for private copying is almost certainly between 5 and 15 per cent. Even the lower figure would mean that two million private copies were made onto these media in 1999. Such a number definitely meets the threshold of ordinariness as the Board interprets it.

Audio recording media that are clearly meant for purposes other than private copying are excluded. A case in point are microcassettes commonly used in dictating machines. Digital audio tapes are another, as for all practical purposes, they are used by professionals, not by individual consumers.

The definition of what is a blank audio recording medium is an open one. As markets evolve, new types may be identified if the Board is satisfied that consumers have found other ways to make private copies of their favourite music.

Discussion Questions

1. Consider the implications of the Tariff 22 and Private Copying decisions on sites such as Napster and its users. Is Napster protected by the ISP exemption outlined in Tariff 22? Are its users protected by the Private Copying decision?

2. Is the posting of songs for download on Napster the equivalent of posting on a Web site? If so, does that constitute an authorization to communicate, which is also an infringement of copyright? Do all Napster users need licenses?

3. The Copyright Board characterizes the private copying regime as compensatory in nature. What do you think that means? If the recording industry actually benefits from private copying as some suggest (arguing that private copying is the equivalent of sampling music and actually results in increased music sales), should the compensation be reduced?

4. The Private Copying decision addresses copying onto blank audio cassettes and blank CDs. Do you think this could be extended to other media such as the Diamond Rio or computer hard drives? Consider the "ordinary use" definition adopted by the Copyright Board. It was the subject of considerable controversy as many commentators suggested that it was too broad and effectively covered any type of media. The Federal Court of Appeal reviewed the definition and provided the following analysis in *AVS Technologies Inc. v. Canadian Mechanical Reproduction Rights Agency (CMRRA).*

AVS Technologies Inc. v. Canadian Mechanical Reproduction Rights Agency (CMRRA)†

The issue in this case is whether this Court should interfere with a decision of the Copyright Board dated December 17, 1999 interpreting a definition provision of the Copyright Act R.S.C. 1985, c. C-42, which reads:

---

† Docket A-19-00 (Fed. Ct. App.), June 14, 2000.

79. In this Part,

> "audio recording medium" means a recording medium, regardless of its material form onto which a sound recording may be reproduced and that is of a kind ordinarily used by individual consumers for that purpose, excluding any prescribed kind of recording medium;

In particular, the issue was whether certain CD's were leviable at the manufacturers' and importers' level, which they would be if they were "of a kind ordinarily used by individual consumers for that purpose", i.e. reproducing a sound recording.

The Board's reasons on the matter, which in total occupied 69 pages and dealt with several other issues, were as follows:

Although the word "ordinarily" is broad, context sensitive and "very fluid", dictionaries and case law greatly help in understanding its meaning. "Ordinary" is used to describe anything from that which is regular, normal or average, to what is merely recurring or consistent. Therefore, the ordinary character of an occurrence is not necessarily a function of quantity, but rather a matter of consistency. One can ordinarily spend Christmas with one's family even though this only occurs once a year: the regularity of a person's visit with kin makes it "ordinary".

Court decisions also tend to emphasize consistency rather than frequency. An ordinary activity need not be a person's main activity, as long as it is one which is not rare or abnormal or minimal, that is, not trivial or insignificant. The use of a secondary residence by a family needs to be consistent, not frequent, in order for it to be ordinary.

Modern statutory interpretation generally gives to an expression the meaning that a reasonable individual would ascribe to it, taking into account the context, linguistic conventions and what we know of the world, including the purpose of the legislation where the expression is found and the policy considerations motivating its use. So the purpose of the regime is of primary importance in interpreting as fluid a notion as "ordinary". One of the purposes of the regime is to legalize private copying. Another is to adequately compensate eligible authors, performers and producers of musical works. This will not happen if the definition of "blank audio recording medium" is interpreted restrictively. Too restrictive an interpretation will strip the regime of any meaning. A broad interpretation of the definition helps to level the playing field for importers and manufacturers by ensuring that only those media that clearly are not used to make private copies are not subject to the levy. Consequently, ordinary use, as that expression is found in the definition of "audio recording medium", ought to be interpreted as including all non-negligible uses.

Therefore, a person who made two copies of sound recordings onto a type of medium in each of the last two years ordinarily uses that type of medium for private copying, even though that same person may well use many more such media for other purposes: a medium can have more than one ordinary use.

Furthermore, since the definition speaks of ordinary use by individual consumers, the analysis must focus on the person who uses the medium for her own enjoyment, to the exclusion of others. Thus, the fact that only five per cent of a given type of medium is sold to individual consumers does not mean that it does not qualify. In fact, all those media, including the 95 per cent sold to "non-consumers", will be subject to the levy as long as a non-marginal number of consumers use them for private copying in a fashion that is not marginal.

By contrast, media essentially reserved for corporate or professional uses will not qualify even if a few individuals use the technology to make private copies of music. The "personal consumer use" must involve more than a few eccentrics.

This Court must now decide whether to interfere with this decision. I am of the view that we should not.

In our view, this issue is mainly a question of law, that is, the interpretation of legislation that the Board administers. Such a determination falls squarely within the jurisdiction of the Board. It is in its home territory. The issue is a polycentric one dealing with the interests of artists, manufacturers, importers, consumers who record sound, consumers who do not record sound and others. The purpose of Part VIII of the Act is mainly an economic one — that is, to fairly compensate artists and the other creative people for their work by establishing fair and equitable levies. These are matters within the expertise of the Board which has been given the authority to decide inter alia the manner of determining the levies, who pays, how much they pay and the terms and conditions of the payment. The Board, therefore, should know the industry it is regulating better than the Court. Hence, applying the "functional and pragmatic" test of Pushpanathan v. Canada, and having looked at the factors outlined, the proper standard of review on this issue, even though there is no privative clause, is patent unreasonableness, as considerable curial deference is due to this Board on this question.

The key point is whether the Board had to decide the meaning of "ordinarily used" by looking at the products generally, as contended for by the applicant, or by considering the use by individual consumers of that product. In my view, it is the usage by individual consumers that must be ordinary, not the use of the product generally, because of the insertion of the words "by individual consumers", which have to be given some meaning. If these words were not there, the applicants' contention would have been more solidly grounded. The French version is consistent with this interpretation as there is also a reference to use by "consommateurs", who are generally considered to be individuals, not corporations or institutions.

It must be recalled that the scheme devised by Parliament was to fairly compensate artists and others for copyright infringement by those who illegally copied their work. It was not an easy task to charge individuals a levy, so that a system was devised to place the levy on importers and manufacturers of products based on an estimate of the value of the copyright which was infringed by individuals who ordinarily copied music on those products. Such a scheme cannot be perfect; it is a rough estimate, involving possible overcharging of some and undercharging of others. The main goal is to be as fair and equitable as possible to both the artists and those who enjoy and profit from their work, and those upon whom the levy may be imposed but who do not copy the work.

The applicants argued that the interpretation of the term "ordinarily" should be guided by dictionary definitions such as "usually" or "commonly" and by certain authorities from other contexts they cited, which indicated it should be defined as "chiefly" or "mainly". Later, they suggested that a number approaching 50 percent of the products used in this way might be considered to be used ordinarily. In my view, these definitions and cases are not very helpful. Nor is the percentage approach, for that would be arbitrary. Moreover, it would mean that the artists would receive no compensation at all for the infringement of their copyrights until nearly one-half of the products are so used. This would hardly be consistent with the object of the legislation.

In short, the applicants have not demonstrated that the Board's approach was obviously or clearly wrong or that another approach would be more obvious.

It should be recalled that the Board, after concluding that the products in question fell within the definition, reduced the levy by some 80 percent to reflect the fact that, according to the research, only a small proportion of the products were actually used to record music. Such a result seems more in harmony with the statutory scheme.

I, therefore, cannot conclude that the Board's decision was patently unreasonable.

18

Electronic Commerce Patents

A business method patent is one awarded for a special technique for doing business, such as improvements to a company's accounting or sales department. The problems began with the 1998 U.S. case, *State Street Bank* v. *Signature Financial Corp.* In that case, the U.S. Court of Appeals for the Federal Circuit ruled that patents could be awarded for business methods.

In the aftermath of the *State Street Bank* decision, companies rushed to file patent claims for a wide range of business practices. Although Canada has yet to embrace the concept of a business method patent, Canadian companies have obtained such patents in the United States. For example, the Royal Bank obtained a U.S. patent in 1998 for its automobile financing buy-back program.

In the e-commerce world, efforts to patent online business methods have met with great success. In 1998, patents were awarded for frequent flier awards for on-line purchases, incentives for consumers to interact with online ads, the Internet shopping cart, and the name-your-own price reverse auction. This last patent, obtained by Priceline.com, generated considerable attention as founder Jay Walker indicated that the company had filed 20 patent applications covering all aspects of its business methods.

Not surprisingly, e-commerce patent awards have now become the basis of a growing number of patent infringement lawsuits.

State Street Bank & Trust Co. v. Signature Financial Group, Inc.†

BACKGROUND

Signature is the assignee of the '056 patent which is entitled "Data Processing System for Hub and Spoke Financial Services Configuration." The '056 patent issued to Signature on 9 March 1993, naming R. Todd Boes as the inventor. The '056 patent is generally directed to a data processing system (the system) for implementing an investment structure which was developed for use in Signature's business as an administrator and accounting agent for mutual funds. In essence, the system, identified by the proprietary name Hub and Spoke (R), facilitates a structure whereby mutual funds (Spokes) pool their assets in an investment portfolio (Hub) organized as a partnership. This investment configuration provides the administrator of a mutual fund with the advantageous combination of economies of scale in administering investments coupled with the tax advantages of a partnership.

State Street and Signature are both in the business of acting as custodians and accounting agents for multi-tiered partnership fund financial services. State Street negotiated with Signature for a license to use its patented data processing system described and claimed in the '056 patent. When negotiations broke down, State Street brought a declaratory judgment action asserting invalidity, unenforceability, and noninfringement in Massachusetts district court, and then filed a motion for partial summary judgment of patent invalidity for failure to claim statutory subject matter under §101. The motion was granted and this appeal followed.

DISCUSSION

. . . .

The following facts pertinent to the statutory subject matter issue are either undisputed or represent the version alleged by the nonmovant. See *Anderson* v. *Liberty Lobby, Inc*. The patented invention relates generally to a system that allows an administrator to monitor and record the financial information flow and make all calculations necessary for maintaining a partner fund financial services configuration. As previously mentioned, a partner fund financial services configuration essentially allows several mutual funds, or "Spokes," to pool their investment funds into a single portfolio, or "Hub," allowing for consolidation of, inter alia, the costs of administering the fund combined with the tax advantages of a partnership. In particular, this system provides means for a daily allocation of assets for two or more Spokes that are invested in the same Hub. The system determines the percentage share that each Spoke maintains in the Hub, while taking into consideration daily changes both in the value of the Hub's investment securities and in the concomitant amount of each Spoke's assets.

In determining daily changes, the system also allows for the allocation among the Spokes of the Hub's daily income, expenses, and net realized and unrealized gain or loss, calculating each day's total investments based on the concept of a book capital account. This enables the determination of a true asset value of each Spoke and accurate calculation of allocation ratios between or among the Spokes. The system

---

† 47 U.S.P.Q.2D (BNA) 1596 (Fed. Cir. 1998).

additionally tracks all the relevant data determined on a daily basis for the Hub and each Spoke, so that aggregate year end income, expenses, and capital gain or loss can be determined for accounting and for tax purposes for the Hub and, as a result, for each publicly traded Spoke.

It is essential that these calculations are quickly and accurately performed. In large part this is required because each Spoke sells shares to the public and the price of those shares is substantially based on the Spoke's percentage interest in the portfolio. In some instances, a mutual fund administrator is required to calculate the value of the shares to the nearest penny within as little as an hour and a half after the market closes. Given the complexity of the calculations, a computer or equivalent device is a virtual necessity to perform the task.

The '056 patent application was filed 11 March 1991. It initially contained six "machine" claims, which incorporated means-plus-function clauses, and six method claims. According to Signature, during prosecution the examiner contemplated a §101 rejection for failure to claim statutory subject matter. However, upon cancellation of the six method claims, the examiner issued a notice of allowance for the remaining present six claims on appeal. Only claim 1 is an independent claim.

The district court began its analysis by construing the claims to be directed to a process, with each "means" clause merely representing a step in that process. However, "machine" claims having "means" clauses may only be reasonably viewed as process claims if there is no supporting structure in the written description that corresponds to the claimed "means" elements. This is not the case now before us.

When independent claim 1 is properly construed in accordance with §112, P 6, it is directed to a machine, as demonstrated below, where representative claim 1 is set forth, the subject matter in brackets stating the structure the written description discloses as corresponding to the respective "means" recited in the claims.

1. A data processing system for managing a financial services configuration of a portfolio established as a partnership, each partner being one of a plurality of funds, comprising:
   (a) computer processor means [a personal computer including a CPU] for processing data;
   (b) storage means [a data disk] for storing data on a storage medium;
   (c) first means [an arithmetic logic circuit configured to prepare the data disk to magnetically store selected data] for initializing the storage medium;
   (d) second means [an arithmetic logic circuit configured to retrieve information from a specific file, calculate incremental increases or decreases based on specific input, allocate the results on a percentage basis, and store the output in a separate file] for processing data regarding assets in the portfolio and each of the funds from a previous day and data regarding increases or decreases in each of the funds, assets and for allocating the percentage share that each fund holds in the portfolio;
   (e) third means [an arithmetic logic circuit configured to retrieve information from a specific file, calculate incremental increases and decreases based on specific input, allocate the results on a percentage basis and store the output in a separate file] for processing data regarding daily incremental income, expenses, and net realized gain or loss for the portfolio and for allocating such data among each fund;
   (f) fourth means [an arithmetic logic circuit configured to retrieve information from a specific file, calculate incremental increases and decreases based

on specific input, allocate the results on a percentage basis and store the output in a separate file] for processing data regarding daily net unrealized gain or loss for the portfolio and for allocating such data among each fund; and

(g) fifth means [an arithmetic logic circuit configured to retrieve information from specific files, calculate that information on an aggregate basis and store the output in a separate file] for processing data regarding aggregate year-end income, expenses, and capital gain or loss for the portfolio and each of the funds.

Each claim component, recited as a "means" plus its function, is to be read, of course, pursuant to §112, P 6, as inclusive of the "equivalents" of the structures disclosed in the written description portion of the specification. Thus, claim 1, properly construed, claims a machine, namely, a data processing system for managing a financial services configuration of a portfolio established as a partnership, which machine is made up of, at the very least, the specific structures disclosed in the written description and corresponding to the means-plus-function elements (a)–(g) recited in the claim. A "machine" is proper statutory subject matter under §101. We note that, for the purposes of a §101 analysis, it is of little relevance whether claim 1 is directed to a "machine" or a "process," as long as it falls within at least one of the four enumerated categories of patentable subject matter, "machine" and "process" being such categories.

This does not end our analysis, however, because the court concluded that the claimed subject matter fell into one of two alternative judicially-created exceptions to statutory subject matter. The court refers to the first exception as the "mathematical algorithm" exception and the second exception as the "business method" exception. Section 101 reads:

Whoever invents or discovers any new and useful process, machine, manufacture, or composition of matter, or any new and useful improvement thereof, may obtain a patent therefor, subject to the conditions and requirements of this title.

The plain and unambiguous meaning of §101 is that any invention falling within one of the four stated categories of statutory subject matter may be patented, provided it meets the other requirements for patentability set forth in Title 35, i.e., those found in §§102, 103, and 112, P2.

The repetitive use of the expansive term "any" in §101 shows Congress's intent not to place any restrictions on the subject matter for which a patent may be obtained beyond those specifically recited in §101. Indeed, the Supreme Court has acknowledged that Congress intended §101 to extend to "anything under the sun that is made by man." Thus, it is improper to read limitations into §101 on the subject matter that may be patented where the legislative history indicates that Congress clearly did not intend such limitations.

The "Mathematical Algorithm" Exception

The Supreme Court has identified three categories of subject matter that are unpatentable, namely "laws of nature, natural phenomena, and abstract ideas." Of particular relevance to this case, the Court has held that mathematical algorithms are not patentable subject matter to the extent that they are merely abstract ideas. In Diehr, the Court explained that certain types of mathematical subject matter, standing alone, represent nothing more than abstract ideas until reduced to some type of practical application, i.e., "a useful, concrete and tangible result."

Unpatentable mathematical algorithms are identifiable by showing they are merely abstract ideas constituting disembodied concepts or truths that are not "useful." From a practical standpoint, this means that to be patentable an algorithm must be applied in a "useful" way. In Alappat, we held that data, transformed by a machine through a series of mathematical calculations to produce a smooth waveform display on a rasterizer monitor, constituted a practical application of an abstract idea (a mathematical algorithm, formula, or calculation), because it produced "a useful, concrete and tangible result" — the smooth waveform.

Similarly, in *Arrhythmia Research Technology Inc.* v. *Corazonix Corp.*, we held that the transformation of electrocardiograph signals from a patient's heartbeat by a machine through a series of mathematical calculations constituted a practical application of an abstract idea (a mathematical algorithm, formula, or calculation), because it corresponded to a useful, concrete or tangible thing — the condition of a patient's heart.

Today, we hold that the transformation of data, representing discrete dollar amounts, by a machine through a series of mathematical calculations into a final share price, constitutes a practical application of a mathematical algorithm, formula, or calculation, because it produces "a useful, concrete and tangible result" — a final share price momentarily fixed for recording and reporting purposes and even accepted and relied upon by regulatory authorities and in subsequent trades.

The district court erred by applying the Freeman-Walter-Abele test to determine whether the claimed subject matter was an unpatentable abstract idea. The Freeman-Walter-Abele test was designed by the Court of Customs and Patent Appeals, and subsequently adopted by this court, to extract and identify unpatentable mathematical algorithms in the aftermath of Benson and Flook. The test has been thus articulated:

> First, the claim is analyzed to determine whether a mathematical algorithm is directly or indirectly recited. Next, if a mathematical algorithm is found, the claim as a whole is further analyzed to determine whether the algorithm is "applied in any manner to physical elements or process steps," and, if it is, it "passes muster under §101."

After Diehr and Chakrabarty, the Freeman-Walter-Abele test has little, if any, applicability to determining the presence of statutory subject matter. As we pointed out in Alappat, application of the test could be misleading, because a process, machine, manufacture, or composition of matter employing a law of nature, natural phenomenon, or abstract idea is patentable subject matter even though a law of nature, natural phenomenon, or abstract idea would not, by itself, be entitled to such protection. The test determines the presence of, for example, an algorithm. Under Benson, this may have been a sufficient indicium of nonstatutory subject matter. However, after Diehr and Alappat, the mere fact that a claimed invention involves inputting numbers, calculating numbers, outputting numbers, and storing numbers, in and of itself, would not render it nonstatutory subject matter, unless, of course, its operation does not produce a "useful, concrete and tangible result." After all, as we have repeatedly stated,

> every step-by-step process, be it electronic or chemical or mechanical, involves an algorithm in the broad sense of the term. Since §101 expressly includes processes as a category of inventions which may be patented and §100(b) further defines the word "process" as meaning "process, art or method, and includes a new use of a known process, machine, manufacture,

composition of matter, or material," it follows that it is no ground for holding a claim is directed to nonstatutory subject matter to say it includes or is directed to an algorithm. This is why the proscription against patenting has been limited to mathematical algorithms....

The question of whether a claim encompasses statutory subject matter should not focus on which of the four categories of subject matter a claim is directed to — process, machine, manufacture, or composition of matter — but rather on the essential characteristics of the subject matter, in particular, its practical utility. Section 101 specifies that statutory subject matter must also satisfy the other "conditions and requirements" of Title 35, including novelty, nonobviousness, and adequacy of disclosure and notice. For purpose of our analysis, as noted above, claim 1 is directed to a machine programmed with the Hub and Spoke software and admittedly produces a "useful, concrete, and tangible result." This renders it statutory subject matter, even if the useful result is expressed in numbers, such as price, profit, percentage, cost, or loss.

The Business Method Exception

As an alternative ground for invalidating the '056 patent under §101, the court relied on the judicially-created, so-called "business method" exception to statutory subject matter. We take this opportunity to lay this ill-conceived exception to rest. Since its inception, the "business method" exception has merely represented the application of some general, but no longer applicable legal principle, perhaps arising out of the "requirement for invention" — which was eliminated by §103. Since the 1952 Patent Act, business methods have been, and should have been, subject to the same legal requirements for patentability as applied to any other process or method.

The business method exception has never been invoked by this court, or the CCPA, to deem an invention unpatentable. Application of this particular exception has always been preceded by a ruling based on some clearer concept of Title 35 or, more commonly, application of the abstract idea exception based on finding a mathematical algorithm. Illustrative is the CCPA's analysis in In re Howard, wherein the court affirmed the Board of Appeals' rejection of the claims for lack of novelty and found it unnecessary to reach the Board's section 101 ground that a method of doing business is "inherently unpatentable."

Similarly, In re Schrader, while making reference to the business method exception, turned on the fact that the claims implicitly recited an abstract idea in the form of a mathematical algorithm and there was no "transformation or conversion of subject matter representative of or constituting physical activity or objects."

State Street argues that we acknowledged the validity of the business method exception in Alappat when we discussed Maucorps and Meyer:

> Maucorps dealt with a business methodology for deciding how salesmen should best handle respective customers and Meyer involved a 'system' for aiding a neurologist in diagnosing patients. Clearly, neither of the alleged 'inventions' in those cases falls within any §101 category.

However, closer scrutiny of these cases reveals that the claimed inventions in both Maucorps and Meyer were rejected as abstract ideas under the mathematical algorithm exception, not the business method exception.

Even the case frequently cited as establishing the business method exception to statutory subject matter, *Hotel Security Checking Co.* v. *Lorraine Co.*, did not rely on the exception to strike the patent. In that case, the patent was found invalid for lack of novelty and "invention," not because it was improper subject matter for a patent. The court stated "the fundamental principle of the system is as old as the art of bookkeeping, i.e., charging the goods of the employer to the agent who takes them." "If at the time of [the patent] application, there had been no system of bookkeeping of any kind in restaurants, we would be confronted with the question whether a new and useful system of cash registering and account checking is such an art as is patentable under the statute."

This case is no exception. The district court announced the precepts of the business method exception as set forth in several treatises, but noted as its primary reason for finding the patent invalid under the business method exception as follows:

> If Signature's invention were patentable, any financial institution desirous of implementing a multi-tiered funding complex modelled (sic) on a Hub and Spoke configuration would be required to seek Signature's permission before embarking on such a project. This is so because the '056 Patent is claimed [sic] sufficiently broadly to foreclose virtually any computer-implemented accounting method necessary to manage this type of financial structure.

Whether the patent's claims are too broad to be patentable is not to be judged under §101, but rather under §§102, 103 and 112. Assuming the above statement to be correct, it has nothing to do with whether what is claimed is statutory subject matter.

In view of this background, it comes as no surprise that in the most recent edition of the Manual of Patent Examining Procedures (MPEP) (1996), a paragraph of §706.03(a) was deleted. In past editions it read:

> Though seemingly within the category of process or method, a method of doing business can be rejected as not being within the statutory classes.

This acknowledgment is buttressed by the U.S. Patent and Trademark 1996 Examination Guidelines for Computer Related Inventions which now read:

> Office personnel have had difficulty in properly treating claims directed to methods of doing business. Claims should not be categorized as methods of doing business. Instead such claims should be treated like any other process claims.

We agree that this is precisely the manner in which this type of claim should be treated. Whether the claims are directed to subject matter within §101 should not turn on whether the claimed subject matter does "business" instead of something else.

CONCLUSION

The appealed decision is reversed and the case is remanded to the district court for further proceedings consistent with this opinion.

The first infringement action relating to Internet commerce inventions involved two well-known American corporations, each with a substantial presence in cyberspace. Amazon.com filed for a preliminary injunction against Barnesandnoble.com, alleging infringement of its U.S. Patent No. 5,960,411 — A Method and System for

Placing a Purchase Order Via a Communications Network. The patent involved a service that allows repeat visitors to move directly to the virtual checkout with one click (completing payment and shipping information in the process). The District Court for the Western District of Washington granted its request for a preliminary injunction, noting the following.

Amazon.com, Inc. v. BarnesandNoble.com, Inc.[†]

On October 21, 1999, Plaintiff Amazon.com filed a complaint in this Court alleging patent infringement by Defendants Barnesandnoble.com Inc. and Barnesandnoble.com LLC (hereinafter referred to collectively as "Barnesandnoble.com"). The patent in question is United States Patent No. *5,960,411* (the *'411* patent), which was issued on September 28, 1999. The *'411* patent describes a Method and System for Placing a Purchase Order Via a Communications Network and includes 26 claims.

The *'411* patent, in essence, describes a method and system in which a consumer can complete a purchase order for an item via the Internet using only a single action (such as a single click of a computer mouse button) once information identifying the item is displayed to the consumer. This method and system is only applicable in situations where a retailer already has in its files various information about the purchaser (such as the purchaser's address and credit card number) and where the purchaser's client system (e.g., a personal computer) has been provided with an identifier that enables the retailer's server system to identify the purchaser.

Amazon.com alleges that Defendants' "Express Lane" ordering feature infringes various claims of the *'411* patent.

· · · ·

Direct Evidence of Nonobviousness

Amazon.com has provided direct evidence of nonobviousness. Jeff Bezos, Amazon.com's founder and an inventor on the *'411* patent, testified that because "many customers were tentative and somewhat fearful of on-line purchasing, conventional wisdom was that they had to be slowly and incrementally led to the point of purchase. In addition, consumers were not acclimated to rely without confirmation on stored personal information for correct shipping and billing."

Professor Eric Johnson of Columbia Business School testified in his declaration that "Amazon.com's 1-Click (R) purchasing was a major innovation in on-line retailing that allows for purchasing without disrupting the consumer's shopping experience; and by eliminating additional confirmation requirements, recasts the default in a way that both maximizes the likelihood that consumers will complete their purchases and minimizes consumer anxiety over real or perceived issues of internet security."

Moreover, despite their experience with prior art shopping cart models of online purchasing, both sides' technical experts acknowledged that they had never conceived of the invention. Mr. Mulligan testified that ordering with one click was "a huge leap from what was done in the past." Mr. Mulligan testified further that: "I've been working in electronic commerce for years now. And I've never thought of the

---

[†] 73 F. Supp. 2d 1228 (W.D. Wash. 1999).

idea of being able to turn a shopping cart or take the idea of clicking on an item and suddenly having the item ship — having the complete process done." Mr. Mulligan also testified that he believed it was "a huge leap of faith for the website and the consumer to implement something like this." Additionally, as noted above, Dr. Lockwood testified that he never thought of modifying Web Basket to provide single-action ordering.

Objective Factors

Plaintiff's single-action ordering method addressed an unsolved need that had been long-felt (at least in the relatively short period of time that e-commerce has existed), namely streamlining the on-line ordering process to reduce the high percentage of orders that are begun but never completed, *i.e.,* abandoned shopping carts. The problem of on-line consumers starting but abandoning shopping carts was acknowledged by both parties and their experts

In the on-line industry in general and at Barnesandnoble.com in particular, over half of the shopping carts started by customers are abandoned before checkout. In an attempt to alleviate the problem of abandoned shopping carts, Barnesandnoble.com attempts to make the checkout process as simple and easy as possible. The single-action ordering invention of the *'411* patent solves the problem by eliminating the checkout process entirely.

Barnesandnoble.com presented evidence that a number of other e-commerce retailers have offered single-action ordering to customers

Amazon.com's single-action ordering is used by millions of customers, indicating the commercial success of the feature. Barnesandnoble.com's Express Lane also accounts for a significant portion of its sales. Further evidence of commercial success of single-action ordering is suggested by the fact that Barnesandnoble.com promoted its Express Lane feature in a press release after it was announced and in its prospectus. Indeed, Barnesandnoble.com described Express Lane as one of its "major enhancements" to its on-line business.

Industry analysts and the popular press also found Amazon.com's single-action ordering process to be innovative. Patricia Seybold, an e-commerce observer and consultant, described Amazon.com's 1-Click (R) purchasing as "legendary." Joseph Gallivan in *The New York Post* described Amazon.com's 1-Click (R) purchasing as a "seductive innovation." *InfoWorld* indicated: "Net retailers are starting to realize that potential customers often don't make it as far as the virtual checkout line — they fill their on-line shopping carts with products, then simply abandon them.... Faced with these problems, it's no surprise that retailers have been eyeing Amazon.com's 1-click purchases with envy for some time now."

. . . .

D. Public Interest

The public is served by innovation on the Internet and in electronic commerce, particularly now while it is still developing rapidly. Competition to provide unique, effective and enjoyable consumer experiences will lead to innovation and diversity in on-line commerce. On the other hand, innovation will be discouraged if competitors are permitted a free ride on each other's patented inventions. Protection of intellectual property rights in innovations will foster greater competition and innovation.

Granting Amazon.com's preliminary injunction will serve the public interest. The public has a strong interest in the enforcement of intellectual property rights. The purpose of the patent system is to reward inventors and provide incentives for further innovation by preventing others from exploiting their work. Encouraging Amazon.com to continue to innovate — and forcing competitors to come up with their own new ideas — unquestionably best serves the public interest.

Defendants' argument that the injunction would not serve the public interest presupposes that the '411 patent is invalid and not infringed. Amazon.com has established that Defendants' defenses lack substantial merit. The Amazon.com inventors are therefore entitled "to reap the benefits of their labor" and "prevent others from practicing what they have invented." This is particularly true in a rapidly developing industry where the window of opportunity to reap the benefits is likely to be short-lived, given the fertile climate for e-commerce inventions.

The Canadian Patent Office has yet to adopt the business method patent, rejecting such applications as non-statutory subject matter. Much of the resistance may stem from the landmark 1982 decision of *Schlumberger Canada Ltd. V. Commissioner of Patents* (56 CPR (2d) 204)), in which the court rejected computer programs as valid subject matter for patents, stating:

In order to determine whether the application discloses a patentable invention, it is first necessary to determine, what, according to the application, has been discovered. Now, it is obvious, I think, that there is nothing new in using computers to make calculations of the kind that are prescribed by the specifications. It is precisely in order to make that kind of calculation that computers were invented. What is new here is the discovery of the various calculations to be made and of the mathematical formulae to be used in making those calculations. If those calculations were not to be effected by computers but by men, the subject-matter of the application would clearly be mathematical formulae and a series of purely mental operations; as such, in my view, it would not be patentable. A mathematical formula must be assimilated to a "mere scientific principle of abstract theorem" for which s. 28(3) of the Act prescribes that "no patent shall issue." As to mental operations and processes, it is clear, in my view, that they are not the kind of processes that are referred to in the definition of invention in s.2. However, in the present case, the specifications prescribe that the calculations be made by computers. As a result, as I understand the appellant's contention, those calculations are not mental operations but purely mechanical ones that constitute the various steps in the process disclosed by the invention. If the appellant's contention were correct, it would follow that the mere fact that the use of computers is prescribed to perform the calculations prescribed in the specifications, would have the effect of transforming into patentable subject-matter what would, otherwise, be clearly not patentable. The invention of the computer would then have the unexpected result of giving a new dimension to the *Patent Act* by rendering patentable what, under the Act as enacted, was clearly not patentable. This, in my view, is unacceptable. I am of opinion that the fact that a computer is or should be used to implement discovery does not the change the nature of that discovery. What the appellant claims as an invention here is merely the discovery that by making certain calculations according to a certain formulae, useful information could be extracted from certain measurements. This is not, in my view, an invention within the meaning of s. 2.

Discussion Questions

1. The patent system is designed to encourage invention and innovation by providing developers with legal protection for a limited time to enable them to fully exploit the value of their work. To be deserving of patent protection a series of criteria must be met, including a requirement that the source of the patent be novel and non-obvious. Does a one-click online purchase system seem sufficiently non-obvious as to merit patent protection?

2. Does the increasing number of e-commerce patent awards present a threat to the growth and development of e-commerce? Who are likely to emerge as the winners and losers under this system?

PART FIVE

INTERNET COMMERCE

19

Online Contracting

With each passing day, e-commerce gains a greater foothold within society. It has become so much a part of mainstream commerce that businesses are now often classified alternatively as "bricks and mortar" businesses or "e-businesses." For businesses to function effectively online, contractual relationships must be established. Online contracting is clearly central to the e-commerce transaction, since without the ability to create enforceable contracts online, e-commerce would grind to a halt.

The formation of a contract in cyberspace raises the fundamental question of enforceability. The new paradigm of establishing contracts through e-mail or by clicking the "I Accept" button on a Web page must fit within the existing body of contract law. In certain respects, the introduction of new technologies has not disrupted the "ebb and flow" of contract law. It has adequately adapted to the Internet predecessors such as post mail, telex machines and fax machines. E-mail and the World Wide Web are simply the newest incarnations along this same evolutionary path.

The Internet does, however, present some novel issues. In many e-commerce situations the parties do not have an underlying relationship, and the contract is consummated "on the fly." Moreover, the favoured approach for contracting online is a controversial one — the clickwrap contract. The clickwrap contract is merely a contract by which terms are assented to through clicking an "I Agree" button. As a result of the implementation of many Web interfaces, it is frequently difficult or even impossible to ascertain the terms of clickwrap contracts. Parallels are often drawn to the software industry and its shrinkwrap contracting practices, in which the terms of the software licence are only available to the purchaser after they open the purchased product.

Can parties be bound to new terms after the exchange of consideration? Are parties bound to the terms of a contract that they have not even read? As a starting point, we first consider the famous Canadian case of *Tilden Rent-A-Car Co.* v. *Clendenning*, followed by a closer look at the legality of shrinkwrap contracting.

Tilden Rent-A-Car Co. v. Clendenning[†]

In modern commercial practice, many standard form printed documents are signed without being read or understood. In many cases the parties seeking to rely on the terms of the contract know or ought to know that the signature of a party to the contract does not represent the true intention of the signer, and that the party signing is unaware of the stringent and onerous provisions which the standard form contains. Under such circumstances, I am of the opinion that the party seeking to rely on such terms should not be able to do so in the absence of first having taken reasonable measures to draw such terms to the attention of the other party, and, in the absence of such reasonable measures, it is not necessary for the party denying knowledge of such terms to prove either fraud, misrepresentation or non est factum.

Intellectual Property and Shrinkwrap Licenses[‡]

MARK LEMLEY

Shrinkwrap licenses have been a fixture in computer software transactions for some time. Shrinkwrap licenses take many forms. The prototypical example is a single piece of paper containing license terms which has been wrapped in transparent plastic along with one or more computer disks. In theory, purchasers of a computer program will read the license terms before tearing open the plastic wrap and using the computer disks. Other examples of the genre include licenses printed on the outside of boxes containing software, licenses simply included somewhere within the box, or licenses shrinkwrapped with the owner's manual accompanying the software.

Wherever they are located, shrinkwrap licenses commonly include language along the following lines:

> [Vendor] is providing the enclosed materials to you on the express condition that you assent to this software license. By using any of the enclosed diskette(s), you agree to the following provisions. If you do not agree with these license provisions, return these materials to your dealer, in original packaging within three days from receipt, for a refund.

The point of such language is simple — the software vendor is attempting to create what some have referred to as a "reverse unilateral contract." This language is the sine qua non of shrinkwrap licenses, because without such a provision there is no license at all. Vendors intend that, by opening the plastic wrap and actually using the software, customers will bind themselves to the terms of the shrinkwrap license.

· · · ·

B.   Judicial Treatment of Shrinkwrap Licenses
Because of the nature of the shrinkwrap license, and because of its potential to re-write the rules of tort and intellectual property law, courts have viewed such licenses

---

† [1978] 18 O.R. (2d) 601 (O.C.A.).
‡   (1995) 68 S. Cal. L. Rev. 1239 at 1241–42, 1248–59. Notes omitted. Reproduced with permission of the Southern California Law Review and the author.

with a skeptical eye. Courts have considered three different legal issues with respect to shrinkwrap licenses: (1) whether the shrinkwrap license is valid at all as a matter of contract law; (2) whether the particular terms discussed in the last section are enforceable, even if the license is considered valid; and (3) whether, even if state contract law would enforce terms that modify intellectual property law, federal intellectual property law preempts such modifications. I will briefly review the law on each of these issues in turn.

1. The Validity of Shrinkwrap Licenses

Shrinkwrap licenses do not follow the normal model of contracts. Black letter contract law sets out three predicates to the formation of a contract: offer, acceptance, and consideration. Behind these requirements is the overarching notion of a bargain between the parties. In the prototypical contract, where the parties meet face to face and discuss the terms before coming to an agreement, the bargain is obvious. But where is the bargain in a standard form shrinkwrap license that is not even signed by the party against whom it will be enforced?

The few courts that have considered this issue have relied on U.C.C. sections 2-207 and 2-209 in concluding that shrinkwrap license terms are not generally enforceable. The most detailed discussion of this issue to date is the Third Circuit's decision in *Step-Saver Data Systems, Inc.* v. *Wyse Technology*. The case involved a breach of warranty claim brought by Step-Saver Data Systems, Inc., the purchaser of a shrinkwrapped computer program, against the vendor, The Software Link, Inc. ("TSL"). The shrinkwrap license disclaimed all express and implied warranties on the software, including certain prior warranties allegedly given by TSL to Step-Saver. The district court directed a verdict for TSL on the warranty claims, holding that the shrinkwrap license terms constituted the complete and exclusive agreement between the parties.

The Third Circuit reversed. The court applied the provisions of U.C.C. sections 2-207 to the contract at issue. It reasoned that a contract was formed when Step-Saver, responding to magazine advertisements by TSL, placed telephone orders for copies of TSL's software, and TSL shipped the software. At this point, the contract was formed by agreement and performance because both parties had acted as if a contract existed. The court concluded that the issue therefore concerned the nature of the terms of the contract.

Because the contract was formed before Step-Saver ever received the shrinkwrap license, the court treated the license provisions as a written confirmation and as an attempt to modify the terms of the contract (under U.C.C. sections 2-202 and 2-209, respectively). Because those provisions require that both parties intend to adopt the additional terms, the court held that the shrinkwrap license did not bind Step-Saver. This conclusion was confirmed by the court's application of U.C.C. section 2-207:

> UCC s2-207 establishes a legal rule that proceeding with a contract after receiving a writing that purports to define the terms of the parties's [sic] contract is not sufficient to establish the party's consent to the terms of the writing.... In the absence of a party's express assent to the additional or different terms of the writing, section 2-207 provides a default rule that the parties intended, as the terms of their agreement, those terms to which both parties have agreed, along with any terms implied by the provisions of the UCC. In other words, because the parties agreed to a contract at the point of telephone order and product shipment, only those terms on which the parties agreed at that point became part of the contract. Other terms could be implied, if necessary, from the U.C.C.'s default rules. But the shrinkwrap

license was ineffective to modify the contract terms unless Step-Saver expressly agreed to such a modification.

The Step-Saver decision has potentially broad applicability to shrinkwrap license cases. While the decision is premised on the formation of a contract through telephone orders before the shrinkwrap license is ever delivered, many commercial sales of software occur in analogous contexts. Often the software is ordered by letter or by telephone. Even if it is purchased over the counter, the purchase transaction is completed — and an agreement between retailer and customer is reached — at the point of sale. A shrinkwrap license contained inside a box cannot be discovered and read until after the customer has returned home, opened the box, and begun the process of installing the software.

The few other cases considering the issue directly have generally lined up with Step-Saver in refusing to enforce shrinkwrap licenses. Two courts reached this result on the grounds that the licenses are "unenforceable contracts of adhesion." This rationale is broader than Step-Saver, because a court would then not enforce any shrinkwrap license terms, whether or not the customer was aware of the license at the time the agreement was made. Rather, the "contract of adhesion" rationale focuses on the weaker bargaining position of the consumer, and the consumer's lack of meaningful choice as to the terms offered.

Only one court has enforced the terms of a shrinkwrap license, and then only in a very limited way. In *Arizona Retail Systems, Inc.* v. *Software Link, Inc.*, the district court enforced the shrinkwrap terms sent along with an "evaluative" copy of the software. The court's decision was based on Arizona Retail Systems, Inc.'s ("ARS") admission that it did not decide to keep the copy until having opened and read the shrinkwrap license and used the software for several hours. Thus, unlike Step-Saver, ARS was aware of the terms of the shrinkwrap license at the time the agreement was formed. However, the court refused to enforce the same license when it accompanied software subsequently purchased by phone and shipped to ARS. The court's reasoning for refusing to enforce the license against telephone orders follows Step-Saver. In addition, the court relied on a number of policy arguments against enforcing shrinkwrap licenses. Because of its schizophrenic result, Arizona Retail is at best limited authority for enforcing shrinkwrap licenses.

The general refusal of the United States courts to enforce shrinkwrap licenses is echoed outside the United States. A number of countries either refuse to enforce shrinkwrap licenses at all, or place restrictive conditions on the form and contents of such licenses. Comparatively fewer countries freely enforce shrinkwrap licenses.

2. The Validity of Particular Terms

Even if courts were to conclude that shrinkwrap licenses are themselves enforceable, there remains the possibility that particular terms contained in those licenses will not be enforceable. Contract law offers three circumstances in which license provisions in an otherwise valid contract will not be enforced.

First, the contract term may be "unconscionable." Unconscionability is governed by U.C.C. section 2-302. Under this provision, unconscionability has two components: the absence of meaningful choice or bargaining power on the part of one party (procedural unconscionability) and contract terms which are unreasonably favorable to the other party (substantive unconscionability). The procedural element is satisfied if the contract was not negotiated, and the party claiming unconscionability lacked meaningful choice in entering into the contract. The substantive element is satisfied by proof of "harsh" or "one-sided" results that unreasonably place contract risks on the party lacking bargaining power. While unconscionability generally arises in form contracts that unfairly bind individual consumers, it has sometimes been applied to protect small businesses as well.

Particular shrinkwrap license terms may be vulnerable to unconscionability claims if they place unfair burdens on licensees. The nature of the shrinkwrap license seems to satisfy the requirement of procedural unconscionability. As a result, substantively unreasonable terms may not be enforced even if the shrinkwrap license is otherwise valid. Terms which purport to alter existing law in significant ways are particularly likely to be invalidated under this rule.

A second legal principle that threatens the enforceability of specific provisions of some shrinkwrap licenses is based on section 211(3) of the Restatement (Second) of Contracts. That section limits the enforceability of standardized contract terms that are not negotiated, even if the contract itself is signed by both parties and some of the terms are bargained over. Such standardized contract terms will not be considered part of the agreement if there is "reason to believe that the party manifesting ... assent [to the form contract] would not do so if he knew that the writing contained a particular term...." Courts have applied Restatement section 211(3) to invalidate standardized contract terms modifying existing law in software transactions. However, application of this rule to shrinkwrap licenses is limited in practice by its requirement that the contract term be unknown and beyond the range of reasonable expectation. An unreasonable rule that was well-known and universally used in shrinkwrap licenses would apparently pass muster under the Restatement test.

Finally, a few courts have been willing to rely on public policy to invalidate license terms. In *Angus Medical Co.* v. *Digital Equipment Corp.*, the court cited public policy in favor of access to the courts as one reason for finding unenforceable a contract term which shortened the applicable statute of limitations. It concluded that a term which violates public policy may be "beyond reasonable expectation" even if it is not "unusual or unexpected."

3. Copyright Preemption and Shrinkwrap Licenses

Shrinkwrap license terms that purport to alter the rights granted to purchasers and licensees under patent or copyright law may also be vulnerable to the charge that they are preempted by federal intellectual property law. Several courts have held or strongly suggested that federal statutes preempt state contract law rules to the extent that those rules permit the parties to "opt out" of some parts of the federal statutory scheme. Other courts have found a continuing role for contract law, even where it conflicts with federal law.

The most celebrated decision on intellectual property preemption is *Vault Corp.* v. *Quaid Software Ltd.* That case involved Vault's copy protection program called Prolok, which was designed to prevent unlawful duplication of other software by "locking" it. Vault sold Prolok with a shrinkwrap license, which provided in relevant part that the purchaser could not copy or reverse engineer any part of the software. Quaid purchased a copy of Prolok and reverse engineered it in order to find a way to defeat the copy protection program. Quaid incorporated its knowledge in an "unlocking" product it sold, called Ramkey. The final version of Ramkey did not contain any material copied from Prolok.

Vault sued Quaid, alleging copyright infringement and violation of the shrinkwrap license provision. The Fifth Circuit found that Quaid had not infringed Vault's copyright by reverse engineering Prolok or producing Ramkey. It then turned to Vault's claims based on the shrinkwrap license. The district court had held that the shrinkwrap license was unenforceable as a contract of adhesion unless it was saved by the Louisiana Software License Enforcement Act. The Louisiana statute, enacted at Vault's urging, specifically authorized contractual terms prohibiting reverse engineering.

The Fifth Circuit found that the Louisiana statute directly conflicted with the rights of purchasers of copyrighted works set out in section 117 of the Copyright Act, and was therefore preempted by copyright law. The court relied on a venerable line of Supreme Court cases for the proposition that "[w]hen state law touches upon the area of [patent or copyright statutes], it is 'familiar doctrine' that the federal policy 'may not be set at naught, or its benefits denied' by the state law."

Vault's conclusion that state law could not expand the rights granted to authors under the copyright law has been endorsed by other courts. Further, several courts have applied Vault's preemption analysis to the interpretation of bargained software license agreements. For example, the court in *SQL Solutions, Inc. v. Oracle Corp.* limited the effect of a choice of law provision, holding that "federalism principles dictate that state rules of contractual construction cannot interfere with federal law or policy. In particular, state law must be applied in a manner that does not conflict with federal copyright law and policy."

It does not follow from this, however, that all contract law provisions relating to the subject matter of copyright are preempted. In *National Car Rental Sys. v. Computer Assocs.*, the court considered whether copyright law preempted a bargained software license that limited the licensee to using the software for internal purposes. The court held that contract law was not preempted because it did not grant rights "equivalent to" those offered by copyright. Contract law was saved from general preemption by the presence of an "extra element" not required by copyright — an agreement between the parties. The court held that the license agreement governed the question of which of the exclusive rights listed in section 106 Computer Associates had granted to National Car Rental Systems. It did not, however, decide whether the license agreement would be preempted if the agreement directly contradicted rights granted to the user under copyright law.

On this point, the Supreme Court's decision in *Goldstein v. California* is particularly relevant. In that case, the Court upheld a California criminal statute penalizing the unauthorized commercial duplication of sound recordings, which at that time were not protected by federal copyright law. The Court identified three classes of cases: those instances in which the federal government intended to provide protection; those instances in which the federal government intended to permit copying; and those instances in which it intended neither. Only in the third instance, the Court held, was state copyright protection permissible:

> [A] conflict would develop if a State attempted to protect that which Congress intended to be free from restraint or to free that which Congress had protected. However, where Congress determines that neither federal protection nor freedom from restraint is required by the national interest, it is at liberty to stay its hand entirely. Since state protection would not then conflict with federal action, total relinquishment of the State's power to grant copyright protection cannot be inferred. Where Congress expressed no intention, the Court held that states are free to legislate. However, Goldstein suggests that this freedom does not permit states to give intellectual property owners rights that the federal government intended to withhold.

A similar set of cases (outside the computer software context) exists in patent law. On the one hand, the Supreme Court has held that patent law does not generally preempt contract law. As a result, it has permitted inventors to charge a royalty for unpatented inventions. On the other hand, it has steadfastly refused to let licensees bargain away the right to challenge the validity of patents, or to extend the patent term by contract.

In short, courts have been skeptical of shrinkwrap licenses for a variety of reasons. Some courts hold that shrinkwrap licenses are entirely unenforceable under contract law. Particular terms of shrinkwrap licenses may also be vulnerable to judicial attack, especially if they are unexpected, unconscionable, or violative of public policy. Finally, some courts have concluded that shrinkwrap licenses are preempted by intellectual property law to the extent that they attempt to change the balance of rights struck by federal policy. But virtually no reported decisions have actually enforced shrinkwrap license provisions as written, especially where those provisions modify federal law.

Professor Lemley's article illustrates the prevailing thought on shrinkwrap contracting for much of the 1980s and 1990s. The tide shifted in 1996, however, with the release of *ProCD* v. *Zeidenberg*.

ProCD v. Zeidenberg[†]

Must buyers of computer software obey the terms of shrinkwrap licenses? The district court held not, for two reasons: first, they are not contracts because the licenses are inside the box rather than printed on the outside; second, federal law forbids enforcement even if the licenses are contracts. The parties and numerous amici curiae have briefed many other issues, but these are the only two that matter — and we disagree with the district judge's conclusion on each. Shrinkwrap licenses are enforceable unless their terms are objectionable on grounds applicable to contracts in general (for example, if they violate a rule of positive law, or if they are unconscionable). Because no one argues that the terms of the license at issue here are troublesome, we remand with instructions to enter judgment for the plaintiff.

I

ProCD, the plaintiff, has compiled information from more than 3,000 telephone directories into a computer database. We may assume that this database cannot be copyrighted, although it is more complex, contains more information (nine-digit zip codes and census industrial codes), is organized differently, and therefore is more original than the single alphabetical directory at issue in *Feist Publications, Inc.* v. *Rural Telephone Service Co.* ProCD sells a version of the database, called SelectPhone, on CD-ROM discs. The "shrinkwrap license" gets its name from the fact that retail software packages are covered in plastic or cellophane "shrinkwrap," and some vendors, though not ProCD, have written licenses that become effective as soon as the customer tears the wrapping from the package. Vendors prefer "end user license," but we use the more common term.) A proprietary method of compressing the data serves as effective encryption too. Customers decrypt and use the data with the aid of an application program that ProCD has written. This program, which is copyrighted, searches the database in response to users' criteria (such as

---

† 86 F. 3d 1447 (7th Cir. 1996).

"find all people named Tatum in Tennessee, plus all firms with 'Door Systems' in the corporate name"). The resulting lists (or, as ProCD prefers, "listings") can be read and manipulated by other software, such as word processing programs.

The database in SelectPhone cost more than $10 million to compile and is expensive to keep current. It is much more valuable to some users than to others. The combination of names, addresses, and sic codes enables manufacturers to compile lists of potential customers. Manufacturers and retailers pay high prices to specialized information intermediaries for such mailing lists; ProCD offers a potentially cheaper alternative. People with nothing to sell could use the database as a substitute for calling long distance information, or as a way to look up old friends who have moved to unknown towns, or just as an electronic substitute for the local phone book. ProCD decided to engage in price discrimination, selling its database to the general public for personal use at a low price (approximately $150 for the set of five discs) while selling information to the trade for a higher price. It has adopted some intermediate strategies too: access to the SelectPhone database is available via the America Online service for the price America Online charges to its clients (approximately $3 per hour), but this service has been tailored to be useful only to the general public.

If ProCD had to recover all of its costs and make a profit by charging a single price — that is, if it could not charge more to commercial users than to the general public — it would have to raise the price substantially over $150. The ensuing reduction in sales would harm consumers who value the information at, say, $200. They get consumer surplus of $50 under the current arrangement but would cease to buy if the price rose substantially. If because of high elasticity of demand in the consumer segment of the market the only way to make a profit turned out to be a price attractive to commercial users alone, then all consumers would lose out — and so would the commercial clients, who would have to pay more for the listings because ProCD could not obtain any contribution toward costs from the consumer market.

To make price discrimination work, however, the seller must be able to control arbitrage. An air carrier sells tickets for less to vacationers than to business travelers, using advance purchase and Saturday-night-stay requirements to distinguish the categories. A producer of movies segments the market by time, releasing first to theaters, then to pay-per-view services, next to the videotape and laserdisc market, and finally to cable and commercial tv. Vendors of computer software have a harder task. Anyone can walk into a retail store and buy a box. Customers do not wear tags saying "commercial user" or "consumer user." Anyway, even a commercial-user-detector at the door would not work, because a consumer could buy the software and resell to a commercial user. That arbitrage would break down the price discrimination and drive up the minimum price at which ProCD would sell to anyone.

Instead of tinkering with the product and letting users sort themselves — for example, furnishing current data at a high price that would be attractive only to commercial customers, and two-year-old data at a low price — ProCD turned to the institution of contract. Every box containing its consumer product declares that the software comes with restrictions stated in an enclosed license. This license, which is encoded on the CD-ROM disks as well as printed in the manual, and which appears on a user's screen every time the software runs, limits use of the application program and listings to non-commercial purposes.

Matthew Zeidenberg bought a consumer package of SelectPhone in 1994 from a retail outlet in Madison, Wisconsin, but decided to ignore the license. He formed Silken Mountain Web Services, Inc., to resell the information in the SelectPhone database. The corporation makes the database available on the Internet to anyone willing to pay its price — which, needless to say, is less than ProCD charges its commercial customers. Zeidenberg has purchased two additional SelectPhone packages, each with an updated version of the database, and made the latest information available over the World Wide Web, for a price, through his corporation. ProCD filed this suit seeking an injunction against further dissemination that exceeds the rights specified in the licenses (identical in each of the three packages Zeidenberg purchased). The district court held the licenses ineffectual because their terms do not appear on the outside of the packages. The court added that the second and third licenses stand no different from the first, even though they are identical, because they might have been different, and a purchaser does not agree to — and cannot be bound by — terms that were secret at the time of purchase.

II

Following the district court, we treat the licenses as ordinary contracts accompanying the sale of products, and therefore as governed by the common law of contracts and the Uniform Commercial Code. Whether there are legal differences between "contracts" and "licenses" (which may matter under the copyright doctrine of first sale) is a subject for another day. Zeidenberg does not argue that Silken Mountain Web Services is free of any restrictions that apply to Zeidenberg himself, because any effort to treat the two parties as distinct would put Silken Mountain behind the eight ball on ProCD's argument that copying the application program onto its hard disk violates the copyright laws. Zeidenberg does argue, and the district court held, that placing the package of software on the shelf is an "offer," which the customer "accepts" by paying the asking price and leaving the store with the goods. In Wisconsin, as elsewhere, a contract includes only the terms on which the parties have agreed. One cannot agree to hidden terms, the judge concluded. So far, so good — but one of the terms to which Zeidenberg agreed by purchasing the software is that the transaction was subject to a license. Zeidenberg's position therefore must be that the printed terms on the outside of a box are the parties' contract — except for printed terms that refer to or incorporate other terms. But why would Wisconsin fetter the parties' choice in this way? Vendors can put the entire terms of a contract on the outside of a box only by using microscopic type, removing other information that buyers might find more useful (such as what the software does, and on which computers it works), or both. The "Read Me" file included with most software, describing system requirements and potential incompatibilities, may be equivalent to ten pages of type; warranties and license restrictions take still more space. Notice on the outside, terms on the inside, and a right to return the software for a refund if the terms are unacceptable (a right that the license expressly extends), may be a means of doing business valuable to buyers and sellers alike. Doubtless a state could forbid the use of standard contracts in the software business, but we do not think that Wisconsin has done so.

Transactions in which the exchange of money precedes the communication of detailed terms are common. Consider the purchase of insurance. The buyer goes to an agent, who explains the essentials (amount of coverage, number of years) and remits the premium to the home office, which sends back a policy. On the district judge's understanding, the terms of the policy are irrelevant because the insured paid before receiving them. Yet the device of payment, often with a "binder" (so that the insurance takes effect immediately even though the home office reserves the right to withdraw coverage later), in advance of the policy, serves buyers' interests by accelerating effectiveness and reducing transactions costs. Or consider the purchase of an airline ticket. The traveler calls the carrier or an agent, is quoted a price, reserves a seat, pays, and gets a ticket, in that order. The ticket contains elaborate terms, which the traveler can reject by canceling the reservation. To use the ticket is to accept the terms, even terms that in retrospect are disadvantageous. Just so with a ticket to a concert. The back of the ticket states that the patron promises not to record the concert; to attend is to agree. A theater that detects a violation will confiscate the tape and escort the violator to the exit. One could arrange things so that every concertgoer signs this promise before forking over the money, but that cumbersome way of doing things not only would lengthen queues and raise prices but also would scotch the sale of tickets by phone or electronic data service.

Consumer goods work the same way. Someone who wants to buy a radio set visits a store, pays, and walks out with a box. Inside the box is a leaflet containing some terms, the most important of which usually is the warranty, read for the first time in the comfort of home. By Zeidenberg's lights, the warranty in the box is irrelevant; every consumer gets the standard warranty implied by the UCC in the event the contract is silent; yet so far as we are aware no state disregards warranties furnished with consumer products. Drugs come with a list of ingredients on the outside and an elaborate package insert on the inside. The package insert describes drug interactions, contraindications, and other vital information — but, if Zeidenberg is right, the purchaser need not read the package insert, because it is not part of the contract.

Next consider the software industry itself. Only a minority of sales take place over the counter, where there are boxes to peruse. A customer may place an order by phone in response to a line item in a catalog or a review in a magazine. Much software is ordered over the Internet by purchasers who have never seen a box. Increasingly software arrives by wire. There is no box; there is only a stream of electrons, a collection of information that includes data, an application program, instructions, many limitations, and the terms of sale. The user purchases a serial number, which activates the software's features. On Zeidenberg's arguments, these unboxed sales are unfettered by terms — so the seller has made a broad warranty and must pay consequential damages for any shortfalls in performance, two "promises" that if taken seriously would drive prices through the ceiling or return transactions to the horse-and-buggy age.

· · · ·

What then does the current version of the UCC have to say? We think that the place to start is §2-204(1): "A contract for sale of goods may be made in any manner sufficient to show agreement, including conduct by both parties which recognizes the existence of such a contract." A vendor, as master of the offer, may invite acceptance by conduct, and may propose limitations on the kind of conduct that constitutes acceptance. A buyer may accept by performing the acts the vendor proposes to treat as acceptance. And that is what happened. ProCD proposed a contract that a buyer would accept by using the software after having an opportunity to read the license at leisure. This Zeidenberg did. He had no choice, because the software splashed the license on the screen and would not let him proceed without indicating acceptance. So although the district judge was right to say that a contract can be, and often is, formed simply by paying the price and walking out of the store, the UCC permits contracts to be formed in other ways. ProCD proposed such a different way, and without protest Zeidenberg agreed. Ours is not a case in which a consumer opens a package to find an insert saying "you owe us an extra $10,000" and the seller files suit to collect. Any buyer finding such a demand can prevent formation of the contract by returning the package, as can any consumer who concludes that the terms of the license make the software worth less than the purchase price. Nothing in the UCC requires a seller to maximize the buyer's net gains.

Section 2-606, which defines "acceptance of goods", reinforces this understanding. A buyer accepts goods under §2-606(1)(b) when, after an opportunity to inspect, he fails to make an effective rejection under §2-602(1). ProCD extended an opportunity to reject if a buyer should find the license terms unsatisfactory; Zeidenberg inspected the package, tried out the software, learned of the license, and did not reject the goods. We refer to §2-606 only to show that the opportunity to return goods can be important; acceptance of an offer differs from acceptance of goods after delivery; but the UCC consistently permits the parties to structure their relations so that the buyer has a chance to make a final decision after a detailed review.

Some portions of the UCC impose additional requirements on the way parties agree on terms. A disclaimer of the implied warranty of merchantability must be "conspicuous." UCC §2-316(2), incorporating UCC §1-201(10). Promises to make firm offers, or to negate oral modifications, must be "separately signed." UCC §§2-205, 2-209(2). These special provisos reinforce the impression that, so far as the UCC is concerned, other terms may be as inconspicuous as the forum-selection clause on the back of the cruise ship ticket in Carnival Lines. Zeidenberg has not located any Wisconsin case—for that matter, any case in any state—holding that under the UCC the ordinary terms found in shrinkwrap licenses require any special prominence, or otherwise are to be undercut rather than enforced. In the end, the terms of the license are conceptually identical to the contents of the package. Just as no court would dream of saying that SelectPhone must contain 3,100 phone books rather than 3,000, or must have data no more than 30 days old, or must sell for $100 rather than $150—although any of these changes would be welcomed by the customer, if all other things were held constant—so, we believe, Wisconsin would not let the buyer pick and choose among terms. Terms of use are no less a part of "the product" than are the size of the database and the speed with which the software compiles listings. Competition among vendors, not judicial revision of a package's contents, is how consumers are protected in a market economy. ProCD has rivals, which may elect to compete by offering superior software, monthly updates, improved terms of use, lower price, or a better compromise among these elements. As we stressed above, adjusting terms in buyers' favor might help Matthew Zeidenberg today (he already has the software) but would lead to a response, such as a higher price, that might make consumers as a whole worse off.

III

The district court held that, even if Wisconsin treats shrinkwrap licenses as contracts, §301(a) of the Copyright Act, 17 U.S.C. §301(a), prevents their enforcement. The relevant part of §301(a) preempts any "legal or equitable rights [under state law] that are equivalent to any of the exclusive rights within the general scope of copyright as specified by section 106 in works of authorship that are fixed in a tangible medium of expression and come within the subject matter of copyright as specified by sections 102 and 103". ProCD's software and data are "fixed in a tangible medium of expression", and the district judge held that they are "within the subject matter of copyright". The latter conclusion is plainly right for the copyrighted application program, and the judge thought that the data likewise are "within the subject matter of copyright" even if, after Feist, they are not sufficiently original to be copyrighted. *Baltimore Orioles, Inc.* v. *Major League Baseball Players Ass'n* supports that conclusion, with which commentators agree. One function of §301(a) is to prevent states from giving special protection to works of authorship that Congress has decided should be in the public domain, which it can accomplish only if "subject matter of copyright" includes all works of a type covered by sections 102 and 103, even if federal law does not afford protection to them.

But are rights created by contract "equivalent to any of the exclusive rights within the general scope of copyright"? Three courts of appeals have answered "no." The district court disagreed with these decisions but we think them sound. Rights "equivalent to any of the exclusive rights within the general scope of copyright" are rights established by law—rights that restrict the options of persons who are strangers to the author. Copyright law forbids duplication, public performance, and so on, unless the person wishing to copy or perform the work gets permission; silence means a ban on copying. A copyright is a right against the world. Contracts, by contrast, generally affect only their parties; strangers may do as they please, so contracts do not create "exclusive rights." Someone who found a copy of SelectPhone (trademark) on the street would not be affected by the shrinkwrap license—though the federal copyright laws of their own force would limit the finder's ability to copy or transmit the application program.

Think for a moment about trade secrets. One common trade secret is a customer list. After Feist, a simple alphabetical list of a firm's customers, with address and telephone numbers, could not be protected by copyright. Yet *Kewanee Oil Co.* v. *Bicron Corp.* holds that contracts about trade secrets may be enforced — precisely because they do not affect strangers' ability to discover and use the information independently. If the amendment of §301(a) in 1976 overruled Kewanee and abolished consensual protection of those trade secrets that cannot be copyrighted, no one has noticed — though abolition is a logical consequence of the district court's approach. Think, too, about everyday transactions in intellectual property. A customer visits a video store and rents a copy of Night of the Lepus. The customer's contract with the store limits use of the tape to home viewing and requires its return in two days. May the customer keep the tape, on the ground that §301(a) makes the promise unenforceable?

A law student uses the LEXIS database, containing public-domain documents, under a contract limiting the results to educational endeavors; may the student resell his access to this database to a law firm from which LEXIS seeks to collect a much higher hourly rate? Suppose ProCD hires a firm to scour the nation for telephone directories, promising to pay $100 for each that ProCD does not already have. The firm locates 100 new directories, which it sends to ProCD with an invoice for $10,000. ProCD incorporates the directories into its database; does it have to pay the bill? Surely yes; *Aronson* v. *Quick Point Pencil Co.* holds that promises to pay for intellectual property may be enforced even though federal law (in Aronson, the patent law) offers no protection against third-party uses of that property. But these illustrations are what our case is about. ProCD offers software and data for two prices: one for personal use, a higher price for commercial use. Zeidenberg wants to use the data without paying the seller's price; if the law student and Quick Point Pencil Co. could not do that, neither can Zeidenberg.

Although Congress possesses power to preempt even the enforcement of contracts about intellectual property — or railroads, on which see *Norfolk & Western*

Ry. v. *Train Dispatchers* — courts usually read preemption clauses to leave private contracts unaffected. *American Airlines, Inc.* v. *Wolens* provides a nice illustration. A federal statute preempts any state "law, rule, regulation, standard, or other provision ... relating to rates, routes, or services of any air carrier." Does such a law preempt the law of contracts — so that, for example, an air carrier need not honor a quoted price (or a contract to reduce the price by the value of frequent flyer miles)? The Court allowed that it is possible to read the statute that broadly but thought such an interpretation would make little sense. Terms and conditions offered by contract reflect private ordering, essential to the efficient functioning of markets. Although some principles that carry the name of contract law are designed to defeat rather than implement consensual transactions, the rules that respect private choice are not preempted by a clause such as §1305(a)(1). Section 301(a) plays a role similar to §1301(a)(1): it prevents states from substituting their own regulatory systems for those of the national government. Just as §301(a) does not itself interfere with private transactions in intellectual property, so it does not prevent states from respecting those transactions. Like the Supreme Court in Wolens, we think it prudent to refrain from adopting a rule that anything with the label "contract" is necessarily outside the preemption clause: the variations and possibilities are too numerous to foresee. National Car Rental likewise recognizes the possibility that some applications of the law of contract could interfere with the attainment of national objectives and therefore come within the domain of §301(a). But general enforcement of shrinkwrap licenses of the kind before us does not create such interference.

Aronson emphasized that enforcement of the contract between Aronson and Quick Point Pencil Company would not withdraw any information from the public domain. That is equally true of the contract between ProCD and Zeidenberg. Everyone remains free to copy and disseminate all 3,000 telephone books that have been incorporated into ProCD's database. Anyone can add sic codes and zip codes. ProCD's rivals have done so. Enforcement of the shrinkwrap license may even make information more readily available, by reducing the price ProCD charges to consumer buyers. To the extent licenses facilitate distribution of object code while concealing the source code (the point of a clause forbidding disassembly), they serve the same procompetitive functions as does the law of trade secrets. Licenses may have other benefits for consumers: many licenses permit users to make extra copies, to use the software on multiple computers, even to incorporate the software into the user's products. But whether a particular license is generous or restrictive, a simple two-party contract is not "equivalent to any of the exclusive rights within the general scope of copyright" and therefore may be enforced.

Discussion Questions

Do you agree with the Court's analysis? Does the market-based approach sufficiently protect the rights of all parties? Do software vendors have other means of bringing license terms to the attention of purchasers? Given the rising popularity of freeware and open source software, are the assumptions made by the Court still valid?

The Alberta Court of the Queen's Bench addressed a similar issue in *North American Systemshops Ltd.* v. *King*. In that case, the issue was whether all copyright restrictions apply at the time of sale or only to those restrictions brought to the attention of the purchaser. Both the indication of copyright and the licensing agreement were not visible on the software packaging or on the disk. Instead, it was hidden inside the software manual.

North American Systemshops Ltd. v. King†

[The court stated:]

On the evidence, I conclude that: the program was sold to the defendants shrink-wrapped; that no copyright symbol was visible to the purchaser, (since the copyright symbol on the booklet is on the inside front cover of the booklet and not on the outside cover and the copyright symbol on the floppy disk is in the same general location on the disk as the registration number and the evidence of the witness Wallace is that the registration number was not visible through the shrink-wrap); and that no licence statement was visible (the licence statement being on the inside back cover of the booklet and not being on the floppy disk). In addition, the evidence establishes that the copyright symbol comes up on the first screen when the program is used, but no licence statement comes up on the screen. Finally, I am satisfied that the user of the program would not have to refer to the booklet for general use of the program as the program was designed to be, and was in fact, "user-useful" [...]

· · · ·

It is true that in every contract, including a contract for the sale of goods, the Court may imply terms. However, it will not imply reasonable terms; it will only imply necessary terms. The law does imply that the purchaser has intended to divest itself of all rights in the article sold, unless restrictions are brought home to the purchaser:

> If a Patentee sells the patented article to a purchaser and the purchaser uses it, he, of course, does not infringe. But why? By reason of the fact that the law presumes from the sale an implied licence given by the Patentee to the purchaser that he shall use that which he has bought, and in the absence of condition, this implied licence is a licence to use or sell or deal with the goods as the purchaser pleases.

The jurisprudence does conclude that patented articles, and I am prepared to find that copyrighted articles belong to a similar category, are different from normal goods in that restrictions not only may be imposed on the sale, but the restrictions will run with the goods:

> [It is] open to the patentee by virtue of his statutory monopoly to make a sale sub modo or accompanied by restrictive conditions, which would not apply in the case of ordinary chattels; secondly, that the imposition, of these conditions in a sale is not presumed, but, on the contrary, a sale having

---

† [1989] A.J. No. 512 (Alta. Q.B.).

> occurred the presumption is that the full right of ownership was meant to
> be vested in the purchaser; while, thirdly, the owner's rights in a patented
> chattel will be limited, if there is brought home to him the knowledge of
> conditions imposed ... upon him at the time of sale.

It appears to me that this general thrust of English jurisprudence is all the
more applicable to the over-the-counter sale of computer software because of the
way in which a computer program must be used, i.e. in order to be used, it must be
copied at least once into the computer's memory. In that way, the sale of computer
software programs differs markedly from the sale of other types of copyrightable
materials such as books.

The Internet equivalent to the shrinkwrap contract is known as a clickwrap contract. Unlike software, which requires removal of the shrinkwrap to manifest acceptance of the terms, the Internet enables parties to be far more explicit in their
consent. The most common approach is the "I Accept" button that is frequently
found at the bottom of the online contract. The Ontario courts became among the
first in North America to address the enforceability of clickwrap contracts in this
1999 decision.

Rudder v. Microsoft Corp.[†]

This is a motion by the defendant Microsoft for a permanent stay of this intended
class proceeding. The motion is based on two alternative grounds, first that the parties have agreed to the exclusive jurisdiction, and venue, of the courts, in King
County in the State of Washington in respect of any litigation between them, and
secondly, that in any event, Ontario is not the appropriate forum for the conduct of
this proceeding and that the service ex juris of the Statement of Claim ought to be
set aside.

The Microsoft Network ("MSN"), is an online service, providing, inter alia,
information and services including Internet access to its members. The service is
provided to members, around the world, from a "gateway" located in the State of
Washington through computer connections most often made over standard telephone
lines.

The proposed representative plaintiffs in this action were subscriber members
of MSN. Both are law school graduates, one of whom is admitted to the Bar in
Ontario while the other worked as a legal researcher. They were associated with the
law firm which originally represented the intended class. The plaintiffs claim under
the Class Proceedings Act, 1992, S.O., C.6 on behalf of a Canada-wide class defined
as:

> All persons resident in Canada who subscribed for the provision of Internet
> access or information or services from or through MSN, The Microsoft
> Network, since September 1, 1995.

This class is estimated to contain some 89,000 MSN members across Canada.

---

† [1999] O.J. No. 3778 (Ont. Sup. Ct.).

The plaintiffs claim damages for breach of contract, breach of fiduciary duty, misappropriation and punitive damages in the total amount of $75,000,000.00 together with an accounting and injunctive relief. The plaintiffs allege that Microsoft has charged members of MSN and taken payment from their credit cards in breach of contract and that Microsoft has failed to provide reasonable or accurate information concerning accounts. The Statement of Claim was served on Microsoft at its offices in Redmond, Washington on January 5, 1998.

The contract which the plaintiffs allege to have been breached is identified by MSN as a "Member Agreement". Potential members of MSN are required to electronically execute this agreement prior to receiving the services provided by the company. Each Member Agreement contains the following provision:

> 15.1 This Agreement is governed by the laws of the State of Washington, U.S.A., and you consent to the exclusive jurisdiction and venue of courts in King County, Washington, in all disputes arising out of or relating to your use of MSN or your MSN membership.

The defendant relies on this clause in support of its assertion that the intended class proceeding should be permanently stayed.

Although the plaintiffs rely on the contract as the basis for their causes of action, they submit that the court ought not to give credence to the "forum selection clause" contained within. It is stated in support of this contention that the representative plaintiffs read only portions of the Member Agreement and thus had no notice of the forum selection clause. Alternatively, the plaintiffs contend, in any event, that the Washington courts are not appropriate for the conduct of this lawsuit.

I cannot accede to these submissions. In my view, the forum selection clause is dispositive and there is nothing in the factual record which persuades me that I should exercise my discretion so as to permit the plaintiffs to avoid the effect of the contractual provision. Accordingly, an order will go granting the relief sought by the defendant. My reasons follow.

Analysis and Disposition

Forum selection clauses are generally treated with a measure of deference by Canadian courts. Madam Justice Huddart, writing for the court in *Sarabia* v. *"Oceanic Mindoro"* adopts the view that forum selection clauses should be treated the same as arbitration agreements. She states:

> Since forum selection clauses are fundamentally similar to arbitration agreements, ... there is no reason for forum selection clauses not to be treated in a manner consistent with the deference shown to arbitration agreements. Such deference to forum selection clauses achieves greater international commercial certainty, shows respect for the agreements that the parties have signed, and is consistent with the principle of international comity.

Huddart J.A. further states that "a court is not bound to give effect to an exclusive jurisdiction clause" but that the choice of the parties should be respected unless "there is strong cause to override the agreement." The burden for a showing of a "strong cause" rests with the plaintiff and the threshold to be surpassed is beyond the mere "balance of convenience". The approach taken by Huddart J.A. is consistent with that adopted by courts in Ontario.

The plaintiffs contend, first, that regardless of the deference to be shown to forum selection clauses, no effect should be given to the particular clause at issue in this case because it does not represent the true agreement of the parties. It is the plaintiff's submission that the form in which the Member Agreement is provided to potential members of MSN is such that it obscures the forum selection clause. Therefore, the plaintiffs argue, the clause should be treated as if it were the fine print in a contract which must be brought specifically to the attention of the party accepting the terms. Since there was no specific notice given, in the plaintiffs' view, the forum selection clause should be severed from the Agreement which they otherwise seek to enforce.

The argument advanced by the plaintiffs relies heavily on the alleged deficiencies in the technological aspects of electronic formats for presenting the terms of agreements. In other words, the plaintiffs contend that because only a portion of the Agreement was presented on the screen at one time, the terms of the Agreement which were not on the screen are essentially "fine print".

I disagree. The Member Agreement is provided to potential members of MSN in a computer readable form through either individual computer disks or via the Internet at the MSN website. In this case, the plaintiff Rudder, whose affidavit was filed on the motion, received a computer disk as part of a promotion by MSN. The disk contained the operating software for MSN and included a multi-media sign up procedure for persons who wished to obtain the MSN service. As part of the sign-up routine, potential members of MSN were required to acknowledge their acceptance of the terms of the Member Agreement by clicking on an "I Agree" button presented on the computer screen at the same time as the terms of the Member Agreement were displayed.

Rudder admitted in cross-examination on his affidavit that the entire agreement was readily viewable by using the scrolling function on the portion of the computer screen where the Membership Agreement was presented. Moreover, Rudder acknowledged that he "scanned" through part of the Agreement looking for "costs" that would be charged by MSN. He further admitted that once he had found the provisions relating to costs, he did not read the rest of the Agreement. [...]

. . . .

It is plain and obvious that there is no factual foundation for the plaintiffs' assertion that any term of the Membership Agreement was analogous to "fine print" in a written contract. What is equally clear is that the plaintiffs seek to avoid the consequences of specific terms of their agreement while at the same time seeking to have others enforced. Neither the form of this contract nor its manner of presentation to potential members are so aberrant as to lead to such an anomalous result. To give effect to the plaintiffs' argument would, rather than advancing the goal of "commercial certainty", to adopt the words of Huddart J.A. in Sarabia, move this type of electronic transaction into the realm of commercial absurdity. It would lead to chaos in the marketplace, render ineffectual electronic commerce and undermine the integrity of any agreement entered into through this medium.

On the present facts, the Membership Agreement must be afforded the sanctity that must be given to any agreement in writing. The position of selectivity advanced by the plaintiffs runs contrary to this stated approach, both in principle and on the evidence, and must be rejected. Moreover, given that both of the representative plaintiffs are graduates of law schools and have a professed familiarity with Internet services, their position is particularly indefensible.

Notes

1. The State of New Jersey similarly upheld the forum selection at issue in *Caspi* v. *The Microsoft Network, L.L.C.*, 732 A.2d 528 (N.J. App. 1999). After resolving that the forum selection clause was valid and did not violate consumer fraud concepts, the court considered whether there was adequate notice of the clause.

    > The scenario presented here is different because of the medium used, electronic versus printed; but, in any sense that matters, there is no significant distinction. The plaintiffs in Carnival could have perused all the fine-print provisions of their travel contract if they wished before accepting the terms by purchasing their cruise ticket. The plaintiffs in this case were free to scroll through the various computer screens that presented the terms of their contracts before clicking their agreement.
    >
    > Also, it seems clear that there was nothing extraordinary about the size or placement of the forum selection clause text. By every indication we have, the clause was presented in exactly the same format as most other provisions of the contract. It was the first item in the last paragraph of the electronic document. We note that a few paragraphs in the contract were presented in upper case typeface, presumably for emphasis, but most provisions, including the forum selection clause, were presented in lower case typeface. We discern nothing about the style or mode of presentation, or the placement of the provision, that can be taken as a basis for concluding that the forum selection clause was proffered unfairly, or with a design to conceal or de-emphasize its provisions. To conclude that plaintiffs are not bound by that clause would be equivalent to holding that they were bound by no other clause either, since all provisions were identically presented. Plaintiffs must be taken to have known that they were entering into a contract; and no good purpose, consonant with the dictates of reasonable reliability in commerce, would be served by permitting them to disavow particular provisions or the contracts as a whole.).
    >
    > The issue of reasonable notice regarding a forum selection clause is a question of law for the court to determine. We agree with the trial court that, in the absence of a better showing than has been made, plaintiffs must be seen to have had adequate notice of the forum selection clause. The resolution of this notice issue, at this stage of the litigation between plaintiffs and defendants must, of course, be seen to be without prejudice to any showing either party may have the opportunity to make in another jurisdiction in a plenary proceeding on the contract regarding issues apart from the validity and enforceability of the forum selection clause.

2. The U.S. courts have been fairly consistent in ruling that forum selection clauses are valid within the Internet context. As a result of the clause, the court in *Decker* v. *Circus Circus Hotel* (49 F. Supp. 2d 743 (D.N.J., 1999))was unable to assert jurisdiction. The court stated:

    > With regard to the defendant's Internet site, the plaintiffs' attorney attached a copy of printed pages from that site to his affidavit in this matter. From those pages it is clear that any customer can reserve a room through the Web site. This activity is certainly commercial in nature. Moreover, by making reservations available on the Internet, the defendants have effectively placed their hotel and its services into an endless stream of commerce. Under the "stream of commerce" theory, a forum state may exercise jurisdiction over a non-resident corporation "that delivers its product into the stream of commerce with expectation that they will be purchased by consumers in the forum state." However, the defendant's Internet site contains a forum selection clause requiring that by

making a reservation over the Internet, customers agree to have their disputes settled in Nevada state and federal courts. This forum selection clause ought to be enforced. "A clause establishing ex ante the forum for dispute resolution has the salutary effect of dispelling any confusion about where suits arising from the contract must be brought and defended, sparing litigants the time and expense of pretrial motions to determine the correct forum and conserving judicial resources that otherwise would be devoted to deciding those motions." This Court will not exercise personal jurisdiction over the defendant based on the maintenance of its Internet site.

Discussion Questions

1. What is reasonable notice? Is it easier to give reasonable notice for clickwrap contracts rather than shrinkwrap contracts?

2. When is an online contract concluded? When the software is purchased? On delivery of software? Once the software is downloaded? Once it is installed?

The *Uniform Electronic Commerce Act* (UECA), a project of the Uniform Law Conference of Canada (ULCC), obtained official approval in 1999, providing Canada with a legal model for electronic commerce transactions. The subject of more than two years of negotiation, the UECA brings much needed certainty to the world of e-commerce. Based largely on the United Nations Model Code on Electronic Commerce, it clarifies issues such as the enforceability and formation of online contracts, the use of electronic agents in the contracting process, and at what point an electronic contract is deemed sent and received.

The governing principle underlying the UECA is the concept of electronic equivalence. Although the Act does not deem electronic communications valid (just as with paper documents, legal validity depends upon more than just a document's form), it promises that information will not be denied legal effect or enforceability solely because it is in electronic form.

The Act is also careful not to compel parties to use electronic communications. In an important deviation from the U.N. model, the Canadian version provides that nothing in the Act requires a person to use or accept information in electronic form without their consent.

Consent to use electronic communication, however, may be inferred from a person's behaviour. For example, providing a business card with an email address could be construed as consent to receive email. Similarly, placing an order on the Web could be treated as consent to deal with a seller electronically.

The most interesting section of the law focuses on online contracts. Although thousands of contracts are entered into daily through e-commerce, some sellers and consumers remain uncertain of the legal implications of clicking the "I Agree" button on a Web site. The law removes any doubt that this popular form of online consent is indeed valid by stipulating that unless the parties agree otherwise, an offer or acceptance of an offer can be expressed in electronic form by clicking on an appropriate icon.

Contracts between an individual and a computer or between two computers also attracted the attention of the law's drafters. This issue has become particularly important with the growing popularity of online stock trading, as well as with other forms of e-commerce, such when a person deals solely with a computer on the other end of a transaction. The concern in this situation lies with the difficulty of correcting a mistake. For example, if someone inadvertently orders 11 copies of a book rather than just a single copy, can they get out of the contract?

The law creates an appropriate compromise by ensuring that consumers have an opportunity to review the terms of their contract before it becomes binding. Under the UECA, computer-based contracts are not enforceable where an individual alleges that a mistake has occurred and the individual was not provided with the opportunity to prevent or correct the error (as long as the individual notifies the other party of the mistake and does not profit from it).

One of the most contentious issues faced by the drafters concerned the point at which an electronic communication is deemed sent and received. In the early days of contract law, a postal acceptance rule was established which deemed a contract accepted from the moment the acceptance was mailed. The UECA seeks to develop an Internet equivalent. An electronic document is deemed sent once it enters an information system outside the control of the originator. For most Internet users, this occurs once their email program actually sends the email (not necessarily when the user clicks the send button).

An electronic document is presumed received by an addressee when it enters their information system, provided the recipient has designated the system for receipt of electronic documents. In other words, the recipient does not actually have to retrieve the message, but merely have the capability of doing so.

Although legislative proposals passed by the ULCC are not binding, they are forwarded to all provincial and territorial governments with a recommendation that they be enacted in order to provide Canada with a harmonized approach to important legal issues.

Uniform Electronic Commerce Act[†]

1. The definitions in this section apply in this Act.
  (a) "electronic" includes created, recorded, transmitted or stored in digital form or in other intangible form by electronic, magnetic or optical means or by any other means that has capabilities for creation, recording, transmission or storage similar to those means and electronically has a corresponding meaning.
  (b) "electronic signature" means information in electronic form that a person has created or adopted in order to sign a document and that is in, attached to or associated with the document.
  (c) "Government" means
      (i) the Government of [enacting jurisdiction];
      (ii) any department, agency or body of the Government of [enacting jurisdiction], [other than Crown Corporations incorporated by or under a law of [enacting jurisdiction]]; and

---

† Online: <http://www.law.ualberta.ca/alri/ulc/acts/eueca-a.htm>. Reproduced with permission of Uniform Law Conference of Canada.

(iii) [any city, metropolitan authority, town, village, township, district or [rural municipality or other municipal body, however designated, incorporated or established by or under a law of [enacting jurisdiction].]

2.(1) Subject to this section, this Act applies in respect of [enacting jurisdiction] law.

(2) The [appropriate authority] may, by [statutory instrument], specify provisions of or requirements under [enacting jurisdiction] law in respect of which this Act does not apply.

(3) This Act does not apply in respect of

(a) wills and their codicils;
(b) trusts created by wills or by codicils to wills;
(c) powers of attorney, to the extent that they are in respect of the financial affairs or personal care of an individual;
(d) documents that create or transfer interests in land and that require registration to be effective against third parties.

(4) Except for Part 3, this Act does not apply in respect of negotiable instruments, including negotiable documents of title.

(5) Nothing in this Act limits the operation of any provision of [enacting jurisdiction] law that expressly authorizes, prohibits or regulates the use of electronic documents.

(6) The [appropriate authority] may, by [statutory instrument], amend subsection (3) to add any document or class of documents, or to remove any document or class of documents previously added under this subsection.

(7) For the purpose of subsection (5), the use of words and expressions like "in writing" and "signature" and other similar words and expressions does not by itself prohibit the use of electronic documents.

. . . .

4. The provisions of this Act relating to the satisfaction of a requirement of law apply whether the law creates an obligation or provides consequences for doing something or for not doing something.

5. Information shall not be denied legal effect or enforceability solely by reason that it is in electronic form.

6.(1) Nothing in this Act requires a person to use or accept information in electronic form, but a person's consent to do so may be inferred from the person's conduct.

(2) Despite subsection (1), the consent of the Government to accept information in electronic form may not be inferred by its conduct but must be expressed by communication accessible to the public or to those likely to communicate with it for particular purposes.

7. A requirement under [enacting jurisdiction] law that information be in writing is satisfied by information in electronic form if the information is accessible so as to be usable for subsequent reference.

8.(1) A requirement under [enacting jurisdiction] law for a person to provide information in writing to another person is satisfied by the provision of the information in an electronic document,

  (a) if the electronic document that is provided to the other person is accessible by the other person and capable of being retained by the other person so as to be usable for subsequent reference, and

  (b) where the information is to be provided to the Government, if

   (i) the Government or the part of Government to which the information is to be provided has consented to accept electronic documents in satisfaction of the requirement; and

   (ii) the electronic document meets the information technology standards and acknowledgement rules, if any, established by the Government or part of Government, as the case may be.

. . . .

Part 2 Communication of Electronic Documents

19. In this Part, "electronic agent" means a computer program or any electronic means used to initiate an action or to respond to electronic documents or actions in whole or in part without review by a natural person at the time of the response or action.

20.(1) Unless the parties agree otherwise, an offer or the acceptance of an offer, or any other matter that is material to the formation or operation of a contract, may be expressed

  (a) by means of an electronic document; or

  (b) by an action in electronic form, including touching or clicking on an appropriately designated icon or place on a computer screen or otherwise communicating electronically in a manner that is intended to express the offer, acceptance or other matter.

   (2) A contract shall not be denied legal effect or enforceability solely by reason that an electronic document was used in its formation.

21. A contract may be formed by the interaction of an electronic agent and a natural person or by the interaction of electronic agents.

22. An electronic document made by a natural person with the electronic agent of another person has no legal effect and is not enforceable if the natural person made a material error in the document and

  (a) the electronic agent did not provide the natural person with an opportunity to prevent or correct the error;

  (b) the natural person notifies the other person of the error as soon as practicable after the natural person learns of the error and indicates that he or she made an error in the electronic document;

  (c) the natural person takes reasonable steps, including steps that conform to the other person's instructions to return the consideration received, if any, as a result of the error or, if instructed to do so, to destroy the consideration; and

  (d) the natural person has not used or received any material benefit or value from the consideration, if any, received from the other person.

23.(1) Unless the originator and the addressee agree otherwise, an electronic document is sent when it enters an information system outside the control of the originator or, if the originator and the addressee are in the same information system, when it becomes capable of being retrieved and processed by the addressee.

(2) An electronic document is presumed to be received by the addressee,

(a) when it enters an information system designated or used by the addressee for the purpose of receiving documents of the type sent and it is capable of being retrieved and processed by the addressee; or

(b) if the addressee has not designated or does not use an information system for the purpose of receiving documents of the type sent, when the addressee becomes aware of the electronic document in the addressee's information system and the electronic document is capable of being retrieved and processed by the addressee.

(3) Unless the originator and the addressee agree otherwise, an electronic document is deemed to be sent from the originator's place of business and is deemed to be received at the addressee's place of business.

(4) For the purposes of subsection (3)

(a) if the originator or the addressee has more than one place of business, the place of business is that which has the closest relationship to the underlying transaction to which the electronic document relates or, if there is no underlying transaction, the principal place of business of the originator or the addressee; and

(b) if the originator or the addressee does not have a place of business, the references to "place of business" in subsection (3) are to be read as references to "habitual residence".

Discussion Questions

1. Consider the definition for "electronic", which is designed to be "technology neutral." Do you think the law will outlive current technologies such as the digital signature?

2. What potential problems are encountered when using electronic agents to form contracts?

Notes

Countries around the world are adopting legislation modeled after the UN standard and thus similar in form to the UECA. As of July 2000, over 20 U.S. states, including Pennsylvania and California, had adopted the U.S. equivalent called the *Uniform Electronic Transactions Act*. In Australia, the *Electronic Transactions Bill* had been adopted in two states. Similar initiatives were under way around the world, including proposals in Singapore, India, Ireland, the U.K. and Ecuador.

E-commerce legislation gained increasing momentum across Canada in the year 2000 as five provinces enacted or proposed enacting e-commerce legislation by July.

Saskatchewan, which became the first province to propose e-commerce legislation in December 1999, also led the way as the first Canadian province to enact e-commerce legislation when the *Information and Documents Act 2000* (Bill 38) received Royal Assent on June 21, 2000. An excerpt is found below.

Ontario, Manitoba, and British Columbia also introduced e-commerce bills that are likely to be enacted by the end of the calendar year. As of July 2000, Ontario's *Electronic Commerce Act, 2000* (Bill 88), had passed its second reading and had been sent to the Justice and Social Policy Committee for review. A copy of the bill can be found online at <http://www.ontla.on.ca/Documents/StatusofLegOUT/b088_ e.htm>.

Manitoba introduced the *Electronic Commerce and Information, Consumer Protection Amendment and Evidence Amendment Act* (Bill 31) on June 6, 2000. The bill, which passed second reading on July 24, 2000, can be found online at <http:// www.gov.mb.ca/chc/statpub/free/pdf/b31-1s00.pdf>.

British Columbia introduced the *Electronic Transactions Act* (Bill 32) on July 5, 2000. The bill can be found online at http://www.legis.gov.bc.ca/2000/1st_read/ gov32-1.htm.

Quebec introduced a draft bill in June 2000 entitled *An Act Respecting the Legal Normalization of New Information Technologies*. An English copy of the draft bill can be found online at <http://www.assnat.qc.ca/eng/publications/ index.html#Draft>.

The Electronic Information and Documents Act, 2000[†]

HER MAJESTY, by and with the advice and consent of the Legislative Assembly of Saskatchewan, enacts as follows:

3. In this Part:

(a) "electronic" means created, recorded, transmitted or stored in digital or other intangible form by electronic, magnetic or optical means or by any other similar means;

(b) "electronic signature" means information in electronic form that a person has created or adopted in order to sign a document and that is in, attached to or associated with the document.

4.(1) This Part does not apply to:

(a) wills;

(b) directives within the meaning of *The Health Care Directives and Substitute Health Care Decision Makers Act*;

(c) trusts created by wills;

(d) powers of attorney, to the extent that they concern the financial affairs or personal care of an individual;

---

† S.S. 2000, Ch. E-7.22.

(e) documents that create or transfer interests in land and that require registration to be effective against third parties; or

(f) any other provisions, requirements, information or documents prescribed in the regulations.

(2) Divisions 2 and 3 do not apply to negotiable instruments, including negotiable documents of title.

(3) This Act does not apply to any matter to which Part III applies or may apply.

.   .   .   .

5(1) Nothing in this Part limits the operation of any law that expressly authorizes, prohibits or regulates the use of information or documents in an electronic form.

(2) For the purpose of subsection (1), the use of "in writing" and "signature" and other similar words and expressions does not by itself prohibit the use of information or documents in an electronic form.

(3) The provisions of this Part relating to the satisfaction of a requirement of any law apply whether or not the law creates an obligation or provides consequences for doing something or for not doing something.

18.(1) Unless the parties agree otherwise, an offer or the acceptance of an offer, or any other matter that is material to the formation or operation of a contract, may be expressed:

(a) by means of information or a document in an electronic form; or

(b) by an action in an electronic form, including touching or clicking on an appropriately designated icon or place on a computer screen or otherwise communicating electronically in a manner that is intended to express the offer, acceptance or other matter.

(2) A contract shall not be denied legal effect or enforceability solely by reason that information or a document in an electronic form was used in its formation.

19.(1) In this section and in section 20, "electronic agent" means a computer program, or any electronic means, used to initiate an action or to respond to electronic information, documents or actions in whole or in part without review by an individual at the time of the response or action.

(2) A contract may be formed by the interaction of an electronic agent and an individual or by the interaction of electronic agents.

20. An electronic document made by an individual with the electronic agent of another person has no legal effect and is not enforceable if the individual made a material error in the document and:

(a) the electronic agent did not provide the individual with an opportunity to prevent or correct the error;

(b) the individual notifies the other person of the error as soon as is practicable after the individual learns of the error and indicates that he or she made an error respecting the electronic document;

(c) the individual takes reasonable steps, including steps that conform to the other person's instructions, to return the consideration received, if any, as a result of the error or, if instructed to do so, to destroy the consideration; and

(d) the individual has not used or received any material benefit or value from the consideration, if any, received from the other person.

21.(1) In this section:

(a) "addressee" means the person to whom any information or document in an electronic form is to be sent;

(b) "originator" means the person sending the information or document in an electronic form.

(2) Unless the originator and addressee agree otherwise, information or a document in an electronic form is sent when it enters an information system outside the control of the originator or, if the originator and the addressee are in the same information system, when it becomes capable of being retrieved and processed by the addressee.

(3) Information or a document in an electronic form is presumed to be received by the addressee:

(a) when it enters an information system designated or used by the addressee for the purpose of receiving information or documents in an electronic form of the type sent and it is capable of being retrieved and processed by the addressee; or

(b) if the addressee has not designated or does not use an information system for the purpose of receiving information or documents in an electronic form of the type sent, when the addressee becomes aware of the information or document in the addressee's information system and it is capable of being retrieved and processed by the addressee.

(4) Unless the originator and the addressee agree otherwise, information or a document in an electronic form is deemed to be sent from the originator's place of business and is deemed to be received at the addressee's place of business.

(5) For the purposes of subsection (4):

(a) if the originator or the addressee has more than one place of business, the place of business is that which has the closest relationship to the underlying transaction to which the information or document in an electronic form relates or, if there is no underlying transaction, the principal place of business of the originator or the addressee; and

(b) if the originator or the addressee does not have a place of business, the references to "place of business" in subsection (4) are to be read as references to "habitual residence".

20

Digital Signatures

The signature, which for hundreds of years has symbolized acceptance of a binding contractual obligation (and before the signature, the seal accomplished the same thing), has proven to be one of the most difficult aspects of traditional commercial relations to replicate in cyberspace. In real space, contracting parties can meet face-to-face to sign a contract. A person's signature is distinctive and can be used to hold them to their bargain. In cyberspace, however, there are no face-to-face meetings, and electronic communication is susceptible to interception and alteration. This presents a significant concern for lawyers, who fear that contractual reliability and enforceability may be compromised.

The commonly accepted solution to this problem is the digital signature. With the establishment of a full-scale electronic signature programme, each person would create their own distinctive digital signature (comprised of a cryptographic key) which would be legally binding and provide contracting parties with the assurance that each person is who they claim to be.

The use of digital signatures extends beyond just signing documents, since they can be designed to verify other information, such as age, residence or credentials, as well as to provide assurances that electronic communications have not been altered while in transit. With a fully developed certificate programme, known as a public key infrastructure, digital certificates could even serve a critical role in limiting pornographic material to adults, providing greater certainty to jurisdictional questions, and enabling the public Internet to match the security of private communications systems.

Notwithstanding the great potential of certificates and signatures, several important legal questions remain. Should certificate issuers be subject to government regulation? Who is liable if a certificate is relied upon that proves to be false? Will users need multiple certificates (one for their health information, another for a professional association, another for their tax returns, etc.), or will a single certificate suffice? If the latter approach is adopted, can a cross-certification process be implemented to ensure that one certificate is recognized by multiple authorities?

We begin our examination of digital signatures with Professor Jane Winn's helpful explanation of their origin and uses.

Couriers Without Luggage: Negotiable Instruments and Digital Signatures[†]

JANE K. WINN

III. WHAT IS THE ORIGIN OF DIGITAL SIGNATURES, AND WHAT BUSINESS OBJECTIVES DO THEY SERVE?

A. Military and Commercial Use of Symmetric Key Cryptography

Digital signatures are a specific application of encryption technology, or cryptography. In turn, cryptography is one element of the larger field of information and computer system security. Computer security takes into account many factors, "including various technical safeguards, trustworthy and capable personnel, high degrees of physical security, competent administrative oversight, and good operational procedures." Until very recently, cryptography has been one of the least used of the available technical safeguards. When it has been used, the mechanics of its deployment have not been widely disseminated. Thus, the appropriate role of cryptographic tools in commercial transaction systems has not been as widely debated or analyzed as other issues at the intersection of information technology and commercial law.

Various forms of encryption have been used to maintain the confidentiality of information for over four thousand years. Encryption involves transforming the information for over four thousand years. Encryption involves transforming the text to be protected into a form that cannot be deciphered without having a copy of the key used to modify the original text. Simple cryptographic systems operate on the same principle as Captain Midnight decoder rings: a "cipher" is established to transform text into a secure form. The original text is called the "plaintext," and the transformed text is known as the "ciphertext." For example, if the cipher is the alphabet in reverse order, then the plaintext "Captain Midnight" becomes the ciphertext "Xzkgzrrn Nrwnutsg." The process of converting plaintext to ciphertext is a function of the encryption algorithm.

In 1949, Claude Shannon established the scientific basis for modern cryptography with the development of information theory which provided a mathematical basis for analyzing cryptographic systems. Modem encryption technology is based on using a complex mathematical function in combination with a unique number which serves as the encryption key to transform plaintext into ciphertext. Once a message has been encrypted, it can be decrypted by running it through a second complex function together with an encryption key. In private key, or symmetric cryptography, the same secret key is used both to encrypt and decrypt. In public key, or asymmetric cryptography, two different but mathematically related keys are used for encryption and de-

---

[†] (1998) 49 South Carolina Law Review 739 at 757–66. Notes omitted. Reproduced by permission of publisher.

cryption. Some of the relevant differences between public key and symmetric key cryptosystems in electronic commerce are discussed below.

The quality of encryption technology security is measured by how resistant an encrypted message is to being decrypted by someone who does not have the secret key. The simplest way to try to break an encoded message is a "brute force" attack, which consists of trying every possible key until the correct key is found. Because of the rapidly decreasing cost of computation, cryptographic systems that cost $1 billion to break in 1945 can be broken for approximately $10 today. Because this trend is expected to continue into the future, cryptographic systems being designed to support electronic commerce applications today should have large safety margins to protect against the effects of future advances in technology.

Although the functions used to encrypt and decrypt messages are available on many computers, controlling access to the encryption key ensures the confidentiality of the encrypted message.

The longer the encryption key, the harder it is for someone without access to the key to decrypt the ciphertext. The length of the number used for the secret key is expressed in bits, such as a 56-bit key. Each bit in a key can be 1 or 0, so for a 56 bit key there are 2, or 72,057,594,037,900,000, possible different keys. The Data Encryption Standard (DES), adopted as a U.S. government standard in 1977 and as an American National Standards Institute Standard in 1981, uses a 56-bit key. If the attacker had the capability to test a billion keys a second, it would take 834 days to test all possible keys. In other words, by using technology available in 1998, it is possible for someone with enough time and money to break a message encrypted with a 56-bit key. In 1996, a computer equipped with an application specific chip could test 30 million DES keys per second. It is estimated that a government agency willing to invest $300 million in an array of such chips could break a DES key in 12 seconds. While it is unlikely that any government in the world currently possesses such equipment, rapidly falling prices for information processing power make it difficult to predict when a government's security or military agencies will possess such capabilities.

A longer key makes the encryption more difficult to crack by several orders of magnitude. According to another estimate, it would take 70,000 years to decrypt a file protected by an 80-bit key using technology available in 1998. To decrypt a message encrypted with a 128-bit key with technology available in 1998, it would take longer than current estimates for the life of the universe. Thus, while cracking any message encrypted with modern encryption technology is not easy, encryption with longer secret keys is significantly more secure. The first applications of computer-based encryption technology in the United States were in the military and financial institutions. In response to military needs, the U.S. Department of Defense (DOD) developed early computer security standards. By the 1980s, the DOD issued Trusted Computer System Evaluation Criteria (TCSEC) as standards for information system security, including the management of cryptosystems. Although systems developed according to TCSEC are considered trustworthy systems, the standards in TCSEC reflect conditions that characterize military rather than private commercial security applications. For example, TCSEC places more emphasis on confidentiality and less emphasis on integrity and availability of resources, issues of greater concern in private information systems. TCSEC also reflects the security concerns of an earlier generation of computer technology, which becomes more apparent as multiuser mainframe computers are displaced by distributed computer networks. Furthermore, compatibility of security standards between users is a crucial issue for electronic commerce that was not addressed in TCSEC. Similarly, secure military messaging systems developed for DOD are poorly suited for commercial applications because they rely on a rigid hierarchy and facilitate top-down communications only.

United States banking and financial institutions have created a vast and highly reliable network of computers that provide electronic funds transfers throughout the world. The movement toward automated financial services began in the 1950s with the expansion of retail banking services and the development of "full service" banking. The automation of the check collection process and the movement of banks into the credit card business reflect this trend. In the 1960s, banks began to develop EFT systems using computer technology that had been acquired to support check processing. A nationwide EFT network was established, including a chain of ACHs and networks of automated teller machines (ATM). The 1970s brought predictions that the checkless society was imminent, based on the assumption that the electronic funds transfer system would expand to include point-of-sale (POS) payment functions. However, the public proved more resistant to the replacement of paper checks with electronic funds transfers than anticipated, and it was not until the 1990s that retail POS EFT services began to achieve significant market share.

During the 1960s and 1970s, the wholesale wire transfer system was developed for the commercial banking services market. In the early 1970s, Fedwire was created to automate funds transfers through the Federal Reserve System. At the same time, the New York Clearinghouse Association established CHIPS. The Society for Worldwide Interbank Fund Transfers (SWIFT) began operations in 1977 as a secure communications network that, unlike the Fedwire or CHIPS, does not provide settlement functions. Through the development of these and other proprietary systems such as the communications networks that provide for central-switch transmission of messages between participants in the credit card system, financial service providers in the United States have built one of the largest electronic commerce networks in the world. In developing these networks and the services they support, financial institutions have developed comprehensive approaches to security. This includes policies to safeguard the financial institution's central processing facilities from physical damage, breaches in employee security procedures, and software failures. In addition, encryption maybe used for communications between remote locations and the central processing facilities. To secure customer access at remote locations, financial institutions will generally issue cards and personal identification numbers to customers which control access to customer funds. In addition, financial remote access providers may take steps in designing the ATM facility, such as installing a surveillance camera, to minimize the risk that customers will be attacked or observed while accessing funds.

With the exception of possessing a magnetic strip card or remembering the personal identification number (PIN) for consumer EFT access devices, security systems are transparent to the retail consumer of electronic financial services. Because of consumer protection regulations, financial service providers absorb the costs of most security failures of retail financial electronic service networks, even if caused by the consumer. This allocation of liability in favor of the institutional transactor has prompted institutional participants in these systems to invest heavily in security technology. Security procedures now used by credit card issuers to combat fraud include mailing inactive cards that require cardholders to make contact with the issuer by telephone to activate the card, placing holograms on the card to make reproduction of the card more difficult, placing a photograph of the cardholder on the card to improve the accuracy of identification checks, and encoding the magnetic strip with algorithms that aid in matching the card with the proper cardholder. In addition, neural network technology can be used to compare cardholder usage with known patterns of fraud, and expert or rules-based systems can be programmed to react when established parameters of activities are exceeded.

In commercial wire transfer services, the customer and the bank must agree to commercially reasonable security procedures for the bank to avoid liability for unauthorized transfers from the customer's account. If a bank has executed an unauthorized funds transfer instruction after the bank has established an economically reasonable security procedure, the bank's customer can avoid liability for the amount of the funds transfer by showing that the bank did not follow the security procedure, or the instruction did not originate with personnel or facilities under the customer's control. The loss allocation rules place the risk of unauthorized payment orders initially on the bank, but permit the bank to shift liability to the customer by insuring that the customer implements a commercially reasonable security procedure. However, if the customer can meet the substantial burden of proving that a loss was not his or her fault, then the bank is forced to absorb the loss.

Symmetric cryptography is commonly employed within well-established electronic financial services networks. The Data Encryption Standard (DES) is the most widely used form of encryption technology in financial services networks. In the early 1970s, when the military accounted for most cryptography research, IBM developed and marketed the DES algorithm. At the same time IBM was independently developing DES, the National Bureau of Standards (NBS), later renamed the National Institute of Standards and Technology (NIST), issued a call for proposals of a standard encryption algorithm. After testing the algorithm to determine its security and suitability for a national standard, the NBS entered into a nonexclusive, royalty-free license that permitted the use of DES as a standard form of encryption. After a period of public comment, DES was adopted as a federal standard in 1976. In 1981, the American National Standards Institute (ANSI) approved DES as a private sector standard. The ANSI Financial Institution Retail Security Working Group developed a DES-based standard for authentication of retail financial messages. The American Bankers Association also adopted a standard recommending DES for encryption. Because the DES algorithm has been widely known and used for decades, financial institutions may use Triple-DES as an alternative to DES to decrease the possibility that a DES could be decrypted by a simple brute-force attack. Triple-DES uses the DES algorithm three times, incorporating two different keys to achieve greater security, and is an appealing choice for financial institutions which have already installed DES equipment.

DES is a symmetric key cryptography system, which means the same key is used to encrypt and decrypt the plaintext. The administration of symmetric key systems within closed systems is a serious but not unmanageable problem. The primary key management problem within symmetric key systems is finding a way to distribute the keys to those who need them without compromising the security of the keys in transit. One solution is to take a page from the old James Bond novels, give the key to a courier in a sealed briefcase, and handcuff the briefcase to the courier. If the courier fails to arrive or the seal is broken, then the key is presumed compromised and not used. The overhead associated with such a distribution system may not be significant in the context of national security during the Cold War, but is obviously too great for mainstream electronic commerce applications today. Another shortcoming of symmetric key cryptography is that it cannot be used between parties with no prior contact because they must first find a way to share copies of the key. One solution is to create a central key distribution system. However, a key distribution system may create more problems than it solves because the individuals who run the key distribution system may not be as trustworthy as they should be. The key management problems of symmetric key cryptography can be avoided by using asymmetric or public key encryption, which is the heart of digital signatures.

B. Public Key Cryptography and Its Promise for Open Network Commerce

The first public key system was described in 1976 by Whitfield Diffie and Martin Hellman. A short time later, Ronald Rivest, Adi Shamir, and Len Adelman developed another public key system. The great advantage of a public key system is that it permits individuals to use two different but related keys to maintain the confidentiality of their communications. One key, the private key, is kept secret by the owner, while the other key, the public key, can be widely distributed. The two keys are mathematically related, but one of the features of public key cryptography is that it is computationally infeasible to derive one key from knowledge of the other.

It is a convention among those who try to explain public key cryptography to the uninitiated to use hypotheticals populated with Alice, Bob, and Carol. In a public key cryptography system, Alice and Bob exchange public keys. When Bob wants to communicate securely with Alice, he uses her public key to encrypt a message, confident that no one other than Alice may decrypt the message. If Alice wants to send Bob a message and provide Bob with confidence that it must have come from Alice, Alice may encrypt her message with her private key. After Bob receives the message, he decrypts it with his copy of Alice's public key, certain that the message originated with Alice.

The most secure system for exchanging keys in a public key cryptography system is like the most secure system for distributing private keys: a face-to-face transaction between parties with a prior acquaintance. If Alice and Bob feel confident of the security of their e-mail communications, they can exchange public keys via e-mail. If Alice and Bob have no prior dealings, however, they may be reluctant to trust simple e-mail.

The usefulness of public key cryptography is not limited to guaranteeing the confidentiality of messages. The digital signature function of public key cryptography can also be used to identify the party sending a message without encrypting the text. A digital signature is produced by first running the message to be signed through a hash function program that produces a digest of the entire message. One characteristic of this message digest is that if any change is made to the message, when the message is run through the hash function again, it will produce a totally different digest. Once this digest has been computed, the digest is encrypted with the private key of the sender, Alice. This encrypted digest is the digital signature. The plaintext of the message is sent to the recipient, Bob, together with the digital signature. Bob, who must already be in possession of Alice's public key, runs the message through the same hash function and produces a message digest independently. Bob then uses Alice's public key (the public key of the signer) to decrypt the digest that was appended by Alice to the message. If the two digests are identical, then Bob can reasonably have a high degree of confidence that only Alice (or someone who obtained control of Alice's key) sent the message, and that the text of the message has not been tampered with in transit.

However, even public key cryptography does not eliminate the problem of how to administer the distribution of keys. Someone might establish a "Get to Know Bill Gates" web site, generate a matched key pair and post the public key to the web site for anyone in the world to download and use in their correspondence with "Bill Gates." Yet no sensible person would believe that the person with whom they were communicating by using this key and the e-mail address on the web site was actually the chief executive officer of Microsoft.

There are various solutions to the problem of distributing public keys in a manner that gives the recipient confidence that the public key belongs to the person to whom it appears to belong. One solution was advanced by Phil Zimmerman, who wrote a public key cryptography program, called Pretty Good Privacy (PGP), for use by private citizens. The "web of trust" allows each person using PGP to have the option of certifiying [sic] that other keys do indeed belong to the individuals who purport to use them. Whenever a PGP user receives a key, the user is given the opportunity to review the other PGP users' certification of the key, and is asked to make a notation in the program regarding the degree to which the user trusts the authenticity of the identity of the purported user. To return to Alice and Bob, Bob may be a complete stranger to Alice, but Bob had his key certified by Carol, who is a good friend of Alice's. When PGP tells Alice that Carol has certified Bob's key, Alice may be willing to trust that the person sending her what purports to be Bob's public key is in fact Bob.

The Digital Signature Guidelines focus on the possibility of using a trusted third party, known as a "certification authority" (CA), to bind the identity of a person in the material world with the use of a specific key pair in an online environment. The Digital Signature Guidelines define a certification authority as "[a] person who issues a certificate." The procedure used by a CA to review an application from a prospective subscriber may be one of the CA practices described in a "certification practice statement" (CPS). In order to issue certificates for subscribers' public keys, the CA must have a "trustworthy system." If the CA operates a trustworthy system, the CA will be able to provide reliable "time stamps" for issuance of certificates, thus allowing relying parties to know with certainty the time when the certificate will expire and reliance on it would no longer be reasonable. What level of system security is appropriate to achieve a trustworthy system is a question that can only be resolved in light of all the circumstances under which the system will be used.

To return to the story of Alice and Bob, we can now introduce Carol, the CA. Assuming that Alice and Bob do not have any prior acquaintance, then Carol can perform an invaluable service of permitting Alice and Bob to make each other's acquaintance in an online environment and to have confidence that they know with whom they are dealing. Bob sends his public key to Alice included in Carol's certificate, which includes, among other things, a copy of Bob's public key signed by Carol's private key. If Alice has a copy of Carol's public key that she believes to be trustworthy, then she can use that public key to verify Carol's signature on the certificate. Once she has successfully verified Carol's public key, Alice can have confidence that Bob's key is what it purports to be. Using Carol's CA services, however, solves one problem — whether to trust that Bob's public key actually has some connection to the human being Bob with whom Alice believes she is dealing — only if two new problems can also be solved. These problems are: (1) whether Alice understands the degree of scrutiny applied by Carol before issuing Bob a certificate and has thought about whether that degree of scrutiny is appropriate for the use Alice has in mind for Bob's key; and (2) whether there is a system for distributing Carol's keys that inspires the confidence of people like Alice and Bob that they do actually have a copy of Carol's key.

Although the privacy provisions receive most of the attention, Canada's *Personal Information Protection and Electronic Documents Act* (formerly Bill C-6) also contains important provisions pertaining to the use of electronic signatures. These provisions are limited to the use of electronic signatures between individuals and government, but the approach provides a hint as to how the private sector might approach the issue as well.

Personal Information Protection and Electronic Documents Act†

PART 2 — ELECTRONIC DOCUMENTS

31.(1) The definitions in this subsection apply in this Part.

"electronic signature" means a signature that consists of one or more letters, characters, numbers or other symbols in digital form incorporated in, attached to or associated with an electronic document.

"secure electronic signature" means an electronic signature that results from the application of a technology or process prescribed by regulations made under subsection 48(1).

. . . .

36. A provision of a federal law that provides that a certificate or other document signed by a minister or public officer is proof of any matter or thing, or is admissible in evidence, is, subject to the federal law, satisfied by an electronic version of the certificate or other document if the electronic version is signed by the minister or public officer with that person's secure electronic signature.

. . . .

42. A requirement under a provision of a federal law for a document to be in its original form is satisfied by an electronic document if

(a) the federal law or the provision is listed in Schedule 2 or 3;
(b) the electronic document contains a secure electronic signature that was added when the electronic document was first generated in its final form and that can be used to verify that the electronic document has not been changed since that time; and
(c) the regulations respecting the application of this section to the provision have been complied with.

43. Subject to sections 44 to 46, a requirement under a provision of a federal law for a signature is satisfied by an electronic signature if

(a) the federal law or the provision is listed in Schedule 2 or 3; and
(b) the regulations respecting the application of this section to the provision have been complied with.

44. A statement required to be made under oath or solemn affirmation under a provision of a federal law may be made in electronic form if

---

† S.C. 2000, c. 5.

(a) the person who makes the statement signs it with that person's secure electronic signature;

(b) the person before whom the statement was made, and who is authorized to take statements under oath or solemn affirmation, signs it with that person's secure electronic signature;

(c) the federal law or the provision is listed in Schedule 2 or 3; and

(d) the regulations respecting the application of this section to the provision have been complied with.

45. A statement required to be made under a provision of a federal law declaring or certifying that any information given by a person making the statement is true, accurate or complete may be made in electronic form if

(a) the person signs it with that person's secure electronic signature;

(b) the federal law or the provision is listed in Schedule 2 or 3; and

(c) the regulations respecting the application of this section to the provision have been complied with.

46. A requirement under a provision of a federal law for a signature to be witnessed is satisfied with respect to an electronic document if

(a) each signatory and each witness signs the electronic document with their secure electronic signature;

(b) the federal law or the provision is listed in Schedule 2 or 3; and

(c) the regulations respecting the application of this section to the provision have been complied with.

. . . .

48.(1) Subject to subsection (2), the Governor in Council may, on the recommendation of the Treasury Board, make regulations prescribing technologies or processes for the purpose of the definition "secure electronic signature" in subsection 31(1).

(2) The Governor in Council may prescribe a technology or process only if the Governor in Council is satisfied that it can be proved that

(a) the electronic signature resulting from the use by a person of the technology or process is unique to the person;

(b) the use of the technology or process by a person to incorporate, attach or associate the person's electronic signature to an electronic document is under the sole control of the person;

(c) the technology or process can be used to identify the person using the technology or process; and

(d) the electronic signature can be linked with an electronic document in such a way that it can be used to determine whether the electronic document has been changed since the electronic signature was incorporated in, attached to or associated with the electronic document.

Notes

1. The Act's provisions are limited to statutorily created signature requirements. Private sector use of digital signatures is addressed in the Uniform Electronic Commerce Act.

2.   The Act adopts a technology-neutral approach by ensuring that any technology that complies with a series of minimum characteristics can receive governmental approval as an approved electronic signature. At the present time, digital signatures are the most common form of electronic signature, but other approaches, such as retinal scans or digital fingerprints, may prove viable in the future.

Uniform Electronic Commerce Act[†]

1. In this Act,

"electronic" includes created, recorded, transmitted or stored in digital form or in other intangible form by electronic, magnetic or optical means or by any other means that has capabilities for creation, recording, transmission or storage similar to those means and electronically has a corresponding meaning.

"electronic signature" means information in electronic form that a person has created or adopted in order to sign a document and that is in, attached to or associated with the document.

10.(1) A requirement under [enacting jurisdiction] law for the signature of a person is satisfied by an electronic signature.

(2) For the purposes of subsection (1), the [authority responsible for the requirement] may make a regulation that,

(a) the electronic signature shall be reliable for the purpose of identifying the person, in the light of all the circumstances, including any relevant agreement and the time the electronic signature was made; and

(b) the association of the electronic signature with the relevant electronic document shall be reliable for the purpose for which the electronic document was made, in the light of all the circumstances, including any relevant agreement and the time the electronic signature was made.

(3) For the purposes of subsection (1), where the signature or signed document is to be provided to the Government, the requirement is satisfied only if

(i) the Government or the part of Government to which the information is to be provided has consented to accept electronic signatures; and

(ii) the electronic document meets the information technology standards and requirements as to method and as to reliability of the signature, if any, established by the Government or part of Government, as the case may be.

---

† Online: <http://www.law.ualberta.ca/alri/ulc/acts/eueca-a.htm>. Reproduced by permission of Uniform Law Conference.

11.(1) A requirement under [enacting jurisdiction] law that requires a person to present or retain a document in original form is satisfied by the provision or retention of an electronic document if

(a) there exists a reliable assurance as to the integrity of the information contained in the electronic document from the time the document to be presented or retained was first made in its final form, whether as a paper document or as an electronic document;

(b) where the document in original form is to be provided to a person, the electronic document that is provided to the person is accessible by the person and capable of being retained by the person so as to be usable for subsequent reference; and

(c) where the document in original form is to be provided to the Government,

(i) the Government or the part of Government to which the information is to be provided has consented to accept electronic documents in satisfaction of the requirement; and

(ii) the electronic document meets the information technology standards and acknowledgement rules, if any, established by the Government or part of Government, as the case may be.

(2) For the purpose of paragraph (1)(a),

(a) the criterion for assessing integrity is whether the information has remained complete and unaltered, apart from the introduction of any changes that arise in the normal course of communication, storage and display;

(b) the standard of reliability required shall be assessed in the light of the purpose for which the document was made and in the light of all the circumstances.

Notes

1. For more on the UECA, see pp. 492–496 in Chapter 19.

2. During the UECA negotiations, the Uniform Law Conference of Canada commissioned several studies on electronic signature and contracting policy issues. The following excerpt from D. Bruce Farrend is taken from his 1998 policy paper, *Policy Considerations Behind Legislation Recognizing Electronic Signatures*. Article 7 of the UNCITRAL Model Law, referred to in the excerpt, provides the following:

    (1) Where the law requires a signature of a person, that requirement is met in relation to a data message if:

    (a) a method is used to identify that person and to indicate that person's approval of the information contained in the data message; and
    (b) that method is as reliable as was appropriate for the purpose for which the data message was generated or communicated, in the light of all the circumstances, including any relevant agreement.

    (2) Paragraph (1) applies whether the requirement therein is in the form of an obligation or whether the law simply provides consequences for the absence of a signature.

    (3) The provisions of this article do not apply to the following: [...].

Policy Considerations Behind Legislation Recognizing Electronic Signatures†

D. BRUCE FARREND

The ULCC is considering model legislation that would recognize electronic signatures for commercial purposes. This paper will set out my views on the policy issues that should be considered in drafting such legislation. I will leave the topic of dealings with or by government per se to others.

As a starting point, I understand there are two constraints which are more or less accepted in connection with model legislation dealing with electronic "writings" in general, to wit:

1. Any such legislation should, to the extent possible, be technology neutral. Any general legislation which is tied to a specific technology or process will be of limited value and may hinder electronic commerce as new technologies or processes develop.
2. Any such legislation should, to the extent possible, recognize electronic writings as functionally equivalent to paper based writings. In other words, rather than providing that a computer-generated document (commonly referred to as a "message") is for all purposes the same as a document written on paper, permitting legislation would provide that electronic messages can perform the same function as tangible documents.

Further, I understand that the starting point for such legislation is article 7 of the UNCITRAL Model Law on Electronic Commerce (the "Model Law"), with which I am assuming all readers are familiar.

Hence, the basic question to be addressed herein is whether article 7 is appropriate for commercial purposes and, if not, how should it be amended.

Functions of Signatures

With constraint number 2 in mind, it becomes necessary to identify the possible functions of a handwritten signature on a piece of paper (hereafter referred to as a "Pen Signature").

The only function of a Pen Signature that can be stated in general terms is to link or "bind" a person to a document. In this regard, I make no distinction between individuals and other types of persons. That is, the only blanket statement that can be made about a Pen Signature is that the signature is objective or tangible evidence that a person, in some manner, is associating him, her or itself with the document. In the context of electronic signatures, this is usually referred to as "authentication".

The Model Law (and the commentary accompanying it) suggests the functions of a Pen Signature are (1) to identify a person, (2) to provide certainty as to the personal involvement of that person in the act of signing, and (3) to associate that person with the content of the document.

With the greatest of respect to UNCITRAL, I do not accept the first function they attach to signatures, namely to identify the signer. Perhaps, if a person's Pen Signature is known to the recipient of the signed document, the signature can be

---

† Online: <http://www.law.ualberta.ca/alri/ulc/current/efarrend.htm> (last modified: July 1998). Reproduced by permission of Uniform Law Conference of Canada.

used to identify the signer. I do not otherwise see how a handwritten mark on a piece of paper identifies someone. In my view, the document itself identifies the signer (or, more precisely, identifies who is intended to be the signer). A mark on a piece of paper is not evidence that a particular person signed, it is only evidence that somebody signed. Proving that a particular person signed a document or, conversely, proving that a particular person did not sign a document is not a function of the mark itself (except to the extent that handwriting analysis is used).

As to the third function identified by the Commission, I suggest that the association between a person and a document exists independently of the signature. In other words, a person first decides to associate him or herself with a document then, to evidence that fact, signs it.

The second function identified by the Commission, to provide certainty (ie. evidence) of a person's association with a document, is, in my view, the only general statement that should be made about Pen Signatures.

The nature of the association with a document, or in other words the reason for signing the document (and thereby establishing evidence of the association between the person and the document), will vary according to the nature of the document. Some examples:

- the primary function of the signature of a party to a contract on the contract is to provide evidence that the signer has agreed to be bound by the contents of the document, ie. the terms of the contract

At law, my understanding is that the signature is not deemed, or even presumed, to be evidence that the signer fully knew or understood the contents of the document, provided that the contents had not been misrepresented to the signer.

> "...I have not been unmindful of the need of the Courts to restrict the plea of mistake within narrow limits because of the dangerous confusion that would ensue if a man were able to disown his own signature merely by proving that he misunderstood the contents or effect of a document. But there is ample authority, founded in good sense, that the Courts will relieve a person of his contract where a misunderstanding as to its true effect was induced, even though innocently, by the other party and where injustice would be done if performance were to be enforced."
>
> *Royal Bank of Canada* v. *Hale* (1961), 30 DLR (2d) 138 at 150 (B.C.S.C.)

> "In the absence of proof of fraud, a person who is informed of the contents of a document the full effect of which he does not understand may be bound by it if he signs it even though illiterate. If, however, the document is of an entirely different nature so that his mind does not accompany his signature, the plea of non est factum applies."
>
> *Sumner* v. *Sapkos* (1955), 17 W.W.R. 21 at 24 (Sask. C.A.)

What these two excerpts suggest is that a signature of a party on a commercial document (in the absence of fraud, forgery, misrepresentation or other such defence) effectively estops the signer from denying or repudiating the legal consequences that flow from that document. The excerpt from Sumner also supports, I suggest, my assertion that the association with a document exists independently from the act of signing it.

- the primary function of the signature of a drawer of a cheque on the cheque or the signature of a credit card holder on a credit card slip is to provide evidence that the signer has authorized the bank or credit card issuer to advance payment to somebody from the signer's account.

- the primary function of the signature on a receipt is to provide evidence that whatever is described in the receipt was, in fact, received.
- the primary function of the signature of a witness to the signature of a party to a commercial document is to provide evidence that the party, in fact, signed the document.

Some U.S. comments on the definition of "signature":

> "The term 'signature' includes any memorandum, mark or sign, written or placed on any instrument or writing, such as a will, with intent to execute or authenticate such instrument or writing."
>
> *In re Romaniw's Will* 296 NYS 925

> "The signature to a memorandum under the Statute of Frauds may be written or printed and need not be subscribed at the foot of the memorandum but must be made or adopted with declared or apparent intent of authenticating the memorandum as that of the signer."
>
> *Joseph Denunzio Fruit Co.* v. *Crane* 79 F. Supp. 117

> "A signature is whatever mark, symbol or device one may choose to employ as representative of himself."
>
> *Griffith* v. *Bonawitz* 103 N.W. 327

Clearly, a document may serve more than one function, in which case a signature on that document would also serve more than one function. A lengthy commercial agreement may contain certifications as to matters of fact (representations), promises to do certain things (covenants), acknowledgements (receipts), authorizations (grant of power of attorney) and other matters. However, the point I am getting at is that the function of the signature is, as a general statement, determined by the document itself. I cannot imagine how a random act of signature may give rise to legal consequences in a commercial setting.

Indicate That Person's Approval
I want to emphasize this point about the association between a person and an electronic document: The nature of the association between a person and a signed document from which consequences can flow has to be ascertainable from the document itself. Recall that the Model Law provides that an electronic signature should "indicate [the signer's] approval of the information contained in the data message." The association with a document evidenced by a signature may be approval of the information contained therein or it may be much more limited. Consider three examples:

1. a document, not a word of which I approve, agree with or even believe. At the end, I might sign where it says I acknowledge having received and read the document. A silly example for sure, but the point is that my signature has a limited purpose, not having to do with approval of the information, but which is apparent from the document.
2. a proxy for a general meeting of a public company. The proxy will give the shareholder choices as to how the proxy should be voted on the various matters before the meeting. A Pen Signature on a proxy where no choices are made would be meaningless, and no consequences would flow from the delivery of that proxy. In other words, the nature of the association between the person and the document (I agree, Yes, No, Abstain or whatever) would not be ascer-

tainable from the document. (To avoid this problem, every proxy has a default rule which typically provides that, where no choices are made, the shareholder is deemed to vote Yes to the identified matters and give discretion to the proxyholder for other matters.)

3. a witness. If I sign a document in the place marked "Witness", my association with the document is simply to provide some assurance that the named person actually signed in the place marked "Party". I am in no way approving or agreeing to the rest of the document, but my association with it is clear on the face of the document.

To beat this dead horse a little longer, in the case of a digital signature, I do not understand how the signature itself, as distinct from the data message, can indicate the signer's approval. You will recall that a digital signature is the hash result of the data message which is encrypted using the signer's private key. In other words, the signature is a product of the message, not an extra message saying "I concur with the attached message."

Where the Law Requires a Signature...
In my view, the qualifying phrase "Where the law requires a signature" decreases, rather than increases, certainty.

There are some obvious examples of the law requiring a signature in commercial and non-commercial situations. Tax returns, wills, bills of exchange and land transfers all must be signed in order to be effective. But even the obvious examples in my previous sentence are not absolute. Electronic filing of income tax returns does not involve delivering a signature to Revenue Canada. In any event, the law (which clearly includes both statutes and common law) does not typically require a signature for commercial matters. A verbal agreement is still an agreement, although proving the existence and terms of that agreement may be difficult. An agreement which has been reduced to writing but not signed is evidence of the existence and terms of the agreement. The law may apply a presumption once the document has been signed (ie. the parol evidence rule), but an unsigned contract does not, in any general way, give rise to any presumptions.

The Ontario courts recently also had the opportunity to consider the role of the signature and the impact of using an electronic signature in *Re Newbridge Networks Corp.*

Re Newbridge Networks Corp.[†]

I have reviewed the interim order requested as to the Newbridge Networks Corporation proposed arrangement pursuant to the Canada Business Corporations Act (CBCA) and particularly s. 192. The procedures requested appear to me to be reasonable and appropriate in the circumstances. The interim order is to issue as per my fiat.

It would be appropriate for me to review the aspect of the permission and authority granted to use an electronic procedure for notice and voting for those

---

† [2000] O.J. No. 1346 (Ont. Sup. Ct.).

holders of Newbridge Options who are current officers, directors or employees of Newbridge. I understand that there are approximately 4,300 such Optionholders based in various locations in Canada and throughout the world.

.   .   .   .

Overall for most intents and purposes and on balance the electronic procedure envisaged is a safer and more reliable system than is that which relies on the mails or other delivery systems. Password integrity has been built in.

Notice of non-delivery is rather instantaneous. What of the signature? I think that aspect is answered by analyzing what is intended to be the signature. In my view it is a device whereby the "signer" can confirm to the intended recipient that he or she is advising as to the choice selected. That this is accomplished by the use of electronic passwords does not detract from that advice, but rather enhances it. I note in that respect that proxy voting by securityholders in Canada has usually (I can think of no instances of exception although I do not preclude the possibility) been by way of a return of a form of proxy in printed form with a "traditional" signature — namely someone signing with a writing instrument leaving an indelible trail of ink. This signature is not a "guaranteed" one in the sense that securities dealers wish to have security certificates signed off for transfer by having a financial institution confirm that the signature affixed is that of the registered holder. Of course if there is a dispute as to the regularity of the vote, there should be some means to verify the authenticity of the signatures (this may involve an expensive, time consuming and tedious process). It would seem to me that an electronic signature with the integrity of passwords would be easier to verify. That does not mean either under the traditional system or the electronic procedure that someone with access to the voting instruments (in the case of electronic procedure that the securityholder has allowed someone else access to his or her passwords) that someone dedicated to the task could not intercept the message and forge the securityholder's signature.

I would note in passing that even with the traditional signature, this is not a fixed or constant thing. My signature at the present time looks usually something like >ultra squiggle<. However, my signature may vary from time to time — in fact signature to signature. In generic terms my signature may be depicted as something like "xxxx" but it may vary and be "xxx", "xx" or "xxxxxx". I give an illustrative anecdote. Some years ago I was a witness to a document which was to be filed in a South Carolina land registry office. That office returned the document explaining that the signature >ultra squiggle< did not accord with my print name "J. M. Farley" and that it should be reexecuted. Tilting at windmills or the bureaucracy in a foreign land is never truly productive. I reexecuted my signature in a more legible squiggle as "J. M. Farley" as I may have signed it a half century ago in grade school. Both >ultra squiggle< and grade school squiggle "J.M. Farley" were my signatures on that document as I intended those writings to be my signature. If I execute an electronic signature, that too is my signature as I intend it to be my signature (and the recipient is so advised of that intention in the context).

I also pause to note that I do not find the distinction in the legislative amendments between "written" or "printed" format to be helpful when contradistincted to the electronic format. When the electronic format is extracted from its envelope sent to me, it is in written form on a screen and may, at my choice, be printed out on a printer for hard copy. One should be as careful here as one ought to be in distinguishing between an oral statement and a written one — but without the careless use of "verbal" for "oral".

The Canadian approach to digital signature legislation has had the benefit of observing similar legislative experimentation elsewhere. One of the first comprehensive digital signature statutes was enacted by the State of Utah in 1996. In addition to codifying the legality of electronic signatures, the statute creates a liability framework for digital signature providers. The statute is generally regarded as a failure so far, since relatively few entities have taken advantage of the statutorily created framework.

Utah Digital Signature Act (1996)[†]

46-3-102. Purposes and construction.
This chapter shall be construed consistent with what is commercially reasonable under the circumstances and to effectuate the following purposes:

(1) to facilitate commerce by means of reliable electronic messages;

(2) to minimize the incidence of forged digital signatures and fraud in electronic commerce;

(3) to implement legally the general import of relevant standards, such as X.509 of the International Telecommunication Union (formerly International Telegraph and Telephone Consultative Committee or CCITT); and

(4) to establish, in coordination with multiple states, uniform rules regarding the authentication and reliability of electronic messages.

46-3-103. Definitions.
For purposes of this chapter, and unless the context expressly indicates otherwise:

(1) "Accept a certificate" means:

  (a) to manifest approval of a certificate, while knowing or having notice of its contents; or
  (b) to apply to a licensed certification authority for a certificate, without canceling or revoking the application, if the certification authority subsequently issues a certificate based on the application.

(2) "Asymmetric cryptosystem" means an algorithm or series of algorithms which provide a secure key pair.

(3) "Certificate" means a computer-based record which:

  (a) identifies the certification authority issuing it;
  (b) names or identifies its subscriber;
  (c) contains the subscriber's public key; and
  (d) is digitally signed by the certification authority issuing it.

---

† Utah Code, Title 46, Ch. 3.

(4) "Certification authority" means a person who issues a certificate.

. . . .

(7) "Certify" means the declaration of material facts by the certification authority regarding a certificate.

. . . .

(10) "Digital signature" means a transformation of a message using an asymmetric cryptosystem such that a person having the initial message and the signer's public key can accurately determine whether:

(a) the transformation was created using the private key that corresponds to the signer's public key; and

(b) the message has been altered since the transformation was made.

(11) "Division" means the Division of Corporations and Commercial Code within the Utah Department of Commerce.

. . . .

(22) "Private key" means the key of a key pair used to create a digital signature.

(23) "Public key" means the key of a key pair used to verify a digital signature.

PART 2 — LICENSING AND REGULATION OF CERTIFICATION AUTHORITIES

46-3-201. Licensure and qualifications of certification authorities.

(1) To obtain or retain a license a certification authority shall:

(a) be the subscriber of a certificate published in a recognized repository;

(b) employ as operative personnel only persons who have not been convicted of a felony or a crime involving fraud, false statement, or deception;

(c) employ as operative personnel only persons who have demonstrated knowledge and proficiency in following the requirements of this chapter;

(d) file with the division a suitable guaranty, unless the certification authority is the governor, a department or division of state government, the attorney general, state auditor, state treasurer, the judicial council, a city, a county, or the Legislature or its staff offices provided that:

    (i) each of the above-named governmental entities may act through designated officials authorized by ordinance, rule, or statute to perform certification authority functions; and

    (ii) one of the above-named governmental entities is the subscriber of all certificates issued by the certification authority;

(e) have the right to use a trustworthy system, including a secure means for controlling usage of its private key;

(f) present proof to the division of having working capital reasonably sufficient, according to rules of the division, to enable the applicant to conduct business as a certification authority;

(g) maintain an office in Utah or have established a registered agent for service of process in Utah; and

(h) comply with all other licensing requirements established by division rule.

(2) The division shall issue a license to a certification authority which:

(a) is qualified under Subsection (1);
(b) applies in writing to the division for a license; and
(c) pays the required filing fee.

(3)   (a) The division may classify and issue licenses according to specified limitations, such as a maximum number of outstanding certificates, cumulative maximum of recommended reliance limits in certificates issued by the certification authority, or issuance only within a single firm or organization.

        (b) A certification authority acts as an unlicensed certification authority when issuing a certificate exceeding the limits of the license.

(4)   (a) The division may revoke or suspend a certification authority's license for failure to comply with this chapter, or for failure to remain qualified pursuant to Subsection (1).

        (b) The division's actions under this subsection are subject to the procedures for adjudicative proceedings in Title 63, Chapter 46b, Administrative Procedures Act.

(5) The division may recognize by rule the licensing or authorization of certification authorities by other governmental entities, provided that those licensing or authorization requirements are substantially similar to those of this state. If licensing by another governmental entity is so recognized:

(a) Part 4 of this chapter, which relates to presumptions and legal effects, applies to certificates issued by the certification authorities licensed or authorized by that governmental entity in the same manner as it applies to licensed certification authorities of this state; and
(b) the liability limits of Section 46-3-309 apply to the certification authorities licensed or authorized by that governmental entity in the same manner as they apply to licensed certification authorities of this state.

(6) Unless the parties provide otherwise by contract between themselves, the licensing requirements in this section do not affect the effectiveness, enforceability, or validity of any digital signature except that Part 4 of this chapter does not apply to a digital signature which cannot be verified by a certificate issued by a licensed certification authority. Further, the liability limits of Section 46-3-309 do not apply to unlicensed certification authorities.

46-3-203. Enforcement of requirements for licensed certificate authorities.

(1) The division may investigate the activities of a licensed certification authority material to its compliance with this chapter and issue orders to a certification authority to further its investigation and insure compliance with this chapter.

(2) As provided in Section 46-3-201, the division may restrict a certification authority's license for its failure to comply with an order of the division, or may suspend or revoke the license of a certification authority.

(3) Any person who knowingly or intentionally violates an order of the division issued pursuant to this section or Section 46-3-204 is subject to a civil penalty of not

more than $5,000 per violation or 90% of the recommended reliance limit of a material certificate, whichever is less.

(4) The division may order a certification authority in violation of this chapter to pay the costs incurred by the division in prosecuting and adjudicating proceedings relative to, and in enforcement of, the order.

(5) Pursuant to Title 63, Chapter 46b, Administrative Procedures Act:

  (a) the division shall exercise its authority under this section in accordance with procedures for adjudicative proceedings;
  (b) a licensed certification authority may obtain judicial review of the division's actions under this section; and
  (c) if the division seeks injunctive relief, as provided in Section 46-3-204, to compel compliance with any of its orders, the division may collect the cost of enforcement as provided in Subsection 63-46b-19(1)(d)(iii).

PART 3 — DUTIES OF CERTIFICATION AUTHORITY AND SUBSCRIBER

46-3-301. General requirements for certification authorities.

(1) A licensed certification authority or subscriber shall use only a trustworthy system:

  (a) to issue, suspend, or revoke a certificate;
  (b) to publish or give notice of the issuance, suspension, or revocation of a certificate; and
  (c) to create a private key.

(2) A licensed certification authority shall disclose any material certification practice statement, and any fact material to either the reliability of a certificate which it has issued or its ability to perform its services. A certification authority may require a signed, written, and reasonably specific inquiry from an identified person, and payment of reasonable compensation, as conditions precedent to effecting a disclosure required in this subsection.

46-3-309. Recommended reliance limits and liability.

(1) By specifying a recommended reliance limit in a certificate, the issuing certification authority and the accepting subscriber recommend that persons rely on the certificate only to the extent that the total amount at risk does not exceed the recommended reliance limit.

(2) Unless a licensed certification authority waives application of this subsection, a licensed certification authority is:

  (a) not liable for any loss caused by reliance on a false or forged digital signature of a subscriber, if, with respect to the false or forged digital signature, the certification authority complied with all material requirements of this chapter;
  (b) not liable in excess of the amount specified in the certificate as its recommended reliance limit for either:
      (i) a loss caused by reliance on a misrepresentation in the certificate of any fact that the licensed certification authority is required to confirm; or
      (ii) failure to comply with Section 46-3-302 in issuing the certificate;

(c) liable only for direct, compensatory damages in any action to recover a loss due to reliance on the certificate, which damages do not include:
   (i) punitive or exemplary damages;
   (ii) damages for lost profits, savings, or opportunity; or
   (iii) damages for pain or suffering.

PART 4 — EFFECT OF A DIGITAL SIGNATURE

46-3-401. Satisfaction of signature requirements.

(1) Where a rule of law requires a signature, or provides for certain consequences in the absence of a signature, that rule is satisfied by a digital signature if:

 (a) that digital signature is verified by reference to the public key listed in a valid certificate issued by a licensed certification authority;
 (b) that digital signature was affixed by the signer with the intention of signing the message; and
 (c) the recipient has no knowledge or notice that the signer either:
   (i) breached a duty as a subscriber; or
   (ii) does not rightfully hold the private key used to affix the digital signature.

(2) Nothing in this chapter precludes any symbol from being valid as a signature under other applicable law, including Uniform Commercial Code, Subsection 70A-1-201(39).

(3) This section does not limit the authority of the State Tax Commission to prescribe the form of tax returns or other documents filed with the State Tax Commission.

46-3-402. Unreliable digital signatures.

Unless otherwise provided by law or contract, the recipient of a digital signature assumes the risk that a digital signature is forged, if reliance on the digital signature is not reasonable under the circumstances. If the recipient determines not to rely on a digital signature pursuant to this section, the recipient shall promptly notify the signer of its determination not to rely on the digital signature.

46-3-403. Digitally signed document is written.

(1) A message is as valid, enforceable, and effective as if it had been written on paper, if it:

 (a) bears in its entirety a digital signature; and
 (b) that digital signature is verified by the public key listed in a certificate which:
   (i) was issued by a licensed certification authority; and
   (ii) was valid at the time the digital signature was created.

(2) Nothing in this chapter precludes any message, document, or record from being considered written or in writing under other applicable state law.

46-3-404. Digitally signed originals.

A copy of a digitally signed message is as effective, valid, and enforceable as the original of the message, unless it is evident that the signer designated an instance of the digitally signed message to be a unique original, in which case only that instance constitutes the valid, effective, and enforceable message.

46-3-406. Presumptions in adjudicating disputes.
In adjudicating a dispute involving a digital signature, a court of this state shall presume that:

(1) a certificate digitally signed by a licensed certification authority and either published in a recognized repository or made available by the issuing certification authority or by the subscriber listed in the certificate is issued by the certification authority which digitally signed it and is accepted by the subscriber listed in it;

(2) the information listed in a valid certificate, as defined in Section 46-3-103, and confirmed by a licensed certification authority issuing the certificate is accurate;

(3) if a digital signature is verified by the public key listed in a valid certificate issued by a licensed certification authority:

(a) that the digital signature is the digital signature of the subscriber listed in that certificate;
(b) that the digital signature was affixed by the signer with the intention of signing the message; and
(c) the recipient of that digital signature has no knowledge or notice that the signer:
  (i) breached a duty as a subscriber; or
  (ii) does not rightfully hold the private key used to affix the digital signature; and

(4) a digital signature was created before it was time stamped by a disinterested person utilizing a trustworthy system.

The European Union is also considering enacting digital signature legislation. As of July 2000, the following draft directive appeared headed for adoption by the end of the calendar year. Compare the standards established by the E.U. directive with those found in the Utah statute. Which do you prefer?

EU Draft Directive on Digital Signatures[†]

Article 1 Scope
This Directive covers the legal recognition of electronic signatures.

It does not cover other aspects related to the conclusion and validity of contracts or other non-contractual formalities requiring signatures.

It establishes a legal framework for certain certification services made available to the public.

Article 2 Definitions
For the purpose of this Directive:

(1) "electronic signature" means a signature in digital form in, or attached to, or logically associated with, data which is used by a signatory to indicate his approval of the content of that data and meets the following requirements:

---

† COM (1998) 297 final, 13.05.98.

(a) it is uniquely linked to the signatory,

(b) it is capable of identifying the signatory,

(c) it is created using means that the signatory can maintain under his sole control, and

(d) it is linked to the data to which it relates in such a manner that any subsequent alteration of the data is revealed.

(2) "signatory" means a person who creates an electronic signature;

(3) "signature creation device" means unique data, such as codes or private cryptographic keys, or a uniquely configured physical device which is used by the signatory in creating an electronic signature;

(4) "signature verification device" means unique data, such as codes or public cryptographic keys, or a uniquely configured physical device which is used in verifying the electronic signature;

(5) "qualified certificate" means a digital attestation which links a signature verification device to a person, confirms the identity of that person and meets the requirements laid down in Annex I;

(6) "certification service provider" means a person who or an entity which issues certificates or provides other services related to electronic signatures to the public;

(7) "electronic signature product" means hardware or software, or relevant components thereof, which are intended to be used by a certification service provider for the provision of electronic signature services.

Article 3 Market access

1. Member States shall not make the provision of certification services subject to prior authorization.

2. Without prejudice to the provisions of paragraph 1, Member States may introduce or maintain voluntary accreditation schemes aiming at enhanced levels of certification service provision. All conditions related to such schemes must be objective, transparent, proportionate and non-discriminatory. Member States may not limit the number of certification service providers for reasons which fall under the scope of this Directive.

3. The Commission may, in accordance with the procedure laid down in Article 9, establish and publish reference numbers of generally recognized standards for electronic signature products in the *Official Journal of the European Communities*. Member States shall presume compliance with the requirements laid down in point (e) of Annex II when an electronic signature product meets those standards.

4. Member States may make the use of electronic signatures in the public sector subject to additional requirements. Such requirements shall be objective, transparent, proportionate, and non-discriminatory, and shall only relate to the specific characteristics of the application concerned.

Article 4 Internal Market principles

1. Each Member State shall apply the national provisions it adopts pursuant to this Directive to certification service providers established on its territory and to the services they provide. Member States may not restrict the provision of certification services which originate in another Member State in the fields covered by this Directive.

2. Member States shall ensure that electronic signature products which comply with this Directive are permitted to circulate freely in the Internal Market.

Article 5 Legal effects

1. Member States shall ensure that an electronic signature is not denied legal effect, validity and enforceability solely on the grounds that the signature is in electronic form, or is not based upon a qualified certificate, or is not based upon a certificate issued by an accredited certification service provider.

2. Member States shall ensure that electronic signatures which are based on a qualified certificate issued by a certification service provider which fulfils the requirements set out in Annex II are, on the one hand, recognized as satisfying the legal requirement of a hand written signature, and on the other, admissible as evidence in legal proceedings in the same manner as hand written signatures.

Article 6 Liability

1. Member States shall ensure that, by issuing a qualified certificate, a certification service provider is liable to any person who reasonably relies on the certificate for:

   (a) accuracy of all information in the qualified certificate as from the date on which it was issued, unless the certification service provider has stated otherwise in the certificate;
   (b) compliance with all the requirements of this Directive in issuing the qualified certificate;
   (c) assurance that the person identified in the qualified certificate held, at the time of the issuance of the certificate, the signature creation device corresponding to the signature verification device given or identified in the certificate;
   (d) in cases where the certification service provider generates the signature creation device and the signature verification device, assurance that the two devices function together in a complementary manner.

2. Member States shall ensure that a certification service provider is not liable for errors in the information in the qualified certificate that has been provided by the person to whom the certificate is issued, if it can demonstrate that it has taken all reasonably practicable measures to verify that information.

3. Member States shall ensure that a certification service provider may indicate in the qualified certificate limits on the uses of a certain certificate. The certification service provider shall not be liable for damages arising from a contrary use of a qualified certificate which includes limits on its uses.

4. Member States shall ensure that a certification service provider may indicate in the qualified certificate a limit on the value of transactions for which the certificate is valid. The certification service provider shall not be liable for damages in excess of that value limit.

5. The provisions of paragraphs 1 to 4 shall be without prejudice to Council Directive 93/13/EEC.

Article 7 International aspects

1. Member States shall ensure that certificates issued by a certification service provider established in a third country are recognized as legally equivalent to certificates issued by a certification service provider established within the Community:

(a) if the certification service provider fulfils the requirements laid down in this Directive and has been accredited in the context of a voluntary accreditation scheme established by a Member State; or

(b) if a certification service provider established within the Community, which fulfils the requirements laid down in Annex II guarantees the certificate to the same extent as its own certificates; or

(c) if the certificate or the certification service provider is recognized under the regime of a bilateral or multilateral agreement between the Community and third countries or international organizations.

2. In order to facilitate cross-border certification services with third countries and legal recognition of electronic signatures originating in third countries, the Commission will make proposals where appropriate to achieve the effective implementation of standards and international agreements applicable to certification services. In particular and where necessary, it will submit proposals to the Council for appropriate mandates for the negotiation of bilateral and multilateral agreements with third countries and international organizations. The Council shall decide by qualified majority.

Article 8 Data protection

1. Member States shall ensure that certification service providers and national bodies responsible for accreditation or supervision comply with the requirements laid down in Directives 95/46/EC and 97/66/EC of the European Parliament and of the Council.

2. Member States shall ensure that a certification service provider may collect personal data only directly from the data subject and only in so far as it is necessary for the purposes of issuing a certificate. The data may not be collected or processed for other purposes without the consent of the data subject.

3. Member States shall ensure that, at the signatory's request, the certification service provider indicates in the certificate a pseudonym instead of the signatory's name.

4. Member States shall ensure that, in the case of persons using pseudonyms, the certification service provider shall transmit the data concerning the identity of those persons to public authorities upon request and with the consent of the data subject. Where according to national law the transfer of the data revealing the identity of the data subject is necessary for the investigation of criminal offences relating to the use of electronic signatures under a pseudonym, the transfer shall be recorded and the data subject informed of the transfer of the data relating to him as soon as possible after the investigation has been completed.

ANNEX I
REQUIREMENTS FOR QUALIFIED CERTIFICATES
Qualified certificates must contain:

(a) the identifier of the certification service provider issuing it;

(b) the unmistakable name of the holder or an unmistakable pseudonym which shall be identified as such;

(c) a specific attribute of the holder such as, the address, the authority to act on behalf of a company, the credit-worthiness, VAT or other tax registration numbers, the existence of payment guarantees or specific permits or licences;

(d) a signature verification device which corresponds to a signature creation device under the control of the holder;

(e) beginning and end of the operational period of the certificate;

(f) the unique identity code of the certificate;

(g) the electronic signature of the certification service provider issuing it;

(h) limitations on the scope of use of the certificate, if applicable; and

(i) limitations on the certification service provider's liability and on the value of transactions for which the certificate is valid, if applicable.

ANNEX II
REQUIREMENTS FOR CERTIFICATION SERVICE PROVIDERS
Certification service providers must:

(a) demonstrate the reliability necessary for offering certification services;

(b) operate a prompt and secure revocation service;

(c) verify by appropriate means the identity and capacity to act of the person to which a qualified certificate is issued;

(d) employ personnel which possesses the expert knowledge, experience, and qualifications necessary for the offered services, in particular competence at the managerial level, expertise in electronic signature technology and familiarity with proper security procedures; they must also exercise administrative and management procedures and processes that are adequate and which correspond to recognized standards;

(e) use trustworthy systems, and use electronic signature products that ensure protection against modification of the products so that they can not be used to perform functions other than those for which they have been designed; they must also use electronic signature products that ensure the technical and cryptographic security of the certification processes supported by the products;

(f) take measures against forgery of certificates, and, in cases where the certification service provider generates private cryptographic signature keys, guarantee the confidentiality during the process of generating those keys;

(g) maintain sufficient financial resources to operate in conformity with the requirements laid down in this Directive, in particular to bear the risk of liability for damages, for example, by obtaining an appropriate insurance;

(h) record all relevant information concerning a qualified certificate for an appropriate period of time, in particular to provide evidence of certification for the purposes of legal proceedings. Such recording may be done electronically;

(i) not store or copy private cryptographic signature keys of the person to whom the certification service provider offered key management services unless that person explicitly asks for it;

(j) inform consumers before entering into a contractual relationship in writing, using readily understandable language and a durable means of communication, of the precise terms and conditions for the use of the certificate, including any limitations on the liability, the existence of a voluntary accreditation and the procedures for complaints and dispute settlement.

Discussion Questions

1. Canada has chosen to not regulate digital signature (also known as certificate) providers, instead relying on market forces to craft a fair liability structure. Should the government increase its regulatory participation in this important commercial arena? What degree of public sector collaboration is appropriate and desirable in developing a common approach to the accreditation of private-sector certification authorities and in capitalizing on market opportunities?

2. How can the tension between competitive market forces and organized, predictable structures be managed in a way that engenders trust and confidence and protects public interests?

3. To what extent should public policy objectives (e.g., protecting public interests, encouraging competition etc.) influence the terms and conditions of the contracts that govern authentication-related services?

21

E-Cash and Payment Systems

The signature is not the only aspect of the modern commercial transaction undergoing significant change as a result of electronic commerce. Payment systems suitable to the electronic format are also required. Since cash is paper based and credit cards are expensive, many companies are racing to develop electronic cash alternatives.

An appropriate e-cash solution is particularly vital in light of the limitations of the current favoured method for electronic commerce payments — the credit card. First, credit cards raise security concerns, as card numbers may be compromised and used fraudulently. Second, credit cards are an expensive payment system, especially for smaller transactions. Third, since few minors own credit cards, the payment system effectively excludes a large segment of the population from electronic commerce. Fourth, credit cards frequently raise privacy concerns since, unlike cash, they create a record of all purchasing activity.

Given these limitations, an effective e-cash system that would allow for anonymous purchasing while facilitating secure payments for the smallest of transactions in a cost-effective manner would provide a huge boost to e-commerce.

Should such e-cash payment systems gain marketplace acceptance, regulators will be forced to address a series of novel legal issues. These include answering the question of who bears responsibility for regulating new payment systems; how, if at all, payment systems affect monetary supply; and how the legal risk allocation should be apportioned to protect e-cash providers and users.

This chapter begins with an excellent examination of the e-cash issue and its legal implications from University of Miami law professor Michael Froomkin.

*Flood Control On The Information Highway: Living With
Anonymity, Digital Cash And Distributed Databases*[†]

A. MICHAEL FROOMKIN

A great number and variety of businesses have announced plans for or prototypes of
Internet-based commercial activities. As many as fifteen percent of consumer purchases may be electronic by the turn of the century. Internet commerce seems
poised to evolve in two complementary directions, which one might call ordinary
commerce in tangible things and information commerce.

In the case of ordinary commerce in tangible things, many transactions that are
currently carried out by telephone, ordinary mail (e.g., catalog sales), and even in
person, may shift to the net. The shopping mall of the future may be on line, and
offer everything from video product demonstrations and recorded customer testimoni-
als to technical specifications for the product. Interactive sales may allow merchants
to question customers as to their needs and budgets and then guide them to particular products; the products could be manufactured to the customer's size, color, and
other specifications based on the customer's specifications. It may even be possible
to haggle with the merchant's computer about the price.

From the most practical standpoint, the challenge of Internet commerce is of
conducting business via a medium that excels at moving information, but provides a
very insecure means of communication. It is not always possible to be certain that
persons are who they claim to be, nor is it certain that no one is eavesdropping.
Digital cash promises to solve the problem of moving value, but it is too early to
say which if any type of digital cash is likely to find wide acceptance in the marketplace. In the mean time, consumer transactions are being conducted by credit/debit
card.

A. INTERNET CREDIT CARD TRANSACTIONS

In the short run, credit and debit cards provide the simplest, if not necessarily the
ideal, means of transferring value over the Internet. These Internet credit card transactions can usefully be divided into three categories:

(1) The customer e-mails the merchant her credit card details (or fills out a
form on a World Wide Web page), much as a person currently sends such
information through the ordinary mail. Although there is some risk that this
information might be copied en route, particularly if the message originates on
Ethernet systems that are vulnerable to in-house packet sniffing, to date such
theft of credit card details seems rare at most. The customer's liability for
fraudulent use in such cases is subject to the same $50 limit as with any other
credit card transaction.

(2) The customer encrypts the credit card data before sending it, e.g., with PGP or
with Netscape's Secure Sockets Layer (SSL) protocol. Subject to the constraint
that a determined attacker armed with enough computers and time can always
break some of the shorter codes in use, this reduces the risk that the credit

---

[†] (1996) 15 U. Pitt. J. of L. & Comm. 395. Notes omitted. Reproduced by permission of the publisher.

card details will be copied by a third party. (Other risks include the danger that the cryptographic system is flawed, badly implemented, or used on an insecure platform, e.g., one which stores the data in an insecure manner.)

(3) The customer enters into an agreement with a third party such as First Virtual Holdings, in which the credit card data is transmitted to the third party by some other means. In the case of First Virtual, an early entrant to this market, each transaction is also confirmed by e-mail; in other cases, the customer may be issued some identifying data, such as a PIN or a public-private key pair with which to digitally sign messages. In both cases participating merchants clear transactions through the third party before the charge is posted to the customer's credit card.

In all three categories, the customer needs to have a valid debit/credit card, e.g., Visa, or MasterCard, to make the transaction work. The charges are sent to the bank, or appear on the credit card, and are settled between the buyer, the seller (or the third party) and the card issuer as if the customer had used the card to buy something in an ordinary transaction.

Despite the variety of options, however, the transfer of ordinary commerce in tangible things from existing retail channels to distributed network sales is likely to raise relatively few new legal problems, although there is no reason to expect any of the existing problems associated with retail sales to disappear. Indeed, ordinary Internet commerce in tangible things may remain well suited to credit card sales, particularly if the customer's potential liability for fraud remains fixed at $50.

In contrast to ordinary commerce in tangible things that simply moves to the Internet, the sale of information is likely to be transformed. This transformation will bring new legal and social problems in its wake, or at the very least amplify old ones. Although today access to most World Wide Web pages is free and open to anyone with a browser, this may change once the pioneers on the information ocean begin creating exclusive economic zones in their virtual real estate and limiting access to users who have either purchased a password for access or have browsers that are pre-configured to pay charges, perhaps up to a pre-defined limit, for access to World Wide Web pages. Web pages are ideally suited to micro-transactions, in which the reader is charged a trifling fee — a penny or less — for each access, so long as the process of payment can be seamlessly integrated into browsing tools. At present, minute charges such as a tenth of a cent cannot economically be processed through existing credit card systems and this seems unlikely to change in the near future. Thus, a digital means to transfer value, preferably one that does not require the participation of a third party such as a credit bureau or credit card issuer, will be required before micro-charges can become part of the new information economy. It is clear that the potential for growth of Internet information commerce is enormous, and that the high fixed costs of credit card transactions makes them particularly unsuited for high-volume low-value transactions.

B. DIGITAL CASH: A TECHNICAL MENU

Cryptologists have worked out methods for creating and transmitting tokens of value the digital equivalent of cash and checks over a network like the Internet. This "digital cash," also known as "electronic cash," "E$," or "e-cash," will allow buying and selling goods or services over the Internet. Any digital cash system vastly expands the commercial possibilities of the Internet, particularly if the system has low transaction costs. With low transaction costs, pay-per-view/pay-per-byte systems in which pennies or less are charged to view an article or picture on the World Wide Web become a real possibility.

Depending on which protocol is adopted, the transaction may or may not result in a record of the buyer's participation in the transaction being maintained by either the seller or the bank. Digital cash can leave the audit trail of a credit card purchase, or can provide greater anonymity than paper currency. Without some form of anonymity built into digital cash, however, each payment creates the possibility of a record which, when combined with other similar records, becomes a detailed consumer profile. If digital cash replaces credit cards for ordinary commerce in tangible things, the consequences of this profiling may be no more severe than those caused by the use of credit cards today. If, however, the availability and ease of use of Internet commerce causes consumers to shift cash sales to Internet credit card sales or traceable digital cash, the effect will be to increase the amount of information available on the consumer's buying habits.

If consumers use a traceable payments mechanism for the purchase of information as well as goods, the potential for consumer profiles grows larger still. If Internet tools such as the World Wide Web become a major national and international communications medium with an embedded micro-charging mechanism, every newspaper article accessed, every online catalog perused, every political debate sampled, will leave an information residue. These data can be collected to form a highly detailed profile of the consumer-citizen. The existence of such detailed dossiers on spending and intellectual preferences would be unprecedented.

We are at a very early stage in the development of Internet commerce. Most payment products and protocols are somewhere between the drawing board and the street; few are beyond their field tests. No standards have emerged, but many large financial corporations and banks are preparing to provide consumer electronic financial exchange products. Each of these implementations requires that decisions be made about inevitable tradeoffs between security, anonymity, cost, and ease of use.

Let us assume that the digital cash is to be provided by a bank, and used in a real-time transaction between Alice, a customer, and Bob, a merchant. In a real-time transaction Alice buys information (software, news, art, the right to view a Web page) on-line. There may be only seconds between Alice's proffer of payment and her expectation that Bob will deliver the goods; Bob must confirm the validity of Alice's payment immediately, or run the risk that there will be little he can do if Alice has cheated him. An Internet transaction might of course take many other forms, and these too receive occasional mention in what follows. The transaction could, for example, be a catalog sale transaction in which Alice places an order, makes a payment, and Bob waits until payment clears before shipping the goods. In this model, Bob's risk that the payment will be bad is relatively low since he need only fail to ship the goods.

Because the digital cash is represented by a series of bits, and there are few things in this life easier to copy than bits, the bank is going to be very anxious to ensure that any copies of the digital cash created by Alice or by Mallet, a hostile third party, will be unspendable, or at least very easy to detect. The bank wishes to prevent, or at very least detect, attempted double-spending of digital cash in order to avoid having to pay twice, and ideally it also wants to be able to figure out who the double-spenders are in order to have them prosecuted for fraud. For example, if the bank's communication with Alice is not encrypted, Mallet might eavesdrop on Alice's telephone line and record the digital cash as it is transmitted and then try to spend it before Alice does. And even if the communication with Alice is secure, the bank wishes to make sure that Alice herself cannot spend a coin more than once.

Bob, the merchant, wishes to be able prove that Alice authorized the transaction, in order to ensure that Alice will not attempt to deny it later ("non-repudiation"). Bob also wants an assurance that Alice has the funds to pay for the transaction, and that the bank will transfer them to him. In some circumstances Bob may also wish to avoid revealing the fact of the transaction. Meanwhile, Alice wishes to ensure that unauthorized payments are impossible, that Bob cannot deny having received her payment, that the fact of transaction is private, and that there is some redress available if Bob defaults or delivers shoddy goods. In some cases, Alice wants the transaction to be fully anonymous — not even Bob should know Alice's identity; in such cases, however, Bob will want to ensure that Alice remains unable to disavow the obligation to pay.

If the transaction is entirely electronic, each of the parties will need a mechanism to ensure the other parties will pay what is required. In a world where fraud is possible, or the transaction has any non-instantaneous aspects (e.g., a warranty, the possibility of product liability suits, the possibility that a party might attempt to repudiate the payment) the parties will want some assurance that the other parties are who they claim to be: bank, Bob, and Alice (the owner of the digital currency). Identity authentication, however, is by far the easiest aspect of the electronic transaction, as it can easily be achieved with digital signatures.

Digital cash can be stored in any one of a number of places: in the financial institution's computer, in Alice's and Bob's computers, or on smart cards carried by the customer and the merchant. The digital cash may be backed by actual funds, or it may not. Depending on the system used, if Alice and Bob hold the digital cash, the bank may issue it in the form of digital "coins" which must be aggregated to reach the total amount of the purchase, or Alice and Bob may hold it in a digital account on a smart card which is debited and credited as needed. The system may require that all transactions are cleared by the issuer, or it may allow funds to circulate freely between customers and merchants.

What follows attempts to be a representative sample of the types of digital cash currently being developed. Few of the digital payment systems discussed below allow unlimited direct transferability between holders of electronic funds: with the single exception of the Mondex digital purse model, in all of the digital coin models the recipient of an electronic payment must always return to the bank for a new coin before being able to spend it, although it is theoretically possible for users to modify at least one digital coin payment scheme to allow the coins to be transferred among third party without returning to the bank.

1. The Debit Card Model

One simple, albeit costly, electronic payment strategy that meets the bank's security needs, but not necessarily all of Alice and Bob's, is to require that every transaction between them be cleared through the bank at the time of the transaction. The highest-security version of this model is not really digital cash at all, and is modeled on debit cards: the bank requires Bob, the merchant, to contact the bank on-line at the time of payment in order to transfer the funds from Alice's account to Bob's account. If Alice has insufficient funds, the bank refuses to allow the transaction. If the client has the funds, they are transferred from the client's account to the merchant's account at time of sale. An alternative form of this model has the "bank" replaced by a clearing service that forwards the payment instructions to the ordinary banks previously selected by members of the scheme.

Alice's and Bob's identity can be verified using unforgeable digital signatures, making the chances of a fraudulent or repudiable transaction remote so long as both parties carefully protect the passphrases (longer, alphanumeric, versions of bankcard PIN numbers) that access their accounts. There is no danger of double-payment or duplication of digital currency because no digital currency ever leaves the banking system.

One disadvantage of this approach is that on-line verification introduces both delay and expense into the transaction akin to that of ordinary credit cards. The transaction costs associated with the debit-card paradigm make it unsuited for low-value/very-high-volume transactions. The basic debit card model would work for buying a car on-line, or even perhaps a t-shirt, but not for charging a tenth of one cent to read a Web page. The debit-card paradigm also does nothing to protect the privacy interests of either Alice or Bob: the bank has a full record of every transaction. This facilitates auditing, and may be of great value to law-enforcement, but it also means that privacy vis a vis the bank is low, and that the bank will find consumer profiling easy.

2.   The Basic Digital Coin

The basic digital coin model is fairly simple: the Bank issues the user a very large, probabilistically unique, random number (the "serial number" of the coin) signed with the Bank's private key. When Alice wants to spend the coin, she sends it to Bob, who turns it in to the bank either on line, or after the fact. The bank checks the serial number against its list of spent coins and, if the coin has not previously been spent, either credits Bob's account or issues him a new coin with a new serial number. So long as the bank is honest, Alice and Bob both have the proof they need that the transaction, and the payment, occurred. The coin model is also computationally simple to implement. Each coin requires a long, unique, random number, but the bank can re-use the same private-public key pair to sign every coin of a given denomination. The basic coin model does not allow coins to circulate freely: every time Alice spends a coin at Bob's shop, Bob must redeem the coin at the issuing bank, either for traditional funds or a new coin, before he can spend the money.

The basic coin model has two problems. First, if the transaction is on-line in real time, but verification is off-line (that is, at some time after the completion of the transaction), Bob may be unable to ensure that the coin Alice is offering him has not previously been spent until it is too late. Bob can check the coin's digital signature against the public key associated with a coin of the purported denomination. This test will distinguish a forged coin from a real one. But without on-line verification Bob cannot tell if a coin already has been redeemed elsewhere at the time Alice wants to buy from him. On-line verification ensures that the coin being proffered is valid, but this verification likely involves delay and expense. Second, since the serial number of the coin is unique and known to the bank, Bob's redemption of the coin links Alice to the transaction, and the bank ends up with a database containing information on all of its customers; as in the credit-card model, the customers have no privacy.

Basic digital coins are likely to have at most a small effect on the money supply. Whether they have any effect at all depends in large part on how banks and customers manage the coins and whether they use on-line or off-line clearing systems. At one extreme, transactions are cleared on-line and the bank allows Alice to avoid purchasing the digital coins until the moment she needs them. As a result, Alice keeps her funds in an interest-bearing account until she needs a coin. When she wants to transact with Bob she contacts the bank, it issues a coin, and she offers it to Bob who redeems it as soon he receives it from Alice. In this scenario, the digital coin's effect on the money supply is negligible.

At the other extreme, transactions are cleared off-line and the bank requires that Alice acquire digital coins in advance of need, much as one buys travellers checks today. Because on-line clearing is not available, or too expensive to be practical, Bob takes some risk of being paid in previously spent coinage when he accepts a coin from Alice. Bob's need to aggregate coins before redeeming them from the bank introduces further delays between before settlement. In this version, digital coins function much like travellers checks. Since both travellers checks and cash are part of M1, the narrowest measure of money commonly used by macroeconomists, this alone is not significant. If, however, people choose to hold digital coins instead of ordinary cash, more of the money in circulation will flow into the banking system, increasing the money supply through fractional reserve lending. Digital coins also could have a small effect on the velocity of money if they enable a greater number of transactions per year, or if the existence of world-wide 24-hour cybermalls encourages people to transact more often.

3.   Blinded Coins

The basic coin model gives the bank confidence at the price of on-line verification and the opportunity for banks to amass customer spending profiles. It is possible, however, to retain the features of the basic coin model that make it either impossible or at least very risky for people to copy their digital cash and spend it twice without giving the bank an opportunity to create a giant database of who spent what where. In this model, payors, but not payees, can remain anonymous.

Using "blinded coins" Alice can acquire digital cash with a unique serial number from a bank without allowing the bank to create a record of the coin's serial number. Despite the bank's ignorance of the serial number, the number's uniqueness helps ensure that Alice cannot spend it twice. The techniques that achieve this, developed and patented by David Chaum and being marketed by a company he founded called DigiCash, are complex. Like a basic digital coin, a blinded coin begins with a large random serial number, but this time the serial number is generated by Alice, the customer who intends to acquire a coin from the bank. Alice multiplies this serial number by another random factor ("the blinding factor"), and sends the product (the "blinded" number) to the bank. As in the basic case, the bank signs the number with its secret key.

Unlike the basic case, however, a bank issuing a blinded coin does not know the true serial number of the coin at the time the bank issues it by affixing its digital signature to the "blinded" number. All that the bank knows is that Alice has purchased a coin of a given denomination, and the "blinded" number Alice submitted. In the absence of anonymous bank accounts, the bank knows Alice's identity, and knows how many coins of each denomination Alice is buying. Armed with this information, the bank should be able to comply with rules designed to control money laundering and tax evasion to the same extent as an ordinary bank. Alice's privacy depends in part on there being a sufficiently large volume of coins in circulation such that Alice's purchase and use of the coins does not stand out.

There is yet another way to hide and retrieve Alice's identity. In this variation, the bank does not know who spent the money so long as it is spent only once, but this information is accessible to a designated organization outside the bank. The inventors of this type of digital cash suggest that the trusted third party which would hold the means of de-annonymizing [sic] the digital cash should be "a consumer rights organization." Nothing in their protocol, however, would prevent a government from requiring that the organization be the police or the courts. In effect, this proto-col opens the door to Clipperized digital cash, in which the government could have access to transactional data subject to Fourth Amendment constraints. It is possible, however, to modify the system of traceable anonymous cash so that the user's identity will only be disclosed if several parties ("trustees") agree. This system of multiple trustees resembles the system of multiple escrow agents envisioned for the keys to the Clipper chip.

All forms of blinded coins are generated as follows. When Alice gets the signed blinded number back from the bank, she performs a mathematical operation that removes the "blinding factor." The result is a coin that looks like a basic digital coin, bears the "true" serial number, and has a digital signature from the bank that authenticates the true — not the blinded — serial number. Alice can now spend the coin in Bob's shop as if it were a basic coin. In the absence of anonymous bank accounts, Bob must still disclose his identity to redeem the coin. (If for some reason Alice later wants to "stop payment" on the coin because Bob defaulted, she can always reveal the true serial number to the bank.)

Like a basic coin, however, the blinded coin is just digitized data. Since the blinding process means that the bank cannot trace the coin's serial number to Alice, some means is required to convince her not to run off and duplicate coins. Pre-venting double-spending is relatively simple for an on-line clearing system; preventing Alice from cheating a system that relies on off-line clearing is more difficult.

a. Preventing Double-Spending of Blinded Coins With On-Line Clearing (DigiCash)

When Alice spends a blinded coin and Bob presents the coin to the bank for settlement, the bank cannot link the coin to Alice because it has no record of the coin's serial number. Without some means of preventing double-spending, the temp-tation might be more than Alice could resist. On-line clearing removes all tempta-tion. Since the bank keeps a record of every serial number redeemed, it can check the coin proffered by Bob against the master list. If the coin was previously spent it denies payment. As the clearing is on-line, Bob then is able to tell Alice that the bank has refused to honor her coin, much like a merchant will tell a customer that a credit card company has refused to authorize a purchase.

On October 23, 1995, Mark Twain Bank of St. Louis, Missouri became the world's first financial institution to issue blinded digital coins backed by value. The bank uses software licensed from DigiCash. The system relies on on-line clearing of blinded coins, but details of the technical specifications of the system were limited at the time this article went to press. Other financial institutions are likely to be providing similar electronic cash services in the near future. For example, DigiCash has licensed its software to the Swedish Post Office, which owns the retail bank that transacts with accounts held by seventy-five percent of Swedish households.

b. Preventing Double-Spending of Blinded Coins With Off-Line Clearing

On-line clearing is potentially expensive in both time and money. Off-line clear-ing is usually much cheaper in both. Unfortunately, off-line clearing creates an opportunity for an unscrupulous party to spend the same coin many times since the party accepting the coin will not know it has been spent until it is too late.

Bob's risk that the coin offered by Alice will prove to be worthless is greatest when neither Bob nor the bank knows who Alice is, since Alice will reasonably believe that her anonymity protects her from the consequences of her double-spending. Even if Bob knows Alice's identity but the bank does not, Bob bears considerable risk when the costs of making Alice pay would be greater than the value of the debt. This may include a large set of transactions if Internet commerce becomes global. Nevertheless, if Alice is aware that Bob or the bank knows her identity, she can reasonably fear that Bob might report her to the appropriate authorities, perhaps for criminal prosecution, which should reduce the temptation to double-spend.

The essence of a blinded coin is that the bank does not know the coin's serial number, and hence cannot deduce the payor's identity when the coin is presented for redemption by the payee. In both the basic coin model and the standard blinded coin model, the coin carries no information about Alice. It is possible, however, to encode information about Alice's identity in such a way that if the coin is spent only once the information remains encrypted on the coin. If someone tries to spend a coin that has previously been redeemed, the second spending will disclose the information encoded on the coin about its original owner. This system works even if Alice spends the coin with two different merchants.

The second spending can only reveal whatever identifying information the bank encoded into the coin at the time it gave the coin to Alice. The issuing bank is responsible for choosing to encode sufficient information, e.g., a unique identification number, to allow it to trace the coin back to the customer. The bank, however, has a problem: the bank cannot read the information about Alice's identity encoded onto a blinded coin unless Alice spends the coin twice. In other words, the blinding prevents the bank from inspecting the coin at the time of issuance to ensure that Alice has in fact supplied the required information. The bank can, however, use probabilistic methods that make it very likely that Alice will encode her identity on the coin at the time the bank issues the coin. For example, the bank might require that Alice generate a hundred blinded numbers and associated encrypted data fields. The bank could then require that Alice reveal the contents of ninety-nine coins of the bank's choice. If all of these coins turn out to have the proper information about Alice, the odds are good that the 100th coin — the only one that will actually be signed by the bank, and the only one for which Alice does not reveal the contents — does too. If Alice tries to cheat by inserting missing or erroneous information into even one of the 100 coins, the odds are good that the bank will detect it. And if the bank detects attempted cheating, the bank will probably refuse to issue digital coins to Alice ever again.

In an off-line clearing scheme, Bob's security against double spending rests on a challenge-response protocol that discloses Alice's identity if she tries to double-spend. Bob thus bears some risk of being stuck with the digital equivalent of a slug in the vending machine because Alice may have spent the coin elsewhere before he gets it to the bank. Unlike the slug in the vending machine, however, the coin can contain information that identifies Alice to the bank. Whether this suffices to find Alice and get civil or criminal remedies depends on whether the information on the coin is accurate and on the jurisdictions involved.

It may be that blinded coins cannot safely be issued in denominations of any significant size in the absence of an efficient on-line clearing system; Alice could spend even a $1 coin many times in a few minutes and then attempt to vanish. However, if the denomination is small enough, Bob can limit his risk if he checks every small-denomination coin Alice offers to make sure that it is not a duplicate of a coin he has personally received in the past, and makes sure to contact the bank for verification whenever he has received as many coins as he cares to risk holding.

c. Preventing Double-Spending of Blinded Coins With Electronic Wallets

In order to feel confident about issuing blinded coins, banks are likely to require considerable assurance that the coins cannot be spent more than once; banks may also want to minimize the chances of third-party money laundering in order to avoid difficulties with national regulatory authorities. From the bank's point of view it may be cold comfort to be able to identify the person who spent a coin a million times if that person cannot be found.

An electronic wallet is a smart card with a microprocessor on it. The wallet interacts with specially designed card readers, somewhat like bank cards are used in Automatic Teller Machines. Embedding the coin, or at least part of the information needed to use the coin, in a smart card with tamper-resistant features provides greatly added security if the tamper-resistant part of the card is programmed to prevent double spending. Banks, merchants, even personal computers, might have the necessary smart card readers.

One extension of this model requires that the tamper-resistant part of the card have an electronic "observer" whose participation is required to spend a coin. The combination protects Alice's privacy by having all communications from the observer go via Alice's computer which is programmed to ensure that no transaction details are disclosed. If anyone breaks the tamper-resistance and attempts to double-spend, the blinded coins protocol still applies and the identity of the coin's original owner is revealed. Perhaps the best example of this is the Conditional Access for Europe (CAFÉ) project, being sponsored by the European Union's ESPRIT program. The CAFÉ protocol promises to offer high security for the customer, a chance of getting unspent money back if the purse is lost, and payer (but not payee) privacy; so far, however, no actual CAFÉ products exist beyond prototypes.

4. The Traveler's Check Model

Coin-based digital cash systems have problems with exact change. Digital coins are not divisible without sacrificing customer privacy and also making the payment system much less efficient to operate. Indivisible coins ordinarily have to be aggregated to get the amount needed for a purchase, just as dimes and pennies might be combined to make a 23-cent acquisition. If coins are in small denominations, a large number of coins may be required to buy anything even moderately expensive. At some point, processing a large enough number of coins can introduce transmission delays and information processing costs. If the coins are to be carried on a smart card, large numbers of coins require a card with a larger memory, which increases the investment required to participate in the system.

Whatever the price of the good being purchased, Bob needs to provide change if Alice does not happen to have the exact coins required. Thus, Bob needs to have a stock of coins on hand to pay Alice (recall that all coins must be returned to the bank each time they are spent), and Alice needs to be able to deposit coins in the bank as well as withdraw them.

In contrast, an electronic traveller's check system allows Alice to spend each check for any amount up to a predetermined maximum. The bank debits Alice for the maximum value when the check is created, and refunds Alice the difference between the maximum and the amount actually expended. If the check system relies on "blinded" checks, akin to blinded coins, it is possible to design the refund system so that when Alice presents the unexpended portion of the check for a refund, nothing in the refund request itself (other than the amount requested) gives the bank any information that would allow it to link the refund request to a particular payment. Unlike traveller's checks, competitive pressures might force banks to pay some interest on the funds set aside to cover the check.

5.   The Electronic Purse (Mondex Money)

The electronic purse is a smart card or a computer program that holds and keeps track of the owner's electronic funds balance, much as a copy card or a telephone card stores value. If the purse is on a smart card, the card can be used either with ATMs or with specialized card readers attached to computers or telephones. In the pure implementation, no backups exist: if the card is lost, or the computer disk crashes, the consumer's money is as gone as if a dollar bill were burnt but the bank gets to keep it. An electronic purse can be designed with whatever privacy, or lack of privacy, the manufacturer desires. If the smart card functioning as the electronic purse has sufficient storage, the card can keep track of every transaction that it touches; the purse can be designed so that this information is accessible only to its owner, or it can be designed so that the information is accessible to others, such as the issuing bank or law enforcement. Similarly, the ATMs and card readers that the smart cards need to communicate with each other and with the bank can also be programmed to keep track of every transaction, but do not have to.

One example of the electronic purse concept is the Mondex system currently being field tested in Swindon, England by a joint venture of NatWest and Midland Bank, in cooperation with British Telecom. The Mondex card is unusual in two respects. First, it is designed to hold up to five different currencies on a single card; second, and more important, it allows direct peer-to-peer fund transfers, without the intervention of a bank.

Little is publicly known about the mechanics of the Mondex system. Mondex representatives have stated that the company intends to restrict information about the workings of its cards, including its public key and the algorithm used, in order to make life that much more difficult for anyone who would be tempted to try to hack the system. The company has stated that it uses digital signatures to distinguish an authentic Mondex transaction from a fraudulent one, and that each card will carry two security systems, one of which will be changed every two years in series. Each card also carries a unique 16-digit identifier that links it to the person who purchased it. The Mondex system has, however, been criticized for relying too heavily on the tamper-resistance of the smart card. According to Mondex's competitors, if an attacker were to manage to break the tamper-resistance of the device, he would be able to introduce new money on the card virtually at will. And if the system of breaking the cards were to be widely published, the issuing bank would be helpless.

Exactly how much privacy the Mondex card provides the user is a subject of considerable dispute. The Chairman of Mondex has stated that the company has not yet decided how much transaction logging the card will do when it graduates from field tests to commercial use. Meanwhile, Simon Davies, a Visiting Professor of Law at Essex University, a well-known privacy advocate and gadfly, has alleged that Mondex card readers keep records of up to the last 500 cards used in the reader, despite Mondex's claim that the cards are as anonymous as cash; Professor Davies has filed a false advertising complaint with the UK Trading Standards Board. Mondex states that the card itself keeps a record of the last ten transactions; there have been allegations that the card is designed to download this information to the central bank every time the card is placed in an ATM.

Digital purses with currency that does not have to be cleared through the issuing bank raise a number of intriguing regulatory problems beyond the scope of this article. Among them are: (1) what regulations might be appropriate to reduce the harmful consequences of the "meltdown scenario" in which someone cracks the security of the electronic smart cards and begins minting her own apparently legitimate digital cash; (2) how to prevent smart cards from becoming a tool of money laundering; (3) how to monitor issuing banks to ensure that they do not issue more card-based currency than customers have actually purchased; (4) transborder regulatory questions including consumer protection, the role of non-bank banks in foreign markets, possible loss of seignorage [sic], and bank exposure to multiple and differing concepts of escheat. More than any other implementation of electronic cash, digital purses such as Mondex threaten to erode the control of central bank authorities over the money supply. Central banks appear to be concerned: "although none of the central banks have pointed the finger at [Mondex] by name, one governor [of the European Monetary Institute] delivering a recent speech on the subject in his native language reportedly dropped into English to declare: 'Purse to purse, No!'"

When Alice pays Mondex to put money on a smart card, the transaction increases the money supply until the credit is redeemed. Unlike other payment schemes such as checking accounts, travellers checks or even digital coins, the Mondex scheme allows, even encourages, participants to refrain from redeeming stored value at the bank. The Mondex card's ability to transfer value from one card to another thus increases the effective money supply. When Alice puts $10 into her checking account, the bank has use of the money (and Alice has a claim on the bank), but Alice does not have the use of the money until she takes it out again. The only time when the bank and Alice both have the use of that $10 is during any float period between when Alice writes a check and the bank honors it. Furthermore, advances in technology have been reducing this float period compared to the past; debit cards eliminate it. In contrast, when Alice purchases $10 worth of credit for her Mondex card, the bank has the use of the $10 (and Alice has a claim on the bank), but Alice also has the use of a $10 store of value. If she purchases something from a merchant who does not return the funds to the bank, but instead either holds the funds or makes another purchase, the money supply has effectively increased because the same $10 is circulating as money on the card and as money that the bank can loan out in its customary manner. An unscrupulous bank, or one based in a country that enjoys a very relaxed regulatory regime, might become tempted to "mint" its own unbacked electronic funds, which it might loan to customers, or use to meet its own obligations. If electronic messages stored on smart cards are not considered "money," however, such actions might even comply with banking laws.

C. REGULATION OF DIGITAL CASH

The policy-maker's perspective on digital cash generally and anonymous digital cash in particular is complicated by uncertainty about the capabilities of the technologies, on the market's reaction to them, and on their effect on privacy and law enforcement. The policy-maker's task is further complicated by the multiple and sometimes conflicting objectives that her policy might be designed to serve.

1. The Privacy Calculus

The effect of a digital cash system on privacy depends on which system is used and, often, the details of how it is implemented. The systems canvassed above range from privacy-destroying to having a mixed effect on privacy. The major privacy-enhancing feature offered by any of these systems as compared to traditional cash is that transactions under most schemes need not be face-to-face, a potentially significant privacy advantage given the prevalence of in-store video cameras. Ordinary cash itself, after all, is less than completely anonymous since it is usually exchanged in person, bears a unique serial number, carries fingerprints, and can easily be marked for identification.

Some digital cash models compare favorably to plastic debit and credit cards; others are no better. The debit card model of digital cash creates a complete accounting record of all transactions. Blinded digital coins provide more privacy than ordinary credit cards, since credit cards create a complete transaction record that is accessible to the issuer; blinded digital coins provide payor, but not payee, anonymity.

In the absence of an installed base of smart card readers on personal computers, digital coins in tiny denominations appear most suited to Internet information commerce. Arguably, the basic digital coin "does not deserve to be called cash ... because it lacks the distinguishing characteristic" of ordinary money — its anonymity. As each transaction is cleared with the bank it leaves a record. In contrast, blinded cash protects the anonymity of the payor, but not the payee. At this writing, only one financial institution offers blinded digital cash backed by ordinary currency. Even blinded coins or checks only anonymize payments, not receipts. In fairness to digital cash, however, it should be noted that paper money is not as anonymous as it may seem. Large transactions in paper currency often trigger reporting requirements designed to detect money laundering.

Truly anonymous digital cash would be possible with an anonymous bank account. If the bank account is anonymous, then withdrawals and deposits cannot be traced to the owner. Digital cash would actually enhance transactional privacy if banks that support digital cash become willing to open anonymous accounts, and to accepts deposits in digital cash. In this scenario, anonymous bank accounts, combined with anonymous purchases and payment, would be even more private than cash, since both the seller and buyer could mask their identity. Even if a bank wanted to offer this service, regulatory authorities would be likely to oppose it.

The electronic purse's effect on privacy is particularly sensitive to how it is implemented. Electronic purses are the only system described above that are designed to allow peer-to-peer funds transfers without requiring the parties to contact a third party. Mondex cards and card readers could be configured to do little transaction logging, which would make them possibly more private than cash, or the hardware could capture and record every transaction. At present, however, Mondex is not well-suited to an Internet payments mechanism because personal computers have no means of accessing Mondex cards without expensive and rare connective hardware. Furthermore, as currently designed, the Mondex system is vulnerable to a "man in the middle" attack when the transacting parties are not face-to-face, making the system more suited to in-store transactions than to Internet transactions. One can imagine ways to use electronic purses to enhance privacy, such as adding value from vending machines paid with ordinary cash; but so long as the card itself is not anonymous, and so long as all cards keep even limited records, the card provides less privacy than traditional cash.

2.   Regulatory Policy Goals and Practical Constraints

All governments and central banks have an obvious interest in retaining control of the money supply. Central banks should be able to achieve this objective by taking three related steps: (1) Ensuring that issuers of digital cash are subject to the rules that apply to existing, regulated, financial service providers. One simple, if restrictive, means of achieving this would be to limit digital cash issuance to banks. (2) Adjusting reserve requirements to neutralize the effects of changes in the stock of pocket cash. (3) Taking whatever steps are possible to reduce the likelihood of the "meltdown scenario" in which someone cracks the security of a digital cash scheme. All these steps are equally applicable whether or not the digital cash is anonymous.

Whether the U.S. or other governments will choose or should choose to regulate anonymous digital cash is more complicated. Citizens are likely to feel, with some reason, that their governments should help create the conditions that make it possible for them to protect their privacy. Data protection laws or changes in property rights over information might contribute to this, but they are uncertain at best. And once information privacy is lost it is difficult to regain as there is almost no way to recall data that are in wide circulation.

On the other hand governments have an interest in preserving their ability to enforce existing laws and regulations, such as tax collection and laws against fraud and illicit transactions. Furthermore, as the enforcer of moral values that have been embodied in legislation or, in some cases, as tyrant, governments may desire to control the purchase or movement of information and of funds. Governments are likely to believe, not without reason, that their enforcement abilities would be threatened by the widespread deployment of anonymous digital cash, although traceable digital cash might often make their work easier.

Only fully anonymous digital cash stands much chance of aiding in financial crimes such as money laundering or tax evasion. Banks will continue to have records of the amounts withdrawn by their clients and will know who is depositing digital cash. Law enforcement will, however, have less information than they would have when tracing a wire transfer, since a wire transfer links payor and payee to a single transaction. In contrast, a DigiCash transfer, for example, does not allow the bank or the police to link the two halves of the transaction. Nevertheless, anyone depositing DigiCash to a bank must disclose their identity, just as they do when depositing cash. Indeed, most digital coins make money laundering more difficult than does traditional cash, since digital coins must be returned to the bank after every expenditure. Similarly, in its current form a Mondex card is unlikely to be of much value in money laundering. Even if Mondex cards do not keep transaction records, the value that can be encoded on a card is likely to be limited to $500 or pounds sterling 500. To the extent the government is concerned about these issues, they point towards either outlawing fully anonymous cash, or otherwise complicating its deployment; one means to achieve this is to tilt the regulatory playing field towards forms of digital cash that are not fully anonymous and hope that they achieve market dominance.

Governments have considerably more power to reduce the liquidity, acceptability, and utility of anonymous digital cash than they do to cut off the flow of anonymous speech. Unlike anonymous speech, which does not require any willing parties inside the country other than a single speaker or listener, anonymous cash requires at least two parties, the buyer and seller, and often also involves a trusted third party as well. If anonymous digital cash is banned by a government, many corporations active in that jurisdiction will be reluctant to use it because they are subject to audit and disclosure requirements, and have assets to lose if subjected to civil or criminal penalties. At a minimum, a ban would raise the cost of using anonymous digital cash, perhaps to the point where few people were willing to trade in it. Even a refusal to enforce contracts or debts based on the exchange of anonymous currency would have a significant deterrent effect.

Widespread use of Internet-tradable digital cash might internationalize money. That day seems far away, if it will ever come; to date, even the Mondex card, the most self-consciously international digital cash to be field tested, is linked to national currencies (up to five on one card). In principle there is no reason why, given the international nature of the Internet, its unit of account needs to be pegged to a particular currency. Trading in Internet-provided information, perhaps starting with micro-charges for access to web pages, is ideally suited to a new unit of account, used initially for the internet only. If the issuance of the new monetary unit perhaps it could be called the "bit"? — could be designed so that the money supply grew at the right speed, one would eventually expect to see transactions in which bits were exchanged for traditional currencies. Amusing as these speculations can be, practice and prudence suggest a different outcome.

Internationalized cash would suffer from a number of serious problems that would have to be resolved before it would be safe to rely on it. First, there is the question of who would issue it. If a single digital currency were to become an international standard, it would require either a central bank or at least an agreed, enforceable, mechanism for controlling the minting of currency. This sort of centralization is unlike the Internet as we know it. More likely, individual issuers around the world would agree on a common protocol for the issuance of "bits," and international banking would be plunged into an electronic repeat of the pre-Civil War financial system. Before the central bank centralization of the mid-19th century, banks commonly issued their own notes, and the discount applied to these notes varied according to the reputation of the bank (which affected the liquidity of the note), and usually the distance the note had travelled from the issuer.

Whether internationalized or simply anonymized, Internet digital cash worries national authorities charged with preventing money laundering. Digital cash is obviously more portable and mobile than ordinary paper currency. So long as funds must clear through a bank, and the payee is not anonymous, the effects of digital cash on money laundering control should be fairly low, since most existing money laundering rules require banks to know who deposits cash. If, however, digital cash that does not have to be cleared through a bank (e.g., a Mondex scheme) becomes widespread, the ability of authorities to control money laundering will depend greatly on the extent to which the scheme allows authorities to trace the funds. The longer the memory on a smart card, and the more information it collects about the smart cards with which it transacts, the more incriminating that card will be if searched or captured by the authorities. Similarly, if smart cards are programmed routinely to dump the contents of their memories to the bank for auditing and verification purposes, then banks will usually have databases that will meet the claimed needs of law enforcement.

If anonymous, untraceable, digital cash without expenditure limits were to be deployed, it would greatly increase the range of interpersonal transactions that could be conducted anonymously, even if it did not become "a heyday for criminals." One can imagine on-line fraud, in which a digital personality provides attestations from hundreds of satisfied customers, each of whom is nothing more than another digital personality created by the author of the fraud. While it is possible to envision sophisticated reputation systems that would reveal many such manufactured attestations, these do not currently exist, and might be cumbersome to use. Other unsavory possibilities include vastly simplified insider trading in securities transactions, the sale of corporate and personal secrets, blackmail and "perfect crimes." Armed with untraceable digital cash, any transaction that Alice can persuade Bob to undertake for a digital payment can be commanded anonymously, with even Bob ignorant as to Alice's identity. Alice might be more willing to hire a contract killer, for example, if she felt secure that the crime could never be traced back to her; on the other hand, if Bob doesn't know who Alice is, he will demand payment in advance. Killer Bob might not be that interested in advertising his true identity either, which might make Alice unwilling to pay an anonymous stranger in advance.

In light of these possibilities, even if they are largely theoretical, it would not be surprising if many governments, including the U.S. government, wish to act to discourage or forbid the issuance and use of completely anonymous digital cash, at least forms that allow it to be exchanged in denominations higher than those proposed by Mondex. Although libertarians and advocates of increased privacy are likely to be disappointed, a decision to ban or discourage fully anonymous digital cash is likely to be politically acceptable in the U.S., for example, because it appears to extend the status quo to the digital age. Small cash transactions are largely anonymous today; neither large cash transactions nor most electronic transactions have any anonymity.

A ban on the use of anonymous digital cash for ordinary tangible commerce appears likely to face few constitutional or practical obstacles as applied to the sale of goods. Even if the ban made anonymous purchases in tangible goods difficult or impossible, it would probably be constitutional because there is no generalized right to shop anonymously. The constitutional difficulties arise when the same rules are applied to the sale of information, i.e., "speech." As explained below, a ban on anonymous digital cash could greatly obstruct the anonymity of speakers and readers. The practical problems arise from the potential constitutional difficulties: there is no way to create anonymous digital cash that could only be used for commerce in information. Any regulation that aims to control the perceived evils of anonymous cash, e.g., money laundering and illicit trade, perforce impinges on anonymous speech as well.

Note

Notwithstanding the generally accepted view that digital cash is needed as a substitute for credit card payments, DigiCash filed for bankruptcy protection in 1998.

With widespread implementation of a digital cash system seemingly several years away, few legal authorities have considered the legal issues raised by such systems. The European Union, which has developed the following proposed directive, is a notable exception.

Proposal for a European Parliament and Council Directive
on the Taking Up, the Pursuit and the Prudential Supervision
of the Business of Electronic Money Institutions†

Whereas within the wider context of the rapidly evolving electronic commerce it is desirable to provide a regulatory framework that assists electronic money in delivering its full potential benefits and that avoids hampering technological innovation in particular;

Whereas, therefore, this Directive introduces a technology-neutral legal framework that harmonises the prudential supervision of electronic money institutions to the extent necessary for ensuring their sound and prudent operation and their financial integrity in particular;

Whereas credit institutions, by virtue of point 5 of the Annex to Council Directive 89/646/EEC as last amended by directive 92/30/EEC, are already allowed to issue and administer means of payment including electronic money and to carry on such activities Community-wide subject to mutual recognition and to the comprehensive prudential supervisory system applying to them in accordance with the European banking Directives;

Whereas the introduction of a separate prudential supervisory regime for electronic money institutions, which although calibrated on the prudential supervisory regime applying to credit institutions and Directives 77/780/EEC and 89/646/EEC in particular, differs from that regime, is justified and desirable because the issuance of electronic money cannot, in view of its specific character as an electronic surrogate for coins and banknotes, be regarded as a deposit-taking activity prohibited pursuant to Article 3 of Directive 89/646/EEC to undertakings other than credit institutions;

Whereas in order to respond to the specific risks associated with the issuance of electronic money this prudential supervisory regime must be more targeted and, accordingly, is less cumbersome than the prudential supervisory regime applying to credit institutions, notably as regards reduced initial capital requirements and the non-application of Directives 89/647/EEC, 92/121/EEC and 93/6/EEC;

Whereas, however, it is necessary to preserve a level playing field between credit institutions issuing electronic money and electronic money institutions and, thus, to ensure fair competition among a wider range of institutions to the benefits of users;

Whereas this is achieved since the above-mentioned less cumbersome features of the prudential supervisory regime applying to electronic money institutions are balanced by provisions that are more stringent than those applying to credit institutions, notably as regards restrictions of the business activities electronic money institutions may carry on and, particularly, prudent limitations of their investments aimed at ensuring that their financial liabilities related to outstanding electronic money are backed at all times by highly liquid low risk assets;

Whereas with a view to the possibility of operational and other ancillary functions related to the issuance of electronic money being performed by undertakings which

---

† COM/98/0461 final; Official Journal (31) of 15/10/98.

are not subject to prudential supervision it is appropriate to afford competent authorities certain powers with respect to these undertakings;

Whereas it is appropriate to afford competent authorities the possibility to waive certain requirements imposed by this Directive for electronic money institutions which operate only within the territories of the respective Member State and whose business activities do not exceed certain thresholds;

. . . .

Article 1
Scope, definitions and restriction of activities

(1) This Directive shall apply to electronic money institutions.

(2) It shall not apply to the institutions referred to in Article 2 (2) of Directive 77/780/EEC.

(3) For the purposes of this Directive:

1.1.(a) 'electronic money institution' shall mean an undertaking, other than a credit institution as defined in article 1, first indent, (a) of Council Directive 77/780/EEC which issues means of payment in the form of electronic money or which invests the proceeds from such activities without being subject to Council Directive 93/22/EEC 15;

1.2.(b) 'electronic money' shall mean monetary value which is
  (i) stored electronically on an electronic device such as a chip card or a computer memory;
  (ii) accepted as means of payment by undertakings other than the issuing institution;
  (iii) generated in order to be put at the disposal of users to serve as an electronic surrogate for coins and banknotes; and
  (iv) generated for the purpose of effecting electronic transfers of limited value payments.

2.(4) The business activities of electronic money institutions other than the issuing of electronic money shall be restricted to:

  (a) the provision of closely related financial and non-financial services such as the administering of electronic money by the performance of operational and other ancillary functions related to its issuance and the issuing and administering of other means of payment within the meaning of point 5 of the Annex to Directive 89/646/EEC; and
  (b) the provision of non-financial services that are delivered through the electronic device.

Electronic money institutions shall not have any holdings in other undertakings except where these undertakings perform operational or other ancillary functions related to electronic money issued or distributed by the institution concerned.

Article 2
Application of Banking Directives

(1) Save where otherwise expressly provided for, references to credit institutions in EC regulations, directives other than Directives 77/780/EEC and 89/646/EEC, recommendations and opinions shall not apply to electronic money institutions.

(2) Articles 2 (5) and (6), 3 (3) b), c) and d) and (7), 4, 6, 7 (2) and (3), 8 (2), (3) and (4), 10 and 14 of Directive 77/780/EEC and Articles 4, 6, 10, 12, 18 (2), 23 and 24 of Directive 89/646/EEC shall not apply. The freedom of establishment and the freedom to provide services according to Articles 18 to 21 of Directive 89/646/EEC shall not apply to electronic money institutions' business activities other than the issuance of electronic money.

(3) Council Directives 91/308/EEC and 92/30/EEC shall apply to electronic money institutions.

(4) For the purpose of applying Article 3 of Directive 89/646/EEC funds received in exchange for electronic money shall not be regarded as deposits within the meaning of that Article if the underlying contractual arrangements:

(a) clearly establish the specific character of electronic money as an electronic surrogate for coins and banknotes; and

(b) do not provide for the possibility of advancing funds with a view to and in exchange for the receipt of electronic money at a later stage.

Redeemability of electronic money is, in itself, not a sufficient reason for considering the funds advanced by the user to be deposits within the meaning of Article 3 of Directive 89/646/EEC. The contract between the issuer and the user shall define if the stored electronic money is redeemable or not, and, if appropriate, the conditions, the formalities and the time period of redeemability.

Article 3
Initial capital and ongoing own funds requirements

(1) Electronic money institutions shall have an initial capital of no less than ECU 500,000. Notwithstanding paragraphs 2 and 3 below their own funds shall not fall below that amount.

(2) Electronic money institutions shall have at all times own funds equal to or above 2% of the higher of the current amount or the average of the preceding 6 months' total amount of their financial liabilities related to outstanding electronic money.

(3) Where an electronic money institution has not completed a 6 months period of business, including the day it starts up, it shall have own funds equal to or above 2% of the higher of the current amount or the 6 months target total amount of its financial liabilities related to outstanding electronic money. The 6 months target total amount of the institution's financial liabilities related to outstanding electronic money shall be evidenced by its business plan subject to any adjustment to that plan having been required by the competent authorities.

Article 4
Limitations of investments

(1) Electronic money institutions shall have investments of an amount of no less than their financial liabilities related to outstanding electronic money in the following assets only:

2.1.(a) asset items which according to Article 6 (1) (a) points 1, 2, 3, 4 and Article 7 (1) of Directive 89/647/EEC attract a zero credit risk weighting and which are highly liquid;

2.2.(b) sight deposits held with Zone A credit institutions and debt instruments, which are

(i) highly liquid;

(ii) not covered by paragraph 1 point (a),

(iii) recognised by competent authorities as qualifying items within the meaning of Article 2 (12) of Directive 93/6/EEC, and

(iv) issued by undertakings other than undertakings which have a direct or indirect holding in the electronic money institution concerned or which must be included in these undertakings' consolidated accounts or in which the electronic money institution concerned has a direct or indirect holding.

(2) Investments referred to in paragraph 1 point (b) may not exceed twenty times the own funds of the electronic money institution concerned and shall be subject to limitations which are at least as stringent as those applying to credit institutions in accordance with Directive 92/121/EEC.

(3) For the purpose of hedging market risks arising from the issuance of electronic money and from the investments referred to in paragraph 1 electronic money institutions may use highly liquid interest-rate and foreign-exchange-related off balance-sheet items in the form of exchange-traded derivative instruments to which Annex II to Directive 89/647/EEC does not apply. The use of derivative instruments according to the first sentence is permissible only if the full elimination of market risks is intended and, to the extent possible, achieved.

(4) Member States shall impose appropriate limitations on the market risks electronic money institutions may incur from the investments referred to in paragraph 1.

(5) For the purpose of applying paragraph 1 assets shall be valued at the lower of cost or market value.

(6) If the value of the assets referred to in paragraph 1 falls below the amount of financial liabilities related to outstanding electronic money the competent authorities shall ensure that the electronic money institution in question takes appropriate measures to remedy that situation promptly. To this end, and for a temporary period only, the competent authorities may allow the institution's financial liabilities related to outstanding electronic money to be backed by assets other than those referred to in paragraph 1 up to an amount not exceeding the lower of 5% of these liabilities and the institution's total amount of own funds.

Article 5
Verification by competent authorities
Competent authorities shall verify compliance with Articles 3 and 4 not less than twice each year on the basis of data supplied by the electronic money institutions.

Article 6
Sound and prudent operation
(1) Electronic money institutions shall have sound and prudent management, sound administrative and accounting procedures and adequate internal control mechanisms. These should respond to the financial and non-financial risks to which the institution is exposed.

(2) If an electronic money institution undertakes business activities of the type referred to in Article 1 (3) point (a) in co-operation with another undertaking which performs operational or other ancillary functions related to these business activities and which, with a view to the risks related to these functions, is subject to no prudential supervision, the contractual arrangements underlying this co-operation shall provide for contractual rights which enable the electronic money institution properly to monitor and contain these risks and immediately and unconditionally to cancel the contractual arrangements underlying the co-operation if the effective exercise of these rights is impaired in practice or upon request of the competent authorities in accordance with paragraph 3 last indent.

(3) In order to ensure the effective supervision of an electronic money institution which co-operates with another undertaking in the manner described in paragraph 2, Member States shall provide that their competent authorities may:

(a) require that other undertaking to supply any information which would be relevant for the purpose of supervising the electronic money institution;
(b) carry out, or have carried out by external inspectors, on-the-spot inspections of that other undertaking to verify such information; and
(c) require as appropriate the electronic money institution promptly to remedy any shortcomings and if necessary immediately to cancel the contractual arrangements underlying the co-operation with that other undertaking.

Article 7
Waiver

(1) Member States may waive the application of Articles 1 (4), 3 (1), and 8 of this Directive and the application of Directives 77/780/EEC and 89/646/EEC to an electronic money institution if the totality of the business activities of the type referred to in Article 1 (3) point (a) it undertakes alone or in co-operation with other electronic money institutions fulfil the following conditions:

(a) it generates a total amount of financial liabilities related to outstanding electronic money that normally does not exceed ECU 10 million and never exceeds ECU 12 million; and
(b) is related to electronic money the underlying contractual arrangements of which provide that the electronic storage device at the disposal of users for the purpose of making payments is subject to a maximum storage amount of no more than ECU 150.

An electronic money institution for which the application of one of the above Articles has been waived shall not benefit from the freedom of establishment and the freedom to provide services as conveyed by Directive 89/647/EEC.

(2) For the purpose of applying this Directive to undertakings which seek for a waiver according to paragraph 1 to be approved or for which the waiver has been approved:

(a) 'competent authorities' shall mean those national authorities which are responsible for the supervision of electronic money institutions; and
(b) 'own funds' shall mean own funds as defined in Council Directive 89/299/EEC.

Article 8
Grandfathering

(1) Electronic money institutions subject to this Directive which have commenced their activity in accordance with the provisions in force in the Member States in which they have their head offices before the entry into force of the provisions adopted in implementation of this Directive shall be presumed to be authorised. The Member States shall oblige such electronic money institutions to submit, within a reasonable period, all relevant information in order to allow the competent authorities to assess whether the institutions comply with the requirements pursuant to this Directive, which measures need to be taken in order to ensure compliance, or whether a withdrawal of authorisation is appropriate.

(2) The presumption according to paragraph 1 first sentence shall not apply to electronic money institutions which benefit from a waiver in accordance with Article 7. If such a waiver is subject to prior approval by competent authorities the presumption shall become void by the time of that approval.

Discussion Questions

1. Do you think the E.U. directive will have the effect of encouraging e-cash providers by creating enhanced legal certainty or discouraging such providers by creating an "overregulated" marketplace?

2. Since the E.U. is the only major jurisdiction to consider enacting e-cash legislation, will it place the E.U. ahead or behind jurisdictions without such legislation?

With credit cards likely to remain the preferred method of payment online for the foreseeable future, the power of credit card issuers and the protections afforded to consumers merit closer consideration. The following Canadian case illustrates the important role played by credit card companies in the development and execution of e-commerce businesses.

Pesoexpress Systems Inc. v. Internetsecure Inc.†

This is a motion by the plaintiff for a mandatory order compelling the defendants to restore Electronic Purchase Service to the plaintiff forthwith and for a mandatory order compelling the defendants to release U.S. $10,464.98 in held back funds to the plaintiff.

The plaintiff established a web site which allows persons to send money to the Philippines in either Canadian or U.S. dollars using their credit cards. The plaintiff applied to the defendant, Internetsecure Inc., to be an approved merchant.

---

† [1999] O.J. No. 4682 (Ont. Sup. Ct. of Justice, 1999).

Internetsecure acts as a facilitator between approved merchants who wish to sell goods and services on the internet and certain financial institutions who authorize merchants to use their credit cards. In this particular case, the financial institution was the defendant, Bank of Nova Scotia.

In making its application for approved merchant status, the plaintiff identified its proposed goods and/or services as "goods & services specifically designed for Filipinos" and then directly thereafter mentioned "books, calendars, Christmas decor, videos, etc." The plaintiff was approved and consequently signed a "Scotiabank Merchant & Provider Visa Agreement - Internet Commerce" (the "Merchant Agreement") which provided the contractual terms between the plaintiff and the defendants for this service.

Apparently, and to my mind quite surprisingly, throughout this approval process, no one at Internetsecure who was in any position of management authority bothered to look at the plaintiff's web site. Internetsecure was therefore unaware at the outset that what the web site actually promoted was a mechanism of providing cash advances to persons rather than selling any actual goods and/or services as otherwise would have fairly been assumed to be the object of the business because of the representation made by the plaintiff on its application form.

The web site began its operations on September 16, 1999. Sometime in early November, 1999, Internetsecure became concerned about the nature of the transactions being engaged in on the plaintiff's web site particularly because of a number of similar transactions with the same individual involving substantial sums. As a consequence of this concern, Internetsecure had a closer look at the plaintiff's web site and discovered that the plaintiff was providing cash advances to persons. As I have already noted, this would have been apparent to anyone who visited the web site and viewed its home page.

Upon learning of this, Internetsecure immediately suspended the plaintiff's participation in the Internetsecure program which meant that the plaintiff could not process any transactions for any of its customers on the web site. Internetsecure took this step because there is, apparently, a policy of the financial institutions with which Internetsecure deals that they do not wish to process cash advance transactions for any of their merchants due, at least in part, to the fact that cash advances are supposed to be recorded and treated differently from ordinary transactions on credit cards in that interest is supposed to accrue on such transactions from the day of the advance. A secondary reason for Internetsecure's action is that there is a different and more stringent approval process by Internetsecure for any merchant that might be approved to offer cash advances assuming that a financial institution was prepared to permit them.

The plaintiff says that the action of Internetsecure has effectively shut down its fledgling business and seeks, at least on an interim basis, a mandatory order requiring Internetsecure to reestablish its ability to offer the services it was providing. In so doing, the plaintiff relies on the fact that there is nothing in the Merchant Agreement which prohibits it from offering cash advances and that, if the defendants had wished to do so, they should have made that an express term of the Merchant Agreement.

The defendants, on the other hand, say that they were misled by the plaintiff's stated intentions for the business that it was going to offer and would never have approved the plaintiff for their services had the actual intended business been made known to them. The defendants also point to the following two provisions in the Merchant Agreement as permitting them to take the steps that they have:

> 3(o) The Merchant agrees that, notwithstanding anything else stated in this Agreement, the Provider and/or Scotiabank reserve the right to decline any requested Transaction, up to the time of the settlement thereof, for any reasons whatsoever without giving notice to or obtaining the consent of the Merchant, and shall not incur any liability as a result thereof.

> 12(k) Scotiabank reserves the right to suspend or completely cancel any portion of the Electronic Merchant Service, at any time, without prior notice to the Merchant.

The test for obtaining a mandatory order is essentially the same as the test for obtaining an interlocutory injunction subject to one proviso I will mention. The test for an interlocutory injunction is well known and is set out in the decision of the Supreme Court of Canada in *RJR-MacDonald Inc.* v. *Canada (A.G.)*, [1994] 1 S.C.R. 311 at p. 334, that is, (i) there must be a serious issue to be tried; (ii) the applicant must establish that it would suffer irreparable harm, and; (iii) an assessment must be made as to which of the parties would suffer greater harm from the granting or refusal of the remedy pending a decision on the merits.

The one proviso that I mentioned is the fact that when a mandatory order is sought the hurdle that the applicant has to clear is stated to be somewhat higher as evidenced by the decision in *Ticketnet Corporation* v. *Air Canada* (1987), 21 C.P.C. (2d) 38 (Ont. H.C.) at p. 43 where White J. quoted with approval the following statement of Megarry J. in *Shephard Homes Ltd.* v. *Sandham*, [1970] 3 All E.R. 402 (Ch. D.) at p. 412:

> Third, on motion, as contrasted with the trial, the court is far more reluctant to grant a mandatory injunction than it would be to grant a comparable prohibitory injunction. In a normal case the court must, inter alia, feel a high degree of assurance that at the trial it will appear that the injunction was rightly granted; and this is a higher standard than is required for a prohibitory injunction.

In my view, the plaintiff cannot, in this case, satisfy the test for an interlocutory injunction so it becomes unnecessary for me to consider whether the higher hurdle for a mandatory order is applicable to these circumstances.

First, I accept that there may be a serious issue to be tried in the sense that the plaintiff's claim is not frivolous or vexatious. However, I must say that in light of what seems to have been a less than frank disclosure of the nature of the business in applying for the approval, and the express provisions of the two clauses of the Merchant Agreement that I have quoted above, I have serious reservations as to whether the plaintiff will be able to sustain its position at a trial.

Secondly, and more importantly, I do not view the harm that is being incurred here as irreparable as that term is normally construed. First, the relief sought in the notice of action is strictly one of damages which would suggest that, in the plaintiff's own view, damages are an adequate remedy. Further, the nature of the plaintiff's loss is a business loss. It has said that it can probably re-establish its business in four months through another service. Assuming it does so, the quantification of the losses in the period between now and then should be capable of being determined.

The plaintiff's other concern is that another business may usurp its idea and enter the market in this interim period. If that happens, the plaintiff says that it would be precluded from re-establishing the business at all. It is not clear to me why that result should necessarily follow. I note that this is not a novel idea. Another web site offered the same type of service to persons wishing to send money to people in Cuba in May, 1998. It apparently suffered the same fate as the plaintiff has here. In any event, just because another business is established does not mean that the plaintiff cannot re-establish its business and then compete with whoever then happens to be in the market. I do not accept that a plaintiff in this situation can elevate its damages to the status of irreparable harm simply by saying that it is not prepared to compete with another entity that may happen onto the scene at the same time as this dispute is unfolding.

Thirdly, while superficially the plaintiff may appear to suffer the greater harm from the refusal of the remedy than the defendants would suffer from it being granted, I am not convinced that the actual balance so clearly favours the plaintiff. While the plaintiff will have an interruption in its business, if the defendants are required to re-establish the service, they then become potentially liable for any of these transactions that subsequently get disputed by the plaintiff's customers. Such amounts might be considerable in a cash advance business and there is no information before me that the plaintiff company has the financial wherewithal to reimburse the defendants for any such losses.

Finally, there has been no undertaking as to damages proffered by the plaintiff. While that deficiency alone would be sufficient to deny the relief sought, I am prepared to assume that such an undertaking would have been made available by the plaintiff as a term of any order if that became the only obstacle to the relief sought — although counsel for the plaintiff did not make such an offer when the issue was raised by counsel for the defendants. However, and in any event, I would still have concerns about the efficacy of the undertaking, in a financial sense, even if it had been given.

In the end result, therefore, and taking all of the aspects of the applicable test into consideration, I conclude that the plaintiff has failed to establish that it is entitled to the relief sought and the motion is therefore dismissed. Since a more proactive approach by Internetsecure to the original application of the plaintiff, or more clearly worded terms in the Merchant Agreement, might well have avoided this entire situation, I would not make any order as to the costs of this motion.

Unlike Canada, which has not enacted statutory protections for consumers arising out of credit card use, the United States has several provisions on point. Regulation Z provides U.S. credit card holders with two very significant protections, including a limitation of liability for fraud over $50 and a right to withhold payment where charges are disputed, a process known as chargebacks.

Truth in Lending Act — Regulation Z[†]

Sec. 226.13 Billing error resolution.

A creditor shall not accelerate any part of the consumer's indebtedness or restrict or close a consumer's account solely because the consumer has exercised in good faith rights provided by this section. A creditor may be subject to the forfeiture penalty

---

† 12 CFR 226.13 — Chargebacks.

under section 161(e) of the Act for failure to comply with any of the requirements of this section.

(a) Definition of billing error. For purposes of this section, the term billing error means:

(1) A reflection on or with a periodic statement of an extension of credit that is not made to the consumer or to a person who has actual, implied, or apparent authority to use the consumer's credit card or open-end credit plan.

(2) A reflection on or with a periodic statement of an extension of credit that is not identified in accordance with the requirements of Secs. 226.7(b) and 226.8.

(3) A reflection on or with a periodic statement of an extension of credit for property or services not accepted by the consumer or the consumer's designee, or not delivered to the consumer or the consumer's designee as agreed.

(4) A reflection on a periodic statement of the creditor's failure to credit properly a payment or other credit issued to the consumer's account.

(5) A reflection on a periodic statement of a computational or similar error of an accounting nature that is made by the creditor.

(6) A reflection on a periodic statement of an extension of credit for which the consumer requests additional clarification, including documentary evidence.

(7) The creditor's failure to mail or deliver a periodic statement to the consumer's last known address if that address was received by the creditor, in writing, at least 20 days before the end of the billing cycle for which the statement was required.

(b) Billing error notice. A billing error notice is a written notice from a consumer that:

(1) Is received by a creditor at the address disclosed under Sec. 226.7(k) no later than 60 days after the creditor transmitted the first periodic statement that reflects the alleged billing error;

(2) Enables the creditor to identify the consumer's name and account number; and

(3) To the extent possible, indicates the consumer's belief and the reasons for the belief that a billing error exists, and the type, date, and amount of the error.

(c) Time for resolution; general procedures.

(1) The creditor shall mail or deliver written acknowledgment to the consumer within 30 days of receiving a billing error notice, unless the creditor has complied with the appropriate resolution procedures of paragraphs (e) and (f) of this section, as applicable, within the 30-day period; and

(2) The creditor shall comply with the appropriate resolution procedures of paragraphs (e) and (f) of this section, as applicable, within 2 complete billing cycles (but in no event later than 90 days) after receiving a billing error notice.

(d) Rules pending resolution. Until a billing error is resolved under paragraph (e) or (f) of this section, the following rules apply:

(1) Consumer's right to withhold disputed amount; collection action prohibited. The consumer need not pay (and the creditor may not try to collect) any portion of any required payment that the consumer believes is related to the disputed amount (including related finance or other charges). If the cardholder maintains a deposit account with the card issuer and has agreed to pay the credit card indebtedness by periodic deductions from the cardholder's deposit account, the

card issuer shall not deduct any part of the disputed amount or related finance or other charges if a billing error notice is received any time up to 3 business days before the scheduled payment date.

(2) Adverse credit reports prohibited. The creditor or its agent shall not (directly or indirectly) make or threaten to make an adverse report to any person about the consumer's credit standing, or report that an amount or account is delinquent, because the consumer failed to pay the disputed amount or related finance or other charges.

(e) Procedures if billing error occurred as asserted. If a creditor determines that a billing error occurred as asserted, it shall within the time limits in paragraph (c)(2) of this section:

(1) Correct the billing error and credit the consumer's account with any disputed amount and related finance or other charges, as applicable; and

(2) Mail or deliver a correction notice to the consumer.

(f) Procedures if different billing error or no billing error occurred. If, after conducting a reasonable investigation, a creditor determines that no billing error occurred or that a different billing error occurred from that asserted, the creditor shall within the time limits in paragraph (c)(2) of this section:

(1) Mail or deliver to the consumer an explanation that sets forth the reasons for the creditor's belief that the billing error alleged by the consumer is incorrect in whole or in part;

(2) Furnish copies of documentary evidence of the consumer's indebtedness, if the consumer so requests; and

(3) If a different billing error occurred, correct the billing error and credit the consumer's account with any disputed amount and related finance or other charges, as applicable.

(g) Creditor's rights and duties after resolution. If a creditor, after complying with all of the requirements of this section, determines that a consumer owes all or part of the disputed amount and related finance or other charges, the creditor:

(1) Shall promptly notify the consumer in writing of the time when payment is due and the portion of the disputed amount and related finance or other charges that the consumer still owes;

(2) Shall allow any time period disclosed under Secs. 226.6(a)(1) and 226.7(j), during which the consumer can pay the amount due under paragraph (g)(1) of this section without incurring additional finance or other charges;

(3) May report an account or amount as delinquent because the amount due under paragraph (g)(1) of this section remains unpaid after the creditor has allowed any time period disclosed under Secs. 226.6(a)(1) and 266.7(j) or 10 days (whichever is longer) during which the consumer can pay the amount; but

(4) May not report that an amount or account is delinquent because the amount due under paragraph (g)(1) of the section remains unpaid, if the creditor receives (within the time allowed for payment in paragraph (g)(3) of this section) further written notice from the consumer that any portion of the billing error is still in dispute, unless the creditor also:

    (i) Promptly reports that the amount or account is in dispute;

(ii) Mails or delivers to the consumer (at the same time the report is made) a written notice of the name and address of each person to whom the creditor makes a report; and

(iii) Promptly reports any subsequent resolution of the reported delinquency to all persons to whom the creditor has made a report.

. . . .

Sec. 226 Special credit card provisions.

(a) Issuance of credit cards. Regardless of the purpose for which a credit card is to be used, including business, commercial, or agricultural use, no credit card shall be issued to any person except:

(1) In response to an oral or written request or application for the card; or

(2) As a renewal of, or substitute for, an accepted credit card.

(b) Liability of cardholder for unauthorized use

(1) Limitation on amount. The liability of a cardholder for unauthorized use of a credit card shall not exceed the lesser of $50 or the amount of money, property, labor, or services obtained by the unauthorized use before notification to the card issuer under paragraph (b)(3) of this section.

(2) Conditions of liability. A cardholder shall be liable for unauthorized use of a credit card only if:

    (i) The credit card is an accepted credit card;

    (ii) The card issuer has provided adequate notice of the cardholder's maximum potential liability and of means by which the card issuer may be notified of loss or theft of the card. The notice shall state that the cardholder's liability shall not exceed $50 (or any lesser amount) and that the cardholder may give oral or written notification, and shall describe a means of notification (for example, a telephone number, an address, or both); and

    (iii) The card issuer has provided a means to identify the cardholder on the account or the authorized user of the card.

(3) Notification to card issuer. Notification to a card issuer is given when steps have been taken as may be reasonably required in the ordinary course of business to provide the card issuer with the pertinent information about the loss, theft, or possible unauthorized use of a credit card, regardless of whether any particular officer, employee, or agent of the card issuer does, in fact, receive the information. Notification may be given, at the option of the person giving it, in person, by telephone, or in writing. Notification in writing is considered given at the time of receipt or, whether or not received, at the expiration of the time ordinarily required for transmission, whichever is earlier.

(4) Effect of other applicable law or agreement. If state law or an agreement between a cardholder and the card issuer imposes lesser liability than that provided in this paragraph, the lesser liability shall govern.

(5) Business use of credit cards. If 10 or more credit cards are issued by one card issuer for use by the employees of an organization, this section does not prohibit the card issuer and the organization from agreeing to liability for unauthorized use without regard to this section. However, liability for unauthorized use may be imposed on an employee of the organization, by either the card issuer or the organization, only in accordance with this section.

(c) Right of cardholder to assert claims or defenses against card issuer

(1) General rule. When a person who honors a credit card fails to resolve satisfactorily a dispute as to property or services purchased with the credit card in a consumer credit transaction, the cardholder may assert against the card issuer all claims (other than tort claims) and defenses arising out of the transaction and relating to the failure to resolve the dispute. The cardholder may withhold payment up to the amount of credit outstanding for the property or services that gave rise to the dispute and any finance or other charges imposed on that amount.

(2) Adverse credit reports prohibited. If, in accordance with paragraph (c)(1) of this section, the cardholder withholds payment of the amount of credit outstanding for the disputed transaction, the card issuer shall not report that amount as delinquent until the dispute is settled or judgment is rendered.

(3) Limitations. The rights stated in paragraphs (c)(1) and (2) of this section apply only if:

    (i) The cardholder has made a good faith attempt to resolve the dispute with the person honoring the credit card; and

    (ii) The amount of credit extended to obtain the property or services that result in the assertion of the claim or defense by the cardholder exceeds $50, and the disputed transaction occurred in the same state as the cardholder's current designated address or, if not within the same state, within 100 miles from that address.

(d) Offsets by card issuer prohibited

(1) A card issuer may not take any action, either before or after termination of credit card privileges, to offset a cardholder's indebtedness arising from a consumer credit transaction under the relevant credit card plan against funds of the cardholder held on deposit with the card issuer.

(2) This paragraph does not alter or affect the right of a card issuer acting under state or Federal law to do any of the following with regard to funds of a cardholder held on deposit with the card issuer if the same procedure is constitutionally available to creditors generally: obtain or enforce a consensual security interest in the funds; attach or otherwise levy upon the funds; or obtain or enforce a court order relating to the funds.

(3) This paragraph does not prohibit a plan, if authorized in writing by the cardholder, under which the card issuer may periodically deduct all or part of the cardholder's credit card debt from a deposit account held with the card issuer (subject to the limitations in Sec. 226.13(d)(1)).

(e) Prompt notification of returns and crediting of refunds.

(1) When a creditor other than the card issuer accepts the return of property or forgives a debt for services that is to be reflected as a credit to the consumer's credit card account, that creditor shall, within 7 business days from accepting the return or forgiving the debt, transmit a credit statement to the card issuer through the card issuer's normal channels for credit statements.

(2) The card issuer shall, within 3 business days from receipt of a credit statement, credit the consumer's account with the amount of the refund.

(3) If a creditor other than a card issuer routinely gives cash refunds to consumers paying in cash, the creditor shall also give credit or cash refunds to consumers using credit cards, unless it discloses at the time the transaction is consum-

mated that credit or cash refunds for returns are not given. This section does not require refunds for returns nor does it prohibit refunds in kind.

(f) Discounts; tie-in arrangements. No card issuer may, by contract or otherwise:

(1) Prohibit any person who honors a credit card from offering a discount to a consumer to induce the consumer to pay by cash, check, or similar means rather than by use of a credit card or its underlying account for the purchase of property or services; or

(2) Require any person who honors the card issuer's credit card to open or maintain any account or obtain any other service not essential to the operation of the credit card plan from the card issuer or any other person, as a condition of participation in a credit card plan. If maintenance of an account for clearing purposes is determined to be essential to the operation of the credit card plan, it may be required only if no service charges or minimum balance requirements are imposed.

Notes

The power wielded by credit card companies became glaringly apparent in May 2000 when American Express announced it would cease accepting merchant accounts from online pornography operators, citing excessively high costs associated with such accounts due to high incidence of chargebacks. With credit cards effectively the only credible method of online payment, merchants must obtain merchant accounts or face extinction on the Web.

22

Consumer Protection and the Internet

Internet fraud, until recently a relatively rare phenomenon, has increased in frequency and importance with the growth of electronic commerce. Although polls indicate that most Internet users find electronic commerce an enjoyable experience, the incidence of fraud online has increased dramatically, revealing a dark side to the benefits of the Internet. Unfortunately, perpetrators of fraud tend to prey on naïve and inexperienced Internet users, who are unable to effectively judge between a legitimate opportunity and a scam.

In many respects, the problems found online mirror those found in real space. Popular Internet scams include securities fraud, pyramid schemes, sales of bogus goods, and credit card manipulation — the types of scams commonly found in real space. The problem may be more serious in the online environment, however, since sophisticated Web sites lend an aura of credibility to perpetrators of fraud. Moreover, the borderless nature of the Internet often renders law enforcement officials powerless to stop fraudulent activity.

Ironically, the Internet is the best source of information on Internet fraud since consumer watchdog groups and other agencies can easily use the medium to disseminate information on the latest fraudulent schemes. Sadly, many Internet users are unaware of these resources and do not conduct the necessary "due diligence" before engaging in electronic commerce.

Consumer groups and industry watchdogs have become particularly active in trying to develop effective consumer protection standards for the online environment. After months of discussions, Canada released its consumer protection guidelines in late 1999.

*Principles of Consumer Protection for Electronic Commerce:
A Canadian Framework, Working Group on Electronic
Commerce and Consumers[†]*

GUIDING PRINCIPLES

Equivalent protection
"Consumers" should not be afforded any less protection in "electronic commerce" than in other forms of commerce. Consumer protection provisions should be designed to achieve the same results whatever the medium of commerce.

Harmonization
Canadian governments should adapt existing consumer protection laws to apply to electronic commerce, and should strive to harmonize provisions across jurisdictions without requiring any jurisdiction to lower its standards.

International consistency
Without compromising the level of protection provided to consumers under the principles in this document or under existing laws, the Canadian consumer protection framework should be consistent with directions in consumer protection established by international bodies such as the Organisation for Economic Co-operation and Development.

PRINCIPLE 1: INFORMATION PROVISION

> **Consumers should be provided with clear and sufficient information
> to make an informed choice about whether and how to make a
> purchase.**

1.1 Information should be provided in a form that is clear and understandable to the consumer. Vendors should:

(a) avoid using jargon and legalese, and use plain language whenever possible;
(b) provide information in a form and manner that allows the consumer to keep the information for future reference;
(c) clearly distinguish the terms and conditions of sale from marketing and promotional material or messages.

1.2 Information required by these principles should be "prominently disclosed."

1.3 The following information should be provided to anyone accessing a vendor's Web site:

(a) vendor identity, location and any accreditation
    (1) vendor's legal identity, business name, full street address and telephone number (sufficient to enable consumers to verify the vendor's legitimacy);
    (2) an electronic method of verifying any accreditation claims;

---

† Office of Consumer Affairs Canada Web site: <http://strategis.ic.gc.ca/SSG/ ca01185e.html>. Source of Information: Industry Canada. Reproduced with the permission of the Minister of Public Works and Government Services Canada, 2000.

(b) any geographic limitations on where a product or service is for sale;

(c) fair and accurate descriptions of products or services for sale;

(d) level of privacy protection (in accordance with Principle 3: Privacy)
    (4) "personal information" that is being collected and for what purposes;
    (5) vendor's privacy policy;

(e) security mechanisms available to consumers to protect the integrity and confidentiality of the information being exchanged;

(f) complaint procedure
    (5) how, where and by whom complaints will be handled;
    (6) any third-party dispute resolution mechanisms to which the vendor subscribes, including contact information and any cost;

(g) types of payment that will be accepted, and the implications of each in terms of any extra charges or discounts applied by the vendor.

1.4 Vendors should disclose all terms and conditions of sale to consumers prior to the conclusion of any "sales transaction." These include:

(a) the full price to the consumer, including the currency and any shipping charges, taxes, customs duties and customs broker fees and any other charges (when unsure of the amount of any potentially applicable charges, vendors must disclose to consumers the fact that such charges may apply);

(b) delivery arrangements, including timing, cost and method of delivery;

(c) any geographic limitations on where a product or service is for sale;

(d) cancellation, return and exchange policies, warranties if applicable, and any associated costs.

All the terms and conditions of sale should be available in one place.

1.5 Vendors should provide consumers with their own record of the transaction, including key details, as soon as possible after the transaction has been completed. In a sales transaction, consumers should be able to obtain their own record of the completed transaction as proof of purchase and a printable record of the terms and conditions of the contract.

1.6 Where there is a delay between the purchase and delivery of goods, or tickets for the use of a service (for example, airline or theatre tickets), vendors should provide the information set out below to consumers at the time of delivery:

(a) cancellation, return and exchange policies, warranties if applicable, and any associated costs;

(b) contact information in the event of a complaint;

(c) payment arrangements, including any vendor credit terms;

(d) applicable safety warnings and care instructions.

PRINCIPLE 2: CONTRACT FORMATION

> **Vendors should take reasonable steps to ensure that the consumer's agreement to contract is fully informed and intentional.**

2.1 Vendors should take reasonable steps to ensure that consumers are aware of their rights and obligations under the proposed contract before they agree to the contract or provide payment information.

2.2 Vendors should make clear what constitutes an offer, and what constitutes acceptance of an offer, in the context of electronic sales transactions.

(a) Vendors should employ a multistep confirmation process that requires consumers to, specifically and separately, confirm the following:

(7) their interest in buying;

(8) the full price, terms and conditions, details of the order, and method of payment;

(9) their agreement to purchase.

(b) If an appropriate multistep confirmation process, such as that set out above, is not used, vendors should allow consumers a reasonable period within which to cancel the contract.

PRINCIPLE 3: PRIVACY

Vendors and intermediaries should respect the privacy principles set out in the CSA International's *Model Code for the Protection of Personal Information.*

These 10 principles form the basis of the *Model Code for the Protection of Personal Information (CAN/CSA-Q830-96).*

1. Accountability
An organization is responsible for personal information under its control and shall designate an individual or individuals who are accountable for the organization's compliance with the following principles.

2. Identifying Purposes
The purposes for which personal information is collected shall be identified by the organization at or before the time the information is collected.

3. Consent
The knowledge and consent of the individual are required for the collection, use or disclosure of personal information, except when inappropriate.

4. Limiting Collection
The collection of personal information shall be limited to that which is necessary for the purposes identified by the organization. Information shall be collected by fair and lawful means.

5. Limiting Use, Disclosure and Retention
Personal information shall not be used or disclosed for purposes other than those for which it was collected, except with the consent of the individual or as required by law. Personal information shall be retained only as long as necessary for the fulfilment of those purposes.

6. Accuracy
Personal information shall be as accurate, complete and up-to-date as is necessary for the purposes for which it is to be used.

7. Safeguards
Personal information shall be protected by security safeguards appropriate to the sensitivity of the information.

8. Openness

An organization shall make readily available to individuals specific information about its policies and practices relating to the management of personal information.

9. Individual Access

Upon request, an individual shall be informed of the existence, use and disclosure of his or her personal information and shall be given access to that information. An individual shall be able to challenge the accuracy and completeness of the information and have it amended as appropriate.

10. Challenging Compliance

An individual shall be able to address a challenge concerning compliance with the above principles to the designated individual or individuals accountable for the organization's compliance.

PRINCIPLE 4: SECURITY OF PAYMENT AND PERSONAL INFORMATION

Vendors and intermediaries should take reasonable steps to ensure that transactions in which they are involved are secure. Consumers should act prudently when undertaking transactions.

4.1 Vendors and intermediaries should safeguard payment and personal information that is exchanged and/or stored as a result of a transaction.

4.2 Consumers should take reasonable steps to conduct transactions safely and securely.

PRINCIPLE 5: REDRESS

Consumers should have access to fair, timely, effective and affordable means for resolving problems with any transaction.

5.1 Vendors should provide adequate resources to handle consumer complaints efficiently and effectively.

5.2 When internal mechanisms have failed to resolve a dispute, vendors should make use of accessible, available, affordable and impartial third-party processes for resolving disputes with consumers. However, vendors should not require consumers to submit to such processes.

5.3 Governments, businesses and consumer groups should work together to develop appropriate standards for dispute resolution mechanisms.

5.4 So that consumers are not disadvantaged, governments should cooperate in the development of clear rules regarding the applicable law and forum, and the mutual enforcement of judgements, in the event of cross-border disputes.

PRINCIPLE 6: LIABILITY

Consumers should be protected from unreasonable liability for payments in transactions.

6.1 Consumers should not be held liable for amounts billed to them for "unauthorized transactions." Vendors should promptly refund consumer payments for unauthorized transactions or sales transactions in which consumers did not receive what they paid for.

6.2 Credit card issuers should make reasonable efforts to help consumers resolve complaints with vendors in the event of non-delivery or unauthorized transactions.

6.3 In inadvertent sales transactions in which consumers acted reasonably, the vendor should allow the consumer a reasonable period of time to cancel the transaction once the consumer has become aware of it.

6.4 When a consumer disputes a sales transaction in which the vendor failed to provide relevant information, the vendor should refund payment provided that the consumer returns the good or declines the service within a reasonable period of time.

PRINCIPLE 7: UNSOLICITED COMMERCIAL E-MAIL

Vendors should not transmit commercial E-mail without the consent of consumers, or unless a vendor has an existing relationship with a consumer.

PRINCIPLE 8: CONSUMER AWARENESS

Government, business and consumer groups should promote consumer awareness about the safe use of electronic commerce.

8.1 Consumer education and awareness initiatives should highlight those circumstances in the use of electronic commerce in which consumers are most vulnerable.

8.2 Consumers should be provided with advice on how to minimize the risks associated with electronic commerce.

8.3 Consumers should be made aware of their rights and obligations with respect to vendors.

8.4 Consumers should take reasonable steps to inform themselves about how to conduct transactions safely and securely.

8.5 Consumers should have access to information identifying disreputable electronic commerce practices.

8.6 Consumers should have access to information identifying those convicted of illegal electronic commerce practices.

GLOSSARY

The following definitions apply in *Principles of Consumer Protection for Electronic Commerce: A Canadian Framework.*

Consumer: an individual who engages in electronic commerce for personal, family or household purposes.

Electronic Commerce: the conduct of commercial activities between vendors and consumers and the solicitation of donations from consumers over open networks, including the Internet. This definition is not intended to cover communications conducted solely over the telephone.

Intermediaries: third parties facilitating a transaction, including those responsible for the storage of information.

Personal Information: information about an identifiable individual that is recorded in any form.

Prominently Disclosed (with respect to information): easily visible and quickly accessible to consumers at the appropriate time. This includes accessibility through clearly labelled hot links.

Sales Transaction: a transaction involving the buying, selling, leasing or licensing of a good or service by electronic commerce.

Transaction: an electronic commerce transaction

Unauthorized Transaction: a transaction not authorized by the consumer due to theft, fraud or vendor error.

Vendor: an organization or an individual marketing, selling, leasing or licensing a good or service or soliciting donations by electronic commerce.

Discussion Questions

1. The Canadian guidelines carry no legal weight and simply provide business with a "best practices" guide to online consumer protection. Do you think this is an effective approach? Is specific consumer protection legislation needed? Since any legislative initiative would fall under provincial jurisdiction, is the threat of differing consumer protection standards nationwide a threat to e-commerce growth?

Notes

1. The OECD released its international consumer protection guidelines soon after Canada. The principles underlying the OECD approach mirror those found in the Canadian document. They can be found online at <http://www.oecd.org/news_and_events/release/guidelinesconsumer.pdf>.

2. The U.S. Federal Trade Commission has been particularly vigilant in targeting online fraud and in developing new standards for online consumer protection. In May 2000, the agency issued comprehensive guidelines that provide marketers with a helpful roadmap to ensure that their online advertising activities fall squarely within the regulations.

    The FTC guidelines begin with the premise that all prevailing advertising regulations — unfair and deceptive practice legislation as well as solicitation restrictions — apply equally offline and online. In fact, it assures the public that regulations that contain phrases such as "in writing" are readily adaptable to the online environment. The belief that the basic principles of advertising regulations, that it be truthful, fair, and easily substantiated, remain inherent in the FTC's approach. However, it admits that the Internet environment is different from the offline one and regulations must be adapted to meet the challenges posed by hyperlinks, banner ads, audio, and video.

    Ensuring that advertising disclosures remain as equally effective on the Internet as they are offline was the most critical issue the FTC faced in this context. Offline advertisers must disclose any limitations to express and implied claims found in their advertisements to ensure that they do not mislead the public. This results in the ever-present "fine print" that typically accompanies advertisements for pharmaceutical products, motor vehicles, sale flyers and contests.

To achieve an equally effective online disclosure, the FTC highlighted several relevant requirements, including the placement and prominence of the disclosure on the Web page, its proximity to the claim and whether the disclosure is rendered ineffective by virtue of too many distractions on the Web page.

Web sites that bury their disclosures out of sight at the bottom of the page were the target of special scrutiny. Sites that discourage scrolling by leaving large sections of blank space — implying that there is nothing further on the page — will not meet the effective disclosure standard.

The use of hyperlinks was also of particular concern. The FTC recognized that disclosures may often be shuffled off to an entirely separate page, connected only by a hyperlink. Accordingly, it cautioned against separating the claim from the disclosure where it is an integral part of the claim. In other instances, it recommended using an obvious label for the link and placing the link in close proximity to the claim.

Although most Internet users have browsers that support features such as frames and Java, the use of such technologies is not yet universal. The FTC feared that consumers might miss pertinent information due to technological limitations if disclosures were encompassed within these newer technologies. It therefore advocated resisting the use of new technologies or features that have not achieved widespread marketplace penetration.

Not surprisingly, the ubiquitous banner ad, probably the most common (and some would say least effective) form of Internet advertising, did not escape the FTC's attention. The guidelines recommended inserting disclosures within banner ads where practicable. Moreover, where a transaction may be conducted within an interactive banner ad without clicking through to the sponsoring Web site, the disclosure *must* appear within the banner ad.

The FTC guidelines can be found online at <http://www.ftc.gov/bcp/conline/pubs/buspubs/dotcom/index.html>.

Consumer Protection Rights in Canada in the Context of Electronic Commerce[†]

ROGER TASSÉ AND KATHLEEN LEMIEUX

1. Legislation of Broader Application

Online purchasing is in its essence like any other purchase of goods/services. Only the means of conducting the transaction differs. Consumers transacting online should

---

[†] Office of Consumer Affairs Canada Web site: <http://strategis.ic.gc.ca/SSG/ca01031e.html>. Part Five: Options and Recommendations. Source of Information: Industry Canada. Reproduced with the permission of the Minister of Public Works and Government Services Canada, 1999.

still be and are still entitled to the same protection as provided by the laws, regulations and practices that apply to existing forms of commerce, especially those laws of general application. However, in the online world, traditional mechanisms to address imbalances in the marketplace fail to provide sufficient protection to consumers. Shortcomings of the SGA [Sale of Goods Act] and UBPA [Unauthorized Business Practices Act] legislative schemes, for example, include 1) the fact that the SGAs apply only to goods; 2) the provision in most SGAs that rights, liabilities and warranties under the SGA can be waived by agreement between the parties; 3) the possibility that other unfair practices which are directly relevant to transactions formed on the Internet are not specifically mentioned in the UBPAs.

Most provinces and the two territories have enacted consumer protection legislation to address the lacunae of this broader legislation with a view to dealing with the particularities of consumer transactions. However, due to the novelty of electronic commerce, many consumers are facing problems which were not anticipated at the time current legislation was enacted. Maintaining the existing focus on court redress mechanisms and merely modifying legislation to include electronic commerce transactions within its ambit of protection, however, may not offer the best or most practical solution.

In the case of DSA [Direct Sales Act], disparity in the protection provided under the provisions of this Act by the different provinces/territories has already been noted. Two provinces and the Yukon require face-to-face encounters between the seller and the buyer in order for the provisions to apply. Further, as mentioned before, the licensing requirements imposed on direct sellers by provincial and territorial legislation would render the application of these provisions to Internet vendors very impractical.

One significant benefit provided to buyers under the DSAs, is the "cooling off" period — the period during which a contract may be cancelled by the buyer, without cause. Under the terms of the 1994 Agreement on Internal Trade, the Provinces agreed to work toward harmonizing their direct sales legislation with respect to rescission rights. In 1996, the provinces agreed to a uniform 10-day "cooling-off" period. Some provinces/territories also provide extended "cancellation" periods in the situation where goods and services have not been supplied or delivered. A legislative update of consumer protection law might include the incorporation of similar provisions applying to online consumer transactions.

2. Consumer Protection Legislation

An overview of Canadian consumer protection legislation revealed inconsistent and unequal levels of consumer protection among the different jurisdictions.

The disparities between the jurisdictions are significant and consumers will be protected in varying degrees depending on the law governing a particular transaction. The discrepancy may be further exacerbated by the fact that courts are not required to enforce the judgments of courts in other provinces/territories.

In some cases, the title of the Act ("CPA") does not appear to adequately reflect its content. We have seen that in the case of Newfoundland and P.E.I., for example, the CPAs focus exclusively on credit transactions and do not apply to consumer transactions not involving credit. In many cases, consumers involved in non-credit or non-direct sale transactions may only effectively seek relief under the SGAs and the UBPAs. Similarly, B.C.'s CPA offers most of its protection to purchasers in the case of executory or direct sale contracts. Other consumers do not appear to have the same kind of protection and must resort to protection provided in other Acts.

On the other hand, six provinces and the two territories have included in their CPA specific provisions relating to conditions and warranties to be implied in every consumer sale transaction or to every sale of consumer products. In all cases the implied conditions specified in the CPA cannot be waived by the parties. The protection in three provinces, New Brunswick, Saskatchewan and Quebec, and of the two territories are even more extensive than that offered by the other three provinces, given their inclusion of additional implied conditions/warranties, (which also cannot be waived), and the provision of a redress mechanism within the CPA itself.

Online consumers will benefit from the current protection under the SGAs in all provinces/territories where the transaction is for a sale of goods. Online consumers can also benefit (in all provinces save New Brunswick, Nova Scotia and the territories) from UBPA-type legislation for relief against any vendor/seller for misrepresentations (of the type listed) made to the consumer; in most cases the consumer will be able to avail her/himself of redress mechanisms provided in the SGAs. In most jurisdictions online consumers will also be able to avail themselves of whatever protection is offered by the respective CPAs. Alberta has incorporated these provisions in its new Fair Trading Practices Act.

Since provincial/territorial laws only operate within the limits of the enacting jurisdiction (except where conflict of laws rules permit otherwise) the difficulty of enforcing applicable remedies may ultimately leave the consumer empty handed and dissatisfied.

Common Issues

Finally, while the common issues raised in Part III are of particular significance in the context of electronic commerce in general, these issues should perhaps, be addressed in a broader commercial context, accommodating both consumer-to-business transactions as well as business-to-business transactions. We refer in particular to issues relating to the definition of "writing", the desirability of defining 'signature', general issues of contract formation (what constitutes an offer, when and where a contract is formed, the issue of acceptance, etc.)

Most of the common issues will need to be addressed in the broader context of online commercial transactions to account for business transactions as well as consumer transactions.

II. IMPORTANT ISSUES IN ONLINE TRANSACTIONS

This part attempts to gather and redefine the questions raised in the second half of the previous part.

1. Contract Formation
2. Formal Requirements
3. Jurisdiction
4. Contents of the Contract
5. Misrepresentations
6. Conditions and warranties
7. Interpretation Rules
8. "Cooling off" Period
9. Delivery
10. Redress Mechanisms

This part proposes to discuss each of these issues and their importance in online consumer transactions. We will also canvass various options that might be considered to ensure that consumers using the Internet to purchase goods and/or services are adequately protected. As will be seen from our analysis, there are issues which might best be addressed through effecting changes in the law, while others might preferably be left to the private sector to address, through, for example, the development of codes of conduct or "best online practices".

1.   Contract Formation

Contract formation issues are likely to arise every time a consumer purchases goods/services online. Consumers may question whether a particular advertisement on a vendor's home page constitutes an offer or an invitation to treat; whether the consumer is the offeror or the offeree; when an offer is deemed to have been accepted; whether the acceptance of an offer will be confirmed or whether the transaction itself will be confirmed.

These questions are not specifically addressed in the legislation and courts are likely to rely on general common law and civil law principles to resolve them. Since an offer stems from a statement or conduct by a person indicating a willingness to enter into a contract on certain terms with another person, one could assume that the vendor is the offeror, offering goods and/or services for sale at a certain price. The consumer would thus be the offeree, accepting to purchase the goods/services under the terms dictated by the vendor. In the case of all online transactions, the contract will be executory in nature, in the sense that the terms of the contract are dictated by one party, the vendor, and the goods/services will be delivered once payment has been effected. Online contracts are also a form of distance selling. Some Canadian jurisdictions have recognized the potential for abuse of consumers where contracts are executory and formed at a distance.

There are also specific issues with respect to acceptance. A contract will be deemed to have been accepted when the offeree signifies that s/he wishes to form a contract on the terms stipulated in the offer. The statements or conduct constituting acceptance are not always obvious when transacting on the Internet. Should amendments be made to legislation to oblige online vendors to indicate within the contract what will constitute acceptance? This indication might then be recognisable by the consumer as an act of purchase.

Perhaps the best way to encourage vendors to resort to this kind of practice would be to develop a model acceptance or transaction confirmation scheme as part of an industry code of conduct, whereby adherents to the code would agree to use such a process.

Contract Formation

Contract formation issues should generally be left to the determination by the courts;

Consideration should be given to the enactment of legislative provisions requiring vendors to specifically indicate what would constitute an acceptance on the part of a purchaser in online transactions;

A model acceptance scheme and/or a model transaction confirmation scheme should be developed as a complement to the legislative provisions referred to above, to guide the private sector;

2. Formal Requirements

While a written contract is not required in the case of all "consumer transactions", executory contracts, direct sales contracts and credit contracts are generally required by law to be in writing and signed by the consumer and/or the vendor. Since most online transactions are credit transactions and are executory in nature, many of these contracts may be in violation of the formal requirements of current legislation. Does such a contract when formed online, constitute a contract "in writing" and under what conditions will it be deemed to have been effectively "signed" by the consumer? Will a computer printout serve as a legally acceptable duplicate original copy of the contract? Current definitions of "writing" in the Interpretation Act of each province and territory might be broad enough to include online contracts. If they are not, are online contracts invalid?

The purpose of requiring that a contract be in writing and that the consumer be provided with a copy of the contract is to ensure that the consumer has a discernable record of the transaction. It is arguable that "fully integrating data into a broad database loses that capacity". Quebec has already recognized this evidentiary question and has incorporated in its Civil Code provisions dealing with computerized records. Documents reproducing a juridical act which was entered on a computer system make proof of the content of the act if it is intelligible and if its reliability is sufficiently guaranteed.

These issues go beyond the narrower situation of the online consumer transaction. While provincial governments have already taken steps to address evidentiary issues with respect to electronic documents, laws will generally have to be updated to be consistent and conducive to the realities of electronic commerce.

Formal Requirements

Consideration should be given to enacting a legislative provision which would define the conditions under which an electronic contract constitutes a contract or document "in writing"; similarly, a definition of what constitutes a "signature" might also be considered.

3. Jurisdiction Issues

The Quebec Civil Code and its CPA addresses the "jurisdiction" issue by expressly adopting the "instantaneous communications" rule for all contracts, regardless of the method of communication used by the parties. According to this rule, all contracts are deemed to have been formed when and where acceptance was received by the offeror.

Assuming the vendor is the offeror, the contract is deemed to have been formed in the jurisdiction of the offeror at the time s/he receives the consumer's acceptance. In the case of contracts formed at a distance, however, the CPA modifies the general principles and the distance sales contract, which may include an online contract in certain circumstances (provided it is not solicited by a consumer), is deemed to be entered into at the address of the consumer.

As a result, under this rule, the contract will, in the context of a consumer transaction, be formed when the vendor receives the consumer's acceptance and the contract will be subject to the jurisdiction of the province/territory in which the consumer resides. The protection afforded by this provision may, in some cases, be illusive, as the consumer residing in Quebec may be transacting with a vendor in Europe or Asia. While the consumer may, in that case, bring an action against the foreign vendor in Quebec, the value of a judgment against the vendor is likely to be limited if the vendor does not have assets in Quebec.

Common law jurisdictions have not set out jurisdiction rules as clearly and there is some debate as to whether online transactions should fall under the "instantaneous communication" rule, and be deemed to be formed at the place and time where the acceptance is received, or under the "mail box" rule, according to which the contract is formed when the acceptance is expedited or mailed by the consumer.

Since online transactions are occurring at increasingly greater speeds, it is likely that the "instantaneous communications" rule will apply and online contracts will be deemed to have been formed when and where the acceptance is received, namely, at the address of the vendor.

None of the common law jurisdictions, save for Saskatchewan and Alberta, in its newly enacted Fair Trading Practices Act, provide an exception in the case of consumer contracts.

Accordingly, consumers residing in the common law provinces and territories may often be subject to the laws of the jurisdiction of the vendor, unless the courts determine otherwise. Even if the consumer had a better chance of obtaining and enforcing a judgment against a vendor under the laws of the vendor's jurisdiction, commencing an action in the foreign vendor's jurisdiction may not appeal to the consumer who would have to incur travel expenses and the cost of "foreign" legal advice to defend his/her rights.

Jurisdiction issues in the context of online transactions present one of the greatest challenges to the current system's way of addressing disputes which involves two or more provinces, territories or countries. As mentioned in the Report on New Approaches to Consumer Law in Canada, "beyond the best intentions and good will, there is no formal way for a province whose citizens are allegedly victims of cross-border scams to receive assistance from a second province where alleged perpetrators are located and where the alleged fraudulent conduct is taking place".

Amendments or additions to legislative schemes already in place may be helpful to address these issues more effectively. It may be preferable to address these questions in a private sector code of conduct or best online practices pursuant to which consumers would refer to an appointed ombudsperson for the resolution of their complaints. Such a code of practices might also include an informal complaint mechanism which in turn, would address situations where vendors and consumers are in different jurisdictions.

Jurisdiction Issues

Consideration should be given to a legislative provision to the effect that online contracts entered into by consumers are deemed to have been entered into at the address of the consumer;

The private sector should be encouraged to develop best practices in dealing with complaints by online consumers; specifically, guidelines might be established for the informal review and efficient resolution of consumer complaints; vendors would be encouraged to provide information on complaint handling services prior to the formation of the contract.

4. Contents of the Contract

Specific content and disclosure requirements are now mandatory in direct sales contracts and credit transactions in most jurisdictions. Required information includes the name and address of the seller and/or salesperson, description of the goods/services, price and terms of payment, etc. Most other transactions do not have similar requirements. Consumers are particularly vulnerable when transacting online since in many instances, the only information available to the consumer is the vendor's home page address (URL). The consumer may not know who s/he is dealing with or where the company is located.

Consumers should at the very least be able to clearly identify the vendor and the location of the business they are transacting with. Other relevant information includes a clear statement of the terms of the contract, details on the products/services provided and information on available methods of payment.

Consumers should be provided with all relevant information pertaining to the transaction. The vendor might, for example, be required to provide information on the following:

1. the vendor's identity and place of business (including full address and contact name);
2. the duration of the offer;
3. date and place the contract is concluded;
4. a complete description of the goods and services offered;
5. since the transaction consists of a sale by description, there should be an implied condition that the goods are of merchantable quality;
6. the total price of the goods including GST, PST, shipping and handling charges and terms of payment; if additional taxes or duties are to be levied, they should be brought to the consumer's attention;
7. a statement of warranties applying to the goods/services;
8. the currency and the exchange rate should also be clearly stated;
9. as many online transactions are paid for via credit cards, the disclosure requirements set out in current legislation should also appear in online contracts;
10. if a cooling-off period is legislated, information about an appropriate cancellation notice should be provided;
11. a date for the delivery of the goods or the performance of the services should be indicated;
12. information pertaining to the possibility of refunds or exchange and the procedure for doing so;
13. information pertaining to possible complaints and the name, telephone number and address of the person to be contacted;
14. information about any informal redress mechanisms adopted by the vendor in case of disputes.

It is for consideration whether a legislative provision should be adopted making some of this information legally mandatory with no possibility of waiver by either party. A contract formed in violation of these requirements would be deemed to be void or voidable.

There could also be a strengthening of the requirements pertaining to sales by description. Under the SGA, there is an implied condition that goods purchased through a sale by description are of merchantable quality. While this condition cannot be waived, the parties can agree that the sale is not a sale by description. In the case of online transactions, it would appear that all sales are sales by description since they are contracts formed at a distance.

A legislative amendment might include a provision whereby parties cannot provide that an online transaction is not a sale by description; there might also be a provision, as there is in many provinces/territories, that goods and services purchased online will correspond to the description made of them.

A non-legislative option may be to include, as part of a code of conduct or best practices, guidelines on the information to be made available to consumers on the vendor's business, the terms of the contract and payment methods. Specific industry guidelines (sector by sector) would mandate the information to be provided on products and services offered for sale. Vendor Associations organized along industry lines might place a "stamp" or "seal of approval" on a member's Web page certifying that the vendor subscribes to the practices established by the association in question and has provided information on its business which is readily accessible by the consumer. The consumer could then access this information by clicking on the seal etc. The Association would reserve the right to remove the seal if the vendor did not comply with disclosure standards.

Contents of Contract

Consideration should be given to a legislative amendment setting out what minimal information vendors should be required to provide consumers prior to the formation of the online transaction;

The private sector should be encouraged to develop sector-by-sector guidelines on information to be provided to consumers on the vendor's business, the terms of the contract, the goods and services sold, payment methods and informal redress mechanisms;

5.   Misrepresentations

All provinces except Nova Scotia, New Brunswick and the territories currently have legislation governing unfair business practices.

Online consumers can already avail themselves of the provisions set out in legislation governing unfair business practices. Examples of unfair practices which might arise in the context of electronic transactions and which are already part of current legislation include:

1. misrepresenting the price or charging a price that is grossly above that being offered for similar products;
2. entering into a transaction in which the consumer is not likely to either receive the goods/services or receive any substantial benefit from the subject matter of the transaction;
3. entering into a transaction which stipulates such harsh and adverse terms as to be inequitable to the consumer;
4. representations that the goods or services have special advantages that they do not have;
5. using misleading or deceptive advertisement;
6. holding out that goods have particular characteristics in appearance, quality or performance which they do not;
7. representing that goods are new or reconditioned when they are not.

Practices which are not currently covered by the UBPAs might include misrepresentations as to the identity or address of the vendor, misrepresentations as to the currency and exchange rates; misrepresentations as to refund policies, misrepresentations as to the time for delivery of goods, etc. In all provinces which have enacted UBPAs or similar provisions, the Lieutenant Governor in Council or the Minister has some authority to make regulations. In the case of Ontario, British Columbia, Alberta (in its new Fair Trading Practices Act) and P.E.I., the Minister or Lieutenant Governor in Council may prescribe or specify practices which are unfair or deceptive. In the case of Manitoba, Saskatchewan and Newfoundland, the Lieutenant Governor in Council may make regulations respecting other matters necessary for carrying out the purpose and intent of the Act or to give effect to the purpose of the Act. Given the fairly broad wording of the UBPAs, this power to make regulations may or may not include the specification of additional unfair practices to which the UBPA would apply. As consumer involvement in the electronic environment increases and more exchanges between consumers and vendors occur online, unfair practices which are particular to the online environment and to a specific industry are likely to become more apparent. Consideration should be given to updating or clarifying current UBPAs to ensure that new unfair practices are included.

Under current legislative schemes where a vendor is suspected of deceptive practices the Director of Trade Practices has powers of investigation and in some provinces has the power to order the cessation of an unfair practice without the requirement of court approval. Saskatchewan is the only province which makes a mediation attempt mandatory. A similar provision might be considered in all jurisdictions.

Misrepresentation

The list of unfair practices covered in provincial legislation should be updated to address new practices adopted by online vendors and to secure online consumer protection; as part of a code of conduct or best practices, private sector vendors should be encouraged to develop industry norms for appropriate behaviour in offering consumer transactions online;

It is for consideration whether mediation should be made mandatory in case of unfair practices;

6. Conditions and Warranties

SGAs provide for basic conditions or warranties to be implied in every contract for the sale of goods. These include 1) condition as to title; 2) warranty as to freedom from encumbrance; 3) warranty as to quiet possession. Some provincial and territorial CPAs have added further warranties in addition to the SGA conditions/warranties which are to be implied in every consumer transaction or to every consumer sale. They include, for example:

(a) a warranty that goods purchased by description will correspond with the description;
(b) a condition that the goods are of merchantable quality except for any described defects;
(c) a condition that the goods are new and unused unless otherwise described;
(d) a condition that the goods will be durable for a reasonable period of time;
(e) a warranty that services will be performed in a skilful and workmanlike manner;
(f) that the product is of such quality, state or condition as to be fit for the purpose for which products of that kind are normally used;
(g) a warranty as to quality (i.e., latent defects).

Consideration should be given to streamlining the conditions or warranties to be implied in a consumer transaction occurring online. In some provinces/territories, the conditions and/or warranties are to be applied to consumer sales of goods; in other provinces, the conditions and/or warranties are to be applied to sales of consumer products and/or services.

As a large number of electronic transactions involve the sale of services, it is for consideration whether current legislation should be amended to harmonize protection across Canada and create greater consistency in levels of protection by having the same conditions and warranties implied in contracts for the sale of both goods and services. It has been noted that some provinces do not have additional warranties/ conditions within their CPA legislation (P.E.I., Alberta and B.C.). Ontario includes only minimal conditions/warranties (those applying to sales of goods under the SGA). Amendments might be considered to provide for similar conditions/warranties to be implied in every consumer transaction.

Warranties and Conditions
Conditions and warranties to be implied in online consumer transactions should be streamlined and should apply to both goods and services;

7. Interpretation of the Contract

Rules of interpretation in common law jurisdictions are fairly general and broad in scope. While few provinces/territories (Alberta is the only common law province to have recently done so in its Fair Trading Practices Act) have enacted specific rules for the interpretation of consumer contracts, the common law rule in cases where a contract is ambiguous and open to more than one meaning is that the meaning which is least favourable to the party that drafted the document governs. Quebec has specific legislative provisions which gives the consumer the benefit of the more advantageous interpretation in certain situations. The consumer is protected where there is doubt or where clauses in a consumer contract are external, ambiguous, illegible, incomprehensible or abusive. Consideration should be given to a legislative provision, perhaps similar to that recently enacted in Alberta, protecting the consumer against external, ambiguous, illegible, incomprehensible or abusive clauses.

Interpretation
A legislative provision should be considered to protect consumers against external, ambiguous, illegible, incomprehensible or abusive clauses.

8. "Cooling-Off" Period

Currently, only the legislative schemes pertaining to direct sales give the consumer/ purchaser the option to cancel a direct sales contract for any reason within a period of time referred to as the "cooling-off" period. Pursuant to harmonization efforts by the provinces/territories, it is expected that a ten-day period will soon be uniformly implemented. Most provinces/territories also provide for cancellation if the goods/services are not supplied within a certain period of time and provided that the purchaser does not accept them when they are delivered. There is no similar provision for non-direct sales contracts.

As consumers purchasing online are expected to purchase immediately, they will not, in most cases, have an opportunity to carefully consider the offer before purchasing the good or service in question. Online consumers should be provided with a reasonable period of time to cancel the contract without cause. The European Commission's Directive on Distance Selling recommends a period of at least seven working days during which the consumer can withdraw from the contract without penalty and without giving any reason(s). The only charge to be born by the consumer would be the cost of returning the goods.

Also for consideration is the enactment in conjunction with a cooling off period, of a provision similar to s. 22 of Quebec's CPA which states that "no merchant may, when soliciting a consumer for the purpose of making a remote-parties contract or when making such a contract, demand total or partial payment by the consumer or propose to collect such payment before performing his principal obligation", namely the delivery of goods. Alternatively, jurisdictions may consider enacting provisions ensuring that if the price of the goods/services are fully or partly covered by credit, the credit agreement can be cancelled without penalty, if the consumer exercises his/her right to cancel the contract.

Cooling-Off

Consideration should be given to the enactment of "cooling-off" periods for online consumer transactions; similarly, if within the "cooling-off" period, the consumer exercises his/her right to cancel the contract, s/he may also cancel, without penalty, any accompanying credit arrangement;

9. Delivery of Goods/Services

Under SGAs, the payment of the price stipulated in the contract and the delivery of the goods must be concurrent conditions unless agreed to otherwise by the parties. If no time for delivery is specified in a contract, the goods must be delivered within a reasonable time. What is 'reasonable' is a question of fact and under the SGAs, stipulations as to time will be treated as warranties. Accordingly, a breach of a stipulation as to time will be determined on a case by case basis and will provide a consumer with the remedies generally available for breach of warranty. In such cases, the purchaser is generally not entitled to reject the goods and treat the contract as repudiated.

A recent OECD report has recognized the physical delivery infrastructure in online transactions as one of the "weakest links in any consumer-oriented Electronic Commerce system involving tangible goods": consumers have no assurance that they will receive the products they have purchased electronically.

Amendments to the legislation may not provide an adequate or satisfactory answer to the question of delivery or prompt delivery of goods or services purchased online.

Codes of conduct along industry lines might offer a more practical approach. They might include a provision stipulating that information pertaining to delivery, including the anticipated delay for the delivery of goods or the supply of services, must be provided in every online consumer transaction prior to its conclusion.

Delivery of Goods and Services

Consideration should be given to a legislative amendment or the development by the private sector of codes of conduct or best practices requiring the provision of information on delivery arrangements, including anticipated delays (or a time limit for the performance of the contract) to consumers in online transactions;

10. Redress Mechanisms

Current legislation provides a number of options for consumers who seek redress: they include rescission/cancellation, damages (both general and punitive), specific performance, and injunction depending on the circumstances. While these measures are available to the consumer transacting online, the difficulty or impracticality of enforcing court redress mechanisms significantly limits, in most instances, the value of any of these remedies.

In other words, legal remedies in the context of online transactions are not the most effective means of redress because of the nature of distance selling, and jurisdiction problems.

An option might include the development of codes of conduct or best practices encouraging vendors to provide informal complaint handling services, including the provision of information on the manner in which complaints will be handled. The Australian Report on "Consumer Protection in Electronic Commerce — Draft Principles and Key issues" recommends that vendors commit themselves to effective complaints handling services. Pursuant to the recommendations of this report, vendors would:

1. demonstrate commitment to handling complaints;
2. provide adequate resources for handling customer complaints;
3. publicise online the existence of their customer complaints services;
4. ensure no costs or charges are levied for the handling of a complaint;
5. handle complaints fairly;
6. deal with complaints quickly and thoroughly;
7. deal with complaints in a manner which would assist any further examination which may be necessary such as referral to a dispute resolution mechanism; and
8. promptly inform the complainant of the outcome.

A system incorporating such guidelines might empower an ombudsperson, some other provincial authority or an impartial industry-specific authority to hear and resolve consumer complaints. Under such non-legal arrangements, mediation or arbitration would be encouraged and costly legal battles avoided.

Redress Mechanisms

Consideration should be given to the development by the private sector of codes of conduct of best practices encouraging vendors to provide complaint resolution services, including the appointment of an ombudsperson; vendors would be encouraged to provide prior to the formation of the contract, any information as to how potential complaints will be addressed and handled by the vendor;

Although guidelines are important, Internet fraud constitutes criminal activity and must addressed as such. The U.S. Federal Trade Commission has been particularly active on the Internet fraud prosecution front. The following brief provides a good illustration of the agency's approach.

Federal Trade Commission v. Hare[†]

COMPLAINT FOR INJUNCTION AND OTHER EQUITABLE RELIEF
Plaintiff, the Federal Trade Commission ("FTC" or "the Commission"), for its complaint alleges:

---

† (S.D. Fla. 1999)

The FTC brings this action under Sections 13(b) and 19 of the Federal Trade Commission Act ("FTC Act"), 15 U.S.C. §§53(b) and 57b, to secure preliminary and permanent injunctive relief, rescission of contracts, restitution, disgorgement, and other equitable relief for defendant's violations of Section 5(a) of the FTC Act, 15 U.S.C. §45(a), and the FTC's "Mail or Telephone Order Merchandise Rule" (the "Rule"), 16 C.F.R. Part 435.

. . . .

Plaintiff

Plaintiff, FTC, is an independent agency of the United States Government created by statute. 15 U.S.C. §§41 *et seq.* The FTC is charged, *inter alia*, with enforcement of Section 5(a) of the FTC Act, 15 U.S.C. §45(a), which prohibits unfair or deceptive acts or practices in or affecting commerce, as well as enforcement of the Mail or Telephone Order Merchandise Rule, 16 C.F.R. Part 435. The FTC is authorized to initiate federal district court proceedings to enjoin violations of the FTC Act in order to secure such equitable relief as may be appropriate in each case, and to obtain consumer redress. 15 U.S.C. §§53(b) and 57b.

Defendants

Defendant CRAIG LEE HARE, a/k/a DANNY HARE ("Hare"), an individual, does business as EXPERIENCED DESIGNED COMPUTERS ("EDC") and C&H COMPUTER SERVICES ("C&H"). EDC and C&H are unincorporated entities. Hare conducts business from his residence located at 64 Plantation Boulevard, Lake Worth, Florida 33467. Defendant Hare offers computers and computer hard drives for sale on the Internet at "auction house" web sites. At all times material to this complaint, acting alone or in concert with others, defendant Hare has formulated, directed, controlled or participated in the deceptive acts and practices set forth in this complaint. Hare transacts or has transacted business in the Southern District of Florida.

. . . .

Commerce

At all times material to this complaint, defendant has maintained a substantial course of trade in or affecting commerce, as "commerce" is defined in Section 4 of the FTC Act, 15 U.S.C. §44.

Defendant's Business Activities

Since at least January 1998, defendant Hare has offered computers and computer hard drives for sale on the Internet at auction house web sites.

An Internet auction house is an online forum that facilitates communications between would-be buyers and sellers of goods and services. Sellers use the auction house's web site to advertise the goods and services they seek to sell. Auctions are conducted on the auction house's web site with would-be buyers sending bids through electronic mail to the web site. At the conclusion of the auction, buyers and sellers typically communicate with each other via electronic mail about the terms of payment and delivery and then complete their commercial transactions through the U.S. mail system.

Defendant Hare places advertisements offering computers and computer hard drives on the web sites of Internet auction houses. Among other things, defendant states in advertisements that he is marketing Micron 266 MHZ Pentium II computers with monitors which are "Brand New in their Original Boxes [and] come standard with a 3 year warranty from Micron" or "Toshiba Satellite Pro 410 CDT" computers which are "Refurbished, and Carry a (1) year Warranty from *Toshiba*." Defendant also states in advertisements that he is marketing computer hard drives that are "brand new" and for which the manufacturer provides a "3 Year Warranty."

Consumers have placed bids for defendant Hare's merchandise which Hare has accepted. Hare has further accepted payment from those consumers who have "successfully" bid for the computer goods he offered for sale on the Internet at auction house web sites. In a number of instances, Hare has failed to provide either the promised merchandise of computers or computer hard drives, or a refund to those consumers whose bids he has accepted and from whom he has received payment.

VIOLATIONS OF SECTION 5 OF THE FTC ACT

Count I

In the course of offering computers and computer hard drives for sale via Internet auction houses, defendant has represented, expressly or by implication, that the consumers who offer the highest bids and send defendant the agreed-on payment for the computers or computer hard drives pursuant to those bids, will receive the promised computers or computer hard drives.

In truth and in fact, in a number of instances, the consumers who offer the highest bids and send defendant the agreed-on payment for the computers or computer hard drives, pursuant to those bids, have not received the promised computers or computer hard drives.

Therefore, defendant's representations set forth in Paragraph 12 are false and misleading and constitute deceptive acts or practices in violation of Section 5(a) of the FTC Act, 15 U.S.C. §45(a).

THE MAIL OR TELEPHONE ORDER MERCHANDISE RULE

The FTC promulgated the Mail or Telephone Order Merchandise Rule, 16 C.F.R. Part 435, on October 22, 1975, and revised the Rule on September 21, 1993. The revised Rule became effective on March 1, 1994, and has remained in full force and effect since that time.

The Rule applies to sales in which the buyer has ordered merchandise from the seller by mail or directly or indirectly by telephone, such as by fax machines and computers. 16 C.F.R. §§435.1 and 435.2 (a) and (b).

The Rule prohibits a seller from soliciting any order for the sale of merchandise to be ordered by the buyer through the mail or telephone, unless, at the time of the solicitation, the seller has a reasonable basis to expect that it will be able to ship any ordered merchandise to the buyer within the time stated on the solicitation, or, if no time is stated, within thirty days of the completion of the order. 16 C.F.R. §435.1(a)(1).

The Rule requires that the seller follow certain procedures if merchandise ordered through the mail or by telephone will not be shipped within the applicable time limit. Specifically, the Rule requires that, when there is a shipping delay, the seller must, prior to the expiration of the applicable time, offer the buyer an option either to agree to the delay or to cancel the order and receive a prompt refund (as defined in 16 C.F.R. §435.2(f)).

The Rule also requires that a seller deem an order canceled and make a prompt refund to the buyer whenever the seller has failed to ship within the specified time period and has failed to offer the consumer the option to consent to further delay or to cancel the order.

Pursuant to Section 18(d)(3) of the FTC Act, 15 U.S.C. §57a(d)(3), and 16 C.F.R. §435.1, violations of the Rule constitute unfair or deceptive acts or practices in or affecting commerce, in violation of Section 5(a) of the FTC Act, 15 U.S.C. §45(a).

. . . .

PRAYER FOR RELIEF
WHEREFORE, plaintiff requests that this Court, as authorized by Sections 13(b) and 19 of the FTC Act, 15 U.S.C. §§53(b) and 57b, and pursuant to its own equitable powers:

1. Award plaintiff such temporary and preliminary injunctive and ancillary relief as may be necessary to avert the likelihood of consumer injury during the pendency of this action and to preserve the possibility of effective final relief, including, but not limited to, temporary and preliminary injunctions and an order freezing defendant's assets;
2. Permanently enjoin defendant from violating the FTC Act and the Mail or Telephone Order Merchandise Rule as alleged herein;
3. Award such relief as the Court finds necessary to redress injury to consumers resulting from defendant's violations of the FTC Act and the Mail or Telephone Order Merchandise Rule, including but not limited to, rescission of contracts, the refund of monies paid, and the disgorgement of ill-gotten monies;
4. Award such relief against relief defendant Herter as the Court finds necessary to protect and return funds and other property that were derived from defendant Hare's violations of Section 5 of the FTC Act and of the Mail or Telephone Order Merchandise Rule, including an asset freeze and an order to disgorge ill-gotten gains or proceeds that relief defendant Herter has received and that relate to the acts and practices complained of herein, and an order imposing a constructive trust on such gains or proceeds; and
5. Award plaintiff the costs of bringing this action, as well as such other and additional relief as the Court may determine to be just and proper.

The Canadian Criminal Code also has provision for this form of fraud.

Canada Criminal Code[†]

(1) Every one who, by deceit, falsehood or other fraudulent means, whether or not it is a false pretense within the meaning of this Act, defrauds the public or any per-

---

† R.S., c. C-34, s. 380.

son, whether ascertained or not, of any property, money or valuable security or any service,

(a) is guilty of an indictable offence and liable to a term of imprisonment not exceeding ten years, where the subject-matter of the offence is a testamentary instrument or the value of the subject-matter of the offence exceeds five thousand dollars; or

(b) is guilty of an indictable offence and liable to imprisonment for a term not exceeding two years, or

(c) of an offence punishable on summary conviction,

where the value of the subject-matter of the offence does not exceed five thousand dollars.

(2) Every one who, by deceit, falsehood or other fraudulent means, whether or not it is a false pretence within the meaning of this Act, with intent to defraud, affects the public market price of stocks, shares, merchandise or anything that is offered for sale to the public is guilty of an indictable offence and liable to imprisonment for a term not exceeding ten years.

In addition to active prosecution of Internet fraud, several jurisdictions worldwide have taken affirmative steps to enact new regulations designed to provide consumers with increased protections in the electronic commerce environment. These initiatives are relatively new and untested but are likely to generate considerable controversy as governments attempt to establish an effective balance between the rights of consumers and those of businesses.

Alberta Fair Trading Act[†]

Marketing through Electronic Media

Regulations

(1) The Minister may make regulations respecting the marketing of goods and services through forms of electronic media, such as telephone, television or the Internet, that are specified in the regulations.

(2) Without limiting subsection (1), the Minister may make regulations

(a) specifying the forms of electronic media and the types of marketing to which the regulation applies;

(b) regulating and prohibiting specified activities involved in marketing of goods and services through electronic media;

(c) setting out the rights and remedies of consumers who enter into consumer transactions wholly or partly through a form of electronic media.

---

† S.A. 1998, F-1.05, s. 42.

California Business and Professions Code[†]

(a) It is unlawful in the sale or lease or offering for sale or lease of goods or services, for any person conducting sales or leases by telephone, Internet or other electronic means of communication, mail order, or catalog in this state, including, but not limited to, the offering for sale or lease on television, radio, Internet, or other electronic means of communication or telecommunications device of goods or services which may be ordered by mail, telephone, internet, or other electronic means of communication or telecommunications device, or for any person advertising in connection with those sales, leases, or advertisements a mailing address, telephone number, or Internet or other electronic address, to accept payment from or for a buyer, for the purchase or lease of goods or services ordered by mail, telephone, Internet, or other electronic means of communication or telecommunications device, whether payment to the vendor is made directly, through the mails, by means of a transfer of funds from an account of the buyer or any other person, or by any other means, and then permit 30 days, unless otherwise conspicuously stated in the offering or advertisement, or unless a shorter time is clearly communicated by the person conducting the sale or lease, to elapse without doing any one of the following things:

(1) Shipping, mailing, or providing the goods or services ordered.

(2) Mailing a full refund or, if payment was made by means of a transfer from an account, (A) crediting the account in the full amount of the debit, or (B) if a third party is the creditor, issuing a credit memorandum to the third party who shall promptly credit the account in the full amount of the debit.

(3) Sending the buyer a letter or other written notice (A) advising the buyer of the duration of an expected delay expressed as a specific number of days or weeks, or proposing the substitution of goods or services of equivalent or superior quality, and (B) offering to make a full refund, in accordance with paragraph (2), within one week if the buyer so requests. The vendor shall provide to the buyer in that letter or written notice a toll-free telephone number or other cost-free method to communicate the buyer's request for a full refund. If the vendor proposes to substitute goods or services, the vendor shall describe the substitute goods or services in detail, indicating fully how the substitute differs from the goods or services ordered.

(4)(A) Shipping, mailing, or providing substitute goods or services of equivalent or superior quality, if the buyer is extended the opportunity to return the substitute goods or services and the vendor promises to refund to the buyer (i) the cost of returning the substitute goods or services and (ii) any portion of the purchase price previously paid by the buyer.

(B) Except as provided in subparagraph (C), a notice to the buyer shall accompany the mailing, shipping, or providing of the substitute goods or services which informs the buyer of the substitution; describes fully how the substitute differs from the goods or services ordered, except that obvious nontechnical differences, such as color, need not be described; and discloses the buyer's right to reject the substitute goods or services and obtain a full refund of the amount paid, plus the cost of returning the substitute goods or services.

---

† §17538.

(C) The vendor may omit from the notice required by subparagraph (B) a description of how the substitute goods or services differ from the ordered goods or services if the notice otherwise complies with subparagraph (B), and if all the following requirements are complied with:

(i) The vendor maintains at least 100 retail outlets located in at least 20 counties in this state that are open to the public regularly during normal business hours where buyers can order catalog goods, pick them up, and return them for refunds.

(ii) The vendor maintains a toll-free telephone number and provides to each buyer, at the time of the buyer's call, a full description of how substitute goods or services differ from ordered goods or services. The toll-free telephone number shall operate and be staffed at all times during which goods or services normally are available for pick up from the vendor's retail outlets.

(iii) If the buyer picks up substitute goods or services from the vendor's retail outlet, the notice required by subparagraph (B) as modified by this subparagraph is placed on, or attached to, the exterior of the package or wrapping containing the substitute, or is handed to the buyer at the time the buyer picks up the substitute.

(iv) The notice contains a reference number or some other means of identifying the ordered goods or services and the substitute goods or services.

(v) The notice contains the vendor's toll-free telephone number and instructions to the buyer that the buyer may call that number to obtain a full description of how the substitute differs from the ordered goods.

.   .   .   .

(d) A vendor conducting business through the Internet or any other electronic means of communication shall do all of the following when the transaction involves a buyer located in California:

(1) Before accepting any payment or processing any debit or credit charge or funds transfer, the vendor shall disclose to the buyer in writing or by electronic means of communication, such as E-mail or an on-screen notice, the vendor's return and refund policy, the legal name under which the business is conducted and, except as provided in paragraph (3), the complete street address from which the business is actually conducted.

(2) If the disclosure of the vendor's legal name and address information required by this subdivision is made by on-screen notice, all of the following shall apply:

(A) The disclosure of the legal name and address information shall appear on any of the following: (i) the first screen displayed when the vendor's electronic site is accessed, (ii) on the screen on which goods or services are first offered, (iii) on the screen on which a buyer may place the order for goods or services or (iv) on the screen on which the buyer may enter payment information, such as a credit card account number. The communication of that disclosure shall not be structured to be smaller or less legible than the text of the offer of the goods or services.

(B) The disclosure of the legal name and address information shall be accompanied by an adjacent statement describing how the buyer may receive the information at the buyer's E-mail address. The vendor shall provide the disclosure information to the buyer at the buyer's E-mail address within five days of receiving the buyer's request.

(C) Until the vendor complies with subdivision (a) in connection with all buyers of the vendor's goods or services, the vendor shall make available to a buyer and any person or entity who may enforce this section pursuant to Section 17535 on-screen access to the information required to be disclosed under this subdivision.

(3) The complete street address need not be disclosed as required by paragraph (1) if the vendor utilizes a private mailbox receiving service and all of the following conditions are met:

(A) the vendor satisfies the conditions described in paragraph (2) of subdivision (b) of Section 17538.5, (B) the vendor discloses the actual street address of the private mailbox receiving service in the manner prescribed by this subdivision for the disclosure of the vendor's actual street address, and (C) the vendor and the private mailbox receiving service comply with all of the requirements of subdivisions (c) to (f), inclusive, of Section 17538.5.

(e) As used in this section and Section 17538.3, the following words have the following meanings:

(1) "Goods" means tangible chattels, including certificates or coupons exchangeable for those goods, and including goods which, at the time of the sale or subsequently, are to be so affixed to real property as to become a part of that real property, whether or not severable therefrom.

(2) "Person" means an individual, partnership, corporation, association, or other group, however organized.

(3) "Buyer" means a person who seeks or acquires, by purchase or lease, any goods or services for any purpose.

(4) "Services" means work, labor, and services, including services furnished in connection with the sale or repair of goods.

(5) "Vendor" means a person who, as described in subdivision (a), vends, sells, leases, supplies, or ships goods or services, who conducts sales or leases of goods or services, or who offers goods or services for sale or lease. "Vendor" does not include a person responding to an electronic agent in connection with providing goods or services to a buyer if the aggregate amount of all transactions with the buyer does not exceed ten dollars ($10).

(6) "Internet" means the global information system that is logically linked together by a globally unique address space based on the Internet Protocol (IP), or its subsequent extensions; and is able to support communications using the Transmission Control Protocol/Internet Protocol (TCP/IP) suite, or its subsequent extensions, or other IP-compatible protocols; and provides, uses, or makes accessible, either publicly or privately, high level services layered on the communications and related infrastructure described herein.

(7) "Electronic agent" means a computer program designed, selected, or programmed to initiate or respond to electronic messages or performances without review by an individual.

(f) Any violation of the provisions of this section is a misdemeanor punishable by imprisonment in the county jail not exceeding six months, or by a fine not exceeding one thousand dollars ($1,000), or by both.

Directive 97/7/EC of the European Parliament and of
the Council of 20 May 1997 on the Protection of Consumers
in respect of Distance Contracts†

Article 4
Prior information

1. In good time prior to the conclusion of any distance contract, the consumer shall be provided with the following information:

  (a) the identity of the supplier and, in the case of contracts requiring payment in advance, his address;
  (b) the main characteristics of the goods or services;
  (c) the price of the goods or services including all taxes;
  (d) delivery costs, where appropriate;
  (e) the arrangements for payment, delivery or performance;
  (f) the existence of a right of withdrawal, except in the cases referred to in Article 6 (3);
  (g) the cost of using the means of distance communication, where it is calculated other than at the basic rate;
  (h) the period for which the offer or the price remains valid;
  (i) where appropriate, the minimum duration of the contract in the case of contracts for the supply of products or services to be performed permanently or recurrently.

2. The information referred to in paragraph 1, the commercial purpose of which must be made clear, shall be provided in a clear and comprehensible manner in any way appropriate to the means of distance communication used, with due regard, in particular, to the principles of good faith in commercial transactions, and the principles governing the protection of those who are unable, pursuant to the legislation of the Member States, to give their consent, such as minors.

3. Moreover, in the case of telephone communications, the identity of the supplier and the commercial purpose of the call shall be made explicitly clear at the beginning of any conversation with the consumer.

Article 5
Written confirmation of information

1. The consumer must receive written confirmation or confirmation in another durable medium available and accessible to him of the information referred to in Article 4 (1) (a) to (f), in good time during the performance of the contract, and at the latest at the time of delivery where goods not for delivery to third parties are concerned, unless the information has already been given to the consumer prior to conclusion of the contract in writing or on another durable medium available and accessible to him.

  In any event the following must be provided:

---

† O.J. No. 166, 04.06.1997.

- written information on the conditions and procedures for exercising the right of withdrawal, within the meaning of Article 6, including the cases referred to in the first indent of Article 6 (3),
- the geographical address of the place of business of the supplier to which the consumer may address any complaints,
- information on after-sales services and guarantees which exist,
- the conclusion for cancelling the contract, where it is of unspecified duration or a duration exceeding one year.

2. Paragraph 1 shall not apply to services which are performed through the use of a means of distance communication, where they are supplied on only one occasion and are invoiced by the operator of the means of distance communication.

Nevertheless, the consumer must in all cases be able to obtain the geographical address of the place of business of the supplier to which he may address any complaints.

Article 6
Right of withdrawal

1. For any distance contract the consumer shall have a period of at least seven working days in which to withdraw from the contract without penalty and without giving any reason. The only charge that may be made to the consumer because of the exercise of his right of withdrawal is the direct cost of returning the goods.

The period for exercise of this right shall begin:

- in the case of goods, from the day of receipt by the consumer where the obligations laid down in Article 5 have been fulfilled,
- in the case of services, from the day of conclusion of the contract or from the day on which the obligations laid down in Article 5 were fulfilled if they are fulfilled after conclusion of the contract, provided that this period does not exceed the three-month period referred to in the following subparagraph.

If the supplier has failed to fulfil the obligations laid down in Article 5, the period shall be three months. The period shall begin:

- in the case of goods, from the day of receipt by the consumer,
- in the case of services, from the day of conclusion of the contract.

If the information referred to in Article 5 is supplied within this three-month period, the seven working day period referred to in the first subparagraph shall begin as from that moment.

2. Where the right of withdrawal has been exercised by the consumer pursuant to this Article, the supplier shall be obliged to reimburse the sums paid by the consumer free of charge. The only charge that may be made to the consumer because of the exercise of his right of withdrawal is the direct cost of returning the goods. Such reimbursement must be carried out as soon as possible and in any case within 30 days.

3. Unless the parties have agreed otherwise, the consumer may not exercise the right of withdrawal provided for in paragraph 1 in respect of contracts:

- for the provision of services if performance has begun, with the consumer's agreement, before the end of the seven working day period referred to in paragraph 1,
- for the supply of goods or services the price of which is dependent on fluctuations in the financial market which cannot be controlled by the supplier,
- for the supply of goods made to the consumer's specifications or clearly personalized or which, by reason of their nature, cannot be returned or are liable to deteriorate or expire rapidly,
- for the supply of audio or video recordings or computer software which were unsealed by the consumer,
- for the supply of newspapers, periodicals and magazines,
- for gaming and lottery services.

4. The Member States shall make provision in their legislation to ensure that:

- if the price of goods or services is fully or partly covered by credit granted by the supplier, or if that price is fully or partly covered by credit granted to the consumer by a third party on the basis of an agreement between the third party and the supplier, the credit agreement shall be cancelled, without any penalty, if the consumer exercises his right to withdraw from the contract in accordance with paragraph 1.

Member States shall determine the detailed rules for cancellation of the credit agreement.

Article 7
Performance

1. Unless the parties have agreed otherwise, the supplier must execute the order within a maximum of 30 days from the day following that on which the consumer forwarded his order to the supplier.

2. Where a supplier fails to perform his side of the contract on the grounds that the goods or services ordered are unavailable, the consumer must be informed of this situation and must be able to obtain a refund of any sums he has paid as soon as possible and in any case within 30 days.

3. Nevertheless, Member States may lay down that the supplier may provide the consumer with goods or services of equivalent quality and price provided that this possibility was provided for prior to the conclusion of the contract or in the contract. The consumer shall be informed of this possibility in a clear and comprehensible manner. The cost of returning the goods following exercise of the right of withdrawal shall, in this case, be borne by the supplier, and the consumer must be informed of this. In such cases the supply of goods or services may not be deemed to constitute inertia selling within the meaning of Article 9.

Article 8
Payment by card

Member States shall ensure that appropriate measures exist to allow a consumer:

- to request cancellation of a payment where fraudulent use has been made of his payment card in connection with distance contracts covered by this Directive,

- in the event of fraudulent use, to be recredited with the sums paid or have them returned.

Article 9
Inertia selling

Member States shall take the measures necessary

- prohibit the supply of goods or services to a consumer without their being ordered by the consumer beforehand,
- where such supply involves a demand for payment, exempt the consumer from the provision of any consideration in cases of unsolicited supply, the absence of a response not constituting consent.

Article 10
Restrictions on the use of certain means of distance communication

1. Use by a supplier of the following means requires the prior consent of the consumer:

- automated calling system without human intervention (automatic calling machine),
- facsimile machine (fax).

2. Member States shall ensure that means of distance communication, other than those referred to in paragraph 1, which allow individual communications may be used only where there is no clear objection from the consumer.

Discussion Questions

1. Considering the borderless nature of e-commerce, what is your view of the effectiveness of these measures? Are international, rather than national or state, measures needed?

2. The E.U. Directive provides consumers with significant new protections for online purchases. Does the directive alter the balance too far in the direction of consumers? Do consumers also now enjoy new powers online by virtue of access to shopping bots that conduct worldwide price comparisons in seconds? Has the balance of power between buyer and seller shifted? If so, is the shift reflected in the directive?

3. Critics suggest that the E.U.'s enthusiastic embrace of regulation is likely to impede the growth of e-commerce. Do you agree?

23

Internet Taxation

Since countries and states frequently rely on sales taxes as an important source of revenue, increasing sales on the Internet raise important taxation policy considerations. Unless the transaction takes place between a buyer and a seller residing in the same taxing jurisdiction, collection of sales or use tax rarely, if ever, occurs. Sensing that the Internet could cause lost tax dollars, some countries and states have begun to consider enacting Internet taxes. Opposition to such schemes is fierce, however, as it is feared that such taxes would severely dampen the growth of electronic commerce.

Proponents of a tax-free Internet fear that governments view the Internet as a lucrative new source of revenue and will rush to impose new taxes on transactions taking place within their jurisdiction. Given the Internet's distinctly non-geographic design, collection of new taxes would pose significant enforcement challenges, since it is frequently unclear precisely where a transaction occurs when it is conducted online. Moreover, consumers and businesses might be dissuaded from embracing the Internet's commercial potential due to concerns with compliance and cost.

Governments typically counter this perspective by pointing to the potential drain on existing revenues should the Internet be declared tax-free. In 1992, the U.S. Supreme Court ruled in *Quill Corp.* v. *North Dakota* [504 U.S. 298 (1992)] that a "physical presence" in the jurisdiction is required for states to assert taxation requirements against out-of-state vendors. With the increasing popularity of mail and telephone ordering, the ruling created a major concern at that time for U.S. states fearing the loss of an important source of taxation revenue. Eight years later, the potential of electronic commerce, most of which would involve out-of-state vendors, exponentially increases those same concerns.

While both the United States and E.U. have adopted aggressive positions on the Internet taxation issue, Canada has been relatively cautious in its approach to the issue. The key government policy document on Internet taxation remains a 1998 study, part of which is found below.

E-Commerce and Canada's Tax Administration[†]

In assessing the impact of electronic commerce on the economy, the Committee has attempted to compare traditional commerce, involving tangible goods and services, with electronic commerce, involving intangible goods and services. Although both types of commerce share many tax-compliance problems, electronic commerce may exacerbate many of them. Governments should carefully study and measure the points at which there is a risk of revenue loss because of electronic commerce and the extent of that loss. Government action should be commensurate with the projected revenue loss and should avoid imposing additional compliance burdens.

4.2.1   Reporting Issues

The unregulated nature of the Internet and the anonymity it provides may make it easier to avoid or evade income tax on profits realized on electronic transactions.

4.2.1.1   Intentional Non-Reporting

ISSUE

Electronic commerce may increase the incidence of non-compliance with the tax system.

ANALYSIS

Taxpayers who now intentionally avoid Canadian federal and provincial taxes do so by going "underground." Avoidance schemes may range from simply not registering as a taxpayer or tax collector, or conducting all transactions with untraceable cash, to more elaborate measures using false names, records, or business systems. The ease of conducting electronic commerce may reduce the number of elaborate schemes, but may increase the number of simple attempts to avoid paying tax.

Revenue Canada is concerned about the magnitude of the underground economy and has established various internal programs to pursue non-filers and ensure compliance with the current tax system. These measures range from an active campaign to locate non-filers to significant penalty and interest charges under the *Income Tax Act*. These programs have been increased over the past few years to encourage greater compliance with the Canadian self-reporting system.

A voluntary disclosure program is in place to encourage current non-filers to come forward. Penalties are waived under this program, provided that disclosure is voluntary and not a result of a Revenue Canada investigation.

Of concern is the potential increase of non-filers as a result of electronic commerce. Specifically, will Revenue Canada require additional effort to maintain the existing level of compliance with the *Income Tax Act*? The Australian Taxation Office believes that increased effort is necessary, and has undertaken to develop Webcrawler software to trace non-filers.

Other concerns with increased non-compliance arise as a result of electronic commerce. They are:

---

† Revenue Canada Web site: <http://www.rc.gc.ca/ecomm/>. Reproduced with permission of Minister of Public Works and Government Services Canada, 1999.

- refillable cash cards and other forms of electronic cash;
- the ability to move cash to and from customers and suppliers without the involvement of banks; and
- the ability to use non-Canadian banks.

These areas are dealt with elsewhere in this report (see sections 4.2.2.9 and 4.5.7, below, as well as Chapter 2).

RECOMMENDATIONS

1. Revenue Canada should extend its active campaign to locate non-filers to include electronic commerce activities. It should consider programs to identify businesses conducting Internet commerce, such as:
   (a) accessing the domain registry and identifying domain names for Canadian businesses;
   (b) establishing a system that identifies Canadians doing business over the Internet;
   (c) developing compliance programs based on the population and results of previous audits of businesses with a presence on the Web (risk management); and
   (d) developing Webcrawler software to trace non-filers to complement existing programs.
2. Revenue Canada should review current penalties for non-compliance under the *Income Tax Act* to ensure that they are a sufficient deterrent to non-reporting opportunities that may be created through electronic commerce. These penalties should apply equally to promoters and intermediaries who knowingly participate in non-compliance schemes.
3. Financial institutions should be required to report to Revenue Canada cash or equivalent transactions over a prescribed limit.
4. Revenue Canada should study, with other interested tax authorities, the benefits of an international organization designed to assist countries (most likely those that are signatories of tax treaties) in the exchange of information in order to minimize tax evasion.

4.2.1.2   Unintentional Non-Reporting

ISSUE

Some taxpayers may not be aware of their taxpayer or tax collector obligations and consequently will not report taxable activities or withhold or remit appropriate taxes.

ANALYSIS

Revenue Canada is concerned about the magnitude of the underground economy and has established various programs to pursue non-filers and to ensure compliance with the current tax system. A voluntary disclosure program eliminates penalties for non-filers who come forward on their own.

Unclear and unknown rules may lead to businesses being subjected to interest and penalty charges once the filing requirements become known. The voluntary disclosure procedure is not useful if a taxpayer's filing status is not known.

Specific concerns include:

- the vendor's inability to identify the purchaser's country of residence;

- the vendor's knowledge, or lack of knowledge, of the tax legislation of the purchaser's country of residence; and
- the purchaser's lack of knowledge of the tax implications of payments to non-residents and related procedures (e.g., the need to withhold and remit).

These concerns are not restricted to Canada. Canadian businesses expanding beyond Canadian borders may have difficulty learning about and complying with tax laws of many foreign jurisdictions. The related filing requirements, especially with a small volume of purchases, could be onerous on businesses if they are subjected to tax in numerous jurisdictions. This problem is international in scope and, to allow business to flourish, it requires international agreement and clarification.

RECOMMENDATIONS

5. Revenue Canada should develop a communication strategy to educate taxpayers on the tax implications of doing business on the Internet or over private networks.
6. Revenue Canada should use its Web site to advertise to residents and non-residents of Canada the implications of doing business in Canada on the Internet and e-mail information to interested parties. Revenue Canada also should link its Web site to Industry Canada's Web site, where information on the implications of doing business in Canada on the Internet already exists.
7. Revenue Canada should approach appropriate organizations (e.g., the CICA/ AICPA and similar organizations) to arrange electronic links to the Revenue Canada Web site to provide users with information on the tax implications of doing business on the Internet.

4.2.2 Interjurisdictional Issues

It is now common for goods and services to be produced in one location and consumed in another. The production of services, in particular, no longer needs to take place where the services are to be consumed. Businesses can set up specialized service centres to provide financial management, marketing, accounting, or other services to different arms of the same MNE or to unrelated third parties. These service centres can easily be separated from the rest of the enterprise and can be located where skilled or low-cost labour, or other commercial or tax advantages, are readily available. This fragmentation of economic activity will make it difficult to determine where a particular activity is carried out, which tax jurisdiction has proper authority to tax the profits or the transaction, and how the profits should be allocated between jurisdictions.

For example, suppose a Canadian corporation owns the worldwide rights to distribute a movie over the Internet. The Canadian corporation establishes an Internet site to distribute the movie worldwide. The Internet site resides on a server that could be located in one of three places: (1) in Canada; (2) in a country with which Canada has negotiated a tax treaty; and (3) in a country with which Canada has not negotiated a tax treaty. Customers interested in the movie sign on to the site, which both advertises and provides the facilities to order the movie. A customer, potentially located in any country in the world, orders the movie through this site. The question then arises as to how such a transaction, and the profits it generates, should be taxed in Canada.

The question is further complicated by the need to determine whether the transaction concerns the provision of services, the sale of goods, or the sale of intellectual property (in the form of digitized media).

Non-residents of Canada generally are liable to pay income tax in Canada under the general rules set out in the *Income Tax Act* only if they carry on business in Canada, dispose of certain types of tangible property, or earn passive income from Canadian sources. However, the general rules of the *Income Tax Act*, even where they apply, may be overridden by provisions of international tax treaties to which Canada is a party. Under these tax treaties, non-residents who carry on business in Canada are taxable only on profits earned in Canada that are attributable to a permanent establishment located in Canada. The emergence of electronic commerce reduces the need for a non-resident to maintain a permanent establishment in order to serve Canadian customers.

Similar concerns arise as well with respect to interprovincial transactions.

4.2.2.1   Residence of a Corporation

ISSUE

Modern communications technology, such as the Internet, may have a significant impact on the determination of a corporation's residency status, potentially resulting in residency and taxation in multiple jurisdictions.

BACKGROUND

Corporations that are resident in Canada are subject to tax in Canada on their worldwide income from all sources — business, property (e.g., rent from real property), and investment (e.g., dividends and interest). A corporation is generally considered to be resident in Canada if it is incorporated under Canadian law (either federal or provincial) or if its central mind and management is in Canada (generally the place where the company's board of directors meets to carry on the company's business).

Since residence is the basis of Canadian taxation, determining the residence of corporations is critical to Canada's ability to impose and collect tax. This is especially critical where corporations incorporated outside Canada appear to be carrying on business in Canada and seek to be exempted from Canadian taxation under applicable tax treaties.

ANALYSIS

Before the advent of modern communications technology, the directors of a company usually had to be physically present for board meetings, thus facilitating the determination of where the company's central mind and management was located. In today's environment, with the use of videoconferencing facilities and other communications technology, the effective management of a corporation no longer requires the physical presence of the directors at board meetings. As a result, determining where the central mind and management of a corporation is located is no longer an easy task.

With modern communications technology, it may be impossible to determine conclusively where the central mind and management resides. In what jurisdiction is a decision by conference call or videoconference made? If corporate decisions are determined by resolutions that are circulated among different countries for execution, where is the decision made? Without tie-breaker rules, competing tax jurisdictions may each assert jurisdiction to tax.

There is an increasing risk that MNEs operating effectively with telecommunications equipment may be considered to be resident in multiple jurisdictions by the tax authorities of each of those jurisdictions.

Where such corporations are incorporated in countries with which Canada has a tax treaty, tie-breaker rules will usually resolve this question. In other cases (e.g., where corporations are incorporated in non-treaty countries), residence must be determined through the use of internal domestic rules and concepts, such as the location of the central mind and management.

Concern has been expressed that some countries may be overly aggressive in collecting taxes that "may or may not be applicable," with the result that taxpayers may be in a position of both double taxation and reduced cash flow pending resolution of matters through the competent authority. Businesses may have difficulty functioning in such an environment. It may be appropriate for taxing jurisdictions to provide temporary relief for taxpayers who are facing a double-taxation situation.

RECOMMENDATIONS

8. Revenue Canada should consider, in cooperation with tax treaty partners, ways to shorten the competent authority process in order to eliminate, or minimize, the impact of double taxation on taxpayers.

9. Revenue Canada should consult with the Department of Finance as to methods for ameliorating the potential adverse effects of the competent authority process for Canadian SMEs entering international trade.

10. Revenue Canada should issue an interpretation bulletin addressing the significance of modern telecommunications technology on the concept of residence (including central mind and management).

4.2.2.2   Carrying On Business in Canada

ISSUE

Electronic commerce raises concerns about where business is transacted electronically and what degree of electronic activity constitutes carrying on business in Canada.

ANALYSIS

A non-resident of Canada is taxable in Canada on employment income earned in Canada, on profits from a business carried on in Canada, and on the disposition of certain defined property, referred to as "taxable Canadian property."

For the purposes of the *Income Tax Act*, the concept of carrying on business is deemed under section 253 to include any activity where a person

(a) produces, grows, mines, creates, manufactures, fabricates, improves, packs, preserves or constructs, in whole or in part, anything in Canada whether or not the person exports that thing without selling it before exportation, [or]

(b) solicits orders or offers anything for sale in Canada through an agent or servant, whether the contract or transaction is to be completed inside or outside Canada or partly in and partly outside Canada.

Electronic commerce raises a number of specific issues with respect to what constitutes carrying on business in Canada:

• Where electronic goods or services are provided to Canadian customers by a non-resident, are these goods and services produced, created, or fabricated in Canada for the purposes of the domestic deeming rule?

- Does the location of a file server, another central computer, or a satellite with storage facilities affect the determination of carrying on business and the concept of selling or soliciting orders in Canada?
- In what jurisdiction is an electronic transaction completed, and which jurisdiction has the right to impose tax on the profits earned by the parties to that transaction?
- Is the transaction manager an agent of the non-resident?

In determining the jurisdiction in which a transaction is completed, established legal principles may continue to apply. Among these principles are:

- the country whose laws the parties specified would govern the transaction;
- the country in which title passed to the purchaser would govern the transaction;
- the country in which possession passed to the purchaser would govern the transaction; and
- the country in which risk of possession or ownership passed to the purchaser would govern the transaction.

It is unclear whether the location of a file server or other computer is determinative of, or even necessarily a factor in determining, the situs of a transaction for tax purposes. The computer may simply be a mutually acceptable facilitator for the parties to the transaction, just like a telegraph or telephone service, facilitating communication between the parties. Legal certainty as to the role of the computer is required.

Similarly, a transaction manager may not be considered an agent of either party any more than the telephone company that connects parties is an agent of either. To the extent that the transaction manager's computer plays a more active role in any particular transaction, its role may be as the controlled tool of one party — but not necessarily as an agent. It is arguable that an agent is proactive, while the computer of today can react only in accordance with its programming. With improving technology and the introduction of computer intelligence, a computer may become proactive and, therefore, its role may be viewed differently.

RECOMMENDATIONS

11. Revenue Canada should issue an interpretation bulletin to clarify its position on the circumstances in which electronic commerce activities may constitute carrying on business in Canada.
12. Revenue Canada should examine the appropriateness of the definition of "carrying on business" under the *Income Tax Act* in an electronic commerce environment, including addressing the roles of various electronic commerce elements (the file server's location, the transaction manager's role, etc.), and, if necessary, convey its concerns to the Department of Finance.

4.2.2.3 Carrying On Business Outside Canada

ISSUE

Electronic commerce may make it difficult to ensure, and verify, that the central mind and management of foreign operations (specifically foreign subsidiaries) is not in Canada and that profits from international transactions are properly and timely reported.

ANALYSIS

With the growth of international trade and electronic commerce, there will be more opportunities and incentives for individuals to shift profits away from high-tax jurisdictions to low-tax jurisdictions.

Recent changes to the *Income Tax Act* have enhanced Revenue Canada's ability to both identify and trace these profits and to ensure that they are properly and timely taxed. Recent international initiatives, such as the cooperation provisions of the Canada-US tax treaty, also aid in Canada's ability to enforce its domestic law.

A simple mechanism for avoiding income tax in Canada is to establish a foreign sales company. This company would be established in a low-tax jurisdiction and would typically be owned by Canadian residents. This company would purchase products for resale from suppliers anywhere in the world, and would resell the products to its customers. In theory, the profit on the sale would be taxed in the low-tax jurisdiction, and only Canadian sales and related profits would be taxable in Canada.

It could be argued that the profits that arise in this example should be taxable in Canada, especially if the Canadian shareholder is active as the salesperson, and is responsible for both purchasing and reselling decisions.

If all business decisions were made in Canada so that it could be demonstrated that the central mind and management of the business was in Canada, the profits arising from these decisions would be taxable in Canada under general tax rules, on the basis that the company was resident in Canada for tax purposes (resident companies are taxed on their worldwide income).

Situations exist where residents using these types of companies to avoid Canadian tax take the position that there is no obligation to report the foreign profits, and thereby avoid compliance with existing law. Customers of and suppliers to these companies have no reporting obligations to Revenue Canada. The Canadian tax system is really protected only by taxpayer self-assessment.

The advent of electronic commerce does not alter this tax-avoidance technique. However, the Internet will make it easier for those who wish to avoid tax to contact offshore suppliers and customers.

A Revenue Canada foreign reporting form (T106) provides considerable penalties for non-compliance, but it does not ask for specific information with respect to electronic commerce activities (such as URLs and other Web site information of related non-resident persons). New foreign reporting rules are being introduced that will increase disclosure of foreign transactions. Because of the existence of these reporting requirements and the related penalties, it is arguable that most transactions will be disclosed to Revenue Canada and be available for scrutiny.

RECOMMENDATION

13. Revenue Canada should issue an interpretation bulletin addressing the significance of modern telecommunications technology on the concepts of residence (including central mind and management) and carrying on business outside Canada.

4.2.2.4   Permanent Establishment Under Tax Treaties

ISSUE

Is the concept of "permanent establishment" valid in the electronic environment? If it is, to what extent do various components of electronic commerce play a part in determining permanent establishment? If it is not, should "permanent establishment" be replaced with an alternative concept?

BACKGROUND

Canada's *Income Tax Act* is subject to the provisions of tax treaties that Canada has entered into with other jurisdictions. One of the major provisions of Canada's tax treaties is that non-residents who are carrying on business in Canada are subject to tax in Canada only if they earn profits that can be attributed to a permanent establishment. In most treaties, a "permanent establishment" means a fixed place of business in which the business of the enterprise is wholly or partly carried on. The term "permanent establishment" is then expanded to include a place of management, a branch, an office, a factory, a workshop, or other tangible place of business activity. However, the concept of permanent establishment generally does not include

- facilities used solely for the purpose of storage, display, or delivery of goods or merchandise belonging to the non-resident;
- the maintenance of a stock of goods or merchandise belonging to the enterprise solely for the purpose of storage, display, or delivery;
- the maintenance of a fixed place of business solely for the purpose of purchasing goods or merchandise or for collecting information for the enterprise; or
- the maintenance of a fixed place of business solely for the purpose of advertising, for the supply of information, or for similar activities that have a preparatory or auxiliary character for the enterprise.

In addition, if a non-resident carries on business through an agent in Canada, the non-resident is deemed to have a permanent establishment only if the agent habitually exercises an authority to conclude contracts in the name of the non-resident. A broker, a general commission agent, or other agent of independent status who acts in the normal course of its business (e.g., a representative agent of a non-resident) will not be considered to create a permanent establishment of that non-resident.

Tax treaties generally prevent double taxation in three ways:

- by defining who is considered a resident for the purposes of claiming treaty benefits (e.g., the tie-breaker rules in modern treaties solve the dilemma of dual-resident corporations);
- by defining concepts or transactions for the purposes of withholding taxes (e.g., the definition of interest or royalties in modern treaties expands or refines those concepts); and
- by providing for a competent authority dispute resolution process, where an aggrieved taxpayer can request that revenue authorities in each country review a double-taxation situation and provide administrative relief.

Unfortunately, these provisions are not guaranteed to provide relief. Canada still has old treaties without tie-breaker rules. Competent authority relief is an extraordinary remedy and aggrieved taxpayers cannot compel action; they have no meaningful remedy if the competing tax jurisdictions cannot reach agreement.

ANALYSIS

Once it is determined that a non-resident carries on business in Canada, relief from Canadian tax may be provided under the terms of treaties that exist with other countries. In the context of treaty provisions, electronic commerce raises issues relating to what constitutes a permanent establishment:

- Do treaties provide sufficient direction and definition of various concepts to ensure that double taxation does not occur?

- Is a file server or other central computer a permanent establishment or fixed place of business for treaty purposes? If it is, is it a fixed place of business solely for the purpose of advertising or one of the other activities excluded from the definition of permanent establishment?
- Is the transaction manager a dependent agent of the non-resident for tax treaty purposes?

Treaties do not provide sufficient direction and definition of various concepts to ensure that double taxation does not occur. The OECD is currently studying issues relating to its model tax treaty and is expected to revise that model treaty to reflect electronic commerce issues.

It must be determined whether the traditional concept of permanent establishment can be applied. In the context of electronic commerce, there are at least two possible sites for a permanent establishment.

The first possible site is the location of the customer signing on to the site to conduct the transaction. However, it is arguable that there is no fixed place of business at the customer's location and no required element of permanence to this location. It is simply where the customer logged on to the site to initiate the entire transaction.

The second possible site is the location of the server. It is arguable that this site has many of the traditional characteristics, or near equivalents, of a permanent establishment. It might be a fixed location and one might argue that it is a fixed place of business. If actual orders are conducted on the site, the fixed place of business argument is much stronger than it would be if the site provided only advertising or information. Various transactions could occur through this site, including the authorization of the contract, arrangement and acceptance of the contract, collection of the fees for the transaction, and even digitized deposits to banks. the site has all the characteristics of a centre of activity: it may be fixed (albeit in the form of electronic information located on some form of computer storage medium in a computer in a building) and its programs may give it the ability to act.

Representatives of Revenue Canada should be cautious when meeting with other OECD member countries before contemplating the replacement of fundamental concepts such as residency, source, and permanent establishment. These concepts have existed for a long time, are well known, and have proved their usefulness. Priority should be given to considering these concepts and their applicability to electronic commerce before choosing to pursue alternative or new concepts.

RECOMMENDATIONS

14. Revenue Canada should continue to be active in the workings of the OECD to address electronic transactions. Priority should be given to considering and applying existing concepts to electronic commerce before choosing to pursue alternative or new concepts.
15. Revenue Canada and the Department of Finance should liaise on an urgent basis as soon as the OECD recommendations with respect to changes to the model tax treaty are known. Revenue Canada and the Department of Finance need to address the taxation of electronic commerce, including prompt renegotiations of or negotiating protocols to existing treaties.
16. Revenue Canada should convey to the Department of Finance and other interested departments the Committee's view that government departments should

consult with regard to the implications and ramifications to Canada of any change in the existing balance between source and residence taxation.

17. Revenue Canada should continue to participate in the OECD discussions on the status of file servers (e.g., as virtual offices, or virtual employees) and transaction managers for permanent establishment purposes. Revenue Canada should consult with other interested government departments on the ramifications to Canada's tax base.

4.2.2.5   International Allocations

ISSUE

Canada's domestic tax rules that allocate revenue and expenses between countries may result in the double taxation of electronic commerce transactions.

ANALYSIS

Continuing developments in electronic commerce have given rise to a number of complex and challenging issues. International taxation laws have generally assumed that a transaction will involve a physical exchange of some sort at some time in the course of the transaction. With the emergence of electronic commerce vendors, customers can conclude agreements without regard to physical or national boundaries.

It is possible that transactions will be subjected to taxation in more than one jurisdiction or that transactions will be subject to differing taxation treatment in different jurisdictions (e.g., subject to business taxation in one jurisdiction and withholding taxes in the other). (For additional comments on the characterization of transactions, see section 4.2.3.)

For example, foreign withholding tax could apply to income received by a resident of Canada and, in the computation of Canadian taxable income, that same income would not be treated as foreign source income. The Canadian taxpayer would then be unable to claim a foreign tax credit for foreign taxes withheld because the Canadian tax system limits the credit to the Canadian taxes that would otherwise apply to foreign source income. Although the *Income Tax Act* allows for a deduction against income for taxes not otherwise creditable against Canadian taxes, this is only a partial relief from double taxation.

RECOMMENDATION

18. Revenue Canada should convey to the Department of Finance the Committee's view that Finance should monitor income-sourcing rules for foreign tax credit purposes to ensure that they continue to provide appropriate relief as electronic commerce grows.

4.2.2.6   Interprovincial Allocations

ISSUE

Do the existing interprovincial allocation rules in the *Income Tax Act* regulations need to be adapted to reflect electronic commerce?

BACKGROUND

The *Income Tax Act* contains provisions to allocate taxable income between the provinces for the purposes of levying provincial tax. Three provinces (Alberta, Ontario, and Quebec) collect their own provincial taxes; however, the formula contained in the legislation of those jurisdictions is similar to that contained in the federal *Income Tax Act* for application to the other provinces.

Regulation 400 of the *Income Tax Act* deals with the concept of "permanent establishment" as well as the allocation of the taxable income earned by a corporation among different provinces. The regulations contain a hierarchy of criteria that will give rise to a permanent establishment.

The first criterion is that a corporation that has a fixed place of business in a province will have a permanent establishment in that province. If the corporation does not possess a fixed place of business, some of the other enumerated factors that should be considered are the location where the corporation principally carries on its business, the location of the corporation's place of management, and the location where the corporation uses substantial machinery and equipment. In certain situations a corporation may also have a permanent establishment in a province if it carries on business in the province through an agent.

The concept of permanent establishment originally was dependent on geographical location; however, its applicability becomes somewhat uncertain in the world of electronic commerce. A business can now carry on a large number of activities in a province without having any real fixed place of business in that province, thereby making the traditional concept of permanent establishment difficult to apply.

The example of distributing movies over the Internet (see section 4.2.2) could also be applied to Canadian provinces and the interaction between different provinces and whether they will attempt to tax this transaction. All provinces rely on the concept of permanent establishment to tax the income of corporations. If more than one province determines that there is a permanent establishment in that province, the issue then becomes the allocation of income between the different provinces.

The regulations under the *Income Tax Act* address the allocation issue, and the various provincial regulations mirror the federal rules. These rules allocate a corporation's taxable income between the different provinces that have a permanent establishment based on the average of the following two items:

• the proportion of a corporation's gross revenue that is attributable to a permanent establishment in that province; and
• the proportion of the corporation's salaries and wages that are paid to employees of a permanent establishment in that province.

Where there are no salaries and wages paid in any province, the allocation will depend solely on the revenue attributable to a permanent establishment. (The opposite also holds true where there are no revenues attributable to a permanent establishment.)

If the file server is maintained by an independent corporation so that there are no wages in either the customer's or the server's province, how will taxable income be allocated based solely on the revenue attributable to transaction? Is it appropriate that the revenue be allocated to the province where the server is located?

If the answer to this last question is yes, corporations could decrease their tax liability by locating the file server in a jurisdiction that has no or low rates of income tax.

The situation is even less clear where the file server is not owned by the corporation but rather is leased from an independent third party.

The United States uses similar concepts to allocate income. However, the United States applies a third factor — assets deployed within the state.

ANALYSIS
Concerns raised by electronic commerce include:

- the implications of the location of file servers;
- the applicability of the concept of permanent establishment (a concern similar to that with the Canadian income tax conventions);
- means of allocating electronic transactions to a permanent establishment; and
- concerns of potentially differing definitions of electronic transactions between the provinces.

It must be determined whether the traditional concept of permanent establishment can be applied. These concerns are similar to those concerning permanent establishment under various international tax treaties (see section 4.2.2.4).

The recent activities and initiatives of various US states to tax electronic commerce transactions is well documented and of concern. Inconsistent treatment of transactions between provinces can be harmful to business and restrict commerce.

The allocation of taxable income between states is based on three factors: salaries, revenues, and assets deployed within the state. The inclusion of the third factor (assets) reduces the impact of the revenue allocation and, to a degree, the distortions that may occur in allocating electronic commerce revenue to a permanent establishment.

RECOMMENDATIONS

19. Revenue Canada should convey to the Department of Finance the Committee's view that Finance and the provinces should review the regulations to the *Income Tax Act* and the provincial allocation formula to ensure that electronic commerce transactions are fairly allocated. Consideration could be given to allocating taxable income between provinces based on more than two criteria (e.g., salaries, revenues, and assets deployed within the province). Such an approach would affect more than electronic commerce transactions and must be considered in the context of neutrality.
20. Revenue Canada, the Department of Finance, and provinces with their own allocation systems should establish a policy related to file servers and whether these file servers would constitute a permanent establishment for the purposes of the *Income Tax Act* and the allocation of provincial taxable income.

4.3.1   Shift in Collection Points

ISSUE

The increased ability to acquire products directly from non-residents may result in the disappearance of some of the collection points on which commodity tax regimes currently rely to collect and remit tax. Although GST/HST is collected by Customs on goods, unless new collection points are identified for some services and intangibles, revenue authorities will have to rely on purchasers to self-assess and remit sales tax.

ANALYSIS

Traditionally, a Canadian purchaser who acquires a product from a foreign supplier does so through a wholesaler or distributor located in Canada. The GST regime, like most commodity tax regimes, imposes the obligation on the vendor to collect GST from the customer and remit the tax to the government. Reporting requirements, handling of remittances, and enforcement/verification processes are all currently focused on the registrant suppliers. With electronic commerce, consumers can order directly from foreign vendors through the Internet. Many of these non-residents will not be required to collect consumption taxes of the state where the purchaser is located. A loss of collection points may therefore result.

Under the GST regime, where a business acquires products or services outside Canada and tax is not collected by the vendor or Customs, the business is required to self-assess and remit the required GST, so long as the business would not be entitled to claim a full input tax credit. Where an individual consumer is involved, self-assessment, although technically required under the GST regime, rarely occurs.

As a result, there is a risk that end-use consumers, primarily individuals, will be tempted to purchase products that can be provided electronically from foreign vendors in order to escape paying the GST.

If a government fears that there is a real risk of lost tax revenues because of this non-compliance, it may be tempted to impose onerous obligations on vendors merely because they provide products to consumers within the jurisdiction of that government.

Many parties who use the Internet to market their products are small to medium-sized vendors. Although electronic commerce allows these vendors to compete in a global marketplace, it may be overly optimistic to believe that these vendors can cope with global consumption tax obligations.

Furthermore, if the Canadian government attempts to force all non-residents who market products to Canadian residents to register as collection agents for Canadian consumption taxes, Canada must anticipate that other countries could respond by requiring Canadian vendors to assume reciprocal obligations. This would serve only to dampen the enthusiasm for doing business on the Internet.

Revenue Canada could take steps to increase compliance with and enforcement of the obligation on consumers to self-assess GST. This would include information campaigns as well as increased verification. This increased enforcement could be relatively straightforward in the case of businesses that, if registered for GST, are required to report self-assessed GST at the same time as they file the "GST net tax" return on which they report GST collected and claim their input tax credits. Businesses that are registered for GST are known to Revenue Canada and can be identified for audit verification.

Businesses that have failed to register, or that otherwise refuse to file returns to self-assess GST, present challenges to Revenue Canada that are similar to those already presented by businesses currently in the so-called underground economy. It is a matter of speculation whether electronic commerce will encourage development of, or shrink (as some commentators have predicted), the tax underground economy.

Self-assessment at the level of individual consumers raises different issues. Typically, the amounts that individuals would be required to self-assess would be relatively small. Revenue Canada would, accordingly, be faced with an increased volume of returns and small remittances to process. It would have to assess whether its form- and remittances-processing facilities could accommodate this increase in volume, and whether it would be cost-effective to implement the changes necessary to deal with this volume.

More significant, perhaps, is the possible consumer resistance to increased enforcement programs that target individuals' obligation to self-assess.

As noted, however, even though some traditional intermediary vendors may disappear as electronic commerce expands, other intermediaries will emerge or extend their existing roles to meet the needs of the electronic commerce environment. One approach that has been suggested would be to make financial intermediaries responsible for collecting sales tax on the transactions that they process for payment. Under this scenario, software could be developed that the financial intermediaries would operate in conjunction with their financial processes. Ideally, this approach would provide a seamless approach to the collection of sales tax on the cross-border sale of digitized products. However, such an approach would represent a fundamental shift in the legal liabilities for tax collection, and also raises a number of important issues. For example, to apply Canadian sales tax structures, financial intermediaries would need to know, at the very least, the location of the supplier and the purchaser, the place of supply, whether tax had already been collected by the supplier, the tax status of the purchaser, and the nature of the product.

It may be feasible to work with financial or transaction intermediaries to develop software to facilitate the collection of sales tax on transactions as they are processed. In this way, the intermediaries would not bear an undue compliance burden, or the risk of being liable for failure to collect and remit the correct taxes.

The feasibility of solutions that involve enlisting financial or transaction intermediaries in collecting sales tax for governments will depend on how electronic commerce processes and information-gathering techniques and capacities expand.

RECOMMENDATIONS

37. Even if faced with loss of GST revenues due to the failure of consumers to self-assess GST on their purchases over the Internet, the Government of Canada should avoid the temptation to react by imposing additional onerous collection and registration requirements on electronic commerce vendors.
38. Revenue Canada should consider the feasibility of developing a communication strategy to make small businesses and consumers aware of their obligations to self-assess GST in situations where it will not be collected by the vendor or Customs.
39. Revenue Canada should develop a communication strategy for non-resident vendors to encourage them to register to collect and remit GST. A description of the benefits of registration should be included, along with a commitment from Revenue Canada that registration, in itself, will not be considered to result in Canadian income tax obligations for the vendor.
40. Revenue Canada should consider the feasibility of developing a new consumer self-assessment process that would make it easier to collect small amounts of tax from a large base of taxpayers.
41. Revenue Canada, in consultation with the Department of Finance, should explore the role transaction intermediaries could play in the collection and remittance of tax.
42. Revenue Canada, in cooperation with the Department of Finance, should consult with industry to evaluate the burden that would be imposed on industry by the mutual enforcement of consumption tax collection obligations between jurisdictions before entering into such international agreements.

4.3.2 Shift in GST Results

ISSUE

There may be distortions in the GST results as products that are provided electronically are recharacterized from goods to services or intangible property, or from services to intangible property.

ANALYSIS

The place-of-supply rules for intangible personal property and services, including the non-resident override, assume an ability on the part of the supplier to determine

- the residency status of the supplier; and
- the place where the supplier performs the service or the place where the intangible can be used.

These can be complex and uncertain determinations. "Non-residents," for example, can be deemed to be "residents" for GST purposes if they have a "permanent establishment" in Canada. Even Canadian residents are deemed to be non-residents for GST purposes where they carry on business through a permanent establishment outside Canada.

In the electronic environment, it is increasingly possible for businesses to fragment their activities and to link remote locations and facilities electronically. With increasing frequency, these different facilities will be located in different jurisdictions. Digitized products or components of products will pass across borders in greater volume and with greater frequency.

As this phenomenon increases, it will become increasingly difficult

- to determine the location where a supply is "made";
- to determine the "resident" or "non-resident" status of the supplier or recipient; and
- to determine where or how the recipient will in fact use or consume the supply.

All three factors affect how the GST place-of-supply rules will apply, and whether an international transaction is brought within the scope of the GST regime. The second factor also affects whether supplies destined for external consumption will be properly zero-rated and relieved from GST.

The Committee is concerned that the current GST rules, when applied in the context of international electronic commerce and business activity, should

- be easy for suppliers to apply and provide the certainty of GST result that businesses require;
- result in functionally similar commodities being subjected to GST in a similar fashion, when provided by traditional or electronic means;
- ensure that GST will appropriately apply to supplies that are for use or consumption in Canada; and
- not result in supplies being subject to GST when they are for use or consumption outside Canada.

Failure to do so could result in

- a loss of GST revenue;
- an adverse impact on the ability of Canadian business to compete in the global marketplace; and
- an adverse impact on the international perception of Canada as a welcoming environment for international electronic business.

These issues must, of course, be viewed in the overall context of the international marketplace. If similar results occur under the commodity tax regimes of all other countries, it is unlikely that Canadian businesses or the Canadian business environment will be at a competitive disadvantage.

As experience accumulates, it may become evident that international negotiation and cooperation between revenue authorities will be required to respond appropriately to the challenges described above.

RECOMMENDATIONS

43. Revenue Canada should convey to the Department of Finance the Committee's view that supplies of intangibles that are provided electronically to non-residents should be zero-rated when no or limited use will be made of these products in Canada.
44. Revenue Canada, in consultation with the Department of Finance, should monitor the GST place-of-supply rules, the tax-relieving rules, and the self-assessment rules to ensure that services and intangibles that are provided to Canadian residents for use in Canada continue to be part of the GST base.
45. Revenue Canada, in consultation with the Department of Finance, should monitor the use of electronic commerce to ensure that the place-of-supply and self-assessment rules continue to operate in a manner such that only those services and intangibles that are consumed or used in Canada are included in the tax base.

4.4 CUSTOMS DUTIES AND TARIFFS

Issues and recommendations common to income taxes, consumption taxes, and customs duties and tariffs are dealt with in section 4.5. The two areas most pertinent to customs duties and tariffs are detailed below.

4.4.1 Accessibility and Reliability

ISSUE

It may be difficult to verify compliance with Revenue Canada customs law in the electronic business environment.

ANALYSIS

Revenue Canada legislation and policy govern the accounting and reporting requirements of import transactions. These requirements specify the data to be submitted to Revenue Canada to determine the duties owing and to support trade requirements, such as the statistical base of commerce in Canada. The required data include the country of origin (critical to meet the obligations under international trade agreements such as NAFTA) and the identity of the importer and the exporter in a transaction.

Although data are submitted for each import transaction, Revenue Canada relies increasingly on periodic verification (audit after the fact) to verify compliance with importing laws and policies.

Electronic commerce may jeopardize the accessibility of data to support compliance verification, and may bring into question the reliability of data.

Revenue Canada customs legislation contains rules with respect to record availability and retention that are designed to ensure that Revenue Canada has access to the information required to verify the propriety of import and export transactions.

Persons who conduct customs business must keep books and records. The books and records must be in appropriate form and contain appropriate information to enable Revenue Canada to verify the details of the transaction. It is the responsibility of the person (importer, exporter, carrier, etc.) to maintain books and records.

New section 8.1 of the *Customs Act*, effective January 1, 1998, provides for electronic filing, addresses certain related evidentiary issues, and provides for related regulatory authority. This new authority reflects the trend toward electronic reporting of goods, and is structured after similar GST-related legislation.

Various regulations made under the authority of the *Customs Act* now require clients who provide information by electronic means to retain records electronically in an electronically readable format for the appropriate retention period.

To support evidentiary requirements, the new *Customs Act* legislation provides that in the normal course of trade a printout of a form received electronically can be accepted as evidence.

RECOMMENDATION

46. Revenue Canada should work with importers and other interested third parties to understand and have input into standards being developed for electronic commerce, especially those standards that establish verifiable data-storage formats and certification authorities.

4.4.2 Transformation of "Tangible Goods"

ISSUE

The transformation of "tangible goods" to electronic products or transactions may result in reduced customs duties and tariffs being levied and collected.

ANALYSIS

The Customs division of Revenue Canada has responsibilities beyond the levying of duties and tariffs. Other responsibilities (such as control of obscene materials) are beyond the scope of this Committee's mandate and are not addressed in this report.

Customs duties and tariffs are levied on tangible goods. Historically, Canada has taken the position that products transmitted electronically are not goods per se. Hence, they are not subject to the valuation provisions of the *Customs Act* and are not assessed duties (except if the transmission is associated with an imported tangible good or is an "assist" and thus part of the value for duty). The transformation of tangible goods to formats that are no longer defined as tangible goods may result in a reduction in the amount of duties and tariffs collected.

Since the mid-1980s Customs has worked with the Department of Finance to update the range of customs tariff provisions related to the trade in goods (and software) packaged principally as electronic media to ensure that it is not impeded during entry into Canada. This trend has highlighted the need for importers, exporters, and suppliers to maintain adequate records so that the origin of goods can be confirmed.

Recently, the Canadian government has pursued agreements (e.g., NAFTA) that have reduced or eliminated duties and tariffs on an increasing number of tangible goods. Consequently, the impact of duties and tariffs on electronic commerce transactions will likewise be reduced.

The Committee, while making no comment on the trend to reduce customs duties and tariffs, is of the view that a change in the nature of a tangible good to an electronic product or transaction should not result in tax treatment that differs from that accorded similar products or transactions that remain tangible goods.

RECOMMENDATIONS

47. Revenue Canada should convey to the Department of Finance the Committee's view that the government should state that customs duties and tariffs will not apply to tangible goods transformed into electronic products or services and, in particular, to transactions conducted through the Internet.

48. Revenue Canada should convey to the Department of Finance the Committee's view that Finance should zero-rate tangible goods that are equivalent to those that can be delivered electronically.

4.5 ISSUES COMMON TO INCOME TAX, CONSUMPTION TAX, AND CUSTOMS DUTIES AND TARIFFS

Electronic commerce and Internet transactions raise practical compliance difficulties from an evidentiary perspective. Although taxing authorities typically have extensive powers to compel disclosure of information and production of documents, their power exists only within their own jurisdiction. If taxing authorities in one jurisdiction seek international information, they must rely on the cooperation of other jurisdictions under applicable tax treaties. However, where there are no treaties, or where the other jurisdiction does not agree to disclose information (as could be the case, for example, with tax-haven jurisdictions), difficulties will arise.

In the context of customs duties and tariffs, the focus has been and continues to be the importer. If the current customs duties and tariff legislation is amended to include electronic transactions as being taxable similar to tangible goods, issues such as identity and location of the parties to a transaction will be an issue to Customs.

Even where the disclosure of information can be compelled, there will be questions as to the form and admissibility of evidence.

4.5.1 Identity and Location of the Parties to a Transaction

ISSUE

It may be difficult to assess compliance with Canadian tax law when little is known about the extent of business being conducted electronically by residents and non-residents, or about who they are.

ANALYSIS

A sound tax administration requires knowledge of the persons who comprise the tax base. For consumption taxes they are registrants, for income tax they are filers, and for customs duties they are importers.

To maintain the integrity of the tax system, tax administrations conduct audits and other activities designed to assess risk and ensure tax compliance by preventing fiscal evasion and avoidance. Transactions over the Internet are not excluded from this activity. To assess compliance of these businesses and to better understand and assist businesses, it is important that Revenue Canada gain an understanding of the Internet, who conducts business over the Internet, and the nature of this business.

Specifically, Revenue Canada needs information on which Canadian businesses are carrying on business over the Internet, the volume of this activity, the business sectors involved, and the goods and services traded. To date, electronic commerce is a relatively small part of the economy, but as it grows in significance and as Canada develops a knowledge-based economy, the need for this information will also increase.

The management and administration of the Internet are undergoing dramatic change. The Internet is moving away from its roots in the academic and research community and is becoming more commercial. As a result, the exact nature of new governance and administrative structures is not yet known.

During this period, Revenue Canada will need to adapt its compliance enforcement measures to the online environment. This will involve exploring how the evolving Internet governance structures may be used to assist Revenue Canada in its activities. One possible structure is the domain name registration system. Given the dramatic changes involving the domain name system, however, it is too early to specify the precise mechanisms Revenue Canada will need to fulfil its mandate in the emerging digital economy.

RECOMMENDATION

49. Revenue Canada should design and implement programs to test the compliance of businesses conducting commerce over the Internet.

Discussion Questions

1. Is the report's recommendation for GST compliance realistic? In light of past opposition to the GST, should Revenue Canada expect that Canadians will self-report online purchases? Consider that in 1999, the State of Michigan added a section to its state income tax form to allow state residents to self-report state sales taxes owing due to online purchases.

2. Do you think the report fully appreciates the impact of the technology underlying the Internet?

Notes

The report recommends following the OECD lead on certain Internet taxation policy matters. In the fall 1999, an OECD Working Group released its proposal for defining "permanent establishment," a key term in international tax treaties, within an Internet context. The proposal included the following discussion and recommendations:

1. There has been some discussion as to whether the mere use of computer equipment located in a country through which electronic commerce operations are carried on in that country could constitute a permanent establishment. That question raises a number of issues in relation to the provisions of the Article.

2. First, whilst fixed automated equipment operated by an enterprise and located in a country may constitute a permanent establishment in that country (see paragraph 10 [of the existing Commentary]), a distinction needs to be made between computer equipment, which could thus constitute a permanent establishment in these circumstances, and the data and software which is used by that equipment. For instance, an Internet web site may be seen as a combination of software and electronic data which is stored on and operated by a server. The web site itself does not involve any tangible property and therefore cannot itself constitute a "place of business" ("installation d'affaires" in the French version) as there is there is "no facility such as premises or, in certain circumstances, machinery or equipment" (see paragraph 2 [of the existing Commentary] above) as far as only the

software and data constituting that web site is concerned. On the other hand, the server through which that web site is operated is a piece of equipment which itself needs a physical location and may thus, if it is fixed within the meaning of paragraph 1, constitute a "fixed place of business" of the enterprise that operates it.

3. That distinction is important since the enterprise that operates a server on which a web site is hosted is often different from the enterprise that carries on business through that web site. Unless the server itself may be said to be a fixed place of business of the latter enterprise, e.g. where a server situated at a particular location is rented to the enterprise that carries on business through the web site, the mere operation of the web site of that enterprise from a server located in that country cannot constitute a permanent establishment for that enterprise. For example, it is common for the web site through which an enterprise carries on its business to be hosted on the server of an Internet Service Provider (ISP). In that case, the server and its location are not at the disposal of the enterprise, even if the enterprise has been able to decide that its web site should be hosted on that particular server; in fact, the enterprise does not even have a physical presence at that place since the web site does not involve tangible assets. Thus, the enterprise cannot be considered to have acquired a place of business by virtue of that arrangement (the possible application of the provisions of paragraph 5 is discussed below).

4. Second, it is not relevant whether the equipment used for electronic commerce operations in a particular country is or is not operated and maintained by personnel who are residents of that country or visit that country for that purpose. Automated equipment that does not require on-site human intervention for its operation may still constitute a permanent establishment.

5. Third, computer equipment may only constitute a permanent establishment if it meets the requirement of being fixed. In the example referred to in paragraph 2, what matters is not the possibility of the server being moved around, but whether it is in fact so moved. Therefore, in order to constitute a fixed place of business, a server will need to be located at a certain place for a sufficient period of time so as to become fixed within the meaning of paragraph 1.

6. Fourth, as already noted, it is common that access to the Internet is provided by Internet Service Providers which, among the services that they provide, host web sites of other enterprises on their own servers. In that case, the issue may arise as to whether paragraph 5 may apply to deem such ISPs to constitute permanent establishments of the enterprises that carry on electronic commerce through web sites operated through the servers owned and operated by these ISPs. While this could be the case in very unusual circumstances, paragraph 5 will generally not be applicable because the ISPs will not constitute agents of the enterprises to which the web sites belong, because these ISPs will not have authority to conclude contracts in the name of these enterprises and will not regularly conclude such contracts or because they will constitute independent agents acting in the ordinary course of their business, as evidenced by the fact that they host the web sites of many different enterprises. It is also clear that since the web site through which an enterprise carries on its business is not itself a "person" as defined in Article 3, paragraph 5 cannot apply to deem a permanent establishment to exist by virtue of the web site being an agent of the enterprise for purposes of that paragraph.

7. Finally, no permanent establishment may be considered to exist where the electronic commerce operations carried on through computer equipment lo-

cated in a country are restricted to the preparatory or auxiliary activities covered by paragraph 4. The question of whether particular activities performed through computer equipment fall within paragraph 4 needs to [be] examined on a case-by-case basis having regards to the various functions performed by the enterprise through the software and electronic data stored or operated through that equipment. Where the functions performed through the computer equipment include activities that form in themselves an essential and significant part of the commercial activity of an enterprise as a whole, these would go beyond the activities covered by paragraph 4 and if the equipment constituted a fixed place of business of the enterprise (as discussed in paragraphs 1 to 5 above), this equipment would therefore be a permanent establishment of the enterprise.

The United States has assumed the leading role as a key proponent for a tax-free Internet. In 1998, the U.S. Congress passed the *Internet Tax Freedom Act*, which established a three-year moratorium on new Internet taxes. That policy came under fire in 2000 when policy makers considered a permanent extension to the moratorium. Although most federal officials supported the moratorium, many state and local officials feared that revenue losses would be substantial, and began to raise the prospect of new Internet taxation schemes. As a final compromise, the moratorium was extended for an additional five years, until 2006, with the prospect of the imposition of new Internet taxes at that time.

Internet Tax Freedom Act[†]

SEC. 1101. MORATORIUM.

(a) *Moratorium.* — No State or political subdivision thereof shall impose any of the following taxes during the period beginning on October 1, 1998, and ending 3 years after the date of the enactment of this Act —

(1) taxes on Internet access, unless such tax was generally imposed and actually enforced prior to October 1, 1998; and
(2) multiple or discriminatory taxes on electronic commerce.

(b) *Preservation of State and Local Taxing Authority.* — Except as provided in this section, nothing in this title shall be construed to modify, impair, or supersede, or authorize the modification, impairment, or superseding of, any State or local law pertaining to taxation that is otherwise permissible by or under the Constitution of the United States or other Federal law and in effect on the date of enactment of this Act.

(c) *Liabilities and Pending Cases.* — Nothing in this title affects liability for taxes accrued and enforced before the date of enactment of this Act, nor does this title affect ongoing litigation relating to such taxes.

---

† Approved as H.R. 4328 by Congress on October 20, 1998. Signed As Public Law 105-277 on October 21, 1998.

(d) *Definition of Generally Imposed and Actually Enforced.* — For purposes of this section, a tax has been generally imposed and actually enforced prior to October 1, 1998, if, before that date, the tax was authorized by statute and either —

(1) a provider of Internet access services had a reasonable opportunity to know by virtue of a rule or other public proclamation made by the appropriate administrative agency of the State or political subdivision thereof, that such agency has interpreted and applied such tax to Internet access services; or

(2) a State or political subdivision thereof generally collected such tax on charges for Internet access.

(e) *Exception to Moratorium.* —

(1) In general. — Subsection (a) shall also not apply in the case of any person or entity who knowingly and with knowledge of the character of the material, in interstate or foreign commerce by means of the World Wide Web, makes any communication for commercial purposes that is available to any minor and that includes any material that is harmful to minors unless such person or entity has restricted access by minors to material that is harmful to minors —
    (A) by requiring use of a credit card, debit account, adult access code, or adult personal identification number;
    (B) by accepting a digital certificate that verifies age; or
    (C) by any other reasonable measures that are feasible under available technology.

(2) Scope of exception. — For purposes of paragraph (1), a person shall not be considered to making a communication for commercial purposes of material to the extent that the person is —
    (A) a telecommunications carrier engaged in the provision of a telecommunications service;
    (B) a person engaged in the business of providing an Internet access service;
    (C) a person engaged in the business of providing an Internet information location tool; or
    (D) similarly engaged in the transmission, storage, retrieval, hosting, formatting, or translation (or any combination thereof) of a communication made by another person, without selection or alteration of the communication.

(3) Definitions. — In this subsection:
    (A) By means of the World Wide Web. — The term "by means of the World Wide Web" means by placement of material in a computer server-based file archive so that it is publicly accessible, over the Internet, using hypertext transfer protocol, file transfer protocol, or other similar protocols.
    (B) Commercial purposes; engaged in the business. —
        (i) Commercial purposes. — A person shall be considered to make a communication for commercial purposes only if such person is engaged in the business of making such communications.
        (ii) Engaged in the business. — The term "engaged in the business" means that the person who makes a communication, or offers to make a communication, by means of the World Wide Web, that includes any material that is harmful to minors, devotes time, attention, or labor to such activities, as a regular course of such person's trade or business, with the objective of earning a profit as a result of such activities (although it is not necessary that the person make a profit or that the making or offering to make such communications

610 / **Part Five:** Internet Commerce

be the person's sole or principal business or source of income). A person may be considered to be engaged in the business of making, by means of the World Wide Web, communications for commercial purposes that include material that is harmful to minors, only if the person knowingly causes the material that is harmful to minors to be posted on the World Wide Web or knowingly solicits such material to be posted on the World Wide Web.

(C) Internet. — The term "Internet" means collectively the myriad of computer and telecommunications facilities, including equipment and operating software, which comprise the interconnected world-wide network of networks that employ the Transmission Control Protocol/Internet Protocol, or any predecessor or successor protocols to such protocol, to communicate information of all kinds by wire or radio.

(D) Internet access service. — The term "Internet access service" means a service that enables users to access content, information, electronic mail, or other services offered over the Internet and may also include access to proprietary content, information, and other services as part of a package of services offered to consumers. Such term does not include telecommunications services.

(E) Internet information location tool. — The term "Internet information location tool" means a service that refers or links users to an online location on the World Wide Web. Such term includes directories, indices, references, pointers, and hypertext links.

(F) Material that is harmful to minors. — The term "material that is harmful to minors" means any communication, picture, image, graphic image file, article, recording, writing, or other matter of any kind that is obscene or that —

    (i) the average person, applying contemporary community standards, would find, taking the material as a whole and with respect to minors, is designed to appeal to, or is designed to pander to, the prurient interest;

    (ii) depicts, describes, or represents, in a manner patently offensive with respect to minors, an actual or simulated sexual act or sexual contact, an actual or simulated normal or perverted sexual act, or a lewd exhibition of the genitals or post-pubescent female breast; and

    (iii) taken as a whole, lacks serious literary, artistic, political, or scientific value for minors.

(G) Minor. — The term "minor" means any person under 17 years of age.

(H) Telecommunications carrier; telecommunications service. — The terms "telecommunications carrier" and "telecommunications service" have the meanings given such terms in section 3 of the Communications Act of 1934 (47 U.S.C. 153).

(f) *Additional Exception to Moratorium.* —

(1) In general. — Subsection (a) shall also not apply with respect to an Internet access provider, unless, at the time of entering into an agreement with a customer for the provision of Internet access services, such provider offers such customer (either for a fee or at no charge) screening software that is designed to permit the customer to limit access to material on the Internet that is harmful to minors.

(2) Definitions. — In this subsection:

    (A) Internet access provider. — The term "Internet access provider" means a person engaged in the business of providing a computer and communications facility through which a customer may obtain access to the Internet, but does not include a common carrier to the extent that it provides only telecommunications services.

    (B) Internet access services. — The term "Internet access services" means the provision of computer and communications services through which a customer using a computer and a modem or other communications device may obtain access to the Internet, but does not include telecommunications services provided by a common carrier.

    (C) Screening software. — The term "screening software" means software that is designed to permit a person to limit access to material on the Internet that is harmful to minors.

(3) Applicability. — Paragraph (1) shall apply to agreements for the provision of Internet access services entered into on or after the date that is 6 months after the date of enactment of this Act.

SEC. 1104. DEFINITIONS.

For the purposes of this title:

(1) *Bit tax.* — The term "bit tax" means any tax on electronic commerce expressly imposed on or measured by the volume of digital information transmitted electronically, or the volume of digital information per unit of time transmitted electronically, but does not include taxes imposed on the provision of telecommunications services.

(2) *Discriminatory tax.* — The term "discriminatory tax" means —

    (A) any tax imposed by a State or political subdivision thereof on electronic commerce that —

        (i) is not generally imposed and legally collectible by such State or such political subdivision on transactions involving similar property, goods, services, or information accomplished through other means;

        (ii) is not generally imposed and legally collectible at the same rate by such State or such political subdivision on transactions involving similar property, goods, services, or information accomplished through other means, unless the rate is lower as part of a phase-out of the tax over not more than a 5-year period;

        (iii) imposes an obligation to collect or pay the tax on a different person or entity than in the case of transactions involving similar property, goods, services, or information accomplished through other means;

        (iv) establishes a classification of Internet access service providers or online service providers for purposes of establishing a higher tax rate to be imposed on such providers than the tax rate generally applied to providers of similar information services delivered through other means; or

    (B) any tax imposed by a State or political subdivision thereof, if —

        (i) except with respect to a tax (on Internet access) that was generally imposed and actually enforced prior to October 1, 1998, the sole ability to access a site on a remote seller's out-of-state computer server is considered a factor in determining a remote seller's tax collection obligation; or

> > (ii) a provider of Internet access service or online services is deemed to be the agent of a remote seller for determining tax collection obligations solely as a result of —
> >
> > > (I) the display of a remote seller's information or content on the out-of-state computer server of a provider of Internet access service or online services; or
> > >
> > > (II) the processing of orders through the out-of-state computer server of a provider of Internet access service or online services.

(3) *Electronic commerce.* — The term "electronic commerce" means any transaction conducted over the Internet or through Internet access, comprising the sale, lease, license, offer, or delivery of property, goods, services, or information, whether or not for consideration, and includes the provision of Internet access.

(4) *Internet.* — The term "Internet" means collectively the myriad of computer and telecommunications facilities, including equipment and operating software, which comprise the interconnected world-wide network of networks that employ the Transmission Control Protocol/Internet Protocol, or any predecessor or successor protocols to such protocol, to communicate information of all kinds by wire or radio.

(5) *Internet access.* — The term "Internet access" means a service that enables users to access content, information, electronic mail, or other services offered over the Internet, and may also include access to proprietary content, information, and other services as part of a package of services offered to users. Such term does not include telecommunications services.

(6) Multiple tax. —

> (A) In general. — The term "multiple tax" means any tax that is imposed by one State or political subdivision thereof on the same or essentially the same electronic commerce that is also subject to another tax imposed by another State or political subdivision thereof (whether or not at the same rate or on the same basis), without a credit (for example, a resale exemption certificate) for taxes paid in other jurisdictions.
>
> (B) Exception. — Such term shall not include a sales or use tax imposed by a State and 1 or more political subdivisions thereof on the same electronic commerce or a tax on persons engaged in electronic commerce which also may have been subject to a sales or use tax thereon.
>
> (C) Sales or use tax. — For purposes of subparagraph (B), the term "sales or use tax" means a tax that is imposed on or incident to the sale, purchase, storage, consumption, distribution, or other use of tangible personal property or services as may be defined by laws imposing such tax and which is measured by the amount of the sales price or other charge for such property or service.

(7) *State.* — The term "State" means any of the several States, the District of Columbia, or any commonwealth, territory, or possession of the United States.

(8) *Tax.* —

> (A) In general. — The term "tax" means —
>
> > (i) any charge imposed by any governmental entity for the purpose of generating revenues for governmental purposes, and is not a fee imposed for a specific privilege, service, or benefit conferred; or

(ii) the imposition on a seller of an obligation to collect and to remit to a governmental entity any sales or use tax imposed on a buyer by a governmental entity.

(B) Exception. — Such term does not include any franchise fee or similar fee imposed by a State or local franchising authority, pursuant to section 622 or 653 of the Communications Act of 1934 (47 U.S.C. 542, 573), or any other fee related to obligations or telecommunications carriers under the Communications Act of 1934 (47 U.S.C. 151 et seq.).

(9) *Telecommunications service.* — The term "telecommunications service" has the meaning given such term in section 3(46) of the Communications Act of 1934 (47 U.S.C. 153(46)) and includes communications services (as defined in section 4251 of the Internal Revenue Code of 1986).

(10) *Tax on Internet access.* — The term "tax on Internet access" means a tax on Internet access, including the enforcement or application of any new or preexisting tax on the sale or use of Internet services unless such tax was generally imposed and actually enforced prior to October 1, 1998.

TITLE XII — OTHER PROVISIONS

SEC. 1201. DECLARATION THAT INTERNET SHOULD BE FREE OF NEW FEDERAL TAXES.

It is the sense of Congress that no new Federal taxes similar to the taxes described in section 1101(a) should be enacted with respect to the Internet and Internet access during the moratorium provided in such section.

SEC. 1203. DECLARATION THAT THE INTERNET SHOULD BE FREE OF FOREIGN TARIFFS, TRADE BARRIERS, AND OTHER RESTRICTIONS.

(a) *In General.* — It is the sense of Congress that the President should seek bilateral, regional, and multilateral agreements to remove barriers to global electronic commerce through the World Trade Organization, the Organization for Economic Cooperation and Development, the Trans-Atlantic Economic Partnership, the Asia Pacific Economic Cooperation forum, the Free Trade Area of the America, the North American Free Trade Agreement, and other appropriate venues.

(b) *Negotiating Objectives.* — The negotiating objectives of the United States shall be —

(1) to assure that electronic commerce is free from —
   (A) tariff and non-tariff barriers;
   (B) burdensome and discriminatory regulation and standards; and
   (C) discriminatory taxation; and

(2) to accelerate the growth of electronic commerce by expanding market access opportunities for —
   (A) the development of telecommunications infrastructure;
   (B) the procurement of telecommunications equipment;
   (C) the provision of Internet access and telecommunications services; and
   (D) the exchange of goods, services, and digitalized information.

(c) *Electronic Commerce.* — For purposes of this section, the term "electronic commerce" has the meaning given that term in section 1104(3).

Discussion Questions

1. At the heart of this policy issue is the question of tax fairness. Does it make sense to tax the purchase of books online differently from offline? Is a tax-free Internet little more than a tax break for the upper and middle classes who constitute the majority of Internet users and e-commerce shoppers? How important is the facilitation of e-commerce as a policy goal?

Notes

The European Union's approach presents a much different perspective. Early European proposals focused on a "bit tax" that would levy tax based on the amount of digital content downloaded. Critics pointed out that the size of download bore little relation to the value of the downloaded content, and thus the tax scheme was inherently unfair.

More recently, the European Union proposed the imposition of Value Added Tax (VAT) for all online purchases. The proposal, described in part below, yielded swift condemnation from U.S. e-commerce businesses, who argued that the plan would harm the development of e-commerce throughout Europe and place an unfair obligation on non-European businesses.

> Proposal for a COUNCIL DIRECTIVE amending Directive 77/388/EEC as regards the value added tax arrangements applicable to certain services supplied by electronic mean[s]
>
> THE COUNCIL OF THE EUROPEAN UNION,
>
> Having regard to the Treaty establishing the European Community, and in particular Article 93 thereof,
> Having regard to the proposal from the Commission
> Having regard to the opinion of the European Parliament
> Having regard to the opinion of the Economic and Social Committee,
>
> Whereas:
> (1) The rules currently applicable to VAT on certain services supplied by electronic means under Article 9 of the Sixth Council Directive 77/388/EEC of 17 May 1977 on the harmonisation of the laws of the Member States relating to turnover taxes — Common system of value added tax: uniform basis of assessment are inadequate for taxing such services consumed within the Community and for preventing distortions of competition in this area.
> (2) In the interests of the proper functioning of the internal market, such distortions should be eliminated and new harmonised rules introduced for this type of activity. Action should be taken to ensure, in particular, that such services where effected for consideration and consumed by customers established in the Community are taxed in the Community and are not taxed if consumed outside the Community.
> (3) To this end, certain services supplied by electronic means to persons established in the Community or to recipients established in third countries should, in principle, be taxed at the place of the recipient of the services. For the purpose of establishing a special rule for determining the place of

supply it has to be defined when services are supplied "by electronic means".

(4) To facilitate the compliance with their fiscal obligations, economic operators established outside the Community should be given the possibility to choose for a single VAT identification in the Community.

(5) Such VAT identification by a non-EU supplier in an EU Member State should be for the purposes of this directive only and does not constitute establishment within the meaning of the Articles 43 or 48 of the EC Treaty or of other Community directives and a non-EU supplier should not benefit from the Internal Market freedoms enshrined in the EC Treaty or in Community directives merely by becoming identified for VAT.

(6) Subject to conditions which they lay down, Member States should allow statements and returns to be made by electronic means.

(7) By reason of administrative simplification supplies of services by electronic means within a threshold indicating a negligible economic activity in the Community should benefit from a special scheme for small undertakings, and this threshold should be reviewed and changed if necessary.

(8) The change of the place of supply involves adjustments in the area of Directive 77/388 as to the modalities of the definition of the person liable to tax and its obligations.

(9) It appears appropriate to ensure certainty on the rate of taxation to be applied to the services supplied by electronic means, which will be in principle the normal VAT rate.

24

Securities Regulation and the Internet

The Internet has revolutionized many business sectors, but few more so than the securities industry. In the span of a few short years, online brokerages have grabbed a large share of consumer stock trades, dot-com companies have become the darling of the stock market, and the Internet has emerged as the primary information source for millions of investors.

Given its growing importance, securities regulators find themselves increasingly preoccupied with Internet-related issues. The rising incidence of online securities fraud, online disclosure issues and jurisdictional complexity have forced securities commissions worldwide to place the Internet at the top of their priority list and to engage in cooperative policy and enforcement exercises.

With the United States still the leader in this sector, its chief regulator, the Securities and Exchange Commission (SEC), has taken a very proactive role in the development of online securities regulation policy. Its approach to issues such as jurisdiction and online disclosure has provided other jurisdictions with a blueprint to follow, and has fostered the development of harmonized (some would say, "Americanized") regulations.

JURISDICTION

Interpretation; Statement of the Commission Regarding Use of Internet Web Sites to Offer Securities, Solicit Securities Transactions, or Advertise Investment Services Offshore†

A. The Global Reach of the Internet

The development of the Internet presents numerous opportunities and benefits for consumers and investors throughout the world. It also presents significant challenges for regulators charged with protecting consumers and investors. Regulators in many countries are attempting to administer their respective laws to preserve important protections provided by their regulatory schemes without stifling the Internet's vast communications potential. We share this goal in our administration of the U.S. securities laws.

Information posted on Internet Web sites concerning securities and investments can be made readily available without regard to geographic and political boundaries. Additionally, the interactive nature of the Internet makes it possible for investors to purchase electronically the securities or services offered. For these and other reasons, we believe that the use of the Internet by market participants and investors presents significant issues under the U.S. securities laws.

Although this release focuses on Internet Web sites, the Internet offers a variety of forms of communication. We distinguish between Web site postings and more targeted Internet communication methods. More targeted communication methods are comparable to traditional mail because the sender directs the information to a particular person, group or entity. These methods include e-mail and technology that allows mass e-mailing or "spamming." Information posted on a Web site, however, is not sent to any particular person, although it is available for anyone to search for and retrieve. Offerors using those more targeted technologies must assume the responsibility of identifying when their offering materials are being sent to persons in the United States and must comply fully with the U.S. securities laws.

B. Regulation of Offers

Many registration requirements under the U.S. securities laws are triggered when an offer of securities or financial services, such as brokerage or investment advisory services, is made to the general public.

*   Under the Securities Act, absent an exemption, an issuer that offers or sells securities in the United States through use of the mails or other means of interstate commerce must register the offering with the Commission. An offering of securities may be exempt from registration if it is conducted as a "private placement," without any general solicitation of investors.
*   Under the Investment Company Act, a foreign investment company may not use the mails or other means of interstate commerce to publicly offer its securities in the United States or to U.S. persons unless the investment company receives an

---

† Securities and Exchange Commission [Release No. 33-7516], online: <http://www.sec.gov/rules/concept/33-7516.htm> (last modified: March 23, 1998). Reproduced with permission.

order from the Commission permitting it to register under the Investment Company Act. A foreign investment company may, however, make a private offer of its securities in the United States or to U.S. persons in reliance on one of the exclusions from the definition of "investment company" under the Investment Company Act.

- Under the Advisers Act, an adviser is prohibited from using the mails or other means of interstate commerce in connection with its business as an investment adviser, unless the adviser is registered with the Commission, or is exempted or excluded from the requirement to register.
- Under the Exchange Act, a broker or dealer generally must register with the Commission if it uses the mails or any means of interstate commerce to effect transactions in, or to induce or attempt to induce the purchase or sale of, any security.
- Under the Exchange Act, an exchange generally must register with the Commission if it uses the mails or any means of interstate commerce for the purpose of using its facilities to effect any transaction in a security or to report any such transaction.

The posting of information on a Web site may constitute an offer of securities or investment services for purposes of the U.S. securities laws. Our discussion of these issues will proceed on the assumption that the Web site contains information that constitutes an "offer" of securities or investment services under the U.S. securities laws. Because anyone who has access to the Internet can obtain access to a Web site unless the Web site sponsor adopts special procedures to restrict access, the pertinent legal issue is whether those Web site postings are offers *in the United States* that must be registered.

III. OFFSHORE OFFERS AND SOLICITATIONS ON THE INTERNET

A. General Approach

Some may argue that regulators could best protect investors by requiring registration or licensing for any Internet offer of securities or investment services that their residents could access. As a practical matter, however, the adoption of such an approach by securities regulators could preclude some of the most promising Internet applications by investors, issuers, and financial service providers.

The regulation of offers is a fundamental element of federal and some U.S. state securities regulatory schemes. Absent the transaction of business in the United States or with U.S. persons, however, our interest in regulating solicitation activity is less compelling. We believe that our investor protection concerns are best addressed through the implementation by issuers and financial service providers of precautionary measures that are reasonably designed to ensure that offshore Internet offers are not targeted to persons in the United States or to U.S. persons.

B. Procedures Reasonably Designed to Avoid Targeting the United States

When offerors implement adequate measures to prevent U.S. persons from participating in an offshore Internet offer, we would not view the offer as targeted at the United States and thus would not treat it as occurring in the United States for registration purposes. What constitutes adequate measures will depend on all the facts and circumstances of any particular situation. We generally would not consider an offshore Internet offer made by a non-U.S. offeror as targeted at the United States, however, if:

- The Web site includes a prominent disclaimer making it clear that the offer is directed only to countries other than the United States. For example, the Web site could state that the securities or services are not being offered in the United States or to U.S. persons, or it could specify those jurisdictions (other than the United States) in which the offer is being made; and
- The Web site offeror implements procedures that are reasonably designed to guard against sales to U.S. persons in the offshore offering. For example, the offeror could ascertain the purchaser's residence by obtaining such information as mailing addresses or telephone numbers (or area code) prior to the sale. This measure will allow the offeror to avoid sending or delivering securities, offering materials, services or products to a person at a U.S. address or telephone number.

These procedures are not exclusive; other procedures that suffice to guard against sales to U.S. persons also can be used to demonstrate that the offer is not targeted at the United States. Regardless of the precautions adopted, however, we would view solicitations that appear by their content to be targeted at U.S. persons as made in the United States. Examples of this type of solicitation include purportedly offshore offers that emphasize the investor's ability to avoid U.S. income taxes on the investments. We are concerned that the advice that we provide to assist those who attempt to comply with both the letter and spirit of the securities laws will be used by others as a pretext to violate those laws. Sham offshore offerings or procedures, or other schemes will not allow issuers or promoters to escape their registration obligations under the U.S. securities laws.

C. Effect of Attempts by U.S. Persons to Evade Restrictions

We recognize that U.S. persons may respond falsely to residence questions, disguise their country of residence by using non-resident addresses, or use other devices, such as offshore nominees, in order to participate in offshore offerings of securities or investment services. Thus, even if the foreign market participant has taken measures reasonably designed to guard against sales to U.S. persons, a U.S. person nevertheless could circumvent those measures.

In our view, if a U.S. person purchases securities or investment services notwithstanding adequate procedures reasonably designed to prevent the purchase, we would not view the Internet offer after the fact as having been targeted at the United States, absent indications that would put the issuer on notice that the purchaser was a U.S. person. This information might include (but is not limited to): receipt of payment drawn on a U.S. bank; provision of a U.S. taxpayer identification or social security number; or, statements by the purchaser indicating that, notwithstanding a foreign address, he or she is a U.S. resident. Confronted with such information, we would expect offerors to take steps to verify that the purchaser is not a U.S. person before selling to that person. Additionally, if despite its use of measures that appear to be reasonably designed to prevent sales to U.S. persons, the offeror discovers that it has sold to U.S. persons, it may need to evaluate whether other measures may be necessary to provide reasonable assurance against future sales to U.S. persons.

D. Third-Party Web Services

An issuer, underwriter or other type of offshore Internet offeror may seek to have its offering materials posted on a third-party's Web site. In that event, if the offeror uses a third-party Web service that employs at least the same level of precautions against sales to U.S. persons as would be adequate for the offshore Internet offeror to employ, we would not view the third-party's Web site as an offer that is targeted to the United States.

When an offeror, or those acting on its behalf, uses a third-party's Web site to generate interest in the Internet offer, more stringent precautions by the offeror than those outlined in Section III.B. may be warranted. These precautions may include limiting access to its Internet offering materials to persons who can demonstrate that they are not U.S. persons. For example, additional precautions may be called for when the Internet offeror:

- Posts offering or solicitation material or otherwise causes the offer to be listed on an investment-oriented Web site that has a significant number of U.S. clients or subscribers, or where U.S. investors could be expected to search for information about investment opportunities or services; or
- Arranges for direct or indirect hyperlinks from a third-party investment-oriented page to its own Web page containing the offering material.

IV. ADDITIONAL ISSUES UNDER THE SECURITIES ACT

Our Securities Act analysis assumes that the information posted on a Web site would, were we to deem it to occur in the United States, constitute an "offer" within the meaning of Section 5(c) of the Securities Act and Regulation S, a "public offering" prohibited under Section 4(2) of the Act, a "general solicitation or general advertising" prohibited under Rule 502(c) of Regulation D, and a "directed selling effort" prohibited under Regulation S. The focus of our analysis, then, is under what circumstances should we deem offshore Internet offers to which U.S. persons can gain access not to occur in the United States.

A. Offshore Offerings by Foreign Issuers

1. Regulations

When a foreign issuer is making an unregistered offshore Internet offer and does not plan to sell securities in the United States as part of the offering, it should implement the general measures outlined in Section III.B. to avoid targeting the United States. Assuming that the offering is made pursuant to Regulation S, the offering must comply with all of the applicable requirements under that regulation, including the requirement that all offers and sales be made in "offshore transactions."

2. U.S. Exempt Component

Foreign issuers commonly make offshore offerings concurrently with private offerings to U.S. institutional buyers. An offering exempt under Section 4(2) of the Securities Act may not involve "any public offering." Regulation D specifically prohibits the offer or sale of securities through a "general solicitation or general advertising." Publicly accessible Web site postings may *not* be used as a means to locate investors to participate in a pending or imminent U.S. offering relying on those provisions. If a Web site posting would be inappropriate for a U.S. private placement, an issuer should not attempt to accomplish the same result indirectly through the posting of an offshore Internet offer.

In addition to implementing the type of precautionary measures previously discussed, foreign issuers could implement other procedures to prevent their offshore

Internet offers from being used to solicit participants for their U.S.-based exempt offerings, including:

- The Internet offeror could allow unrestricted access to its offshore Internet offering materials, but not permit persons responding to the offshore Internet offering to participate in its exempt U.S. offering, even if otherwise qualified to do so. In that situation, the offeror would keep a record of all persons responding over the Internet and all persons who otherwise indicate that they are responding to the offshore Internet offering; *or*
- The Web site offeror could ensure that access to the posted offering materials is limited to those viewers who first provide their residence information and, in doing so, do not provide information such as a U.S. area code or address that indicates that they are a U.S. person. Thus, U.S. persons could obtain access only by misrepresenting their residence information.

We believe that it would not be advisable for us to dictate the use of any one particular technology or screening method to protect against general solicitation in these instances. Any less costly, less intrusive method that is equally or more effective than those that we have suggested would be adequate as well.

In addition, the posted offering materials should relate only to the offshore offering. The materials should contain only that information (if any) concerning the private U.S. offering that is required by foreign law to be provided to investors participating in the offshore public offering.

B. Offshore Offerings by U.S. Issuers

Our approach to the use of Web sites to post offshore securities offerings distinguishes between domestic and foreign issuers. For the following reasons, additional precautions are justified for Web sites operated by domestic issuers purporting not to make a public offering in the United States:

- The substantial contacts that a U.S. issuer has with the United States justifies our exercise of more extensive regulatory jurisdiction over its securities-related activities;
- There is a strong likelihood that securities of U.S. issuers initially offered and sold offshore will enter the U.S. trading markets; and
- U.S. issuers and investors have a much greater expectation that securities offerings by domestic issuers will be subject to the U.S. securities laws.

Our experience with abusive practices under Regulation S indicates that we should proceed cautiously when giving guidance to U.S. issuers in the area of unregistered offshore offerings. As a result, we would not consider a U.S. issuer using a Web site to make an unregistered offer to have implemented reasonable measures to prevent sales to U.S. persons unless, in addition to the general precautions discussed above in Section III.B., the U.S. issuer implements password-type procedures that are reasonably designed to ensure that only non-U.S. persons can obtain access to the offer. Under this procedure, persons seeking access to the Internet offer would have to demonstrate to the issuer or intermediary that they are not U.S. persons before obtaining the password for the site.

In the context of broader Securities Act reform, we have been considering whether the current general solicitation and other offering communications restrictions on issuers and other offering participants should be modified to create greater flexibility. To the extent that we reform those restrictions on offering communications in the future, we also will consider the implications of those changes for unregistered offshore Internet offerings.

C.   Concurrent U.S. Registered Offering

A registered offering in the United States that takes place concurrently with an unregistered offshore Internet offer presents concerns because of the Securities Act's restrictions on making offers prior to the filing of a registration statement or, in the case of written or published offers, outside of the statutory prospectus. Consistent with these requirements, therefore, premature posting of offering information must be avoided. Existing Commission rules that provide a safe harbor for announcements of anticipated offerings provide guidance in this respect. The Commission is considering whether to provide further guidance or to make further changes concerning concurrent U.S. registered offerings and offshore Internet offers in the context of broader Securities Act reforms.

D.   Underwriters

Just as an issuer must take reasonable steps to avoid offers of unregistered securities in the United States, so too must persons acting on behalf of the issuer, such as underwriters or distributors. These persons, for purposes of the Securities Act, stand in the place of the issuer. Thus, regardless of whether the underwriter is foreign or domestic, what constitutes measures reasonably designed to prevent sales to U.S. persons will depend on the status of the issuer. For example, if the issuer is domestic and precautionary measures would call for its Web site containing offshore offering information to be password-protected, so too should the information be protected on the underwriter's Web site.

Canadian regulators have followed the SEC's lead by adopting a similar approach to jurisdiction.

Trading in Securities Using the Internet and Other Electronic Means[†]

CSA Approach to Trading in Securities Using the Internet and Other Electronic Means

The CSA has decided that statutory requirements relating to trading and offering securities should not change as a result of the involvement of the Internet or other electronic means. That is to say that in the absence of the Policy, a trade or offering involving the Internet or other electronic means could still take place, provided that appropriate securities legislation is complied with. The Policy represents the CSA views on how best to comply with securities legislation when electronic media is used and points out issues that a market participant should consider when conducting trades or offerings on the Internet.

[†] British Columbia Securities Commission [Notice NIN#98/72], online: <http://www.bcsc.bc.ca/Policy/Nin98-72.pdf> (last modified: December 31, 1998). Reproduced with the permission of the B.C. Securities Commission.

Summary of the Policy
Part 2 addresses a number of issues relating to the use of the Internet for trading in securities.

Section 2.1 notes the interjurisdictional nature of the Internet, and the resulting need for issuers and other market participants to consider how they will satisfy the registration and prospectus requirements contained in Canadian securities legislation, as well as similar requirements under the securities laws of foreign jurisdictions.

Section 2.2 states that the CSA generally consider a person or company to be trading in securities in a jurisdiction if that person or company posts on the Internet a document that offers, or solicits trades of, securities, if that document is accessible to persons or companies in that jurisdiction. Under certain circumstances, however, such a posting of a document on the Internet is not considered by the CSA to be a trade or, if applicable, a distribution in a jurisdiction. These circumstances exist if

(a) the document contains a prominent disclaimer that identifies the jurisdictions or foreign jurisdictions in which the offering or solicitation is qualified to be made, not including that particular jurisdiction; and

(b) reasonable precautions are taken by all persons or companies offering or soliciting trades of securities through the document not to sell to anyone resident in that particular jurisdiction.

Section 2.2 also reminds market participants that registration requirements apply to the posting of a prospectus or other offering document on the Internet in connection with a distribution in a jurisdiction. The act of posting the prospectus or offering document in those circumstances is an act in furtherance of a trade in that jurisdiction, and the person or company posting the prospectus or offering document must satisfy the registration requirements of the jurisdiction, or refer all inquiries concerning the document to a registered dealer.

Section 2.3 states that a person or company located in British Columbia, Alberta or Quebec that is distributing securities entirely outside of those jurisdictions through the Internet is considered to be trading within those jurisdictions, and is therefore subject to applicable registration and prospectus requirements in those jurisdictions.

Section 2.4 reminds Canadian issuers and other market participants to consider the requirements of securities laws of foreign jurisdictions when they post materials on a Web site that can be accessed by persons or companies there. Section 2.4 notes that some foreign securities regulators have informed the market on their views concerning these matters, and issuers and other market participants are referred to a recent report of the Technical Committee of the International Organization of Securities Commissions that references the rules, policies and guidelines of various international securities regulators on these matters.

Section 2.5 notes the requirement contained in Canadian securities legislation for persons and companies distributing securities under a prospectus to record the name of all persons or companies that have received a copy of the preliminary prospectus, whether in paper form or distributed by electronic means. Section 2.5 states that this requirement can be satisfied in connection with the electronic distribution of a prospectus if a person or company monitors who has had access to information or requires a written or electronic consent form from each recipient of a preliminary prospectus.

Section 2.6 states that the posting of new information on a Web site during a period of distribution may be construed as advertising, which is subject to restrictions in certain jurisdictions.

Section 2.7 deals with a number of issues relating to the use of the Internet to transmit road shows. The section notes that, in principle, the Canadian securities regulatory authorities do not object in principle to an issuer or underwriter transmitting roadshows electronically over the Internet during the waiting period prescribed by Canadian securities legislation in connection with a distribution of securities. Section 2.7 sets out guidelines that are recommended to ensure that the transmission of a roadshow complies with the waiting period requirements and Canadian securities legislation generally. The guidelines include a reminder that information provided in the roadshow not be inconsistent with the information contained in the applicable preliminary prospectus; that a copy of the preliminary prospectus be made available to all viewers of the transmission; that electronic access to the Internet transmissions of a roadshow be controlled by the issuer or underwriter conducting the roadshow to ensure that all viewers are identified and have been offered a preliminary prospectus; and that all viewers of the transmission should agree not to copy, download or further transmit the transmissions.

The Alberta Securities Commission became one of the first securities regulators in North America to address the jurisdictional issue in the following case, which was discussed in Chapter 3 but is worth reviewing in this context as well.

World Stock Exchange (Re)[†]

(A) Origins of the World Stock Exchange
At all relevant times, Orest Rusnak and Tom Seto both resided in Edmonton, Alberta. Tom Seto described himself as a salesman, business consultant and the founder of the WSE. Orest Rusnak, a former lawyer, is president of Academy Financial Planners & Consultants Inc. ("Academy Financial"). The letterhead of Academy Financial says, "International Business, Legal & Financial Consulting".

In September or October of 1997, Tom Seto came up with the idea of setting up an Internet stock exchange. He discussed the idea with Orest Rusnak, who prepared most of the written material relating to the WSE, with editorial input from Tom Seto. Mr. Rose, an Edmonton businessman, also provided some comments on the material.

At that time, there was no formal organization to the WSE. Tom Seto described Mr. Rose as an "extremely competent and conscientious type businessman" whose advice he respected. Tom Seto described Orest Rusnak's role with the WSE "basically as a consultant and advisor, and in some ways a friend and business cohort".

In late October of 1997, Tom Seto registered a domain name (worldstock.com) and opened a website under the name "World Stock Exchange on the Internet". A website is a collection of web pages stored on a single computer that is connected to, and accessible through, the Internet. The WSE website was stored on and acces-

---

† Alberta Securities Commission Decision, February 15, 2000.

sible through an Internet service provider whose computer was located in Edmonton, Alberta.

At that time, the website was still under construction and, although it is clear that no companies were then listed, the website included information on how a company could become listed on the WSE. Not all the information on the website was consistent, but it appeared to include a requirement that the listing company purchase shares in the WSE. A printed copy of the website as it existed on November 5, 1997 was entered in evidence.

By November 5, 1997 Commission staff had learned of the website and issued an Investigation Order pursuant to section 28 of the Act. On November 10, 1997 a Commission investigator, Mr. Kimak, met with Tom Seto and advised him to "take the website down" pending further investigation. Tom Seto removed everything except the title page, and advised Mr. Kimak that he was going to the Cayman Islands the next day to set up the website there.

On November 11, 1997, Tom Seto, Orest Rusnak and Mr. Rose went to the Cayman Islands. On that trip, WSE was incorporated in the Cayman Islands, as were Valle Los Reyes Island Resort Ltd. ("Valle Los Reyes") and Canroc International Ltd. ("Canroc"), two of the companies to be listed on the WSE.

Tom Seto was named as a director of WSE. Mr. Rose was, as he described it, "a director and the nominal president". According to Mr. Rose, Orest Rusnak was essentially running the show during their time in the Cayman Islands, while Mr. Rose "sort of toddled around behind everybody". Mr. Rose resigned his positions with the WSE in May 1998 because, as he described it:

> I was concerned that Orest Rusnak was doing some things, and even though I was nominal president and director I wanted to know what was going on. And I didn't know that our website had been shut down, I didn't know that our lawyer had ceased to act for us and things like that that had to do with this problem with the Cayman Stock Exchange and with the government getting on our case. And a month had gone by and Orest who had all of this information didn't pass it on to me. I thought there is no communication here and, therefore, I can't be left in a position where I am a director of a company and I don't know what is happening. So that is when I resigned.

The WSE website was stored on and accessible on the Internet through a computer located in the Cayman Islands for some time. The Cayman Island authorities had some problems with the WSE website and, as Mr. Rose described it, "the government, the police shut it down". The WSE website was then moved to a computer located in Antigua. Mr. Kimak downloaded a copy of the Antigua website as it existed on September 28, 1998 and the printed version of that was entered in evidence.

(B) Soliciting listings for the WSE and other activities of the respondents

Orest Rusnak and Tom Seto both solicited a number of Albertans and Alberta companies to raise money on the WSE. The Commission investigator, Mr. Kimak, testified that "somewhere between 30 and 40 people were engaged in conversations concerning the WSE and concerning the possibility of getting listed on the WSE", all of whom were Alberta residents. According to Mr. Kimak, every one of those people who discussed the WSE with either Orest Rusnak or Tom Seto was told about the WSE website.

Everyone understood that, in order to become listed on the WSE, companies had to be incorporated "offshore", which apparently meant in the Cayman Islands or another similar jurisdiction.

The November 1997 trip to the Cayman Islands was financed by Mr. Wall, a retired businessman residing in Edmonton. Mr. Wall paid $16,500 to Orest Rusnak, for which he expected to have Valle Los Reyes incorporated in the Cayman Islands and listed on the WSE. He also expected to receive shares in Valle Los Reyes and in the WSE. Mr. Wall understood that Tom Seto, Orest Rusnak and Mr. Rose were the directors of the WSE. Orest Rusnak passed the $16,500 to Tom Seto, who used it to obtain travelers cheques for himself and Orest Rusnak. All the money was spent during the trip to the Cayman Islands.

Mr. Ziegler, president of an Alberta company, was contacted by Tom Seto in March 1998. Tom Seto told him about the WSE website and offered to help him "raise capital in a public venue". They discussed the $5,000 listing fee for the "Speculative Trading Board" on the WSE, and were negotiating a "Management Agreement" whereby Tom Seto would, among other things, "prepare an Offering Memorandum ... for listing on the WSE".

Mr. Ziegler wanted Tom Seto to raise $200,000 for the company. They discussed the possibility of listing Mr. Ziegler's company on other exchanges or the OTC Bulletin Board in the U.S., but "narrowed it down to the WSE because of the cost of the other exchanges". Mr. Ziegler was not asked to purchase shares in the WSE and he stopped dealing with Tom Seto after talking to Commission Staff.

Mr. Lalsin, principal of an Alberta company named Lombard Developments Inc., first met Orest Rusnak sometime late in 1997. Mr. Lalsin wanted to raise capital. Orest Rusnak suggested the WSE, and told Mr. Lalsin that he was a "partner in the WSE". Mr. Lalsin asked Orest Rusnak several times whether he was a director of the WSE, but never received an answer.

On January 21, 1998, Orest Rusnak sent a proposal to Lombard Developments Inc. through Mr. Lalsin's lawyer. The covering letter and proposal are both on Academy Financial letterhead. The covering letter describes the WSE, gives its website address, and advises that the WSE "is currently setting up an information site that will be listed on all the search engines, which domain address is: worldstock.com".

The proposal is entitled "INTERNATIONAL FINANCING FOR LOMBARD WORLD HOUSING CORPORATION through the WORLD STOCK EXCHANGE". It says, in part:

> 1. That you will retain my services to incorporate LOMBARD WORLD HOUSING CORPORATION in the Cayman Islands and then to prepare and file the proper documents to list this company on the WSE in the Cayman Islands.
>
> 2. That in addition to the estimated disbursements of $10,000 to complete the above services, you have agreed to pay me compensation for my services in the amount of $5,000 plus 2% of the shares issued to the promoters in the above company....
>
> 5. That the Offering Memorandum to be filed with the WSE will be organized to raise a total of $15 million (U.S. Funds). It is proposed that these funds will be raised in three separate stages to enhance the promotional efforts for the company [$5 million in each stage, at issue prices of $1.00, $2.00 and $3.00 per share]....

The time frame for completing the set-up of this program to the stage of having the shares listed on the World Stock Exchange and ready for trading would be approximately 2 weeks. During that time, the promotion of the company can be launched to arrange interested investors. It is my assessment that this project should proceed immediately as the circumstances are ideal to create the necessary excitement to generate the initial capital required in a short time frame.

Mr. Lalsin signed and accepted the proposal. On January 27, 1999 he paid $10,000 to Academy Financial, which he understood to be the listing fee for the WSE. The listing fee quoted on the WSE website was $15,000 (U.S.), but Mr. Lalsin told Orest Rusnak:

I said like we are going in as a guinea pig on these things and I wasn't going to give him the $15,000, we would give him the ten. Plus, they were getting a piece of the company.

Lombard World Housing Corporation ("Lombard") was incorporated in the Cayman Islands on February 13, 1998, and listed on the WSE some time later. Mr. Lalsin understood that prospective investors would be able to locate the WSE through search engines, that investors could purchase shares through the WSE and that the WSE would take a percentage of the money coming to Lombard from investors. Mr. Lalsin said that The WSE initially wanted 10%, but he negotiated this down to about 5% with Orest Rusnak and Tom Seto.

Mr. Lalsin was not asked to purchase shares in the WSE. Tom Seto indicated that the WSE only received $5,000 of the $10,000 paid by Mr. Lalsin to Academy Financial.

(C) Contents of the WSE website
We have two snapshots of the contents of the WSE website: one from November 5, 1997, when the website was stored on a computer in Edmonton (the "Edmonton website"); and one from September 28, 1998, when the website was stored on a computer in Antigua (the "Antigua website"). Each website contained a large amount of information, not all of which was consistent. Some of that information is described below.

(i) general descriptions of the WSE
Under the heading "How the WSE Operates", the Antigua website says, in part:

What Security Regulations control the listing of companies?

The World Stock Exchange was incorporated and established in a manner that ensures that it does not fall under the Securities Regulations of any country. Only the regulations and policies of the World Stock Exchange control the listing of companies on the various Trading Boards of the World Stock Exchange.

The World Stock Exchange was established on the principle that its role is simply to provide a mechanism for full disclosure of relevant financial information for each company listed. It is up to the investors to review the information filed in the Company's web page and to decide whether to invest in the company. There are no standards or regulations that preclude any company from being listed, but companies are distinguished by the Administrator of Filings based on the length of business operations and assigned to specific Listing Boards. Furthermore, Warning Handles are attached to companies where there is relevant information which poses a risk to prospective investors.

Aside from requiring the listing companies to provide full disclosure, making the information easily accessible to interested investors, and requiring the company's directors, lawyer and accountant accessible [sic] for information on the company, the World Stock Exchange does not interfere with the rights of investors to invest in any company. The recourses of investors to sue the company and its directors for providing false or misleading information remains the only recourse of the investors (similar to all other jurisdictions).

Where is the World Stock Exchange Situated?

The World Stock Exchange is incorporated offshore in a tax free haven. The server for the web site of the World Stock Exchange is located offshore, and all financial transactions are finalized through offshore banks....

NOTE: The World Stock Exchange charges fees of between 3% and 10% on buy and sell orders. Of this amount, 1% in each case will be retained by the World Stock Exchange to pay for operational costs. The World Stock Exchange may charge fees for their services that they must provide in the course of serving their customers.

The Antigua website contained detailed information about how to apply for listing on the WSE. The "Procedures for Listing" include the requirement for "Confirmed arrangements for the payment of the Filing Fees, as required, together with the further investments for the purchase of shares in the World Stock Exchange." At some places in the Antigua website, only a "Listing Filing Fee" is mentioned, but another part of the website refers to both the Listing Filing Fee and a minimum or maximum WSE stock purchase.

There were four "trading boards" on the WSE:

- speculative ("for start up companies with no proven record of earnings");
- growth ("for companies that have a minimum of two years research or activity");
- established ("for companies with three years of profitable operations"); and
- blue chip ("for companies with five years of profitable operations").

The Antigua website shows three listed companies on the WSE, Valle Los Reyes and Canroc on the "growth" trading board and Lombard on the "established" trading board. Each of these companies was recently incorporated in the Cayman Islands, and the operations of each were apparently conducted through what are described as subsidiary or affiliate companies. Canroc had a subsidiary company in Alberta. Lombard had an affiliate company in Alberta. Valle Los Reyes had a subsidiary company incorporated in Costa Rica.

Each listed company had its own web page on the Antigua website containing information relating to the company. For Valle Los Reyes and Canroc, there was a certificate of incorporation, a "lawyer's letter", an "accountant's letter", an "offering memorandum", and each company's application for listing on the WSE. Lombard's web page contained everything except the accountant's letter, plus additional information on Lombard including its own website and the address of the company's president in Edmonton, Alberta.

(ii) buying and selling shares on the WSE

The Antigua website included "buttons" labeled "TO BUY/SELL SHARES CLICK HERE", and electronic forms to be filled in to buy or to sell. These forms included a "certificate" whereby the buyer or seller applied to become "registered" with the "ISBC", which is identified elsewhere on the website as the International Stock Brokerage Corporation. It appears that the ISBC would act as some type of designated agency for the WSE, and the website notes:

> There are NO stock certificates issued for any companies listed exclusively on the World Stock Exchange, and the records and letters of confirmation (which, if desired, include an electronically generated share certificate to be used for record purposes only) by the International Stock Brokerage Corporation will be the only proof of ownership.

. . . .

4. ANALYSIS AND FINDINGS

. . . .

(B) Did the WSE "carry on business as an exchange in Alberta", contrary to section 52(1) of the Act?

Section 52 of the Act says:

> 52(1) No person or company shall carry on business as an exchange in Alberta unless the person or company is recognized by the Commission as an exchange.
>
> (2) The Commission may, on the application of a person or company proposing to carry on business as an exchange in Alberta, recognize the person or company as an exchange if the Commission considers that it would not be prejudicial to the public interest to do so.
>
> (3) The recognition of an exchange under this section shall be made in writing and is subject to any terms and conditions that the Commission may impose.

We were referred to no decisions interpreting section 52 or any of the similar provisions in other provinces' securities legislation.

Staff urged the Commission to adopt a broad interpretation of "carry on business as an exchange in Alberta" for enforcement purposes, suggesting that it might encompass any exchange activity occurring in Alberta. Such a broad interpretation of section 52(1) may, however, be inconsistent with the way these provisions have actually been applied to exchanges until now.

At the time of the hearing, the Alberta Stock Exchange ("ASE") was the only exchange recognized by the Commission under this section. During the hearing, a restructuring of Canadian stock exchanges was announced and, recently, the ASE and the Vancouver Stock Exchange ("VSE") merged to form the Canadian Venture Exchange ("CDNX"). CDNX was recognized as an exchange by the commissions in both Alberta and British Columbia on November 26, 1999. In this decision, we generally refer to the ASE, VSE and other exchanges as they were prior to the restructuring.

It is an historical fact that section 52 has never been applied to exchanges, such as the VSE, that are recognized elsewhere or are otherwise subject to a regulatory scheme comparable to that in Alberta, but are not recognized in Alberta. We will call these "regulated exchanges". This category would clearly also include the Toronto Stock Exchange ("TSE"), the Montreal Exchange and a number of foreign exchanges such as the New York Stock Exchange. Regulated exchanges may be distinguished from those exchanges that are recognized in Alberta such as the ASE, and now CDNX, which we will refer to as "recognized exchanges".

It is easy to see why, historically, section 52 of our Act and the equivalent provisions in other provinces applied only to the "local" exchange. The ASE, like most other stock exchanges, existed long before the advent of the modern Canadian Securities Acts. In Alberta, a provision similar to section 52(1) first appeared in The Securities Act, 1967. At that time, the ASE and other exchanges each operated a physical trading floor. The location of the trading floor was an obvious indicator of where the exchange carried on business.

Since then, the exchange business has changed dramatically. Trading floors have disappeared and have been replaced by computer systems. As these proceedings demonstrate, modern technology gives almost anyone the operational capacity to set up a new type of exchange. That raises important issues about whether and how the law applies to such exchanges.

Tom Seto argued that the WSE's trading-floor equivalent is located either in "Cyberspace, or Antigua where the correspondence is received, or where the transaction is completed, the Cayman Islands". He argued that the WSE should be subject to regulation only by its incorporating jurisdiction, the Cayman Islands.

Tom Seto urged the Commission to compare the activities of the WSE to those of regulated exchanges like the VSE and TSE, which actively and successfully solicit listings in Alberta. Tom Seto argued that, since the Commission does not apply section 52(1) to the VSE and TSE, they are not carrying on business as an exchange in Alberta, so the less extensive activities of the WSE in Alberta cannot reasonably be construed as carrying on business here.

Tom Seto indicated that he intends to carry on with the WSE and, apparently, market it on the basis of the WSE's lack of regulation and low listing cost in relation to other exchanges. He suggested in argument that "the [Alberta Securities Commission] should not be held in greater esteem than myself in making regulations as a securities regulator".

The essence of Tom Seto's position is that the WSE is not subject to section 52(1) of the Act. As Tom Seto's arguments suggest, there is no question here about whether the WSE meets Alberta's regulatory standards. It does not. It falls far below the standards imposed on exchanges recognized by Alberta or by any other major commercial jurisdiction. The WSE appears to accept that, because it does not attempt to meet those standards and it freely admits taking deliberate steps to avoid such rigorous regulation. The WSE wants to be an "unregulated exchange", by which we mean an exchange that is not recognized or otherwise subject to a regulatory scheme comparable to that in Alberta. The fundamental question here is whether the WSE, as an unregulated exchange, is subject to section 52(1) of the Act. Due to the lack of existing authority on this issue and the range of potential consequences that may flow from our interpretation of section 52(1), we must undertake a comprehensive analysis of this provision before attempting to apply it to the particular circumstances of the WSE.

(i) is the WSE an "exchange"?

Although Tom Seto did not dispute staff's allegation that the WSE was an exchange, it is useful to review current developments relating to this question. "Exchange" is not defined in the Act. It is clear that traditional exchanges like the ASE are examples of exchanges but that does not provide much guidance in determining whether less traditional organizations are exchanges.

The functional characteristics of exchanges are described in proposed National Instrument 21-101 Marketplace Operation ("NI 21-101") and Companion Policy 21-101CP. These were published for comment by the Commission on July 2, 1999 at (1999), 8 A.S.C.S. 1830. NI 21-101 and Companion Policy 21-101CP are intended to regulate all marketplaces operating within any Canadian jurisdiction including exchanges, quotation and trade reporting systems, and alternative trading systems ("ATSs"). Section 1.1 of NI 21-101 defines "marketplace" to mean:

(a) an exchange,

(b) a quotation and trade reporting system, and

(c) any other person or company that
  (i) constitutes, maintains or provides a market or facilities for bringing together purchasers and sellers of securities,
  (ii) brings together the orders for securities of multiple buyers and sellers, and
  (iii) uses established, non-discretionary methods under which the orders interact with each other, and the buyers and sellers entering the orders agree to the terms of a trade.

Section 3.1(2) of Companion Policy 21-101CP says, in part:

> The Canadian securities regulatory authorities generally consider a marketplace to be an exchange for purposes of securities legislation, if the marketplace
> (a) requires an issuer to enter into an agreement in order for the issuer's securities to trade on the marketplace, i.e., the marketplace provides a listing function;

Although these provisions are not authoritative in this proceeding, we find that they accurately describe the defining functions of an exchange that are applicable regardless of the exchange's other physical, organizational or technological characteristics. It is not necessary for us to explore the limits of the definition because the WSE falls squarely within them.

The WSE actually provided a listing function and a market or facilities for bringing together purchasers and sellers of securities. It set non-discretionary methods for trading. The fact that no one actually bought or sold securities through the WSE means that we do not know whether the WSE actually had the capacity to consolidate orders of multiple parties, but it clearly wanted to. We find that the WSE is an exchange within the meaning of the Act.

(ii) what is "carrying on business as an exchange in Alberta"?
The interpretation of this phrase is the most difficult issue raised by these proceedings. There is apparently no authority that deals directly with the question of what constitutes carrying on business as an exchange.

. . . .

(D) PURPOSES OF SECTION 52(1)
In our view, the over-arching purpose of section 52(1) is to ensure that no exchange operates contrary to the public interest in Alberta. We note, however, that the application of section 52(1) to an exchange will trigger either of two distinctly different regulatory responses.

. . . .

This helps explain why section 52(1) has never been interpreted to apply to the activities in Alberta of regulated exchanges like the VSE or TSE. Their activities are not contrary to the public interest in Alberta precisely because they are already subject to small-r regulation in what may be described as their "home" jurisdiction. It seems evident that it is not the purpose of section 52(1) to capture regulated exchanges, provided the small-r regulation in their home jurisdiction is satisfactory. That appears to be why each regulated exchange has traditionally been viewed as carrying on business only in its home jurisdiction. Functionally, this is similar to many situations where statutory or discretionary exemptions recognize the effectiveness of regulatory requirements imposed by other jurisdictions.

(E) PUBLIC INTEREST CONSIDERATIONS RELATING TO THE WSE

The purpose and function of section 52 is directly related to public interest considerations. Section 52(2) provides that the Commission may recognize an exchange only if it "considers that it would not be prejudicial to the public interest to do so". The public interest considerations relating to the WSE may be seen by comparing the WSE to recognized and regulated exchanges.

. . . .

[...] WSE raises so many fundamental concerns by failing to meet the most basic requirements of exchange operations. It is not financially responsible, its corporate structure is false, it has no clearance and settlement system, and so on. Any of these factors, alone, would present a significant public interest concern. In this case, however, these factors must be considered as part of the background to the two most striking characteristics of the WSE's operations: 1) its lack of credible listing and disclosure requirements; and 2) offering direct trading access to the public through the Internet.

1) listing and disclosure requirements

The requirement for listed companies (and other issuers) to provide full and accurate disclosure of financial and business information is central to our system of securities regulation and investor protection. Regulated exchanges generally play a significant role in setting and enforcing such requirements, so that a listing on a regulated exchange connotes compliance with certain listing and disclosure standards.

The WSE has no credible listing standards or disclosure requirements for its listed companies. A sophisticated investor who closely examined the WSE website would probably recognize this and shun the WSE. However, a less-sophisticated investor might think that a WSE listing connotes compliance with meaningful listing or disclosure standards, which would be a dangerous mistake. The overall presentation of information on the WSE website seems to be crafted to lure the unwary investor to make that mistake.

It is significant that, although the website says that the WSE's "role is simply to provide a mechanism for full disclosure of relevant financial information for each company listed", there were no financial statements whatsoever on the website. Although financial statements could be requested from the companies, the companies' statements were mainly projections. We find that the apparent purpose and effect of this is to obscure the fact that there is no reliable financial information about the listed companies.

Similar considerations apply to the excessively promotional descriptions of listed companies' business plans and prospects on the website. Together, these create a definite risk that prospective investors would be misled.

2) direct trading access

Perhaps the most unorthodox characteristic of the WSE is that it offers direct trading access to anyone through the Internet.

We are not aware of any regulated exchange that offers such access to anyone who is not a member of that or another regulated exchange. All members of regulated exchanges are normally registrants under the Act and members of SROs, subject to a wide range of regulatory requirements intended to protect the public interest. The transactions on regulated exchanges are trades by registrant/members (who will often be acting as agents for other persons). Regulated exchanges do not trade. Their members trade (exempted by section 54(1) of the Act) and their members' customers trade (exempted by section 65(1)(j) of the Act).

The WSE is radically different in that it has no members. The core of the WSE's intended business is the primary distribution of securities by direct sales through the Internet. Anyone with Internet access could buy shares through the WSE. By offering to sell securities directly through its website, the WSE trades in securities. Although the WSE website referred to the ISBC having some role in these transactions it is clear that the ISBC's role was in no way comparable to the function of registrant/members of regulated exchanges.

This aspect of the WSE's business violates one of the fundamental tenets of the Act, which is that no one may trade in securities unless they are registered or exempt from the registration requirement. In addition, since the securities of the companies listed on the WSE were not qualified for sale in Alberta, this trading by the WSE also constitutes an illegal distribution of securities, thereby violating another fundamental tenet of the Act. It is self-evident that these aspects of the WSE's business are contrary to the public interest because they could be the subject of enforcement action as violations of sections 54(1) and 81(1) of the Act. They are considered as public interest issues here in the context of section 52(1) because they are an integral part of the WSE's unique method of carrying on business as an exchange.

Almost every aspect of the WSE's structure and operations presents a substantial threat to prospective investors and we find that its overall business is utterly contrary to the public interest.

(F) TERRITORIALITY OF SECTION 52(1)

The WSE is active in and has connections to many jurisdictions, including Alberta. Our jurisdiction under the Securities Act is basically territorial, and we must consider whether the WSE's activities fall within that jurisdiction.

We find that the same territoriality considerations apply in this case as discussed by the Supreme Court of Canada in Libman v. The Queen. Libman involved a fraud charge under the Criminal Code where the accused conducted activities in several countries, including Canada. La Forest J. reviews the history of English and Canadian law in relation to transnational offences and distills it down to a concise rationale and conclusion which we find directly applicable to the case at hand.

La Forest J. describes the basic rationale for territoriality as follows:

> [T]he territorial principle in criminal law was developed by the courts to respond to two practical considerations, first, that a country has generally little

direct concern for the actions of malefactors abroad, and secondly, that other states may legitimately take umbrage if a country attempts to regulate matters taking place wholly or substantially within their territories. For these reasons the courts adopted a presumption against the application of laws beyond the realm....

. . . .

La Forest J. summarized his approach to the limits of territoriality as follows:

As I see it, all that is necessary to make an offence subject to the jurisdiction of our courts is that a significant portion of the activities constituting that offence took place in Canada. As it is put by modern academics, it is sufficient that there be a "real and substantial link" between an offence and this country, a test well known in public and private international law....

La Forest J. also described the need to adopt an evolving concept of comity, saying:

Just what may constitute a real and substantial link in a particular case, I need not explore. There were ample links here. The outer limits of the test may, however, well be coterminous with the requirements of international comity.

As I have already noted, in some of the early cases the English courts tended to express a narrow view of the territorial application of English law so as to ensure that they did not unduly infringe on the jurisdiction of other states. However, even as early as the late 19th century, following the invention and development of modern means of communication, they began to exercise criminal jurisdiction over transnational transactions as long as a significant part of the chain of action occurred in England. Since then means of communications have proliferated at an accelerating pace and the common interests of states have grown proportionately. Under these circumstances, the notion of comity, which means no more nor less than "kindly and considerate behaviour towards others", has also evolved. How considerate is it of the interests of the United States in this case to permit criminals based in this country to prey on its citizens? How does it conform to its interests or to ours for us to permit such activities when law enforcement agencies in both countries have developed cooperative schemes to prevent and prosecute those engaged in such activities? To ask these questions is to answer them. No issue of comity is involved here. In this regard, I make mine the words of Lord Diplock in Treacy v. Director of Public Prosecutions cited earlier. I also agree with the sentiments expressed by Lord Salmon in Director of Public Prosecutions v. Doot, supra, that we should not be indifferent to the protection of the public in other countries. In a shrinking world, we are all our brother's keepers. In the criminal arena this is underlined by the international cooperative schemes that have been developed among national law enforcement bodies.

Although the Libman decision addresses territoriality in the context of criminal law, in our view the same principles are applicable to the Act, including section 52(1).

(G) CONCLUSION

We find that the WSE did carry on business as an exchange in Alberta, contrary to section 52(1) of the Act.

We find that any similarity between the activities in Alberta of the WSE and of regulated exchanges is entirely superficial. The most important distinguishing characteristic of the WSE is its general lack of regulation, manifested in business practices that are contrary to the public interest. We find that the purpose of section 52(1) is [sic] protect the public interest by prohibiting such practices.

We interpret the phrase "carry on business as an exchange in Alberta" to mean, in effect, "conduct any exchange activity in Alberta that requires the Commission to act to protect the public interest". Although this makes the application of section 52(1) somewhat nebulous, that is a natural consequence of the fact that it is impossible to precisely define the public interest in the context of innovative or evolving exchange activity. While the public interest remains relatively constant, and is quite clearly reflected in the regulatory requirements imposed upon the actual activities of recognized exchanges, exchange activities are almost infinitely variable. Every exchange must be assessed individually and it is the combined effect of all its activities that must be weighed against the public interest to determine whether section 52(1) should apply. It would be inappropriate to focus on particular operations or activities as determinative because these are easily manipulated (as this case shows), and to do so would enable such manipulation to succeed in avoiding public-interest regulation.

. . . .

With the passage of physical trading floors and the evolution of technology, the location of exchange operations has become increasingly flexible and notional. That makes the location of exchange operations less significant, and the functional linkage between an exchange and its recognizing regulator more significant, in determining where that exchange carries on business. To some extent, exchanges may choose where they want to be regulated and so assert where they believe that they carry on business within the meaning of the Act, as CDNX did recently when it sought recognition from the Commissions in both Alberta and British Columbia. In our view, as long as the connection between a regulated exchange and its home jurisdiction is reasonable and substantial, and the exchange's activities do not raise public interest concerns in Alberta (generally, by the home jurisdiction maintaining regulatory standards comparable to ours), section 52(1) should be interpreted to say that the regulated exchange carries on business only in its home jurisdiction.

We see clear distinctions between the connection of a typical regulated exchange to its home jurisdiction and the situation of the WSE. The WSE tried to choose its regulator by deliberately seeking the minimum possible amount of regulation. When the authorities in the Cayman Islands shut down the WSE's operations there, it moved to Antigua. In our view, this flag-of-convenience approach demonstrates the lack of any substantial connection between the WSE and either of its purported home jurisdictions. Even if the WSE had much closer links to its purported home jurisdictions, the lack of significant regulation by those jurisdictions would, in our view, preclude them from being considered home jurisdictions comparable to those of regulated exchanges. In this sense, unregulated exchanges are homeless. They may therefore be seen as carrying on business wherever they set foot and subject to enforcement action by any jurisdiction with standards comparable to ours.

The WSE has real and substantial links to Alberta, more than sufficient to justify the application of Alberta law. The WSE was established in and run from Alberta. Tom Seto and Orest Rusnak were both Alberta residents who spent much of their time here promoting the WSE to Albertans. The real and substantial nature of these links is evident by comparing them to the artificial and insignificant links between the WSE and the Cayman Islands (place of incorporation) or Antigua (location of computer).

We also find that the Commission has a legitimate interest in applying Alberta law to the WSE merely because its activities have unlawful consequences here. If the WSE had operated entirely "offshore", as it wanted to, we would still have jurisdiction to take enforcement action against anyone in Alberta with a sufficient connection to the WSE. Similar considerations would apply in every other jurisdiction with securities laws comparable to ours. As a practical issue, it may be necessary to wait until someone comes from offshore to such a jurisdiction before effective enforcement action can be taken. The prospect of such action by any of a number of major commercial jurisdictions should be a deterrent to anyone associated with offshore entities who conduct unlawful securities market activities through the Internet. Such deterrent is only effective if individual jurisdictions take action wherever possible, and we see no reason in comity to prevent that. There would be no purpose in having an elaborate framework of securities regulation to protect the public interest if the law permitted entities like the WSE to circumvent it all by using modern technology and communications to step beyond our jurisdiction.

The WSE's potential victims include anyone with Internet access so, in this situation, comity encourages us to apply Alberta law because the WSE's links to Alberta allow us to act and because we would want other jurisdictions to take a similar approach.

IPOs AND INVESTOR COMMUNICATION

With the proliferation of online corporate myths such as Neiman Marcus (alternatively circulated as Mrs. Fields) charging $250 for a cookie recipe or Snapple supporting the Klu Klux Klan, corporations and their advisors must actively monitor online discussion and move quickly to dispel unfounded rumours and misinformation. This task is particularly challenging given the thousands of chat sites, Usenet groups, news sources and independent Web sites currently online. Consider whether the following disclosure guidelines from the Toronto Stock Exchange meet the needs of investors in the current frenzied marketplace.

Proposed Electronic Communications Disclosure Guidelines†

II. APPLICABLE DISCLOSURE RULES

Dissemination of information via a Web site, e-mail or otherwise via the Internet is subject to the same laws as traditional forms of dissemination such as news releases. In establishing electronic communications, a company should have special regard to disclosure requirements under applicable securities law. Companies should refer to the TSE Policy Statement on Timely Disclosure and Related Guidelines and

---

† Toronto Stock Exchange Web site: <http://www.tse.com/mregs/pdf/web_proposed.pdf> (last modified: August 13, 1998). Source: The Toronto Stock Exchange (all rights reserved). Reproduced with permission.

National Policy No. 40 Timely Disclosure. Companies must comply with the disclosure requirements in all jurisdictions in which they are reporting issuers.

These rules apply to all corporate disclosure through electronic communications and must be followed by each company.

1. Electronic communications cannot be misleading

A company must ensure that material information posted on its Web site is not misleading. Material information is misleading if it is out of date, incomplete, incorrect or omits a fact so as to make another statement misleading.

a. Duty to correct and update

A Web site should be a complete repository of current and accurate investor relations information. Viewers visiting a Web site expect that they are viewing all the relevant information about a company and that the information provided to them by the company is accurate in all material respects. A company is, therefore, obligated to correct any misleading information on its Web site. It is not sufficient that the information has been corrected or updated elsewhere, for example, in documents filed with SEDAR.

It is possible for information to become inaccurate over time. A company must regularly review and update or correct the information on the site.

b. Incomplete information or material omissions

Providing incomplete information or omitting a material fact is also misleading. A company must include all material disclosed information. It must include all news releases, not just favourable ones. Similarly, documents should be posted in their entirety. If this is impractical for a particular document, such as a technical report with graphs, charts or maps, care must be taken to ensure that an excerpt is not misleading when read on its own. In such circumstances, it may be sufficient to post the executive summary.

2. Electronic communications cannot be used to "tip" or leak material information

A company's internal employee trading and confidentiality policies should cover the use of electronic forms of communication. Employees must not use the Internet to "tip" or discuss in any form undisclosed material information about the company.

A company must not post a material news release on a Web site or disseminate it by e-mail or otherwise on the Internet before it has been disseminated on a news wire service in accordance with the TSE Policy Statement on Timely Disclosure and Related Guidelines.

. . . .

3. Electronic communications must comply with securities laws

A company should have special regard to securities laws and, in particular, registration and filing requirements, which may be triggered if it posts any document offering securities to the general public on its Web site. If a listed company is considering a distribution of securities, it should carefully review its Web site in consultation with the company's legal advisors in advance of and during the offering. The release of information and promotional materials before or during a public offering is subject to restrictions under securities laws. Documents related to a distribution of securities should only be posted on a Web site if they are filed with and receipted by the appropriate securities regulator. Promotional materials related to a distribution of securities may contravene advertising restrictions and should only be posted on a Web site if such materials are permitted to be disseminated.

Anyone, anywhere in the world can access a Web site. Special regard should be made to foreign securities laws that may be stricter than Ontario laws. Foreign securities regulators may take the view that posting offering documents on a Web site that can be accessed by someone in their jurisdiction constitutes an offering in that jurisdiction unless appropriate disclaimers are included on the document or other measures are taken to restrict access. Reference should be made to the guidelines issued by the U.S. Securities and Exchange Commission for issuers who use Internet Web sites to solicit offshore securities transactions and clients without the securities being registered in the United States.

III. ELECTRONIC COMMUNICATIONS GUIDELINES

The TSE recommends that listed companies follow these guidelines when designing a Web site, establishing an internal e-mail policy or disseminating information over the Internet.

Unlike the disclosure rules which are applicable to all electronic communications, these guidelines are not hard and fast rules which must be followed. Aspects of these guidelines may not be appropriate for every company. A company should tailor these guidelines to create an internal policy that is suitable to its particular needs and resources.

Each listed company should establish a clear written policy on electronic communications as part of its existing policies governing corporate disclosure, confidentiality and employee trading. Please refer to the TSE Policy Statement on Timely Disclosure and Related Guidelines. The TSE suggests that the policy describe how its electronic communications are to be structured, supervised and maintained. The policy should be reviewed regularly and updated as necessary. To ensure that the policy is followed, it should be communicated to all individuals in the company to whom it will apply.

1. Who should monitor electronic communications?

The TSE recommends that one or more of the officers appointed under the company's disclosure policy be made responsible for the company's policies on electronic communications. Reference should be made to page 13 of the TSE Policy Statement on Timely Disclosure and Related Guidelines. These officers should ensure that all investor relations information made available by the company on the Web site, broadcast via e-mail or otherwise on the Internet complies with applicable securities laws and internal policies. This responsibility includes ensuring the company Web site is properly reviewed and updated.

2. What should be on the Web site?

a. All corporate "timely disclosure" documents and other public documents filed with securities regulators

A company may either post its own investor relations information or establish links to other Web sites that also maintain publicly disclosed documents on behalf of the company such as news wire services, SEDAR and stock quote services. "Investor relations information" includes all public documents required to be filed with securities regulators or the TSE such as: the annual report; annual and interim financial statements; the Annual Information Form; news releases; material change reports; declarations of dividends; redemption notices; management proxy circulars; and any other communications to shareholders.

The TSE recommends that a company post its own investor relations information on its Web site, rather than linking to other sites carrying that information (e.g. SEDAR and news wires). There is usually a delay, sometimes up to 24 hours, if the information is posted and updated by third party providers. If a company posts and updates its own information, it has more control over the timing and can be more comprehensive in the type of information it includes on its site.

If a company chooses to link to SEDAR or to a news wire Web site, it is recommended that the link be directly to the company's page on that site. If a company merely links to the other site's home page, the investor may find navigating the other site to find the information to be frustrating and time consuming. Links to other Web sites should be checked regularly to ensure they still work.

b. All supplemental information provided to analysts and other market observers but not otherwise distributed publicly

The TSE recommends that a company that disseminates non-material information to analysts and institutional clients make such information available to all investors. Supplemental information includes such materials as fact sheets, fact books, slides of investor presentations and transcripts of management investor relations speeches and other materials distributed at investor presentations. Posting supplemental information on a Web site is a very useful means of making it generally available.

This recommendation is consistent with the recommendations made in the Final Report of the Committee on Corporate Disclosure: Responsible Corporate Disclosure (March 1997) and the Canadian Investor Relations Institute: Standards and Guidance for Disclosure (February 1998). Each recommends that any supplementary information that is disseminated on a selective basis be made available generally.

The TSE suggests that a company should post all supplemental information on its Web site, unless the volume or format makes it impractical. If this is the case, the company should describe the information on the Web site and provide a contact for the information so that an investor may contact the company directly either to obtain a copy of the information or to view the information at the company's offices.

In addition to any supplemental information provided by the company to analysts, the TSE suggests that a company also consider posting on its Web site or otherwise making available transcripts or recordings of all analyst conference calls.

c. Investor relations contact information

The TSE suggests that a company provide an e-mail link on its Web site for investors to communicate directly with an investor relations representative of the company. The company policy should specify who may respond to investor inquiries and should provide guidance as to the type of information that may be transmitted electronically.

To assure rapid dissemination of material information to Internet users who follow the company, a company may consider establishing an e-mail distribution list, permitting users who access its Web site to subscribe to receive electronic delivery of news directly from the company. Alternatively, a company may consider using software that notifies subscribers automatically when the company's Web site is updated.

d. On-line Conferences

A company may choose to participate on an on-line news or investor conference. The TSE suggests that participation by the company in such on-line conferences should be governed by the same policy that the company has established in respect of its participation in other conferences such as an analyst conference call.

3. What should not be disseminated via electronic communications?

a. Employee misuse of electronic communications

Access to e-mail and the Internet can be valuable tools for employees to perform their jobs, however, the TSE suggests that clear guidelines should be established as to how employees may use these new media. These guidelines should be incorporated into the company's disclosure, confidentiality and employee trading policy. Employees should be reminded that their corporate e-mail address is a company address and that all correspondence received and sent via e-mail is to be considered corporate correspondence.

Appropriate guidelines should be established about the type of information that may be circulated by e-mail. A company should prohibit its employees from participating in Internet chat-rooms or news groups in discussions relating to the company or its securities.

b. Analyst reports and third party information

As a general practice, the TSE recommends that a company should not post any investor relations information on its Web site that is authored by a third party, unless the information was prepared on behalf of the company, or is general in nature and not specific to the company. For example, if a company posts an analyst report on its Web site, it may be seen to be endorsing the views and conclusions of the report. By posting such information on its site, a company may become "entangled" with the report and be legally responsible for the content even though it did not author it. This could also give rise to an obligation to correct the report if the company becomes aware that the content is or has become misleading (for example, if the earnings projection is too optimistic).

Instead of posting analyst reports on its Web site, the TSE suggests that a company provide a list of all analysts who follow the company together with contact information so that investors may contact the analyst's firm directly. The list should be complete and include all analysts that the company knows to follow it, regardless of their recommendations.

If a company chooses to post any analyst reports on its Web site, the TSE recommends that extreme caution be exercised. A company's policy on posting analyst reports should address the following concerns:

* permission to reprint a report should be obtained in advance from the analyst, since reports are subject to copyright protection;
* the information should clearly be identified as representing the views of the analyst and not necessarily those of the company;
* the entire analyst report should be reproduced so that it is not misleading;

- any updates, including changes in recommendations, should also be posted so the company's Web site will not contain out-of-date and possibly misleading information;
- all analyst reports should be posted; if the company posts only some of the available reports, it should list all of the other reports that are available on the company and provide contact information so that such reports may be obtained directly from the analyst.

c. *Third Party Links and "Framing"*

A company may establish hyper-links between its Web site and third party sites. If a company creates a hyperlink to a third party site, there is a risk that a viewer will not realize that he or she has left the company's Web site. The TSE suggests that the company include a disclaimer that the viewer is leaving the company Web site and the company is not responsible for the contents of the other site. The risk that a viewer will not realize that he or she has left the company's site is much greater if a company "frames" the third party site. A "frame" is a distinctive design or border that surrounds each Web page and does not materially change from page to page within the site. A company should only frame its own pages to minimize the possibility of confusion.

d. *The blurred line between investor and promotional information*

The TSE recommends that a company clearly identify and separate its investment information from other information on its Web site. In particular, promotional, sales and marketing information should not be included on the same Web pages as investor relations information. A company's homepage should clearly distinguish sections containing investor relations information from sections containing other information.

When should information be removed from a Web site? Care should be taken to make sure that information that is inaccurate or out-of-date no longer appears on the Web site. Companies may delete or remove inaccurate information from the Web site, as long as a correction has been posted. In addition, companies may establish an archiving system to store and access information that is no longer current. To assist investors in determining the currency of the information on the site, the TSE suggests that a company date each page of each document as they are posted on the Web site.

The TSE recommends that the company's policy establish a minimum retention period for material corporate information that it posts on its Web site. Different types of information may be retained for a different period of time. For example, the company may decide to retain all news releases on the site for a period of one year from the date of issue. In contrast, the company may decide that investors would want to access its financials for a longer period (e.g. two years for quarterlies and five years for annuals).

5. **Rumours on the Internet**

Rumours about the company may appear on chat-rooms and newsgroups. Rumours may spread more quickly and more widely on the Internet than by other media. Market Surveillance monitors chat-rooms and news groups on the Internet to identify rumours about TSE listed companies that may influence the trading activity of their stocks. The TSE Policy Statement on Timely Disclosure and Related Guidelines addresses how a company should respond to rumours. A company is not expected to monitor chat-rooms or news groups for rumours about itself. Nevertheless, the TSE recommends that the company's standard policy for addressing rumours apply to those on the Internet.

Whether a company should respond to a rumour depends on the circumstances. The TSE suggests that the company should consider the market impact of the rumour and the degree of accuracy and significance to the company. In general, the TSE recommends against a company participating on a chat-room or news group to dispel or clarify a rumour. Instead, it is preferable for the company to issue a news release to ensure widespread dissemination of its statement.

If a company becomes aware of a rumour on a chat-room, news group or any other source that may have a material impact on the price of its stock, it should immediately contact Market Surveillance. If the information is false and is materially influencing the trading activity of the company's securities, it may consider issuing a clarifying news release. The company should contact Market Surveillance so that the TSE can monitor trading in the company's securities. If Market Surveillance determines that trading is being affected by the rumour, it may require the company to issue a news release stating that there are no corporate developments to explain the market activity.

Discussion Questions

1. Do you agree with the policy approach that exempts companies from actively monitoring online chat room activity? Given the effects online rumours can have on the market, is a positive obligation preferable?

2. Online chat sites such as Silicon Investor or Yahoo! have developed into critical sources of information for thousands of investors with unsubstantiated rumours capable of altering share prices instantly. Should the chat sites bear some measure of responsibility for their users?

3. The Ontario courts also addressed the issue of investor communication through electronic means in *Re Newbridge Networks Corp.* ([2000] O.J. No. 1346, Ont. Sup. Ct.). Consider whether the court seems to suggest that electronic disclosures may actually be better than traditional methods. The focus seems to be on the security of the system — what other considerations might be important in determining whether to approve an electronic disclosure system?

   > I have reviewed the interim order requested as to the Newbridge Networks Corporation proposed arrangement pursuant to the Canada Business Corporations Act (CBCA) and particularly s. 192. The procedures requested appear to me to be reasonable and appropriate in the circumstances. The interim order is to issue as per my fiat.
   >
   > It would be appropriate for me to review the aspect of the permission and authority granted to use an electronic procedure for notice and voting for those holders of Newbridge Options who are current officers, directors or employees of Newbridge. I understand that there are approximately 4,300 such Optionholders based in various locations in Canada and throughout the world.
   >
   > At the present time the CBCA is silent as to electronic notice and voting. There are some amendments now being proposed (first reading March 21,

2000). I note that the Business Corporations Act (Ontario) (OBCA) has been recently amended (March 27, 2000 effective) to provide for an electronic procedure. I understand that the by-laws of Newbridge are silent as to electronic procedure. Newbridge prides itself (and I understand with justification) that it is an electronic company — after all that is the business it is in.

I have reviewed the proposed amendments to the CBCA and the OBCA actual amendments. They appear to be in response to the increased functional use of computer technology. However, I would observe in passing that perhaps they focus a little too much on the present state of technology and not enough on the concepts behind notice and voting. Thus their specificity may be overrestrictive for "mechanical" reasons and without the necessary and desirable flexibility to accommodate advances in technology which are rapidly developing with the promise of more to come. The key to the matter in my view is whether the notice and voting concepts can utilize the present technology and retain the integrity required. Technology should be the handmaiden of the law and not vice versa.

Thus I have reviewed the procedures envisaged for the Optionholders to elect to receive notice and vote in the electronic mode, as well as the electronic notice and voting procedure. I am satisfied that the election and procedures are reliable and sufficiently safeguarded and that there will be a record maintained and available for possible further analysis and scrutiny. Functionally, the electronic procedure herein is the equivalent of receiving notice through the mail or delivery with that notice being in printed form on paper; similarly the voting procedure as to proxy. An Optionholder will be able to record his or her choice and transmit this choice by electronic proxy. This will be transmitted via Newbridge to the Montreal Trust Company, Newbridge's Registrar and Transfer Agent with appropriate safeguards. I note in this respect that Montreal Trust Company is agreeable to the electronic procedure overall and specifically this transmission arrangement. Further there is no impediment of a legal nature to prohibit a corporation from being its own registrar and transfer agent nor from the corporation acting as an agent for an outside registrar and transfer agent.

Overall for most intents and purposes and on balance the electronic procedure envisaged is a safer and more reliable system than is that which relies on the mails or other delivery systems.

4.   Consider the following Australian case involving the prosecution of a Web site owner involved in illegally touting stock online. Is the court's characterization of the Web site reasonable?

Australian Securities And Investments Commission v. Matthews[†]

As I have already pointed out, the respondent has conceded that he does not hold a licence and he is not an exempt investment adviser. The respondent did not provide any evidence for the court to consider in opposing the interlocutory orders, however, he made a number of submissions. The first of them was that the provision of material on the screen of an internet of the kind which is reproduced in the affidavits is not a publication of this material and, after some inter-

---

† [1999] FCA 164 (19 February 1999).

change with him, he agreed that the description of what he was doing was equivalent to having an "electronic sandwich board".

I do not think that (even putting what he said at its highest) the use of an "electronic sandwich board" falls outside the description of publishing and, more particularly, a publishing business because Mr Matthews also concedes that his website is conducted continuously and systematically so that it does fit within the description, "to carry on business" as explained in Hyde v Sullivan & Anor [1956] 56 NSWLR 113, a decision of the New South Wales Court of Appeal. No quarrel was taken by Mr Matthews with that definition and it is my view that in relation to the activity taken by Mr Matthews in respect of his website, as he describes it, he is carrying on a business.

The question of whether this business is carried on for profit does not arise because that is not necessary to be demonstrated for the purpose of the application. It, however, certainly fits within the definition of carrying on a business contained in Hyde v Sullivan (supra). Mr Matthews put to me that he wasn't in a commercial relationship with subscribers but, as I said, he has admitted to all the other characteristics of carrying on a business.

He also submitted that he was not giving advice in the conduct of his electronic site. I do not accept that submission. The parts of the evidence presented by the applicant to which counsel referred, used phrases and words that are all directed to evaluation and encouragement to those reading the site to deal in the share market. It is certainly couched in the ordinary terminology of advice, and I so find.

I therefore find that the respondent, who is not licensed or authorised to do so, is carrying on an investment advice business without determining whether that is being done for profit and in the course of conducting the website, 'The Chimes', is holding himself out as an investment adviser. Unless he is licensed or given an exemption as an investment adviser, this activity is, in my view, prima facie in contravention of the Corporations Law and it was for that reason, having taken into account all of the material to which I was referred, that I made the orders sought by the applicant.

If Mr Matthews, of course, had been earning his living in conducting the site or could have demonstrated today that there were serious financial or other consequences to him in making the orders, it might have been necessary to have considered both in relation to making interlocutory orders and also the consequences of them. For example expedition or other orders could have been made to prevent any damage being too acute. Counsel for the applicant rightly points out that his client is exempt from any order as to undertaking for damages should Mr Matthews be successful in the main proceeding.

However, I am comforted by Mr Matthews' submissions that this activity, in conducting the website, is done for pleasure only and the consequences of him complying with the orders will be to curb that pleasurable activity. The only other consequence he could point to was perhaps press comment on the activities that have been restrained by the order which I described in the context of the hearing of only having an effect on Mr Matthews' ego and would not, in my view, create too much of a burden upon him.

The respondent, apart from the submissions about publishing advice and other matters that I have already referred to in these reasons gave no other reason for resisting the injunctive relief. What I have particularly been concerned about and have put great weight upon is the incident which is part of the evidence in relation to the engine company CSY and the serious consequences which are deposed to from that acknowledged mistake contained in Mr Matthews' web site. For those reasons I have made the orders.

I propose to make a further order and that is that this matter be now referred to the registrar to be assigned, in the ordinary course, to a docket of a judge of the court for hearing of the application for final relief. The applicant has assured me that it is ready to proceed. It really will be a matter for Mr Matthews to consider any application he may care to make.

ONLINE FRAUD

The SEC plays the leading role in combating online securities fraud. It recently established the Internet Enforcement Office headed by John Reed Stark. Staffed by a number of Internet and securities experts who actively monitor Internet activity in an effort to exert the SEC's muscle against securities law violators, the Office has succeeded in uncovering several major Internet securities scams. Charges were laid against over 50 individuals in 1998 and 1999.

Canadian securities regulators have also faced their share of online securities fraud. The following case provides a sense of how the Canadian legal system addresses fraudulent activity.

American Technology Exploration Corp. (Re)[†]

Philip Lieberman has been the subject of several previous Commission proceedings and is currently subject to two sets of enforcement orders. On March 4, 1988, the Superintendent of Brokers (now called the Executive Director) made an order removing Philip Lieberman's exemptions under the Act for 10 years. The order was based on findings that he had made misrepresentations, in public disclosures by issuers he controlled, concerning the mineral prospects of a property in California. That order was confirmed by the Commission following a hearing and review of the Superintendent's decision.

On March 7, 1994, the Commission found that Philip Lieberman had contravened the 1988 order and imposed new orders prohibiting him from being a director or officer of a reporting issuer for 8 years, removing his exemptions for 8 years, and ordering him to pay an administrative penalty of $10,000 and hearing costs of $1,000. He has failed to pay either the administrative penalty or the costs.

Marc Lieberman is the son of Philip Lieberman.

ATEC is a Nevada corporation and was incorporated in August 1993. It operates from an office in British Columbia. It is not a reporting issuer under the Act. Its shares trade over the counter in the United States and are quoted on the NASDAQ OTC bulletin board. The original list of directors and officers filed with the Nevada Secretary of State showed Philip Lieberman and his daughter, Peppa Martin, as the only directors and officers of ATEC. The most recent list so filed showed Philip Lieberman as president and treasurer and Marc Lieberman as secretary. No directors were shown. However, disclosure statements filed and

---

[†] COR #98/013, B.C.S.C. Weekly Summary, Edition 98:4, p. 7.

promotional material issued by ATEC showed Philip Lieberman as chairman of the board and chief executive officer and Marc Lieberman as president, treasurer and a director.

None of ATEC, Philip Lieberman or Marc Lieberman is registered under the Act.

A British Columbia company with the same name, American Technology Exploration Corporation, was incorporated in October 1994. Corporate registry records show Philip Lieberman as president and a director and Marc Lieberman as secretary and a director. No other directors or officers are shown. This company was not directly involved in these proceedings.

Evidence presented by Commission staff shows that, in October 1996, Philip Lieberman contracted on behalf of ATEC with Stock Research Group Inc. ("SRG"), for SRG to develop and maintain for ATEC a World Wide Web site accessible through the Internet (the "Web site"). ATEC was responsible for the content of the Web site. Lieberman provided SRG with a diskette containing information in a word processing format. SRG converted it to the "hyper text" format used in Web sites. The site was easily accessed from British Columbia and contained nothing to suggest that it was not directed at investors in this province. The Web site displayed two telephone numbers, both in British Columbia. The number for the "Executive Office" was recorded by BC Tel as being in the name of Marc Lieberman. The "Private line Chairman of the Board" was a number recorded by BC Tel as being in the name of Philip Lieberman.

The Web site contained a description of ATEC and its mineral property, hot links to stock quotations and charts for ATEC shares and an inquiry form that could be sent by E-mail to obtain more information.

The Web site began by describing ATEC as "An innovative resource company developing major US gold deposits" and stated that it "trades on the NASDAQ small cap bulletin board". It went on to describe ATEC's business prospects in glowing terms, making a series of extraordinary claims about the Moapa property, a set of mineral claims in Nevada held by ATEC, and stated that "The company plans to begin production late spring 1997." Readers were advised that "Shares can easily be purchased anywhere in the world through any securities house."

The description of the property stated or implied in several places that considerable work had been done on the property, including assays using a "proprietary procedure". Most notably, ATEC said that the property contained "232,734,870 tons of blocked out ore reserves, containing 76 million ounces of gold in place." This statement implied that sufficient work had been done on the property to estimate the tonnage and grade of mineralized material. This work would have involved drilling many holes and assaying thousands of samples. ATEC also claimed that a U.S. government study and work on an adjacent property supported the presence of gold on the Moapa property. The description concluded by saying that ATEC had tested the property sufficiently to "guarantee" a mine life of over 30 years. The net revenue projected from the mine was more than $20 billion.

If the Web site description of the Moapa claims were to be believed, ATEC had the largest gold deposit in the world, larger even than the 71 million ounce deposit that had been reported falsely to be located on the famous Busang property of Bre-X. Furthermore, this vast deposit was not buried in a remote jungle on a tropical island, but was accessible from an interstate highway and mineable at the surface.

In fact, there is no basis to support ATEC's description of the Moapa property. None of the required permits have been sought or obtained from the U.S. government or Nevada state agencies in order to authorize exploration or development work on the property. ATEC's financial statements as at June 30, 1996, show that nothing had been spent on exploration or development of the Moapa property and ATEC had no resources to fund any meaningful work on the property. Nevada state officials indicate that there has never been any precious metals production in the Moapa area. The U.S. government study referred to in the Web site, which was produced more than a century ago, in 1890, does not even refer to Nevada, let alone the Moapa area.

In a page dealing with the management of ATEC, the Web site described Philip Lieberman as "a highly successful Chairman of many companies." It made no reference to his past regulatory problems or the orders to which he is currently subject. The page also described a member of ATEC's advisory team, Evaldo L. Kothny, Ph. D., and said that he "is listed in 'Who is Who in the West'". In fact, Who's Who in the West, a bi-annual catalogue containing biographies of prominent individuals in the Western U.S. and Western Canada, listed Kothny in its editions from 1976 to 1982 but has not listed him since.

The reference on the Web site to ATEC shares being traded on the "NASDAQ small cap bulletin board" is also misleading. There is, in fact, no market by that name. The NASDAQ Stock Market Inc. operates both the NASDAQ Stock Market and the OTC (over the counter) Bulletin Board. The NASDAQ Stock Market is divided into the NMS (national market system) and the Small Cap market. The NMS has substantial listing requirements. The Small Cap market has lower listing requirements, including a public float of $5 million and either net tangible assets of $4 million, market capitalization of $50 million or net income of $750,000. (All these figures are in U.S. dollars.) By contrast, the OTC Bulletin Board, on which ATEC shares are quoted, is a quotation service for issuers that do not qualify for the NASDAQ Stock Market. An issuer is not required to meet any financial or other requirements, other than having a market maker apply on its behalf, in order to have bids and offers by dealers for its shares quoted on the OTC Bulletin Board.

On June 4, 1997, after locating the ATEC Web site and reviewing its contents, Commission staff member Dennis Paulley called both telephone numbers shown on the Web site and left messages under an assumed name. Marc Lieberman called him back. In response to Paulley's questions, Marc Lieberman said that ATEC was a very small company, that Paulley should call his broker if he wished to purchase shares, that he should keep his eye on the Web site for more details about ATEC and that he should fax his name and address to Marc Lieberman in order to be put on the mailing list.

The Executive Director issued temporary orders against ATEC and both Liebermans on June 6. On June 10, Philip Lieberman faxed a hand written note to SRG, on ATEC letterhead, instructing that the ATEC Web site be suspended. Lieberman's note said he intended to resume the service at a later date.

3. FINDINGS

Commission staff allege that ATEC, Philip Lieberman and Marc Lieberman

- made or caused to be made statements that were misrepresentations while they were engaging in investor relations activities, in contravention of section 50(1)(d) of the Act;
- traded in securities without being registered, in contravention of section 34 of the Act.

Staff acknowledged at the hearing that Marc Lieberman (and presumably ATEC) could rely on the registration exemption in section 42(2)(7) of the Act for trading through a registered dealer. However, they noted that, because of the outstanding orders made against Philip Lieberman in the earlier proceedings, the exemptions do not apply to Philip Lieberman, with the result that any trading by him was in contravention of the previous orders.

The sections of the Act relevant to these allegations are as follows:

Section 1 definition of investor relations activities
"investor relations activities" means any activities or oral or written communications, by or on behalf of an issuer or security holder of the issuer, that promote or reasonably could be expected to promote the purchase or sale of securities of the issuer, but does not include

(a) the dissemination of information provided, or records prepared, in the ordinary course of the business of the issuer
(i) to promote the sale of products or services of the issuer, or
(ii) to raise public awareness of the issuer,
that cannot reasonably be considered to promote the purchase or sale of securities of the issuer,

(b) activities or communications necessary to comply with the requirements of
(i) this Act or the regulations, or
(ii) the bylaws, rules or other regulatory instruments of a self regulatory body or exchange,

(c) communications by a publisher of, or writer for, a newspaper, news magazine or business or financial publication, that is of general and regular paid circulation, distributed only to subscribers to it for value or to purchasers of it, if
(i) the communication is only through the newspaper, magazine or publication, and
(ii) the publisher or writer receives no commission or other consideration other than for acting in the capacity of publisher or writer, or

(d) activities or communications that may be prescribed for the purpose of this definition;

No activities have been prescribed under paragraph (d) of the definition.

Section 1 definition of material fact
"material fact" means, where used in relation to securities issued or proposed to be issued, a fact that significantly affects, or could reasonably be expected to significantly affect, the market price or value of those securities;

Section 1 definition of misrepresentation "misrepresentation" means
(a)   an untrue statement of a material fact, or
(b) an omission to state a material fact that is
(i) required to be stated, or

(ii) necessary to prevent a statement that is made from being false or misleading in the circumstances in which it was made;

Section 1 definition of trade
"trade" includes

(a) a disposition of a security for valuable consideration whether the terms of payment be on margin, installment or otherwise, but does not include a purchase of a security or a transfer, pledge, mortgage or other encumbrance of a security for the purpose of giving collateral for a debt,

(b) entering into an exchange contract,

(c) participation as a trader in a transaction in a security or exchange contract made on the floor of or through the facilities of an exchange,

(d) the receipt by a registrant of an order to buy or sell a security or exchange contract,

(e) a transfer of beneficial ownership of a security to a transferee, pledgee, mortgagee or other encumbrancer under a realization on collateral given for a debt, and

(f) any act, advertisement, solicitation, conduct or negotiation directly or indirectly in furtherance of any of the activities specified in paragraphs (a) to (e);

Section 34(1) registration requirement
A person must not

(a) trade in a security or exchange contract unless the person is registered in accordance with the regulations as
(i) a dealer, or
(ii) a salesperson, partner, director or officer of a registered dealer and is acting on behalf of that dealer,

Section 50(1) prohibited representations
A person, while engaging in investor relations activities or with the intention of effecting a trade in a security, must not do any of the following:

(d) make a statement that the person knows, or ought reasonably to know, is a misrepresentation.

Our analysis of each of the allegations is as follows.

Investor Relations Activities

The evidence is clear that ATEC, on the direction of Philip Lieberman, contracted to have the Web site set up and provided the written content of the site. The site was accessible to anyone, in British Columbia or elsewhere, who had access to the Internet. The glowing descriptions of ATEC's Nevada mineral property and its future prospects, together with the information about ATEC shares and how to buy them, clearly communicated information (and misinformation) that promoted the purchase of ATEC shares. The contents of the Web site did not fit within any of the exclusions in paragraphs (a) to (d) of the definition of investor relations activities. On this basis, we find that, in communicating to potential investors through the Web site, ATEC was engaging in investor relations activities.

As detailed in the background, the descriptions in the Web site of ATEC, its property and its management were riddled with false and misleading statements. The following are the most egregious examples:

- ATEC stated that it had blocked out reserves containing 76 million ounces of gold on the Moapa property, had tested the property sufficiently to guarantee a mine life of over 30 years, and projected net revenues from the mine of more than $20 billion, when in fact it had done little or no exploration work on the property and had no basis to support these statements.
- ATEC stated that it planned to "begin production late spring 1997" when in fact it had done little or no exploration work to establish the feasibility of a mine and had not applied for or obtained any of the numerous government permits or approvals that would be required before mining could begin. ATEC stated that work on an adjacent property supported the presence of gold on the Moapa property, when in fact there has never been any precious metals production in the Moapa area. ATEC falsely stated that a particular U.S. government study indicated the presence of gold in the Moapa area.
- ATEC described Philip Lieberman as the "highly successful Chairman of many companies", while omitting to state that he had been subject to serious regulatory sanctions.
- ATEC stated that Evaldo Kothny "is listed in 'Who's Who in the West'", when in fact Kothny has not been listed in that catalogue since 1982.
- ATEC stated that its shares were traded on the "NASDAQ small cap bulletin board", which gave the misleading impression that its shares were listed on the NASDAQ Small Cap market, when in fact its shares were quoted only on the OTC Bulletin Board, a quotation service with much lower standards.

These statements all relate to ATEC's business or to persons connected with ATEC. ATEC must be taken to have known that the statements about the Moapa property and about Philip Lieberman were false and misleading. The statements about the U.S. government study, the purported work on an adjacent property and Evaldo Kothny could easily have been checked, and therefore ATEC ought to have known they were false and misleading. The misleading reference to the "NASDAQ small cap bulletin board" could have been an honest mistake, but it is consistent with the reckless disregard for the truth that is reflected throughout the Web site contents.

Most of these statements concerned material facts, that is matters that could reasonably be expected to affect the market price or value of ATEC's shares. The false and misleading statements as to material facts were misrepresentations as defined in the Act.

We find that ATEC, while engaging in investor relations activities, made statements that it knew or ought to have known were misrepresentations and, in so doing, contravened section 50(1)(d) of the Act.

Trading
The contents of the ATEC Web site were designed to excite the reader about the prospects for ATEC and its shares and to interest potential investors in buying ATEC shares. The reader of the Web site is told (misleadingly) that the shares trade on the "NASDAQ small cap bulletin board" and that "Shares can easily be purchased anywhere in the world through any securities house." The material on the Web site could therefore be described as an advertisement or solicitation for investors to purchase ATEC shares, which would thereby create demand and allow others to trade their ATEC shares.

Philip Lieberman and ATEC were responsible for setting up the Web site and for the written material contained on it. Marc Lieberman may not have had the same degree of involvement in setting up the Web site or placing the contents on it, but he responded to Paulley's telephone call, made to a number listed on the Web site, by telling him to call his broker if he wished to purchase ATEC shares. We find that, in their activities related to the Web site, Philip Lieberman, Marc Lieberman and ATEC engaged in acts, advertisements or solicitations directly or indirectly in furtherance of trading in ATEC shares and, therefore, they were trading in securities.

ATEC and Marc Lieberman could, at least arguably, rely on the exemption from registration in section 45(2)(7) of the Act for "a trade in a security by a person acting solely through a registered dealer". However, under the orders issued by the Superintendent in 1988 and the Commission in 1994, neither that exemption nor any other applies to Philip Lieberman. Accordingly we find that, in trading in securities through the ATEC Web site, Philip Lieberman has contravened those orders.

4. DECISION

ATEC used the modern technology of the Internet for an old fashioned purpose promoting its shares with outrageous misrepresentations. Information is the lifeblood of a securities market. A misinformed market lacks integrity and presents inappropriate risks to investors who are invited to trade in the promoted shares. Furthermore, ATEC is not a reporting issuer. Although staff did not allege or prove that ATEC contravened the prospectus requirements of the Act, it is difficult to imagine how a company based in British Columbia, like ATEC, could become publicly traded and promote its shares in this province while avoiding the need to comply with these requirements. We consider it in the public interest to cease all trading in ATEC shares until ATEC has filed a prospectus and obtained a receipt for it.

Despite some confusion in the corporate records, it is clear that Philip Lieberman and his son Marc Lieberman were the directors of ATEC and the individuals responsible for conducting its business. They must be held accountable for ATEC's use of misrepresentations in its Web site promotion.

Philip Lieberman bears primary responsibility. He was undoubtedly the moving force behind ATEC. As in previous cases where he has been subject to discipline by this Commission, his activities reflect his total disregard for the truth in conducting his business affairs. In this case, he also violated two sets of orders already outstanding against him. In order to protect investors against his repeated misconduct, we consider it in the public interest to permanently remove him from the market and activities related to issuers and to require him to pay a substantial penalty.

Marc Lieberman was Philip Lieberman's assistant, helping to run ATEC and to inflict its misrepresentations on potential investors. We consider it in the public interest to remove him from the market and activities related to issuers for a significant period.

We order:

* under section 161(1)(b) of the Act that all persons cease trading in the shares of ATEC until ATEC has filed a prospectus and obtained a receipt for it from the Executive Director;
* under section 161(1)(c) of the Act that the exemptions described in sections 44 to 47, 74, 75, 98 and 99 do not apply to Philip Lieberman for the rest of his

natural life or to Marc Lieberman for a period of 5 years from the date of this decision;

- under section 161(1)(d)(ii) of the Act that Philip Lieberman is prohibited from becoming or acting as a director or officer of any issuer for the rest of his natural life and that Marc Lieberman is prohibited from becoming or acting as a director or officer of any issuer until the later of 5 years from the date of this decision and the date he successfully completes a course of study satisfactory to the Executive Director on the duties of directors;
- under section 161(1)(d)(iii) of the Act that Philip Lieberman is prohibited from engaging in investor relations activities for the rest of his natural life and that Marc Lieberman is prohibited from engaging in investor relations activities for a period of 5 years from the date of this decision;
- under section 162 of the Act that Philip Lieberman pay an administrative penalty of $50,000 within thirty days of the date of this decision; and
- under section 174 of the Act that ATEC, Philip Lieberman and Marc Lieberman pay prescribed fees or charges for the costs of or related to the hearing, in an amount to be determined following further submissions from the parties.

We note that, despite the previous decisions of the Commission, Philip Lieberman was able to set up ATEC and have its shares quoted on the OTC Bulletin Board in the United States. This gave him the opportunity, once again, to conduct his brand of business, wildly misrepresenting to public investors the prospects of a mineral property. In an effort to forestall further activities of this type, we direct Commission staff to provide copies of this decision to the relevant securities and mining authorities in the United States and to alert them to the nature of Philip Lieberman's business practices.

25

CRTC Internet Regulation

The target of intense criticism from many quarters in Canada, the Canadian Radio-television and Telecommunications Commission (CRTC) is responsible for Canadian broadcasting and telecommunications regulation. In upholding its mandate, established by the federal government, the CRTC is responsible for maintaining Canadian content laws, setting telecom price increases and developing broadcast policy.

Although the CRTC's mandate is limited to broadcast and telecommunications, the Commission is widely perceived as the most likely Canadian source for "Internet regulation." In fact, during the CRTC's controversial New Media Hearings in 1998–99, many observers suspected that the Commission would take the opportunity to create a new series of Internet regulations. The CRTC surprised the critics by adopting a "hands off" approach to the Internet.

This chapter examines three areas of CRTC competence that overlap with the Internet. It begins with the broadcasting component of the Commission's mandate and continues with telecommunications and Internet access issues.

BROADCAST
Any examination of the CRTC's role in regulating Internet broadcasting must begin with the federal *Broadcast Act*, which establishes the limits of CRTC broadcast regulatory power.

Broadcast Act[†]

2.(1) In this Act,

"broadcasting" means any transmission of programs, whether or not encrypted, by radio waves or other means of telecommunication for reception by the public by means of broadcasting receiving apparatus, but does not include any such transmission of programs that is made solely for performance or display in a public place;

"broadcasting receiving apparatus" means a device, or combination of devices, intended for or capable of being used for the reception of broadcasting;

"Commission" means the Canadian Radio-television and Telecommunications Commission established by the Canadian Radio-television and Telecommunications Commission Act;

"encrypted" means treated electronically or otherwise for the purpose of preventing intelligible reception;

(2) For the purposes of this Act, "other means of telecommunication" means any wire, cable, radio, optical or other electromagnetic system, or any similar technical system.

PART II OBJECTS AND POWERS OF THE COMMISSION IN RELATION TO BROADCASTING

5.(1) Subject to this Act and the Radiocommunication Act and to any directions to the Commission issued by the Governor in Council under this Act, the Commission shall regulate and supervise all aspects of the Canadian broadcasting system with a view to implementing the broadcasting policy set out in subsection 3(1) and, in so doing, shall have regard to the regulatory policy set out in subsection (2).

(2) The Canadian broadcasting system should be regulated and supervised in a flexible manner that (a) is readily adaptable to the different characteristics of English and French language broadcasting and to the different conditions under which broadcasting undertakings that provide English or French language programming operate; (b) takes into account regional needs and concerns; (c) is readily adaptable to scientific and technological change; (d) facilitates the provision of broadcasting to Canadians; (e) facilitates the provision of Canadian programs to Canadians; (f) does not inhibit the development of information technologies and their application or the delivery of resultant services to Canadians; and (g) is sensitive to the administrative burden that, as a consequence of such regulation and supervision, may be imposed on persons carrying on broadcasting undertakings.

(3) The Commission shall give primary consideration to the objectives of the broadcasting policy set out in subsection 3(1) if, in any particular matter before the Commission, a conflict arises between those objectives and the objectives of the regulatory policy set out in subsection (2).

6. The Commission may from time to time issue guidelines and statements with respect to any matter within its jurisdiction under this Act, but no such guidelines or statements issued by the Commission are binding on the Commission.

---

† R.S.C. 1985, c. B-9.01.

CRTC New Media Report[†]

Introduction

On 31 July 1998, in Broadcasting Public Notice CRTC 1998–82 and Telecom Public Notice CRTC 98-20 (the Public Notice), the Commission announced that it was initiating a proceeding under both the Broadcasting Act and the Telecommunications Act calling for comments on the rapidly expanding and increasingly available range of communications services collectively referred to as "new media."

The Commission held a three-phase process for the submission of written comments by interested parties. This proceeding was unprecedented in terms of the broad spectrum of individuals, industries, and interest groups from whom the Commission received comments. The call for comments produced well in excess of 1000 contributions from individuals, multimedia companies involved in the production and distribution of new media products and services, as well as the traditionally regulated industries and their industry associations that are familiar and active participants in Commission proceedings.

. . . .

The Commission's approach to new media

Many parties to this proceeding agreed that there is a need for greater regulatory clarity and certainty regarding services that are being offered by way of the Internet. In this respect, parties submitted that there is a need for the Commission to move beyond the statements included in its 19 May 1995 report to Government entitled Competition and Culture on Canada's Information Highway: Managing the Realities of Transition (the Convergence Report).

In the Convergence Report, the Commission noted, among other things, that the current Broadcasting Act will likely capture many of the new and emerging services. Since that report was released, neither the Commission nor other government bodies have clarified what approach or treatment should be applied to such services.

Parties differed on whether the Broadcasting Act applies at all to new media undertakings and the services they provide. Some parties argued that most new media services are beyond the scope of "broadcasting" as defined in the Broadcasting Act and that the Commission should settle any uncertainty to that effect. Others argued that none of the services delivered over the Internet are consistent with any notion of broadcasting that would have been contemplated by the Broadcasting Act.

Interpretations on this point were varied. For instance, the vast majority of individual Canadians who participated in the on-line forum that was initiated at the outset of this proceeding, as well as the numbers of individuals who e-mailed the Commission during the course of the proceeding, submitted, in essence, that there should be no regulatory oversight of these services by the Commission pursuant to the Broadcasting Act.

Certain parties, however, argued that most new media services would qualify as "broadcasting" and the undertakings that provide them as "broadcasting undertakings" under the definitions set out in the Broadcasting Act.

---

† CRTC, Telecom Public Notice CRTC 99-14, "New Media" (May 1999). © Canadian Radio-television and Telecommunications Commission. Reproduced with permission.

Putting those differing interpretations aside, parties were generally consistent in the view that there is a compelling need for the Commission to provide more clarity and certainty as to the approach that it intends to develop with regard to new media. They argued that the uncertainty surrounding this issue creates difficulties for developers and distributors of such services in accessing capital markets and in bringing new and innovative services to the Canadian market.

The Commission agrees that there has been uncertainty as to whether new media services constitute broadcasting in light of the breadth of the definitions of "program" and "broadcasting" under the Broadcasting Act. The Commission also agrees that such uncertainty could be problematic for the developers and providers of new and emerging services. In the following section, the Commission provides its views as to the scope of the definition of "broadcasting" in the Act and sets out its approach to new media.

Is new media "broadcasting"?

Statutory Definitions
"Broadcasting" is defined in section 2 of the Broadcasting Act as follows:

> [a]ny transmission of programs, whether or not encrypted, by radio waves or other means of telecommunication for reception by the public by means of broadcasting receiving apparatus, but does not include any such transmission of programs that is made solely for performance or display in a public place.

The term "program" is in turn defined in section 2 of the Act as:

> [s]ounds or visual images, or a combination of sounds and visual images, that are intended to inform, enlighten or entertain, but does not include visual images, whether or not combined with sounds, that consist predominantly of alphanumeric text.

Explicit statutory exclusions from the definition of broadcasting
The Commission notes that, as stated above, much of the content available by way of the Internet, Canadian or otherwise, currently consists predominantly of alphanumeric text and is therefore excluded from the definition of "program". This type of content, therefore, falls outside the scope of the Broadcasting Act. Accordingly, the remainder of this section contemplates Internet content that consists only of audio, video, a combination of audio and video, or other visual images including still images that do not consist predominantly of alphanumeric text.

It was submitted, among other things, that information displayed on the Internet can be considered to be solely for display in a public place and therefore excluded from the definition of "broadcasting". Certainly, the Canadian public expressed its view that the Internet has a unique ability to foster citizen engagement and public discourse. While the Commission agrees, it considers that the Internet is not in and of itself a "public place" in the sense intended by the Act. Programs are not transmitted to cyberspace, but through it, and are received in a physical place, e.g. in an office or home.

The Commission considers, however, that the exception to the definition of "broadcasting" for programs transmitted for display in a public place would apply, as suggested by one participant, to a particular service delivered via the Internet that is accessible by end-users only in a terminal or kiosk located in a public place, such as a public library.

Technological neutrality of "broadcasting"

The Commission notes that the definition of "broadcasting" includes the transmission of programs, whether or not encrypted, by other means of telecommunication. This definition is, and was intended to be, technologically neutral. Accordingly, the mere fact that a program is delivered by means of the Internet, rather than by means of the airwaves or by a cable company, does not exclude it from the definition of "broadcasting".

Some parties argued that there is no "transmission" of content over the Internet, and therefore, there is no "broadcasting". The fact that an end-user activates the delivery of a program is not, in the Commission's view, determinative. As discussed below, on-demand delivery is included in the definition of "broadcasting". Further, the Commission considers that the particular technology used for the delivery of signals over the Internet cannot be determinative. Based on a plain meaning of the word, and recognizing the intent that the definition be technologically neutral, the Commission considers that the delivery of data signals from an origination point (e.g. a host server) to a reception point (e.g. an end-user's apparatus) by means of the Internet involves the "transmission" of the content.

Some parties submitted that the definition of "broadcasting receiving apparatus" was not intended to capture devices such as personal computers or Web TV boxes when used to access the Internet. The Commission notes that the definition of "broadcasting receiving apparatus" includes a "device, or combination of devices, intended for or capable of being used for the reception of broadcasting". The Commission considers that an interpretation of this definition that includes only conventional televisions and radios is not supported by the plain meaning of the definition and would undermine the technological neutrality of the definition of "broadcasting". In the Commission's view, devices such as personal computers, or televisions equipped with Web TV boxes, fall within the definition of "broadcasting receiving apparatus" to the extent that they are or are capable of being used to receive broadcasting.

Transmission of programs for reception by the public

It is therefore necessary to consider whether the transmission of sounds or visual images (or a combination of sounds and visual images) that do not consist predominantly of alphanumeric text by means of the Internet can be said to involve the transmission of programs for reception by the public.

A number of parties submitted that content that is "customizable" does not constitute "broadcasting". The Commission notes that parties have used the term "customizable" to mean different things. For example, some parties cited the non-simultaneous characteristic of Internet services as a basis for which such services cannot be considered to be "broadcasting".

The Commission considers it important to distinguish between the ability to obtain Internet content "on-demand" — the non-simultaneous characteristic of Internet services — and the ability of the end-user to "customize", or interact with, the content itself to suit his or her own needs and interests.

In the Commission's view, there is no explicit or implicit statutory requirement that broadcasting involve scheduled or simultaneous transmissions of programs. The Commission notes that the legislator could have, but did not, expressly exclude on-demand programs from the Act. As noted by one party, the mere ability of an end-user to select content on-demand does not by itself remove such content from the definition of broadcasting. The Commission considers that programs that are transmitted to members of the public on-demand are transmitted "for reception by the public".

The Commission considers, however, that some Internet services involve a high degree of "customizable" content. This allows end-users to have an individual one-on-one experience through the creation of their own uniquely tailored content. In the Commission's view, this content, created by the end-user, would not be transmitted for reception by the public. The Commission therefore considers that content that is "customizable" to a significant degree does not properly fall within the definition of "broadcasting" set out in the Broadcasting Act.

By contrast, the ability to select, for example, camera angles or background lighting would not by itself remove programs transmitted by means of the Internet from the definition of "broadcasting". The Commission notes that digital television can be expected to allow this more limited degree of customization. In these circumstances, where the experience of end-users with the program in question would be similar, if not the same, there is nonetheless a transmission of the program for reception by the public, and, therefore, such content would be "broadcasting". These types of programs would include, for example, those that consist of digital audio and video services.

Proposal to exempt all new media broadcasting undertakings

Section 9(4) of the Broadcasting Act requires the Commission to exempt broadcasting undertakings from the licensing requirements in the Act if the Commission is satisfied that compliance by these undertakings with these requirements will not contribute in a material manner to the implementation of the broadcasting policy for Canada.

The record of this proceeding indicates that the Internet has given rise to new avenues and forms of expression and communication for Canadians, amongst themselves and others in both French and English. The proceeding also highlighted the often local and regional nature of many of the services. They provide valuable sources of information and other services to many Canadians that are otherwise unavailable. Moreover, the demand for Canadian information and other services has led to the development of search engines and aggregation sites that facilitate access to Canadian services.

Furthermore, the Commission considers that to impose licensing on new media would not contribute in any way to its development or to the benefits that it has brought to Canadian users, consumers and businesses.

In light of the foregoing, the Commission is satisfied that compliance with Part II of the Act, and any applicable regulations made thereunder, by persons carrying on new media broadcasting undertakings will not contribute in a material manner to the implementation of the policy objectives set out in section 3(1) of the Act.

Accordingly, the Commission will issue a proposed exemption order without terms or conditions in respect of all undertakings that are providing broadcasting services over the Internet, in whole or in part, in Canada.

In addition, in light of the Commission's view with respect to "customizable" content delivered by the Internet expressed above, it considers it appropriate to review in the near future its current exemption order with respect to video game programming undertakings.

. . . .

A Canadian presence in new media

Under its mandate to implement the policy objectives set out in the Broadcasting Act, the Commission has imposed Canadian exhibition and expenditure requirements on traditional broadcasters, as well as requirements for distribution undertakings to contribute financially to the production of Canadian programming. This was done in recognition of the fundamental importance of broadcasting to Canadian sovereignty and cultural identity and the realization that market forces alone would not provide a significant amount of Canadian broadcasting content. Canada's small domestic market makes it difficult to finance the creation of competitive Canadian programs. Whereas U.S. producers can recover the majority of their production costs through domestic license fees, the license fees earned in Canada by most Canadian program producers represent only a fraction of their total production costs.

The economies of scale that exist in the United States make American programming less expensive for Canadian broadcasters to acquire than Canadian programming. At the same time, American programming has tended to attract larger Canadian audiences than Canadian programming because of its higher production values and well-established star system. This has particularly been the case for English-language television. American broadcasters cannot provide their programming directly to Canadian viewers except in situations where off-air signals are directly receivable. This has resulted in a system whereby profitable non-Canadian programming is purchased by Canadian broadcasters to subsidize the cost of Canadian programming.

Similarly, in English-language radio, before the advent of Canadian content regulations, it was difficult for Canadian sound recordings to get airplay in Canada because they were competing against more heavily-financed and promoted "hits" from the United States and other countries.

The Commission confirms that its policies and regulations for conventional broadcasting services remain appropriate.

Availability of Canadian Content

In the Public Notice, the Commission set out a number of questions related to Canadian content on the Internet. Specifically, the Commission was interested in participants' views on the availability and visibility of Canadian new media content and whether any incentives or regulatory measures were needed to prompt existing or new industry participants to develop, produce, promote and distribute Canadian new media content and services.

Differing views on the need for public intervention to foster the development and production of Canadian new media content were discussed at the hearing. Some parties saw no need for any intervention at all, arguing that government should not interfere in any way because there is no shortage of Canadian new media content, no access problems for producers or consumers, and the new media industry is developing rapidly.

Other participants, however, favoured some form of support for the production and distribution of new media content, although the majority of these participants clearly preferred an incentive-based approach to one involving regulation. To increase the level of support for Canadian new media content, a number of initiatives were recommended. Among these were direct funding programs targeted specifically at Canadian new media content, various tax incentives to support the new media industry, content-specific industry development initiatives, and activities to stimulate consumer demand for new media content.

A few parties argued that a regulatory approach is the only way to ensure that Canadian new media content is produced, promoted and guaranteed a place of prominence on the Internet. The main suggestions for regulatory measures included: (1) requiring ISPs to contribute a portion of their annual revenues to content development funding; (2) requiring ISPs and/or content aggregators to ensure shelf space and a place of prominence for Canadian new media content; and (3) requiring Canadian ISPs to provide links to Canadian web sites.

In the Commission's view, the circumstances that led to the need for regulation of Canadian content in traditional broadcasting do not currently exist in the Internet environment. Market forces are providing a Canadian presence on the Internet that is also supported by a strong demand for Canadian new media content. Participants provided statistics indicating that Canadian web sites represent about 5% of all Internet web sites.

Admittedly, the sheer amount of content available on the Internet makes it difficult to measure Canadian-based content. However, parties demonstrated that a strong Canadian presence exists on the Internet through reference to some of the following: (1) the impressive number of Canadian web sites that exist; (2) key partnerships that have developed between some ISPs and Canadian content creators for the specific purpose of generating a supply of Canadian content; (3) the expansion of many traditional Canadian media businesses to the Internet; and (4) the search tools available that make it easier to locate Canadian content on the Internet.

Further, during the hearing, many broadcasters illustrated how they use their web sites to cross-promote their traditional Canadian broadcasting services. There also appears to be a significant demand for local and regional Canadian content on the Internet. Many Canadian television and radio stations distribute some of their local news programming through their web sites.

In light of the above, the Commission concurs with the majority of participants that there is a significant amount of Canadian new media content and services available on the Internet today and ample business and market incentives for its continued production and distribution. In fact, many parties submitted that regulation would serve to hinder, not help, the production and distribution of Canadian new media content. Therefore, there is no policy rationale for the Commission to impose regulatory measures to stimulate the production and distribution of Canadian content.

Visibility of Canadian Content

The issue of how Canadian new media content producers will acquire visibility for their content was discussed at the hearing. Concern was expressed that a few large content aggregators who might gain dominant positions could act as gatekeepers to the most heavily trafficked web sites on the Internet.

Parties disagreed on the urgency of this threat. Some producers claimed to have already been asked to pay for access to search engines or portals. However, many of the content aggregators that appeared before the Commission denied that anyone is charging for access. Instead, they indicated that Canadian content is always in demand because of the Internet's virtually limitless capacity to carry it. Others have argued that producers are demanding and receiving significant compensation in return for the right to mirror or cache their sites on a particular portal or server. Many also noted that there are a number of Canadian content aggregators and portal sites that are being established that could lead Canadian consumers easily to Canadian content.

In the Commission's view, there was no convincing evidence submitted throughout the hearing process to suggest that visibility of Canadian content on the Internet is a problem and, therefore, no policy rationale to pursue regulatory measures to support access to Canadian content on the Internet.

The Commission is aware that the likely explanation as to why Canadian content is flourishing on the Internet today is because the Internet is still primarily a text-based information medium with a strong appeal to local and regional interests. The type of content that is predominant on the Internet has low production values; it is relatively inexpensive to produce; and it is in demand by Canadians who want access to local, regional and national information in such areas as weather, sports, current affairs and social services. If the Internet remains primarily a text-based, information medium, then it is likely that market forces alone will continue to provide an adequate supply of Canadian content.

Many expressed concern about the preservation of funding resources for high quality Canadian programming in the future new media environment. A broad spectrum of participants recommended different funding initiatives to support Canadian new media content. These included direct government funding of new media content, in the form of grants, loans, and equity investments. A number of refundable tax credits were also recommended to cover such new media expenses as investment in new media production, labour, research and development, and capital costs. Several parties also recommended that Section 19 of the Income Tax Act, which provides advertisers in Canadian publications with deductions equal to the costs of their advertisements, should be applied to new media.

The Commission notes that a number of funds have already been developed in both the public and private sectors to help finance Canadian new media content. Funds such as The Multimedia Fund administered by Telefilm Canada, the Stentor and Bell New Media funds and recent funds announced by Industry Canada have been targeted toward Canadian new media content in the entertainment and educational genres.

The Commission also acknowledges the work that is being done to develop initiatives to support Canadian new media content and to nurture the Canadian new media industry by such government departments as Canadian Heritage, Industry Canada and the Department of Foreign Affairs and International Trade. Among a number of noteworthy initiatives has been the government's "Connecting All Canadians" agenda, which was announced in the 1998 Budget. This agenda has six pillars or areas of emphasis for national leadership in new media which are intended to ensure that, among other things, all Canadians will have access to new media, Canada will be a leader in electronic commerce, and Canadian content will occupy a place of prominence on the Internet.

Funding initiatives may be particularly necessary for the French-language new media market, which is significantly smaller than the English-language market. Francophone new media developers are faced with higher production costs than English-language producers because they often have to create a product in both languages and develop more costly marketing and distribution strategies to expand their market. Export options are also more limited in the francophone market. Not surprisingly, the level of French-language content on the Internet is quite low when compared with English-language content.

Nevertheless, it is worth noting that the federal and Quebec governments have been working to address this issue and have established funds that are targeted specifically at French-language new media production. In addition, despite the challenges it has faced, the new media industry in Quebec is one of the most vibrant and well-developed in Canada. The Commission also notes the availability of a number of French-language search engines that provide access to information in French.

The Future of Canadian Content on the Internet

There was a wide divergence of views among parties on how the future of the Internet might unfold and the impact that this will have on traditional media and on Canadian content.

Many predicted that the future new media environment could differ greatly from that of traditional broadcasting. For one thing, the notion that the Internet might some day be a substitute for traditional television and radio broadcasting is predicated on the assumption that it will be capable of delivering broadband content. As mentioned previously, this will depend upon, among other things, significant advances in bandwidth and processing speeds as well as the resolution of major intellectual property issues. Several parties also pointed out that no new medium has ever completely displaced a previous medium and it could be that television and radio will continue to co-exist with the Internet, although perhaps in altered forms.

Even if the Internet does become the dominant medium for reaching mass audiences, it cannot be taken for granted that the economic model that governs traditional broadcasting, whereby Canadian broadcasters can acquire discrete Canadian rights for American programming, will exist on the Internet. This will depend on, among other things, whether or not geographic rights markets for content on the Internet will emerge.

Some feel that it is more likely that production companies such as Disney, Fox or MGM will have their own servers located in the United States that will distribute video products cheaply and effectively direct to other countries around the world. If there is no need for intermediaries, then Canadian programmers or distributors may not be able to access the rights to non-Canadian intellectual property. This could have an impact on the production of Canadian programming if revenues from the exhibition of American programming are no longer available to Canadians. In any case, the business model for the Internet would be significantly different from that of traditional television. The business model could be driven by Canadian content, eliminating the need for the regulation of Canadian content although not necessarily the need for public funding of this content.

By contrast, other parties predicted that the emergence of geographic boundaries for intellectual property rights on the Internet is imminent. Several parties also pointed out that some fundamental differences in the new media environment are likely to provide Canadians with advantages that did not exist in conventional broadcasting. For instance, some argued that the economies of scale in distribution that have existed for U.S. content creators in traditional broadcasting will not exist to the same extent in the new media environment. The advantage of the Internet is that anyone can place their product or program on a server and immediately gain access to a global audience. Similarly, technologies such as computer animation are already resulting in lower costs for some types of production and further technological innovations may continue this trend.

There will also be many more outlets for alternative voices and niche services that may be able to develop an audience or market base. An example was given at the oral hearing of a Canadian artist who developed a following in Japan where he sold some of his paintings via the Internet.

Many Canadians will increasingly have access to a diversity of content and services that might not have been available to them through conventional broadcasting. This may benefit Canadians who belong to communities of interest that have not been well-represented by mainstream media. This also raises the question of whether the Internet will ever have the ability to create mass audiences in a manner similar to that of conventional television, which is driven by mass-oriented entertainment programming, or whether the sheer number of "channels" offered by the Internet will always result in fragmentation. While some spoke of mass market Internet services, others were of the view that the successful content creators on the Internet will be the ones who target narrower communities of interest such as sports fans, art and music lovers, youth culture, and so on.

Finally, many consider Canada is ideally positioned to achieve success in the new media market because of its expertise and strengths in several of the creative and knowledge-based industries that fuel this growing industry including telecommunications, software development, digital animation and multicultural/multilingual content creation.

In light of all of the above, the Commission does not consider that it needs to impose any regulatory measures to support the development, production, promotion and distribution of Canadian new media content and services. On balance, while there may be both advantages and disadvantages in the future new media environment, the Commission is confident, based on the record of this proceeding, that the industry is moving in a direction that will result in a strong Canadian new media industry and a strong Canadian presence on the Internet. Most noteworthy was the expression of excitement and energy that was communicated by those who discussed their work in new media. The Commission does not intend to impede this creative energy through unnecessary regulatory measures but rather to encourage the continued leadership and innovation of the Canadian new media sector.

How conventional broadcasting and telecommunications are
affected by new media

One of the issues raised by the Commission in its Public Notice was whether, and if so, to what extent new media are now, or may be expected to become substitutes for existing broadcasting services and their distribution systems. It was argued by some parties that a high degree of substitutability could threaten regulated broadcasters' revenue sources and significantly impede their ability to fulfil their obligations under the Broadcasting Act.

The vast majority of participants agreed that, in the short term, traditional media and new media services should be considered to be complementary rather than substitute services. Participants noted key differences from both a consumer's and a supplier's point of view when comparing traditional and new media.

From the consumer's perspective, new media services provide interactive and mostly unscheduled access, while traditional media offer mostly one-way point-to-multipoint programming. Many participants also noted that the quality of new media video is not of the quality available from traditional media. That situation is expected to remain until extensive technological developments allow for improved quality.

From a supplier's perspective, new media offer a market where basic content can be produced and distributed at relatively little cost. New media offer, among other things, consumer-specific messaging, an unlimited number of distribution channels and a borderless distribution system through the Internet. This is in contrast to the traditional media industry which is characterized by limited channel capacity, a high degree of mass appeal programming, and high distribution costs and barriers to entry. The Internet, which today has a penetration rate of approximately 20%, compared to the much higher penetration rates of television and radio, cannot yet deliver mass Canadian audiences.

There was considerably less consensus among participants regarding the longer term substitutability of new and traditional media services and distribution systems. Some argued that there is no evidence that the Internet will be capable of supporting the delivery of anything near broadcast quality video within the next decade.

Still other participants were of the view that new media services will become substitutes for traditional media services within a shorter time frame. Some suggested this could possibly occur within seven years.

While views vary considerably, the Commission agrees with most participants that key technological developments must take place before new media services and distribution systems compete more directly with traditional media. Should broadcast quality video and audio services become available, other factors need to be considered before new media services and distribution systems can be considered to be substitutes. Such factors include the cost of exhibition devices, the general appeal of the service offerings, customers' willingness to pay, as well as PC and Internet access penetration rates.

The Commission notes, however, that new media may evolve in ways that are entirely different from the current forms of conventional broadcasting. For example, they may simply co-exist with and complement conventional media, as in the cases of books, radio and television.

.   .   .   .

Offensive and illegal content

Most parties to the proceeding acknowledged the presence of both offensive and potentially illegal content on the Internet. Where parties differed to some extent was in how best to deal with this type of content. Most agreed that Commission regulation of participating undertakings and the services they provide is either inappropriate or unnecessary. While the majority argued that issues of social concern, such as hate propaganda and obscenity, are most appropriately dealt with under existing Canadian laws, they also supported industry self-regulation as an effective means of addressing offensive content, either through codes of conduct or other self-regulatory mechanisms. They also pointed to a number of tools currently on the market, such as content filters and blocking devices, which exist to protect children from content that might be harmful to them.

However, a number of parties expressed concern about the ease with which both offensive and potentially illegal content can be accessed and disseminated. Some called upon the Commission to regulate this type of content. Of those expressing concerns, a number agreed that while the Criminal Code contains tools for dealing with illegal content, using those tools can be a lengthy and arduous process. A number of parties suggested that additional powers should be given to the Canadian

Human Rights Commission to combat certain hate propaganda and other activities prohibited by the Canadian Human Rights Act. Some argued that stronger codes of conduct, including procedures for notice and take down of offending web sites, should be developed by industry groups.

Most parties, while concerned about offensive and potentially illegal content on the Internet, were reluctant to endorse regulation that would restrict access to information or rights of rebuttal on the medium.

It was also suggested that the Commission and Government work with a variety of partners, in both the public and private sectors and on both domestic and international levels, to deal with the issue of "illegal and undesirable activity" on the Internet. The Commission notes that government agencies and ISP industry representatives are currently discussing these matters.

The Commission acknowledges the expressions of concern about the dissemination of offensive and potentially illegal content over the Internet. It also acknowledges the views of the majority of parties who argued that Canadian laws of general application, coupled with self-regulatory initiatives, would be more appropriate for dealing with this type of content over the Internet than either the Broadcasting Act or Telecommunications Act. The vast majority of such content, particularly hate propaganda, is beyond the regulatory jurisdiction of the Broadcasting Act because it consists predominantly of alphanumeric text. As such, it falls outside of the definition of a "program" set out in the Act. In keeping with the overall policy stated earlier, significantly customized content does not fall within the definition of broadcasting and that content which is broadcasting will be exempt from regulation.

The Commission also notes that Internet service providers and their industry associations, in conjunction with both government agencies and other organizations, have made efforts to develop codes of conduct that would assist in combating the dissemination of offensive and potentially illegal material. The Commission encourages these groups to continue their work in developing standards and procedures for dealing with such content. The Commission considers that more can likely be done in the area of illegal content by, for example, establishing complaint lines and industry ombudsmen as well as developing international arrangements. Such arrangements could include co-operation between law enforcement agencies for providing notice and take down of web sites disseminating such content.

The Commission also believes that users can assist in controlling access to web sites that may be inappropriate for children. The existence of content filtering software that is relatively inexpensive and, in some cases, free of charge, is a useful tool for controlling access by children to unsuitable material. The Commission notes that, like most other aspects of new media, effective content filtering software is developing rapidly.

Lastly, the Commission notes that, as with most other media, awareness and knowledge of the benefits that can be obtained from the rich diversity of content available on the Internet, as well as of the existence of offensive content, can be a powerful tool in the hands of users. Organizations such as the Media Awareness Network, a Canadian not-for-profit organization, are dedicated to media education and media issues affecting children and youth. Useful information can be obtained from such groups. The Media Awareness Network, for example, can be accessed on the Internet at http://www.media-awareness.ca.

Discussion Questions

1. The headlines in the Canadian media the day after the release of the New Media report trumpeted the CRTC's decision to not "regulate the Internet." How accurate was this characterization?

2. How important is the distinction between "can't regulate" and "won't regulate"?

3. Many critics suggested that the CRTC adopted a *laissez faire* approach to the Internet largely because it could not practically regulate Internet activity. Do you agree? Should the CRTC have simply conceded that Internet regulation is beyond its jurisdictional mandate?

4. The CRTC argued that certain types of Internet transmissions, such as streaming audio and video, remain under its regulatory purview under the *Broadcast Act*. The majority of Internet content (characterized as "alphanumeric text"), however, is not broadcast and thus beyond the CRTC's jurisdictional competence. Does this distinction make sense? Do you think Parliament even considered such differences when it enacted the *Broadcast Act*?

5. Is there a place for CRTC regulation of broadcasting in light of the New Media decision? Considering the convergence occurring between media, do you think these distinctions will remain relevant in the years ahead?

As promised, the CRTC passed Exemption Order 1999-197 in December 1999, exempting new media businesses from CRTC regulation. The order provided as follows:

> The Commission is satisfied that compliance with Part II of the Broadcasting Act (the Act) and applicable regulations made thereunder by the class of broadcasting undertakings described below will not contribute in a material manner to the implementation of the broadcasting policy set out in subsection 3(1) of the Act.
>
> Therefore, pursuant to subsection 9(4) of the Act, the Commission exempts persons who carry on, in whole or in part in Canada, broadcasting undertakings of the class consisting of new media broadcasting undertakings, from any or all of the requirements of Part II of the Act or of a regulation thereunder. New media broadcasting undertakings provide broadcasting services delivered and accessed over the Internet, in accordance with the interpretation of "broadcasting" set out in Broadcasting Public Notice CRTC 1999-84 / Telecom Public Notice CRTC 99-14, Report on New Media, 17 May 1999.

The exemption was quickly tested by iCraveTV, a Canadian Webcaster that provided Internet users with the opportunity to watch television in real-time directly on their personal computers. In doing so, the company created a firestorm of protest from broadcasters and content creators across North America. Those parties, who only months earlier had vehemently opposed Internet regulation, now watched in horror as an unregulated Internet hatched new business models that caught many of them by surprise. The reaction in both the United States and Canada was swift — legal actions demanded an immediate cessation of all unauthorized Webcasts on both sides of the border with massive damage claims sought for alleged infringement.

In the United States, a group of broadcasters, studios, and sports leagues succeeded in obtaining an injunction that effectively shut down iCraveTV. Highlighting the conflict between Canadian and U.S. approaches to Webcasting, the Court adopted the following reasoning.

Twentieth Century Fox Film Corp. v. iCraveTV†

This is a civil action for money damages and equitable relief, filed by the National Football League ("NFL"), National Basketball Association ("NBA"), and NBA Properties, Inc. ("NBA Properties") (collectively "the Sports Leagues"), Twentieth Century Fox Film Corporation, Disney Enterprises, Inc., Columbia Tristar Television, Inc., Columbia Pictures Television, Inc., Columbia Pictures Industries, Inc., Metro-Goldwyn-Mayer Studios Inc., Orion Pictures Corporation, Paramount Pictures Corporation, Universal City Studios, Inc., Time Warner Entertainment Company, L.P. (collectively "the Studios"), and ABC, Inc., CBS Broadcasting Inc., and Fox Broadcasting Company (collectively "the Networks"). Plaintiffs seek a preliminary injunction, contending that defendants violated the Copyright Act, 17 U.S.C. §106, the Lanham Act, 15 U.S.C. §1125(a), and various state laws.

Defendants William R. Craig, George Simons and William R. Craig Consulting are residents of the Commonwealth of Pennsylvania. William Craig is a dual citizen of the United States and Canada. Defendant iCraveTV is a private Canadian company, and Defendant TVRadioNow Corp. is a Canadian company incorporated under the laws of Nova Scotia, with its principal place of business in Ontario, Canada.

The gravamen of this dispute concerns the public performance of plaintiffs' copyrighted programming from Toronto, Canada, to computer users in the United States since November 30, 1999, over the Internet. Specifically, defendants have streamed copyrighted professional football and basketball games as well as copyrighted programs such as "60 Minutes," "Ally McBeal," and "Star Trek Voyager," framed with advertisements obtained by defendants. Plaintiffs allege that defendants have captured United States programming from television stations in Buffalo, New York and elsewhere, converted these television signals into computerized data and streamed them over the Internet from a website called iCraveTV.com. According to plaintiffs, any Internet user may access iCraveTV.com by simply entering three digits of any Canadian area code, one of which is provided to the user on the site itself, and by clicking two other buttons. Further, Internet users from the United States and elsewhere easily may revisit the site because iCraveTV causes a small file, or cookie, to be deposited in a user's computer during his or her initial visit so that the user can automatically bypass defendants' screening process. Although defendants have ceased streaming of plaintiffs' copyrighted programming since entry of the temporary restraining order on January 28, 2000, there is no dispute that defendants streamed plaintiffs' programming continuously from November 29, 1999 through January 28, 2000, despite several requests from plaintiffs that defendants cease doing so.

---

† No. 00-120 (W.D. Pa. February 8, 2000)

. . . .

As a threshold question, the Court must first determine whether it has subject matter jurisdiction. Pursuant to 28 U.S.C. §1338, Congress has provided that the district courts shall have original jurisdiction of every civil action arising under any Act of Congress relating to copyrights and trademarks. Although the trademark laws of the United States have enjoyed extraterritorial application, the Court is mindful of the long-standing precept that the United States copyright laws do not have extraterritorial operation.

Defendants argue that their website is for Canadian viewers only and it is not intended for citizens of the United States and elsewhere. Thus, the argument continues, the alleged improper acts are limited to Canada.

Plaintiffs have presented testimony, sworn affidavits and declarations establishing that Pennsylvania residents have accessed defendants' website and viewed the programs which were streamed thereon. Further, defendants posted an article on the website by a United States citizen noting that access to defendants' website could be obtained by any United States citizen with little or no difficulty.

Accordingly, when an allegedly infringing act occurring without the United States is publicly performed within the United States, the Copyright Act is implicated and a district court possesses jurisdiction. Subject matter jurisdiction exists because, although the streaming of the plaintiffs' programming originated in Canada, acts of infringement were committed within the United States when United States citizens received and viewed defendants' streaming of the copyrighted materials. These constitute, at a minimum, public performances in the United States.

. . . .

The plaintiffs have established without rejoinder from the defendants that they have copyright and trademark ownership of several items, including, among others, the Super Bowl, the NBA Finals, and the NFL playoff games and regular League games, "The Simpsons", "Married With Children", "Frasier", "Babe", "Twentieth Century Fox", "Disney", and "The Drew Carey Show".

Defendants do not deny that they have copied these items, represented themselves as the authors and that they have publicly performed them over the Internet. Rather, defendants argue that there is no desire on the part of defendants for any United States residents to access iCraveTV. Notwithstanding defendants' intentions, the Court finds that plaintiffs have presented sufficient facts to establish their claims of copyright and trademark infringement and therefore likely success on the merits.

Indeed, on January 17, 2000, John Trickey of iCraveTV reported to Cox that roughly "45 percent of the traffic impressions on the iCraveTV website" had come from Internet users based in the United States. Trickey said that he knew this from iCraveTV's "log books." A January 25, 2000 breakdown of "impressions" and "clicks" onto the iCraveTV website, generated by a private ad serving system (DART) utilized by Cox, reported 1.6 million impressions (page views) from United States visitors on the iCraveTV website. This figure was second only to the figure for Canada, which was 2.0 million.

Defendants also use a "Real Video" server to stream video programming through their website. This server maintains "logs" of the Internet Protocol addresses of computers that contact defendants' server to obtain access to video programming. An analysis of the Real Video server logs shows that substantial numbers of persons in the United States received the streaming of programming, including programming in which plaintiffs own copyrights.

The evidence set forth above and other evidence in the record shows that plaintiffs are likely to succeed in showing that defendants are unlawfully publicly performing plaintiffs' copyrighted works in the United States. Defendants do so by transmitting (through use of "streaming" technology) performances of the works to the public by means of the telephone lines and computers that make up the Internet. This activity violates plaintiffs' rights to perform their works publicly and to authorize others to do so. These infringements occur in the United States and violate the U.S. Copyright Act. Defendants have also engaged in contributory infringement by making plaintiffs' copyrighted programming available on the Internet with the knowledge that third parties (such as streambox.com) could and would further infringe plaintiffs' copyrights by further transmitting (and publicly performing) the programming. Defendants' streaming of plaintiffs' programming through the Internet, even with supposed security controls, materially contributes to these further infringements.

Plaintiffs are also likely to succeed in showing that defendants have violated plaintiffs' rights under Section 43(a) of the Lanham Act, 15 U.S.C. §1125(a), by, among other things, (1) using the plaintiffs' trademarks without permission in a manner likely to cause confusion as to sponsorship or affiliation; (2) offering a search engine with special links about the Networks' and the Studios' programs, creating (in this context) the impression of some special sponsorship; (3) falsely claiming to be the copyright owner of plaintiffs' programming; and (4) conveying the erroneous impression that plaintiffs' programming lacks closed captioning and other information.

Defendants have submitted a declaration of a Canadian law professor, Michael Geist, which argues that defendants' activities are permissible under Canadian law. However, because plaintiffs seek relief under U.S. law for infringements of the U.S. Copyright Act, there is no need for this Court to address any issue of Canadian law.

On February 28, 2000, approximately one month after it put a temporary stop to its Webcasting activities under the judicial order from a federal court in Pittsburgh, iCraveTV announced that it had reached a settlement with the broadcasters and content creators on both sides of the border, agreeing to permanently stop its unauthorized Webcasting activities.

INTERNET TELEPHONY

Internet service providers (ISPs) are rapidly becoming much more than just providers of Internet access. In addition to providing Web content of their own, many ISPs are moving toward providing telephone service to subscribers. Since the backbone of the Internet runs along telephone lines, many believe that there is great potential to provide low cost, long distance telephone service using the Internet.

Early implementation of Internet-based telephony was relatively primitive. Access required the user to have both a personal computer and compatible software. The reception was often less than satisfactory, with background echoes, lost transmissions, poor audio quality. Technology is rapidly improving, however, as the need for a personal computer is eliminated and sound quality at least approximates that of a cell phone call.

The technological capability of providing phone service over the Internet raises significant new regulatory issues. In pre-Internet telephony times, telephone carriers were few in number and the CRTC's regulatory task was relatively straightforward. With the advent of Internet-based telephone carriers, the number of businesses capable of providing phone service has become virtually unlimited, leaving the CRTC with the prospect of reforming a regulatory framework that may not adequately address these new market participants.

The CRTC has indeed begun with a series of public orders and decisions on Internet telephony. Of particular concern to current and potential telephone service providers is the question of contribution charges. Since regulated telephone companies pay annual contribution charges (the equivalent of license fees), the CRTC must determine whether ISPs providing Internet telephony services must also make similar contributions.

CRTC Telecom Order 97-590[†]

On 29 May 1996, London Telecom Network Inc. (London Telecom) requested clarification of whether this proceeding would examine all services which access the Public Switched Telephone Network (PSTN) or would be confined to IX services only, leaving the consideration of other services accessing the PSTN to other proceedings.

. . . .

The principal issues in this proceeding were the appropriateness of the existing treatment of DALs and whether contribution should be payable with respect to the following uses or services: paging; wireless e.g., cellular, enhanced switched mobile radio and personal communications services (PCS); Alternate Providers of Long Distance Services' (APLDS') internal administrative use of line-side connections; data service provided through line-side connections (excluding Internet); Internet; and Centrex one-hop services.

The Commission notes that, with respect to its determinations set out below, there are differences in the contribution regime set out in Regulatory Framework for Québec-Téléphone and Télébec ltée, Telecom Decision CRTC 96-5, 7 August 1996 (Decision 96-5), and Regulatory Framework for the Independent Telephone Companies in Quebec and Ontario (Except Ontario Northland Transportation Commission, Québec-Téléphone and Télébec ltée, Telecom Decision CRTC 96-6, 7 August 1996 (Decision 96-6), for the independent telephone companies.

. . . .

With respect to Internet traffic, Stentor submitted that, because it is difficult to distinguish line-side local traffic from IX traffic, all voice and data services should be

---

subject to contribution charges, unless the Internet Service Provider (ISP) can demonstrate that the traffic is not interexchange.

Stentor was of the view that, if the Commission determines that line-side data attracts contribution, then ISPs should also be required to pay contribution charges.

AT&T Canada LDS stated that all Internet traffic originated over public dial-up access or through line-side connections should be contribution-eligible as it is likely IX traffic.

fONOROLA stated that ISPs should pay contribution based on the number of switched minutes.

The Commission notes that ISPs typically lease line-side connections to the PSTN such as local business lines, Centrex or ISP Link services in order to provide access from customers to the ISP and that traffic from the ISP outward to the Internet is carried on dedicated facilities to and from the data backbones of the Internet.

The Commission notes that parties provided limited evidence addressing the appropriateness of applying contribution charges to Internet services; for example, most parties did not address the argument that ISPs are customers of the IXCs as opposed to being resellers of leased facilities.

Further, the impact of Internet usage on the PSTN is rapidly evolving as a result of, among other things, the development of new technology, including separate networks, used to deliver a greater number of services over the Internet.

In the circumstances, the Commission is not persuaded that it is appropriate at this time to extend the application of the existing contribution scheme to Internet Services.

The Commission considers, however, that given the rapid evolution of Internet services, the above determination may have to be revisited in the future.

The Commission notes that, where the Internet network is used as the underlying transmission facility by a service provider to provide public switched IX voice or data services, the service provider is to register as a reseller and to pay contribution.

CRTC Telecom Order 97-1471[†]

By letter dated 3 April 1997, Call-Net Enterprises Inc. (Call-Net), acting on behalf of Sprint Canada Inc. (Sprint Canada), noted that the Commission's practice is to exempt from contribution payments interconnecting line-side access circuits used for providing Internet access service. Call-Net therefore requested an order exempting from contribution payments the interconnecting circuits listed in the affidavit submitted with its application. Call-Net filed the application and attached affidavit and schedule in confidence with the Commission, providing an abridged version to BC TEL, Bell Canada (Bell) and TELUS Communications Inc. (TCI).

Call-Net stated that Sprint Canada's Internet network is technically and operationally configured separately from its switched voice services. Call-Net stated that in accor-

---

dance with the test established in Competition in the Provision of Public Long Distance Voice Telephone Services and Related Resale and Sharing Issues, Telecom Decision CRTC 92-12, 12 June 1992, Sprint Canada's Internet service is not and will not be used significantly for joint-use interexchange voice service. Call-Net stated that moreover, the technical and operational distinctiveness of Sprint Canada's Internet service network is apparent to and can be easily verified by the local telephone companies providing the local access circuits.

By letter dated 30 April 1997, Stentor Resource Centre Inc. (Stentor) responded on behalf of BC TEL, Bell and TCI (collectively, the companies). Stentor noted that in accordance with Applications for Contribution Exemptions, Telecom Decision CRTC 93-2, 1 April 1993 (Decision 93-2), where a service provider provides both voice and data services, an exemption for data services should be supported by a technical audit confirming that the data circuits are separate from the voice network and cannot be used to carry voice traffic. Stentor therefore submitted that Sprint Canada has failed to satisfy the evidentiary requirements. However, Stentor agreed that, subject to the provision of satisfactory evidence, circuits used solely to carry data traffic would qualify for an exemption from contribution charges. Accordingly, Stentor submitted that Sprint Canada's application should be approved on an interim basis, with final approval subject to the provision of satisfactory evidence, in the form of a technical audit, within a reasonable period of time.

By letter dated 9 May 1997, Call-Net submitted that the affidavit filed in support of the application provides satisfactory evidence consistent with the Commission's requirements in Decision 93-2, and that the application should be given final approval on that basis.

Call-Net submitted that Internet services do not pay contribution as a general rule. Call-Net submitted that this policy was confirmed in the Commission's recent ruling with respect to the scope of IX contribution paying services in Telecom Order CRTC 97-590, 1 May 1997 (Order 97-590). Call-Net stated that in that Order, the Commission determined that: "it is [not] appropriate at this time to extend the application of the existing contribution scheme to Internet services". Accordingly, Call-Net submitted that there is no requirement that Internet Service Providers (ISPs) or communication service providers who also provide Internet services file an application for exemption with the Commission as a pre-condition to exemption.

By letter dated 11 June 1997, Call-Net withdrew its confidentiality request and included unabridged versions of its application and reply comments for the public record.

The Commission is of the view that there are three issues.

The first issue is whether ISPs (including telecommunications service providers who provide Internet access as but one of several services) are currently required to file contribution exemption applications if they wish not to pay contribution.

The Commission disagrees with Sprint Canada that Order 97-590 relieved ISPs of the requirement to file contribution exemption applications.

The second issue is whether the requirement for ISPs to file exemptions for contribution is appropriate on a going-forward basis. The Commission is of the preliminary view that, the current regime should, in the case of ISPs, be replaced by a lighter regime in which the Commission would only be involved to the extent that disputes arise between the parties. The Commission intends shortly to initiate an expedited proceeding by way of a public notice to seek comments on, among other things, this proposal. The Commission notes that ISPs would be required to file contribution exemption applications pending disposition of this proceeding.

The third issue is whether Sprint Canada's application should be approved, and if so, on what basis. With respect to Sprint Canada's submission that carrier verification, as distinct from a technical audit, is sufficient, the Commission notes that currently, an Internet network is considered a data network, and that, as required by Decision 93-2 regarding competitors that provide both switched voice and data (which is the case here), Sprint Canada should be required to file a technical audit in order to ensure that voice and data are carried on different networks. Moreover, the Commission notes that contrary to Sprint Canada's submission, the local telephone company cannot determine that the two networks are separate. Accordingly, the Commission is of the view that Sprint Canada's application should be approved on an interim basis effective the date of application, 3 April 1997, with final approval subject to the provision of a technical audit within 30 days of the Order.

CRTC Telecom Decision 98-17†

As noted earlier, section 2(1) of the Telecommunications Act, as amended by Bill C-17, establishes a new definition, that of "telecommunications service provider", and empowers the Commission to require that specified classes of basic telecommunications service providers obtain a license in order to provide international telecommunications services within a class specified by the Commission. By virtue of the definition of telecommunications service provider, the new licensing power extends to resellers.

In PN 97-34, the Commission requested comment on which classes of international services and service providers, if any, should be subject to licensing requirements. The Commission also stated the view that license conditions should not constitute a barrier to entry, but rather should ensure that the regulatory regime put in place with regard to international services is respected by service providers. In that context, it requested comment on the conditions to be incorporated into licenses. Other licensing issues on which the Commission requested comment include the following: (a) possible reporting requirements; (b) the appropriate term of the license; (c) the information that should be provided upon application for a license; and (d) procedures for issuing and renewal of licenses.

· · · ·

The Commission notes that some parties considered that, by virtue of the terms of Bill C-17, the Commission would have no alternative but to implement some form of licensing regime. The Commission considers that the recently enacted section 16.1 of the Telecommunications Act empowers but does not require it to specify and require licenses for certain classes of international telecommunications services and service providers. Therefore, it is open to the Commission to determine that licensing is unnecessary.

---

† Regulatory Regime for the Provision of International Telecommunications Services. © Canadian Radio-television and Telecommunications Commission. Reproduced with permission.

. . . .

The Commission notes that various proposals were advanced with regard to which class or classes of services and service providers should require licenses.

. . . .

Finally, Stentor considered that, consistent with its proposals in Proposed New Contribution Exemption Regime for Internet Service Providers, Telecom Public Notice CRTC 97-37, 3 November 1997, Internet service providers (ISPs) should be exempt from licensing requirements, as long as they are offering contribution-exempt Internet services only and no other service provider is offering PSTN voice or any other contribution-eligible telecommunications services from the same service location(s).

. . . .

The Commission has also determined that it would not be appropriate to subject certain ISPs to a licensing regime at this time, as described below. The Commission considers Internet telephony to be in the development stage. At present, Internet telephony does not afford a mechanism to manipulate international settlements on a significant scale. The Commission notes that this situation may change in the future.

In Telecom Order CRTC 98-929, 17 September 1998, the Commission is providing for automatic exemptions from contribution charges for certain ISPs, generally consistent with Stentor's submissions in the proceeding. In particular, subject to certain requirements, the Commission concluded that ISPs should be exempt from contribution, and not be required to register with the Commission, if the ISP offers only contribution-exempt ISP services and no other service provider offers PSTN voice or any other contribution-eligible telecommunications services from the same location. The Commission considers that such ISPs should similarly be excluded from any licensing requirement. However, the Commission puts ISPs on notice that this may change in the future as Internet telephony develops.

Discussion Question

Considering the convergence of telephone providers and Internet service providers, does distinguishing between traditional phone service and Internet-based telephony still seem viable?

The European Union has also addressed the issue of Internet telephony in the following directive. It provides a helpful starting point for assessing whether Internet telephony should be considered equal to traditional phone services and thus subject to the same regulatory framework.

Notice by the Commission concerning the status of voice on the Internet under Directive 90/388/EEC

Supplement to the Communication by the Commission to the European Parliament and the Council on the status and implementation of Directive 90/388/EEC on competition in the markets for telecommunications services

The Commission has approved a draft position on the status of voice on the Internet under Directive 90/388/EEC.

The Commission intends to adopt the draft position as a Supplement to the Communication by the Commission to the European Parliament and the Council on the status and implementation of Directive 90/388/EEC on competition in the markets for telecommunications services after having heard any comments from interested parties.

STATUS OF VOICE ON THE INTERNET UNDER DIRECTIVE 90/388/EEC

Regulatory position of voice on Internet

Directive 90/388/EEC on competition in the markets for telecommunications services defines in detail the service which the Member States may continue to reserve to their telecommunications organisations.

According to Article 1 of Directive 90/388/EEC "'voice telephony' means the commercial provision for the public of the direct transport and switching of speech in real-time between public switched network termination points, enabling any user to use equipment connected to such a network termination point in order to communicate with another termination point."

On 20 October 1995 the Commission published a Communication to the European Parliament and the Council on the status and implementation of Directive 90/388/EEC on competition in the markets for telecommunications services ("the Communication"). This set out the Commission's approach on the implementation of the definition in Article 1 of Directive 90/388/EEC. Since then due to the development of specific software it has become possible to code, compress and transmit voice communications in such a way that it has become viable and to send them via the Internet — at local call tariffs — to other Internet subscribers using the same or interoperable software. This is a new issue and the Commission should therefore adopt a Supplement to the Communication on this matter.

The Commission considers that under the definition of voice telephony in Directive 90/388/EEC, voice communication between Internet users could only be considered as voice telephony if each of the following criteria are met:

Such communications are the subject of a commercial offer
This requires that the simple technical non-commercial provision of a telephone connection between two users should be authorised. "Commercial" should be understood in the common sense of the word, i.e. that the transport of voice is provided as a commercial activity with the intention of making a profit. In the case of the Internet, the commercial provision of the transport of voice is, at least for the time being, not the aim of access providers. Such telephone calls are established by users

who procured themselves the required software without referring to the access provider to which they subscribe.

It is provided for the public

Although only users who subscribed to a server providing access to the Internet and who used compatible software would be able to use the Internet for calling other users, it could be argued that the service is provided "for the public" since the service would be available to all members of the public on the same basis.

To and from public switched network termination points on
the fixed telephony network

"[B]etween public switched network termination points" means that, to be reserved, the voice service not only has to be offered commercially and to the public, but also it has to connect *two* network termination points on the *switched* network at the same time. If access to the Internet is obtained via leased circuits, the service could never be considered as voice telephony, even if the call terminates on the public switched network. However, as a large number of internet users gain access to the Internet via the PSTN, such use would fall within this definition. One future development which would affect this would be the introduction of equipment which would allow Internet access via the cable television networks. Such cable modems are already on sale in the United States. This would allow widespread Internet voice telephony with data never travelling via the PSTN.

If the Internet user can only call other Internet subscribers whose computers are connected via a modem and who are using similar software, then this is also not "voice telephony" because it is not "enabling *any user* ... to communicate with *another* termination point".

It involves direct transport and switching of speech in real time

Given the technique used for the first voice communications between Internet users and the early state of development of Internet technology (mainly bandwidth and compression techniques) Internet telephony could not, originally be considered to take place in real-time. According to this basic technique, the voice is digitally encoded, packed and sent by a user from a termination point to a server and on to the reception server which in turn sends it to the receiver equipment, connected to a termination point, which assembles the packets to be delivered as voice via the loudspeaker. The time period required for processing and transmission from one termination point to the other was such that the voice service could not be and still cannot be considered as a real-time service. However, with the evolution of the available software and bandwidth, this assessment may well need to be reviewed.

In summary therefore, it would seem that the definition of voice telephony in Directive 90/388/EEC taken together with existing precedents can provide good guidance for assessing the regulatory position of voice on the Internet in the pre-liberalisation situation. Voice on the Internet cannot be considered as "voice telephony" in the sense of this Directive and therefore falls within the liberalised area may therefore not be reserved to the telecommunications organisations. The situation will, however, have to be kept under review in the light of technological and market developments. It may be, however, that if Internet service providers began marketing their service on the basis of the voice telephony capability, this conclusion would have to be reversed.

Consequences

a) licensing

The fact that a telecommunications service may not be reserved, does not prevent Member States from making its supply subject to licensing, general authorisation or declaration procedures aimed at compliance with the essential requirements.

Directive 90/388/EEC sets out a basic framework as regards the extent of such authorisation procedures.

According to the Directive:

- the provision of telecommunications services other than voice telephony, the establishment and provision of public telecommunications networks and other telecommunications networks involving the use of radio frequencies, may be subjected to only a general authorisation or a declaration procedure. *A priori* authorisation may therefore not be imposed on Internet access/service providers;

- the authorisation procedures may only contain conditions which are objective (i.e. linked to the essential requirement involved), non-discriminatory, proportionate and transparent. This implies that no specific authorisation scheme should be drafted for Internet access/service providers which is different from the one applicable to other data transmission providers;

- where a Member State wants to discontinue the supply of a non-reserved service, reasons must be given and there must be a procedure for appealing against such a decision;

- the relevant authorisation schemes must have been communicated to the Commission.

Internet service providers now typically operate under a data transmission or value-added service license. Where some customers use the service for voice telephony (often the Internet service provider will not even know about it), this remains essentially within the Internet service provider's license, in the same way as calling card services are considered to be outside the reserved area: the voice telephony ability is an additional feature of a service which is chosen by the customer for other reasons, such as browsing, downloading etc. In that sense, the voice telephony application is subsumed under the broader license which covers the Internet service provider's operation.

The consequence of that argument is that Internet service providers would even in the future, when voice telephony applications improve, not require voice telephony licenses, thereby avoiding the need to apply for individual licenses and the requirement to contribute to the funding of universal service.

b) contribution to Universal Service

A further issue is whether Internet access/service providers should contribute to the burden of Universal Service.

Community law provides a framework according to which contributions to universal service may be required from organisations providing publicly available telecommunications networks and publicly available voice telephony services. As Internet Voice is not considered to be "*voice telephony*" within the meaning of the directive, no contribution can be required from Internet Access providers.

The answer is given in Article 3 of Directive 90/388/EEC which only allows Member States to subject public network and voice telephony providers to licensing conditions encompassing possible "financial obligations with regard to universal service". This provision is mirrored by Article 5(1) of the draft ONP Interconnection Directive, allowing the imposition of contributions to universal service costs on organisations providing "publicly available voice telephony services".

In relation to Article 5(1) of the common position on the proposal for a Directive on interconnection in telecommunications, the Commission recalled in a declaration to the minutes of the Council of Ministers' meeting of 21 March 1996 that Article 4c of Commission Directive 96/19/EC of 13 March 1996 amending Directive 90/388/EEC regarding the implementation of full competition in telecommunications markets states that, where Member States set up mechanisms for sharing the net cost of universal service obligations, they should apply these mechanisms to undertakings providing public telecommunications networks.

The Commission concluded that it will interpret both Article 4c of the Commission Directive and 5(1) of this common position as allowing contributions only to be imposed on voice telephony providers in proportion to their usage of public telecommunications networks. Given that, as mentioned above, Internet access/service providers cannot, for the time being, be considered as voice telephony providers, they should not be subject to the payment of such contributions.

c) regulatory consequences of technical evolution

As shown in the above analysis, the regulatory position of voice on the Internet depends on an analysis of the actual service provided as regards the various elements of the definition of voice telephony in Article 1 of Directive 90/388/EEC.

The current position of voice on Internet under Community law may change in due course if, for example, the following conditions are met:

- Internet service providers start providing a service whereby an Internet user can connect to a local Internet service, log on with his PC or other terminal equipment, input the destination telephone number, have the call routed over the Internet to any telephone number (including to users without a modem) at the far end (with payment by credit card, pre-paid card or electronic cash for the local interconnection rates plus a margin); and
- a decisive drive for Internet subscription becomes the telephony feature as the quality of service improves and in particular is provided in real-time.

Those Internet service providers offering a dial out service to any telephone number — and only those — could then be considered as "voice telephony providers" under Community law. This description is by way of example and does not exclude other possible interpretations of future developments. Technical developments will have to be periodically reviewed by the Commission.

This could have significant consequences for the relevant undertakings. Indeed, according to Article 3 of Directive 90/388/EEC, Member States could then subject the operation in their territories of Internet service providers' voice telephony services to individual licensing procedures.

Indeed, if in the future Internet voice is considered voice telephony, then providers could be asked to contribute to universal service funding in accordance with the principles set out in Community law and with the guidelines on the costing and financing of universal service set out in the Commission's Communication of 27 November 1996 (COM(96) 608).

Moreover the conditions in such licensing schemes must be objective, non-discriminatory, proportionate and transparent, and the schemes must have been notified to the Commission.

As soon they reach a significant market share of the relevant geographical voice telephony market, the concerned Internet providers could — under the proposed amendment to the Article 100(a) Voice Telephony Directives now being discussed before the European Parliament and Council by Council and Parliament regarding interconnection and the scope of voice telephony — be subject to interconnection obligations as well as the obligation to provide a voice telephony service at [sic] under the conditions set out in Directive 95/62/EC, as amended.

Finally, if in the future Internet voice is considered voice telephony, this will also be of relevance in the Member States to which the Commission has granted additional implementation periods for the liberalisation of voice telephony.

INTERNET ACCESS

Given the importance of the Internet in virtually every aspect of modern communications and information dissemination, Internet access emerges as a critical policy issue. Studies suggest that a large segment of the Canadian population still does not have Internet access, and that a very small portion enjoys high speed Internet access. The CRTC has become involved in this issue as well. It has worked to create a competitive marketplace for Internet access services in the hope of delivering lower access prices and greater market penetration.

CRTC New Media Report[†]

TELECOMMUNICATIONS ISSUES

Competitors' access to carriers' facilities that are closest to the end user
Internet service providers consider that the most immediate need is for Commission involvement in resolving access issues remaining with respect to facilities that are closest to the customer ("last mile facilities"), including higher speed access. It was submitted by others that the Commission must ensure that such Internet service providers understand that tariffing such access is a transitional step, and that Internet service providers should invest in their own facilities. With respect to this position, it was stated that, under current legislation, this approach would effectively require Internet service providers to be Canadian-owned to supply high speed Internet services. Further, this would also amount to the government assuming what should appropriately be business investment decisions by forcing investment to be made in "transmission facilities" and away from "exempt transmission apparatus" such as routers, servers, and software.

---

† CRTC, Telecom Public Notice CRTC 99-14, "New Media" (17 May 1999). © Canadian Radio-television and Telecommunications Commission. Reproduced with permission.

The Commission agrees that it is important that potential providers of competitive retail level Internet services have access to the facilities of carriers that are dominant with respect to such facilities. For example, the Commission has addressed such issues in Telecom Decision CRTC 98-9, Regulation under the Telecommunications Act of Certain Telecommunications Services Offered by "Broadcast Carriers", 9 July 1998. In that Decision, the Commission decided it would approve ("tariff") the rates and terms on which incumbent cable and telephone companies provide higher speed access to their telecommunications facilities with respect to competitive providers of retail level Internet services. The Commission anticipates that it will issue, by 30 July 1999, its decision on the general regulatory approach to such higher speed access services when they are offered by cable carriers.

However, in light of the nature of the arguments made, the Commission wishes to clarify that it does not agree with parties suggesting that the Commission's objective is that all ISPs, providers of local exchange services or other service providers must own or operate transmission facilities and so become "facilities-based" carriers. The Commission has stated its objective of promoting facilities-based entry in respect of switched services in particular (such as local exchange and long distance services). However, this objective does not exclude resale. While the Commission considers that facilities-based competition is important to the realization of sustainable competition, it also recognizes that not all service providers will invest in the transmission facilities that qualify them as "telecommunications common carriers" under the Telecommunications Act.

CRTC Telecom Decision 99-11[†]

The independent members of the Canadian Association of Internet Providers (CAIP) have asked for relief under the *Telecommunications Act* (the Act) against various incumbent cable carriers that offer higher speed retail Internet services (IS or retail IS). CAIP's concern is that these carriers do not provide access for competing ISPs to their higher speed telecommunications facilities even though the carriers offer their own retail IS using these facilities. CAIP considers that this is anti-competitive and allows cable carriers to establish themselves in this emerging market before they provide access to competitors.

CAIP requested relief against: Canadian Cable Television Association (CCTA) members including Rogers Communications Inc., Shaw Communications Inc., Cogeco Inc., Vidéotron ltée and their affiliates, or other broadcast carriers presently providing retail IS. More specifically, CAIP requested that the Commission direct cable carriers (a type of broadcast carrier) to provide access now to competing ISPs and, until access is available, to stop promoting and marketing their own retail IS. As an alternative, CAIP requested that the Commission direct cable carriers to make retail IS available for resale until access is provided.

The Commission addressed issues relating to access in *Regulation under the Telecommunications Act of Certain Telecommunications Services Offered by "Broadcast*

---

† (September 1999). Application concerning access by Internet service providers to incumbent cable carriers' telecommunications facilities. © Canadian Radio-television and Telecommunications Commission. Reproduced with permission.

Carriers", Telecom Decision CRTC 98-9, 9 July 1998 (Decision 98-9). In that Decision, the Commission directed that access to the higher speed telecommunications facilities of incumbent cable carriers offering higher speed retail IS be provided pursuant to a tariff approved by the Commission. Cable carriers began to offer retail IS in 1996. At the time of the proceeding leading to Decision 98-9, cable carriers did not provide competing ISPs with access to their telecommunications facilities for technical reasons. In that proceeding they undertook to implement access as soon as possible.

In the current proceeding CCTA stated that it expects that cable companies will be in a position to implement commercial access service by mid-2000. Representatives of CAIP and the CCTA have established the CAIP/CCTA Technical Working Group (Working Group) to achieve this objective. The Commission notes efforts made by ISPs and cable carriers, especially since 1998, to implement access and expects all parties to make every effort to ensure that access is implemented according to the current schedule.

Overview of positions of parties
CAIP alleged in its application that CCTA members are deliberately delaying the implementation of access. It considered that this delay is causing irreparable harm to the independent members of CAIP, and that CCTA members in the retail IS market are benefiting from the delay. CAIP further argued that CCTA members are aggressively marketing their higher speed retail IS, which CAIP argued has become a separate market, while preventing ISPs from entering this market through delay. CAIP submitted that, as a result, cable carriers are conferring an undue preference on themselves or subjecting ISPs to an unreasonable disadvantage, contrary to section 27(2) of the Act.

CCTA denied CAIP's allegations and argued that access cannot currently be provided in a way that meets CAIP's requirements. CCTA stated that the Commission determined in Decision 98-9 that cable carriers could offer higher speed retail IS before access is available, and that such retail IS could be offered without a requirement for resale of that service. CCTA also disagreed with CAIP's claim that the IS market has evolved into two markets at the retail level since the Commission issued Decision 98-9.

MTS Communications Inc., NBTel Inc., Maritime Tel & Tel Limited and Island Telecom, as well as TELUS Communications and BC TEL commented on and generally supported CAIP's position.

Characterization of the retail IS market
In Decision 98-9, the Commission determined that the retail IS market, regardless of speed and the facilities over which the services are carried, constitutes a single market. In that Decision, the Commission stated that it considered that lower and higher speed retail level ISs share sufficient attributes to be considered as reasonable substitutes.

The Commission is of the opinion that the higher speed segment of that market has increased materially in importance since the proceeding which led to Decision 98-9. The Commission does not consider that the evidence submitted by CAIP demonstrates that the retail IS market has evolved into two markets and concludes that the retail IS market remains one market.

Request that cable carriers provide immediate access

In support of its position that access to cable carriers' facilities be provided immediately, CAIP referred to two situations where access was, or is being, provided. One of these service offerings is a trial being conducted by a cable company in the Timmins area. The other was a trial conducted in the United States by GTE, the results of which were announced recently.

Among other points, CCTA submitted that the Timmins and GTE trials do not respond to CAIP's own requirements that access provide the capability to handle large volumes of subscribers in a multi-ISP environment through standard industry-wide implementation.

CAIP stated that the access technology used in the Timmins trial is scalable, and meets many of its members' specifications. CAIP did not elaborate and also did not specifically address operational issues such as manual versus automated billing. The Commission also notes that, through the Working Group, CAIP and CCTA have recently taken steps to trial an approach to access which will be responsive to CAIP's requirements.

Based on the record of this proceeding, the Commission considers that the two approaches cited by CAIP would not provide comparable alternatives to the approach to access being developed by the Working Group. In all the circumstances, the Commission denies CAIP's request that cable carriers be required to provide access immediately.

Resale of retail IS

The Commission forbore from regulating the rates for cable carriers' retail IS in Decision 98-9, but determined that it would not be appropriate to forbear from section 24 of the Act. It therefore retained the power under section 24 to impose such conditions on the offering and provision of retail IS services as may be necessary in the future.

In Decision 98-9, the Commission did not mandate resale of retail IS because it considered that the supply of underlying access services had continued to increase and had contributed to creating a workably competitive market for retail IS. In this proceeding, the issue arises as to whether resale should now be mandated because of the continued lack of access to incumbent cable carriers' telecommunications facilities. Resale is being considered in this proceeding as a proxy for a service that provides such access through interconnection with incumbent cable carriers' facilities.

As noted above, the higher speed segment of the retail IS market has increased materially in importance since the release of Decision 98-9. Further, a period of over three years has passed since cable carriers first offered retail IS commercially without providing access. Cable carriers first offered retail IS in 1996; in 1998 they undertook to implement access as soon as possible, and access is now expected to be available commercially no earlier than mid-2000.

In this proceeding CCTA argued that the supply of access services has continued to increase since the release of Decision 98-9 with, in particular, the introduction of access to telephone company Asymmetrical Digital Subscriber Line (ADSL) services. In the Commission's view, considering all the circumstances, the supply of underlying access services has not increased to the extent that it continues to be in the public interest for incumbent cable carriers to offer higher speed retail IS without providing access through interconnection or resale as a proxy for access. The Commission concludes that, until cable carriers are in a position to provide access, it is in the public interest to advance the competitiveness of IS by providing for the resale of incumbent cable carriers' higher speed IS.

The Commission notes that resale of retail IS would allow competitor ISPs to bill and collect from their customers. It also anticipates that, as outlined by CAIP, ISPs would customize and brand the IS by providing their own customer software (browser and e-mail package) as well as the e-mail address and home page for the customer.

Therefore, pursuant to section 24 of the Act, the Commission imposes, as a condition of the provision of higher speed retail IS by incumbent cable carriers, the requirement that such a carrier make its higher speed retail IS available for resale to provide IS at a 25% discount from the lowest retail IS rate charged by that carrier to a cable customer in the applicable serving area during any one month period. Service charges typically charged by the cable carrier to its customer will be paid by the ISP and are not subject to the discount. Cable carriers must not establish higher service charges for ISPs than for their own IS customers. This condition will apply 90 days from the date of this Decision and will continue to apply until access is provided pursuant to an approved tariff. The specific rates charged by the cable carriers do not require Commission approval.

If an incumbent cable carrier wishes to charge an ISP at a different discount rate, it may file a proposed alternative discount for approval with the Commission, supported by appropriate costing information. In such cases, the Commission emphasizes that the carrier must make its higher speed retail IS available for resale at the discount set out in this Decision, until it has received approval to modify it.

Discussion Questions

Should the CRTC be in the business of setting high speed access rates for the marketplace? Do you think that a market-based solution would prove more effective?

The issue of access to high speed cable lines is also being hotly contested in the United States. The U.S. debate has taken a decidedly local flavour, as cable access rights are typically allocated by city or county. Several cities have voted to force cable providers to provide open access for competitive purposes, an approach the cable companies reject and one which is currently being fought in the courts.

Most recently, the 9th Circuit Court of Appeals rejected Portland, Oregon's attempt to force open access in *AT&T Corporation* v. *City of Portland*.

AT&T Corporation v. City of Portland[†]

This appeal presents the question of whether a local cable franchising authority may condition a transfer of a cable franchise upon the cable operator's grant of

---

† 2000 U.S. App. LEXIS 14383 (9th Cir. 2000).

unrestricted access to its cable broadband transmission facilities for Internet service providers other than the operator's proprietary service. We conclude that the Communications Act prohibits a franchising authority from doing so and reverse the judgment of the district court.

I

Distilled to its essence, this is a struggle for control over access to cable broadband technology. In broadband data transmission, a single medium carries multiple communications at high transmission speeds. The allure of broadband technology is that it allows users to access the Internet at speeds fifty to several hundred times faster than those available through conventional computer modems connected to what is commonly referenced in the telecommunications industry as "plain old telephone service." Broadband allows transmission, or "streaming," of live video and audio communications, as well as video and audio data files. To satisfy consumer demand for broadband Internet access, cable television operators have replaced coaxial wires with fiber-optic cable, telephone companies have initiated high-frequency digital subscriber line ("DSL") services over standard twisted-pair copper wires, fixed wireless providers have upgraded their microwave transmission capacities, satellite providers have launched global two-way digital networks, and researchers have explored the use of quantum communication methods.

The race to acquire broadband transmission systems has, in part, prompted a number of corporate mergers. This appeal concerns the merger between AT&T, at the time the nation's largest long distance telephone provider, and Telecommunications, Inc. ("TCI"), one of the nation's largest cable television operators. In addition to providing traditional cable television programming, TCI provided cable broadband Internet access to consumers in certain geographic areas. Since acquiring TCI, AT&T has continued to offer cable broadband access as part of its "@Home" service, which bundles its cable conduit with Excite, an Internet service provider ("ISP") under an exclusive contract. Like many other ISPs, @Home supplements its Internet access with user e-mail accounts and a Web portal site, a default home page gateway offering Internet search capabilities and proprietary content devoted to chat groups, interactive gaming, shopping, finance, news, and other topics. @Home subscribers also may "click-through" to other free Web portal sites, and may access other Internet service providers if they are willing to pay for an additional ISP; however, subscribers cannot purchase cable broadband access separately from an unaffiliated ISP, and have no choice over terms of Internet service such as content and bandwidth restrictions.

The @Home cable broadband infrastructure differs from that of most ISPs. A typical ISP connects with the Internet via leased telecommuncations [sic] lines, which its consumers access through "dial-up" connections over ordinary telephone lines. @Home operates a proprietary national "backbone," a high-speed network parallel to the networks carrying most Internet traffic, which connects to those other Internet conduits at multiple network access points. This backbone serves regional data hubs which manage the network and deliver Excite's online content and services, including multimedia content that exploits broadband transmission speeds. Each hub connects to local "headend" facilities, cable system transmission plants that receive and deliver programming, where "proxy" servers cache frequently requested Internet data, such as Web sites, for local delivery. Each headend connects to cable nodes in neighborhoods, each of which in turn connects via coaxial cable to the user's cable modem and computer.

To effect the merger, AT&T and TCI sought three types of regulatory approval. The Department of Justice approved the merger on antitrust grounds, subject to TCI's divestiture of its interest in Sprint PCS wireless services. The Federal Communications Commission ("FCC") approved the transfer of federal licenses from TCI to AT&T, after addressing public interest concerns in four service areas, including residential Internet access.

One of the issues that the FCC considered forms the undercurrent of the present controversy: whether to impose a requirement of open access to cable broadband facilities. A variety of interest groups and competitors argued that allowing AT&T to restrict cable broadband access to the proprietary @Home service would harm competition and reduce consumer choice. In its order approving the license transfer, the FCC rejected any open access condition, citing the emergence of competing methods of high-speed Internet access, and @Home customers' "ability to access the Internet content or portal of his or her choice." It found "that the equal access issues raised by parties to this proceeding do not provide a basis for conditioning, denying, or designating for hearing any of the requested transfers of licenses and authorizations." The FCC concluded that "while the merger is unlikely to yield anti-competitive effects, we believe it may yield public interest benefits to consumers in the form of a quicker roll-out of high-speed Internet access services."

The last regulatory hurdle that AT&T and TCI faced was the approval of local franchising authorities where required by local franchising agreements. TCI's franchises with Portland and Multnomah County (collectively, "Portland") permitted the city to "condition any Transfer upon such conditions, related to the technical, legal, and financial qualifications of the prospective party to perform according to the terms of the Franchise, as it deems appropriate." This language parallels the text of *47 U.S.C. §541*(a)(4)(C), which describes the conditions a locality may impose on a franchise.

Portland referred the transfer application for recommendation by the Mount Hood Cable Regulatory Commission, an intergovernmental agency overseeing cable affairs in the Portland region. In response to Portland's preliminary questions, AT&T confirmed that TCI was in the process of upgrading its cable system to support @Home over cable broadband, and maintained that @Home was a proprietary product "not subject to common carrier obligations." At public hearings, the incumbent local telephone exchange carrier US WEST and the Oregon Internet Service Providers Association called for open access to TCI's cable broadband network, citing — in addition to consumer welfare — the need for "a level playing field" with US WEST's common carrier obligations and a "very real potential that consumer [Internet] access businesses could go out of business." The Mount Hood Commission recommended that the city and county approve the transfer of franchise control subject to an open access requirement.

On December 17, 1998, Portland and Multnomah County voted to approve the transfer, subject to an open access condition expressed in a written acceptance:

Non-discriminatory access to cable modem platform. Transferee shall provide, and cause the Franchisees to provide, non-discriminatory access to the Franchisees' cable modem platform for providers of Internet and on-line services, whether or not such providers are affiliated with the Transferee or the Franchisees, unless otherwise required by applicable law. So long as cable modem services are deemed to be "cable services," as provided under Title VI of the Communications Act of 1934, as amended, Transferee and the Franchisees shall comply with all requirements regarding such services, including but not limited to, the inclusion of revenues from cable modem services and access within the gross revenues of the Franchisees' cable franchises, and commercial leased access requirements.

AT&T refused the condition, which resulted in a denial of the request to transfer the franchises. AT&T then brought this action, seeking declarations that the open access condition violated the Communications Act of 1934, as amended by the Telecommunications Act of 1996, Pub. L. No. 104-104, 110 Stat. 56 (1996), codified at *47 U.S.C. §151, et seq.* (collectively, the "Communications Act"), the franchise agreements, and the Constitution's Commerce Clause, Contract Clause, and First Amendment. The district court rejected all of AT&T's claims and granted summary judgment to Portland. We review de novo a grant of summary judgment; there being no disputed factual issues, we face only a question of statutory interpretation.

II

The parties, and numerous amici, forcefully urge us to consider what our national policy should be concerning open access to the Internet. However, that is not our task, and in our quicksilver technological environment it doubtless would be an idle exercise. The history of the Internet is a chronicle of innovation by improvisation, from its genesis as a national defense research network, to a medium of academic exchange, to a hacker cyber-subculture, to the commercial engine for the so-called "New Economy." Like Heraclitus at the river, we address the Internet aware that courts are ill-suited to fix its flow; instead, we draw our bearings from the legal landscape, and chart a course by the law's words. To that end, "we look first to the plain language of the statute, construing the provisions of the entire law, including its object and policy." We note at the outset that the FCC has declined, both in its regulatory capacity and as amicus curiae, to address the issue before us. Thus, we are not presented with a case involving potential deference to an administrative agency's statutory construction pursuant to the *Chevron* doctrine.

A

Because Portland premised its open access condition on its position that @Home is a "cable service" governed by the franchise, we begin with the question of whether the @Home service truly is a "cable service" as Congress defined it in the Communications Act. We conclude that it is not.

Subject to limited exceptions, the Communications Act provides that "a cable operator may not provide cable service without a franchise." The Act defines "cable service" as "(A) the one-way transmission to subscribers of (i) video programming, or (ii) other programming service, and (B) subscriber interaction, if any, which is required for the selection or use of such video programming or other programming service." For the purposes of this definition, "video programming" means "programming provided by, or generally considered comparable to programming provided by, a television broadcast station," and "other programming service" means "information that a cable operator makes available to all subscribers generally." The essence of cable service, therefore, is one-way transmission of programming to subscribers generally.

This definition does not fit @Home. Internet access is not one-way and general, but interactive and individual beyond the "subscriber interaction" contemplated by the statute. Accessing Web pages, navigating the Web's hypertext links, corresponding via e-mail, and participating in live chat groups involve two-way communication and information exchange unmatched by the act of electing to receive a one-way transmission of cable or pay-per-view television programming. And unlike transmission of a cable television signal, communication with a Web site involves a series of connections involving two-way information exchange and storage, even when a user views seemingly static content. Thus, the communication concepts are distinct in both a practical and a technical sense. Surfing cable channels is one thing; surfing the Internet over a cable broadband connection is quite another.

Further, applying the carefully tailored scheme of cable television regulation to cable broadband Internet access would lead to absurd results, inconsistent with the statutory structure. For example, cable operators like AT&T may be required by a franchising authority to set aside cable channels for public, educational or governmental use, must designate some of their channels for commercial use by persons unaffiliated with the operator, and must carry the signals of local commercial and non-commercial educational television stations. We cannot rationally apply these cable television regulations to a non-broadcast interactive medium such as the Internet. As our sister circuit concluded in the context of the abortive "video dialtone" common carrier television technology, regulating @Home as a cable service "simply makes no sense in any respect, and would be infeasible in many respects."

Thus, because the Internet services AT&T provides through @Home cable modem access are not "cable services" under the Communications Act, Portland may not directly regulate them through its franchising authority.

B

Although we conclude that a cable operator may provide cable broadband Internet access without a cable service franchise, we must also determine whether Portland may condition AT&T's provision of standard cable service upon its opening access to the cable broadband network for competing ISPs. To do so, we must determine how the Communications Act defines @Home.

Under the statute, Internet access for most users consists of two separate services. A conventional dial-up ISP provides its subscribers access to the Internet at a "point of presence" assigned a unique Internet address, to which the subscribers connect through telephone lines. The telephone service linking the user and the ISP is classic "telecommunications," which the Communications Act defines as "the transmission, between or among points specified by the user, of information of the user's choosing, without change in the form or content of the information as sent and received." A provider of telecommunications services is a "telecommunications carrier," which the Act treats as a common carrier to the extent that it provides telecommunications to the public, "regardless of the facilities used."

By contrast, the FCC considers ISP itself as providing "information services" under the Act, defined as "the offering of a capability for generating, acquiring, storing, transforming, processing, retrieving, utilizing, or making available information via telecommunications." As the definition suggests, ISPs are themselves users of telecommunications when they lease lines to transport data on their own networks and beyond on the Internet backbone. However, in relation to their subscribers, who are the "public" in terms of the statutory definition of telecommunications service, they provide "information services," and therefore are not subject to regulation as telecommunications carriers. Indeed, "information services" — the codified term for what the FCC first called "enhanced services" — have never been subject to regulation under the Communications Act.

Like other ISPs, @Home consists of two elements: a "pipeline" (cable broadband instead of telephone lines), and the Internet service transmitted through that pipeline. However, unlike other ISPs, @Home controls all of the transmission facilities between its subscribers and the Internet. To the extent @Home is a conventional ISP, its activities are one of an information service. However, to the extent that @Home provides its subscribers Internet transmission over its cable broadband facility, it is providing a telecommunications service as defined in the Communications Act.

Under this taxonomy, the Communications Act bars Portland from conditioning the franchise transfer upon AT&T's provision of the @Home transmission element that constitutes telecommunications:

> (3)(A) If a cable operator or affiliate thereof is engaged in the provision of telecommunications services —
>
>> (i) such cable operator or affiliate shall not be required to obtain a franchise under this title for the provision of telecommunications services; and
>> (ii) the provisions of this title shall not apply to such cable operator or affiliate for the provision of telecommunications services.
>
> (B) A franchising authority may not impose any requirement under this title that has the purpose or effect of prohibiting, limiting, restricting, or conditioning the provision of a telecommunications service by a cable operator or an affiliate thereof.
>
> (C) A franchising authority may not order a cable operator or affiliate thereof —
>
>> (i) to discontinue the provision of a telecommunications service, or
>> (ii) to discontinue the operation of a cable system, to the extent such cable system is used for the provision of a telecommunications service, by reason of the failure of such cable operator or affiliate thereof to obtain a franchise or franchise renewal under this title with respect to the provision of such telecommunications service.
>
> (D) Except as otherwise permitted by sections 611 and 612, a franchising authority may not require a cable operator to provide any telecommunications service or facilities, other than institutional networks, as a condition of the initial grant of a franchise, a franchise renewal, or a transfer of a franchise.

Pub. L. No. 104-104, §303(a), 110 Stat. 56, 124–25 (1996), codified at *47 U.S.C. §541*(b)(3); *see also* §101(a), 110 Stat. at 70, codified at *47 U.S.C. §253*(a) ("No State or local statute or regulation, or other State or local legal requirement, may prohibit or have the effect of prohibiting the ability of any entity to provide any interstate or intrastate telecommunications service."). Subsection 541(b)(3) expresses both an awareness that cable operators could provide telecommunications services, and an intention that those telecommunications services be regulated as such, rather than as cable services.

The Communications Act includes cable broadband transmission as one of the "telecommunications services" a cable operator may provide over its cable system. Thus, AT&T need not obtain a franchise to offer cable broadband; Portland may not impose any requirement that has "the purpose or effect of prohibiting, limiting, restricting or conditioning" AT&T's provision of cable broadband; Portland may not order AT&T to discontinue cable broadband; and Portland may not require AT&T to provide cable broadband as a condition of the franchise transfer. Therefore, under the several provisions of §541(b)(3), Portland may not regulate AT&T's provision of @Home in its capacity as a franchising authority, and the open access condition contained in the franchise transfer agreement is void.

C

Beyond the domain of cable-specific regulation, the definition of cable broadband as a telecommunications service coheres with the overall structure of the Communications Act as amended by the Telecommunications Act of 1996, and the FCC's existing regulatory regime. Elsewhere, the Communications Act contemplates the provision of telecommunications services by cable operators over cable systems. In the Telecommunications Act, Congress defined advanced telecommunications capability "without regard to any transmission media or technology," in terms that describe cable broadband: "high-speed, switched, broadband telecommunications capability that enables users to originate and receive high-quality voice, data, graphics, and video telecommunications using any technology." Consistent with our view, the FCC regulates DSL service, a high-speed competitor to cable broadband, as an advanced telecommunications service subject to common carrier obligations.

Among its broad reforms, the Telecommunications Act of 1996 enacted a competitive principle embodied by the dual duties of nondiscrimination and interconnection. Together, these provisions mandate a network architecture that prioritizes consumer choice, demonstrated by vigorous competition among telecommunications carriers. As applied to the Internet, Portland calls it "open access," while AT&T dysphemizes it as "forced access." Under the Communications Act, this principle of telecommunications common carriage governs cable broadband as it does other means of Internet transmission such as telephone service and DSL, "regardless of the facilities used." The Internet's protocols themselves manifest a related principle called "end-to-end": control lies at the ends of the network where the users are, leaving a simple network that is neutral with respect to the data it transmits, like any common carrier. On this rule of the Internet, the codes of the legislator and the programmer agree.

Thus far, the FCC has not subjected cable broadband to any regulation, including common carrier telecommunications regulation. We note that the FCC has broad authority to forbear from enforcing the telecommunications provisions if it determines that such action is unnecessary to prevent discrimination and protect consumers, and is consistent with the public interest. Congress has reposed the details of telecommunications policy in the FCC, and we will not impinge on its authority over these matters.

III

We hold that subsection 541(b)(3) prohibits a franchising authority from regulating cable broadband Internet access, because the transmission of Internet service to subscribers over cable broadband facilities is a telecommunications service under the Communications Act. Therefore, Portland may not condition the transfer of the cable franchise on non-discriminatory access to AT&T's cable broadband network. We need not reach AT&T's other statutory and constitutional arguments.

26

Legal Services and the Internet

The introduction of new technologies into law practice presents both an unparalleled opportunity and a difficult challenge for the profession. The Internet's potential for both a worldwide client base and greater law practice efficiencies must be balanced against the plethora of legal considerations and issues raised by online legal practice.

As with most Internet-related issues, the question of jurisdiction remains in the forefront. The legal profession has always been controlled and regulated on a jurisdictional basis, while online legal practice does not conform to those traditional borders. Reconciling global legal practices with local regulatory environments is a complex issue that law societies and bar associations are only beginning to address.

Solicitor-client privilege, the hallmark of a legal profession, depends upon client trust. The use of new technologies such as email and the Web creates a series of security-related issues and threatens to jeopardize the client-solicitor privilege, so fundamental to the legal profession. The promotional side of the Web also raises concerns, as the legal profession grapples with the parameters of acceptable online advertising and promotional conduct.

Canadian law societies have generally been slower than their U.S. counterparts in addressing these issues. The Law Society of Alberta is a notable exception. It has seized the opportunity, and recently released guidelines on ethics and the use of the Internet in the legal practice.

Guidelines on Ethics and the New Technology†

Technology and The Duty of Competence

The Code of Professional Conduct of the Law Society of Alberta deals with Competence in Chapter 2. Chapter 2 Rule 1 provides:

> A lawyer must maintain a state of competence on a continuing basis in all areas in which the lawyer practises.

Commentary G.1 (page 12) of Chapter 2 contains a list of characteristics encompassed by the term "competence". List item (h) reads:

> maintenance and improvement of knowledge and skills

With the ever-increasing impact of technology on the practice of law, a lawyer using technology must either have reasonable understanding of the technology used in the lawyer's practice, or access to someone who has such understanding. As well, certain endeavours in the practice of law may require a lawyer to be technologically proficient. For example, it might be impossible to competently handle a complex child/spousal support case without recourse to support calculation software; similarly, it might be impossible to competently handle a complex litigation matter involving a large number of documents without litigation support software.

. . . .

PART II — LAW ON THE INTERNET

1. Upholding the law of other jurisdictions

Chapter 1 of the Code of Professional Conduct deals with The Relationship of the Lawyer to Society and the Justice System. Rule 1 reads:

> A lawyer must respect and uphold the law in personal conduct and in rendering advice and assistance to others.

The Commentary on this Rule states, on page 3:

> "The law" for the purposes of Rule #1 is to be broadly interpreted and includes common law, such as tort law, in addition to criminal and quasi-criminal statutes.

An Alberta lawyer who practises law in another jurisdiction by providing legal services through the Internet must respect and uphold the law of the other jurisdiction, and must not engage in unauthorized practice in that jurisdiction.

2. Privileged communications

Chapter 4 of the Code, Relationship of the Lawyer to other Lawyers, Rule 8 reads:

> A lawyer who comes into possession of a privileged written communication of an opposing party through the lawyer's own impropriety, or with knowledge that the communication is not intended to be read by the lawyer, must not use the communication nor the information contained therein in

---

† Law Society of Alberta, February 1998. Reproduced with permission.

any respect and must immediately return the communication to opposing counsel, or if received electronically, purge the communication from the system.

Chapter 4, Rule 8 includes communications received through e-mail.

3. Conflict of Interest

Chapter 6 of the Code deals with Conflict of Interest. To ensure that there is no breach of the obligations to avoid conflict of interest when delivering legal services using the Internet or e-mail, a lawyer must determine the actual identity of parties with whom the lawyer is dealing.

4. Capacity in which Lawyer is Acting

Chapter 15 of the Code, The Lawyer in Activities Other than the Practice of Law, Rule 1 states:

> Where there may be confusion as to the capacity in which a lawyer is acting, the lawyer must ensure that such capacity is made as clear as possible to anyone with whom the lawyer deals.

A lawyer who communicates with others in chat rooms, discussion groups or otherwise through electronic media such as the Internet must advise others participating in the communication when the lawyer does not intend to provide legal services.

PART III — CONFIDENTIALITY AND THE INTERNET

Chapter 7 of the Code, Confidentiality, contains a statement of principle as follows:

> A lawyer has a duty to keep confidential all information concerning a client's business, interests and affairs acquired in the course of a professional relationship.

The relevant Rules in this section of the Code are as follows:

> **1.** A lawyer must not disclose any confidential information regardless of its source and whether or not it is a matter of public record.
>
> **2.** A lawyer must not disclose the identity of a client nor the fact of the lawyer's representation.
>
> **4.** A lawyer must take reasonable steps to ensure the maintenance of confidentiality by all persons engaged or employed by the lawyer.

The Commentary section of Chapter 7 does not specifically deal with the use by a lawyer of e-mail, whether via the Internet, internal e-mail or otherwise, or the use of cellular telephones or fax machines to transmit confidential client information. However, a lawyer using electronic means of communication must ensure that communications with or about a client reflect the same care and concern for matters of privilege and confidentiality normally expected of a lawyer using any other form of communication.

First, both the lawyer and the client can choose to use an electronic means of communication, including the Internet, cellular telephones and fax machines, as a means of communication in the solicitor-client relationship. The use on the part of the client or the lawyer may be said to be an implied invitation to use or respond via the same electronic means.

Second, while initially there seems to have been much debate on this topic, the better view today is that there is no basis to conclude that Internet communications are any less private than those using traditional land-line telephones. There does not seem to be a ready and apparent danger that e-mail is less confidential than fax machines or cellular telephones, so anyone using the Internet to communicate has a reasonable and justified expectation of privacy, and it cannot be said as a simple rule that a lawyer must encrypt anything that the lawyer believes the client would not want to read in the local newspaper.

Third, lawyers communicating on the Internet without encrypting their transmissions do not violate the principle of confidentiality. While encryption makes theft or interception more difficult, even strong encryption can be technically defeated. The vulnerability to theft and interception therefore remains. However, in ordinary circumstances, a lawyer is not expected to anticipate the criminal activity of theft of solicitor-client communications on the Internet any more than mail theft.

The use of e-mail and other electronic media presents opportunities for inadvertent discovery or disclosure of messages, given the manner in which information:

(a) is transmitted within the network systems of an Internet;
(b) is kept as a permanent record if conscious efforts are not made to delete those messages and thereby destroy the prospect of discovery or inadvertent disclosure.

A lawyer using such technologies must develop and maintain a reasonable awareness of the risks of interception or inadvertent disclosure of confidential messages and how they can be minimized.

Encryption software is available and must be used, if electronic means of communication are used, for those confidences that may be so valuable or sensitive that it is in the client's interest to take the extraordinary step of encrypting to protect them. The challenge, as in so many ethical areas, is to recognize those extraordinary situations and exercise sound judgment in relation to them.

When using electronic means to communicate in confidence with clients or to transmit confidential messages regarding a client, a lawyer must:

(a) develop and maintain an awareness of how technically best to minimize the risks of such communications being disclosed, discovered or intercepted;
(b) use reasonably appropriate technical means to minimize such risks;
(c) when the information is of extraordinary sensitivity, advise clients to use encryption software to communicate with their lawyer, and use such software;
(d) develop and maintain such law office management practices as offer reasonable protection against inadvertent discovery or disclosure of electronically transmitted confidential messages.

Notes

As of July 2000, the Federation of Law Societies, an umbrella organization for all Canadian provincial law societies, was engaged in a policy discussion on the merits of adopting national guidelines similar to those found in Alberta. For more on the Federation's initiative, consult its Web site at <http://www.flsc.ca>.

ONLINE LEGAL PRACTICE

The quintessential illustration of the impact of the Internet on the legal profession is the power to provide legal services directly online. The State of Texas Unauthorized Practice of Law Committee confronted this issue within the context of a novel question — can a computer software program constitute legal practice?

Unauthorized Practice Of Law Committee v. Parsons Technology, Inc. D/B/A Quicken Family Lawyer[†]

The Plaintiff, the Unauthorized Practice of Law Committee ("the UPLC"), is comprised of six Texas lawyers and three lay citizens appointed by the Supreme Court of Texas. The UPLC is responsible for enforcing Texas' unauthorized practice of law statute, TEX. GOV'T CODE §§. 81.101–.106 (Vernon's 1998) ("the Statute").

The Defendant, Parsons Technology, Inc., ("Parsons") is a California corporation, whose principal place of business is Iowa, and is engaged in the business of developing, publishing and marketing software products, such as Quicken Financial Software, Turbo Tax, and Webster's Talking Dictionary. Parsons has published and offered for sale through retailers in Texas a computer software program entitled Quicken Family Lawyer, version 8.0, and its updated version Quicken Family Lawyer '99 ("QFL").

QFL is the product at the center of this controversy. In its more recent version, QFL offers over 100 different legal forms (such as employment agreements, real estate leases, premarital agreements, and seven different will forms) along with instructions on how to fill out these forms. QFL's packaging represents that the product is "valid in 49 states including the District of Columbia;" is "developed and reviewed by expert attorneys;" and is "updated to reflect recent legislative formats." The packaging also indicates that QFL will have the user "answer a few questions to determine which estate planning and health care documents best meet [the user's] needs;" and that QFL will "interview you in a logical order, tailoring documents to your situation." Finally, the packaging reassures the user that "[h]andy hints and comprehensive legal help topics are always available."

.   .   .   .

The first time a user accesses QFL after installing it on her computer the following disclaimer appears as the initial screen:

> This program provides forms and information about the law. We cannot and do not provide specific information for your exact situation.
>
> For example, we can provide a form for a lease, along with information on state law and issues frequently addressed in leases. But we cannot decide that our program's lease is appropriate for you.
>
> Because we cannot decide which forms are best for your individual situation, you must use your own judgment and, to the extent you believe appropriate, the assistance of a lawyer.

[†] 1999 U.S. Dist. LEXIS 813 (N.D. Texas).

This disclaimer does not appear anywhere on QFL's packaging. Additionally, it does not appear on subsequent uses of the program unless the user actively accesses the "Help" pull-down menu at the top of the screen and then selects "Disclaimer."

On the initial use of QFL, or anytime a new user name is created, QFL asks for the user's name and state of residence. It then inquires whether the user would like QFL to suggest documents to the user. If the user answers "Yes," QFL's "Document Advisor" asks the user a few short questions concerning the user's marital status, number of children, and familiarity with living trusts. QFL then displays the entire list of available documents, but marks a few of them as especially appropriate for the user based on her responses.

. . . .

When the user accesses a document, QFL asks a series of questions relevant to filling in the legal form. With certain questions, a separate text box explaining the relevant legal considerations the user may want to take into account in filling out the form also appears on the screen. As the user proceeds through the questions relevant to the specific form, QFL either fills in the appropriate blanks or adds or deletes entire clauses from the form. For example, in the "Real Estate Lease — Residential" form, depending on how the user answers the question regarding subleasing the apartment, a clause permitting subleasing with the consent of the landlord is either included or excluded from the form.

If a user selects a "health care document" (i.e., a living will, an advance health care directive, or a health care power of attorney) the following screen appears:

> Health Care laws vary from state to state. Your state may not offer every type of health care document.
>
> Family Lawyer assumes that you wish to have a health care document based on the laws of your state.
>
> When you select a living will, health care power of attorney, or advance health care directive, Family Lawyer will open the appropriate document based on your state.

When a Texas user selects a health care document a form entitled "Directive to Physicians and Durable Power of Attorney for Health Care" appears.

In addition to the separate text boxes providing question and form specific information, at any time throughout the program, the user may access various other help features which provide additional legal information. One such feature is "Ask Arthur Miller," where the user selects a general topic and then a specific question, after which either a text-based answer is provided or, if the user's computer has a CD-ROM player, a sound card and a video card, a sound and video image of Arthur Miller answering the question appears.

. . . .

The UPLC filed this action in state court alleging that the selling of QFL violates Texas' unauthorized practice of law statute, TEX. GOV'T CODE Sec. 81.1015 and seeking, among other things, to enjoin the sale of QFL in Texas. Parsons subsequently removed this case to this Court. Both parties now seek summary judgment. The UPLC argues that Parsons has violated the Statute as a matter of law. Parsons responds that the mere selling of books or software cannot violate the statute because some form of personal contact beyond publisher — consumer is required by a plain reading of the Statute. Alternatively, if the statute is not construed to require some form of personal relationship, Parsons argues that the application of the Statute to the mere sale and distribution of QFL would infringe upon Parsons' speech rights under the United States and Texas Constitutions. Parsons also argues that the Statute if utilized to prevent the sale and distribution of QFL, should be void for vagueness.

. . . .

In this case, there are no genuine issues or material fact or disputed acts. Parsons' act of publishing QFL is undisputed. The contents of QFL are undisputed. All that remains to be determined is the legal consequences, if any, of these undisputed acts, and according to Cortez, the power to make this determination ultimately resides with the Court. Therefore, under both Texas law and the traditional federal summary judgment standards, this case is ripe for decision on summary judgment.

B. The Violation of the Texas Unauthorized Practice of Law Statute.

The UPLC moves for summary judgment because it claims, as a matter of law, the sale and distribution of QFL violates the Statute. The UPLC argues that QFL gives advice concerning legal documents and selects legal documents for users, both of which involve the use of legal skill and knowledge, and this constitutes the practice of law. Additionally, the UPLC argues that the Defendant's forms arc misleading and incorrect. In sum, the UPLC alleges that QFL acts as a "high tech lawyer by interacting with its 'client' while preparing legal instruments, giving legal advice, and suggesting legal instruments that should be employed by the user." In other words, QFL is a "cyber-lawyer."

. . . .

No one disputes that the practice of law encompasses more than the mere conduct of cases in the courts. See In re Duncan, 65 S.E. 210 (S.C. 1909) (finding that the practice of law includes "the preparation of legal instruments of all kinds, and, in general, all advice to clients, and all action taken for them in matters connected with the law."). However, a comprehensive definition of just what qualifies as the practice of law is "impossible," and "each case must be decided upon its own particular facts." Palmer v. Unauthorized Practice of Law Committee.

The UPLC, in arguing that the publication and sale of QFL constitutes the unauthorized practice of law, relies on two Texas Court of Appeals cases, Palmer v. Unauthorized Practice of Law Committee, 438 S.W.24 374 (Tex. App. — Houston 1969, no writ), and Fadia v. Unauthorized Practice of Law Committee, 830 S.W.2d 162 (Tex. App. — Dallas 1992, writ denied).

Palmer held that the sale of will forms containing blanks to be filled in by the user, along with instructions, constituted the unauthorized practice of law. The Palmer court observed that the form sold by Mr. Palmer was "almost a will itself" and that the form purported to make specific testamentary bequests. The court feared that the unsuspecting layman "by reading defendants' advertisements, by reading the will form, and by reading the definitions that are attached,... [would be] led to believe that defendants' will 'form' is in fact only a form and that all testamentary dispositions may be thus standardized." Id. at 376. The Palmer court held that the preparation of legal instruments of all kinds involves the practice of law. The Palmer court further held that the exercise of judgment in the proper drafting of legal instruments, or even the selecting of the proper form of instrument, necessarily affects important legal rights, and thus, is the practice of law.

In Fadia, the pro se defendant sold and distributed a manual entitled "You and Your Will: A Do-it-Yourself Manual." The defendant in Fadia attempted to get around Palmer's conclusion that the selling of a will manual constitutes the unauthorized practice of law, by arguing that the court should reject Palmer in light of recent state court decisions requiring some form of personal contact or relationship between the alleged unauthorized lawyer and the putative client in order to violate the unauthorized practice of law statute. The court rejected the defendant's argument, stating that it would not overrule Palmer and if there were to be a pre-requisite of personal contact between the parties, such a change to the Statute would have to come from the legislature and not the courts. The Fadia court went on to hold that because a will secures legal rights and its drafting involves the giving of advice requiring the use of legal skill or knowledge, the preparation of a will involves the practice of law. Since the selection of the proper legal forms also affects important legal rights, the court reasoned that it too constituted the practice of law. Therefore, since the will manual both purported to advise a layman on how to draft a will and selected a specific form for the layman to use, the court determined that the Defendant's selling of a will manual qualified as the unauthorized practice of law.

As already mentioned, the Palmer court found that the preparation of legal instruments of all kinds involves the practice of law. The Texas Supreme Court has since held that the mere advising of a person as to whether or not to file a form requires legal skill and knowledge, and therefore, would be the practice of law.

Based on the interpretations of the Statute by the Texas courts, QFL tails within the range of conduct that Texas courts have determined to be the unauthorized practice of law. For instance, QFL purports to select the appropriate health care document for an individual based upon the state in which she lives. QFL customizes the documents, by adding or removing entire clauses, depending upon the particular responses given by the user to a set of questions posed by the program. The packaging of QFL represents that QFL will "interview you in a logical order, tailoring documents to your situation." Additionally, the packaging tells the user that the forms are valid in 49 states and that they have been updated by legal experts. This creates an air of reliability about the documents, which increases the likelihood that an individual user will be misled into relying on them. This false impression is not diminished by QFL's disclaimer. The disclaimer only actively appears the first-time the program is used after it is installed, and there is no guarantee that the person who initially uses the program is the same person who will later use and rely upon the program.

QFL goes beyond merely instructing someone how to fill in a blank form. While no single one of QFL's acts, in and of itself, may constitute the practice of law, taken as a whole Parsons, through QFL, has gone beyond publishing a sample form book with instructions, and has ventured into the unauthorized practice of law.

Parsons attempts to avoid the conclusion that it is guilty of the unauthorized practice of law by arguing that the Statute requires personal contact or a lawyer-client relationship. Parsons bases its argument first on the language of the Statute, which it contends requires that the prohibited services must be provided "on behalf of a client" in order to be the practice of law.

Even assuming that Parsons is correct that paragraph (a) of the Statute requires the prohibited services to be completed "on behalf of" a client, paragraph (a) of the Statute is not an exclusive definition of the unauthorized practice of law. Paragraph (b) of the Statute gives the Court the authority to determine that other acts constitute the unauthorized practice of law. Therefore, a judge could legitimately determine, under the authority granted in paragraph (b), that services provided to the public as a whole, as opposed to a singular client, qualify as the practice of law.

Next, Parsons argues that this Court should require a personal relationship between the party charged with the unauthorized practice of law and the party who benefits from the "advice" since this is the logic of almost every other court to consider the issue. However, as noted above, the pro se defendant in Fadia made this exact argument and the Texas Court of Appeals rejected it.

Nonetheless, Parsons contends that if the Texas Supreme Court were to consider the issue it would follow the lead of the other states. Although this Court is not Erie bound to follow the Fadia decision, it believes the Texas Supreme Court would find the Fadia decision a persuasive precedent. For this Court to be the first to impose a new interpretation of a state statute which has been on the books in its current form since 1987, and some form since 1939, would fly in the face of generally accepted notions of federal-state comity. If Parsons believes such a personal contact requirement should be included in the Statute, it should address these concerns to the Texas legislature. It is not appropriate for this Court to be the first to read such a requirement into the Statute.

Parsons' arguments to the contrary notwithstanding, QFL is far more than a static form with instructions on how to fill in the blanks. For instance, QFL adapts the content of the form to the responses given by the user. QFL purports to select the appropriate health care document for an individual based upon the state in which she lives. The packaging of QFL makes various representations as to the accuracy and specificity of the forms. In sum, Parsons has violated the unauthorized practice of law statute.

Unauthorized Practice of Law Comm. v. Parsons Tech., Inc.[†]

Defendant-appellant Parsons Technology, Inc. appeals the district court's grant of summary judgment in favor of plaintiff-appellee, The Unauthorized Practice of Law Committee, and the court's subsequent order permanently enjoining defendant-appellant from selling and distributing its software programs, Quicken Family Lawyer Version 8.0 and Quicken Family Lawyer '99, within the state of Texas. The district court based its decision on its determination that the sale and distribution of the software constitutes the "practice of law" under Texas Government Code Annotated §81.101 (1998).

Subsequent to the filing of this appeal, however, the Texas Legislature enacted an amendment to §81.101 providing that "the 'practice of law' does not include the design, creation, publication, distribution, display, or sale ... [of] computer software,

---

[†] 179 F. 3d 956 (5th Cir. Tex. 1999).

or similar products if the products clearly and conspicuously state that the products are not a substitute for the advice of an attorney," effective immediately. We therefore VACATE the injunction and judgment in favor of plaintiff-appellee and REMAND to the district court for further proceedings, if any should be necessary, in light of the amended statute. Each party shall bear its own costs.

Discussion Questions

1. How would the Alberta guidelines address this issue?

2. Is the Texas statutory amendment a reasonable solution to this issue or does it swing the pendulum too far in the opposite direction by removing restrictions on activities that ought to be regulated?

3. Whose interests are being protected in these cases — the legal profession, the public, or both?

The ability of a Canadian court to assert jurisdiction over lawyers from another jurisdiction, yet practicing within the province was recently addressed in the following adoption case. How do you think the court should have treated the use of the Web site for jurisdictional purposes?

Re K.†

David Leavitt is a California attorney whose practice is almost exclusively devoted to adoptions. In declarations filed with the court he indicated that both birth and adoptive parents consult him, seeking his assistance in arranging adoptions. Leavitt's services to adoptive parents can be summarized by the statement contained on his Internet site: "I do not expect adopting parents to advertise or find a baby themselves. I do that for them" (http://www.adoptionlawcenter.com/adinfoap.html; visited December 1, 1998). He charges prospective adoptive parents a fee, which is in addition to medical expenses and support for the birth mother. Leavitt stated that the arrangement of direct placement, private adoptions by attorneys and persons other than licensed adoption agencies is lawful in California and accounts for the majority of adoptive placement in that state.

In each case the adoptive parents are residents of Alberta. One couple had retained Leavitt previously, when they adopted their first child. Both sets of adoptive parents contacted Leavitt and indicated their desire to adopt. In each case, he told the birth mother about the prospective adopting couple. When the birth mother expressed interest in the couple, he provided telephone numbers, resulting in a successful contact between the adoptive parents and the birth mother. In each case, the birth mother came to Alberta, where she delivered the baby, signed the consent,

---

† [1998] A.J. No. 1373 (Q.B.).

placed the baby in the care of the adoptive parents and departed. The adoptive parents paid the birth mother's expenses. They also paid a fee to Leavitt.

The adoptions were processed in accordance with the procedures set out in Alberta law. A licensed adoption agency completed a home assessment and post-placement assessment. Both couples retained the same Alberta lawyer and paid him a fee for his services. The birth mothers were independently represented by different legal counsel.

Eventually both couples applied to the court for orders approving the adoptions. In both cases the legal work was sloppy. Various consents were not in the appropriate form, and when the adoptive parents' lawyer attempted to file the applications for approval of the adoptions, the paperwork was rejected by the court clerks. Fiats, signed by judges, were eventually obtained to permit the filing of the material notwithstanding the deficiencies. Ultimately I heard the applications for orders approving the adoptions.

No one opposed the applications or made a competing claim for either child. Although the Director asked the court for guidance, he did not suggest that these adoptions should not proceed. In both cases the children have been well placed. The home studies paint a picture of loving families and of babies who are happy and secure. The children have adapted well to their homes and are deeply cared for. It is abundantly clear that it is in their best interests that the adoption orders be granted and I have granted them.

ISSUES

In Alberta adoptions are governed by Part 6 of the Child Welfare Act, S.A. 1984, c. C-8.1 and the Adoption Regulation (Alberta Regulation 3/89 as amended). The statute sets out the requirements for an adoption in Alberta. Sections 68.1 and 68.11 restrict the ability to facilitate the placement of a child for the purpose of an adoption, and prohibit the payment or receipt of fees for facilitation, except in narrow circumstances. One exception permits a lawyer to charge reasonable fees, expenses and disbursements for legal services provided in connection with an adoption.

The Director of Child Welfare asks for the court's advice on the following issues:

. . . .

c. If the facilitation provisions of the Act have been contravened, does Alberta have jurisdiction to pursue any recourses against a facilitator who is not a resident of Canada, and if so, what recourses does the Director have?

The Current Alberta Legislation

The Alberta legislation was introduced in 1994. The amendments restricted facilitation and entrusted most adoptive placements to adoption agencies licensed in Alberta. In part, the amendments addressed concerns identified by Mason J. in the baby boy "M" case, S.(J.W.) v. M.(N.C.) at 432:

> There are benefits to private adoption placement. But situations such as this point out that some legislative safeguards and guidelines appear necessary from my perspective based on this case. I would urge an immediate government study to assess the current situation and, if necessary, legislative action to prevent abuse.

In Alberta, s. 68.11(1) of the Act determines who can place or facilitate the placement of a child for the purpose of an adoption:

(a) a parent of the child;

(b) a director;

(c) a licensed adoption agency;

(c.1) the Central Authority for Alberta as designated in Part 6.1 or any person authorized by the Central Authority for Alberta;

(d) a person authorized by the Minister in accordance with the regulations.

Section 25 of the Adoption Regulation allows any adult who maintains his usual residence in Alberta to facilitate an adoption with the prior authorization of the Director. Section 27 lists the factors the Director must consider before authorizing a person to facilitate a placement.

Section 68.1 deals with payments for facilitating an adoption:

(1) No person shall give or receive or agree to give or receive any payment or reward, whether direct or indirect,

(a) to procure or assist in procuring, or

(b) to place or facilitate the placement of

a child for the purpose of adoption in or outside Alberta.

Section 68.1(2) recognizes four exceptions to the general prohibition against payment for adoption:

(2) Subsection (1) does not apply to reasonable fees, expenses or disbursements paid to

• a qualified person in respect of the preparation of a home assessment report pursuant to this Part,

• a lawyer in respect of legal services provided in connection with an adoption,

• a physician in respect of medical services provided to a child who is the subject of an adoption, or

• a licensed adoption agency, if the fees, expenses or disbursements are prescribed in the regulation. [Emphasis added.]

Section 69 provides the sanction. A person who violates ss. 68.1 or 68.11 is liable to a fine not exceeding $10,000 or, in default of payment, to imprisonment for a term not exceeding 6 months. A prosecution may be commenced only with the written authorization of the Minister of Family and Social Services (s. 69(2)).

. . . .

Jurisdiction And Recourses

I next consider the recourses the Director has in the case of improper facilitation by a person who is not a resident of Canada. The first issue is one of jurisdiction.

An adoptive parent who maintains his usual residence in Alberta, or maintained it at the time he received custody of a child, may apply for an adoption order under the Act, provided the child is a Canadian citizen or a permanent resident of Canada (s.58). Alberta then has jurisdiction over the adoption. Facilitating the placement of a child for the purpose of an adoption in Alberta is prohibited, as is receipt of a fee directly or indirectly for facilitation. The fact that the facilitation resulted in an adoptive placement in Alberta or that the facilitator received a fee, even indirectly, from adoptive parents in Alberta, may be sufficient to confer jurisdiction over the facilitator.

While the jurisdictional hurdle is not high, it is also possible that to confer jurisdiction, elements of the prohibited facilitation must have actually occurred in Alberta. Direct solicitation in Alberta by the facilitator is not required. It is the provision of services, even in response to inquiries, or the payment and receipt of a fee, directly or indirectly, which is prohibited. One does not have to leave the comfort of one's own home to violate the law of another jurisdiction [See Note 9 below]. Elements of facilitation in Alberta might include the execution of a retainer agreement by the adoptive parents in Alberta, payment of fees drawn on an Alberta bank, or even the receipt of information in Alberta by mail, telephone, fax or e-mail.

While I have defined facilitation and have decided that Leavitt's activities fit squarely within that definition, I make no finding of guilt against him. Subject to any limitation periods, it is within the discretion of the Director to determine whether to prosecute under s. 69 of the Act. The written authorization of the Minister would be required. The court hearing the trial would have to consider jurisdiction and be satisfied that the criminal standard of guilt beyond a reasonable doubt had been met.

Section 68.1(1) does not confine its prohibition to the person who receives a payment for facilitating a placement. The person who pays also violates the section. Therefore, subject to any limitation periods, the adoptive parents, as the payers, may also be prosecuted for contravening the Act. It is questionable whether such prosecutions would achieve the goal of the legislation. The adoptive parents are generally one or two time participants. The facilitator, who arranges multiple adoptions and profits from the activity, would seem to be the better target.

Section 68.1(1) prohibits giving or receiving a payment for facilitating the placement of a child for the purposes of an adoption in or outside Alberta. The result is that Albertans who engage in the practice, even for the purpose of facilitating adoptions outside the province, would be caught by the section and subject to prosecution.

In the case of a facilitator who is not a Canadian resident, the prohibition against facilitation may be more theoretical than real. While Alberta may choose to prosecute the facilitator, the facilitator may choose not to attorn to Alberta's jurisdiction. The offence of facilitation under the Act is not one which would require a California facilitator to be extradicted to Canada to answer for his actions.

The legislation in its present form has not and seems unlikely to curtail unlawful facilitation by people outside Canada who are not deterred by laws, but only by sanctions. A state can prevent people from entering its borders and can restrict the flow of goods. But facilitation services involve little more than providing information to put willing parties in touch with each other. It is notoriously difficult to erect stop signs on the information super-highway. Neither the vigilance of the Alberta regulators nor the strength of its legislation can be faulted for a failure to stop a flow of information whose supply is not criminalized in the jurisdiction from which it emanates. This issue is broader than the geographical boundaries of Alberta. It may require international co-operation and legal solutions.

Notes

Mark Hicken, a lawyer practicing in B.C., laid claim to the title of Canada's first "virtual lawyer" when he began offering his legal services exclusively through his Web site. The site, located at <http://www.electriclawyer.com>, provides basic legal services such as incorporations as well as wills and estate work.

EMAIL CONFIDENTIALITY

With lawyers and their clients using email as a common form of communication ever more frequently, questions have been raised as to whether email enjoys the same level of confidentiality protection as other forms of communication. The answer would appear to lie with whether email carries a reasonable expectation of privacy. If it does, there is little doubt that email correspondence enjoys full protection. If email is treated as something akin to a postcard, however, the reasonable expectation to privacy diminishes.

As discussed above, the Law Society of Alberta has weighed in on the matter by arguing that not only does email correspondence enjoy confidentiality protection, but that lawyers are typically not required to encrypt their correspondence to better ensure that it remains confidential in transit. Although this approach conforms with recent American Bar Association guidance, some members of the legal profession remain unconvinced.

The experience in South Carolina illustrates the perils of regulating with only limited understanding of the underlying technology. In Decision 94-27, the State bar questioned the confidentiality of email communications. That position was reversed soon after in Decision 97-08, as the state adopted the position described above.

In Canada, the leading case on email and the reasonable expectation of privacy is *R. v. Weir*, a 1998 Alberta decision. As of July 2000, the decision was under appeal with some speculation that it might find its way to the Supreme Court sometime in 2001.

R. v. Weir†

Does E-Mail Carry A Reasonable Expectation Of Privacy?

The defence suggests that e-mail carries an expectation of privacy much like the level of privacy accorded to first class mail or a telephone call. Therefore, the police performed an unlawful search while the e-mail was at the ISP. A search warrant was obtained by the police to search the e-mail box of Mr. Christenson (christed) at his ISP, and they should have done the same with Supernet.

In order to explore this argument further, the question of the expectation of privacy needs to be addressed.

† [1998] A.J. No. 155 (Q.B.).

I have no Canadian case law making a finding that e-mail carries a reasonable expectation of privacy. Nor do I have opinion surveys demonstrating the opinion of Canadians on the topic.

All of the witnesses who testified on this voir dire indicated that it was their expectation, personally, that their e-mail would remain private. Mr. Hasson and Mr. Murray from Supernet testified it was the ISP's goal to keep the customer's e-mail private, but they acknowledged it was not always possible. Mr. Verheijen testified e-mail customers could expect at least the same level of privacy as telephone users. Mr. Boeske agreed the ISP's goal is to keep e-mail private, but he acknowledged the nature of the technology is such that some entry into the message may be necessary in certain situations. An example of such a situation is "mail bombing". When dealing with the aftermath of a mail bomb the objective is to take the minimum information needed from the customer's e-mail in order to restructure the e-mail box. Sometimes, however, file names have to be looked at. Mr. Boeske summarizes that although e-mail privacy is important, he never thinks of it as guaranteed. He advises e-mail users to not send via e-mail anything they consider very private. Therefore, although e-mail communications are expected to be private, the nature of the technology leaves it vulnerable to exposure. Exposure arises in repair situations.

Mr. Boeske testified that he is aware of government documents which hold out a "pious hope" that e-mail privacy interests can be protected. Mr. Boeske uses the label pious hope because individual governments are largely powerless to implement the objective of privacy in e-mail communications. The difficulty lies in the nature of the technology. ISP's number in the tens to hundreds of thousands. They are located in most countries and on every continent. Because of their geographical diversity, individual governments can do little that is effective to regulate the ISPs used by their citizens. International agreements would be required to make headway on regulation but such agreements between governments are at this stage nonexistent. The nature of any e-mail transmission is that it goes from the sender's computer to the sender's ISP. At that ISP various searches are done by the computer to conduct an electronic route in order to ensure the sender's message gets to the recipient. That route may include a number of Internet nodes before the recipient's ISP is reached. The message can be tampered with and the internal headers modified by any node in the system. Generally, e-mail messages are not viewed by ISPs simply because they are far too numerous to be bothered with and only troublesome messages attract attention. The bottom line, however, is that e-mail messages are easy to invade, and a normal user would be none the wiser if invasion occurred.

The question of the expectation of privacy and e-mail messages has been explored by Megan Connor Berton in her article Home is Where Your Modem Is: An Appropriate Application of Search and Seizure Law to Electronic Mail. Ms. Berton argues that e-mail should carry a similar privacy interest to that of first class mail. She compares e-mail with first class mail and with telephone communication.

Ms. Berton lists the similarities of e-mail to first class mail at p.182. They both support powerful one to one communications, encourage users to express their thoughts to others in print, feature private mailboxes controlled by the person receiving the mail, support delivery of written documents in a timely manner directly to the addressee, allow for large amounts of additional material to be included, can be easily copied and sent to others or saved indefinitely, involve a delay between transmission and reception as well as between reception of the message and any response, support the communication of a message by the sender uninterrupted by the recipient, enhance communication between people who have never met, are relatively cheap and the cost of domestic transfer is not usually affected by the location of the recipient, allow a recipient to know either who a communication is from or where it originated before reading it, wait for the recipient and can be read on the recipient's own time, once sent cannot be retrieved, make bulk mailings and junk mail easy to send to unwanting recipients, with neither [sic] can a sender know immediately if a message has received its intended destination, both are sent out in batches, and, last, both can be subject to fraudulent use.

Next Ms. Berton outlines the similarities between e-mail and telephone communication. The primary similarity between the two is technology. Both e-mail and telephone calls travel over the same wires and require little effort on the part of the sender. Both can be transmitted essentially with the stroke of a few keys. There is no need to leave the house. Both may be received more than once a day. Neither requires manpower for delivery. Technology and an infrastructure is required to use both. Without it, messages can neither be sent or received. And last, e-mail can be used for the same type of simultaneous discussion that telephone communications are intended to be.

At p. 185 of her article, Ms. Berton comments on the unique characteristics of e-mail. It is one of the most cost efficient forms of communication available. E-mail address systems allow for anonymity if desired by the sender. The address system allows for automatic reply with little effort. Also, Netiquette, a body of generally accepted rules of behaviour, has been developed for e-mail and Internet communications in general. For example, uppercase letters signify the sender is yelling. Netiquette behaviours imply that replying to e-mail messages is easier than replying to other communications.

Ms. Berton's argument is that e-mail is most similar to first class mail and it deserves protection similar to that now afforded to first class mail. A conclusion in her article, which is based on Fourth Amendment law in the United States, is that until the law catches up with technological developments, the existing law provides a sufficient basis for protecting the privacy of rights of individuals who utilize e-mail. She also concludes that the objective of minimization in the interference of the privacy of individuals should mould the style of vehicle which courts should entertain for allowing interference in e-mail. That vehicle should be modelled after that which is now used to interfere with privacy interests in first class mail.

In Canada, that vehicle would be the search warrant which particularizes what the authorities are looking for. In the telephone call environment, wiretaps collect everything that is said and therefore are a greater invasion of the individual's privacy. In the postal environment, checking every letter is not usually warranted. Rather, the police are required to set out reasonable grounds to believe that a particular package is of interest in relation to a crime being investigated. Ms. Berton argues that permitting searches of e-mail, only after delivery of the mail and with a properly supported search warrant, would eliminate the extended invasion allowed by wiretaps. Not only would the application of the traditional warrant type of search limit the time within which information can be seized, but it would also limit the amount of information that could be seized through the requirement of particularization.

While I see the merit in Ms. Berton's suggestion, my view is that both the search warrant and a form of wiretap lend themselves to the e-mail environment.

Both procedures as they now exist require that the police take steps to ensure the right to privacy is not unreasonably infringed.

I am mindful that engaging in this discussion presupposes a finding of a reasonable expectation of privacy in e-mail. The following case supports such a finding.

In United States v. Maxwell 42 M.J. 568 the U.S. Air Force Court of Criminal Appeals made such a finding. Like the case at bar, the server, America Online, notified the FBI that a number of subscribers of America Online were using the service to transmit and receive visual images portraying child pornography. A confirmatory disk was passed by America Online to the FBI. The FBI opened an investigation. They contacted America Online in an effort to ascertain the identities of those involved with the child pornography. America Online advised the FBI a search warrant was needed to obtain e-mail transmissions. A search warrant was obtained. Anticipating a warrant would issue, America Online withdrew the information from their computers before the warrant was executed. On execution of the warrant, America Online turned over to the FBI 39 high density computer disks containing information in excess of that particularized by the warrant. The disks contained e-mail messages and visual transcriptions linked to Colonel Maxwell. Upon learning that Maxwell was a member of the Air Force, the FBI turned the investigation over to Air Force Special Investigations. Armed with this information Special Investigations obtained a warrant authorizing a search of Colonel Maxwell's quarters. Among the items seized during the search was Colonel Maxwell's personal computer. In deciding this case under Fourth Amendment law, the Chief Justice indicated at p. 575 "the underlying issue in a case involving an asserted violation of the Fourth Amendment is whether the person making the claim has a legitimate expectation of privacy in the invaded place." In the discussion that ensues the Chief Justice found:

> However, we find appellant definitely maintained an objective expectation of privacy in any e-mail transmissions he made so long as they were stored in the America Online computers. In our view, the appellant clearly had an objective expectation of privacy in those messages stored in computers which he alone could retrieve through the use of his own assigned password. Similarly, he had an objective expectation of privacy with regard to messages he transmitted electronically to other subscribers of the service who also had individually assigned passwords. Unlike transmissions by cordless telephones, or calls made to a telephone with six extensions, or telephone calls which may be answered by anyone at the other end of the line, there was virtually no risk that the appellant's computer transmissions would be received by anyone other than the intended recipients.

On the evidence before me, together with Ms. Berton's article and the finding in Maxwell, I am persuaded that e-mail with the ISP carries a reasonable expectation of privacy. Therefore, judicial pre-authorization (a warrant) will usually be required to search and seize it.

Warrantless searches are permitted under certain circumstances. The admissibility of evidence which emerges from a warrantless search can sometimes depend on the nature of the privacy invaded. Invasion of one's body without warrant (blood) may be seen as more serious than invasion of one's car without warrant. Therefore, I wish to briefly address the nature of e-mail privacy while the e-mail is with the ISP.

Before moving to the e-mail message I will address the cover. The envelope on first class mail shields the contents of the message. The information on the cover carries a lower expectation of privacy than does the message inside.

In the e-mail environment, the headers (hidden and exposed) can be likened to the information on the envelope. The message is directed by its headers. Much repair work to e-mail can be done through headers. Like the outside of the envelope, the headers have a lower expectation of privacy.

The difference between the two types of cover is that in first class mail the cover is respected. In e-mail, the cover is (or was in June of 1996) routinely violated in order to repair the technology. There are two or three levels of violation depending on the type of repair done and excluding a repair done by deleting the message or by enlarging the e-mail box. The size of the attachments may be viewed. The list of attachment names may be viewed. The message itself may be opened which can include looking at the message and the attachments or either. These facts about the technology help me to conclude the e-mail message is unlike first class mail in the level of privacy that it can attract.

Another difference between e-mail and first class mail is that in order to make an e-mail message truly private, one can encrypt it.

The evidence of Mr. Boeske is that encryption, although readily available, is not yet widely used by the general public. However, the debate in the United States over whether there should be publicly regulated bodies for deposit of encryption keys to permit reading of encrypted e-mail, suggests that encrypted mail is, for all practical purposes, unreadable and, therefore, privacy is secured. That encryption is relied on by some e-mail users to ensure privacy, and that it is not yet used widely by the general public underscores the need for legal protections.

In summary, I am satisfied e-mail via the Internet ought to carry a reasonable expectation of privacy. Because of the manner in which the technology is managed and repaired that degree of privacy is less than that of first class mail. Yet the vulnerability of e-mail requires legal procedures which will minimize invasion. I am satisfied that the current Criminal Code and Charter of Rights protections are adequate when applied in the e-mail environment.

Notes

The following sites are invaluable for the latest information on state bar association ethics activities as they relate to the Internet:

* Legal Ethics.com — <http://www.legalethics.com>
* Georgia State Bar, Computer Law Section — <http://www.computerbar.org/netethics/>

INTERNET ADVERTISING AND PROMOTION

With virtually every law firm now maintaining a Web site, the Internet has emerged as an accepted form of lawyer advertising. As the following case illustrates, some online activities stretch the bounds of accepted practice (not to mention good taste).

In Re: Laurence A. Canter[†]

On or about April 13, 1994, Respondent engaged in placing an advertisement that appeared on more than 5,000 Internet groups and thousands of E-Mail lists. The posting was unsolicited.

The posting read in totality:

> Green Card Lottery 1994 May Be The Last One! THE DEADLINE HAS BEEN ANNOUNCED.
>
> The Green Card Lottery is a completely legal program giving away a certain allotment of Green Cards to persons born in certain countries. The lottery program was scheduled to continue on a permanent basis. However, recently, Senator Alan J. Simpson introduced a bill into the U.S. Congress which could end any future lotteries. THE 1994 LOTTERY IS SCHEDULED TO TAKE PLACE SOON, BUT IT MAY BE THE VERY LAST ONE.
>
> PERSONS BORN IN MOST COUNTRIES QUALIFY, MANY FOR FIRST TIME.
>
> The only countries NOT qualifying are: Mexico, India, P.R. China; Taiwan, Philippines, North Korea, Canada, United Kingdom (except Northern Ireland), Jamaica, Dominican Republic, El Salvador, and Vietnam.
>
> Lottery registration will place soon. 55,000 Green Cards will be given to those who register correctly. NO JOB IS REQUIRED.
>
> THERE IS A STRICT JUNE DEADLINE. THE TIME TO START IS NOW!!
>
> For the next FREE, information via Email, send request to cslaw@indirect.com******
>
> Canter & Siegel, Immigration Attorneys 3333 E Camelback Road, Ste 250, Phoenix AZ 85019 USA cslaw@indirect.com telephone (602) 661-3911 Fax (602) 451-7617

The posting appeared on computer screen unsolicited, and each reader was required to read at least the introduction of each message. The posting appeared on Bulletin Boards having no relevance to immigration law. It was, therefore, an improper intrusion into the privacy of the recipient, in violation of DR 1-102(A)(1),(5) and (6), and DR 2-103.

Internet users/readers generally pay by the minute for access to the various Bulletin Boards. They, therefore, had to pay for the time they so viewed it. The recommendation for legal retention and employment was, therefore, not only unsolicited, but also at the recipient's expense. This was violation of DRI-102(A)(5) and (6), and DR 2-103(A).

At the time of this advertisement, DR 2-1O1(N) required the words: "This Is An Advertisement" to be included on communications soliciting professional employment. The posting placed by Respondent did not contain this language and thereby violated DR 2-1O1(N).

The Respondent's firm, particularly describing itself as "Immigration Attorneys", presented itself as a specialist. However, the posting did not contain the disclaimer required by DR 2-1O1(C).

[†] Docket No. 95-831-O-H (Tenn. Sup. Ct., Bd. Of Prof. Responsibility, February 1997).

Respondent did not deliver to the Board of Professional Responsibility a copy of this posting within three days of its distribution as required by DR2-1O1(F).

Degree Of Discipline To Be Imposed Relative To The Internet Matter
ABA Standards For Imposing Sanctions, 7.1, 7.2, 7.3, and 7.4 provide the standards for imposing discipline in lawyer advertising cases. Standard 7.3 states that a reprimand (censure), "is generally appropriate when a lawyer negligently engages in conduct that is a violation of a duty owed to the profession and causes injury or potential injury to a client, the public, or the legal system." Standard 7.2 states that a suspension is appropriate if the conduct is "knowingly."

This posting caused injury to the public by intruding improperly into the privacy of computer users by compelling recipients to pay for an advertisement they did not want nor solicit. The advertisement has further damaged the reputation of the legal profession and thereby the legal system.

The following are aggravating factors to be utilized in assessing discipline in the Internet case: (ABA Standards For Imposing Sanctions. 9.2).

• prior disciplinary offenses,
• dishonest or selfish motive,
• bad faith obstruction of the disciplinary proceedings, and
• refusal to acknowledge wrongful nature of misconduct.

There are no mitigating factors appropriate to the Internet case.

Judgment Of The Hearing Committee
Based upon the pleadings, the evidence and testimony, the argument of counsel and the entire record in this cause,
It is therefore ORDERED, ADJUDGED and DECREED:

2. That the Respondent, Laurence A. Canter, be suspended from the practice of law for one (1) year for those violations of the Disciplinary Rules set forth above in reference to Docket #95-831-O-H (the "Internet matter").
3. That the Respondent, Laurence A. Canter, be disbarred from the practice of law for those violations of the Disciplinary Rules set forth in reference to [specific on-Internet matters].
4. That these disciplines run concurrently.

Notes

New Internet business models regularly pose new ethical challenges for the legal profession. One of the more popular new business models is referral sites that refer prospective clients to lawyers for a fee. This approach raises significant ethical concerns, with several state bar associations finding that such conduct is unethical. For example, in Arizona Decision 99-06, the Committee found that:

> ER 7.1 (j) prohibits a lawyer from giving "anything of value to a person for recommending the lawyer's services, except that a lawyer...may pay the usual charges of a lawyer referral service or other legal service organization." ER 7.1 (j) "must be read in conjunction with ER 7.1 (r)(3)," which permits a lawyer to be recommended by or to cooperate with a lawyer referral service only where the organization is operated, sponsored or approved by a bar association. Ariz. State

Bar Committee on the Rules of Professional Conduct, Op. 98-03, p. 6. In short, before a lawyer may pay the usual charges of a referral service or be recommended to clients by the service, that service must satisfy the requirement of ER 7.1 (r)(3). See generally Ariz. State Bar Committee on the Rules of Professional Conduct, Ops. 90-09 and 85-8. In its earlier opinion on use of the Internet by lawyers, the Committee concluded that a lawyer "probably" could not join an on-line referral service "unless the service is in compliance with ER 7.1 (r)(3) ... At present that would require approval by the State Bar of Arizona. The are no on-line services currently approved by the State Bar." Ariz. State Bar Committee on the Rules of Professional Conduct, Op. 97-04, p. 5. Here, it does not appear that the service has been approved by any bar association much less by the State Bar of Arizona. Accordingly, the on-line service described in the e-mail communication to the inquiring attorney does not comply with ER 7.1 (r)(3)....

Other state bar rulings of interest include: Illinois treating Web sites like yellow page advertisements (Decision 96-10); Ohio ruling that a lawyer need not use a firm's name as part of the domain name for the firm's Web site, but that the name used must not be false, fraudulent or deceptive or imply special competence or experience (Decision 99-4); and Tennessee ruling that newsgroup postings constitute improper solicitation (Decision 95-A-570).

27

Telemedicine and the Law

The delivery of medical services via the Internet, often referred to as telemedicine, raises significant new legal issues for the medical profession. Alongside the potential for new levels of service to remote regions borderless, interactive medical care, as well as greater medical efficiencies and lower costs, comes the challenge of updating outmoded health care legislation to meet these new realities.

The introduction of telemedicine raises several key legal issues. How can health information privacy be maintained in an electronic environment? Which medical board may assert jurisdiction over a physician who conducts diagnosis over the Internet — the province where the patient resides, or the one where the doctor resides? May a pharmacist sell pharmaceuticals online?

An assessment of these issues begins with a major Health Canada study concerning the potential and challenges of telemedicine.

Canada's Health Infoway: Paths to Better Health, Health Canada, 1999†

Improving Privacy Protection

The Canadian Medical Association (CMA), in its comments on our interim report, stated, "We believe that the development of a robust health infostructure is essential to better health system planning and research and ultimately better patient care. However, in developing this structure it is important to ensure that the privacy of patients and the physician's duty of confidentiality is adequately safeguarded." The Council agrees completely. It is also convinced that the Canada Health Infoway can and must lead to improved privacy protection within Canada's health sector.

To this end, the Council considers privacy protection one of the four strategic goals for, and a key design feature of, the Canada Health Infoway. The three previous chapters, which focus on the realization of other strategic goals, also contain a discussion of privacy. Chapter 3 in particular contains an extensive recommendation on how to ensure the privacy of electronic health records. To fully appreciate the Council's position of personal privacy protection, it is necessary to read Chapters 2 to 4.

This chapter focuses on the key mechanisms that should be in federal, provincial and territorial privacy protection legislation relating to health information. As an introduction to this discussion, we shall draw heavily on our interim report to lay out some key privacy concepts and considerations.

We wish to thank Canada's federal, provincial and territorial privacy commissioners for their comments and helpful feedback on our interim report. Their recommendations have helped us make privacy protection an even more pivotal concern in our broad strategy to develop and implement the Canada Health Infoway.

In considering the Council's approach to privacy in this report, it is important to consider what it is not. We have not spelled out specific legislative provisions or offered instructions for drafting privacy legislation. Nor do we lay out all of the rules and procedures that should govern the protection of personal health information, confidentiality obligations and effective security arrangements. Privacy is a very complex issue, and such detail is beyond the scope of this report. As with the other basic strategic goals for the Canada Health Infoway, our mandate is to present broad strategic directions, general principles and approaches that would improve privacy protection within Canada's health sector. It will be the responsibility of those who come after — including Canada's privacy community — to bring about sound privacy protection.

Privacy Concepts

As noted in our interim report, Canadians in survey after survey have expressed concern about loss of privacy in the new electronic environment and, more specifically, their control over personal information. Few such categories are more sensitive than personal health information. In its own consultations, the Council also found much

† Health Canada Web site: <http://www.hc-sc.gc.ca/main/hc/web/datapcb/ohih/htdocs/achis/fin-rpt/intro_e.html> [Chapter 5]. Source of Information: Health Canada. Reproduced with permission of the Minister of Public Works and Government Services Canada, 1999.

anxiety about this issue among stakeholders in the health sector and representatives of the general public.

Privacy is often defined as the right to be free from intrusion or interruption. It is linked with other fundamental human rights such as freedom and personal autonomy. In relation to information, privacy involves the right of individuals to determine when, how and to what extent they share information about themselves with others.

Privacy can also be a concern for groups such as Aboriginal and immigrant communities. These communities worry that research on their members could be released to the media without notice and used in a negative way. This emerging issue is growing in importance and, in the Council's view, should be a serious consideration in the context of ethical reviews of proposed research projects.

Safeguarding privacy for individuals includes protecting information about oneself — that is, any information that can be linked to a person who can be identified. Protection of personal information requires adherence to fair information practices in managing such information.

Confidentiality refers to the obligations on one person to preserve the secrecy of another's personal information. Security refers to the procedures and systems used to restrict access and maintain the integrity of that information.

As noted in our interim report, privacy, although a fundamental value and right, is not an absolute right in law and in Canadian society. For example, in criminal cases or in matters affecting public health, there are justifiable circumstances in which privacy must be weighed against the public good. Such balancing should never involve considering the sacrifice of personal privacy on a broad scale, even to achieve some overwhelming public benefit. Rather, the consideration might relate to a case-by-case review to assess whether a presumed public benefit is of sufficient value to warrant — in that case and for that purpose — a limited intrusion of privacy with specific restrictions and safeguards.

Key Legislative Mechanisms

Significant variations now exist in provincial and territorial laws, regulations and guidelines for privacy and the protection of personal health information in the public sector. Quebec has legislation which also applies to the private sector. The federal government also brought forward in October 1998 legislation (Bill C-54, the Personal Information and Electronic Documents Act) that would apply to those parts of the private sector under federal jurisdiction for the next three years. Three provinces have introduced or passed new legislation intended to protect personal health information. However, compatible approaches are not always taken.

In the Council's view, as noted in its interim report, a real danger exists that Canada could end up with many different approaches to privacy and the protection of personal health information. Different approaches could make it difficult, if not impossible, to improve the portability of services or create information resources needed for accountability and continuous feedback on factors affecting the health of Canadians. In some cases, any exchange of information might be prohibited by law in those jurisdictions that do not provide adequate protection for personal health information. Refusal to share information in such circumstances would be entirely defensible. However, it is to be hoped that the circumstances justifying such a refusal can be avoided in Canada.

For these reasons, in its interim report the Council called on the federal Minister of Health to take the lead in encouraging an accord among provincial, territorial and federal governments to harmonize the approaches in their respective jurisdictions to privacy and the protection of personal health information taking into account best practices internationally. The Council also recommended that all governments in Canada should ensure that they have legislation to address privacy protection specifically aimed at protecting personal health information through explicit and transparent mechanisms.

Several key principles, approaches and mechanisms should be incorporated in such legislation. In depicting them, however, we are aware that our list is not comprehensive, all-inclusive or definitive, either here or within Recommendation 3.4. In responding to our interim report, the CMA drew attention to its recent officially announced privacy code which addresses the seriousness of the association's commitment to privacy. The code represents an important contribution to the deliberations of Canadians and legislators on how to safeguard privacy across the health domain. In keeping with our mandate, we have set out broad legislative directions relevant to the electronic health infostructure without specifically endorsing a particular set of proposed codes.

It is critical that privacy protection legislation define health information in broad terms to include information collected by both the public and private sectors. Obligations to protect health information should apply equally to both.

Such legislation should contain a clear definition of personal health information and address the differences in the degree to which data can be made personally identifiable, as described in Chapter 3.

Within the legislation, there should be a transparent definition for custodians or trustees of personal health information — the persons responsible for ensuring the protection, confidentiality and security of personal health information. Their obligations should be precisely defined. They should apply equally to public and private sector organizations, as well as to organizations acting as an agent or contractor for the custodian. The definitions of guardians (e.g. for minors) and their obligations should also be clearly set down in the legislation.

The legislation should also contain a precise definition of free and informed consent, as well as a statement of principle that informed consent should be the basis for sharing personal health information.

"Exemptions" to this requirement for informed consent should also be clearly set out in law. More specifically, legislative guidance should be provided on how to balance the right of privacy with the public good for research purposes to implement the coherent and harmonized pan-Canadian system for independent, ethical review recommended in Chapter 3. The legislation should also contain a clear prohibition against all secondary commercial use of personal health information.

Provisions regulating secondary uses of non-identifiable health information must form part of the legislation. Such provisions should address privacy concerns surrounding the degree to which such data might be linked back to an identifiable individual, as described in Chapter 3.

To prevent such potential abuses, the legislation should set clear limits on access to and use of health information by third parties outside the health care system. To prevent the serious invasions of privacy that can result from the unrestricted linking of personal health information with other kinds of information on the same individual, the legislation should contain provisions prohibiting the use for any another [sic] purpose of unique personal identifiers in health information systems.

Finally, such legislation should include measures to remedy breaches of privacy, including criminal sanctions and civil law remedies.

Recommendation

In harmonizing and strengthening the protection of personal health information across jurisdictions, governments should ensure that their privacy legislation for health embodies the following mechanisms and principles:

(a) a clear definition of health information, broad enough to incorporate health information collected in public and private systems and to ensure that equal obligations and penalties apply to both public and private sectors;

(b) a definition of personal health information, which takes into account the spectrum of potential identifiability in the case of health information;

(c) a definition of a custodian or trustee of personal health information, and a custodian or trustee's obligations, including provisions for ensuring that these obligations apply equally to private sector organizations and organizations acting as an agent or contractor for the custodian;

(d) definitions of a guardian (e.g. for a minor child or a mentally incompetent person) and of a guardian's obligations;

(e) a definition of what constitutes informed consent, as well as a clear statement of principle to the effect that informed consent should be the basis for sharing information;

(f) a precise definition of "exemptions" to this requirement for informed consent — specifically provisions that give clear guidance on how to balance the right of privacy with the public good for research purposes;

(g) provisions prohibiting all secondary commercial use of personal health information;

(h) provisions setting clear limits on access and use of health information by third parties outside the health care system;

(i) provisions regulating secondary uses of non-identifiable health information, taking into account the spectrum of potential identifiability of such information;

(j) provisions prohibiting the use of personal health identifiers for other purposes, to prevent the potential serious invasions of privacy attendant upon potential access to personal health information beyond the health domain or the combination of records from several different areas to assemble a comprehensive profile; and

(k) provision for remedies in the case of breaches of privacy.

Discussion Questions

1. The federal government clearly has big plans for telemedicine in Canada. What legal infrastructure is needed? Is the *Personal Information and Electronic Documents Act* examined earlier adequate to deal with the privacy concerns raised in the Health Canada report? Given that health falls primarily under provincial jurisdiction, is a national legal framework a realistic alternative?

2. Notwithstanding the report's recommendation that provinces work together to develop national standards, several provinces have already developed legislative protections and standards. Manitoba's *Personal Health Information Act* provides as follows:

18(1) In accordance with any requirements of the regulations, a trustee shall protect personal health information by adopting reasonable administrative, technical and physical safeguards that ensure the confidentiality, security, accuracy and integrity of the information.

(2) Without limiting subsection (1):

(c) if the trustee uses electronic means to disclosure of personal health information or to respond to requests for disclosure procedures to prevent the interception of the communication information by unauthorized persons;

(3) A trustee who maintains personal health information in electronic form shall implement any additional safeguards for such information required by the regulations.

19. In determining the reasonableness of security safeguards required under section 18, a trustee shall take into account the degree of sensitivity of the personal health information to be protected.

What level of security protection do you think is adequate for safeguarding personal health information? In light of recent high-profile hacking attacks on government sites, it appears that no system is foolproof. Does the vulnerability of electronic information raise concerns for the federal government's plans to create a Health Infoway? Does legislation addressing security concerns adequately address privacy issues?

Saskatchewan addressed the concerns about electronic storage of personal health information by providing provincial residents with the option of opting-out of an electronic system. In particular, the *Saskatchewan Health Information Protection Act* provides as follows:

2.(l) "networked electronic health record" means an electronic health record containing personal health information collected by one or more trustees for the purpose of creating a comprehensive profile of an individual's personal health history to be made available, in whole or in part, over an electronic network to one or more trustees, but does not include electronic mail or other office or systems support services that may be provided over an electronic network;

. . . .

8.(1) An individual may require a trustee not to store a record or a portion of a record of the individual's personal health information on the networked electronic health record maintained by the Saskatchewan Health Information Network or on any other prescribed network.

(2) Where an individual's personal health information is stored on the networked electronic health record maintained by the Saskatchewan Health Information Network, the individual may require a trustee to prevent access by other trustees to all or part of that information from the network.

(3) Where a trustee has entered into an agreement with the Saskatchewan Health Information Network for the purpose of storing and making available personal health information, the trustee must take reasonable steps to inform individuals from whom the trustee collects personal health information that the trustee has entered into such an agreement.

In contrast to the Manitoba statute, no specific provision was made for the security of electronic records.

Considering that two differing statutes have already been enacted, is a national harmonized model law, much like the *Uniform Electronic Commerce Act*, the best approach for future development of Canadian telemedicine privacy protections?

LICENSING AND TELEMEDICINE

In most jurisdictions, individual provinces or states are responsible for regulating the practice of medicine through the licensing of physicians by medical boards. Physicians not licensed by the forum state may be subject to civil suits or criminal prosecution under an "unauthorized practice of medicine" statute. In addition, authorities in the forum state may report unauthorized practice to the offending physician's home state licensing board.

For example, the educational and competency requirements for obtaining an initial medical license in the United States are relatively uniform, but are ultimately determined by medical boards to whom the state delegates licensing authority. Those requirements include: graduating from an accredited medical school; passing the United States Medical Licensing Exam (USMLE); and residency at a teaching hospital or other post-graduate training.

The advent of telemedicine has prompted several U.S. states to amend their medical licensing statutes to cover the delivery of medical services through electronic media. No Canadian province has enacted similar legislation, though the following two proposed bills may provide useful examples should regulators choose to venture into this area.

An Act Relating To Medical Practice[†]

A bill to be entitled an act relating to medical practice; creating s. 458.351, F.S.; requiring licensure of any physician, wherever located, who has primary authority over the care or diagnosis of a patient located in this state; providing an exception; providing applicability with respect to transmission of radiographic images; providing an effective date.

Be It Enacted by the Legislature of the State of Florida:

Section 1. Section 458.351, Florida Statutes, is created to read:

> In addition to any other provision of this chapter defining or otherwise regulating the practice of medicine, any physician, wherever located, who has primary authority over the care or diagnosis of a patient located in this state is practicing medicine in this state and shall be subject to licensure as required by this chapter. A physician lawfully licensed in another state or territory of the United States or in a foreign country who engages in consultation with a physician duly licensed in this state and does not exercise primary authority over the patient's care and diagnosis is exempt from licensure, as provided

---

[†] (1999 HB 1703), Florida House of Representatives.

in s. 458.303(1)(b). In the case of electronic transmission of radiographic images, a physician who provides, through an ongoing regular arrangement, official authenticated interpretations of radiographic images to any health care
practitioner or patient located in this state shall be regarded as exercising
primary authority over the diagnosis of the involved patient and is subject to
licensure as required by the chapter.

Montana House Bill No. 399 (1999)[†]

An Act Prohibiting The Practice Of Telemedicine Without A Telemedicine Certifi-
cate Issued By The Board Of Medical Examiners; Providing Legislative Findings;
Providing A Definition And Exceptions; Providing Qualifications For A Telemedicine
Certificate; Specifying Powers And Duties Of The Board; Providing For Disciplinary
Action By The Board; Establishing Jurisdiction For The Medical Legal Panel And
The Courts; Amending Section 37-3-301, Mca; And Providing Effective Dates.

Be It Enacted By The Legislature Of The State Of Montana:

Section 1.   Legislative findings.

The Montana legislature previously found, in 37-3-101, that the practice of medicine
in Montana is a privilege, not a natural right, and that the regulation of the practice
of medicine is necessary to ensure the health, happiness, safety, and welfare of the
people of Montana. The legislature now finds that because of technological advances
and changing patterns of medical practice, medicine is increasingly being practiced by
electronic means across state lines. Although access to technological advances is in
the public interest, the legislature also finds that regulation of the practice of medicine across state lines is necessary to protect the public against the unprofessional,
improper, unauthorized, and unqualified practice of medicine. Accordingly, the legislature finds that physicians outside the boundaries of Montana who enter the state
by electronic or other technological means to practice medicine for compensation on
patients inside Montana are seeking the benefit and protection of the laws of
Montana and are subject to the licensure and regulatory requirements provided in
[sections 1 through 9].

Section 2.   Definition — scope of practice allowed by
telemedicine certificate.

(1) As used in [sections 1 through 9] and 37-3-301, "telemedicine" means the practice of medicine, as defined in 37-3-102, by a physician located outside the state who
performs an evaluative or therapeutic act relating to the treatment or correction of a
patient's physical or mental condition, ailment, disease, injury, or infirmity and who
transmits that evaluative or therapeutic act into Montana through any means,
method, device, or instrumentality under the following conditions:

(a) The information or opinion is provided for compensation or with the expectation of compensation.

(b) The physician does not limit the physician's services to an occasional case.

---

† Montana House Bill No. 399 (1999).

(c) The physician has an established or regularly used connection with the state, including but not limited to:

(i) an office or another place for the reception of a transmission from the physician;

(ii) a contractual relationship with a person or entity in Montana related to the physician's practice of medicine; or

(iii) privileges in a Montana hospital or another Montana health care facility, as defined in 50-5-101.

(2) As used in [sections 1 through 9] and 37-3-301, telemedicine does not mean:

(a) an act or practice that is exempt from licensure under 37-3-103;

(b) an informal consultation, made without compensation or expectation of compensation, between an out-of-state physician and a physician or other health care provider located in Montana;

(c) the transfer of patient records, independent of any other medical service and without compensation;

(d) communication about a Montana patient with the patient's physician or other health care provider who practices in Montana, in lieu of direct communication with the Montana patient or the patient's legal representative;

(e) diagnosis of a medical condition by a physician located outside the state, based upon an x-ray, cardiogram, pap smear, or other specimen sent for evaluation to the physician outside the state by a health care provider in Montana; or

(f) a communication from a physician located outside Montana to a patient in Montana in collaboration with a physician or other health care provider licensed to practice medicine in Montana.

Section 3. Practice of telemedicine prohibited without certificate — scope of practice limitations — violations and penalty.

(1) A physician may not practice telemedicine in this state without a telemedicine certificate issued pursuant to [sections 1 through 9] and 37-3-301.

(2) A telemedicine certificate authorizes an out-of-state physician to practice telemedicine only with respect to the specialty in which the physician is board-certified or meets the current requirements to take the examination to become board-certified and on which the physician bases the physician's application for a telemedicine certificate pursuant to [section 5(2)].

(3) A telemedicine certificate authorizes an out-of-state physician to practice only telemedicine. A telemedicine certificate does not authorize the physician to engage in the practice of medicine while physically present within the state.

(4) A physician who practices telemedicine in this state without a telemedicine certificate issued pursuant to [sections 1 through 9] and 37-3-301, in violation of the terms or conditions contained in the certificate, in relation of the scope of practice allowed by the certificate, or without a physician's certificate of licensure issued pursuant to 37-3-301(2)(a), is guilty of a misdemeanor and on conviction shall be sentenced as provided in 37-3-325.

Section 4. Application for telemedicine certificate.

(1) A person desiring a telemedicine certificate shall apply to the department and verify the application by oath, in a form prescribed by the board.

(2) The application must be accompanied by:

  (a) a certificate fee prescribed by board rule; and

  (b) documents required by the board that establish that the applicant possesses the qualifications prescribed by [sections 1 through 9] and the rules of the board. The burden of proof is on the applicant, but the department may make an independent investigation to determine whether the applicant possesses the requisite qualifications.

(3) The application must include a clear statement that the applicant consents to the jurisdiction of the state as specified in [section 9].

(4) The applicant shall provide to the board authorizations necessary for the release of records and other information required by the board.

Section 5.   Qualifications for telemedicine certificate — basis for denial.
The board may not grant a telemedicine certificate to a physician unless the physician has established under oath that the physician:

(1) has a full, active, unrestricted certificate to practice medicine in another state or territory of the United States or the District of Columbia;

(2) is board-certified or meets the current requirements to take the examination to become board-certified in a medical specialty pursuant to the standards of, and approved by, the American board of medical specialties or the American osteopathic association bureau of osteopathic specialists;

(3) has no history of disciplinary action or limitation of any kind imposed by a state or federal agency in a jurisdiction where the physician is or has ever been licensed to practice medicine;

(4) is not the subject of a pending investigation by a state medical board or another state or federal agency;

(5) has no history of conviction of a crime related to the physician's practice of medicine;

(6) has submitted proof of current malpractice or professional negligence insurance coverage in the amount to be set by the rules of the board;

(7) has not paid, or had paid on the physician's behalf, on more than three claims of professional malpractice or negligence within the 5 years preceding the physician's application for a telemedicine certificate;

(8) has identified an agent for service of process in Montana who is registered with the secretary of state and the board and who may be a physician certified to practice medicine in this state;

(9) has paid an application fee in an amount set by the rules of the board; and

(10) has submitted as a part of the application form a sworn statement attesting that the physician has read, understands, and agrees to abide by Title 37, chapters 1 and 3, and the administrative rules governing the practice of medicine in Montana.

Section 6.   Certificate renewal — fee.

(1) A physician certified to practice telemedicine shall renew the telemedicine certificate every 2 years.

(2) The physician shall complete and return an application for renewal provided by the board by a date established by board rule.

(3) The physician shall pay an application renewal fee in an amount established by board rule.

Section 7.   Reasons for denial of certificate — alternative route to licensed practice.

(1) The board may deny an application for a telemedicine certificate if the applicant:

  (a) fails to demonstrate that the applicant possesses the qualifications for a certificate required by [sections 1 through 9] and the rules of the board;
  (b) fails to pay a required fee;
  (c) does not possess the qualifications or character required by this chapter; or
  (d) has committed unprofessional conduct.

(2) A physician who does not meet the qualifications for a telemedicine certificate provided in [section 5] may apply for a physician's license in order to practice medicine in Montana.

Section 8.   Discipline of physician with telemedicine certificate.

A physician granted a telemedicine certificate may be subject to investigation and discipline on the grounds that the physician has:

(1) committed unprofessional conduct, as described in 37-1-316 or in a board rule; or

(2) failed to:

  (a) maintain the qualifications provided in [section 5] or in a board rule;
  (b) maintain complete, legible patient records in written or readily retrievable electronic form;
  (c) make complete, legible patient records available to the board during an investigation or disciplinary proceeding concerning the physician's practice of telemedicine; or
  (d) appear and testify at a deposition within the state in the course of an investigation or disciplinary proceeding conducted under Montana law that concerns the physician's practice of telemedicine.

Section 9.   Consent to jurisdiction. A physician granted a telemedicine certificate shall, pursuant to [section 4], consent to the jurisdiction of:

(1) the courts of Montana for the purpose of civil actions, including but not limited to tort, contract, and equitable actions, related to the physician's practice of telemedicine;

(2) the courts of Montana for the purpose of criminal actions related to the physician's practice of telemedicine;

(3) the board for the purposes of licensing and disciplinary action by the board; and

(4) the Montana medical legal panel for matters within the panel's jurisdiction, as provided in Title 27, chapter 6.

Discussion Questions

The Florida and Montana bills present two potential approaches to telemedicine licensing regulation. The Florida approach suggests that existing rules are sufficient to adequately regulate out-of-state physicians providing medical care online with only a statutory clarification needed. Montana has opted to create a specific telemedicine license that defines permitted and prohibited activities and seeks to bring all out-of-state physicians within the state regulations by issuing a license.

Which approach do you prefer? Is there a danger in relying on existing regulations that rarely contemplated online medical care? Is the Montana proposal sufficiently comprehensive? Would a Canadian physician be eligible for a telemedicine license? Does a state-by-state license approach obstruct telemedicine growth? Is a national or international solution needed?

SALE OF PHARMACEUTICALS ONLINE

With billions of dollars spent every year on prescription drugs, many Internet companies are anxious to garner a portion of that market. In recent months the issue has attracted widespread attention as regulators become increasingly concerned with the proliferation of Web sites providing online pharmaceutical sales.

In fact, the American Medical Association has recommended that doctors actually see patients face to face before prescribing any form of medication. Some question whether such a policy directly contradicts the practice of permitting doctors to dispense medical advice over the phone, a practice which is permitted in many states. Undeterred by the policy debate, several states, including Connecticut, Nevada, Wyoming, Maryland and Kansas, have already chosen to ban online prescriptions.

Walgreen Co. v. Wisconsin Pharmacy Examining Board And Wisconsin Department Of Regulation And Licensing†

The Wisconsin Pharmacy Examining Board appeals from an order reversing its ruling that the Walgreen Company, the owner and operator of several pharmacies in Wisconsin, violated various regulatory statutes and administrative rules relating to pharmacies when, as part of a test program, it accepted prescription orders from physicians via a computer electronic mail system, and provided used computers

---

† 1998 Wisc. App. Lexis 201 (Court Of Appeals Of Wisconsin, District Four, 1998).

for some of the physicians participating in the test. The board concluded that: (1) the use of computer-transmitted prescriptions violated §450.11(1), STATS., which requires written prescription orders to be signed by the prescribing physician; and (2) Walgreen's provision of computers to some of the participating physicians violated WIS. ADM. CODE §PHAR 10.03(14), which prohibits pharmacies from participating in "rebate or fee-splitting arrangements" with physicians.

While we pay due deference to the board's decision, we are satisfied that its interpretation of §450.11(1), STATS., while reasonable, is overcome by a more reasonable interpretation and that its determination that Walgreen's program violated the "rebate" rule lacks any reasonable basis in the record. We therefore reverse the board's decision and affirm the circuit court's order.

In determining that Walgreen's program violated §450.11(1), STATS., the board reasoned that, because the statute does not specifically mention electronic transmissions, but rather defines a "prescription order" as simply "a written or oral order by a [physician] for a drug or device for a particular patient," §450.01(21), STATS., an electronic transmission is the equivalent of a written order and thus subject to the signature requirement of the statute. The board determined that the program also violated the "rebate" rule because Walgreen received a financial benefit by providing free computer equipment to several of the participating physicians — although it never estimated either the value of the equipment or the nature of the "benefit" to Walgreen. Having so found, the board assessed a forfeiture of $89,200 against Walgreen.

Walgreen sought judicial review of the board's decision and the circuit court reversed, concluding with respect to the §450.11(1), STATS., violation that prescriptions transmitted electronically were more analogous to prescriptions ordered by telephone, which, under the statute, a physician need not sign. The court also rejected the board's determination that Walgreen's program violated the "rebate" rule because the board failed to determine the extent of any financial benefit to either Walgreen or the participating physicians.

The board appeals, reasserting the arguments it raised before the trial court.

. . . .

II. THE STATUTORY VIOLATION

Emphasizing that §450.11(1), STATS., on its face, deals with only written and "oral" prescriptions, the board maintains that a computer electronic mail system is more analogous to a written prescription order than an oral one because "the communication between the doctor and the pharmacist is textual," involving the use of letters and numbers typed at one computer and read on another computer. Thus, according to the board, because a computer transmission lacks the prescribing physician's signature, Walgreen's system violates §450.11(1).

It is in the nature of things that statutes must at times be applied to situations unforeseen at the time of their enactment. When this occurs, the statute can and should be considered in terms of its manifest intent to see, in Professor Hurst's words, whether the "pictures actually drawn by the statutory text ... [are] sufficient to cover the new type of situation that the course of events has produced." According to Hurst, if the legislature has supplied "sufficient specifications to provide a discernible frame of reference within which the situation now presented quite clearly fits, even though it represents in some degree a new condition of affairs unknown to the lawmakers," the statute may be interpreted accordingly.

The circuit court, disagreeing with the board's conclusion that a computer-transmitted prescription was so analogous to a written prescription that it must be treated as such under the statute, ruled that it was more closely akin to a prescription transmitted orally — by telephone — which the legislature, in the concluding lines of §450.11(1), STATS., expressly stated may be filled without being signed. That is, to us, a more reasonable interpretation than the board's in light of the simple facts of computer transmission: The prescription is put into a computer as text and the message is then electronically transmitted to the pharmacy's terminal, much as a telephone call — or a facsimile — would be.

Finally, we note that the circuit court's interpretation appears to be consistent with the board's own rule allowing electronic transmission of renewal prescription orders on a one-time basis between two pharmacies. See WIS. ADM. CODE §PHAR 7.05(3) and (5).

We are thus satisfied that the circuit court properly reversed the board's conclusion that Walgreen's test program violated §450.11(1), STATS.

Effective regulation of the online sales of pharmaceuticals is directly linked to international regulatory cooperation. Since pharmaceuticals may be lawfully sold in one jurisdiction but not approved for sale in another, regulators face the dilemma of "global pharmacies" capable of selling virtually any approved pharmaceutical anywhere in the world. Although border and customs agents may succeed in preventing some pharmaceuticals from entering their jurisdiction, total enforcement of local pharmaceutical laws is rendered virtually impossible.

Sensing the new challenge posed by online pharmaceutical sales, regulators have engaged in several cooperative "Internet sweeps" aimed at uncovering the illegal sale of pharmaceuticals online. For example, a sweep by U.S. and Thailand officials in March 2000 resulted in the arrest on criminal charges of eleven Thai nationals selling pharmaceuticals online.

Despite some willingness to engage in regulatory cooperation, differing legal systems often pose a significant barrier. This 1999 New Zealand case illustrates the challenge in shutting down online pharmaceutical sales targeted outside the home jurisdiction.

Bell v. Med Safe New Zealand Medicines and Medical Devices†

The applicant, Kerry Donald Bell, is a duly qualified and registered pharmacist and is a member of the NZ Pharmaceutical Association. He carries on a retail pharmacy business from premises at 491 New North Road, Kingsland, Auckland trading as Kingsland Pharmacy.

Mr Bell has made application to the Court pursuant to s 65 of the Medicines Act 1981 (the Act) seeking an order that the seizure of certain medicines, taken from him by the respondent pursuant to the powers of seizure contained in s 63 of the Act be wholly disallowed, and a direction that the medicines concerned be returned to him.

---

† [2000] DCR 60 (Dist. Ct. Auckland 1999).

This application is resisted by the respondent which contends that the seizure was proper and lawful and should be upheld.

Formal appearances were entered by counsel for two pharmaceutical companies Roche Pharmaceuticals (NZ) Ltd and Douglas Pharmaceuticals (NZ) Ltd as parties having an interest in the goods seized. Neither company took any active part in the proceedings.

Since some time in 1993 the applicant has, as an adjunct to his retail pharmacy business in Kingsland, been in the business of advertising medicines for sale to overseas buyers by means of the Internet. This aspect of the applicant's business involves the retail sale of medicines to individual purchasers overseas, mainly in the USA. In many instances the medicines so supplied have included prescription medicines as defined in the Act, that is to say medicines which in terms of the Act may only be supplied in accordance with a prescription from a registered medical practitioner, veterinarian or other authorised professional.

Affidavits sworn by Alan Roy Freshwater, and Marie Therese Scott, who are both "officers" in terms of the Act, disclose that on 23 November 1999 those two officers detained some six bags of mail held at the NZ Post depot at Auckland Airport. These mail bags contained 178 parcels, addressed to different persons at what appear to be private addresses overseas, 173 of the addressees being in the USA and five in the United Kingdom. All of these parcels were despatched by the applicant, Kerry Bell.

Later the same day the officers visited Mr Bell's pharmacy at Kingsland. Mr Bell took the officers to a separate room in the basement of the premises in which he explained was his "Internet Pharmacy". That part of the premises contained a substantial quantity of prescription medicines. The list of addresses taken from the parcels detained at the airport was compared with the business records held by the applicant at the Kingsland premises, and from a perusal of invoices the contents of some of the parcels was able to be identified, indicating that the parcels contained various prescription medicines including medicines known as Viagra, Xenical, Prosac and Propetia. No prescriptions for any of these drugs were located amongst the applicant's business records. When interviewed by the officers Mr Bell acknowledged that no prescriptions had been issued in respect to the prescription medicines posted in the various parcels intercepted. Later on 24 November the officers formally seized the parcels at the airport, and also seized a quantity of prescription medicine held in the Internet Pharmacy part of the applicant's premises at Kingsland. Written notices of seizure and a schedule of the medicines seized were given to Mr Bell at the time of seizure.

As to the medicines seized from the post, Mr Freshwater in his affidavit deposes "as Mr Bell had admitted that he had sold and was selling prescription medicines without a prescription from a medical practitioner, and once we had found prescription medicines both at his premises and at the airport bound for overseas addresses, I had a reasonable belief that an offence against s 18(2) of the Medicines Act had been committed".

Similarly as to the medicines seized from the Kingsland premises Ms Scott in her affidavit deposes "after examining the documentation, in particular invoices, orders and packaging records and after Mr Bell acknowledged that there were no doctor's prescriptions, I reasonably believed that an offence against s 18 of the Act had been committed".

The respondent also filed in opposition to the application, an affidavit sworn by Stuart Sinclair Jessamine, a duly registered medical practitioner and Senior Medical

Adviser to the Ministry of Health. Dr Jessamine's affidavit deals with the purpose and scheme of the Medicines Act as the respondent understands it to be. It also deals in some detail with the specific health risks associated with the indiscriminate use of certain prescription medicines, which are seen as requiring that access to those medicines be limited to supply on medical prescription only.

Dr Jessamine refers in his affidavit to a publication approved by The Ministry of Health giving detailed medical and pharmacological information concerning drugs for the information of prescribers known as "The Data Sheet". Detailed medical and pharmacological information from this source in relation to Viagra and Propetia set out in the affidavit clearly shows that in certain persons, and particularly in those with cardiovascular disease, serious cardiovascular events, urino-genital disorders and ocular disorders can be associated with the inappropriate use of Viagra. it is also shown that Viagra is incompatible with certain other medications, particularly with some commonly prescribed for cardiovascular conditions.

Similarly information provided in the affidavit in relation to Propetia, indicates that the male foetus of a pregnant woman exposed to this drug faces a serious risk of deformity.

There are therefore sound reasons in the interests of public health safety for restricting indiscriminate public access to medicines of this kind and requiring that they be available only on a proper medical prescription.

It is clear that the sale of such medicines within New Zealand otherwise than upon prescription is prohibited.

The respondent contends that the sale of prescription medicines to overseas buyers without medical prescription is also unlawful being proscribed by s 18(2) of the Act.

The relevant provisions of s 18 state:

18. Sale of medicines by retail

(1) Except as provided in sections 25, 27, and 30 to 33 of this Act, or as may be permitted by regulations made under this Act, no person shall, in the course of any business carried on by that person, sell by retail, or supply in circumstances corresponding to retail sale, or distribute by way of gift or loan or sample or in any other way,

(a)   Any prescription medicine or restricted medicine, unless he is a pharmacist and sells, supplies, or distributes the medicine in a pharmacy or a hospital; or

(b)   Any pharmacy-only medicine, unless he sells, supplies, or distributes the medicine —
    (i) In a pharmacy or a hospital; or
    (ii) In any shop described in section 51(2) of this Act and in accordance with a licence issued under Part III of this Act.

(2) Except as provided in sections 25, 30, 31, and 69 of this Act, or as may be permitted by regulations made under this Act, no person shall sell by retail, or supply in circumstances corresponding to retail sale, any prescription medicine otherwise than pursuant to a prescription given by a practitioner, registered midwife, or veterinary surgeon and conforming with the provisions of any such regulations relating to prescriptions.

The terms "sale by retail" and "prescription medicine" used in the section are the subject of extensive definitions elsewhere in the Act. It is common ground that the Internet sales made by the applicant with which this case is concerned were sales by retail and were sales of prescription medicine, within the meaning of the Act, and that no prescriptions had been given in respect to any of the medicines so sold.

The respondent further contends that well prior to the seizures the applicant had been put on notice as to the unlawful nature of such sales by means of articles published in the journal of the NZ Pharmaceutical Society which is distributed to its members, and further, by direct contact with the respondent's staff.

The applicant contends that the seizure was unexpected, and was made without warning. He says that he was unaware of the articles published in the pharmaceutical journal, and says that so far as his contacts with staff of the respondent are concerned, he had made it quite clear at all times that in his view the activity complained of by the respondent is not in breach of the Act. He says that he was not given any warning about the matter as such but rather told to rely upon his own legal advice which he has done. He says that he has at all times maintained that his export sales via the Internet do not offend against the Medicines Act as a matter of law.

. . . .

The sole question for determination is whether upon a proper construction of the provisions of the Medicines Act what the applicant has admittedly done, is as a matter of law an offence against the Act.

The applicant's position is that it is not, having regard to the provisions of s 33 of the Act, and that hence, since no offence has been or will be committed on the present state of the law, the only proper order is for the seized goods to be returned.

The respondent contends that s 33 does not have the effect contended for by the applicant, but accepts that if the Court finds that the Act should be read in the manner contended for by the applicant then the goods should be returned.

Section 33 provides:

> 33. Exemptions in respect of procuring and exporting medicines
>
> Notwithstanding sections 17 to 24 of this Act or anything in any licence, but subject to the other provisions of this Act and to any regulations made under this Act, —
>
> (a) Any person may procure a medicine if the person from whom he procures that medicine is authorised by or under this Act to sell or supply the medicine to him:
>
> (b) Any person may export, in the course or for the purpose of sale, any medicine that, at the time when it is exported, might lawfully be sold by a pharmacist to a person in New Zealand, whether pursuant to a prescription or otherwise.

Mr Asher QC for the applicant says that this means just what it says. The word "notwithstanding" he says has the effect of setting aside the provisions of ss 17 to 24 and in particular s 18(2) of the Act in so far as the activity under consideration is in compliance with s 33.

A fair reading of the plain words of s 33 it is said shows it to be directed to authorising the export in the course of sale or for the purpose of sale of any medicine that may lawfully be sold by a pharmacist in New Zealand. This authority extends to "any person" and is to be seen as being enacted for the purpose of enabling the export of medicines for commercial purposes to proceed without restriction, provided such medicines are of the kind that may be lawfully sold by a pharmacist within New Zealand. There are three restricted classes of medicines defined in s 18 of the Act, namely, prescription medicines, pharmacist only and pharmacy only medicines all of which may only be sold through a pharmacy. The words "whether by prescription or otherwise" are in counsel's submission added to make it clear that prescription medicines are intended to be included within the categories of medicines to which s 33 refers.

Hence it is said that in as much as the applicant's Internet sales of prescription medicines are all export sales to persons in the USA and the United Kingdom, no offence is committed against s 18(2).

While s 33 is not in itself a penal provision, the consequences of breach of s 18(2) are penal and hence counsel submits a strict approach to the interpretation issue is appropriate.

In the course of a careful submission in reply Mr Hamlin sought to persuade me that a consideration of the scheme of the Medicines Act overall and the mischief at which s 18 is directed, justifies and requires a purposive reading of s 33.

The Act classifies medicines into four categories placing different restrictions upon the manner of their sale according to the risks which they are perceived to present if misapplied. Prescription medicines are the most closely controlled, being available only in accordance with a prescription in terms of s 18(2). The policy reasons for such restrictions in the interests of public health and safety are well demonstrated by the material traversed in Dr Jessamine's affidavit.

Other sections such as s 47, which deals with storage and delivery of medicines, and s 19 which deals with the administration of prescription medicines it is submitted are seen to fortify the legislative intent that prescription medicines are to be closely controlled.

Counsel referred to s 26(3)(b) as a further indication of Parliamentary intent towards strict control of the sale of prescription medicines.

It was submitted that a purposive approach is appropriate, given that s 33 is permissive in character and is not in itself a penal section.

For all of these reasons it is said that s 33 should be read so that the words "might lawfully" should be treated as referring not only to the nature of the medicine sold (ie something capable of being lawfully sold in New Zealand) but also as to the manner of the sale in New Zealand (ie a lawful sale within New Zealand).

The Court was invited to conclude that the legislation is intended to proscribe the unrestricted export of prescription medicines as a measure of international comity in the control of such commodities. The argument in favour of such a purposive construction was however purely formulated upon the basis of a consideration of the Act itself, and the material as to the specific drugs traversed in Dr Jessamine's affidavit. No supportive material detailing any concluded international treaty obligations, or reference to Hansard, Parliamentary White Paper, or the like was introduced to support such a contention.

It would be dangerous for the Court to speculate upon such matters.

. . . .

I am not of the opinion that the purpose for which the medicines seized from the applicant are intended to be put will probably involve the commission of an offence against the Act, or that the continued detention of those medicines is expedient for the purpose of their production in any pending proceedings under the Act.

I direct that the items seized be restored to the applicant accordingly.

Discussion Questions

Does this case suggest that an international accord is needed on this issue? If countries permit the online sale of pharmaceuticals outside their jurisdiction, is there any realistic hope of curtailing this activity?

Case Law Index

Index

About the Author

Michael Geist is a law professor at the University of Ottawa specializing in Internet and e-commerce law and Director of E-commerce Law at the law firm Goodman Phillips & Vineberg.

Professor Geist graduated with an LL.B. from Osgoode Hall Law School in Toronto in 1992, conducted graduate legal research at Kobe University School of Law in Japan as a Monbusho Scholar, and obtained Master of Laws degrees (LL.M.) from Cambridge University in the U.K. and Columbia Law School in New York, the latter while a Fulbright Scholar and SSHRC Doctoral Fellow. Professor Geist taught at Dalhousie Law School and the Columbia Law School before joining the University of Ottawa law faculty in 1998. At the University of Ottawa he has established a number of innovative Internet and e-commerce law courses including the Regulation of Internet Commerce, the Regulation of Internet Communication, an E-commerce Law Workshop, and a Technology Law Internship program.

He has written numerous academic articles and government reports on the Internet and law, is national columnist on cyberlaw issues for the *Globe and Mail*, editor of the monthly newsletter, *Internet and E-commerce Law in Canada* (Butterworths), the creator and founder of BNA's Internet Law News, served as an expert on several landmark Canadian Internet law cases, and sits on the advisory boards of several leading Internet law publications including *Electronic Commerce & Law Report* (BNA), the *Journal of Internet Law* (Aspen) and *Internet Law and Business* (Computer Law Reporter). He is regularly quoted in the national and international media on Internet law issues and has appeared before government committees on e-commerce policy.

Professor Geist lives in Ottawa with his wife Allison and two children, Jordan and Ethan.